Psychology

HENRY GLEITMAN

UNIVERSITY OF PENNSYLVANIA

W · W · NORTON & COMPANY · NEW YORK · LONDON

Published simultaneously in Canada by George J. McLeod Limited, Toronto.
Printed in the United States of America
All Rights Reserved
First Edition

Library of Congress Cataloging in Publication Data
Gleitman, Henry.
Psychology.

Includes bibliographical references and index.
I. Title.   [DNLM: 1. Psychology.   BF38 G557p]
BF121.G58 1981   150   80-21380
ISBN 0-393-95102-2

Designed by Antonina Krass

Makeup by Ben Gamit

Photo research by Ruth Mandel and Donna Seldin

Acknowledgments and copyrights appear on pages A66–A71 which
constitute a continuation of the copyright page.

W. W. Norton & Company, Inc. 500 Fifth Avenue, New York, N.Y. 10110
W. W. Norton & Company Ltd. 25 New Street Square, London EC4A 3NT

1 2 3 4 5 6 7 8 9 0

To three who taught me:

Edward Chace Tolman, to cherish intellectual passion
Hans Wallach, to recognize intellectual power
Lila Ruth Gleitman, to admire intellectual elegance

Contents

CHAPTER 10   **Language** 353

BY LILA R. GLEITMAN AND HENRY GLEITMAN

Preface

It is widely believed that one of the best ways to learn something is to teach it, for in trying to explain it to others you first have to clarify it to yourself. This holds for the subject matter of every course I have ever taught, but most especially for introductory psychology. Students in an advanced course will come at you with tough and searching questions; they want to know about the evidence that bears on a theory of, say, color vision or language acquisition, and about how that evidence was obtained. But students in an introductory course ask the toughest questions of all. They ask why anyone would want to know about color vision (or language acquisition or whatever) in the first place. And they also ask what any one topic in the course has to do with any other. They ask such questions because they—unlike the advanced students—have not yet accepted the premises of the field. They wonder whether the emperor is really wearing clothes. As a result, they made me ask myself what the field of psychology is all about and how it hangs together—what the emperor's clothes are really like when you look at them closely.

This book grew out of my attempts to answer such questions over the years in which I taught the introductory course, to answer them not only to satisfy the students but also to satisfy myself. My goal in writing it was to present psychology in all its diversity while yet conveying the sense in which it is a coherent intellectual enterprise. Toward this end I have done the following:

1. To present the different sub-areas of psychology, I organized the book around four main questions: How do humans (and, where relevant, animals) act, how do they know, how do they interact, and how do they differ from each other?

2. To provide some intellectual cohesion, I considered each topic (usually a chapter) against the backdrop of one or two major ideas that could serve as an

organizing and unifying framework. Thus the chapter on the biological bases of behavior opens with Descartes' conception of the organism as a machine, the next chapter treats various aspects of motivated behavior as manifestations of negative feedback. To relate the material across chapters I used several overarching themes. For example, the various chapters that deal with cognition (Sensory Processes, Perception, Memory, Thinking, and Language) can all be regarded as variations on the twin controversies, nature versus nurture and psychological atomism versus organization.

3. In many cases, the attempt at integration required taking a step backward to look at psychology's intellectual history, for a number of psychological endeavors are hard to explain unless one points to the paths that led up to them. Why did Thorndike study cats in puzzle boxes? Why did his conclusions have such an important effect on American psychology? Why were they challenged by Köhler and Tolman? It still pays to take a serious look at the work of such pioneers before turning to the present. Much as a river's water is clearer when it is taken from its spring, so issues which have become more and more complex as detail has piled upon detail and qualification upon qualification become very much clearer when we trace them back to their origin.

4. To gain still more cohesion, I have tried to show the connection between aspects of psychology and other fields of inquiry. To the extent that this contact is made, psychology can be better understood, for it will then be seen as it fits within the broad scope of human knowledge. In this book, I have tried to underscore such contacts: to philosophy, in which many of psychology's central questions were first asked; to biology, to which we turn when we try to understand the physiological underpinnings of behavior and the evolutionary origin of built-in characteristics; to anthropology, which serves as a necessary corrective to a cultural parochialism; to the visual arts which gave the first impetus to the study of perception; to history, which provides the context for many of psychology's key conceptions.

As to the way the topics are presented, the overall structure of the book stresses the idea that psychological phenomena can be regarded from various perspectives: as mental events, as overt behaviors, as manifestations of underlying physiological processes, as cognitions, as social interactions, as expressions of individual differences. By way of an introduction to the field as a whole, the first chapter takes up one phenomenon, dreaming, and shows how it can be considered from each of these vantage points. The rest of the book is divided into four parts: Action, Cognition, Social Behavior, and Individual Differences. In brief outline, they cover the following topics:

Part One, *Action* focuses on overt behavior and its physiological basis. It begins by asking about the biological underpinning of human and animal action. These questions lead to a discussion of the nervous system and its operation (Chapter 2), and to a consideration of motivation (Chapter 3). Another issue is how organisms can modify their behavior to adapt to new circumstances. It is approached through a discussion of classical and instrumental conditioning, of modern behavior theory, and of various reactions to this theoretical view (Chapter 4 and 5).

Part Two, *Cognition,* deals with knowledge and how it is gained and used. We begin by asking how the senses provide us with information about the world outside (Chapter 6), and how this information is organized and interpreted to lead to the perception of objects and events (Chapter 7). Further questions concern the way this knowledge is stored in memory and retrieved when needed (Chapter 8), the way it is reorganized through thinking, both in adulthood and in the course of the cognitive development that leads to it (Chapter 9), and the way knowledge is communicated to others through the medium of language (Chapter 10).

Part Three, *Social Behavior,* takes up three kinds of factors that determine interaction with others. One concerns built-in social tendencies in both humans and animals, a topic to which modern ethology has made major contributions (Chapter 11). A second is the effect of childhood on personality development, which is considered in terms both of psychoanalytic concepts and of modern approaches to socialization (Chapters 12 and 13). A third set of factors pertains to the present and to the way social situations are interpreted and coped with in the light of our social role (Chapter 14).

Part Four, *Individual Differences,* begins with a chapter on mental testing in general and intelligence testing in particular, paying special attention to the nature-nurture issue (Chapter 15). It then turns to various issues in personality assessment (Chapter 16). It continues with psychopathology. After looking at several varieties of psychopathology and asking how they arise (Chapter 17), Part Four concludes by examining various methods of treatment and therapy (Chapter 18).

How does this organization compare with standard treatments of the subject matter? By and large, it contains all the traditional topics, of the field. There are also a few additions and changes:

1. There is a separate chapter on language, considered as an integral part of human cognition, discussed with particular emphasis on language acquisition and written by Lila R. Gleitman and myself.

2. The part on social behavior departs from traditional treatments by emphasizing a number of topics and placing them all under one roof. It features a whole chapter (Chapter 11) on the biological foundations of social behavior, and two chapters (Chapters 12 and 13) on the process of socialization, of which the first is a discussion of Freud's contributions to psychological thought. The last chapter in this part (Chapter 14) focuses on modern social psychology, which is here put in a context of related topics rather than floating in comparative isolation.

3. There is no separate chapter on developmental processes. Instead, developmental issues are raised within the context of the particular topic at hand, as in a discussion of perceptual development (Chapter 7), language acquisition (Chapter 10), and personality development (Chapters 12 and 13). A detailed discussion of cognitive development and of the contributions of Piaget forms a substantial part of the chapter of thinking (Chapter 9).

4. To help serve the needs of instructors, teaching assistants, and students, several supplementary materials are available with the textbook. First, there is a full *study guide* for students, prepared by John Jonides of the University of Michigan and Paul Rozin of the University of Pennsylvania. Second, the *instructor's manual,* prepared by Alan Silberberg of The American University, offers specific suggestions for using the text and also includes an annotated

film and media guide prepared by James B. Maas of Cornell University. Third, Susan Scanlon of the University of Pennsylvania and Harvey Weingarten of McMaster University have carefully constructed a *test item file* which includes questions for all chapters and the statistical appendix.

To conclude. It is sometimes said that students in the introductory course want to learn about things that are relevant to themselves and to their own lives. But why is this a problem? When you come right down to it, there is something odd about the idea that psychology is *not* relevant to anyone's particular life history, specialist and nonspecialist alike. Psychology deals with the nature of human experience and behavior, about the hows and whys of what we do, think, and feel. Everyone has perceived, learned, remembered, and forgotten; has been angry and afraid and in love; has given in to group pressure and has been independent—in short, has experienced most of the phenomena that psychology tries to explain. This being so, psychology cannot fail but be relevant.

It surely is, but its relevance has to be pointed out. By a liberal use of examples from ordinary experience and a frequent resort to metaphors of one kind or another, I have tried to show the direct relation of many psychological phenomena to the reader's own life. In the process I have often oversimplified—as in making analogies between short-term memory and loading platforms. The introductory course often calls for what amount to caricatures to convey the essence of a topic to those who come to it for the first time—exaggerations of the major features that let the student see the larger picture before confronting its separate parts.

Acknowledgments

There remains the most pleasant task of all: to thank the persons who helped me so greatly in the various phases of writing this book. Friends, students, editors, colleagues—never has one author owed so much to so many.

I have received a great deal of assistance from many colleagues and friends. They read parts of the manuscript and gave invaluable advice and criticism, or they talked to me at length about various issues in the field which I saw much more clearly because of them. I am very grateful to them all. Many are at my institution at the University of Pennsylvania, whose Department of Psychology has provided me with a valued intellectual community for more than a dozen years. These many helpers, and the main areas in which they have advised me, are as follows:

BIOLOGICAL FOUNDATIONS

Norman T. Adler *University of Pennsylvania* Robert C. Bolles *University of Washington* Brooks Carder John D. Corbitt *Brown University* Alan N. Epstein *University of Pennsylvania* Charles R. Gallistel *University of Pennsylvania* Harvey J. Grill *University of Pennsylvania* Jerre Levy *University of Chicago* Martha K. McClintock *University of Chicago* Allen Parducci *University of California at Los Angeles* Paul Rozin *University of Pennsylvania* W. John Smith *University of Pennsylvania* Paul G. Shinkman *University of North Carolina* Edward M. Stricker *University of Pittsburgh*

LEARNING	Frank Costin *University of Illinois* Richard B. Day *McMaster University* Richard C. Gonzalez *Bryn Mawr College* Werner K. Honig *Dalhousie University* Francis W. Irwin *University of Pennsylvania* Nicholas J. Mackintosh *University of Sussex* Robert A. Rescorla *Yale University* Barry Schwartz *Swarthmore College* Richard L. Solomon *University of Pennsylvania*
SENSATION AND PERCEPTION	Duncan R. Luce *Harvard University* Julian E. Hochberg *Columbia University* Leo M. Hurvich *University of Pennsylvania* Dorothea Jameson-Hurvich *University of Pennsylvania* Neil A. Macmillan *Brooklyn College* Jacob Nachmias *University of Pennsylvania* Edward Pugh *University of Pennsylvania* Irvin Rock *Rutgers University* Burton S. Rosner *University of Pennsylvania* Robert Steinman *University of Maryland* D. Varner *University of Pennsylvania* James L. Zacks *Michigan State University*
COGNITION	Justin Aronfreed *University of Pennsylvania* Edwin Boswell *University of Pennsylvania* Lynn A. Cooper *University of Pittsburgh* Rochel Gelman *University of Pennsylvania* Francis C. Keil *Cornell University* Deborah Kemler *Swarthmore College* Stephen M. Kosslyn *Harvard University* John Jonides *University of Michigan* Ellen Markman *Stanford University* Ulric Neisser *Cornell University* Daniel N. Osherson *Massachusetts Institute of Technology* Myrna Schwartz *University of Pennsylvania* Elizabeth Spelke *University of Pennsylvania* Rose T. Zacks *Michigan State University*
LANGUAGE	Sharon L. Armstrong *Wesleyan University* John Gilbert *University of British Columbia* Lila R. Gleitman *University of Pennsylvania* Barbara Landau *University of Pennsylvania* Elissa L. Newport *University of Illinois* Ted Supalla *University of Illinois*
PERSONALITY	Lewis R. Goldberg *Institute for the Measurement of Personality, Portland, Oregon* Ruben Gur *University of Pennsylvania* Lester B. Luborsky *University of Pennsylvania* Carl Malmquist *University of Minnesota* Jerry S. Wiggins *University of British Columbia*
SOCIAL PSYCHOLOGY	Solomon E. Asch *University of Pennsylvania* Joel Cooper *Princeton University* Frederick J. Evans *Carrier Foundation, Bellemead, N.J.* Larry Gross *University of Pennsylvania* Michael Lessac *Colonnade Theater, New York, N.Y.* Martin T. Orne *University of Pennsylvania* Albert Pepitone *University of Pennsylvania* John P. Sabini *University of Pennsylvania* Phillip R. Shaver *University of Denver*
INTELLIGENCE	Jonathan Baron *University of Pennsylvania* Daniel B. Keating *University of Minnesota*
PSYCHPATHOLOGY	Lyn Abramson *University of Wisconsin* John P. Brady *University of Pennsylvania* Leonard M. Horowitz *Stanford University* Anne Premack *University of Pennsylvania* Martin E. P. Seligman *University of Pennsylvania* Larry Stein *University of California, Irvine* Hans H. Strupp *Vanderbilt University* Paul L. Wachtel *City College of the City University of New York* Richard Warner *University of Pennsylvania* David R. Williams *University of Pennsylvania* Julius Wishner *University of Pennsylvania*
INTELLECTUAL HISTORY	Mark B. Adams *University of Pennsylvania* Alan C. Kors *University of Pennsylvania* Elisabeth Rozin Harris B. Savin

ACKNOWLEDGMENTS

To detail how each of these persons has helped me is impossible. But I do want to express special thanks to a few of them.

Several friends and colleagues saved me from egregious errors. Charles R. Gallistel and Jerre Levy performed such acts of intellectual good Samaritanism in the area of physiological psychology; Martin E. P. Seligman did the same in the fields of learning and psychopathology. Others helped to repair various sins of omission, in particular Jonathan Baron, who made me aware of important new developments in the fields of memory and intelligence, and W. John Smith who taught me the elements of ethology.

I owe special thanks to still others who read all or most of the manuscript: to Richard Day and Paul Shinkman who read every chapter, not only as specialists but also as experienced teachers who helped me to assess its suitability for undergraduates; to Leo Hurvich and Dorothea Jameson-Hurvich for their careful, scholarly critique of many chapters, especially those on vision, and for enlightening discussions of the psychology of art; to Francis W. Irwin for finding all the places where I had tried to paper over difficult issues with platitudes and embarrassing me into doing something about them; to Duncan R. Luce for reading over a dozen chapters with an unerring eye for inconsistencies and errors of fact and logic; to Jacob Nachmias for his advice on matters sensory and his wise counsel on all phases of the manuscript from its inception; to Elisabeth Rozin for encouragement and help with style and clarity; to John Sabini for perceptive and critical comments on the chapters on social behavior; to Elizabeth Spelke for incisive comments on many chapters, particularly those on cognition, and for countless and invaluable discussions of the book's overall organization.

Several friends and colleagues helped me to see whole topics in a new light, and read successive drafts of the relevant chapters as they were reorganized accordingly. They include: Julian E. Hochberg, whose vigorous arguments and counterarguments forced me to reevaluate my thoughts on perception and rewrite the chapter appropriately, as they have forced me to reconsider my thoughts on so much else since we first met at CCNY thirty-five years ago; John Jonides whose sharp, yet balanced, comments were extremely helpful for the book as a whole and were indispensable for the chapter on memory, which was recast because of them; Ellissa Newport, whose lucid, lengthy, and telephonic discussions of many chapters, especially that on language, were even more profitable to me and Lila Gleitman than they were to the Bell Telephone Company; Barry Schwartz who has elevated the practice of common sense to a fine art, which he liberally shared with me in several long discussions that led me to reorganize the chapters on animal learning; Edward Stricker who generously gave of his time and his hospitality to teach me a few rudiments of modern neuropsychology which he did with amazing skill and patience, resulting in major changes in the treatment of these topics.

One person contributed in a special way. This is Neil Macmillan of Brooklyn College who wrote the appendix, "Statistics: The Collection, Organization and Interpretation of Data," with a fine sense of balance between the demands of the subject matter and the demands of expositional clarity.

All of the preceding clearly went way beyond the call of friendship and colleagial duty. Two other colleagues at the University of Pennsylvania went beyond "beyond." One is Paul Rozin, who served as general advisor on all stages, recasting old ideas and tossing off new ones, understanding everything

ACKNOWLEDGMENTS

I ever said and making me say it better than I would have otherwise. His emphasis on the role of evolutionary factors on psychological processes has affected me greatly and is reflected in many chapters. I owe him much and so does this book.

What can I say about the one colleague I have not yet thanked—my wife, colleague, collaborator, and, above all, friend—Lila R. Gleitman. What didn't she do? She co-authored the chapter on language (that is, wrote four-fifths of it), helped with issues of organization and expositional clarity, discussed and read and edited just about every chapter in an (undoubtedly futile) effort to make my prose sound like that of a native English-speaker, she read galleys, checked for grammatical ambiguities and typos—the list is endless. That someone so brilliant and productive as she was so encouraging throughout made and makes the whole effort worthwhile.

Several persons helped in other ways. My thanks go to: Claire Gleitman and Ellen Gleitman who read parts of the manuscript to provide an undergraduate's perspective; to Felice Bedford who did much the same and also helped to check the references; to Judith Stewart who helped with the glossary; to Edwin Boswell, who performed herculean labors in gathering and organizing illustration material, working on references, and taking photographs of preschool children in the developmental laboratory. Special thanks are due to Ada Katz who transcribed an early draft and was always ready to help thereafter. I owe a special debt to Brigitta Howe, calm and imperturbable, who typed draft after draft for over five years and somehow managed to find order in a chaos of innumerable papers, references, illustration outlines and God knows what else, always knowing where something was that I was sure I'd lost. I also thank Patricia Moisan for her excellent job at performing a similar function during the past six months and for using her fine artist's eye to help select art illustrations.

Further thanks go to my publisher, Norton, in particular to staff artist Antonina Krass for designing the book and making it look attractive, to layout specialist Ben Gamit for bringing the appropriate text next to the appropriate illustration and making it look uncluttered, and to photo researchers Ruth Mandel and Donna Seldin for obtaining the unobtainable and making it look easy.

To end I will go back to the beginning and acknowledge my debt to the man who first gave me the idea which led to this book: Donald Lamm of Norton. He served as sharp-eyed critic, brilliant advisor, occasional psychotherapist, and patient (oh, how patient) literary midwife; in the course of this long enterprise he has become my friend. He and two incisive and utterly indefatigable Norton editors, Donald Fusting and Mary Shuford, have made me come to realize, that, at their best, publishers do more than print and even sell a book—they help to make it.

H. G.

Merion, Pennsylvania
September 1980

Psychology

CHAPTER 1

Introduction

What is psychology? It is a field of inquiry that is sometimes defined as the science of mind, sometimes as the science of behavior. It concerns itself with how and why organisms do what they do. Why wolves howl at the moon and sons rebel against their fathers; why birds sing and moths fly into the flame; why we remember how to ride a bicycle twenty years after the last try; why humans speak and make love and war. All of these are behaviors and psychology is the science that studies them all.

The Scope of Psychology

The phenomena that psychology takes as its province cover an enormous range. Some border on biology, others touch on social sciences such as anthropology and sociology. Some concern behavior in animals, many others pertain to behavior in humans. Some are about conscious experience, others focus on what people do regardless of what they may think or feel inside. Some involve humans or animals in isolation, others concern what they do when they are in groups. A few examples will give an initial sense of the scope of the subject matter.

HUNGRY FLIES

Some psychological phenomena involve relatively simple, automatic processes that are based on built-in mechanisms of the nervous machinery. These are often best studied in primitive animals. Consider the black blowfly, a small

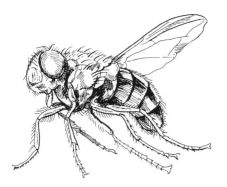

1.1 The blowfly *(After Dethier, 1976)*

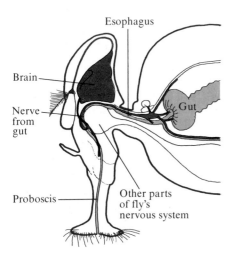

1.2 Feeding mechanisms in the blowfly
The fly's digestive (gray) and nervous systems (color) drawn schematically. (After Dethier, 1972)

insect barely one centimeter long with a total life-span of at most two months (Figure 1.1). This creature's intellect is as puny as its size, for it seems to be unable to learn. But even so, it manages to do one thing: It can regulate its food intake appropriate to its needs. The question is how. At first glance, the blowfly's behavior appears to be an exercise in aeronautical aimlessness; it flies about, lands somewhere, takes off, lands, takes off again—all in apparently random fashion. But a closer look shows an underlying pattern. Sometimes, the fly lands in a drop of sugary liquid. When this happens, the creature feeds. It extrudes its proboscis, an elongated tube through which the liquid is sucked up. Eventually, the fly has had its fill; it withdraws its proboscis and flies off (Figure 1.2). What makes the fly start to eat and what makes it call a halt?

To understand what triggers eating, one has to look at the animal's legs. At the bottom of the fly's feet are small taste hairs which contain nerve cells that are activated by sugar. This arrangement permits the fly to taste with its feet. If it steps into a sugary solution, the taste hairs send a message upward to the animal's tiny brain, the proboscis descends and sucking begins. As the fly continues to suck, more and more liquid accumulates in a portion of the gut. This gradually swells and its distension stimulates other nerve cells which countermand the original feeding impulse so that feeding stops. Proof came from studies in which these nerves from the gut were cut by delicate microscopic surgery. Now the fly lost its inability to regulate its food intake. When it stepped into a sugary puddle, its proboscis descended and it sucked and sucked until it—literally—burst apart.

ELECTRICALLY TRIGGERED IMAGES

The relation between biological mechanisms and psychological phenomena is not confined to primitive processes of the sort found in blowflies. Some investigators developed a technique of electrically stimulating the brains of human patients who were about to undergo brain surgery. Such operations are generally conducted under local rather than general anesthesia. As a result, the patients are conscious and their reports may guide the neurosurgeon in the course of the operation (Figure 1.3).

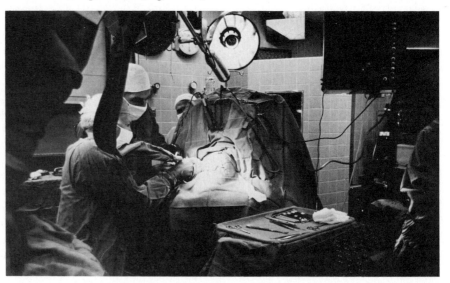

1.3 A brain operation *(Photo by James H. Karales/Peter Arnold Inc.)*

1.4   An ambiguous figure   *(After Bugelski and Alampay, 1961)*

1.5   Perceptual bias   *The ambiguous figure above can be seen either as (A) a rat or (B) a man with glasses. (After Bugelski and Alampay, 1961)*

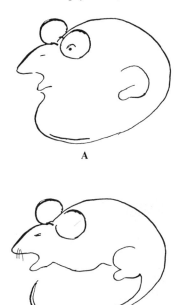

A

B

These procedures have turned up a fascinating fact. When stimulated in a certain portion of the brain, a few of the patients suddenly experienced extraordinarily vivid visual and auditory memory images. One heard a church concert as she had heard it years ago, a flashback so gripping that it seemed almost real, enacted at the tempo of normal life. Another patient reported, "Oh, a familiar memory—in an office somewhere. I could see the desks. I was there and someone was calling to me—a man leaning on his desk with a pencil in his hand" (Penfield and Roberts, 1959; Penfield, 1975).

Just why stimulation of certain brain sites evokes such images is still unknown. Nor is it at all clear that these effects have much to do with remembering as we encounter it in ordinary life. For now, they merely serve as a dramatic illustration of the intimate relation between psychological phenomena and events in the brain.

AMBIGUOUS SIGHTS AND SOUNDS

Many psychological phenomena are much further removed from issues that might be settled by biological or medical investigation. To attack them, one proceeds at the psychological level alone. An example is the effect of the immediately preceding context on what we hear or understand. Some visual patterns are ambiguous; they can be interpreted in two or more different ways. Consider Figure 1.4 which can be seen as either a rat or as the face of an amiable gentleman with glasses. Which do we see? In part it depends on what we have seen just before. If we are first shown a relatively unambiguous rat, the ambiguous picture will be perceived as a rat. If we are first exposed to an unambiguous face, we will see a face (Figure 1.5).

What holds for visual patterns also holds for language. Many utterances are ambiguous. If presented out of context, they can be understood in several different ways. An example is the sentence

The mayor ordered the police to stop drinking.

This sentence may be a command to enforce sobriety among the population at large. It may also be a call to end drunkenness among the police force. Just how it is understood depends on the context. A prior discussion of panhandlers and skid row probably would lead to the first interpretation; a comment about alcoholism among police officers is likely to lead to the second.

CHANGING SEX ROLES

The reactions to ambiguous patterns illustrate the effects of the immediately preceding past upon our interpretation of the present. But behavior is obviously affected by the individual's entire past of which the just preceding recent past is only a small fraction. An example is sex roles. Our biological makeup determines whether we are male or female, but society—which initially exerts its effects through the family—has much to do with how we play the parts of man and woman into which we are cast in infancy. In some cultures, women are the no-nonsense breadwinners, while the men gossip and practice dance steps. In our own society, new attitudes toward sex roles are rapidly transforming work and family life.

As an illustration consider working mothers. During the last ten years almost half of all mothers in the United States who live with their husbands

3

and have children over three have been employed. What effect did this employment have on their children? The clearest answer concerns the daughters, at least in middle-class families. Daughters of working mothers tend to be somewhat more independent, are more oriented toward achievement, and perform better at school than do daughters whose mothers are not employed. In addition, they tend to think more highly of themselves (and indeed of women generally), are more outgoing, and seem somewhat better adjusted socially. These differences suggest that the working mother may well give the child something that it might otherwise lack, especially if the child is a girl—a female model for the development of independence, personal competence, and a feeling of self-esteem (Hoffman, 1979).

PANICKY CROWDS

Phenomena such as sex roles indicate that much of the subject matter of psychology is inherently social. Humans, as well as many animals, are social creatures. To do full justice to their behavior, psychology must study them not just alone but also in their interactions with each other: bees in their swarms, lions in their prides, and humans in their various cultures. When it does this, psychology necessarily overlaps with the various social sciences.

Some phenomena of social interaction involve the behavior of groups. Under some circumstances, people in crowds behave differently from the way they do when alone. An example is panic. When someone shouts "Fire" in a tightly packed auditorium, the resulting stampede may claim many more victims than the fire itself would have. At the turn of the century, a Chicago theater fire claimed over six hundred victims many of whom were smothered or trampled to death by the frantic mass behind them. In the words of a survivor, "The heel prints on the dead faces mutely testified to the cruel fact that human animals stricken by terror are as mad and ruthless as stampeding cattle" (Brown, 1965). The task for psychology is to try to understand why the crowd behaved differently from the way each of its members would have acted alone.

A Science of Many Faces

These illustrations document the enormous range of psychology, whose territory borders on the biological sciences at one end and touches on the social sciences at the other. This broad range makes psychology a field of multiple perspectives, a science of many faces.

To make this point concrete, we will focus upon one psychological phenomenon and show how it can be approached from several different vantage points. This phenomenon is *dreams*. Dreaming is a topic interesting in its own right, but it is also an especially good illustration of how psychology approaches any single phenomenon—not just from one point of view but from several.

Let us start out by describing dreaming as we all experience it. A dream is a kind of nocturnal drama to which the only price of admission is falling asleep. It is usually a series of scenes, sometimes fairly commonplace, sometimes bizarre and disjointed, in which the dreamer often figures as a participant. While this dream play unfolds, it is generally experienced as real. It seems so

Henri Rousseau, **The Sleeping Gypsy**
(Collection, The Museum of Modern Art, New York. Gift of Mrs. Simon Guggenheim)

real in fact, that on waking one sometimes wonders whether the dream events might have happened after all. As a Chinese sage wrote over two thousand years ago, "Once upon a time, I, Chuang-tzu, dreamed I was a butterfly, fluttering hither and thither. . . . Suddenly I was awakened. . . . Now I do not know whether I was a man dreaming I was a butterfly, or whether I am a butterfly now dreaming I am a man" (MacKenzie, 1965).

How can such delicate, transient events ever become a suitable topic for scientific inquiry?

DREAMS AS MENTAL EXPERIENCES

One way of looking at dreams is as conscious, mental experiences. According to an old account which goes back to the Greek philosopher Aristotle, the dream happenings are mental re-evocations of sights and sounds that occurred during the dreamer's waking life. Aristotle believed that the succession of these dream images from the past is experienced as real while it occurs because during sleep there is no competition from the clamor of waking reality and because the intellect is "dulled" during sleep (Aristotle, ca. 330 B.C.).

Later investigators tried to relate what people dream about to what happens to them both before and during sleep. One question concerns the effect of recent waking experiences. Aristotle was apparently correct in his belief that such recent events often re-emerge in dreams. This is especially so when the recent waking experience was highly emotional. For example, soldiers who have just gone through intense battle stress may relive their combat terrors in nightmare dreams (Pai, 1946).

Some writers have suggested that the dream images from the past are supplemented by external events that impinge upon the sleeper in the present. A widely cited example is the alarm clock which is often said to turn into a peal of church bells or a fire engine in the dream.

To test this hypothesis, several investigators have studied the effects of applying various forms of external stimulation during sleep. Numerous sleepers have been shaken, tickled, splashed with water, and shouted at—all to discover whether they would later report a dream that referred to these expe-

A

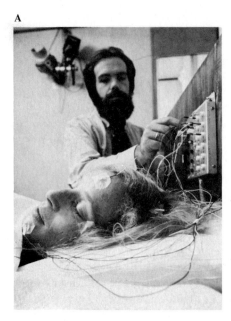

B

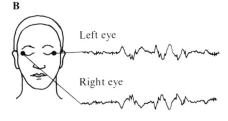

Left eye

Right eye

1.6 Quiet and active sleep (A) Subject
in a sleep laboratory with electrodes re-
cording pulse, respiration, brain waves,
and eye movements. (Photograph by
Chris Springmann, Black Star) (B) Re-
cord of eye movements picked up by
electrodes at the side of each eye. The
record shows the eye-movement pattern
during active sleep, the period when
sleepers dream. Both eyes move rapidly
and in synchrony. (After Dement, 1974)

riences. Sometimes they did. An example is a dream reported on awakening
after an experimenter shouted "Help" into the sleeper's ears: "I was driving
along the highway at home. Heard yelling and we stopped. A car was turned
sideways in the road. I went down and saw the car was turned over on the side
of the road. . . . There was a woman badly cut. We took her to the hospital"
(Hall, 1966, p. 6). It is hard to resist the conclusion that, at some level, the
dreamer heard and understood the shout "Help" even while asleep and then
incorporated it within his dream narrative.

DREAMS AS BEHAVIOR

Dreams as conscious, mental experiences are essentially private; they go on
"inside" the individual. As such, dreams can be regarded as a form of behavior that is looked at from within, as if the actor were observing his own actions.
Yet psychologists study most aspects of behavior from "outside," for much of
what we do is directly apparent and overt and can therefore easily be seen by
others. Humans and animals act. They run and fly and scurry about; they eat
and fight and mate; they often perform new acts to attain their ends.

OVERT BEHAVIOR

Can we study dreaming by taking this action-oriented view from the outside? On the face of it, the prospects don't seem too bright, for during sleep the
body is by and large immobile. Even so, there is a way. For there is one thing
which the sleeper does while dreaming that is overt and can be observed from
the outside: He moves his eyes.

This fact emerged after it became clear that there are two kinds of sleep:
quiet sleep and active sleep. During quiet sleep, both breathing and heart rate
are slow and regular while the eyes are motionless. But during active sleep the
pattern is different. Breathing and heart rate accelerate, and—most characteristic of all—the eyes move back and forth behind closed eyelids in quick
irregular darts. Periods of quiet and of active sleep (often called REM sleep
because of the rapid eye movements) alternate throughout the night, with a
total of perhaps ninety minutes devoted to REM (Figure 1.6).

The crucial fact about REM sleep is that this is the period during which
dreams occur. When subjects—the persons whose behavior is being studied—
are aroused during REM sleep, about 85 percent of the awakenings lead to
reports of a vivid dream. In contrast, subjects awakened from non-REM sleep
recall dreams much less often (Dement, 1974).

There is little doubt that the rapid eye movements go along with dreaming.
But some investigators take a further step. They suggest that these movements
provide a clue to what the sleeper is dreaming of. In their view, the eye
movements indicate that the sleeper is "looking at" whatever he sees in his
dream world. Some evidence for this intriguing (though quite controversial)
hypothesis comes from studies which show that the direction of the eye
movements observed during a given REM period is appropriate to what the
subject recalls having seen while dreaming. For example, when the predominant direction of eye movements was up and down, one subject dreamed that
he had thrown basketballs, looking up at the net and shooting, then looking
down to pick another ball off the floor. In contrast, another REM period in
which the eye movements were mostly from side to side, produced a dream in

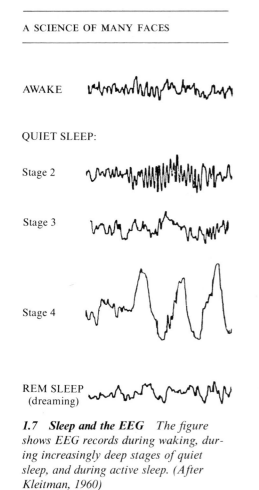

AWAKE

QUIET SLEEP:

Stage 2

Stage 3

Stage 4

REM SLEEP
(dreaming)

1.7 Sleep and the EEG *The figure shows EEG records during waking, during increasingly deep stages of quiet sleep, and during active sleep. (After Kleitman, 1960)*

which the subject watched two people throwing tomatoes at each other (Dement and Kleitman, 1957).

BIOLOGICAL UNDERPINNINGS OF BEHAVIOR

Evidence based on eye movements is one clue to the nature of dreaming. Another clue concerns its biological basis. Most psychologists take it for granted that whatever we do or think has some physical basis in the activity of our brains. Some promising first steps in this direction pertain to dreams. These came after the development of a number of methods for monitoring what people do when they are fast asleep. An important tool is the electroencephalogram, or EEG, which measures the overall activity of the sleeper's brain. The EEG traces the quick fluctuations of electrical activity over time, whose graphic record is sometimes called brain waves. Happily for sleep investigators, it soon proved possible to attach the multitude of required electrodes to the subjects without disturbing their sleep (Figure 1.7).

The results showed that the EEG patterns of sleep and waking differ markedly. As the subject falls into deeper and deeper stages of sleep, the brain waves become slow, large, and rather regular, indicating a lower level of brain activity. But this only holds for periods of quiet sleep. As this is interrupted by active (that is REM) sleep, the EEG becomes quite similar to that found when the subject is awake. This makes good sense, for it suggests that during REM sleep the brain is reasonably aroused and active—as well it should be since this is the time when we are busily engaged in dreaming.

DREAMS AS COGNITION

Like many other psychological phenomena, dreams reflect what we know, or have experienced, or have thought about, activities which psychologists call cognition. To be sure, the dream happenings didn't really take place. We didn't really fly through the air or have tea with Queen Elizabeth. But the components of the dream were surely drawn from the dreamer's own knowledge which contains information about flying and Queen Elizabeth. How was this knowledge retrieved and woven into the dream story? How was the dream recalled on later awakening? And, most relevant of all, why is it that we are so sure that we didn't really have tea with the queen, that our dreams are not a piece of waking reality?

Some psychologists approach such questions by studying the cognitive development of children. They ask how young children acquire certain basic intellectual operations—to count, to understand that events have causes, and so on. In the case of dreams, the question is how children come to distinguish between two realms of phenomena, those we call subjective (thoughts, beliefs, feelings, and of course dreams) and those we call objective (the world of things "out there"). To ask how this distinction is made is another way of asking how we attain our adult notion of objective reality, how we come to know that the tree in the garden—unlike a dream—will still be there after we blink our eyes.

This distinction is by no means clear in early childhood. Thus young children initially have great trouble in distinguishing dreams from waking life. A three-year old awakes and tells her parents how much she loved the elephants at the circus yesterday. The parents correct her; she had not been at the circus yesterday. But the child indignantly sticks to her story and appeals to her

7

That very night in Max's room a forest grew

and grew—

The distinction between dreams and waking reality is not always clear in childhood *(From Sendak, 1963)*

brother for corroboration for "he was there too." When her brother shakes his head in denial, she begins to cry, angrily insisting that she told the truth. Eventually she learns that there is a whole group of experiences that older people call "just dreams," no matter how real they seem to her (Levy, J., 1979).

The fact that the child finally recognizes the circus elephants—and the nightmare robbers and witches—as dreams does not mean that it has acquired an adult conception of what dreams are. Young children tend to think of them as physical objects. When asked whether dreams can be tall, a four-year old replied, "*Yeah.* How tall? *Big, big, big* (spreads arms). Where are dreams? *In your bedroom.* In the day time? *No, they're outside.* . . . What are they like. *They're made of rock.* Could they be heavy? *Yeah; and they can't break either*" (Keil, 1979, pp. 109–10).

It's quite a while before children think of dreams the way adults do. By six or seven, they believe that dreams are sent through the air, perhaps by the wind or by pigeons. Eventually of course they recognize that, as one eleven-year old put it, "You dream *with the head* and the dream is *in the head*" (Piaget, 1972).

This realization that dreams are subjective events is no mean achievement. As we will see later, it is not limited to dreams, but extends to many other conceptual attainments about the basic nature of the physical and psychological universe.

DREAMS AND SOCIAL BEHAVIOR

Human life is rarely solitary but is spent among a world of others—strangers and friends, partners and rivals, potential and actual mates. What holds for waking existence, holds for dreams as well. Most of them involve interaction with others. Some feature themes of aggression, such as competition, attack, and submission. Others concern friendship and sometimes sex. But whatever the plot, the cast usually includes some others. More than 95 percent of our dreams are peopled with others and most revolve around our relations with them (Hall and Van de Castle, 1966).

DREAMS AND THE CULTURE

Dreams concern major themes in the person's own life, but they take place within a larger framework, the dreamer's own culture. In our own society, a common dream is of appearing naked among strangers and being embarrassed. But such a dream would be unlikely among Australian aborigines who wear no clothing. Nor are many urban Americans likely to have nightmares in which they are chased by cows, which happens to be a common dream in western Ghana (Barnouw, 1963).

The culture affects not only what the dream is about but also how the dreamer thinks about it when she recalls it later on. In some societies, including our own, dreams are generally dismissed as nonsensical fancies, irrelevant to real life. Many preliterate cultures have a different view (Figure 1.8). Some regard dreams as supernatural visions and behave accordingly. Others take dreams very seriously even though they think of them as naturally occurring events. The Senoi, a tribe in Malaya, act as if they had all taken several courses in psychoanalysis. They believe that dreams indicate something about their inner lives and can provide clues for heading off problems before they become serious. Every morning Senoi children tell their father what they had dreamed about the night before. The father then helps the children interpret their dreams. These may reveal some incipient conflict with others, as in a dream of being attacked by a friend. If so, the father may advise the child on how to correct matters, for example, by making his friend a present (Stewart, 1951).

DREAMS AND INTERNAL CONFLICT

The social aspect of dreaming lies at the heart of a famous (and controversial) theory of dreams proposed by Sigmund Freud. According to Freud, dreams are the product of an elaborate clash between two contending forces—the unconscious primitive urges of our biological heritage and the civilizing constraints imposed by society. In dreams we sometimes see one, sometimes the other side of the battle. Various forbidden impulses—mostly sex and aggression—emerge, but they are soon opposed by the thou-shalt-nots of our early upbringing. The result is a compromise. The forbidden material breaks through but only in a stealthy, censored masquerade. This disguise explains why dreams are so often odd and senseless. Their senselessness is only on the surface, a cunning mask that lets us indulge in the unacceptable wish without realizing that it is unacceptable (Freud, 1900).

According to Freud, some distortions involve various transformations of the unacceptable themes. One is symbolism. For example, he believed that sexual urges often emerge in symbolic guises. Thus in his view, dreams of riding horses or walking up a staircase often mask erotic wishes. Here the symbols presumably bear some resemblance to that which they symbolize. The rhythmic movements of rising and falling in the saddle are similar to those of sexual intercourse, while ascending a staircase may be reminiscent of the way in which sexual passion mounts to a peak (Figure 1.9).

1.8   Iroquois cornhusk mask for dream ceremony   *The Iroquois Indians regarded dreams as an important means for revealing hidden desires and held formal dream-remembering ceremonies during which special masks were worn. (Courtesy the American Museum of Natural History)*

1.9   Symbolism in dreams   *A film about Freud's early career includes a dream sequence in which he enters a deep tunnel that eventually leads him to a cavern where his mother sits, smiling, on a Cleopatra-like throne. The dream is a compact symbolic expression of how Freud saw himself: an explorer of subterranean unconscious motives who uncovered the hidden childhood lusts of all men and women. (From John Huston's 1963 film,* Freud, *with Montgomery Clift. Courtesy The Museum of Modern Art/Film Stills Archive)*

Freud argued that these and many other symbolic transformations are the dreamer's way of smuggling the forbidden wish past the inner censor's eye. He believed that such defenses refer back to early childhood when the parents set up the various prohibitions that still haunt the adult in the present. Seen in this light, dreams reflect important social processes that pertain to the past, to the way in which the major social commandments were instilled in each of us by society's first agents, our parents.

DREAMS AND INDIVIDUAL DIFFERENCES

There is a further aspect of dreams: they are a reflection of the fact that people are different. People vary in what they characteristically do and think and feel. And some of these differences between people are reflected in their dreams. Some simply pertain to the differing circumstances in the dreamers' lives. This point was made some two thousand years ago by the Roman poet Lucretius who noted that at night lawyers plead their cases, generals fight their battles, and sailors wage their war with the winds (Woods, 1947).

More interesting are differences that reveal something about the personalities of the dreamers. An example is a comparison between the dreams of normal people and of patients with a diagnosis of schizophrenia, a condition generally regarded as the most serious psychiatric disorder in our time. The differences between the two groups was enormous. The schizophrenics reported dreams which were highly bizarre and often morbid. The dreamer is eaten alive by an alligator; there are nuclear wars and world cataclysms. Themes of bodily mutilation were fairly common, as in a dream in which a woman killed her husband and then stuffed parts of his body into a camel's head. In contrast, the normals' dreams were comparatively mild and ordinary (Figure 1.10). This result fits in with what we know about schizophrenia.

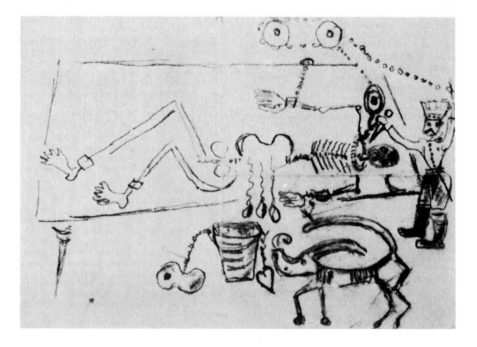

1.10 A schizophrenic's daytime fantasies *This picture was drawn by a forty-year-old male schizophrenic and depicts various elaborate fantasies of bodily torture and bizarre details. Such preoccupations are not uncommon in patients with this diagnosis. Given this pattern of daytime fantasy, the fact that the dreams of schizophrenics are more bizarre and morbid than those of normals is not too surprising. (From Lehmann, 1975)*

Wilhelm Wundt (1832–1920) *(Courtesy Historical Pictures Service, Inc.)*

William James (1842–1910) *(Courtesy The Warder Collection)*

Schizophrenics often jump from one idea to the other without maintaining a firm line of thought. As a result, their behavior often appears bizarre. It seems that their extremely bizarre and morbid dreams are simply an exaggeration of a condition already present in their waking life (Carrington, 1972).

The Task of Psychology

We have seen that dreams can be looked at as conscious, mental experiences, as overt behaviors, as reflections of underlying psychological events, as aspects of cognition, as indications of social patterns, and as expressions of the dreamer's individuality. What holds for dreams holds for most other psychological phenomena: They can all be viewed from several perspectives. Each perspective is valid but none is complete without the others. For psychology is a field of many faces and to see it fully, we must see them all.

Given the many-faceted character of psychology, it is not surprising that those who have contributed to it came from many quarters. Some had the proper title of psychologist with appropriate university appointments in that discipline, including two of its founding fathers, Wilhelm Wundt of Germany and William James of the United States. But psychology was not built by psychologists alone. Far from it. Among its architects are philosophers, beginning with Plato and Aristotle and continuing to our own time. Physicists and physiologists played important roles and still do. Physicians contributed greatly, as did specialists in many other disciplines, including anthropology, and more recently, linguistics and computer science. Psychology, the field of many faces, is by its very nature a field of many origins.

In presenting the subject matter of psychology as it is today, we must try to do justice to this many-sidedness. In an attempt to achieve that, this book has been organized around four topics which emphasize somewhat different perspectives on the field as a whole. These four mirror the different ways in which we have just looked at dreams: action, cognition, social behavior, and individual differences.

GENERAL PRINCIPLES AND UNIQUE INDIVIDUALS

Before starting, a word about a widespread misunderstanding. Psychology is sometimes popularly regarded as a field that concentrates on the secret inner lives of individual persons—why Mary hates her mother and why George is so shy with girls. But questions of this sort are really not psychology's main concern. To be sure, there is an applied branch of psychology that deals with various adjustment problems, but it is only a special part of the field. The primary questions psychology asks are of a more general sort. Its purpose is not to describe the distinctive characteristics of a particular individual. Its main goal is to get at the facts that are general for all of humankind.

The reason is simple. Psychology is a science and, like all other sciences, it looks for general principles—underlying uniformities that different events have in common. A single event as such means little; what counts is what any one event—or object or person—shares with others. Ultimately of course, psychology—again, like all other sciences—hopes to find a route back to under-

11

stand the individual event. It tries to discover, say, some general principles of adolescent conflict or parent-child relations to explain why George is so shy and why Mary is so bitter about her mother. Once such explanations are found, they may lead to practical applications: to help counsel and guide, and perhaps to effect desirable changes. But, at least initially, the science's main concern is with the discovery of the general principles.

Is there any field of endeavor whose primary interest is in individual persons, with the unique George and Mary who are like no other persons that ever lived or ever will live? One such field is literature. The great novelists and playwrights have given us portraits of living, breathing individuals who exist in a particular time and place. There is nothing abstract and general about the agonies of a Hamlet or the murderous ambition of a Macbeth. These are concrete, particular individuals, with special loves and fears that are peculiarly theirs. But from these particulars, Shakespeare gives us a glimpse of what is common to all humanity, what Hamlet and Macbeth share with all of us. Both science and art have something to say about human nature, but they go about it from different directions. Science tries to discover general principles and then applies them to the individual case. Art focuses on the particular instance and then uses this to illuminate what is universal in us all.

Science and art are complementary. To gain insight into our own nature we need both. Consider Hamlet's description:

> What a piece of work is a man, how noble in reason, how infinite in faculties; in form and moving how express and admirable, in action like an angel, In apprehension like a god: the beauty of the world, the paragon of animals! (*Hamlet,* Act II, scene ii).

To understand and appreciate this "piece of work" is a task too huge for any one field of human endeavor, whether art, philosophy, or science. What we will try to do here is to sketch psychology's own attempts toward this end, to show what we have come to know and how we have come to know it. And perhaps even more important, how much we have not learned as yet.

We will begin with the topic of action. Our first question is what makes humans and animals move.

PART I

Action

The study of mind has many aspects. We may ask what human beings know, we may ask what they want, and we may ask what they do. Much of psychology is an attempt to answer the last question: What is it that humans do and why do they do it? In this section we will deal with the approach to mind that grows out of an interest in what all animals do, an approach that emphasizes behavior as the basic subject matter of psychology. We will focus on the particular version of this approach that is based on the notion that mind can be understood as a reflex machine. We shall see how the reflex notion has led to impressive achievements in our understanding of the structure and function of the nervous system, and how this notion has been modified to encompass the phenomena of motivation and of learning in animals and humans.

CHAPTER 2

Biological Bases of Behavior

The ancients, no less than we, wondered why men and beasts behave as they do. What is it that leads to animal movement, impels the crab to crawl, the tiger to spring? Prescientific man could only answer *animistically:* There is some inner spirit in the creature that impels it to move, each creature in its own fashion. Today we know that any question about bodily movement must inevitably call for some reference to the nervous system; for to us it is quite clear that the nervous system is the apparatus which most directly determines and organizes an organism's reactions to the world in which it lives. We will soon ask many detailed questions about the structure of this apparatus and the way it functions. But we begin with a more general question. Broadly speaking, what must such a system accomplish?

The Organism as Machine

This question was first raised seriously by the French philosopher René Descartes (1596–1650), and his answer provides the broad outline within which we think about such matters even now. Descartes lived in a period that saw the beginning of the science of mechanics. Kepler and Galileo were beginning to develop ideas about the movements of the heavenly bodies which some thirty years later led to Newton's *Principia.* Radically new views of man and his universe were being put forth. There were laws of nature that determined the fall of stones and the motions of planets: rigid, precise, and immutable. The universe was run by a system of pushes and pulls originally set in motion by God, the Great Watchmaker. At a more lowly level, these natural laws were

René Descartes *(Courtesy National Library of Medicine)*

15

mirrored in the workings of ingenious mechanical contrivances that were all the rage in the wealthy homes of Europe: clocks with cuckoos that would call the hour, water-driven gargoyles with nodding heads, statues in the king's garden that would bow to the visitor who stepped on a hidden spring. The action of a lever, the release of a spring—these could explain the operation of such devices. Could human thought and action be explained in similar mechanical terms?

DESCARTES AND THE REFLEX CONCEPT

To Descartes all action, whether human or animal, was essentially a response to some event in the outside world. His human machine would work as follows. Something from the outside excites one of the senses. This in turn excites a nerve which transmits the excitation upward to the brain, which then relays the excitation downward to a muscle. The excitation from the senses thus eventually leads to a contraction of a muscle and thereby to a reaction to the external event which started the whole sequence. In effect, the energy from the outside is *reflected* back by the nervous system to the animal's muscles—the term **reflex** finds its origin in this conception (Figure 2.1).

Of course, Descartes' neurology was necessarily limited by the anatomical knowledge of the time. For example, he thought that the nerves conducted excitation hydraulically. He accepted the then-prevailing view that the nerves are hollow containers of "animal spirits" that are agitated by external action, and that the nerves transmit this agitation as pipes transmit water. His specific conception of the mechanism was primitive, but the overall view is certainly not. The Cartesian conception of the reflex is still with us, as is the conception of behavior as a mechanical reaction to physical energies impinging from outside.

Conceived thus, human doings could be regarded as the doings of a machine. But there was a problem. The same external event produces one reaction today and another tomorrow. The sight of food leads to reaching movements, but only when we are hungry. In short, the excitation from one of the senses will excite a nerve leading to one muscle on one occasion, but on another occasion it will excite a different nerve that may innervate an entirely different muscle. This means that Descartes' hydraulic piping system must have a central switching system, supervised by some operator who sits in the middle to decide what incoming pipe to connect with which pipe leading to the outside.

To describe these behavioral options mechanically was very difficult. Descartes was deeply religious and he was extremely concerned over the theological implications of his argument should he bring it to its ultimate conclusion. In addition he was prudent—Galileo had difficulties with the Inquisition because his scientific beliefs threatened the doctrines of the Church. So Descartes proposed that human mental processes were only semiautomatic. To handle the switching function—the behavior options under varying circumstances—he provided a soul which would affect the choice of possible nervous pathways through the **conarium** (literally, "the seat of the will"). A specific anatomical structure, the **pineal body,** was assumed to carry this function. The pineal body was chosen as the residence of the soul, or more pre-

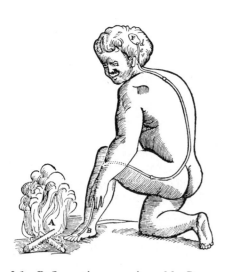

2.1 Reflex action as envisaged by Descartes *In this sketch by Descartes, the heat from the fire, A, starts a chain of processes that begins at the affected spot of the skin, B, and continues up the nerve tube until a pore of a cavity, F, is opened. Descartes believed that this opening allowed the animal spirits in the cavity to enter the nerve tube and eventually travel to the muscles which pull the foot from the fire. While the figure shows that Descartes anticipated the basic idea of reflex action, it also indicates that he did not realize the anatomical distinction between sensory and motor nerves. (From Descartes, 1662)*

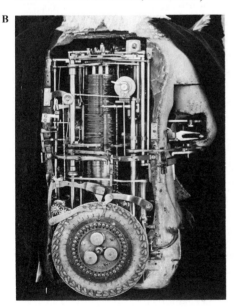

2.2 Automata in the eighteenth century *(A) A mechanical "scrivener" who could dip a pen into an inkwell and write a number of words. (B) The scrivener's mechanical insides. (Courtesy Musée d'Art et d'Histoire, Neuchâtel)*

cisely as the specific point where the soul and the body interact, because of its strategic location in the center of the brain.

Descartes shrank from taking the last step in his own argument, the reduction of human beings to the status of machines. Animals might be machines, but by virtue of the conarium, humans were more than mere robots. Later thinkers went further. They felt that the laws of the physical universe could ultimately explain all action, whether human or animal, so that a scientific account required no further "ghost in the machine"—that is, no reference to the soul. This position was vehemently defended by one of Descartes' own followers, Julian Offray de La Mettrie (1709–51), less than a century after Descartes' death (La Mettrie, 1748). La Mettrie's *L'homme machine* ruthlessly extended Descartes' logic to human beings, arguing that humans differ from animals only in being more finely constructed mechanisms (Figure 2.2).

THE BASIC NERVOUS FUNCTIONS: RECEPTION, INTEGRATION, REACTION

Psychologists today agree with Descartes that much of behavior can be understood as reactions to outside events: The environment poses a question and the organism answers it. This approach, like Descartes', must lead to a tripartite classification of nervous functions: *reception* through the senses, *reaction* from the muscles and glands, and a *conduction* and *integration* system that mediates between these two functions.

THE ACTION SEQUENCE

The chain of events that leads to action typically begins outside of the organism. A particular physical energy impinges upon some part of the organism sensitive to it. This event we call a *stimulus,* (a term that derives from the name of a wooden implement with a nail at one end used by Roman farmers some two thousand years ago to goad their sluggish oxen). The stimulus excites *receptors,* specialized structures capable of translating some physical energy into a nervous impulse. Once a receptor is stimulated, the excitation is conducted farther into the nervous system. Bundles of nerve fibers that conduct excitation toward the brain or spinal cord are called *afferent nerves* (from the Latin, *affere,* "to bring to"). These fibers transmit their message still farther; in the simplest case, to other fibers that go directly to the *effectors,* the muscles and glands that are the organs of action. Nerve fibers that lead to the effectors are called *efferent nerves* (from the Latin, *effere,* "to bring forth").

The transmission path from receptors to effectors is usually more circuitous than this, however. The afferent fibers often bring their messages to intermediate nerve cells, or *interneurons,* in the brain or spinal cord. These interneurons may transmit the message to the efferent nerve cells or send it on to yet other interneurons. Typically, very many central nerve cells have been "consulted" before the command to action is finally issued and sent down the path of the efferent nerve fibers.

FROM AMOEBA TO VERTEBRATE

The analysis of an action sequence into the three components of *reception, transmission-integration,* and *reaction* is quite useful even in animals that lack

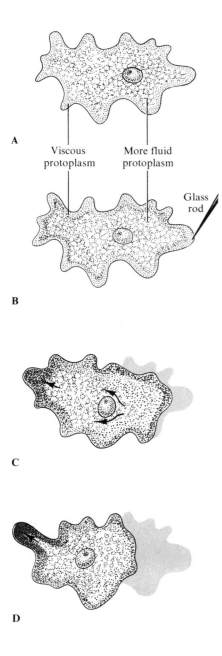

A

Viscous   More fluid
protoplasm   protoplasm

Glass
rod

B

C

D

anatomical structures that are specialized for these three functions. Take the case of an amoeba, an exceedingly unspecialized, unicellular creature, whose one cell is forced to be a jack of all biological trades. An amoeba moves by changes in the nature of the protoplasm of which it is composed (Figure 2.3). A weak stimulus, such as a mild touch, causes the protoplasm in the region of the stimulation to become more fluid, mechanically creating a bulge in the outer wall, a pseudopod. If stimulation persists, fluid protoplasm from elsewhere will flow into the pseudopod; the resulting enlargement of the pseudopod has the mechanical effect of moving the amoeba toward the stimulus. The exact opposite occurs if the stimulus is very strong. When the forward end of an advancing amoeba is prodded by a glass rod, the protoplasm nearby becomes more viscous (reception). As a result, the forward flow of protoplasm within the cell is first stopped and then reversed (transmission-integration). As the flow reverses, pseudopodia are formed on the opposite side; the formerly hindmost region becomes the foremost, and the amoeba oozes away from the offending stimulus (reaction).

As we go up the evolutionary ladder we find ever-increasing specialization of these functions. In vertebrates, well-developed musculatures operate the various levers of the skeletal mechanism; intricate sense organs give precise information about the external world; and, most advanced of all, a nervous system made up of billions of cells not only transmits but also integrates the messages that come to it from the outside. Although exceedingly more complex, the essential function of the total reacting system of more advanced organisms can still be analyzed along the same tripartite plan appropriate to more primitive organisms: reception, transmission-integration, and reaction.

We now turn to a more detailed discussion of the nervous system. We will deal with progressively larger units of analysis, first discussing the smallest functional and structural units of nervous activity (the nerve impulse and the nerve cell), then the interaction among different nerve cells (the synapse), and, finally, the functional plan of the major gross structures of the nervous system.

Nerve Cell and Nerve Impulse

Neuroscientists know that the basic building block of the nervous system is the nerve cell or **neuron,** and that the basic unit of nervous function is the **nerve impulse,** the firing of an individual neuron. This impulse is today considered in

2.3 Reaction of the amoeba to strong external stimulation *Under normal conditions, the cellular liquid within the amoeba is composed of an outer, viscuous portion and an inner, more freely flowing one. This is shown schematically in Part (A) of the figure. When a strong external stimulus, such as a vigorous prod from a glass rod, is applied to one part of the amoeba, the protoplasm in that region and those nearby becomes more viscuous, as shown in Part (B). The viscuous mass in the affected area exerts pressure on the more fluid material in the center and squeezes it in the opposite direction. As a result, the protoplasm in the center begins to flow away from the stimulus. When it reaches the opposite side of the cell, it becomes more viscuous again and exerts a push against the cell wall there. This leads to the formation of a pseudopod, a temporary organ of locomotion, shown in Part (C). In Part (D) the pseudopod is fully formed and the amoeba is well on its way from the offending stimulus (Buchsbaum, 1948; Keeton, 1980).*

physical and chemical terms. But this conception was not attained for centuries. Animistic conceptions of nerve function were not easily abandoned and the ghost in the machine was not exorcised until the nineteenth century.

FROM ANIMAL SPIRITS TO NERVE IMPULSE

It was known even in ancient times that bodily motion depends upon the muscles. But what makes the muscles move? The Greeks proposed an immaterial soul *(anima)* that "animated" the body but was made of different stuff. By 100 A.D. it was clear enough that the whitish threads called nerve fibers were somehow critical. The Roman physician Galen proposed that the critical agent was a gaseous substance, the **animal spirits,** distilled from the blood in the brain and transmitted through the nerves to the muscles.

Galen's views were frozen into a medical dogma which prevailed until the seventeenth century. This doctrine was accepted even by Descartes, although evidence against it was gradually being accumulated. The most convincing argument was raised finally by the Dutch naturalist Jan Swammerdam (1637–80), who excised a frog's leg muscle together with a piece of the nerve connected to it. He found that if the nerve is pinched or irritated, the muscle will contract. Swammerdam then asked whether the muscle increases in volume while contracting. After all, if contraction is caused by animal spirits that enter the muscle, there should be an increase of volume; the muscle should expand as does a balloon when inflated by air. But nothing of the kind took place (Figure 2.4). Given this finding, the concept of animal spirits became difficult to entertain.

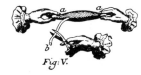

2.4 Swammerdam's nerve-muscle preparation *The sketch is taken from Swammerdam's original account in 1737. (From Fearing, 1930)*

THE SPEED OF THE IMPULSE

Animal spirits were rejected, but what was to take their place? No one could deny that muscular contraction depended on transmission of an impulse via the nerves—no matter how strong the stimulus, a muscle whose nerves were cut would not contract But if no "substance" was transmitted through these nerves, how then did they carry their message to the muscles? For nearly two more centuries physiologists proposed new variants of the old idea that the transmission was accomplished by some "subtle fluid" with special properties. Part of the problem arose from the mistaken belief that the nerve impulse moves at a speed so fast as to be immeasurable. This view was logically acceptable since mental processes were thought to occur on a different plane from those of the physical world. After all, what is faster than a thought? But in actual fact this argument proved to be false.

The critical experiment which showed that the speed of the nerve impulse is finite was performed in 1850 by the German scientist Hermann von Helmholtz. Contrary to then-prevailing speculations, the velocity of the impulse turned out to be remarkably slow. It was nowhere near the order of the speed of light; it was actually slower than the speed of sound waves—in humans, a mere 50 to 100 meters per second. Enormous mystery still surrounded the process that caused the nervous impulse, but von Helmholtz had at least shown that nerve transmission takes some measurable time to occur and thus does not have to be conceived in spiritual, nonsubstantial terms (Figure 2.5).

2.5 Measuring the velocity of the nerve impulse *This is a schematized account of Helmholtz' procedure. A nerve-muscle preparation is set up so that, when the muscle contracts, it pulls a pen upward. This leaves a mark on a recording drum. On one occasion, the nerve is stimulated at point A. On another occasion, the nerve is stimulated at point B which is d centimeters farther from the muscle than is point A. Helmholtz showed that when the nerve is stimulated at the more distant point B, the muscle will twitch later than if the stimulus is applied at point A. By measuring the actual time difference, T, he was able to calculate the impulse velocity. This velocity is obtained by dividing d (the distance between A and B) by T (the extra time it takes for the muscle to twitch if the nerve is stimulated at B rather than at A).*

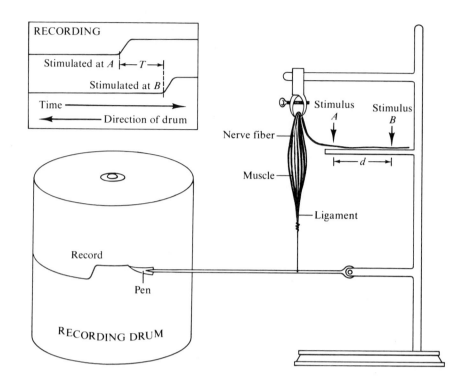

REACTION TIME

Related findings came from a surprising source—the astronomer's observatory. Until the middle of the nineteenth century, precise calibrations of clocks depended upon the observation of a stellar transit, that is, the exact moment when a star was seen to cross over a thin line built into the field of view of the telescope. But what was this exact moment? The astronomers found that a time interval, quite short but still noticeable (usually of the order of fractions of a second) occurred between the observation of the transit and the depression of some response key by the observer. This interval between the presentation of a signal and the observer's response to it is now called ***reaction time.*** In part, this time interval is simply another reflection of the finite velocity of the nervous impulse. We are all certainly familiar with reaction time in ordinary life. An obvious example is provided by the driver who brakes his car as he suddenly sees a child dart out on to the road. Here the modern automobile can give tragic proof that the driver's reaction is not instantaneous. In fact, a driver's minimum reaction time to visual stimulation is about .2 seconds, and a car traveling at 60 miles per hour will move at least 18 feet before the driver even starts to apply the brakes.

HOW A NEURON FIRES

Von Helmholtz had shown that the speed of the nerve impulse was measurable. But what was its nature? We must take a brief detour into anatomy to consider the microscopic structure in which this impulse occurs—the neuron.

THE NEURON

The **neuron** is the simplest element of nervous action. It is a single cell with three important subdivisions: the **dendrites,** the **cell body,** and the **axon.** The dendrites are usually branched, sometimes enormously so. The axon often extends for a very long distance; at its end it may fork out into several **collaterals.** Impulses from other cells are received by the dendrites; the axon transmits the impulse to yet other cells or to effector organs such as muscles and glands. Thus the dendrites are the receptive units of the neuron, while the axon endings may be regarded as its effector apparatus (Figure 2.6).

The gap between the axon terminals of one neuron and the dendrites of another is called the **synapse;** this is the gap the nerve impulse must cross for one neuron to stimulate the next. Such junctions often involve more than two cells. Especially in the brain, the dendrites of any one cell may receive impulses from axons of many different cells, while the axon endings of a particular cell may contact dendrites of many different neurons.

TYPES OF NEURONS

Different kinds of neurons are specialized for different tasks. We will mention only a few of the varieties. Some neurons are attached to, or are extensions of, **receptor cells** that can respond to various external energies, such as pressure, chemical changes, light, and so on. These cells can translate (more technically, **transduce**) such physical stimuli into a nervous impulse which they can then transmit to other neurons. Receptor cells are like money changers, exchanging the various energies impinging from the outer world into the only currency acceptable within the nervous system—the neural impulse.

A

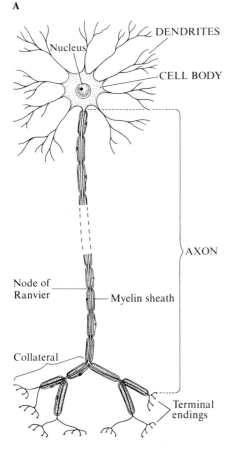

2.6 Neurons *(A) A schematic diagram of the main parts of a "typical" neuron. Part of the cell is myelinated; that is, its axon is covered with a segmented, insulating sheath. (After Katz, 1952) (B) Several neurons with dendrites in a mouse brain, magnified about 400 times. (Courtesy Manfred Kage—Peter Arnold, Inc.)*

B

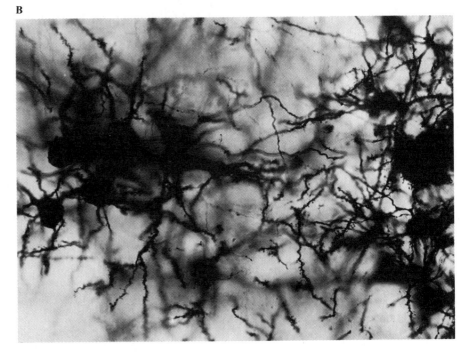

21

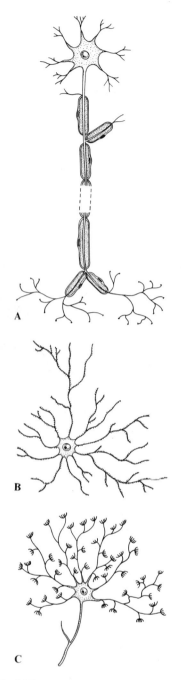

Neurons that convey impulses from receptors toward the rest of the nervous system are called **sensory neurons.** Sometimes the receptor is a specialized part of the sensory neuron; an example is the neurons that are responsible for sensing pressure on the skin. But in many cases, transduction and transmission are separate functions that are entrusted to different cells. In vision and hearing there are receptor cells which transduce optic stimulation and air pressures into electrical changes in the cell. These changes in the receptors trigger impulses in sensory neurons that then transmit their information to other neurons in the nervous system.

Other neurons have axons that terminate in effector cells. An important example is the **motoneurons** which activate the **skeletal musculature,** the muscles which control the skeleton such as those of the arms and legs. The cell bodies of the motoneurons are in the spinal cord, and their long axons have terminal branches whose final tips contact individual muscle cells. When a motoneuron fires, a chemical event is produced at its axon tips which causes the muscle fibers to contract. Sensory neurons and motoneurons handle the beginning and end of the action cycle—reception and reaction.

In complex organisms, the vast majority of neurons are **interneurons** whose functional position is between sensory neurons and motoneurons. Interneurons come in many shapes and forms; they usually show considerable branching, often of both dendrites and axons, producing an enormous number of synaptic contacts (Figure 2.7).

A few details about neurons will give a feeling for their size and number. The diameter of an individual neuron is very small; cell bodies vary from 5 to about 100 microns in diameter (1 micron = 1/1,000 millimeter). Dendrites are typically short, say, a few hundred microns. Axons can be very long; some extend from the head to the base of the spinal cord, others from the spinal cord to the fingers and toes. To get a sense of the relative physical proportions of the cell body to the axon in a motoneuron, visualize a basketball attached to a garden hose that stretches the whole fourteen-mile length of Manhattan Island. The total number of neurons in the human brain is about 10 billion. While this number seems prodigious, it is somewhat sobering to realize that there is no way of getting more; a neuron, once lost, can never be replaced.

2.7 Different kinds of neurons in the human nervous system *(A) A motor neuron of the spinal cord. (B) A short interneuron with a large number of axon branches which hook up many neurons with each other. (C) A bushy interneuron with many dendrites that collect impulses from many different cells and then convey their output through one single axon. (After Morgan, 1965)*

THE ELECTRICAL ACTIVITY OF THE NEURON

The description of the electrical events that occur when a neuron fires required several advances in scientific instrumentation. One of these was the development of ever-finer **microelectrodes,** some of which have tips tapered to a diameter of 1 micron. Such electrodes can pick up currents from within a neuron without squashing the cell they are supposed to study. Equally important was the development of the **oscilloscope,** a galvanometer whose electrical response is amplified by vacuum tubes which send forth a stream of electrons that are swept across a fluorescent screen, leaving a glowing line in their wake. The pattern on the screen indicates what happened electrically during the entire (very brief) interval of the cell's activity. The final contribution was made by evolution, which provided the squid, an animal whose axons have giant diameters up to 1 millimeter—a great convenience for electrophysiological work on the nervous impulse (Figure 2.8).

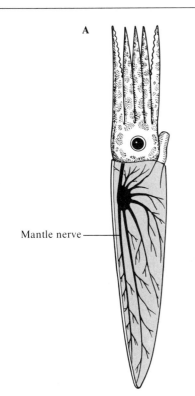

A

Mantle nerve

2.8 The nerve impulse and the squid
*(A) A drawing of the nerve in the squid
that contains the giant axons. When
dissected from the animal and placed
in sea water, the axons will conduct
nerve impulses for 12 hours or so.
(Eccles, 1973) (B) Photograph of a
squid. (Photograph by V. B. Scheffer)
(C) A schematic drawing of how the impulse is recorded. One electrode is inserted into the axon, the other records
from the axon's outside. (Eccles, 1958)*

Resting and action potentials Figure 2.8 shows how one microelectrode is inserted on the inside of a squid axon while the other records from the surface of the fiber. In this manner one can record the *electrical potential* (the difference in electrical charge) across the cell membrane. One fact emerges immediately. There is a difference in potential between the inside and the outside of the fiber when the cell is at "rest" (that is, not firing). The inside is electrically negative with respect to the outside. This *resting potential* is about –60 millivolts relative to the outside of the cell. Put differently, this means that in its normal state the cell membrane is *polarized.* Its outside and inside are like the electrical poles of a miniature battery, with the outside positive and the inside negative.

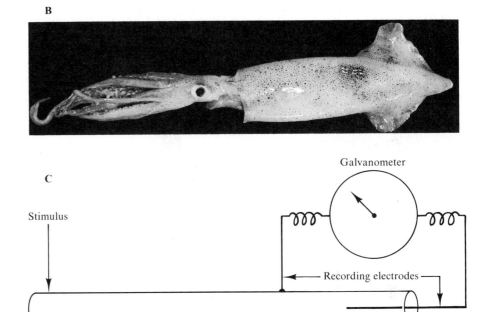

B

C

Galvanometer

Stimulus

Recording electrodes

Axon

What happens when the neuron is aroused from rest? To find out, the surface of the fiber is stimulated by means of a third microelectrode which applies a brief electrical pulse. This pulse reduces the potential across the membrane for a brief instant. If the pulse is weak, nothing further will happen; there is no impulse. If the strength of the pulse is slowly increased, the resting potential drops still more, but there is still no impulse. This continues until the pulse is strong enough to decrease the potential to a critical point, the *threshold.*

Now a new phenomenon occurs. The potential suddenly collapses; in fact, it overshoots the zero mark and for a brief moment the axon interior becomes positive relative to the outside. This brief flare lasts about 1 millisecond and quickly subsides. The potential then returns to the resting state. This entire sequence of electrical events is called the *action potential* (Figure 2.9).

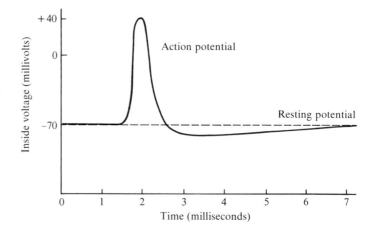

2.9   The action potential   *Action potential recorded from the squid giant axon. (After Thompson, 1967)*

The action potential is recorded from only one small region of the axon. What happens elsewhere in the fiber? Consider Figure 2.10. An **adequate stimulus**—that is, one which is above threshold—is applied to point *S* and the potential is measured at points *A, B,* and *C.* At first, an action potential is observed at *A;* at that time *B* and *C* are still at rest. A bit later, *A* returns to normal, while *B* shows the action potential. Still later, *B* returns to normal but

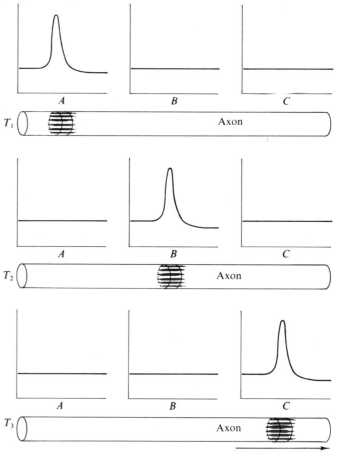

2.10   The action potential as it travels along the axon   *The axon is shown at three different moments in time—*T_1, T_2, *and* T_3*—after the application of a stimulus. The electrical potential is shown at three different points along the axon, A, B, and C.*

an action potential is found at *C*. (Of course, these time intervals are exceedingly brief.) The change of potential is evidently infectious: each region sets off its neighbor much as a spark travels along a fuse.

The all-or-none law   One point must be stressed. The size of the reaction is unaffected by the intensity of the stimulus, once the stimulus is at threshold level or above. Increasing the stimulus value above this level will not increase the intensity of the action potential or affect its speed of conduction to other points in the fiber. This phenomenon is sometimes referred to as the **all-or-none law** of neuron stimulation. The all-or-none law clearly implies that the stimulus does not provide the energy for the nervous impulse. It serves as a trigger and no more. Given that the trigger is pulled hard enough, pulling yet harder has no effect. Like a gun, a neuron either fires or does not fire. It knows no in-between.

Explaining the action potential   How do we explain these phenomena? Modern neurophysiology proposes a model based on physical and chemical interactions at the cell membrane. The neuron is enclosed in a very thin membrane which serves as a gatekeeper governing the entrance and egress of various particles into the cell and out of it. The particles are **ions,** atoms or molecules that have gained or lost electrons, thus acquiring a negative or positive electric charge. The membrane is selectively permeable; it tends to keep certain ions inside the cell and others out. The result is the resting potential. Stimulation of a neuron to its threshold value produces "holes" in the membrane through which ions (especially positive ions) can pass readily. The consequence is a quick collapse of the potential. But the holes close almost as soon as they open and the potential is restored. The loss of polarization across the membrane (that is, the **depolarization**) that occurs as the ions rush in and out through the membrane holes is the action potential which initiates the nerve impulse's progress along the axon.

Why does this excitation spread to neighboring regions? The new potentials across the disturbed regions of the membrane probably lead to electric currents which depolarize adjacent regions. These develop holes in their turn. The final step is to restore the cell to its original condition. This is accomplished (at least in part) by biochemical "pumps" which pump some ions back into the cell and others out of it. As a result, the resting potential is restored and the neuron is ready for the next stimulus.

STIMULUS INTENSITY

We have seen that the axon obeys the all-or-none law. It appears that stimulus intensity has no effect once threshold is passed. Does this law make sense? Much of our everyday experience seems to deny it. We can obviously tell the difference between the buzz of a mosquito and the roar of a jet plane, even though both sounds are above threshold. How can we square such facts with the all-or-none law?

The number of neurons stimulated   In many cases what happens is that the more intense stimulus excites a greater number of neurons. This is precisely what we should expect, for we know that different neurons vary enormously in their thresholds. Thus, a strong stimulus will stimulate more neurons than a weak stimulus. The weak stimulus will stimulate all neurons whose thresholds are below a given level; the strong stimulus will stimulate all of those, plus others whose threshold is higher. Under the circumstances, we are not surprised to find that the all-or-none law does *not* apply when we stimulate a nerve (that is, a whole collection of axons) rather than an individual neuron.

Frequency of impulse   While remaining strictly obedient to the all-or-none law, the individual neuron is nevertheless affected by stimulus intensity. This becomes apparent when we apply a continuous stimulus for somewhat longer intervals. Now we obtain not one impulse but a whole volley. We notice that the size of the action potentials remains the same whatever the stimulus intensity. What changes instead is the impulse frequency. The stronger the stimulus, the more *often* the axon will fire. This effect holds until we reach a maximum rate of firing, after which further increases in intensity have no effect (Figure 2.11). Different neurons have different maximum rates; the highest in man is of the order of 500 impulses per second.

To explain the relationship between stimulus intensity and impulse frequency we must bring up another characteristic of the nervous impulse—the **refractory phase.** Consider a neuron that has just fired in response to a momentary stimulus pulse. Can it fire again if stimulated immediately thereafter? Not quite. Like a musket, the neuron needs a moment for reloading; the resting potential must be restored, and this takes a little time. There is a brief period after stimulation during which no stimulus whatever can excite the neuron—the **absolute refractory period.** This period ranges from .5 to 2 milliseconds, depending upon the individual nerve cell. After this period has passed, the neuron can fire once again, but for a while it needs special coaxing. Its threshold has bccn raised, and it now requires a stronger stimulus than before to set off an impulse. This is the **relative refractory period** which continues for a few milliseconds until the threshold returns to normal.

The existence of the relative refractory period is one of the reasons why impulse frequency increases with increasing stimulation. As stimulus intensity

2.11 Stimulus intensity and firing frequency   *Responses of a crab axon to a continuous electric current at three levels of current intensity. The records are on an oscilloscope but the time scale is relatively slow. As a result, the action potentials show up as single vertical lines or "spikes." Note that while increasing the current intensity has no effect on the height of the spikes (the all-or-none law) it leads to a marked increase in the frequency of spikes per second. (After Eccles, 1973)*

CURRENT STRENGTH:

At threshold

At 160% of
threshold intensity

At 270% of
threshold intensity

|← 1 second →|

increases beyond the threshold level, firing can occur during the relative refractory phase and impulse frequency rises.

Increasing impulse velocity   There are enormous variations among neurons in thresholds, action potentials, refractory periods, speed of conduction, and so on. Some of these differences seem to be a function of fairly simple physical characteristics. For example, impulse velocity increases with axon diameter. But thick axons are only one means for speeding up the impulse, a means found in many invertebrates. Vertebrates have another mechanism: Many axons are encased in a fatty insulating tissue called the **myelin sheath.** This sheath is interrupted at regular intervals by the so-called **nodes of Ranvier.** These nodes are critical in helping to accelerate the impulse; they are relay stations for the impulse which jumps from node to node across the sheath between them, permitting a tenfold increase in conduction speed (see Figure 2.6).

Interaction among Nerve Cells

As we look back, it is quite clear that we have come a long way from the doctrine of animal spirits. We may still have questions about many details, but today there is no doubt that nerve conduction is a phenomenon whose explanation requires no special principles over and above those that govern the physical and chemical processes of the material world. What matters to psychologists is the fact that each nerve cell is capable of firing an impulse, which is usually triggered by impulses from other cells, and which in turn is capable of triggering impulses in yet others.

THE REFLEX ARC

In a way, the neurons of our nervous system are like 10 billion speakers, endlessly prattling and chattering to one another. But each of them has only one word with which to tell its story, the one and only word it can utter. It can choose only whether to speak its word or keep silent, and whether to speak it often or more rarely. Looked at in isolation, the individual speakers seem like imbeciles with a one-word vocabulary, babbling and being babbled at. But when taken as a whole, this gibbering becomes somehow harmonious. The trick is in the integration of the individual messages, the interplay of the separate components. The really interesting question for psychology, then, is not how a neuron manages to produce its word, but rather how it can talk to others and how it can listen.

To deal with this question we now discuss the interactions among different neurons. We begin with the simplest illustration of such interaction, the **reflex.** Descartes had pointed out that some of our actions are automatic—controlled by mechanical principles and not by the "will." Later progress in neuropsychology was made by studying animal motion that persists after the brain is gone. (What farmer had not seen a chicken running around the barnyard after its head was cut off?) Around 1750, the Scottish physician Whytt showed that such movements are controlled by the spinal cord. He found that a decapitated frog will jerk its leg away from a pinprick; but when deprived of *both* brain and spinal cord it no longer responded. Presumably, the frog's leg movement depended on the spinal cord.

The study of reflexes received some additional impetus during the French Revolution. Pierre Cabanis, friend and physician to some of its leaders, was asked to determine whether consciousness survives beheading. He concluded that it does not and that the body's twitches after execution are mere reflex actions, automatisms without consciousness. This grim business was taken up again some forty years later by the German scientist Theodor Bischoff who performed a series of rather macabre experiments on the freshly separated head of an executed criminal. Even fairly intense stimuli produced no effects during the first minute after decapitation. Among the stimuli Bischoff employed, with perhaps greater devotion to science than human sensitivity, was the word "Pardon!" shouted into the ears of the severed head (Fearing, 1930).

Today we can list a host of reflexes, built-in response patterns executed automatically, without thought and without will. Vomiting, the rhythmic contraction of the intestines (peristalsis), erection of the penis, blushing, limb flexion in withdrawal from pain, sucking in newborns—the catalog is very large.

Can we classify these reflexes in any sensible fashion? There are several criteria. We can ask how many steps are part of the **reflex arc**—the reflex pathway that leads from stimulus to response. Some reflexes represent a chain of only two components, as in the case of an afferent neuron which contacts a motoneuron directly. More typically the chain is longer, and one or more interneurons are interposed between the afferent and efferent ends. We can also ask whether the reflex involves the brain (and if so, which part) or the spinal cord. When considering **spinal reflexes** we may want to distinguish further between those of **flexion** and those of **extension,** representing reflexive innervations of flexor and extensor muscles respectively. Flexion reflexes are typically associated with withdrawal, as when one pulls back one's arm from a burning fire. Extensor reflexes are often involved in postural reactions which uphold the body against gravity. Pressure on the soles of the feet stimulates the extensors, which thrust the leg upright.

INFERRING THE SYNAPSE

Most of these facts were known by the end of the nineteenth century. What was not understood was the underlying neuronal organization. It was by no means obvious that a reflex pathway comprised *separate* neurons; on the contrary, some of the most distinguished neurologists of the time believed that the path of the impulse was across a long and essentially continuous strand of nervous tissue. The notion of the **synapse,** a gap between neurons across which they must communicate, is relatively modern. Once the synapse is taken as a fact, it is perfectly obvious that transmission across it must be a major concern of present-day neurophysiology, for it is at the synapse that the interaction between neurons occurs. It is a more prosaic small-scale replica of the switching system that Descartes had housed in the pineal body.

The critical studies which established the existence of the synapse and its role in nerve interaction were performed at the turn of the century by the

Sir Charles Sherrington (Courtesy National Library of Medicine)

English physiologist Sir Charles Sherrington (1857–1952). Sherrington's work was conducted at the level of behavior rather than that of electrophysiology. What he observed directly was reflex action in dogs, cats, and monkeys. How the synapse worked, he inferred. Today we know that his inferences were amazingly correct, for the functional properties of the synapse can now be studied directly by electophysiological techniques.

Sherrington set out to study the **simple reflex,** that is, the reflex considered in splendid neurological isolation, unaffected by activities elsewhere in the nervous system. Of course he was well aware that such simplicity does not really exist, for even the lowliest spinal reflex is modified by higher centers in the spinal cord or the brain. An itch in your side will initiate a scratch reflex, but if you are the catchman in a trapeze act you will probably inhibit it. To remove the effect of higher centers, Sherrington used the **spinal animal,** usually a dog whose spinal cord had been completely transected in the neck region. This severed all connections between the body (from the neck down) and the brain, so that spinal reflexes could be studied pure.

CONDUCTION WITHIN AND BETWEEN NEURONS

Sherrington's method was simple. He applied mild electric shocks to some point on the spinal animal's skin and observed whether this stimulus evoked a particular reflex response (Figure 2.12). His results indicated that there had to be conduction across at least two neurons—a sensory neuron from the skin receptor and a motoneuron that activates muscle fibers. Sherrington had asked whether conduction across neurons had the same characteristics as conduction within neurons. He discovered that it did not. Reflex conduction turned out to have some new properties altogether.

Reflex latency   One can easily measure the time between the application of the stimulus and the occurrence of the response, the **reflex latency.** Sherrington pointed out that those latencies are larger than they should be considering the velocity of the nervous impulse, that is, the speed of the impulse within the neuron. With fairly mild but still effective stimuli, the latency for a flexion reflex is about 100 milliseconds. Assuming a velocity of 200 feet per second and estimating that the reflex roundtrip measures about 2 feet in the dog, the

2.12   Saddle-shaped area of spinal dog that elicits scratch reflex   When a stimulus whose strength is above threshold is applied at any point in the "saddle," the animal will perform a scratching movement. (After Sherrington, 1906)

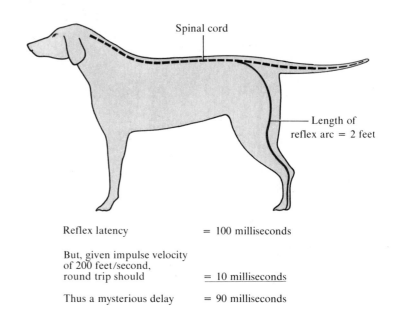

2.13 **An argument for synaptic transmission—reflex latency** *The time between the application of the stimulus and the occurrence of the reflex response is considerably longer than it ought to be when calculated on the basis of the speed of the nervous impulse. Sherrington argued that the excess time is caused by the fact that conduction across neurons is a different and slower process than conduction within neurons—that is, synaptic transmission.*

Spinal cord

Length of
reflex arc = 2 feet

Reflex latency	= 100 milliseconds
But, given impulse velocity of 200 feet/second, round trip should	= 10 milliseconds
Thus a mysterious delay	= 90 milliseconds

total travel time should be only 10 milliseconds. What accounts for the extra 90 milliseconds? The delay must be attributed to the fact that there is transmission across neurons as well as conduction within them. Some new (and presumably very much slower) process must be operating when the impulse crosses from one nerve cell over to the other (Figure 2.13).

Summation Another difference from conduction within the cell is indicated by **temporal summation.** Sherrington showed that while one stimulus below threshold will not elicit the reflex, two or more of them (all equally subthreshold) may do so if presented in succession. The important point was that such temporal summation effects occurred even when the individual stimuli were spaced at intervals of up to half a second or thereabouts. But summation over such comparatively long time intervals does not occur within an individual axon fiber. The fact that temporal summation takes place anyway suggests that the summation process occurs somewhere else, presumably at the crossover point between neurons.

A CENTRAL EXCITATORY STATE

The differences between conduction in reflex arcs and conduction in individual nerve fibers point to different mechanisms operating at the synaptic junction. Sherrington supposed that there is some kind of excitatory process (presumably caused by the liberation of a then still undiscovered chemical substance from the ends of the axon) which accumulates at the synapse and builds up until it reaches a level high enough (the threshold level) to trigger the next neuron into action. This hypothesis clearly accounts for **temporal summation.** Every time cell *A* fires, a tiny amount of the excitatory substance is liberated into the synaptic gap between cell *A* and cell *B*. With enough repetitions of the stimulus, the total quantity of what Sherrington called the **central excitatory state** (**CES**) exceeds the threshold of cell *B* which then fires. Since

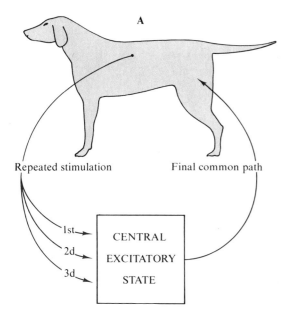

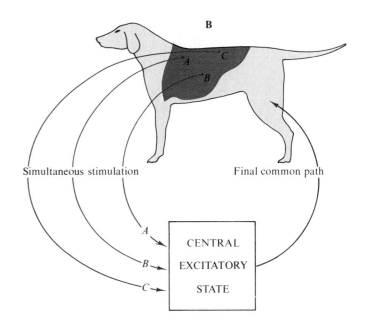

2.14 Further arguments for synaptic transmission (A) Temporal summation. A subthreshold stimulus will not elicit the reflex but two or more stimuli will, if presented successively at intervals of up to half a second. This indicates that the effects of the first stimulus were somehow stored and added to the effects of the second (or third or fourth). Sherrington believed that the stored effects produced a central excitatory state, or CES, that determines transmission between neurons—that is, synaptic transmission. (B) Spatial summation. Subthreshold stimuli applied to different points in the saddle area will not evoke a reflex if presented separately, but they will if presented simultaneously. This indicates that the excitatory effects from different regions are all funneled into the same common path and add to the CES which will then be large enough to evoke the reflex.

reflex conduction is invariably in one direction, Sherrington supposed that the excitatory substance is produced only at the axon endings and that the dendrites and cell body are sensitive to this substance while the axon is not.

Further evidence for Sherrington's general approach derives from the phenomenon of **spatial summation** which highlights the fact that several neurons may funnel in upon one output. Consider two fairly adjacent points on a dog's flank, *A* and *B*, such that stimulating either of them alone will elicit a particular reflex if the stimulus is intense enough. Sherrington showed that subthreshold stimulation at *both* points will yield the reflex, even though this same weak stimulation would not suffice for either of these points in isolation. This indicates that two groups of nerve fibers converge upon one neural output—the **final common path**. At this juncture, the several converging neurons generate excitatory processes whose effects summate (Figure 2.14).

INHIBITION

So far it would appear that neurons either vote "aye," thus adding to the central excitatory state at the synapse, or else abstain altogether. However, some neurons may signal "nay" and set up an inhibitory effect, actively opposing and preventing excitation.

One of the clearest demonstrations of such an effect is the phenomenon of **reciprocal inhibition.** Skeletal muscles typically come in antagonistic pairs— flexor and extensor (Figure 2.15). What happens to the flexor muscle when the extensor is excited and conversely? Patently, the antagonists must not both contract at the same time, like wrestlers straining against each other. For maximum mechanical efficiency, the force of the excited muscle should encounter no opposition whatever from its antagonist.

Some mechanism of this sort was envisaged by various seventeenth-century writers, including Descartes, but it remained for Sherrington to provide a brilliant experimental demonstration. Using a spinal animal, Sherrington

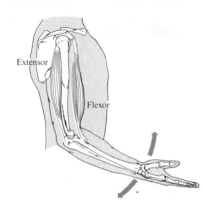

2.15   An example of muscle antagonists
The figure shows how the members of an antagonistic muscle pair oppose each other in flexing and extending the forearm.

severed the various tendons of the flexor muscle to the knee but kept all the nerves intact; the flexor could contract but this contraction could produce no skeletal movement. Even so, stimulation of a sensory site that caused the flexor to contract had a further effect. It also caused the extensor to relax so that it actually became limp—limper in fact than it was in the normal resting state. Sherrington concluded that this subzero level of muscular contraction could only be explained by assuming that there was a counteracting process that nullifies the excitatory messages to the muscle fibers—*inhibition.*

These facts suggest that the same final common path can receive both excitatory and inhibitory messages. The two processes summate algebraically; they pull in opposite directions and thus have opposite signs (with excitation positive, inhibition negative). Whether an efferent neuron fires (and thus activates a muscle fiber) depends upon many other neurons that form a synapse with it. Each of these cells gives a positive or negative signal or remains neutral and thereby determines whether the excitatory threshold of the efferent neuron is to be reached, whether it is to fire or not.

DISINHIBITION

Impulses that have an inhibitory effect may derive from centers higher up than the spinal cord. The inhibitory effect of such brain centers is often discovered indirectly, by noting an *increase* in the strength of a reflex after the influence of this higher center is removed. Such an effect is called *disinhibition.* A classic example is spinal reflexes in frogs, which are more vigorous when all brain structures have been removed.

Some very dramatic demonstrations of inhibition and disinhibition are found in insects. Many insects (as well as other animals) feign death when confronted by danger—no doubt a useful trick in a world where predators are more likely to detect prey that is moving. The relevant mechanism appears to be the inhibition of bodily reflexes, which is typically exerted by cerebral ganglia (that is, clusters of neurons) in the organism's head.

A rather ghoulish instance of disinhibition is provided by the love life of the praying mantis. The female mantis is a rapacious killer. She seizes and devours any small creature unfortunate enough to move across her field of vision. Since the male mantis is smaller than the female, he too may qualify as food. This cannibalism is not infrequent and is quite puzzling. How can the mantis survive as a species given a behavior tendency that counteracts successful fertilization?

As it happens, the female's predatory pattern is triggered almost exclusively by moving visual stimuli. The courting male's behavior is delicately attuned to this fact. As soon as he sees her he becomes absolutely immobile, keeping his eyes utterly fixed upon her. Whenever she looks away for a moment he stalks her ever so slowly, but immediately freezes as soon as her eyes wheel back toward him—an inhibitory effect upon overall reflex activity. When close enough to her, he suddenly leaps upon her back and begins to copulate. Once squarely upon the female's back he is reasonably safe (her normal killer reflexes are elicited only by moving visual stimuli and he is mostly out of sight). But the dangers he must surmount to reach this place of safety are enormous. He must not miss her when he jumps; he must not slip while upon her. Should he fall, he will surely be grasped and eaten. Fairly often he does

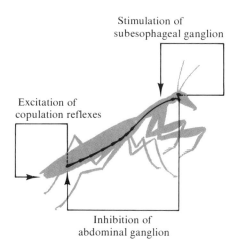

2.16 Reproductive behavior in the praying mantis *(A) Copulating pair of mantises in which the male has not been attacked. (B) The female devouring the male's head while his abdomen shows the bending movements of copulation. (C) The decapitated male copulating. (The insects normally hang upside down from the underside of a leaf or twig. For clarity, their positions are here reversed. From Roeder, 1967)*

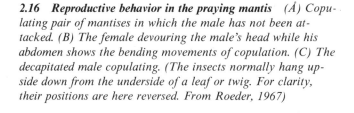

Stimulation of
subesophageal ganglion

Excitation of
copulation reflexes

Inhibition of
abdominal ganglion

lose his balance, but even then all love's labour is not lost—for the species, if not for him. The female commences to eat her fallen mate from the head on down. In almost all instances, the abdomen of the male now starts vigorous copulatory movements that are often successfully completed (Figure 2.16). Clearly, the male performs his evolutionary duty whatever his own private fate. But what is the mechanism?

It appears that the intact male's copulatory reflexes are inhibited by the subesophageal ganglion, located in his head. When this nerve cluster is removed, the animal will engage in endless copulatory movements even when no female is present (Roeder, 1935). The same thing happens if the female chances to seize her mate and eat him. She first chews off his head and with it the subesophageal ganglion, thus disinhibiting the male's copulatory pattern which now resumes in full force—proof positive that love can survive beyond the grave (Figure 2.17).

2.17 The disinhibitory mechanism in the praying mantis *Excitation of the abdominal ganglion leads to copulatory movements in the male. But the sight of the moving female stimulates the subesophageal ganglion in the male's head. This in turn inhibits the abdominal ganglion so that copulation stops. Decapitation removes the subesophageal ganglion and its inhibitory effect. The result is disinhibition and copulation resumes. (After Roeder, 1967)*

THE SYNAPTIC MECHANISM

Sherrington could only guess at the specific physical mechanism that governs transmission across the synapse, but he did sketch some general guidelines. There had to be excitatory and inhibitory processes, accumulating over time yet eventually dissipating, pooling effects from various neural inputs, and adding algebraically. Some fifty years later, several neurophysiologists were finally able to tackle the problem directly.

Let us begin with a bit of anatomy. The electron microscope has shown *synaptic knobs,* tiny swellings of the axon terminals that contact the dendrite (and sometimes part of the cell body) of another cell, separated by a fantastically narrow space of perhaps .02 microns, the *synaptic cleft.* Within the knobs are numerous tiny sacs, *synaptic vesicles,* which contain chemical substances called *transmitters.* When the neuron fires, the vesicles move down to the *presynaptic membrane* and release their transmitter load. The transmitters diffuse across the synaptic cleft and act upon the *postsynaptic membrane* below. Diffusion is a fairly slow process, and this partially accounts for synaptic delay (Figure 2.18).

How do the transmitters transmit? Essentially, by changing the potential of the dendrites and cell body. These substances stream across the gap between the two cells and create some depolarization of the postsynaptic membrane just below them, a so-called *excitatory postsynaptic potential* (mercifully abbreviated to *ESP).* The EPSPs can summate, over time and over space. As more transmitter molecules are hurled over more synaptic bridges, there will be more and greater EPSPs which will spread and summate until they reach the initial segment of the second cell's axon. When this region is reached by EPSPs which have summed up to a critical level, the action potential is triggered and this will now speed down the rest of the axon.

Modern neurophysiologists believe that a similar analysis applies to inhibitory processes. At some synapses a presynaptic impulse leads to postsynaptic hyperpolarization (a polarization considerably greater than usual). The

2.18   The synapse   *(A) Electron micrograph of synaptic knobs, magnified 11,250 times. (Lewis, 1969) (B) Schematic outline of the synaptic transmission mechanism. Transmitter substances stored in special vesicles move through the synaptic cleft and stimulate sensitive sites of the dendrite of the adjacent cell. (After Eccles, 1965)*

A

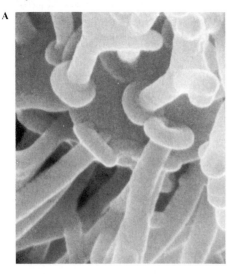

B

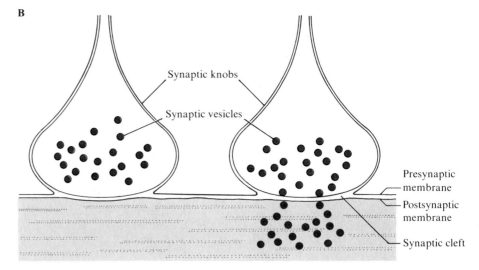

membrane interior becomes even more negative than it was to begin with, and thus even further away from the critical threshold value required to trigger the impulse. Such *inhibitory postsynaptic potentials (IPSP)* are caused by transmitter substances liberated by the firing of the presynaptic cell; these summate in time and over space as do EPSPs. They also summate with EPSPs but of course algebraically. It appears that some neurons produce only EPSPs and others only IPSPs, while at least some others seem capable of generating both.

This general view of synaptic transmission has emerged from a convergence of anatomical, electrophysiological, and pharmacological evidence. In one study, microelectrodes were inserted on both sides of a synapse in an anesthetized cat. One electrode was placed in the axon of an afferent neuron and the other in the cell body of the motoneuron with which it made contact. By this means, the investigators could simultaneously observe the presynaptic cause (in the afferent neuron) and the postsynaptic effect (in the motoneuron). When the afferent neuron was stimulated, the presynaptic electrode registered an action potential. Shortly afterward, an EPSP showed up on the other postsynaptic electrode. The EPSP does not begin until the action potential of the first cell has nearly run its course, a delay that is just what we would expect, since it will take some time for the transmitter substances to cross the synaptic gap (Eccles, 1973).

The Main Structure of the Nervous System

Our general approach has been to move from the simple to the increasingly complex. We first looked at the operation of the smallest functional unit of the nervous system, the neuron, and then considered the way in which two or more neurons may interact. We now turn to a third and still more complex level of analysis to discuss the function of large aggregates of neurons. What can we say about the function of those clumps of nervous tissue, each made up of millions of neurons, that comprise the gross structures of the brain and spinal cord? The attempts to answer this question go far back into psychology's history, and little wonder. If man is indeed a machine, the secret of its running is surely hidden in that mass of folds and convolutions that is the human brain.

THE EVOLUTION OF CENTRAL CONTROL

The nervous system is analogous to a government, and its evolution can be understood as the gradual imposition of central control over local autonomy. A first step was the establishment of regional rule. Early in evolutionary history the cell bodies of many interneurons began to clump together to form *ganglia* (singular, *ganglion*). At first, these ganglia served primarily as relay stations that passed on sensory messages from the receptors to the muscles. But eventually they became much more than mere relay stations. The close proximity of the cells within these clumps of neural tissue allowed an ever-increasing number and complexity of synaptic interconnections. As a result, the ganglia became local control centers which integrated messages from different receptor cells and coordinated the activity of different muscle fibers. These

35

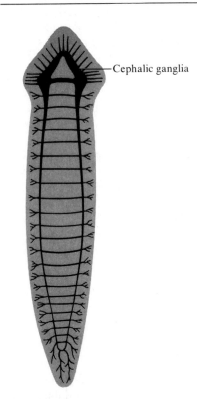
—Cephalic ganglia

2.19   The flatworm   *The first steps toward neurological centralization— cephalic ganglia in the flatworm. (After Buchsbaum, 1948)*

regional centers were usually located close to the sites where important sensory information is gathered or where vital activity takes place.

As evolution progressed, the initial loose federation of ganglia gradually became increasingly centralized; some ganglia began to control others. The dominant ganglia were those that were located in the head. Their eventual preeminence grew out of the fact that the head contains the major receptors. This location naturally followed from the body plan organized around a front-to-end axis that is first seen in worms. Even the lowly flatworm has a head that contains its mouth and a tail that more or less corresponds to the end of its digestive tube. Given this body plan, one can see why the flatworm is better off with taste and vision receptors in the head than elsewhere. Taste receptors are obviously more useful near the entrance to the digestive tube; they signal edibility and determine whether food is accepted or rejected. Distance receptors such as vision are also more effective if situated at the animal's front end. The flatworm already knows something about its rear, for it was there just a moment ago; but what is ahead is still unknown (Figure 2.19).

To integrate the messages from the various receptors in the head, more and more neural machinery was required and the ganglionic centers which processed the incoming information became increasingly complex. They eventually started to coordinate the activity of ganglia elsewhere in the body until they finally emerged as the head ganglia in status as well as location—in short, they became the brain.

This tendency toward increasing centralization continued within the brain itself. The various structures of the brain tend to function hierarchically; there are higher centers which command lower centers, which in turn command still lower centers, and so on. The evolutionary tendency toward increasing dominance of the higher cerebral centers is called **encephalization** (from the Greek *encephalon,* "brain"). A comparison of the brains of different vertebrate animals shows increasing encephalization with ascending rank on the evolutionary scale. Figure 2.20 shows that the most pronounced changes involve an expansion of the more frontward (anterior) parts. These new structures, especially the outer mantle of the two **cerebral hemispheres,** the **cerebral cortex,** allowed a vastly more complex level of behavioral functioning to the animals lucky enough to be so endowed. They now could respond to subtle patterns in their environment and learn new ways of coping with the world that their more primitive forebears were unable to perceive or to learn.

But as central government grows, local governments must inevitably lose some of their autonomy. Concurrent with the enormous development of the higher centers is a decline in the independent functioning of the lower ones. An example is the cerebral control of vision. Suppose we remove a cat's **visual cortex,** the part of the cortex that receives afferent signals from the eyes (by way of an intermediate relay station, the **thalamus**). The cat can no longer distinguish between two forms such as a square and a circle, but it can still discriminate between dark and light. If the same operation is performed on a chimpanzee, the loss of vision is total. The same holds for humans whose visual cortex is destroyed by a stroke or by an accident—they are blind. Vision is evidently less encephalized in cats than in apes or humans. Some aspects of the cat's vision seem to be still handled by a lower cerebral center which can function even in the absence of central supervision (Marquis, 1935).

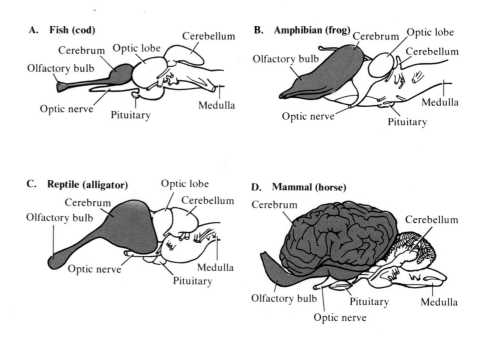

2.20   Increasing encephalization in different vertebrates   *Note the increasing expansion of the forebrain (color) in the sequence from (A) fish through (B) amphibian, (C) reptile, and (D) mammal. (After Keeton, 1980)*

THE PERIPHERAL AND CENTRAL NERVOUS SYSTEMS

The end product of encephalization is the human nervous system. Taken as a whole, it consists of a fine network of fibers that gradually merge into larger and larger branches which converge upon a central trunk line, like the tributaries of a stream. This system is composed of the central and peripheral nervous systems. The ***central nervous system*** (usually abbreviated ***CNS***) is made up of the brain and spinal cord. The ***peripheral system,*** as its name implies, comprises all nervous structures that are outside of the CNS.

Anatomists distinguish between two divisions of the peripheral nervous system—the somatic and the autonomic. The ***somatic division*** is primarily concerned with the control of the skeletal musculature and the transmission of information from the sense organs. It consists of various nerves that branch off from the CNS—efferent fibers to the muscles and afferent fibers from the skin, the joints, and the special senses. The ***autonomic nervous system (ANS)*** serves the many visceral structures that are concerned with the basic life processes, such as the heart, the blood vessels, the digestive system, the genital organs, and so on. Its name derives from the fact that it operates with some degree of independence from CNS control. The largely involuntary character of many autonomically governed activities is apparent from the fact that they continue even during sleep. Breathing and the contractions of stomach and intestines are two obvious examples. This autonomy is not complete, however, a point to which we will return later when we discuss this system more fully (see Chapter 3).

The central nervous system is in essence a long tube that is very much thickened at the front end. The lower portion of the tube is the ***spinal cord,*** which becomes the ***brainstem*** as it enters the skull. Two pairs of hemispheres are attached to the thickened front end. One pair, the ***cerebral hemispheres,*** is

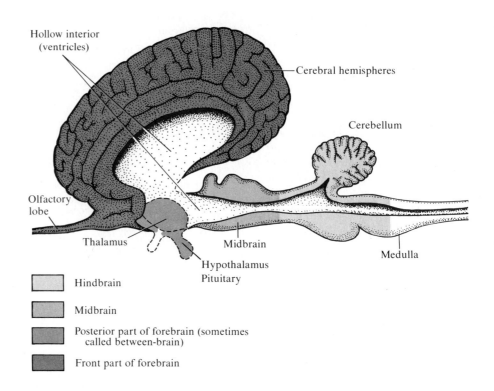

Hollow interior
(ventricles)

Cerebral hemispheres

Cerebellum

Olfactory
lobe

Thalamus

Midbrain

Medulla

Hypothalamus
Pituitary

Hindbrain

Midbrain

Posterior part of forebrain (sometimes
    called between-brain)

Front part of forebrain

2.21   The central nervous system   This diagram is a highly schematic representation of the main parts of the brain. (After Morgan, 1965)

very large and envelops the central tube completely; the other pair, the **cerebellum** (literally, "little brain"), is located lower down and is much smaller (Figure 2.21).

One general point holds for virtually all regions of the CNS. Any of its anatomical structures usually contain two kinds of subcomponents—**integration centers** and **transmission tracts.** Integration centers are made up of the gray, unmyelinated portions of nerve cells—axon terminals, dendrites, and cell bodies, all clumped together in close proximity. Their function follows from the fact that such clumpings allow many synaptic junctions. They serve to coordinate sensory information or motor commands, a coordination that is usually modulated by other centers which outrank them in the neurological hierarchy. Transmission tracts are bundles of myelinated axons that conduct information from one region to another. Since the myelin sheath has a whitish appearance, the tracts are often described as **white matter,** in contrast to the integration centers that are **gray matter.**

THE SPINAL CORD

Like most structures in the CNS below the level of the cerebral hemispheres, the spinal cord has two functions. First, it acts as a relay station for tracts coming down from and going up to the brain. Second, it serves as a control center in its own right; specifically, it is responsible for **spinal reflexes.**

THE ANATOMY OF THE BRAIN

Neuroanatomists like to consider the brain in terms of three major subdivisions; the **hindbrain, midbrain,** and **forebrain** (Figures 2.21 and 2.22).

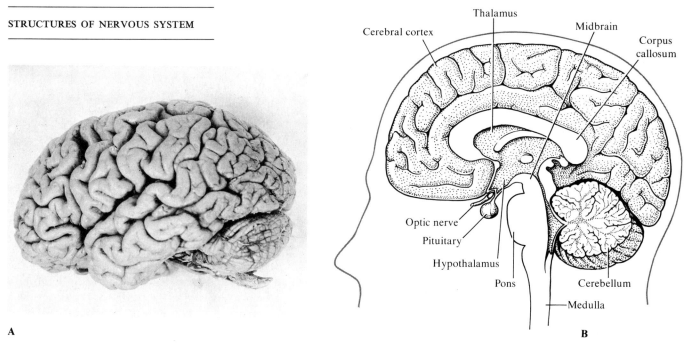

A

B

2.22   The human brain   *(A) A photograph of the brain taken from the side. (Courtesy The American Museum of Natural History) (B) A diagram of the brain, cut lengthwise. (After Keeton, 1980)*

The hindbrain   The hindbrain includes the **medulla** and the **cerebellum.** The medulla is a control center for several critical bodily processes, of which respiration and heartbeat are the most important. The cerebellum consists of two deeply convoluted hemispheres attached to the lower brainstem. It controls bodily balance and motor coordination.

The midbrain   The midbrain contains several neural centers which act as relay stations for the auditory or visual systems, and which, especially in some lower mammals, control certain visual or auditory functions (for instance, eye movements) on their own. Of particular interest is a rather diffuse structure known as the **reticular formation** which extends through the entire length of the brainstem from medulla to thalamus, but is particularly prominent in the midbrain region. It acts as a general activator whose excitation arouses other parts of the brain, particularly the cerebral hemispheres. Its deactivation seems related to sleep. We will return to these issues in a later section (see Chapter 3).

Forebrain: Thalamus and hypothalamus   Two of the forebrain structures represent the topmost part of the brainstem (which is sometimes called the "between-brain"). They are the **thalamus** and the **hypothalamus.** The thalamus is the great relay station for sensory information. Fibers from the eyes, the ears, and the skin, all deliver their messages at the thalamus, to be forwarded upward from there to the cerebral cortex. The hypothalamus is intimately involved in the control of behavior patterns that stem from the basic biological urges (e.g., feeding, drinking, sexual activity, and so forth; see Chapter 3).

39

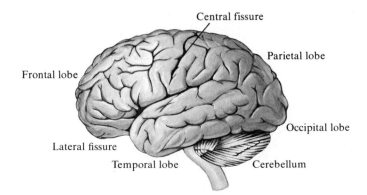

2.23 The cerebral hemispheres, side view *(After Gray, 1948)*

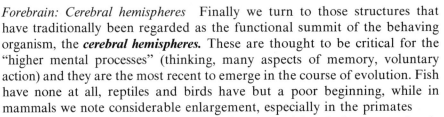

2.24 The limbic system in various mammals *(A) Rabbit, (B) cat, (C) monkey, (D) man. (After Thompson, 1967)*

Forebrain: Cerebral hemispheres   Finally we turn to those structures that have traditionally been regarded as the functional summit of the behaving organism, the *cerebral hemispheres.* These are thought to be critical for the "higher mental processes" (thinking, many aspects of memory, voluntary action) and they are the most recent to emerge in the course of evolution. Fish have none at all, reptiles and birds have but a poor beginning, while in mammals we note considerable enlargement, especially in the primates

The most casual glance shows that the cerebral hemispheres are deeply folded and convoluted (Figure 2.23). Thus crumpled up, the cerebral surface that can be packed into the cranial cavity is very much increased. Anatomists usually distinguish several large parts within each hemisphere, called *lobes.* There are four such lobes, each named for the cranial bone nearest to it: the *frontal, parietal, occipital,* and *temporal.*

If we slice through a hemisphere and look at the cross-section, we immediately note an important structural feature—there is an outer layer of gray matter with white matter underneath. This outer layer is called the *cerebral cortex* and it is really this region rather than the hemispheres as a whole that is thought to represent the pinnacle of neural integration. There are good *a priori* reasons for such a view. The cells in the cortex are unmyelinated, densely packed, and intricately interconnected; they are therefore capable of the most complex synaptic interactions. In contrast, the subcortical white matter consists of myelinated tracts that interconnect with the structures below. Even more persuasive is the sheer number of neurons in the human cortex—an incredible 5 billion, half of all the cells of the entire brain.

A word or two should be added about the subcortical regions of the cerebral hemispheres. As already noted, much of this area is taken up by ascending and descending tracts, but there are some other structures located near the center of the hemispheres in a region that borders upon the brainstem. These are often grouped together under the term *limbic system* (from *limbique,* "bordering"). Many limbic structures are part of what in evolutionary terms is an older unit, the "old cortex," that is more prominent in lower mammals than in man (Figure 2.24), has close anatomical ties with the hypothalamus, and is almost surely involved in the control of emotional and motivational activities. Another subcortical structure is the *corpus callosum,* a large band of fibers that connects the two hemispheres and plays an important role in integrating their function (see pp. 47–50).

Localization of Function in the Cerebral Cortex

What are the functions of the various parts of the cerebral cortex? While we are still very far from an adequate answer, some first steps toward understanding have begun to emerge.

PROJECTION AREAS

Among the first discoveries in the study of cortical localization was the existence of the so-called *projection areas.* These serve as receiving stations for sensory information or as dispatching centers for motor commands. *Sensory projection areas* are those regions of the cortex where the messages from the various senses are first received and upon which the sensory input is "projected." *Motor projection areas* are those from which the final directives to the muscles are issued.

Motor areas The discovery of the cortical motor areas dates back to 1870 when two German physiologists, Fritsch and Hitzig, opened the skull of a lightly anesthesized dog and then applied mild electric currents to various portions of its cerebral cortex. They discovered a region in the frontal lobe that controls movement. Stimulating a given point led to motion of the forelimb, stimulating another point led to motion of the trunk, and so forth. The effect was always on the side of the body opposite to the site of stimulation. Exciting the left hemisphere led to movements on the right side of the body; exciting the right hemisphere caused movements on the left. This made good anatomical sense because most of the major efferent pathways from the brain cross over to the opposite side just as they leave the hindbrain.

Similar studies have been conducted on human subjects by the Canadian neurosurgeon, Wilder Penfield. The stimulation is administered in the course of a brain operation. Such operations are usually administered under local rather than general anesthesia and patients are therefore able to report their experiences. Electrical stimulation applied to the open brain produces no pain. While pain receptors are located throughout the body and send their messages upward to the brain, the brain itself contains no such receptors.

The results of Penfield's studies showed that the cortical motor area in humans is in a region of the frontal lobe that is quite similar to that found in dogs by Fritsch and Hitzig. Stimulation there led to movement of some parts of the body, much to the surprise of patients who had no sense of "willing" the action, or of "performing it themselves." Systematic exploration showed that for each portion of the motor cortex, there was a corresponding part of the body that moved when its cortical counterpart was stimulated, with each hemisphere controlling the side of the body opposite to it. The results are sometimes expressed graphically by drawing a "motor homunculus," a schema of the body as it is represented in the motor projection area (Figure 2.25).

Inspection of the motor homunculus shows that equal areas of the body do not receive equal cortical space. Instead, parts of the body that are very mobile and capable of precisely tuned movement (for instance, the fingers, the

41

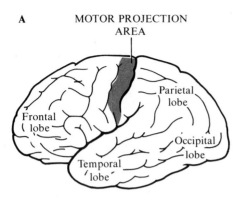

A MOTOR PROJECTION AREA

Parietal lobe

Frontal lobe

Occipital lobe

Temporal lobe

2.25 The motor projection area of the human cortex *(A) The location of the motor projection area in a side view of the brain. (B) The motor projection area of one hemisphere shown in a cross-section of the brain. The location and relative amount of cortical space allotted to each body region is graphically expressed as a motor homunculus. (C) The head shows the plane of the cross-section of both this and the following figure. (After Penfield and Rasmussen, 1950)*

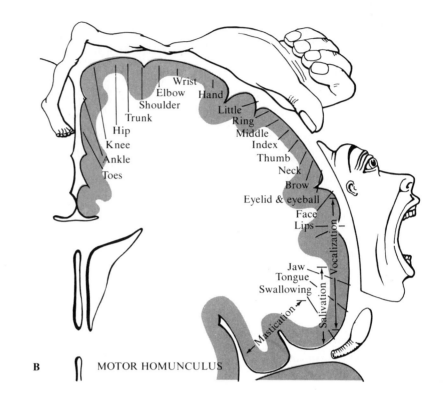

B MOTOR HOMUNCULUS

Wrist
Elbow
Shoulder   Hand
Trunk   Little
Hip   Ring
Knee   Middle
Ankle   Index
Toes   Thumb
            Neck
            Brow
Eyelid & eyeball
            Face
            Lips

Jaw
Tongue
Swallowing
Mastication
Salivation
Vocalization

C

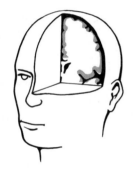

tongue) are assigned greater cortical space compared to those employed for movements that are more gross and undifferentiated (for instance, the shoulder). What matters is evidently function, the extent and complexity of use (Penfield and Rasmussen, 1950).

Some related findings with various animals fit neatly into this picture. For example, the spider monkey has an elegant prehensile tail, much used as a manipulative organ and thus much favored in cortical allotment (Gray, 1948). Or compare the cortical representations of the forepaw in dogs and raccoons. Unlike the dog, the raccoon is a "manual" creature which explores the world with its forepaws; neatly enough, the forepaw cortical area in raccoons dwarfs its counterpart in the dog (Welker, Johnson, and Pubols, 1964).

Sensory areas Analogous stimulation methods have demonstrated the existence of cortical sensory areas. The **somatosensory area** is located in the parietal lobes. Patients stimulated at a particular point of this area report a tingling sensation somewhere on the opposite side of their bodies. (Less frequently, they will report experiences of cold, warmth, or of movement.) Again, we find a neat topographic projection. Each portion of the body's surface is mapped onto a particular region of the cortical somatosensory area as summarized by the "sensory homunculus" (Figure 2.26). Here too we note an unequal assignment of cortical space: The parts of the body that are most sensitive to touch such as the index finger and the tongue enjoy a disproportionately larger space allotment in the brain.

Similar projection areas exist for vision and for hearing. They are located in

A SOMATOSENSORY PROJECTION
AREA

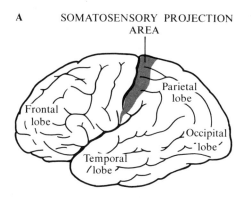

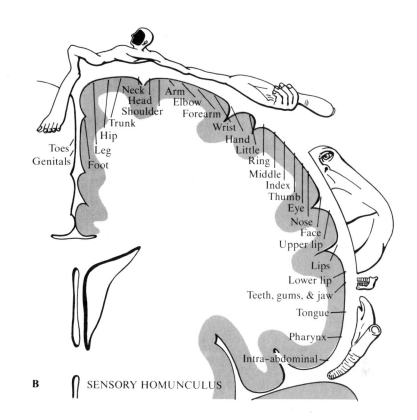

B SENSORY HOMUNCULUS

2.26 The somatosensory projection area of the human cortex (A) The location of the somatosensory projection area in a cross-section of the brain. (B) A sensory homunculus, analogous to the motor homunculus of Figure 2.25 B, which shows the location and relative cortical space allottment of different body regions. The plane of this cross-section is a bit behind that shown in Figure 2.25 C. (After Penfield and Rasmussen, 1950)

the occipital and temporal lobes respectively (Figure 2.27). Patients stimulated in the visual projection area report optical experiences, vivid enough, but with little form or meaning—flickering lights, formless colors, streaks. Stimulated in the auditory area, they hear things, but again the sensation is meaningless and rather chaotic—clicks, buzzes, booms, hums. Some psychologists might argue that here we have "pure" visual and auditory input, the crude, disembodied raw materials of sensation, to be shaped and interpreted as the excitation is transmitted to other areas.

The visual projection area provides yet another example of topographic mapping of the sensory surface. Each region on the *retina* (the visual receptor system; see Chapter 6), projects to a corresponding region on the visual cortex, but once again more space is devoted to the functionally more sensitive area:

2.27 Auditory and visual projection areas of the human cortex (After Morgan, 1965)

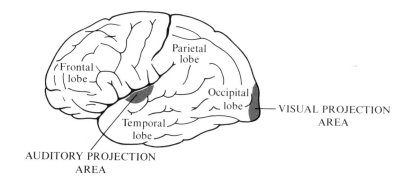

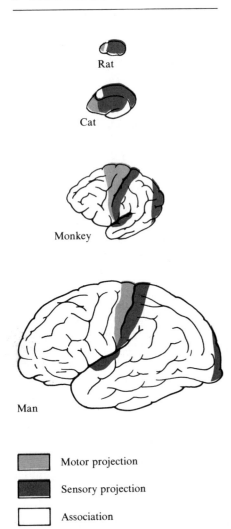

Rat

Cat

Monkey

Man

■ Motor projection

■ Sensory projection

□ Association

2.28 Projection and association areas in rat, cat, monkey, and man *There is an orderly progression in the amount of cortex comprising the association area. As we go up the series from rat to man, both the absolute amount of cortical association area and the ratio of association to projection areas increases dramatically. In rats, cats, and to some extent even monkeys the bulk of the cortex is devoted to being agile and perceptive; humans devote most of it to being smart. (After Thompson, 1973)*

The center of the retina (where the image of an object falls as the eye turns to look at it) is represented by a disproportionately larger cortical area than is the periphery.

A similar pattern holds for the auditory cortex. There is evidence which suggests that its organization is **tonotopic,** with response to high-frequency tones in one region, low ones in another, and middle ones in the regions in between.

ASSOCIATION AREAS

Less than one-quarter of the human cortex is devoted to the projection zones. The remaining regions have traditionally been called **association areas,** a term that grew out of an earlier notion that these areas somehow link events arising in different projection zones, whether motor or sensory. There is good reason to believe that these areas are implicated in the higher mental processes such as planning, remembering, thinking, and speech. One source of this belief stems from a comparison of the anatomy of the cortex found in different mammals. In the rat, the bulk of the cortex is taken up by projection zones; in the cat, more space is devoted to the association areas; more yet in monkeys; and most in man (Figure 2.28).

Apraxia and agnosia Most of the evidence on the function of the association areas comes from studies of human patients who have incurred cortical damage (technically, **lesions**) through tumors, hemorrhage or blockage of cerebral blood vessels (popularly known as a stroke), or accident. Lesions in the association areas seem to impair the organization of messages that come from the sensory projection areas or that go to the motor areas.

An example is **apraxia** (Greek, "inability to act"), a serious disturbance in the organization of voluntary action. In one form of apraxia, actions that normal persons regard as quite simple and unitary become utterly fragmented and disorganized. When asked to light a cigarette, the patient may strike a match against a match box, and then strike it again and again after it is already burning; or he may light the match and then put it into his mouth (Luria, 1966). These defects are in no sense the result of a motor paralysis, for the patient can readily perform each constituent of the sequence in isolation. His problem is in selecting the right components and fitting them together. In many apraxias, movements that cannot be performed voluntarily can still be executed when they occur as parts of an automatic routine. Thus, while unable to stick out his tongue when asked, a patient may use it perfectly well in semi-involuntary acts such as swallowing (Jackson, 1884).

Apraxia is evidently some impairment of a neurological system that organizes individual movements into coherent, larger actions, and also initiates them. This system is analogous to the command post of a regiment that draws up the battle plan and orders the attack. If the command post falls (and no other takes its place) there can be no organized attack, despite the fact that the individual soldiers are still able to fire their guns and throw their hand grenades. There is considerable debate over just where this neural command center is localized, or for that matter, whether there is one such center or several. Some neurologists argue that the relevant regions are roughly adja-

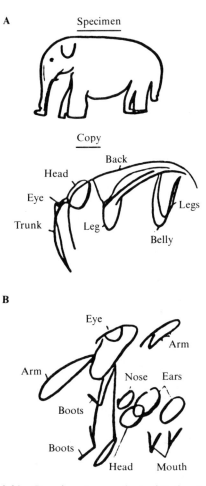

2.29 Drawings by a patient with visual agnosia (A) Trying to copy an elephant. (B) Production when asked to draw a man. (From Luria, 1966)

cent to the motor projection zone in the frontal lobe. As evidence, they point to the fact that certain apraxias are caused by lesions in the association areas of the frontal lobe (Luria, 1966). But this cannot be the whole story, for other kinds of apraxia are evidently produced by lesions elsewhere in the cortex.

Another disorder caused by lesions in certain association areas is **agnosia** (Greek, "ignorance"). Whereas apraxia represents a disrupted organization of action, agnosia is characterized by a disorganization of various aspects of the sensory world. In visual agnosia, patients can see, but are often unable to recognize what they see. They may have 20/20 vision, but they nevertheless suffer from what neurologists have called "psychic blindness." In less severe cases, patients may be able to perceive each separate detail of a picture, but be unable to see the picture as a whole. When shown a drawing of a monkey, one patient painstakingly identified several parts and then ventured an appropriate guess: "Eyes . . . mouth . . . of course, it's an animal." Or for a picture of a telephone: "A dial . . . numbers . . . of course, it's a watch or some sort of machine!" (Luria, 1966, p. 139). He had similar difficulties when asked to copy a drawing he was shown. The individual parts were rendered reasonably well, but they couldn't be integrated into a coherent whole (Figure 2.29).

It is perhaps not surprising that visual agnosias of this sort are usually produced by lesions of the association areas surrounding the visual projection zone, for it is not implausible to believe that the elaboration and organization of messages from a given projection area is the primary business of neighboring association regions.

Aphasia Certain lesions of cortical association areas lead to serious disruptions of the most distinctively human of all human activities—the production and comprehension of language. A disorder of this kind is called **aphasia** (Greek, "lack of speech").

In one form of aphasia, **expressive aphasia,** the patient's primary difficulty is with the expression of speech—in effect, a language apraxia. In extreme cases, a patient with expressive aphasia becomes virtually unable to utter or to write a word. Less extremely, a few words or phrases survive. These may be routine expressions such as "hello" or emotional outbursts such as "damn it!" They may also be words uttered just prior to the event that caused the lesion. An example is a woman who suffered a cerebral stroke while ordering boiled beef and subsequently could express her entire range of ideas in only one word—"horseradish" (Ruch, 1965). In less severe cases, more of the spoken vocabulary remains intact but the patient's speech becomes fragmented, as finding and articulating each word requires a special effort. The result is a staccato, spoken telegram: "Here . . . head . . . operation . . . here . . . speech . . . none . . . talking . . . what . . . illness" (Luria, 1966, p. 406).

The similarity to the apraxias we have discussed before is very striking. There is no paralysis of speech muscles, for the patient is perfectly able to move lips and tongue. What is impaired is the ability to organize and plan these movements into a unified sequence, the ability to synthesize individual movements so as to form a word or to put one word after another so as to create a coherent sentence.

Expressive aphasias of the kind described here are generally produced by lesions in a region of the left frontal lobe called **Broca's area** (after a French

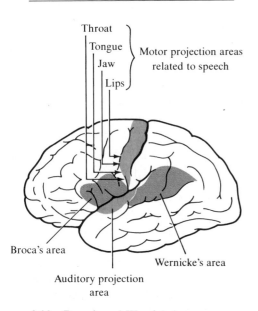

Throat
Tongue
Jaw
Lips

Motor projection areas
related to speech

Broca's area

Auditory projection
area

Wernicke's area

2.30 Broca's and Wernicke's areas
*The schematic shows the two associa-
tion areas most relevant to language.
Destruction of Broca's area generally
leads to expressive aphasia; destruction
of Wernicke's area leads to receptive
aphasia. Note the proximity to the
relevant projection areas: Broca's is
close to the regions that control the various speech muscles, while Wernicke's
borders on the auditory projection zone.*

physician, Paul Broca, who first noted its relation to speech in 1891; see Figure 2.30). This is an association area that borders on the part of the motor projection zone which controls the various speech muscles (jaw, tongue, lips, larynx, and so on) and presumably plays an important role in orchestrating their separate functions.

(What happens to left-handers will be discussed later on; see p. 51.) This sphere is damaged. In right-handed persons, aphasia results from damage to an appropriate region of the left hemisphere; destruction of the corresponding region of the right hemisphere rarely impairs language functions. (What happens to left-handers will be discussed later on; see p. 51.) This assymetrical localization holds for all forms of aphasia; at least in right-handers, language is under the jurisdiction of the left hemisphere.

In expressive aphasia, patients understand what they hear but cannot answer. In *receptive aphasia,* the patients' problem is that they don't understand, though they often try to answer anyway—in effect, a language agnosia. In consequence, they are usually impaired in both comprehension and expression. A relatively mild version of receptive aphasia is sometimes called word deafness. Patients can hear but they can no longer differentiate the complex acoustic patterns that make up speech. These are now perceived as a disorganized jumble, much as we perceive a rapid conversation in a language we don't know. As one patient described his condition, "Voices come, but no words. I can hear, sounds come, but words don't separate" (Brain, 1965, p. 106).

Other cases of receptive aphasia are even more catastrophic, for in them the patient has an impaired appreciation of the meaning of the words she hears (or sees in print). She can perceive the sound patterns, for she can repeat them; but they often lack their former symbolic value. Thus, when asked to point to a spoon, one patient said, "Spoon, poon, yes," and then pointed to an irrelevant object. When asked to touch her nose, she replied, "Stuch, tux news, nose," and then did nothing (J. W. Brown, 1972, p. 65).

The previous examples illustrate the fact that severe receptive aphasia affects speech production as well as comprehension, for one can hardly speak normally if one doesn't understand one's own utterances. In marked contrast to expressive aphasia, patients with receptive aphasia talk very freely and very fast, but while there are many words, they say very little. The sentences are reasonably grammatical but they are largely composed of filler words that provide little information. A typical example is, "I was over the other one, and then after they had been in the department, I was in this one" (Geschwind, 1970, p. 904).

In many cases, there are substitutions of one sound for another ("spoot" for "spoon") or of one word for another ("fork" for "spoon"). Occasionally, the entire speech output becomes an almost unintelligible jargon. In some cases, most of the key words are incomprehensible: "Then he graf, so I'll graf, I'm giving ink, no, gefergen, in pane, I can't grasp, I haven't grob the grabben, I'm going to the glimmeril, let me go" (J. W. Brown, 1972, p. 64). In others, each individual word is clear enough but the phrase as a whole is gibberish, as in the reply of a patient when shown a bunch of keys and asked to name it: "Indication of measurement of pieces of apparatus or intimating the cost of apparatus in various forms" (Brain, 1965, p. 108).

Receptive aphasia is usually associated with left-hemisphere lesions (in right-handers) in various association areas of the temporal and parietal lobes. Many authorities believe that the crucial locus is **Wernicke's area,** a region that borders on the auditory projection zone and is named after a nineteenth-century neurologist who first described word deafness and other receptive aphasias (Figure 2.30).

ONE BRAIN OR TWO?

Anatomically, the two cerebral hemispheres appear to be mirror-image twins, but there is abundant evidence that their functions are by no means identical. This asymmetry of function is called **lateralization** and its manifestations include such diverse phenomena as language, spatial organization, and the superior dexterity of one hand over the other.

Evidence for lateralization We have already seen that in right-handers aphasia is usually associated with lesions in the left hemisphere. Until recently, neuropsychologists interpreted this fact to mean that one hemisphere is **dominant** over the other. They called the (right-hander's) right hemisphere the **minor hemisphere,** for they believed that it is essentially a left hemisphere without language functions and with a lesser capacity for fine motor control.

More recent evidence has rescued the right hemisphere from this poor relation status, for it now appears that it has some important functions of its own. Right-handers with lesions in the right hemisphere seem to suffer from various difficulties in the comprehension of space and form, a point already noted in our discussion of agnosia. Some are deficient in the perception of complex forms; they concentrate on details but cannot grasp the overall pattern. Some have trouble recognizing faces. Some have great difficulties in dressing themselves; they put their arms in a pants leg or put a shirt on backward. Such disorders are much more common when the lesion is in the right than when it is in the left hemisphere (Bogen, 1969).

The results are more ambiguous in left-handers. Some are lateralized in mirror image to right-handers. Their right hemisphere is more specialized for language, their left for visual-spatial functions. But in many other left-handers, there is less lateralization altogether; the functional capacities of their two hemispheres are more on a par. In this group, aphasia may be produced by lesions to either hemisphere. There is also a greater likelihood of recovery from aphasia, for the intact hemisphere is better able to take over the responsibilities formerly assigned to the one that suffered damage (Brain, 1965).

Further evidence for lateralization comes from studies on persons with **split brains.** These are people whose **corpus callosum** has been surgically severed. The corpus callosum is a massive bundle of nerve fibers that interconnects the two hemispheres so that they can pool their information and function as a harmonious whole. This neurological bridge (and some other less important ones) is sometimes cut in cases of severe epilepsy so that the seizure will not spread from one hemisphere to the other. Once confined to a small cortical area, the seizures are much less severe and, in fact, much less frequent. The operation clearly relieves suffering, but it has a side effect—the two hemispheres of the split brain become functionally isolated from each other and essentially act as two separate brains (Figure 2.31).

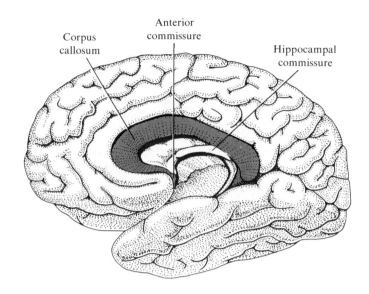

Corpus
callosum

Anterior
commissure

Hippocampal
commissure

2.31 The split brain *To control epi-lepsy, neurosurgeons sometimes sever the two hemispheres. This is accomplished by cutting the corpus callosum and a few other connective tracts. The corpus callosum is shown here in a lateral cross-section.*

The effect of the split-brain operation is best demonstrated by setting a task which poses a question to one hemisphere and requires the answer from the other one. One method is to expose a picture so that the neural message reaches only one hemisphere. This is done by flashing the picture for a fraction of a second to either the right or the left side of the patient's field of vision. If it is to the right, it is projected to the left hemisphere; if to the left, to the right hemisphere (Figure 2.32). The patient simply has to say what he sees. When the picture is on the right, he easily does so, for the information is transmitted to the same hemisphere that can formulate a spoken answer—the left. This is not so when the picture is flashed on the left. Now the visual image is sent to the right hemisphere, but this hemisphere can neither provide a spoken (or for that matter, written) reply, nor can it relay the news to the left hemisphere which has the language capacity. In consequence the patient is unable to answer. Sometimes, there is a haphazard guess. When this happens, the patient may frown or shake his head immediately after he has given the incorrect answer. The right hemisphere evidently does have some limited language capacity after all. It sees the pictured object, and while it cannot produce the correct name, for instance, "ashtray," it at least understands that this name is not "coffee pot."

Another demonstration of the fact that the right hemisphere understands what is shown even though it cannot talk about it, comes from the observation of a patient who was unexpectedly shown a picture of a nude girl. When this picture was flashed to the left hemisphere, the patient laughed and correctly described what she had seen. When the same picture was presented to the right hemisphere, the patient said that she saw nothing, but immediately afterward she smiled slyly and began to chuckle. When asked what was so funny, she said, "I don't know . . . nothing . . . oh—that funny machine" (Gazzaniga, 1967, p. 773). The right hemisphere knew what it was laughing at; the left hemisphere heard the laughter but couldn't tell its cause.

An elegant demonstration of hemispheric differences uses stimuli that are

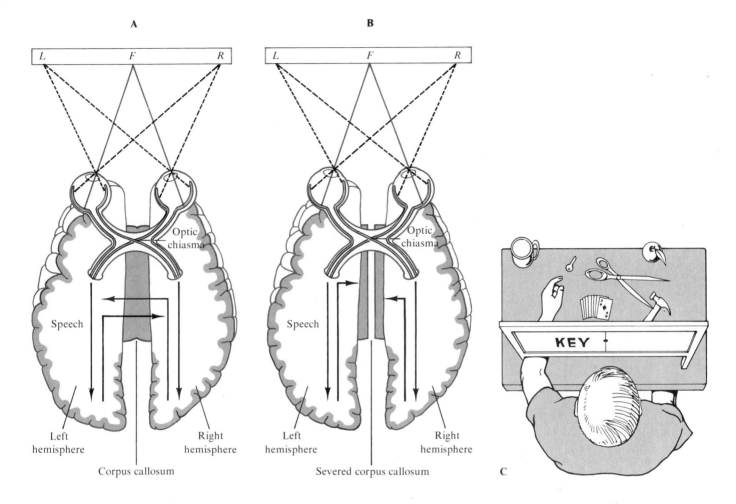

A   **B**   **C**

2.32 Restricting visual input to only one hemisphere   *(A) This illustration shows how visual information is sent to the brain in normals. A person looks at a point—the so-called fixation point or F—of a picture. Points to the left of F, such as L, will fall on the right side of each retina (the receptor region of each eye). Points to the right of F, such as R, will fall on the left side of each retina. The reason is simple optics: Our lens reverses up and down, right and left. We next have to consider a special anatomical fact. As the figure shows, half of each retina sends its information to the hemisphere on the same side. But the other half feeds into a part of the optic nerve that crosses over to the opposite side of the hemisphere. This arrangement guarantees that if the eyes are fixed at F, the entire left side of the field (including point L) will be sent up to the right hemisphere; the entire right side of the field (including point R) will be dispatched to the left hemisphere.*

As a result of all this, point L goes to the right hemisphere; point R to the left one. But this only works if the eyes stay fixed at point F. In actuality, it is hard to keep the eyes stationary. To get around this, investigators use a special trick. They flash the picture very briefly, say, for 150 milliseconds. They can now be sure that there are no eye movements while the picture is exposed, for such eye movements take longer to execute (about 200 milliseconds) than the time the picture is in view.

(B) These procedures ensure that certain points in the visual field go to only one hemisphere. This hardly matters in normals who have an intact corpus callosum which serves as a bridge between the two hemispheres over which information can be passed in both directions. But this isn't so in split-brain patients whose corpus callosum is cut so that their right and left hemispheres can't exchange information. As the figure shows, in a split-brain patient point L only gets to the right hemisphere and can't be relayed back to the left which has the language capacity. As a result, the patient is unable to say what he saw on the left side of the field.

(C) A setup sometimes used in split-brain studies. The subject fixates a center dot and then sees a picture or a word on the right or left side of the dot. He may be asked to respond verbally, by reading the word or naming the picture. He may also be asked to respond without words, for example by picking out a named object from among a group spread out on a table and hidden from view, so that it can only be identified by touch. (After Gazzaniga, 1967)

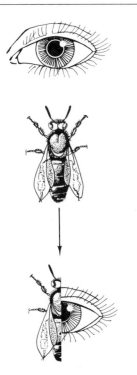

2.33 Composite figures used to test for hemispheric differences in split-brain patients *(After Levy, Trevarthen, and Sperry, 1972)*

composites of two pictures, in which the left half of one is joined to the right half of the other (Figure 2.33). These are briefly exposed, with their midline centered in the field of vision. Normal subjects see such pictures as they really are—bizarre monstrosities, such as the left half of a bee stuck onto the right half of an eye. In contrast, split-brain patients never seem to notice anything unusual. They either see a bee or they see an eye, but never both.* Which of the two they choose depends upon which hemisphere is asked. Suppose the stimulus is the bee-eye combination, with the bee on the left (thus in the right hemisphere), the eye on the right (hence in the left hemisphere). In one condition, the subjects have to indicate what they just saw by pointing to one of several objects that are shown to them after the brief flash of the bee-eye combination. The choice objects include both a bee and an eye (drawn in complete form) and can be inspected at the subjects' leisure. In this task, language is irrelevant, for the subjects have to recognize only the similarity between two forms, regardless of the names. We have already seen that the right hemisphere is probably more critical for the perception of complex forms than the left. If so, the patients should point to the bee, for that is the only stimulus that the right hemisphere saw. This is just what happens.

In another condition, the task calls on language functions. Patients are again presented with a brief flash of the bee-eye combination. They are then shown pictures of several objects, such as a key and a pie, and they have to select the one whose name *rhymes* with the object they just saw. When tested in this manner, the patients will almost invariably choose the pie, an object whose name rhymes with the name of the only stimulus that was shown to the left hemisphere, the eye (Levy, Trevarthen, and Sperry, 1972; Levy, 1974).

Two modes of mental functioning The preceding discussion indicates that language and spatial organization are usually handled in two different areas of the brain. Many psychologists regard this fact as support for a view they held previously—the notion that verbal and spatial processes represent two radically different modes of thought. That such a difference exists is in line with our everyday observations. We often think in words—about scientific problems, about politics, about who likes whom; the list is endless. But no less often do we mentally manipulate the world with little benefit of language, as when we visualize our living room with rearranged furniture or work on a jigsaw puzzle. Many problems can be solved by either mode. We may find our way to a friend's home by referring to a mental map, or by memorizing a verbal sequence such as "first right after the third traffic light." But sometimes the two modes are not intersubstitutable. How a corkscrew works is hard to describe in words; the pros and cons of a two-party system are impossible to get across without them.

The difference between verbal and spatial modes of thought is explicitly recognized in the construction of many tests of intelligence. Different sets of test items are provided to assess each mode separately. Verbal aptitude may be gauged by questions that involve comprehension ("Why do married people

---

* Interestingly enough, the patients don't see just half an object, whether half a bee or half an eye. Instead, they tend to complete whichever half they see, and never report that anything is missing.

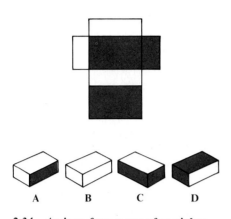

2.34 An item from a test of spatial relations *The subject has to decide which of the figures, A, B, C, or D, can be made by folding the pattern above. (The correct answer is* D. *After Cronbach, 1970b)*

who want a divorce have to go to court?") or vocabulary ("What does *formulate* mean?") or the abstraction of underlying similarities ("In what ways are waterpipes and streets alike?").

Spatial ability may be tested by items that require the subject to construct a design by arranging a set of variously colored blocks, or to visualize how a two-dimensional shape will appear when folded into a box (Figure 2.34). When we look at the test scores obtained from a large number of normal subjects, we find that verbal and spatial scores do not go together as much as do their component subtests. For instance, given vocabulary scores, one can predict comprehension scores with a fair degree of accuracy. The prediction is much less accurate if it is made from a verbal to a spatial subtest; for example, from vocabulary to block design (Cronbach, 1970b).

This result is a further argument for the view that verbal and spatial abilities represent two different clusters of intellectual functioning. In line with our previous discussion, these tend to be localized in different hemispheres—verbal test scores are more impaired by lesions to the left hemisphere; spatial test scores by lesions to the right (Levy, 1974).

Is the verbal-spatial distinction a sufficiently basic description of the modes of functioning associated with each hemisphere? One problem concerns the role of the left hemisphere. In right-handers, this is dominant for language, but it is also superior in the organization of skilled motor acts. The left hemisphere controls bodily movement on the side of the body opposite to it, which in right-handers is obviously more dexterous. (The Latin adjective *dexter* means "situated on the right" and thus also "skillful.") The superiority of the right is not confined just to the hand. If a right-hander tries to write with his toes, he does better with his right than with his left foot.

Is it just an accident that the same hemisphere that handles language is also the one that is responsible for fine motor control? Some neuropsychologists feel that it is not. In their view, the difference in hemispheric functions is a matter of space versus time. The right hemisphere is specialized for the organization of space, whereas the left hemisphere concentrates upon organization in time. This formulation of the left hemisphere's functions is relevant both to language and motor dexterity, for both require a precise appreciation of temporal order. The person who is insensitive to what comes first and what comes second cannot possibly speak or understand the speech of others. *Tap* is not the same word as *pat,* and the sentence "Wellington beat Bonaparte" is crucially different from "Bonaparte beat Wellington." This is also true for skilled manual acts, which consist of organized sequences of wrist and finger movements whose order must not be disrupted. To summarize this view, the right hemisphere is concerned with what goes where, the left with what comes when (Bogen, 1969).

SOME PROBLEMS IN LOCALIZING FUNCTION

The preceding discussion has sketched some recent advances in our understanding of the localization of function in the human brain. But the picture is not as neat as we have presented it thus far, for there are various problems of both method and interpretation that complicate the analysis of any correlation between anatomical site and psychological function.

Where is the anatomical locus?   One problem is anatomical. Much of our knowledge of human cerebral function comes from the study of lesions. But the exact locus of a lesion is hard to determine while a patient is alive. The results are sometimes ambiguous even if postmortem inspection is possible. There may be other lesions elsewhere in the brain in addition to those the neurologist considers critical. Did those others contribute to the disorder?

Another problem is that the relevant functional disturbance is often accompanied by others. Which disorder was caused by which lesion? Neuropsychologists have described lesions as cruel experiments performed by nature, but nature is not a scientist and her experiments are rarely neat and precise. None of these difficulties is insurmountable. One way of coping with many of them is to study a large number of patients all of whom share one lesion but not others. If they all show a similar loss of function, it is very likely that the relevant anatomical loss is the one shared by all.

Further complications arise from the fact that many functions are represented not in one area of the brain but in several. For example, vision, hearing, and the somatic senses each have *secondary projection areas* in the cortex, in addition to the primary ones we have discussed before. In one study the cortical representation of vision in the cat was determined by electrical recording during visual stimulation (Hubel and Wiesel, 1965). No less than three areas could be mapped in which neural responses were in neat topographical relationship to each other and to the retina.

What is the psychological function?   Suppose we have overcome the difficulties in specifying the precise anatomical locus that corresponds to a particular psychological effect. Does this mean that we have localized a function? Not necessarily, for we must first be sure that we understand what the underlying function really is. Sometimes this is fairly clear, as in lesions of sensory projection areas which cause defects in vision or hearing. In other cases, the explanation is less obvious.

A good example is a famous case reported by the French neurologist Dejerine in 1892 (Geschwind, 1972). Dejerine's patient woke up one morning to discover that he could no longer read. He could speak and understand speech as before; in fact, he could write, though he could not read what he had written. His vision was unaffected with one exception—he could no longer see the right half of his visual field. Given the anatomical arrangement of the visual pathways, one neurological inference was inescapable: There was serious damage to the visual projection area of the left hemisphere (see Figure 2.32). Should we conclude that this region is a "reading center"? Such an interpretation is wildly improbable. Man roamed earth for eons before the advent of writing and we could hardly expect the evolutionary process to provide neurological machinery for a purpose some million years ahead.

To explain the phenomenon we must first consider what reading is. In virtually all modern writing systems, the written word is a visual transcription of the spoken one. (The great exception is Chinese.) The child learns to read by associating certain visual forms with speech sounds and, through them, with meanings. Since the speech sounds and meanings are dealt with in the language areas of the left hemisphere, it is plausible to assume that these areas must participate in the act of reading. According to this view, the visual information has to be passed on to the language areas of the left hemisphere

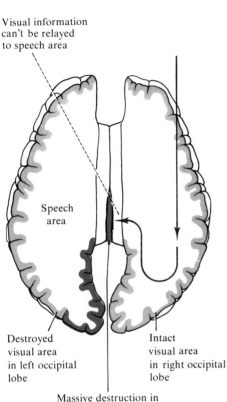

Visual information
can't be relayed
to speech area

Speech
area

Destroyed
visual area
in left occipital
lobe

Intact
visual area
in right occipital
lobe

Massive destruction in
posterior corpus callosum

*2.35 A disconnection effect The sche-
matic shows lesions in the left occipital
cortex and the posterior corpus callosum. Given these effects, vision depends
entirely on the visual projection area in
the right hemisphere. But this information can't be relayed to the speech area
of the left hemisphere because the hemispheric bridge for visual messages is the
posterior corpus callosum. As a result,
the patient sees the word, but only as a
meaningless set of forms. (After Geschwind, 1972)*

in order to be interpreted as language symbols—in order to be read. But
suppose the pathway between the visual and the speech areas is no longer
there? At postmortem examination, Dejerine found that his patient suffered
such a disconnection. A large portion of his corpus callosum was destroyed, as
was the visual projection area of the left hemisphere. This solved the riddle.
The *right* visual cortex was unimpaired and so the patient could see. The
language areas of the left hemisphere were intact, and so he could speak and
comprehend. The motor system was unaffected, so he could write. But the
destruction in the corpus callosum isolated the visual cortex of the right
hemisphere from the language areas of the left. As a result, the patient saw
printed text but could not read it (Figure 2.35). This effect is obviously quite
similar to what is observed in split-brain patients.

This example highlights the fact that we must try to understand both terms
of a psychoanatomical correlation. To understand the neural underpinnings
of some aspect of behavior, whether language, memory, or whatever, we must
understand something about that behavior itself, quite apart from its relation
to cerebral anatomy. To take another example, certain studies have shown
that stimulation of certain regions of the temporal lobes in some epileptic
patients leads to vivid recollections of past events (Penfield and Roberts, 1959;
see Chapter 1). This result is fascinating, but we won't be able to explain it
until we know more about memory as such (or perhaps about epilepsy, for the
result may be specific to patients with this disorder). In summary, psychology
and neurophysiology go hand in hand. To claim that psychology will not
progress until we know more about the brain is to assert only half the truth
because the search for a neurophysiological underpinning necessarily requires
some knowledge of what it is an underpinning of.

Summary

1. Since Descartes, many scientists have tried to explain human and animal movements within the framework of the *reflex* concept: A stimulus excites a sense organ,
which transmits the excitation upward to the spinal cord or brain, which in turn
relays the excitation downward to a muscle or a gland, thus producing action. Descartes' general classification of nervous function is still with us as we distinguish
between *reception, transmission-integration,* and *reaction.*

2. Descartes saw reflex action as analogous to the operation of a machine. Subsequent investigators extended this machine conception by demonstrating that nervous activity is subject to the same physical and chemical laws that govern the rest of
the universe. A high point in this endeavor was Helmholtz' measurement of the *speed
of the nervous impulse.*

3. Later investigators showed that the smallest unit of the nervous system is the
neuron, whose primary anatomical subdivisions are the *dendrites, cell body,* and *axon.*

4. The main function of a neuron is to produce a *nervous impulse.* This is an
electrochemical disturbance that is propagated along the membrane of the axon. The
impulse is triggered by stimuli that are above some *threshold* value. The impulse obeys
the *all-or-none law* of neuron stimulation: Once threshold is exceeded, further increases of stimulus intensity have no effect on the magnitude of the impulse. But the
nervous system can nevertheless distinguish between stimulus intensities. One means
is *impulse frequency;* the more intense the stimulus, the more often the neuron fires.

5. To understand how neurons communicate, investigators have studied *reflex action,* which is necessarily based on the activity of several neurons. Results of studies with *spinal dogs* led Sherrington to infer the processes that underlie conduction across the *synapse,* the gap between the axon of one neuron and the dendrites of the next. Conduction within neurons was shown to obey different laws than conduction between neurons (across the synapse). Evidence included the fact that *reflex latency* was too slow to be accounted for by the speed of the nervous impulse and by the phenomena of *temporal and spatial summation.* Such studies showed that excitation from several neurons funnels into a common reservoir to produce a *central excitatory state.*

6. Further studies argued for a *central inhibitory state.* Evidence came from *reciprocal inhibition* found in antagonistic muscles. Further work showed that a reflex can be activated either by increasing excitation or by decreasing inhibition. An example of the latter is the *disinhibition* produced by destruction of higher centers which inhibit the reflex.

7. Sherrington's inferences of synaptic functions have been confirmed and extended by modern electrical and chemical studies. Today we know that transmission across the synapse is accomplished by *neurotransmitters,* chemical substances which are liberated at the axon terminals of one neuron and exert excitatory or inhibitory effects on the dendrites of another.

8. As the nervous system evolved, there was more and more *encephalization,* an ever-increasing dominance of the higher brain centers over lower portions of the nervous system.

9. A crude anatomical outline of the vertebrate nervous system starts out with the division between the *peripheral (somatic* and *autonomic)* and *central nervous systems.* The central nervous system consists of the *spinal cord* and the *brain.* Important parts of the brain are the *hindbrain* (including *medulla* and *cerebellum*), *midbrain* (including the *reticular formation*), and *forebrain* (including *thalamus, hypothalamus, cerebral hemispheres,* and *cerebral cortex*).

10. The cerebral cortex is generally believed to underlie the most complex aspects of behavior. The *projection areas* of the cortex act as receiving stations for sensory information or as dispatching centers for motor commands. The remaining regions of the cortex are called *association areas.* Their function seems to relate to such higher mental processes as planning, remembering, thinking, and speech.

11. Certain lesions of association areas lead to *apraxia,* a serious disturbance in the organization of voluntary action. Other lesions produce *agnosia,* a disorganization of perception and recognition. Still others cause *aphasia,* a profound disruption of language function, which may involve speech production, speech comprehension, or both.

12. In many ways, the two cerebral hemispheres are mirror images of each other. But to some extent, their function is not symmetrical. In most right-handers, the left hemisphere handles most of the language functions, while the right hemisphere is more relevant to spatial comprehension. Thus aphasia is generally associated with lesions in the left hemisphere, while many spatial agnosias are likely to result from right hemisphere lesions. Further evidence for this difference in hemispheric function, or *lateralization,* comes from studies of *split-brain patients.* In such persons the main connection between the two hemispheres, the *corpus callosum,* has been surgically cut.

CHAPTER 3

Motivation

In this chapter we examine some of the simple motives that human beings share with other animals, such as thirst, hunger, and fear. These motives steer our behavior in certain directions rather than others; toward food, say, rather than toward shelter. But motives also have a further effect, especially as they become more pressing. They arouse us to increasing levels of activity. A hungry tiger, for instance, is wide-awake and capable of enormous exertions as it tries to capture its prey. Thus motives have a dual function. On the one hand, they direct behavior, like a radio tuner that is used to select the channel. On the other hand, they mobilize the organism so that its behavior will be more aroused and energetic, somewhat analogous to the radio's volume control. We will consider both the directional and the activating function of motives and we will look at the biological basis of each.

Our main concern will be with motives that are essentially unlearned and which pertain to the individual alone rather than in interaction with others. Examples are hunger and thirst, the desire for safety, the need for rest. We will later take up two other kinds of motives. One concerns desires that are mainly acquired through learning, such as the need to achieve, to attain prestige, or to amass possessions (see Chapters 13 and 14). The other group is no less biologically based than hunger and thirst, but it involves motives that transcend the individual alone and focus on his interactions with others. Examples are sex, filial love, and aggression. While these have biological roots, they are best studied in the context of social rather than individual behavior (see Chapter 11).

Motivation as Direction

Most human and animal actions are directed. We don't simply walk, reach, shrink, or flee; we walk and reach *toward* some objects, shrink and flee *away from* others. The objects that are approached or are withdrawn from may be in the organism's here and now, as when a kitten jumps toward a rolling ball or when a mouse darts away from a sudden noise. But often enough, the object that defines the direction of an action exists in an as yet unrealized future. The hawk circles in the sky in search of prey but there is none in sight as yet. In such a case, the direction of behavior is set from inside, there is an inner *motive* (in popular terms, a purpose, a desire) which leads to actions that bring the hawk closer to food.

Directed action seems difficult to reconcile with Descartes' notion of humans and animals as reflex machines, however complex their internal wiring. This problem is most pronounced for actions that are directed toward some future goal, for it is hard to see how an automaton can be imbued with purpose or desire. But difficulties arise as well even in the simplest case in which the direction is toward (or away from) an immediately present object. Consider the kitten reaching for the ball. What matters is not whether this flexor muscle is contracted or that extensor muscle is relaxed, but rather whether the overall pattern of muscular activity gets the creature closer to the final end state—near the ball. The response cannot really be defined in specific muscular terms. The kitten may swipe at the ball with its right paw or its left, it may crouch more on one side or the other—all that matters is that, whatever the specific motor response, it will be toward the ball. Can a reflex automaton produce such directed actions? Descartes' statues walked out and bowed when a visitor stepped on a hidden spring, but did they bow *to* the visitor? Suppose the visitor were to push the spring and then to jump quickly to the left. The statue would surely lumber through its prescribed routine exactly as before, in stony disregard of the altered circumstance.

It is evident that a simple automaton is incapable of directed action. Can the machine be modified to overcome this lack? The answer is yes. There are mechanisms which have the capacity for directed action and they include both machines developed by modern technology and neurological systems developed by evolution.

Control Systems

Modern engineers have developed an immense technology based on machines that control their own activities and are in that sense directed. The basic principle upon which these devices are built is the notion of a *feedback system.* When a machine is in operation it performs some kind of action which may be mechanical, electrical, thermal, or whatever, but which in all cases engenders some changes in the external environment. If these changes in turn influence the further operation of the machine—if they feed back upon the machine—we have a control system based on feedback.

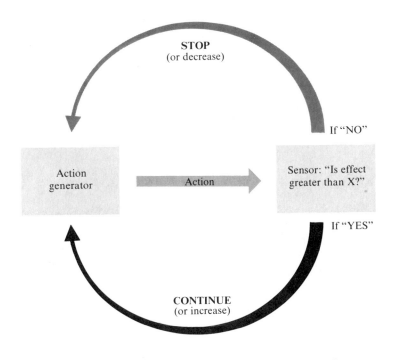

3.1 Positive feedback *In positive feedback systems, the feedback strengthens the response that produces it. A sensing device indicates the level of a certain stimulus. If that level is greater than some set point, the action continues and usually intensifies. The result is an increasing escalation of response intensity.*

NEGATIVE AND POSITIVE FEEDBACK

In ***positive feedback systems,*** the feedback strengthens the very response that produced it. The result is an ever-increasing level of activity (Figure 3.1). A technological example is a rocket that homes in on airplanes. It is designed to increase its velocity the closer it gets to its target.

Of greater relevance to our present concern is ***negative feedback*** in which the feedback stops, or even reverses, the original response of the machine that produced the environmental change. Negative feedback underlies a large number of industrial devices called ***servomechanisms*** that can maintain themselves in a particular state. A simple example is the system that controls most home furnaces. A thermostat closes an electric contact for all temperatures below a given setting and opens it for all that are above it. The contact controls the furnace, which only operates when the contact is closed. In the winter, the result is a steady house temperature, for the furnace will burn fuel only if the temperature is below the critical level; once this is reached, the furnace shuts off, deactivated by its own negative feedback (Figure 3.2). Vastly more complex servomechanisms keep naval guns fixed on target whatever the ship's roll; the list of industrial and military applications is virtually endless. In all cases, the servomechanisms provide the capacity for direction and for self-regulation. In a sense, the thermostatically controlled furnace has a goal: It "aims" at a particular temperature.

Negative feedback systems exist at all levels of the nervous system and are responsible, at least in part, for directed action. In this chapter we will see how such systems underlie motivated actions of many kinds. Some concern the organism's regulation of various vital functions—temperature maintenance, food and water intake, and the like. Others involve the organism's reaction to

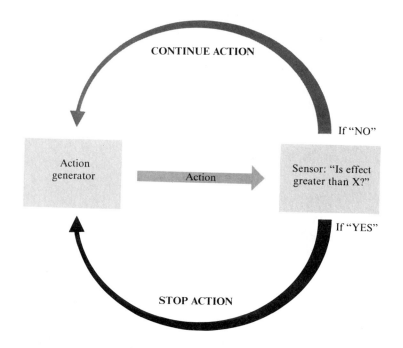

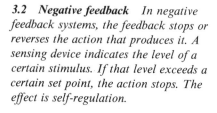

3.2 Negative feedback In negative feedback systems, the feedback stops or reverses the action that produces it. A sensing device indicates the level of a certain stimulus. If that level exceeds a certain set point, the action stops. The effect is self-regulation.

threats from outside, whether fearful escape or raging attack. We will begin with a simpler example, a neurological feedback system that controls orienting reactions in rather primitive organisms. Such orienting reactions are reflexive and automatic but they are nevertheless directed, like the blind flight of the moth into the flame.

TAXES

Many lower animals show strong orientation responses to certain of the stimulus energies that impinge upon them, for example, gravity, light, temperature, or mechanical stimulation. Such an orienting reaction is a ***taxis*** (plural, *taxes*). The taxis is said to be positive if the stimulus leads to approach, negative if it leads to withdrawal. Examples abound. Slugs and starfish show negative ***geotaxis.*** They invariably crawl upward (withdraw from the pull of gravity) when placed on an inclined plane. More familiar are the ***phototaxes*** of the moth and the cockroach—positive for the moth that beats its wings against the shining lantern, and negative for the cockroach that scurries into darkness. Unlike many reflexes, these taxes involve the entire musculature of the creature, but just like them they are unaware and unreasoning. It is not that the moth *chooses* the light because it likes it. It cannot help itself.

The automatic nature of such reactions is neatly illustrated by studies in which two taxes are pitted against each other. Consider a slug that is placed on an inclined plane with light shining from one side. The creature is impelled upward by a negative geotaxis and sideward by a negative phototaxis. Its actual path is a diagonal compromise between these two (Figure 3.3). When the strength of one of these forces is increased while the other is unaltered, the animal's reaction changes accordingly. The figure shows the slug's progress when the light intensity is varied while the inclination of the plane is held

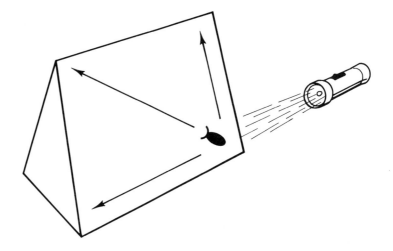

3.3 The interaction of two taxes *A slug with a negative geotaxis and a negative phototaxis is placed on an inclined plane and stimulated by a beam of light. The black arrows show the paths the slug would take if impelled by either of the two taxes in isolation: upward in response to gravity, sideways in response to light. The actual path (the color arrow) is a compromise, with the angle dependent upon the light intensity—the more intense the light, the more the path will incline toward the horizontal.*

constant—the brighter the light, the less the upward slope of the animal's path (Crozier and Hoagland, 1934).

What is the mechanism that underlies such taxes? A well-known account emphasizes the fact that taxes are mostly found in creatures whose body plan is bilaterally symmetrical, that is, in which both sides of the body are essentially mirror images (Loeb, 1918). Two assumptions are critical. The first is that receptors from one side of the body conduct excitation primarily to the muscle groups of only one side, typically the opposite one. The second assumption is that the vigor of muscular contraction depends directly upon the intensity of receptor stimulation. In positive taxes, receptor stimulation excites the relevant muscle groups; in negative taxes, it inhibits them. Given these assumptions, the relevant orientation patterns follow.

Consider a moth's positive phototaxis. Initially, the light is at the creature's right (*A* in Figure 3.4) so that its right photoreceptors are more excited than are those on its left. As a result there is unequal motor innervation, which leads to a turning movement. The wings on one side will beat faster than those on the other. This produces a turning pattern, familiar enough to anyone who has ever tried to row a boat (*B* in Figure 3.4). The turning movement continues until both right and left photoreceptors are equally stimulated. Once this point is reached, the negative feedback circuit has accomplished its mission and the creature is properly oriented: It faces the light (*C* in Figure 3.4).

A curious question remains. What is the biological utility of these behavior patterns? They are obviously based on built-in neurological feedback systems and are surely the product of evolutionary selection. The survival value of some taxes is clear enough. The cockroach finds food and safety in dark, inaccessible crevices and so its negative phototaxis serves it well. But some of these automatic behaviors have clear drawbacks—many a moth has met a fiery death because of them. Some biologists suggest that the moth's positive

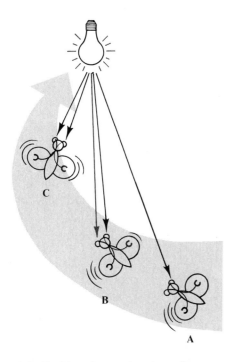

3.4 Positive phototaxis *According to one proposal, the more intense the light on one side of a moth's body, the more vigorous will be the contraction of the muscles on the opposite side. In (A), the light hits only the right side, resulting in more vigorous wing movements on the left. This leads to a turning movement which orients the animal toward the light, at first partially (B), then completely (C). When the orientation is complete, the two wings beat equally vigorously and the animal flies more or less directly toward the light.*

phototaxis is critical for its reproduction and is thus of overriding species utility. The male moth is guided to the female by scent, but this cue only indicates the general region he has to approach. Once in this region, he must rely on vision in order to find her. But the moth is a nocturnal animal; under the circumstances, how can the sexes see each other in the dark? The answer is moonlight and positive phototaxis. Both sexes will fly toward whatever lit-up areas there are at night and will thus have a greater chance of meeting. According to Shelley's poetic fancy, the moth has a quixotic, romantic "desire for the star." Shelley may have been more accurate than he guessed. The insect is utterly possessed by a built-in feedback system, and the most likely purpose of that system is indeed romance.

Self-Regulation

Control by feedback explains the rudimentary form of directed action seen in taxes. Here, the direction comes from the outside. Can we apply the same principles to the understanding of motivated action in which the direction is imposed from within? We will begin by considering those motives which grow directly out of the organism's regulation of its own internal state, such as its temperature, its water level, and its supply of food nutrients.

HOMEOSTASIS

Some two hundred years after Descartes, another Frenchman, the physiologist Claude Bernard (1813–78), emphasized the fact that the organism exists in an internal environment as well as an external one—the organism's own body fluids, its blood and its lymph. Bernard pointed out that this *internal environment* is kept remarkably constant despite considerable fluctuations of the environment outside. The striking constancy is shown by the salt and water balance of the body, its oxygen concentration, its pH (a measure of acidity), its concentration of various nutrient substances such as glucose, and its temperature (in warm-blooded animals). In healthy organisms, all of these oscillate within very narrow limits, and these limits define the organism's conditions for health and survival. Thus 60 to 90 milligrams per 100 cubic centimeters of blood is the acceptable range for the glucose concentration in the bloodstream of a healthy person. A drop below this level means coma and eventual death; a prolonged rise above it indicates disorders such as diabetes. The modern term for this stable internal equilibrium is **homeostasis** (literally, "equal state") and the mechanisms whereby it is achieved are sometimes said to reflect the "wisdom of the body" (Cannon, 1932).

HOMEOSTATIC BALANCE: TEMPERATURE REGULATION

A rather simple example of homeostatic balance is temperature regulation in birds and mammals. These animals are called warm-blooded because they maintain their internal body temperature at a fairly constant level, despite wide temperature variations in the surrounding environment. To achieve this internal equilibrium, a large repertoire of reflexive, **homeostatic adjustments** is brought into play. If the internal temperature is too high, various reactions

Claude Bernard (Courtesy National Library of Medicine)

produce heat loss. One of these is peripheral **vasodilatation,** a widening of the diameter of the skin's capillaries. This sends warm blood to the body surface and results in heat loss by radiation. Other reactions which lead to cooling are sweating (in humans), panting (in dogs), and fur-licking (in rats), all of which produce heat loss by evaporation.

An opposed pattern occurs when the internal temperature is too low. There is no sweating and no panting, and instead of peripheral vasodilatation there is **vasoconstriction.** The capillary diameters narrow so that the blood is squeezed away from the cold periphery and heat is conserved. Other reflexive reactions include a ruffling of fur *(piloerection)* which creates a thick envelope of protective air. (The gooseflesh feeling is our feeble remnant of this reflex response, of little use to us now in our naked condition.) In addition to these various reflexive mechanisms for preventing heat loss, the body also has a few tricks for generating heat when required. One of these is shivering, in which muscular movement expends mechanical energy which is transformed into heat. Another reaction is an increase in the rate at which the body burns up its nutrient fuel and converts part of it into heat.

The homeostatic mechanisms we have just described are essentially involuntary. They may be actions, but we don't feel that they are *our* actions; in fact, some of them concern only a fraction of the body's subsystems. For example, vasodilatation and vasoconstriction do not involve the skeletal musculature at all. If the need arises, such involuntary reflex mechanisms are supplemented by *voluntary* actions that do involve the organism as a whole. If a rat is placed in a cold cage, it will search for suitable materials and build a nest. These voluntary actions are still in the service of that same internal environment whose constancy is so vital, but there is one important difference: Now the organism actively changes its external environment so that its internal environment may stay the same.

There are, then, two main ways in which the internal environment is maintained at a stable level. One is a set of reflexive, homeostatic adjustments, such as vasodilatation in response to heat. Such reflexive mechanisms typically change the internal environment directly and often have little or no effect on the external world. A second means of maintaining homeostasis is behavior that involves the whole organism and that is often voluntary. Such behavior is ultimately in the service of homeostasis, but its effect on the internal environment is indirect. The activity is directed toward some change in the external world which will then produce the appropriate adjustment in the internal environment. In both cases, the ultimate control is by negative feedback. If the bloodstream gets too hot, various adjustment mechanisms are triggered and will serve to cool it. They are then shut off by their own success.

CONTROLLING THE INTERNAL ENVIRONMENT:
THE AUTONOMIC NERVOUS SYSTEM

What controls the various reactions of the internal organs that are so critical for reflexive, internal homeostatic regulation? The most direct control is exerted by the autonomic nervous system (ANS), which sends commands to the **glands** and to the **smooth muscles*** of the viscera (internal organs) and the

---

* The individual fibers of these muscles look smooth when observed under the microscope, in contrast to the fibers of the skeletal muscles which look striped.

blood vessels. The ANS has two divisions: the **sympathetic** and the **parasympathetic.** These two divisions often act as antagonists. Thus, the excitation of the sympathetic division leads to acceleration of heart rate and inhibition of peristalsis (rhythmic contractions) in the intestines. Parasympathetic activation has effects that are the very opposite: cardiac deceleration, stimulation of peristalsis. The two systems do not uniformly stand in opposition (for instance, salivation is determined jointly by both). But even so, the notion of the two great autonomic divisions engaged in a continual tug-of-war is probably a fairly valid picture.

The endocrine system   The smooth muscles are obviously important effector agencies for the control of the internal environment. But the **endocrine system** is no less important (Figure 3.5 and Table 3.1). Various endocrine glands (e.g.,

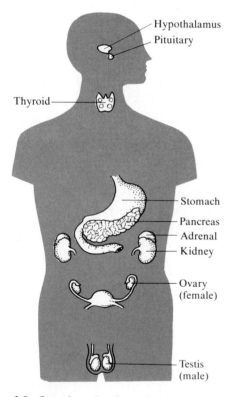

3.5   Location of major endocrine glands   *(After Keeton, 1972)*

Table 3.1   THE MAIN ENDOCRINE GLANDS, THEIR SECRETIONS AND FUNCTIONS

Gland	Hormone	Some major functions
Anterior pituitary	Among others, adrenocorticotropic hormone (ACTH), luteinizing hormone (LH)	Often called the body's master gland because it triggers hormone secretion in many of the other endocrine glands. ACTH stimulates secretions of the adrenal cortex, LH stimulates development of testes and ovaries, and so on.
Posterior pituitary	Among others, antidiuretic hormone	Prevents loss of water through kidney.
Thyroid	Thyroxin	Affects metabolic rate.
Islet cells in pancreas	Insulin	Affects utilization of glucose.
Adrenal cortex	Cortical steroids	Various effects on metabolism; some effects on sexual behavior.
Adrenal medulla	Primarily epinephrine (adrenalin)	Increases sugar output of liver; stimulates various internal organs in the same direction as the sympathetic branch of the ANS (e.g., accelerates heart rate).
Ovaries	Estrogen	Produces female primary and secondary sex characteristics. Necessary for sexual behavior in mammals other than humans.
Ovaries	Progesterone	Prepares uterus for implantation of embryo.
Testes	Androgen (testosterone)	Produces male primary and secondary characteristics. Relevant to sexual arousal.

adrenal, pituitary, pancreas) release their secretions directly into the bloodstream and thus exert effects upon structures often far-removed from their biochemical birthplace.* Because of the endocrine glands, the bloodstream represents an additional form of integration between various parts of the organism (of course, the nervous system is the other), an integration system based on chemical means. Many reactions of this system are in the service of homeostasis. For example, the *pancreas* helps to control the sugar level in the blood by the secretion of *insulin.* This hormone stimulates the liver to convert blood sugar into another biochemical form which is then held in storage.

SENSING THE INTERNAL ENVIRONMENT: THE HYPOTHALAMUS

The ultimate neural control of the internal environment is lodged in the hypothalamus (see Figure 3.6). This control is twofold. First, the hypothalamus functions as the head ganglion of the autonomic nervous system which governs the viscera and various glands. Second, it has a major share in the control of the endocrine system, for it exerts an enormous influence on the *pituitary* which serves as a kind of master gland. Secretions of the pituitary trigger the secretions of many other glands.

The hypothalamus represents a certain triumph of biological miniaturiza-

* In addition to the endocrine glands there are also *duct glands* (for example, salivary and tear glands) which have ducts that channel their secretions to the proper region of application.

3.6   The hypothalamus and pituitary
Cross-section of the human brain, with the hypothalamus and pituitary indicated in color. (After Keeton, 1980)

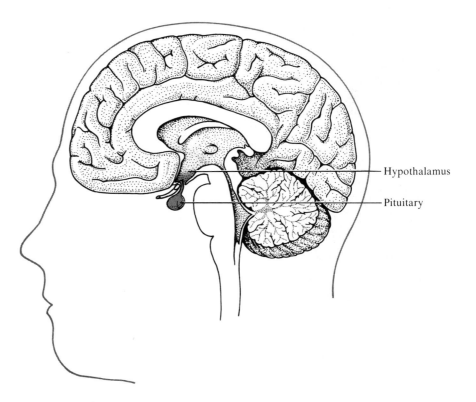

Hypothalamus

Pituitary

tion, for within its few cubic millimeters are the controls for virtually all of the biological motives. As an example, consider temperature regulation. Two regions within the hypothalamus are the efferent control centers for temperature regulation: One cools the body down, the other heats it up. Stimulation of the anterior region leads to panting and vasodilatation; its destruction may cause death by overheating (Andersson, Grant, and Larsson, 1956). Under normal conditions, of course, temperature regulation is nearly perfect. This means that the organism somehow knows its own body temperature, can sense deviations from the normal level, and can decide in which direction it must throw the neural two-way switch (that is, vasodilatation versus vasoconstriction) to restore the thermal balance. How does it do this?

The answer is that the hypothalamus contains its own thermometer: receptor cells which respond to the temperature of the body fluids in which the brain is bathed. These thermoreceptors are hooked up to the reflex controls so as to yield negative feedback—a hypothalamic thermostat. If this is so, one should be able to fool the hypothalamus by changing its temperature independently of the temperature of the skin and body; a hot hypothalamus should then cause sweating, regardless of the actual body temperature. This is just what happens. When a cat's anterior hypothalamus is heated by a warm wire, there is panting and vasodilatation despite the fact that the cat's body temperature may be well below normal (Magoun et al., 1938). The effect is analogous to what happens when a burst of hot air is directed at a home thermostat. The furnace will shut itself off, even though the house is actually freezing.

The reflex operations that lead to heating and cooling are carried out by the autonomic nervous system. The anterior part of the hypothalamus excites the parasympathetic division. This leads to panting and vasodilatation, mechanisms that tend to cool body temperature. Another part of the hypothalamus excites the sympathetic division of the ANS. This results in shivering, fur-ruffling, and vasoconstriction—reflexive devices that serve to push body temperature up. The two branches of the ANS evidently act as the hypothalamus' executive agents to keep body temperature in fine adjustment.

Vasoconstriction and vasodilatation are involuntary reflexes, more in the domain of physiology than that of behavior. Does the hypothalamic feedback device have similar effects upon actions that reach out into the external world (for instance—wearing a fur coat)? Indeed it does. As one example, consider a study that utilized the fact that rats in a cold chamber will press a bar for a brief burst of heat (Weiss and Laties, 1961; see Figure 3.7). The question was whether rats that had learned this skill in a cold environment would bar-press for heat if one cooled their brains rather than their bodies. The test was to run cold liquid through a very thin U-shaped tube implanted in the anterior hypothalamus (Satinoff, 1964). The rats turned on the heat lamp when their brains were cooled even though the outside temperature was reasonably neutral.

Tricking the hypothalamus can evidently affect integrated behavior patterns just as it does autonomic reactions like vasodilatation. The hypothalamus defines an internal need state for the rest of the nervous system, and this need state will then become an important criterion for the appropriateness of any given act.

3.7 Performing a learned response to keep warm *A rat kept in a cold environment will learn to press a lever which turns on a heat lamp for a few seconds after each lever press. (Weiss and Laties, 1961)*

What holds for temperature holds for certain other homeostatic regulations as well. An example is the body's water supply. The organism continually loses water—through the kidneys, the sweat glands, the digestive tract, and occasionally, by hemorrhage. The loss is generally twofold. On the one hand, there is simply a drop in the total *volume* of body fluid, most importantly, of blood. On the other hand, there is typically a change in the *concentration of certain minerals,* such as sodium and potassium salts, that are dissolved in the body's liquids.

How does the system act to offset these disturbances? One set of reactions is entirely internal. Thus a loss of water volume leads to a secretion by the pituitary gland that instructs the kidneys to reabsorb more of the water that passes through them. In consequence, the animal loses less of its water in its urine.

But as so often, internal readjustments can only restore the bodily balance up to a point. Eventually, the corrective measures must involve some behavior by which the organism reaches out into the external world so as to readjust its internal environment. In the case of water loss, this behavior of course is drinking. Just what the organism drinks depends upon the particular disturbance of the water balance; the animal will seek water that is more or less salty as its need dictates. This explains why athletes prefer slightly salty drinks such as *Gatorade* to clear tap water after strenuous exercise—they have to replenish the salt lost through sweating.

How does the organism know that it lacks water or that its sodium concentration is too high or too low? Most modern investigators believe that the stimuli that produce drinking are intimately tied up with the body's general fluid system. Some arise from within the veins that contain receptors which detect drops in blood pressure set off by lowered fluid volume (Stricker, 1973). Other receptors are located within the hypothalamus and respond to a chemical messenger produced by the kidneys which signals a decrease of the body's water level (Epstein, Fitzsimons, and Rolls, 1970). Still other cells in the brain respond to the salt concentration of the body fluids and initiate drinking whenever this concentration rises above some critical level.

Arousing The Body: The Autonomic Nervous System

Thus far our primary focus has been on the **directive** function of motives. But as we have noted, motives have another function as well. They arouse the organism, which then becomes increasingly alert and vigorous. A given motive will thus act like both the tuner and the volume control of a radio. A thirsty animal seeks water rather than food or a sexual partner. But the thirstier it is, the more intensely will it pursue its goal.

Psychologists have used various terms to describe this facet of motivation. Some call it **activation;** others prefer the term **drive.** They all agree that increased drive states generally lead to increased behavioral vigor. Thus rats will run faster to water the longer they have been water-deprived. They will also pull more energetically at a harness that holds them away from the water source, will be willing to tolerate more intense electric shocks in order to get to the water, and so on.

We will now look at some of the biological mechanisms that underlie this activation system. It is convenient to regard this system as composed of two subparts. One concerns the arousal of the autonomic nervous system and represents part of the biological basis of such violent reactions as fear and rage. The other concerns the activation of structures within the brain, and represents the biological basis of sleep and wakefulness.

THE BIOLOGICAL BASIS OF FEAR AND RAGE

We will begin our discussion of activation by considering the arousal functions that are handled by the autonomic nervous system (Figure 3.8). We have previously seen how the interaction of sympathetic and parasympathetic excitations permits adjustments of the visceral bodily machinery in the control of temperature. This delicate tuning of the internal environment depends in large part upon the antagonism between the two autonomic branches which oppose each other in the specific control of various organs. But this is only part of the story.

3.8   The sympathetic and parasympathetic branches of the autonomic nervous system   *The parasympathetic system (shown in black) facilitates the vegetative functions of the organism: It slows the heart and lungs, stimulates digestive functions, permits sexual activity, and so on. In contrast, the sympathetic system (shown in color) helps to place the organism on an emergency basis: It accelerates heart and lung actions, liberates nutrient fuels for muscular effort, and inhibits digestive and sexual functions. Note that the fibers of the sympathetic system are interconnected through a chain of ganglionic fibers outside of the spinal cord. As a result, sympathetic activation has a somewhat diffuse character; any sympathetic excitation tends to affect all of the viscera rather than just some. This is in contrast to the parasympathetic system whose action is more specific. (After Cannon, 1929)*

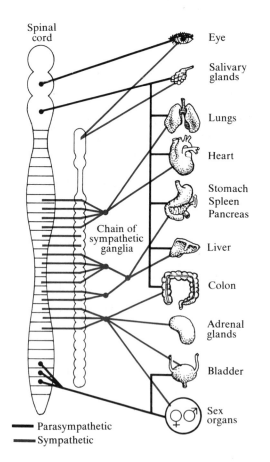

Spinal cord

Eye

Salivary glands

Lungs

Heart

Stomach
Spleen
Pancreas

Chain of sympathetic ganglia

Liver

Colon

Adrenal glands

Bladder

Sex organs

— Parasympathetic
— Sympathetic

PARASYMPATHETIC SYSTEM

Constriction of pupil

Secretion of tear glands

Salivation

Inhibition of heart action

Constriction of respiratory passages

Stomach contraction: secretion of digestive fluids

Intestinal peristalsis

Contraction of bladder

Erection

SYMPATHETIC SYSTEM

Dilation of pupil

Inhibition of tear glands

Inhibition of salivation

Acceleration of heart action

Opens respiratory passages

Inhibits stomach contractions and digestive secretion

Inhibits intestinal peristalsis

Relaxes bladder

Inhibits erection

Walter Cannon (Courtesy National Library of Medicine)

THE SYMPATHETIC AROUSAL SYSTEM

Some fifty years ago, the American physiologist Walter Cannon (1871–1945) argued that the opposition between the sympathetic and parasympathetic systems is more fundamental yet. In his view, they serve two basically different biological functions. The parasympathetic system handles the *vegetative functions* of ordinary life: the conservation of bodily resources, reproduction, and the disposal of wastes. When we consider some of the consequences of parasympathetic excitation, they indeed reflect an organism's functions during times of peace—a lowered heart rate, peristaltic movements of stomach and intestines, secretion of digestive glands, emptying of colon and of bladder. The parasympathetic system also controls many aspects of sexual activity. In contrast, the sympathetic system has an *activating* function. It serves to mobilize the body's resources and gets the organism ready to act (Cannon, 1929).

As an example, take food metabolism. During the process of digestion, various foods are converted into a number of utilizable substances. One of these is *glucose,* a sugar that is the main source of energy for muscles and for the brain. But most of the glucose delivered from the intestines is not used up immediately. A considerable portion is converted into other, more durable forms and cached away for later use. The parasympathetic branch tilts the reaction toward this energy storage. The sympathetic branch has the opposite effect. It accelerates the conversion of these potential energy sources into usable glucose. To put it another way, the sympathetic branch prepares the body to spend the energy which the parasympathetic division worked so diligently to save up.

A similar opposition of function characterizes the role of the sympathetic and parasympathetic divisions in governing the delivery of nutrient fuels and oxygen and the removal of waste products to and from the body's musculature. Parasympathetic excitation slows down heart rate and respiration and reduces the blood pressure. Sympathetic excitation has the opposite effects and also inhibits digestion and sexual activity. The effects of sympathetic arousal are boosted by the action of the *adrenal medulla* (the inner core of the adrenal gland). One consequence of sympathetic excitation is the stimulation of the adrenal medulla which pours *adrenalin* (often called epinephrine) into the bloodstream. Adrenalin has precisely the same effects as sympathetic stimulation—it accelerates the heart, speeds up metabolism, and so on. As a result, the sympathetic effects are amplified still further.

The upshot is a mobilization of the entire body which is now prepared for action. This mobilization is quick and rather diffuse. The entire bodily system—heart, liver, lungs and so on—is alerted more or less simultaneously. A last point concerns the transmitter substance that is released at the sympathetic neurons' axon terminals and through which the target organs (such as the blood vessels) are affected. This substance is *norepinephrine* (usually abbreviated *NE).* NE belongs to a family of chemically related neurotransmitters called *catecholamines.* Other members of this family are epinephrine, which we have already encountered, and *dopamine (DA).* As we will see, catecholamine-releasing neurons are found not only in the autonomic nervous system but also within the brain where they seem to have an analogous activating function.

Cannon pointed out that intense sympathetic arousal has a special function. It serves as an **emergency reaction** that mobilizes the organism for conditions of war and crisis. To survive, an animal must do more than meet the normal demands of day-to-day homeostatic regulation. It must also be able to cope with sudden external threats, to flee from an enemy or to fight it when cornered. We will now discuss the reaction patterns that come into play during such emergencies, the overt reactions of escape and defense and the violent emotions of fear and rage that usually accompany them.

Flight or fight   Consider a grazing zebra, placidly maintaining homeostasis by nibbling at the grass and vasodilatating in the hot African sun. Suddenly it sees a lion approaching rapidly. The vegetative functions must now take second place, for if the zebra does not escape it will have no internal environment left to regulate. The violent exertions of the skeletal musculature require the total support of the entire bodily machinery and this support is provided by intense sympathetic activation. There is more nutrient fuel for the muscles which is now delivered more rapidly. At the same time, waste products are removed more quickly and all unessential organic activities are brought to a halt. If the zebra does not escape, it is not because its sympathetic system did not try.

Cannon produced considerable evidence suggesting that a similar autonomic reaction occurs when the pattern is one of attack rather than of flight. A cat about to do battle with a dog shows accelerated heartbeat, piloerection (normally a heat-conserving device), and pupillary dilation—all signs of diffuse sympathetic arousal, signs that the body is girding itself for violent muscular effort (Figure 3.9). But some later studies have suggested that, despite their many similarities, the autonomic reactions that accompany fear and anger may not be entirely identical. In one experiment, human subjects were either frightened by the possibility of an intense electric shock or were angered by a rude technician who insulted them. Both fear and anger led to intense sympathetic arousal, but the hormonal secretions were not the same. In frightened subjects, there was a high level of epinephrine, but in angered subjects there was an increase in norepinephrine, which has similar but not identical physiological effects (Ax, 1953).

Cannon emphasized the biological utility of the autonomic reaction but his principle cannot tell us which choice the animal will make—whether it will choose fight or flight. This depends in part upon built-in predispositions, in part upon the specific situation. For example, a rat first tries to escape, but fights when finally cornered. Emergency situations may produce still different reactions from those we have already seen. Some animals become paralyzed by fright and stand immobile—an adaptive reaction since predators are more likely to detect a prey that is in motion. Other animals have even more exotic means of self-protection. Some species of fish pale when frightened, which makes them harder to spot against the sandy ocean bottom. This effect is produced by the direct action of epinephrine upon various pigmented substances in the animal's skin (Odiorne, 1957).

Bodily concomitants of intense emotion are of course found also in humans. In fear, our hearts pound, our palms sweat, and we sometimes shiver—all

3.9   Sympathetic emergency reaction in a kitten   (© Walter Chandoha, 1979)

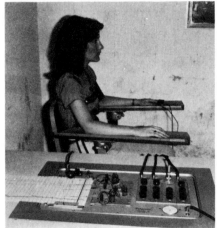

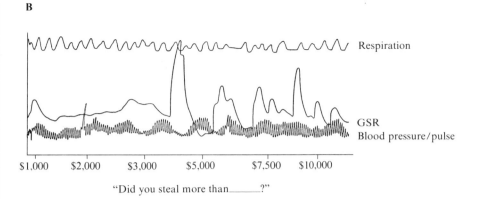

3.10   Lie detection by use of autonomic measures   *(A) Various devices measure autonomic arousal—a tube around the chest measures respiration rate, electrodes attached to the hand measure GSR, and an armband measures blood pressure and pulse. (Photograph by Mary Shuford) (B) A recording of respiration, GSR, and a measure of blood pressure and pulse. The record was obtained from a store employee caught stealing merchandise. At issue was the amount of the theft. To determine this, all parties agreed to be guided by the results of a lie-detector test. The subject was asked questions about the amount, such as "Did you steal more than $1,000?" and "Did you steal more than $2,000?" The record shows a high peak just after $3,000 and before $4,000. Later the subject confessed that the actual amount was $4,000. (After Inbau and Reid, 1953)*

sympathetic activities. It is hardly surprising that such autonomic responses (for example, pulse rate, respiration, and the so-called galvanic skin response) are often used as indicators of emotional states. The **galvanic skin response (GSR)** is a particularly favored measure. It is a drop in the electrical resistance of the skin, particularly of the palm (related to, but not identical with, the activity of the sweat glands), that is a sensitive index of general arousal. This phenomenon is used in lie-detector technology. Lie detectors obviously cannot detect lies as such, but they can uncover autonomic arousal to certain questions or key phrases (Figure 3.10).

CENTRAL CONTROLS

The autonomic nervous system is by no means as autonomous as its name implies, but is in large part guided by other neural centers. Some of these are among the oldest and most primitive portions of the cerebral cortex. These primitive cortical structures, together with the hypothalamus and some surrounding regions, comprise the so-called **limbic system** which is intimately involved in the control of the emotional reactions to situations that call for flight, defense, and attack (Figure 3.11). Electrical stimulation of certain portions of the limbic system transforms a purring cat into a spitting, hissing Halloween figure, with arched back, bared teeth, and all the signs of intense sympathetic arousal—blazing eyes (pupillary dilation), piloerection, and violent heartbeat (Magnus and Lammers, 1956). Stimulation of the same region in humans often produces feelings of great anxiety or of rage, as in a patient who said that she suddenly wanted to tear things to pieces and to slap the experimenter's face (King, 1961).

There are different control centers for predatory attack and for the kind of counterattack which is essentially self-defense (and may be related to what we call rage). Stimulation of certain regions of a cat's hypothalamus leads to quiet stalking, followed by quick deadly attack. The Halloween pattern is produced

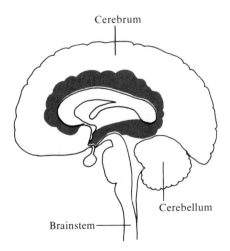

Cerebrum

Cerebellum

Brainstem

3.11   The limbic system of the human brain   *The limbic system (shown in color) is composed of a number of anatomically different structures of the brain, including relatively primitive parts of the cortex. These structures are intimately related in the control of various emotional reactions, especially those that concern flight and attack. (After Keeton, 1980)*

69

by the stimulation of different areas. When these are excited, the cat ignores a nearby mouse or rat but will spring viciously at the experimenter, by whom, no doubt, it feels attacked (Egger and Flynn, 1963). The lion who pounces on the zebra is presumably not enraged but is simply engaged in the matter-of-fact business of food gathering (a fact that is probably of little comfort to the zebra).

STIMULUS CONTROLS

What are the stimuli that produce fear and lead to flight or to counterattack? Some of them obviously acquire their significance through learning. However, some stimuli seem to produce fear without any prior experience. We will briefly note two such innate triggers of fear.

Stimulus intensity   By and large, animals flee from any stimulus that is very intense, especially if its onset is sudden. These tendencies are probably built into the organism's reaction system and do not depend upon experience. They are certainly found at a very early age. Puppies and human infants are terrified by loud, sudden noises, young rats by high-pitched sounds, and colts by the sight of an abrupt movement. Another fear-evoking stimulus is pain. This may simply be a special case of stimulus intensity, for pain sensations are generally quite intense.

According to the American psychologist, T. C. Schneirla, the fear response to sudden, intense stimulation is only one facet of a broader, biopsychological principle: Weak stimuli lead to approach, strong ones to withdrawal (Schneirla, 1959). Thus infants smile and gurgle on hearing a soft tone; a loud, sudden noise produces crying and colic. Toads lunge at small moving targets but retreat from larger ones (Eibl-Eibesfeldt, 1970). Even unicellular creatures seem to fit the general pattern. As we have already seen, an amoeba forms pseudopodia at the site of weak stimulation, and thus approaches the stimulus; the exact opposite occurs when the stimulus is intense.

The biological utility of a general tendency to approach weak stimuli and to withdraw from strong and sudden ones is self-evident. Generally speaking, weak stimuli correspond to the good things in the environment, those that are safe and are often desirable (for instance, food, mates). The opposite holds true for stimulation that is strong. If the weak stimulus is likely to be something that can be eaten, the strong one may well be something that can eat you.

Stimulus novelty   Both animals and humans are afraid of the unknown. Infant monkeys shake with fright when placed in a large, empty room or when confronted by a strange, mechanical toy that makes clanking noises; they immediately run to their mothers and cling desperately (Harlow and Zimmerman, 1959). Similarly, chimpanzees go into paroxysms of terror when they come across an unfamiliar object such as a stuffed toy animal, or—eerier yet—the trunkless head of a chimpanzee (actually a plaster cast; Hebb, 1946). In humans, there is the well-known fear of strangers observed in most infants between eight and twelve months of age. A built-in disposition to fear novelty and change makes good biological sense, given a world full of myriad, hidden dangers in which it generally pays to keep the unknown at a safe and healthy distance (Figure 3.12). This fear is most apparent in the young who have had

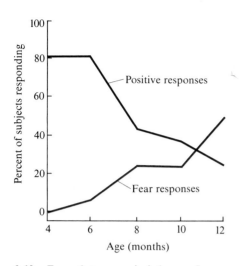

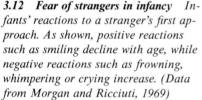

3.12 Fear of strangers in infancy *Infants' reactions to a stranger's first approach. As shown, positive reactions such as smiling decline with age, while negative reactions such as frowning, whimpering or crying increase. (Data from Morgan and Ricciuti, 1969)*

little opportunity to get used to new situations and to learn that they are safe enough. The unfamiliar, however, is only feared if recognized as a change from the familiar. To the newborn, all faces are strange but she fears none of them. The fear of strangers begins only *after* the child recognizes and responds to one or both parents (Schaffer, 1966).

DISRUPTIVE EFFECTS OF AUTONOMIC AROUSAL

Our preceding discussion emphasized the biological value of the emergency system. But strong autonomic arousal can also be disruptive and even harmful to the organism. This negative side of the matter is especially clear in humans. In our day-to-day lives we rarely encounter emergencies that call for violent physical effort. But our biological nature has not changed just because our modern world contains no sabertooth tigers. We still have the same emergency system that served our primitive ancestors and its bodily consequences may take serious tolls.

SOME SIDE-EFFECTS OF INTENSE EMOTION

The disruptive effect of fear and anger upon digestion or upon sexual behavior is a matter of common knowledge. During periods of marked anxiety there are often complaints of constipation and other digestive ills. The same holds for impotence and frigidity. This is hardly surprising since both the digestive and the sexual functions are largely controlled by the parasympathetic system and are thus inhibited by sympathetic arousal.

A more difficult question is why there is a loss of bladder and bowel control during states of intense terror. In humans this occurs only under extreme conditions (for instance, on the battlefield), but in animals the effect is so common that urination and defecation are often utilized as objective indices of emotional agitation (Hall, 1934). The phenomenon is puzzling because parasympathetic arousal leads to the *relaxation* of the relevant sphincter muscles. But if so, shouldn't intense fear with its violent sympathetic concomitants lead to parasympathetic inhibition and thus to the very opposite effect? Cannon tried to resolve the paradox by suggesting that when the excitations get intense enough, the pattern of mutual inhibition between the two autonomic systems breaks down and both of them may discharge more or less simultaneously.

Another puzzling phenomenon is weeping. This is usually a concomitant of the more unpleasant emotions; by and large, tears are shed in grief and sadness. But this is not the whole story. A bereaved person rarely weeps when most depressed by the loss; weeping comes later, when there is some relief or comfort mingled with the grief. A common example is a man whose wife dies suddenly. For several days he shows no emotion except deep depression, but he breaks into tears when a friend brings a beautiful wreath. A similar pattern holds in various forms of psychopathology. The most depressed and agitated patients rarely weep; tears are much more likely when the patient's condition is transitional, moving from a depressed to a more elated state (Lund, 1930).

These phenomena are by no means understood, but some of their aspects may reflect the interaction of parasympathetic and sympathetic excitation. The tear glands are activated by parasympathetic fibers. Their uncontrollable discharge seen in weeping may be in part the result of a neural ***rebound effect,***

71

specifically, a ***parasympathetic overshoot.*** Given strong sympathetic excitation (for instance, the fear that someone we love may die) and the concomitant inhibition of parasympathetic action, what happens when this excitation is suddenly withdrawn? The effect is analogous to a tug-of-war in which one of the contestants abruptly lets go of the rope—the opponent falls backward. Thus the parasympathetic division overshoots its normal level after the inhibition from its sympathetic antagonist is suddenly lifted.

BODILY DAMAGE DUE TO AUTONOMIC AROUSAL

The aftereffects of emotional arousal sometimes cause profound and long-lasting bodily harm. Various disorders such as peptic ulcer, colitis, asthma, and hypertension can often be traced back to emotional patterns in the patient's life and are then considered ***psychosomatic*** ailments in which a psychological cause produces a bodily, a somatic, effect (see Chapter 18). But the wages of autonomic arousal can be even more grievous and irrevocable; they may be death.

Anthropologists have long noted instances of mysterious and sudden death in members of various preliterate cultures who believed that they were victims of sorcery. Some of these cases were examined by competent physicians who found no signs of ordinary disease or of poisoning. Under the circumstances, there was some reason to believe that death was brought on by psychological factors, including the victim's belief in his persecutor's supernatural powers. Several such cases were studied by Walter Cannon. He describes a vivid example:

> I have seen more than one hardened old Haussa soldier dying steadily and by inches because he believed himself to be bewitched; no nourishment or medicines that were given to him had the slightest effect either to check the mischief or to improve his condition in any way, and nothing was able to divert him from a fate which he considered inevitable. In the same way, and under very similar conditions, I have seen Kru-men and others die in spite of every effort that was made to save them, simply because they had made up their minds, not (as we thought at the time) to die, but that being in the clutch of malignant demons they were bound to die (Cannon, 1942).

Needless to say, such reports have to be viewed with considerable caution; they are essentially anecdotes, whose details are difficult to check. But a similar effect has been observed in some animal studies—sudden death that is somehow linked to violent fear.

In one experiment, wild rats were placed in large vats filled with water (Richter, 1957). To survive, the animals had to keep on swimming. Some of them died within a few minutes after they were placed in the vat. Instead of swimming (which should be no problem, for rats are very good swimmers) they gave up, dropped to the bottom of the vat, and died. A few rats died even before immersion, when held in the experimenter's hand. Why did these animals die so suddenly? No doubt they were intensely frightened, but surprisingly enough they did not die because of sympathetic overstimulation. Quite the contrary. Autopsy showed that at death the heart was *over*expanded (a parasympathetic effect) rather than constricted (a sympathetic effect). Death was therefore produced by an excess of parasympathetic activity, by an excess of cardiac relaxation. A further fact fits in neatly. If the rats were first injected with atropine, a drug that blocks the parasympathetic division, they generally continued to struggle and did not die a sudden death.

This effect may well be the result of a more violent form of the parasympathetic overshoot we have already discussed. Initially, the organism is in utter terror and its sympathetic emergency apparatus operates at its absolute peak. When this system comes to a sudden halt, there is a correspondingly massive rebound in the other direction. But why this sudden stop in sympathetic action? One possibility is that the animal has given up hope and stops struggling. In line with this interpretation is what happened to rats that were first immersed in the water, then taken out, then immersed again, and so on. When later tested in the same situation that produced sudden death in the others, these rats did not succumb. They had learned that they could cope in the situation by swimming; in consequence they kept on struggling and managed to survive.

Arousing the Brain: Waking and Sleeping

The sympathetic fibers represent an arousing system for the more primitive physiological processes of the body. A similar system operates to alert the brain. It activates the cortex so that it is fully responsive to incoming messages. In effect, it awakens the brain.

WAKING

The arousal of the brain is the function of the ***reticular activating system*** or ***RAS.*** This neurological structure has its origin in the upper portion of the reticular formation, a network of interconnected cells that extends throughout the brainstem and has branches which ascend to much of the rest of the brain (Figure 3.13). Sleeping cats whose RAS is electrically stimulated will awaken; cats whose RAS is destroyed are somnolent (Lindsley, 1960). RAS activity not

3.13 The reticular activating system
The figure indicates the location and function of the reticular structures in the hind- and midbrain. When a sense organ is stimulated, one effect is specific. The sensory message is relayed to a particular region of the cortex, typically a projection area. A second effect is nonspecific. The sensory stimulation triggers the reticular system which then arouses the cortex. As a result, the areas of the brain that receive the specific sensory message are sufficiently activated so that they can interpret it. (After French, 1957)

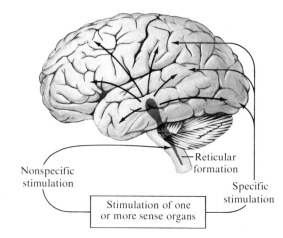

only leads to awakening but it also produces increased levels of arousal once awake. Stimulation of the RAS in waking monkeys jolts them into a highly alert state of attention in which they look around expectantly.

THE EFFECT OF RETICULAR ACTIVATION

What triggers the RAS? One factor is sensory stimulation. On the face of it, this is hardly surprising, for we all know that sleep comes more readily when it is quiet and dark. But the neurological chain of events that explains why intense stimuli lead to awakening is fairly complex. Oddly enough, the direct input from the sensory pathways to the cortex is not the primary cause of wakefulness. In one study, the investigators severed virtually all of the sensory tracts to the cortex in cats (Lindsley et al., 1950). When the cats were asleep the experimenters presented a loud tone and the cats woke up. But how could this be, if the path from ear to cortex was cut so that the cortex was isolated from any auditory input? The answer is that there is another, indirect pathway that leads through the RAS. All of the sensory pathways to the cortex send collateral side branches to the RAS. The information the RAS receives in this manner is very meager and unspecific; it amounts to no more than a statement that a sensory message is on its way up to the cortex without any further indication of what that message might be. But this is enough for the RAS which now functions as a general alarm. It arouses the cortex which can then interpret the specific signals sent over the direct sensory pathway. In effect, the RAS is like a four-year old who has just been handed a telegram while its mother is asleep. The child cannot read but it awakens the mother who can.

Sensory stimulation is not the only source of RAS activation. Another comes from the cortex itself. There are descending fibers from the cortex that may excite the RAS which will then activate the cortex more fully. This circuit—cortex to RAS to cortex—probably plays an important role in many phenomena of sleep and waking. We sometimes have trouble in falling asleep because we "can't shut off our thoughts." Here cortical activity triggers the RAS which activates the cortex which again excites the RAS and so on. The importance of cortical activation of the RAS is also shown by the fact that some stimuli are more likely to wake us than others, regardless of their intensity—a baby's cry, the smell of fire, the sound of one's own name.

THE TWO AROUSAL SYSTEMS COMPARED

Both the sympathetic system and the RAS are activating mechanisms. One mobilizes the viscera while the other arouses the brain. But is the analogy any deeper than this? A few other similarities suggest that it may be.

To begin with, we should note that both arousal systems are comparatively diffuse. Sympathetic activity is triggered by any number of stimuli that signal the need for bodily action. The RAS is similarly nonspecific. Any reasonably intense stimulus—sound and light from without, thirst or hunger sensations from within, cortical messages from above—will stimulate the RAS which will then arouse other regions of the brain and thus prepare them to react.

Another point of similarity concerns the transmitter substances by means of which the neurons of the two arousal systems achieve their activation effect. In both cases, the transmitters are catecholamines. In the RAS, the relevant substances are norepinephrine and dopamine. These are liberated at the axon terminals of RAS fibers and activate other neurons at synapses higher up. What the RAS does naturally, humans sometimes try to do artificially. A number of drugs such as the ***amphetamines*** are close relatives of the catecholamines and mimic many of their effects, producing a heightened sense of alertness, extra energy, and a sense of being "high." Unfortunately they have drawbacks, including the fact that users often develop tolerance for the drug and therefore take it in ever-increasing amounts (see p. 93).

Yet another similarity between the sympathetic and reticular activating systems is the fact that both have antagonists. In the first case, the antagonist is the parasympathetic branch which acts to conserve the energy that the sympathetic division does everything to spend. In the case of the RAS, the tug-of-war is with another set of neurological structures that originate within the brainstem, a system whose activation leads to drowsiness and sleep.

These points suggest that there is a genuine parallel between the arousing functions of the sympathetic fibers and of the RAS. In effect, the sympathetic system activates the body, while the RAS activates the mind.

SLEEP

The primary focus of this chapter is on motivation, and thus on the direction and activation of behavior that motives bring about. In this context, phenomena such as rest and sleep are largely side issues whose main interest derives from the fact that they serve as antagonists to arousal. But, since all humans sleep, as indeed do most vertebrate animals, we will take a detour to consider sleep as a topic in its own right.

How can we tell that someone is sleeping? We cannot ask the person directly since, by definition, sleep is a condition of which the sleeper is unaware. We may have conscious experiences in the form of dreams, but we do not know them as dreams while they occur. This even applies to the occasions when we create a nocturnal play within a play and dream that we are dreaming. The internal dream is recognized as such but the framework dream is not.

SLEEP AND BODILY ACTIVITY

Since we cannot observe sleep from within, we perforce must study it from without. One way of doing so is by observing the sleeper's bodily activity. The sleeper's eyes are closed, her heart rate and respiration are lowered, her position is generally prone and relaxed, and there is marked decrease in the sensitivity to external stimulation (Kleitman, 1963). A corresponding stillness descends upon virtually all members of the animal kingdom during at least one period of the twenty-four-hour day. Lobsters become immobile, fish remain motionless at the ocean bottom, and various birds tuck their heads under one wing while their toes are curled around a perch, held in place by special bumps on their legs. Some animals sleep at night and others during the day; some sleep for a few hours and others for sixteen; but all show some alternation between activity and rest.

SLEEP AND BRAIN ACTIVITY

Eavesdropping on the brain is made possible by the fact that the language of the nervous system is electrical. When electrodes are placed at various points on the skull, they pick up the electrical changes that are produced by the

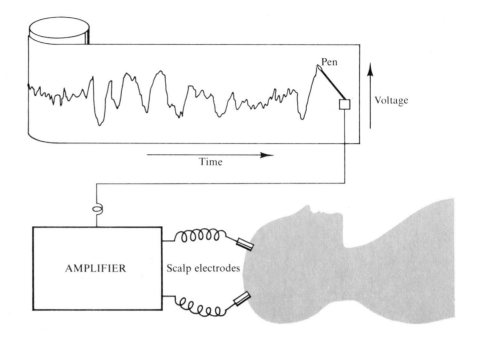

3.14 Schematic diagram of EEG recording *A number of scalp electrodes are placed on a subject's head. At any one time, there are small differences in the electrical potential (that is, the voltage) between any two of these electrodes. These differences are magnified by an amplifier and are then used to activate a recording pen. The greater the voltage difference, the larger the pen's deflecion. Since the voltage fluctuates, the pen goes up and down, thus tracing a so-called brain wave on the moving paper. The number of such waves per second is the EEG frequency.*

summed activity of the millions of nerve cells in the cerebral cortex that is just underneath. In absolute terms these changes are very small; they are therefore fed to a highly sensitive amplifier whose output in turn activates a series of pens. These pens trace their position on a long roll of paper that moves at a constant speed (Figure 3.14). The resulting record is an ***electroencephalogram*** or EEG, a picture of voltage changes over time occurring in the brain.

Figure 3.15 shows two EEG records. This first was taken while the subject was relaxed, "not thinking about anything in particular," and had his eyes closed. The record shows ***alpha waves,*** a rather regular waxing and waning of electrical potential, at some eight to twelve cycles per second. This alpha rhythm is very characteristic of this state (awake but resting), and is found in most mammals. When the subject attends to some stimulus with open eyes, or when he is involved in active thought (for instance, mental arithmetic) with his eyes closed, the picture changes. Now the alpha rhythm is ***blocked;*** the voltage

3.15 Alpha waves and alpha blocking *(After Guyton, 1966)*

Relaxed, eyes closed

Alpha blocking, eyes open

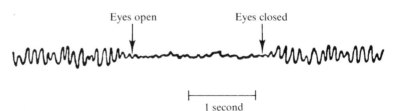

is lower, the frequency is much higher, and the pattern of ups and downs is nearly random.

How does the alpha rhythm arise? The EEG records the electrical composite produced by the millions of neurons just beneath the scalp electrodes, and one might well expect a pattern that is essentially random over time. Instead there is a rhythm which indicates that many cells fire in synchrony. Some cerebral pacemaker evidently drives the cortical nerve cells to make them act in concert, at roughly ten times per second. Alpha blocking is often thought to be caused by the superimposition of a focused cortical pattern which destroys the synchrony. Thus far we don't really know what causes the rhythm and what conceivable biological function it might serve.

There is some evidence that people can learn to induce the alpha state in themselves. Some investigators claim success through *biofeedback* (Kamiya, 1969). Subjects receive a signal, such as a tone, that is activated by the EEG record and tells them whether they are in an alpha state. This is said to help the subjects recognize their own internal states so that they can eventually attain them at will. Whether such biofeedback techniques really work is still a matter of debate; some experimenters have argued that the subjects merely learn to reduce their visual input by defocusing their open eyes (Orne and Wilson, 1978).

The issue derives much of its interest from the claim that the alpha state is a concomitant—or even the prime ingredient—of the experience of *meditation.* This practice has long been advocated by various Eastern sects, such as the Yogi and Zen Buddhists, who regard it as a way of attaining "a higher consciousness achieved through a fully rested and relaxed body and a fully awake and relaxed mind." Different sects propose different means to achieve the meditation state; one technique is to concentrate upon one word (the so-called mantra) to the exclusion of all else. In experienced practitioners, the meditation state seems to have objective, physiological correlates. While in this state, alpha waves are predominant. In addition, there are various metabolic changes, such as a decrease in oxygen consumption. Some studies suggest that meditation represents a state of partial quiescence while yet awake. This state is presumably the very opposite from the violent arousal level produced by the fight-or-flight reaction of the sympathetic nervous system (Wallace, 1972).

The stages of sleep Several decades of work involving continuous, all-night recordings of EEGs and other measures have shown that there are several stages of sleep and that these vary in depth. Just prior to sleep, there tends to be an accentuated alpha rhythm. As the subject becomes drowsy, the alpha comes and goes; there are increasingly long stretches during which the pattern is random. The subject is now in a light, dozing sleep, from which she is easily awakened (Stage 1 in Figure 3.16). Over the course of the next hour she drifts into deeper and deeper stages, in which the EEGs are characterized by the complete absence of alpha and by waves of increasingly higher voltage and much lower frequency (Stages 2 through 4 in Figure 3.16). In the last stages, the waves are very slow. They occur about once every second and are some five times greater in amplitude than those of the alpha rhythm. At this point the sleeper is virtually immobile and will take a few seconds to awaken, mumbling incoherently, even if shaken or shouted at. During the course of the night, the sleeper's descent repeats itself several times. She drops from dozing to deep, slow-wave sleep, reascends to Stage 1, drops back to slow-wave sleep, and so on for some four or five cycles.

Apart from dreams, a topic to which we will turn presently, is there any mental activity during sleep, especially in its deeper stages? Some commercial enterprises advertise special tape recorders with loudspeakers that fit under the pillow and gently whisper lists of irregular French verbs into the sleeper's ear. Their claim is the lazy man's wish, that we can learn while asleep. Unfortunately evidence for *sleep learning* is negative. In one study, sleeping subjects were presented with a tape recording of ten words, played over and over through the night. The tape was only played when the subject had a sleeping EEG and was turned off at all other times. When tested in the morning, the subjects showed not the slightest benefit of their nocturnal exposure to the word list (Emmons and Simon, 1956).

While sleep learning does not occur, a certain degree of mental activity is nevertheless possible. In all but perhaps the very deepest stages of sleep, there is still some capacity to analyze and classify certain incoming sensory inputs. Parents are said to sleep through thunderstorms but wake at their baby's soft whimper. If so, the sleeping brain must maintain the capacity to discriminate between the one stimulus that matters and the many which do not. Some experimental evidence suggests that this is indeed the case. Subjects are more likely to respond (usually by awakening) to the sound of their own name rather than to the names of others presented on a tape recording during even the deeper stages of sleep (Oswald, Taylor, and Treisman, 1960).

TWO KINDS OF SLEEP

The oscillations between different sleep stages are not merely changes in depth. When the sleeper reascends into Stage 1, he seems to enter a qualitatively different state entirely. This state is sometimes called *active sleep* to distinguish it from the *quiet sleep* found during the other stages, Stages 2 through 4. Active sleep is a paradoxical condition with contradictory aspects. In some ways it is as deep as sleep ever gets. The sleeper's general body musculature is more flaccid and he is less sensitive to external stimulation (Williams, Tepas, and Morlock, 1962). But judged by some other criteria, the level of arousal during active sleep is almost as high as during alert wakefulness. One sign is the EEG, which in humans is rather similar to that found in waking (Jouvet, 1967).

3.16   The stages of sleep   *The figure includes EEG records taken from three different regions of the brain, during waking, quiet sleep, and active sleep. (After Kleitman, 1960)*

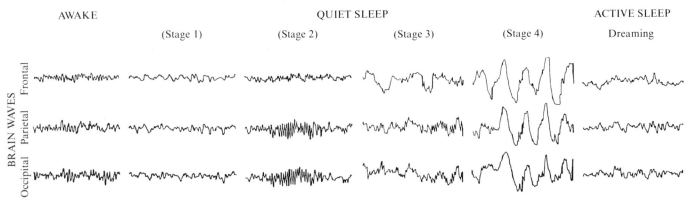

| AWAKE | (Stage 1) | QUIET SLEEP | | | ACTIVE SLEEP |
| | | (Stage 2) | (Stage 3) | (Stage 4) | Dreaming |

BRAIN WAVES
Occipital Parietal Frontal

3.17 REM and non-REM sleep *(A) A subject in a sleep laboratory. Note the head electrodes for recording EEG as well as electrodes at each side of the head for monitoring movements of the eyes. (Courtesy New York University School of Medicine) (B) Eye movements during non-REM and REM sleep. The REM periods are associated with dreaming. (C) The alternation of non-REM and REM periods throughout the course of the night (REM periods are in color). Rapid eye movements and dreams begin as the person repeatedly emerges from deeper sleep to the level of Stage 1. (Both after Kleitman, 1960)*

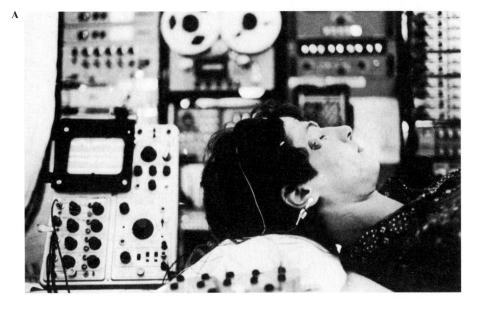

A

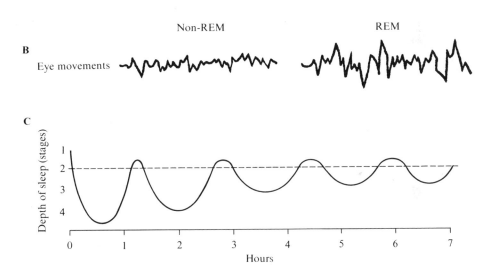

B

Non-REM   REM

Eye movements

C

Depth of sleep (stages)

1
2
3
4

0   1   2   3   4   5   6   7

Hours

Of particular interest are the sleeper's eye movements which can be recorded by means of electrodes attached to the sides of each eye. During quiet sleep, the eyes drift slowly and no longer move in tandem. But during active sleep a different pattern suddenly appears. The eyes move rapidly and in unison behind closed lids, as if the sleeper were looking at some object outside. These jerky, rapid eye movements (REMs) are one of the most striking features of active sleep, which is often called ***REM sleep*** for this reason. Young human adults enter this stage about four times each night (Figure 3.17).

DREAMS

Active sleep and dreaming REM sleep was discovered fairly recently but its discoverers almost immediately related it to a phenomenon known to humans

79

since prehistoric times: dreaming. When sleeping subjects are awakened during REM sleep they generally report a dream whose content they can describe in some detail. Not so for quiet (that is, non-REM) sleep. When awakened then, subjects are much less likely to relate dream episodes. Further evidence links the duration of the dream events to the length of the REM period. Subjects who are awakened five minutes after the onset of REM tend to describe shorter dreams than subjects who are awakened fifteen minutes after the REM period begins (Dement and Kleitman, 1957). This result argues against the popular notion that dreams are virtually instantaneous, no matter how long they take to relate when later recalled while awake. In actual fact, the dream seems to take about as long as the dream episode might have been in real life (Dement and Wolpert, 1958).

These findings suggest that the average adult dreams for about 1.5 hours every night, the time spent in REM sleep. How can we square this assertion with the fact that in everyday life, most people seem to experience dreams only occasionally and that some deny that they ever dream? The answer is that dreams are generally forgotten within minutes after they have occurred. In one study, subjects were awakened either during REM sleep or five minutes after a REM period had ended. In the first condition detailed dream narratives were obtained on 85 percent of the awakenings; in the second, there were none.

Why dreams leave such fragile memories is as yet unknown. One possibility is that the memories as such are unscathed but that they are ordinarily inaccessible. This might be caused by a failure to relate the dream episode (while it occurs) to the many other memories of waking life (see Chapter 8). This interpretation may perhaps explain some odd experiences in which we seem to remember something that we know did not occur. These may be fleeting recollections of a dream but without the recognition that it was a dream and not a real event. One such phenomenon may be the experience of *déjà vu,* the feeling that what is happening now has happened before, that one is somehow reliving the past, but without any knowledge of its when and where.

What is a dream?   An old theory of dreams is that they are sleepers' responses to external or internal stimuli which become intense enough to bring them near awakening. According to this view, the dream is triggered by these stimuli which then provide the original starting point around which the dream content is organized. Plausible as it may seem, this conception is false. Dreams are rarely initiated by sensory input, whether from within or without. In one study, the experimenters sprayed cold water on the sleeping subject's face. If he continued to sleep (which he often did), he was awakened a few minutes later and asked for his dream report. On many occasions, the stimulus seemed to have modified the dream, but there was no evidence that it ever triggered it. It was apparently incorporated within an already ongoing dream episode. For example, one subject described an intricate dream sequence in which he took part in a play: "I was walking behind the leading lady, when she suddenly collapsed and water was dripping on her." The external stimulus is evidently woven into a dream tapestry that was already unfolding, but it does not cause the dream in the first place (Dement and Wolpert, 1958).

What then causes the dream? Our best guess is that the dream is a reflection of the brain's aroused state during active sleep. During this period, the cerebral cortex is active and its activity is manifested in conscious experience—the dream. But this dream experience necessarily has a special form. The cortex may be active but it is largely shut off from sensory input. Under the circumstances, its activity is not constrained by the demands of external reality. Memory images become more prominent than they are in waking life, for they do not have to compete with the insistent here and now provided by the senses. The recent experiences of the day are evoked most readily and they will then arouse a host of previous memories and intermingle with them. The cortex is sufficiently active to connect and interpret these basic materials so that we experience a running, inner narrative. But this is often accomplished in a primitive, disjointed way; perhaps the cortex is not active enough to provide more than a crude organization. Thought proceeds at a much less abstract level than it does in waking life and is often embodied in a very concretized form. For example, during the day, a subject met some women that struck him as haughty and statuesque; at night, he dreamed that he saw them as statues (Foulkes, 1966).

The conscious events of active sleep have one further characteristic: While they occur, they are "real." The apparent reality of our dreams is caused at least in part by the lack of sensory input during sleep. The brain is active, but it only looks within its own storehouse of memories and thoughts. Since there is no external reality against which this dream activity can be checked, this internal experience is real for a while.

Since cerebral activity is relatively unconstrained by sensory reality during sleep, the content of dreams is likely to reflect the individuality of the dreamer. The raw materials of the dream are peculiarly hers: *her* thoughts, *her* memories, *her* emotions. Since objective sensory input is absent, these subjective sources are more prominent. Under the circumstances, it is not surprising that dreams have often been thought to have a deeper meaning (see Chapter 12).

The limitations of looking in from without   The electrorecording techniques of sleep research have opened a window through which we can observe what goes on within a person while asleep. But we must realize that this window is very clouded; it does not really permit us to look into the sleepers' minds. Given the appropriate EEG and REM equipment we can determine whether subjects are asleep. We can even tell whether they are dreaming. But neither the EEG nor the REM records can tell us what they are dreaming about. If that's what we want to know, we must wake the sleepers and ask.

The EEG and REM records are devices which indicate the general arousal level, whether the brain's activity is low as in quiet sleep, high but focused inward as in active sleep, or high and directed outward as in alert wakefulness. But they do not tell us what the particular activity is at any moment. An EEG record can indicate that a person is thinking but not what he is thinking about. This is not really surprising. EEG recording is like attaching a microphone to the roof of the Empire State Building. Could we possibly reconstruct the conversations in any of the offices below from the aggregate babble on the tape? On the other hand, we might well expect to get some general indication of the overall activity level within the building. The babble will surely drop to a whisper between 2:00 and 6:00 A.M.

What function is served by sleep, whether in its active or quiet form? Surprisingly enough, the answer is still unknown.

Sleep deprivation　One way of trying to assess the benefits that sleep may bring is to observe what ills befall if it is prevented. This is the logic of **sleep-deprivation** experiments in which humans and animals are kept awake for days on end. Many authors believe that the results of such studies demonstrate that there is a need for sleep. If deprived of sleep, the organism seeks it, just as it seeks food when it is starved. If sleep is forbidden, there are snatches of **microsleep** during which the subjects doze off for a second or two without knowing that they do. When sleep is finally allowed, the subjects sink down upon the nearest vacant cot and try to make up the sleep they lost. Fortunately for them, the sleep-debt does not have to be repaid on a strict hour-by-hour basis. After three days without sleep, young adults generally sleep for twelve to fourteen hours on the first recovery night and may sleep an hour more than usual on one or two nights thereafter; subsequent to this they seem to be fully recovered (Hartmann, 1973).

The need of the sleep-deprived person is not just for sleep in general but for the two major sleep-states that comprise it. The demonstration of such specific needs comes from studies on **selective sleep deprivation** in which the experimenter prevents one kind of sleep (for instance, REM) but not the other. If he wants to deprive the subjects of REM sleep selectively, he simply awakens him whenever the EEG and eye-movement records signal the beginning of a REM period. After the subject wakes up, he goes back to sleep, is reawakened when he next enters the REM state, goes back to sleep, is reawakened, and so on through the night. After a few nights of this, the subject is allowed to sleep freely. He will now spend more time in REM than he normally does, as if to make up for the state of which he was deprived (Figure 3.18). The same holds for selective deprivation of the deep, slow-wave sleep of Stages 3 and 4. If lost one night, it is made up on another (Webb, 1972).

Restorative function　The sleep-deprivation experiments suggest that there is a need for sleep, but they do not explain why. One possibility is that sleep is restorative, that it is a period during which some vital substance is resynthesized in the nervous system. In some form or other, this view was held at least as early as Renaissance. To Shakespeare, sleep was "nature's soft nurse," a "balm of hurt minds" that "knits up the ravel'd sleave of care." That sleep has some such restorative function seems probable even though we have only a sketchy idea of what might be restored and how.

According to one author, the basic revitalizing function is served by the deep, slow-wave stages of quiet sleep, Stages 3 and 4 (Hartmann, 1973). Slow-wave sleep is enhanced under conditions in which there is a greater need for bodily restoration such as physical fatigue or minor illness. It is also the stage of sleep during which growth-hormone secretion takes place. Under the circumstances, it is not surprising that slow-wave sleep enjoys a certain priority. When sleep is shortened, the other sleep states suffer most but the duration of Stages 3 and 4 is largely unaffected.

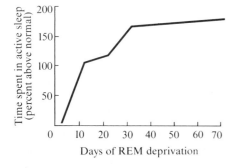

3.18　The effect of lost REM sleep
The figure shows an increase in the time cats spend in REM sleep after various periods of REM-sleep deprivation. The animals were deprived of REM sleep (but not non-REM sleep) for from 5 to 72 days by being awakened as soon as their EEG indicated the beginning of a REM period. On the first day when the animals were finally allowed to sleep undisturbed, there was an increase in the proportion of time spent in REM sleep rather than non-REM sleep. (Data from Cohen, 1972)

The functions of REM sleep   Some authors believe that REM sleep also has a restorative function. They suggest that while slow-wave sleep heals the exhaustion of the body, REM sleep heals the exhaustion of the mind. For instance, REM sleep seems to go up after a day of intense mental preoccupation or emotional stress. In one study, subjects wore prisms that turned the world upside down so that they had to adjust to a topsy-turvy environment. At night, there was a sharp increase in active sleep time. A similar effect seems to occur after a day of worry or depression. According to restoration theorists, learning (and perhaps various emotional reactions) requires the presence of certain transmitter substances in particular areas of the brain. The most likely candidates are the **catecholamines.** According to the theory, these substances are depleted when the organisms learns—or tries to learn—new modes of adjustment. They are resynthesized during REM sleep. This claim is still mostly conjecture. Some supporting evidence comes from the effects of various drugs. Drugs which deplete catecholamine levels seem to enhance active sleep; those which augment the available catecholamine supply have the opposite effect (Hartmann, 1973).

The restorative hypothesis is an attempt to understand the biological function of REM state within the depletion-repletion model that seems to fit many other bodily motives. The idea stems from the assumption that we need REM sleep. This in turn is based on the results of REM deprivation. When finally allowed to sleep the subject engages in a veritable orgy of REM. But it is worth noting that this doesn't really prove that there is a need for REM. There is some evidence that the neurological underpinnings for REM and non-REM sleep inhibit each other reciprocally (Morgane and Sterne, 1974). But this would have the result that suppression of the one system is likely to be followed by a rebound of the other. An example of such a rebound in another area is parasympathetic overshoot. When intense sympathetic stimulation is withdrawn, the heart rate drops below its normal level. But this rebound effect is simply a result of the way in which the two systems are hooked up; it is certainly not an attempt to make up for missed parasympathetic excitation. The same analysis may well apply to excess REM activity after REM deprivation. But if this is so, it is misleading to speak of a need for REM (though there may well be a need for sleep in general). If no such need exists, attempts to explain REM as a form of restoration may be off the mark.

A Motive Looked at in Detail: Hunger

Most biological motives involve direction by internal as well as external factors. They also involve arousal and its antagonist, quiescence. This interplay of factors is especially clear in the case of the motive which psychobiologists have studied most extensively: hunger.

THE SIGNALS FOR FEEDING

There is no doubt that feeding is ultimately in the service of homeostasis. No matter what food an animal eats or how it gets it, the final biological consequence of eating is always the same—to maintain appropriate nutrient supplies in the internal environment. But what are the actual mechanisms that determine whether humans and animals eat or stop eating? To put it another way, what is hunger and what is satiety?

SIGNALS FROM WITHIN

There are numerous signals that control food intake. Among the most important of these are stimuli that arise from within the animal's own body and somehow inform the brain of the current state of the nutrient supplies. That some such messages are sent is certain. Without them, neither humans nor animals would be able to control their food intake, and they generally do. If food is freely available, they usually tend to eat just about the right amount to keep a roughly constant weight as adults. What is regulated is calorie intake rather than the total volume of food that is eaten. This was demonstrated in a study in which the experimenter varied the calorie level of the diet he fed to rats by adulterating their food with nonnutritive cellulose. The more diluted the food, the more of it was eaten, in a quantity roughly adequate to keep the total calorie content constant (Adolph, 1947).

This self-regulation of food intake persists even when there is no guidance from taste and smell receptors. One experiment used rats whose food was always delivered directly into the stomach. The animals learned to press a bar that squirted a few drops of liquid food through a special tube which led into the stomach. The rats injected themselves with just about the right number of squirts to keep a level weight. When the food was diluted with an equal amount of water, they doubled their intake (Epstein and Teitelbaum, 1962).

Receptors in the brain How does the animal manage to adjust its food intake to its calorie needs? From the start, investigators focused on **glucose** (or blood sugar) which is the major source of energy for bodily tissues. They believed that somewhere in the body are receptors which detect changes in the way this metabolic fuel is utilized.

Many authors believe that some of the relevant receptors are in the brain itself, most likely the hypothalamus. These **glucoreceptors** are thought to sense the amount of glucose that is available for metabolic use (Mayer, 1955). Evidence comes from studies in which the hypothalamus was injected with a chemical that made its cells unable to respond to glucose. The result was ravenous eating. This treatment presumably silenced the glucoreceptors whose failure to fire was then interpreted as a fuel deficiency, which led to feeding (Miselis and Epstein, 1970).

Receptors in the digestive organs Signals from within the brain, such as those which come from the glucoreceptors, cannot provide the sole information about the nutrient levels in the bloodstream. In actual fact, the nutrient supplies to the brain are kept remarkably constant even under conditions of near-starvation. In the body's economy, the brain is a privileged organ; it gets its glucose supply ahead of all other parts of the body and will therefore be the last to notice that metabolic fuel is in short supply. This means that there has to be some other source of information about the body's nutrient levels. The most important source turns out to be the organ that acts as the manager of the body's food metabolism—the liver.

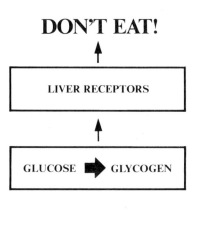

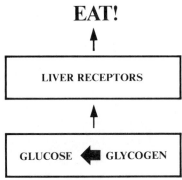

3.19 *The relation between the glucose-glycogen balance in the liver and eating*

Immediately after a meal glucose is plentiful. Since the body can't use it all, much of it is converted into other forms and put in storage. One such conversion goes on in the liver where glucose is turned into *glycogen* (often called animal starch). Glycogen cannot be used up as a metabolic fuel. This is fine right after a meal, but eventually the stored energy has to be tapped. At that time, the chemical reaction goes the other way. Now the glycogen is turned into usable glucose.

Several recent studies suggest that the liver contains receptors that can sense in which direction the metabolic transaction goes, from glucose cash to glycogen deposits, or vice versa. If the balance tips toward glycogen manufacture, the receptors signal satiety and the animal stops eating. If the balance tips toward glucose production, the receptors signal hunger and the animal eats (Figure 3.19). The evidence that this happens in the liver comes from hungry dogs that were injected with glucose. If the injection was into the vein that goes directly to the liver, the dogs stopped eating. If the injection was anywhere else, there was no comparable effect (Russek, 1971).

Such evidence suggests that the internal stimuli for hunger and satiety arise at a rather earlier stage in the process of food extraction and storage than had been traditionally believed. If so, food-related homeostasis is not a last-ditch affair in which the system waits until the internal environment is already in precarious imbalance. Instead, the built-in hunger mechanism seems to be more prudent. It has an anticipatory character that corrects metabolic insufficiencies before they can possibly affect the internal environment that bathes the brain.

SIGNALS FROM WITHOUT

The self-regulation of food intake is remarkable, but it is not perfect. Humans and animals eat to maintain nutritive homeostasis; put another way, they eat because they are hungry. But they sometimes eat because they like the taste of a particular food. We eat dessert even though we may be "full"; our hunger is gone, but not our appetite.

Such facts show that eating is not solely determined by stimuli that come from within. These are supplemented by various external signals. Clearly we do not eat for calories alone. Taste—and also smell and texture—is a powerful additional determinant of food intake for humans as well as animals. Many animals prefer sweet tastes and tend to reject bitter ones, a pattern which seems to be built into the feeding system, for it is found even in early infancy. This selectional bias tends to be adaptive for it leads to the best nutritional bet: In general, sweet substances have more nutritional value than others. The bet sometimes loses. Saccharin is sweet, is generally preferred to less sweet substances, and contains no calories whatsoever.

Palatability is not the only external signal for eating. Other signals are developed through learning. The expected mealtime is one example; the company of fellow-eaters is another. A hen who has had her fill of grain will resume her meal if joined by other hens who are still hungry (Bayer, 1929). Further examples are provided by learned food preferences (Mother's apple pie) and learned aversions and taboos (pork to Muslims and Jews). Some culturally transmitted food aversions may have their origins in digestive biology. Chinese cuisine shuns most milk products, an aversion which probably arises from the fact that many adult Chinese lack the enzyme that digests milk sugar (Johnson, Kretchmer, and Simoons, 1974).

HYPOTHALAMIC CONTROL CENTERS

We have seen that there are many different signals for food intake. It was natural to suppose that these various messages are all integrated at one point in the nervous system where a final decision is made to eat or not to eat. The natural candidate for such a "feeding center" was the hypothalamus which was already known to house controls for temperature regulation and water balance and which gave evidence of containing glucoreceptors. Psychophysiologists soon devised a theory of hypothalamic control of feeding that was analogous to the temperature system. It postulates two antagonistic centers, one corresponding to hunger, the other to satiety.

DUAL-CENTER THEORY

According to dual-center theory, the hypothalamus contains an "on" and an "off" command post for eating. Two anatomical regions are implicated. One is located in the *lateral zone* of the hypothalamus; it was said to function as a "hunger center" whose activation leads to food search and eating. The other is the *ventromedial region* which was thought to be a "satiety center" whose stimulation stops eating (Figure 3.20).

A

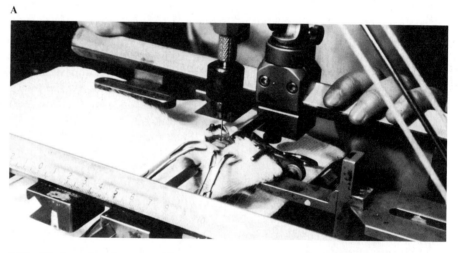

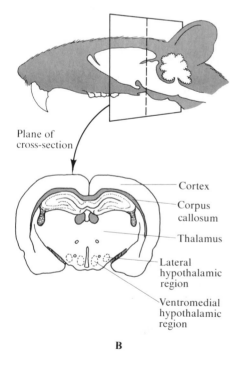

Plane of
cross-section

Cortex

Corpus callosum

Thalamus

Lateral hypothalamic region

Ventromedial hypothalamic region

B

3.20 The lateral and ventromedial hypothalamic regions   To create a lesion, or to implant an electrode in the interior of an animal's brain, one needs a device that can reach a point in the brain specified in three dimensions: the stereotaxic instrument. The animal is anesthetized, its head is firmly clamped, and a small opening is made in its skull. A very thin wire—insulated except at its tip—is inserted to the desired point in the brain. Certain kinds of currents will create a lesion; others will simply stimulate that region of the brain. (A) A rat in the stereotaxic device. (Photograph by Ed Boswell) (B) A schematic of the lateral and ventromedial regions of the hypothalamus. The top part of the figure shows a side view of a rat's head and indicates the plane of the bottom figure, which is an ear-to-ear section of the brain showing the two hypothalamic regions. (After Hart, 1969)

A

B

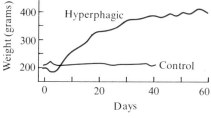

3.21 Hyperphagic rat   (A) Photograph of a rat after an operation creating a hypothalamic lesion. (Courtesy Neal E. Miller) (B) Curve showing the weight gain of hyperphagic rats after the operation. The weight eventually stabilizes at a new level. (After Teitelbaum, 1955)

To buttress their claims about the function of these regions, dual-center theorists pointed to the effects of lesions. Rats whose lateral hypothalamus has been destroyed suffer from ***aphagia*** (Greek, "no eating"). They refuse to eat and drink and will starve to death unless forcibly tube-fed for weeks (Teitelbaum and Stellar, 1954). Interestingly enough, eventually there is some recovery of function. After a few weeks the animals begin to eat again, especially if tempted by such delectables as liquid eggnog (Teitelbaum and Epstein, 1962). The reverse occurs after lesions to the ventromedial zones. Animals with such lesions suffer from ***hyperphagia*** (Greek, "excess eating"). They eat voraciously and keep on eating. If the lesion is large enough, they may become veritable mountains of rat obesity, finally reaching weights that are three or four times as great as their preoperative levels (Figure 3.21). Tumors in these hypothalamic regions (though very rare) have the same effect in humans.

Dual-center theorists saw such results as confirmation of their general position. They regarded the two hypothalamic regions as mutually inhibitory centers, of which one serves as an on-switch for eating, the other as an off-switch. These switches are in turn activated by a number of internal and external signals. All of these signals act upon the feeding centers—some to trigger eating, others to inhibit it. Whether the organism eats will then depend upon the summed value of them all: the level of various available nutrients in the bloodstream, gastric distension, satiety signals from the intestines, food palatability, learned factors, and so on (Stellar, 1954).

Several features of this approach are not unique to the dual-center approach, but are shared by other theories of hunger. One is the conception of the entire system as a negative feedback device. By eating or by not eating, the organism necessarily changes the overall pattern of signals that act upon it. As this changes, so does the organism's behavior. A related assumption is that there is a trade-off between the various signals. If one set is very strong, it may tilt the balance toward, say, eating, even if the others are fairly weak. For example, after a two-day fast, we gratefully eat foods that we would ordinarily not touch. But if we are already full, we will continue to eat only if tempted with unusually tasty delicacies. It is no accident that sweets are generally the last course in a meal and rarely the first.

DUAL CENTERS RECONSIDERED

The dual-center theory of feeding has held center stage for several decades. But it has been seriously questioned in recent years. The main grounds concern the effects of hypothalamic lesions. Some recent critics believe that what matters is not the destruction of certain hypothalamic loci. As they see it, the effects are instead produced by damage to some important nerve tracts that happen to run through these regions. In this view, the presumed "on" and "off" centers aren't really feeding centers at all. They are only way-stations through which some vital neural rail lines pass (Stricker and Zigmond, 1976).

As an example, consider the voracious overeating brought about by lesions of the ventromedial hypothalamus. According to the dual-center view, rats with such lesions overeat because of damage to some off-switch for feeding. But critics of this theory lay the blame on a disruption of fat metabolism.

Under normal conditions, animals store some of their unused nutrients as fats. This tendency to save for later use can sometimes go too far. One effect of ventromedial lesions is that they produce an overreaction of certain branches of the parasympathetic system. This in turn increases the proportion of usable nutrients, especially glucose, that are turned into fat and cached away as adipose tissue. The trouble is that so much is stored not enough is left over to serve as metabolic fuel. As a result, the animal stays hungry; it has to eat more to get the fuel that it needs. But since most of what it eats is turned into fat and stored away, the process continues and the animal has to keep on eating. It is in the position of a rich miser who has buried all of his possessions and has therefore no money to live on.

Evidence in favor of this general approach comes from studies which show that animals with ventromedial lesions get fatter than normals even when both groups are fed the identical amount. Whether such results are a decisive disproof of the dual-center theory is still a matter of debate (Friedman and Stricker, 1976).

FEEDING AND ACTIVATION

Some authors believe that hunger and satiety are aspects of the opposition between general activation and quiescence that we have already discussed. To feed, an animal has to be reasonably aroused. This involves the participation of the reticular activating system (RAS) and its catecholamine-containing fibers. In this view, the aphagia produced by lesions to the lateral hypothalamus is caused by damage to some of the fibers from the RAS that pass through that particular site. One line of evidence comes from the fact that animals so afflicted show deficits that are not confined to feeding. They are generally somnolent and apathetic; they neither eat nor drink, nor do much of anything else. According to this position, what is impaired is not an "on" center for feeding. It is rather the arousal system whose partial destruction diminishes the drive to do anything at all (Stricker, 1976).

If feeding is related to activation, satiety is related to quiescence and sleep. All of us know that a good meal tends to make us drowsy. One possible reason is that the biochemical changes which occur during the absorptive phase of food metabolism lead to an increase in the level of a neurotransmitter, *serotonin,* which is responsible for producing quiet sleep (Jouvet, 1969). These neurons inhibit the catecholamine neurons of the activating system (Stricker, 1978). If this analysis is correct, then one of the major tenets of the dual-center theorists is upheld, though in a new form. Hunger and satiety do reflect some underlying tug-of-war in the nervous system. But the basic antagonism may not be between eating and not eating, but rather between being aroused and being somnolent.

OBESITY IN RATS AND PEOPLE

The affluence of modern industrial society has created a problem that prior eras would have suffered only too gladly: Many of its members are fat. Obesity is generally defined as a body weight that exceeds the average for a given height by 20 percent. Judged by this criterion, about one-third of all Americans are obese. Most of them would rather be slim, and their wistful desires offer a ready market for a vast number of diet foods and fads. In part, the reason is health. But more important are social standards of physical attractiveness. There are no corpulent matinee idols, no fat sex goddesses (Stunkard, 1975).

Most authorities agree that there are several different reasons why people become obese. In some cases, the cause is a bodily condition. In others, it is a matter of eating too much.

BODILY FACTORS IN OBESITY

One reason for obesity is a metabolic malfunction. For whatever reason, some persons secrete too much insulin. As we have seen, this leads to excess fat storage. People with this condition are in the position of rats with ventromedial hypothalamic lesions, at least as seen from an anti-dual-center point of view. They are continually hungry because they can't help converting most of what they eat into fat. They don't become fat because they eat too much. They eat too much because they are becoming fat.

A related bodily factor pertains to the fat cells within the body. In obese adults, their number is some three times larger than that found in normals (Hirsch and Knittle, 1970). To the obese person, these cells are an adipose albatross that cannot be removed. If a fat person diets, the fat cells will shrink in size but their total number remains unchanged. Some investigators suspect that the brain receives some signals that urge further eating until the shrunken fat cells are again refilled. If this is so, the once-fat can never truly escape their obese past. They may rigorously diet until they become as lean as a friend who was never fat, but their urge to eat will always be greater.

Some recent studies suggest that the number of fat cells in the body (and thus one cause of obesity) is determined by feeding patterns during early childhood. If rats are overfed before weaning, they grow many more fat cells. In contrast, overfeeding in adulthood leads to an enlargement of the fat cells that are already there but does not change their number (Knittle and Hirsch, 1968). These results fit in with the fact that obesity often begins in childhood: The fat boy is the father to the fat man (Abraham et al., 1971).

BEHAVIORAL FACTORS

For some groups, obesity is evidently produced by a bodily malfunction. But for others, the cause lies in behavior: These people eat too much and exercise too little. The question is why. It is virtually certain that there is no one answer, for there are probably many reasons for chronic overeating.

One suggestion comes from an odd fact about rats with ventromedial lesions. If offered normal food, they consume much more than unoperated animals. But if their food is made relatively unpalatable—for example, by adulterating it with a bitter substance such as quinine—they hardly touch it, even after fasts of one or two days (Miller et al., 1950). They have become finicky rat gourmets who devour foods that are tasty and disdain those that are not. Normal rats behave differently. When food-deprived, they will gratefully eat quinine-adulterated food if none else is available.

One interpretation of this phenomenon is that the ventromedial lesion (for whatever reason) leads to a change in the relative weighting of external and internal feeding signals. The notion is that the hyperphagic rat becomes more responsive to external signals and less responsive to internal ones than a

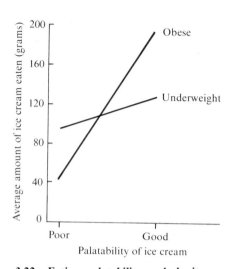

3.22 Eating, palatability, and obesity
In the experiment, obese and under-weight subjects were given the oppor-tunity to eat ice cream. If the ice cream tasted good, the subjects ate more than the underweight ones. The reverse was true if the ice cream did not taste good. (After Nisbett, 1968)

normal rat. A normal animal will eat quinine-laced food when starved; the negative external signals are overriden by positive internal ones. But the rat with a ventromedial lesion does not balance the feeding equation in the same manner. For it, the external signals count more than the internal ones, so it will refuse to eat.

Some authors argue that what holds for rats with hyperphagia, holds also for obese humans (Schachter, 1971). Several lines of evidence suggest that obese people are comparatively unresponsive to their own internal hunger state. When normal persons are asked how hungry they are, their response depends on the time since their last meal. In obese people, there is no such correlation between the subjective experience of hunger and deprivation in-terval (Nisbett, 1968).

The obese person's insensitivity to the signals from within is accompanied by an enhanced susceptibility to signals from without. When offered a mixture of quinine and vanilla ice cream, some obese subjects are as finicky as hyper-phagic rats; they eat much less of the mixture than do normals. But if the ice cream is an excellent variety of vanilla, they consume considerably more (Figure 3.22). A related factor is whether the food looks as if it can be con-sumed immediately and without effort. In one study, subjects were left alone in a room for 15 minutes, ostensibly to fill out a questionnaire. On the desk at which they worked was a bag of almonds from which they were invited to help themselves if they wanted to. For half of the subjects, the almonds were already shelled and ready to eat; for the other half, the almonds were still in their shells. The results show that obese people respond most avidly to food that can be eaten right then and there, with no pause or effort. Normal subjects were as likely to eat whether the almonds were shelled or were not; their reaction was probably triggered mostly by their internal state. Not so for obese subjects. Virtually all of them ate if the almonds were shelled; virtually none of them did when the shells were still on the almonds (Schachter, 1971).

Just why some obese people are more sensitive to external than to internal hunger signals is by no means clear. Nor is it clear how all of this is related to ventromedial hypothalamic lesions. There is obviously a parallel between the lesioned rats and obese persons, but it is far from being understood. The parallel becomes even more shaky in light of the fact that in lesioned animals, finickiness and obesity don't always occur together. If the lesion is small, one can create obesity without finickiness and vice versa (Graff and Stellar, 1962). But even so, the similarity between many obese people and rats with ven-tromedial lesions is sufficiently striking to merit serious attention (Rodin, 1977).

What Different Motives Have in Common

The preceding sections have dealt with a number of motives that impel to action—hunger, thirst, fear and so on. For each of these motives there is a different goal toward which the organism strives, be it food or water or escape from threat. Do these different goals have anything in common? Our everyday experience suggests that they do. Thus food seems satisfying if one is hungry, water if one is thirsty, and safety if one is fearful. But what is common to these and other satisfactions?

DRIVE-REDUCTION THEORY

An influential attempt to answer this question was the theory of **drive reduction** proposed by Clark L. Hull some forty years ago. Hull and his students were impressed by the fact that many motives seem directed at the reduction of some internal state of bodily tension which if continued would lead to injury or even death. Examples are food deprivation, water deprivation, pain, and so on. Hull believed that this is true for all motives. In his view, all built-in rewards produce some reduction of tension (or, as he called it, of drive).

Hull's theory is a homeostatic conception carried to an extreme form. As Hull saw it, anything an organism does is ultimately directed at getting rid of some noxious state—pain, nutrient deficit, or whatever. This leads to the assertion that at bottom there is no difference between what we usually call pleasure and what we call relief from pain or discomfort. One immediate difficulty is posed by sex, a motive which is clearly not homeostatic in the sense in which hunger and thirst are. To explain sexual satisfaction in drive-reduction terms, Hull and his students argued that what is rewarding about sexual activity is the drop in tension that occurs during orgasm (Hull, 1943).

SEEKING STIMULATION

Hull's theory seems contrary to our everyday observations. Some experiences seem to be intrinsically sought after, such as the taste of sweets or erotic stimulation. These are felt to be a positive pleasure rather than a mere removal of an irritant. Several experiments have produced results that fit these intuitions. One example concerns saccharin, a sweet substance that has no nutritive value and thus no effect on the biological deficit that underlies hunger. But rats and other animals will nevertheless drink a saccharine solution avidly (Sheffield and Roby, 1950).

Another example concerns sexual activity. In one study, male rats were run in a maze that had two end boxes. One was empty, while the other contained a sexually receptive female. When the male encountered the female, he usually mounted her. But an unsympathetic experimenter invariably separated the pair before ejaculation could occur. This meant that sexual tension was increased rather than decreased. But the males nevertheless chose the side of the maze that held the female. This shows that sexual stimulation is rewarding in its own right. Whether this point really required experimental substantiation is debatable, considering that so many humans engage in sexual foreplay and try to lengthen the time before orgasm (Sheffield, Wulff, and Backer, 1951).

Such evidence suggests that drive reduction is not the only goal. Similar conclusions emerge from work on curiosity and manipulation. Monkeys will evidently go through considerable lengths to puzzle out how to open latches that are attached to a wooden board. But when the latches are unlocked, nothing opens, because the latch never closed anything in the first place (Figure 3.23). Since unlatching the latch gets the animal nothing, the response is presumably its own reward. In this regard, the monkeys acted much like human beings who, in countless ways, indicate that they often do things as ends in themselves rather than as means to other ends.

What is a means sometimes becomes an end and vice versa. Thus rats can be trained to run on a treadmill in order to eat, but they can also be trained to

3.23 Mechanical puzzles which monkeys solve without special reward The complex puzzle presented to monkeys was basically a hinge which was restrained by a variety of devices: a bar, a pin, a bolt, and so on. The monkeys received no special reward for their labors, but even so, learned to open many of these devices "for the fun of it." (After Harlow, 1950)

91

eat in order to get the chance to run on the treadmill (Premack, 1962). Similarly, children will play a pinball machine to get candy, but if required, will also eat candy to be allowed to play the pinball machine. Such facts were well known to Tom Sawyer, who made his friends pay him for the opportunity to paint his fence.

Can Hull's theory handle any of these criticisms? One approach has been to argue that certain apparent contradictions, such as the rewarding effects of saccharin, are based on prior learning. According to this view, long previous experience with real foods has made the animal associate sweetness and the cessation of bodily hunger tension. But this line of argument is rather implausible. For one thing, the preference for sweet tastes is found very early in life. Thus in one study, some animals were shown to like saccharin before they ever had any experience with sweet foods (Foster, 1968).

ELECTRICAL BRAIN STIMULATION

The preceding section suggested that animals and humans often seek out stimulation. A related finding concerns the rewarding effect of *electrical stimulation of the brain,* usually abbreviated *ESB* (Olds and Milner, 1954).

The basic phenomenon is simple enough. Electrical stimulation of certain subcortical areas (the lateral hypothalamus is one such region) acts as a reward. Rats, cats, dogs, and monkeys will avidly perform various responses to obtain this stimulus again and again. This kind of reward can be quite powerful. To obtain it, rats will press a lever at rates of up to a thousand presses per hour for hours on end. When forced to choose between food and ESB, hungry rats will typically opt for ESB even though it literally brings starvation (Spies, 1965).

What is the mechanism that underlies the rewarding effect of ESB? One hypothesis is that ESB provides something akin to pleasure (Olds and Olds, 1965; Stein, 1964). But this can't be the whole story. One reason is that the same rats which initially respond with such wild frenzy, will ignore the lever altogether when put back in the experimental chamber after an interval of an hour or less. The rats will resume pressing if given a few free ESB pulses; this priming seems to reinstate the desire for the ESB, but the reasons are still unclear (Gallistel, 1973).

As yet we don't know the mechanisms that underlie ESB. But whatever its ultimate explanation, the rewarding effect of ESB constitutes one further argument against the notion that all rewards are tension reducing. Electrical stimulation of certain areas of the brain evidently produces a desirable state of affairs that animals try to obtain rather than to get rid of.

AN OPTIMUM AROUSAL LEVEL

One can reinterpret Hull's drive-reduction theory as a statement about desirable arousal levels. In effect, his theory asserts that organisms always seek to diminish their level of arousal. But as we have seen, the evidence says otherwise. To be sure, we do try to reduce arousal if our arousal level is unduly high as in intense hunger or fear or pain. But this doesn't mean that the aim is an arousal level of zero. There seems to be an above-zero optimum (which probably varies from person to person and from time to time). If we are below this optimum, we seek stimulation to ascend to it.

DRUGS

Occasionally, we are aroused to rather high-pitched levels—by prolonged sex play, by watching "Jaws," by riding on roller coasters. These are ways of inducing high arousal states by external stimulation. But there is another way of getting "high." One can use drugs that artificially excite the brain's arousal system.

Examples of drugs that have this effect are the **amphetamines** ("speed") and **cocaine.** They boost the activity of the reticular arousal system by artificially increasing the amount of available catecholamine transmitters at the relevant synaptic sites. The result is greater activation. The individual is almost literally "turned on"—alert, sensitive, and extremely energetic. This overactivation is often experienced as very pleasurable, sometimes to the point of euphoria.

ADDICTION

Of course the confirmed drug user pays a substantial price. To begin with, the arousing drugs have certain unpleasant side-effects. If the activation is intense enough, there may be high anxiety and extreme suspiciousness. Even more important is the fact that in many individuals repeated drug use leads to **addiction.** The consequences of this are twofold. One is an increased **tolerance** for the drug so that the addict requires ever-larger doses to obtain the same effect. A second consequence of addiction goes hand in hand with increased tolerance. When the drug is withheld, there are certain **withdrawal symptoms.*** In general, these are the precise opposites of the symptoms produced by the drug itself. For instance, amphetamine addicts deprived of their drug often feel intensely depressed and sluggish.

THE OPPONENT-PROCESS THEORY OF MOTIVATION

According to a recent proposal, the phenomena of drug addiction can be considered as a special case of a more general psychological principle. The idea is that the nervous system has a general tendency to counteract any deviation from motivational normalcy. If there is too much of a swing toward joy and ecstasy, an **opponent process** is called into play that tilts the balance toward the negative side.† Conversely, if the initial swing is toward terror or revulsion, there will be an opponent process toward the positive side. The net effect is an attenuation of the emotional state one happens to be in so that ecstasy becomes mild pleasure and terror loses some of its force. A further result occurs when the situation that originally led to joy or to extreme fear is withdrawn. Now the opponent process is unopposed by the motivational condition that at first evoked it. The consequence is a shift toward the opposite side of the emotional spectrum (Solomon and Corbit, 1974).

* Some writers reserve the term *withdrawal symptoms* for the more severe reactions that occur after addiction to certain depressant drugs such as barbiturates and to opiates such as heroin. We use the term more broadly, to underline some general principles that seem to apply not only to different addictions but also to other motivational conditions in which one gets used to a certain emotional state.

† The term *opponent process* was originally used by psychologists who studied sensory processes, especially color vision (see Chapter 6).

This general approach may be able to account for the tolerance and withdrawal effects observed in drug addiction. The drug leads to a particular emotional reaction, say, euphoria in the case of amphetamine. An opponent process is set up that pulls in the opposite direction; as a result, there is increased tolerance. This opponent process is revealed more starkly when the drug is withheld. Now there are withdrawal reactions in the form of depression (Solomon, 1977).

Another example is based on a study of sky divers. They presumably parachute for the fun of it, but not on their first jump. Judging from photographed facial expressions and autonomic measures, they are initially in a state of panic. When they land safely, they act stunned and stony-faced. But after several successful jumps, their reaction changes. Prior to the jump, they are no longer terrified; at worst, they are somewhat tense. And when they land safely, they feel exuberant and intensely happy (Epstein, 1967).

This pattern of results fits in with the opponent-process view. With repeated experiences, the parachutists' original terror is counteracted by an opponent process that tilts the scale toward the positive side. As a result, there is less and less fear prior to the jump (a phenomenon presumably akin to drug tolerance). The opponent process reveals itself even more clearly following several safe landings. This is the analogue of withdrawal, but in this case it is all to the good, since what is withdrawn is the occasion for the initial terror. All that is now left is the opponent process. Since this pulls toward the positive side of the emotional axis, there is exhilaration.

Opponent-process theory points to an interesting similarity between a number of motivational phenomena such as drug addiction and the gradual adjustment to fears. But this doesn't mean that the specific physiological mechanisms that underlie these different effects are equivalent. The best guess is that they are not. But even so, there may be a more general principle of neurological action that holds true for many areas even though it is not always implemented by the same means.

Summary

1. Most human and animal actions are motivated. *Motives* have a twofold function. They *direct* behavior toward or away from some goal. They also serve to *activate* the organism which becomes more aroused the greater the strength of the motive.

2. The biological basis of directed action is *negative feedback* in which the system "feeds back" upon itself to stop its own action. Built-in, negative feedback systems are the basis of various automatic orientation responses to external stimuli, or *taxes,* found in lower organisms.

3. Built-in negative feedback is also responsible for many reactions that maintain the stability of the organism's internal environment or *homeostasis.* Special cells in the hypothalamus sense the body's internal state, for example, its temperature. If this is above or below certain *set points,* various self-regulatory reflexes are triggered (such as shivering) in addition to directed, voluntary acts (such as putting on a sweater). Similar homeostatic mechanisms underlie a number of other biological motives such as *thirst.*

4. Activation of behavior depends in part upon the *autonomic nervous system* which consists of two antagonistic branches. One is the *parasympathetic system* which serves

SUMMARY

the vegetative functions of everyday life, such as digestion and reproduction. The other is the *sympathetic system* which activates the body and mobilizes its resources. It increases the available metabolic fuels and accelerates their utilization by increasing heart rate and respiration. Intense sympathetic activity represents an *emergency reaction* which underlies the overt reactions of *fight or flight* and their usual emotional concomitants, rage or fear.

5. The sympathetic emergency reaction is not always biologically adaptive. It is sometimes disruptive and harmful as in psychosomatically produced ailments and certain cases of "sudden death."

6. While the sympathetic system activates the body, a structure in the brainstem, the *reticular activating system* or RAS, arouses the brain. The RAS exerts its effects through a number of chemical transmitters called *catecholamines*. The RAS awakens the cortex and is opposed by an antagonistic system which leads to sleep.

7. During sleep, brain activity changes as shown by the *electroencephalogram* or EEG. Each night, we oscillate between two kinds of sleep. One is *quiet sleep* during which the cortex is relatively inactive. The other is *active sleep,* characterized by considerable cortical activity and *rapid eye movements* or REMs, a pattern of internal activity which is experienced as *dreams. Sleep-deprivation* studies show that when one or the other kind of sleep is prevented, it is to some extent made up later on. This suggests that there is a need for each of the two sleep states, but the biological functions served by either is as yet unknown.

8. The biological motive that has been studied most extensively is *hunger.* Some stimuli for feeding come from the internal environment, the nutrient levels in the bloodstream and metabolic processes in the liver. Other stimuli are external, including the *palatability* of the food and learned food preferences and aversions.

9. Many authors believe that the control of feeding is lodged in two antagonistic centers in the hypothalamus whose excitation gives rise to hunger and satiety respectively. As evidence, they point to the effects of lesions. Destruction of the supposed hunger center leads to *aphagia,* a complete refusal to eat and drink. Destruction of the so-called satiety center produces *hyperphagia,* a vast increase in food intake.

10. A feeding-related disorder is *obesity.* Some cases are produced by bodily disorders including an oversecretion of insulin and an overabundance of fat cells. Others are a result of behavioral factors. Among them is a comparative insensitivity to internal hunger signals and an oversensitivity to external ones such as palatability.

11. According to *drive-reduction theory,* all built-in motives act to reduce stimulation and arousal. Evidence against this view comes from sexual activity and the rewarding nature of electric stimulation of certain regions of the brain. Today most authors believe that organisms strive for an *optimum level of arousal.* If below this optimum, they try to increase it by various means, including the use of certain drugs. The *opponent-process theory of motivation* points out that all shifts of arousal level produce a counteracting process which acts to moderate the ups and downs. When the original instigator of the shift is removed, the opponent process is revealed more clearly, as in the *withdrawal effects* in a drug addict.

CHAPTER 4

Learning I: Classical and Instrumental Conditioning

Thus far our discussion has centered on the built-in facets of human and animal behavior, the general neural equipment that provides the underpinning for everything we do and the specific, innate feedback systems that underlie directed action. But much of what we do and are goes beyond what nature gave us. It is acquired through experience in our own lifetimes. People learn—to grasp a baby bottle, to eat with knife and fork, to read and write, to make a living, to love or hate their neighbors, and eventually, to face death. In animals, the importance of learning is less dramatic but it is still perfectly obvious.

Can learning be incorporated into Descartes' and LaMettrie's reflex-machine conception, which holds that behavior is determined by events in the organism's environment? Many influential writers insist that it can, provided that we consider events in the past as well as in the present. Adherents of this general approach, whose modern exponents are sometimes called **behavior theorists,** believe that the organism's *prewired* repertory of behaviors is supplemented by continual *rewirings* that are produced by experience. Some of these rewirings consist of new connections between stimuli. Thus the sight of the mother's face may come to signify the taste of milk. Other rewirings involve new connections between acts and their consequences, as when a toddler learns that touching a hot radiator is followed by a painful burn.

According to behavior theorists, such rewirings are the fundamental building blocks of any learning whatever, be it a dog learning to sit on command or a college student learning integral calculus. As they see it, even the most involved learned activities are composed of simpler ones, much as complex chemical compounds are made up of simpler atoms. Given this belief, behavior theorists have concentrated their efforts on trying to understand learning in simple situations and in simple creatures like dogs, rats, and pigeons. They sought to strip the learning process down to its bare essence so that its basic, atomic laws might be revealed. They were sure that once these laws were known, it was just a matter of detail to explain more complex situations; all one had to do then was to show how the simpler constituents are put together to yield increasingly complex forms of behavior. This search led to major discoveries to which we now turn.

We will begin by considering two forms of simple learning which occur in humans and most animals: classical and instrumental conditioning. That these two kinds of learning exist is a matter of fact, not of theory. What is at issue, as we shall see in both this and the next chapter, is whether *all* learning can be understood in these terms.

Before turning to the main topic, note that not all modifications of behavior are learned. Learning produces behavioral changes, but so does physical *maturation.* In many cases, the distinction between the two is perfectly clear. When a tadpole becomes a frog it starts to croak, yet no one imagines that the change is brought about by learning. But sometimes the point is less obvious. An example is walking. Human infants don't walk until about fifteen months of age. But they don't learn to do this; they walk when they are physically good and ready.

Classical Conditioning

The first serious attempt to relate the reflex conception and learning was made by I. M. Sechenov (1829–1905), a Russian physiologist. Sechenov was convinced that ultimately all psychological reactions can be explained in reflex terms. As he saw it, whatever people do or think comes down to skeletal reflexes. "Whether it's the child laughing at the sight of toys . . . or Newton creating universal laws and inscribing them on paper—the ultimate fact in all cases is muscular movement" (Sechenov, 1863, p. 3). This reflex-is-all position required some provision for the effects of experience since, after all, even Newton had to learn to read and write. Sechenov's solution was that there are learned modifications of reflexes which result from **association.** Like most of his contemporaries, he thought that initially unrelated mental events become associated if they occur together often enough; eventually, the one will elicit the other. Sechenov felt that a similar association occurs between reflexes which somehow become linked and thus modified.

Sechenov's proposal would have granted considerable plasticity to Descartes' machine; this now became a robot that could learn. But the specific how and why of this were left quite vague. It remained for another Russian scientist, I. P. Pavlov, to deliver on Sechenov's promise.

PAVLOV AND THE CONDITIONED REFLEX

Ivan Petrovich Pavlov (1849–1936) had already earned the Nobel Prize for his work on digestion before he embarked upon the study of conditioning which was to gain him even greater fame. His initial interest was in the built-in nervous control of the various digestive reflexes in dogs; most important to us, the secretion of saliva. He surgically diverted one of the ducts of the salivary gland, thus channeling part of the salivary flow through a special tube **(fistula)**

Ivan Petrovich Pavlov (Courtesy Sovfoto)

97

Pavlov watching an experiment *(Courtesy Sovfoto)*

4.1 Apparatus for salivary conditioning
The figure shows an early version of Pavlov's apparatus for classical conditioning of the salivary response. The dog was held in a harness, sounds or lights functioned as conditioned stimuli, while meat powder in a dish served as the unconditioned stimulus. The conditioned response was assessed with the aid of a tube connected to an opening in one of the animal's salivary glands. The rate at which saliva was secreted was one of Pavlov's measures of response strength. It was recorded on a revolving drum by a stylus activated by the saliva that came through the tube. (After Yerkes and Morgulis, 1909)

to the outside of the animal's body where it could be easily measured and analyzed. Pavlov demonstrated that salivation was produced by several innate reflexes, one of which prepares the food for digestion. This is triggered by food (especially dry food) placed in the mouth.

In the course of this work a new fact emerged. The salivary reflex could be set off by stimuli which at first were totally neutral. Dogs that had been in the laboratory for a while would soon salivate to a whole host of stimuli that had no such effect on their uninitiated fellows. Not only the taste and touch of the meat in the mouth, but its mere sight, the sight of the dish in which it was placed, the sight of the person who usually brought it, even that person's footsteps—eventually all of these might produce salivation. Pavlov soon decided to study such effects in their own right, for he recognized that they provided a means of extending the reflex concept to embrace learned as well as innate reactions. The approach was simple enough. Instead of waiting for accidental events in each animal's history, the experimenter would provide those events himself. Thus he would repeatedly sound a buzzer and always follow it with food. Later he observed what happened when the buzzer was sounded and no food was given (Pavlov, 1927).

The experiment was simpler in principle than in practice. To eliminate extraneous stimulation, the animal was isolated in a soundproof room during experimental sessions, with all stimulus-presentation, food-delivery, observation, and measurement handled by remote control. Another problem was to minimize extraneous activity. Accordingly, the dog was trained to stand quietly on a table, harnessed to an overhead beam by straps looped under its limbs, prevented insofar as was possible from doing anything that might interfere with its primary job—to salivate (Figure 4.1).

THE ORIENTING REFLEX

Pavlov found that the first step in noting the new significance of a hitherto neutral stimulus such as a buzzer is to pay attention to it. When faced with a new stimulus, the dog's initial reaction was an *orienting reflex.* Pavlov sometimes called this reaction the "What-is-it? reflex." The dog turned its head and shoulders toward the new stimulus, pricked up its ears, and looked attentive.

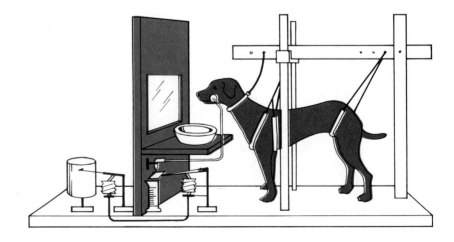

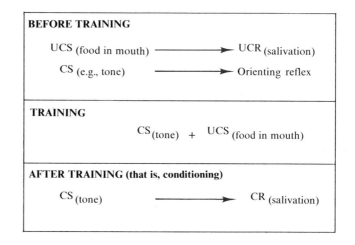

BEFORE TRAINING

UCS (food in mouth) ⟶ UCR (salivation)

CS (e.g., tone) ⟶ Orienting reflex

TRAINING

CS (tone) + UCS (food in mouth)

AFTER TRAINING (that is, conditioning)

CS (tone) ⟶ CR (salivation)

4.2   Relationshps between CS, UCS, CR, and UCR in classical conditioning

CONDITIONING

The next step was the most important: Repeated buzzer-food pairings led to salivation to the buzzer alone. To explain this, Pavlov proposed a distinction between unconditioned and conditioned reflexes. ***Unconditioned reflexes*** he held to be essentially inborn; these would be unconditionally elicited by the appropriate stimulus regardless of the animal's history. An example is salivating to food in the mouth. In contrast, ***conditioned reflexes*** were acquired, thus conditional upon the animal's past experience, and, according to Pavlov, based upon newly formed connections in the brain. An example is salivating to the buzzer. Every unconditioned reflex is based upon a connection between an ***unconditioned stimulus (UCS)*** and an ***unconditioned response (UCR);*** in our example, food-in-the-mouth (UCS) and salivation (UCR). The corresponding terms for the conditioned reflex are ***conditioned stimulus (CS)*** and ***conditioned response (CR).*** The CS is an initially neutral stimulus (here, the buzzer) that is paired with the UCS; the CR (here, again salivation) is the response elicited by the CS after some such pairings of CS and UCS. Typically, the CR is very similar to the UCR but the two are not necessarily identical, a point we shall return to later on. These various relationships are summarized in Figure 4.2.

THE SCOPE OF CLASSICAL CONDITIONING

Classical conditioning* goes well beyond salivary reaction as it occurs in dogs. It is found in many other response systems and in many other species, including humans. Some of the different reactions that can be conditioned in humans include such diverse responses as the ***galvanic skin response*** or ***GSR*** (with UCS a loud noise or electric shock and UCR a drop in skin resistance associated with sweating) and the blink-reaction of the eyelid (where UCS is typically a puff of air on the open eye; Kimble, 1961).

* The adjective *classical* is used, in part, as dutiful tribute to Pavlov's eminence and historical priority; in part, to distinguish this form of conditioning from another kind which we will discuss later, *instrumental conditioning.*

We can only guess at the actual scope of classical conditioning in human everyday life, but it is likely to be large indeed. Many of our internal feelings and urges are probably conditioned in just this sense. We tend to feel hungry at mealtimes and less so during the times between; this is so even if we fast a whole day. Another example is falling asleep. At least in some of us this requires a fairly precise stimulus arrangement which can be violated only at the cost of insomnia, as in the case of the child's "security blanket." Still another instance is sexual arousal which is often produced by a word or gesture whose meaning is very private and surely learned.

CONDITIONED EMOTIONS

Even more important is the role of classical conditioning in the formation of various emotional reactions, especially those concerned with fear. Fear is readily conditioned in the laboratory, a fact known all too well to scores of rats, cats, and dogs that have been exposed to a neutral CS paired with a painful UCS (typically, electric shock). After several such trials, the CS will produce various bodily reactions appropriate to fear—crouching, trembling, urination, defecation, and similar indications that the animal has learned that the CS is a signal for impending shock.

It is a plausible guess that many adult fears are based upon classical conditioning, acquired in much the way that fear is acquired in the laboratories. These fears may be relatively mild or very intense (if intense enough, they are called *phobias*). They may be acquired in early childhood or during particularly traumatic episodes in later life. Examples are usually drawn from clinical case histories of patients with severe fear reactions, as in the case of an Air Force pilot who bailed out of his plane but whose parachute failed to open until the last five seconds before he hit the ground (Sarnoff, 1957). In such traumatic episodes, conditioning apparently occurs in a single trial. This seems reasonable enough, for it would certainly be unadaptive if the pilot had to bail out on ten separate occasions, each time barely escaping death, before finally developing conditioned fear.

CONDITIONING IN LOWER ANIMALS

Conditioning has also been demonstrated in creatures much lower on the evolutionary ladder than mammals. With electric shock as UCS and light as CS, fish have been conditioned to thrash about, cockroaches to move restlessly, and crabs to twitch their tail spines. In the octopus (with touch as UCS) the conditioned response is more exotic. Presented with CS, the creature changes color. Even the lowly flatworms show signs of conditionability. They turn or contract their bodies when subjected to electric shock. If shock is repeatedly paired with light, eventually that CS (light) will elicit the same response (Jacobson, Fried, and Horowitz, 1967).

Thus classical conditioning is evidently a rather ubiquitous process. Salivation can be conditioned, so can the eye blink, heart rate, the knee jerk, the GSR, and a number of other reflexes. That human beings show classical conditioning is hardly anything to be especially proud of, since the flatworm shows it too. There can be little doubt that Pavlov had discovered a phenomenon of considerable generality.

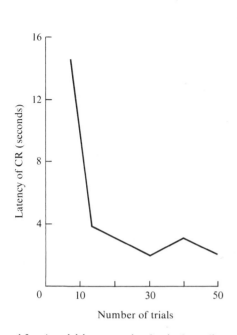

4.3 Acquisition curve in classical conditioning *The acquisition of a classically conditioned salivary response. The CS was a tone, the UCS was meat powder, and the measure of response strength was latency of the CR; that is, the time between the onset of the CS and the start of salivation. Increasing response strength is indicated by a* decline *in the response measure; the stronger conditioning, the shorter the latency. As a result, the acquisition curve goes down as trials proceed. (After Anrep, 1920)*

THE MAJOR PHENOMENA OF CLASSICAL CONDITIONING

Pavlov regarded the conditioned reflex as the basic building block of all learning, no matter how complex; whether the skill was bicycle riding or chess playing, he felt that at bottom it could be analyzed into its component conditioned reactions. It is for this reason that we will consider the phenomenon in detail.

ACQUISITION OF CONDITIONED RESPONSES

Reinforcement Pavlov noted that the tendency of CS to elicit CR goes up the more often CS and UCS have been paired together. Clearly then, presenting UCS together with (or more typically, subsequent to) CS is a critical operation in classical conditioning. Such a pairing is said to **reinforce** the connection; trials on which UCS occurs and on which it is omitted are called **reinforced** and **unreinforced** trials respectively.

Figure 4.3 is a typical **acquisition** or **learning curve** in which magnitude of CR is plotted against successive test trials. In all such learning curves the vertical or *y*-axis represents some measure of response strength while the horizontal or *x*-axis represents learning trials. Note that the figure shows results for a single dog and for relatively few test trials. The data show a clear trend, but even so there is a certain irregularity, with minor ups and downs that presumably reflect small chance effects. Perhaps on a given trial the dog was bitten by a flea and was distracted. The assumption is that, given enough observations (more dogs, more test trials), such chance effects will even out.

The general trend of the conditioning curves is very clear and unsurprising: Response strength increases with reinforced trials. We also see that, at least in these situations, the curves of acquisition are **negatively accelerated.** More is gained from the first ten reinforced trials than from the next ten, and so on throughout acquisition.

Higher-order conditioning Once the CS-UCS relation is solidly established, the CS can serve to condition yet further stimuli. To give one example, Pavlov first conditioned a dog to salivate to the beat of a metronome, using meat powder as the UCS. After many such pairings, he presented the animal with a black square followed by the metronome beat, but without ever introducing the food. Eventually the sight of the black square alone was enough to produce salivation. This phenomenon is called **higher-order conditioning.** In the present case, conditioning was of the second-order. The metronome which served as the CS in first-order conditioning functioned as the UCS for a second-order conditioned response. In effect, the black square had become a signal for the metronome, which in turn signaled the appearance of food.

In most cases, higher-order conditioning is fairly weak. Pavlov found that the second-order response was about half the strength of the first-order one, that third-order responses could be established only with great difficulty, while fourth-order conditioning was impossible altogether. We can readily understand why, if we consider the specifics of the experimental procedure. The black square is paired with the metronome, but on these occasions the metronome is never followed by food. The square becomes indeed a signal for

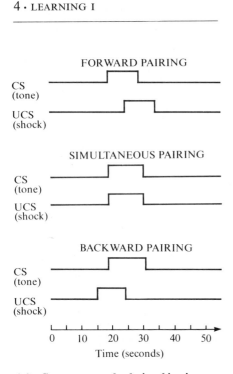

FORWARD PAIRING

CS (tone)

UCS (shock)

SIMULTANEOUS PAIRING

CS (tone)

UCS (shock)

BACKWARD PAIRING

CS (tone)

UCS (shock)

0   10   20   30   40   50

Time (seconds)

4.4 Some temporal relationships in classical conditioning

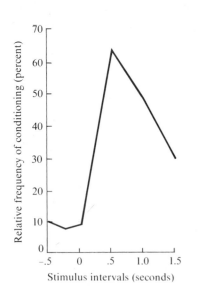

4.5 The role of the CS-UCS interval in classical conditioning   *The figure shows the results of a study on the effectiveness of various CS-UCS intervals in humans. The CR was a finger withdrawal response, the CS a tone, and the UCS an electric shock. The time between CS and UCS is plotted on the horizontal axis. Negative intervals mean that the UCS was presented before the CS (backward pairing), a zero interval means that the two stimuli were presented simultaneously, and a positive interval means that the CS began before the UCS (forward pairing). The vertical axis indicates the degree of conditioning. This was weakest for backward pairing and strongest for forward pairing with half a second interval between CS and UCS. (After Spooner and Kellogg, 1947)*

the metronome, but while this happens the metronome loses *its* signal relationship to food. Put more precisely, the CR to the metronome *extinguishes* (see below). Since higher-order CRs stand upon the shoulders of now unreinforced lower-order ones, the pyramid can never attain any appreciable height. As the higher-order CRs are established, the ones below necessarily start to crumble.

Temporal relations between CS and UCS   In pairing CS and UCS, we can vary the time between these two stimuli and also the order of their presentation. CS may precede UCS *(forward pairing),* it may follow UCS *(backward pairing),* or it may occur at exactly the same time *(simultaneous pairing)* (Figure 4.4). What is the effect of these different procedures upon the strength of the conditioned response?

Figure 4.5 plots the results of two experiments on conditioned finger withdrawal, with electric shock as UCS and sound as CS, using forward, backward, and simultaneous pairing procedures (Spooner and Kellogg, 1947). As the figure shows, conditioning was best when CS *preceded* UCS by about half a second. Presenting CS and UCS simultaneously is much less effective; the backward pairing procedure is just as bad or worse. On the other hand, the effectiveness of forward pairing rapidly declines when the (forward) CS-UCS interval increases beyond .5 seconds. Though the specific shapes of the curves vary somewhat, the general trend of the results is substantially similar for other animals (for instance, dogs, rabbits) and other responses (for instance, eyelid conditioning, galvanic skin response; Schneiderman and Gormezano, 1964; Moeller, 1954).*

How do we make sense of these facts? Pavlov suggested that the CS serves a signaling function: It prepares the organism for a UCS that is to come. Let us consider forward, simultaneous, and backward pairing in this light by likening the subject's situation to that of a driver setting out upon an unfamiliar road. Suppose our driver wants to go from Denver to Salt Lake city, and that some 150 miles out of Denver there is a dangerous hairpin turn over a ravine. How should the driver be warned of the impending curve? Presumably there will be a sign, "Hairpin Turn," which should obviously appear just a bit before the turn (analogous to forward pairing with a short CS-UCS interval). If the interval is too long it will be almost impossible to connect the sign with that which it signifies. We will lose some of our faith in the Highway Department if it sets up the sign, "Hairpin Turn," just outside the Denver city limits while the turn itself is three hours away (forward pairing with a long CS-UCS interval). Our faith will be really shaken if we see the sign prominently displayed just at the sharpest bend of the turn (simultaneous pairing). We finally begin to suspect a degree of malevolence if we discover the sign innocently placed on

* There is one important exception. As we shall see, when animals eat something and then get sick hours later they seem to be able to connect the taste of the ingested substance with the later illness (see Chapter 5).

the road a hundred feet or so beyond the turn (backward pairing) though we should probably be grateful that we did not find it at the bottom of the ravine.

It is clear that in classical conditioning an organism learns something about the relationship between stimuli. As Pavlov saw it, what was learned was an association between two stimuli. The exact how and why doesn't matter at the moment. The important point is that to Pavlov associative conditioning was a glue that could bind just about anything to anything else. All that mattered was that the two stimuli were contiguous in time, with the CS preferably a bit before the UCS. We will later return to these two assumptions of Pavlovian doctrine, that classical conditioning is an association and that any CS will be linked to any UCS as long as the two occur together in time (see Chapter 5).

EXTINCTION

The adaptive value of conditioning is self-evident. A zebra's chance of future survival is enhanced by conditioning. There's much to be gained by a conditioned fear reaction to a place from which a lion has pounced some time before (assuming, of course, that the zebra managed to survive the CS-UCS pairing in the first place). On the other hand, it would be rather inefficient if a connection once established could never be undone. The lion may change its lair and its former prowling place may now be perfectly safe for grazing.

Pavlov showed that in fact a conditioned reaction can be undone. He demonstrated that the conditioned response will gradually disappear if the CS is repeatedly presented without being reinforced by the UCS; in his terms, the conditioned reflex undergoes *experimental extinction.* Figure 4.6 presents an extinction curve from a salivary extinction experiment. As usual, response strength is measured along the *y*-axis, while the *x*-axis indicates the number of extinction trials (that is, trials without reinforcement). As extinction trials proceed, the salivary flow dries up. In effect, the dog has learned that the CS is no longer a signal for food.

What accounts for extinction? Pavlov thought that there are two antagonistic processes upon which the various phenomena of conditioning are based. One of these is *excitation,* a hypothetical process in the nervous system which triggers the conditioned response. This is opposed by *inhibition,* another nervous process somehow produced by nonreinforcement which he believed was the basis of extinction. Given this theoretical framework, Pavlov assumed that the strength of the original conditioning could be measured indirectly, by the resistance it offered to later extinction. As he saw it, excitation and inhibition exert forces in opposite directions, so one can be measured in terms of the other (just as an object is weighed by determining how many pounds must be used as a counterweight to keep the scales in balance).

Reconditioning A conditioned response that has been extinguished can be resurrected. One means is through *reconditioning,* that is, by presenting further reinforced trials. Typically, reconditioning requires fewer reinforced trials to bring the CR to its former strength than were necessary during the initial conditioning session, even if extinction trials had been continued until the animal stopped responding altogether. The conditioned response was evidently not really abolished by extinction but instead was somehow masked. In Pavlov's terms, the excitation was still present but its effect was nullified by inhibition; once this inhibition was removed, the underlying excitatory process showed up again.

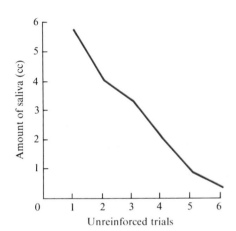

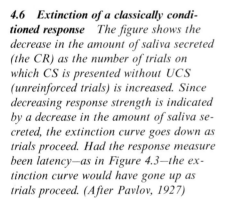

4.6 Extinction of a classically conditioned response *The figure shows the decrease in the amount of saliva secreted (the CR) as the number of trials on which CS is presented without UCS (unreinforced trials) is increased. Since decreasing response strength is indicated by a decrease in the amount of saliva secreted, the extinction curve goes down as trials proceed. Had the response measure been latency—as in Figure 4.3—the extinction curve would have gone up as trials proceed. (After Pavlov, 1927)*

103

Spontaneous recovery   The continued presence of excitation—masked but not abolished by extinction—is also shown by the phenomenon of **spontaneous recovery.** A thoroughly extinguished CR will usually reappear after a rest period during which the animal is left to its own devices. Here is another indication that the CR is not really abolished but is only covered up by the extinction procedure. Typically, the recovery is greater the longer the rest interval.

Pavlov interpreted spontaneous recovery in the light of his belief that inhibition is more transitory than excitation, but one may well question whether this is a genuine explanation or merely a restatement of the phenomenon. To date there is no really adequate theory of the effect.

THE ROLE OF THE STIMULUS

Generalization   So far our discussion has been confined to situations in which the animal is tested with the *identical* stimulus which had served as CS during training. But of course in the real world the stimuli are never really identical. The master's voice may signal food, but the exact intonation will surely vary from one occasion to another; can the dog still use whatever it has learned before? If not, its conditioned response will be of little benefit. Similarly, schoolchildren must be able to apply what they have learned to situations other than those in which they were taught. Learning to read is not simply being able to read *My First Reader.* In fact, animals do respond to stimuli other than the original CS, so long as these are sufficiently similar.

This phenomenon is called **stimulus generalization.** A dog may be conditioned to a tone of 1,000 hertz (cycles per second); nevertheless, the CR will be obtained not just with that tone, but also with tones of different frequencies. The CR evoked by such new stimuli is weaker than that elicited by the original CS, diminishing progressively the greater the difference between the new stimulus and the original CS. The resulting curve (typically more or less symmetrical) is called a **generalization gradient.** Fairly similar gradients have been obtained using variations along different stimulus dimensions (Figure 4.7). One of Pavlov's favorites was tactual stimulation. If a touch on the small of the back had served as the CS, then stimulation of other regions would produce less and less salivation the greater the distance from the original point.

Discrimination   Stimulus generalization is not always beneficial. A kitten may be similar to a tiger; but a man who generalizes from one to the other is likely to be sorry. What he must do instead is discriminate.

The phenomenon of **discrimination** is readily demonstrated in the conditioning laboratory. A dog is first conditioned to salivate to a CS, for example, a black square (CS+). After the CR is well established, reinforced trials with the black square are randomly interspersed with nonreinforced trials with another stimulus, say, a gray square (CS−). This continues until the animal discriminates perfectly, always salivating to CS+, the reinforced stimulus, and never to CS−, the nonreinforced stimulus. Of course the dog does not reach this final point immediately. During the early trials it will be confused, or more precisely, it will generalize rather than discriminate. It will tend to salivate to CS− (which, after all, is quite similar to CS+); by the same token, it will often fail to salivate when presented with CS+. Such errors gradually become fewer and

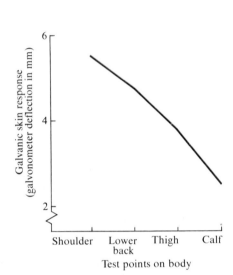

4.7   Generalization gradient of a classically conditioned response   *The figure shows the results of an experiment in which the CR was the galvanic skin response in a human subject, the UCS was electric shock, and the original CS was being touched on the shoulder. After original conditioning, the subject was presented with four test stimuli: He was touched on the shoulder (the original CS) and at three other bodily locations. As the figure shows, the response fell off with increasing distance from the point of original stimulation. (Based on data in Bass and Hull, 1934)*

fewer until perfect discrimination is finally achieved. Not surprisingly, the discrimination gets harder and harder the more similar the two stimuli are. As similarity increases, the tendency to respond to CS$^+$ will increasingly generalize to CS$^-$, while the tendency not to respond to CS$^-$ will increasingly generalize to CS$^+$. As a result, the dog will require many trials before it finally responds without errors.

One might think that the difficulty in forming discrimination is that the animal has trouble telling the two stimuli apart. But that is generally not the reason. The dog's problem is not that it can't form a sensory discrimination between CS$^+$ and CS$^-$. What is at fault is not its eyesight, for it can distinguish between the dark-gray and light-gray squares visually. Its difficulty is in discovering and remembering which stimulus is *right,* which goes with UCS and which does not. Eventually the animal learns, but this doesn't mean that it has learned to see the stimuli differently. What it has learned is their significance; it now knows which stimulus is which.

WHAT IS LEARNED DURING CLASSICAL CONDITIONING?

A STIMULUS-STIMULUS (S-S) CONNECTION

Pavlov believed that conditioning is based on a linkage between the CS and the UCS (an S-S connection). This position presumes that after many pairings, excitation of the cerebral center that corresponds to CS will eventually stimulate the center that is normally aroused directly by UCS. This in turn arouses the efferent control centers of the UCR. In effect then, the CS will gradually come to substitute for the UCS.

Many psychologists would agree that in classical conditioning the animal learns something about the relationship between two stimuli, but not all of them believe that this relation is necessarily a simple association. The question is whether the CS really comes to *substitute* for the UCS, as the S-S position would seem to imply. If it does, then a well-conditioned dog should respond to the CS just as it does to the UCS. Put another way, the CR should be identical to the UCR. But this is usually not the case. In salivary conditioning, for example, the response is quite different depending upon whether it occurs as UCR or as CR; the UCR is more copious and richer in digestive enzyme than is the CR. The difference is even more pronounced for other aspects of behavior. Given the UCS, the animal lunges forward to the food pan; given the CS it looks as if it is "expecting" the UCS, but it "does not appear to be eating an imaginary food" (Zener, 1937, p. 393). All of this makes good biological sense. The CR prepares the organism while the UCR actually performs the task for which the organism is now so well prepared.

A particularly interesting demonstration of the fact that UCR and CR are not identical comes from studies on the conditioning of drug effects. Suppose a person gets many doses of insulin, which depletes blood sugar. It turns out that after many such insulin injections, the bodily reaction to various conditioned stimuli that accompany the drug is precisely the opposite of the response to the drug itself: The blood-sugar level goes up (Siegel, 1977). It is as if the body prepares itself for the chemical agent it is about to receive and does so by adopting a compensatory reaction that tilts the other way. Here the CR is the precise opposite of the form taken by the UCR, which is another argument against the notion that the CS becomes a substitute for the UCS.

105

Facts like these have led some psychologists to believe that what is acquired in classical conditioning is an *expectancy.* Given one stimulus, the animal expects the other. Instead of substituting for the UCS, the CS becomes a sign that the UCS is to follow (Tolman, 1932).

This view of classical conditioning circumvents some of the problems we have raised previously but it encounters problems of its own. In at least some cases the CR will be made even when the subject knows perfectly well that the UCS will no longer follow the CS. An example is conditioned fear. Consider a concentration camp survivor who visits the site of the camp three decades later. He probably will still feel his heart race and his mouth dry up. He knows that Hitler is dead and that the camp is in ruins; in the usual sense of the word he certainly does not now *expect* any of the horrors that he once had so much cause to fear. But this does not change his actual reaction.

Classical conditioning is a rather primitive form of learning, in many ways quite mechanical and involuntary. If we try to describe it as *expectation,* we must realize that we have changed the normal sense of the word. Classical conditioning may be a primordial predecessor of true expectation. It does share the anticipatory character we find in genuine expectation, in which one event signals another further off in time. On the other hand, it is not as readily modified by other items of information, and is thus a more rudimentary version of what we usually call expectation, primitive as befits a mechanism shared by man and flatworm both.

Instrumental Conditioning

Classical conditionings is one of the two main forms of simple learning. The other is instrumental learning.* An example of instrumental learning comes from the zoo. When a seal learns to turn a somersault to get a fish from the zoo attendant, it has learned an *instrumental response.* The response is instrumental in that it leads to a sought-after effect; in this case, the fish.

On the face of it there are many similarities between this form of learning and classical conditioning. (This is one reason why instrumental learning is often called *instrumental conditioning.*) Compare the seal with a dog that has acquired a salivary CR to a bell while meat powder served as the UCS. In both cases we have a response which occurs more frequently with increased training (on the one hand, salivation, on the other, the somersault). In both cases, we have a stimulus that is somehow important in determining whether the response is made (the bell and the sight of the attendant). In both cases, finally, we have reinforcement without which the response will soon disappear (the meat powder and the fish).

Yet, despite these many similarities, there are some important differences. Perhaps most important is the fact that in instrumental learning, reinforcement (that is, reward) depends upon the proper response. For the seal the rules of the game are simple: no somersault, no fish. This is not true for

* As we will see, this form of learning is also called *operant conditioning.*

classical conditioning. There the UCS is presented regardless of what the animal does. Another difference concerns response selection. In instrumental learning, the response must be selected from a sometimes very large set of alternatives. The seal's job is to select the somersault from among the numerous other things a seal could possibly do. Not so in classical conditioning. There the response is forced, for the UCS unconditionally evokes it.

We could loosely summarize the difference between the two procedures by a rough description of what is learned in each. In classical conditioning the animal must learn about the relation between two stimuli, the CS and the UCS: Given CS, UCS will follow. In instrumental learning, the animal has to learn the relation beween a response and reward: Given this response, there will be reinforcement. But such statements are only crude descriptions. To get beyond them we must discuss instrumental learning in more detail.

THORNDIKE AND THE LAW OF EFFECT

The experimental study of instrumental learning began a decade or two before Pavlov. It was an indirect consequence of the debate over the doctrine of evolution. Darwin's theory was buttressed by impressive demonstrations of continuity in the bodily structures of many species, both living and extinct. But his opponents could argue that such evidence was not enough. To them the essential distinction between humans and beasts was elsewhere: in the human ability to think and reason, an ability that animals did not share. To answer this point it became critical to find proof of mental as well as of bodily continuity.

For evidence, the Darwinians turned to animal behavior. At first, the method was largely anecdotal. Several British naturalists (including Darwin himself) collected stories about the intellectual achievements of various animals as related by presumably reliable informants. Taken at face value, the results painted a flattering picture of animal intellect, as in accounts of cunning cats scattering bread crumbs on the lawn to entice the birds (Romanes, 1882). But even if such observations could be trusted (and they probably could not) they did not prove that the animals' performances were achieved in the way a human might achieve the same thing: by reason and understanding. To be sure of that, one would have to study the animals' learning processes from start to finish. To see a circus seal blow a melody on a set of toy trumpets is one thing; to conclude from this observation that it has musical understanding is quite another.

There was clearly a need for controlled experimental procedures whereby the entire course of learning could be carefully scrutinized (Morgan, 1894). That method was provided in 1898 by Edward L. Thorndike (1874–1949) in a brilliant doctoral dissertation that became one of the classic documents of American psychology (Thorndike, 1898).

Edward L. Thorndike (Courtesy The Granger Collection)

CATS IN A PUZZLE-BOX

Thorndike's method was to set up a problem for the animal. To gain reward the creature had to perform some particular action determined by the experimenter. Much of this work was done on hungry cats. The animal was placed in a so-called *puzzle box,* an enclosure from which it could escape only

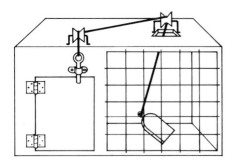

4.8 Puzzle box much like those used by Thorndike *The animal steps on a treadle which is attached to a rope, thereby releasing a latch that locks the door. (After Thorndike, 1911)*

by performing some simple action that would unlatch the door, such as pulling a loop or wire or pressing a lever (Figure 4.8). Once outside, the animal was rewarded with a small portion of food and then placed back into the box for another trial. This procedure was repeated until the task was mastered.

On the first trial, the typical cat struggled valiantly; it clawed at the bars, it bit, it struck out in all directions, it meowed, and it howled. This continued for several minutes until the animal finally hit upon the correct response by pure accident. Subsequent trials brought gradual improvement. The mad scramble became shorter and the animal took less and less time to perform the correct response. By the time the training sessions were completed the cat's behavior was almost unrecognizable from what it had been at the start. Placed in the box, it immediately approached the wire loop, yanked it with businesslike dispatch, and quickly hurried through the open door to enjoy its well-deserved reward. The cat had certainly learned.

How had it learned? If one merely observed its final performance one might credit the cat with reason or understanding, but Thorndike argued that the problem was solved in a very different way. For proof he examined the learning curves. Plotting the time required on each trial (that is, the **latency**) over the whole course of training, he usually found a curve that declined quite gradually (Figure 4.9). Had the animals "understood" the solution at some point during training, the curves should have shown a sudden drop with little change thereafter (for one would hardly expect further errors once understanding was reached).

Related work led to the same conclusion. Thorndike tried to teach several cats the solution by holding their paws over the lever and then pressing it down for them. If the cats learned by reason, they would surely find their way

4.9 Learning curve of one of Thorndike's cats *To get out of the box, the cat had to move a wooden handle from a vertical to a horizontal position. The figure shows the gradual decline in the animal's latency. Note that the learning curve is by no means smooth but has rather marked fluctuations. This is a common feature of the learning curves of individual subjects. Smooth learning curves are generally produced by averaging the results of many individual subjects. (After Thorndike, 1898)*

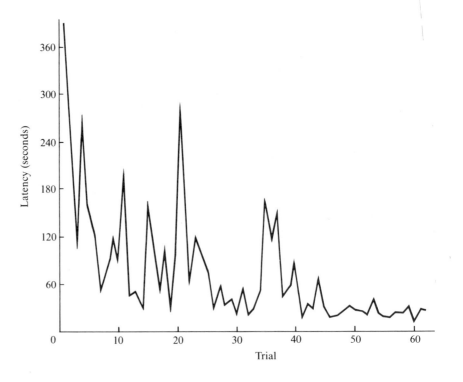

out of the box once Thorndike had shown them the method. But such **passive training** had no effect. To learn, the animal evidently had to perform the response itself. The results argue that the cats did not really understand what led to what.

S-R BONDS AND THE LAW OF EFFECT

Thorndike proposed that what the animal had learned was an association between the total stimulus situation (including the box and its own hunger) and a motor reaction, an **S-R bond.** Initially, the stimulus calls out a large set of responses, perhaps because of prior learning, perhaps because of built-in predispositions. As it happens, virtually all of these lead to failure. As trials proceed, the bonds between the stimulus and the incorrect reactions gradually weaken. This is in contrast to the bond between the stimulus and the correct response, which at first is weak or totally absent but which increasingly grows in strength. In Thorndike's terms, the correct response is gradually "stamped in" while futile ones are correspondingly stamped out. The improvements in the learning curves "represent the wearing smooth of a path in the brain, not the decisions of a rational consciousness" (Thorndike, 1911).

Thorndike's view is an **S-R theory** of learning. In such a theory, the basic components of learning are stimuli and responses which become forged together as training proceeds. The question is how the appropriate connections are established.

Thorndike's answer was a bold formulation called the **law of effect.** The relevant features of his analysis are schematized in Figure 4.10, which indicates the bonds between stimulus and the various responses, whether correct

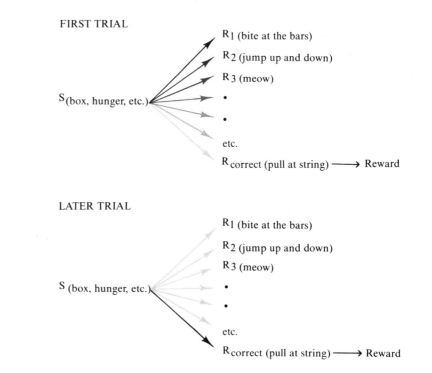

4.10 Thorndike's law of effect *The figure is a schematic presentation of Thorndike's theory of instrumental learning. On the first trial, the S-R bonds linking the stimulus situation (the box, being hungry, and so on) and various incorrect responses (biting the bars, jumping up and down) are very strong while the link between the stimulus situation and the correct response (pulling the string) is weak or nonexistent. As trials proceed, the strengths of these S-R bonds change. The bonds between the stimulus situation and the incorrect responses become weaker and weaker, for none of these responses are immediately followed by reward. In contrast, there is a progressive strengthening of the S-R bond that links the stimulus situation and the correct response since that response is followed more or less immediately by reward.*

FIRST TRIAL

$S_{(box, hunger, etc.)}$

R_1 (bite at the bars)
R_2 (jump up and down)
R_3 (meow)
·
·
etc.
$R_{correct}$ (pull at string) ⟶ Reward

LATER TRIAL

$S_{(box, hunger, etc.)}$

R_1 (bite at the bars)
R_2 (jump up and down)
R_3 (meow)
·
·
etc.
$R_{correct}$ (pull at string) ⟶ Reward

(R_c) or incorrect (R_1, R_2, R_3, etc.). The critical question is how the correct S-R bond gets strengthened until it finally overwhelms the incorrect ones that are at first so dominant. Thorndike's proposal, the law of effect, held that the consequences (that is, the effect) of a response determine whether the tendency of the stimulus to produce that response again is strengthened or weakened. If the response is followed by reward, the corresponding S-R connection will be strengthened; if it is followed by the absence of reward (or worse yet, by punishment) it will be weakened. There was no need to postulate any further intellectual process in the animal, no need to assume that the animal noticed a connection between act and consequence, no need to believe that it was trying to attain some goal. If the animal made a response in the presence of a stimulus, and reward followed shortly, that stimulus would be more likely to evoke the respone at a subsequent time.

This proposal neatly fits into the context of evolutionary thinking so dominant at the time. Thorndike emphasized the adaptive nature of the animal's activity which is gradually shaped to serve its biological ends. But the relationship·to evolutionary theory is even closer for, as Thorndike pointed out, the law of effect is an analogue of the law of the survival of the fittest. In the life of the species, the individual whose genetic makeup fits it best for its environment will survive to transmit its characteristics to its offspring. In the life of the individual, learning provides another adaptive mechanism through the law of effect which decrees that only the fittest *responses* shall survive. As Thorndike put it, "It is a process of selection among reactions . . . by eliminating the unsuitable reaction directly by discomfort, and also by positively selecting the suitable one by pleasure. . . . It is of tremendous usefulness. . . . 'He who learns and runs away, *will live* to learn another day'" (Thorndike, 1899, p. 91).

As we have seen, the anecdotalists tried to support their evolutionary convictions with accounts of high animal intelligence. But Thorndike seemed to show that animal learning proceeds in another way altogether, without reason or understanding. Did this do violence to the evolutionist's belief in an ultimate continuity between the mental processes of humans and animals?

The eventual upshot was ironic. The belief that humans and animals learn in much the same way won many adherents among psychologists of Thorndike's general persuasion, but hardly in a way that Darwin or the anecdotalists had in mind. These thinkers had suggested that animals learn like humans; S-R theorists proposed that humans learn like animals! Eventually many psychologists began to believe that the laws of learning discovered with cats in a puzzle box (or dogs in Pavlov's harness) hold for all other situations and for all animals including human beings. This belief in the essential equivalence of both learners and learning tasks dominated much of the research on learning produced during the five or six decades following Thorndike's original work and commands considerable allegiance even now.

METHODS FOR STUDYING INSTRUMENTAL LEARNING

Thorndike's puzzle box was of course only one means whereby instrumental learning could be studied experimentally. Many other methods have been developed since. Animals have been trained to make a sequence of turns in a **maze,** jump at one of two windows in a **jumping stand,** sprint back and forth in

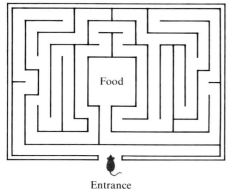

Food

Entrance

A

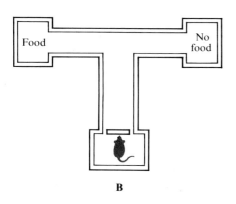

Food

No food

B

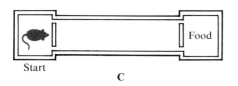

Start

Food

C

4.11 Methods for studying instrumental learning: From maze to runway (A) In the maze, an animal—usually a rat—has to find its way from a starting point to the reward. Initially, psychologists used rather elaborate multiple-unit mazes in which many choices had to be made. This is a floor plan of one such device. (After Stone and Nysander, 1927)

(B) Later developments led to simplifications. One favorite tool was the T-maze, as shown in the figure. Here, the rat only had to make one choice.

(C) Some investigators took away even this last choice and placed the animal in a runway in which instrumental learning is measured by the speed with which the animal runs from start to finish.

a *shuttle box,* peck at a lighted key or press a lever in an *operant chamber*—always to obtain reward, whether a pellet of rat chow or a piece of grain or the cessation of a painful shock. The number of possible methods is legion, limited only by the imagination of the experimenter and the organism's capacity to perform a given response. (However much one rewards it, a dog cannot learn to meow.)

Despite the huge variety of possibilities, a few methods have become favorite tools. In general, the criterion was simplicity. Those methods were preferred in which the phenomenon of instrumental learning appeared stripped to its essence. One example is the *T-maze* in which the animal has to make only one choice, and in which the index of response strength is typically the probability of error. Another is the *runway* in which the animal is required to run from one end of an alley to the other where it obtains reward and in which response strength is measured by the time it takes the animal to traverse the path (Figure 4.11).

Many contemporary psychologists prefer a method which does not depend upon the use of *discrete trials.* In most experiments with the puzzle box (or the maze or the runway) the animal is placed in the apparatus, left there until it makes the response, and is then taken out until the next trial. An alternative method allows the animal to respond regardless of trials. This is the *free operant* procedure, developed by B. F. Skinner for the study of instrumental behavior. An animal is placed in a box (popularly called a *Skinner box*) that requires a particular response to bring reward—for a rat, pressing a lever; for a pigeon, pecking at a lighted disk (Figure 4.12). The animal remains in the box for a lengthy session (say, one or two hours) pressing or pecking as it chooses.

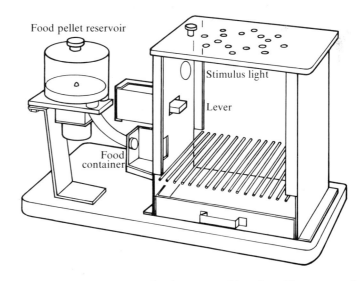

Food pellet reservoir

Stimulus light

Lever

Food container

4.12 Methods for studying instrumental learning: The operant chamber The figure shows an operant chamber (often called a Skinner box) designed for a rat. The animal presses a lever which delivers food by activating a device that releases a small food pellet into a food container. (Ralph Gerbrands Co., Arlington, Mass.)

A

B

4.13 Methods for studying instrumental learning: The jumping stand (A) With the jumping stand, the animal's task is discrimination. The rat has to jump to one of two cards, say, a triangle or a square, behind which is a ledge that contains food. If the choice is correct, the card gives way and the animal gets to the food. If the choice is incorrect, the card stays in place, the rat bumps its nose and falls into a net below. (after Lashley, 1930) (B) A rat performing such a jump. (Photograph by Frank Lotz Miller—Black Star)

The results of numerous studies with these and other techniques made it clear that many of the phenomena of instrumental learning parallel those found in conditioning. Consider *reinforcement.* In classical conditioning, the term refers to an operation (pairing CS and UCS) which strengthens the CR. In the context of instrumental learning, reinforcement refers to an analogous operation: having the response followed by a condition that the animal "desires." This may be the presentation of something "good," such as grain to a hungry pigeon. It may also be the termination of something "bad" (usually called an *aversive stimulus*) such as the cessation of an electric shock. As in classical conditioning, the probability of responding increases with an increasing number of reinforcements. And, again as in classical conditioning, the response suffers from *extinction* if reinforcement is withdrawn. Furthermore, the extinguished response can be reconditioned and is subject to spontaneous recovery. Finally, there are numerous procedures that document stimulus *generalization* and *discrimination* in instrumental learning (Figure 4.13).

SECONDARY REINFORCEMENT

It was perfectly clear to both Thorndike and his successors that his law of effect required some amendments. One of these concerned the extension of the law to include learned as well as unlearned reinforcers.

So far, our examples of reinforcement have been food, or water, or the termination of an electric shock. These are instances of *primary reinforcement* whose capacity to reinforce responses is presumably based upon a built-in mechanism. But instrumental learning is not always reinforced by events of such immediate biological consequence. For example, piano teachers rarely reinforce their pupils with food or the cessation of electric shock; a nod or the comment "good" is all that is required. How does the Thorndikian approach explain why the word *good* is reinforcing?

The answer given is that a stimulus can acquire reinforcing properties if it is repeatedly paired with a primary reinforcer. It will then provide *secondary reinforcement* (or *conditioned reinforcement*) if administered after a response has been made. In one representative experiment rats were first trained in a runway whose end box contained food on some trials but not on others. The end boxes were different, depending upon whether food was present or absent; for example, black on food trials and white on others. After several days on the runway, the rats were placed on a simple maze that offered a choice between two empty end boxes: one black and the other white. The animals quickly learned the path that ran to the black box which now served as a secondary reinforcer (Saltzman, 1949).

Numerous other experiments give further evidence that hitherto neutral stimuli may acquire reinforcing properties. Thus chimpanzees were first trained to insert poker chips into a vending machine to obtain grapes, and they then learned to operate another device which delivered poker chips (Cowles, 1937; Figure 4.14).

Examples of this kind indicate that the critical factor in establishing the secondary reinforcing properties of a stimulus is its association with primary reinforcement. It is then not surprising that the effect increases the more frequently the two have been paired. As we might also expect, a secondary

4.14 Secondary reinforcement in chimpanzees *An example of secondary reinforcement is a chimpanzee using a token to obtain food. (The device in which this token is inserted is sometimes called the "chimpomat".) The apes work to obtain the tokens, but they also try to get them from each other by begging, and occasionally, by stealing. (Courtesy Yerkes Regional Primate Research Center of Emory University)*

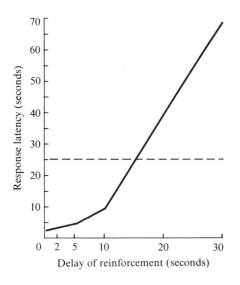

reinforcer will gradually lose its powers if it is repeatedly unaccompanied by primary reinforcement. All of this argues that secondary reinforcement is established by a process that is akin to, if not identical with, classical conditioning. The secondary reinforcer serves as a CS that signals some motivationally significant UCS.

If secondary reinforcers are so readily extinguished in the laboratory, why do they seem so much more permanent in human life? Nods do not lose their reinforcing value just because they have not been paired with any primary reinforcer for a month or more. In part, the answer may be that the nod or the smile has enormous generality. Unlike the black end box, it is associated not with one but with many different desirable outcomes. Even if extinguished in one context, it would still be maintained in countless others.

DELAY OF REINFORCEMENT

The law of effect requires a second amendment. This concerns the role of the time interval between the response and the reinforcement that follows it.

During an early trial in a puzzle box a cat performs many incorrect responses (for instance, clawing at the bars) before it finally performs the correct one and obtains reward. But this means that reward eventually follows all responses (both the correct ones and the incorrect ones). Given the law of effect, all of these responses should therefore gain in strength. But if so, how does the correct response ever outstrip its rivals? This question shows that the law of effect requires an amendment: A reinforcer becomes less and less effective the longer its presentation is delayed after the response is made. In the puzzle box this interval is necessarily shorter for the correct response than for the others. (After all, the cat doesn't pull the wire loop and then run back for another bite at the bars before it finally leaves the box.)

The relation between the delay and the effectiveness of a reward has been experimentally studied in various ways. One experimenter trained several groups of rats to press a lever which was withdrawn from the box immediately after the correct response. Food was delivered after different delays of reinforcement ranging from 0 to 30 seconds for the various groups. Learning was clearly faster the shorter the interval. These results are summarized in Figure 4.15 which shows the declining effectiveness of reinforcement with increasing delay, a relationship often called the ***gradient of reinforcement.*** Note that in this study there was no learning at all when the interval was as large as 30 seconds; in instrumental learning, late is sometimes no better than never (Perin, 1943).

The gradient of reinforcement has been applied to the interpretation of more complex phenomena. One example concerns the runway. What does the animal learn here? Clark L. Hull (1884–1952), a very influential S-R theorist during the thirties and forties, proposed that the rat's behavior is best under-

4.15 The effect of a delay in reinforcement *The graph shows the response latency for rats pressing a lever after 50 trials on which they received food reward after a delay of 0, 2, 5, 10, or 30 seconds. The dotted line indicates the animals' average latency at the very first trial. It is clear that animals trained with delays up to 10 seconds improved over trials, and the shorter the delay the greater was their improvement. But animals trained with a delay of 30 seconds did not improve; on the contrary, their performance was markedly worse after 50 trials than it was initially. (Data from Perin, 1943)*

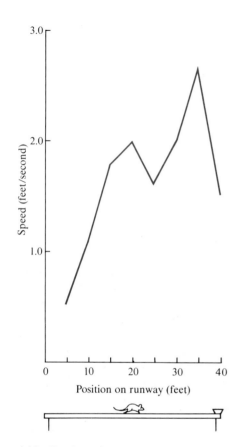

3.0

2.0

Speed (feet/second)

1.0

0   10   20   30   40

Position on runway (feet)

4.16 Rats' running speed on a runway
The figure shows the running speed of rats on a forty-foot runway. The animals' speed increases the closer they get to the goal. The exception is toward the very end of the runway where the animals slow down. This final slowdown is hardly surprising. If it did not occur, the rats might overshoot the end of the runway. (After Hull, 1934)

stood as a sequence of separate responses: one step, then another, and so on until the goal is reached. Reinforcement is food, presented at the very end. It is clear that the delay of reinforcement is less for responses at the very end of the chain than for those at its beginning. If so, then response strength should be greatest at the end of the alley, and lowest at its start. This seems to be what happens (Hull, 1934). Rats show a progressive increase in running speed on a runway; at the start they amble but they eventually get faster and faster as they approach the goal (Figure 4.16).

THE GRADIENT OF REINFORCEMENT IN HUMAN BEHAVIOR

To what extent does the delay of reward principle apply to humans? It depends upon which aspects of human behavior we consider. At one level there is an enormous gap between what we see in the rat and what we know of ourselves. Rats and humans live according to different time scales entirely. Reinforcement may come months or even years after an action and still have effect, because humans can relate their present to their past by all sorts of symbolic devices. A politician wins a close election, looks carefully at the returns, and realizes that a speech he gave a month ago turned the tide. Unlike the rat, humans can transcend the here and now.

The fact that people sometimes overcome the gradient of reinforcement should not blind us to the fact that they often do not. Many of our actions are dictated by immediate reward, regardless of the long-term outcome. To give only one example, consider cigarette smoking. By now, most smokers are probably convinced of the ultimate dangers they are courting. In fact, they may experience some discomfort: They may cough and have trouble breathing when they wake up. Yet, despite all this, they continue to smoke. The problem is that the *immediate* reinforcement of the act is positive while discomfort or worse comes later. Transcending the gradient of reward is no easy task.

CONFLICT AND APPROACH-AVOIDANCE GRADIENTS

A suitable modification of the gradient-of-reinforcement concept we have just discussed may help us to explain another phenomenon found in both rats and humans: *conflict.*

Our main interest is in *approach-avoidance* conflicts in which the same goal attracts but also repels. In such situations, a common effect is *oscillation.* A little child wants to pet a dog but is afraid of doing so. As a result, he extends his hand, withdraws it, reaches out again, and so on. According to some accounts, these back-and-forths reflect the fact that the degree to which the goal attracts or repels changes as one gets closer to it. From afar, the animal the child wants to pet is a lovable doggie. Once closer, it seems a dangerous creature that might bite.

These informal conceptions of what might go on in approach-avoidance conflicts have been systematized by one of Hull's early associates, Neal Miller. Miller believes that both reward and punishment become more effective the closer one gets to them. The closer one is to a desired object, the greater one's tendency to approach. Conversely, the closer one gets to a feared object, the

4.17 Conflict and gradients of approach and of avoidance *The figure illustrates Neal Miller's theory of conflict behavior. If the goal is both desirable and frightening (such as an end box in which a rat has found food but has also been shocked) it elicits both approach and avoidance reactions. Both tendencies increase the closer the animal gets to the goal. But according to Miller, the tendency to avoid rises more steeply than the tendency to approach. As a result, the animal continues to approach the goal until it gets beyond the point where the gradients of approach and avoidance intersect. Now the avoidance tendency is greater than the tendency to approach so the animal retreats. This brings it to a region where the approach tendency is greater than the tendency to avoid, so the animal approaches again, and so on. (Miller, 1959)*

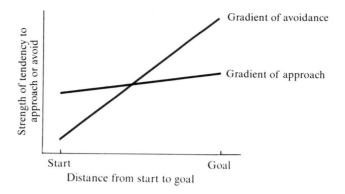

greater one's tendency to flee. These changes in response strength as a function of distance from the goal are called **gradients of approach** and **gradients of avoidance** respectively. The assumption is that these tendencies add algebraically. If the tendency to approach is greater than that of avoidance, the organism will approach, and conversely (Miller, 1959).*

Miller's major assumption is that the gradient of avoidance is steeper than that of approach. Put another way, every step closer to a desired object makes it more desirable while every step closer makes a feared object more frightening. But each step increases the fear more than the desire.

With these assumptions, we can explain some of the phenomena of approach-avoidance conflict. Consider a hungry rat who has found food at the end of an alley but has also been shocked there. It is now placed at the alley's start. Figure 4.17 shows the strength of both approach and avoidance tendencies as a function of the distance from the end of the alley. At the runway start there is no avoidance tendency but there is some tendency to approach. Since this is so, the rat will run. But as it proceeds, the avoidance tendency gets stronger and stronger. The approach tendency also rises, but not as quickly. As a result, the rat starts to slow down and falter, takes one or two more tentative forward steps, draws back, approaches gingerly and withdraws again. It has now reached the point where the avoidance tendency is as strong or even stronger than the tendency to approach. One might think that the rat would just stand still at the point where the two gradients intersect, since here both pull and push are of equal strength. But instead, it presents a rat's version of Hamlet, vacillating back and forth in the critical region. One possibility is that it is pushed beyond the point of intersection by sheer momentum. Once beyond this point, it is in the region where the avoidance tendency predominates. It now withdraws, overshoots again, approaches and overshoots, and so on.

How can we be sure that the approach and avoidance gradients really vary in steepness? To find out, the two gradients have to be independently mea-

* Gradients of approach and avoidance are analogous to generalization gradients. The tendency to approach is greatest when one is close to the goal and falls off the greater one's distance. In much the same way, the tendency to perform the conditioned response is greatest when presented with the original CS; when presented with another stimulus, the tendency to respond as before will decrease the more dissimilar this new stimulus is to the old CS.

sured. This was done in an ingenious study by J. S. Brown (Brown, 1948). Some rats were trained to run in an alley to reach food. Another group was trained to run the alley so as to avoid an electric shock. While in the alley, the animals wore a harness which was connected to a spring by strings and pulleys. This device allowed the experimenter to measure how strongly the rat strained at the harness at different distances from the desired or the feared place. The results were in accordance with Miller's theory. The pull away from shock rose much more sharply than the pull toward the food.

From S-R Theory to Operant Analysis

To Pavlov and Thorndike, as well as to many of their successors, the terms *stimulus* and *response* meant pretty much what they had always meant within a reflex framework: The stimulus was defined as some excitation of a sense organ and the response as a muscular or glandular reaction. Even more important, the basic law that dictated the behavior of Descartes' robot still held: no stimulus, no response.

This reflex-oriented way of looking at learned behavior was a feature of most S-R theories and continued to be influential through the thirties and forties. But as time went on, more and more arguments were raised against this extreme S-R position. The main charge was that it was unable to account for many of the phenomena of learning, especially instrumental conditioning. As we shall see, some of these challenges led to the development of a **modified behavior theory,** whose chief proponent is B. F. Skinner.*

SOME PROBLEMS OF S-R THEORY

Some of the more serious criticisms of simple S-R theory grew out of the question, What is learned? Suppose an animal has mastered some instrumental task such as a puzzle box or a maze. What has it really learned after it manages to perform without further error? One issue concerns the definition of the response in instrumental learning.

THE PROBLEM OF THE RESPONSE: MOLAR OR MOLECULAR

What do we mean by the term *response?* According to the reflex scheme, it is a particular set of muscular or glandular reactions. Described in this manner, the behavior of the rat in a lever box consists of various movements of its legs, head, and trunk. A description cast in these terms is often called **molecular,** to emphasize that the units of analysis are relatively small. But behavior can also be described in terms of larger units. Thus rats working in a Skinner box may depress the lever in various ways. Sometimes they use one paw, sometimes another, and occasionally they yank the lever with their teeth. At the muscular (molecular) level these responses are radically different. But if we define the rat's response by the way in which it changes its environment rather than by

---

* Another upshot of this critique was an alternative view of animal learning which endowed the animal with more reason and intelligence than Thorndike had. (Of this, more will be said in Chapter 5.)

John B. Watson (Courtesy The Bettmann Archive)

the specific movements it employs in so doing, then all these responses can be regarded as identical. In every case the lever has been pulled down. This is sometimes called a ***molar*** description of behavior.*

As we have seen, two responses may differ according to a molecular analysis (different muscle movements) and yet be identical in molar terms (the lever is depressed). Conversely, two responses may be the same on the molecular level while very different from a molar point of view. Consider two men, each slapping a third person. Each uses the same movement: the same wrist action, the same follow-through. Suppose we learn that the first man slapped in anger while the second tried to squash a tarantula on the victim's cheek. In molar terms, the two men performed two very different acts.

Any behavior can be described in both molar and molecular terms, but for certain purposes one level of description may be more illuminating than the other. An example comes from the study of maze learning in rats. One of the earliest interpretations of maze learning was proposed by J. B. Watson (1878–1958), the founder of American behaviorism. Watson offered an S-R theory in which R was conceived as completely molecular. He argued that the rat learns a certain sequence of motor acts (say, turning right, then left, then left again, and so on). Each of these molecular responses is chained to a specific pattern of sensory stimulation, a vital component of which is the feedback from the preceding response (J. B. Watson, 1914).

To test the adequacy of this description, we ask what the animal does if the situation is changed. A representative experiment is one performed in the laboratory of Edward C. Tolman, a major American critic of S-R theory. Rats were first trained to run in an alley maze. After the rats had learned their way to the food box, the alleys were flooded with eight inches of water (Macfarlane, 1930). Now the animals could no longer run through the maze but had to swim instead, using an entirely different set of muscle movements. Nevertheless, they swam to the food box with hardly an error. (For some related findings, see Figure 4.18). This and other experiments showed that Watson's "muscle-twitch" theory was clearly in error. The rats learned a response that required a broader description—getting to the place where the food was located. Today it is generally agreed that a molecular definition

---

*The term *molar* is taken from the physical sciences where it refers to large masses of matter and is often used in contrast with *molecular*.

4.18   Muscle twitch or molar response? *A number of studies show that learned responses are more than a set of muscle twitches. (A) In one experiment, human subjects were conditioned to withdraw their finger at the sound of a bell by pairing the bell with a mild shock to the finger. They sat with the palm down, so that the response was finger extension. (B) In a later test, the subject turned his hand over. When the bell was now sounded, the typical response was finger flexion. From a molecular (that is, muscular) point of view, the two responses are exact opposites. But in a molar sense they are the same—they both involve finger withdrawal. (After Wickens, 1943)*

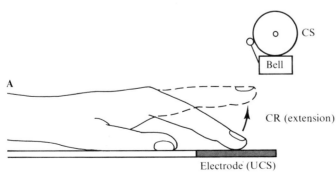

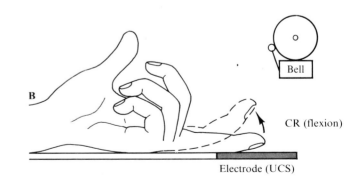

which emphasizes specific muscular movements does not easily square with the facts of instrumental learning.

THE PROBLEM OF THE STIMULUS: WHAT IS THE S IN THE S-R BOND?

Another issue concerns the stimulus term in the S-R formula. The trouble is that in instrumental learning this stimulus is generally inferred rather than observed directly. Take Thorndike's puzzle box. What was the stimulus to which responses such as string pulling were presumably connected? Since Thorndike argued that the animal learned an S-R bond, some stimulus had to be postulated. This was usually said to be the total situation in which the cat found itself in the box, including both external stimuli (the bars, the string) and the internal ones (fear, hunger). But this vaguely described "stimulus" is certainly a far cry from the neatly defined CS encountered in classical conditioning.

THE OPERANT APPROACH

The modified behavior theory developed by B. F. Skinner (1904–) sidesteps many of the difficulties we have just discussed. Skinner starts out by underlining the distinction between classical and instrumental conditioning. In classical conditioning, the animal's behavior is elicited by the CS; the salivation appears to be set off from the outside, thus justifying the reflex analogy to some extent. But in instrumental conditioning, the organism appears to be less at the mercy of the external stimulation. Its reactions seem to come from within, as if they were what we normally call **voluntary.** And the best way of describing such instrumental reactions is at a molar level of analysis. Skinner calls such molarly defined instrumental responses **operants;** they *operate* on the environment to bring about some change that leads to reward (Skinner, 1938).

While Skinner denied that operants are elicited by external stimuli, he did not abandon the idea that behavior is controlled by environmental events. Far from it. What he did was to assert that in the case of instrumental learning the important external events are in the *past.* They involve the organism's prior reinforcement history—what it did and what it was rewarded for. The basic law was much like Thorndike's law of effect. But unlike Thorndike, Skinner does not believe that reinforcement creates an association between the response and the stimulus. In his view, what gets strengthened—just as blindly and just as mechanically as Thorndike argued—is the operant itself which is now more likely to be emitted in the future. Thus the basic association is that between the response and the reinforcement that follows it.

The operant is not elicited by external stimuli, but this doesn't mean that such stimuli have no effect. They do exert considerable control over behavior, for they may serve as **discriminative stimuli.** Suppose a pigeon is trained to hop on a treadle to get some grain. When a green light is on, hopping on the treadle will pay off. But when a red light is on, the treadle-hopping response is of no avail, for the pigeon gets no access to the food container. Under these circumstances, the green light becomes a positive discriminative stimulus and the red light a negative one (here designated S^+ and S^- respectively). The pigeon will hop in the presence of the first and not when presented with the

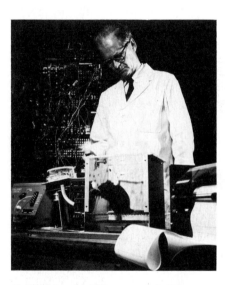

B. F. Skinner   *(Photograph by Nina Leen—Life Magazine, Time, Inc.)*

second. But this discrimination is made in an operant and not a classical conditioning context. The green light doesn't signal food the way a CS⁺ might in Pavlov's laboratory. Instead, it signals a particular relationship between the operant and the reinforcer, telling the pigeon as it were, "If you hop now, you'll get food." Conversely for the red light, the S⁻, which tells the animal that there is no point in going through the treadle-hopping business just now.

STUDYING THE OPERANT

As we've already noted, a basic assumption of all behavior theories is that the laws of learning are the same for all conditions and most species. This assumption has prompted a search for ever-simpler situations in the hope that the true laws will show up there. Skinner's way of simplifying the study of operant behavior was to create a situation in which the same instrumental response could be performed repeatedly. The most common example is the experimental chamber (popularly called the Skinner box) described before, in which a rat presses a lever or a pigeon pecks at a lighted key. In these situations, the animal remains in the presence of the lever or key for, say, an hour at a time, pressing and pecking at whatever rate it chooses. As we have noted, Skinner and his followers prefer this free-responding setup to procedures such as Thorndike's in which the animal is tested on discrete trials. They argue that the discrete-trials method is artificial and does not mirror what happens in real life. A dog sits up and begs for food and then may beg again; for him, the occasion for responding is set by himself, not by the experimenter. In Skinner's view, the essence of this situation is better captured by the free operant procedure than any other (Figure 4.19).

Considerable precautions are taken to create a controlled environment. The chamber is usually soundproofed and the experimenter never handles the animal except to place it in the chamber at the beginning of the session and to

4.19 Animals in operant chambers
(A) A rat trained to press a lever for water reinforcement. (Courtesy Pfizer, Inc.) (B) A pigeon pecking at a lighted key for food reinforcement. Reinforcement consists of a few seconds' access to a grain feeder which is located just below the key. (Photo by W. Rapport, courtesy B. F. Skinner)

A

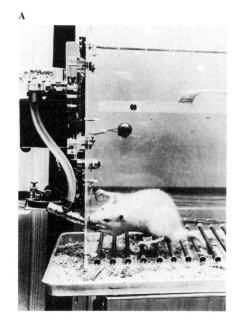

B

A

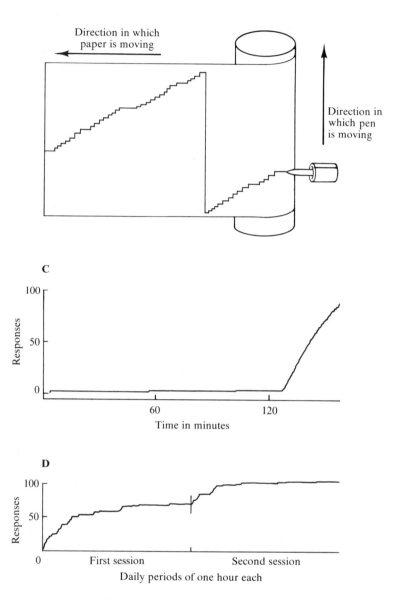

B

Direction in which paper is moving

Direction in which pen is moving

C

D

4.20   The cumulative recorder   *(A) The device. (Courtesy Ralph Gerbrands Co., Arlington, Mass.) (B) Schematic of the recorder's operation. The paper moves at a constant speed. A pen traces its record on the paper. Every time the animal makes a response, the pen moves a step upward. Its position at any time indicates all the responses the animal has made thus far—it cumulates (adds) all the responses. When the pen reaches the top of the paper, it automatically returns to the bottom so it can resume its upward movement. Since the paper moves at a constant speed, the slope of the record indicates the rate at which the animal responds: the steeper that slope, the higher the response rate. (C) A typical cumulative record of acquisiton. Initially, the animal doesn't respond, so the record is flat. It responds once or twice, and then picks up the tempo of responding until it presses at a fairly high rate. (After Skinner, 1938) (D) A typical record of extinction and spontaneous recovery, showing the performance of a previously conditioned rat on two one-hour sessions with no reinforcement. On the first extinction session, the rate of responding gradually declines until the animal virtually stops responding and the record is flat. The second session was given 47 hours later. There is a short period of spontaneous recovery followed by near-zero responding. (After Skinner, 1938)*

take it back to the home cage when the session is over. All of the animal's responses are automatically recorded; stimuli and reinforcements are presented automatically by automatic programming devices. The measure of response strength is ***response rate,*** that is, the number of responses per unit time. Response rate is often depicted graphically by a so-called ***cumulative recorder*** (Figure 4.20).

STRENGTHENING OPERANTS

Shaping behavior   How does the animal first get to make the desired response? Once the response is made, reinforcement can act to strengthen it; but suppose the animal does not perform it even once? As it happens, pecking and lever pressing are fairly easy as such responses go; many animals hit upon them on their own accord. But we can make the response much more difficult. For example, we could set the rat's lever so high on the wall that it must stretch up on its hindlegs to depress it. Now the animal may never make the response on its own. But it can learn this response and even ones more outlandish if its behavior is suitably shaped. This is accomplished by the method of *successive approximations.*

Take the problem of the elevated lever. The first step is to train the animal to approach the tray in which the food is delivered whenever the food-dispensing mechanism gives off its characteristic click. At random intervals, the click sounds and a food pellet drops into the tray; this continues until the rat shows that it is properly trained by running to pick up its pellet as soon as it hears the click. Shaping can now begin. We might first reinforce the animal for walking into the general area where the lever is located. As soon as it is there, it hears the click and devours the pellet. Very soon it will hover around the neighborhood of the lever. We next reinforce it for facing the lever, then for stretching its body upward, then for touching the lever with its paws, and so on until we finally complete its education by reinforcing it for pressing the lever down. The guiding principle throughout is immediacy of reinforcement. If we want to reinforce the rat for standing up on its hindlegs we must do it the instant after the response; even a one-second wait may be too long, for by then the rat may have fallen back on all fours and if we reinforce it then we will reinforce the wrong response.

By means of this technique, animals have been trained to perform exceedingly complex response chains. Pigeons have been trained to play Ping-Pong and dogs to plunk out four-note tunes on a toy piano. Such successes encouraged some enterprising psychologists to develop live advertising exhibits, featuring such stars as "Priscilla, the Fastidious Pig" to promote the sale of certain farm feeds (Breland and Breland, 1951). Priscilla turned on the radio, ate breakfast at a kitchen table, picked up dirty clothes and dropped them in a hamper, vacuumed the floor, and finally selected the sponsor's feed in preference to Brand X—a convincing tribute to the sponsor and to the power of reinforcement. In such sequences, one generally begins at the end and works backward toward the beginning. The response just before reinforcement (say, picking the right feed) is established first, then the one just before (moving the vacuum around) and so on back to the start (Figure 14.21).

Superstitious behavior Our discussion of reinforcement has stressed its adaptive role in shaping behavior. But this role can be otherwise. A classic demonstration was provided by Skinner. He placed pigeons in experimental chambers and gave them access to food every fifteen seconds *no matter what they did.* Since the pigeons' behavior brought no reward, one might think that no responses would be learned. But in fact, the birds gradually acquired highly distinctive behavior patterns. One pigeon executed several pirouettes between reinforcements, another swung head and body like a pendulum, still another tossed its head toward one of the corners of the box (Skinner, 1948).

Skinner argued that the peculiar reactions of his birds were produced by the joint action of reinforcement and accident. One pigeon happened to hop just before food was delivered; another happened to flap its wings. According to

4.21 The little pig that went to market *The figure shows a pig trained by means of operant techniques to push a market cart. The animal was first taught to push with its snout, a response which it is innately prepared to perform, and was then trained to use its forelegs and stand upright. Some of the implications of this mixture of instinctively given response patterns and learned modifications of such responses will be discussed in Chapter 5. (Courtesy Animal Behavior Enterprises)*

Skinner, the effect of reward was to increase the one bird's tendency to hop, the other's to wing-flap. As a result, these responses were more likely to recur when food was delivered the next time. This in turn would strengthen these responses still more, which would make it even more likely that they would be reinforced again, and so on. The end result would be the gradual emergence of a motor pattern that was peculiar to each bird, each tossing or hopping or wing-flapping depending upon what they happened to do on the first few occasions when food appeared.

Skinner called these odd motor reactions **superstitious behaviors.** He regarded them as analogous to superstitious rituals in humans. Like animals, people are sometimes reinforced by accident which will then strengthen superstitious responses. From his point of view, his pigeons' behavior wasn't too very different from that of a witch doctor dancing to bring rain. After all, it surely rains *sometimes* after a dance.*

SCHEDULES OF REINFORCEMENT

So far we have dealt only with cases in which reinforcement follows the response every time it is made. But outside of the laboratory this arrangement is surely the exception and not the rule. The fisherman does not hook a fish with every cast, and even a star tennis player occasionally loses a match to one of her less accomplished rivals. All of these are cases of **partial reinforcement,** (sometimes called **intermittent reinforcement**) in which a response is reinforced only some of the time.

One way of studying phenomena of this kind is in the free-responding situation. Here reinforcement can be easily *scheduled* in different ways—after every response, after some number of responses, after some interval, and so on. The **schedule of reinforcement** is simply the rule set up by the experimenter which determines the occasions on which a response is reinforced. We have already encountered two schedules that represent the extremes: reinforcement after every response **(continuous reinforcement)** or after none **(extinction).** Let us turn to some others.

Behavior when the schedule is in force We might decide to reinforce every second response, or every fourth or fiftieth or whatever. All of these are examples of **fixed-ratio schedules** (abbreviated FR 2, FR 4, FR 50, as the case may be) in which the subject has to produce a specified number of responses for every reward, like a factory worker on piecework. Such schedules can generate very high rates of responding but to get the organism to that level requires some finesse. The trick is to increase the ratio very gradually, beginning with continuous reinforcement and slowly stepping up the requirement. By such procedures, pigeons (and probably factory workers) have been led to perform at schedules as high as FR 500 (Figure 4.22).

When the fixed-ratio gets high enough, a new pattern develops. Following a reinforcement, the pigeon will pause for a while before it starts to peck again.

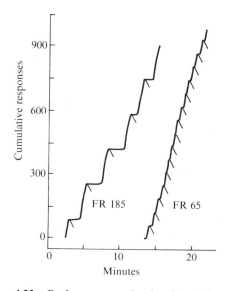

4.22 Performance on fixed-ratio schedules *Cumulative records of a piegon's performance on two fixed ratios, FR 185 and FR 65. The small diagonal slashes indicate times when the animal received reinforcement. Note the characteristic pause after the fixed ratio has been run off, a pause whose duration increases with increasing ratios. (After Ferster and Skinner, 1957)*

* Whether these results really prove Skinner's claim that reinforcement has an automatic effect is still a matter of debate. According to some critics, the pigeons' motor rituals were not operants at all. They were instead a by-product of the fact that the animals had to wait for food and therefore engaged in certain irrelevant activities characteristic of their species, much as we bite our nails or pull our hair when mildly anxious (Staddon and Simmelhag, 1971).

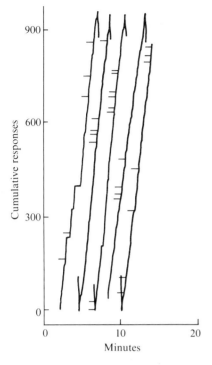

4.23 Performance on a variable-ratio schedule *The cumulative record of a pigeon's performance on a variable ratio, VR 173. Again, the small slashes indicate reinforcements. As the record shows, response rates are very high and there are no pauses after reinforcement. (After Ferster and Skinner, 1957)*

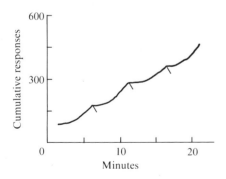

The higher the ratio, the longer the pause (see Figure 4.22). In a way, the pigeon is like a student who has just finished one term paper and has to write another. It is very hard to start again, but once the first page is written, the next ones come more readily. In part, this effect is the result of a discrimination. A peck (or a page) is only reinforced if it is preceded by other pecks (or pages). Not having pecked before is then a stimulus associated with lack of reinforcement, an S⁻ which inhibits the response. The pause following reinforcement can be eliminated by changing the schedule to a ***variable-ratio*** (VR). In VR schedules, reinforcement still comes after a certain number of responses but that number varies irregularly, averaging out to a particular ratio (for example VR 50). Now there is no way whereby the pigeon can know which of its pecks will bring reward. It might be the first, the tenth, or the hundredth peck following the last reinforcement. Since the number of prior pecks is no longer a clue, the pause disappears and behavior can be maintained at enormously high rates (Figure 4.23). A glance at a gambling casino gives proof that VR schedules affect humans much as they do pigeons. The slot machines are set to pay off occasionally, just enough to maintain the high rate of behavior that keeps the casino lucrative to its owners and not to its clients.

Ratio schedules are based on *numbers* of responses. Another set of schedules is defined by intervals of *time*. In a ***fixed-interval schedule*** (FI), the animal is reinforced for the first response performed after a certain interval has passed following the last reinforcement but not for any response before then. For example, if the interval is two minutes (FI 2) our pigeon may peck all it wants after any reinforcement, but it will be to no avail until the two minutes are up. After this, its first peck will be rewarded and the cycle begins again.

An animal that has been on an FI schedule for a while shows a typical response pattern known as the ***FI scallop.*** Immediately after reinforcement, its response rate is low but it gradually picks up and gets faster and faster as the end of the interval approaches, thus generating a scalloped curve on the cumulative record (Figure 4.24). It has acquired a temporal discrimination, having learned that immediately after reinforcement the outlook for reward is bleak.

We can readily remove the scallop by changing the schedule so that it no longer provides a basis for a temporal discrimination. This is accomplished by a ***variable-interval schedule*** (VI) which differs from the FI schedule in that the interval varies irregularly around some average period (say, VI 4 minutes). Such a schedule leads to very stable and uniform response rates. Unpleasant examples of such schedules in ordinary life involve negative reinforcers such as surprise quizzes in the classrooms and speed traps on the highway.

Partial reinforcement and extinction Some of the most dramatic effects of partial reinforcement are seen during subsequent extinction. The basic fact can be stated very simply: A response will be much harder to extinguish

4.24 Performance on a fixed-interval schedule *The cumulative record of a pigeon's performance on a fixed-interval schedule, FI 5. The small diagonal slashes are reinforcements. Note the scalloped shape which is characteristic of performance on FI after the animal has been on that schedule for a few sessions. (After Ferster and Skinner, 1957)*

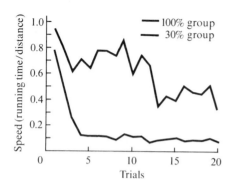

4.25   The partial-reinforcement effect
The figure shows runway speeds during extinction of two groups of rats. One had previously been reinforced on every trial; the other had only been reinforced on 30 percent of the trials. The figure shows that the group trained under full reinforcement stops running considerably before the groups that were trained under partial reinforcement. (After Weinstock, 1954)

if it was acquired during partial rather than continuous reinforcement. This phenomenon is often called the ***partial-reinforcement effect*** (Humphreys, 1939).

A good illustration is provided by an experiment in which several rats were trained on a runway for food (Weinstock, 1954). All animals received the same number of trials but not the same number of reinforcements. One group was reinforced on every trial, another only on 30 percent of the trials. Figure 4.25 shows what happened to these two groups during extinction. The rats reinforced 100 percent of the time gave up very much sooner than their partially reinforced fellows. Numerous other experiments have given substantially the same result, on all manner of subjects, including humans.

On the face of it, the partial-reinforcement effect is paradoxical. If the strength of an instrumental response increases with increasing reinforcements, we should expect that groups reinforced 100 percent of the time would continue to respond for longer than those reinforced only partially. In fact, the very opposite is true. The question is why? Speaking loosely, we might suggest that the rat has come to expect that reward may occur even after several unrewarded trials; it has learned that "if you don't succeed, try, and try again." In contrast, the rat reinforced 100 percent of the time has never encountered unreinforced trials before. If this interpretation of the partial reinforcement effect is correct, we would expect an irregular sequence of reinforcements to be harder to extinguish than a regular one, even if the proportion of reinforcements is the same in both cases. This is precisely what happens. Thus ratio schedules engender greater resistance to extinction if they are variable rather than fixed. In discrete-trial studies, a simple alternation of reinforced and unreinforced trials leads to faster extinction than a random sequence (Capaldi, 1967).

To see the partial-reinforcement effect in action, consider a simple problem in child-rearing. Many parents find that their six-month old does not want to go to sleep; put into his crib at night, he howls his vehement protests until he is lifted out again. Sooner or later his parents resolve that this has to stop. The baby is put away and the wails begin. The parents stay firm for a while but eventually they weaken (after all, the baby might be sick). Brought out of his crib, the baby gurgles happily and the process of partial reinforcement has begun. Next time, the parents will have an even harder time. According to one study (and to common sense) the answer is consistent nonreinforcement. Two determined parents plotted an extinction curve for their twenty-one-month-old child's bedtime tantrums. One day they simply decided to put their little tyrant to bed and then leave the bedroom and not go back. On the first occasion, the child howled for forty-five minutes; the next few times the cries were much diminished, until finally after ten such "trials," the child went to sleep smiling and with no complaints at all (Williams, 1959).

THE ROLE OF THE STIMULUS

Free-operant techniques have been widely used to study the role of the stimulus in affecting learned behavior. Many of the results mirror those obtained in the study of generalization and discrimination of classical conditioning. We will only give a few examples here.

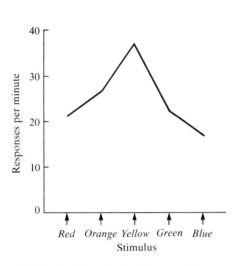

4.26 Gradient of stimulus generalization of an instrumental response *Pigeons were originally reinforced to peck at a yellow light. When later tested with lights of various colors, they showed a standard generalization gradient, pecking more vigorously at colors more similar to yellow (such as green and orange) than at colors farther removed (such as red and blue). Prior to being reinforced on the yellow key, their tendency to peck was minimal and roughly equal for all colors. (After Reynolds, 1968)*

Generalization gradients A number of investigators have investigated generalization for color in pigeons. Figure 4.26 shows a typical generalization gradient. The animals were trained to peck at a key illuminated with yellow light, after which they were tested with lights of varying wavelengths. The resulting gradient is orderly: As the test light became less similar to the original S+, the pigeons were less inclined to peck at it (Guttman and Kalish, 1956). Somewhat more involved procedures showed corresponding inhibitory gradients for stimuli associated with nonreinforcement. The tendency not to respond to S− generalized to stimuli that were similar to it (Honig et al., 1963).

SKINNER AND EARLIER BEHAVIOR THEORIES

Where do we stand after Skinner's reformulation of behavior theory? Skinner had abandoned the insistence of the older S-R theories that all behavior must be understood in molecular, muscle-oriented terms. His own approach requires a more molar conception in which the instrumental response is defined by its consequences. Skinner had also abandoned the S-R credo that all behavior is elicited by stimuli in the present. In his view, this is true enough for classical conditioning but is not for instrumental behavior, which he regards as *emitted* rather than *elicited*.

In these regards, Skinner obviously departs from the S-R model set up by such predecessors as Thorndike. But in many other respects, he accepts much of the spirit of the Thorndikian enterprise. Like Thorndike, he insists that instrumental learning is a process in which responses are mechanically stamped in by subsequent reinforcement; that this is the way in which instrumental learning occurs, no matter how simple or how complex the task; and that this learning process is the same in such diverse species as pigeons, rats, and humans. For him, the necessary and sufficient conditions for instrumental learning are those specified by the law of effect—contiguity of response and reinforcer. If an instrumental response is immediately followed by a reinforcer, that response will be strengthened.

In the following chapter, we will consider various criticisms of this general approach to instrumental learning. Many of these raise the possibility that animals and humans don't learn as blindly and automatically as Pavlov, Thorndike, and Skinner say they do—at least not always. But for now, we will consider some phenomena that suggest that such blind and automatic learning does occur—sometimes. The areas to which we will turn are the instrumental conditioning of involuntary responses and some applications of classical and instrumental conditioning in behavior therapy.

Instrumental Conditioning of Involuntary Responses

So far in our discussion, we have only considered examples of instrumental conditioning in which the response is of the kind that is loosely called voluntary rather than involuntary. There is obviously a world of difference between an apologetic gesture and a blush. The first act could surely be instrumentally trained; it seems to come from inside and is something the person wants to do. The second seems to stem from some internal reaction system outside of the person's own control (specifically, vasodilatation of the facial blood vessels); the blush occurs regardless of the blusher's wishes. Can involuntary reactions like a blush be brought under instrumental control?

The experimental investigation of this question has typically dealt with the conditionability of autonomic or glandular responses. Blushing is one of these; changes in the heart rate, contractions of the stomach walls, alterations of the concentration of the urine would be some others. Responses such as these had been the traditional CRs in classical conditioning studies. The question is whether such responses can also be conditioned instrumentally and strengthened by reward. The general belief originally was that they could not, but subsequent developments led to a reconsideration of this view (Rescorla and Solomon, 1967).

There is little doubt that some humans—such as Yogis—manage to control such apparently involuntary reactions as heart rate. But that is not the issue. The real question concerns the mechanism whereby such feats are achieved. Studies of several Yogis have shown that their control over autonomic reactions is indirect, exerted through responses that involve the skeletal musculature. For example, they slow down their heartbeats by retaining their breath and exercising considerable muscular tension in the chest and abdomen (Kimble and Perlmuter, 1970). This is certainly no mean trick, but it is not the trick we are interested in now. Our present question is whether autonomic responses can be instrumentally conditioned directly, when all skeletal intermediaries have been ruled out.

This problem has been experimentally attacked by Neal E. Miller and his associates at Rockefeller University (Miller, 1969). These investigators performed a truly heroic series of studies on rats injected with *curare,* a drug which completely paralyzes the entire skeletal musculature but which does not affect the visceral reactions such as the heartbeat and intestinal peristalsis. (Since the skeletal muscles used in breathing are paralyzed as well, such an experiment requires artificial respiration.) In one such study, the response was a change in heart rate. For some animals the correct response was an increase in heart rate; for others, it was a decrease. The animals learned just what the experimenters asked them to. As Figure 4.27 shows, their heart rates changed in the desired direction. Similar results were obtained for other autonomic or glandular reactions. Thus some curarized rats learned to relax or contract their lower intestines when the reward was direct electrical stimulation of a

4.27 Instrumental conditioning of autonomic responses (A) An experimental apparatus used to study instrumental conditioning of autonomic responses in a rat. The animal is injected with curare to paralyze the skeletal muscles. This control rules out various skeletal intermediaries but necessitates some further elaborations. One is artificial respiration; since the rat cannot breathe on its own, a respirator provides air through a face mask fitted to the rat's snout. Other elaborations concern the reinforcer. Since ordinary reinforcers such as food and water cannot be used, given the rat's paralyzed state, reinforcement consists of a brief stimulation of a "rewarding center" in the hypothalamus. (B) The curves illustrate heart rate changes in rats rewarded for increasing the heart rate (black) or decreasing it (color). (After DiCara, 1970)

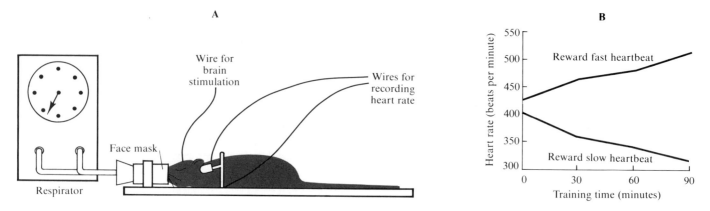

rewarding area in the brain (see Chapter 3). Other rats increased or decreased the rate at which their stomach contracted, altered various aspects of their kidney functions, raised or lowered their blood pressure (independent of their heart rate), and dilated or constricted the capillaries in their tails (DiCara, 1970). The experimenters had evidently succeeded in bringing autonomic reactions under instrumental control.*

Miller's findings may have considerable practical implications. To begin with, they suggest that some physiological reactions to stress often found in humans may be learned instrumentally. Miller gives the example of a child who has a queasy stomach on the day of an examination and is told to stay home by her solicitous parents; after many such experiences, she may well acquire a gastrointestinal escape response to similar situations. Even more interesting are the possibilities for effecting therapeutic change. Perhaps some cases of hypertension or asthma can be alleviated by training the patients to change their autonomic reactions, say, by reducing their heart rates. Such procedures are still in their infancy, but they indicate the exciting possibilities of this line of research.

Behavior Therapy

We have previously seen that there are good reasons to suppose that various human emotions, especially fears, are acquired through classical conditioning. Of particular importance are the intense, irrational fears known as phobias. A number of clinical psychologists, called **behavior therapists,** believe that the principles of classical conditioning help us understand how such phobias arise and also provide the tools by which they can be eliminated (Wolpe and Lazarus, 1969).

CLASSICAL CONDITIONING TECHNIQUES

As an example, take an irrational fear of snakes. Behavior therapists believe that this phobia is a classically conditioned response which they try to remove by **counterconditioning.** The idea is to combat the original CR, fear, by connecting the stimuli that presently evoke it to a new response that is incompatible with fear and will displace it. The response that is usually picked to serve this competing role is **muscular relaxation.** This is a pervasive untensing of the entire musculature which is presumably incompatible with the autonomic and muscular reactions that underlie fear. The patients are first trained to achieve this deep relaxation on command. Once they can do this, they are repeatedly exposed to various stimuli that evoke the phobia. Concurrently, they are asked to relax. According to behavior therapists, the same stimuli that serve as CS for fear will now become CS for relaxation:

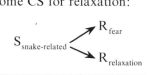

$$S_{snake\text{-}related} \begin{cases} \nearrow R_{fear} \\ \searrow R_{relaxation} \end{cases}$$

---

* Unfortunately these effects are not always as robust as one might wish. Some more recent studies have verified the fact that autonomic reactions can be instrumentally controlled, but the degree of control was disappointingly weak (Miller and Dworkin, 1973).

As the link to relaxation becomes stronger and stronger, the fear response will presumably become gradually displaced.

There is one important qualification: The desensitization process has to be gradual. The behavior therapist sneaks up on the phobia rather than confronting it directly in its full-blown state. The therapist doesn't start out by asking the patient to fondle a rattlesnake. On the contrary. She first has the patient construct an **anxiety hierarchy,** in which fear-provoking situations are arranged in order, from most frightening to least. She then asks the patient to expose himself to these stimuli, starting with the least frightening (say, the sight of an earthworm) and gradually working up to more and more anxiety-provoking stimuli. Moreover, all of this occurs only in the patient's mind. He is asked to *imagine* the fear-arousing scene as vividly as possible while in a state of deep relaxation.

These and related techniques drawn from the conditioning laboratory are by now the preferred methods for dealing with certain irrational fears. Their main area of application is in phobias, but they are also used to treat certain sexual disturbances such as impotence and frigidity (see Chapter 18).

OPERANT TECHNIQUES

Desensitization and other behavior therapies based on classical conditioning try to alter the significance of various stimulus events, as in making a patient recognize that snakes are not really threatening. Another set of behavior-modification techniques comes from the operant laboratory and emphasizes the relation between acts and consequences. Its theme is the same as that which underlies the entire operant approach—the control of behavior through reinforcement.   •

ELIMINATING RESPONSES

Suppose a person does something that is regarded as maladaptive. A behavior therapist will tend to assume that this undesirable behavior is somehow getting reinforced. He will try to find the reinforcement and remove it, sure that once this is done extinction will necessarily follow. One method is to give so much of a reinforcer that the recipient gets sick of it; after all, a food pellet won't serve as a reinforcer for a rat which has just gorged itself.

An example of this **satiation principle** is the case of a severely disturbed patient in a mental hospital who hoarded towels. On the average, she collected about twenty-five towels in her room, frustrating all attempts of the nurses to get them back. This hoarding pattern had gone on for nine years. The treatment was a surfeit of towels. The nurses stopped taking her towels away. On the contrary, they gave her seven towels a day, without comment, and gradually increased this number to thirty. Initially, the patient was grateful; she folded the towels and stacked them neatly away. But upon accumulating over six hundred towels that spilled all over her room, she complained ever more bitterly, telling the nurses that the incessant work of folding and stacking towels was getting completely out of hand. At this point, no more towels were given, and the patient gradually divested herself of her now unwanted riches until she was finally down to a normal one or two towels a day. The towel hoarding stopped and never returned (Figure 4.28).

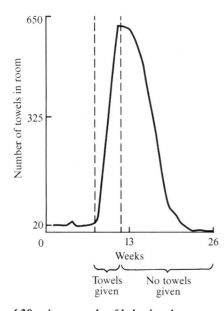

4.28 An example of behavior therapy based on operant techniques *A response, towel hoarding, was eliminated by providing the patient with an overabundance of towels. When the number of towels got up to 625, the patient started to discard them until the average number of towels in her room reached 1.5 compared to the previous average of 20. (After Ayllon, 1963)*

STRENGTHENING DESIRED BEHAVIORS

Elimination of undesirable behaviors is one objective of behavior modification. Another is to get patients to perform certain desirable acts. To accomplish this end, the operant behavior therapist tries to provide an appropriate reinforcer. An example is provided by *token economies* which have been set up in hospital wards, some of which house chronic patients given up as hopeless. These tokens function much as money does in our economy; they can be exchanged for desirable items within the hospital situation such as snacks, cigarettes, or watching TV. But again, like money, they must be earned by the patients, perhaps by being neatly dressed or talking to others or performing various ward chores. The overall effect seems to be salutary. While the patients are not cured, they become less apathetic and the general ward atmosphere is much improved (Ayllon and Azrin, 1968).

EVALUATING OPERANT BEHAVIOR MODIFICATION

It's hard to evaluate these applications of the operant approach. There is little doubt that the various reinforcement regimens we have described affected the patients: One stopped hoarding towels, others performed ward chores, and so on. While these effects fell far short of a cure, they were surely changes for the better. But even so, some worries remain.

One question concerns the relation between application and theory. Is the one really derived from the other? Are the various behavior-modification systems really based on principles discovered in the animal laboratory? Consider the civil engineers who build a bridge. They certainly need an intimate knowledge of the laws of mechanics developed by physicists. But do the behavioral engineers who set up a token economy require an equivalent knowledge of the principles of classical and instrumental conditioning? Do they really have to know all the ins and outs of, say, interval and ratio schedules? Or is what they do simply an elaboration of common sense, dressed up in the fancy language of behavior theory? After all, many parents have long known that certain childish outbursts are best handled by being ignored. In effect they advocated the extinction procedure developed by behavior modifiers, but without calling it extinction.

A very different question concerns the nature of the changes that behavior modification produces. In the case of severely disturbed mental patients, these changes were on the whole beneficial. But with other groups, these gains are accompanied by certain drawbacks. An example is the use of token reinforcement in young elementary school or preschool children. These tokens—which can be exchanged for trinkets or candy—are very effective in keeping children working at such school tasks as reading or counting. But unfortunately, there is a side-effect. To be sure, the children work considerably harder than they would have otherwise, but they now do so merely to earn tokens—they have lost their interest in reading or counting for their own sakes. Nursery school children who received gold stars for drawing stopped drawing when gold stars were no longer given. Drawing was no longer fun; it was work. And, at least within an operant framework, work is not its own reward (Lepper, Greene, and Nisbett, 1973). As one team of critics put it, "Token rewards may lead to token learning" (Levine and Fasnacht, 1974).

It is probably too early to evaluate behavior-modification techniques. Some may prove to be ineffective. Some may prove to have undesirable consequences. Some may prove not to be derived from the theories from which they claim descent. But the data so far suggest that some of the techniques behavior modifiers use do work and that some of these techniques are related—however vaguely—to the general operant approach.

To the extent that all of this is true, the conditioning approach does describe some genuine facets of human and animal behavior. To some extent we are creatures of habit. And we often enough do work for gain.

Summary

1. One of the simplest forms of learning is *classical conditioning,* first studied by I. P. Pavlov. Prior to conditioning, an *unconditioned stimulus* or UCS (such as food) elicits an *unconditioned response* or UCR (such as salivation). After repeated pairings of the UCS with a *conditioned stimulus* or CS (such as a buzzer), this CS alone will evoke a *conditioned response* or CR (here again, salivation) that is normally similar to the UCR. Classical conditioning has been found for responses as varied as salivation, fear, and sexual excitement and in species as diverse as humans and flatworms.

2. The strength of conditioning is measured by the readiness with which CS elicits CR. This strength increases with the number of *reinforced trials,* that is, pairings of CS and UCS. Such pairings are most effective when CS precedes UCS by about half a second. If original conditioning is strong enough, a new stimulus can be paired with CS to produce *higher-order conditioning* to this new stimulus.

3. Nonreinforced trials, during which CS is presented without the UCS, lead to *extinction,* as manifested by a decreased tendency of CS to evoke CR. An extinguished CR can be resurrected by *reconditioning* during which CS is again paired with UCS, or by *spontaneous recovery* after a rest period.

4. The CR will be elicited not only by CS but also by stimuli that are similar to it. This effect, *stimulus generalization,* increases the greater the similarity between CS and the new stimulus. To train the animal to respond to CS and not to other stimuli, one stimulus (CS+) is presented with the UCS, another (CS−) is presented without UCS. The greater the similarity between CS+ and CS−, the greater the difficulty of this *discrimination training* will be.

5. According to Pavlov, classical conditioning is based on a learned link between CS and UCS, which eventually allows CS to serve as a *substitute* for UCS. This position is challenged by the fact that CR and UCR are often not identical. An alternative view is that classical conditioning is a primitive form of an *expectation.*

6. In classical conditioning, the UCS is presented regardless of whether the animal makes the CR or not. In another form of simple learning, *instrumental conditioning* (or *operant conditioning*), something analogous to UCS, the *reward,* is only delivered upon performance of the appropriate instrumental response.

7. An early study of instrumental conditioning was performed by E. L. Thorndike, using cats who learned an arbitrary response to escape from a *puzzle box.* According to Thorndike, what the animals learned involved no understanding but was rather based on the gradual strengthening of an *S-R bond.* To explain this bond, Thorndike proposed his *law of effect.* This law states that the connection between a stimulus and a response made in its presence is strengthened if that response is followed by reward (or *reinforcement*) and weakened if it is not.

8. Thorndike's successors pointed out that S-R bonds can be strengthened by both *primary reinforcers,* whose reinforcing power is unlearned and *secondary* (or *conditioned*) *reinforcers,* whose abilities to reinforce a response comes from prior pairings with primary reinforcers.

9. A further supplement to the law of effect concerns the *delay of reinforcement gradient:* the shorter the interval between the response and reinforcement, the stronger the S-R bond. An extension of this principle may explain *approach-avoidance conflicts* on the assumption that gradients for avoidance are steeper than gradients for approach.

10. B. F. Skinner's *operant approach* is similar to Thorndike's S-R theory of instrumental learning but differs from it in several ways. Skinner's definition of the response, which he calls the *operant,* is explicitly *molar* rather than *molecular.* In his view, reinforcement strengthens this operant itself, rather than strengthening an S-R bond. Thus the operant is seen as *emitted* rather than *elicited.*

11. Skinner developed various procedures for studying the operant by a *free-responding method,* using special operant chambers in which *response rate* is recorded as a critical measure. Initial acquisition of the operant sometimes requires *shaping* by the *method of successive approximation.* Under some conditions, reinforcement may be delivered by accident which may lead to *superstitious behavior.*

12. Reinforcement may be *continuous* or *partial.* Different *schedules of reinforcement*—such as *fixed* and *variable ratio, fixed* and *variable interval*—lead to characteristic response patterns while the schedule is in force. Responses that were originally acquired during partial reinforcement are harder to extinguish than those learned when reinforcement is continuous.

13. There is some evidence that involuntary responses which depend on the action of the autonomic nervous system, such as changes in heart rate, can be conditioned instrumentally. This finding may have implications for the understanding and therapy of psychosomatic ailments.

14. A group of clinical practitioners, the *behavior therapists,* try to apply the principles of conditioning to the cure or alleviation of various psychological disorders. Some stress classical conditioning and try to cure *phobias* and related conditioning by gradual *counterconditioning* of fear. Others use operant techniques to eliminate unwanted behaviors and strengthen desirable ones, often by the use of *token economies.*

CHAPTER 5

Learning II: Behavior Theory Reconsidered

The ultimate purpose of behavior theory was very ambitious. Eventually, all of animal and human behavior was to be reduced to one or another variant of the behavior theory model. In the last chapter, we have considered some phenomena that fit this conception rather well, at least at first glance. The effects of various behavior therapies are a case in point. Here learning seems to be just as blind and mechanical as behavior theorists hold it to be. But there are other instances of learning whose essence seems very different, as in the cases of a student who "gets the point" of a mathematical demonstration or of a garage mechanic who figures out why an engine stalls. These examples represent manifestations of reason or intelligence of a kind that Pavlov, Thorndike, and Skinner largely ignored. The issue is whether such phenomena can be explained by the principles of behavior theory.

This question has occupied critics of behavior theory since its inception. The starting point for their investigations was the study of animal learning. If they could show that behavior theory faced major difficulties even there, then it was surely plausible to assume that it would encounter yet more serious problems when extended to the human realm.

Insightful Behavior

We will start by considering another investigation of animal intelligence, undertaken only a decade or so after Thorndike's. Its author was a young

Wolfgang Köhler (*Courtesy The Warder Collection*)

German psychologist, Wolfgang Köhler (1887–1968), who in 1913 arrived at Tenerife, a small island off the west coast of Africa, in order to take charge of an institute for the study of anthropoid apes. When World War I broke out, Köhler was forced to remain on the island and he spent the war years in an intensive study of the chimpanzee's intellectual gifts.*

CHIMPANZEES WITH STICKS AND BOXES

Köhler believed that animals can behave intelligently. To be sure, Thorndike's cats had shown little signs of understanding, but perhaps cats are not the best subjects if one wants to determine the upper reaches of animal intellect. A closer relative of man, such as a chimpanzee, might prove a better choice. Even more important, Köhler believed that Thorndike had loaded the dice in favor of blind trial and error, for the problems he had posed his cats were often impossible to solve in any other way. Thus, even an intellectual supercat could never hit on the idea of yanking the wire that pulled the door latch except by pure chance; there was no other way, for all the strings and pulleys were hidden from the animal's view. To Köhler the real question was whether animals would behave intelligently if the conditions were optimum—when all of the ingredients of the solution were visibly present.

Köhler's procedure was simple. The chimpanzee was placed in an enclosed play area. Somewhere out of its reach was a desirable lure (usually some fruit, such as a banana). To obtain it, the ape had to employ some nearby object as a tool. In this the animals were remarkably successful. They learned to use sticks as rakes to haul in bananas placed on the ground just outside the cage, but beyond the reach of their arms. Sticks were equally useful to club down fruit which was hung too high overhead. Some chimpanzees used the sticks as a pole; they stood it upright under the banana, frantically climbed up its fifteen-foot length, and grasped their reward just as the stick toppled over (a considerable intellectual as well as gymnastic feat, demonstrating the virtues of a healthy mind in a healthy body). The chimpanzees also learned to use boxes as footstools and makeshift ladders, dragging them under the banana and then stepping on top to claim their prizes. Eventually they even became builders, piling boxes on top of boxes and finally erecting structures that went up to four (rather shaky) stories, as Köhler spurred them on to ever-greater architectural accomplishments by progressively raising the height of the lure (Figure 5.1).

Occasionally the apes became toolmakers as well as tool-users. For example, when in need of a stick, they might break off a branch of a nearby tree. Even more impressive was the manufacture of a double stick. A particularly gifted chimpanzee called Sultan was faced with a banana far out of his reach. There were two bamboo sticks in his cage, but neither of them was long enough to rake in the lure. After many attempts to reach the banana with one

---

* The short-run effect of this work was to contribute to the harassment of several British intelligence agents who were certain that the professor's experiments were part of some devious scheme of German espionage and who carefully examined each shipment of freshly caught animals, convinced that whatever the purpose of Köhler's work, it was not just to find out how a chimpanzee learns to get a banana.

A   B   C   D

5.1 Tool using in chimpanzees
(A) Using a stick as a pole to jump up to a banana. (B) Using a stick as a club to beat down a banana. (C and D) Erecting three- and four-story structures to reach a banana. (From Köhler, 1925)

stick or another, Sultan finally hit upon the solution. He pushed the thinner of the two sticks into the hollow inside of the thicker one and then drew the banana toward himself, his reach now enlarged by the length of two sticks (Figure 5.2).

THE EVIDENCE FOR INSIGHT

Köhler denied that such achievements could be understood in S-R terms. On the contrary, the animals behaved as if they had attained some ***insight*** into the relevant relationships, as if they comprehended the organizing principles that underlie the solution of the problem: It is as if they *saw* what led to what.*

Köhler offered several lines of evidence. To begin with, when the problem was once solved, the animals usually performed smoothly and continuously thereafter as if they "knew what they were doing," in marked contrast to Thorndike's cats who went on fumbling for many trials. In further opposition to Thorndike's findings was the fact that often the insightful solution came quite suddenly, sometimes after a pause during which the chimpanzee only moved its head and eyes as if to study the situation. Thus Sultan, when first faced with the box as a potential stepping-stone to the banana, soon gave up the attempt to reach the fruit by leaping up from the ground and then "paced restlessly up and down, suddenly stood still in front of the box, seized it, tipped it hastily straight towards the object . . . began to climb upon it . . . and springing upwards with all his force, tore down the banana" (Köhler, 1925, p. 40). Once the correct response was made, further errors were rare. On the very next day, Sultan dragged the box directly under the banana; the box had

5.2 Tool making in chimpanzees
Sultan making a double stick. (From Köhler, 1925)

* The fact that intellectual understanding is often expressed by a visual metaphor is perhaps no accident: Smart people are "bright," ignorant ones "stumble in the dark" until "their eyes are opened" and they "see daylight," and cartoonists invariably indicate a sudden solution by a flashing lightbulb.

become a "climb-upon-able" which would bring him physically closer to the desired goal.

The most convincing evidence for the view that the chimpanzees had learned by insight rather than by blind trial and error came from tests in which the situation was changed to determine what the animals could *transfer* from the original task. This is a method that serves to define what has been learned in any given situation. Teachers use just this approach to find out what their students have understood. Consider a young child who quickly answers "7" when confronted by the symbols "3 + 4 = ?" Has he really grasped the notion of addition? A simple test might be to present him with another problem, "4 + 3 = ?" If he is now bewildered, he presumably has learned merely to give a specific answer to a specific question, but if his reply again is "7," he may be on the way to genuine arithmetic insight. Köhler used similar tests on his chimpanzees. For example, he took animals who had previously learned to use a box as a platform and presented the high lure again, but now with all boxes removed. The animals were quick to find other objects, such as a table or a small ladder, which they promptly dragged to the proper place. These were not the only substitutes. On one occasion, Sultan came over to Köhler, pulled him by the arm until he was under the banana, and then showed that in a pinch even the director of the Prussian anthropoid station would do as a climb-upon-able.

KÖHLER AND BEHAVIOR THEORY

The differences that Köhler saw between the insightful behavior of his chimpanzees and the blind trial and error of Thorndike's cats are still of interest, for they foreshadow the major points of controversy between contemporary behavior theorists and their opponents: What is learned, how it is learned, and who does the learning.

A behavior theorist might argue that Köhler's chimpanzees simply learned to perform certain responses, such as shoving boxes underneath bananas. But Köhler felt that this description does not do justice to what really happened. As he saw it, the new responses were a side-effect of what the animals learned. What was really acquired seemed to be a new set of internal "representations" of the situation, a knowledge of what led to what, and some expectations of which actions would yield which consequences. Put in other words, what was learned was a change in what the animals *knew* rather than in what they *did*.

Another difference concerns Köhler's view of how his animals learned. Köhler rejected the notion that they learned by a blind, mechanical process in which various elements—stimuli, responses, rewards—are connected with each other merely by virtue of having occurred together. He believed that the animals learned more intelligently than that. In his view, they actively reorganized the way in which they perceived the situation and thus acquired certain general insights that could then be applied more widely.

A final difference concerns the species that Köhler studied. Köhler's animal subjects, chimpanzees, are presumably higher on the evolutionary ladder than Thorndike's cats and Pavlov's dogs. Perhaps some of the difference in the results pertained to who the learners were. This flies in the face of the behavior theorists' claim that the laws of learning are identical for all animal species, or at least for all mammals and birds.

We now turn to a discussion of these issues as they have occupied investigators in this field since Köhler's time

What Is Learned?

Early behavior theorists, including Pavlov and most of Thorndike's followers, understood such central terms as *stimulus, response,* and *reinforcement* within a biological framework. They regarded a response as a particular motor or glandular reaction, a stimulus as a certain physical energy impinging on a sense organ, and reinforcement as an event that restores a disturbed biological equilibrium, such as the ingestion of food after a period of starvation. But as we have seen, molecular descriptions of this sort are much too narrow to capture what animals are really learning and doing.

THE RESPONSE

That a molecular conception is an inadequate description of what goes on in instrumental learning was already apparent in Tenerife. Köhler's pole-vaulting, box-stacking, and stick-doubling chimpanzees had surely learned more than the particular set of muscle movements required in any one situation. These and other findings represented a serious attack on early S-R theory, though not on Skinner's operant approach which incorporated a molar response definition from the very outset.

THE STIMULUS

Somewhat similar questions can be raised about the stimulus to which the organism responds. One may argue that this is not simply the physical stimulus that is presented by the experimenter. For we surely don't react to everything we see (or hear or touch). On the contrary, we focus on some features of the world while ignoring others. According to Köhler, a chimpanzee who looks for something to climb on is less likely to notice a box if another ape is already sitting on it; it is now a sit-upon-able rather than climb-upon-able, even though its physical appearance is exactly the same. The same holds for humans. We select some aspects of the stimulus and disregard others. Thus, when introduced to people, we try to connect their names with their faces, rather than associating their faces with the color of their neckties. There is evidently some internal process that helps to preselect the stimulus features to which we give special weight and that filters out other features we want to ignore. In ordinary language, this selective process is called ***attention.***

ATTENTION AND DISCRIMINATION

Relevant and irrelevant stimulus dimensions Attentional selection plays an important role in discriminative learning. The reason is that discrimination does not only concern stimuli that are always associated with reward (S+) and nonreward (S−). It also involves stimuli that are irrelevant. Consider a rat who learns to jump to a circle (S+) and not to a triangle (S−). A heartless experimenter has arranged to make the discrimination more difficult. On half the

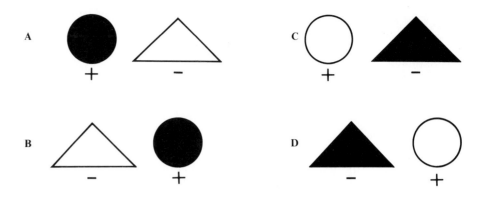

5.3 The effect of irrelevant dimensions on learning a discrimination *The figure illustrates the problem posed by irrelevant dimensions in learning a discrimination. A rat has to learn to discriminate between a circle and a triangle with the circle serving as S⁺ and the triangle as S⁻. Two other dimensions are irrelevant: relative position (that is, right versus left) and black versus white. On half of the trials (trials B and D), the circle appears on the right side; thus the right side is rewarded 50 percent of the time. On half of the trials, (trials A and B), the circle is black; thus black is rewarded 50 percent of the time. Part of the difficulty that animals (and humans, for that matter) have in solving discriminations of this sort is caused by these irrelevant dimensions. To solve the task, the animals must first learn that these dimensions* are irrelevant.

trials, the circle will be black while on the other half it will be white. Similarly for the triangle. But the black-white difference is irrelevant. Black is rewarded half of the times (when the circle is black) and not the other half (when the triangle is black). The trouble is that the rat doesn't yet know that the color difference has nothing to do with the discrimination. Until it learns that this

rat's problem is much like that facing a child who is learning when it is safe to cross at an intersection. She must first learn that the relevant dimension is the color of the traffic lights. Once this is learned, it is easy enough to learn which particular value of the dimension—that is, red or green—is associated with stop and which with go.

Teaching which dimension is relevant Learning which dimension is relevant, and which is not, is especially important for difficult discriminations. This point was already known to Pavlov (Pavlov, 1927). Suppose a dog has to learn a discrimination between two quite similar stimuli, such as two gray pieces of cardboard of only slightly different shades. The animal may fail to discriminate between them, even after hundreds of trials. But there is a way to make the dog's task easier: First teach it to discriminate between black and white. Once this easier discrimination is mastered, the dog has much less trouble with the more difficult one. Similar results have been found for rats in an instrumental discrimination task (Lawrence, 1952). These findings are yet another demonstration that discrimination depends on knowing what stimulus differences are relevant. What we do for the dog by first training it on the easy discrimination is analogous to what good teachers do for their classes with a well-chosen example—they highlight the point that is crucial. The dog's problem was not to see the difference between the two shades of gray; it was to *attend* to brightness differences rather than other stimulus features.* The easier black-white discrimination tells the animal that the brightness dimension is the one that counts. The rest is easy.

COGNITIVE THEORY OF ANIMAL LEARNING

The preceding discussion dealt with the molar-molecular issue as it applies to the characterization of both stimulus and response. But there was also another

* Needless to say, the difference cannot be so small that this is physically impossible.

Edward C. Tolman *(Courtesy Psychology Department, University of California, Berkeley)*

5.4 Learning without doing (I) Rats were ferried from place A to place B in a transparent trolley car, all the while suffering electric shock. The two places were highly differentiated. At A, there was a large screen with vertical stripes; at B, the screen had horizontal stripes. (II) After a number of trips from A to B, the rats were made hungry and tested in the same spatial situation but an elevated T-maze was substituted for the trolley, with its choice point midway between A and B. About three-quarters of the animals chose B, where shock had ended previously. This suggests that the animals had formed a cognitive map of the room layout without motor performance. (After Gleitman, 1963)

point at issue. According to behavior theory, instrumental learning consisted of the strengthening of responses. A number of critics disagreed.

Both Köhler and later writers such as Edward C. Tolman (1886–1959) argued that in instrumental learning an animal acquires various items of knowledge or *cognitions* (Tolman, 1932). These bits of knowledge are organized so that they can be utilized when needed. This is very different from asserting that the animal acquires a tendency to perform a particular response. To the *cognitive theorist,* the response an animal acquires in the course of a learning experiment is only an index that a given cognition has been gained. It is an indispensable measuring stick, but it is not the thing that is being measured. The essence of what is learned is something within the animal, a private event which will only become public when the animal acts upon its newly acquired knowledge.

COGNITIVE MAPS

Evidence that animals acquire cognitions comes from a number of experiments designed to determine whether instrumental learning can occur without performance of the relevant response. Many behavior theorists claim that performance is an indispensable ingredient for instrumental learning. They assert that the animal "learns by doing" and in no other way. However, several studies suggest that this is not the case. Rats have been ferried from one end of a large room to another in transparent trolley cars. Later tests showed that they had learned something about the general features of the room even though they had not performed any relevant instrumental responses during their trolley-car ride (Figure 5.4). They had acquired what Tolman called a "cognitive map" that indicates what is where and what leads to what (Tolman, 1948).

In another study, rats were run in an enclosed *T*-maze that had a black end box on one side and a white one on the other (Figure 5.5). Both ends contained food and the animals chose indifferently between them on several trials. Subsequently, the animals were placed into each box by hand without actually running the maze. In one end box they now found food as before; in the

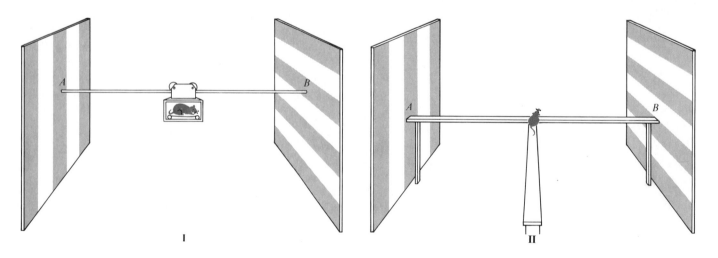

I

II

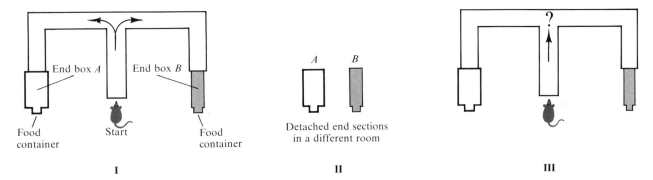

I   **II**   **III**

5.5   Proving that rats learn what leads to where   *(I) Floor plan of a maze in the first phase of an experiment during which rats could learn that a left turn leads to end box* A, *a right turn to end box* B. *(II) The second phase of the experiment in which the two end boxes were detached from the rest of the maze and the animals were shocked in one of them, say,* A. *(III) In the third phase of the experiment, the animals were returned to the original situation. If they could put the two experiences together, then, having learned that a left turn led to* A *and that* A *led to shock, they should turn right—that is, away from shock. The results showed that they did. (After Tolman and Gleitman, 1949)*

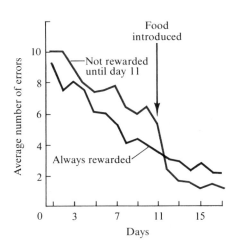

other they were shocked. After all this, the animals were again allowed to run down the original *T*-maze. Now virtually all of them chose the side away from the end box in which they had been shocked. Clearly, the rats had learned which turn led to which box, but this cognition led to selective action only after the two boxes had acquired their new significance. In effect, the animals had to combine two experiences. During the first phase of the experiment, they presumably learned to associate a particular turn with a particular end box. During the second phase, they further learned that a particular end box brought shock. The results of the final test indicate that they were able to put these two experiences together—an argument against the view that all instrumental learning depends on the strengthening or weakening of particular response tendencies (Tolman and Gleitman, 1949).

Similar **latent learning effects** have been obtained in a number of other studies. A classic example is an experiment in which rats were run through a maze without a reward for ten days. When food was finally placed in the goal box, there was an abrupt decline in errors. Presumably the rats had learned something about the maze during the preceding days. But they did not show that they had learned until the reward was introduced. Before then, what they had learned was only latent but not yet manifest (Tolman and Honzik, 1930; Figure 5.6).

5.6   Latent learning   *The figure shows the results of an experiment in which two groups of rats were run in a multiple-unit maze. One group found food in the end box on every daily trial. The other found an empty end box for the first ten days. As one would expect, the results for the first ten days showed that the rewarded groups made fewer errors than the nonrewarded group. On the eleventh day the previously nonrewarded group found food in the end box. The results showed that on the subsequent day this group performed as well (in fact, somewhat better) than the group that had always been rewarded. This finding suggests that the rats had learned something about the maze during the ten days in which they had run through it without reward. To be sure, they had entered many blind alleys, but this makes good sense since they had no particular reason to get to the end box in which there was no reward. Once they found reward in the end box, they had a motive to get there quickly. (After Tolman and Honzik, 1930)*

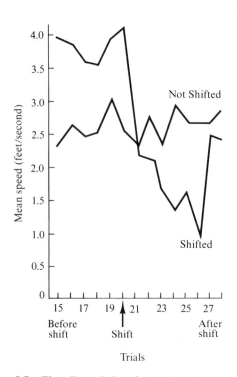

5.7 The effect of changing the level of reward *The figure shows the runway performance of two groups of rats. For the first nineteen trials, one group received a large reward, the other a small reward. From the twentieth trial on, both groups received the small reward. The initially well-rewarded group ran much more quickly during the first nineteen trials. But from the twenty-first trial on, its performance declined below that of the group that had received the smaller reward all along. This shows that the effective value of a present reward depends upon the prior level the animal had become "accustomed to," which implies that animals had developed an expectation of the level of reward. (After Crespi, 1942)*

EXPECTANCIES

According to Thorndike and Skinner, instrumental learning occurs because reward strengthens an immediately preceding response. But cognitive theorists have a different conception of the role of reward. They don't regard reward as an automatic strengthener, but rather as something the animal learns *about.* * It learns that there are dog biscuits or bananas and comes to expect that such and such an act will produce them.

How can one show that animals have expectations? One line of attack is to observe what happens when a normal—and thus presumably expected—sequence of events is violated. An illustrative study compared different groups of rats which were run on an alley to different amounts of food reward. Not too surprisingly, the well-rewarded rats ran more quickly than their less fortunate fellows. The question was what would happen when rats who were first trained with the large reward were switched to a smaller one. The results showed that they will perform more poorly than those who had been run to the smaller reward all along (Figure 5.7).

This result demonstrates a **contrast effect.** Relative to the riches they were used to, the rats that were switched downward suffered a loss. This shows that the psychological value of a reward does not merely depend upon its absolute magnitude; it is also relative. But relative to what? Presumably, to what the animal expected. There is no way in which a downward shift can lead to a contrast effect unless there is some knowledge—cognition, expectation—of the original value from which the shift was made.

Another illustration is provided by an experiment on rhesus monkeys (Tinklepaugh, 1928). The experimenter placed a lure under one of two containers while the animal was watching. A moment later, the animal was permitted to choose one or the other of the two containers. Sometimes the reward was a lettuce leaf, a reward that was only moderately desirable; sometimes it was a piece of banana, which was immensely prized. The animals worked for both rewards, though with much greater enthusiasm if bananas were used instead of lettuce leaves. All went well until the experimenter did the unforgivable. In full sight of the monkey he baited the container with a piece of banana; then, while a screen was down, he substituted a lettuce leaf in its place. When the monkey discovered the lettuce leaf, he disdained to touch it. Instead he searched vigorously, examining the containers and the place around them, occasionally shrieking his rage at the experimenter, until he finally withdrew in a sulk, an innocent victim of the reinforcement contrast effect. Had he not expected a piece of banana, he would have calmly accepted the lettuce leaf.

Similar contrast effects are a continual feature of human life. The identical paycheck will seem larger or smaller depending upon whether it represents a salary raise or a salary cut; the identical course grade may mean success or failure depending upon the grade the student aspired to. To a large extent, the rewarding effect of an event is relative; it is determined, not only by the event itself, but also by what is expected.

---

* Cognitive theorists avoid the use of the term *reinforcement* because of this implication of an automatic strengthening effect. They prefer neutral terms such as *reward* instead.

Frustration   Contrast effects that result from downward reward shifts provide evidence that animals have expectations. But they also tell us something about the animals' emotions. Generally speaking, there is an adverse emotional reaction whenever an expectation of reward is not fulfilled: The monkey anticipates a banana and is "disappointed" when he receives a lettuce leaf, let alone nothing at all. This negative emotional state is generally called *frustration.* Several psychologists have emphasized the fact that frustration is an unpleasant state of affairs (Amsel, 1962). To be without water in the desert is bad enough; to find a well and *then* discover that it has dried up is unendurable. It appears that rats also find frustration painful. They are more likely to try to escape from an empty goal box in which they had previously found food than from an empty goal box that had always been empty previously (Adelman and Maatsch, 1956).

Another reaction to frustration is aggression. Pigeons will peck at each other when they are shifted from a food-reinforced schedule to extinction (Azrin, Hutchinson, and Hake, 1966). Similarly, rats will attack other rats when they fail to receive expected rewards (Thompson and Bloom, 1966).

TWO-FACTOR THEORY OF AVOIDANCE

Results such as those in the preceding discussion show that animals can learn what is where (cognitive maps) and what leads to what (expectancies). Do these findings embarrass behavior theory? They do represent a challenge to at least one of its versions—the S-R approach. Phenomena such as latent learning, frustration effects, and insightful problem solving suggest that what is acquired in instrumental learning is not a set of S-R bonds but rather some knowledge about certain relationships between events, in space and in time. To cope with this challenge, advocates of S-R theory have come up with several schemes that allow them to reinterpret some of the troublesome phenomena in terms of their basic conceptual framework. We shall consider one such endeavor, the two-factor theory of avoidance learning.

ESCAPE LEARNING

Thus far our discussion has largely centered on cases where reinforcement is positive, of the kind we normally call reward. Examples are food, water, and the company of a willing sexual partner, given that the organism is hungry, thirsty, or sexually aroused. There is another class of events that is no less relevant to instrumental learning than is reward; it represents the opposite side of the coin—the stick rather than the carrot, punishment rather than reward. These are *aversive stimuli* (Thorndike called them "annoyers") which the organism does everything to avoid and nothing to attain. Examples are loud noises and swats on the rear for infants, electric shock for laboratory rats. There is little doubt that both animals and humans learn to do whatever they must to minimize such unpleasantries, to get as few shocks, swats, and insulting reproofs as they possibly can. The question is how.

We will start with a concrete example. A rat is placed in a *shuttle box* which consists of two compartments separated by a hurdle (Figure 5.8). After a moment the floor of the box is electrified. The animal jumps, squeals, and runs

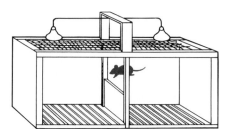

5.8   A method for studying escape and avoidance learning: The shuttle box   *In the shuttle box, the animal's task is to escape or avoid an electric shock by jumping over a hurdle to get from one compartment to another. If the animal is trained to avoid, the impending shock is usually signaled by a warning stimulus, such as a lamp or a buzzer. (After Solomon and Wynne, 1953)*

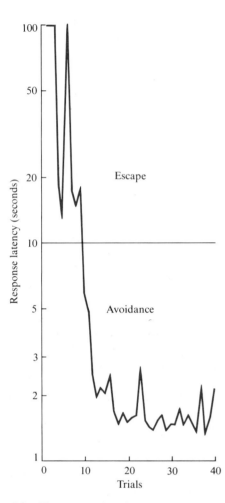

5.9   The course of avoidance learning in a dog   *The figure shows response latencies in a shuttle box. A warning stimulus indicated that shock would begin 10 seconds after the onset of the signal. For the first nine trials the dog escaped. It jumped over the hurdle* after *the shock began. From the tenth trial on, the dog avoided: It jumped* before *its 10 seconds of grace were up. The jumping speed increased even after this point until the animal jumped with an average latency of about 1½ seconds. (Note that latency is plotted on a logarithmic scale. This compresses the time scale so as to put greater emphasis on differences between the shorter response latencies.) (After Solomon and Wynne, 1953)*

142

about frantically; eventually it clambers over the hurdle to the other compartment where it is momentarily safe. But a bit later, shock is applied to the second compartment and continues until the animal climbs over the hurdle in the opposite direction. After a number of trials the animal masters the task by jumping over the hurdle as soon as the shock is turned on. This is **escape learning,** a species of instrumental learning in which the organism is required to perform a response which terminates or reduces an aversive stimulus.

Escape learning poses no special problems for S-R theory. All the necessary ingredients for the formation of an S-R bond are readily identified. There is a response: jumping over the hurdle. There is a stimulus: the onset of shock in one or the other compartments. Most important of all, there is reinforcement: the termination of shock.

THE PROBLEM OF AVOIDANCE LEARNING

The theorist's job becomes more difficult if we change our experimental procedure in just one respect, by permitting the animal to *avoid* the shock instead of merely escaping it. One way is to provide a warning signal, such as a light over each compartment that turns on, say, five seconds before the floor is electrified. If the animal jumps before its five seconds of grace are up, it averts the shock altogether. (In such studies the light usually goes off as soon as the animal jumps.) The animal typically begins by first learning to escape. Its latencies become shorter and shorter, but for a while at least they do not fall below the five-second mark; it usually jumps a fraction of a second after shock begins. But eventually the latencies drop below the critical point; the animal *anticipates* the shock and jumps faster and faster as soon as the light appears. It has learned to avoid.

How can we analyze avoidance learning in Thorndikian terms? Thorndike and other S-R theorists would say that the animal has acquired an S-R bond. The stimulus is the light, the response is jumping over the hurdle. But what is the reinforcement? It certainly can't be *cessation* of shock for, if the animal avoids, it doesn't get shocked to begin with. It is not that the shock stops; it is rather than no shock is given. But this event, not getting a shock, seems to act like a reinforcer, for it strengthens the response. Consider Figure 5.9 which shows jumping speeds for a dog learning an avoidance response in a shuttle box. As the figure shows, this animal avoided without error after the first ten trials. Even so, its speed of jumping increased on the trials following. This means that successful avoidance produces some reinforcement. But what is this reinforcement?

The first answer that comes to mind is *absence of shock.* But this is clearly wrong. For *not* receiving a punishment is only a source of satisfaction if punishment has been threatened. After all, most of us spend our entire lives without being drowned, beaten, or otherwise put to bodily harm, but we don't therefore regard ourselves in a state of perpetual bliss. It follows that the real reward cannot be the absence of shock as such. It is rather the *absence of shock when shock is expected.**

---

* There is a parallel between the reactions to frustration and to avoidance. In frustration, the animal's emotional reaction is produced by the absence of an expected reward. In avoidance, the reaction is caused by the absence of an expected punishment. The two emotional reactions go in opposite directions. In frustration, the reaction is negative (humans might call it *disappointment*); in avoidance, it is positive (an everyday term might be *relief*).

The trouble is that this analysis of avoidance learning is not one that an S-R theorist will happily accept. The whole thrust of Thorndike's position had been that the organism acts blindly and without recognition of what leads to what. If we now claim that the animal "expects shock" we violate the entire spirit of the S-R theoretical enterprise. But if we can't make this claim, we still have no answer to the question of what reinforces avoidance learning?

AVOIDANCE INTERPRETED AS ESCAPE FROM FEAR

Attempts to answer this question in S-R terms led to the ***two-factor theory*** of avoidance learning. It is so called because it argues that avoidance learning is based on both classical and instrumental learning (Mowrer, 1947; Rescorla and Solomon, 1967).

Let us return to the rat in the shuttle box. At least on the initial trials, the animal suffers painful shock. But as we know already, intense pain has profound effects upon the autonomic nervous system, especially its sympathetic branch—heartbeat and respiration are accelerated, peristaltic movements are inhibited, the animal may urinate and defecate (see Chapter 3). Since this pattern of sympathetic arousal usually occurs in situations in which humans experience the emotion fear, it is often called the fear response, whether it occurs in animals or in man. In the shuttle box the UCS (shock) for this fear response is repeatedly paired with the warning signal (the CS, light). This leads to classical conditioning: Eventually, the light alone evokes the fear response.

Learning to fear the warning signal is the first step in learning to avoid, for it provides the mechanism whereby the instrumental hurdle-jumping response is reinforced. According to two-factor theory, fear acts as an aversive stimulus. If so, then its termination or reduction will be reinforcing. In this regard, fear is rather similar to motive states like hunger and thirst whose reduction also constitutes reinforcement.

Given these assumptions, we can account for avoidance learning in S-R terms. Since fear reduction is reinforcing, any response which follows it will be strengthened. This includes any response that terminates the warning signal. By jumping the hurdle, the rat gets away from the stimulus to which fear is connected—the light above the dangerous compartment. As a result, fear is reduced and the jumping response is strengthened.

Let us summarize the steps in this analysis. The animal has learned two associations. First, it acquires a fear response to the light, presumably by classical conditioning:

Second, it learns to jump over the hurdle when the light over the compartment is turned on. This is instrumental learning, reinforced by fear reduction—an indirect result of the instrumental response (jumping the hurdle) which gets the animal away from the light:

$$CS_{light} \longrightarrow R_{jump} \text{ (which reduces fear)}$$

Put another way, avoidance learning as here described is really a species of escape learning, but instead of escaping from pain, the animal escapes from fear.

How adequate is two-factor theory as an account of avoidance learning? There is certainly something elegant about its core assumption that avoidance is reinforced by escape from fear. This explains how the absence of something—that is, nonshock—can be a reinforcer without invoking the concept of an expectation. But is this assumption correct?

One problem concerns the nature of the hypothetical fear response during avoidance. What exactly is it? One answer is that it is the sympathetic arousal that accompanies fear—accelerated heart rate, increased blood pressure, and so on. If so, we would expect a close relation between avoidance and such autonomic measures. But, in fact, this relation is far from clear. In one study, dogs were trained to press a panel to avoid shock. Simultaneously, their heart rates were monitored. The results showed that the dogs' heart rates went up after they performed the avoidance response and did not subside until a few seconds later (Black, 1959). But if the avoidance response is really reinforced by fear reduction, shouldn't the heart rate have gone down immediately after the panel was pressed? Two-factor theorists reply that the fear response should not be too closely identified with the peripheral autonomic reaction. It should instead be regarded as a central (presumably cerebral) state that is only imperfectly indexed by outer signs such as heart rate (Rescorla and Solomon, 1967).

All of this makes one wonder whether two-factor theory of avoidance learning is really preferable to cognitive accounts. These are often criticized because they rely on terms such as *expectancy,* which refer to internal events that are hypothetical and inferred. But two-factor theory is not exactly immune to this kind of criticism either, considering that central fear states are just as hypothetical and inferred as expectations.

The problems of two-factor theory highlight the difficulties of trying to account for cognitions in S-R terms. These difficulties loom all the larger considering that the two-factor interpretation of avoidance learning is the most systematic venture of this sort. Attempts to provide an S-R account of latent learning and related phenomena have been even less convincing.

Contingency

Cognitive theorists argue that the building blocks of learned behavior are not what the early behavior theorists thought they were. But whatever these basic building blocks may be, many modern behavior theorists still adhere to Pavlov's and Thorndike's beliefs about *how* they are put together. They maintain that learning involves the connection between certain elements—between stimuli for classical conditioning, and between responses and reinforcers for instrumental conditioning. And they further assert that these connections are established by one factor—***contiguity*** or togetherness in time. We will now turn to several lines of fairly recent evidence which suggest that these assertions are untrue.

Is learning the result of connections that are created by contiguity in time? Consider classical conditioning. According to Pavlov, the important condition is the *pairing* of CS and UCS. Each such pairing was said to add to the strength of the bond that is gradually forged between them. But cognitive theorists such as Köhler and Tolman would argue that the learning process is much less mechanical. In their view, the CS becomes a signal that allows the animal to *predict* whether or not a UCS is about to occur.

Is this view really different from Pavlov's account? A modern theoretical treatment by Robert Rescorla suggests that it is. The difference hinges on the distinction between **contiguity** and **contingency.**

Contiguity in time simply means that two events occur together. Pavlov's experimental arrangement certainly provides this, since CS and UCS are generally presented in close succession. But Rescorla points out that there is another aspect of Pavlov's procedure that has generally been overlooked. To be sure, the dog gets meat when the tone is sounded. But no less important is the fact that when the tone is not sounded the dog gets nothing. Such no-tone, no-meat occasions occur during the intervals between trials. The dog remains in its harness but no CS is given nor is there a UCS.

According to Rescorla, conditioning occurs precisely because the dog gets both experiences. If tone, then meat; if no tone, then no meat. These two experiences allow the animal to discover that the occurrence of the UCS is **contingent** (loosely speaking, is dependent) upon the occurrence of the CS. But to discover this, the dog must put together information provided by both kinds of experiences. The fact that a CS always occurs together with a UCS is not enough. For example, it is well known that experienced dogs don't salivate when put in the conditioning harness. To be sure, getting meat is contiguous with being in the harness. But it is not contingent upon it for the dog is in the harness both when it gets food and when it doesn't. As a result, being in the harness provides no information on the basis of which the dog can forecast what is going to happen next.

Contingency need not be perfect. In nature it rarely is. A dark cloud generally precedes a storm but it doesn't always. The same holds for the laboratory in which we can arrange whatever relationship between CS and UCS we choose. To recognize such imperfect contingencies, the organism must somehow integrate four possible stimulus combinations. Given the tone as CS and the meat as UCS, these combinations are: tone/meat, tone/no meat, no tone/meat, and no tone/no meat. To determine whether there is a tone/meat contingency, the organism must compare two probabilities—the probability of getting meat when the tone is sounded and the probability of getting meat when the tone is not sounded. If the first is greater than the second, then getting meat is contingent upon the tone. If the first is smaller than the second, then the meat is contingent upon the absence of the tone. Finally, if the two probabilities are identical, then the two events are independent (see Table 5.1). According to the hypothesis, conditioning will occur only if there is a positive meat/tone contingency.

To prove his point, Rescsorla pitted contiguity against contingency. Using tones and shock, he exposed dogs to different kinds of CS-UCS relationships.

Table 5.1 CONTINGENCY IN CLASSICAL CONDITIONING

The table shows the number of trials on which each of the four stimulus combinations were offered. Each table presents a different tone/meat contingency based on twenty trials for each of the three conditions. The column labeled p shows the probabilities that meat will occur under a particular stimulus condition.

Meat contingent upon tone

	Meat	No meat	*p*
Tone	8	2	.80
No tone	2	8	.20

Meat contingent upon absence of tone

	Meat	No meat	*p*
Tone	3	7	.30
No tone	7	3	.70

Meat and tone independent

	Meat	No meat	*p*
Tone	5	5	.50
No tone	5	5	.50

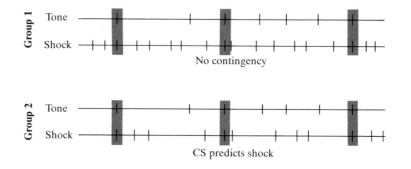

5.10 Contingency in classical conditioning *The figure is a schematic outline of Rescorla's experiment on contingency. Two groups of dogs were run. Both received tones and shock. Sometimes the tone and shock occurred together; such pairings are indicated in color. Note that the number of such CS-USC pairings is identical in the two groups. Note also that the total number of shocks is less in Group II than in Group I. The tone-shock contingency is created by making a shock more probable after a tone than at other times. It is not achieved by increasing the absolute number of shocks. (After Rescorla, 1967)*

For one group, the tones and shocks occurred randomly and independently. Pure accident produced a number of CS-UCS pairings but the CS had no predictive power. Shock was equally likely during or after a tone as at any other time. A second group received the same number of CS-UCS pairings as did the animals in the first group. The important difference was that for this group, the CS had predictive power; for them, shock was more likely shortly after the tone than at other times. But this difference was not created by adding more shocks. On the contrary. The second group received the same number of shocks as the first group during the half-minute or so after the tone went off (Figure 5.10).

According to the contiguity theory of conditioning, both groups should come to fear the tone equally since both were exposed to an equal number of tone-shock pairings. In contrast, a contingency approach would lead one to expect that there would be no conditioned fear of the tone in the first group, for which this CS had no predictive value. Conditioned fear should be shown by the animals of the second group, for whom the tone predicted an increased likelihood of shock. This should be so despite the fact that these dogs received fewer shocks overall than the animals in the first group.

To decide between these alternatives, Rescorla first trained his dogs to jump back and forth in a shuttle box to avoid unsignalized shock. Then, while the animals were jumping steadily, he introduced the tone. If the CS was conditioned to fear, one would expect the jumping rate to go up. The CS would increase the animal's fear and this should enhance the vigor of the avoidance reaction.

The results were in line with the contingency approach. If the CS was previously associated with an increased likelihood of shock, its introduction made the dogs jump twice as often as they had before. But if shock had been just as likely during or after the tone as at other times, the jumping rate was unaffected. It appears that conditioning depends on contingency rather than on contiguity alone.

The contingency approach is a serious challenge to the notion that conditioning is produced by a simple, mechanically established connection. Instead, it suggests that the learning process that underlies conditioning may not be drastically different from that which was manifested by Köhler's chimpanzees. As the contingency view has it, the animal acts as if it were trying to evaluate the events of the past so as to decide just what was different on UCS occasions and no-UCS occasions and finally concludes, "Well, it must have been the tone."

CONTINGENCY IN INSTRUMENTAL LEARNING: CONTROL

The same reasoning that led to the contingency analysis of classical conditioning also applies to instrumental (operant) learning. Here, too, the issue is between contiguity and contingency. According to Thorndike and Skinner, the critical factor is whether the response is immediately followed by a reinforcer. In their view, it makes little difference whether the response actually produces the reward or precedes it only accidentally. All that counts is the temporal contiguity between them.

Cognitive theorists see instrumental learning differently. In their view, it occurs because animals learn about the relation between acts and outcomes. This cognitive position can be recast in contingency terms. As in classical conditioning, the determination of the contingency requires the comparison of two probabilities. Suppose the relevant outcome is a food pellet and the response is lever-pressing. If so, the comparison is between the probability of getting a pellet when the lever has been pressed and getting it when the lever has not been pressed. If the first probability is greater than the second, getting the food is contingent upon lever-pressing. If the two probabilities are equal, there is no contingency—lever-pressing and getting pellets are independent.*

Do animals and people respond to such response-outcome contingencies? Proof that they do comes from studies which compare the effects of response-independent outcomes.

RESPONSE CONTROL IN INFANTS

One line of evidence concerns human infants. A group of two-month-old infants was provided with an opportunity to make something happen. The infants were placed in cribs above which a colorful mobile was suspended. Whenever the infants moved their heads, they closed a switch in their pillows. This activated the overhead mobile which promptly turned for a second or so and did so every time the pillow switch was closed. The infants soon learned to shake their heads about, thus making their mobiles turn. They evidently enjoyed doing so; they smiled and cooed happily at their mobiles, clearly delighted at seeing them move. A second group of infants was exposed to the same situation. There was one difference—they had no control over the mobile's movement. Their mobile turned just about as often as the mobile for the first group, but it was moved for them, not by them. After a few days, these infants no longer smiled and cooed at the mobile nor did they seem particularly interested when it turned. This suggests that what the infants liked about the mobile was not that it moved but that they made it move. This shows that the infants can distinguish between response-controlled and response-independent outcomes, which is a strong argument for the contingency approach. It also shows that infants, no less than we, prefer to exercise some control over their environments. The reason for this is by no means clear, but it appears that even a two-month-old infant wants to be master of its own fate (J. S. Watson, 1967).

---

* If the second probability is greater than the first, then getting the pellet is contingent upon not pressing the lever. This kind of contingency is common whenever one wants the learner to refrain from doing something, for example, "I'll give you a cookie if you stop whining."

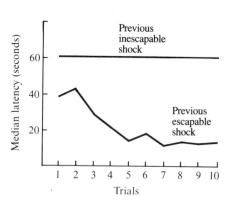

5.11 Learned helplessness *The curves show the shuttle box performance of two groups of dogs. At the start of each trial, there was a 10-second signal after which one compartment was electrified. The dog could escape the shock by jumping over the barrier. If the animal did not jump after 60 seconds, the trial was terminated. Both groups of animals had previously experienced shock in a hammock. One group (black) was able to escape this shock by performing an instrumental response. The second group (color) was yoked to the first; it received the same number of shocks and for the same duration but was unable to do anything about them. As is shown, the dogs that had previously exerted some control, learned to escape in the shuttle box as indicated by the quick decrease in their escape latencies. In contrast, the animals who had received inescapable shocks had become helpless and were unable to learn to escape. (After Maier, 1969)*

HELPLESSNESS IN DOGS

The mobile-turning infants illustrate the joys of mastery. Another, highly influential series of studies demonstrates the despair when there is no mastery at all. Their focus is on ***learned helplessness,*** an acquired sense that one can no longer control one's environment so that one gives up trying (Seligman, 1975).

The classic experiment on learned helplessness employed two groups of dogs, *A* and *B*, who received strong electric shocks while strapped in a hammock. The dogs in group *A* were able to exert some control over the situation. They could turn the shock off whenever it began by pushing a panel that was placed close to their noses. The dogs in group *B* had no such power. For them, the shocks were inescapable. But the number and duration of these shocks was exactly the same. For each dog in group *A* there was a corresponding animal in group *B* whose fate was "yoked" to that of the first dog. Whenever the group *A* dog was shocked, so was the group *B* dog. Whenever the group *A* dog turned off the shock, the shock was turned off for the group *B* dog. This arrangement guaranteed that the actual physical punishment meted out to both groups was precisely the same. What was different was what they could do about it. Group *A* was able to exercise some control; group *B* could only endure.

The question was how the group *B* dogs would fare when presented with a new situation that provided them with an opportunity to help themselves. To find out, both groups of dogs were presented with a standard avoidance learning task in a shuttle box (Figure 5.11). The dogs in group *A* learned just about as quickly as did naïve dogs who had no prior experimental experience of any kind. During the first trials, they waited until the shock began and then scrambled over the hurdle; later, they jumped before their grace period was up and thus avoided shock entirely. But the dogs in group *B,* who had previously suffered inescapable shock in the hammock, behaved very differently. Initially, they behaved much like other dogs; they ran about frantically, barking, and howling. But they soon became much more passive. They lay down, whined quietly, and simply took whatever shocks were delivered. They neither avoided nor escaped; they just gave up trying. In the hammock setup they had been objectively helpless; there really was nothing they could do. But in the shuttle box, their helplessness was only subjective, for there was now a way in which they could make their lot bearable. But they never discovered it. They had learned to be helpless (Seligman and Maier, 1967).

HELPLESSNESS AND DEPRESSION

Martin Seligman, one of the discoverers of the learned helplessness effect in animals, has recently proposed that a similar mechanism underlies the development of certain kinds of depression in human patients. (For further discussion of depression, see Chapter 17.) He believes that such patients share certain features with animals who have been rendered helpless. Both fail to initiate actions but "just sit there"; both are slow to learn that something they did was successful; both lose weight and have little interest in others. To Seligman and his associates these parallels suggest that the underlying cause is the same in both cases. Like the helpless dog, the depressed patient has come to feel that his acts are of no avail. And like the dog, the depressed patient was brought to this morbid state of affairs by an initial exposure to a situation in which he was objectively helpless. While the dog received inescapable shocks in its hammock, the patient found himself powerless in the face of bereavement, business failure, or serious illness (Seligman, Klein, and Miller, 1976).

Whether learned helplesness turns out to be relevant to depression or does not, there is little doubt that it is relevant to questions about the nature of learning. It is a strong argument for the contingency approach to instrumental learning. It clearly shows that animals (much as human infants) react differently to situations in which their responses have an effect than to those in which they don't. This indicates that animals learn something about the relationship between their acts and these acts' outcomes. If they are dogs who received inescapable shocks, they learn something still more general; namely, that no such relationship exists.

Belongingness

The preceding discussion suggested that both classical and instrumental (operant) conditioning involve the integration of a number of different experiences by means of which the animal decides which of the many things it saw, heard, or smelled is the best predictor of the UCS, and which of the many things it did is the one that led to reinforcement. We now consider another group of phenomena that are even more challenging to behavior theory. They indicate that the relationship between CS and UCS or between response and reinforcer is not arbitrary.

BELONGINGNESS IN HUMAN LEARNING

One of the central tenets of behavior theory is that the connections that are established by classical or instrumental (operant) conditioning do not depend upon the relationship between the elements that are connected. Put another way, these connections are said to be *arbitrary*. To give an example, take names and faces. Suppose we have two female faces and two female names, say, Joan and Carol. Which connection is more reasonable? Should it be as in Figure 5.12*a*? Or should it be as in Figure 5.12*b*?

It is obvious that both sets of pairings are equally plausible. Neither face is more Carolish or Joanlike than the other. As a result, the face-name pairing is indeed arbitrary. Much the same holds for virtually all of the sounds by which our language designates the objects in the world around us. Except for a few onomatopoeic terms like *buzz* and *hiss* the relation between the sound of a word and its meaning is completely arbitrary. The same holds for many other associations we pick up in the course of ordinary life, such as addresses, telephone numbers, and the like.

Behavior theorists believe that this arbitrariness is a basic feature of all learning. In their view, events are linked together by an associative process that acts like a universal glue which bonds just about anything to anything else. But there is some evidence to the contrary, even in humans. While we are marvelously gifted at associating arbitrary items, these associations are more

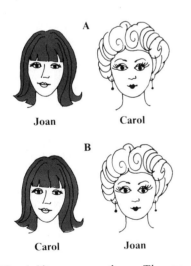

5.12 Arbitrary connections *The connection between faces and names is largely arbitrary. The names fit just as well in (A) as in (B).*

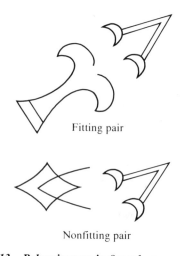

Fitting pair

Nonfitting pair

5.13 Belongingness in figural perception *Pairs of nonsense figures which "fit" are much easier to associate than those which do not. (Köhler, 1941)*

readily formed if the two members of the pair seem to fit together. An example was provided by Köhler who asked human subjects to associate pairs of figures. In a subsequent test, the subjects were presented with one member of the pair and had to produce the other. They did twice as well if the pairs "fit" than if they did not (Figure 5.13).

Similar effects have been found with verbal materials. Ironically enough, one of the best demonstrations was provided by the man who some thirty years earlier had helped to found behavior theory, E. L. Thorndike. Thorndike showed that subjects can associate two words more easily when both occur within the same sentence than when they don't. This is true even when the temporal contiguity between the two items is equated. An example is a list of sentences such as

Larry is a tailor.
Henry is a butcher.
Frank is a grocer.

The subjects are read a list of, say, twenty such sentences and are then tested for either within-sentence or across-sentence associations. To test for the former, they have to answer questions like, "What words followed *Larry?*" To get at the latter, they were asked, "What words followed '. . . *is a tailor?*'" The results showed much better recall for within- than across-sentence pairs. To use Thorndike's own term, it is evidently much easier to connect items that already seem to *belong* together than items which do not (Thorndike, 1931).

BELONGINGNESS IN ANIMAL LEARNING

Whether such results contradict behavior theory's insistence of the arbitrariness of association is debatable. A behavior theorist could argue that the belongingness which Thorndike and Köhler noted is a result of prior learning. Perhaps the subjects had previously learned that certain kinds of visual forms go together or that words have more to do with each other if they occur within the same sentence than if they don't. This argument becomes rather less plausible when we consider analogous belongingness effects at the animal level.

Behavior theorists have typically maintained that the relations which are acquired in classical and instrumental conditioning are essentially arbitrary. They believed that any CS can be conditioned to any UCS and any operant can be reinforced by any reinforcer. To be sure, one can't use a CS the animal isn't sensitive to (dogs have no color vision), nor should one require an animal to perform a response it is not equipped for (rats can't fly), nor should one provide a reinforcer that isn't reinforcing (cats don't eat bananas). But once these and similar provisos are granted, the relation between the particular elements should have little if any effect. As it turns out, the facts say otherwise.

CS-UCS RELATIONS IN CLASSICAL CONDITIONING

In classical conditioning, subjects learn to relate a CS and a UCS. A number of recent studies show that certain conditioned stimuli are more readily related to certain unconditioned stimuli than to others. The bulk of the evidence comes from **learned taste aversions.**

It has long been known that rats are remarkably adept at avoiding foods they ate just before falling sick. This is the reason why it is very difficult to exterminate wild rats with poison: The rat takes a small bite of the poisoned food, becomes ill, generally recovers, and thereafter avoids the particular flavor. The animal has become bait shy. Similar effects are easily produced in the laboratory. The subjects (usually rats) are presented with a given flavor, such as water containing saccharin. After drinking some of this water, they are exposed to X-ray radiation—not enough to kill them, but enough to make them quite ill and nauseous. After they are recovered, they are given a choice between, say, plain water and a saccharine solution. They will now refuse to drink the saccharin even though they had much preferred this sweet-tasting drink prior to their illness.

Such learned taste aversions are usually believed to be based on classical conditioning in which the CS is a certain flavor (here, saccharine) and the UCS is being sick. The question is whether other stimuli such as colors or tones serve equally well as CSs for such taste aversions.

The test was a study in which thirsty rats were allowed to drink saccharine-flavored water. The water came from a drinking tube; whenever the rat licked the nozzle, a bright light flashed and a clicking noise sounded. Subsequently, some rats received a shock to their feet. Others were exposed to a dose of illness-producing X-rays. All of the animals developed a strong aversion. When again presented with water that was sweet and was accompanied by bright flashes and clicks, they hardly touched the drinking nozzle. All rats had presumably acquired a classically conditioned aversion. The UCS was either shock or illness. The CS was a stimulus compound comprised of the flavor, the light, and the noise. But did the rats learn to avoid all of these stimulus features or only some?

To find out, the experimenters tested the rats in a new situation. They either gave them water that was saccharine flavored but unaccompanied by either light or noise. Or they gave them plain, unflavored water that was accompanied by the light and sound cues that were present during training. The results showed that what the rats had learned to avoid depended upon the UCS. If they had been shocked (and felt pain) they refused water that was accompanied by light and noise but they had no objection to the sweet flavor. If they had been X-rayed (and became ill) the opposite was true—they avoided the saccharine flavor but were perfectly willing to drink when the water was preceded by light and noise (Table 5.2).

Table 5.2 BELONGINGNESS IN CLASSICAL CONDITIONING

In all groups: CS = saccharine taste + light + sound

TRAINING UCS:	Shock		X-ray illness	
TEST Water with:	Saccharine taste	Light + sound	Saccharine taste	Light + sound
RESULTS	No effect	Aversion	Aversion	No effect

These results indicate that rats tend to link stimuli in certain fitting ways: Taste goes with illness, sights and sounds with externally induced pain. These effects may well reflect a built-in belongingness relationship. This would make good biological sense. In the world of the rat, an omnivorous creature that selects its food mainly on the basis of its flavor, taste may well be the most reliable cue that warns of impending illness. If so, a natively given bias to associate sickness with preceding tastes is likely to have survival value. In effect, the rat cannot help but ask itself, "What did I eat?" whenever it has a stomach ache (Garcia and Koelling, 1966).

If this is so, one might expect rather different results for animals who select their food on the basis of cues other than taste. An example are many species of birds that rely heavily on vision when choosing food. In one study, quail drank blue, sour water and were then poisoned. Some of the birds were later tested with blue, unflavored water; others were tested with water that was sour but colorless. The quail developed a drastic aversion to blue water. But they drank just about as much sour water as they had prior to being poisoned. Here, the learned food aversion was evidently based on color rather than on taste (Wilcoxin, Dragoin, and Kral, 1971). It appears that the built-in belongingness relation is species-specific. Certain birds have a natively given bias to link sickness with visual cues, while rats and other mammals link it to taste. This bias *prepares* them to learn certain relations rather than others (Seligman, 1970). In both cases, the preparedness fits in with the way the animal identifies food in its native habitat.

RESPONSE-OUTCOME RELATIONS IN INSTRUMENTAL CONDITIONING

The preceding discussion has shown that the CS-UCS relation in classical conditioning is not always arbitrary. A similar nonarbitrariness characterizes many instrumental learning situations.

Pigeons, pecking, and food   Consider a pigeon pecking away in a Skinner box. Here surely is the very prototype of arbitrary instrumental learning. But in fact, the relation between peck and what is pecked at is far from arbitrary. One line of evidence comes from the fact that it is exceedingly hard to train pigeons to peck so as to escape or avoid electric shock (Hineline and Rachlin, 1969). This doesn't mean that shock escape or shock avoidance are inadequate reinforcers for pigeons. Far from it. The birds readily learn to fly or hop or flap their wings in order to get away from shock. What they have trouble learning is to peck to bring about the same outcome. According to Robert Bolles, this is because many animals have built-in defense reactions to danger that are specific to their species. The pigeon is no exception. Its species-specific defense reaction is speedy locomotion, preferably airborne flight. Like all other animals, the bird can learn new avoidance responses, but only to the extent that these fit in with its natively given danger reaction. Hopping, flying, and wing-flapping qualify, for they are merely modifications of the basic defense pattern. But pecking does not and it is therefore very hard to learn as an escape or an avoidance response (Bolles, 1970).

If pigeons have so much trouble learning to peck to escape or avoid, why are they so readily trained to peck for food? The reason is that pecking is what pigeons do naturally when they consume food. This makes it extremely easy

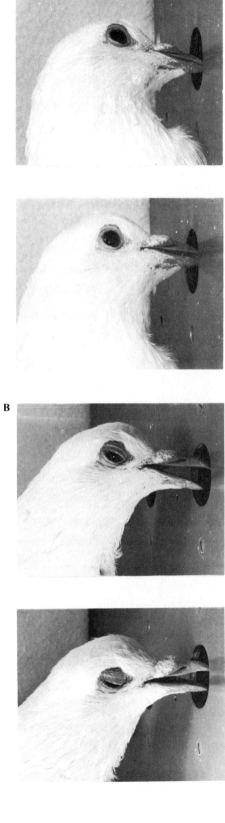

A

B

for them to peck as a way of getting food. In effect, they are simply performing an anticipatory eating response. That something of this sort goes on is shown by how they peck when other reinforcers are used. In one study, thirsty pigeons had to peck at a key to obtain water. Their pecks were quite different from those seen with food reinforcement; they resemble the beak-movements they make while drinking (Figure 5.14). In another study, key-pecking brought access to a sexually receptive mate. Now the pigeons cooed as they pressed the key. All of this means that key-pecking is not an arbitrary instrumental response. In effect, the pigeon "eats" the key when working for food, "drinks" it when working for water, and "courts" it when working for sex. There clearly is an intimate relation between response and reinforcer (Schwartz, 1978).*

GENERALIST AND SPECIALIST

To sum up, it becomes clear that the way in which animals associate events is not arbitrary. Different species seem to come biologically prepared to acquire certain linkages rather than others. For instance, rats connect illness with taste but not with sights and sounds. Such built-in belongingnesses have the virtue of helping the animal to adapt to its particular ecological niche. But they have the drawback of making the animal into an intellectual specialist whose unusual gifts in noting certain relations are counterbalanced by its sluggishness in responding to others (Rozin and Kalat, 1971).

In any case, natively given belongingness represents a major challenge to behavior theory. It highlights the importance of species differences in learning. And by showing that rats, pigeons, and many other animals don't relate CS and UCS, or response and outcome, arbitrarily, it undercuts one of the cornerstones on which behavior theory rests.

There is something ironic about all of this. For the arbitrariness which both Pavlov and Skinner regarded as basic is something which people are more capable of than rats and pigeons. For people, a Skinner-box lever would indeed be an indifferent means to an end, as readily pressed for food as for anything else. To this extent, the box might be suitable to study them rather

* A number of psychologists have interpreted such findings as evidence that key-pecking in a Skinner box is a classically rather than an instrumentally conditioned response. To some extent, this may be true. One line of evidence comes from a study in which naïve pigeons were left in a box whose key lit up periodically. The pigeons received food if they did *not* peck at the key during a six-second interval. But if they did peck, the key-light went out and no food was presented. Here, food-reward was contingent upon not pecking. But the pigeons pecked anyway. They simply couldn't help themselves (Williams and Williams, 1969). The CS-UCS contingency (here, lit key and food) evidently outweighed the response-outcome contingency (here, not pecking and food), which may be another way of saying that the response was in part a classically conditioned CR (Schwartz and Gamzu, 1977).

5.14 Key pecking for food and water (A) The pictures show a pigeon's beak movements as it pecks a key to obtain water. The movements resemble those the bird makes when it drinks. (B) These pictures show quite different beak movements made when the bird is hungry and pecks a key for food. Now the movements resemble those the animal makes when it eats. (Photographs by Bruce Moore, from Jenkins and Moore, 1973)

than the animal subjects for which it was designed (Schwartz, 1974). This is not to say that the behavior theorists' devices can begin to do justice to the human intellect. After all, a Skinner box is hardly a place in which Plato or Shakespeare would show to full advantage. But while not remotely adequate to assess our intellectual maximum, it is an apparatus that seems to fit one fact of human learning: We are generalists who can relate just about anything to anything else. *We* can learn arbitrary relations.

Many psychologists believe that this is not the end of the story. Compared to animals, we are indeed generalists who can learn arbitrary relations. But we are also specialists, with built-in predispositions to learn certain relationships very quickly. One of these species-specific predispositions is for language. That language is learned is indubitable. Eskimo children come to speak Eskimo and Chinese children speak Chinese. But the question is how it is learned. It is something that virtually all human children acquire, without fuss or effort and within the first few years of life. By the time they are four or five, they all know how to speak their native tongues, uttering sentences of considerable complexity, many of which they could never have heard before. This is not because they are taught explicitly, for most children aren't. Instead, it probably reflects a built-in tendency to fit sounds, words, and larger units into a very general framework with which the organism comes already equipped. How this process works is as yet unknown (see Chapter 10). But it seems to be the counterpart of other specializations of the learning functions found elsewhere in the animal kingdom.

Higher-Order Concepts in Higher Animals

The preceding discussion has shown that in some ways, behavior theory has overestimated the intellectual flexibility of many animal species. Rats and pigeons are unable to associate quite as arbitrarily as Pavlov and Skinner had maintained. But according to many critics, beginning with Köhler, behavior theory is no less guilty of the opposite error. It underestimates the capacity of many animals, especially that of the primate family to which we ourselves belong. If appropriately tested, these animals manifest a degree of intelligence that is hard to account for within the framework of behavior theory. We have already considered some of the early evidence collected by Köhler. We now turn to some recent studies of higher-order intellectual performance in primates. We will consider only two manifestations of this intelligence—the fact that these animals seem to use abstract concepts and the fact that they seem to know something about their own mental processes.

ABSTRACT CONCEPTS IN ANIMALS

We have previously seen that an important criterion for insight is wide and appropriate transfer. The child who responds "6" to both "$2 + 4 = ?$" and to "$4 + 2 = ?$" is a case in point. But is this kind of transfer really so hard to explain in behavior theory's terms? Can't one say that it is simply some form of stimulus generalization? A dog who has been conditioned to a tone of 1,000 hertz will also salivate when presented with 4,000 hertz. This is certainly transfer. How is it different from the kind of transfer which we regard as a sign of understanding?

The answer is that in stimulus generalization, transfer is only based on perceptual similarity. A variety of stimuli are seen as more or less alike and so they are responded to in a similar fashion. But in the case of the "2 + 4" example, the transfer is based on something else, on a common principle, on an abstract conceptual relationship. The important thing is not that "2 + 4" and "4 + 2" look alike. The important thing is that they are alike in meaning.

A number of studies have shown that various primates can respond to some abstract, conceptual aspects of a situation that transcend their perceptual characteristics.

LEARNING TO LEARN IN MONKEYS

A simple example of transcending perceptual characteristics is **learning to learn**. This phenomenon has been extensively studied by Harry Harlow. Harlow trained rhesus monkeys on a long series of different discriminations. Each discrimination involved two stimulus objects that were never used again on any further problem. Thus, in the first discrimination, the monkey might have to choose between a small red square and a large blue circle; in the second, between a white line and a yellow dot; in the third, between a green pyramid and a black hemisphere. In one such study, the animals were trained on 344 separate discrimination problems (Figure 5.15). The results were dramatic. Learning the first few discriminations was difficult, but the animals became better and better the more new problems they encountered. After 300 of them, they solved each new problem in just one trial. In Harlow's terms, the mon-

5.15 A device for studying discrimination learning in monkeys The figure shows the so-called Wisconsin General Test Apparatus. A monkey is presented with a stimulus tray that contains two (sometimes three or more) wells. In one of the wells is a desirable food reward, such as a raisin or a grape. The wells are covered with various objects, such as the sphere and cube shown in the figure. One of these objects is designated as the correct stimulus. The animal's task is to learn which of these objects is correct, push it aside, and pick up its reward from the well below. (After Harlow, 1949)

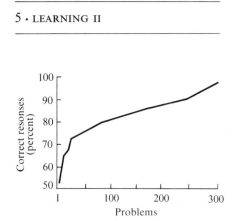

5.16 Discrimination learning sets *Monkeys were given 344 different discrimination problems, each for 6 trials. The curve shows the animals' average performance on the second trial. (After Harlow, 1949)*

keys had acquired a ***learning set;*** they had learned how to learn a certain kind of problem (Figure 5.16; Harlow, 1949).

What did the animals learn during this long series of different discrimination problems that finally enabled them to solve such tasks so efficiently? At first, each monkey was prone to certain kinds of errors that it made quite systematically—choosing the right side, or alternating sides from trial to trial, or always choosing the larger of the two objects. Such errors gradually dropped out, as if the monkey realized that none of these factors was relevant to the solution. Once these error tendencies were eliminated, the animals could eventually adopt a new strategy, appropriate not just to one discrimination problem but to all of them. If you find food under some object, choose it again; if you don't, switch to the other. This "Win-stay, lose-shift" strategy obviously does not depend upon the specific stimuli employed in the task. It is based on a conceptual, not a perceptual, relationship (Harlow, 1959).

SYMBOL MANIPULATION IN CHIMPANZEES

The most impressive demonstrations of abstract concepts in animals have been obtained as a side-product of attempts to teach some form of language to chimpanzees and other apes (Gardner and Gardner, 1971; D. Premack, 1976). We will consider only one such language-teaching enterprise, conducted by David Premack.

Premack's prize student is Sarah, a fifteen-year-old female chimpanzee who was taught a visual "language." The "words" of the language are small pieces of plastic made into arbitrary shapes with a metal backing by means of which they can be attached to a magnetized board. The "sentences" are strings of these plastic tokens arranged vertically, such as "No Sarah take chocolate" (Figure 5.17).

A

B

C

5.17 Symbol manipulation by chimpanzees *(A) David Premack and pupil. (B) Photograph of young chimpanzee obeying command on the symbol board. (C) "No Sarah take chocolate." (Photographs courtesy of A. J. Premack; after Premack and Premack, 1972)*

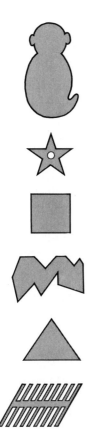

5.18 Complex string of symbols Sarah can respond to correctly *(After Premack and Premack, 1972)*

The first step in acquiring this minilanguage was the formation of simple token-object associations. The trainer placed, say, a piece of apple next to the plastic *apple* token. Sarah had to attach the *apple* token to the magnetized writing board before she was allowed to take the apple. By similar procedures, she was taught to use the tokens for *orange, banana,* and *fig,* and she demonstrated her proficiency with the visual vocabulary by picking the correct token from among several alternatives when presented with a particular fruit. Later on, Sarah learned to use special tokens to designate particular trainers. She then had to form two-word sentences such as "Mary apple" by placing both the *Mary* token and the *apple* token on the board in the correct order. Still later, her vocabulary was expanded to include several verbs (*wash, insert*), other nouns (*pail*), adjectives (*red*), and general class terms (e.g., *color of*). Eventually, she was able to respond to a sentence such as Figure 5.18, which, freely translated from the original Premackese, reads,

Sarah Insert Banana Pail Insert Apple Dish

By and large, Sarah dutifully complied by putting the banana into the pail and the apple into the dish. Nor did she always have to be rewarded with tangible reinforcers. The trainer's "That's very good, Sarah" was usually quite enough.

A few methodological provisos were added to make sure that Sarah's performance was genuine. There was always the possibility that she had responded to some inadvertent cues given by the trainer—perhaps an involuntary gesture, or an uncontrolled facial expression. To check on this and other confounding factors, Premack ran a control with a trainer who did not know the chimpanzee "language." This "dumb" trainer was told how to proceed by means of a code sheet which listed tokens by number, but he had no idea what any of the tokens meant. When this was done, Sarah's performance declined somewhat; perhaps she did use some social cues, perhaps she was upset that her old trainer was no longer with her. But her performance was still sufficiently good to rule out the possibility that she had not learned the communication system at all and was responding solely on the basis of social cues.

Sarah's accomplishments are evidently not an artifact. She has acquired a genuine, visual communication system. The question is whether this system deserves the title "language" in the human sense. Many authors, including Premack himself, doubt that it does. One reason is that chimpanzees seem to be unable to learn a richly structured system of rules for putting words together. Such a rule-system, or **syntax,** is characteristic of all human languages, and the fact that chimpanzees seem unable to acquire anything like it suggests that language is specific to humans alone (see Chapter 10). But our present concern is not with the linguistic capacities of the chimpanzee as such. It is rather with what attempts to teach them language have told us about the concepts these animals can form. And in this regard the results are unambiguous. They point to a level of conceptual abstraction that is hard to reconcile with a behavior theorist's view of what animals can learn.

Same-different   An example of such an abstract concept is the notion same-different. Consider a situation in which an animal is shown three items. One is a sample, while the other two are alternatives. The animal's task is to choose

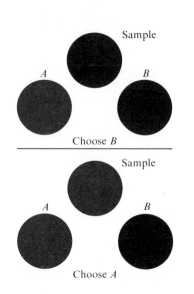

5.19 Matching to sample *The figure shows the procedure of a typical matching-to-sample experiment. The top circle in each panel represents the sample. The subject's task is to choose the one circle among the two at the bottom which matches the sample in color. In the top panel of the figure, the correct choice is B; in the bottom panel, it is A.*

5.20 The same-different problem *(After A. Premack, 1976)*

that alternative which matches the sample. Suppose that alternatives are a triangle and a square. If so, the triangle is correct if the sample is a triangle; conversely, if the sample is a square. This procedure is called **matching to sample** (Figure 5.19). There is little doubt that virtually all vertebrates can be taught to match if they are given enough trials to learn. Pigeons can be trained to peck at a green rather than a yellow key if the sample is green, and to peck at the yellow key if the sample is yellow. But does that mean that they understand what sameness means?

The question is whether they somehow understand that the relation between two red keys is the same as the relation between two equal tones or two identical triangles; that in all cases, the two items are the same. To test whether the animal has this abstract concept of sameness, we have to determine whether there is any transfer from one matching-to-sample situation to another one in which the particular stimulus items are quite different. Take the pigeon that has learned to match green-green. Does this training facilitate learning to match red-red, or better yet, triangle-triangle? By and large, the answer seems to be no (Premack, 1978; but see also Zentall and Hogan, 1974). It can recognize that two reds are the same. But it does not recognize that this sameness is the identical relation that exists between two other equal stimulus items.

The situation is quite different in chimpanzees. Having matched to sample on only three prior problems, Sarah and a few other animals readily handled new problems, performing perfectly on the very first trial. Even more impressive is the fact that Sarah learned two new words to indicate *same* and *different.* She was first shown two identical objects, such as two cups, and was then given a token whose intended meaning was *same.* Her task was to place this *same* token between the two cups. She was then presented with two different objects, such as a cup and a spoon, was given yet another token intended to mean *different,* and was required to place this *different* token between the cup and the spoon. After several such trials, she was tested with several pairs of items, some identical and some different, and had to decide whether to place the *same* or the *different* token between them (Figure 5.20).

With time, the tests became more sophisticated. Eventually the experimenters taught Sarah a question format. A token was invented that served as a question mark; it required Sarah to pick an answering token from among

Means *same*

Means *different*

158

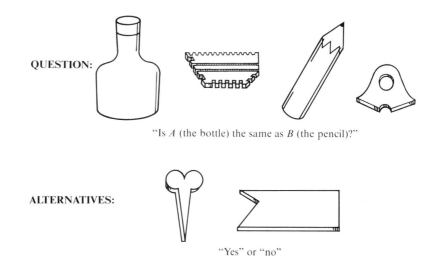

QUESTION:

"Is *A* (the bottle) the same as *B* (the pencil)?"

ALTERNATIVES:

"Yes" or "no"

5.21   Question-and-answer test for chimpanzees   *(After Premack, 1976)*

several available alternatives. Two other tokens became *yes* and *no*. This allowed Premack to ask his student questions such as the one shown in Figure 5.21. By and large, his pupil performed rather commendably.

Name of   Further evidence for abstract concepts is provided by Sarah's use of a token whose meaning is *name of.* The plastic word for *apple* was put side by side with an actual apple. Then Sarah was given the *name of* token which she had to place in between the two. After a number of such trials she caught on and was able to pick out the appropriate token of a (previously named) object when presented with that object (for instance, a cup), the *name of* token, and the token which served as a question mark (Figure 5.22).

5.22   The symbol "name of"   *These are combinations of tokens and real objects used to teach Sarah the proper use of the symbol "name of." (A) The symbol which means "name of" is placed between the token for apple (a triangle) and an actual apple. (B) The symbol "name of" is placed between the token for banana (a square) and an actual banana. (C) The "name of" symbol is combined with the symbol for "not" (a wedge-shaped token). These two combine to yield the symbol "not name of" which is placed between the token for banana and an actual apple. (After Premack and Premack, 1972)*

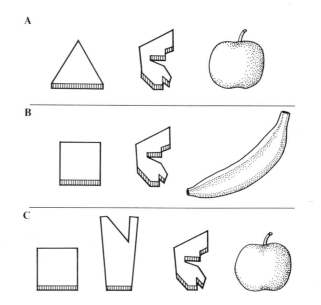

A

B

C

First- and second-order relationships   Such accomplishments show that chimpanzees can develop a way of thinking about the world that goes beyond the specific perceptual relations of the concrete moment. Like pigeons, they can of course respond to these concrete **first-order relationships** as Premack calls them—the relationships between, say, red and red, circle and circle, A-flat and A-flat. But unlike pigeons, chimpanzees can also deal with some **second-order relationships,** the relations that hold between the various first-order relationships. They can therefore recognize that the relation between red and red is identical to that between circle and circle, and for that matter between hippopotamus and hippopotamus—that in all of these the relation is *sameness*. Similarly for the abstract concept of *is the name of,* which also holds regardless of which particular token-object relation we are talking about.

Presumably humans are capable of yet higher levels of abstraction than are chimpanzees. Thus humans would surely be able to recognize certain **third-order relationships** among the tokens themselves. To give an example, consider various adjectives Sarah knows, such as *red* and *square*. Humans would have no trouble in noting that these words share one third-order relationship: They all describe an attribute—albeit a different one—that is found in many objects. This third-order relationship (which we describe with the label *adjective*) is different from that which characterizes the tokens for *give, take, insert,* and so on. All of these describe actions and we would call them verbs. Could Sarah learn to put the adjective tokens and the verb tokens into two different groups and describe each with its own supertoken? More important, could she apply these supertokens correctly after being taught certain new words, say, *bitter* and *climb,* indicating that she recognized their status as adjectives and verbs respectively? Thus far, the experiment has not been run so we don't know. The best guess is that Sarah will fail this test since many preschool children would probably fail it too. But even if she should pass, she will surely fail at some higher level of abstraction where humans—or at least adult humans—would not. Human intelligence can operate on *n*th-order abstract relationships that are very distant indeed from their perceptual base. Sarah knows the word for *square* and could probably be taught a token for *triangle*. But it is utterly certain that she could never attain the *n*th-order relationships that are implied in the Pythagorean statements about the squares of a triangle's sides.

ACCESSING WHAT ONE KNOWS

The formation and use of abstract concepts is certainly one of the characteristics of what we normally call intelligence. But it is not the only one. Another criterion is whether the animal has some **access** to its own intellectual operations.

Consider a pigeon who finds its way home over large distances. That bird is a brilliant navigator. It refers to the stars, to the sun, to a number of landmarks, and somehow calculates the correct path with remarkable accuracy. But we don't therefore regard the bird as especially intelligent. The reason is that we are convinced that it doesn't really know what it is doing. Its brain constitutes a marvelous navigational computer. But the bird can't use that computer for any purpose other than that for which it was installed by evolution. It has no access to its own intellectual machinery.

In this regard, the pigeon is quite different from a human being. At least to some extent, we do have access to our own mental functioning. We think and remember and know that we think and remember. And we can use these and other intellectual capacities very broadly. This access to our own intellectual functions is by no means total; as we will see later on, it is especially limited in childhood (see Chapters 9 and 10). Our present point is only that this access is one of the defining features of intelligent behavior and is a characteristic of that intellectual generalist, man (Rozin, 1976a).

Some recent studies by Premack and his collaborators suggest that intellectual access is not confined to humans. They showed Sarah several videotaped scenes of a trainer struggling with different problems. In one scene, he tried to reach a banana suspended high above him. In another, he vainly stretched his arm toward a banana on the floor outside of a cage. After Sarah saw the tapes, she was shown different photographs of the trainer engaged in one of several actions. In one picture he was climbing on a box, in another he was shoving a stick under the wire mesh of the cage, and so on. Sarah's job was to pick the photograph that depicted the appropriate problem solution. Thus, if she was first shown a scene in which the trainer struggled to reach an overhead banana, she had to choose the picture of a man stepping on a box. Sarah did quite well, succeeding in 21 out of 24 trials (Figure 5.23).

Sarah's success in this task suggests that the chimpanzee's problem-solving ability goes further even than Köhler had thought. To be sure, Sarah can solve a variety of spatial problems and can do so insightfully. But her ability may go beyond this. She not only solves problems, she also seems to know something *about* problem solving. She recognizes that the trainer has a problem, what this problem is, and how it should be solved. To this extent, she has some access to her own intellectual processes.

Reevaluating Behavior Theory

What is the upshot of the behavior theorists' efforts, which began with the studies of Pavlov and Thorndike some eighty years ago? They clearly uncovered some basic phenomena of human and animal behavior: the laws of classical and instrumental conditioning which, despite some recent qualifications, are still recognized as valid. What is much more debatable is the generality of these laws of learning. Behavior theorists had claimed that their formulations could account for all of learning and all of behavior. But it now appears that this claim was premature. Behavior theory seems to have overemphasized the role of blind, arbitrary learning and to have ignored the built-in tendencies that differentiate various species. As a result, it tends to overestimate the intellectual flexibility of comparatively lower animals. And it

5.23 Knowing about problem solving (A) End of brief videotaped segment showing Sarah's trainer reaching for bananas that are too high for him. (B) Two pictured alternatives. One shows the trainer stepping on a box. The other shows him reaching along the ground with a stick. Sarah tended to choose the picture that showed the correct solution; in the present case, the trainer stepping on top of the box. This suggests that she has some concept of what problem solving is, whether the problem is posed to her or to another organism. (After Premack and Woodruff, 1978)

likewise underestimates the kind of learning the primates, and especially humans, are capable of.

Many of the critiques of behavior theory hinge on the fact that animals—and of course, humans—are capable of cognition. Rats learn what leads to where in a maze, while chimpanzees solve problems insightfully and can acquire certain abstract concepts. Such phenomena suggest that psychological functions concern not just what animals and humans do but also what they *know*. This runs counter to behavior theory's primary emphasis, which is on overt action. That action must be a major focus of psychology goes without saying. But it should not be the only one. Knowledge and the ways in which it is acquired—that is, cognition—are no less important as subjects of psychological inquiry. And these are the topics which we take up next.

Summary

1. Whatever their many differences, Pavlov, Thorndike, Skinner, and their followers—here collectively described as *behavior theorists*—were all agreed that learning is essentially a blind and mechanical process. An important challenge to this view was Köhler's work on problem solving in chimpanzees. Köhler found that these animals often performed *insightfully*. His strongest evidence was that the apes showed wide and appropriate *transfer* when tested in novel situations.

2. A major difference between Köhler and many behavior theorists is in their conception of *what* animals learn. He believed that the presumed building blocks of behavior are not as molecular as early behaviorists assumed. An example is the stimulus to which the instrumental response is made. This is not equivalent to the physical stimulus presented by the experimenter, as shown by studies of *relevant and irrelevant dimensions* in discrimination learning that point to the role of *selective attention*.

3. Even more fundamental is Köhler's belief that what animals learn is best regarded as a change in what they *know* rather than (as behavior theorists assert) a change in what they *do*. Because of this emphasis on knowledge or *cognition*, Köhler and like-minded investigators such as Tolman, are called *cognitive theorists*. Evidence for cognition comes from phenomena such as *latent learning* which show that animals learn what is where, suggesting that they acquire *cognitive maps*. They also acquire expectancies, for they learn what leads to what, as shown by *frustration effects* following the receipt of a lesser reward than they had obtained previously.

4. Some authors have tried to reinterpret these and other troublesome phenomena in S-R terms. One such theoretical attempt concerns *avoidance learning*. This requires an animal to perform an instrumental response (for instance, jumping across a hurdle) to avoid an aversive event (for instance, electric shock) before it occurs. What is the reinforcement for this response? One answer is that it is the absence of an expected shock. But this won't do, for the term *expect* is incompatible with an S-R view. *Two-factor theory of avoidance* is an attempt to get around these difficulties while yet remaining within the S-R framework.

5. According to two-factor theory, avoidance learning is based on two learned components. One is *classical conditioning of fear*. The fear response (rapid heart beat) becomes connected to the stimulus that signals shock (a flashing light) because the animal has experienced that stimulus and shock-produced pain together. The second component is the *instrumental conditioning of the avoidance response*. Since fear is

aversive, its removal constitutes reinforcement. The instrumental response (jumping) gets the animal away from the warning stimulus (the light) and thus reduces the level of fear.

6. Critics of behavior theory dispute not only its views of *what* is learned but also its conceptions of *how* this learning is accomplished. One target of criticism is the assertion that conditioning depends on *contiguity* alone: of CS and UCS (in classical conditioning) and of response and reinforcement (in instrumental conditioning). Recent evidence suggests that the crucial factor is *contingency* rather than contiguity. In classical conditioning, the crucial factor is the extent to which CS *predicts* the occurrence of UCS.

7. Related effects have been found for instrumental conditioning. What matters here is the extent to which reinforcement is contingent upon the response. When this contingency is absent, the animal will learn that it has no *response control.* Threatening conditions in which there is no response control may engender *learned helplessness* which generalizes to other situations.

8. Still another criticism of behavior theory concerns its belief that the connections established by classical or instrumental conditioning are *arbitrary;* that is, independent of the relations between the elements to be connected. This view is challenged by the fact that certain CSs are more readily associated with some UCSs than with others, as shown by studies of *learned taste aversions* in rats. Similar effects occur in instrumental conditioning. Some responses are more readily strengthened by certain reinforcers than by others. Many animals can't learn an avoidance response unless it fits in with a *species-specific defense reaction,* such as flying in birds.

9. A final criticism of behavior theory is that it underestimates the intellectual capacity of higher species. Recent studies of monkeys and apes demonstrate that these animals can learn to respond to abstract, *conceptual* relationships. An example is provided by monkeys who acquire *learning sets.* Another example is symbol manipulation in chimpanzees. One chimpanzee has been taught a number of *second-order concepts* such as "same-different" and apparently has some *access* to its own cognitive operations.

PART II

Cognition

The approach to mental life we have considered thus far emphasizes action, whether natively given or modified by learning. It is an approach that always asks what organisms do and how they do it. We now turn to another approach to mental functioning that asks what organisms know and how they come to know it.

Both humans and many animals are capable of knowledge, though in our own species, knowing (or cognition*) is vastly more refined. We know about the world directly around us,* perceiving *objects and events that are in our here and now, like the rose that we can see and smell. We also know about events in our past at least some of which are stored in our* memory *and can be retrieved at some later time; the rose may fade, but we can recall what it looked like when it was still in bloom. Our knowledge can be transformed and manipulated by* thinking*; we can somehow sift and analyze our experiences to emerge with new and often abstract notions, so that we can think of the faded rose petals as but one stage in a reproductive cycle which in turn reflects the procession of the seasons. Finally, we can communicate our knowledge to others by the use of* language, *a uniquely human capacity which allows us to accumulate knowledge across the generations, each building upon the discoveries of the preceding.*

CHAPTER 6

Sensory Processes

To survive, we must know the world around us. For most objects in the world are charged with meaning. Some are food, others are mates, still others are mortal enemies. The ability to distinguish between these—say, between a log and a crocodile—is literally a matter of life and death. To make these distinctions, we have to use our senses. We must do our very best to see, hear, and smell the crocodile so that we can recognize it for what it is and can do so before it sees, hears, smells, and (especially) tastes and touches us.

The Origins of Knowledge

The study of sensory experience grows out of an ancient question: Where does human knowledge come from? Modern attempts to answer this question have their origins in the work of the English philosopher, John Locke (1632–1704). Locke is generally regarded as the founder of **British empiricism,** a school of thought that takes its name from its insistence that knowledge comes by way of (empirical) experience.

THE EMPIRICIST VIEW

Locke maintained that all knowledge comes through the senses. There are no innate ideas; at birth, the human mind is a blank tablet, a *tabula rasa* (a metaphor that goes back to Aristotle) upon which experience leaves its stylus marks.

Let us suppose the mind to be, as we say, a white paper void of all characters, without any ideas:—How comes it to be furnished? Whence comes it by that vast store which the busy and boundless fancy of man has painted on it with an almost endless variety? Whence has it all the materials of reason and knowledge? To this I answer, in one word, from *experience*. In that all our knowledge is founded; and from that it ultimately derives itself (Locke, 1690).

John Locke   *(Courtesy National Library of Medicine)*

Locke's view fit in well with the emerging liberalism that was the dominant sentiment of the rising middle classes during the eighteenth century. The merchants and manufacturers of Western Europe had little use for the hereditary privileges of a landed aristocracy or the divine right of kings to govern (and worse, to tax) as they chose. Under the circumstances, they readily grasped at any doctrine that proclaimed the essential equality of all men. If all men enter life with a *tabula rasa,* then all distinctions among them must be due entirely to a difference in their environments. By 1776 this basic conviction was found on both sides of the Atlantic. The men who signed the American Declaration of Independence held certain truths to be self-evident, among them "that all men are created equal."

Once the premises of empiricism are granted, the role of learning becomes paramount. If all knowledge comes through experience, then in principle, men and women should be infinitely perfectable by proper changes in their environment, especially through education. In our own century, this faith in the near-limitless plasticity of human beings is well illustrated by much of behavior theory (see Chapters 4 and 5). As John B. Watson, one of the founders of this approach, has put it,

Give me a dozen healthy infants, well-formed, and my own specified world to bring them up in and I'll guarantee to take any one at random and train him to become any type of specialist I might select—doctor, lawyer, artist, merchant-chief, and, yes, even beggar-man thief, regardless of his talents, penchants, tendencies, abilities, vocations, and race of his ancestors (J. B. Watson, 1925).

DISTAL AND PROXIMAL STIMULI

Given the assumption that all knowledge comes through the senses, it was natural enough to ask about the kind of knowledge that the senses can give us. What is the information that the senses receive? Consider vision. We look at a tree some distance away. Light reflected from the tree's outer surface enters through the pupil of the eye, is gathered by the lens, and is cast as an image upon the photosensitive region at the rear of the eye called the **retina.** The stimuli that are involved in this visual sequence can be described in either of two ways. We can talk about the **distal stimulus,** an object or event in the world outside, such as the tree. (This is typically at some distance from the perceiver, hence the term *distal.*) We can also talk about the **proximal stimulus,** the pattern of stimulus energies that takes its origin at the distal stimulus and finally impinges on a sensory surface of the organism (hence, the term *proximal*). In our example, this proximal stimulus would be the optical image the tree casts on the retina. As perceivers, our interest obviously centers upon the distal stimulus, the real object in the world outside. We want to know about the tree, not its retinal image. Our interest is in the tree's real size, its distance away from us, the kinds of leaves it has, and so on. But we can only learn

Bishop George Berkeley (*Detail from* The Bermuda Group *by John Smibert; courtesy Yale University Art Gallery, gift of Isaac Lothrop of Plymouth, Mass.*)

about the distal stimulus through the proximal stimuli to which it gives rise. There is no way of really seeing the tree out there without a retinal image of the tree. The same holds for the other senses. We can only smell a rotten egg (the distal stimulus) because of hydrogen sulfide molecules suspended in the air which eddies over the sensory cells in our nasal cavities (the proximal stimulus).

If the senses are the only portals we have to the world outside, the proximal stimuli are the only messengers that are allowed to pass information through them. Such heirs of Locke as Bishop George Berkeley (1685–1753) were quick to show that this fact has enormous consequences. For one thing, the sensory information provided by the proximal stimulus seems to lack many of the qualities that presumably characterize the external object (that is, the distal stimulus) to which this information refers.

Berkeley pointed out that we cannot tell the size of the physical object from the size of its retinal image. Our tree might be a miniature plant nearby or a giant one in the distance. By the same token, we cannot tell whether an object is in motion or at rest from its retinal image alone, for motion of the image may be caused by motion of the external object or by movements of the observer's eye. It appears that the knowledge that comes by way of the retinal image is very meager.

SENSATIONS

Considerations of this sort led the British empiricists to assume that the raw materials out of which knowledge is constructed are **sensations.** These are the primitive experiences that the senses give us and upon which we must then build. Green and brown are examples of visual sensations. An example of an auditory sensation would be a loud A-flat. An example of a gustatory (that is, taste) sensation would be a bitter taste. According to the empiricists, our perceptual experience is ultimately composed of such sensations—a mosaic of colored patches, tones of different pitch and loudness, sweets and sours, and so on.

Can this description possibly do justice to the richness of our perceptual world? The fact is that we do see trees (and innumerable other objects) and not mere patches of green and brown. While Bishop Berkeley might argue that our vision cannot inform us about depth or true size, in actual life we seem to have little difficulty in telling how far an object is away from us. (Were it otherwise, every automobile would become a wreck within minutes of leaving the showroom.) And we can in fact perceive the true size of an object. After all, even Berkeley would have had little trouble in distinguishing between a tiger in the distance and a kitten close by.

How did the empiricists reconcile these facts with their assumptions about the nature of sensation? Their answer was learning.

THE ROLE OF ASSOCIATION

The empiricists assumed that the organized character and the meaningfulness of our perceptual world are achieved by prior experience. The key to this accomplishment was held to be **association,** the process whereby one sensation is linked to another. The basic idea was very simple: If two sensations occur

169

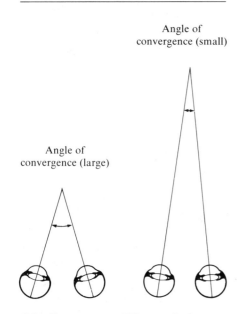

Angle of
convergence (small)

Angle of
convergence (large)

6.1 Convergence *When we look at an object, our eyes turn so as to converge upon it. The closer the object is to us, the more the eyes will have to turn, thus producing a larger angle of convergence. This angle of convergence may then provide some information about the object's distance. (After Coren, Porac, and Ward, 1978)*

together often enough, eventually one of them alone will evoke the idea of the other. According to the empiricists, associative linkage was the cement that bound the separate components of the perceptual world to each other. Complex ideas were thought to be combinations of simpler ones joined together by association.*

An example of how the associative principle was applied to problems of perception is Berkeley's explanation of perceived depth. In his view, the perception of distance is not directly based upon vision but results rather from associations between certain visual signs (which later psychologists called **cues**) and sensations of touch and motor movement. Consider **convergence,** the angular motion of the two eyes as they focus upon an object. The closer the object, the more the eyes will swivel toward each other; the farther the object is removed, the more they will approach a parallel position (Figure 6.1). Is this enough for the perception of distance? Berkeley thought not. He agreed that we could sense the angle of convergence, but how could we know that such and such an angle meant such and such a distance? This knowledge had to be provided by experience (Berkeley, 1709).

According to Berkeley, the important events date back to the crib. The infant reaches out for various objects, such as a toy. Sometimes the toy is close by; if so, a small arm movement is enough to grasp it. Sometimes the toy is farther off; the infant must then reach farther out. In both cases, the arm (and leg) movements are preceded by a particular angle of convergence. If the angle is sharp and inward (toy nearby), the subsequent arm movement will be small. If the two eyes are closer to a parallel position (toy far), the arm will extend farther out. This state of affairs will occur again and again, finally forging an association between particular sensations of convergence and the memory of certain reaching movements. Eventually, the child no longer has to reach for an object to know how far it is away. She sees it, senses a given angle of convergence, and remembers a certain reaching movement. It is this memory that is the basis of the distance we perceive visually according to Berkeley.

Berkeley was well aware that there were cues for distance other than sensations of convergence. Some of these had been noted by the painters of the Renaissance who discovered several techniques for rendering a three-dimensional world on a two-dimensional canvas. Among them was **linear perspective;** objects appear to be farther away as they decrease in size (Figure 6.2). To Berkeley, the explanation was again a matter of prior association. Visual cues of perspective generally precede reaching or walking; eventually, the visual cue alone will produce the memory of the appropriate movement and thus the experience of depth.

THE NATIVIST REJOINDER

The empiricist view was soon challenged. The most influential rejoinder came from the German philosopher Immanuel Kant (1724–1804) who argued that knowledge cannot come from sensory input alone; there must also be certain preexisting "categories" according to which this sensory material is ordered

---

* It is obvious that the notion of association is at the root of many of the theories of learning we have described in previous chapters. For instance, Pavlov's conceptions of classical conditioning are in many ways derived from the views of the early associationists.

6.2 The use of linear perspective in Renaissance art. *The School of Athens by Raphael, 1509–11. (Courtesy Stanza della Segnatura, Vatican [*St. Louis*])*

Immanuel Kant (Courtesy National Library of Medicine)

and organized. Examples are space, time, and causality—categories which, according to Kant, are ***a priori,*** built into the mind (or, as we would now say, into the nervous system). In Kant's view, there was no way in which we can see the world except in terms of these categories. It is as if we looked at the world through colored spectacles that we can never take off; if they are red, then redness is necessarily a part of everything we see. A position like Kant's is often called ***nativism*** since it holds that various aspects of our perception of the world are natively given, in contrast to empiricism which argues for an enormously greater role of learning.

Of course neither nativism nor empiricism can exist in absolute, pure form. Ultimately, the structure of our perceptual world surely depends upon both "nature" (our innate endowment) and "nurture" (learning). What is at issue is the *relative* contribution of these two factors.

Psychophysics

Given the assumption that all knowledge comes through the senses, it is hardly surprising that later investigators directed more and more effort toward discovering how these senses function. Their question can be stated very simply. What is the chain of events that begins with a stimulus and leads up to reports such as "a bitter taste," a "dull pressure," or a "brightish green." The details of this sequence are obviously very different for the different senses. Vision differs from hearing, and both differ from taste—in the stimuli that normally excite them, in their receptors, in the qualities of their sensations.

171

Even so, we can analyze the path from stimulus to sensory experience in quite similar ways, whatever the particular sense may be.

In all cases, one can crudely distinguish three steps in the sequence. First, there is the proximal stimulus. Second, there is the neural chain of events that this stimulus gives rise to. The stimulus is translated (technically, **transduced**) into the only language that all neurons understand, the nervous impulse. Once converted into this form (typically by specialized receptor cells), the message is transmitted farther and often is modified by other parts of the nervous system. Third, there is some sort of psychological response to the message, often in the form of a conscious, sensory experience (or sensation).

The sensory sequence can be looked at from several points of view. One concerns the **psychophysical** relations between some property of the (physical) stimulus and the (psychological) sensory experience it ultimately gives rise to, quite apart from the intervening neural steps. Another approach concerns the **psychophysiology.** Here the questions concern the neural consequences of a given stimulus input—how it affects the receptors and the neural structures higher up in the brain. For now, we will confine our discussion to psychophysical matters, leaving psychophysiological issues for later on.

The object of **psychophysics** is to relate the characteristics of physical stimuli to attributes of the sensory experience they produce. There are a variety of stimuli to which the human organism is sensitive. They include chemicals suspended in air or dissolved in water, temperature changes on the skin, pressure on the skin or within various parts of the body, pressure in the form of sound waves, and electromagnetic radiations within the visible spectrum. In each case, the sensory system will not respond unless the stimulus energy is above some critical level of intensity, the so-called **absolute threshold.**

The range of stimuli to which a given sensory system reacts is actually quite limited. Human sight is restricted to the visible spectrum and human hearing to sound waves between 20 and 20,000 hertz (that is, cycles per second). But there are many organisms that respond to different ranges of stimulation and thus see and hear a world different from ours. Many insects see ultraviolet light, while dogs and cats hear sound waves of much higher frequency than we can. The bat has carried high-frequency hearing to a point of exquisite perfection. As it glides through the night it emits high-pitched screams of about 100,000 hertz which are used as a kind of sonar. They bounce off small objects in the air such as insects, echo back to the bat, and thus enable it to locate its prey.

SENSORY QUALITY

The different senses obviously produce sensations of different quality. For example, the sensations of pressure, A-flat, orange, or sour clearly belong to altogether different sensory domains (technically, to different **sense modalities).** To what factor shall we ascribe these differences in experienced quality? Is it the difference in the stimuli that produce these sensations? In 1826, the German physiologist Johannes Müller (1801–58) argued that this answer was false. To be sure, visual sensations are usually produced by light waves, but occasionally other stimuli will serve as well. Strong pressure on the eyeballs leads us to see rings or stars (to the chagrin of boxers and the delight of cartoonists). Similarly, we can produce visual sensations by electric stimulation of various parts of the nervous system. Such facts led Müller to formulate his famous *doctrine of specific nerve energies.** According to this law, the differences in experienced quality are caused not by differences in the stimuli but by the different nervous structures which these stimuli excite, most likely in centers higher up in the brain. Thus, were we able to rewire the nervous system so as to connect the optic nerve to the auditory cortex and the auditory nerve to the visual cortex we might be able to see thunder and hear lightning.

Some of Müller's successors extended his doctrine to cover qualitative differences within a given sense modality. For example, blue, green, and red are qualitatively different even though all three are colors. To the heirs of Müller, such a qualitative difference could only mean one thing: There had to be some decisive difference in the neural processes that underlie these different sensations, perhaps at the level of the receptors, perhaps higher up. This belief ultimately led to some fundamental discoveries about the physiological basis of various sensory experiences, such as color and pitch (Boring, 1942).

SENSORY INTENSITY

Measuring the magnitude of a stimulus is in principle easy enough. We measure the physical stimulus energy—in pounds, in degrees centigrade, in footcandles, in decibels, or whatever. But matters become more difficult when we try to assess *psychological intensity,* the magnitude of a sensation rather than that of a stimulus.

MEASURING SENSORY INTENSITY

Gustav Theodor Fechner (1801–87), the founder of psychophysics, believed that sensations cannot be measured directly. In his view, sensations and the stimuli that produce them belong to two totally different realms—to use the terms many philosophers employ, that of the body and that of the mind. If this is so, how can one possibly describe them by reference to the same yardstick? Fechner recommended a roundabout way. He argued that while sensations can't be compared to physical stimuli, they can at least be compared to each other. A subject can compare two of his own sensations and judge whether the two are the same or are different.

Consider the sensation of visual brightness produced by a patch of light projected on a certain part of the eye. We can ask, what is the minimal amount by which the original light intensity of the patch must be increased so that the subject experiences a sensation of brightness *just* greater than the one he had before. This amount is called the *difference threshold.* It produces a *just-noticeable difference,* or *j.n.d.* The j.n.d. is a psychological entity, for it describes a subject's ability to discriminate. But it is expressed in the units of the physical stimulus that produced it. (In our example, this would be millilamberts, a unit of illumination.) Fechner had found an indirect means to relate sensory magnitude to the physical intensity of the stimulus.

Before proceeding we should note that the absolute threshold may be con-

Gustav Theodor Fechner (Courtesy National Library of Medicine)

* Müller used the term *energy* for what we now call *quality.*

sidered as a special case of a difference threshold. Here the question is how much stimulus energy must be added to a zero stimulus before the subject can tell the difference between the old stimulus ("I see nothing") and the new ("Now I see it").

Fechner's methods　The specific procedures Fechner devised to determine thresholds were all based on recording subjects' same-or-different judgments. Fechner and his successors generally took a large number of such judgments, for they believed that the threshold (whether absolute or difference) fluctuates from moment to moment. This might be because of changes in the responsiveness of receptor cells or because of shifts in what the subject attends to. Whatever the cause, these fluctuations force us to treat the threshold as a statistical average of many measurements.

One of Fechner's procedures is called the **method of limits.** Our example will use weights. The subject is asked to lift two weights on each trial, the **standard stimulus** (say, 100 grams,) and one of a series of **comparison stimuli** (ranging from, say, 92 to 108 grams in steps of 2 grams). The subject's task is to indicate whether the first weight feels lighter than, equal to, or heavier than the second. This procedure is repeated many times, sometimes starting with the lightest weight and working up, sometimes starting with the heaviest and working down. Our interest is in the two points where the subject's judgments shift, first, from "lighter" to "equal," and then from "equal" to "heavier." These two points represent the upper and lower limits of an **uncertainty interval.** This interval is comprised of two different thresholds—the number of grams that has to be added to create a just noticeably heavier weight and the number that has to be subtracted to yield a just noticeably lighter one.

The same method can be used for the determination of absolute thresholds. For example, subjects might be presented with tones of gradually increasing or decreasing intensity and asked to indicate whether they hear or don't hear the tone. The absolute threshold is then the average point at which the judgments shift from "Yes, I hear" to "No, I don't" and vice versa.

The Weber fraction　To Fechner, measuring j.n.d.s was only the means to a larger goal—the formulation of a general law relating stimulus intensity to sensory magnitude. He believed that such a law could be built upon an empirical generalization first proposed by the German physiologist E. H. Weber (1795–1878) in 1834. Weber proposed that the size of the difference threshold is a constant ratio of the standard stimulus. Suppose that we can just tell the difference between 100 and 102 candles burning in an otherwise unilluminated room. If Weber is right, we would be able to just distinguish between 200 and 204 candles, 400 and 408, and so forth. Fechner was so impressed with this relationship that he referred to it as **Weber's law,** a label by which we still know it. Put algebraically, Weber's law is usually written as

$$\frac{\Delta I}{I} = C$$

where ΔI is the increment in stimulus intensity (that is, the j.n.d.) to a stimulus of intensity I (that is, the standard stimulus) required to produce a just-noticeable increase, and where C is a constant. The fraction $\Delta I / I$ is often referred to as the **Weber fraction.**

Fechner and his successors performed numerous studies to determine

E. H. Weber　*(Courtesy National Library of Medicine)*

whether Weber's law holds for all of the sensory modalities. In a rough sort of way, the answer seems to be yes, at least for much of the normal range of stimulus intensity within each sense.* The nervous system is evidently geared to notice relative differences rather than absolute ones.

Weber's law allows us to compare the sensitivity of different sensory modalities. Suppose we want to know whether the eye is more sensitive than the ear. How can we tell? We certainly cannot compare j.n.d.s for brightness and for loudness. To mention only one problem, the values will be in different units—millilamberts for the first, decibels for the second. The problem is avoided if we consider the Weber fractions for the two modalities. If $\Delta I/I$ is small, the discriminating power of the sense modality is great; proportionally little must be added to the standard for a difference to be observed. The opposite holds when $\Delta I/I$ is large. It turns out that we are keener in discriminating brightness than loudness; the Weber fraction for the first is 1/62, for the second it is only 1/11. Weber fractions for other sense modalities are presented in Table 6.1.

Table 6.1 REPRESENTATIVE (MIDDLE-RANGE) VALUES FOR THE WEBER FRACTION FOR THE DIFFERENT SENSES

Sensory Modality	Weber fraction ($\Delta I/I$)
Vision (brightness, white light)	1/60
Kinesthesis (lifted weights)	1/50
Pain (thermally aroused on skin)	1/30
Audition (tone of middle pitch and moderate loudness)	1/10
Pressure (cutaneous pressure)	1/7
Smell (odor of India rubber)	1/4
Taste (table salt)	1/3

SOURCE: Schiffman, 1976.

FECHNER'S LAW

Weber's law indicated that the more intense the stimulus, the more the stimulus intensity has to be increased before the subject notices a change. By making a number of further assumptions, Fechner generalized Weber's finding to express a broader relationship between sensory and physical intensity. The result was ***Fechner's law*** which states that the strength of a sensation grows as the logarithm of stimulus intensity,

$$S = k \log I$$

where S stands for psychological (that is, subjective) magnitude, I for stimulus intensity, and k is a constant.

* Weber's law tends to break down at the two extremes of the intensity range, especially at the lower end (for example, for visual stimuli only slightly above absolute threshold). At these intensities, the Weber fraction is larger than it is in the middle range.

This law has been challenged on several grounds which are taken up in a special section at the end of this chapter (see the Appendix). For now, we only note that a logarithmic law such as Fechner's makes good biological sense. The range of stimulus intensities to which we are sensitive is enormous. We can hear sounds as weak as the ticking of a watch twenty feet away and as loud as a pneumatic drill operating right next to us. The same holds for vision. We can see a candlelight miles away if the night is clear but we can also see the brilliant white of an ocean beach at high noon. Our nervous system has to have a mechanism to compress this huge range into some manageable scope, and this is precisely what a logarithmic transformation does for us.

An Overview of the Senses

The development of psychophysical methods, coupled with various physiological techniques, gave psychology a powerful set of tools with which to study the various senses. Our primary focus will be on just one of these senses, namely vision. But before turning to the detailed study of visual sensation, we will cast a look at several other sensory systems that provide information about various aspects of the world and about our position within it.

KINESTHESIS AND THE VESTIBULAR SENSES

One group of senses informs the organism about its own movements and its orientation in space. Skeletal movement is sensed through **kinesthesis,** a collective term for information that comes from receptors in the muscles, tendons, and joints. Receptors in the joints tell the organism about the position of any part of the skeleton relative to another. Receptors in the muscles give information about the degree to which various muscle fibers are stretched. Their signals are the basis of a delicate control system for achieving different degrees of tension in any part of the musculature.

A different group of receptors signals the body's overall position in space. These receptors respond to the force of gravity and provide information about the orientation of the head. They are located within the two **inner ears** which are embedded in bone on both sides of the skull. The specific structures that contain these receptors are the **vestibules.** Each vestibule contains two main systems, the **vestibular sacs** and the **semicircular canals** (Figure 6.3). The vestibular sacs signal the position the head is in when at rest. The bottom of each vestibular sac contains small crystals which press down on hairlike receptor cells. As the head tilts, the crystals shift and so does the pressure exerted on the receptors.

The semicircular canals perform a different function; they signal rotation of the head. There are three such canals which lie in three roughly perpendicular planes. The canals contain a viscuous liquid that moves when the head rotates.

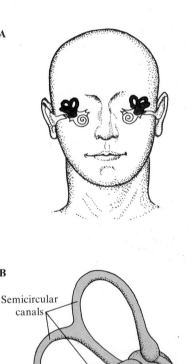

A

B

Semicircular
canals

Vestibular
sacs

6.3   The vestibular apparatus   (A) The location of the inner ear in the head. The vestibular canals are indicated in color, the rest of the inner ear is devoted to the sense of hearing. (After Krech and Crutchfield, 1958) (B) One of the two vestibular canal systems, with the three semicircular canals and two vestibular sacs. (After Mueller, 1965)

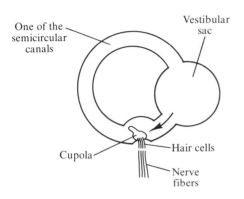

6.4   The action of the semicircular canals   *One of the semicircular canals. Each canal has an enlarged chamber which contains a sensory structure, the cupula. When the fluid contained within the canal is set in motion by head rotation it exerts pressure upon the cupula causing it to bend in one direction or another, depending upon the direction and force of the head rotation. This bending stimulates the hair cells at the base of the cupula, generating impulses which are then transmitted to the brain. (After Schiffman, 1976)*

This motion bends hair cells that are located at one end of each canal. These hair cells are part of the receptor system; when bent, they give rise to a neural impulse. The liquid's movement (and the consequent deformation of the hair cells) is most pronounced in the canal that lies closest to the plane in which the head's rotation takes place (Figure 6.4). Since there are three canals, the receptor discharge from them all provides an accurate description of the nature and extent of this rotation.

One vital function of the semicircular canal system is to provide a firm base for vision. As we walk through the world, our head moves continually. To compensate for this endless rocking, the eyes have to move accordingly. This adjustment is accomplished by a reflex system which automatically cancels each rotation of the head by an equal and opposite motion of the eyes. These compensatory eye movements are initiated by messages from the three semicircular canals which are relayed to the appropriate muscles of each eye. As a result, the visual system is effectively stable and can operate as if it rested on a solid tripod.

THE SENSE OF TASTE

The sense of taste has a simple function. It acts as a gatekeeper for the organism's digestive system in that it provides information about the substances that may or may not be ingested. Its task is to keep poisons out and usher foodstuffs in. In most land-dwelling mammals, this function is performed by specialized receptor organs, the *taste buds,* which are sensitive to chemicals dissolved in water. The average person possesses about 10,000 such taste buds, located mostly in the tongue, but also in other regions of the mouth.

TASTE SENSATIONS

Most investigators believe that there are four basic taste qualities: *sour, sweet, salty,* and *bitter.* In their view, all other taste sensations are produced by a mixture of these primary qualities. Thus grapefruit tastes sour and bitter, while lemonade tastes sweet and sour. One widely held hypothesis is that each of these primary taste qualities is associated with a different kind of taste receptor. In line with this view is the fact that the sensitivity of these qualities is not equally distributed throughout the tongue (Figure 6.5). For instance, thresholds for sweet are lowest at the tip of the tongue, while those for bitter and sour are lowest at the back and the sides respectively (Bartoshuk, 1971).

What are the stimuli that produce these four basic qualities? As yet, we don't have a full answer. Consider the experience "sweet." This is produced by various sugars, but also by saccharin, a chemical compound that is structurally very different from sugar. Just what these substances have in common so that they activate the same taste receptors is still unknown.

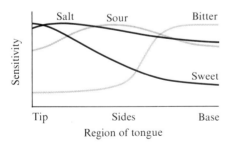

6.5   Taste sensitivity on different regions of the edge of the tongue   *The figure plots sensitivity of the four primary taste sensations: sweet, salty, sour, and bitter. Sweet is detected most readily at the tip of the tongue, bitter at its base, sour at the sides, with salty roughly equal throughout. This result is an argument for the view that these qualities are produced by different receptors that are distributed in different regions of the tongue. (After Boring, 1942)*

The sense of taste provides several illustrations of a rather pervasive principle that holds for most (perhaps all) of the other senses and which we will here call *sensory interaction.* This principle is based on the fact that a sensory system's response to any given stimulus rarely depends on that stimulus alone. It is also affected by other stimuli that impinge, or have recently impinged, upon that system.

One kind of interaction involves the effect of simultaneously presented stimuli. Suppose two regions of the tongue were stimulated by two different solutions. For example, one might be exposed to sucrose, another to ordinary table salt. The effect will be a form of contrast. The sweet taste produced by the sucrose will make the salt taste saltier (Bartoshuk, 1971).

A second kind of sensory interaction occurs over time. Suppose one taste stimulus is presented continuously for 15 seconds or more. The result will be *adaptation,* a phenomenon that is found in virtually all sensory systems. If a particular region of the tongue is continually stimulated with the identical taste stimulus, sensitivity to that taste will quickly decline. For example, after continuous exposure to a quinine solution, the quinine will taste less and less bitter and may finally appear to be completely tasteless. This adaptation process is reversible. If the mouth is rinsed out and left unstimulated for, say, half a minute, the original taste sensitivity will be restored in full.

Still another kind of interaction involves the relation between different sensory systems. This is especially clear in the realm of taste. The normal experience of tasting food involves many sensory experiences in addition to those provided by the taste buds; these include texture, temperature, and—most important of all—smell. When our nose is completely stuffed up by a bad cold, food appears to be without any flavor. While we can still experience the basic taste sensations, the aroma is lost and thus the food seems tasteless. If smell is gone, we can no longer distinguish between vinegar and a fine red wine or between an apple and an onion. A gourmet needs not only taste buds but also a sensitive nose.

THE SKIN SENSES

Stimulation of the skin informs the organism of what is directly adjacent to its own body. Not surprisingly, skin sensitivity is especially acute in those parts of the body that are most relevant to exploring the world that surrounds us directly: the hands and fingers, the lips and tongue. An important measure of this sensitivity is the *two-point threshold.* This is the minimum distance by which two pressure-producing stimuli must be separated so that a subject experiences two touch sensations rather than one. On the arms and legs, this two-point threshold is about forty millimeters, while it is only three millimeters on the index finger (Figure 6.6). These differential sensitivities are reflected in the organization of the cortical projection area for bodily sensations. As we have seen, the allocation of cortical space is quite unequal, with a heavy emphasis on such sensitive regions as face, mouth, and fingers (see Chapter 2).

How many skin senses are there? Aristotle believed that all of the sensations from the skin could be subsumed under just one rubric, that of touch. But

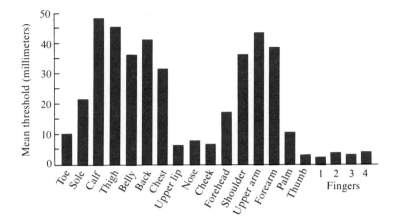

6.6 Skin sensitivity in different regions of the body *Two-point-thresholds—the minimum distance between two points pressing on the skin that yield two touch sensations rather than one—are lowest (and the sensitivities highest) for the face, hands, and fingers. (After Weinstein, 1968)*

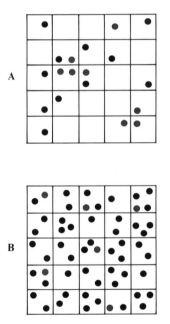

today we know that there are at least four different skin sensations: ***pressure, warmth, cold,*** and ***pain.*** The fact that these sensory qualities are so very different has led to the belief that they are produced by different underlying receptor systems. In support of this view is the finding that different spots on the skin are not uniformly sensitive to the stimuli which produce the various sensations. Suppose we draw a small grid on a part of a blindfolded subject's skin and then touch different squares of the grid with a hair, the tip of a warmed or cooled rod, or with a needle point. These stimuli presumably evoke sensations of pressure, warmth, cold, and pain respectively. By this means we can map the skin's sensitivity for these four sensory qualities. The results show that the four maps are not identical. Some spots are sensitive to pressure but not to warmth, others to warmth but not to pressure, and so on (Figure 6.7).

What are the receptors that correspond to these different sensations? For pressure, a number of different receptors have been discovered in the skin. Some of them are capsules made up of onionlike layers wrapped around a neuron. This capsule is easily bent by slight deformations of the skin and its bending fires the enclosed neuron. Less is known about the underlying receptor systems for temperature and pain.

Pain in particular has been the subject of much controversy. Some investigators believe that there are specialized pain receptors which are activated by tissue injury and produce an unpleasant sensation. Others hold that pain results from the overstimulation of any skin receptor. But whatever its receptor basis, there is little doubt that pain has a vital biological function. It warns the organism of potential harm. This point is vividly brought home by persons who have a congenital insensitivity to pain. On the face of it, the inability to experience this unpleasant sensation might seem to be a blessing, but nothing could be further from the truth. People who lack pain sensitivity often sustain

6.7 Sensitivity of different spots on the skin to warmth, cold, pressure, and pain *(A) A map of temperature sensitivity on a 1 centimeter square area of the upper arm. To determine warm spots (color), each location was gently touched with a very thin copper tip heated to 110 degrees Fahrenheit. To determine cold spots (black), the tip was cooled to 50 degrees Fahrenheit. As the map shows, the warm and cold spots do not coincide, some evidence for the view that these two temperature sensations are produced by different receptor systems. (B) A map of the sensitivity to pain and pressure on a 2.5 millimeter square area of the forearm. Pressure spots (color) were determined by a touch with a hair, pain spots (black) by a light prick with a needle. (After Boring, Langfeld, and Weld, 1939)*

extensive burns and bruises, especially in childhood; they never receive the first signals of danger so they don't withdraw the affected body parts. As a child, one such patient bit off the tip of her tongue while chewing food and sustained serious burns when she kneeled on a hot radiator. Another patient walked on a leg with a cracked bone until the bone broke completely (Melzack, 1973).

THE SENSE OF SMELL

Thus far, our discussion has centered on the sensory systems that tell us about objects and events close to home: the movements and position of our own body, what we put in our mouth, and what we feel with our skin. But we clearly receive information from much farther off. We have three main receptive systems that enlarge our world by responding to stimuli at a distance: smell, hearing, and vision. Of these, smell is in many ways the most primitive.

Smell, or to use the more technical term, **olfaction,** provides information about chemicals suspended in air which excite receptors located at the top of our nasal cavity (Figure 6.8). There is still considerable debate about the nature of the chemicals that act as olfactory stimuli and the way in which they set off the olfactory receptors. Several classification schemes exist for describing all odors by reference to a number of primary smell sensations, for example, *fragrant* (rose), *spicy* (cinnamon), and *putrid* (rotten egg). But as yet, there is no agreement about the underlying principle that makes certain chemicals arouse one of these olfactory experiences rather than another.

In any case, smell is a minor sense in humans. To be sure, it can warn us of impending danger as when we sniff escaping gas; it greatly adds to our enjoyment of food; and it provides the basis of the perfume and deodorant industries. According to some reports, it even helps to sell cars; used cars that are given a "new car" odor are said to bring a higher price (Wenger, Jones, and Jones, 1956). Nevertheless, smell is clearly less important to us than it is to many other species. In this regard, we are similar to our primate cousins and to birds in that these animals all left the odor-impregnated ground to move up into the trees, an environment in which other senses, especially vision, became more critical. In contrast, smell is of vital importance to many ground dwellers such as dogs. For them, it furnishes a guide to food and to receptive mates, and it may give warning against certain predators. Smell often provides the sensory basis whereby members of a species (and among many mammals, individuals within a species) recognize each other.

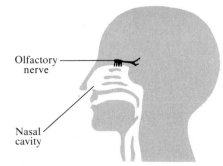

Olfactory nerve

Nasal cavity

6.8   The olfactory apparatus   *Chemicals suspended in the air that flows through the nasal passages stimulate olfactory receptors which connect with the olfactory nerve. (After Geldard, 1972)*

PHEROMONES

In a number of species, olfaction has a further function: It represents a primitive form of communication. Certain animals secrete special chemical substances called **pheromones** which trigger particular reactions in other members of their own kind. Some pheromones affect reproductive behavior. In many mammals, the female secretes a chemical (often in the urine) that signals that she is sexually receptive. This arouses the male, but only if his sense of smell is functioning. If his olfactory sense is surgically destroyed, he shows no sign of sexual interest (Gleason and Reynierse, 1969). In some species, the male sends chemical return messages to the female. For example, boars apparently secrete a pheromone which renders the sow immobile so that she stands rigid during mating (Michael and Keverne, 1968).

Other pheromones signal alarm. It appears that some animals can smell danger. To be more exact, they can smell a substance secreted by members of their own species who have been frightened. An experimental demonstration comes from a study of laboratory rats trained to press a bar in a Skinner box. While the rats worked on the bar, a whiff of air was introduced into the box. This air came from the vicinity of either of two groups of rats, one from a group which suffered electric shock and the other from a group which did not. The air sample from the shocked group seriously disrupted the trained animals' bar-pressing performance; the air from the unshocked group had no effect. The rats who suffered pain presumably exuded a chemical which alarmed their fellows in the experimental chamber (Valenta and Rigby, 1968).

Are there pheromones in humans? There may be some vestigial remnants. One line of evidence comes from olfactory thresholds to certain musklike substances. Sexually mature women are vastly more sensitive to the smell of these compounds than are men or sexually immature girls. This sensitivity fluctuates with the menstrual cycle, reaching a peak when the level of the female hormone estrogen is at its maximum. Musklike odors characterize the sex pheromones secreted by the males of several mammalian species. An intriguing speculation is that the human female's greater sensitivity to this odor points to the existence of a human male sex pheromone. This pheromone may be in our evolutionary past. It may also be still present, though in greatly attenuated form, and in any case masked by the application of modern deodorants (Vierling and Rock, 1967).

HEARING

The sense of hearing, or *audition,* is a close relative of other receptive senses that react to mechanical pressure, such as the vestibular senses or touch. Like these, hearing is a response to pressure, but with a difference—it informs us of pressure changes in the world that may take place many meters away. In effect, then, hearing is feeling at a distance.

SOUND

What is the stimulus for hearing? Outside in the world there is some physical movement which disturbs the air medium in which it occurs. This may be an animal scurrying through the underbrush or a rock dropping from a cliff or a set of vibrating vocal cords. The air particles directly adjacent to the movement are agitated, push particles that are ahead of them, and then return to their original position. Each individual air particle moves back and forth for just a tiny bit, but this is enough to set up a series of successive pressure variations in the air medium. These travel in a wave form analogous to the ripples set up by a stone thrown into a pond. When these *sound waves* hit our ears, they initiate a set of further mechanical pressure changes which ultimately trigger the auditory receptors. The reaction of these receptors is then eventually interpreted by the brain as something that is heard rather than felt.

181

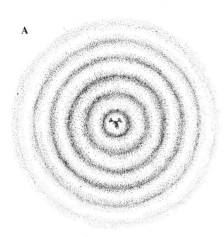

A

B

Wavelength

Amplitude

6.9 The stimulus for hearing *(A) depicts a momentarily frozen field of vibration in air. An insect vibrating its wings rapidly leads to waves of compression in the surrounding air. These waves travel in all directions like ripples in a pond into which a stone has been thrown. (B) The corresponding wave pattern is shown in simplified form. The amplitude of the wave is the height of each crest; the wavelength is the distance between successive crests. (From Gibson, 1966)*

Sound waves can vary in both *amplitude* and *wavelength.* Amplitude refers to the height of a wave crest: the greater the intensity of the vibration, the higher this crest will be. Wavelength is simply the distance between successive crests. Investigators in the field of audition usually describe sound waves by their *frequency,* which is the number of waves per second. Since the speed of sound is constant within any given medium, frequency is inversely proportional to wavelength (Figure 6.9).

Both amplitude and frequency are physical dimensions. Our brain translates these into the psychological dimensions of *loudness* and *pitch.* Roughly speaking, a sound will appear to be louder as its amplitude increases and will appear more high-pitched as its frequency goes up.

Amplitude and loudness The range of sound amplitudes to which humans can respond is enormous. Investigators have found it convenient to use a scale which compresses this unwieldy range into a more convenient form. This scale describes sound intensities in *decibels* (Table 6.2). Perceived loudness approximately doubles every time the physical intensity goes up by 10 decibels (Stevens, 1955).

Table 6.2 INTENSITY LEVELS OF VARIOUS COMMON SOUNDS

Sound	Intensity level (decibels)
Manned spacecraft launching (from 150 feet)	180
Loudest rock band on record	160
Pain threshold (approximate)	140
Loud thunder; average rock band	120
Shouting	100
Noisy automobile	80
Normal conversation	60
Quiet office	40
Whisper	20
Rustling of leaves	10
Threshold of hearing	0

Frequency and pitch The frequency of a sound wave is generally measured in *hertz,* or waves per second, (so called after the nineteenth-century German physicist Heinrich Hertz). The highest note on the piano has a frequency of 4,180 hertz, the lowest one of 27.5 hertz, with middle C at 261.6 hertz. Young adults can hear tones as low as 20 hertz and as high as 20,000 hertz, with maximal sensitivity to a middle region in between. As people get older, their sensitivity to sounds declines, especially at the higher frequencies.

Simple and complex waves Thus far we have only dealt with simple wave forms. These are made up of waves that have only one frequency. Such waves are very rare in nature; they are produced by special electronic devices or by tuning forks. When such simple waves are expressed graphically, with pressure change plotted against time, they yield curves that correspond to the plot of the trigonometric sine function. Accordingly, such curves are called *sine waves* (Figure 6.10).

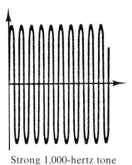

| Weak 100-hertz tone | Strong 100-hertz tone | Weak 1,000-hertz tone | Strong 1,000-hertz tone |

6.10   Simple wave forms vary in frequency and amplitude   *Simple sound waves can be graphically expressed by plotting air-pressure change over time. The result is a so-called sine curve. These curves show the sine waves for a weak and a strong 100-hertz tone (relatively low in pitch) and a strong and a weak 1,000-hertz tone (comparatively high pitch). (After Thompson, 1973)*

The sounds encountered in normal life are virtually never as simple as this. Instead, they are composed of many different waves, which differ in both frequency and amplitude. An example is this (relatively simple) **complex wave:**

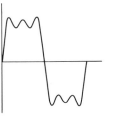

The complex wave is physically produced by the acoustic mixture of three simple sine waves:

The important point is that the auditory system can analyze the complex wave into its component parts. We can hear the separate notes that make up a chord; the tones are mixed but we can unmix them. This ability to sort out the component parts of a complex wave form has its limits. If the sound is made up of a great number of unrelated waves, it is perceived as **noise,** which we can no longer analyze (Figure 6.11).

Explosion

6.11   An irregular sound wave—an explosion   *As in the previous figures, pressure change is plotted against time; but now there is no more regularity, so the wave form cannot readily be analyzed into its simpler components. (From Boring, Langfeld, and Weld, 1939)*

183

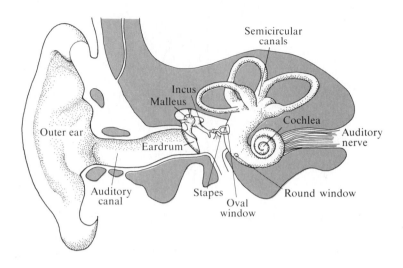

6.12 **The human ear** *Air enters through the outer ear, stimulates the eardrum which sets the ossicles in the middle ear in motion. These in turn transmit their vibration to the membrane of the oval window which causes movement of the fluid in the cochlea of the inner ear. Note that the semicircular canals are anatomically parts of the inner ear. (After Lindsay and Norman, 1977)*

THE EAR AS AN ACCESSORY DEVICE

Most of the ear is made up of various accessory structures whose function is to conduct and amplify sound waves so that they can affect the auditory receptors (Figure 6.12). Sound waves collected by the external ear are funneled toward a taut membrane which they cause to vibrate. This is the **eardrum** which transmits its vibrations across an air-filled cavity, the **middle ear,** to another membrane, the **oval window,** that separates the middle from the **inner ear.** This transmission is accomplished by way of a mechanical bridge built of three small bones connected by ligaments: the **malleus** (hammer), **incus** (anvil) and **stapes** (stirrup), collectively known as the **ossicles.** The vibrations of the eardrum move the malleus, which then moves the incus, which in turn moves the stapes, which completes the chain by imparting the vibratory pattern to the oval window to which it is attached. The movements of the oval window set up waves in a fluid which fills the **cochlea,** a coiled tube in the inner ear which contains the auditory receptors.

Why did nature choose such a roundabout method of sound transmission? The major reason is that the cochlear medium is a fluid which like all liquids is harder to set into motion than air. To overcome this difficulty, the physical stimulus must be amplified. This amplification is provided by various features of the middle-ear organization. One involves the relative sizes of the eardrum and of that portion of the oval window which is moved by the stapes; the first is about twenty times larger than the second. The result is the transformation of a fairly weak force that acts on the entire eardrum into a much stronger force concentrated upon the (much smaller) oval window.

TRANSDUCTION IN THE COCHLEA

What happens in the cochlea when the oval window is set into motion? To deal with this question, we need some more anatomy. Throughout most of its length the cochlea is divided into an upper and a lower section by several structures including the **basilar membrane.** The auditory receptors are **hair cells**

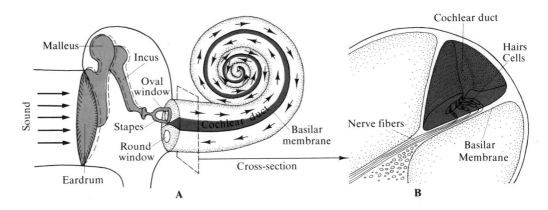

6.13 *Detailed structure of the middle ear and the cochlea* *(A) Movement of the fluid within the cochlea deforms the basilar membrane and stimulates the hair cells that serve as the auditory receptors. (After Lindsay and Norman, 1977) (B) Cross-section of the cochlea showing the basilar membrane and the hair cell receptors. (After Coren et al., 1978)*

which are lodged between the basilar membrane and other membranes above it. Motion of the oval window produces pressure changes in the cochlear fluid which lead to deformations of the basilar membrane. Such deformations bend the hair cells and provide the immediate stimulus for their activity (Figure 6.13).

THE PERCEPTION OF PITCH

The preceding discussion has given a general idea of how sound waves lead to the excitation of auditory receptors. But another question comes up immediately. How does this receptor discharge lead to different sensory qualities? In hearing, the relevant quality is *pitch* which depends upon the frequency of the stimulating sound wave. Pitch is a matter of quality and not of intensity. Consider the difference between, say, A-flat and C-sharp. To say that one tone sounds "lower" than the other is *not* to say that it appears either stronger or weaker. The question is how the auditory system deals with sound frequency to give rise to the experience of pitch.

Basilar place and pitch According to the *place theory* of pitch, first proposed by Hermann Helmholtz, different parts of the basilar membrane are responsive to different sound frequencies. In Helmholtz' view, the nervous system will then interpret basilar place as pitch. The stimulation of receptors at one end of the membrane will lead to the experience of a high tone, while that of receptors at the other end leads to the sensation of a low tone.

Today we know that Helmholtz was correct, at least in part. Much of the relevant evidence comes from the work of Georg von Békésy (1899–1972) whose studies of auditory function won him the Nobel Prize in 1961. Some of Békésy's experiments utilized cochleas taken from fresh human cadavers. Békésy removed part of the cochlear wall so that he could actually see (through a microscope) what happened to the basilar membrane when the oval window was vibrated. For a stimulus, he used a small electrically pow-

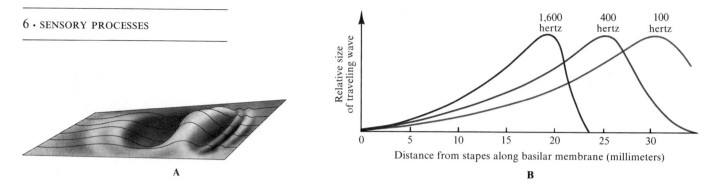

6.14   The deformation of the basilar membrane by sound   *(A) In this diagram, the membrane is schematically presented as a simple, rectangular sheet. In actuality, of course, it is much thinner and coiled in a spiral shape. (B) The relation between sound frequency and the location of the peak of the basilar membrane's deformation. The peak of the deformation is located at varying distances from the stapes (that sets the membrane in motion by pushing at the oval window). As the figure shows, the higher the frequency of the sound, the closer to the stapes this peak will be. (After Lindsay and Norman, 1977; Coren et al., 1978)*

ered piston (which here took the place of the stapes). He observed that such stimulation led to a wavelike motion of the basilar membrane (Figure 6.14A). When he varied the frequency of the vibrating stimulus, the peak of this deformation occurred in different regions of the basilar membrane: high frequencies corresponded to regions close to the oval window, low ones to regions close to the cochlear tip (Figure 6.14B; Békésy, 1957).

Sound frequency and frequency of neural firing   The place theory of pitch faces a major difficulty, however. When the sound frequency is low enough, say, below 400 hertz, the traveling wave set up by the tone deforms the entire membrane equally. In this case, all receptors will be equally excited. But since we can discriminate low frequencies down to about 20 hertz, there must be a second mechanism (in addition to basilar location) whereby pitch is sensed by the nervous system.

It is generally believed that this second mechanism for sensing pitch is related to the firing frequency of the auditory nerve. For lower frequencies the basilar membrane vibrates at the frequency of the stimulus tone and this vibration rate is then directly translated into the appropriate number of neural impulses per second, as evidenced by gross electrical recordings taken from the auditory nerve. The impulse frequency of the auditory output is further relayed to higher centers which somehow interpret it as pitch.

A further fact leads to some complications. A neuron cannot fire more often than about 1,000 times per second (see Chapter 2). While this would suggest that the impulse-frequency mechanism does not apply to tones higher than 1,000 hertz, its potential range has been extended to tones of still higher frequency by the **volley theory.** This proposes that impulse frequencies above 1,000 per second are generated by different squads of neurons, each of which is firing at a slightly different pace. For example, consider two neurons, both responding at a uniform rate of 1,000 impulses per second. If the second neuron starts to respond half a millisecond after the first, then the combined firing rate for both of them will be 2,000 impulses per second. In principle, this arrangement may allow even higher firing rates for the auditory nerve considered as a whole. Various lines of evidence suggest that some such mechanism may operate up to frequencies of about 4,000 hertz.

It appears then that pitch perception is based upon two separate mechanisms: higher frequencies are coded by the place of excitation on the basilar membrane, lower frequencies by frequency of the neural impulse (which may involve the volley principle). It is not clear where the one mechanism leaves off and the other takes over. Place of excitation probably has no role below about 400 hertz; impulse frequency has none for impulses above 4,000 hertz. It may well be that sound frequencies in between are jointly handled by both mechanisms (Green, 1976).

THE SENSES: SOME COMMON PRINCIPLES

In our discussion of the various senses, we have come across many ways in which they differ. We have also encountered a number of important phenomena that are not specific to any one sensory system but are found more generally.

First, in most sense modalities, the processing of external stimulus energies begins with various *accessory structures* which gather and amplify these physical energies and thereby fashion a "better" proximal stimulus for the receptors to work on. An example is provided by the semicircular canals which contain a liquid that is set in motion by head rotation and then stimulates the hair cell receptors of the vestibular system.

Second, in all sense modalities, the next step involves the receptors which achieve the *transduction* of the physical stimulus energy into a neural impulse. In some sensory systems, particularly hearing and vision, the nature of this transduction process is reasonably well understood. In other systems, such as smell, it is still unknown.

Third, the processing of stimulus input does not stop at the receptor level. There are typically further neural centers at which *coding* occurs. The stimulus information is coded (so to speak, translated) into the various dimensions of sensation that we actually experience. Some of these dimensions involve intensity. Thus in taste, we have more or less bitter, while in hearing we have more or less loud. Other dimensions involve differences in quality. In taste, we have the differences between bitter, sweet, sour, and salty. In hearing, we have differences in pitch.

Fourth, any part of a sensory system is in *interaction* with the rest of that system. This process of interaction pertains both to the immediate past and to present activity in neighboring parts of the system. We considered some examples of sensory interaction in the taste system, including the phenomena of adaptation (with continued exposure, quinine tastes less bitter) and taste contrast (sugar) on one side of the tongue makes salt on the other side taste saltier).

We now turn to a detailed discussion of vision, which in humans is the distance sense *par excellence*. The organization of this account will reflect the four characteristics just considered which are common to most of the senses. Specifically, we will (1) describe the eye as an accessory structure for gathering the visual stimulus, (2) examine the transduction of light energies by the visual receptors, (3) discuss a number of interaction processes found in vision, and (4) consider the coding processes that are involved in seeing color.

The Stimulus for Vision

Most visual sensations have their point of origin in some external (distal) object. Occasionally, this object will be a light source which *emits* light in its own right; examples (in rather drastically descending order of emission energy) are the sun, an electric light bulb, and a glow worm. All other objects can only give off light if some light source illuminates them. They will then *reflect* some portion of the light cast upon them while absorbing the rest.

LIGHT

The stimulus energy we call light comes from that relatively small band of radiations to which our visual system is sensitive. These radiations travel in a wave form which is somewhat analogous to the pressure waves that are the stimulus for hearing. This radiation can vary in its *intensity,* the amount of radiant energy in unit time, which is a major determinant of perceived brightness (as in two bulbs of different wattage). It can also vary in *wavelength,* the distance between the crests of two successive waves, which is a major determinant of perceived color. The light we ordinarily encounter is made up of a mixture of different wavelengths. The range of wavelengths to which our visual system can respond is the *visible spectrum,* extending from roughly 400 ("violet") to about 750 ("red") nanometers (1 nanometer = 1 millionth of a millimeter) between successive crests.

THE EYE

The next stop in the journey from stimulus to visual sensation is the eye. Except for the *retina,* none of its major structures has anything to do with the transduction of the physical stimulus energy into neurological terms. Theirs is a prior function: to fashion a proper proximal stimulus for vision, a sharp retinal image, out of the light that enters from outside.

Let us briefly consider how this task is accomplished. The eye has often been compared to a camera and in its essentials the analogy holds up well enough (Figure 16.5). Both eye and camera have a *lens* which suitably bends

6.15   Eye and camera   As an accessory apparatus for fashioning a sharp image out of the light that enters from outside, the eye has many similarities to the camera. Both have a lens for bending light rays to project an inverted image upon a light-sensitive surface at the back. In the eye a transparent outer layer, the cornea, participates in this light-bending. The light-sensitive surface in the eye is the retina, whose most sensitive region is the fovea. Both eye and camera have a focusing device; in the eye, the lens can be thickened or flattened. Both have an adjustable iris diaphragm. And both finally are encased in black to minimize the effects of stray light; in the eye this is done by a layer of darkly pigmented tissue, the choroid coat. (After Wald, 1950)

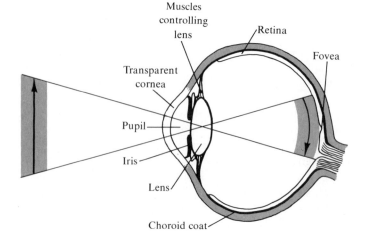

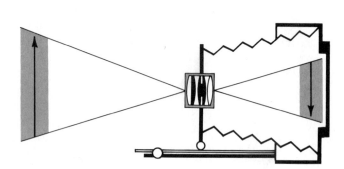

light rays passing through it and thus projects an image upon a light-sensitive surface behind—the film in the camera, the retina in the eye. Both have a focusing mechanism. In the eye this is accomplished by a set of muscles that changes the shape of the lens. It is flattened for objects at a distance and thickened for objects closer by, a process technically known as *accommodation.* Finally, both camera and eye, have a *diaphragm* which governs the amount of entering light. In the eye this function is performed by the *iris,* a smooth, circular muscle which surrounds the pupillary opening, and which contracts or dilates under reflex control when the amount of illumination increases or decreases substantially.

THE RETINAL IMAGE

The image of an object that falls upon the retina is determined by simple optical geometry. Its size will be inversely proportional to the distance of the object, while its shape will depend on its orientation. Thus a rectangle viewed at a slant will project as a trapezoid. In addition, the image will be reversed with respect to right and left and will be upside down.

The reversal of the retinal image was the subject of centuries of controversy that was not resolved until the time of Locke and Berkeley. How could we see the world as it really is if its retinal projection is upside down? Early students of vision, such as Leonardo da Vinci, were so preoccupied by this question that they assumed the existence of a further optical process within the eye which reverses the image once again and thus restores it to its erect position. No such re-reversal occurs but, as we now know, the issue is only a pseudo-problem. The inversion of the image will cause trouble if we think of the mind as a little person inside our head who looks at the image of the retina as if it were a television screen and who simultaneously sees the outside world directly. Then of course, the image would be seen as inverted, because it is indeed inverted with respect to the things outside. But in fact, all of our visual information comes from the retina, so there is no visual contradiction.

The Visual Receptors

We have arrived at the point where the path from distal object to visual sensation crosses the frontier between optics and psychophysiology—the transformation of the physical stimulus energy into a nervous impulse. We now consider the structures which accomplish this feat: the visual receptor organs.

THE RETINA

First, a few words about the anatomy of the retina. The retina is made up of several layers of nerve cells, one of which is the receptor layer. Microscopic inspection shows two kinds of receptor cells, whose names describe their different shapes—the *rods* and the *cones.* The cones are more plentiful in the *fovea,* a small roughly circular region at the center of the retina approximately

6.16   The visual angle   *The visual angle is measured in degrees and is determined by both the size of the distal object and the distance of that object from the eye. In the figure, object A is shorter than B but nearer to the eye. In this case, the sizes and distances are such that the two objects give rise to the same visual angle—and produce the same retinal size. Examples of visual angles include ½ degree for the sun and the moon, 2 degrees for a quarter held at arm's length, and 1/60 degree for a quarter at a distance of 90 yards. (Cornsweet, 1970)*

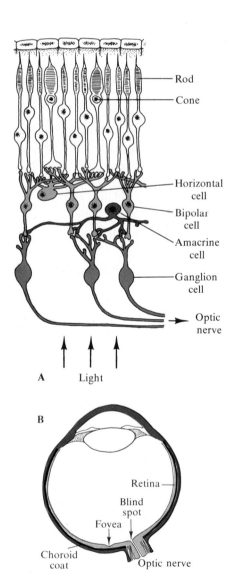

2 degrees in diameter. (Retinal distances are often expressed in terms of the so-called **visual angle;** Figure 16.16.) While very densely packed in the fovea, the cones occur with rapidly decreasing frequency the farther out one goes toward the periphery. The opposite is true of the rods; they are completely absent from the fovea and are more frequent in the periphery. In all, there are some 120 million rods and about 6 million cones.

The receptors do not report to the brain directly, but relay their message upward by way of two intermediate neural links—the **bipolar cells** and the **ganglion cells.** The bipolar cells are stimulated by the receptors. In the foveal region, each bipolar cell responds to only one cone. There is less privacy in the periphery where several receptors typically converge upon one bipolar cell. The last retinal layer consists of the ganglion cells which are excited by the bipolars. The axons of these ganglion cells are collected from all over the retina, converging into a bundle of fibers that finally leaves the eyeball as the **optic nerve.** The region where these axons converge contains no receptors and thus cannot give rise to visual sensations; appropriately enough, it is called the **blind spot** (Figure 6.17).

VISUAL ACUITY

One of the most important functions of the visual sense is to enable us to tell one object from another. A minimum precondition for doing so is the ability to distinguish between separate points that are projected on the retina so that we do not see a blur. The ability to make such distinctions is called **acuity.** It is measured by such devices as the optician's familiar eye chart or by asking a subject to identify the orientation of a ring that has a small gap in it. In the normal eye, the acuity threshold is about 1/60 of a degree, which corresponds to a separation of half an inch at a distance of 150 feet from the observer.

6.17   The retina   *(A) There are three main retinal layers: the rods and cones, which are the photoreceptors; the bipolar cells; and the ganglion cells whose axons make up the optic nerve. There are also two other kinds of cells, horizontal cells and amacrine cells, that allow for sideways (lateral) interaction. As shown in the diagram the retina contains an anatomical oddity. As it is constructed the photoreceptors are at the very back, the bipolar cells are in between, and the ganglion cells are at the top. As a result, light has to pass through the other layers (they are not opaque so this is possible) to reach the rods and cones whose stimulation starts the visual process. (After Coren et al., 1978) (B) The fovea is the region on the retina in which the receptors are most densely packed. The blind spot is a region where there are no receptors at all, this being the point where the optic nerve leaves the eyeball. (After Cornsweet, 1970)*

Under normal daylight conditions, acuity is greatest in the fovea, for it is there that the receptors are most closely bunched and thus provide the sharpest optical resolution. To "look at" an object means to move the eyes so that the image of that object falls upon both foveas. In peripheral vision we often see something without quite knowing what it is. To see it clearly, we swivel our eyes so that the image of the as yet unidentified something falls upon the foveal regions where our resolving power is greatest.

THE DUPLICITY THEORY OF VISION

The fact that rods and cones differ in structure suggests that they also differ in function. Some seventy years ago, this notion led to the development of the **duplicity theory of vision,** a theory that by now has the status of established fact. The essential idea is that rods and cones handle different aspects of the visual task. The rods are the receptors for night vision; they operate at low light intensities and lead to **achromatic** (colorless) sensations. The cones serve day vision; they respond at much higher levels of illumination and are responsible for sensations of color. The biological utility of such an arrangement becomes apparent when we consider the enormous range of light intensities encountered by organisms like ourselves who transact their business during both day and night. In humans, the ratio between the stimulus energy at absolute threshold and that transmitted by a momentary glance at the midday sun is 1 to 100,000,000,000. Evolution has evidently provided a biological division of labor, assigning two separate receptor systems to the upper and lower portions of this incredible range.

Several facts provide important evidence in support of the duplicity theory. Sensitivity to dim light is much greater in the periphery where rods are prevalent than in the center of the fovea where they are absent. This fact is familiar to sailors who know that the way to detect a faint star in the night sky is to look at it not directly, but to look off at an angle from where they think it might be. The quality of the visual sensation produced by such dim light is invariably achromatic, much like a black-and-white film. Related evidence comes from comparative anatomy. The retinas of nocturnal creatures such as mice, bats, and owls are largely made up of rods. The opposite holds for animals such as hens and pigeons, who rise with the sun, retire as it sets, and sensibly enough, possess nothing but cones. Two further phenomena complete the case for the duplicity theory: **spectral sensitivity** and **dark adaptation.**

Spectral sensitivity curves The human eye is insensitive to light waves shorter than about 350 and longer than about 750 nanometers. What is its sensitivity to the wavelengths in between? We know that photographic film (whether chromatic or achromatic) is more responsive to some regions of the visible spectrum than to others. Is the same true for the eye?

To answer this question, we ask subjects to detect a faint test light that is projected on a retinal region which contains mostly rods. The light can be independently varied in physical intensity and in wavelength. If the light is seen, it will necessarily appear gray, since only the rods are stimulated. The question is whether these rods are more sensitive to some wavelengths than to others.

To answer this question we determine the absolute thresholds for each separate wavelength. The result is the **spectral sensitivity curve** in which ab-

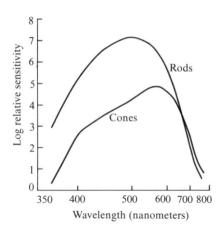

6.18 Sensitivity of rods and cones to light of different wavelengths *Sensitivity was measured by determining the threshold for different frequencies of light projected on retinal areas rich in rods or cones. Sensitivity was then computed by dividing 1 by the threshold (the lower the threshold, the greater the sensitivity). Since sensitivity varied over an enormous range, the range was compressed by using logarithmic units. Note first that the cones, overall, are less sensitive than the rods. Note also that the point of maximal sensitivity is different for the two receptor systems. The cone maximum (560 nanometers) is closer to yellow, the rod maximum (510 nanometers) closer to green. (After Cornsweet, 1970)*

solute threshold is plotted against wavelength (Figure 6.18). Maximal sensitivity is toward the short-wave region with a peak at about 510 nanometers.

What about the cones? We determine their spectral sensitivity by performing the same experiment, but now with the test patch at the fixation point and thus on the all-cone fovea (Figure 6.18). We immediately see that the cones have much higher absolute thresholds than do the rods. Equally important, their region of maximal sensitivity is toward the longer wavelengths, with a peak at about 560 nanometers (which is seen as a yellowish green). Rods and cones evidently differ in their relative sensitivity to different wavelengths. For rods, the blues are easier to detect than the yellows and reds (though of course they all appear gray); the opposite holds for the cones. This difference in relative sensitivity accounts for the so-called **Purkinje shift,** named after a nineteenth-century Czech physiologist who noticed that the relative brightness of reds and blues changes with the onset of twilight. Take a red rose and a blue aster that appear to be equally bright at noon; as dusk falls, the rose will look progressively darker compared to the aster. We increasingly shift from cone to rod vision as the illumination dims, and thus move from one region of maximal sensitivity to another.

The difference between the two spectral sensitivity curves is yet another argument in support of the duplicity theory. These curves presumably reflect some characteristic of the photochemical substances in the receptor cells which are altered more rapidly by some wavelengths than by others. Since the curves differ, we have reason to believe that the photochemicals differ also.

Dark adaptation   When we first enter a movie theater from a sunlit street we can barely find our seats, but we gradually adjust and eventually we see rather well. This phenomenon is called ***dark adaptation,*** an increased sensitivity to light following a period of darkness. The opposite effect occurs after an interval of light exposure. Now the eye becomes ***light adapted*** and grows insensitive to weaker light intensities.

Dark adaptation can be studied experimentally by measuring absolute thresholds after different periods spent in the dark. One experiment used a test patch of short-wave light which was projected on an area which contains both rods and cones (Figure 6.19). The most dramatic result is a tremendous increase in sensitivity. After thirty minutes in the dark, the subject can detect a light whose intensity is only 1/100,000 of that which was required before dark adaptation began.

An important further feature of the dark-adaptation curve is its shape. It is discontinuous, reaching a first plateau within five or ten minutes, and then sharply descending once again. This discontinuity further supports the duplicity theory. The first portion of the curve represents the dark adaptation of the cones, the second that of the rods. Proof comes from studies which varied retinal position. If the test patch is projected on a cone-free region well to the side of the fovea, the resulting dark-adaptation curve has no break in it and looks just like the second (that is, the rod-produced) segment of the usual

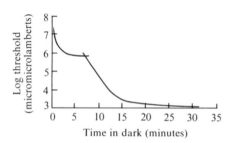

6.19   Dark adaptation   *The curve shows thresholds for light with increasing periods of time spent in the dark. The longer that time, the lower the threshold. This increase in sensitivity is called dark adaptation. Thresholds are here measured in micromicrolamberts, a unit of illumination; logarithmic units are again used to compress the huge range over which sensitivity changes. (After Hecht and Shlaer, 1938)*

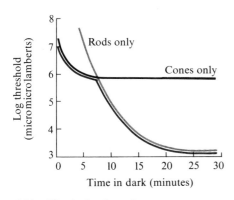

6.20 **The dark adaptation curve as a composite of two separate processes**
The figure shows separate dark adaptation curves for cones and rods. The black curve is for a light patch projected into the rod-free fovea and represents the cone-produced portion of the standard dark adaptation curve (as shown in Figure 6.19). The gray curve is for a light patch projected well off the fovea into a cone-free region and represents the rod-produced component of the standard adaptation curve. The colored curve is the characteristic two-part adaptation curve, obtained when the test patch stimulates both rods and cones so that both rod-produced and cone-produced effects come into play. (After Cornsweet, 1970)

curve. The opposite result is obtained if the test patch is projected entirely within the rod-free fovea. Now we only obtain the first (cone) portion of the adaptation curve (Figure 6.20).

VISUAL PIGMENTS

When light hits a visual receptor, its energy somehow triggers a nervous impulse. Many of the details of how this happens are still unknown, but one thing at least is clear. The first stage of this energy conversion involves a photochemical process. We are again reminded of the camera. In a photographic plate the sensitive elements are grains of silver salt such as silver bromide. When light strikes the film, some of it is absorbed by the silver bromide molecules with the result that the silver is separated from the compound (and eventually becomes visible after several darkroom manipulations). The visual receptors contain several *visual pigments* which perform an analogous function for the eye. Like ordinary pigments they absorb some wavelengths more than others, reflecting only a portion of the spectrum so that they appear colored.

BLEACHING THE PIGMENTS

Until recently, most work on the photochemistry of vision concentrated upon the rods. Their visual pigment is *rhodopsin,* a complex protein whose normal color is reddish-purple but which is gradually bleached into transparency when exposed to light. The most convincing proof that this is indeed the visual pigment contained by rods comes from the fact that rhodopsin has the same spectral sensitivity curve as rod vision. If we take a test tube of dissolved rhodopsin and expose it to light of different wavelengths we can measure the proportion of light absorbed as a function of wavelength (Figure 6.21). This provides an index of the pigment's sensitivity to different parts of the spectrum, for the energy that causes the photochemical alteration is delivered by the light which is absorbed rather than that which is reflected. The resulting function is virtually identical to the spectral sensitivity curve obtained with dark-adapted (and hence, rod-using) human subjects.

In both rods and cones, the breakdown of visual pigments presumably leads to neural excitation. This is then transmitted to the next link in the neural chain.

REGENERATING THE PIGMENTS

Unlike a photographic emulsion, the visual pigments constantly renew themselves. Were it otherwise, a newborn infant would open her eyes, look at the bustling world around her, and never see again—her retina would be bleached

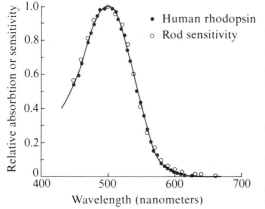

6.21 **The chemical sensitivity of rhodopsin compared to the sensitivity of human rod vision** *The figure shows the relative extent to which rhodopsin is bleached by light of different wavelengths (colored dots). As the figure shows, the chemical and visual sensitivity curves are essentially identical, proof that rhodopsin is the chemical substance whose reaction to light is the basis of rod vision. (After Alpern, Lawrence, and Wolsk, 1967)*

forever. The bleached pigments are somehow reconstituted to permit an unbroken succession of further retinal pictures.

The details of this chemical regeneration process have been worked out for rod vision by George Wald and his collaborators. In crude outline, their analysis indicates the simultaneous operation of two opposed chemical reactions. Rhodopsin disintegrates into two end products, *retinene* and *opsin,* but at the same time, retinene and opsin recombine to form rhodopsin (Wald, 1959). Resynthesis also requires the presence of vitamin A which is converted into retinene by another set of chemical reactions that occur more readily with decreasing illumination. Under the circumstances, it is not surprising that vitamin A deficiency is known to produce night blindness.

Sensory Interaction

We now turn to a set of phenomena which prove that the visual system (as indeed all sensory systems) is much more than the passive observer which Locke and Berkeley had assumed it to be. On the contrary, the visual system actively shapes and transforms the optic input; its components never function in isolation, but constantly interact.

INTERACTION IN TIME

Suppose we present a subject with a lighted patch, thus stimulating a particular region of the retina. What the subject sees will obviously depend upon how this region is stimulated. But the appearance of the patch will also depend upon how this region was stimulated immediately before. The general finding can be summarized in one simple rule: There will be a gradual decline in the reaction to any stimulus that persists unchanged. For example, after continued inspection of a green patch, its greenness will eventually fade away.

SENSORY ADAPTATION

As we have already seen, such phenomena are found in most other sensory systems. The cold ocean water feels warmer after we have been in it for a while; the foul odor of hydrogen sulfide is virtually unnoticeable in a matter of minutes. The physiological mechanisms that underlie these adaptation processes vary depending upon the particular sensory system. In touch, adaptation seems to occur at the receptor level; a constant pressure stimulus leads to quick decline in the impulse frequency recorded from the sensory nerve. In taste, the pattern is different. While the absolute threshold to salt concentration quadruples in about 30 seconds, there is no corresponding decline in the discharge of the gustatory nerves. Presumably this is a case of *central adaptation* which takes place in some higher neural link.

What does the organism gain by sensory adaptation? One advantage is the likelihood that stimuli which have been around for a while tend to be safe and of lesser relevance to the organism's survival; under the circumstances, it pays to give them less sensory weight. What is important is change, especially

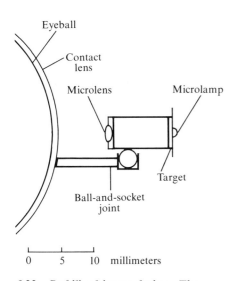

Eyeball

Contact lens

Microlens

Microlamp

Target

Ball-and-socket joint

0   5   10   millimeters

6.22 Stabilized-image device *The subject wears a contact lens on which a tiny projector is mounted. At the rear of the projector is the stimulus target which is projected onto the retina. This target will remain fixed at one point of the retina, for as the eyeball moves, so does the contact lens and its attached projector. As a result, the image on the retina remains stabilized. (After Pritchard, 1961)*

sudden change, for this may well signify food to a predator and death to its potential prey. Adaptation is the sensory system's way of pushing old news off the neurophysiological front page.

THE STABILIZED IMAGE

In normal vision, the eyes constantly move. In consequence, no retinal region ever suffers prolonged exposure to the same stimulus; one moment, it will be stimulated by a dark object, the next, by a lighter one. Since every change of gaze leads to a change in the visual stimulus, there will be no visual adaptation. Even if one tries to hold one's eyes steady to fixate a stationary picture, adaptation effects will be rather minor. The fact is that we cannot truly hold our eyes motionless. Small tremors in the eye muscles lead to involuntary eye movements, and these necessarily alter the stimulus input for any given retinal region.

Several contemporary investigators have developed a technique which achieves a truly stationary retinal image. The basic idea is as clever as it is simple. Since you can't stop the eye from moving, move the stimulus along with the eye. This is accomplished by means of a contact lens to which a tiny projector is attached. This projects a stimulus pattern upon the retina. The contact lens moves with every motion of the eyeball but the projector moves with it. The result is a *stabilized image.* However the eye moves, so does the stimulus; thus each retinal region is continually exposed to the identical portion of the stimulus pattern (Figure 6.22). At first, the stabilized retinal image is seen very sharply, but after some seconds it fades away completely—a dramatic demonstration of the system's adaptation to unchanging stimulation. Interestingly enough, the image will reappear if the stimulus pattern is somehow altered, whether in intensity or in its retinal location (the latter by slippage of the contact lens). We can conclude that, in humans, continual involuntary eye movements serve the biologically useful purpose of keeping the visual world intact (Riggs et al., 1953).

Gordon Walls, an authority on the visual systems of vertebrates, once suggested that certain birds—unlike man—may find a momentary fading of the image useful. Many birds who prey on worms or insects alternate frozen postures with abrupt movements while searching for food. Since birds have only rudimentary eye muscles and probably no involuntary eye movements, the periods of immobility presumably lead to a stabilized image. This would quickly wash out all visual signals from the stationary environment, thus emphasizing the signals produced by the moving prey. According to Walls, birds who feed on stationary objects like seeds or berries behave very differently. These birds could only lose from a stabilized image, and they apparently conduct their food search in a way that will avoid it, continually hopping, pecking, or flying as they feed (Cornsweet, 1970).

INTERACTION IN SPACE

Temporal interaction effects show that sensory systems respond to change over time. If no such change occurs, the sensory response diminishes. What holds for time, holds for space as well. For here, too, the key word is *change*. In vision (as in some other senses), the response to a stimulus applied to any one

195

6.23 Brightness contrast *A gray patch on a light gray background looks darker than the (objectively) identical gray on a black background.*

region partially depends on how the neighboring regions are stimulated. The more the difference, the greater the sensory effect.

BRIGHTNESS CONTRAST

It has long been known that the appearance of a gray patch depends upon its background. The identical gray will look much brighter on a black background than it will on a white background. This is ***brightness contrast,*** an effect which increases the greater the intensity difference between the two contrasting regions. Thus, gray appears brighter on black than on dark gray and darker against white than against light gray (Figure 6.23).

Contrast is also a function of the distance between the two contrasting regions—the smaller that distance, the greater the contrast (Figure 6.24). Theatrical lighting experts use brightness contrast by lighting the stage backdrop brilliantly without changing the light that falls upon the actors in front of it. The actors will then appear as silhouettes.

Such contrast effects serve a vital biological function. They accentuate the edges between different objects in our visual world and thus allow us to see them much more clearly. To explain why this is so, we must consider some further facts about the optics of the eye and about brightness contrast.

ACCENTUATION BY CONTRAST

In previous sections we have ignored some defects of the eye as an optical instrument. The lens and cornea have serious optical aberrations which cause some blur of the retinal image. This blur is further aggravated by light which is dispersed as it passes through the liquid medium of the eye, scattering a diffuse haze over the entire retina. The result is a retinal image in which there

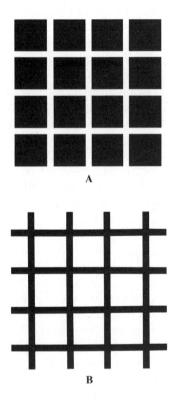

A

B

6.24 The effect of distance between contrasting regions *(A) The white lines in the grid are physically homogeneous, but they don't appear to be—each of the "intersections" seems to contain a gray spot. The uneven appearance of the white strips is caused by contrast. Each strip is surrounded by a black square which contrasts with it and makes it look brighter. But this is not the case at the intersections which only touch upon the black squares at their corners. As a result, there is little contrast in the middle of the intersections. This accounts for the gray spots seen there. (B) The same point is made by the second grid. Here there seem to be whitish spots at the intersections. The explanation is the same. The black lines are bounded by white and thus look darker by contrast. There is less contrast operating on the regions in the middle of the intersections. As a result, they don't appear as dark as the streets, looking like whitish spots. (After Hering, 1920)*

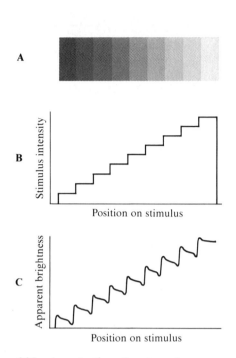

6.25   Accentuation of contours by contrast   *(A) The series of gray strips is arranged in ascending brightness, from left to right. Physically, each strip is of uniform light intensity. This is graphically expressed in (B) which plots stimulus position against the physical light intensity, showing a simple series of ascending steps. But this is not what is seen, for the strips do not appear to be uniform. For each strip, the left edge (adjacent to its darker neighbor) looks brighter than the rest, while the right edge (adjacent to the lighter neighbor) looks darker. This is graphically shown in (C) which plots stimulus position against apparent brightness, showing a scalloped series. The explanation is contrast. The edges are closer to their darker or lighter neighbors, and will thus be more subject to contrast than the rest of the strip. The result is an accentuation of the contours that separate one strip from the next. (After Cornsweet, 1970 and Coren et al., 1978)*

are no distinct outlines but only fuzzy fringes. How then do we see the sharp contours of the world around us? The answer is that brightness contrast accentuates intensity differences between adjacent retinal areas, so much so that it sometimes creates perceived boundaries where physically there are none. This point was demonstrated by Ernst Mach (1838–1916) a physicist-philosopher of the nineteenth century, best known for his discovery of the speed of sound.

Mach's stimuli were surfaces in which the physical light intensity varies from place to place according to some prearranged function (Figure 6.25). Part A contains strips of grays that range from very dark to very light. Within each strip, the physical light intensities are equal. But that is not how they appear. Within each strip, there appears to be a band brighter where that strip borders on a darker strip and a darker band where it borders on a lighter one. Parts B and C summarize the results. Part B shows the physical light intensities plotted against spatial position. This is the figure as it actually is. Part C plots the apparent light intensities against spatial position, showing the figure as it appears.

These effects are a result of the same contrast phenomenon we have discussed before. Contrast accentuates the difference between two regions. But this sharpening is maximal at the borders where the distance between the two contrasting areas is smallest. The bands (which are sometimes called **Mach bands**) are the result.

It is generally agreed that essentially the same phenomenon explains the sharpening of contours in the retinal image cast by ordinary objects in the real world. As we have seen, the optical imperfections of the eye produce gradual transitions of intensities even if the external stimulus is sharply defined. But the visual system recreates, and even exaggerates, these boundaries by the same processes that generate Mach bands. As Mach put it, the retina "schematizes and caricatures," emphasizing those aspects of the visual information that are of the greatest significance to the organism, the distinctions between one object and another.

A PHYSIOLOGICAL ACCOUNT OF SPATIAL INTERACTION

What is the physiological mechanism that underlies spatial interaction? Today we know that the effect is based on the mutual inhibition of cells in the retina and higher up. The conclusive demonstration that this is so had to await the techniques of modern electrophysiology. But more than fifty years before this, such sensory psychologists as Ernest Mach and Ewald Hering (1834–1918) had postulated precisely such a process on the basis of what they observed in the sensory laboratory. In their view, the phenomena of contrast and Mach bands could be explained in no other way. In this regard, Mach and Hering resemble Sherrington who inferred the synapse on the basis of behavioral data alone, many decades before there was any means for providing physiological proof.

RECEPTIVE FIELDS

The modern physiological account of contrast effects is based on single-cell recording methods. The first step is to place a microelectrode in a cat's optic

Microelectrode

Stimulus projected
on screen

Oscilloscope

Amplifier

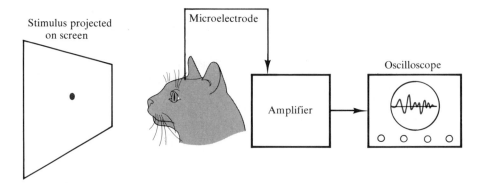

6.26 Recording from the visual system of a cat *The experimental setup for record-ing neural responses from the visual system of a cat. An anaesthesized cat has one eye propped open so that visual stimulation can be directed to particular regions of the ret-ina. A microelectrode picks up neural impulses from a single cell in the optic system, amplifies them, and displays them on an oscilloscope. (After Schiffman, 1976)*

Stimulus   Oscilloscope record

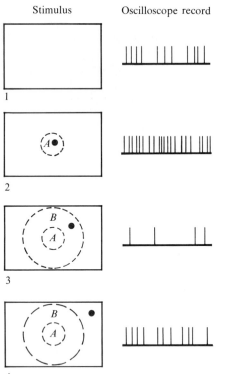

nerve so that it picks up electrical activity from only one cell. The eye of an anesthetized animal is propped open and is stimulated by spots of light of varying intensities and at different locations (Figure 6.26). We find that there is a small region of the retina the stimulation of which leads to an increase in the cell's normal firing rate. The more intense the light, the greater the cell's response. But this central region is surrounded by a region in which illumina-tion has the opposite effect. Here, illumination depresses the cell's firing rate, and this depression increases with increases in the light intensity (Figure 6.27). The entire area of the retina in which stimulation by light affects the cell's firing rate—whether up or down—is called the ***receptive field*** of that cell.

LATERAL INHIBITION

The results show that neighboring regions in the retina tend to inhibit each other. The reason is a process called ***lateral inhibition*** (in effect, it is inhibition exerted sideways). A simplified version of how this mechanism works is as follows: When any visual receptor is stimulated, it transmits its excitation upward to other cells that eventually relay it to the brain. But this excitation has a further effect. It also stimulates some neurons that extend sideways along the retina. These lateral cells make contact with neighboring cells whose activation they inhibit.

To see how lateral inhibition works, consider the retinal image produced by a gray patch surrounded by a lighter ring (Figure 6.28). For the sake of sim-plicity, we will only look at two neighboring receptor cells, *A* and *B*. *A* is stimulated by the gray patch and receives a moderate amount of light. *B* is

6.27 Receptive fields on the cat's visual system *Using the setup shown in Figure 6.26, stimuli are presented to various regions of the retina. The panels show the firing frequency of a particular ganglion cell. Panel 1 shows the base-level firing rate when no stimulus is presented anywhere. Panel 2 shows the effect when a stimulus is presented anywhere within an inner, central region, A, on the retina. When stimulated in A, the cell's firing rate goes up. Panel 3 shows what happens in response to a stimulus presented anywhere within the ring-shaped re-gion, B, surrounding region A. Stimulation in B causes the cell's firing rate to go down. Panel 4, finally, shows what happens when a stimulus is presented outside of either A or B, the regions that together comprise the cell's receptive field. Now there is no significant change from the cell's normal base level. (From Kuffler, 1953)*

stimulated by the lighter ring and receives much more light. Our primary interest is in the excitation which cell *A*, the one stimulated by the gray patch, relays upward to the brain. The more cell *A* is stimulated, the more excitation it will relay further, and the brighter the patch will appear to be. The important point is that the excitation from cell *A* will not be passed on unimpeded. On the contrary. Some of this excitation will be cancelled by inhibition from neighboring cells. Consider the effect of cell *B*, whose stimulation comes from the lighter ring. That cell is intensely excited. One result of this excitation is that it excites a third cell *C* whose effect is inhibitory and exerted sideways (in short, a lateral inhibitor). The effect of this lateral cell *C* is to block the excitation that *A* sends upward.

Now consider what happens if we look at the same gray patch when it is surrounded by a black ring (Figure 6.29). We again focus on the same two receptors *A* and *B*. Cell *A* is stimulated to the same extent that it was before, for the gray patch from which it receives its light reflects just as much light as it did before. What is different is the amount of excitation that this cell relays upward. For now this excitation is no longer blocked by inhibition from

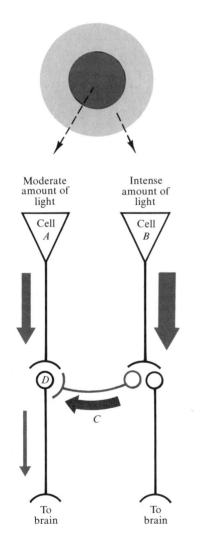

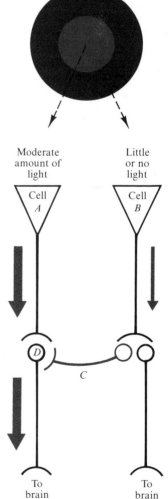

6.28 Lateral inhibition and contrast *Two receptor cells, A and B, are stimulated by neighboring regions of a stimulus. A receives moderate stimulation; B receives an intense amount of light. A's excitation serves to stimulate the next neuron in the visual chain, cell D, which transmits the message further toward the brain. But this transmission is impeded by cell B, whose own intense excitation exerts an inhibitory effect on its neighbors. B excites a lateral cell, C, which exerts an inhibitory effect on cell D. As a result, cell D fires at a reduced rate. (Excitatory effects are shown by gray arrows, inhibitory ones by color arrows.)*

6.29 The effect of reducing lateral inhibition *This shows what happens when A's neighbor, cell B, is stimulated very little or not at all. Now B will not excite the lateral inhibitor C. As a result, A's excitatory message to the next neuron, D, will proceed unimpeded. (For simplicity, both diagrams only show what happens to the message from A. Other effects of B, and irrelevant lateral inhibitors, have been omitted.)*

199

neighboring cells. Cell *B* is in the dark and is thus relatively unexcited. As a result, it won't stimulate the lateral inhibitor cell *C*, which therefore does not impede the message cell *A* sends upward.

The upshot of all this is contrast. The brain gets a visual message that is an exaggeration. What is dark gets darker, what is light gets lighter.

Color

Despite their many differences, the sensory systems of hearing and of vision have some things in common. In both, the relevant stimulus energy is in wave form. And in both, wavelength is related to a qualitative psychological dimension—in one case pitch, in the other color. Much of the research in both domains has revolved around the question of how these sensory qualities are coded. We will here consider only one of these domains, that of color.

There is little doubt that color perception concerns sensory quality rather than intensity. The sensation red is different from green or blue in a way that cannot be described as a matter of more or less. Since Müller's formulation of the doctrine of specific nerve energies, sensory psychologists have assumed that such qualitative differences in sensation imply a difference in the neural processes that underlie these qualities. In their search for the color mechanism, they were guided largely by psychological facts, using them to infer neurological processes which could not be verified directly given the techniques of their time. As in the case of lateral inhibition, some of these inferences have ultimately been confirmed by physiological evidence, in some cases a century after they were first proposed.

THE PHENOMENA OF COLOR

Since qualitative differences are at the heart of the color experience, we will begin by describing some of these. Our first step is classification.

CLASSIFYING THE COLOR SENSATIONS

A person with normal color vision can distinguish over seven million different color shades. Before we can begin to ask questions about the processes that underlie human color vision, we must devise a system of classification that will allow us to describe any of these millions of perceived shades by reference to a few simple dimensions. In this task we concentrate on what we see, classifying our color sensations instead of classifying the physical stimuli which produce them.

The dimensions of color Imagine seven million or so colored paper patches, one for each of the colors we can discriminate. We can classify them according to three perceived dimensions: hue, brightness, and saturation.

Hue is a term whose meaning is close to that of the word *color* as used in everyday life. It is a property of the so-called ***chromatic colors*** (for example, red and blue) but not of the ***achromatic colors*** (that is, black, white, and all of the totally neutral grays in between). Hue varies with wavelength (Figure 6.30). Thus ***unique blue*** (a blue which is judged to have no trace of red or green

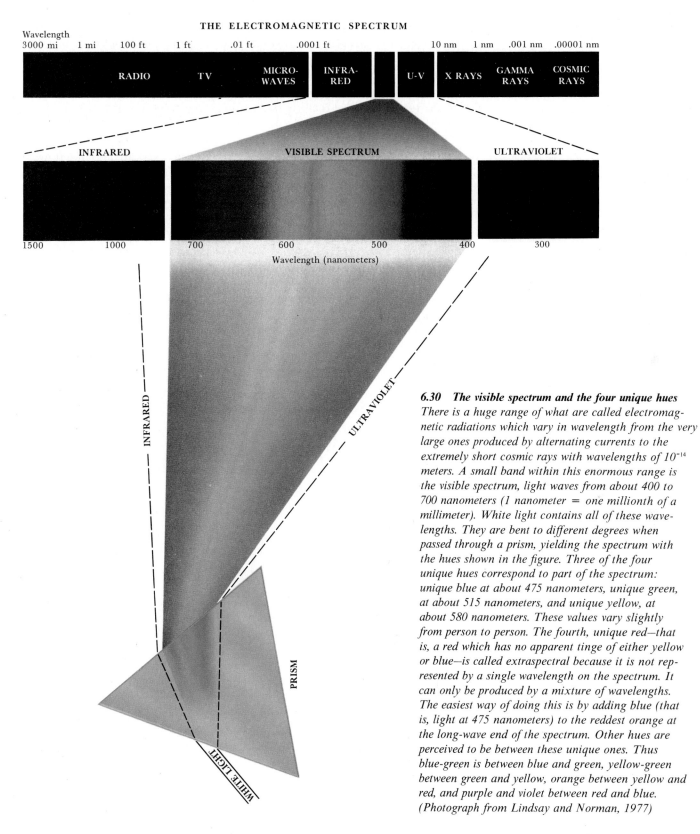

THE ELECTROMAGNETIC SPECTRUM

Wavelength

| 3000 mi | 1 mi | 100 ft | 1 ft | .01 ft | .0001 ft | | 10 nm | 1 nm | .001 nm | .00001 nm |

| RADIO | TV | MICRO-WAVES | INFRA-RED | | U-V | X RAYS | GAMMA RAYS | COSMIC RAYS |

INFRARED **VISIBLE SPECTRUM** **ULTRAVIOLET**

| 1500 | 1000 | 700 | 600 | 500 | 400 | 300 |

Wavelength (nanometers)

INFRARED

ULTRAVIOLET

PRISM

WHITE LIGHT

6.30 The visible spectrum and the four unique hues
There is a huge range of what are called electromagnetic radiations which vary in wavelength from the very large ones produced by alternating currents to the extremely short cosmic rays with wavelengths of 10^{-14} meters. A small band within this enormous range is the visible spectrum, light waves from about 400 to 700 nanometers (1 nanometer = one millionth of a millimeter). White light contains all of these wavelengths. They are bent to different degrees when passed through a prism, yielding the spectrum with the hues shown in the figure. Three of the four unique hues correspond to part of the spectrum: unique blue at about 475 nanometers, unique green, at about 515 nanometers, and unique yellow, at about 580 nanometers. These values vary slightly from person to person. The fourth, unique red—that is, a red which has no apparent tinge of either yellow or blue—is called extraspectral because it is not represented by a single wavelength on the spectrum. It can only be produced by a mixture of wavelengths. The easiest way of doing this is by adding blue (that is, light at 475 nanometers) to the reddest orange at the long-wave end of the spectrum. Other hues are perceived to be between these unique ones. Thus blue-green is between blue and green, yellow-green between green and yellow, orange between yellow and red, and purple and violet between red and blue. (Photograph from Lindsay and Norman, 1977)

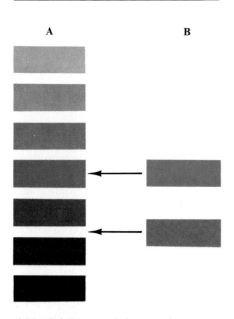

6.31 Brightness *Colors can be arranged according to their brightness. (A) This dimension is clearest in a series of grays, which are hueless and vary in brightness only. (B) Chromatic colors, such as the light blue and the dark green shown here, can also be classified according to their brightness as indicated by the arrows.*

in it), occurs on the spectrum at about 475 nanometers, **unique green** (which has no blue or yellow) at about 515 nanometers, and **unique yellow** (which has no green or red) at about 580 nanometers.

Brightness varies among both the chromatic and achromatic colors. Thus ultramarine is darker than light blue and charcoal gray is darker than light gray (Figure 6.31). But the brightness dimension stands out most clearly if we consider achromatic colors alone. These differ in brightness only, while the chromatic colors may differ in hue (as we have seen) and in saturation (which we will discuss next). Note that white and black represent the top and bottom of the brightness dimension. Thus white is hueless and maximally bright; black is hueless and minimally bright.

Saturation is the "purity" of a color, the extent to which it is chromatic rather than achromatic. The more gray (or black or white) is mixed with a color, the less saturation it has. Consider the various blue patches in Figure 6.32. All have the same hue (blue). All have the same brightness as a particular, achromatic gray (which is also the same gray with which the blue was mixed to produce the less saturated blue patches, *A, B, C,* and *D*). The patches only differ in one respect: the proportion of blue as opposed to that of gray. The more gray there is, the less the saturation. When the color is entirely gray, saturation is zero. This holds for all colors.

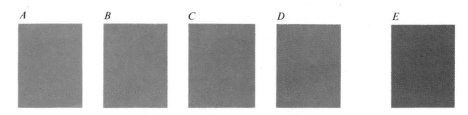

6.32 Saturation *The four patches A–D are identical in both hue and brightness. They only differ in saturation, which is greatest for patch A and decreases from A to D. The gray patch, E, on the far right matches all the other patches in brightness; it was mixed with the blue patch A in varying proportions to produce patches of less and less saturation.*

The color circle and the color solid Some hues appear to be very similar to others. Suppose we only consider the color patches that look most chromatic—that is, those whose saturation is maximal. If we arrange these on the basis of their perceptual similarity, the result is a circular series, the so-called **color circle,** such that red is followed by orange, orange by yellow, yellow-green, green, blue-green, blue and violet, until the circle finally returns to red (Figure 6.33).

The color circle embodies the perceptual similarities among the different hues. To complete our classificatory schema, we construct the so-called **color solid** which incorporates the color circle with the other two dimensions of perceived color, brightness and saturation. Each of our original seven million color patches can be fitted into a unique position in this solid (Figure 6.34). Our classificatory task is thus accomplished.

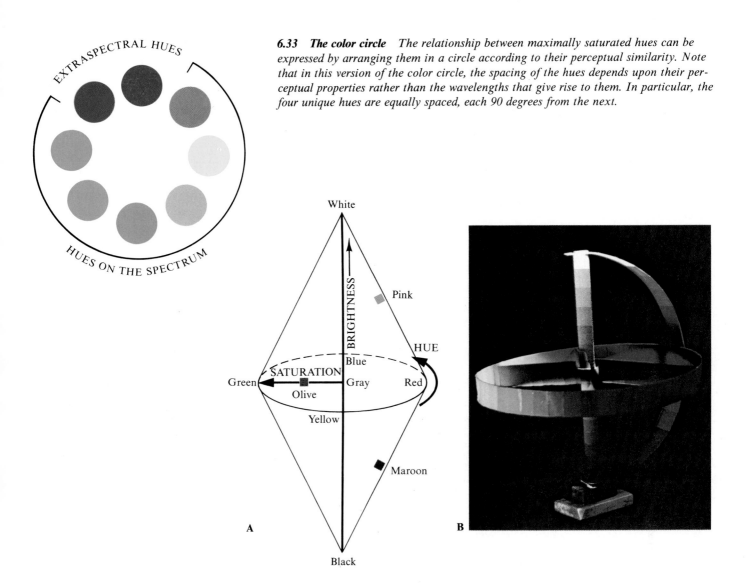

6.33 **The color circle** *The relationship between maximally saturated hues can be expressed by arranging them in a circle according to their perceptual similarity. Note that in this version of the color circle, the spacing of the hues depends upon their perceptual properties rather than the wavelengths that give rise to them. In particular, the four unique hues are equally spaced, each 90 degrees from the next.*

6.34 **The color solid** *(A) The color solid is constructed by first taking the series of achromatic grays and arranging them as a column, with black at the bottom and white at the top. The next step is to take the hue circle and slip it around the black-white column until the midpoint of this circle coincides with middle gray (the midpoint of the black-white series). The final step is to connect all points of the circle's circumference to the top and bottom of the black-white column. The result is a spindle-shaped solid. In this color solid, the vertical axis corresponds to brightness. The angular position relative to the circle corresponds to hue. Saturation is the distance from the central vertical axis: the farther a color is from this axis, the more saturated it is. Every color can now be placed within the solid. Examples are olive, pink, and maroon, whose approximate locations on the solid are shown. Note that for maximal saturation, brightness has to be at a medium value. If a color becomes too bright or too dark, it necessarily becomes desaturated. Pink is a very bright red and maroon a very dark one; both are much less saturated than red at a medium brightness and are therefore shown closer to the middle axis. (B) A full-color construction that schematically shows the relations between the three dimensions of the color solid. (Courtesy School of Art, Bowling Green State University)*

203

COLOR MIXTURE

With rare exceptions, the objects in the world around us do not reflect a single wavelength; rather, they reflect different ones, all of which strike the same region of the retina simultaneously. Let us consider the results of some of these mixtures.

Subtractive mixture Before proceeding, we must recognize that the kind of mixture sensory psychologists are interested in is very different from the sort artists employ when they stir pigments together on a palette. Mixing pigments on a palette (or smearing crayons together on a piece of paper) is **subtractive mixture.** In subtractive mixture, one set of wavelengths is subtracted from another set. The easiest demonstration is with colored filters, such as those used in stage lighting, which allow some wavelengths to pass through them while holding others back. Take two such filters, *A* and *B*. Suppose filter *A* allows passage to all light waves between 400 and 540 nanometers but no others. The broad range of light that comes through this filter will be seen as blue. We next turn to filter *B*, which passes light waves between 520 and 620 nanometers but excludes all others. The band of light waves that comes through this filter will be seen as yellow (Figure 6.35).

We now ask how we see light that has to pass through *both* filters. Filter *A* (the blue filter) blocks all light above 540 nanometers, while filter *B* (the yellow filter) blocks all light below 520 nanometers. As a result, the only light waves that can pass through this double barricade are those that can slip through the narrow gap between 520 and 540 nanometers, the only interval left unblocked by *both* filters. As it happens, light in this interval is seen as green. Thus, when the mixture is subtractive, mixing blue and yellow will yield green.

Thus far we have dealt with filters which let some wavelengths through while blocking others. The same account also applies to artist's pigments. Any pigment reflects only a certain band of wavelengths while absorbing the rest. Suppose we mix pigment *A* (say, blue) to pigment *B* (say, yellow). The result is a form of subtraction. What we will see is the wavelengths reflected by the blue pigment (400 to 540 nanometers) minus the wavelengths absorbed by the yellow pigment (everything below 520 nanometers). The effect is exactly the same as if we had superimposed a blue filter over a yellow one. All that is reflected is light between 520 and 540 namometers, which is seen as green.

6.35 Subtractive mixture *In subtractive mixture, the light passed by two filters (or reflected by two pigments) is the band of wavelengths passed by the first minus that region which is subtracted by the second. In this example, the first filter passes light between 400 and 540 nanometers (a broad-band blue filter), the second light between 520 and 620 nanometers (a broad-band yellow filter). The only light which can pass through both is in the region between 520 and 540 nanometers, which appears green.*

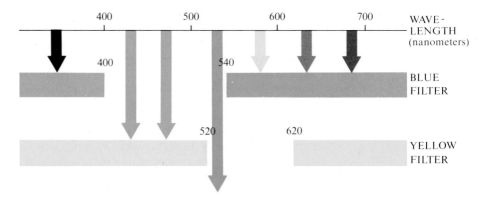

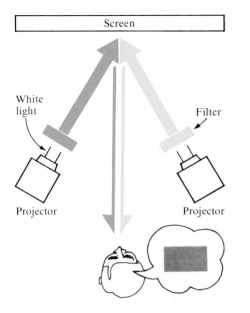

6.36 Additive mixture *In additive mixture, the light passed by two filters (or reflected by two pigments) impinges upon the same region of the retina at the same time. The figure shows two projectors throwing blue-yellow filtered light upon the same portion of the screen from which it is reflected upon the same region of the retina. In contrast to what happens in subtractive mixture, the result of adding these two colors is gray.*

6.37 Additive mixture by rotating a color wheel *(A) A stationary color wheel, partially blue and partially yellow. (B) The same wheel, in motion. Note the colors mix additively and yield gray. (Photographs by Ed Boswell)*

Additive mixture In subtractive mixture, we alter the optic stimulus before it ever hits the eye. There is another kind of mixture that goes on in the eye itself. This is ***additive mixture*** which occurs when different bands of wavelengths stimulate the same retinal region simultaneously. Such additive mixtures can be produced in the laboratory by using filtered light from two different projectors which are focused on the same spot. As a result, the light from each filtered source will be reflected back to the same retinal area (Figure 6.36). Another technique is to present both colors to the same retinal area in very fast succession, typically by rapid rotation of a color wheel (Figure 6.37).

In real life, additive mixture has many uses. One is color television, in which the additive mixture is accomplished by three different sets of photosensitive substances. Another example is provided by the Pointillist painter Georges Seurat (1859–91). He used dots of different colors that are too close together to be seen separately, especially when the picture is viewed from a distance (Figure 6.38, page 206).

Complementary hues One of the most important facts of additive color mixture is the fact that every hue has a ***complementary,*** another hue which if mixed with the first in appropriate proportions will produce the color gray. An easy way to find complementaries is by reference to the color circle. Any hue on the circumference will yield gray if mixed (additively) with the hue on the opposite side of the color circle (see Figure 6.39, page 206). Of particular interest are the complementary pairs that involve the four ***unique colors,*** red, yellow, green, and blue. Blue and yellow are complementaries which produce gray upon additive mixture; the same holds for red and green. Hues that are not complementary produce mixtures which preserve the hue of their components. Thus the mixture of red and yellow leads to orange (which still looks

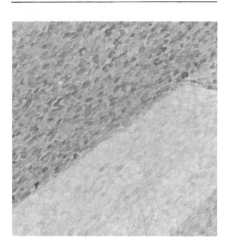

6.39 Complementary hues   Any hue will yield gray if additively mixed (in the correct porportion) with a hue on the opposite side of the color circle. Such hue pairs are complementaries. Some complementary hues are here shown linked by a line across the circle's center. Of particular importance are the two complementary pairs that contain the four unique hues: red-green and blue-yellow.

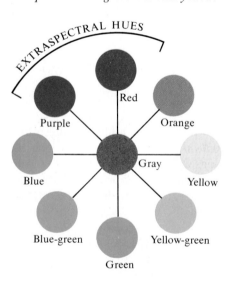

6.38 Additive mixture in Pointillist art   The Port of Gravelines (1890) by Georges Seurat. A detail of the painting (on the left) shows the separate color daubs which, when viewed from a distance, mix additively. The pointillists employed this technique instead of mixing pigments to capture the bright appearance of colors outdoors. Pigment mixture is subtractive and darkens the resulting colors. (Courtesy Indianapolis Museum of Art, gift of Mrs. James W. Fesler in memory of Daniel W. and Elizabeth C. Marmon)

like a yellowish red) while that of blue and red yields a violet (which looks like a reddish blue).

At the risk of repetition, note that all of this holds only for additive mixture. When blue and yellow are additively mixed in the right proportions—for example, by rotating a color wheel—the observer sees gray. This is in contrast to what happens when the mixture is subtractive, as in drawing a blue crayon over a yellow patch. Now the result is green. The same holds for red and green. Additive mixture of the two yields gray; subtractive mixture will produce a blackish brown.

COLOR ANTAGONISTS

The color-mixture effects we have just described suggest that blue and yellow on the one hand, and red and green on the other, are two pairs of mutually opposed antagonists which cancel each other's hue. There are some further phenomena which lead to a similar conclusion.

One effect is the chromatic counterpart of brightness contrast. In general, any region in the visual field tends to induce its color antagonist in adjoining

6.40 Color contrast *The gray patches on the blue and yellow backgrounds are physically identical. But they don't look that way. To begin with, there is a difference in perceived brightness: the patch on the blue looks brighter than the one on the yellow, a result of brightness contrast. There is also a difference in perceived hue, for the patch on the blue looks somewhat yellowish, while that on the yellow looks bluish. This is color contrast, a demonstration that hues tend to induce their antagonists in neighboring areas.*

areas. The result is **simultaneous color contrast.** For example, a gray patch will tend to look bluish if surrounded by yellow, yellowish if surrounded by blue, and so on (Figure 6.40).

In simultaneous contrast, the antagonistic relation involves two adjoining regions in space. In a related phenomenon, the contrast is with an immediately preceding stimulus; it is a contrast in time rather than in space. Suppose we stare at a green patch for a while and then look at a white wall. We will see a reddish spot. This is a **negative afterimage** (Figure 6.41). Negative afterimages have the complementary hue and the opposite brightness of the original stimulus (which is why they are called negative). Thus fixation of a brightly lit red bulb will make us see a dark greenish shape when we subsequently look at a white screen.*

* Lengthy fixation of any color may also lead to a **positive afterimage,** especially if the inspection stimulus was fairly intense. This positive afterimage will have the same hue and brightness as the original stimulus, such as the bright, yellowish disk we see after looking at the sun. The usual interpretation of this effect is that it represents some kind of retinal inertia, a continuation of the original retinal excitation which persists for a while even after the original stimulus is withdrawn.

A

B

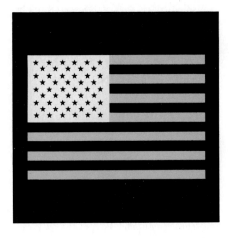

6.41 Negative afterimages *(A) Stare at the center of the figure for about a minute or two, and then look at a white piece of paper. Blink once or twice; the negative afterimage will appear within a few seconds showing the rose in its correct colors. (B) Do the same for the color-reversed picture of the flag.*

207

Afterimages are caused by events that occur in the retina and associated visual mechanisms. This is why, when the eye moves, the afterimage moves along with it. One reason for the effect is retinal adaptation. When we fixate a white disk on a black background, the pigments in the retinal region that corresponds to the disk will be bleached more intensely than those in surrounding areas. During subsequent exposure to a homogeneous white surface, the more deeply bleached regions will respond less vigorously and will thus report a lesser sensory intensity. The result is a dark gray negative afterimage. But peripheral adaptation is probably not the whole story. In addition, there may be a **rebound phenomenon.** While the inspection stimulus was still present, the excited regions may well have inhibited an antagonistic process. White held back black, blue inhibited yellow, and so on. When the stimulus is withdrawn, the inhibited processes rebound, like a coiled spring that is suddenly released.

COLOR RECEPTORS

What is the neurological mechanism that underlies color vision? A more useful way of reformulating this question is to divide it into two parts: (1) How are the relevant light energies transduced into a receptor discharge? (2) How is the resulting receptor message converted so as to yield the psychological properties of the color experience?

THE TRANSDUCTION OF WAVELENGTH

The raw material with which the visual system must begin is light of various intensities and wavelengths. Since we can discriminate among different wavelengths, there must be different receptors (that is, different types of cones) which are somehow differentially attuned to this physical dimension.

It turns out that normal human color vision depends on only three different kinds of color elements (which is why it is called **trichromatic).** Each of these three cone types is a **broad-band receptor.** That is, each responds to a very broad range of wavelengths in the visible spectrum. The main difference between these three cone elements is in their sensitivity curves. One cone type is most sensitive to wavelengths in the short-wave region of the spectrum, the second to wavelengths in the middle, and the third to the larger wavelengths (Figure 6.42).

The overlap between the three sensitivity curves is so extensive that any wavelength must necessarily stimulate each of the three receptor elements. This being so, how do we manage to discriminate wavelengths? The reason we can is inherent in the three sensitivity curves. Each receptor element will respond in differing degree depending upon the stimulating wavelength. If the light is from the blue end of the spectrum, there will be maximal output from

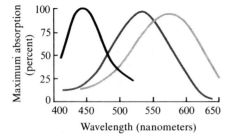

6.42 Sensitivity curves of three different cones in the primate retina *There is evidence that the retina of humans and monkeys contains three different kinds of cones, each with its own photopigments. These photopigments differ in their sensitivity to different regions of the spectrum: one absorbs more of the shorter wavelengths (and is thus more sensitive to light in this spectral region), a second more of the middle wavelengths, a third more of the longer ones. The resulting sensitivity curves are shown here. In this figure, the sensitivity curve of the cone most responsive to the short-wave end of the spectrum is in black, that of the cone most sensitive to the middle region is in light gray, that of the cone most sensitive to the longer wavelengths is in dark gray. (After MacNichol, 1964)*

the cone element whose sensitivity is greater in the short-wave region. If the light is from the orange end, it will elicit maximum activity from the cone element whose sensitivity is greatest in the long-wave region. As a result, each wavelength will produce a different ratio of the outputs of the three receptor types. Assuming that the nervous system can tell which receptor type is sending which message, wavelength discrimination follows.

THE EYE AS AN INTEGRATOR

A trichromatic receptor system such as ours allows wavelength discrimination, but it is not always able to discriminate between wavelength mixtures. We can readily duplicate the receptor output produced by a single wavelength with an appropriate wavelength mixture. Speaking most generally, any given wavelength can be matched by the mixture of no more than three suitably balanced others. Since the receptor outputs are exactly equal, the system has no way of knowing how the color was generated. A given receptor that is stimulated by several wavelengths will pool their individual contributions into one output that gives no clues as to its origin, like an adding machine which records total sums but does not keep track of the component figures. The brain is only informed of the sums on the three different adding machines. If the sum on one of these machines is 9, the brain will never know whether this came about by adding 5 and 4 or adding 2 and 7.

The preceding discussion has shown that the receptors for color vision behave like integrators. They are sensitive to the final sum of a wavelength mixture (they integrate it), but they don't keep track of the individual components. In this regard, the perception of color is quite different from its counterpart in hearing, pitch perception. In hearing, we do perceive the separate notes that make up a chord; we hear a mixture, but we still keep track of the individual components. Unlike the eye which acts as an integrator, the ear behaves like an analyzer.

COLOR CODING

The receptor mechanisms may explain why any color can be *matched* by the proper mixture of three single wavelengths. But these receptor mechanisms alone cannot explain why we *see* a color the way we do, nor can they account for certain perceived relations among perceived colors. For example, some colors appear pure or primary (for example, unique blue) while others do not (for example, violet). Furthermore, these primary colors form two complementary and antagonistic pairs (red-green and blue-yellow). To explain phenomena of this kind we must assume some further neural mechanisms which work on the three receptor outputs and ultimately code them into the sensory qualities we know as color. We will describe a modern version of a conception which dates back to the nineteenth-century visual psychophysiologist, Ewald Hering.

THE OPPONENT-PROCESS THEORY

This version of Hering's position is the **opponent-process theory** formulated by Leo Hurvich and Dorothea Jameson. Hurvich and Jameson adopt Hering's

Ewald Hering *(Courtesy National Library of Medicine)*

premise that there are six psychologically primary color qualities—red, green, blue, yellow, black, and white. They assume that there must be six different neural processes which correspond to each. These six processes are not independent, but instead are organized in three opponent-process pairs: red-green, blue-yellow, and black-white. The two members of each pair are antagonists. Excitation of one member automatically inhibits the other (Hurvich and Jameson, 1957).

The two hue systems According to the opponent-process theory, the experience of hue depends upon two of three opponent-process pairs—red-green and blue-yellow. (As we will see, the black-white system is not relevant to perceived hue.) Each of these opponent-process pairs can be likened to a balance scale. If one arm (say, the blue process) goes down, the other arm (its opponent, yellow) necessarily comes up. The hue we actually see depends upon the position of the two balances. If the red-green balance is tipped toward red and the blue-yellow balance toward yellow (excitation of red and yellow with concomitant inhibition of green and blue), the perceived hue will be orange. This follows, because the resulting hue will be a combination of red and yellow, which is seen as orange. If either of the two scales is evenly balanced, it will make no contribution to the hue experience. This will occur when neither of the two antagonists is stimulated, and also when both are stimulated equally and cancel each other out. If both hue systems are in balance, there will be no hue at all and the resulting color will be seen as achromatic (that is, without hue).

How can we determine the effect of any given wavelength on the two hue systems? Hurvich and Jameson have developed a technique that follows directly from the opponent-process concept. According to the theory, the blue process and the yellow process cancel each other out if both are stimulated equally. The same holds for the red and the green processes. This cancellation effect was the basis of a measurement procedure.

Suppose we want to determine the sensitivity of the yellow-blue system to a test light of, say, 650 nanometers. This test light looks orange, so it presumably tilts the yellow-blue process toward the yellow side. But by how much? To find out, the investigators added another wavelength to the test light—light at about 475 nanometers whose color (when looked at in isolation) is unique blue. The addition of this blue light tended to cancel out the yellow process. (Remember, this is *additive* mixture). The investigators now varied the intensity of this added blue light until the resulting mixture had no trace of either blue or yellow in it. When this point was reached, the light mixture looked red. (Now the yellow-blue system was in complete balance so that the appearance of the mixture was determined by the red-green system alone). By measuring the intensity of blue light that accomplished this, Hurvich and Jameson could measure the degree to which the original test stimulus, 650 nanometers, tilted the yellow-blue process toward the yellow side. They measured the amount of the yellow tilt by determining how much blue had to be added to cancel the yellow out. In effect, the principle is exactly analogous to the use of a balance for measuring weights. To determine the weight of an object, we determine how many grams we must place on the other side of the scale to bring the two arms back in balance.

By similar procedures, Hurvich and Jameson determined the extent to

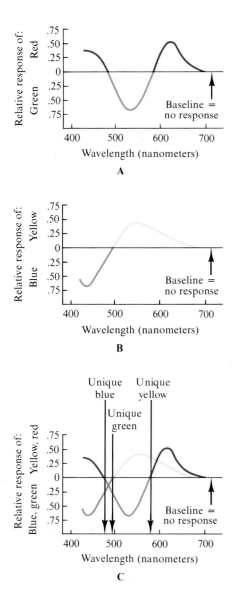

6.43 The cancellation experiment (A) The red-green process. Here the horizontal axis represents the wavelength of the stimulus, while the vertical axis indicates the strength of the red-green process. We arbitrarily decide to plot the strength of the red process as positive and the green process as negative. Since red and green are antagonists, the strength of the green process is indicated by the amount of red that has to be added to a given wavelength to cancel any green hue in the appearance of that light. Similarly, the strength of the red process is indicated by the amount of green that has to be added to the wavelength to cancel any red hue. We now go through the entire visible spectrum, wavelength after wavelength, and perform the necessary cancellations. The results show that the red process is activated at both ends of the spectrum: the violets at the short end, the oranges at the long end. The green process on the other hand is activated in the middle region of the spectrum. (B) The blue-yellow process. The strength of the blue-yellow process is plotted by similar procedures. We arbitrarily decide to plot yellow as positive and blue as negative. To measure the strength of the blue process we determine how much yellow has to be added to a given wavelength to cancel all of the blue in its hue. By an analogous process we measure the strength of the yellow process by determining how much blue we have to add to cancel all the yellow. The results show that the blue process is activated toward the shorter wavelengths while the yellow process is evoked by the longer ones. (C) The two hue-processes considered jointly. In this figure, the curves for the red-green and the blue-yellow process are plotted on the same axis. Several points emerge. Note that the red-green curve crosses the horizontal axis at two points. At these two points, the activity of the red-green is at zero, for here red and green are in complete balance. At these points, the only contribution to perceived hue is made by the blue system. These two points therefore appear as unique blue (at about 475 nanometers) and as unique yellow (at 580 nanometers). Now turning to the blue-yellow process, we see that it crosses the horizontal axis at just one point. Here the blue-yellow system is in perfect balance and the only contribution is made by the red-green system. At this point, this system is tilted toward green, and this point therefore appears as unique green (at about 515 nanometers). (After Hurvich and Jameson, 1955)

which any given wavelength affects either the yellow-blue or the red-green process. The extent to which the yellow-blue system is affected was measured by the intensity of blue required to cancel yellow (or of yellow needed to cancel blue). A similar procedure was used to assess the activity of the red-green system by determining the intensity of red light required to cancel green or of green light necessary to cancel red (Figure 6.43).

The black-white system The brightness or darkness of a visual experience is determined by the activity of a third pair of antagonists, black and white. Every wavelength contributes to the excitation of the white system, in proportion to its intensity and the sensitivity of daylight vision to this point of the spectrum. The black process is produced by inhibition of the antagonistic white process. This is best exemplified by some phenomena of brightness contrast. A black paper placed against a dark gray background will look not black but a darker shade of gray. We can make it look pitch-black by presenting it against a brilliantly illuminated background. By doing so, we inhibit the white process within the enclosed region, which necessarily enhances the activity of its antagonist.*

* One may object that the sensation of black is also produced by the mere absence of visual stimulation. But this is not so: a prolonged stay in total darkness leads to a nondescript sensation of gray, as would be predicted by the opponent-process theory.

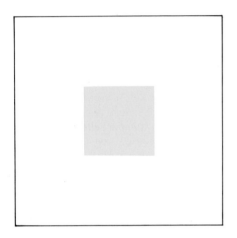

6.44 The black-white process and saturation One yellow patch is surrounded by black, the other (physically identical) by white. To most subjects, the two yellows do not appear to be identical. The one on black seems washed out (that is, desaturated) compared to the one on white. Because the yellow is rather bright to begin with, the patch activates not only yellow but a considerable amount of white; the result is a tendency toward desaturation. When this already bright yellow is placed on a black background, this tendency is magnified. The black induces its opposite, white in the yellow patch, and this adds to the already present white to desaturate the color even further. The opposite happens when the patch is seen against white. The white induces its opposite, black, which cancels some of the white in the yellow patch. As a result, the patch appears more saturated.

Opponent-process theory and saturation   Hue is determined by the tilt of the blue-yellow and red-green balances and brightness by the tilt of the black-white scale. We have not yet accounted for the attribute of saturation. According to Hurvich and Jameson, saturation depends upon the relationship between the activities of the two hue-systems on the one hand and the black-white system on the other. Maximum saturation will occur if one (or both) of the two hue systems is tilted all the way while the black-white system is as near equilibrium as possible. Saturation will decline as the hue systems swing closer to equilibrium (for example, if we add green and yellow to neutralize red and blue). It will also decline if we radically tilt the black-white system to either side: to white by increasing the stimulus intensity, or to black, by adding white light to the area surrounding the stimulus (which induces the black process by contrast; Figure 6.44).

Other color phenomena   The opponent-process theory is readily extended to cover the facts of chromatic contrast and negative afterimages. Chromatic contrast can be interpreted as lateral inhibition between identical processes. For example, the activation of the red mechanism in one retinal region presumably inhibits red processes in neighboring areas, thus tilting the red-green system toward green. Negative afterimages may be understood in similar terms. Inspection of a red light produces inhibition of its green antagonist. When the red light is withdrawn, the green process rebounds.

THE PHYSIOLOGICAL BASIS OF OPPONENT PROCESSES

When the opponent-process theory was first developed, its authors could only speculate about its concrete physiological embodiment. At that time, the opponent processes were only an inference, based upon the perceptual phenomena of color vision. Today there is evidence that this inference was close to the neurophysiological mark. The proof comes from single-cell recordings (in the retina or higher up) which show that some neurons behave very much as an opponent-process theory would lead one to expect.

As an example, take a study of single-cell activity in the visual pathway of the rhesus monkey, whose color vision is known to be very similar to ours. Some of its visual cells behave as though they were part of a red-green system. If the retina is stimulated by red light, these cells fire more rapidly. The opposite holds true if the same area is exposed to green light—the firing rate is inhibited (Figure 6.45). This is exactly what should happen if the underlying color mechanism mirrors the perceptual phenomena. Red should have one effect and green the opposite. Other cells have been discovered which show a similar antagonistic pattern when stimulated by blue or by yellow light (De-Valois, 1965).

COLOR BLINDNESS

A small proportion of the total population consists of people who do not respond to color as most others do. Of these the vast majority are men, since many such conditions are inherited and sex-linked. Some form of color defect is found in 8 percent of all males as compared to only .03 percent of females.

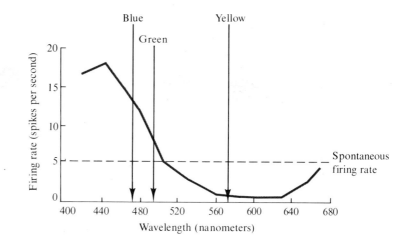

6.45 **Opponent process cells in the visual system of a monkey** *The figure shows the average firing rate of "blue-yellow cells" to light of different wavelengths. These cells are excited by shorter wavelengths and inhibited by longer wavelengths, analogous to the cells in the human system that signal the sensation "blue." As the figure shows, shorter wavelengths lead to firing rates that are above the spontaneous rates obtained when there is not stimulus at all. Longer wavelengths have the opposite effect, depressing the cell's activity below the spontaneous firing rate. (Data from DeValois and DeValois, 1975)*

Color deficiencies come in various forms, some of which involve a missing visual pigment, others a defective opponent process, and many involve malfunction at both levels. Most common is a defect in which reds are confused with greens; least common is total color blindness in which no hues can be distinguished at all. Color defects are rarely noticed in everyday life, for color-blind persons ordinarily use color names quite appropriately. They call blood red and dollar bills green, presumably on the basis of other cues such as form and brightness. To determine whether a person has a color defect he or she must be tested under special conditions in which such extraneous cues are eliminated (Figure 6.46).

How do people with color defects see colors? We may know that a particular person cannot distinguish between red and green, but that does not tell us how these colors look to him. He cannot tell us, for he cannot know what sensory quality is lacking. The question would have remained unanswerable had it not been for a subject who was red-green color blind in one eye and had normal color vision in the other. This subject (who happened to be one of the rare females with a color defect) was able to describe what she saw with the defective eye by using the color language of the normal one. With the color-blind eye she saw only grays, blues, and yellows. Red and green hues were altogether absent, as if one of the opponent-process pairs was missing (Graham and Hsia, 1954).

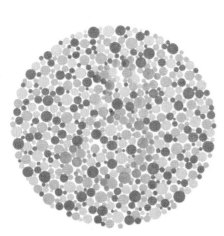

6.46 **Testing for color blindness** *A plate used to test for color blindness. To pick out the number in the plate, an observer has to be able to discriminate certain hues. Normals can do it and will see the number 3. Persons with red-green color-blindness cannot do this. (Courtesy American Optical Corporation)*

Let us take stock. We have looked at the way in which the different sensory systems respond to external stimuli, how they transduce the proximal stimulus and convert it into a neural impulse, how they code the incoming message into the various dimensions of our sensory experience, and how activity in any part of a sensory system interacts with the activity of other parts. All of this has led us to some understanding of how we come to see bright yellow-greens and hear high-pitched noises. But it has not yet addressed the question with which we started. How do we come to know about the objects and events outside—not just bright yellow-greens but grassy meadows, not just high-pitched noises but singing birds? That the sensory systems contribute the raw materials for such knowledge is clear enough. But how do we get from the sensory raw materials to a knowledge of the world outside? This question is traditionally dealt with under the heading of *perception,* the topic to which we turn next.

APPENDIX TO CHAPTER 6
Special Topics in Psychophysics:
Psychophysical Laws and Detection Theory

This chapter has dealt with several essential issues in the realm of psycho-physics. We now turn to some more advanced topics in psychophysical theory and method.

THE SEARCH FOR A PSYCHOPHYSICAL LAW

One important question in the area of psychophysics concerns the relationship between stimulus intensity and sensory magnitude. Can this relationship be expressed by a general equation that holds for all the senses? As we have seen, G. T. Fechner believed that such a general psychophysical law does exist. His own proposal (which we now call *Fechner's law)* was that the relationship is logarithmic. As one author paraphrased it, "The sensation plods along step by step while the stimulus leaps ahead by ratios" (Woodworth, 1938). We will now take a closer look at the reasoning that led Fechner to formulate his law.

FECHNER'S LAW

Fechner's starting point was *Weber's law.* As we saw, that law relates the difference threshold to the physical intensity of the stimulus. According to Weber's law, the amount, ΔI, that must be added to a stimulus of intensity I to produce a just noticeable increase (a j.n.d.) is a constant fraction of that stimulus intensity, I. Put algebraically, this asserts that

$$\frac{\Delta I}{I} = C$$

where C is a constant.

Fechner believed that Weber's law was the basis of a general quantitative relationship between sensory and physical intensity. But there was a crucial gap. Is there a scale of subjective sensory intensity that has some of the same properties which characterize physical dimensions? Consider temperature. Its units remain equal throughout the scale. The difference between 6 and 7 degrees centigrade is identical to that between 1,000 and 1,001 degrees centigrade. Could one devise a psychological scale for sensory magnitude that satisfies the same criterion?

Fechner thought he could. The unit of his proposed scale was the j.n.d. His critical assumption was that all j.n.d.s within a given sensory dimension (for example, loudness) are subjectively equal. Given this assumption, we have a psychological scale. Take any dimension of sensory intensity, for example, heaviness. The psychological scale has an obvious zero point, the absolute threshold. We can then go up in j.n.d steps. We find the weight that is just heavier than the absolute threshold, then the weight just heavier than this, and so on. The resulting set of weights is a series of physical intensities, presumably in grams: $W_1, W_2, W_3, \ldots$ and so on, each separated from the next by one j.n.d.

Corresponding to each of these weights are different sensations, $S_1, S_2, S_3,$

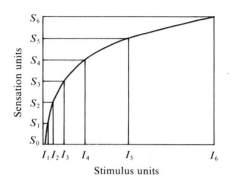

6.47 Fechner's law The relationship between sensation and stimulus intensity according to Fechner. As sensation goes up in equal steps, the corresponding steps in physical stimulus intensity go up geometrically. The result is the logarithmic relationship shown in the figure. (After Guilford, 1954)

S. S. Stevens (Courtesy Harvard University News Office)

... and so on. The important point is that the subjective magnitude of these sensations is assumed to go up in equal steps since, according to Fechner, all j.n.d.s are subjectively equal. The result is a subjective scale that has many of the admirable qualities of scales such as temperature; the difference between, say, S_4 and S_5 is the same as that between S_8 and S_9.

$S_1, S_2, S_3, \ldots$ and so on go up in equal steps, at least according to Fechner. But this is not the case for $W_1, W_2, W_3, \ldots$ and so on, the physical intensities that produced these sensations. These weights are each separated by one j.n.d., and Weber's law tells us that each just noticeable stimulus increment is a constant fraction of the stimulus to which it is added. In consequence, we must mark off ever-larger intervals on the physical scale to correspond to equal intervals on the psychological dimension: The sensations go up by an arithmetic series, the stimuli by a geometric series (Figure 6.47). Fechner derived an equation which expresses this relationship in a more general form,

$$S = k \log I,$$

where S stands for subjective magnitude, I for the intensity of the physical stimulus, and k is a constant. This equation, now called Fechner's law, asserts that the strength of a sensation grows as the logarithm of stimulus intensity.

Fechner's formulation was very influential, especially in psychology's early days. He had shown that it was possible to relate things of the mind to things of the body and to do so in precise, quantitative terms. His law seemed to follow neatly from his premises, and for many decades the facts available seemed to bear it out. But later investigators have raised some serious objections.

ALTERNATIVES TO FECHNER'S LAW

As we have seen, the validity of Weber's law is only one of the assumptions upon which Fechner had built his formulation. What about the others? Is it really true that sensory magnitude can only be assessed indirectly as Fechner had claimed?

Stevens' power law The Harvard psychologist S. S. Stevens (1906–1973) argued that there is a more straightforward method. He asked subjects to estimate sensory magnitude *directly*. The subjects were presented with a series of stimuli to which they had to assign numbers that were proportional to the corresponding subjective impressions. Thus, if one tone sounds three times louder than another, the subject had to assign a number to the first that was three times larger than the number given to the second (Stevens, 1961 *a* and *b*).

There were two main findings. First, the subjects had little trouble in performing the task. They could evidently rate or judge their own subjective experiences, thereby producing a direct scale of subjective magnitude. The second finding concerns the relation between this scale and physical intensity. The function Stevens obtained was not logarithmic, as Fechner proposed. Instead, it was a power function,

$$S = kI^N,$$

where S stands for subjective magnitude, I for stimulus intensity, and where k and N are constants. In effect, this exponential function asserts that the inten-

215

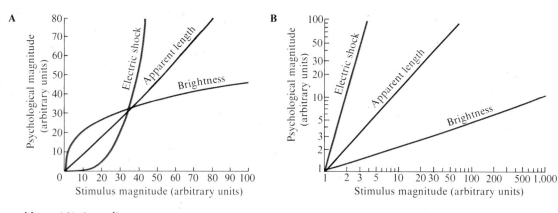

6.48 Stevens' law *(A) According to Stevens, the perceived magnitude of a stimulus is a power function of the physical intensity of that stimulus. When subjective magnitude is plotted against physical magnitude, the power function will be concave upward if the exponent of the power function is greater than 1, as in the case of electric shock. Here, a small range of physical intensities is expanded into a wider range of subjective values. The function will be concave downward when the exponent is less than 1, as in the case of visual brightness. Here, a wide range of stimulus intensities is compressed into a smaller span of subjective values. A final case occurs when the exponent is 1, as with the apparent length of lines. Here, the function that relates subjective and physical magnitude is a straight line, and there is neither compression nor expansion. (B) The power functions are here replotted so that both subjective magnitude and physcial intensity are expressed in logarithmic units. If the curves are indeed power functions, this replotting should yield straight lines. Generally speaking, this seems to be the case. Note that the slope of the lines is determined by the exponent N. If N is larger than 1 (as in the case of electric shock), the slope is relatively steep; if it is smaller than 1 (as in visual brightness), the slope is relatively flat. (Stevens, 1961)*

sity of a sensation is proportional to stimulus intensity raised to a certain power.

The value of the exponent N in the power function evidently depends upon the sensory dimension. For many of these (such as brightness, for which $N = .33$), N is smaller than 1. The result is a function in which sensation grows more slowly than stimulus intensity and which, in this respect, is similar to Fechner's: A wide range of stimulus intensities is compressed into a small span of subjective values. But for a few dimensions, N seems to be larger than 1. This produces the opposite effect: Sensation grows more rapidly than stimulus intensity, thus expanding a smaller stimulus range into a wider range of subjective magnitudes (Figure 6.48). An cxample is pain produced by electric shock ($N = 3.5$). Here, the organism is obviously better served by expansion than by compression. When the stimulus is noxious and already quite intense, even a small increment in its intensity may spell the difference between survival and destruction. Expansion of the subjective scale incites the victim to flee before serious harm is done.

The lasting contributions What can we say about the relative merits of Fechner's and Stevens' laws? On balance, the evidence seems to be in favor of Stevens' formulation, though the issue is still unsettled. Yet in retrospect, the lasting contributions are probably not the specific psychophysical laws themselves. To be sure, it was worth pointing out that the nervous system compresses (and occasionally expands) the enormous range of physical stimulus energies it has to cope with. But what was much more important was the development of methods for studying sensation. Until the middle of the nineteenth century, scientists had despaired of ever measuring psychological processes. Fechner showed that it could be done. He did it indirectly, by sneaking up on sensory intensity and measuring it with a same-different judgment technique. In doing so, he gave the study of sensation its first tools. Later investigators, especially Stevens, extended Fechner's pioneering effort and showed that it was possible for subjects to deal with sensations head-on and to scale them directly.

DETECTION AND DECISION

Up to now, we have carefully swept one troublesome problem under the rug. We have tacitly assumed that psychophysical measures are unaffected by the subject's wishes or expectations. But this is untrue.

RESPONSE BIAS

We have already seen that subjects fluctuate in their reactions to the same physical stimulus intensity. On some trials they can hear it (or see it or feel it); on others they cannot. Since this is so, beliefs and attitudes come into play. Consider a study of absolute thresholds. On every trial, the harried subject is forced into a decision. Is a stimulus there or isn't it? This decision is often difficult, for at times the stimulus is so weak that the subject is quite uncertain of his judgment. Under the circumstances, any *response bias* the subject has, will exert an effect. Such a response bias is a preference for one response over another (here "yes" or "no"), quite apart from the nature of the stimuli. Thus some subjects will approach the task with a free-and-easy attitude, cheerfully offering "yes" judgments whenever they are in doubt. Others will take a more conservative line and will never respond with a "yes" unless they are quite certain. This will produce a difference in obtained thresholds which will necessarily be lower for the subjects who are more liberal with their "yes" responses. But this only reflects a difference in response bias, not in sensory sensitivity. Both groups of subjects can presumably hear or see or feel the stimuli equally well. They only differ in their willingness to report a stimulus when they are unsure.

SIGNAL DETECTION

Such considerations make it clear that thresholds obtained by traditional techniques (such as Fechner's) reflect two factors, sensitivity and response bias. How can these be separated?

The early psychophysicists tried to cope with this problem by using subjects who were highly trained observers. In absolute threshold studies, such subjects would be models of conservatism; they would never say "yes" unless they were completely certain. To maintain this attitude, the experimenters threw in an occasional *catch trial* on which there was no stimulus at all (Woodworth, 1938).

A recent approach to psychophysics, usually described under the heading *signal-detection theory,* has dealt with response bias of attitude more systematically. Its first step was the development of a somewhat different testing technique in which catch trials are a regular part of the procedure rather than just an occasional check to keep the subjects on their toes. This method is called the *detection experiment* (Green and Swets, 1966).

In one version of this procedure, the question is whether the subject can detect the presence of a stimulus. We take a fairly weak stimulus and present it on half of the trials. On the other half of the trials (obviously in random order) we present no stimulus at all. Now the subject may commit two very different kinds of errors. One is a *miss,* not reporting a stimulus when one is presented.

Table 6.3   THE FOUR POSSIBLE OUTCOMES OF THE DETECTION EXPERIMENT

	Responds "yes"	Responds "no"
Stimulus present	Hit	Miss
Stimulus absent	False alarm	Correct negative

Table 6.4   PAYOFF MATRIX THAT WILL PRODUCE A "YES" BIAS

	Subject says "yes"	Subject says "no"
Stimulus present	+ 10¢	− 10¢
Stimulus absent	− 1¢	+ 5¢

Another is a ***false alarm,*** reporting a stimulus when in fact none is present. By the same token there are two different kinds of correct responses: reporting a stimulus when it is actually there ***(hit)*** and not reporting it when none is present ***(correct negative)*** (Table 6.3).

THE PAYOFF MATRIX

The detection experiment provides a basis for getting at the nonsensory factors that underlie response bias. One such factor is differential payoff. Suppose we (literally) pay a subject for every hit and correct negative and penalize her for every miss and false alarm, according to a prescribed schedule of gains and losses called a ***payoff matrix.*** Thus the subject might gain 10 cents for every hit and 5 cents for every correct negative, while losing 10 cents for every miss and only 1 cent for every false alarm. Such a payoff matrix will lead to a bias toward "yes" judgments (Table 6.4). Suppose there are, say, 50 trials on which the subject has no sensory information on the basis of which she can decide whether the stimulus is present or not. If she consistently says "yes," she will on the average be correct on 25 trials (thus collecting ($2.50) and wrong on the other 25 (thus losing $0.25) for a net gain of $2.25. In contrast, consistent "no" judgments will lead to a net loss (+$1.25 for the correct negatives and −$2.50 for the false alarms).

If the stimulus is presented on half of the trials, the payoff bias can be calculated easily by comparing the sum of the values under the Says "yes" column with the sum under the Says "no" column. In this example, these sums are + 9¢ and − 5¢ respectively. Under the circumstances, the subject will do well to adopt a liberal criterion and give a "yes" judgment whenever she is in doubt.

Illustrations of the effect of payoff matrices abound in real life. There the differential payoff is usually reckoned in units larger than pennies. Consider a team of radiologists poring over an X ray to look for a tiny spot that indicates the start of a malignant tumor. What are the penalties for error here? If the physicians decide there is no spot when there actually is one, their miss may cost the patient's life. If they decide that they see a spot when in fact there is none, their false alarm has other costs, such as the dangers of more elaborate clinical tests, let alone those of an operation. What the physicians ultimately decide will depend, both on what their eyes tell them as they inspect the X ray and also on the relative costs of the two possible errors they may commit.

SEPARATING SENSITIVITY AND RESPONSE BIAS: THE ROC CURVE

The preceding discussion showed that psychophysical results are jointly determined by sensitivity and response bias. Is there any way in which the two can be disentangled? The procedure of the detection experiment does provide a means.

The first step is to vary response bias while keeping sensitivity constant. This can be done by changing the payoff matrix. Another way is to vary the proportion of trials on which no stimulus is presented—the fewer such trials, the greater the yes bias.

When response bias is varied in this fashion, the results are quite systematic. If we induce the subject to be more conservative, we find a reduction in the

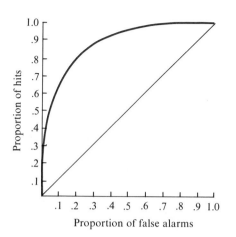

6.49 **The ROC curve** *The proportion of hits is plotted against the proportion of false alarms. The stimulus is kept constant but the response bias is systematically varied by asking subjects to adopt a more liberal attitude with their yeses. This bias becomes progressively larger as we move upward on the vertical axis (proportion of hits) and to the right on the horizontal axis (proportion of false alarms). Note that as the proportion of hits increases, so does the proportion of false alarms.*

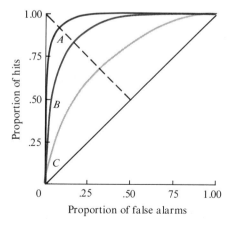

proportion of trials on which he is guilty of a false alarm. But at the same time, we also find a reduction in the proportion of hits. Similarly, upward shifts in the yes bias lead to an increase in the proportion of both hits and false alarms. These effects can be expressed graphically by plotting the two proportions against each other. The resulting function is known by the rather arcane designation of *receiver-operating-characteristic curve,* which is almost always abbreviated *ROC curve* (Figure 6.49).

The next step is to get an index of sensitivity that is uncontaminated by response bias. To do so, we obtain separate ROC curves for different levels of stimulus intensity (with each curve based on a separate detection experiment). The results are very striking. The stronger the stimulus, the more its ROC curve is bowed away from the main diagonal (Figure 6.50).

Why should this be so? To answer this question, consider a hypothetical detection experiment using a visual stimulus but a blind subject. Here the subject's sensitivity is obviously zero, so that his judgments must be based entirely upon response bias. For this blind subject, the stimulus does not exist, so that he is just as likely to obtain a hit as to strike a false alarm. In consequence, his ROC curve is necessarily the *main diagonal.* His yes bias can go up or down, but his proportion of hits and of false alarms will always be equal. Evidently, the main diagonal represents total insensitivity, an absolute inability to distinguish the presence of a stimulus from its absence. As sensitivity goes up, the ROC curve moves away from the diagonal. Thus, the displacement of the ROC curve from the main diagonal provides a pure measure of sensitivity for the stimulus on which the ROC curve is based; it is measured along the second diagonal (Figure 6.50).

SIGNAL DETECTION AND THE DECISION PROCESS

There is one question that we have not really considered. Why does the subject have so much trouble distinguishing between the presence of a stimulus and its absence? Signal-detection theory proposes an intriguing answer. It asserts that there really is no such thing as a zero stimulus.

The theory begins by assuming that psychophysical judgments are based on some underlying neural activity in the sensory system (whose exact nature is for now irrelevant) which can vary in magnitude. Let us call this hypothetical activity the *sensory process.* A sensory process can of course be produced by an actual, external stimulus (the *signal).* But signal-detection theory proposes that a sensory process will occur even when in fact no stimulus is administered. The factors responsible for this are collectively described as *background noise.* Take an experiment in hearing and suppose that no sound is actually presented. This does not guarantee the absence of activity in the auditory system. Some sources of stimulation come from within the subject, such as the throbbing of the pulse. In addition, there is spontaneous activity in the nervous system, with many cells firing at random intervals without any external trigger. Under the circumstances, to say that there is no stimulus only means

6.50 **ROC curves for stimuli of different intensities** *The figure shows ROC curves for three stimuli of increasing intensity (with A the strongest and C the weakest). Note that the stronger the stimulus, the more its ROC curve is displaced from the main diagonal. We can think of this diagonal as the ROC curve produced by a stimulus to which the subject is utterly insensitive. The displacement of the ROC curve from the main diagonal provides a pure index of sensitivity. It is measured along the second diagonal (dotted lines).*

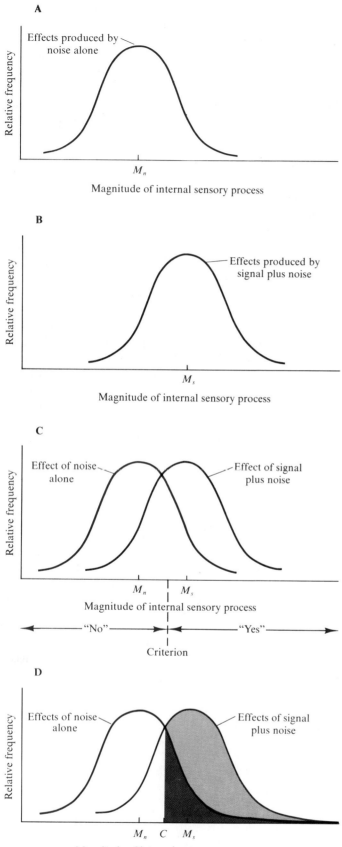

A

Relative frequency

Effects produced by noise alone

M_n

Magnitude of internal sensory process

B

Relative frequency

Effects produced by signal plus noise

M_s

Magnitude of internal sensory process

C

Relative frequency

Effect of noise alone

Effect of signal plus noise

M_n M_s

Magnitude of internal sensory process

"No"   "Yes"

Criterion

D

Relative frequency

Effects of noise alone

Effects of signal plus noise

M_n C M_s

Magnitude of internal sensory process

6.51   The decision process envisaged by signal-detection theory   *(A) Consider the (hypothetical) internal sensory process produced by noise alone, with no stimulus actually presented. The magnitude of this process will sometimes be smaller, sometimes larger. (A) is a frequency distribution, in which the magnitude of the internal process is plotted on the horizontal axis and the frequency with which it occurs is plotted on the vertical. Frequency is here defined in relative terms, by the proportion of trials on which a given magnitude occurs. The most likely magnitude of the internal sensory process is M_n, which is the mean or average of the frequency distribution of these magnitudes produced by noise alone. (B) shows what happens when a stimulus is actually presented. Here too the magnitude of the internal sensory process will sometimes be smaller and sometimes larger. But the values obtained now will in general be larger, since we are dealing with trials in which there is both a signal as well as background noise. As a result, the mean of this frequency distribution, M_s, will be larger than M_n, the mean of the frequency distribution produced by noise alone. (C) How does the subject decide whether she heard a stimulus or not? To see how signal detection theory deals with this issue, we plot the noise-alone and the signal-plus-noise distribution on the same axis. As (C) indicates, the two distributions overlap. This means that on some trials, the magnitude of the internal process produced when there is no stimulus (noise-alone) exceeds that which is generated when a stimulus is there (signal-plus-noise).*

What can the subject do now? Her task, in effect, is to decide whether a given internal experience comes from the signal-plus-noise frequency distribution or the noise-alone distribution. According to signal-detection theory, the subject arrives at this decision by setting herself a criterion. She acts according to a decision rule. If the magnitude of the sensory process exceeds this criterion, C, she decides that it came from the signal-plus-noise distribution and makes a "yes" judgment. If the value of the internal process is less than C, she decides that it was produced by noise alone and gives a "no" judgment. (D) Since the noise-alone and the signal-plus-noise distributions overlap, there is no way in which the subject can avoid some errors. The nature of these errors depends partially on the criterion. As (D) shows, all judgments to the left of the criterion, C, are "nos" while all judgments to the right are "yeses." We can now read off the relative proportion of hits and false alarms directly from the figure. The proportion of hits is given by the portion of the area under the signal-plus-noise curve which falls to the right of C (here indicated in color). The proportion of false alarms is given by the portion of the area under the noise-alone curve which falls to the right of the same criterion point (here indicated in darker color). Exactly where the criterion is placed, depends on the subject's response bias. If she wants to minimize misses (saying "no" when a signal was actually presented), she has to shift her criterion to the left. This will decrease the number of misses but must necessarily increase the number of false alarms.

that the experimenter did not present one. From the subject's point of view, some stimulation is always there.

We can now state the subject's task in a detection experiment in another way. He must decide whether a given sensory process should be attributed to the signal superimposed on background noise or to the background noise alone; whether what he hears is a faint tone outside or his own heartbeat (or spontaneous neural firing or whatever) within. On the average, the signal (plus background noise) produces a process of greater magnitude than does the noise alone, an average value which rises with increasing signal strength. The subject's decision problem arises because the magnitude of the two sets of sensory processes fluctuates. Occasionally, one's heartbeat sounds louder than the experimenter's stimulus tone. But the more intense the stimulus, the less likely it is that such a confusion will occur (Figure 6.51).

To sum up, contemporary investigators using a signal-detection approach have a somewhat different conception of what a sensation is than did earlier psychophysicists. Neither Fechner nor Stevens had any doubt that people have sensations and can report certain things about them. They differed mainly in their beliefs as to how much can be reported and how directly. But according to signal-detection theorists, sensations are not directly given. Instead, these theorists postulate an internal sensory process that can be produced by both signal and by background noise alone. This means that there is always some sensory-process activity. The implication is that subjects have no privileged information about their own mental states. They can't simply *report* that they have a sensation, as Fechner and Stevens thought they could. The best they can do is to *decide* that they have a sensation—that their internal sensory experience is produced by a signal rather than by noise alone. And in this decision they can be wrong.

Summary

1. The study of sensory processes grew out of questions about the origin of human knowledge. John Locke and other *empiricists* argued that all knowledge comes through stimuli that excite the senses. We can distinguish two kinds of stimuli. One is the *distal stimulus,* an object or event in the world outside. The other is the *proximal stimulus,* the pattern of physical stimulus energies that impinges on a given sensory surface. The only way to get information about distal stimuli outside is through the proximal stimuli these give rise to. This leads to theoretical problems, for we perceive many qualities—depth, constant size and shape—that are not given in the proximal stimulus. Empiricists try to overcome such difficulties by asserting that much of perception is built up through learning by *association.* This view has been challenged by *nativists* such as Immanuel Kant who believe that the sensory input is organized according to a number of built-in categories.

2. The path to sensory experience or *sensation* begins with a proximal stimulus. This is *transduced* into a nervous inpulse by specialized receptors, is usually further modified by other parts of the nervous system, and finally leads to a sensation. One branch of sensory psychology is psychophysics which tries to relate the characteristics of the physical stimulus to both the quality and intensity of the sensory experience.

3. Qualitative differences in sensory experience occur both between *sensory modalities* (e.g., A-flat versus red) and within them (e.g., green versus red). According to the *doctrine of specific nerve energies* such qualitative differences are ultimately

caused by differences between the nervous structures excited by the stimuli rather than by differences between the stimuli as such.

4. The founder of psychophysics, Gustav T. Fechner, studied sensory intensity by determining the ability of subjects to discriminate between stimulus intensities. Important measures of this ability are the *absolute threshold* and the *difference threshold*. The difference threshold is the change in the intensity of a given stimulus (the so-called *standard* stimulus) that is just large enough to be detected, producing a *just noticeable difference* or *j.n.d.* According to *Weber's law,* the j.n.d. is a constant fraction of the intensity of the standard stimulus. Fechner generalized Weber's law to express a wider relationship between sensory intensity and physical intensity. This is *Fechner's law,* which states that the strength of a sensation grows as the logarithm of stimulus intensity.

6. Different sense modalities have somewhat different functions and mechanisms. One group of senses provides information about the body's own movement and location. Skeletal motion is sensed through *kinesthesis,* bodily orientation by the *vestibular organs* located in the *inner ears.*

7. The sense of taste acts as a gatekeeper to the digestive system. Its receptors are the *taste buds* whose stimulation generates the four basic taste qualities of *sour, sweet, salty,* and *bitter.*

8. The various *skin senses* inform the organism of what is directly adjacent to its own body. There are at least four different skin sensations: *pressure, warmth, cold,* and *pain.* Whether each of these four is produced by separate receptors is still a matter of debate, though there is no doubt that these experiences are evoked in different spots of the skin.

9. Smell or *olfaction* is the most primitive of the distance senses. In humans, it is relatively minor but in many animals it is a vital guide to food, mates, and danger. In many species it permits a primitive form of communication based on *pheromones.*

10. The sense of hearing or *audition* informs us of pressure changes that occur at a distance. Its stimulus is a disturbance of the air which is propagated in the form of *sound waves.* These can vary in *amplitude* and *frequency,* and may be *simple* or *complex.*

11. A number of accessory structures help to conduct and amplify sound waves so that they can affect the auditory receptors. Sound waves set up vibrations in the *eardrum* which are then transmitted by the *ossicles* to the *oval window* whose movements create waves in the *cochlea* of the inner ear. Within the cochlea is the *basilar membrane* which contains the auditory receptors that are stimulated by the membrane's deformation. According to the *place theory,* the sensory experience of pitch is based on the place of the membrane that is stimulated; each place being responsive to a particular wave frequency and generating a particular pitch sensation. According to the *frequency theory,* the stimulus for pitch is the firing frequency of the auditory nerve. Modern theorists believe that both mechanisms operate: Higher frequencies depend upon the place of the basilar membrane, while lower frequencies depend upon neural firing frequency.

12. Vision is our primary distance sense. Its stimulus is light, which can vary in *intensity* and *wavelength.* Many of the structures of the eye, such as the *lens* and the *iris,* serve mainly as accessory devices to fashion a proper proximal stimulus, the *retinal image.* Once on the retina, the light stimulus is transduced into a neural impulse by the visual receptors, the *rods* and *cones. Visual acuity* is greatest in the *fovea* where the density of the receptors (here, cones) is greatest.

13. According to the *duplicity theory of vision,* rods and cones differ in function. The rods operate at low light intensities and lead to colorless sensations. The cones function at much higher illumination levels and are responsible for sensations of color. Further evidence for the duplicity theory comes from different *spectral sensitivity curves* and different curves of *dark adaptation.*

14. The first stage in the transformation of light into a neural impulse is a photochemical process that involves the breakdown of various *visual pigments* that are later resynthesized. One such pigment is *rhodopsin,* the photochemically sensitive substance contained by rods.

15. The various components of the visual system do not operate in isolation but interact constantly. One form of interaction occurs over time, as in various forms of *adaptation.* Visual adaptation is usually counteracted by eye movements, but their effects can be nullified by the *stabilized image* procedure.

16. Interaction also occurs over space, between neighboring regions on the retina. An example is *brightness contrast.* This tends to enhance the distinction between an object and its background and also *accentuates contours.* The physiological mechanism that underlies this is *lateral inhibition,* as deduced from studies of *receptive fields.*

17. Visual sensations have a qualitative character—they vary in color. Color sensations can be ordered by reference to three dimensions: *hue, brightness,* and *saturation.* Colors can be mixed, *subtractively* (as in mixing pigments) or *additively* (as in simultaneously stimulating the same region of the retina with two or more stimuli). The results of additive mixture studies show that every hue has a *complementary hue* which, when mixed with the first, yields gray. Two important examples are red and green, and blue and yellow. These two color pairs are color antagonists, a fact shown by the phenomena of the *negative afterimage* and *simultaneous color contrast.*

18. The first question about the mechanisms that underlie color vision concerns the way in which the different light waves are transduced into a receptor discharge. There is general agreement that this is done by the joint action of three different cone types, each of which has a somewhat different sensitivity curve.

19. A second question concerns the way the receptor message is converted into our color experience. A leading approach is the *opponent-process theory* of Hurvich and Jameson. This assumes that there are three neural systems, each of which corresponds to a pair of antagonistic sensory experiences: red-green, blue-yellow, and black-white. The first two determine perceived hue; the third determines perceived brightness. To develop the theory further, Hurvich and Jameson mapped out the sensitivity of the red-green and blue-yellow systems to different wavelengths, using a *cancellation procedure.* Further evidence for the opponent-process view comes from single-cell recordings of monkeys and some phenomena of *color blindness.*

CHAPTER 7

Perception

In the previous chapter, we discussed some of the simpler attributes of sensory experience, such as red, A-flat, and cold. Locke and Berkeley thought that these experiences were produced by a passive registration of the proximal stimulus energies which impinge upon the senses. But, as we have seen, the eye is more than a camera, the ear more than a microphone, for both sensory systems actively transform their stimulus inputs at the very start of their neurological journey, emphasizing differences and minimizing stimulation that remains unchanged. This active organization of the stimulus input is impressive enough when we consider the experience of simple sensory attributes, but it becomes even more dramatic when we turn to the fundamental problem traditionally associated with the term *perception:* how we come to apprehend the objects and events in the external reality around us; how we come to see, not just a brightish red, but an apple.

The Problem of Perception

What must be explained to understand how we see the apple? Our initial reaction might be that the only problem is the perceptual meaning of the visual input, how it is interpreted as an edible fruit—which grows on trees, which keeps the doctor away, which caused the expulsion from Eden, and so on. But how objects acquire perceptual meaning is by no means the only question, or even the most basic one, for the student of perception. The fundamental issue is not why a given stimulus is seen as a particular kind of object, but rather why it is seen as any object at all. Suppose we show the apple to someone who has never seen any fruit before. He will not know its function, but he will certainly see it as some round, red thing of whose tangible existence he has no doubt—in short, he will perceive it as an object.

GOING BEYOND THE PROXIMAL STIMULUS

Our discussion of the sensory systems thus far does not explain this basic phenomenon of object perception, the fact that we see the apple as it really is: of constant form and size, in depth, and stationary. But this reality is the reality of the distal stimulus, the actual apple in the external world. The problem is that the distal stimulus is known to us only through the proximal stimulus that it projects upon our retina, and this proximal stimulus is two-dimensional and is constantly changing. It gets smaller or larger depending upon our distance from it; it stimulates different regions of the retina; it moves across the retina as we move our eyes. How does the organism manage to perceive the constant properties of the external object despite the variations in the proximal stimulus?

The attempts to answer this question are best understood as parts of the continuing debate between the heirs of Locke, Berkeley, and Hume on the one hand, and those of Kant on the other. This controversy between empiricists and nativists will serve as an organizational framework for much of the discussion in this chapter.

EMPIRICISM AND NATIVISM REVISITED

Most of the phenomena perception psychologists deal with involve some apparent discrepancy between what the proximal stimulus gives us and what we actually see. The question is how to resolve this discrepancy.

THE EMPIRICISTS' ANSWER

Empiricists handle the problem by asserting that the sensation produced by a particular stimulus is modified and reinterpreted in the light of what we have learned through past experience. Consider perceived size. People five feet away look just about as tall as those at a fifty-foot distance. This is not merely because we *know* them to be average-sized rather than giants or midgets. The fact is that they really *look* equally tall provided there are cues which indicate their proper distance (Figure 7.1).

How can we explain this and similar phenomena? The most influential version of the empiricists' answer was formulated by Hermann von Helmholtz in the late nineteenth century. According to Helmholtz, the perceiver has two sources of information. To begin with, there is the sensation derived from the

A

B

7.1 Perceived size and distance (A) The actual image of the two women in the picture—which corresponds to the size of their retinal image—is in the ratio of 3 to 1. But this is not the way they are perceived. They look roughly equal in size, but at different distances, with one about three times farther off than the other. In (B) there are no cues that indicate that one woman is farther away than the other. On the contrary. The figure was constructed by cutting the more distant woman out of the picture, and pasting her next to the other woman, with the apparent distance from the viewer equal for the two. Now they look very different in size. (From Boring, 1964)

size of the object on the retina. In addition, there are a number of depth cues that indicate how far away the object is. Prior learning has taught the perceiver a general rule: the farther away things are, the smaller will be the sensation derived from the retinal image. The perceiver can now infer the true size of the object, given its retinal size, its distance, and the learned rule that relates the two. As a result she adjusts her perception of size, shifting it downward if the object is seen as close by and upward if it is seen farther off. Helmholtz of course knew full well that we don't go through any *conscious* calculation of this sort when we look at objects and perceive their size. But he believed that some such process was going on anyway and he therefore called it **unconscious inference** (Helmholtz, 1909).

THE NATIVISTS' ANSWER

The nativists' reply is that the perception of true size is directly given. They argue that the stimulus for the perceived size of an object is not the size of its retinal image as such. It is rather some relationship between that size and certain other visual attributes that pertain to depth.

Let's go back to Figure 7.1A. The two women look equally large, even though the two retinal images they give rise to are very different. But this phenomenon is only a problem if we believe that the stimulus for the perceived size of an object is the size of that object's retinal image, without reference to anything else on the retina. Suppose that this stimulus is actually some relationship—between the retinal image of that object and the retinal image of its background. An example of such a relationship is the ratio between the height of the person and the height of the door she sits next to. As the figures show, this ratio is constant. It represents an **invariant** relationship in the stimulus pattern itself which stays unchanged despite changes in distance from the observer. If this ratio is really the stimulus for perceived size, then the problem is solved. Perception is constant, but so is the stimulus (now redefined as the appropriate ratio).

Actually, the situation is more complex. For in fact, distant objects often appear to be of about the right size even in the absence of simple perspective cues of the kind shown in the figure. But our present concern is not with the specifics of perceived size (for that, see pp. 256–59). It is rather to illustrate what the nativists try to do. To explain the phenomena of perceptual organization—the way in which we see space and form and movement—they don't appeal to learning. Instead, they try to look for some more complex characteristic of the stimulus pattern (such as the person-to-door ratio of our example) to which observers respond directly.

As we shall see, the nature-nurture controversy is still with us. Some of its skirmishes have been resolved in favor of one or the other combatant, but this doesn't mean that the conflict is over. Perception psychologists are still divided over such issues as whether visual size and form are directly given or are learned. We cannot take up these matters until we've discussed some of the phenomena in the perception of form, depth, and movement. But we should nevertheless keep them in the backs of our minds, for many of the specific questions we will take up are really subquestions within the great debate between the empiricists and their nativist opponents.

Perceptual Organization

An organism that looks at the world is in effect asking three perceptual questions, the answers to which may be the key to its own survival: What is it? Where is it? What is it doing? Reflecting these questions, we now will discuss some aspects of the perception of form, of depth, and of movement.

THE PERCEPTION OF FORM: WHAT IS IT?

FIGURE-GROUND

Before we can ask what an object is, we must first see it as a coherent whole which stands out against its background, as a tree stands out against the sky and the clouds. This segregation of *figure* and *ground* can easily be seen in two-dimensional pictures. In Figure 7.2, the bright splotch appears as the figure which seems to be cohesive and articulated. On the other hand, the darker region is normally perceived as the ground, which is relatively formless and seems to extend behind the figure.

The differentiation between figure and ground is a perceptual achievement which is accomplished by the perceptual system. It is not in the stimulus as such. Consider the contours that separate the two regions of Figure 7.2. Physically, this contour is simply the transition between one level of stimulus intensity and another; in this sense, the contour belongs to one region as much as to the other. But perceptually the situation is very different. We see the contour as belonging to the figure. (This is why the ground does not seem to stop at the figure's edge but rather seems to extend behind it.) This point is made very strikingly by *reversible figures* in which either of two figure-ground organizations is possible. A classical demonstration is shown in Figure 7.3 which can be seen either as a white vase on a black background or as two black profile faces on a white background. Note that the contour looks different depending upon the figure-ground organization and that it is always seen as part of the figure and never as belonging to the ground. This reversibility of figure-ground patterns has fascinated various artists, especially in recent times.

7.2 Figure and ground   The first step in seeing a form is to segregate it from its background. The part seen as figure appears to be more cohesive and sharply delineated. The part seen as ground is perceived to be more formless and to extend behind the figure.

7.3 Reversible figure-ground patterns (A) is a classic example of a reversible figure-ground pattern. It can be seen as either a pair of silhouetted faces or a white vase.

Figure-ground reversal and art   Victor Vasarely uses the reversible pattern in his print of two lovers embracing. Either lover can be seen as figure or ground (© SPADEM, Paris/VAGA, N.Y. 1980.)

Max Wertheimer   *(Courtesy Omikron)*

PERCEPTUAL GROUPING

Reversible figure-ground formations demonstrate that the same proximal pattern may give rise to different perceptual organizations. The same conclusion follows from the related phenomenon of perceptual **grouping.** Suppose we look at a collection of dots. We can perceive the pattern in various ways depending upon how we group the dots: as a set of rows, or columns, or diagonals, and so on. In each case, the figural organization is quite different even though the proximal stimulus pattern is always the same.

What determines how a pattern will be organized? Some of the factors that determine visual grouping were first described by Max Wertheimer (1880–1943), the founder of **Gestalt psychology,** a school of psychology that believes that organization is basic to all mental activity, that it is unlearned, and that it reflects the way the brain functions. Wertheimer regarded these factors as the laws of **perceptual organization** (Wertheimer, 1923). A few of these are discussed below.

Proximity   The closer two figures are to each other **(proximity)** the more they will tend to be grouped together perceptually (Figure 7.4). Proximity may operate in time just as it does in space. The obvious example is auditory rhythm: four drum beats with a pause between the second and third will be heard as two pairs.

7.4   Proximity as a factor in perceptual organization   *The six lines in the figure will generally be perceived as three pairs of lines.*

Similarity   Other things equal, we tend to group figures according to their **similarity.** Thus in Figure 7.5, we group black dots together with black dots and colored dots with colored dots. As a result, we see columns rather than rows in one case, and rows rather than columns in the other. Equivalent effects are produced by similarities in such other major visual attributes as line orientation (Beck, 1966).

7.5   Similarity as a factor in perceptual organization   *Similarity often determines grouping. Here, the dots are grouped by color, leading to a perception of columns in the upper panel, and of rows in the lower panel.*

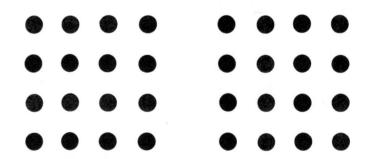

Good continuation   Our visual system seems to "prefer" contours that continue smoothly along their original course. This principle of grouping is called **good continuation** (Figure 7.6). Good continuation is a powerful organiza-

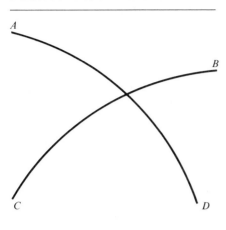

7.6 Good continuation as a factor in perceptual organization *The line segments in the figure will generally be grouped so that the contours continue smoothly. As a result, segment* A *will be grouped with* D, *and* C *with* B.

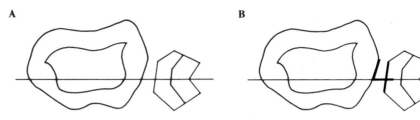

7.7 Good continuation pitted against prior experience *In (A), virtually all subjects see two complex patterns intersected by a horizontal line. Hardly anyone sees the hidden 4 contained in that figure—and shown in (B)—despite the fact that we have encountered 4's much more often than the two complex patterns which are probably completely new. (After Köhler, 1947)*

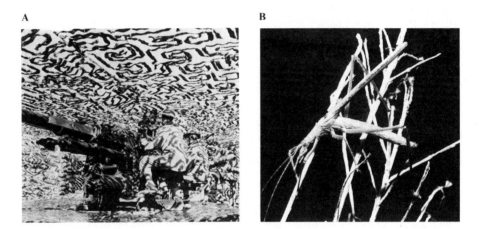

7.8 Good continuation as the basis of camouflage *(A) Camouflage is achieved in the situation shown here by artificial contours that break up the outlines of the soldiers and their military installation. (Courtesy Warder Collection) (B) In this case, good continuation helps to conceal the insect from predators who tend to see various parts of the insect's body as continuations of the twigs on which it stands. (Photograph by David C. Rentz, Bruce Coleman, Inc.)*

7.9 Closure *There is a tendency to complete—or close—figures that have a gap in them, as in the incomplete triangle shown here.*

tional factor which will often prevail even when pitted against prior experience (Figure 7.7). This common principle of camouflage used by the military is also seen in nature (Figure 7.8). This suggests that the use of good continuation as an organizing principle cannot be attributed simply to such artificial habits as looking at line drawings; it also operates in the perceptual systems of the predators whose prey use this means to achieve concealment.

Closure We often tend to complete figures that have gaps in them. Figure 7.9 is seen as a triangle despite the fact that the sides are incomplete.

A closurelike phenomenon yields **subjective contours.** These are contours that are seen, despite the fact that they don't physically exist (Figure 7.10, page 230). Some theorists interpret subjective contours as a special case of good continuation. In their view, the contour is seen to continue along its original path, and, if necessary, jumps a gap or two to achieve the continuation (Kanizsa, 1976).

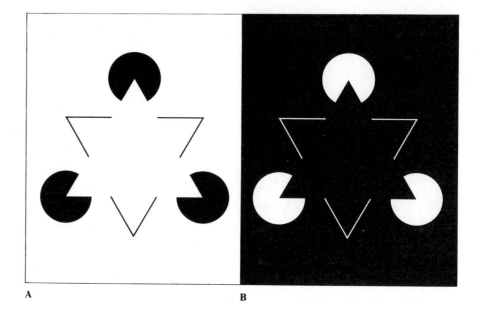

7.10 Subjective contours *Subjective contours are a special completion phenomenon in which contours are seen even where none exist. In (A), we see a white triangle whose vertices lie on top of the three black circles. The three sides of this white triangle (which looks brighter than the white background) are clearly visible, even though they don't exist physically. In (B), we see the same effect with black and white reversed. Here, there is a black triangle (which looks blacker than the black background) with subjective black contours. (From Kanizsa, 1976)*

A   B

FORM EQUIVALENCE

The first step in seeing an object is to see it as something—a figure that stands out against its background and whose parts seem to belong together. But the organism must also determine whether this figure is similar to figures it has seen just before. The major problem of the psychology of **form perception** is to determine how this is accomplished.

Suppose a person looks at two triangles and realizes that they are identical in form or suppose he recognizes a face he has seen before. It is easy to show that this cannot be done by scanning each retinal point of stimulation in isolation. As the retinal image shifts, so do the points that are excited by the visual pattern; but even so, the subject sees the same triangle. No more does it matter whether the pattern is black on white or white on black, whether it is large or small, drawn as a solid or a line drawing, made up of dots or dashes or even American flags. The perceived form remains the same (Figure 7.11). This phenomenon is known as the **transposition of form.** A triangle is a triangle is a triangle, whatever the elements of which it is composed. Similar effects occur in temporal patterning. A melody remains the same even when all of its notes are changed by transposing to another key. The same rhythm will be heard whether played on a kettledrum or a glockenspiel.

Facts such as these were among the chief arguments of the Gestalt psychologists who insisted that perceived forms do not arise as some amalgam of localized sensations corresponding to individual retinal points of excitation (Koffka, 1935; Köhler, 1947). Perceptually, a form is experienced as a *Gestalt,* a whole which is different from the sum of its parts.* To perceive a form, we perceive certain relations among the component parts which remain intact despite alterations of the parts of a figure.

The phenomenon of transposition is not a simple one, for in many instances there is more than one relationship among component parts to which the

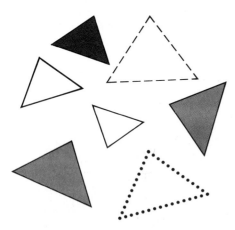

7.11 Form equivalence *A triangle is a triangle regardless of the parts of which it is composed.*

---

* The term *Gestalt* is derived from a German word which means "form" or "entire figure."

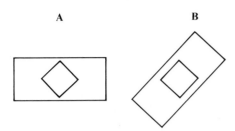

A   B

7.12 The effect of context upon perceived form *The same form may appear different depending upon the surrounding context. The frame drawn around the quadrilateral provides an orientation, which makes the quadrilateral appear like a diamond in (A), like a square in (B). (After Koffka, 1935)*

7.13 The rabbit-duck figure *An ambiguous figure, first used in 1900 by Joseph Jastrow. (After Attneave, 1971)*

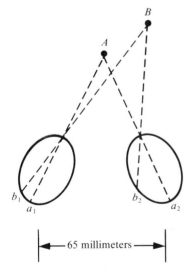

← 65 millimeters →

7.14 Retinal disparity *Two points, A and B, at different distances from the observer, present somewhat different retinal images. The distance between the images on one eye, a_1b_1, is different (disparate) from the distance between them on the other, a_2b_2. The binocular disparity is a powerful cue for depth. (After Hochberg, 1978)*

perceiver may respond. Usually, the perceptual organization chosen will depend upon the context. This context may be within the stimulus pattern itself. For example, the same figure may appear as a square or as a diamond, depending on its orientation (Figure 7.12). The context may also be provided by the subject's expectations. Thus Figure 7.13 can be seen as either a rabbit or a duck. If we have been talking about bird watching, it is very likely that the figure will be seen as a duck.

THE PERCEPTION OF DEPTH: WHERE IS IT?

To know *what* a thing is, is not enough. Whether an object is a potential mate or a sabertooth tiger, the perceivers can hardly take appropriate action unless they also locate it in the external world. Much work on this problem of *visual localization* has concentrated on the perception of depth. Many philosophers (notably Berkeley) and scientists have asked: How can we possibly see the world in three dimensions when only two of these dimensions are given in the image that falls upon the eye? This question has led to a search for *depth cues,* features of the stimulus situation which correspond to the physical distance of the object from the observer or from other objects.

BINOCULAR CUES

Our two eyes look out on the world from slightly different positions; they thus obtain a somewhat different view of any solid object they converge on. This *binocular disparity* inevitably follows from the geometry of the physical situation. Obviously, the disparity becomes less pronounced the farther the object is from the observer. Beyond thirty feet the two eyes receive virtually the same image (Figure 7.14).

Binocular disparity alone can induce perceived depth. If we draw or photograph the two different views received by each eye while looking at a nearby object and then separately present each of these views to the appropriate eye, we can obtain a striking impression of depth. To achieve this stereo effect, the two eyes must converge as they would if they were actually looking at the solid object at the given distance. The appropriate convergence is most readily produced when the pictures are viewed through a special device called a stereoscope (Figure 7.15).

7.15 A stereoscope *(Photograph by Ed Boswell)*

7.16 Interposition *When one figure interrupts the contour of another figure, it provides a monocular cue for depth: interposition. Because of interposition, the colored rectangle in the figure is perceived to be in front of the gray one.*

James J. Gibson *(Courtesy E. J. Gibson)*

7.17 Linear perspective as a cue for depth *(Photograph by Herbert Gehr, © Time, Inc.)*

Binocular disparity is a very powerful (and probably innate) determinant of perceived depth. Yet we can perceive depth even with one eye closed. Even more important, many people who have been blind in one eye from birth see the world in three dimensions. Clearly then, there are other cues for depth perception that come from the image obtained with one eye alone—the ***monocular depth cues.***

Pictorial cues Many of the monocular depth cues have been exploited for centuries by artists, and are therefore called ***pictorial cues.*** Examples include ***linear perspective, relative size,*** and ***interposition*** . In each case, the effect is an optical consequence of the projection of a three-dimensional world upon a flat surface. Objects that are farther away are also inevitably blocked from view by any other opaque object which obstructs their optical path to the eye (interposition; see Figure 7.16). Far-off objects necessarily produce a smaller retinal image than do nearby ones (linear perspective and relative size; Figures 7.17 and 7.18).

A very powerful set of pictorial cues is ***texture gradients.*** These are ultimately produced by perspective. Consider what meets the eye when we look at cobblestones on a road or clumps of grass in a meadow. James Gibson pointed out that the retinal projection of such objects must necessarily show a continuous change, a texture gradient, that depends upon the spatial layout of the relevant surfaces (Figure 7.19). Such texture gradients are powerful determinants of perceived depth. Discontinuities in texture gradients provide information about further spatial relationships between the various textured surfaces. Thus the abrupt change of texture density in Figure 7.20 produces the impression of a sharp drop, a "visual cliff" (J. Gibson, 1950, 1966).

How artificial are pictorial cues? Several psychologists have suggested that the impression of depth that is obtained from pictures may be partially based on cultural conventions. One way of investigating this issue is to study populations that have had little or no experience with pictures. In one experiment,

A
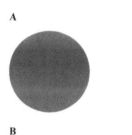
B
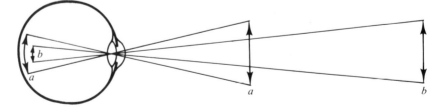

7.18 Relative size *(A) All other things equal, the larger of two identical figures will seem to be closer than the smaller one. This is a consequence of the simple geometry of vision illustrated in (B). Two equally large objects, a and b, that are at different distances from the observer, will project retinal images of different size.*

A

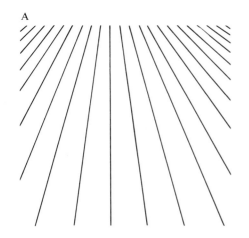

7.19 Texture gradients as cues for depth
A uniformly textured surface at a slant from the observer will produce a retinal projection that shows a texture gradient: as the surface recedes, the texture density increases. Such gradients are a consequence of optic geometry. The effectiveness of such monocular cues for depth is shown in (A) a diagram of a lined, flat surface receding from the observer (After Gibson, 1950) and in the photographs of (B) an expanse of grass (Photograph by Stephen J. Krasemann, Photo Researchers, Inc.) and (C) a large shipment of barrels. (From Gibson, 1950)

7.20 The effect of changes in texture gradients *Such changes provide important information about spatial arrangements in the world. Examples are (A) an upward tilt at a corner and (B) a sudden drop. (After Gibson, 1950)*

A   B

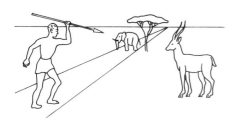

7.21 A drawing used to study the use of pictorial cues in other cultures *The subjects were asked, "Which is nearer to the man, the elephant or the antelope?" (From Hudson, 1960)*

African natives were shown sketches of a man, an antelope, and an elephant whose relative spatial positions were indicated by a few strokes of linear perspective (Figure 7.21). The subjects were asked, "Which is nearer to the man, the elephant or the antelope?" The results seemed to show that the African natives did not utilize the perspective cues effectively, particularly if they had never attended school (Hudson, 1960).

Do results of this kind provide evidence that some pictorial cues are learned, as empiricists such as Berkeley had believed? Not at all. In the first place, this and similar studies have been criticized on a number of methodological grounds (Miller, 1973). One objection is that the question, "Which animal is nearer to the man?" is necessarily ambiguous. It could mean "nearer in the three-dimensional world that is pictured" or "literally nearer, on the—flat—piece of paper on which the picture is drawn." As a result, the effect may simply reflect a difference in the way the subjects interpreted the question rather than a difference in the way they saw the picture.

But even if this and other methodological objections were met, the findings still don't prove that monocular depth cues are learned. At most, they suggest that one has to learn to look at a picture with a certain attitude. The simple fact is that any pictorial representation of a three-dimensional scene is necessarily ambiguous. On the one hand, we see the picture as flat; any number of depth cues provide the information that it is all in one plane. On the other hand, we do see the depth in the scene the artist has depicted on paper or canvas. It may be that one has to learn to ignore those features of the stimulus situation that indicate that the picture is flat and to attend to those that imbue depth to the world shown in the picture.

MOTION PARALLAX

Thus far we have considered situations in which both the observer and the scene observed are stationary. But in real life we are constantly moving through the world we perceive. Motion provides a vital source of visual information about the spatial arrangement of the objects around us, a pattern of cues which once again follows from the optical geometry of the situation. As we move our heads or bodies from right to left, the images projected by the objects outside will necessarily move across the retina. The direction and speed of this motion is an enormously effective monocular depth cue, ***motion parallax*** (Helmholtz, 1909).

As we move through space, nearby objects seem to move very quickly and in a direction opposite to our own; as an example, consider the trees racing backward as one looks out of a speeding train (Figure 7.22). Objects farther

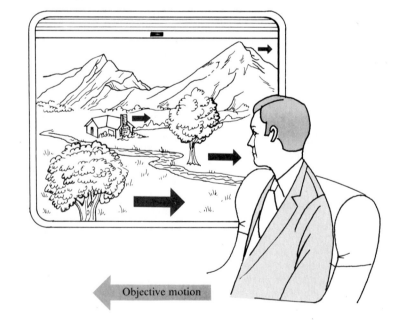

*7.22 **Motion parallax** When an observer moves relative to a stationary environment, the objects in that environment will be displaced (and will therefore seem to move) relative to him. This is motion parallax. The rate of motion parallax depends upon the distance of the objects from the observer. The closer they are, the faster they will seem to move in the opposite direction. Differences in the rate of this displacement are a powerful cue for depth. (The rate of relative displacement is indicated by the thickness of the colored arrows. The thicker these arrows, the more quickly the objects seem to move. The observer's movement is indicated by a gray arrow.) (After Coren et al. 1978)*

Objective motion

7.23 Gradient of motion parallax produced by movement in three dimensions
When a jet pilot lands, different parts of the world pass by at different rates. To land safely, he must respond to this overall optical flow pattern which tells him where he is relative to the landing field. (After Gibson, 1950)

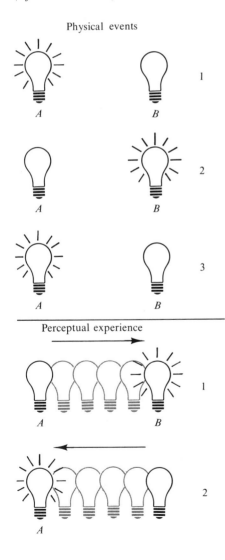

away also seem to move in the opposite direction, but at a lesser velocity. These patterns of motion are a powerful factor in providing us with the experience of depth.

According to James Gibson, the really important factor in motion parallax is not the relative motion of just a few objects, say the trees moving backward. It is the overall pattern of movement in the entire visual field. He regards this overall movement pattern as a ***gradient of motion parallax*** and believes that such gradients are among the most important determinants of perceived depth (Figure 7.22 and 7.23).

THE PERCEPTION OF MOVEMENT: WHAT IS IT DOING?

To see a large, unfriendly Doberman in front of you is one thing; to watch him bare his teeth and rush directly toward you is quite another. We want to know what an object is and where it is located, but we also want to know what it is doing. The basic ingredient of the perception of events is the perception of movement. In our discussion of motion parallax we saw that movement contributes to the perception of depth. We now turn to the perception of movement itself.

APPARENT MOVEMENT

What leads to the perception of movement? One might guess that one sees things move because they produce an image that moves across the retina. But this answer is too simple. For in fact, we sometimes perceive movement even when retinally none occurs.

Suppose we briefly turn on a light in one location of the visual field, then turn it off, and after an appropriate interval (somewhere between 30 and 200 milliseconds) turn on a second light in a different location. The result is ***apparent movement*** (sometimes called ***stroboscopic movement***). The light is seen to travel from one point to the other, even though there was no stimulation (let alone movement) in the intervening region (Figure 7.24). This phenomenon is perceptually overwhelming; given the right time intervals, it may be indistinguishable from real movement. It is an effect that has countless technological applications, ranging from animated neon signs to motion pictures (Wertheimer, 1912).

These results suggest that the stimulus for movement is relative displacement over time. Something is here at one moment and there at the next. If the time intervals are right, the nervous system interprets this as evidence that this something has moved. But suppose that the two stimuli which appear at the two locations are not identical? This question has been experimentally investigated by presenting subjects with two alternating forms, such as a square and a triangle. The subjects will now see a figure that shuttles back and forth, but which somehow changes its form as it moves between the two points (Rock, 1975).

7.24 Apparent movement *The sequence of optical events that produce apparent movement. Light A flashes at time 1, followed by light B at time 2, then back to light A at time 3. If the time intervals are appropriately chosen, the perceptual experience will be of a light moving from left to right and back.*

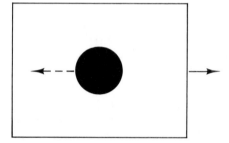

7.25 Induced movement *Subjects in an otherwise dark room see a luminous dot surrounded by a luminous frame. When the frame is moved to the right, subjects perceive the dot moving to the left, even though it is objectively stationary. (Duncker, 1929)*

INDUCED MOVEMENT

How does the perceptual system react when one of two objects is moving while the other is (physically) stationary? Consider a ball rolling on a billiard table. We see the ball as moving and the table at rest. But why not the other way around? To be sure, the ball is being displaced relative to the table edge, but so is the table edge displaced relative to the ball. One might guess that the reason is learning. Perhaps experience has taught us that balls generally move around while tables stay put. But the evidence indicates that what matters is a more general perceptual relationship between the two stimuli. The object that encloses the other tends to act as a *frame of reference* which is seen as stationary. Thus the table serves a frame against which the ball is seen to move.

In this example, perception and physical reality coincide, for the frame provided by the table is truly stationary. What happens when the objective situation is reversed? In one study subjects were shown a luminous rectangular frame in an otherwise dark room. Inside the frame was a luminous dot. In actual fact, the rectangle moved to the right while the dot stayed in place. But the subjects saw something else. They perceived the dot as moving to the left, in the opposite direction of the frame's motion. The physical movement of the frame had induced the perceived movement of the enclosed figure (Figure 7.25).

The *induced movement* effect is familiar from everyday life as well. The moon apparently drifts through the clouds; the base of a bridge seems to float against the flow of the river current. In the second case, there may also be *induced motion of the self.* If the subject stands on the bridge which she perceives as moving, she may perceive herself to move along with it.

PERCEIVED STABILITY

Thus far, we have asked why things are seen to move. A related question is why they are generally seen as stable. The issue arises because our eyes are constantly moving, so that the retinal image shifts all the time. But if so, why do we perceive the world as stationary? One interpretation follows from the fact that eye movements don't produce relative displacements. When we move our eyes as we look at a chair, the retinal image of the chair is displaced, but so is the image of the room which serves as its framework; as a result, there is no relative displacement. But this cannot be the whole story. As Helmholtz showed a century ago, movement will be seen if the eyes are moved by muscles other than their own. Close one eye and jiggle the outside corner of the other eye (gently!) with a finger. Now the world will move around, even though all relationships within the retinal image are kept intact. This shows that the perceptual system can respond to absolute displacement. But if it can do so when the eyes are pushed by a finger, why doesn't it when they are moved by the eye muscles that normally do the job?

Many students of visual perception believe that the nervous system achieves visual stability by compensating for retinal displacements which are produced by voluntary eye movements. Thus when the brain signals the eye muscles to move, it computes the retinal displacement that such a movement would produce and then cancels out this amount in interpreting the visual

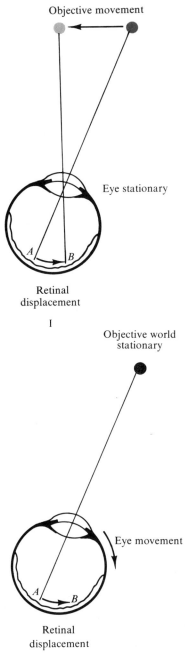

Objective movement

Eye stationary

Retinal
displacement

I

Objective world
stationary

Eye movement

Retinal
displacement

II

input it receives. As a result, we will see a stationary point at rest, even though our eyes are moving. The brain evidently keeps track of what it told the eyes to do; say, to move 10 degrees to the right. It knows that the eye movement should produce a retinal displacement of 10 degrees in the opposite direction, and subtracts this from the visual signal (Figure 7.26).

Innate Factors in Perceptual Organization

The common theme that runs through most of the phenomena we have just described is the same one with which we began our discussion of the entire field. What we perceive does not directly correspond to what the proximal stimulus gives us. Our perception is organized even though this retinal stimulation gives us only a mosaic.

EVIDENCE FOR INNATE FACTORS

How can we discover which aspects of perceptual organization (if any) are innately given? The problem has been approached in two major ways. One involves the study of very young (preferably newborn) organisms; the other asks what happens when function is restored to an organism that has been deprived of certain sensory experiences from birth.

PERCEPTUAL OGANIZATION IN THE VERY YOUNG

Space   In some organisms, important features of the perception of space are apparently built into the nervous machinery. An example is the localization of sounds in space. One investigator studied this phenomenon in a ten-minute-old baby. The newborn consistently turned its eyes in the direction of a clicking sound, thus demonstrating that some spatial coordination between eye and ear exists prior to learning (Michael Wertheimer, 1961).*

A number of authors believe that some aspects of our visual depth perception are also unlearned. A demonstration was provided by R. D. Walk and E. J. Gibson who noted that crawling infants are surprisingly (though by no means perfectly) successful in avoiding the precipices of their everyday lives (Walk and Gibson, 1961). The investigators studied infant behavior on the **visual cliff** which simulates the appearance of a steep edge but is safe enough

* Appropriately enough for this nativist finding, the investigator was Max Wertheimer's son, the subject his newborn grandchild.

7.26 Compensation for eye movements   *When the retinal image of some object is displaced, it may be because the object has moved, because the eye has moved, or both. In panel I, there is objective movement which produces a retinal displacement, as the dot's projection shifts from point A to point B on the retina. But panel II shows that the same retinal displacement can be produced by moving the eye (in the opposite direction from that of the dot in panel I) while the object remains stationary. From the retinal point of view, the displacements in panel I and II are identical. Fortunately, our brain allows us to see motion independent of eye movements by compensating for the displacements caused by changes in eye position. In panel II, the brain would decide that there was no movement because the motion of the eye is precisely equal (and opposite) to the displacement on the retina.*

7.27 *An infant on the visual cliff* The infant is placed on the center board laid across a heavy sheet of glass and his mother calls to him. If she is on the "deep" side, he pats the glass, but despite this tactual information that all is safe, he refuses to crawl across the apparent cliff. (Photograph by William Vandivert)

to mollify the infants' mothers, if not the infants themselves. This device consists of a large glass table, about three feet above the floor, which is divided in half by a wooden centerboard. On one side of the board, a checkerboard pattern is attached directly to the underside of the glass; on the other side, the same pattern is placed on the floor (Figure 7.27). The apparent drop-off is perceived by adults, in part because of a sudden change in texture density, in part because of motion parallax and binocular disparity. But will six-month-old infants respond to any of these cues? The babies were placed on the centerboard, and their mothers called and beckoned to them. When the mother beckoned from the shallow side, the baby usually crawled quickly to her. But only a very few infants ventured forth when called from across the apparent precipice.

An empiricist might well argue that these findings are inconclusive, because the babies had six months of previous experience. Unfortunately, there is no easy way of studying visual cliff behavior in younger infants. You can't very well ask where an infant will crawl to if it cannot get up on its knees. But motor coordination matures much earlier in many species, and various very young animals show appropriate cliff-avoidance as soon as they are old enough to move around at all. Kids and lambs were tested as soon as they were able to stand. They never stepped onto the steep side. Chicks tested less than twenty-four hours after hatching gave the same result.

Events It appears that neither man nor beast starts out in life with a perceptual *tabula rasa*. This holds for the perception of space. It may also be true for the perception of certain events. An example is the response to impending collision.

When an object suddenly comes directly at us, we duck or turn away to avoid its impact. The stimulus that signals the impending impact is the rapid magnification of some form in the visual field. As this form expands, it seems to loom up and to approach suddenly. The result is the avoidance response.

The **looming** effect has been studied experimentally by simulating the visual consequences of rapid approach. A shadow is cast on a screen and is rapidly magnified. Although there is no real object that is actually advancing, such looming shadows nevertheless produce avoidance reactions in humans and in animals. When exposed to these expanding patterns, crabs flatten out, frogs jump away, turtles withdraw their heads into their shells, infant monkeys leap to the rear of their cages, and infants as young as two weeks of age stiffen and cry. None of these reactions occurs when the size of the shadow is decreased. After all why should they? One is rarely afraid of things that withdraw (Ball and Tronick, 1971; Hayes and Saiff, 1967; Schiff, 1965). It is hard to resist the conclusion that the response to looming is based on a widely shared, built-in characteristic of the visual system.

Form Innate mechanisms may also be relevant to form perception. A one-day-old chick will peck at small spheres in preference to small pyramids, even if kept in darkness from hatching to the time of the test. A prewired preference for round shapes together with the capacity to distinguish them is presumably useful to a creature whose primary foods are grain and seed (Fantz, 1957). Human form perception is less ready-made than the chick's; but even so, the

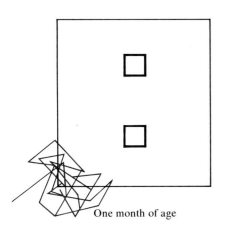

One month of age

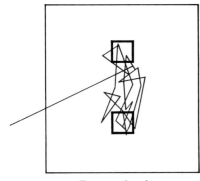

Two months of age

7.28 Contour scanning in very young infants *One-month- and two-month-old infants were presented with various forms, such as the one shown here which has both an external contour (the outer frame) and internal features (the two squares). The infants' eye movements were recorded by photographing the corneas. They are here shown in color and superimposed upon the figure. At one month, the infants usually scan whatever contour feature their eyes first encounter, which is usually part of the external frame. By two months of age, they scan more of the figure's features. (After Salapatek, 1975)*

visual world of a newborn infant is not a chaotic jumble of color and light. When a three-day-old infant is presented with a simple form, such as a triangle, its eyes do not move randomly. Photographs of the infant's cornea show that its eyes tend to orient toward those features of the pattern that help to define it, such as its edges and its vertices (Salapatek and Kessen, 1966; Salapatek, 1975).

Of special interest is the infant's very early tendency to look at forms that resemble a human face, in preference to others (Fantz, 1961; Freedman, 1971). This tendency is probably based on a preference for certain visual components that comprise a face, such as curved rather than straight contours (Fantz, 1970). Whatever its basis, such a built-in predisposition to look at facelike forms must have considerable survival value in an organism whose period of infantile dependence is so long and so intense.

Findings of this sort suggest that very young infants come equipped with some of the basic organizational ingredients for form perception. But up to two months or so, they show little signs of responding to forms as a whole. The eyes of a one-month old gravitate to individual features—an edge, an angle. In contrast, the two-month old scans figures more broadly (Figure 7.28). While it appears that there are no figural wholes but only parts until two months of age or later, this does not prove that the wholes are built up through learning. It is certainly possible that the improvement at two months reflects the maturation of certain brain structures that contribute to form perception.

PERCEPTION AFTER SENSORY DEPRIVATION

Another approach to the problem dates back to a question first raised by William Molyneux, a friend of John Locke's, who wondered how a man born blind would see the world were his vision suddenly restored: "Suppose a man *born* blind, and now adult, and taught by his *touch* to distinguish between a cube and a sphere. Suppose then the cube and sphere placed on a table, and the blind man to be made to see. . . . [Would he] now distinguish, and tell, which is the globe, which the cube?" (Locke, 1690, p. 121).

Molyneux was an empiricist and so to him (as to John Locke who quoted him approvingly) the self-evident answer was an emphatic no. "Though he has obtained the experience of how a globe, how a cube affects his touch, yet he has not yet attained the experience that what affects his touch so or so must affect his sight so or so" (Locke, 1610, p. 121).

Cases of the sort Molyneux had regarded as only imaginary do in fact occur. Persons with cataracts (an opaqueness or translucency of the lens) from birth have had them successfully removed, allowing vision—sometimes after many years of blindness. But the results are not as clear-cut as Molyneux had envisioned. In some cases, there seemed to be great difficulties in perceiving form equivalence. The patients could distinguish figure from ground and could discriminate objects on the basis of their size and color, but they had considerable trouble in distinguishing a triangle from a circle (von Senden, 1932). In other cases, there was some form recognition within a short time after the operation. One patient was able to recognize form by using some of his previously acquired touch experience. For example, he could tell time by looking at a large wall clock in a hospital corridor without any special training.

This feat was based on his prior experience with a pocket watch he had carried all his life. This watch had no glass so that he could feel the time by touching its hour and minute hands (Gregory and Wallace, 1963).

What can we conclude from these cases? The answer is, not much. One reason is that there are various postoperative disturbances, such as severe eye muscle cramp, which make proper assessment of the patient's visual abilities very difficult. Another is that different patients have different degrees of preoperative visual experience. Some cataracts may have blocked out all vision; others may have allowed the perception of some diffuse, cloudy shapes. Given all of these problems, the evidence from cataract removals must be regarded as inconclusive (Zuckerman and Rock, 1957).

THE SEARCH FOR THE BUILT-IN MECHANISMS

We have concluded that some aspects of perceptual organization are innately given. But we have not yet specified the actual mechanisms by which the nervous system reacts to the complex stimulus relations which result in the perceptual response. The last two or three decades have seen some important strides in this direction.

FEATURE ANALYZERS

Electrophysiologists often record from single nerve cells (see Chapter 2). By such techniques they have discovered how particular cells in a sensory system respond to simple stimuli such as light of a given wavelength (see Chapter 6). More recently, they have applied the same approach using stimuli that are much more complex and relational.

In many animals a great deal of perceptual processing occurs in the retina itself. In a classic study, records were taken from different ganglion cells of a frog's optic nerve while the animal was presented with various visual stimuli (Lettvin et al., 1959). Certain ganglion cells were shown to respond only to particular and quite complex patterns of stimulation. For example, one kind of cell reacts most intensely to a small, dark object that is moved into a particular retinal region and is then moved around within it. Moving stimuli that lack the appropriate shape have little or no effect, nor does a change in the general level of illumination. To a frog, the stimulus pattern which excites this particular kind of ganglion cell (a "bug detector") represents its livelihood, for it is normally produced by a flying insect. It represents an uncanny demonstration of prewired perceptual abstraction, a response to buglike objects that move in a buglike manner, with a concomitant disregard for all other features of the stimulus. Could a frog ask for anything more?

Feature analyzers in the brain   The bug detector is one example of a **feature analyzer** (also called feature detector) which selectively responds to certain (usually relational) characteristics of a stimulus pattern. Other analyzers have been found which detect such perceptual features as direction of movement, lines and edges, and so on. In higher animals such as cats and monkeys (and undoubtedly man as well) most of this analysis takes place at a level beyond the retina, primarily in the cortex.

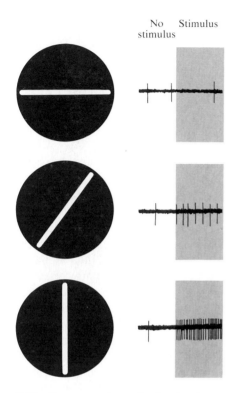

No stimulus   Stimulus

7.29   Feature analyzers in the visual system of the cat   *The response of a single cortical cell when stimulated by a slit of light in three different orientations. This cell, a simple unit, was evidently responsive to the vertical. A horizontal slit led to no response, a tilted slit led to a slight response, while a vertical slit led to a marked increase in firing. (After Hubel, 1963)*

Two physiologists, David Hubel and Torsten Wiesel, studied the activity of single cortical cells of cats in response to various visual stimuli. They found some cells, the so-called **simple units,** which react to lines or edges of a particular orientation. Such a cell would be excited by a thin sliver of light slanted at, say, 45 degrees, but not otherwise. There is a further proviso. To be effective, the stimulus must fall on a very specific region of the retina (Figure 7.29).

Another kind of cell is the **complex unit** which yields a higher degree of perceptual abstraction. Like the simple unit, it is excited by lines of a certain orientation; but unlike the simple unit it fires whether the line is moving or is stationary and it is rather indifferent to the line's specific retinal location. Still other cells, the so-called **hypercomplex units,** seem to generate a yet higher level of abstraction. Some seem to respond to the conjunction of several perceptual features. An example is a cell that reacts to right angles. In effect, this cell reacts to two line orientations, but only if both lines are present and if they are put together in a certain way (Hubel and Wiesel, 1959).*

FEATURE ANALYZERS AND PERCEPTUAL EXPERIENCE

Most psychophysiologists believe that the excitation of feature analyzers leads to such perceptual experiences as movement, angular orientation, and the like. But they have no direct proof. To provide it one would have to find detector cells in (unanesthesized) human subjects and ask them to describe what they perceive while the cell is firing. Such an experiment is obviously out of the question. Nevertheless, most investigators continue to believe that what they pick up with their electrodes is somehow implicated in what we perceive.

One reason for this belief is based on an old conception; the doctrine of specific nerve energies (see Chepter 6). Over 150 years ago, Johannes Müller argued that the quality of sensory experience should be attributed, not to the stimulus, but rather to the nervous structure that was excited by it. The faith that this is so was a guiding force directing the work of generations of scientists who generally assumed that whenever one encounters two different perceptual qualities, two different neural processes must be responsible for them. Originally, these neural underpinnings were sought in the receptors. Thus nineteenth-century sensory psychologists were convinced that the skin must contain different receptors for warmth, cold, pressure, and pain since these experiences seem qualititatively different. Later investigators argued that the law of specific nerve energies holds beyond the receptor level. As we have seen, there are four qualitatively different chromatic colors, and two opponent-process pairs beyond the retina that correspond to them. Many modern

---

* Originally, Hubel and Wiesel believed that these detector cells operate in a hierarchical fashion. Lower level analyzers report to analyzers higher up, and these in turn transmit their message to yet higher analyzers above them. Thus complex cells were thought to receive their input from several simple cells, responding to that feature which their subordinate units had in common. In a similar manner, hypercomplex cells were believed to receive the information relayed to them by the complex cells. This hypothesis seemed very plausible, but recent evidence suggests that it is false. If complex cells are in fact triggered by simple ones, then their latency in response to stimuli should be longer. This follows from the assumption that complex cells are further along the message chain. But in fact, some complex cells respond more quickly than do simple cells. This and related findings throw doubt upon the hierarchical notion (Blakemore, 1975).

psychophysiologists believe that the feature analyzers which react to such stimulus properties as movement or orientation perform a similar function still further up in the nervous system.

The adaptation of analyzers   One means of studying feature analyzers from the psychological perspective is by utilizing the phenomenon of **adaptation.** We have previously encountered adaptation effects in the case of such a relatively simple sensory quality as hue. After prolonged fixation of a green patch, its apparent greenness will fade away and a neutral gray projected upon the same retinal region will look reddish (see Chapter 6). Effects of this sort laid the foundations for a theory of the opponent processes that underlie color. The same logic motivates the study of adaptation effects in more complex perceptual attributes (Anstis, 1975).

An example is the ***aftereffect of visual movement.*** If one looks at a waterfall for a while and then turns away to look at the riverbank, the bank and the trees upon it will be seen to float upward, a dramatic effect which is readily produced in the perceptual laboratory (Figure 7.30). We might expect just this result on the assumption that the direction of perceived movement is signaled by the activity of movement detectors which operate as opponent-process pairs. For example, one such pair might be composed of two kinds of movement detectors: one sensitive to upward, the other to downward movement. If these two detectors interact like the members of the color opponent-process pairs, then the stimulation of either one will automatically lead to the inhibition of the other. If one has been stimulated for a long time (say, by exposure to a downward moving pattern), it will gradually adapt. As a result, the balance will swing toward the other member of the pair (that is, the upward movement detector). This changed balance is revealed when the moving target is withdrawn and the subject looks at a stationary pattern. This (objectively stationary) pattern is now seen to move upward. The effect is analogous

7.30 Aftereffect of movement   *(A) The subject looks at a band of striped lines which moves downward. After inspecting this moving pattern for a minute or two, he looks at a horizontal line (B). This line is objectively stationary but will now appear to be moving up. This effect is generally thought to be produced by the adaptation of one of a pair of mutually antagonistic movement detectors, which signal upward and downward motion.*

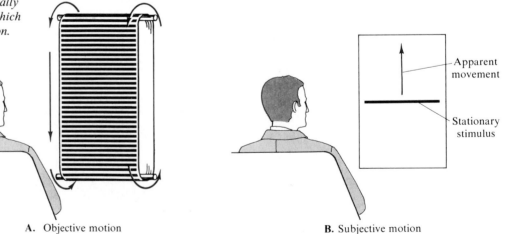

A. Objective motion   B. Subjective motion

Apparent movement

Stationary stimulus

to the red afterimage that follows prolonged fixation of a green patch. In both cases, there is adaptation of one member of an opponent-process pair.

This general interpretation of movement aftereffects is buttressed by some physiological evidence. Single-cell records from the rabbit's retina have yielded adaptation effects to prolonged movement in one direction that are very much in line with this conception (Barlow and Levick, 1965).

FROM FEATURES TO ORGANIZED WHOLES

The organism is evidently endowed with appropriate neural devices that allow it to respond to such stimulus features as directional motion, edges, and orientation. But how does it organize these features into the organized wholes of our perceptual experience?

To take one example, how do we get from edges and orientations to the perception of a triangle? The fact that three angle detectors signal their excitement cannot by itself guarantee that we will perceive a triangle, for a triangle is not just three angles, but three angles in a particular mutual relationship (Figure 7.31). In this sense, the problem raised by the Gestalt psychologists is still with us. Such features as angles and edges and orientations are certainly broader and more relational (put another way, more *molar*) than the discrete sensory atoms proposed by the early empiricists; but the basic issue is still the same. A whole is determined by the relations among its parts, whatever these parts may be. How do we get to this configuration?

One possibility is that the nativist solution works even at this level. Perhaps prewired systems exist which can detect complex shapes of various kinds, particularly those which have a special significance in the life of a given species. Something of this sort may well be true for many lower animals whose analyzers are apparently tuned to the detection of the relatively few objects that matter to them; the frog's bug detector is a case in point.

But it is inconceivable that such built-in mechanisms can account for all of the phenomena of form perception, especially in higher animals. Unlike frogs, humans must discriminate among a multitude of patterns, and it is hardly possible that we carry specialized analyzers for all of them—triangles, squares, apples, apple pies, champagne bottles, B-52s, cabbages, kings—the list is endless. But we do guess that the feature analyzers are the raw materials out of which we construct the infinity of discriminable shapes by a process that somehow involves learning.

Under the circumstances, we conclude that neither extreme nativism nor extreme empiricism can wholly describe the phenomena of human form perception. The truth lies somewhere in between. At this stage, we do not know precisely where the natively given ends and experience takes over. Edges, corners, and the like may indeed be the ultimate innate units, but it is also possible that there are some higher level units above them. For all we know,

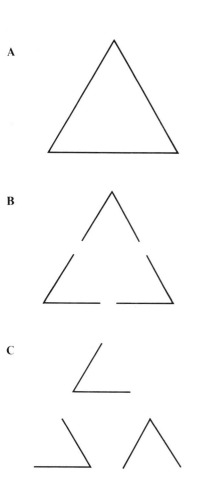

A

B

C

7.31 Features and form *The fact that there are nerve cells that can detect such features as edges and angles does not yet explain how we come to see forms. Consider the triangle in (A). It is made up of three corners. There are probably feature analyzers that can detect the presence of these corners. But the mere activation of these analyzers is not enough. For they would be activated by both (B) and (C). In (B), the corners stand in the proper relationship to each other and constitute a triangle. In (C) this relationship is missing and there is no triangle form.*

subsequent research may turn up some special cell geared to detect a more complex stimulus relationship. (For example, there might be a primitive something-like-a-face detector which would be useful in establishing the reaction to the mother at an early stage of infancy.) But it is certainly clear that at least some constellations are generated by the experience of the organism. We next turn to a discussion of what this experience can contribute.

The Modification of Perceptual Organization

Up to now, we have discussed those aspects of perceptual organization that are relatively unaffected by an observer's past or his expectations of the future. But there is little doubt that perception is often altered by just such factors. We will discuss such modifications of what we perceive under four major headings: perceptual adaptation, perceptual construction, differentiation, and selective attention.

PERCEPTUAL ADAPTATION

How modifiable is perception? One question concerns the relation between different aspects of the perceptual world such as vision and bodily orientation. Can these be realigned? One of the first attempts to find out was performed by the American psychologist George Stratton (1865–1957) just before the turn of the century. He wore an optical device which inverted the entire visual scene, turning right to left and up to down for over a week. (He was thus the first man on earth whose retinal image was right side up.)

For a while, Stratton was seriously handicapped. His environment was utterly bewildering. He reached up for an object that was down; he turned left to enter a doorway that was to the right. But as time went on there was **adaptation.** He gradually readjusted, so that after eight days his motor coordination was perfect and his world seemed no longer strange and incongruous. When he finally removed the inverting lens system, he suffered an ***aftereffect of adaptation.*** Having adjusted to his upside-down existence, he had trouble returning to visual normalcy. At first, the uninverted world looked odd, and there was some difficulty in motor adjustment (Stratton, 1897).

Since Stratton's time, several other psychologists have studied the adaptation to various optical distortions which disrupt the normal relation between vision and the spatial order of the physical world. Some inverted the entire scene as had Stratton; others imposed less drastic distortions. The Austrian psychologist Ivo Kohler has carried such efforts to the level of virtuosity. He and his students have worn all kinds of distorting goggles for months on end and have then shown their faith in the power of adaptation by skiing in the Alps with inverting lenses and riding a motorcycle through the streets of Innsbruck with right-left reversing ones (Kohler, 1964).

Such results are clear evidence for adaptation; but is this adaptation perceptual? Of course Stratton and Kohler came to act appropriately, but did they finally see the world as it really is? For distortions as drastic as total inversion, the results are rather ambiguous. When asked how things looked to him and whether they appeared upside down, one subject replied, "I wish you hadn't asked me. Things were all right until you popped the question at me. Now, when I recall how they *did* look before I put on these lenses, I must answer that they do look upside-down *now*. But until the moment you asked me, I was absolutely unaware of it" (Snyder and Pronko, 1952, p. 113). Reports such as this suggest that the effect was not really perceptual. The subject learned to behave appropriately in the altered world, but he still saw that it was altered.

Milder optical rearrangements produce more clear-cut perceptual effects. Examples are prisms that tilt the world in one direction or that shift the image to the right or the left. Here, there is no doubt that the world does change its appearance. In one study, subjects wore prisms that tilted the image by 20 degrees. Two hours later some of them hardly saw the tilt. When the prisms were removed there was a strong perceptual aftereffect. Asked to adjust a luminous line in an otherwise dark room, they chose a setting of 20 degrees—in a direction opposite to the rotation imposed by the prisms (Mikaelian and Held, 1964).

THE CAUSES OF ADAPTATION

Such results show that the relationship between various aspects of the perceptual world is modifiable. But how is this realignment achieved? Thus far we have only some tentative hypotheses. Some of these center on the information subjects derive from their own voluntary movements in the optically altered world. What happens if such movements are prevented? Some authors believe such active movements are an important factor in bringing perceptual adaptation about. In one study, some subjects were allowed to walk freely while wearing prisms which displaced the image to one side. Others wore the same prisms for the same period of time, but were passively transported over the same path in wheelchairs. When the prisms were removed, the subjects who had moved about on their own showed the usual aftereffect of adaptation; for them, "straight ahead" was shifted to the side opposite to the prismatic displacement. No such aftereffect was found for the subjects who had only been wheeled around. The investigators concluded that, to adapt, the subject must learn a new correlation between self-produced movements and their visual consequences (Held and Bossom, 1961).

According to Held, self-produced movement is important not only in altering the perceptual world of an adult, but it is critical in producing that world in the first place. This notion was tested in an experiment on dark-reared kittens. The animals were run in pairs in a kitten carousel. One kitten was in a harness which allowed it to walk under its own power. The other kitten was strapped into a gondola which was mechanically yoked to the other animal's harness; it was unable to move of its own accord but was wheeled around passively by its active partner (Figure 7.32). Through this arrangement, the stimulation both kittens received was identical in all respects but one—only the active kitten was shown how its own movements affect the visual input (Held and Hein, 1963).

7.32 Self-produced movement and perceptual development One kitten walked about freely; the other received essentially the same visual stimulation as it was wheeled around by its active partner. When later tested, the active kittens showed normal depth reactions; the passive ones did not. (After Held, 1965)

When tested after some thirty hours in the carousel (the rest spent in darkness) the active kittens showed superior depth reactions. They moved to the shallow side of the visual cliff and demonstrated appropriate visual-motor coordination, such as extending their forepaws when lowered onto the floor. In contrast, the passive kittens were quite retarded. This result suggests that self-produced motion may play a role in perceptual development. To perceive the visual world, we must react not only to the optic input, but also to the way in which this changes when we move our eyes, head, or body.

Which changes, vision or touch?   Perceptual adaptation (and aspects of perceptual development) is evidently based on the establishment of a new correlation between visual input and bodily orientation. But exactly what do the subjects learn as they readjust? What is changed? Vision or touch?

Empiricists since Locke and Berkeley have usually maintained that vision is educated by touch. But one can also argue that the teacher-pupil relationship may be the other way around. In one experiment, a subject looked at a square object through an optical device which squeezed the image along one axis, thus projecting the square as a rectangle. Simultaneously, the subject grasped the square with his hand, so that vision and touch were pitted against each other. Almost invariably, vision won out: most subjects said that the object "felt just like it looked," a rectangle rather than a square (Rock and Victor, 1964). Berkeley notwithstanding, the world of touch seems to be more easily altered than that of vision.

PERCEPTUAL CONSTRUCTION

Perceptual adaptations are dramatic enough when they occur in the laboratory, but they are not an ordinary feature of everyday experience. Nor are they the main concern of psychologists who ask how learning affects perception. To them, the primary question is the way in which we come to perceive and recognize new patterns.

Learning new patterns is a pervasive phenomenon of human life, perhaps especially so in infancy. Even as adults we sometimes manage to reorganize something we see or hear so that it looks and sounds completely new. Thus a foreign language often sounds like gibberish before we learn to speak it. Similar effects are found in visual perception. Consider Figure 7.33. At first glance the patches look disorganized; but they take on a new appearance once we discover that they represent a dog and a horseman respectively.

Such examples show that the perception of patterns can be profoundly affected by experience. The question is how this effect arises. According to one group of theorists, including Julian Hochberg and Ulric Neisser, all patterns are **constructions** created by the perceiver. They are pieced together through experience from smaller building blocks which may be given by nature or by prior experience (Hochberg, 1978*a*; Neisser, 1967).

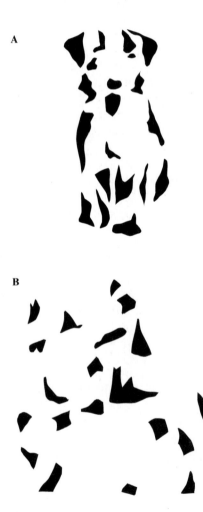

A

B

7.33 Perceptual reorganization   *At first glance, (A) and (B) look like disorganized patches. But after looking at them for a few moments, they take on a new appearance as we see them as a dog (A) and a man on a horse (B). After they have been reorganized in this manner, it is difficult to see them as we did at first. (After Street, 1931)*

VISUAL FORM AS A CONSTRUCTION

We will consider the perceptual construction hypothesis as it applies to visual form. Why is a triangle seen as a triangle, regardless of its size, its color, or its retinal location? How do we perceive the spatial relation between the parts of the figure that defines the triangle?

According to Hochberg's version of the construction hypothesis, the form equivalence is originally based on a sequence of eye movements. The observer looks at a triangle. In so doing, she necessarily has to scan from one vertex to another. As this happens over repeated viewings, she develops a series of expectations about what she'll see when she moves her eyes in a certain way: "If I scan downward, I'll see a corner; if I move my eyes sideways, I'll see a line." According to this hypothesis, to see a triangle is simply to refer to such perceptual expectations—to use them, test them, and confirm them. These expectations are not in the perceiver's awareness. They are instead a direct descendant of Helmholtz' inferences, and just like those, they are unconscious (Hebb, 1949; Hochberg, 1970).

A similar approach may help to explain one aspect of perception that we have thus far ignored. Normally, the eye shifts fixation three or four times per second; yet even so, we have the impression of a single, stable form. We can understand why the image is stationary, for we know that there is an automatic compensation system that allows for eye movements. But why should there be one image rather than a series of visual snapshots? Our perceptual system somehow manages to integrate these separate images. At one moment, the fovea receives the image of a nose, then of an eyebrow, then of an upper lip. But the end result is that we see a face, not just an anatomical jumble. What accounts for this integration? One answer is that what we call a face is really a set of visual expectancies, a perceptual construction built up from the elements provided by the feature analyzers and seen "in the mind's eye."

To test this general notion, Hochberg has devised a technique which provides successive glimpses artificially. Subjects are shown outline figures that are moved around behind a small aperture in a masking cardboard, so that they can only see a small portion of the figure at a time. But they nevertheless recognize the shape (Figure 7.34). This implies that the subject has some kind of perceptual schema of the figure into which the separate, piecemeal glimpses are fitted.

This general position has to cope with a problem: Forms can be recognized even if they are exposed in brief glimpses that are no longer than 150 milliseconds. This period is too short to allow eye movements, but nevertheless the subjects can recognize forms, letters, and words. But how can they, if pattern perception is a sequence of eye movements? Some theorists answer that after a lifetime of practice the physical eye movements are no longer necessary. All that remains is a mental plan that specifies what eye movements will yield which images.

7.34 Form built up by successive glimpses *Subjects look at a circular aperture. Through this aperture they receive a number of successive glimpses, each of which corresponds to a small portion of a figure (here, a cross) that is being moved around behind it. The subjects recognize the shape of the figure, even though they never saw it as a whole. The successive glimpses enabled them to develop a perceptual schema of the form, in analogy to the way we integrate the separate images provided by our eye movements. (After Hochberg, 1970)*

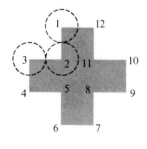

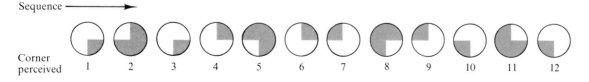

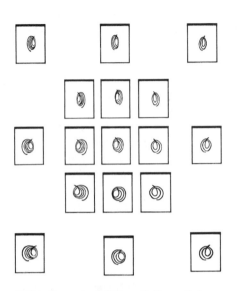

7.35 Perceptual differentiation *Subjects had to learn to differentiate between the curlicues here shown. In the figure, the curlicues are arranged according to distinguishing features such as number of coils, expansion or compression, coiled to right or left. Initially, all of these curlicues looked alike. With increasing experience, they became perceptually differentiated. (After Gibson and Gibson, 1955)*

DIFFERENTIATION

Perceptual construction theorists ask why different stimulus arrangements are perceived to be alike in pattern, why different triangles are all perceived to be the same in form. Another group of psychologists concerned with perceptual learning emphasizes another question. It asks how we come to see differences that we did not see at first.

Common observation tells us that our perceptual world is often refined by further experience. To most of us, all gorillas look alike; to the zookeeper, each of them is utterly distinctive. The same holds for fingerprint experts, X-ray specialists, and wine tasters; they all have learned to perceive differences to which the rest of us are oblivious. This phenomenon has been called *perceptual differentiation* by Eleanor and James Gibson. In one of their studies subjects were shown a series of meaningless curlicues that had to be discriminated from one another (Figure 7.35). After mastering this task, the subjects were presented with a new set of curlicues. The new set was learned more quickly than the old, suggesting that the subjects were well on their way to becoming curlicue connoisseurs; they had learned what to look for to distinguish among such patterns (Gibson and Gibson, 1955).

According to the Gibsons, perceptual differentiation is produced by a process that is akin to discrimination (see Chapters 4 and 5). The subject learns to look for those attributes of the object that distinguish it from others in its class. These distinguishing characteristics are the *distinctive features* to which the subject learns to attend. While doing so, the subject also learns to ignore features that are irrelevant. Thus experienced airplane spotters can tell one plane from another by noting (often without awareness) whether it has a tapered wing or a stubby nose. According to the Gibsons, perceptual differentiation is brought about by attending to an ever more precisely delineated set of such distinguishing hallmarks. In terms of the aircraft example, the learner will gradually progress to ever finer distinctions such as "tapered with a slight upward slant," and so on (E. J. Gibson, 1969).

To James Gibson, the perceptual differentiation concept had still further implications. It allowed him to maintain that the key to all perception is entirely in the stimulus. In his view, this holds for whatever we perceive, whether it is a relatively simple attribute such as depth or motion or a complex one like geometrical form or facial expression. All of these are invariant relationships that are available within the stimulus pattern. It is up to the observer to extract them, to lift the relevant distinctive features from among the welter of irrelevant others. The observer is preequipped to respond to these features. All the observer has to learn is how to find them, how to attend to them, and how to disregard all the rest.

SELECTIVE ATTENTION

Thus far our emphasis has been on modifications of perception that are relatively long-lived. To be sure, some perceptual learning can be unlearned, as in perceptual adaptation effects. But many other instances are hard to reverse. A case in point is differentiation. The experienced wine taster can't go back to the undifferentiated ways of his youth when all white wines tasted alike. The same probably holds for most acquired perceptual schemas.

Such long-term modifications are obviously very useful. But they have to be supplemented with some more flexible means whereby our perception can be affected by past experience and future expectations. This is provided by how we select what we preceive. To a considerable extent, we determine what we look at, what we focus upon, and what we interpret it as. All of these means for perceiving selectively are often grouped under the collective label, **attention.**

ORIENTING MOVEMENTS

The most direct means of selecting the input is to physically orient the various sensory systems toward one set of stimuli and away from another. The organism does not passively touch, see, or hear; it actively feels, looks, and listens. It turns its head and eyes, converges and accommodates, explores the world with its hands (or paws or lips or prehensile trunk), and if it has the necessary motor endowment, pricks up its ears. These orienting adjustments of the sensory machinery are the external manifestations of attention and have been studied in a variety of contexts. An important example is Pavlov's discussion of the **orienting reflex** (see Chapter 4).

In humans the major means of physically selecting the stimulus input are movements of the eyes. Peripheral vision informs us that something is going on, say, in the upper left of our field of vision. But our peripheral acuity is not good enough to tell us what it is precisely. To find out, our eyes move so that this region falls into the fovea. A number of investigators have developed techniques for recording eye movements made when looking at pictures. The records show that the subjects glance most frequently at the regions that are visually most informative (Figure 7.36). This gaze pattern may be different for different observers, since what interests one person, may not interest another.

A

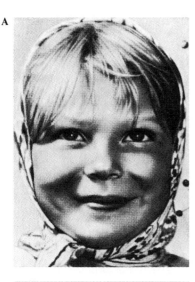

B

7.36 Eye-movement records when looking at pictures *Both (A) and (B) are pictures that were looked at for 3 and 10 minutes respectively. Below each picture is the record of the eye movements during this period. As the records show, the bulk of the eye movements are directed toward the most visually informative regions. As a result, the eye movement record is a crude mirror of the main contours of the picture. (From Yarbus, 1967)*

249

These results suggest that the act of looking is purposeful. People don't scan the world at random in the wistful hope that their foveas will by chance hit on some interesting bit of visual news. They pick up some information from what they've vaguely seen in the periphery and from their general notions of what the scene is about. They then move their eyes to check up on what they've seen and to refine their visual knowledge further.

CENTRAL SELECTION

Physical orientation determines the sensory input the perceptual system receives. But this is only the initial step in the selectional control of perception. From here on, central processes take over. They determine whether a particular portion of the sensory input will be dealt with further, and if so, how it will be interpreted.

Selective listening　A widely used method for studying selectional attention is modeled on a phenomenon often observed in real life, the ***cocktail-party effect.*** During conversations at a noisy party, one tunes in on the voice of the person one is talking to. The many other voices are somehow filtered out and are consigned to a background babble. This effect has been studied experimentally by asking subjects to attend to one of two simultaneously presented verbal messages. The usual procedure is ***dichotic presentation.*** The subject wears two earphones and receives different messages through each of them. To guarantee selective attention, the subject is generally asked to ***shadow*** the to-be-attended message. This means that he has to repeat it aloud, word for word, as it comes over the appropriate earphone. Under these conditions, the irrelevant message tends to be shut out almost entirely. The subject can hear speechlike sounds, but notices little else. He is generally unable to recall the message that came by way of the unattended ear. In fact, he often does not even notice if the speaker on the unattended ear shifts into a foreign language or if the tape is suddenly played backward (Cherry, 1953).

The filter theory of attention　Results of this sort suggested that selective attention acts as a kind of filter. This filter is presumably interposed between the initial sensory registration and later stages of perceptual analysis. If the information is allowed through the attentional filter (that is, if it is fed into the attended ear), it can then be further analyzed—recognized, interpreted, and stored in memory. But if it does not pass through, it is simply lost. Early versions of this theory suggested that the filtering effect is all or none. Subjects in a dichotic listening experiment were thought to understand no part of the message that entered by way of the unattended ear (Broadbent, 1958).

This all-or-none theory turned out to be false, for there is good evidence that information which has some special significance is registered even if it is carried as part of the unattended message. The best example is the sight or sound of one's own name. No matter how intently we concentrate on the person next to us, we can't help but hear our own name in another conversation held on the other side of the room.

This everyday experience has been documented with the shadowing method. When subjects are forced to repeat a message that comes over one ear, word for word, they are almost completely oblivious of the irrelevant message that is fed into the other ear. But they do take notice when that

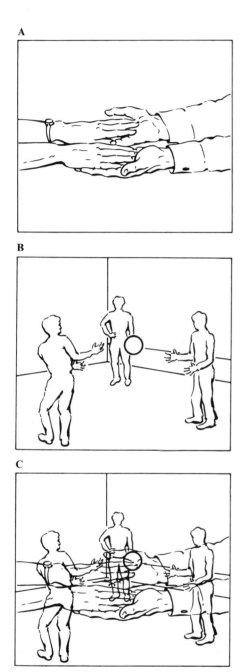

irrelevant message contains the sound of their own name (Moray, 1959). This result suggests that the attentional filter only **attenuates** irrelevant messages, but does not block them completely, like a volume control that is turned down but not off. If the item is important enough (or perhaps familiar enough) then it may pass through the filter and be analyzed to some extent (Treisman, 1964).

Related evidence comes from a study in which subjects had to shadow sentences such as "They threw stones at the bank yesterday." Concurrently, the other ear was presented with either of two words: *river* or *money*. When questioned directly, the subjects couldn't recall which of the two words they had heard, if either. But some part of the meaning of these words must have come through nevertheless. The shadowed sentence contained the ambiguous word, *bank*, which can be understood as either a financial institution or as the side of a river. Which interpretation was chosen depended upon whether the unattended ear was presented with the word *money* or *river*. This shows that the subjects extracted some meaning from the unattended message even though they never knew they did (McKay, 1973).

Selective looking   The filter concept has come in for some serious criticisms. It is essentially a metaphor, but is it apt? It argues that selective attention works by partially blocking information that is carried on the extraneous input channels. This analysis may be appropriate for dichotic listening (though this too is debatable). But there are some other selective attention phenomena that are difficult to interpret in filter-theory terms.

A striking example is provided by studies on **selective looking.** The subject is shown two visual scenes that are superimposed upon each other on a video screen. Each of the two scenes depicts a "game." In one, several players throw a ball around. In another, two people slap each other's hands (Figure 7.37). The subjects are asked to attend to one of the two games. To guarantee that they do, they are required to monitor the relevant scene closely, for example, by pressing a key whenever the ball is thrown (which happens almost once per second). The results are analogous to those found for dichotic listening. The unattended scene is ignored and is essentially not seen (Neisser and Becklen, 1975).

These findings pose problems for filter theory. For it is hard to imagine what the filters could be in the selective looking situation. Do we have perceptual filters that block out information about ball throwing or hand slapping? Such arguments show some of the limitations of the filter approach to attention, but there is as yet no consensus on the alternative (Kahneman, 1973; Neisser, 1976).

SET

We have seen that our concerns and expectations help to determine which aspects of the stimulus world we pay attention to. But they have a further

7.37 Selective looking   Two kinds of "games" were videotaped: (A) handslapping and (B) ball throwing. The two games were then shown simultaneously on a screen (C). The subject's task was to attend to one of the two games and ignore the other. The results were similar to those found in selective listening—the events on the unattended game were essentially not seen. (After Neisser and Becklen, 1975)

effect as well. They influence the way we interpret the sensory information that we have chosen to focus on. To quote William James, "Every stir in the wood is for the hunter his game; for the fugitive his pursuers. Every bonnet in the street is momentarily taken by the lover to enshroud the head of his idol" (James, 1890, vol. 1, p. 442).

Such phenomena are sometimes described (though by no means explained) as the result of a **mental set.** The subject is **set** to think of a particular object or event and is thus more likely to see or hear related matters and less likely to see those that don't fit in. The set is a form of mental preparation, analogous to the **motor set** we see in the athlete whose every muscle is tensed for a particular lunge (and who is carefully schooled to hide the telltale signs of an anticipatory motor set from an opponent).

The effect of set on perception   The effect of set on perception is often studied by the use of ambiguous figures. Thus Figure 7.38 can be seen as either an old woman in profile or a young woman whose head is turned slightly away. In one study, the subjects were first shown either of two *un*ambiguous versions of the figure (Figure 7.38B and C). When later presented with the ambiguous figure (Figure 7.38A), they perceived it in line with the unambiguous version they had seen (Leeper, 1935).

We are typically unaware of our mental sets. We are predisposed toward one particular perceptual organization without knowing that we are. Such unwitting predispositions are especially common in the perception of language, whether read or heard. In Figure 7.39, the two middle "letters" are physically identical, but they are usually seen as an *H* in *THE* and an *A* in *CAT*. A similar point applies to words that sound alike, such as *EYE* and *I*. Their interpretation depends entirely on a linguistic context of which we are hardly ever aware.

7.38   An ambiguous figure: old woman or young woman   *(A) This is ambiguous and is just as likely to be seen as a young woman or as an old woman. (B) and (C) are essentially unambiguous, and depict the young woman and old woman respectively. If the subjects are first shown one of the unambiguous figures, they are almost sure to see the ambiguous picture in that fashion later on. (After Boring, 1930; Leeper, 1935)*

THE CAT

We have seen that some aspects of perceptual organization are innately given. Examples are many of the factors that determine perceived depth and movement. Other facets of perceptual organization are acquired or modified through learning, such as certain realignments of visual space and of touch. In addition, perception is affected by some of the conditions of the immediately preceding context, as shown by various phenomena of attention and mental set.

What then remains of the nature-nurture issue that motivated so much of the initial inquiry into the nature of perception? In some ways the controversy is still with us, though it has moved to a new level. Today, all disputants agree that we start with much larger building blocks than the early empiricists had envisaged, for we now know there are built-in mechanisms that underlie the perception of such units as contours and edges. What is at issue is whether some of the building blocks are even larger, whether we come preequipped to respond to such complex stimulus patterns as triangles, faces, or smiles. As yet, we don't know the answer, though the best bet is that most of these larger perceptual units are built up out of smaller ones by some process of learning. Whether this process is one of perceptual construction or of differentiation or is based on some other mechanism, is still unclear.

The Perception of Reality

Seeing depth and form and movement all serve toward the attainment of a larger goal—the perception of the real world outside. How is this perception of reality achieved?

THE PERCEPTUAL CONSTANCIES

To see the real world is to see the properties of distal objects: their color, form, and location, their movement through space, their permanence or transience. But we have noted previously that organisms cannot gain experience about the distal stimulus directly; all information about the external world comes to us from the proximal stimulus patterns which distal objects project upon the senses. Of course the same distal object will produce different proximal stimulus patterns, but the perceptual system somehow "sees through" the different masks. It responds to the permanent features of the real object outside regardless of the illumination that falls on it and the distance and orientation from which it is viewed. The best proof is provided by the ***perceptual constancies.*** A crow looks black even in sunlight; an elephant looks large even at a distance; and a postcard looks rectangular even though its retinal image is a trapezoid, unless viewed directly head on. In all of these cases, we manage to transcend the vagaries of the proximal stimulus and react to certain constant attributes of the distal object such as its shape and its size.

How does the organism accomplish this feat? We will see that it does so by means of several quite different mechanisms. Some are based on simple, built-in sensory processes of the kind we discussed in the previous chapter. Others are probably the result of perceptual learning. And yet others may involve more complex processes still.

Virtually all objects reflect a certain proportion of the light that falls upon them. The exact proportion depends upon a physical property of the object itself, its **reflectance.** Some objects have a high reflectance (snow), others a low reflectance (coal). To say that an object is perceived as light or dark is really to say that we can tell something about its reflectance. Yet we cannot possibly see the reflectance directly; all we get from the object is the amount of light it actually reflects on any given occasion, the **luminance.** But this luminance depends not only upon the object's reflectance but also upon the **illumination** that falls upon it. A white shirt in shadow may well reflect less light than does a gray shirt in brilliant sunlight. Under the circumstances, can we ever tell that the first is lighter than the second?

The fact is that we can, at least to some extent. A swan will not suddenly seem to turn gray when a cloud hides the sun; it appears just as white, but in shadow. This effect is called **lightness constancy.** The apparent lightness of an object remains fairly constant despite rather drastic changes in the illumination that falls upon it. Lightness constancy is readily demonstrated in the laboratory. Subjects are shown gray papers of known reflectance values. One is a paper whose reflectance is at, say, 50 percent. This paper, *A,* receives twice the illumination of another paper, *B,* which is in shadow (Figure 7.40). What must be the reflectance of *B* so that subjects judge it to be just as light as *A?* To get equal luminance, *B* should be entirely white (its reflectance would then be twice that of paper *A,* thus compensating for the fact that it receives only half as much illumination). But in fact, the subjects show nearly perfect lightness constancy. They judge the two papers to be equally light if *B*'s reflectance is virtually identical to *A*'s.

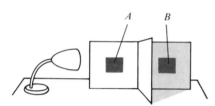

7.40 Lightness constancy *The figure shows schematically the setup in which two identical gray papers,* A *and* B, *are shown to subjects.* A *is illuminated while* B *is in shadow. As a result,* A *reflects much more light than* B. *Even so, the two are perceived to be about equal in lightness, a manifestation of lightness constancy. (After Rock, 1975)*

Learning and lightness constancy   How does lightness constancy come about? To the empiricists, the answer was learning. One suggestion was that our prior knowledge of the lightness of a familiar object might affect the way we see it. But this can't be the answer, for lightness constancy is found even for unfamiliar objects. A more plausible approach is Helmholtz'. He assumed that prior experience has taught us how illumination affects the luminance of different objects. We use this experience to compensate for present illumination levels by a perceptual process similar to an inference. Helmholtz believed that the perceiver tacitly reasons: "This object looks gray. But since I can see that it is very dimly illuminated, it must be lighter than it appears to be. I will therefore adjust my perception accordingly and *see* it as light gray." None of this is conscious, which is why Helmholtz called this hypothetical process **unconscious inference** (Helmholtz, 1909).

Helmholtz' theory faces a number of problems. One concerns his assertion that the observer compensates for the illumination. But how can the observer tell what that illumination is, considering that the only information he has comes from the light that is reflected by objects whose reflectance he doesn't know?

Built-in factors and lightness constancy   A nativist alternative to a learning theory was first suggested by Ewald Hering, who pointed out that lightness constancy might be caused (at least in part) by the same processes that are

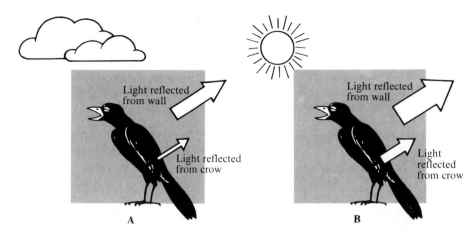

7.41   Lightness constancy and brightness contrast   *Lightness constancy is at least partially caused by the same processes that lead to brightness contrast. In (A) the illumination on both bird and wall is moderate; in (B) it is much greater. The fact that illumination goes up increases the amount of light reflected by the bird but it also increases the amount of light reflected by the wall that serves as its background. The two increases tend to cancel each other. Any increase in the light intensity of the background tends to inhibit the apparent lightness of the figure. This compensation effect acts in the direction of lightness constancy: The crow continues to look black even in brilliant sunshine.*

responsible for brightness contrast (see Chapter 6). The basic idea is that illumination changes normally affect both the object in the foreground and the background against which it is seen. Consider a black crow that stands in front of a gray garden wall (Figure 7.41). The sun is democratic; it will shine equally on the crow and on the garden wall. If it suddenly emerges from behind a cloud, the illumination on the crow (and hence its luminance) will go up. But the same holds for the wall. Its luminance will also increase and will cause a decline in the apparent lightness of the crow. This is just another example of brightness contrast which makes objects appear darker as the luminance of their background goes up. The result is an automatic compensation effect that works in the direction of lightness constancy.

The brightness ratio   Brightness contrast will tend to offset the luminance changes brought about by increases or decreases in the illumination. Is this effect alone large enough to produce lightness constancy? Hans Wallach argued that the effective stimulus for the perceived brightness of any region is the *ratio* of the luminance of that region to the luminance of its surrounding area. If this is so, lightness constancy should be perfect as long as both figure and background are illuminated equally.*

The question is whether perceived lightness is in fact a simple function of the luminance ratio. To get at this issue, Wallach presented subjects with two disks surrounded by rings. The two disk-ring combinations were projected on a screen in an otherwise dark room; the luminance of each ring and disk could be adjusted separately (Figure 7.42). Suppose disk *A* is set at 200 millilamberts (a unit of luminance), while the ring around it is set at 400 millilamberts. If the

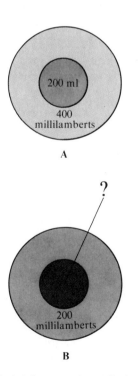

* This follows from the definition of luminance. Let L_F stand for the luminance of the figure, and L_B for the luminance of the background. Let R_F and R_B stand for the reflectances of figure and background respectively, and let I stand for the illumination. Then,

$$L_F = I \times R_F \text{ and } L_B = I \times R_B$$

If the same illumination falls on both figure and background, the ratio of their luminances, L_F/L_B, will remain constant regardless of the value of I:

$$\frac{L_F}{L_B} = \frac{I \times R_F}{I \times R_B} = \frac{R_F}{R_B} = \text{a constant}$$

7.42   The brightness ratio   *(A) A ring with a luminance of 400 millilamberts surrounds a disk at 200 millilamberts. (B) A ring at 200 millilamberts surrounds a disk whose luminance is adjustable. When subjects are asked to adjust the luminance of the disk in (B) so that it looks just as bright as the disk in (A), they set it at about 100 millilamberts, matching the two-to-one luminance ratio between ring and disk in (A).*

255

7.43 Shape constancy *When we see a door frame at various slants from us, it appears rectangular despite the fact that its retinal image is often a trapezoid. (After Gibson, 1950)*

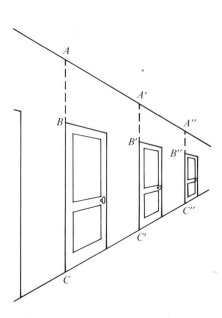

7.44 Invariance and size constancy *One might argue that size constancy is based on an invariant size ratio between the retinal size of the object and of its surrounding framework. In the figure, this would be the ratio between the heights of each door and its surrounding wall which is constant regardless of the distance to the observer. (Thus BC/AC = B'C'/A'C', and so forth.) But this size ratio cannot account for all (or even most) of the size constancy effects, for size constancy is found even when there is no readily available framework.*

ring around disk *B* is set at 200 millilamberts, what must be the luminance of disk *B* so that the subject perceives it to be exactly as bright as disk *A*? Wallach found that the subjects tended to adjust the luminance in accordance with the ratio principle. They set disk *B* at 100 millilamberts, a two-to-one luminance ratio equal to that which holds between disk *A* and the ring surrounding it (Wallach, 1948).

Further evidence suggests that the brightness ratio is only a first approximation. But even so, it seems safe to assume that lightness constancy is for the most part produced by the same built-in visual interaction processes—presumably based on lateral inhibition—that are responsible for brightness contrast and related phenomena.

SIZE AND SHAPE CONSTANCY

Lightness constancy is evidently due in the main to built-in mechanisms. Is the same true for other perceptual constancies, such as those for size and shape? *Size constancy* is a term which describes the fact that the perceived size of an object is the same whether it is nearby or far away. A Cadillac at a distance of 100 feet will look larger than a Volkswagen 20 feet away (a phenomenon we have described before). An analogous phenomenon is *shape constancy.* This refers to the fact that we perceive the shape of an object independent of the angle from which it is viewed. A rectangular door frame will appear rectangular even though most of the angles from which it is regarded will produce a trapezoidal retinal image (Figure 7.43).

The search for an invariant In lightness constancy, there is a stimulus relation that remains invariant throughout an illumination change—the brightness ratio. Are there analogous invariant relations that underlie size and shape constancy? If there are, they may point the way to natively given underlying mechanisms, as in the case of lightness constancy and lateral inhibition.

The primary focus of inquiry has been size constancy. One possible stimulus factor is the relation between the retinal size of the object and of its surrounding framework. A door does not seem to grow in size as we approach it in a hallway even though its retinal image is expanding. But one thing stays unchanged: the ratio between the size of the images of the door and the hallway (Figure 7.44). Does such a constant size ratio underline all size constancy effects? The facts say otherwise, for size constancy is found even when there is no framework that can provide the basis for a size ratio. An example is a room in which the only visible object is a luminous disk. That disk will look about equally large whether it is moved closer or farther off from the subject.

An empiricist approach to size constancy   An invariant size ratio will not explain size constancy. What then will? The most plausible hypothesis derives from Helmholtz. We somehow take account of the object's distance and compensate for it. According to Helmholtz, the size-distance relationship is acquired through long experience. He pointed out that young children sometimes mistake objects at a considerable distance for miniatures; looking down from a tower, they see the people below as tiny dolls (Helmholtz, 1909).

Some evidence for the role of learning in the acquisition of size constancy comes from a study of rats reared in complete darkness for the first month of life. Immediately thereafter, they were unable to tell the difference between the sight of a 1-inch diameter circle 1.5 feet away and a 2-inch diameter circle 3 feet away, even though there were adequate depth cues. These animals could respond to visual depth, as shown by the fact that they ran to the shallow side of a visual cliff. They could respond to the size of the retinal image, as shown by the fact that they could discriminate between the 1-inch and 2-inch circles when they were at the same distance (Heller, 1968). What they could not do was to relate depth and size appropriately. To do this, they presumably have to learn how the two visual attributes change together as one approaches or withdraws from objects. And this necessarily requires visual experience (Rock, 1975).

This finding suggests that Helmholtz was right in asserting that size constancy is learned. But he was wrong in believing that it is learned slowly. In the case of the dark-reared rats, size constancy was restored after only seven days in normal light. In the case of humans, a series of studies by T. G. Bower of the University of Edinburgh provide evidence for size constancy in the second month of life (Figure 7.45). In one of his studies the subjects were infants

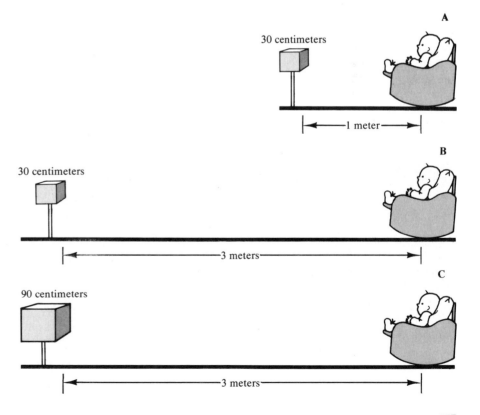

7.45 Size constancy in infants   *(A) Two-month-old infants were trained to turn their heads at the sight of a 30-centimeter cube at a distance of 1 meter. They were then tested with a stimulus at a distance of 3 meters. In one condition, (B), the stimulus was the same 30-centimeter cube. Here, the distal stimulus was unchanged, but the retinal size was drastically diminished. In another condition, (C), they were tested with a 90-centimeter cube. Here, the distal stimulus was altered, but the retinal stimulus was kept the same. The infants responded more vigorously in (B) than in (C), an indication that some degree of size constancy is present very early. (After Bower, 1966)*

7.46 The moon illusion *In (A), the moon is at the horizon. Here, depth cues such as perspective and interposition indicate that the moon is far away. The perceptual system takes the apparent distance into account and, as a result, the moon seems larger. In (B), the moon is overhead. Here, depth cues are less prominent. As a result, the apparent distance to the moon seems less, and the moon appears smaller. In both figures, the basic principle is the relation between retinal size and apparent distance. If an object casts a certain retinal size, it will be perceived to be larger if it appears to be at a greater distance; smaller if it seems to be closer by. This effect works much better in real life where depth cues are more pronounced. (After Kaufman and Rock, 1962a) The general principle that underlies the moon illusion is illustrated in (C). The black rectangle resting at the horizon seems to be larger than the one in the foreground, although both are objectively identical in size. Again, the reason is apparent distance. Since the rectangle at the horizon seems farther off, it is perceived to be larger than the one that has the same retinal size but appears to be nearer. (After Rock and Kaufman, 1962b)*

between six and eight weeks of age who were trained to turn their heads a centimeter or more to the right or to the left. The reinforcement was a "peek-a-boo"; a concealed experimenter popped up cooing and smiling when the infant turned its head, and then disappeared again. When the headturning response was well established (an easy task since the infants dearly loved the peek-a-boos), a discriminative stimulus was introduced. A cube with 30 centimeter sides was placed 1 meter away from the infant's head. When the cube was present, the peek-a-boo was delivered; when it was not, no reinforcement occurred. After the infants acquired this discrimination (they now responded only in the presence of the cube), the critical tests were begun. Sometimes the infant was shown a 30 centimeter cube at a distance of 3 meters (thus changing the retinal size of the original cube, but not its distal size), sometimes a 90 centimeter cube at a distance of 3 meters (thus changing the distal size but not the retinal size). The infants responded much more frequently to the stimulus whose true size was unaltered than to the one whose size was increased so as to produce the same retinal image. This indicates that some measure of size constancy is present even at this early age (T.G. Bower, 1966).

All in all then, current evidence suggests that size constancy is based on some learning process that relates two sources of information that are innately given—retinal size and distance. To this extent, the Helmholtzian view is born out. But the kind of learning that goes on here is remarkably fast, as if it were based on a **biologically prepared disposition** (see Chapter 5).

Inappropriate compensation and illusions The preceding discussion shows that we compensate for distance when perceiving size. By and large, this perceptual strategy works. It leads to size constancy, one of the ways we have for seeing the world as it really is. But occasionally, this policy backfires and produces illusions.

A well-known example is the **moon illusion.** The moon looks considerably larger at the horizon than it does when up in the sky, even though its retinal image is equal in both cases (Figure 7.46). The main reason is that the horizon looks farther away than the overhead sky. But since the perceptual system compensates for perceived distance, the horizon moon is seen as larger. To test

A

B

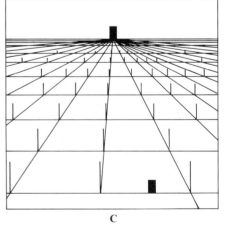

C

A

B

7.47 A size illusion *(A) An Example of an illusion produced by the effect of perceived distance upon perceived size. The two horizontal bars seem to be unequal, with the one on top apparently larger than the one below. In actuality, the two horizontal lines are perfectly identical. shown in (B) where they appear alone. (After Gregory, 1968) This illusion is produced by perspective cues which make the top bar appear to be farther away and thus larger, an effect similar to that which leads to the moon illusion. For a photographic version of the same illusion, see (B). (Photograph by Don Ball)*

this hypothesis, subjects viewed artificial moons through special optical devices. They experienced the standard moon illusion. In line with the size-distance hypothesis, the illusion was greater the farther off the visible horizon appeared (Kaufman and Rock, 1962*a*).

A number of other illusions of size may be caused by a similar effect of perceived distance upon perceived size. Some examples are shown in Figures 7.47 and 7.48. In every instance, perspective cues indicate that one part of the figure is more distant than another. This leads to a faulty compensation in which the part that seems farther away is perceived to be larger than it really is (Gregory, 1963).

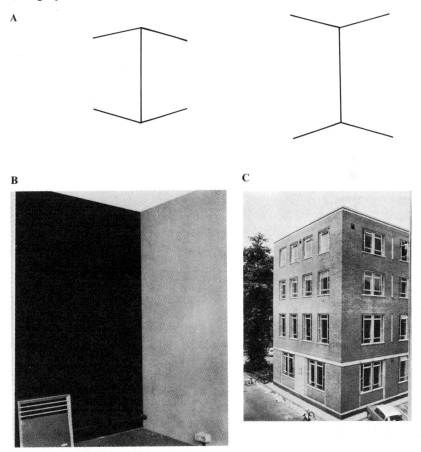

7.48 The Müller-Lyer illusion *(A) In the Müller-Lyer illusion (named after its discoverer), the center line in the left figure seems to be shorter than its counterpart on the right. In actual fact, the two center lines are identical. According to a hypothesis by R. L. Gregory, the illusion is yet another effect of misleading perspective cues. Gregory argues that the ingoing fins make the center line look like an outside corner, which is nearer to the viewer. The outgoing fins, on the other hand, make the line look like an inside corner, which is farther away from the viewer. Since the ingoing fins make the line appear to be nearer, there is a compensatory decrease in it apparent size. The reverse holds for the outgoing fins (Gregory, 1966, 1968). Some examples from the real world illustrate Gregory's argument. The center lines of the inside corner of the room (B) and the outsider corner of the building (C) are objectively identical in height (From Gregory, 1966)*

259

OBJECT PERMANENCE

The various constancies assure the appropriate perception of different attributes of a distal object. This holds even for the infant whose rattle presumably maintains its apparent lightness, size, and shape regardless of change in illumination, distance, and angle of regard. These constancies are certainly necessary for the perception of a real, stable world, but they are not sufficient to assure it. The various attributes of the infant's rattle may be perceptually stable, but what about the rattle itself? To an adult it is an object, a *thing,* of whose existence he has no doubt, whether he looks at it or looks briefly away. The adult is sure of its existence, for he is certain that he will see it once more when he looks at it again.* Does the rattle exist as a thing in the same sense to the infant?

Put somewhat differently, the question is whether an object remains perceptually constant over time. This kind of constancy has been called **object permanence** by the Swiss psychologist Jean Piaget. According to Piaget, there is little object permanence in the first few months of life. His description of his own seven-month-old daughter is illuminating:

> Jacqueline tries to grasp a celluloid duck on top of her quilt. She almost catches it, shakes herself, and the duck slides down beside her. It falls very close to her hand but behind a fold in the sheet. Jacqueline's eyes have followed the movement, she has even followed it with her outstretched hand. But as soon as the duck has disappeared—nothing more! (Piaget, 1951, pp. 36–37).

To Piaget, the fact that Jacqueline did not search for the duck when it was out of sight was proof enough that it was also out of mind. But other psychologists have shown some rudiments of object permanence in very young infants by using more sensitive response indicators. Bower measured increases in heart rate, which at least in adults generally accompanies surprise. His subjects were infants between 20 and 100 days old. They were shown objects, such as a small sphere, which were then covered up with a screen. After an interval the screen was removed, but the sphere was no longer there. When the interval was very short (1.5 seconds) even the youngest subjects showed surprise. Their heart rate increased, suggesting that for a second or so the sphere was still psychologically present, that a tiny bridge had been built between past and present. In three-month-old infants, this bridge spans intervals as long as 15 seconds (T.G. Bower, 1971).

Needless to say, children eventually come to live in a world whose objects do not capriciously appear and disappear with the movements of their eyes.

---

* This point has led some philosophers to define external objects as "permanent possibilities of sensation" (J.S. Mill, 1865, Chapter 11). Helmholtz put it very concretely: "We notice that we can get various images of the table in front of us simply by changing our position; and that we can sometimes have one view and sometimes another. . . . and that the table may vanish from sight and then be there again at any moment we like, simply by turning our eyes. . . . We explain the table as having existence independent of our observation, because at *any moment we like,* simply by assuming the proper position with respect to it, we can observe it" (Helmholtz, 1909, p. 31).

At about ten months of age, they start to search for toys that have been hidden or have fallen out of their cribs. According to Piaget, the infant develops the *object concept* (that is, the notion that things exist independently of its own senses) by gradually interrelating its various sensory experiences and motor reactions; he therefore called the period during which this happens the stage of *sensory-motor development* (the first two years of life). At the end of this period, the child has coordinated the various sensory spaces provided by the different modalities—of vision, touch, bodily movement, and so on—into one real space in which all of the world's objects—himself included—exist.

It is obvious that even in early stages object permanence involves a perceptual achievement that is much more complex than the constancies of brightness, size, or shape. But, at least in principle, some aspects of all these achievements are essentially alike. In each case, perceivers must abstract some aspect of the total stimulus pattern that pertains to a stable characteristic of the object; and they must disregard features of the stimulus that tend to obscure it. To perceive lightness, they must compensate for illumination; to perceive size and shape, they must compensate for their own distance and angle of regard; to perceive a permanent object, they must compensate for the various stimulus changes that occur over time. Some of these abstractions (such as lightness constancy) are essentially built into the system by a kindly evolutionary process that provides an initial starting point for the perception of reality. Others (such as size and shape constancy) are probably developed through learning which builds upon an innately given foundation. Still others (such as object permanence) are primarily learned. The specific mechanisms which underlie these achievements differ considerably. But in all cases the overall effect of these mechanisms is essentially the same—to perceive the enduring properties of the real world outside so that a swan looks as bright in shade as it does in sunlight, so that a hippopotamus seems equally imposing regardless of the size it projects on the viewer's retina, so that a rattlesnake remains dangerously real even when it slithers behind a rock.

A final point. One may well question whether object permanence is really a matter of perception rather than of conception, whether the effect is on seeing or on knowing. According to Piaget, what has changed is the way the child "thinks" about the world and what she "knows" about it, not how the world "looks" to her. Whether such a sharp distinction between perception and conception can be drawn is debatable. But as we have seen, even the simplest perceptual phenomena are affected by such cognitive processes as attention and memory. We therefore should not be too surprised to find that when perception becomes complex enough, it merges into thinking.

The Representation of Reality in Visual Art

Our discussion of object permanence led us to the shadowy region where perception and conception join; where it's not quite clear at what point seeing ends and knowing begins. Another illustration of this overlap is found in the psychology of visual art. We will see that many of the phenomena we have encountered in our discussion of visual perception are part of the equipment of the artists who try to represent this perceptual world on paper or canvas.

Consider Figure 7.49, a mural painted in an Egyptian tomb some four thousand years ago. Why did the artist depict the various figures as he did, with eyes and shoulders in front view and the rest of the body in profile? His fellow Egyptians were surely built as we are. But if so, why didn't he draw them "correctly"?

The answer seems to be that Egyptian artists drew, not what they could see at any one moment or from any one position, but rather what they knew was the most enduring and characteristic attribute of their model. They portrayed the various parts of the human body from the vantage point that shows each form in its most characteristic manner: the front-view for the eyes and shoulders, the profile for the nose and feet. The fact that these orientations are incompatible was evidently of no concern; what mattered was that all of the components were represented as the artist knew them to be (Gombrich, 1961).

On a much more humble level, the same preoccupation with representing the known may explain certain aspects of children's art. Figure 7.50 shows a boy's drawing of a town square. The square is shown from above, yet the people and houses are drawn upright all around it. But this is reasonable enough if we assume that the boy's purpose is to represent what he knows about the world. After all, people and houses are at right angles to the street on which they stand. And if so, why not let the drawing say so?

7.49   Carved tomb relief of a government official, ca. 2350–2280 B.C.   *The conventions of Egyptian art required the main parts of the human body to be represented in its most characteristic view. Thus heads are shown in profile, arms and legs from the side, but eyes are depicted in full-face view, as are the shoulders and the chest. (Courtesy Norbert Schimmel)*

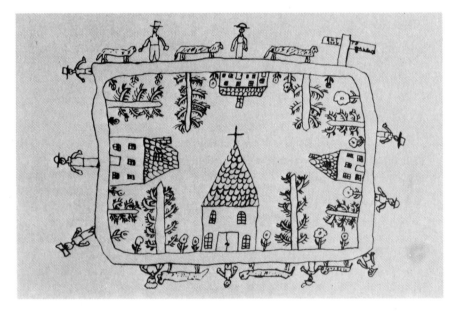

7.50   A child's drawing   A Square of a Town in Connecticut *drawn by a twelve-year-old boy. (From Lewis, 1966)*

THE RENAISSANCE: SCENES THROUGH A WINDOW FRAME

The illustrations of Egyptian art (as well as the lesser masterpieces produced by children) show the enormous role of the known in the visual representation of the seen. One may argue that this simply reflects the fact that these artists never set themselves the task of mirroring nature as it appears to the eye. Does the artist copy more precisely if his purpose is to do just that?

The most striking examples come from the Renaissance masters who conceived the notion that a picture should look just like a real scene that is viewed through a window from one particular orientation. The painting's frame is then the frame of this window into the artist's world. One major step toward achieving this end was the discovery of the geometrical laws of perspective, the way in which all objects are foreshortened as the perspective lines converge toward a vanishing point at the horizon (Figure 7.51). This was supplemented by the systematic use of other pictorial cues for depth such as interposition.

In effect, the Renaissance masters seemed to believe that to catch visual reality, one's picture should correspond to the image the model casts on the eye also. This motivated their search for means to portray depth on a flat

7.51 **The laws of perspective** *An illustration in a 1505 treatise by Viator. (From Ivins, 1975)*

7.52   Early teaching manuals for artists
An illustration of schematic heads in a sixteenth-century artist's manual by Schoen. The spatial grids help the novice to learn the relevant proportions of the object he tries to draw. As he learns this, he develops a schema for representing the object visually. If drawing were simply a matter of copying, no such schema would be necessary. (From Gombrich, 1961)

canvas (Figure 7.53). The same conception also served as the starting point for such empiricists as Locke and Berkeley, whose concern was with the nature of perception. The empiricists asked how the painters' means of portraying depth—the pictorial cues—could lead to the experience of depth if the image on the eye is two-dimensional.

One may question whether these Renaissance artists really copied nature as they set out to do. The art historian E. H. Gombrich argues that they did not. In his view, "The 'Egyptian' in us can be suppressed, but he can never be quite defeated," for the artist can never create a genuine optical replica of his model, can never paint the world independently of what he knows about it.

Gombrich believes that the artist interprets his model through various visual schemas in terms of which he then renders it in pictorial form. Such schemas are like the rules whereby we read a map. A certain kind of line corresponds to a river, another to a road, and so on. The map certainly resembles the terrain in some important ways, but it is not a genuine copy.

Some evidence comes from the teaching manuals published by the artists themselves. They exhort the student to learn what a face, a hand, a foot, really are like, to study their relative proportions and their visual appearance in different bodily postures (Figure 7.52). But why bother to learn all this if you can simply draw what you see? The fact is that what you "see" is in part what you know.

THE IMPRESSIONISTS: HOW A SCENE IS PERCEIVED

The Renaissance painters tried to represent a scene as it is projected on the eye (though to be sure they did very much more than that). Other schools of painting set themselves a different task. Consider the French Impressionists of the late nineteenth century. They tried to recreate certain perceptual experiences that the scene evokes in the observer, the impression it makes rather than the scene itself. One of their concerns was to render color as we see it in broad daylight. Their method was to create a seeming patchwork of different daubs of bright colors (Figure 7.54). These are clearly separate when looked at directly. But when viewed from the proper distance they change appearance, especially in the periphery where acuity is weak. The individual patches now blur together and their colors mix. But when the eyes move again and bring that area of the picture back into the fovea, the mixtures come apart and the individual patches reappear. Some authors believe that this continual alternation between mixed colors and separate dots gives these paintings their special vitality (Jameson and Hurvich, 1975).

This patchwork technique has a further effect. It enlists the beholder as an active participant in the artistic enterprise. Her active involvement starts as soon as she tries to see the picture as a whole rather than as a meaningless jumble of colored patches. This happens when the separate patches blur: when they are viewed from the periphery or from a few steps back. Now the picture suddenly snaps into focus and a whole emerges. This is both similar to and different from what happens in ordinary life. There we move our eyes to bring some part of the world to a region of greater acuity, the fovea. In the museum, we sometimes move our eyes (or our entire body) to bring a picture to a region of lesser acuity, away from the fovea. In either case, active movement leads to the perception of a figural whole (Hochberg, 1978b, 1980).

7.53 Perspective in Renaissance art
The Annunciation *by Crivelli (ca. 1430–95). Note the loving attention to perspective detail, such as roofs and arches extending far back. (Courtesy the National Gallery, London)*

7.54 Bend in the Epte River, near Giverny (1888) by Claude Monet
Monet, one of the leaders of Impressionism, was engaged in a life-long attempt to catch the fleeting sensations of light in nature. If the painting is viewed from farther back or out of foveal vision, the form becomes clearer and less impressionistic. What is lost is the brilliant shimmer of light and color. The oscillation between these two modes of appearance contributes to the total aesthetic effect. (Courtesy Philadelphia Museum of Art: The William L. Elkins Collection)

265

7.55 The Races at Longchamp, Paris (1864) by Eduard Manet *Manet's painting captures the color, bustle, and movement of the scene, in part, by omitting details and letting the beholder fill them in. (Courtesy The Art Institute of Chicago)*

The artist often requires even more activity on the part of the beholder who is often asked to fill in various details, to complete a landscape or a facial expression for which the artist has provided only a sketchy outline. But the net result tends to be that the picture is more rather than less lifelike because of this (Figure 7.55).

THE MODERNS: HOW A SCENE IS CONCEIVED

The Impressionists tried to engender some of the perceptual experiences a scene evokes in the observer. Later generations went further and tried to capture not just how the scene is *perceived* but how it is *conceived;* how it is known as well as seen. Modern art provides many examples, as in Pablo Picasso's still life showing superimposed fragments of a violin (Figure 7.56). Here perception and knowledge are cunningly merged in a sophisticated return to some of the ways of Egyptian artists (Gombrich, 1961).

Some modern artists are not satisfied to add conceptual elements to their visual representations. They want to create ambiguity by setting up visual puzzles that can't be solved. One way is to pit knowledge against visual perception, as in Picasso's faces that are seen in profile and front-face at the same time. Another is to build contradictions within the perceptual scene itself. An example is a painting by the turn-of-the-century Italian Giorgio de Chirico (Figure 7.57). One reason for the disturbing quality of this picture is the fact that de Chirico used incompatible perspectives. The structure on the left converges to one horizon, that on the right to a horizon far below the other, while the wagon in the middle does not converge at all. The result is an insoluble visual problem, an eerie world which cannot be put in order.

7.56 Violin and Grapes *by Pablo*
Picasso, 1912 (Courtesy Museum of
Modern Art, New York, Mrs. David M.
Levy bequest)

7.57 Melancholy and Mystery of a Street
by Georgio de Chirico, 1914 (Courtesy
Mr. and Mrs. Stanley R. Resor)

De Chirico's streets do not look like real streets and Picasso's violins are a far cry from those one sees in a concert hall. In this regard, these modern painters appear quite different from many of their predecessors whose representations were closer to the world as it appears to the perceiver. But we have to realize that no artists, whether Renaissance masters, Impressionists, or moderns, ever try to fool the observer into thinking that he is looking at a real scene. They neither can nor want to hide the fact that their painting is a painting. It may spring to life for a moment and look like a real person or a real sunset, or it may briefly conjure up a vivid memory of what a face or a violin looks like when viewed from several angles. But whether it emphasizes the seen or the known, it is also recognized as a flat piece of canvas daubed with paint.

According to some authors, this perceptual duality is an important part of the beholder's esthetic experience as he looks at a work of representational art. In a well-known poem by Robert Browning, a duke points to his "last duchess painted on the wall,/Looking as if she were alive." The key words are *as if*. One reason why visual art leads to an esthetic experience may be because it provides us with a halfway mark between seen reality and painted appearance, because it presents a visual *as if* (Hochberg, 1980).

In our discussion of visual art we have taken yet another step across the wide, shadowy region where perception and conception, seeing and knowing merge. In the next chapter we cross the boundary altogether and consider how we remember objects and events that no longer stimulate our senses.

Summary

1. Most of the phenomena perception psychologists study, hinge on the apparent discrepancy between what the proximal stimulus gives us and what we actually see. Attempts to resolve this discrepancy have traditionally taken either of two approaches, the *empiricist* and the *nativist*. An example is perceived size, which remains roughly constant whether the object is far off or nearby. Empiricists explain this by referring to *unconscious inference* based on a learned rule that farther objects lead to smaller retinal sensations. Nativists argue that the perception of true size is directly given and is based on some *invariant relationship* in the stimulus pattern, such as certain size ratios in the retinal image. This *nature-nurture controversy* forms the background of much of the discussion in this chapter.

2. The perception of visual form depends on some prior phenomena of *perceptual organization*. One is the segregation of *figure and ground*. This is not inherent in the proximal stimulus but is imposed by the perceptual system, as shown by *reversible figure-ground patterns*. A related phenomenon is *perceptual grouping*, which depends upon such organizational factors as *proximity, similarity, good continuation,* and *closure*.

3. A crucial fact in form perception is *transposition of form*. A perceived form may remain the same even if all of its constituent parts are altered. This phenomenon is the keystone of *Gestalt psychology*, a theory which emphasizes the importance of wholes created by the relationship between their parts.

4. The visual world is seen in three dimensions even though only two of these are given in the image that falls upon the eye. This fact has led to an interest in *depth cues*.

SUMMARY

Among these are *binocular disparity,* and the *monocular, pictorial cues* such as *interposition* and *linear perspective.* Of special interest are various *texture gradients* which are powerful determinants of perceived depth. Even more important is *motion parallax* which depends upon the observer's movements.

5. Organizational factors play a considerable role in the perception of movement, as shown by such phenomena as *apparent movement* and *induced movement* and also by the fact that the nervous system compensates for retinal displacements produced by movements of the eyes.

6. Some of the phenomena of perceptual organization are innately based. Some evidence comes from studies of very young organisms tested on the *visual cliff* and on *looming.* Less conclusive are studies of perception after *sensory deprivation,* as in cases of cataract removal after blindness since birth.

7. Attempts to find the physiological mechanisms that underlie built-in perceptual organization have concentrated on *feature analyzers* both within the retina and in the brain. These are cells that respond to certain relational aspects of the stimulus, as shown by single-cell recordings. The adaptation of such feature analyzers may explain certain changes of perceptual experience after prolonged exposure to a certain kind of stimulus, as in the *aftereffect of visual movement.*

8. Perceptual organization is affected by experience. One example is *perceptual adaptation* to various optical distortions. They are based on learned realignments of several perceptual systems which probably occur more readily when the organism is involved in active movement.

9. Perceptual learning as it normally occurs in adulthood is probably the result of processes that are quite different from those of perceptual adaptation. According to some authors, the key is a process of *perceptual construction* which produces organized sets of expectations about eye movements and their perceptual consequences. A different approach emphasizes *perceptual differentiation,* a process whereby relevant *distinctive features* in the stimulus are gradually singled out and attended.

10. Perceptual organization is affected by expectations which can change from moment to moment as shown by the effects of *selective attention.* This may be by means of *orienting movements* that determine the physical selection of the stimuli that reach the organism's senses. It may also be the result of a *central selection* process as in cases of *selective listening,* of *selective looking,* and of *mental set.*

11. The ultimate function of perceptual organization is to help the organism see the outside world as it really is. An illustration is the *constancies* in which the perceiver responds to certain permanent characteristics of the distal object despite various contextual factors—illumination, distance, and orientation—which lead to enormous variations in the proximal stimulus. In *lightness constancy,* the perceiver responds to the object's *reflectance* and tends to ignore the level of the illumination that falls upon it. This phenomenon is in large part based upon the same built-in process that produces *brightness ratio.* In *size and shape constancy,* the perceiver responds to the actual size and shape of the object more or less regardless of its distance and its orientation, an effect that may be based on learning in very early life. This compensation for distance leads to size constancy but sometimes produces misperceptions, as in the case of the *moon illusion.*

12. Another kind of constancy is *object permanence,* the idea that an object continues to exist even when it is temporarily out of sight. According to Jean Piaget, this *object concept* emerges toward the end of the first year of life, during the *sensory-motor stage* of cognitive development.

13. The psychology of visual art is a further illustration of the overlap between perception and thinking. The artist represents both what he sees and what he knows. *Renaissance* painters represented scenes seen through a window frame; the *Impressionists* tried to recreate certain perceptual experiences the scene creates in the beholder; while many modern artists try to represent the scene as it is conceived and thought about.

CHAPTER 8

Memory

Our discussion of perception, and especially of visual perception, has emphasized the way in which psychological events are organized in space. Locke and Berkeley to the contrary, our perceptual world is not a jumbled mosaic of isolated sensory fragments, but an organized, coherent whole in which every piece relates to every other. We now turn to the subject of *memory,* in which organization plays an equally prominent part.

Memory is the way in which we record the past and later refer to it so that it may affect the present. It is hard to think of humans (or any animal that is able to learn) without this capacity. Without memory, there would be no then but only a now, no ability to utilize skills, no recall of names or recognition of faces, no reference to past days or hours or even seconds. We would be condemned to live in a narrowly circumscribed present, but this present would not even seem to be our own for there can be no sense of self without memory. Each individual wakes up every morning and never doubts that he is *he* or she is *she.* This feeling of continuous personal identity is necessarily based upon the continuity of memories which links our yesterdays to our todays.

Such considerations underline the crucial importance of memory as a psychological process. How can this process be studied?

Acquisition, Retention, Retrieval

To begin with, we must distinguish among three stages which are implied by any act of remembering. Consider a person working on a crossword puzzle who is trying to recall an eight-letter word meaning "African anteater." If she does, we can be sure that she succeeded in all three stages of the memorial process. The first is *acquisition.* To remember, one must first have learned; the subject must somewhere have encountered this particular item of biological exotica. During this acquisition stage, the relevant experiences presumably left some enduring record in the nervous system, the *memory trace.* Next comes *retention,* during which the information is filed away for later use (until the next crossword puzzle). The final stage is *retrieval,* the point at which one tries to remember, to dredge up this particular memory trace from among all others. Many failures to remember are failures of retrieval and not of storage. Our subject may be unable to come up with the correct answer at the time, but when she later sees the solution she realizes that she knew it all along. "Of course, Aardvark!"

A previously acquired item of information can be retrieved in two ways: *recall* and *recognition.* An individual who is asked to recall must produce an item or a set of items. "Where did you park your car?" or "What is the name of the boy who sat next to you in the third grade?" are examples of recall questions. The experimental psychologist typically tests for the recall of materials that were learned in the laboratory; this assures that any failures in recall are not simply failures of original acquisition. Thus a subject might have to learn a dozen unrelated adjectives which he will later be asked to recite. Recall need not be verbal. An example is the retention of a motor skill such as playing golf; here memory is best assessed by observing how the subject hits a golf ball and not by how he talks about his swing. Another example is the memory of visual patterns. This is sometimes tested by the method of reproduction in which the subject tries to draw what he has seen. (Unfortunately, such reproduction failures may only prove that he cannot draw and not that he cannot remember.)

A memory trace can also be tapped with a recognition test. A person who is shown an item must indicate whether he has encountered it before, either in general ("Did you ever see this face before?") or in a particular context ("Is this one of the girls who played on your high school field hockey team?"). In the laboratory the subject is usually asked to pick out the previously learned item from among several false alternatives. Examples are multiple-choice or true-false tests which clearly put a greater premium on recognition than do essay or short-answer fill-in examinations, which emphasize recall.

The Sensory Registers

We usually think of memory in terms of a past that is reckoned in hours, days, or years. But memory actually comes into play as soon as the stimulus is registered on the senses. An example is a telephone number we look up and retain just long enough to complete the dialing; here the interval between acquisition and retrieval is a matter of mere seconds. Similarly, to understand speech one must still remember the beginning of a sentence by the time one hears its end. Clearly, we use memory to reach back both into the remote and the quite immediate past. Many psychologists believe that several different memory systems are involved in such acts. We will consider the three that figure in most theoretical proposals: the sensory register, short-term memory, and long-term memory.

The first link between an organism's present and its past is forged by its *sensory registers.* These hold incoming sensory information for fractions of a second after the stimulus is withdrawn. Such registers probably exist for all the senses. The ones studied thus far are for vision and audition.

THE ICON

An elegant series of studies by George Sperling dealt with some of the properties of the sensory register in vision. Sperling presented his subjects with a very brief exposure (50 milliseconds) of an array of nine letters arranged in three rows of three letters each, as shown below:

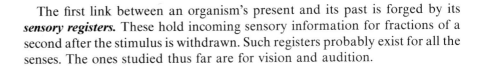

Immediately after the array was shown, the subjects were asked to recall the letters. They reported about half of them. But Sperling believed that they saw many more letters than they were able to report. In his view, the subjects had a vivid mental picture, or *icon,* of the array immediately after the stimulus went off. But this icon fades away very rapidly. This explains why the subjects' recall scores were only 50 percent even though they started to report the letters as soon as the stimulus was withdrawn. When they began to report, the icon was still vivid. But the letters could not be named instantaneously. By the time the subject had named the fourth letter, the rest of the icon had totally faded.

To prove his point, Sperling devised a partial report procedure. He asked the subjects to recall the letters in only one of the rows in the array. This cut down on the letters that had to be named so that the report could be completed before the icon had faded. To make sure that the subject consulted his memory rather than the stimulus itself, the critical row was designated *after* the stimulus had disappeared. The subjects were informed by means of tone signals: a high tone for the first row, a medium-pitched tone for the second, and so on. In Sperling's view, the recall score on these partial reports was an adequate index of the state of the whole icon at that point in time. His logic was similar to that used in many school tests. To test everything the student has learned in a course is very tedious; an adequate approximation can be obtained by an appropriate sample.

The results showed that when the signal was sounded immediately after the visual stimulus disappeared, recall was nearly 100 percent. But even tiny delays impaired recall seriously. If the tone was sounded 300 milliseconds later, recall dropped to about 75 percent. After one second, it was indistinguishable from the results obtained by the usual method (Figure 8.1).

These findings support the notion of a visual sensory register which carries a good deal of information but for only fractions of a second. There is evidently a visual image which subjects can read as if it were a printed page. Unfortunately the page turns blank within a second or so (Sperling, 1960).

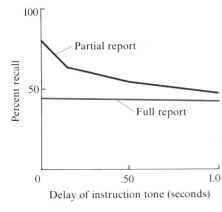

8.1 ***The fading icon*** *Performance of one of Sperling's subjects when tested by the method of partial report, in which a tone indicates which row in the array is to be recalled. The colored line shows the percent recall obtained by this procedure, plotted against the interval between the presentation of the array and the sounding of the tone. As the figure shows, performance drops markedly in the first half a second or so after the array was presented. The gray line indicates performance under full report instructions. This is inferior to partial report performance with short array-tone intervals, presumably because the icon fades while the subject is still reporting. (After Sperling, 1960)*

THE ECHO

Similar techniques have demonstrated that there is a sensory register for audition. The procedure was modeled on Sperling's. Subjects listened to simultaneously presented letters that came over different loudspeakers. On each one-second presentation, there were nine letters in all, three from each speaker. After each presentation, the subjects had to recall what they heard. In one condition, they had to report on all of the items. In the other condition, their report was partial. They had to recall only the items that came over one of the speakers. As in Sperling's experiment, the cue that told them which set of items to report on came after the stimuli were no longer present. The results were analogous to Sperling's. Partial report was superior to complete report, a difference which shows that there is an auditory analog to the icon, a mental echo. Like the icon, the echo fades away very quickly. This is shown by the fact that, in further analogy to Sperling's findings, the difference between partial and complete report diminishes as the interval between stimulus and partial report signal increases. When that interval reaches four seconds, the difference disappears (Darwin, Turvey, and Crowder, 1972).

ICON AND ECHO AS UNPROCESSED INFORMATION

The icon and the mental echo last for only a short moment, but what are they like while they exist? The consensus is that they represent as yet unanalyzed sensory information that is little more than a copy of what the receptors provide. However brief their storage, it is long enough to allow the cognitive system to perform various operations upon them. One is to extract features and assemble them into patterns. Another is to compare these patterns to those already stored in memory. Thus the icon may contain the visual item *A*, but while it is in the visual register this item is not yet recognized as a letter, let alone a vowel, a high course grade, and so on. These and further operations represent ways in which the incoming information is ***processed.*** This information processing begins with the contents of the sensory registers that represent the crude raw materials out of which the world of our knowledge is eventually fashioned.

Short-Term Memory

When we call on memory in ordinary life, we require much more than the sensory register can give us. We normally reach back for longer than the second or so that the icon and echo last. Remembering things like telephone numbers or people's names or where we parked the car are all cases that involve a level of processing vastly beyond anything that the sensory registers can hold. We clearly have to assume an additional memory system. But is one more enough?

Many psychologists have argued for the existence of at least two further systems beyond the sensory registers. One is ***short-term memory*** which holds information for fairly short intervals, say up to a minute. The other is ***long-term memory*** in which materials are stored for much longer periods, perhaps a lifetime.

This distinction is sometimes called the ***duplex theory of memory.*** As we shall see, some of its assumptions can be questioned, but it still provides a useful framework for an initial presentation of some important phenomena of human memory.

THE DUPLEX THEORY

According to the duplex theory, memory for relatively recent and remote events differs in some important ways. One pertains to the manner in which these memories are consciously experienced. A second concerns the form in which they are stored. A third relates to the storage capacity of the two postulated memory systems.

MEMORY AND CONSCIOUS EXPERIENCE

The distinction between short-term and long-term memory appears to fit the way in which we consciously experience our remembered past. The remote past is experienced as gone and done with. The movie seen last night, the dinner enjoyed an hour ago, are in the past tense; they are remembered but not perceived. This is not so for events that happened just a few seconds ago. We hear a melody and seem to perceive much or all of it in the present, even though the first chord has already ebbed away by the time the last note of the musical phrase reaches our ears. This distinction based on conscious experience was described ninety years ago by America's first psychologist, William James:

> An object which is recollected, is one which has been absent from consciousness altogether, and now revives anew. It is brought back, recalled, fished up, so to speak, from a reservoir in which, with countless other objects, it lay buried and lost from view. But an object of primary memory is not thus brought back; it never was lost; its date was never cut off in consciousness from that of the immediately present moment. In fact it comes to us as belonging to the rearward portion of the present space of time, and not to the genuine past (James, 1890, pp. 646–47).

WHAT IS STORED?

According to duplex theory, items generally enter long-term storage by first passing through the short-term system. Short-term memory is thus like the loading platform of a warehouse; incoming packages are first stacked on the platform and eventually carried from there to their more permanent storage place. But this analogy is in some ways inaccurate, for the packages are transformed as they are transferred from one storage system to another.

Acoustic storage in short-term memory   Duplex theorists believe that items in long-term memory are stored in a "processed" form; thus words are stored primarily in terms of their meanings rather than as sounds. In contrast, items in short-term memory are not as fully processed; they often remain as incompletely analyzed acoustic patterns. To be sure, the material in short-term memory is not as raw and unprocessed as the contents of the sensory register. It is in an intermediate form. When we try to hold onto a telephone number we just looked up, we are certainly aware that we're dealing with a set of digits. But these items seem to exist mostly as a sequence of sounds that we frantically repeat to ourselves while rummaging through our pockets for a dime in the telephone booth.

275

Some confirming evidence for these views comes from studies on the effect of similarity on remembering. The idea is that when items are similar, they tend to get confused with each other in memory. In one study, subjects were asked to remember sequences of words. Some were similar *acoustically* (they sounded similar, as in *man, can, fan,* etc.); while others were dissimilar. Acoustic similarity was harmful when the subjects had to recall the sequence immediately, but it had no effect when recall was delayed. The reverse effect was found when the similarity was *semantic* (they were similar in meaning as in *great, huge, large,* etc.). Here, similarity led to sizable disruptions when recall was delayed, but none when it was immediate (Baddeley, 1966). All of this suggests that different characteristics of an item tend to be stored in the two memory systems—an acoustic pattern in short-term memory, semantic meaning in long-term memory.

Acoustic recoding of visual items   Interestingly enough, short-term memory for verbal materials tends to be in acoustic form even when the material is presented visually. If a subject is shown a series of letters, his immediate recall shows acoustic rather than visual confusions. Thus an *E* is hardly ever misremembered as an *F* despite the fact that the two letters are visually very similar. Instead, the errors will be letters like *B* and *D*, similar to *E* in how they sound if spoken (that is, "dee" as opposed to "eff") though not in visual appearance. Presumably the subject **recodes** (that is, translates) the visual material into acoustic form, probably by rehearsing the letters in inner speech, and it is in this form that it is stored in short-term memory (Conrad, 1964).

What accounts for the fact that short-term memories are coded acoustically? One reason is that we have discovered that saying things to ourselves (by and large, silently) is a good strategy for holding onto them in memory, at least for the short run. Young children don't know how to do this. Evidence comes from a study in which children were shown a number of pictured objects. They were subsequently asked to pick out the items they had seen from among a number of alternatives. In one condition, all of the objects had names whose sound was very similar (e.g., *cat, rat, hat,* etc.). In the other case, the objects had dissimilar sounding names (*fish, spoon, girl,* etc.). If the child coded the items acoustically, one would predict worse performance on those that sounded alike. This is exactly what happened to children of seven and older. But at earlier ages, there was no such difference. The best guess is that the younger children had not yet learned how to use speech—that is, inner speech—as an aid to memory (Conrad, 1972).

STORAGE CAPACITY

Another difference between short- and long-term memory is in storage **capacity.** The capacity of long-term memory is enormous; the size of an average college student's reading vocabulary (about 50,000 words, according to one estimate) is documentation enough. In contrast, the capacity of short-term memory is very limited, much like the loading platform that can hold only a tiny fraction of what the warehouse can store.

One way to determine the capacity of the short-term storage is to measure the **memory span,** the number of items an individual can recall after just one presentation. For normal adults this span is remarkably consistent. Whether the items are digits, letters, or unrelated words, whether they are presented visually or orally, the result is essentially the same—the subject can recall about 7 items, give or take about 2. This quantity, 7 plus or minus 2, is sometimes called the *magic number,* a term taken from an influential paper by George Miller (Miller, 1956). According to Miller, this number represents the capacity limit of the short-term system, the number of packages that can be on the platform at any particular time. It is sometimes regarded as the major bottleneck in passing information into the permanent memory store, for many theorists believe that it is difficult or impossible to bypass the short-term system with its restricted memory span.

THE PATHS FROM SHORT-TERM MEMORY

What happens to information after it has entered short-term memory? For the vast majority of items, the answer is simple: They are forgotten, perhaps irrevocably so. While reading the morning newspaper we briefly note all kinds of extraneous matters: the coffee tastes bitter, a child is crying next door, there is a printer's error on the editorial page. But only a few moments hence these experiences are as if they had never been.

FORGETTING OF RECENT MEMORIES

The exceedingly quick forgetting of short-term memories was demonstrated by a study that required subjects to recall a set of three consonants such as *RLZ* after *retention intervals* (that is, intervals between acquisition and retrieval test) of 2 to 20 seconds. The trick was to find a procedure that would prevent *rehearsal.* After all, if the subject is allowed to say *RLZ* to herself over and over again during the 20 seconds after the item is presented, then her real retention interval is obviously much shorter than 20 seconds. Equally serious is the possibility that an item may be transferred from short-term to long-term storage if it is rehearsed. The solution was to fill the retention interval with a very demanding mental activity which presumably left little time for rehearsal (Peterson and Peterson, 1959). Immediately after the subjects heard the consonants, they were presented with a three-place number. Their task was to count backward from that number by threes (that is, 684, 681, 678, and so on) until they received the signal to recall. Under these conditions there was little or no recall after an interval of only 15 seconds (Figure 8.2).

What accounts for forgetting from short-term memory? One possibility is *decay.* The memory trace may be eroded over time by some unknown physiological process so its details become progressively less distinct. Another view is *interference.* Items are somehow pushed out of short-term memory by other items, perhaps those that enter later or those already there. (In the previous study, the interference may have been produced by the backward counting task.) The best evidence to date indicates that both factors play a role, that the packages on the loading platform rot away (decay) and also are shoved off by other packages (interference). In either case, it is clear that they are not allowed to remain on the platform for very long (Reitman, 1974).

This rapid forgetting from short-term memory may be a blessing in disguise. The Bell Telephone Company would be in poor shape if its switchboard operators were unable to forget a number immediately after they had dialed it. Given its limited capacity, the loading platform has to be cleared very quickly to make room for new packages as they arrive.

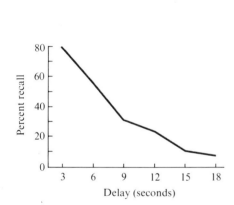

8.2   Forgetting of short-term memories
Subjects hear three consonants and then have to count backward by threes from a given number. After an interval, they are asked to recall the consonants. As the figure shows, forgetting under these conditions is quite rapid. (Peterson and Peterson, 1959)

While most of the parcels on the loading platform disappear forever, a few find their way into long-term storage. Just why this transfer occurs will be taken up later (see pp. 290–91). For now, our main concern is the fact that such a transfer sometimes happens, and that the recall of an item may thus indicate retrieval from either short-term or the long-term storage. Is there any way of telling from which storage system the item was taken?

Attempts to answer this question have provided yet another demonstration that short-term and long-term memories have different properties. Most of the relevant studies utilized the method of *free recall.* The subject is presented with a list of unrelated items, such as common English words, and is asked to recall them in any order she wants to. If the items are presented only once and if their number exceeds the memory span, the subject cannot possibly produce them all. Under these circumstances, the likelihood that any one item will be recalled depends upon where in the list it was originally presented. Items that were at the beginning or at the end of the list will be produced much more often than those in the middle. The *primacy effect* describes the enhanced recall of the items presented at the beginning of the list. The *recency effect* designates the greater recall for items at the end (Figure 8.3).

It is reasonable to assume that the last few items are retrieved from short-term memory; after all, they are the ones the subject heard most recently.* In contrast, items at the beginning are probably retrieved from long-term rather than short-term storage. One reason for this supposition is that the early items have had more opportunity for rehearsal and thus for transfer into long-term memory. For example, if the first three items are "camera," "boat," and "zebra," the subject might rehearse "camera" after hearing that item; then "camera," "boat" after hearing the next; then "camera," "boat," "zebra" on hearing the third, and so on.

Supporting evidence comes from various manipulations of the primacy and recency effects. One important factor is the interval between the last item on the list and the signal to recall (assuming that some rehearsal-preventing task is interposed between them). If this interval is increased to 30 seconds the primacy effect remains unchanged but the recency effect is completely abolished; this is just what we should expect if the last items are stored only in short-term memory from which forgetting is very rapid (Figure 8.4). Other procedures diminish the primacy effect. An example is the rate at which the items are presented. If this rate is very fast the subject has less time for rehearsal so that there will be less transfer to long-term storage. We should therefore expect a reduced primacy effect but no particular change in the recency effect, and this is exactly what happens (Figure 8.5).

* The very last item may even have been retrieved from the sensory register.

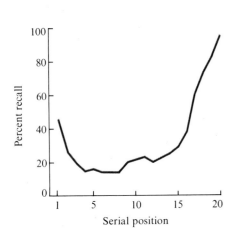

8.3   Primary and recency effects in free recall   *Subjects heard a list of twenty common words presented at a rate of one word per second. Immediately after hearing the list, the subjects were asked to write down as many of the words on the list as they could recall. The results show that the words at the beginning (primacy effect) and at the end (recency effect) were recalled more frequently than those in the middle. (After Murdock, 1962)*

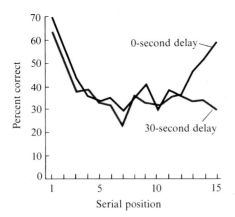

8.4   The recency effect and short-term storage   *Subjects heard several fifteen-word lists. In one condition, free recall was tested immediately after they heard the list. In the other condition, the recall test was given after a thirty-second delay during which rehearsal was prevented. The long delay left the primacy effect unaffected but abolished the recency effect, indicating that this effect is based on retrieval from short-term storage. (After Glanzer and Cunitz, 1966)*

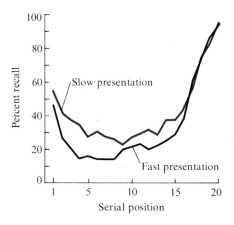

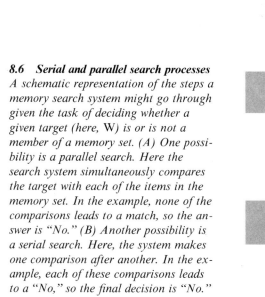

8.5   The primacy effect and long-term storage *The figure compares free-recall performance when item presentation is relatively slow (two seconds per item) and fast (one second per item). Slow presentation enhances the primacy effect but leaves the recency effect unaltered. The additional second per item presumably allowed more time for rehearsal which leads to long-term storage. (After Murdock, 1962)*

RETRIEVAL FROM SHORT-TERM MEMORY

Suppose an item is still in short-term memory, having been neither forgotten nor transferred to the long-term store. How do we retrieve it? Many psychologists feel that there is no problem at all. In their view, there is no need for any kind of mental search, for the relevant memories are already in consciousness. In fact, the situation is not quite so simple. Retrieval from short-term memory is not instantaneous, but requires some mental search and comparison.

The evidence comes from a series of elegant experiments by Saul Sternberg. His subjects were first shown a short list of letters, the memory set, which might contain as few as one or as many as seven items. Suppose the memory set was *C, F,* and *M.* The subjects were then shown a single item (e.g., *W*) and had to indicate whether it was or was not a member of that memory set. What are the retrieval processes that allow the subject to accomplish this task? One thing is clear. To decide whether the target item was or was not presented a moment before, it must be compared with the items that are now in short-term memory. For each comparison, the memory system must decide whether the target stimulus is an adequate match for the trace. How are these comparisons conducted? One possibility is **parallel search.** This proposes that the stimulus letter *W* is simultaneously compared to each of the three items in the memory set. The second alternative is **serial search.** In serial search the comparisons occur successively. The stimulus *W* is first compared to *C,* then to *F,* and finally to *M* (Figure 8.6).

8.6   Serial and parallel search processes *A schematic representation of the steps a memory search system might go through given the task of deciding whether a given target (here, W) is or is not a member of a memory set. (A) One possibility is a parallel search. Here the search system simultaneously compares the target with each of the items in the memory set. In the example, none of the comparisons leads to a match, so the answer is "No." (B) Another possibility is a serial search. Here, the system makes one comparison after another. In the example, each of these comparisons leads to a "No," so the final decision is "No."*

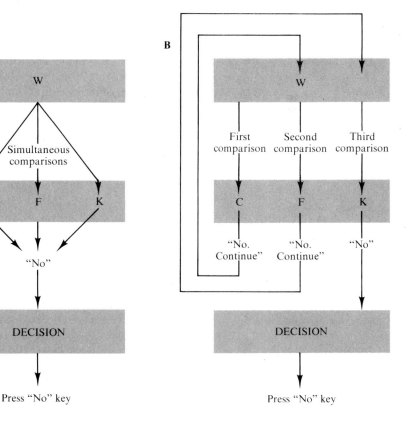

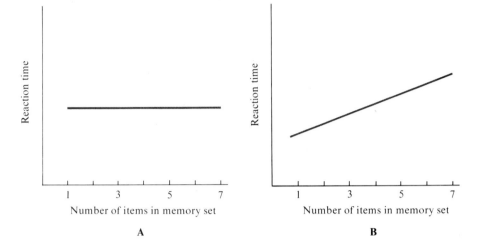

A

B

8.7 Predicted results in Sternberg's experiment (A) If the search through short-term memory is parallel, the time to decide whether a given item is a member of the memory set should be the same regardless of the numbers of items (at least with numbers up to seven, which is the presumed limit of short-term memory's capacity). If so, the curve that relates reaction time and the size of the memory set would be a horizontal line. The height of this reaction-time function would depend on the time required for processes other than the comparison, such as the time required to recognize the target letter, the time to press the key, and so on. (B) If the search is serial, reaction time must increase with the size of the memory set, since each additional item in the set requires an additional comparison. The slope of the predicted line is the increase in reaction time added by any one comparison.

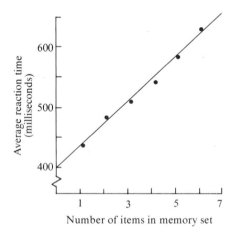

8.8 Actual results of Sternberg's study The figure shows the actual results of one of Sternberg's experiments. The average reaction time over all trials at a given memory set size is shown by the circles. The results clearly support the prediction made by the serial search hypothesis. (After Sternberg, 1970)

To decide between these alternatives, Sternberg measured the reaction time from the moment the target stimulus appeared until the subject made his response (pressing either a "Yes" or a "No" key). To find out whether the search process is conducted serially or in parallel, he determined how reaction time is affected by the number of items in the memory set. Suppose the process is handled in parallel. If so, then the size of the memory set should have no effect, for the various comparisons between the target and the items in memory are assumed to proceed simultaneously (Figure 8.7A).

The results should be quite different if the search is serial, for now the comparisons are assumed to occur one after the other. On the assumption that each comparison takes the same amount of time, reaction time should be a linear function of the size of the memory set (Figure 8.7B).

The results actually obtained fit the hypothesis that the search process is serial: The relation between reaction time and size of memory set is best rendered by a straight line (Figure 8.8). As Sternberg sees it, the slope of this line corresponds to the time it takes to compare the target stimulus to one of the items in the memory set. This slope has generally been found to have a value of about 30 milliseconds. It appears that the search process is serial but is conducted at an exceedingly rapid rate (Sternberg, 1969).

Comparisons of the kind that Sternberg studied may go on in many recognition situations of everyday life. We see a face and either recognize it as familiar or as not, an apparently simple phenomenon that seems a far cry from the tortuous internal rummaging that occurs when we try to recall the name of our high school geometry teacher. But a search process probably goes on whether we are conscious of it or not, for the present stimulus has to be compared to the memorial representations of other faces we have seen. Sternberg's findings may explain why we are ordinarily unaware of such internal question-and-answer processes—they occur at very high speeds.

PHYSIOLOGICAL EVIDENCE

Thus far our discussion has been confined to the behavioral level. We considered how people remember what they see and hear without reference to any underlying neurological processes. But there are several physiological findings which also point to a distinction between short-term and long-term memory.

All of these concern defects in memory that are produced by certain assaults on the brain (Rozin, 1976*b*).

ANTEROGRADE AMNESIA

Certain lesions in the human temporal cortex, (specifically in the *hippocampus* and other structures near the base of the brain) produce a memory disorder called *anterograde amnesia* (anterograde, "in a forward direction"). The patient often has little trouble in remembering whatever he had learned prior to the injury; his difficulty is learning anything new thereafter. Such lesions can occur in various ways. They are found in certain chronic alcoholic patients who suffer from *Korsakoff syndrome* (named after the Russian physician who first described it). They sometimes accompany senility. In a few instances they are a tragic side-effect of neurosurgery such as that undertaken to minimize seizures in severe epilepsy.

A famous example is the case of H.M., whose hippocampal lesion was the result of surgery performed when he was twenty-nine. After the operation, his short-term memory was unaffected. For example, he had a normal memory span. But he seemed to be incapable of adding any new information to his long-term storage. He could not recognize anyone he had not met before the surgery, no matter how often they met afterward. He was unable to find his way to the new house his family subsequently moved into. When told that his uncle had died he was deeply moved, but then forgot all about it and repeatedly asked when this uncle would come for a visit. On each occasion he was informed once more of his uncle's death and every time his grief was as intense as before; to him, each time he was told was the first.

While H.M.'s long-term storage system became almost completely closed to any new memories, his memories prior to the operation remained largely intact, especially for events that happened more than a year or so before the surgery. He could still read and write and engage in lively conversation. In many ways, his intellectual functioning was unimpaired. This is not uncommon in patients suffering damage to the hippocampus and related systems. For example, Korsakoff's original patient could still play a competent game of chess though he could not remember how any given position on the chess board came about. (Needless to say, he had learned the rules of the game previously.)

H.M. also had excellent recall for scenes from his earlier past. It is not too surprising that such memories are brought up endlessly. To quote from Brenda Milner, a psychologist who has studied H.M. over many years:

> He is also apt to tell long anecdotes from his school days, repeating them to the same person on different occasions, since he does not realize that he has told them before. These stereotyped stories which resemble the reminiscences of an elderly person, are presumably all he has with which to occupy his thoughts when he is not actively engaged in some task, so that their persistent intrusion into his conversation can be regarded as a natural consequence of the loss of memory for more recent events (Milner, 1966, pp. 115–16).

Since he still has access to his preoperative past, H.M. is aware that something is now badly amiss. Milner records some of his comments to give us an idea of what such an amnesic state is like:

281

"Right now, I'm wondering. Have I done or said anything amiss? You see, at this moment everything looks clear to me, but what happened just before? That's what worries me. It's like waking from a dream; I just don't remember." [And on another occasion:] "... Every day is alone in itself, whatever enjoyment I've had, and whatever sorrow I've had" (Milner, 1966, p. 115; and Milner, Corkin, and Teuber, 1968, 6: 217).

RETROGRADE AMNESIA

The consolidation hypothesis The studies of H.M. and other patients with anterograde amnesia are yet further evidence for a distinction between short-term and long-term memory. In humans, the hippocampus and related areas seem to play a crucial role in shifting memories from short-term storage and firmly stamping them into the long-term system. But what is the process which leads to this result? According to one hypothesis it is ***trace consolidation.*** A newly acquired memory trace may undergo a gradual change that establishes it more and more firmly. Until thus consolidated, the trace is as vulnerable as a cement mixture before it has hardened; thereafter, its place in long-term storage is reasonably assured.

Adherents of the consolidation theory are still unsure about the underlying physiological mechanisms which might produce such an effect. There have been various proposals, such as a gradual synthesis of certain proteins which some theorists regard as the basic carriers of memorial information (e.g., Booth, 1973). But whatever their divergent views regarding the physiological underpinnings of the memory trace, all these investigators agree on one thing: to consolidate, a trace must not be disturbed for some period of time after acquisition. All of the evidence for consolidation hinges on this point.

Retrograde amnesia in humans It has long been known that various head injuries and brain concussions may lead to ***retrograde amnesia*** (retrograde, "in a backward direction") in which the patient suffers a loss of memories for some period prior to the accident. Immediately after the injury, this loss may be a matter of months or even years. As the patient recovers, the memories come back—first, those that are farthest back in time, then, those that are progressively nearer. But the recovery from amnesia is generally incomplete. The few seconds or minutes just preceding the injury are typically lost forever. The driver who was hit by another car may remember approaching the intersection, but from there on, all is blank (Russell, 1959).

The permanent loss of memories for events just preceding the cerebral assault is a strong argument for consolidation theory. Various events were no doubt entered into short-term memory just before the accident—the yellow light changed to red, a passenger screamed, the brakes pulled to the right. But the shock to the brain occurred before any of these memory traces had a chance to settle firmly; their consolidation was disrupted so that they failed to survive. On the other hand, there is as yet no satisfactory explanation of the initial extensive amnesia and the fact that it gradually shrinks.

Retrograde amnesia in animals Retrograde amnesia can be produced in the laboratory on animal subjects, usually rats or mice. To disrupt consolidation, the animals are typically subjected to a brief but fairly intense pulse of electric

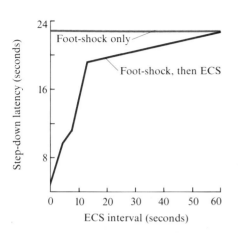

8.9 Electroconvulsive shock and trace consolidation *Mice were placed on a platform and then subjected to a shock to the feet when they stepped down. Mice who received foot-shock only showed high step-down latencies on a second test trial (24 seconds was the maximum latency allowed). Mice who received electroconvulsive shock (ECS) immediately after the first trial had much shorter step-down latencies when tested a second time, as if they had forgotten the shock to the feet. The shorter the interval between the first trial and electroconvulsive shock, the more pronounced was this effect—an argument for the hypothesis that memory traces need time to consolidate. (After Chorover, 1965)*

current passing directly through the brain. This is ***electroconvulsive shock*** (so-called because it produces a convulsive seizure), a violent assault on the nervous system which instantly knocks the animal unconscious and might be expected to have memorial effects similar to those we saw in brain concussions.

In one study, mice were placed on a raised platform. Their normal tendency is to step down quickly, but when they did so they received a mild electric shock to the feet. After this experience, the animals would normally be loath to descend from the platform when tested the following day. But if subjected to electroconvulsive shock immediately after receiving the mild foot-shock, their test performance on the next day was quite different. They nonchalantly stepped down with no more hesitation than they had shown on the day before, as if they had never learned that the floor spells danger. On the other hand, there was no such effect when electroconvulsive shock was administered several minutes after the training trial (Figure 8.9). These results are in line with the consolidation hypothesis. Young memory traces are vulnerable to disruption but older traces are not, for they have already consolidated (McGaugh, 1966).

Long-Term Memory and Associationism

The sensory registers and short-term memory provide a bridge to our very recent past. But their importance is secondary when compared to that much vaster system that holds everything else: our long-term memory. It is this memory system to which we refer when we speak, read, recognize faces, play tennis, and suddenly remember where we put the car keys that we couldn't find before. What governs the acquisition, storage, and retrieval of such long-term memories?

Most of what we know comes from experiments on the memorization of various verbal materials. The two major theoretical approaches mirror the opposing viewpoints we have already encountered in our study of animal learning and of perception: association and organization.

THE HISTORICAL BACKGROUND

We are often forced to commit large bodies of verbal materials to memory. The schoolchild memorizes the multiplication tables, the actor his lines, the medical student the sundry parts of the human anatomy. The heirs of Locke and Berkeley believed that these feats are accomplished by association. By repeated joint occurrence, *4 × 4* becomes linked with *16, To be or not to be* with *that is the question,* until eventually the presentation of the one member of each associative pair is enough to evoke the other. Remembering is then simply a matter of triggering the appropriate associative connections.

Locke and Berkeley, as well as other philosophers dating back to Aristotle, believed that the associative principle was demonstrated by the train of thought. We often jump from idea to idea until we arrive at a point that seems altogether different from where we started. According to the associationists, the intervening ideas are connected through associative links. An example

Hermann Ebbinghaus *(Courtesy Historical Picture Services, Inc.)*

might be a visit to the zoo where one sees a camel. The sight of the camel evokes a mental image of an Arab, which in turn makes one think of the Middle East, which brings up the thought of oil, of oil prices, and of the possibility of gas rationing. According to the associationists, the successive constituents of this train of thought are chained together by associations which were established previously. In their view, there were some prior occasions when the relevant components were experienced together: camels and Arabs, the Middle East and oil, and so on. But this argument hinges on a hypothetical past during which the critical associations were said to have been formed. But were they really? We can't be sure. To determine the role of associations in memory, we have to do more than study how a memory is evoked in the present. We must examine how the memory was formed in the first place. To do this, one first needs an experimental technique.

EBBINGHAUS AND NONSENSE SYLLABLES

The birth of an association was first studied experimentally in 1885 by the German psychologist Hermann Ebbinghaus (1850–1909) who acted as both midwife and mother, serving as the experimenter as well as his own subject. Ebbinghaus developed an experimental technique to investigate how associations are established and utilized. His procedure was to memorize unrelated verbal materials and later to test his own recall. The materials had to be carefully chosen, for Ebbinghaus wanted to study new associations uncontaminated by prior linkages. To this end he invented the ***nonsense syllable***, two consonants with a vowel in between that do not constitute a word, such as *zup* and *rif*.

In all, Ebbinghaus constructed 2,300 such syllables, wrote each on a separate slip of paper, shuffled the slips, and then randomly drew from 7 to 36 of them to create syllable lists of various lengths. He then set himself the task of memorizing each list serially. One of his methods was ***serial anticipation***. At a signal from a metronome, he had to recall the first item (say, *zup*). At the next beat of the metronome, that slip of paper was turned face up. This was the signal to produce the next syllable (say, *rif*) which would be exposed at the next beat, which was his signal to produce the following item, and so on through the list. This sequence was repeated over and over again until the entire list was finally mastered to some predetermined criterion, say, one errorless repetition (Ebbinghaus, 1885). Ebbinghaus learned over several thousand such lists in three or four years, an unbelievable record of the human capacity to withstand boredom if the desire is sufficiently intense. Remarkably enough, his experimental findings still stand up a century later, a fact that is all the more impressive considering that Ebbinghaus used only one subject and had virtually no apparatus beyond his slips of paper and a metronome. For example, he showed the relationship between the number of trials required to learn a list and its length, and he anticipated the distinction between short-term and long-term memory by noting that a list of six or seven items is learned in only one presentation (Figure 8.10). He was also the first to plot a

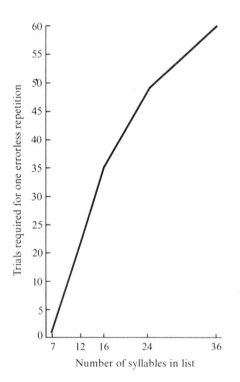

8.10 *The relation between list length and the number of trials required to learn a list of nonsense syllables* The longer the list, the more trials are required for memorization. (After Ebbinghaus, 1885)

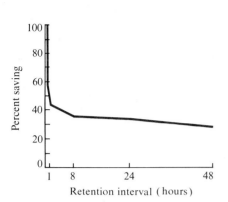

8.11 Forgetting curve *The figure shows retention after various intervals since learning. Retention is here measured in percentage saving, that is, the percent decrease in the number of trials required to relearn the list after an interval of no practice. If the percentage saving is 100 percent, retention is perfect—no trials to relearn are necessary. If the percentage saving is 0 percent, there is no retention at all, for it takes just as many trials to relearn the list as it took to learn it initially. As the figure shows, retention declines (that is, forgetting increases) as the interval between original learning and retention test increases. (After Ebbinghaus, 1885)*

forgetting curve. He tested himself at various intervals after learning (using different lists for each interval) and then asked how much effort he had to expend in order to relearn the list to the level previously achieved. He found that there was *saving:* Relearning the list took less time (or fewer trials) than original learning. As one might expect, the saving declines as the retention interval increases. The decline is sharpest immediately after learning and becomes ever more gradual thereafter (Figure 8.11). Ebbinghaus also showed that there is much less forgetting when the lists are **overlearned,** receiving further repetitions after criterion is achieved. This fact would hardly surprise the professional actor who continues to rehearse lines long after the first errorless performance. To Ebbinghaus, it was an argument for the role of frequency in fixing the associations in memory.

Ebbinghaus assumed that his nonsense syllables were essentially meaningless, so that any associations among them were truly virginal and must reveal the laws of associative learning in their pure form. This assumption is questionable: While *mer* is not a word (at least in English) it certainly resembles some (e.g., *mare*). One may well doubt whether there is any verbal material that is completely meaningless; associative virginity is hard to find. Contemporary workers in the field of verbal memory see no reason to restrict themselves to nonsense syllables, drawing their materials from a wide variety of additional sources, including sets of consonants (like *TQF*), words, digits, and the like.

ASSOCIATIONISM IN S-R TERMS

According to nineteenth-century psychologists such as Ebbinghaus, associations link ideas. Twentieth-century S-R theorists such as Thorndike and his descendants accepted the association concept but held that the connection is between two objectively observable units, stimulus and response. Ebbinghaus' findings can be interpreted in these terms by regarding each syllable in the serial list as both a stimulus and a response, a stimulus for the syllable that follows and a response for the one that precedes. Thus in the series *zup-rif-meb . . .*, *rif* is a response to *zup* and a stimulus for *meb.*

A more natural procedure for analyzing the phenomena of verbal memorization in S-R terms is the **method of paired associates,** which was developed shortly after Ebbinghaus' classic work. Here the subject has to learn pairs of verbal items. When presented with the first member of each pair (the stimulus) the subject must say the second (the response). This procedure is familiar to anyone who has ever tried to learn a foreign-language vocabulary list. Given pairs like Bread-*Brot,* Knife-*Messer,* one tests oneself by trying to respond with the German equivalent of each English stimulus word.

THE INTERACTION BETWEEN ASSOCIATIONS

S-R associationists believe that all learning can be described as the establishment of associative bonds and all remembering as their appropriate evocation. Some of the factors which either help or hinder learning and recall are those which pertain to the particular bond in question: how often the constituent members have been paired, whether the appropriate stimulus item is presented at the moment of recall, and so on. Additional factors also enter.

They involve other associations both at the time of acquisition and the time of recall.

Transfer of training Learning one task will often affect the difficulty of learning another. This phenomenon is **transfer of training,** which we have already discussed in the context of animal learning studies. (Stimulus generalization is one of the simplest cases; see Chapter 4.) If learning the first task aids in learning the second, we talk of **positive transfer;** if it impedes learning the second, we call this **negative transfer.** Examples of positive transfer include learning to play the organ after having learned to play the piano or learning to read one Slavic language after having mastered another. The hope that positive transfer will occur underlies all educational systems. The ultimate aim of the teacher is that the student will be able to apply what he has learned in school to the world he encounters outside; that he will be able to read books and newspapers, not just the first-grade primer. Examples of negative transfer are also common, especially for learned patterns with a large motor component. Many tennis players have trouble with the badminton swing; many Americans have experienced some harrowing moments while driving in England where traffic moves on the left.

To assess transfer, psychologists generally use two groups of subjects. The experimental group first learns task *X* (e.g., swinging a baseball bat) followed by task *Y* (e.g., swinging a golf club). The control group spends the initial period in some unrelated activity and then learns task *Y*. A comparison of the speed with which the two groups master task *Y* will indicate the transfer effect, if any (Table 8.1).

Table 8.1 TRANSFER EXPERIMENT

	Initial period	Test period
Experimental group	Learns *X*	Learns *Y*
Control group	Unrelated activity	Learns *Y*

Paradigms of transfer S-R associationists argue that transfer can be explained through a detailed comparison of the associations that are acquired in the two interacting tasks. They ask how quickly the second association (or set of associations) is learned and if its stimulus is the same, similar to, or different from the stimulus of the second association. The same questions are asked concerning the response.

In one experimental design, the stimuli are changed while the response terms stay constant. (This is often called the *A-B, C-B* procedure.) This procedure generally leads to positive transfer. This is especially true if the response items are very difficult. For example, a subject may learn paired-associate lists in which the stimuli are common adjectives and the response terms are sequences of six consonants. Once a subject has staggered through *fatigued-GBZVKL, joyful-DRWQCH,* and the like, a second list with items like *evil-GBZVKL* and *frightened-DRWQCH* will be comparative child's play. In effect, the subject can carry over specific bits and pieces from the first situation and apply them ready-made to the second task. Imagine being introduced to someone with a difficult last name and then later meeting his wife. Having memorized the name *Harry Zazyczny,* can *Alice Zazyczny* prove much of a challenge?

In another procedure, the stimuli remain constant but the responses change. (This is the *A-B, A-C* procedure.) The general result is negative transfer. Consider a subject who learns one list of paired associates (*zup-rif, meb-wak*) and subsequently learns another with identical stimuli but new responses (*zup-cor, meb-fim*). Now the old associations will markedly interfere with the acquisition of the new ones. Sometimes the old response emerges as an overt intrusion error so that the subject blurts out *rif* when he should have responded with *cor;* sometimes it merely blocks the correct response but does not surface on its own so that the unhappy subject cannot think of any answer. Very similar principles probably apply to such other examples of negative transfer as learning to drive on the left.

Long-Term Memory and Organization

S-R associationists believe that a detailed analysis of human verbal rote learning will ultimately lead to the understanding of human memory in general. This hope grows out of their firm conviction that the basic laws of association underlie all forms of learning and that these laws are best revealed through the study of standardized situations in which learning is especially simple. Their colleagues in the animal laboratory reason similarly when they employ the lever box or the Pavlovian harness.

Most modern investigators in the field of human memory no longer share the associationists' conviction. They admire some of the associationists' achievements—their development of the main methods for studying memory, their detailed analysis of some laboratory phenomena such as the transfer paradigms in verbal rote learning. But they doubt that this approach can provide a foundation for a general theory of human memory.

A very different theoretical approach to long-term memory is based on the concept of ***memory organization.*** We have already encountered numerous instances of organization in the realm of perception; as the Gestalt psychologists pointed out, we do not see a world of unconnected colored patches, but rather group the various elements into interrelated patterns. Many modern psychologists maintain that what is true for perception holds also for memory. As evidence they cite the fact that materials that are organized are much more easily learned and remembered than those that are not. We have little trouble remembering sentences twenty words long; the same twenty words arranged in random order offer a considerable memorial challenge. As another example, suppose a subject is asked to memorize the series

$$1\ 4\ 9\ 1\ 6\ 2\ 5\ 3\ 6\ 4\ 9\ 6\ 4\ 8\ 1.$$

If she treats it as a series of fifteen unrelated digits, she will have to struggle for many trials before reaching mastery. But once she sees that the digits form a pattern,

$$1\ 4\ 9\ 16\ 25\ 36\ 49\ 64\ 81,$$

her task has become absurdly easy. She only has to remember the underlying relationship, "the squares of the digits from 1 to 9," and the fifteen components of the series are readily recreated.

Adherents of the organizational view argue that such examples are representative of how human memory functions generally. In their view, organization affects both acquisition and retrieval, both the form in which the memories are entered into the storehouse and the manner in which they are eventually brought back.

LONG-TERM MEMORY ACQUISITION

One recurrent theme of the organizational approach is that organization enlarges memorial capacity. To enter long-term storage, items must first pass through short-term memory. But as we have seen, the short-term loading platform has a limited capacity. It can handle only a small number of memorial packages at any one time. In view of this bottleneck, how do we manage to deposit so much material in the long-term store? The answer is organization. The capacity limit of the loading platform is on the number of packages, which generally does not exceed 7 plus or minus 2; but what these packages contain is up to us. If we can pack the input more efficiently, we may squeeze more information into the same number of memorial units. The person who interprets the series 1 4 9 . . . 8 1 as "the first nine squares" has done precisely this: he has *recoded* the inputs into larger units, sometimes called *chunks.* Each chunk imposes about the same load on memory as did each of the uncoded units that previously comprised it; but when eventually unpacked, it yields much more information.

CHUNKING IN VERBAL MEMORY

Organization by grammatical units   Much of the job of recoding items into larger chunks has occurred in our early life. To an adult, a word is already a coherent whole, not merely a sequence of sounds. Still higher units of memorial organization are involved in the memory of sentences. The memory span for unrelated words is about 7 items, but we may well recall a 20-word sentence after only a single exposure. This fact holds even for sentences that make little sense, such as *The enemy submarine dove into the coffee pot, took fright, and silently flew away.* This dubious bit of naval intelligence consists of 14 words, but it clearly contains fewer than 14 memorial packages: *the enemy submarine* is essentially one unit, *took fright* is another, and so on.

One way of finding out whether higher order units such as words and phrases have any genuine psychological reality is to consider whether their constituent parts cohere in any special manner. One investigator did this by asking subjects to learn sentences such as *The tall boy saved the dying woman.* Here there are two higher order units: *The tall boy* and *saved the dying woman.* The demonstration that these phrases served as organizational units for memory came from an analysis of recall errors. The two phrases tended to be recalled—or forgotten—as units. A subject who recalled the words *The tall* was fairly likely to recall *boy.* If he recalled *saved,* he was likely to recall *the dying woman.* But the fact that he recalled *The tall boy* did not provide a similar guarantee that he would come up with the appropriate next word of the sentence, *saved*. It appears that the seven words of the sentence were not stored as independent items, but were rather organized as subparts of two higher order syntactic units (Johnson, 1965; for a further discussion of syntactic issues, see Chapter 10).

Organization by semantic categories　We often organize a set of items we want to remember by pigeonholing them under several appropriate rubrics. Sometimes the categories are essentially ready-made. In a shopping list we will obviously file the items under such categories as fruits, vegetables, and meats, and we will tend to remember them in clusters that reflect these categories. This effect has been demonstrated repeatedly in the laboratory. In one study, subjects were presented with lists of items that were drawn from four different categories—animals, vegetables, professions, and first names. The order in which they were presented was random, but the way in which they were recalled was not. There was **recall clustering;** members of the same category tended to be brought up together (Bousfield, 1953).

SUBJECTIVE ORGANIZATION

It is clear then that we tend to remember by using the organization that is already inherent in the material. But we often go a step further by imposing an organization of our own.

Such **subjective organizations** have a powerful effect on recall. An example is a series of studies in which subjects were presented with over fifty common English nouns, each printed on a separate index card. The subjects first had to sort the cards into different piles. They could use any category system they chose and could utilize as many rubrics as they wished. This sorting task continued over several trials until the subjects had demonstrated a stable categorization criterion by placing each card into the same pile from one trial to the next. A short time thereafter they were asked to recall as many of the words as they could.

The results showed that the larger the number of categories into which the subjects had sorted the words, the more words they remembered (Figure 8.12). According to the investigators, each of these categories represents a higher order memorial unit into which the lower order units (that is, the words) are packed; thus many more words can be recalled than could be without the categorization procedure (Mandler and Pearlstone, 1966). Such organizational packaging can probably proceed still further when a hierarchy of categories is used so that higher order categories (e.g., animal) contain subordinate ones (e.g., mammal) and so on down to the lowest level in the memorial hierarchy (e.g., raccoon). At least in principle we ought to be able to memorize a virtually endless list of items by appropriate hierarchical schemes of this sort (Mandler, 1967).

These findings underline the fact that memorial organization is generally an active process. The would-be memorizer is rarely lucky enough to have all of the material pre-chunked; she has to perform some of the chunking herself if she wants to remember successfully.

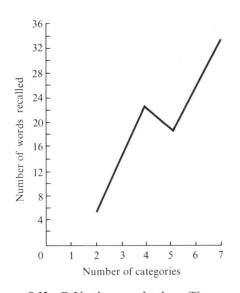

8.12　Subjective organization　*The larger the number of categories into which unrelated words are grouped, the more of them can be recalled. (After Mandler, 1967)*

The role of rehearsal   The phenomenon of subjective organization may help us to answer a question we passed over previously: What is the role of rehearsal in affecting transfer from short-term to long-term memory? We now know that it depends on the kind of rehearsal that the subject engages in.

One form of rehearsal turns out to produce no long-run benefits. This is **maintenance rehearsal** in which the subject merely holds material in short-term memory for a while. Again, the best example is the telephone number which we repeat to ourselves long enough to complete the call and then promptly forget. Experimental evidence comes from an ingenious study that varied the time in which items remained in short-term memory. The subjects were presented with a fairly long list and had to report the last word on the list that began with a certain letter. Suppose the letter was *G* and that the list began with the following words:

> Daughter
> Oil
> Rifle
> Garden
> Grain
> Table
> Football
> Anchor
> Giraffe

In this situation, the subject has to hold one *G*-word in short-term memory until the next one appears which will then replace it until it is replaced in turn. Thus *Garden* will be replaced by *Grain* which will make way for *Giraffe* and so on until the final critical word on the list is reached. This arrangement guarantees that some of the *G* words are held longer in short-term memory than others; thus *Grain* will stay longer than *Garden*. The question was whether this increased the chance that *Garden* would be transferred to long-term memory. To find out, the investigators gave a final—and unexpected—test after many such lists had been presented. The subjects were simply asked to report as many of the words that they had heard in all the sessions as they could. The results showed that there was not the slightest effect of the time an item had been in short-term memory—*Garden* was recalled just as often as was *Grain* (Craik and Watkins, 1973).

Pure maintenance in short-term memory is evidently not enough to produce transfer to long-term memory. But there is another kind of rehearsal that does tend to have this effect. We will call this **active rehearsal** through which the subject organizes the items during the time they are in the short-term store. He may group them or recode them or relate them to each other and to other information already in his memory—all of these are ways of organizing the material by which he enhances its chances for long-term recall. In sum, whether rehearsal does or does not confer lasting benefits depends upon whether the subject uses it as a means to organize the items in memory (Figure 8.13).

Intentional and incidental learning   Memorial organization may help to explain another phenomenon of verbal learning: Memorization usually pro-

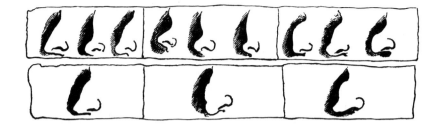

8.13 Memorial organization of visual forms by artists *While rehearsal has been studied mostly for verbal memory, similar organizational methods are sometimes used for visual material. To retain the visual forms they encounter and later have to draw from memory, many artists use organizational aids. In his treatise,* The Art of Painting, *Leonardo da Vinci describes "the method of retaining in the memory the likeness of a man, so as to draw his profile, after having seen him only once." He exhorts the young artist to "observe and remember well the variations of the . . . principal features in the profile. . . . First, of the nose, of which there are three different sorts, straight, concave and convex." Leonardo distinguishes further subvarieties, for example among concave noses that have the concavity at the top, the middle, and the end of the nose. The upshot of such a classification scheme is a method of categorizing facial forms, which is a major aid in memory. The figure is a reproduction of Leonardo's sketch of the varieties of noses. (Leonardo da Vinci, ca. 1500, p. 27; diagram reproduced from Gombrich, 1961)*

ceeds much more efficiently if the learner actively tries to learn. This fact is well-known from everyday experience. A similar effect is readily demonstrated in the laboratory. Two groups of subjects are exposed to the identical material, such as a tape-recorded list of words, for the same period of time. One group consists of **intentional learners** who are asked to memorize the words and who know that they will be tested later. The subjects in the other group are **incidental learners** who are forced to attend to the list (in an indirect way) by engaging in a suitable cover task; for example, they may be asked to rate how well the speakers pronounced each word. To their surprise (and occasional chagrin) they too are subsequently tested for recall of the list. The typical result is a massive superiority in the recall scores of intentional learners (Gleitman and Gillett, 1957).

What accounts for this difference? A plausible hypothesis is that the intentional learners rehearsed while the incidental learners did not. But their rehearsal was presumably of the active variety. The subject who intends to learn, groups items in various categories, forms higher order chunks and integrations, and is thus able to recall the material better.

Some evidence for this hypothesis comes from a study in which subjects were again asked to sort words into various categories. Some of the subjects were told they would be tested later (intentional learners); others were not so informed (incidental learners). When later tested for recall, the usual superiority of intentional to incidental learning did not appear; both groups did equally well. This result makes good sense once we grant that the desire to learn has only an indirect effect: it typically leads to better memorial organization which in turn is the direct cause of improved recall. Since the incidental learners necessarily organized the word list in the course of sorting the words into different categories, they suffered no disadvantage when compared to the intentional learning group (Mandler, 1967).

RETRIEVAL FROM LONG-TERM MEMORY

We have considered the role of organization in determining how long-term memories are acquired. We will now consider the effect of organization on the way these memories are retrieved from storage.

TRACE ACCESSIBILITY

The distinction between memory storage and retrieval has been noted since antiquity. St. Augustine, writing around 400 A.D., likened memory to a storehouse:

And I enter the fields and roomy chambers of memory, where are the treasures of countless images. . . . When I am in this storehouse, I demand that what I wish should be brought forth and some things immediately appear; others require to be longer sought after, and are dragged, as it were, out of some hidden receptacle (St. Augustine, 397 A.D., p. 174).

Retrieval cues   The storehouse metaphor implies that an item may be stored and yet not found. We may know (that is, have stored) a name, a fact, an event, and still be unable to retrieve it on a particular occasion. In such a case, the memory trace is said to be presently **inaccessible.** Access to the trace may be restored by an appropriate **retrieval cue.** This point has often been demonstrated experimentally. Subjects are presented with a list of words that belong to various categories and are then tested for free recall. They may neglect to recall any word from a particular rubric. If now prompted by the category name, they readily produce several of the appropriate items (Tulving and Pearlstone, 1966).

The phenomenon of retrieving a memory that at first seemed altogether lost is well-known. The very words in which we describe our memorial functions testify to the distinction between storage and retrieval: We are *re*minded, we *re*member, we *re*collect—even our vocabulary suggests that what is now brought up was not available before. The recollection of temporarily inaccessible memories by appropriate retrieval cues is usually a rather humdrum event. We can't recall where we parked on a shopping trip, are reminded that our first stop was in a drugstore, and suddenly remember squeezing the car into a narrow space just across the street. But occasionally the effect is much more dramatic. Some persons have reported being unable to recall some of the simplest geographical features of the hometown they left years before. They finally returned for a visit, barely reached the outskirts, and suddenly all of the memories flooded back, often with a sharp pang of emotions that had been felt years before. Physical places are only one source of retrieval cues that may bring back the past. A word, a mood, a smell, a visit from a school friend not met for decades—any of these may trigger memories we thought were utterly lost. A famous retrieval cue in literature is the taste of a little cake which initiates a series of recollections that comprise Marcel Proust's "Remembrance of Things Past":

And once I had recognized the taste of the crumb of madeleine soaked in her decoction of lime-flowers which my aunt used to give me . . . immediately the old grey house upon the street, where her room was, rose up like the scenery of a theatre to attach itself to the little pavilion, opening on to the garden . . . and with the house the town . . . and the whole of Combray and of its surroundings, taking their proper shape and growing solid, sprang into being, town and gardens alike, from my cup of tea (Proust, 1913, p. 58).

Retrieval cues and organization   What are the characteristics of an effective retrieval cue? It is obvious that not every reminder will in fact *re*mind us, will help us retrieve what is stored. The critical requirement seems to be an adequate match between the retrieval cue and the way the material was organized at the time it was stored.

The relation between retrieval and memorial organization is exemplified in a study that used two different lists of forty-eight word pairs each. List *A* was composed of word pairs that could be grouped into several semantic categories, such as birds (e.g., *chirping cardinal, homing pigeon*) and foods (e.g., *roast ham, lamb chop*). In list *B,* the second members of each pair were physically identical to the corresponding items in list *A,* but their meaning was drastically altered, for they were preceded by very different words: for example, *church cardinal, stool pigeon, karate chop, theatrical ham.* When subjects were later tested for the recall of the second members, the category label helped only if it was appropriate to the way in which the words were coded at the time that they were stored. When prompted by *bird,* subjects came up with *cardinal* only if they had originally been presented with *chirping cardinal.* If instead they had originally heard *church cardinal,* the category label *bird* was simply a hindrance. Thus retrieval cues are a vital means of recovering what we have once placed in storage, but they can work only if they fit the organization imposed when the trace was stored originally (G. Bower, 1970a).

MEMORY SEARCH

Many investigators assume that retrieval is generally preceded by an internal process called **memory search.** A possible line of evidence for such a process is to recall something almost but not quite, to "have it on the tip of the tongue" and still be unable to go beyond. There is no better description of what this experience feels like than that by William James:

> Suppose we try to recall a forgotten name. The state of our consciousness is peculiar. There is a gap therein; but no mere gap. It is a gap that is intensely active. A sort of wraith of the name is in it, beckoning us in a given direction, making us at moments tingle with the sense of our closeness, and then letting us sink back without the longed-for term. If wrong names are proposed to us, this singularly definite gap acts immediately so as to negate them. They do not fit into its mold. And the gap of one word does not feel like the gap of another, all empty of content as both might seem necessarily to be when described as gaps (W. James, 1890, vol. 1, p. 251).

There is evidence that the tip-of-the-tongue experience described by James is a good reflection of how close to the mark we had actually come in our memory search, that we were really "getting warm," though unable to reach the exact spot. In one study college students were presented with the dictionary definitions of uncommon English words such as *apse, sampan,* and *cloaca.* The subjects were asked to supply the words that fit these definitions. The experimenters were concerned with those occasions on which subjects were unable to recall the target word but felt that they were on the verge of finding it. Whenever this happened, they were asked to venture some guesses about what the target word sounded like. These guesses turned out to be closely related to the target. Given that the target word was said to be at the tip-of-the-tongue, its initial letter was guessed correctly over 50 percent of the time. Similar results were found when the subjects were asked to guess at the number of syllables. When asked to supply some other words which they thought sounded like the target, the subjects were usually in the correct phonological neighborhood. Presented with the definition "a small Chinese boat" for which the proper answer is *sampan,* subjects who said they almost remembered but not quite, supplied the following as sound-alikes: *Saipan, Saim, Cheyenne,* and *sarong* (Brown and McNeill, 1966).

RETRIEVAL AND RECONSTRUCTION

The term *retrieval* implies the recovery of the same material that was originally stored. But memorial retrieval is sometimes different, for we may **reconstruct** the past from partial knowledge in the process of trying to remember it.

The most influential experiments on memorial reconstruction, were performed by the British psychologist Frederic Bartlett over forty years ago. Bartlett's subjects were asked to reproduce stories taken from the folklore of other cultures; thus their content and structure were rather strange to Western ears. The reproductions showed many changes from the original. Some parts were subtracted, others were overelaborated, still others were additions that were completely new. In effect, the subjects had built a new story upon the memorial ruins of the original. This memorial reconstruction was generally more consonant with the cultural conceptions of the subjects than with the story they had actually heard. For example, certain supernatural plot elements were reinterpreted along more familiar lines.

In another variant of the same experiment, Bartlett used the method of **serial reproduction.** The original was presented to one subject, who reproduced it from memory for the benefit of a second, whose reproduction was shown to a third, and so on for a chain of up to ten subjects (Bartlett, 1932). With this technique (an experimental analogue of rumor transmission) each subject's memorial distortions become part of the stimulus for the next one down the line; the effect was to grossly amplify the reconstructive alteration (Figure 8.14).

Memorial reconstruction has often been noted by lawyers concerned with the accuracy of testimony. Witnesses are sometimes quite confident of various circumstances that fit their assumptions but do not fit the actual facts. An accident occurred months ago and its details have dimmed over time; as he tries to retrieve this past event the witness may fill in the gaps by an inference of which he is quite unaware. Did he really see the impact? All he may have seen are the effects of the impact a few seconds later, but this may be quite enough to lead to a false recollection of the impact itself.

An important factor is the way in which recall is questioned. In one study,

8.14 Remembering studied by the method of serial reproduction *Ten subjects were used in the experiment. Subject 1 saw the original figure and was asked to reproduce it after half an hour. It's reproduction was shown to subject 2 whose reproduction was shown to subject 3, and so on through subject 10. The figure shows the original drawing and the 10 serial reproductions, illustrating a massive reconstruction process. (After Bartlett, 1932)*

Original drawing Reproduction 1 Reproduction 2 Reproduction 3 Reproduction 4

Reproduction 5 Reproduction 6 Reproduction 7 Reproduction 8 Reproduction 9 Reproduction 10

subjects viewed a brief film segment of a car accident. Immediately afterward they were asked a number of questions that were in either of two forms:

"Did you see the broken headlight?"

or

"Did you see a broken headlight?"

The results showed that subjects who were questioned about *the* headlight were more likely to report having seen one than subjects who were asked about *a* headlight. This was so whether the film actually showed a broken headlight or did not. In effect, the use of the definite article, *the,* made the query a leading question, one which implied that there really was a broken headlight and that the only issue was whether the subject had noticed it. No such presupposition is made when the indefinite article, *a,* is used (Loftus and Zanni, 1975).

Another study showed that suitable leading questions during a first interrogation may lead to a reinterpretation of a recently witnessed account. When later questioned again, the witness will recall this reinterpretation. Subjects were again shown film segments of a car accident. Shortly afterward some were asked leading questions such as, "Did you see the children getting on the school bus?" A week later, all subjects were asked the direct question, "Did you see a school bus in the film?" In actual fact, there was no school bus. But when compared to controls, subjects who were originally asked the leading question that presupposed the school bus, were three to four times more likely to say that they had seen one (Loftus, 1975).

These results are of considerable relevance both to the legal process and to the psychology of memory. To legal scholars they reemphasize the crucial importance of how questions are worded, not only in the courtroom but also in prior interrogations. To students of memory, they underline the fact that remembering is in part a reconstructive process in which we sometimes re-create the past while we try to retrieve it.

MNEMONICS

Psychologists have lately begun to reconsider a very practical endeavor whose roots go back to Greece and Rome—the development of devices for improving one's memory, often called **mnemonics.** Until about twenty years ago, mnemonic techniques were largely ignored by American psychologists. Upon reexamination, however, some of these techniques are found to be surprisingly effective. The secret of their success seems to involve the same principle that figured so prominently in recent laboratory investigations of memorization—the active organization of the material by the learner. Small wonder, then, that these devices and tricks were of little interest to a generation of psychologists who believed that memory was merely a matter of association or conditioning.

MNEMONICS THROUGH VERBAL ORGANIZATION

The ancients were aware that it is much easier to remember verbal material if it is organized. They were particularly partial to the use of verse, a phonological organization of word sequences which maintains a fixed rhythm and often rhyme or alliteration. Without such aids, preliterate societies might never have transmitted their oral traditions intact from one generation to the next.

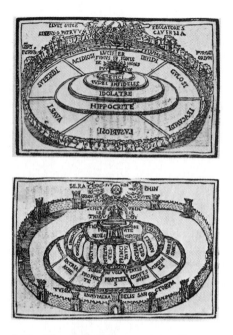

8.15 The medieval conceptions of heaven and hell used as memory systems *Sixteenth-century treatises on mnemonics relied on vivid pictures of hell (above) and heaven (below). Both were conceived as a series of concentric circles, arranged in accordance to the degree of vice or of virtue. Used with the method of loci, these pictures probably were used to help preachers remember parts of their sermons. As one author put it, "The variety of punishments, inflicted in accordance with the diverse nature of the sins, the different situations of the damned, their varying gestures, will much help memory and give many places [that is, loci]." (From Rossellius, 1579, reproduced in Yates, 1966)*

Homeric bards could recite the entire *Iliad,* but could they have done so had it been in prose? Verse is still used as mnemonic when it seems necessary to impose some sort of order upon an otherwise arbitrary set of items (e.g., "Thirty days hath September/April, June, and November").

MNEMONICS THROUGH VISUAL IMAGERY

The methods of loci and pegs Some of the most effective mnemonics ever devised involve the deliberate use of mental imagery. One such technique is the **method of loci** which requires the learner to visualize each of the items she wants to remember in a different spatial location (locus). In recall, each location is mentally inspected and the item that was placed there in imagination is thus retrieved. This method was first described in Roman treatises on oratory, including one by Cicero. (Training in memory was regarded as an indispensable part of the study of oratory, for public speeches were generally delivered from memory alone.) The first step is the careful selection of the different loci, which must be well-known and easily distinguishable. The second is to locate each item in its proper place. If any item is an abstract concept that is hard to visualize, it must be translated into an object that can be visualized in its stead; for example, an anchor might be a fair substitute for "navigation." To quote from one such text, written about 50 A.D.:

> The first notion is placed, as it were, in the forecourt; the second, let us say, in the atrium; the remainder . . . committed not only to bedrooms and parlours, but even to statues and the like. This done, when it is required to revive the memory, one begins from the first place to run through all, demanding what has been entrusted to them, of which one will be reminded by the image. . . . As Cicero says: "We use places as wax and images as letters" (quoted from *Institution Oratoria* by Quintillian, in Yates, 1966, p. 23).

Later authors advocated a somewhat different approach which became known as the **peg method.** The first step is the creation of a set of mental pegs, such as numerals, to which the items to be memorized could be attached. The student begins by memorizing a set of rhymes, such as *one-bun, two-shoe, three-tree,* up to perhaps twenty numbers. Once these pairs are mastered (not too hard a task considering the rhymes) they are ready to serve as mental pegs. To learn a serial list of items (e.g., *college, earthworm, top hat,* etc.) the student must form different compound images that connect each item with its cue word. The first two images might be a bun receiving a college diploma and an earthworm wriggling out of a shoe. When later asked to name an item that was in a particular position, the student must first retrieve the appropriate cue word (e.g., *bun, shoe,* etc.). This presumably triggers the compound image which carries the appropriate answer.

The underlying principles of the methods of loci and pegs are obviously quite similar. Both methods provide a scheme which allows orderly retrieval; a spatial layout for the method of loci, a well-learned system of arbitrary cues for the method of pegs. Both require a deliberate effort to relate the items that must be memorized to distinctive features of the retrieval scheme, and to do so through visual imagery (Figure 8.15).

Several recent studies have tested the efficacy of these mnemonic systems. Subjects who recalled by the method of loci recalled up to seven times more than their counterparts who learned in rote manner. In one such study, college students had to learn lists of forty unrelated concrete nouns. Each list was presented once for about ten minutes, during which the subjects tried to visualize each of the forty objects in one of forty different locations around the college campus. Tested immediately, they recalled an average of thirty-eight of the forty items; tested one day later, they still managed to recall thirty-four (Ross and Lawrence, 1968). In another study the subjects were instructed to learn standard noun-noun paired associates by forming a mental picture that linked the items of each pair. Starting with lists of twenty-five pairs they gradually worked up to much longer lists, achieving recall scores of 100 percent for lists up to three hundred and 95 percent for lists of seven hundred pairs—scores that vastly exceed any level one could possibly hope to attain by the usual Ebbinghausian means (Wallace, Turner, and Perkins, 1957). It is rather sobering to realize that modern psychology had to rediscover a phenomenon that was already known to Cicero.

Why does imagery help? There is reason to believe that mental images will facilitate recall only if they tend to unify the items to be associated into a coherent whole. Consider a subject who has to learn a list of paired associates such as *eagle-locomotive* and is instructed to use imagery as a memorial aid. She can construct mental pictures that bring the items into some kind of unitary relationship, for example, an eagle winging to his eyrie with a locomotive in his beak. But she may form an image whose constituents are merely adjacent and do not interact, such as an eagle at the side of a locomotive. Several recent experiments demonstrate that unifying mental images produce much better recall than non-unifying images (Wollen, Weber, and Lowry, 1972). A similar effect is found when the test items are real pictures. If shown a drawing of a doll standing on a chair waving a flag, subjects quickly reply "chair and flag" when asked to recall the objects that were pictured with the doll. Their recall score is substantially lower if they were shown a picture of the doll, chair, and flag, drawn as separate, unrelated objects (Figure 8.16).

A

8.16 The effect on memory of a unitary relation between elements *Subjects shown related elements, such as a doll standing on a chair and waving a flag (A) are more likely to associate the words* doll, flag, *and* chair *than subjects who are shown the three objects next to each other but not interacting (B). (After G. Bower, 1970b)*

B

These results suggest that the role of imagery in aiding recall is one further manifestation of the general phenomenon of memorial organization. By creating a mental image that unifies a set of initially unrelated items, the subject imposes organization; he constructs a chunk. When part of the chunk (the imagined locus or peg word) is presented, the entire chunk is retrieved, yielding the part required for recall.

The usefulness of mnemonic devices in everyday life Mnemonic systems provide effective means for imposing organization upon otherwise disparate materials, such as a foreign vocabulary list or nonsense materials developed in the psychological laboratory. But we are not often confronted by such arbitrary pairings. A student reading a history text does not have to impose an organization. His job is to discover the organization that is already inherent in the material. When he does so, the various treaties and battles will fall into an appropriate mental scheme, linked to each other and to relevant historical matters that have been learned before. But imagery mnemonics will not help to provide this scheme. A visual image that links, say, General Custer and Chief Sitting Bull, will be of little use in helping the student understand the conflict between the American Indians and the encroaching settlers.

In short, the best prescription for recall is to organize the material at the time it is learned. If this material is devoid of inherent organization, some organization must be imposed upon it. In that case mnemonic devices, especially imagery, are a useful tool. If the material is already organized, the best approach is to discover that organization and to chunk the various items in terms of it.

FORGETTING FROM LONG-TERM MEMORY

In popular usage, the word **forgetting** is employed as a blanket term which is invoked whenever memory fails. But memorial failures have different causes, as we have already seen. Some arise from faulty storage procedures (e.g., inadequate organization) while others are produced by conditions at the moment of recall (e.g., lack of appropriate retrieval cues). We now turn to the relation of memory failure to the **retention interval** which intervenes between original learning and the time of test. At least on the face of it, forgetting increases with increasing retention interval. Yesterday's lesson is fresher today than it will be tomorrow. There are several theories designed to explain this and related phenomena, which we will now discuss.

DECAY

The most venerable theory of forgetting holds that memory traces gradually *decay* as time passes, like mountains that are eroded by wind and water. The erosion of memories is presumably caused by normal metabolic processes whose impact wears down the memory trace until it fades and finally disintegrates.

While this theory has considerable intuitive appeal, there is so far little direct evidence in its favor. Several studies have tried to provide an indirect test by varying body temperature. Like most chemical reactions, metabolic processes increase with increasing temperature. If these reactions are responsible for memorial decay, then forgetting should be a function of the body temperature during the retention interval. This prediction has been tested with cold-blooded animals such as the goldfish whose body takes on the temperature of its surroundings. By and large, the results have been in line with the hypothesis: the higher the temperature of the tank in which the fish is kept during the retention interval, the more forgetting takes place (Gleitman and Rozin, as reported in Gleitman, 1971).

But some other findings complicate this picture considerably. There is good evidence that forgetting is determined not simply by the duration of the retention interval, but by what happens during this time. Experiments on human subjects have shown that recall is substantially worse after an interval spent awake than after an equal period while asleep (Jenkins and Dallenbach, 1924). At a more lowly level, a similar effect has been found in the common cockroach. These creatures were first taught to run from a region of an apparatus in which they received electric shock. Some of them were subsequently placed in a moderate-sized dark cage in which they could move about as they chose. Others were placed in a small box filled with tissue paper which rendered them virtually immobile. When tested twenty-four hours later, the immobilized cockroaches showed much better retention than the active ones (Minami and Dallenbach, 1946).

Such results pose serious difficulties for a decay theory that assigns all of the blame for forgetting to decay, for they show that time itself does not cause all of the loss. To explain such findings within a theory of decay, one would have to assert that the relevant metabolic processes which erode the memory trace are slowed down during sleep or unusual states such as immobilization in insects, an argument for which there is no evidence as yet.

INTERFERENCE

A very different theory of forgetting is **interference**. According to this view, a forgotten memory is neither lost nor damaged, but is only misplaced among a number of other memories which interfere with the recovery of the one that was sought. Seen in this light, our inability to remember the name of a high-school friend is analogous to what happens when a clerk cannot find a letter he received a year ago. The letter is still somewhere in his files but it has been hopelessly buried in a mass of other letters that he filed both before and since.

Retroactive and proactive inhibition Memorial interference is easily demonstrated in the laboratory. A major example is **retroactive inhibition** in which new learning hampers recall of the old. In a typical study, a control group learns some rote material such as a list of nonsense syllables (list *A*) and is tested after a specified interval. The experimental group learns the same list as the control group and is tested after the same retention interval. But in addition it must also learn a second list (list *B*) that is interpolated during the retention interval (Table 8.2, page 300). The usual result is a marked inferiority in the performance of the experimental group; the interpolated list interferes with (inhibits) the recall of list *A*.

A similar effect is **proactive inhibition** in which interference works in a forward (proactive) direction. The usual procedure is to have an experimental

Table 8.2   RETROACTIVE INHIBITION EXPERIMENT

	Initial period	Retention interval	Test interval
Control group	Learns list *A*	———————	Recalls list *A*
Experimental group	Learns list *A*	Learns list *B*	Recalls list *A*

group learn list *A* followed by list *B,* and then test for recall of list *B* after a suitable retention interval. The critical comparison is with a control group which learns only list *B* (Table 8.3). In general, the experimental group does worse on the recall test.

Table 8.3   PROACTIVE INHIBITION EXPERIMENT

	Initial period		Retention interval	Test period
Control group	———————	Learns list *B*	———————	Recalls list *B*
Experimental group	Learns list *A*	Learns list *B*	———————	Recalls list *B*

A critical factor for the occurrence of both retroactive and proactive inhibition is the similarity between the original and the interpolated task. If these are utterly dissimilar, there will be no effect. But as the similarity between the first and second tasks increases, interference goes up correspondingly. Thus a list of adjectives is least affected by an interpolated list of nonsense syllables, somewhat more by a list of nouns, still more by a list of different adjectives, and most of all by a list of synonyms.

Interference and ordinary forgetting   The phenomena of retroactive and proactive inhibition show that one set of memories may interfere with the retrieval of another. But can these effects explain what happens in ordinary forgetting where no explicit source of interference is deliberately introduced by the experimenter? Why does the subject show any forgetting of a paired-associate noun list after a twenty-four-hour interval? According to interference theory, the answer is **extra-experimental interference.** The idea is that during the retention interval the subject is likely to encounter some of the list items in another context. This will produce new associations which will interfere with the evocation of the appropriate item when the subject is finally tested. The longer the retention interval, the more competing associations are likely to be picked up. According to interference theory, it is this, rather than decay, that explains why forgetting increases with longer intervals after acquisition (Postman, 1961).

There is, however, a major stumbling block to this hypothesis. As we have already seen, both proactive and retroactive inhibition depend upon the similarity between the two interfering tasks. But a good deal of forgetting seems to occur even for materials that seem very different from whatever competing habits one might reasonably expect the subject to have acquired during the retention interval. Thus chess players seem to lose their sharpness if they have not played for a while; what could they possibly have learned during the interval that is similar enough to the chess situation to make them forget the nuances of a Queen's Pawn opening?

A more formal test of the hypothesis involves the comparison of two kinds of paired-associate lists. In one, the items were pairs of high-frequency words such as *house-cloud*. In another, they were pairs of low-frequency words, such as *machete-aphid*. If extra-experimental interference plays a major role in forgetting, there should be less retention of the high-frequency than the low-frequency list. By definition, the high-frequency words are more likely to be encountered in ordinary life. As a result, they will be seen in different pairings, such as *house-painter* or *rain-cloud,* and these will interfere with the original pair. In contrast, subjects who learned the low-frequency list are unlikely to run up against them outside of the laboratory. After all, how often does one hear *aphid* or *machete?* In consequence, lists made up of such low-frequency items should be relatively well protected against extra-experimental interference and should therefore be better retained. In actual fact, there is no difference in the levels of retention. If both lists were learned to the same degree of proficiency, they are forgotten at the same rate (Postman, 1969).*

Interference certainly plays a role in forgetting. But it cannot explain all of it. In particular, it cannot explain why forgetting increases with increasing retention interval.

CHANGE OF RETRIEVAL CUES

Decay theory holds that the memory trace gradually fades away with time, while interference theory asserts that the trace gets lost among other traces acquired both before and after. There is a further alternative which argues that memorial success or failure is primarily determined by the retrieval cues presented at the time of recall.

We have already seen that a change in retrieval cues disrupts remembering. But can this effect explain why forgetting increases with an increasing retention interval? To maintain the hypothesis that the critical factor is cue alteration, one must argue that such alteration becomes ever more likely with the passage of time. There are some cases for which this may be true. Certain memories may have been acquired in a particular locale; over the years the neighborhood changes as some houses are torn down and new ones are built, thus altering the physical cue situation and thereby decreasing the chance of retrieval.

This kind of interpretation may explain some of the difficulties we have in recalling the events of our childhoods.† The world of the young child is utterly

---

* Interference theory is actually considerably more involved than this. During the past two decades, it has stressed proactive rather than retroactive inhibition, so that the extra-experimental interference is thought to arise from habits acquired prior to the acquisition of the list (Underwood and Postman, 1960). But this version of the theory is also seriously embarrassed by the fact that high- and low-frequency pairs are forgotten at the same rate.

† Some of these difficulties undoubtedly represent failures of acquisition rather than of retrieval. There is no question that the child—especially the very young child—codes the events of its life in a rather fragmentary manner, especially during the first two or three years when language development is still at an early stage.

different from the world it occupies some ten or fifteen years later. It is a world in which tables are hopelessly out of reach, in which chairs can be climbed upon only with great effort, in which adults are giants in size and gods in ability. Whatever memories the child may store at this time are formed within this context; thus the appropriate retrieval context is usually absent from the adult's environment (Schachtel, 1949).

The retrieval-cue hypothesis is a very plausible account of some aspects of forgetting. But it probably cannot explain them all. Forgetting increases as a function of the time since learning even when the retrieval conditions appear essentially unchanged. Some evidence comes from studies with animal subjects where all facets of the situation are under the experimenter's control (Gleitman, 1971). In one study, rats were trained to run an alley for food reward. Some of them were tested one day after original learning; others, after sixty-eight days. All of the physical conditions of the experiment—the location and illumination of the alley, the home cages, the animal's own weight—were kept identical throughout the entire period. Even so, there was a massive effect of the retention interval. The animals tested some two months after training were much more hesitant on the alley than they were before, as if they had forgotten what they were supposed to do (Figure 8.17).

In summary, we must conclude that each of the theories of forgetting proposed thus far can account for some of the aspects of the phenomenon but not all. Interference and change of retrieval cues play a major role, but neither of them can explain why forgetting increases with the passage of time. While the evidence for decay is by no means solid, it nevertheless seems reasonable to suppose that some such process does occur and is responsible for the effect of retention interval.

What is the upshot of all of this for our own attempts to remember? We cannot avoid all of the conditions that lead to forgetting. To do so, we would have to abstain from all other learning both before and after memorizing the items we want to retain, spend the retention interval asleep (preferably in a refrigerator), and refuse to take any recall test unless the retrieval situation is certified to be identical to the one in which we learned. Under the circumstances, what can we do if we want to remember? We have given the answer before. The path to recall goes through memorial organization. The clerk who

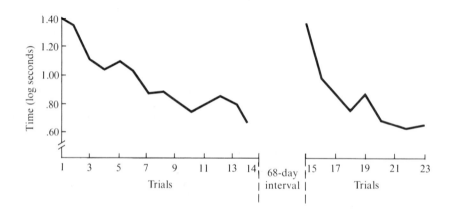

8.17 Forgetting of a running response in a runway The performance of rats on a runway before and after an interval of approximately two months. Note that running times increased considerably on the first day after the interval. (After Gleitman and Steinman, 1964)

must retrieve a letter cannot change the fact (if it is a fact) that some of the ink gradually fades on the paper (decay), or that he has other letters to file both before and after (proactive and retroactive interference), or that the letter he is asked for is sometimes identified by date and sometimes by name (change of retrieval cue). The best he can do is to file the letter in an organized fashion.

Varieties of Long-Term Memory

We have discussed long-term memory as if it were all of a piece, one huge warehouse in which all our memories are stored, regardless of their form and content. Some recent authors have tried to make some further distinctions that may provide a clue to the way this warehouse is arranged.

GENERIC MEMORY

One important distinction is between episodic and generic memory. *Episodic memory* is the memory for particular events (episodes) of one's own life; what happened when and where, as when recalling that one ate fried chicken the other night. This contrasts with *generic memory,* which is memory for items of knowledge as such, independent of the particular occasion in which we have learned them: the capital of France, the square root of 9, and so on. In effect, generic memory is the sum total of a person's acquired knowledge—the meanings of words and symbols, facts about the world, what objects look like.

Most of the studies on memory we have described thus far are primarily about episodic memory. Consider an experiment in which subjects have to memorize a list of nouns such as *submarine, typewriter, elephant,* and so on. When the experimenter tests for later recall, his interest is in what the subjects-learned at the time of the experiment, their episodic memories—that the list they were presented included *elephant* and *typewriter* but not *gazelle* and *thermometer.* This is not to say that there were not many generic memories which the subjects brought to bear on the task. After all, they all knew and understood all the words on the list. But the experimenter was not interested in these generic memories. Had he been, he would have asked questions such as, "What is an elephant?" (Tulving, 1972; Hintzman, 1978).

SEMANTIC MEMORY

One of the most important components of generic memory is *semantic memory,* the memory that concerns the meanings of words and concepts (Tulving, 1972). What first comes to mind in describing semantic memory is its sheer enormity. Our entire vocabulary is in this store; every word together with its pronunciation, all of its meanings, its relations to objects in the real world, the way it is put together with other words to make phrases and sentences. How do we ever find any one bit of information in this near-infinity of verbal knowledge? One thing is certain. When we search for an item—say, a synonym for *quiet*—we don't go through all of the items in the semantic store. If we did, the hunt might last for days or weeks. The fact that we can come up with *silent* in a second or less, shows that we make use of a much more efficient retrieval system. To use a library analogy, the person who takes out a book doesn't have to rummage through all of the volumes on each shelf in order to find the one he wants. He can obtain his book much faster because there is an organized system according to which the books are arranged in the stacks.

Memory activation   What holds for episodic memory holds all the more for semantic memory: It is organized. How can we describe what this organization is? One way is through the study of **memory activation.** A subject is asked to think of a word that begins with a certain letter and belongs to some semantic category. Suppose she is asked for a word that is a *G-fruit.* The experimenter measures the reaction time from the presentation of the category term *fruit* and the response (say *grapes*). Shortly thereafter the subject gets tested once more. On some occasions, the same category is again called for, though with a different initial letter, as in *S-Fruit.* Now, the time to retrieve a suitable word (say, *strawberries*) is quite a bit shorter than it was the first time. What seems to have happened is that a semantic category is activated and remains that way for a while, like a section in a library that is lit up by a previous user who leaves the lights on when she departs. This part of the library will now become easier to find (Loftus, 1973).

Hierarchical search   Memory activation demonstrates that in searching through semantic memory we utilize broad categories in terms of which the items are organized. Other investigators have tried to show that this search is **hierarchical.**

The strategy resembles the one called for by the familiar game of Twenty Questions. The skillful player does not begin by trying to guess the final answer; she narrows the field down by progressive steps. She asks, "Is it a human being?" "Is it a man or a woman?" "Is he still alive?" "Was he born before 1000 A.D.?" Each question leads to a further branch on a decision tree that immediately eliminates all of the other twigs on the other branches. Some authors believe that retrieval from semantic memory proceeds along similar lines. According to this view, subjects, when asked to recall a particular word, search (whether consciously or not) along a decision tree whose branches correspond to semantic categories.

Some evidence comes from studies on the verification of sentences. The subjects were shown short sentences such as "A canary can fly" or "A canary is blue" and had to decide whether these sentences were true or false. To reach a decision, the subject presumably first has to retrieve the meaning of each word. How are these meanings stored? Consider the various facts that most of us know about canaries. Some properties distinguish canaries from other birds: They are yellow; they can sing. Others fit all birds: They have wings and feathers. Still others describe the superordinate category *animal* of which *birds* are a subordinate: They must eat. It is not unreasonable to suppose that the memorial dictionary is organized hierarchically. In such a dictionary, two kinds of entries would be stored with canary. First, that it is a bird (the immediate superordinate category). Second, that it is characterized by whatever properties are particular to it and not to birds in general (its defining properties). For example, the properties of birds as a class (wings, feathers, etc.) would be stored under *bird* but would not appear again and again with *canary, eagle, toucan,* and *chicken,* thus avoiding a prohibitive amount of duplication. So it follows for still higher categories such as animal, living thing, and so on.

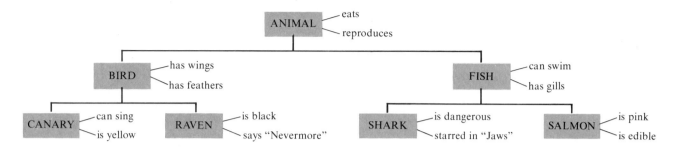

**8.18   The hierarchical theory of seman-
tic memory**   *A schematic of a hierarchical theory of some aspects of semantic
memory. To decide whether the sentence
"Ravens have feathers" is true, given the
organization of the entries here pictured,
one has to "look up" the information at
the second level, under* bird.

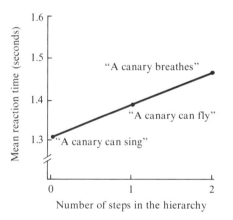

**8.19   Retrieval time from semantic
memory**   *The figure shows the times required to decide whether certain sentences are true or false. In terms of a
hierarchical theory of semantic memory,
different sentences require stepping up 0,
1, or 2 levels in the hierarchy to retrieve
the information that is necessary for a
decision. The reaction times increased
with each additional step. (After Collins
and Quillian, 1969)*

Consider the implications of such a hierarchical scheme for retrieval. If the
subject is asked a question about those characteristics of a canary that are
presumably stored under *canary* ("Does a canary sing?") the retrieval system
is only required to "look up" *canary* in the memorial dictionary. Once there,
the relevant entries are searched, and the answer is found. But suppose the
question is about some aspect of a canary that is really a characteristic of birds
as a class; for example, "Does a canary have feathers?" Now the subject must
look up two words in semantic memory. He starts with *canary* but nothing is
said about feathers. He now moves up one step in the hierarchy to get to *bird*
and finds a relevant entry. Indeed, birds are feathered. A further step is
required if the sentence refers to properties of the higher order category
animal, as in the question "Can a canary breathe?" Here retrieval begins with
canary, moves up one level to *bird,* and one more level to *animal* (Figure 8.19).

To test this conception, the investigators looked at the subject's reaction
times in verifying the sentences. According to the hierarchical scheme, it
should take a certain amount of extra time to move up from one level of the
hierarchy to the next. The results seemed to bear this out. The time required
to arrive at a yes-or-no decision was shortest for sentences that required no
shift in the hierarchy level, such as "A canary can sing." When the sentence
required one step up, as in "A canary has wings," its verification took an
additional 75 milliseconds. When the sentence called for two steps, as in "A
canary can breathe," its verification took yet another 75 milliseconds (Figure
8.20). The authors reasoned that each move up in the hierarchy takes a certain
amount of time; here, 75 milliseconds (Collins and Quillian, 1969). The underlying logic involves the same reaction time method we have already encountered in our discussion of serial search procedures in short-term memory
retrieval.

This hierarchical scheme is very neat but, as so often, nature is much less
neat than theorists would have her be. To mention only one problem, membership in many semantic categories does not seem to be all or none. When
subjects are asked to rate various birds according to the degree to which they
were "typical birds," *robins* were judged to be the most typical, *chickens* less
so, and *penguins* birds by courtesy only (Rosch, 1973). While the evidence is
not all in, the best guess is that these differences in typicality are reflected in
verification times. Thus subjects seem to be faster in agreeing that "*X* is a
bird," if *X* is a typical bird like a canary or a robin rather than a marginal case
like a penguin or an ostrich. Such effects suggest that the relation between
items of information in the semantic memory is not as tidy as the hierarchical
position had supposed (for further discussion, see Chapter 10).

VISUAL MEMORY

Important as words and the abstract concepts that underlie them may be, they are not all that we remember. We also seem to have memory systems that preserve some of the characteristic attributes of our senses. The idea is not just that we know that, say, people's waists are between their head and their toes. Of course we do, but that isn't all. We also seem to be able to somehow retrieve this between-ness from a mental image that has some of the characteristics of the original visual experience. As some authors (beginning with Shakespeare) have put it, we see it in "our mind's eye." While similar claims have been made for other senses—hearing with the mind's ear (composers), feeling with the mind's fingers (blind persons)—our primary concern will be with visual memory.

RATING ONE'S OWN IMAGES

The first attempt to study visual imagery goes back a hundred years ago when Sir Francis Galton (1822–1911), the founder of the field of individual differences, asked people to describe their own images and to rate them for vividness (Galton, 1883). The results showed that individuals differed widely. Some people said they could call up past scenes at will and see them with the utmost clarity. Others (including some well-known painters) denied ever having had any images at all. But these differences in how people described their own experiences have surprisingly little to do with how they actually performed on tasks that seemed to call for visual memory. One study showed that there was no correlation between self-rated image vividness and performance on an objective test that measured memory for spatial designs (Di Vesta, Ingersoll, and Sunshine, 1971). Nor is there any relationship between the way subjects rate their own images and the degree to which they benefit from imagery mnemonics (Baddeley, 1976).

EIDETIC IMAGERY

Since self-judgments of imagery seemed to be of little use, psychologists turned to more sophisticated procedures. In addition to asking what the image appeared to be like, they asked what it enabled the subject to do. For example, is the image a mental picture from which we can read off information as if it were an actual visual scene outside? By and large, the answer is no. But there are some exceptions. One is *iconic memory* which we have encountered before. It is certainly picturelike, but it is obviously not part of long-term storage since it only lasts a fraction of a second. A more pertinent phenomenon is *eidetic imagery,* which is characterized by relatively long-lasting and detailed images of visual scenes that can sometimes be scanned and "looked at" as if they had real existence outside. In one study, a group of schoolchildren was shown a picture for 30 seconds. After it was taken away, the subjects were asked whether they could still see anything and, if so, to describe what they saw (Leask, Haber, and Haber, 1969). Evidence for eidetic imagery is contained in the following protocol of a ten-year-old boy, who was looking at a blank easel from which a picture from *Alice in Wonderland* had just been removed (Figure 8.20).

8.20　Test picture for study of eidetic imagery　*This picture from* Alice in Wonderland *was shown for half a minute to elementary schoolchildren, a few of whom seemed to have an eidetic image of it. (Illustration by Marjorie Torrey)*

EXPERIMENTER:　Do you see something there?

SUBJECT:　I see the tree, gray tree with three limbs. I see the cat with stripes around its tail.

EXPERIMENTER:　Can you count those stripes?

SUBJECT:　Yes (pause). There's about 16.

EXPERIMENTER:　You're counting what? Black, white or both?

SUBJECT:　Both.

EXPERIMENTER:　Tell me what else you see.

SUBJECT:　And I can see the flowers on the bottom. There's about three stems but you can see two pairs of flowers. One on the right has green leaves, red flower on bottom with yellow on top. And I can see the girl with a green dress. She's got blond hair and a red hair band and there are some leaves in the upper left-hand corner where the tree is (Haber, 1969, p. 38).

Eidetic imagery is relatively rare. Only 5 percent or so of tested schoolchildren seemed to have it, and the proportion is almost surely smaller in adults. Nor does it seem to be an especially useful form of mental activity. Contrary to popular lore, memory experts don't generally have eidetic imagery (or photographic memory as it is sometimes popularly referred to); their skill is in organizing material in memory, rather than in storing it in picture form.

OTHER FORMS OF VISUAL MEMORY

Eidetic imagery may be a rare case of an unusually persistent sensory memory. If so, it is the one case in which visual memory corresponds to a picture in the head. But except for this, visual memory is not a simple reembodiment of stored visual sensation. Our perceptions are not like photographs, and so our visual memories can't be either. But they may nevertheless contain certain pictorial attributes that are also found in visual perception. A number of studies suggest that this is indeed the case.

Mental rotation　One line of evidence comes from studies on mental rotation. The subjects were shown a digit or a number, either normally or in mirror-reversed form (that is, *R* or Я). But in addition, the figures were tilted so that the subject might encounter an *R* rotated by, say, 120 degrees, to yield ⅄ . Or he might be presented with the Я figure, rotated by, say, 60 degrees, as in ⅃ . The subjects' task was to press one button if the stimulus was normal, another if it was mirror-reversed.

The reaction times proved to be a regular function of how far the characters were tilted away from the upright. As the orientation of the letters changed from 0 degrees (*R*) through 60 degrees (⅃) to 180 degrees (Я), reaction times increased. The same was true for the mirror-reversed letters. Reaction times were shortest for Я, longer for ⅃ and longest for Я.

The authors interpret their results as evidence for a separate visual memory system. In their view, the subjects mentally rotated an image of the stimulus they were presented with until it was upright. Once they had brought it to this position, it could be compared to the visual memory of the normal and backward characters. The fact that reaction time was a function of angle shows that this mental rotation takes time; in the present case, about 30 milliseconds for every 10 degrees (Cooper and Shepard, 1973).

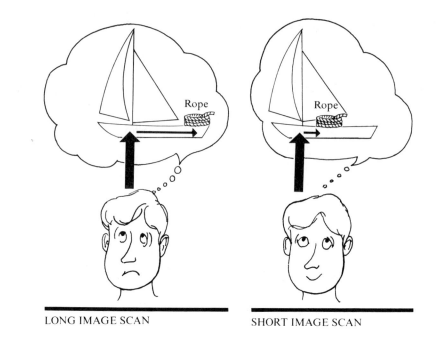

8.21 Image scanning *Subjects asked to look mentally at an image of a drawing they had just seen and to decide whether this contained a particular object responded faster when they had to traverse a shorter distance in their mind's eye. (Kosslyn, 1973)*

LONG IMAGE SCAN   SHORT IMAGE SCAN

Image scanning   Another line of evidence comes from studies on image scanning. Here the subjects were asked to conjure up an image of a drawing they had previously studied. They were asked to focus upon one end of the object they had imaged. For example, if the image was of a boat, they might be asked to take a "mental look" at the bow (Figure 8.21). After this, an object was named, say a *rope,* and the subject had to decide whether this object was present in the picture he had been shown previously. The results showed that the reaction times depended on the distance the subject had to scan along the image before the object was "found." If the subject was initially directed to focus at the boat's bow, reaction times were longer when the rope was in the stern than when it was in the boat's middle. This result would be no surprise had the subject scanned a physical object with his real eye. That the same holds when he scans an image with his mind's eye is rather remarkable (Kosslyn, 1973).

The Memory System as a Whole

We have made several distinctions among different aspects of memory: sensory registers, short-term memory, and the several aspects of long-term memory. In concluding, we want to make a few points about the way human memory works as a whole.

INTERACTION AMONG MEMORY SYSTEMS

It is important to realize that such terms as *short-term memory, semantic memory,* and the like are labels for different aspects of what goes on in memory. But these aspects are all interrelated (Figure 8.22). Initially, investigators

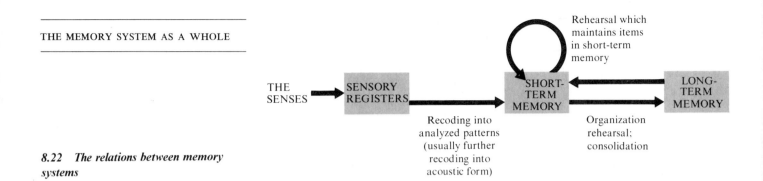

8.22   The relations between memory systems

assumed that the interrelation between these components of memory was quite simple. In their view, the information flow in memory followed a simple one-way traffic pattern with no bypasses: from sensory registers to short-term memory and from there to the long-term store. But, as we've already seen, the information flow in memory is considerably more complex than this. Consider short-term memory. It sends information to the long-term store, but the message stream also goes in the other direction. After all, short-term memory holds meaningful chunks, so that *bear, wolf, tiger* are three items rather than thirteen. But how could this be, unless the unprocessed material had first made contact with the long-term system? This contact may be more or less extensive. If there is a conscious attempt to organize, both semantic and visual memories are called on. One may notice that all three are predatory animals, or one may construct a visual image that relates all three, and so on. Seen in this light, short-term memory is much more than a simple loading platform from which material is lifted into the long-term store. It also serves as a mental workbench on which the material that is to enter long-term memory is sorted, organized, and related to other items already in memory (Baddeley, 1976).

The complex interactions between short- and long-term memory are an example of how memory functions more generally. Much of the research effort of the last twenty-five years has gone into proving that there are genuine distinctions between various memory components. These distinctions are no doubt valid; but the components do interact and do work as a smoothly orchestrated whole.

REMEMBERING AS AN ACTIVE PROCESS

A second point concerns the fact that memory is generally active. During acquisition, we deliberately organize the material and fit it into our preexisting schemas. During retrieval, we hunt and search and sometimes reconstruct. Psychologists still have much to learn about human memory but of one thing at least they are already sure—it is not analogous to a passive wax tablet on which experience leaves its stylus marks.

What we have just said has to be qualified. For memory is not always as organized and active as we have described it. There is one group of subjects in whom the memory process looks much less systematic—young children. Young children have not yet learned the strategies for remembering that adults use as a matter of course. For example, they don't tend to rehearse. In one study, children saw an experimenter point to three objects. Their job was to indicate these same objects after a fifteen-second delay during which they couldn't look at them. A trained lip reader noted that while over 80 percent of the ten-year olds mouthed the names of the objects silently, only 10 percent of the five-year olds did so (Flavell, Beach, and Chinsky, 1966). Similar results are found for category ordering. When children are asked to study a number of objects for later recall, the older children physically group same-category objects together, and later recall them by these category clusters. Younger children don't use this strategy (Moely et al., 1969).

To sum up, memory is an active process. But much of this activity—rehearsal and organization during acquisition, systematic search during retrieval—develops with increasing maturity.

Summary

1. Any act of remembering implies success in each of three phases: *acquisition,* during which a *memory trace* is formed, *retention* over some time interval, and *retrieval,* which may be by *recognition* or *recall.*

2. A widely held assumption is that there are several memory systems. One is a group of *sensory registers* which hold sensory information for fractions of a second. For vision, this register seems to produce a fast-fading *icon,* as shown by studies using *partial recall.*

3. Many psychologists believe that there are at least two further memory systems: *short-term memory* (*STM*) which holds material for a minute or so, and *long-term memory* (*LTM*) in which information is stored for much longer periods. The contents of STM tend to be stored in a rather less processed form than those of LTM, as shown by the fact that immediate recall is more likely to lead to *acoustic confusions,* delayed recall to *semantic confusions.* Another difference between STM and LTM pertains to their *capacity.* That of LTM is enormous, while that of STM is only about seven items, as shown by studies of *memory span.*

4. Material in STM can be forgotten or can be transferred to LTM. Forgetting is fairly rapid as indicated by work with brief *retention intervals* filled with some activity to prevent *rehearsal.*

5. Since there is transfer from STM to LTM, the recall of an item may reflect retrieval from STM or from LTM. Studies of *free recall* with lists of unrelated items have provided a way of indicating the origin of recalled items. The *primacy effect* obtained by use of this procedure is associated mostly with retrieval from long-term storage; the *recency effect* reflects retrieval from short-term storage.

6. Retrieval from STM has been studied by *reaction time* procedures. The results suggest that this retrieval is based on a *serial* rather than on a *parallel search* process. The evidence is the relation between reaction time and the number of items in the *memory set:* each additional item adds a constant time increment.

7. A number of physiological findings fit in fairly well with the STM-LTM distinction. One concerns *anterograde amnesia,* a condition produced by various brain injuries which damage the patient's ability to fix material in LTM. Further evidence comes from *retrograde amnesia,* a loss of memories for events just prior to a head injury. This is often attributed to a disruption of *consolidation.* Retrograde amnesia has been artificially induced in animals by *electroconvulsive shock* administered shortly after learning.

8. One major theoretical approach to the nature of long-term memory is *associationism*. Hermann Ebbinghaus and others developed a number of techniques to study how associations are formed, such as memorizing *serial lists* of *nonsense syllables*. The use of the *paired-associate* technique provided an analysis of *transfer of training* in S-R terms. When subjects learn two paired-associate lists, there will generally be *positive transfer* if the response terms in the two lists are identical (*A-B,* then *C-B*); there will be *negative transfer* if the stimulus terms are identical but the response terms are different (*A-B,* then *A-C*).

9. A different theoretical approach to long-term memory emphasizes *memory organization*. An example is the enlarging of memory capacity by appropriate *recoding* of material into larger *chunks*. In verbal memory, this is often accomplished through the use of *semantic categories,* as demonstrated by studies of *recall clustering* and of *subjective organization*.

10. Organizational factors may explain the role of rehearsal in memorization. An important distinction is between *maintenance rehearsal,* which merely holds material in STM, and *active rehearsal,* which produces memorial organization and thus leads to effective transfer into LTM. Similar factors may account for the typical superiority of *intentional* over *incidental learning:* the first generally leads to memory organization, the second doesn't.

11. Recall depends partially on *trace accessibility* which in turn depends upon proper *retrieval cues*. When these are not immediately present, there is often an attempt at *memory search*. Evidence for such a search process comes from the *tip-of-the-tongue phenomenon*.

12. In some cases, retrieval is essentially *reconstruction,* whose nature depends in part upon the recall instructions, as shown by studies using leading questions to ask for recall.

13. *Mnemonics* are techniques designed to improve memory. Some go back to classical times and rely on the use of *imagery,* as in the *method of loci* and the *method of pegs*. These are quite effective, in part because they force the subject to organize the material into larger units.

14. Other things equal, forgetting increases the longer the time since learning. The reason is still a matter of debate. One theory holds that traces gradually *decay*. Another argues that forgetting is caused by interference produced by other, inappropriate memories. This approach leans heavily on two forms of interference produced in the laboratory, *retroactive* and *proactive inhibition*. Still another theory asserts that forgetting is primarily caused by changes in the retrieval cues at the time of the recall.

15. A distinction is often made between two varieties of LTM, *episodic* and *generic*. An important component of generic memory is *semantic memory,* whose organization has been studied by various techniques for assessing memory search, including *memory activation*. Some investigators believe that this search is *hierarchical,* a claim based on results of various studies on the *verification of sentences*.

16. Some LTM systems seem to be essentially visual. An extreme and rather rare example is *eidetic memory*. More common are other forms of visual memory that are not a simple reembodiment of the original visual impression but still preserve some of the pictorial properties of the original. Evidence comes from studies of *mental rotation* and of *image scanning*.

CHAPTER 9

Thinking and Cognitive Development

In ordinary language, the word *think* has a wide range of meanings. It may be a synonym for *remembering* (as in "I can't think of her name"), or for *attention* (as in the exhortation "Think!"), or for *belief* (as in "I think sea serpents exist"). It may also refer to a state of vague and undirected reverie as in "I'm thinking of nothing in particular." These many uses suggest that the word has become a blanket term which can cover virtually any psychological process that goes on within the individual and is essentially unobservable from without.

But thinking also has a narrower meaning which is graphically rendered in Rodin's famous statue of "The Thinker." Here, the meaning of thinking is best conveyed by such words as *to reason* or *ponder* or *reflect*. Psychologists who study thinking are mainly interested in this sense of the term. To distinguish it from the others, they refer to ***directed thinking,*** a set of internal activities that are aimed at the solution of a problem, whether it be the discovery of a geometric proof, of the next move in a chess game, or of the reason why the car doesn't start. In all of these activities, the various steps in the internal sequence are directed and dominated by the ultimate goal, the solution of the problem.

The Elements of Thought

One of the oldest endeavors in the study of thinking is the search for the elements which make up thought. We will begin by considering two early hypotheses. One claims that the ultimate constituents of thought are mental images; the other asserts that they are small muscle movements.

THOUGHT AS MENTAL IMAGERY

According to Berkeley and other British empiricists, all thought is ultimately comprised of mental images, which enter and exit from the stage of consciousness as the laws of association bid them. But later investigations have shown that it is very unlikely that thought is the simple kaleidoscope of mental pictures (or sounds or touches) that this view claims. As we have already seen, some of Galton's subjects, including several well-known painters, described themselves as altogether lacking in imagery (see Chapter 8). Furthermore, imageless thought is found even in persons who are perfectly capable of vivid images. Around the turn of the century, several psychologists asked subjects to describe everything that "went through their minds" as they tried to solve various intellectual problems. The solution frequently came without a trace of imagery (and also without words). The subjects reported that when their thought was both wordless and imageless they often had a sense of certain underlying relationships, such as the experience of "this doesn't go with that" or a "feeling of *if* or *but*" (Humphrey, 1951).

None of this is to deny the fact that imagery exists and sometimes plays an important role in mental life. What is at issue is whether mental images are a *necessary* ingredient of the thought process. The answer is evidently no. Since this is so, images cannot be the ultimate stuff of which thought is made.

THOUGHT AS MOTOR ACTION

A very different approach to the nature of thinking was advocated by J. B. Watson, the founder of American Behaviorism (see Chapters 4 and 5). To Watson, psychology was the science of what organisms do. While this position may be suitable to the study of such overt activities as maze-running and lever-pressing, one might wonder how it can be extended to include thinking, which is after all a very private sort of thing known only to the thinker and easily hidden from public view.

Watson believed that at bottom there is no distinction, that thinking is a bodily activity like all other behaviors and that it involves motor reactions just as they do. He granted only one difference—the muscle movements that constitute thinking were presumed to be much smaller and thus much harder to observe than those of overt behaviors. Watson attached particular importance to the small movements of the tongue and larynx, for he regarded such ***implicit speech*** reactions as the basis of most human thinking. According to this view, thinking is largely a matter of silently talking to oneself (Watson, 1925).

EVIDENCE FOR THE MOTOR THEORY

Several investigators have tried to buttress Watson's theory by evidence that thinking is typically accompanied by motor activity. To measure muscle action invisible to the naked eye, they recorded the slight changes in electrical potential caused by contracting muscle fibers. By and large, the results were positive. Subjects who were trying to solve problems in logic or arithmetic showed increased motor tension, especially in the region of the speech apparatus (Jacobson, 1932). Of particular interest is a study on a group of deaf-mutes whose major means of communication was by sign language. When these subjects were asked to solve problems, the motor reaction was mainly found in their fingers (Max, 1937).

Such evidence suggests that thought and action are somehow related, but Watson's theory went further than that. To Watson, the motor reaction was not just a concomitant of the thought process, but was essentially equivalent to it. If so, then motor movements should be a necessary condition for thought. This has been shown not to be the case.

One line of evidence comes from several studies in which the relevant implicit speech movements were somehow interfered with. Subjects were asked to read while saying "la, la, la," to translate mentally from a foreign language while clamping their tongue between their teeth, or to find square roots while gargling. In all of these cases, the subjects were still capable of performing the required task. Even more persuasive are the results of a study in which all muscle movements were abolished by curare, a drug which paralyzes the entire skeletal musculature. One of the investigators was injected with curare; his collaborators supplied artificial respiration and other vital necessities while impatiently waiting for the paralysis to wear off so that they could hear their colleague's report. There was no interruption of consciousness. On the contrary, upon recovery the subject said that he was "clear as a bell" throughout and recalled questions that were put to him during the period of total paralysis (Smith et al., 1947).

THOUGHT AS DESCENDED FROM ACTION

Watson notwithstanding, the seat of thought is evidently not in the muscles. But this is not to say that thought and action are unrelated. As we have seen, motor action often accompanies mental effort. In adults, the discovery of this relationship typically requires sophisticated gadgetry. In children, it sometimes appears without any need for magnification. A young child faced by a particularly difficult puzzle often engages in violent contortions, twisting and turning and biting his tongue. It is generally believed that this bodily effort represents a sort of motor overflow produced by the frustration of not being able to solve the problem quickly. The adult confines this overflow to wrinkling his brow and scratching his head; the child is as yet unable to control it.

In overflow reactions the bodily activity has only an indirect relation to the thinking process that goes on concurrently. Sometimes, however, the relation may be more direct. It is not unreasonable to suppose that at least some thought processes grow out of action patterns adopted at an earlier stage of life. In early childhood, trial and error is quite overt. The child who tries to reach a cookie jar acts just like one of Thorndike's cats (see Chapter 4), groping and stretching and clambering unsuccessfully until he finally pulls the right stool under the cupboard. With increasing age, he approaches new problems by **implicit trial and error** in which the response alternatives are no longer enacted in full but are rather tried out "in his head." The process of testing hypotheses thus becomes internalized, but some psychologists claim that the motor origin of these thoughts can still be discerned—a child's hands twitch just a bit in the direction of a possible tool as she considers and then

Motor overflow (Photograph by Suzanne Szasz)

9.1 Motor empathy *Two members of the Girls' Boxing League in Houston, Texas, sparring. Note their trainer's motor involvement. (Photograph by Abigail Heyman, Magnum Photos)*

discards the idea of using it. In adults, visible implicit reactions are often seen in sports. The experienced golfer precedes his swing with an anticipatory little waggle of the club and thus tries out his stroke in miniature. ***Motor empathy*** while watching an athletic event may be an example of a similar process. We see a pole-vaulter at the peak of his jump and go through an abbreviated version of his motor reactions, grimacing and stretching and clenching, as if we were on the field rather than in the stands (Figure 9.1).

Such considerations suggest that while thought may not be motor action, it may in part be descended from it. We will discuss this possibility more fully at a later point in this chapter when we take up Jean Piaget's theories of the development of directed thinking during childhood (see pp. 333–51).

THOUGHT AS A CENTRAL ACTIVITY

On the surface, the two hypotheses we have just considered seem to be polar opposites. But the hypotheses are alike in one important regard—both treat thinking as the resuscitation of a relatively peripheral psychological process. The image hypothesis views thought as the resurrection of old sensory memories. The implicit action hypothesis treats it as the rearousal of a previous pattern of motor movement. Both views appear to be false. This suggests that thinking involves processes that are more central than those which characterize either the passive resurrection of previous perceptions or the contractions of the muscle system.

What are these central processes that underlie thinking? They should presumably be described at a more abstract level than any we have considered thus far. Thinking may well be accompanied by language, by implicit motor action, or by images; but it *is* none of these. It involves processes that are further removed from the concrete world of sensory experiences or motor acts or specific speech utterances. The attempt to describe this deeper, more abstract level is a relatively recent undertaking, at least for psychologists. (We have encountered some of its aspects in our discussion of semantic memory in Chapter 8.) However, some of the key terms of this description are already in the vocabulary of related disciplines such as logic and linguistics. Examples are *concept* and *proposition*.

CONCEPTS

The term ***concept*** is generally used to describe a class that subsumes a number (sometimes an infinite number) of individual instances. One kind of concept is a ***collection.*** Here all instances that are members of the class share one or more characteristics. An example is *dwelling* which includes *hut, house, tent, apartment,* and *igloo*. Other concepts designate qualities or dimensions. Examples are *length* and *age*. Still others are relational such as *taller than*. Relational concepts don't apply to any one item in isolation. One can't be *taller than* except in relation to something else to which one's height is being compared.

PROPOSITIONS

Concepts describe classes of events or objects or relations between them. They are what we generally think about. In so doing, we tend to combine them in various ways. The British empiricists emphasized one such mental combination: the simple associative train of thought in which one idea leads to another. A more important way of relating concepts is by asserting something about them, for example, "dogs generally bite postmen." Such statements are called **propositions.** They make some assertion that relates a subject (e.g., *dogs*) and a predicate (e.g., *generally bite postmen*) in a way that can be true or false.

That much of our thought is propositional requires little proof. The propositions we entertain may be true or false, profound or silly—what matters is that they are propositions, that they link mental elements in certain ways. In what form do such propositions exist psychologically? One possible hypothesis is that they are elaborate images. But as the philosopher Jerry Fodor has shown, this cannot be. Consider the proposition "Napoleon is dead." Can this be expressed by way of a mental image? A vivid imager might conjure up an image of the emperor in an open coffin, with weeping veterans of his wars passing by to pay their last respects. But is this image equivalent to the proposition? By no means. This image implies many propositions other than the one at hand: "Napoleon was buried with his sword," "Napoleon was rather fat when he died," "Napoleon's veterans loved him," and so on. The trouble with pictures (whether real or imagined) is that one can say so many things about them. The proposition is a way of singling out the aspects of the world that one wants to make some assertion about (Fodor, 1975).

It appears that propositions cannot be based on images. But they are not equivalent to the sentences in which they are expressed either, as shown by the fact that the same proposition can be expressed in several forms. People who speak both English and German know that "The dog bites the cat" and "Der Hund beisst die Katze" mean precisely the same thing. The same holds within the same language. Consider "The dog bites the cat" and "The cat is bitten by the dog." Again, the same proposition is asserted. Something is being said (and presumably thought) about the hapless cat that does not depend upon the particular form in which this expression is cast.

To sum up, our search for the elements of thought has shown that these elements are not images, nor implicit motor acts, nor specific speech utterances. They are more abstract mental structures such as concepts and propositions whose psychological nature we are just beginning to investigate. We will discuss them in greater detail when we take up language and meaning as topics in their own right (see Chapter 10).

Problem Solving

Thus far our concern has been with what thought is. We now turn from the question of *what* to that of *how*. How does thinking operate as we try to solve the myriad problems encountered in life, whether trying to fix a broken lawn mower, smoothing over an awkward social situation, or solving a cryptogram?

Regarded in this context, thinking is an activity. It is something an organism does. This activity is central rather than peripheral, but it is an activity nonetheless. Hobbes, Locke, and their many descendants believed that this stream of activity is produced by a chain of associated ideas, each triggered by the one before. The fundamental difficulty of this position is that thinking, like other cognitive processes, is organized.

The items in a mental sequence typically do not stand in isolation but take their meaning from the overall structure in which they are embedded. A famous paper by Karl Lashley on the serial organization of behavior illustrates this point with examples from the psychology of language (Lashley, 1951). Uttering a sentence is not just a matter of stringing one word after another, for the selection of a word often depends not only on the immediately preceding word but upon others spoken much before or upon still others not yet uttered. In English, we say "The dog run*s*" rather than "The dog run," for verb and subject must agree with each other. This agreement rule governs our speech even when the subject comes many words after the verb, as in "Down the street run*s* the excited, barking, hungry, flea-bitten dog." The fact that we produce the verb replete with a third person singular *s* indicates that there is a broad, mental scheme that precedes the actual utterance and determines it. In effect, there was a mental plan that provided the outline according to which the specific speech acts were produced (Miller, Galanter, and Pribram, 1960).

What holds for speech, holds for many other activities, including problem solving. The problem solver goes through a sequence of internal steps. These steps are organized in a special way: they are directed. Consider a taxi driver who is trying to decide on the best route from the city to the airport. According to a simple chain-association hypothesis, the initial stimulus ("Get me to the airport in time for a 9:15 flight") triggers various internal responses (such as "superhighway," "crosstown express," etc.) until the correct solution is finally evoked (Figure 9.2). But this interpretation cannot readily explain why the would-be solutions that come to mind, whether right or wrong, are usually relevant to the problem at hand. Nor can it explain how such potential solutions are accepted or rejected. If they were merely aroused by associative connections, the problem solver would be adrift in a sea of irrelevancies: "crosstown express" might evoke "uptown local" or "crossword puzzle" or

9.2 Schematic outline of taxi driver's approach to solving his problem Note *that the goal (stated at the very outset) determines the thought processes throughout. Some would-be solutions are considered and rejected as inappropriate to the goal. Others (e.g., crossword puzzle), while perhaps associatively related, aren't even called to mind.*

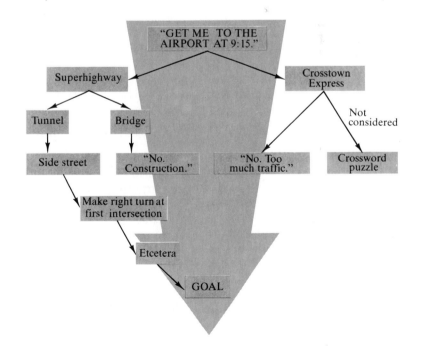

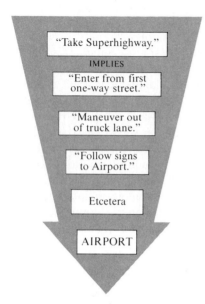

9.3 Hierarchical organization of a plan *Plans have subcomponents which have subcomponents below them, as here illustrated by the taxi driver's task.*

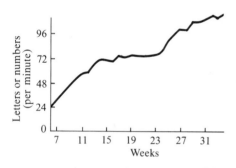

9.4 An apprentice telegrapher's learning curve *The curve plots the number of letters or digits the operator can receive per minute against weeks of practice. Note the plateau in the learning curve. The curve stays level from weeks 15 to 25 and then starts to rise again. According to Bryan and Harter, the new rise indicates the use of larger chunks. (After Bryan and Harter, 1899)*

what have you. Instead, each mental step is determined not just by the step before but by the original problem. This sets the overall direction which dominates all of the later steps and determines how each of them is to be evaluated. The taxi driver considers the superhighway and rejects it as he recalls some road construction along the way, thinks of the crosstown express and dismisses it because of rush-hour traffic, and so on. The original problem acts like a schematic frame, waiting to be filled in by a "fitting" alternative.

HIERARCHICAL ORGANIZATION IN THOUGHT AND ACTION

We have encountered the notion of hierarchical organization while discussing the role of chunking in memory (see Chapter 8). A similar principle governs directed thinking. To the taxi driver, the idea "take the crosstown express" is a sort of master plan which implies various subsidiary actions: entering from the appropriate one-way street, maneuvering out of the truck lane, following the signs to the airport exit, and so on. To the experienced driver all of these substeps require no further decision, for they are a consequence of a hierarchical organization which resembles that of a disciplined army. The colonel who orders his regiment to attack does not have to specify the detailed commands his second lieutenants issue to their platoons. Given the order from above, the subcommands follow (Figure 9.3).

The ability to subsume many details under a larger chunk is one of the crucial features of directed activity, including the internal activity we call thinking. As we shall see, much of the difference between master and apprentice is in the degree to which subcomponents of the activity have been chunked hierarchically. To the master, the substeps have become automatic.

THE DEVELOPMENT OF SKILLS

The role of chunking in directed activity is particularly clear when we study how people become proficient at various skills such as typing, driving a car, or playing golf. In all such activities, becoming skillful depends upon a qualitative change in how the task is performed.

TRANSFORMING THE TASK

The first experimental study in this area was done about eighty years ago by Bryan and Harter. These psychologists were trying to discover how telegraph operators master their trade. Their subjects were Western Union apprentices whose progress at sending and receiving Morse code messages was charted over a period of about forty weeks. Figure 9.4 plots one student's improvement at receiving, measured in letters per minute. What is interesting about this learning curve is its shape. Following an initial rise, the curve flattens to a *plateau* that lasts about ten weeks, after which the curve goes up again. According to Bryan and Harter, such plateaus are an indication that the learner gradually transforms his task. At first he merely tracks individual letters. With time, the effective units he deals with become larger and larger: first syllables and words, then several words at a time, then simple phrases, and perhaps

A	B
YNHRE	GRAY
VDAIX	WHITE
BPOMS	TAN
FWECG	BLACK
FWECG	BROWN
YNHRE	GRAY
ZRQUT	TAN
VDAIX	WHITE
FWECG	BLACK
ZRQUT	TAN
BPOMS	BROWN
YNHRE	WHITE
VDAIX	WHITE
ZRQUT	GRAY
FWECG	BLACK
BPOMS	BROWN

9.5 **The Stroop effect** *The two lists, (A) and (B), are printed in four colors—black, gray, brown, and tan. To observe the Stroop effect, name the colors (aloud) in which each of the nonsense syllables in list (A) is printed as fast as you can, continuing downward. Then do the same for list (B), calling out the colors in which each of the words of the list is printed, again going from top to bottom. This will probably be easier for list (A) than for list (B), a demonstration of the Stroop effect. This effect is usually studied using full colors, but it tends to show up even with just the four colors used here.*

eventually short sentences. The plateau represents the best the learner can do given a unit of a lower level (say, letters); once this lower level is completely mastered, a higher level of organization—a larger chunk—is possible and the learning curve shoots up once more (Bryan and Harter, 1897).

Similar effects are observed in the acquisition of many other skills. To the novice, typing proceeds letter by letter; to the expert, the proper units are much larger, including familiar letter groupings, words, and occasionally phrases. Similarly, the beginning driver laboriously struggles to harmonize clutch, gas pedal, steering wheel, and brake, to the considerable terror of innocent bystanders. After a while, those movements come quite routinely and are subsumed under much higher (though perhaps equally dangerous) chunks of behavior, such as overtaking another car. An even simpler example is dressing. To the small child every article of clothing represents a major intellectual challenge; she beams with pride when she finally gets the knack of tying her shoelaces. To an adult the unit is "getting dressed" and its various components are almost completely submerged within the larger chunk. We decide to dress and before we know it we are almost fully clothed. Somehow our shoes get laced but we never notice, unless the laces break.

AUTOMATIZATION

The automatization of subcomponents in skilled activities has a side-effect. Once the plan is set into motion, its execution may be difficult to stop. An example is reading. When we see a billboard on a highway, we can't help but read what it says, whether we want to or not. The forms on the sign proclaim that they are letters and words; this is enough to trigger our automatized reading routines (La Berge, 1975). A striking demonstration of this phenomenon is the so-called **Stroop effect** (Stroop, 1935). Subjects are asked to name the colors in which groups of letters are printed and to do so as quickly as they can (Figure 9.5). In one case, the letter groups are unrelated consonants or vowels. In this condition, the subjects have little trouble. After a little practice, they become very proficient at rattling off the colors, "red, green . . ."

The subjects' task becomes vastly more difficult in a condition in which the letters are grouped into words, specifically, color names. Diabolically enough, these are not the names of the colors in which the words are printed.

Now the subjects respond much more slowly. They are asked to say "green, red, yellow . . . " But they can't help themselves from reading the words "yellow, black . . . " for reading is an automatized skill. As a result, there is violent response conflict. This conflict persists even after lengthy practice. One way subjects finally manage to overcome it is by learning to unfocus their eyes. By this maneuver, they can still see the colors but can no longer recognize what the letters are (Jensen, 1965).

THE CHUNKING PROCESS

At present we know very little about the mechanisms that underlie the chunking process. Associationists propose that the explanation involves *chaining.* In their view, many skilled acts are highly overpracticed stimulus-response chains in which the first movement provides the kinesthetic stimulus for the second, which produces the stimulus for the third, and so on. This

NAGMARA

BOLMPER

SLEVO

STIGNIH

TOLUSONI

9.6 Anagrams *Rearrange the letters on each line to form a word. (For the solution, see next page.)*

9.7 Concrete object problem *Assemble all six matches to form four equilateral triangles, each side of which is equal to the length of one match. (After Scheerer, 1963; for solution, see Figure 9.21)*

9.8 Nine-dot problem *Nine dots are arranged in a square. Connect them by drawing one continuous line without lifting your pencil from the paper. (After Scheerer, 1963; for solution, see Figure 9.18)*

interpretation is almost certainly false. As Karl Lashley pointed out, a trained pianist may reach a rate of sixteen successive finger strokes a second when playing an arpeggio. This speed is too high to allow time for a sensory message to reach the brain and for a motor command to come back to the fingers. We can only conclude that there is a learned neural program that allows the successive finger movements to occur without interpolated sensory monitoring (Lashley, 1951).

We may not understand precisely how this complex chunking is acquired but there is little doubt of its importance. It is hard to imagine any organized, skilled behavior in which this process does not play a role. In Bryan and Harter's words, "The ability to take league steps in receiving telegraphic messages, in reading, in addition, in mathematical reasoning and in many other fields, plainly depends upon the acquisition of league-stepping habits ... The learner must come to do with one stroke of attention what now requires a half a dozen, and presently, in one still more inclusive stroke, what now requires thirty-six." The expert can, if necessary, attend to the lower-level units of his skill, but for the most part these have become automatic. This acquired automatism, the submergence of lower level units in the higher chunk, frees him to solve new problems. "Automatism is not genius, but it is the hands and feet of genius" (Bryan and Harter, 1899, p. 375).

CHUNKING IN PROBLEM SOLVING

Psychologists have devised a large number of experimental situations for the study of human problem solving. Subjects have been asked to decipher anagrams (Figure 9.6), to manipulate various concrete objects so as to produce a desired result (Figure 9.7), or to find the solution to various geometrical problems (Figure 9.8). Considering this variety of tasks, it is hardly surprising

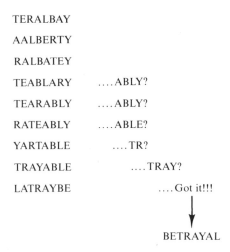

9.9 Steps in solving anagram puzzle *Given the anagram TERALBAY one subject progressively rearranged the letters to approximate English word components until he hit upon the solution. Note that the rearrangements are not random but focus upon common suffixes (ly, able) and consonant combinations (bl, tr). (After Cohen, 1971)*

that there are differences in the way in which they are attacked; a subject who tries to join nine dots with one continuous line will call upon a somewhat different set of mental skills than one who has to rearrange the letters *TERALBAY* into an English word (Figure 9.9). The question is whether there is a common thread that runs through all attempts at problem solving, no matter what the problem may be. Many psychologists believe that hierarchical organization is such a common feature.

OBSERVING THE PROBLEM SOLVER

The role of organization in problem solving was highlighted in a classic study by the Gestalt psychologist Karl Duncker, who asked his subjects to "think out loud" while they tried to find the solution (Duncker, 1945). One of Duncker's problems was cast in medical terms:

> Suppose a patient has an inoperable stomach tumor. There are certain rays which can destroy this tumor if their intensity is large enough. At this intensity, however, the rays will also destroy the healthy tissue which surrounds the tumor (e.g., the stomach walls, the abdominal muscles, and so on). How can one destroy the tumor without damaging the healthy tissue through which the rays must travel on their way?

Duncker's subjects typically arrived at the solution in several steps. They first reformulated the problem so as to produce a general plan of attack. This in turn led to more specific would-be solutions. For example, they might look for a tissue-free path to the stomach and then propose to send the rays through the esophagus. (A good idea which unfortunately will not work—rays travel in straight lines and the esophagus is curved.) After exploring several other general approaches and their specific consequences, some subjects finally hit upon the appropriate general plan. They proposed to reduce the intensity of rays on their way through healthy tissue and then turn up this intensity when the rays reach the tumor. This broad restatement of what is needed eventually led to the correct specific means, which was to send several bundles of *weak* rays from various points outside so that they meet at the tumor where their effects will summate (Figure 9.10).

Duncker's results show that the specific would-be solutions grow out of broader solution classes, much as tactics follows from strategy on the battlefield. Figure 9.11 is a schematic representation of one subject's efforts; it is arranged in the form of a tree diagram which highlights the hierarchical nature of the underlying organization.

Similar effects have been obtained with many other problem situations. For example, Duncker asked subjects to explain why all six-place numbers whose first three digits are identical to their last three digits (e.g., 276276, 692692, 112112, and so on) are divisible by 13. Those subjects who arrived at the correct solution did so by way of several broader solution classes (in effect, chunks). They first asked themselves whether numbers of the general form *abcabc* have a common factor that is divisible by 13. Looking for this factor led them to express *abcabc* as a sum, specifically, $1,000\ abc + abc$. This sum in turn can be rewritten, $1,001 \times abc$. Once here, the next step is clear if somewhat tedious. A bit of long division establishes that $1,001 = 77 \times 13$, the subject mutters QED, and the problem is solved.

9.10   The solution to the ray-tumor problem   *Several weak rays are sent from various points outside so that they will meet at the tumor site. There the radiation of the rays will be intense, for all the effects will summate at this point. But since they are individually weak, the rays will not damage the healthy tissue that surrounds the tumor. (After Duncker, 1945)*

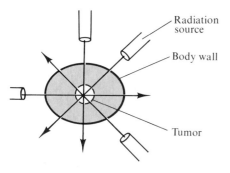

Radiation source

Body wall

Tumor

ANAGRAM

PROBLEM

SOLVE

INSIGHT

SOLUTION

9.6   Solution

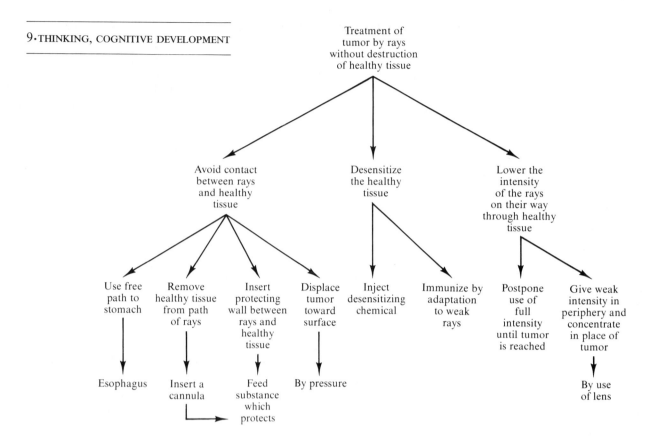

9.11 A summary of one subject's solution process *One subject, given Duncker's medical problem, puzzled about it for thirty minutes. His attempted solutions are schematized in hierarchical form. (After Duncker, 1945)*

MASTERS AND BEGINNERS

Some people solve certain problems better than others do. One of the reasons is simply a matter of experience; the trained mechanic is more likely to hit on the why and wherefore of automotive failure than is his young apprentice. But what exactly does experience contribute? A major factor is chunking, which plays a similar role in problem solving to that played in the execution of various skills. Experts approach a problem in different ways than beginners. They think in larger units whose components are already contained within them and thus require no further thought. To mathematicians, the proof that *abcabc* is divisible by 13 is virtually routine. They immediately "see" that any number can be expressed as so many units plus so many tens plus so many hundreds and so on. Given this chunk, the fact that *abcabc* is 1,001 times *abc* follows quickly, and with it, the desired solution.

An interesting demonstration of how chunking makes the master comes from a study of chess players conducted by the Dutch psychologist Adrian de Groot whose findings have been corroborated and extended by several American investigators (de Groot, 1965; Chase and Simon, 1973). The chess world ranks its members according to a ruthlessly objective hierarchy of merit based on a simple record of who beats whom. Grandmasters are at the very top, followed by masters, experts, and so on, down to Class *D* players at the lower rungs of the chess ladder. De Groot, himself a chess master, posed various chess problems to members of each merit category (including two former world champions) and asked them to select the best move. Contrary to what might have been expected, the grandmasters and masters did not look further ahead. They considered about the same number of moves and calculated about as far into the future as the lower-ranked players. Their superiority was not in quantity, but in quality. All of them chose continuations that would have won the game, while few of the other players did. The difference is in the way the problem is organized. The chess master structures the chess position in terms of broad strategic concepts (e.g., a king-side attack with pawns) from which many of the specific moves follow naturally. Given that his chunks are larger, one would expect the chess master to grasp the position in a shorter time. Some further studies indicate that this is indeed the case. Players of different ranks were shown various chess positions for five seconds each and were then asked to reproduce them a few minutes later. Grandmasters and masters did so with hardly an error; lesser players (including mere experts) performed much more poorly (Figure 9.12). This is not because the chess masters have "better visual memory." When presented with bizarre positions that would hardly ever arise in the course of a well-played game, they recalled no better than novices. Their superiority is in the conceptual organization of chess, not in the memory for visual patterns as such.

The essence of mastership is then an organization of the relevant subcomponents that allows fewer but vastly larger steps. The process of creation is in part just this—the development of newer and better chunkings. In part, this is a matter of experience. But in part, it is surely a matter of talent, for some people can see chunks where the rest of us simply cannot. When the mathematician Karl Friedrich Gauss was a young boy in grammar school, his

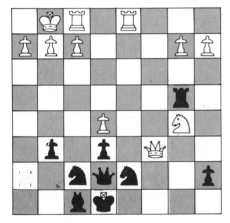

A. Actual position

9.12   Memory for chess positions in masters, experts, and average players   (A) An actual chess position which was presented for five seconds after which the positions of the pieces had to be reconstructed. Typical performances by masters, experts, and average players are shown in (B), (C), and (D) respectively, with errors indicated in color. (After Hearst, 1972)

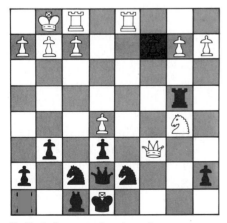

B. Typical master player's performance

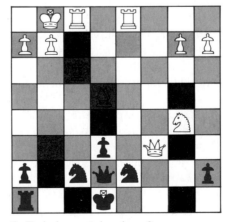

C. Typical expert player's performance

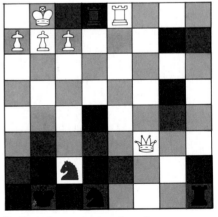

D. Typical average player's performance

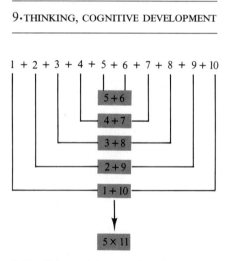

$$1 + 2 + 3 + 4 + 5 + 6 + 7 + 8 + 9 + 10$$

5 + 6

4 + 7

3 + 8

2 + 9

1 + 10

5 × 11

9.13   Reorganizing a series of sums
Young Gauss' solution amounts to the insight that in a series of numbers $1 + 2 \ldots + 10$, the numbers increase by one going from left to right and decrease by one going from right to left. As a result, the sum of the extreme pairs $(1 + 10)$ must equal the sum of the next-to-extreme pair $(2 + 9)$ and so on. Given this insight, it can be generalized to series of any length. Thus $1 + 2 \ldots + 1,000 = 500 (1 + 1,000)$. (After Wertheimer, 1945)

teacher asked the class to add all the numbers from 1 to 10. Young Gauss got the answer almost immediately. Unlike his classmates, he did not chug through all of the tedious steps of the summation. He recognized that the series $1 + 2 + 3 \ldots + 10$ can be rewritten as a sum of 5 pairs each of which equals 11. (His reorganization of the series is rendered graphically in Figure 9.13.) Given this insight, he quickly came up with the correct answer, 55, no doubt to the considerable amazement of the teacher.

This process of reorganizing bits and pieces so that they form a unified whole is also found in artistic creation. Mozart describes it in one of his letters:

> Those ideas that please me I retain in memory, and am accustomed, as I have been told, to hum them to myself. If I continue in this way, it soon occurs to me how I may turn this or that morsel to good account, so as to make a good dish of it, that is to say agreeably to the rules of counterpoint, to the peculiarities of the various instruments, etc. All this fires my soul, and provided that I am not disturbed my subject enlarges itself and becomes methodized and refined, and the whole, though it be long, stands almost complete and finished in my mind, so that I can survey it, like a fine picture or a beautiful statue—at a glance. Nor do I hear in my imagination the parts successively, but I hear them, as it were, all at once. What a delight this is, I cannot tell. . . . What has been thus produced, I do not easily forget, and this is perhaps the best gift I have my divine maker to thank for (Quoted in Humphreys, 1951 p. 53).

ARTIFICIAL INTELLIGENCE

The preceding discussion has emphasized the role played by hierarchical organization in thinking. But how does this organization come about? How does the problem solver hit upon the right plan of attack and how does she recognize that it is right when she thinks of it? These questions are as yet unanswered, but there have been some promising leads.

One hopeful avenue of research comes from attempts to program computers so as to simulate certain aspects of human thinking. The impetus to this work stems from the belief, held by many psychologists, that humans and computers are similar in one important regard—they are both ***information-processing systems.*** We have already seen several examples of the information-processing approach in our discussion of memory. When we talk of items that are temporarily stored in short-term memory, recoded into fewer and more compact chunks, transferred into long-term memory, and then retrieved by various hierarchical search procedures, we are describing a system in which information is systematically converted from one state into others. There is a formal similarity between this sequence of inferred events in human memory and the actual steps of a computer program that handles the storage and retrieval of various materials (e.g., library titles, tax returns, etc.).

To be sure, the underlying physical machinery is very different. Computers use hardware made of magnetic cores and transistors, while biological systems are built of neurons. But this difference does not prohibit a similarity in their operations. Computers may be built of relays or electronic tubes or transistors, but they can be fed the identical program even so. If it doesn't matter whether the components are tubes or transistors, then—for at least some purposes—it may not matter whether they are transistors or neurons. To students of ***artifi-***

cial intelligence, the important point is that both computers and human beings are information processing systems. They therefore regard it as likely that the study of one will help in the understanding of the other.

A further advantage of computer simulation comes from the fact that machines are painfully literal. The program must be spelled out in absolutely precise detail, for the computer will balk if presented with vague or overgeneralized instructions. This limitation is a blessing in disguise. It forces the scientist to formulate his notions in completely rigorous and explicit terms.

ALGORITHMS AND HEURISTICS

Several investigators have deliberately forced their programs to be as humanlike as possible. The most prominent among these are Allen Newell and Nobel laureate Herbert Simon, who have programmed computers to play chess, to discover and prove theorems in symbolic logic, and to decipher cryptograms. They began by studying how human subjects deal with these problems, discovered their typical strategies by use of the think-aloud technique, and then incorporated these problem-solving plans into the instructions fed to their computer. Interestingly enough, the computer does fairly well if it attacks these problems as human subjects say they do (Newell and Simon, 1972).

Newell and Simon found it useful to distinguish between two major kinds of solution strategies. One is an *algorithm,* a procedure in which all of the operations required to achieve the solution are specified step by step. Examples are the various manipulations of arithmetic. An algorithm guarantees that a solution will be found in time, but this time may be very slow in coming. Consider a person working on a crossword puzzle who is trying to find a synonym for "sharp-tongued" that will fit into _c__bi_. An algorithm exists: Insert all possible alphabetic combinations into the four empty spaces and check each result in an unabridged dictionary. While this procedure is certain to produce "acerbic," it should appeal to few puzzle solvers, for it will require the inspection of nearly 460,000 possibilities.

In actual practice, crossword puzzles are solved by procedures which, though not as sure, are much less slow. These are *heuristics* which are various tricks and rules of thumb that have often worked in the past and may do so again, such as guessing at a suffix given the word's grammatical class (*ic* is a good bet for an adjective), forming hypotheses on the basis of likely letter sequences in the language (the first letter is probably an *s* or a vowel), and so on. The great majority of problems people face are solved by such heuristic procedures rather than by algorithms, for human life is short and human processing capacity is limited. Physicians reach their diagnoses by first considering a few hypotheses that seem most plausible and then testing those. If they systematically looked at every possibility, the patient would be dead before being diagnosed.

If the problem is complex enough, even high-speed computers must resort to heuristics. Consider the analysis of a chess position some ten moves ahead. The total number of possibilities (based on moves, replies, replies to replies, and so on) has been estimated at an astronomical billion billion billion. Under the circumstances, an algorithm is out of the question. (If the inspection of each possibility takes one-millionth of a second, the inspection of all of them

9.14   An advice-taking chess computer
Man-versus-machine chess game played between Charles I. Kalme, an American master, and a computer that has been programmed to take advice. This computer program should eventually produce machine chess of a higher order. (Zobrist and Carlson, 1973; photograph by Mervyn Lew)

would be completed after 1,000 billion years.) On the other hand, heuristics work reasonably well. One of Newell and Simon's programs requires the computer to search for moves that satisfy fairly immediate subgoals such as material superiority (e.g., give a pawn for a queen but not vice versa) and occupation of the center squares (which limits the opponent's mobility and enhances one's own). Such an approach resembles that of the human player. His ultimate goal is to checkmate the opponent, but he is not likely to achieve it unless he proceeds hierarchically; instead of evaluating each move in terms of the final goal, he considers it in terms of the subgoals that usually lead up to it. Chess programs that employ heuristics of this sort give a fair account of themselves. While they cannot hope to beat a master, they might hold their own against, say, the average player on a good college team (Figure 9.14).

Programs based on heuristics have scored similar successes in other fields. An example is a program that can prove theorems in symbolic logic (Newell, Shaw, and Simon, 1958). Its general scheme is to work backward from the desired end. The program tries to find a means to the final goal, then a means to achieve that means (which now becomes a subgoal), and so on. To accomplish this, it considers whatever state it "desires" (the goal or subgoal), and then tries to minimize the difference between this and the present state by various operations (e.g., algebraic transformations). Newell and Simon give a simplified example of how a similar strategy might be used by people faced with the ordinary problems of everyday life:

> I want to take my son to nursery school. What's the difference between what I have and what I want? One of distance. What changes distance? My automobile. My automobile won't work. What is needed to make it work? A new battery. What has new batteries? An auto repair shop. I want the repair shop to put in a new battery; but the shop doesn't know I need one. What is the difficulty? One of communication. What allows communication? A telephone . . . and so on (Newell and Simon, 1972, p. 416).

SOME PROBLEMS OF ARTIFICIAL INTELLIGENCE

Computer simulation has added a new and exciting dimension to the study of cognitive processes. But so far at least, it still has some serious limitations as an approach to human problem solving.

Well-defined and ill-defined problems   The problems which existing computer programs can handle are **well-defined.** There is a clear-cut way to decide whether a proposed solution is indeed the right one. Examples are algebraic proofs (Are the terms identical on both sides of the equation?), chess problems (Is the opposing king checkmated?), and anagrams (Is the rearranged letter sequence a word that appears in the dictionary?).

In contrast, many of the problems people face in real life are **ill-defined.** Consider an architect who is asked to design a modern college dormitory? Exactly what is a correct solution? Some proposals can obviously be rejected out of hand—for example, if there are no provisions for bathrooms—but there is no definite criterion for what is acceptable. Similarly for many other problem activities, such as completing a sonnet or organizing a lecture or planning a vacation. In all of these cases, the critical first step is to define the problem so that it can be answered and so that the answer can be evaluated. The architect begins by asking questions about the number of students who are to be housed, the facilities that must be included, the surrounding terrain, the available budget—all in an attempt to render an ill-defined problem well-defined. The progress of human knowledge is often a matter not of problem solution but of problem definition and redefinition. The alchemist looked for a way to change lead into gold; the modern physicist tries to discover the atomic structure of matter.

As of yet, computer programs do not define their own problems. People do, but so far we know little about how they accomplish this.

Loosening the program's direction   As we have seen, computers can be programmed to be purposive; they can have goals and subgoals just as we do. But "when a program is purposive, it is too purposive" (Neisser, 1963). The computer is fanatically single-minded. When set a problem, it drives toward the solution with neither pause nor conflict, never forgetting its goal nor its partial solutions achieved en route. Human thinkers may be directed, but they are never quite as directed as that. They get bored and distracted, they forget, they start to work on other problems. These human frailties may sometimes prevent the discovery of the solution, but they may occasionally help rather than hinder. Some problems—perhaps the most important ones—can only be solved by adopting a completely new approach, an altogether new set of heuristics. Faced with such problems, one might well want to loosen the direction of the thought process, or to forget a prior step which may ultimately prove to be well-forgotten.

Several recent programs have tried to avoid some of the single-mindedness of their predecessors by allowing the machine to consider all sorts of things simultaneously and to forget what it has done unless special circumstances intervene (Reitman, 1965). One of these programs can solve simple word analogies, such as "Bear is to pig as chair is to ____? (foot, table, coffee, strawberry)." It is too early to judge whether such deliberate attempts to build human imperfection into computers will produce an artificial intelligence that is more similar to its human counterpart.

Mental Set

So far, we have primarily dealt with situations in which problem solvers succeed. How can we explain their all too many failures? In many cases, the solution is simply out of reach. The problem solver lacks some necessary informational prerequisites or relevant chunkings or heuristics—as when a ten-year old is unable to solve a problem in integral calculus. But failure often occurs even when all the necessary ingredients for solution are known perfectly well, for the would-be problem solver may get stuck in a wrong approach and cannot get unstuck. When finally told the answer, his reaction shows that he was blind rather than ignorant: "How stupid of me. I should have seen it all along." He was victimized by a powerful *mental set* that was inappropriate for the problem at hand.

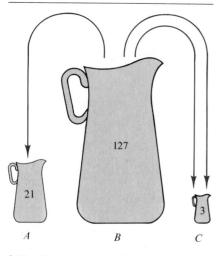

9.15   The standard method for solving the three-container problem   *(After Luchins, 1942)*

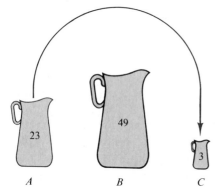

9.16   A simpler method for solving certain three-container problems   *(After Luchins, 1942)*

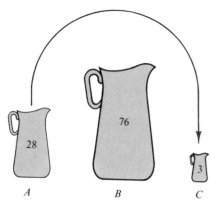

9.17   A case where only the simple method works   *(After Luchins, 1942)*

SET AND PROBLEM SOLVING

We have already seen that people can be predisposed (that is, *set*) to perceive ambiguous situations in one way rather than another (see Chapter 7). Similar effects are commonplace in other cognitive spheres as well.

MECHANIZATION

A well-known study of mechanization in problem solving showed how set can make people rigid. The subjects were presented with a series of problems. They were told that they had three jars of known volume. Their job was to use these to obtain (mentally) an exact quantity of water from a well. In one problem, for example, the subjects had three containers—*A, B,* and *C*—which held 21, 127, and 3 quarts respectively. Their task was to use these three jars to obtain exactly 100 quarts. After a while, they hit upon the correct method. This was to fill jar *B* (127 quarts) completely, and then pour out enough water to fill jar *A* (21 quarts). After this, they would pour out more water from jar *B* to fill jar *C* (3 quarts), empty jar *C* and fill it again from jar *B*. The remaining water in jar *B* was the desired quantity, 100 quarts (Figure 9.15).

On the next few problems, the numerical values differed (Table 9.1). But

Table 9.1   THE THREE-CONTAINER PROBLEM

Desired quantity of water (quarts)	Volume of empty jar (quarts)		
	A	*B*	*C*
99	14	163	25
5	18	43	10
21	9	42	6
31	20	59	4

in all cases, the solution could be obtained by the same sequence of arithmetical steps, that is, Jar *B* − Jar *A* − 2 Jar *C*. Thus, $163 - 14 - 2 \times 25 = 99$; $43 - 18 - 2 \times 10 = 5$; and so on.

After five such problems, the subjects were given two critical tests. The first was a problem that required them to obtain 20 quarts, given jars whose volumes were 23, 49, and 3 quarts. Now most of the subjects showed the mechanization effect. They dutifully performed the laborious arithmetical labors they had used before, computing $49 - 23 - 2 \times 3 = 20$. They did so, even though there was a simpler method that takes only one step (Figure 9.16).

Subsequent to this was a second critical problem. The subjects were now asked to obtain 25 quarts, given jars of 28, 76, and 3 quarts. Note that here the only method that will work is the direct one; that is, $28 - 3 = 25$ (Figure 9.17). But the mechanization induced by the set was so powerful that many subjects failed to solve the problem altogether. They tried the old procedure which is inappropriate ($76 - 28 - 2 \times 3$ does not equal 25) and could not hit on an adequate alternative. The set had made them so rigid that they were blind (Luchins, 1942).

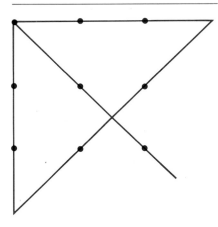

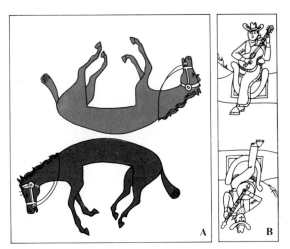

9.19 Horse-and-rider problem *The task is to place (B) on (A) in such a way that the riders are properly astride the horse. (After Scheerer, 1963; for solution, see Figure 9.22)*

9.18 The solution of the nine-dot problem *The problem (Figure 9.8) is solved by going outside of the square frame into which the dots are perceptually grouped. The line has to be extended beyond the dots as shown. Most subjects fail to hit on this solution because of a perceptual set imposed by the square arrangement. (After Scheerer, 1963)*

A

B

Similar effects have been demonstrated in other problem situations. In many of these there is no need to induce the misleading set by instructions or by prior practice, for it is usually engendered by the perceptual arrangement of the problem situation. Examples are the nine-dot problem (Figure 9.18) and the horse-and-rider problem (Figure 9.19).

SET AND MOTIVATION

In fairy tales, the hero is sometimes required to solve a riddle or suffer death and, being a fairy-tale hero, he invariably succeeds. In real life, he would have a harder time, for problem solution, unfairly enough, becomes more difficult when the need for it is especially great. The reason stems from the relation between set and motivation. The greater the motivation toward solution, the stronger are the sets with which the problem is approached. If these sets happen to be appropriate, well and good. But if they are inappropriate, increased motivation will be a hindrance, for these sets will be that much harder to break. Since difficult problems—almost by definition—are problems which tend to engender the wrong set, their solution will be impeded as motivation becomes intense.

Evidence for these assertions comes from several experiments which show that flexibility goes down when motivation becomes intense enough. In one such study, the subjects were posed a practical problem. The problem was to mount two candles on a wall, given only the candles, a box of matches, and some thumbtacks (Figure 9.20). The solution is to empty one of the boxes, tack it to the wall, and then place the candles upon it. The difficulty is caused by *functional fixedness.* This is a set to think of objects in terms of their normal function: a box is to put things in and not on top of. The tendency to maintain this set (that is, functional fixedness) was enhanced by motivation. Subjects who expected no particular reward solved the problem more quickly than subjects who were told that they might win a $20 reward (Glucksberg, 1962).

9.20 Functional fixedness *(A) The problem is to mount two candles on the wall, given the objects shown. (B) To solve the problem, one has to think of a new function for the box. (After Glucksberg, 1962; photograph by Ed Boswell)*

Similar results have been obtained with animals. The simplest example is **detour problems** in which animals are required to take a roundabout path to a goal. Köhler and others have observed that such problems are especially difficult when the lure is very attractive. Consider a dog who is trying to get to a crisply fried piece of sausage on the other side of a fence. To reach the goal he must first turn his back upon it and take as many steps as will bring him around the fence; this is more than dog can bear.

A more formal experimental study on chimpanzees makes a similar point. The apes were confronted by various insight problems of the kind used by Köhler, such as string-pulling, stick-using, and the like (see Chapter 5). The lure was food, and the animals were tested after different periods of fasting. Their probability of success was greatest when the motivation was moderate (Birch, 1945). In small doses, motivation helps. A sated chimpanzee will not expend his intellectual efforts to gain more bananas, but after an hour of abstinence he eagerly engages in the task. But like humans, chimpanzees can get too eager. If starved for a full day, they become frantic and inflexible. They cannot turn away (detour) from the solution they initially hit on even if it doesn't work. If their first attempts lead to failure, they either persist with increasing frenzy or scream in impotent rage. It seems clear that overmotivated chimpanzees are unlikely to get bananas.

RESTRUCTURING

The solution of a difficult problem often involves a dramatic shift in the way in which the problem is viewed. This shift may be very sudden and is then experienced as a flash of insight, a sense of "aha" that occurs when the misleading set is finally broken. Restructuring is especially clear in problems which impose a false perceptual set. To solve the nine-dot problem, the subject has to move out of the square frame imposed by the dots (see Figure 9.18). In a similar vein, the match problem requires working in three dimensions rather than two (Figure 9.21), while the horse-and-rider problem can only be solved by a 90-degree rotation of the drawing which recombines the fore- and hindquarters of the misshapen horses to form two new animals entirely (Figure 9.22).

Gestalt psychologists have proposed that this kind of perceptual restructuring lies at the heart of most problem solving in both animals and humans and they have regarded such effects as a powerful argument against an S-R approach to learning (see Chapter 5). So far, little is known about the mechanisms that underlie the restructuring effect, but there can be little doubt that it is a central phenomenon in the psychology of thinking.

CREATIVE THINKING

The creative thinker is one who generates a problem solution that is both new and appropriate. At the top of the pyramid are such giants as Archimedes, Descartes, and Newton, whose creations define whole chapters of intellectual

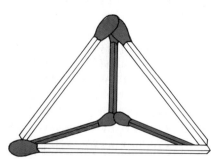

9.21 Solution of the matchstick problem *To arrange six matches (see Figure 9.7) into four equilateral triangles, the matches have to be assembled into a three-dimensional pyramid. Most subjects implicitly assume the matches must lie flat. (After Scheerer, 1963)*

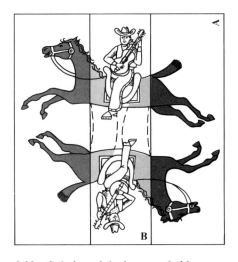

9.22 Solution of the horse-and-rider problem *To solve the horse-and-rider puzzle (see Figure 9.19) requires a change of perceptual set. (A) must be rotated 90 degrees so that the two old nags are in the vertical position. One can now see that the head of each (vertical) can join (horizontally) with the hindquarters of the other. The final step is to slide (B) over the middle of (A) and the problem is solved. (After Scheerer, 1963)*

history. On another level are the anonymous copywriters who develop new advertising slogans for spray deodorants. But whether great or humble, these real-life achievements are quite similar to those of the problem solver in the psychological laboratory. They represent a conceptual reorganization of what was there before.

Some suggestions on how creative solutions arise come from the letters and biographies of various artists and scientists. Almost all refer to unanticipated, sudden illuminations which seem almost to originate from the outside. To Goethe, the German poet, they were like "foreign guests." Gauss, writing of mathematical creation, makes the same point: "Finally, two days ago, I succeeded, not on account of my painful efforts, but by the Grace of God. Like a sudden flash of lightning, the riddle was solved" (Koestler, 1964, p. 117). A similar point was made by Mozart about the origin of his ideas. "*Whence* and *how* they come, I know not; nor can I force them" (Vernon, 1970, p. 53). Under the circumstances, one can understand why such insights were once regarded as divine (or sometimes demonic) inspirations.

According to the creators' own accounts, the critical insights typically occur at unexpected times and places. There is usually a period of intense preparation during which the thinker is totally immersed in the problem and approaches it from all possible angles. But illumination tends not to come then. Quite the contrary. After the initial onslaught fails, there is usually a period of retreat during which the problem is temporarily shelved. Rest or some other activity intervenes, and then suddenly the solution arrives, not at the writer's desk or the composer's piano, but elsewhere entirely—while walking in the woods (Helmholtz), or riding in a carriage (Beethoven, Darwin), or stepping onto a bus (the great mathematician Poincaré), or, in the most celebrated case of all, while sitting in a bathtub (Archimedes; Figure 9.23).

Such effects have sometimes been attributed to a process of **incubation** (Wallas, 1926). According to this view, a thinker does not ignore the unsolved problem altogether when she turns away from it in baffled frustration; she continues to work on it, but does so unconsciously. This hypothesis adds little to our understanding, for it merely substitutes one mystery for another. Unless we know the why and wherefore of unconscious thought (whatever that may be), we know no more than we did before. A possible answer relates to mental set. To find the solution, the problem solver must shake off one or more false sets. These become ever more constricting the longer she stays at the task, all the more so since her motivation is very intense. Leaving the problem for a while may very well break the set which is less likely to be reinstated when the retrieval cues have been drastically altered, as in the woods or in the bathtub. Once the false set is dropped, the true solution has a chance to emerge. It may then appear to be quite obvious, a characteristic reaction whenever a set is broken. In the words of one writer, "The more original a discovery the more

9.23 Archimedes in his bathtub *A sixteenth-century engraving celebrating a great example of creative restructuring. The Greek scientist Archimedes tried to determine whether the king's crown was made of solid gold or had been adulterated with silver. Archimedes knew the weight of gold and silver per unit volume but did not know how to measure the volume of a complicated object such as a crown. One day, in his bath, he noticed how the water level rose as he immersed his body. Here was the solution: the crown's volume is determined by the water it displaces. Carried away by his sudden insight, he jumped out of his bath and ran naked through the streets of Syracuse, shouting "Eureka! I have found it!" (Engraving by Walter H. Ryff, courtesy Burndy Library)*

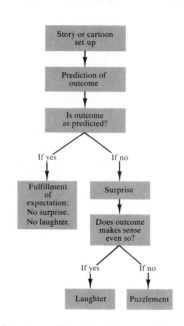

Story or cartoon set up

↓

Prediction of outcome

↓

Is outcome as predicted?

If yes → Fulfillment of expectation: No surprise. No laughter.

If no → Surprise

↓

Does outcome makes sense even so?

If yes → Laughter

If no → Puzzlement

9.24   A cognitive analysis of the appreciation of humor   *The joke or cartoon sets up an expectation. The experience of humor will arise (1) if this expectation is not fulfilled and (2) if the outcome nevertheless makes sense. (After Suls, 1972)*

obvious it seems afterwards. The creative act is not an act of creation in the sense of the Old Testament. It does not create something out of nothing: it uncovers, selects, re-shuffles, combines, synthesizes already existing facts, ideas, faculties, skills. The more familiar the parts, the more striking the new whole" (from Koestler, 1964, p. 120).

RESTRUCTURING AND HUMOR

At least on the face of it, there is a certain similarity between insightful problem solution and humor. A joke does not strike us as funny unless we "get the point." (The "shaggy dog" story is a special case. Its point is that, contrary to our expectation, there is no point.) Conversely, insights often have a comic aspect, especially when one recognizes how absurdly simple the solution actually is.

Several writers suggest that the essential similarity lies in the fact that both insight and humor involve a dramatic shift from one cognitive organization to another (Figure 9.24). The joke-teller creates one expectation during the early stage of the narrative and then betrays it when he comes to the punch line. There is surprise followed by the realization that the unexpected ending does make sense after all. Consider an example from an attempt to treat humor in information-processing terms: "One prostitute says to another, 'Can you lend me ten dollars until I get back on my back?'" (from Suls, 1972, p. 83). The listener presumably expects the ending ". . . until I get back on my feet." The actual ending is quite different, but it does make sense even so. Humor can only occur if there is a viable cognitive alternative into which the unexpected ending fits. If the prostitute had asked for a loan until she got back on her ears, there would be no joke at all, but only bewilderment.

Surprise and reinterpretation are probably not the only cognitive factors required for humor to occur. Another ingredient is the comparison of the two cognitive structures that are juxtaposed. The critical element can be seen in *both* contexts: "on my back" means out of work in one reading, and enjoying the economic benefits of full employment in the other. This simultaneous membership of an item in two radically different cognitive contexts seems to be a crucial aspect of humor. Thus, one of Oscar Wilde's dowagers, on interviewing a potential son-in-law, asks,

LADY BRACKNELL: . . . Now to minor matters. Are your parents living?
JACK: I have lost both my parents.
LADY BRACKNELL: Both? . . . That seems like carelessness.
(Wilde, *The Importance of Being Earnest,* Act 1)

The humor derives from the sudden jolt caused by the second meaning of "lost" which is then contrasted with the first.

While cognitive restructuring is an important and perhaps a necessary condition for the production of humor, it is clearly not a sufficient one. A whole variety of emotional and motivational factors are also involved. Thus humor can serve as a relatively harmless outlet for aggressive or sexual wishes that can't be indulged directly, as in sarcastic wit and "dirty jokes." A further condition is that the new and unexpected meaning (the point of the joke) has to be emotionally acceptable to the listener. Jokes about Hitler's extermination camps are not funny to anyone. This point holds even for the so-called "sick joke." We can (barely) accept, "Yes, yes, Mrs. Lincoln, but how did you like the play?" because 1866 is over a hundred years in the past. An equivalent line about Mrs. John F. Kennedy would be unspeakable.

Cognitive Development: The Views of Jean Piaget

Our discussion of set and restructuring has taken us away from the main theme of this chapter—the hierarchical organization of both thought and action, and the role which chunking plays in making us more proficient at both. As we saw, masters and novices differ in the kind of conceptual units they bring to their tasks. They chunk at different levels: masters type by words rather than by letters, see chess positions as constellations rather than as individual pieces, and play whole musical phrases rather than separate notes. As a result, there is a qualitative difference in the way masters and apprentices ply their trades. The chess champion doesn't merely play a better game than the beginner. He plays a different game.

A similar theme may apply to *cognitive development,* the intellectual growth that accompanies the progress from infancy to adulthood. Few of us develop into expert typists, all-star athletes, or chess champions. But the qualitative differences that accompany the attainment of mastery in these and other fields may provide a useful analogy for the cognitive development that we all do undergo as we grow up. For compared to the child, all adults are masters. Adults live in a world that contains real objects which exist independently of the observer, a world that is ordered in terms of such basic conceptual categories as space, time, number, and causality, and a world which can be conceived abstractly. These conceptual categories are the basic foundations upon which all further intellectual activity rests—they are so basic, indeed, that we have come to take them for granted. We do not congratulate ourselves on the fact that we have well-organized categories of space, time, number, and so on. We hardly even notice that we have them, but these are the categories that make us masters at the trade we are all engaged in—understanding the world.

According to many investigators, these same conceptual categories are far from self-evident in childhood. Children may not think about space and time and causality the way we do as adults, and for this reason cannot figure out many problems whose solution we find self-evident in later life. Thus the conceptual basics may well be analogous to the hierarchical chunkings that make for expertise at such skills as sending telegrams and seeing chess moves. To the extent that the child lacks these basics, its mind may be as qualitatively different from the adult's as the master's performance is from that of the novice.

We will organize our discussion of the child's mental growth around the views of the most influential figure in the field, the Swiss psychologist Jean Piaget (1896–1980).

Jean Piaget *(Photograph by Yves De-Braine, Black Star)*

STAGES OF MENTAL DEVELOPMENT

The hypothesis that mental growth involves major qualitative changes is relatively recent. According to the early empiricists, the child's mental machinery is fundamentally the same as the adult's, the only difference being that the child has fewer associations. Nativists like Kant also minimized the distinction between the child's mind and the adult's, for they viewed the basic categories of time, space, number, and causality as given *a priori,* as part of the native equipment which all humans have at birth. Thus both empiricists and nativists regarded the child as much like an adult; the first saw him as an adult-in-training, the second as an adult-in-miniature. In contrast, Piaget and other developmental psychologists usually look for qualitative differences and try to chart the orderly progression of human intellect as the child grows into an adult.

Piaget regarded intellectual development somewhat the way an embryologist thinks of the development of anatomical structures. Embryological development goes through various stages which are qualitatively different from each other. The human embryo doesn't just get larger between, say, two and seven months; its whole structure changes drastically. Piaget argued that mental development is characterized by similar qualitative changes. In his view, intellectual growth involves the gradual emancipation from the here and now of the immediate, concrete present to a conception of the world in symbolic and abstract terms. As he saw it, this progression proceeds by distinct stages that are manifested during different periods. In crude outline, Piaget's four main periods are as follows. (The age ranges are very approximate and successive stages are often thought to overlap and blend into each other.)

The first major epoch of cognitive development is the period of **sensory-motor intelligence** (0 to about 2 years), during which children achieve the conception of a stable, physical world which they gradually come to distinguish from their own sensory impressions and motor manipulations. The second is the **preoperational** stage (2 to 7 years), during which the child can think of objects and events in their absence but does not as yet possess a system of rules by which it can manipulate its ideas about them. Such a system of rules is found during the next stage, the period of **concrete operations** (7 to 11 years), but this system is still relatively primitive and overly bound to concrete reality. Genuine symbolic and abstract modes of thought are finally attained during the period of **formal operations** (from 11 years on) when reasoning and conceptual judgment are qualitatively no different from those found in adults.

SENSORY-MOTOR INTELLIGENCE

A favorite topic in philosophical discussion is the doctrine of **solipsism** which asserts that the only real object in the universe is oneself, all others being figments of one's own imagination. If Piaget's interpretation is correct, the very young infant goes beyond even the wildest solipsist, for in the infant's world there are neither real objects nor any conception of a self. According to Piaget, there is nothing at first but a succession of transient, unconnected sensory impressions and motor reactions, for mental life during the first few months on earth contains neither past nor future, no distinction between stable objects and fleeting events, and no differentiation between the *me* and the *not me*. The critical achievement of the first two years is the development of these distinctions through which the infant becomes progressively emancipated from his supersolipsism. At the end of this period, the child has attained the notion of **object permanence,** the awareness that objects exist independent of his own sensory experiences and motor manipulations and that they endure even when he neither sees them nor moves them around (see Chapter 7). More generally, the young child has become capable of **representations:** he can "re-present" objects or events to himself in their absence rather than merely reacting to their immediately given, sensory here and now. He has, however primitively, begun to "think" as adults do.

We will consider two aspects of the sensory-motor period—the development of broadly organized action patterns and the beginnings of representational thought.

SENSORY-MOTOR SCHEMAS

The coordination of directed action   The newborn starts life with a rather limited repertoire of built-in reactions such as gross bodily movements in response to distress, sucking and swallowing reflexes, and after a few days such orienting responses as head and eye movements. These recurrent action patterns are the first mental elements—or in Piaget's phrase, *schemas*—in terms of which infants organize the world that impinges upon them. At first, these various schemas operate in isolation. A one-month-old infant can grasp a rattle and can also suck it or look at it. But she will perform these actions only if the stimulus object is directly applied to the relevant sensory surface. She will suck the rattle if it touches her mouth and will grasp the rattle if it is pressed into her palm. But she is as yet unable to grasp whatever she is sucking or to look at whatever she is grasping. The coordination of all of these patterns is not complete until about five months of age. By then, looking, reaching, grasping, sucking have all merged into one unified exploratory schema (Piaget, 1952).

The coordination between the two hands is achieved even later. In some recent studies, various attractive objects were presented to infants sitting in a high chair. If the toy was placed on the right side of an imaginary midline, the children reached for it with their right hand; if it was presented on the left, they reached with the left hand. But for quite a while the two hands seemed unable to work in harmony. Suppose a five-month old is already grasping a toy in his left hand and another toy is then presented on the same side. One might expect the right hand would come to the rescue by reaching over the midline, but this does not happen. The left hand stays clenched around its treasure and ineffectively bangs away at the new toy that it cannot grasp. All this while the right hand remains unoccupied. According to one author, infants have to be at least seven months before their right hand knows what their left is doing (Bruner, 1969).

Imitation   As adults, we tend to consider imitation as a mental activity of a lower order and have little regard for those who merely ape what others do. Compared to creative invention, imitation is indeed of baser coin. But upon reflection, it represents no mean intellectual achievement, especially on its first appearance in infancy. To imitate, a child must grasp the relation between its own movements and those produced by others. This expansion of sensory-motor schemas does not come to full flower until the child is about nine months old. The resulting growth in the capacity for imitation is a vital

Playing pat-a-cake *Imitating an adult playing pat-a-cake is easy because the infant can see its own hands do just what the parent's hands do. (Photograph by Suzanne Szasz)*

prerequisite for many further aspects of intellectual development including the acquisition of language (see Chapter 10) and the adoption of various social roles (see Chapter 13).

During the first few months infants are only capable of ***pseudoimitation.*** If the mother does something the baby has just done a moment before (such as saying "ba-ba") it is likely to resume this activity. This phenomenon probably represents an extension of a ***circular reaction.*** Such reaction patterns are a pervasive feature of early infancy—the child scratches at an object and then gropes at it, scratches and gropes again, repeating the sequence over and over. Similarly for babbling, reaching, and so on. The sensory feedback from each behavior sequence seems to prime its own immediate recurrence. In pseudo-imitation, the cycle is reactivated from the outside: The infant treats the mother's "ba-ba" as if it were a "ba-ba" of his own.

With increasing age, imitation becomes more genuine. From about four months on, infants can imitate actions that they did not perform themselves just moments previously. But they can only do so if their parent's action leads to sights or sounds that are similar to those the infants encounter when they perform that action themselves. Examples are squeezing a pillow or hitting a toy. What the infant sees when she watches her parent's hands is very similar to what she sees when her own hands go through the same motions. The problem becomes much more difficult when imitation requires movements that are invisible to the imitator. Consider a child who tries to imitate someone sticking out the tongue. Not being a frog, the child cannot see her own tongue. Under the circumstances, she can only copy her elders if she has some rather well-developed notions of the what and how of her own facial anatomy, and of the correspondence of her own anatomy to the anatomy of others. By eight or nine months of age the infant's sensory-motor schemas are sufficiently well organized to allow imitations of this kind.* But even then, the schemas are still quite crude. When Piaget tried to get his eleven-month-old daughter to imitate him as he alternately opened and closed his eyes, she did indeed imitate the action of closing and opening, but not of the eyes: "When I opened and closed my eyes, she first opened and closed her hands, very slowly and systematically. Then, equally slowly, she opened and closed her mouth, saying *tata*" (Piaget, 1951, p. 39).

Imitation may be difficult even in adulthood. To be sure, adults have no trouble copying simple movements like sticking out the tongue or closing the eyes. But when they try to imitate a more complex movement pattern like a dance step or a golf swing, their initial attempts are only crude approximations—reminiscent of the fumbling efforts of Piaget's daughter who understood that something had to be opened and closed but didn't know what. Successful imitation requires a well-developed comprehension of what the model is doing, together with a schema that allows the translation of a desired perceptual outcome into motor patterns that bring it about. Consider a woman who knows very little about ballet and watches a ballerina dance. This untutored observer will not "see" what an expert does, even though they are both watching the same performance. Until she can see what the expert sees,

---

* A recent study shows that some modicum of facial imitation (including tongue protrusion) is found in infants as young as two weeks of age. Whether this is imitation in Piaget's sense or some primitive precursor is unknown (Meltzoff and Moore, 1977).

she cannot possibly imitate the ballerina's pirouettes, even if her muscles are every bit as strong and supple. Were it otherwise, we could all become dancers, actors, or bullfighters just by watching the experts perform.

In short, imitation is an active process that requires the development of increasingly differentiated sensory-motor schemas, a process that starts in early infancy but continues into adulthood. Imitation is only easy when the appropriate schemas are already formed. Like all mental activities it requires little further effort once the relevant mental chunks are there.

REPRESENTATIONAL THOUGHT

The end of the sensory-motor period (about 18 to 24 months) marks a momentous change in intellectual development. Children begin to conceive of objects and events that are not immediately present by representing (that is, "re-presenting") some prior experience with these to themselves. Such representations may be internalized actions, images, or words; in all cases they function as symbols which stand for whatever they may signify but are not equivalent to it. Given the tools of representational thought, the two-year old has taken a gigantic step. A year ago, he could interact with the environment only through direct sensory or motor contact; now he can carry the whole world in his head.

One demonstration of this change is the achievement of object permanence. At eighteen months or so, children actively search for absent toys and are surprised (and sometimes outraged) if they don't find them under the sofa cover where they saw the experimenter hide them; it is reasonable to infer that they have some internal representation of the sought-for object. Even more persuasive are examples of *deferred imitation* in which children imitate actions that occurred in the past, such as a playmate's temper tantrum observed a day before. A related phenomenon is make-believe play which is often based on deferred imitations. The eighteen-month old who holds a telephone conversation with a doll (assuming the doll's voice in an appropriate falsetto) has obviously achieved some internalized representation of her experiences.

What is the origin of symbolic representation? According to Piaget, all intellectual processes are ultimately based on action. In the early stages of the sensory-motor period, this action is overt; toward its end, it becomes increasingly covert and internalized. This position is obviously related to various "motor theories of thought" such as Watson's. But unlike Watson, who maintained that thought *is* motor action, Piaget holds that thought is *descended* from motor activity. An overt action is more and more abbreviated, until it finally becomes covert. This covert fraction of the original response serves as the first form of symbolic representation. Eventually even this is no longer necessary, as the child's internal schemas become ever more abstract. But no matter how abstract the thought processes may become eventually, according to Piaget, their parentage can always be traced to the concrete sensory-motor activities of early childhood.

In support of his views, Piaget cited some observations of his sixteen-month-old daughter. She watched him place a small chain in a half-open matchbox and then quickly managed to insert her finger through the opening to extract the chain. Piaget complicated the problem by replacing the chain in the box which he then closed almost completely, leaving only a small slit that was too narrow to remove the chain. The obvious solution is to open the matchbox further, but is it obvious to a toddler who had never opened or closed any boxes before? Piaget's comments are a good illustration of his position:

> She looks at the slit with great attention; then, several times in succession, she opens and shuts her mouth, at first slightly, then wider and wider! Apparently Lucienne understands the existence of a cavity . . . and wishes to enlarge it. The attempt at representation which she thus furnishes is expressed plastically; that is to say, due to [her] inability to think out the situation in words or clear visual images she uses a simple motor indicator as "signifier" or symbol. . . . Lucienne, by opening her mouth thus expresses, or even reflects, her desire to enlarge the opening of the box. . . . Soon after this phase of plastic reflection, Lucienne unhesitatingly puts her finger in the slit and, instead of trying as before to reach the chain, she pulls so as to enlarge the opening. She succeeds and grasps the chain (Piaget, 1952, p. 338).

Up to now we have hardly mentioned language, the primary mode of symbolic function in humans. Where does language come in? Many psychologists maintain that symbolic thought is impossible without language; others believe that language is merely a vehicle in which thought is conveyed (see Chapter 10). For the time being, we only note that language begins to emerge at just about the point that marks the beginning of representational thought, that is, the later half of the second year. Which is cause and which effect? According to Piaget, the ability to form representations precedes linguistic expression and is a prerequisite for it. At sixteen months, Lucienne did not yet know such words as *open* so that her only recourse was to symbolize the situation by some private motor token; in her case, by opening her mouth.

THE PREOPERATIONAL PERIOD

The world of the two-year old contains stable objects and events that can be represented internally, but it still is a far cry from the world of adults. The child has overcome the initial chaos of separate sensations and motor impressions, but only to exchange it for a chaos of ideas (that is, representations) which he is as yet unable to relate in any coherent way. The achievement of the next five years is the emergence of a well-organized world of ideas, a conceptual world that is as ordered and coherent as the concrete world of objects had been since the age of two. According to Piaget, such a conceptual system of thought can only be constructed by means of higher order schemas he calls **operations,** which allow the internal manipulation of ideas according to a stable set of rules. Genuine operations begin to emerge at about seven or so, hence the term *preoperational* for the period from two to seven.

CONSERVATION

Conservation of quantity and number   A revealing example of preoperational thought is the young child's failure to **conserve quantity.** One of Piaget's experimental procedures uses two identical glasses, *G*-1 and *G*-2, which stand side by side and are filled with the same amount of a colored liquid such as orangeade. A child is asked whether there is more orangeade in the one glass

A

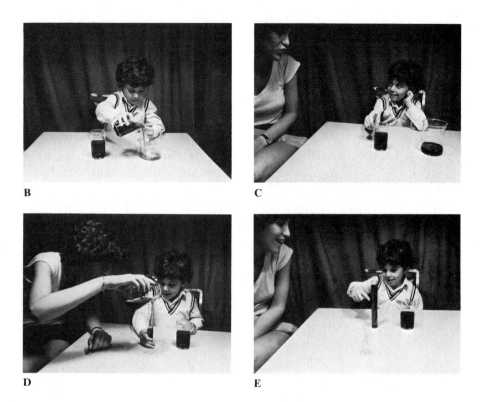

B

C

D

E

9.25 Conservation of liquid quantity
(A) Bobby, aged five years and one month, is asked by the experimenter, "Do we both have the same amount of juice to drink?" Bobby says: "Yep." (B) Bobby pours his juice into a large beaker. (C) When asked, "Do I have as much to drink as you?" Bobby answers, "You have more." (D) The experimenter pours the juice from the beaker into a new, thin glass. (E) Bobby is now asked, "Now do we both have the same amount of juice to drink or does one of us have more?" Bobby answers, "You have more." (Photographs by Ed Boswell)

or in the other and the experimenter obligingly adds a drop here and pours off a drop there until his subject is completely satisfied that there is "the same to drink in this glass as in that." Four-year-olds can easily make this judgment. The next step involves a new glass, *G*-3, which is much taller but also much narrower than *G*-1 and *G*-2 (Figure 9.25). While the child is watching, the experimenter pours the entire contents of *G*-1 into *G*-3. He now points to *G*-2 and *G*-3 and asks, "Is there more orangeade in this glass or in that?" For an adult the question is almost too simple to merit an answer. The amounts are obviously identical since *G*-1 was completely emptied into *G*-3, and *G*-1 and *G*-2 were set to equality at the outset. But four- or five-year olds don't see this. They insist that there is more orangeade in *G*-3. When asked for their reasons, they explain that the liquid comes to a much higher level in *G*-3. They seem to think that the orangeade has somehow increased in quantity as it was transferred from one glass to another. They are too impressed by the visible changes in appearance that accompany each transfer (the changing liquid levels) and do not yet realize that there is an underlying reality (the quantity of liquid) that remains constant throughout.

By the time children are about seven, they respond much like adults. They hardly look at the two glasses, for their judgment needs little empirical support: "It's the same. It seems as if there's less because it's wider, but it's the same." The experimenter may continue with further glasses of different sizes and shapes, but the judgment remains what it was: "It's still the same because it always comes from the same glass." To justify their answer, the children point to the fact that one can always pour the liquid back into the original glass (*G*-1) and thus obtain the same levels. They have obviously understood the basic principle, that the various transformations in the liquid's appearance are **reversible.** For every transformation that changes the way the liquid looks, there is another which restores its original appearance. Given this insight, children at this age recognize that there is an underlying attribute of reality, the quantity of liquid that remains constant (is conserved) throughout the various perceptual changes.

Comparable results are obtained with malleable solids like clay or plasticene. The child is first shown two equal balls of plasticene, one of which is then rolled into a long sausage (Figure 9.26). Until about seven, the children deny that there is the same amount of plasticene in both ball and sausage. Some say that the sausage contains more because it is longer, others insist that it contains less because it is thinner.

Similar results are obtained for **conservation of number.** The child is first shown a row of six evenly spaced bottles, each of which has a glass standing next to it. The child agrees that there are as many bottles as there are glasses. The experimenter now rearranges the six glasses by setting them out into a much longer row while leaving the six bottles unchanged (Figure 9.27). Six or seven years is again the turning point. Up to that age, children generally assert that there are more glasses (or disks, checkers, or whatever) because "they're more spread out." From about seven on, there is conservation; the child has no doubt that there is just as much plasticene in the ball as in the sausage, and that there are just as many bottles in the tightly spaced row as there are glasses in the spread-out line. As with the liquid problem, the older child's explanation emphasizes reversibility—the plasticene sausage can be remolded into a ball, and the long line of glasses can be reassembled into a compact row.

Attending to several factors simultaneously   Why are preschool children unable to appreciate that the amount of a substance remains unaffected by changes of shape or that the number of objects in a given set does not vary with changes in spatial arrangement? According to Piaget, the problem is the child's inability to attend to all of the relevant dimensions simultaneously.

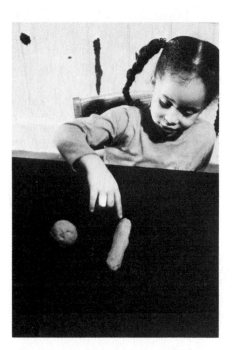

9.26   Conservation of mass quantity
Jennifer, aged four years and four months, is shown two clay balls which she adjusts until she is satisfied that there is the same amount of clay in both. The experimenter takes one of the balls and rolls it into a "hot dog." When now asked which is more, Jennifer points to the hot dog. (Photograph by Ed Boswell)

A   B

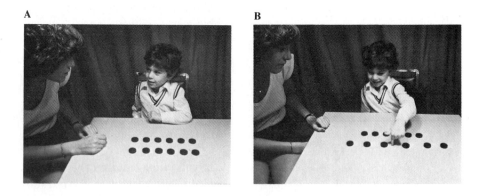

9.27   Conservation of number   *(A) The experimenter points to two rows of "cookies," one hers, the other Bobby's. She asks, "Do I have as many cookies as you?" Bobby says, "Yes." (B) One row of "cookies" is spread out and the experimenter asks, "Now do we still have the same?" Bobby says no and points to the row he says has more. (Photographs by Ed Boswell)*

Consider conservation of liquid quantity. To conserve, the children must comprehend that there are two relevant factors: the height of the liquid column and the width. Initially, they center their attention only on the height and do not realize that the change in height is compensated for by a corresponding change in width. Later on, say at five, they may well attend to width on one occasion and to height on another (with corresponding changes in judgment), but they cannot attend to both dimensions at the same time. To attend to both dimensions concurrently and relate them properly requires a higher order schema which reorganizes initially discrete perceptual experiences into one conceptual unit, a process which may well be akin to chunking.

In Piaget's view, this reorganization occurs when the child focuses on the transformations from one experience into another, rather than on the individual experiences by themselves. The child sees that these transformations are effected by various reversible overt actions, such as pouring the contents of one glass into another. The overt action eventually becomes internalized as a reversible operation so that the child can mentally pour the liquid back and forth or remold the plasticene. The result is conservation of quantity (Piaget, 1952).

In summary, the preoperational child is the prisoner of its own immediate perceptual experience and tends to take appearance for reality. When a seven-year old watches a magician, she can easily distinguish between her perception and her knowledge: she *perceives* that the rabbits come out of the hat, but *knows* that they couldn't possibly do so. Her four-year old brother has no such sophistication. He is delighted to see rabbits anytime and anywhere, and if they want to come out of a hat, why shouldn't they do so?

EGOCENTRISM

Points of view The inability of preoperational children to consider two physical dimensions simultaneously has a counterpart in their approach to the social world. They cannot understand another person's point of view for they are as yet unable to recognize that different points of view exist. This characteristic of preoperational thought is often called **egocentrism.** As Piaget uses this term it does not imply "selfishness." It is not that children seek to benefit at the expense of others; it is rather that they haven't fully grasped that there are other selves.

An interesting demonstration of egocentrism involves a literal interpretation of "point of view" (Piaget and Inhelder, 1956). If two adults stand at opposite corners of a building, each of them knows that the other sees a different wall. Preoperational children don't really understand this. In one study, children were shown a three-dimensional model of a mountain scene. While the children viewed the scene from one position, a teddy bear was placed at various other locations around the model. The child's job was to decide what the bear saw from *its* vantage point (Figure 9.28). To answer, the child had to choose one of several drawings which depicted different views of the mountain scene. Up to four years of age, the children didn't even understand the question. From four to seven their response was fairly consistent: they chose the drawing that showed what they saw, regardless of where the bear was placed.

9.28 The three-mountain test of egocentrism *The child is asked to indicate what the teddy bear sees. The results suggest that the child thinks the teddy sees the scene just as he does, including the little house which is of course obstructed from the teddy bear's vantage point. (After Piaget and Inhelder, 1967)*

Moral judgment and intention Yet another manifestation of egocentrism concerns moral judgment. Our adult conceptions of crime and punishment place great emphasis upon the perpetrator's intention, and carefully distinguish between accident and design. But this requires an ability to take account of another person's motives. Young children cannot do this, anymore than they can take account of width in a liquid conservation task while attending to height. In consequence, they consider only the extent of the injury produced by the deed, regardless of motives. In one of Piaget's studies, children had to judge which of two boys was the naughtier. John accidentally tripped, fell against a cupboard, and smashed fifteen cups. In contrast, Frank only broke one cup which he knocked to the floor while climbing the cupboard to steal some forbidden jam. Younger children generally judged John to be the greater villain who should be punished more severely; after all, he had broken fifteen cups! Older children were much more likely to consider intent (Piaget, 1932).

Preoperational conceptions of reality Since preschool children lack the mental operations to abstract the essential differences and uniformities from the welter of their perceptual experience, it is hardly surprising that their conceptions of the world are still quite primitive. Their notions of causality are yet further testimony to their egocentrism. For example, many six-year olds seem to believe that the sun and moon follow them around: "What does the sun do when you are out for a walk?—*It moves.*—How?—*It goes with me.*—Why?—*To make it light, so that you can see clearly*" (Piaget, 1929, p. 216).

As children get older, they try to reconcile some of the contradictions in this account when they are pushed. One of Piaget's eight-year-old subjects was willing to grant that clouds follow other people and even animals, but was sure that they have to follow somebody: "*When we move along, they move along too.*—Can *you* make them move?—*Everybody can, when they walk.*—When I walk and you are still, do they move?—*Yes.* And at night, when everyone is asleep, do they move?—*Yes.*—But you tell me that they move when somebody walks.—*They always move. The cats, when they walk, and then the dogs, they make the clouds move along*" (Piaget, 1930, p. 62).

A related observation points to a pervasive **animism,** a belief that inanimate objects are alive. This mainly holds for things that move—streams, clouds, and bicycles are alive while trees, walls, and tables are not. These objects also have conscious awareness. The sun knows that it shines; the bicycle, that it runs fast or slowly. The objects move because they want to and their motives are centered on the child's own affairs. The moon comes out to show us the road and the sun follows us to "see if we are good."

Such examples suggest that preoperational children have not yet achieved a complete conceptual separation of self and object. Objects exist in their own right, but they are still endowed with many attributes that belong to the perceiver and not to them. A similar misconception concerns the relation between the name of a thing and the thing itself. Preoperational children (and even somewhat older ones) tend to regard the name of an object as if it were one of the object's intrinsic properties. When asked why a pig is called "pig," a six-year old may answer, "Because it is dirty." The sun is called "sun" because it shines, a mountain is named mountain because it is white, and so on. Romeo was well aware that a rose by any other name would smell as sweet, but seven-year olds are not as sure: "Could the Saleve have been called 'Jura' and the Jura 'Saleve'? [Both are names of Swiss mountains.]—*No.*—Why not?—*Because they are not the same thing.*—And could the moon have been called the 'sun' and the sun 'moon'?—*No.*—Why not?—*Because the sun makes it warm and the moon gives light*" (Piaget, 1930, p. 81).

CONCRETE AND FORMAL OPERATIONS

Seven-year olds have acquired mental operations which allow them to abstract some of the essential attributes of reality such as number and substance. But according to Piaget, these operations are primarily applicable to the relations between concrete events (hence the term *concrete operations*). They do not really suffice when these relations must be considered entirely in the abstract. Eight- or nine-year olds can perform various simple manipulations on specific numbers they are given, but they typically fail to understand that certain results will hold for any number whatsoever. They may realize that 4 is an even number and 4 + 1 is odd, and similarly for 6 and 6 + 1, 8 and 8 + 1, and so on, but they are by no means sure that the addition of 1 to any even number must always produce a number that is odd. According to Piaget, the comprehension of such highly abstract and formal relationships requires ***formal operations,*** operations of a higher order which emerge at about eleven or twelve years of age. Given formal operations, the children's thought can embrace the possible as well as the real. They can entertain hypothetical possibilities, can deal with what *might be* no less than what *is.*

An illustration of the role of formal operations comes from a study in which children had to discover what makes a pendulum go fast or slow. They were shown how to construct a pendulum by hanging some object from a string. They were also shown how to vary the length of the string, the weight of the suspended object, and the initial force which set the pendulum in motion. Children between seven and eleven typically varied several factors at a time. They might compare a heavy weight suspended from a long string with a light weight suspended from a short string, and would then conclude that a pendulum swings faster the shorter its length and the lighter its weight. Needless to say, their reasoning was faulty, for the way to determine whether a given factor (e.g., weight) has an effect is to hold all others (e.g., length) constant. Children below eleven cannot do this, for they can only operate upon the concretely given. They are unable to consider potential cause-and-effect relationships which must first be deliberately excluded and then tested for later on. In contrast, older children can plan and execute an appropriate series of tests. Their mental operations proceed on a more formal plane so that they can grasp the notion of "other things being equal" (Inhelder and Piaget, 1958).

A variety of other findings give further evidence of thought processes that have jumped to a higher order of abstraction. Eleven-year olds can play games like Twenty Questions in a manner similar to adults. If they are trying to determine which of a large number of objects the experimenter has in mind, they first ask some very general questions which narrow the range of alternatives such as "Is it alive?" or "Is it a toy?" Such questions lay the groundwork for further questions and thus imply a broad conception of the range of potential answers. Six-year olds never ask groundlaying questions of this sort.

They immediately guess at a specific object with questions like "Is it the dog?" Eight-year olds are somewhat in the middle. They typically begin with a broadly framed question (e.g., "Is it a tool?") but then move straight to the specific guess (e.g., "Is it the hammer?"). Eleven-year olds usually proceed in a hierarchical manner by a progressive restriction of the field of alternatives. They first ask "Is it a tool?" and then "Can you cut things with it?" (Mosher and Hornsby, 1966).

The period of formal operations is the last important milestone in the child's intellectual progression that Piaget and his co-workers have described in some detail. Their account of the developmental steps that led up to this point has been enormously influential and is a major achievement in psychology's attempt to understand human intelligence. But this does not mean that it has gone unchallenged. We will now consider some efforts to look at Piaget's description of human cognitive development with a more critical eye.

Cognitive Development: A Second Look

Modern discussions of Piaget focus on two questions. One concerns the validity of his description of cognitive development. The other centers on his attempts to explain why the child progresses from one stage to the other.

A REEVALUATION OF PIAGET'S DESCRIPTION

As Piaget's account is often understood, many cognitive capacities that mark one period of development are totally absent at prior periods. Thus there should be no conservation of mass or number at five or below, nor any ability to take another person's perspective. These capacities are instead thought to emerge, virtually full-blown, at about seven when the curtain finally opens on the next act of the developmental drama, the period of concrete operations. A number of modern investigators disagree, for they deny that cognitive development is essentially all or none. As these critics see it, various cognitive achievements such as conservation have primitive precursors that predate the traditional Piagetian calendar by several years. For the most part, these critics have focused on the preschooler's abilities, which they feel have been seriously underestimated by Piaget (Gelman, 1978).

REASSESSING PRESCHOOLERS

Egocentrism revisited One area of reevaluation concerns Piaget's concept of egocentrism. According to Piaget, young preschool children are quite unable to appreciate the difference between another person's point of view and their own. But recent studies show that some modicum of this ability is found in children between two and four.

One study used a picture-showing task. Children from one to three years of age were asked to show a photograph to their mother who was seated opposite them. At two and a half and three, all children turned the picture so that it faced the mother. This implies that they have some conception of the differ-

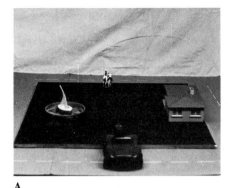

A

B

C

9.29 A simplified test of egocentrism
A recent study suggests that the three-mountain task may overestimate egocentrism in children. Their poor performance may have resulted from the fact that the spatial layout used by Piaget is relatively complicated. When simpler setups were employed, children as young as three and four had little trouble. They were shown various three-dimensional displays, such as (A) and (B), as well as a three-mountain scene (C). Grover, a doll, was shown to drive a toy car around each layout. When he stopped to park his car, the child was asked to turn an identical display on another table until "you are looking at it the same way Grover is." The children did quite well with all displays except (C), the three-mountain scene. This probably caused trouble because the children couldn't distinguish the mountains as readily as the toy objects on the other displays. (Borke, 1975; photographs courtesy of H. Borke)

ence between one person's angle of regard and another's. If they had been totally egocentric, they should have shown their mothers the back of the picture, while continuing to look at its front themselves (Lempers, Flavell, and Flavell, 1977; see also Figure 9.29).

Related findings concern adjustments in speech by young children to the person to whom they are talking. When trying to explain the workings of a toy truck to a two-year old, four-year olds used much shorter and simpler sentences than when talking to their peers. This again shows that the preschooler is not totally egocentric. He can evidently appreciate that a two-year old is a creature with linguistic capacities less developed than his own (Shatz and Gelman, 1973).

A second look at conservation   Another phenomenon whose reexamination suggests that preschoolers are less inept than Piaget supposed is conservation, especially conservation of number. We have previously described the standard Piagetian finding: When preschoolers are asked to compare two rows that contain the same number of, say, toy soldiers, they often say that the longer row contains more soldiers, in an apparent confusion of length and number. But recent studies show that children as young as three can conserve number if the test conditions are suitably arranged.

In one procedure, the children were shown two toy plates, each with a row of toy mice attached to it with velcro. One plate might have two mice, while the other had three. One plate was designated the winner, the other the loser. Each plate was then covered by a can and shuffled around while the children were instructed to keep track of the winner—a small-fry version of the venerable shell game. After each trial, the plates were uncovered and the children received a prize if they could correctly identify the "winner" and "loser." After several such trials, the real test was conducted. The experimenter surreptitiously substituted a new plate for the original winner. In one case, the new plate contained the same number of mice as the original, but the row was made longer or shorter. In the other case, the row length stayed unchanged but a mouse was added or subtracted. The results showed that spatial rearrangement made little difference. But changes in number had dramatic consequences even at three and four years of age. The children were surprised, asked where the missing mouse was and searched for it (Gelman, 1972).

It appears that three- and four-year olds have a better understanding of number than Piaget had suggested. They can evidently distinguish, at least to some extent, between the number of items that comprise a set and the way these items are spatially arranged. As an indignant four-year old put it to the experimenter on confronting a lengthened row of mice on the winner plate (the subject's comments are in italics): *"What you did!* What happened? *Look at that!* What? *Spreaded it out!* I did? *Yep.* Okay, is this the plate that wins a prize? *Yep.* How do you know that plate wins a prize? *Cause it has five"* (Gelman and Gallistel, 1978, p. 168).

Such findings show that the number concepts of later periods are built upon foundations established much earlier. One such foundation is counting. Some initial rudiments of this skill appear as early as two and a half. At this age, children may not yet know the conventional number terms. But they may nevertheless have grasped some aspect of what the counting process is all about. An example is provided by children who employ an idiosyncratic number series. Thus one two-year old consistently used, "one, two, six.": "How many on this [the three-item] plate? *One, two, six!* You want to do that again? *Ya, one, two, six!* Oh! is that how many were on at the beginning of the game? *Ya"* (Gelman and Gallistel, 1978, p. 91).

Other two-year olds had still other private number series. What is important is that they used these series consistently. They realized that each of these number tags has to be applied to each object in the set on a one-to-one basis, that the tags must always be used in the same order, and that the last tag applied is the number of items in the set. At first glance we may be puzzled by the two-year old who looks at three toy animals and triumphantly announces that there are nineteen. But the grounds for his triumph are much clearer when we realize that he operates on the basis of the idiosyncratic series *one, thirteen, nineteen.* In due time he will use more conventional tags. But he has already grasped some of the essential concepts that underlie the counting process (Gelman and Gallistel, 1978).

Phenomena of this kind argue against the notion that cognitive development proceeds by sudden, dramatic leaps. The achievements of the concrete-operational period do not come out of the blue. If we look carefully enough we see that they have preludes in much earlier childhood years. It may well be true that there are stages in intellectual growth that have to be passed in ordered sequence. But there are no neat demarcations between stages and no sharp transitions. The stages of cognitive development are not as all or none as the changes from tadpole to frog (let alone from frog to prince).

REEVALUATING CONCRETE OPERATIONS

Increasing generality of understanding   Does any of this mean that Piaget's cognitive milestones have no psychological reality? Emphatically not. Despite all the precursors of concrete operations at four or even earlier, there is no question that seven- or eight-year olds have something preschoolers lack—the ability to apply their insights to a much wider range of problems (Fodor, 1972). Gelman's three-year olds can tell the difference between two and three mice regardless of how they are spaced on the toy plate. To the extent that they can do this, they have taken the first step toward an understanding of number, but they still have quite a way to go. They are able to count one set and then another (assuming that the numbers are very small) and then compare the two counts to see if they are the same. But they have not fully grasped the idea that number and spatial arrangement are independent and that this is so for all numbers and all spatial rearrangements. Four-year-olds comprehend this only dimly. As a result, they fail the standard Piagetian test for conservation of number in which they have to recognize that two rows of, say, nine buttons contain the same number of buttons regardless of how the rows are expanded or compressed. This task puzzles four-year olds. They find the number of items in each row too large to count, get lost in the count, and become confused. Seven-year-olds have an easier time. They can count higher, but that's not the issue. They know that there is no need to count, that the number of buttons in each row has to be identical, regardless of the way they are arranged. In consequence, they can conserve number in general.

What holds for conservation of number, holds for many other intellectual achievements that are generally associated with the first school years. Most of them have precursors, often at much earlier ages than Piaget might have led us to suppose. But these preschool abilities usually represent isolated pockets of knowledge that can't be applied very widely. The seven- or eight-year old's understanding of physical, numerical, and social reality is considerably more general, so much so, that it seems qualitatively different from what went on before. Consider conservation of liquid quantity. By simplifying the task in various ways, preschoolers can be made to perform much more creditably. But the interesting fact remains that by the time the child is seven or eight, no such simplification is necessary. A seven or eight-year old conserves with barely a glance at the containers in which the liquid is being sloshed around. He doesn't have to look. He *knows* that the liquid quantity is unaffected no matter how the containers are shaped.

Conservation and chunking   Seen from this perspective, the cognitive attainments characteristic of the period of concrete operations (and, later on, of formal operations) are analogous to the higher order chunkings of the master telegrapher, pianist, or chess player. These masters don't have to plod through a message letter by letter, or look at each chess piece individually—as a result, they can take giant steps. The ability to conserve number and quantity confers a similar advantage. The child who can truly conserve sees that there are certain underlying invariant qualities that remain intact despite all sorts of apparent deformations. As a result, she can disregard various superficial differences; she doesn't have to count the items in each row, or worry about the shape of the two jars. Her cognitive task has been simplified, for one concept can now subsume many individual instances. She is on the road to becoming master at the game of understanding reality that all of us must play.

THE CAUSES OF COGNITIVE GROWTH

What produces the changes that characterize cognitive development? Thus far, there is no satisfactory answer. As so often in the field of cognition, the attempts to come up with an adequate explanation fluctuate between the two poles of the nature-nurture controversy.

9.30   Learning, maturation, and walking
*An Indian child strapped into a cradle.
(Courtesy the J. A. Shuck Collection in
the Western History Collections, University of Oklahoma Library)*

THE ROLE OF MATURATION

Many investigators are inclined toward a nativist interpretation. They believe that development is largely based on *maturation,* a pre-programmed growth process based on changes in some underlying neural structures that is relatively independent of environmental conditions. Examples are flying in sparrows and walking in humans. These are behavior patterns that are characteristic of all adult members of the species. They emerge as the organism matures, but their development is relatively unaffected by environmental changes (except those extreme enough to cripple or kill). Human infants start to walk at about fifty weeks of age, but this is a matter of maturation rather than of learning. Practice has little to do with being able to walk. Many American Indians restrict their infants' activity by strapping them to a cradle which the mother carries on her back throughout her daily labors (Figure 9.30). But the onset of sitting, creeping, and walking is not retarded by this practice (Dennis and Dennis, 1940).

A number of authors suspect that mental growth reflects similar maturational processes. In their view, there is something inexorable about cognitive development, especially up to seven or eight (Wohlwill, 1973). This view is buttressed by the fact that at least in broad outline, mental growth seems rather similar in children of different cultures or nationalities. While children of different cultures master intellectual tasks such as conservation at somewhat different ages, they usually pass these landmarks in the same order. Thus Arab, Indian, Somali, and British children show the same progression from nonconservation of quantity to conservation (Hyde, 1959). This is reminiscent of physical maturation. Different butterflies may emerge from their chrysalis at slightly different times, but none is a butterfly first and a chrysalis second. The timing of the transitions may well be affected by environmental conditions (say, temperature), but the order of the stages is predetermined in the genetic code.

THE ROLE OF LEARNING

The simplest alternative to a maturation-centered approach is one that emphasizes learning. But what kind of learning could explain the systematic patterns of cognitive development that Piaget and other investigators have chronicled?

Piaget argued that simple learning theories of the kind espoused by associationists will not do. According to such theories, learning is the acquisition of relatively specific patterns which in principle could be mastered at any age. But this is precisely what Piaget denied. According to Piaget, four-year olds cannot possibly be taught how to use a measuring cup correctly, no matter how attractive the reinforcements or how many trials. They lack the prerequisite concepts of number and quantity (which they cannot attain at the preoperational level) so that any attempt to teach them to measure is as fruitless as trying to build the third story of a house without a second story underneath it. This point of view has obvious relevance to educational policy. If Piaget is right, then there is little point in efforts to teach children this or that aspect of a curriculum before they are "ready" for it; in fact, it may actually do some harm by turning the child against the subject.

In an attempt to test this claim, several investigators have tried to determine whether children can be trained to reach certain cognitive landmarks such as conservation ahead of schedule. The evidence suggests that relatively specific training has little impact. Some investigators have managed to speed up the emergence of conservation by special coaching, but later checks revealed that the children hadn't really understood the underlying principles and quickly reverted to their previous, nonconserving ways (e.g., Smedslund, 1961).

Such considerations suggest that cognitive development is not primarily based on specific learning. This—and the fact that it proceeds in such a near-universal, orderly progression—has often been taken as evidence for the maturation-centered approach. But the point doesn't follow. Just about all children conserve (and proceed beyond egocentrism and so on), but this may not be caused by the fact that they share the same human genetic blueprint. It may instead reflect the fact that they all live in the same world. It doesn't matter whether they dwell in a high-rise apartment or a nomad's tent; in both environments the quantity of a liquid is unchanged by the shape of its container. The principles which eight-year olds understand and which four-year olds do not, concern the basic dimensions of space, time, number, mass, and causality. These principles describe certain invariant properties of the world in which all children live. And as such, they may perhaps be learned.

Can this learning-oriented approach explain why cognitive development occurs in a certain order? It might, by analogy with chunking in the development of skills. The apprentice telegraph operator goes through successive stages of mastery: letters, then letter sequences, then familiar words. This is presumably because each successive chunking level is based on lower levels in the hierarchy. The fact that all apprentice telegraphers go through similar stages suggests two things. First, that all of them were exposed to the same linguistic world in which they could not help but encounter the same letter clusters. (In English, combinations such as *th* and *ly*.) Second, that they all have the same ability to learn by hierarchical chunking.

It may be that the developing child is in the same situation as the apprentice telegrapher. Like the telegrapher, the child is capable of learning by chunking. And like him, the child is faced with a world of complex relations whose mastery probably requires a stage-by-stage progression in which higher order concepts (such as conservation of number) are based on lower order ones (like object permanence). Seen in this light, intellectual growth is largely produced by the acquisition of increasingly efficient techniques for overcoming the limited capacity of the human cognitive system (e.g., Case, 1974; Shatz, 1978). Whether this position will ultimately prevail over the maturation-based conception is as yet an open question.

PIAGET'S ACCOUNT: ASSIMILATION AND ACCOMMODATION

Piaget's own view is that neither maturation nor specific learning can by themselves account for mental development. As he saw it, development involves a constant interchange between the organism and its environment. To be sure, the child can only interpret external events in terms of the mental schemas he has at the time; in Piaget's phrase, the environment is **assimilated** to the schema. But the schemas change as the child continues to interact with the world around him; they **accommodate** to the environment. Without active involvement with the outer world there will be no such accommodation and hence no mental growth.

Piaget's conception of the two opposite processes, assimilation and accommodation, may be a useful way of emphasizing the fact that organism and environment interact in mental growth. But many psychologists doubt that it is a good explanation, for Piaget offered no mechanism whereby schemas are changed through accommodation. Lacking such a mechanism, we do not really understand why children go from one stage of thought into another.

A similar theoretical problem plagues those psychologists who feel that mental development is in principle analogous to the development of skills such as telegraphy and chess. Piaget's account does not really explain why children move from one cognitive stage to another. But cognitive psychologists concerned with learning in adulthood are no less able to explain how higher level chunks are created during the acquisition of a skill. It may be that when we do know how a typist reorganizes his task so that his units are letter clusters and words rather than isolated letters, we will then have a clue as to why a child changes from one stage to another. In both cases, the achievements of the later stage depend upon those of an earlier one. In both cases, there are qualitative changes that seem to depend upon the reorganization of mental structures into higher level units, upon some process akin to chunking. The how and why of this process is one of the major unsolved riddles of the psychology of memory and thinking and—perhaps—of cognitive development as well.

EVALUATING PIAGET'S ACCOUNT

In summary, how do we evaluate Piaget's contribution to our understanding of cognitive processes? He has not provided a viable explanation of cognitive development. (Nor for that matter has anyone else.) What he has done instead is to chronicle this development in a depth and detail no one remotely approached before him. In effect, his contribution is a broad classification of children's intellectual processes at different levels of development. His overall scheme is akin to the taxonomy of a biologist who sees the underlying family resemblance among bears, wolves, and lions, and therefore groups them together under the class of carnivores. In similar fashion, Piaget offers a developmental taxonomy summarized by his various stages. For example, the failure of conservation and the different indexes of egocentrism are all seen as manifestations of an underlying intellectual pattern, the preoperational mode of thought. To the biologist, the several classes, orders, and families of animals are related through evolutionary ancestry. To Piaget, the relation between stages is also developmental: The later intellectual structures grow out of earlier ones, and the general rule of progression is an increasing emancipation from the concrete here and now and a growing development of ever more abstract modes of thought.

Piaget's taxonomy may have to be revised by later investigators. As we have seen, there is some question whether his stages are as neatly distinct as originally thought. Nor is it clear that all the cognitive achievements that he grouped together (for example, failure to conserve and egocentrism) are indexes of the same underlying pattern. But none of this really matters in evaluating Piaget's stature. The first attempt to classify animals put whales together with fish. But this mistake was minor compared to the giant step of undertaking a systematic classification to begin with. In science, description and classification must precede explanation. One can only explain something if one knows what it is one wants to explain.

A Backward Look at Perception, Memory, and Thinking

In looking back over the three broad domains of cognition—perception, memory, and thinking—one is struck by the extent to which they merge into one another. In describing perception, we often cross over the border into memory. For the way we perceive familiar objects—let alone such ambiguous figures as the young woman-old woman picture—is based in part on how we perceived them in the past. But perception also shades into thinking. We look at the moon at the horizon, decide that it must be larger than it first appears since it looks farther off, and promptly perceive it in line with this (presumably unconscious) inference. Nor is it clear where memory leaves off and thinking begins. Much of remembering seems like problem solving. We try to recall to whom we lent a certain book, conclude that it has to be Joe for we know no one else who is interested in the book's topic, and then suddenly have a vivid recollection of the particular occasion on which he borrowed it (and the way he swore that he'd return it right away). But if remembering is sometimes much like thinking, thinking can hardly proceed without reference to the storehouse of generic memory. Whatever we think about—which route to take on a vacation trip, how to fill out a tax form—requires retrieval of items from various memory systems.

All of this shows that there are no exact boundaries between perception, memory, and thinking. These areas are not sharply separated intellectual domains, with neat lines of demarcation between them. They are simply designations for somewhat different aspects of the general process of cognition. We will now turn to the one aspect of cognition that we have thus far discussed only in passing—language and its development. It, too, is intertwined with the other domains of cognition, but unlike perception, memory, and thinking, found in many animals, language is unique to human beings.

Summary

1. A classical issue in the study of thinking concerns the *elements* that make up thought. An early hypothesis held that all thought is necessarily comprised of *mental images,* a view seriously challenged by findings that there is imageless thought. Another approach is exemplified by J. B. Watson's *motor theory of thought* which holds that thinking consists of very small muscle movements, particularly those of *implicit speech.* While there is evidence that thinking is often accompanied by bodily activity, there is little doubt that thinking is not equivalent to motor action and can proceed even during paralysis.

2. Given the failure of both the image theory and the implicit-action theory of thought, virtually all modern psychologists accept the view that the units of thought are best conceived at a more *central* and abstract level than either sensory experiences or motor acts. Attempts to describe this more abstract level include terms such as *concept* and *proposition.*

3. Considered as an activity, thinking is *directed.* In problem solving, all steps are considered as they fit into the overall structure set up by the task. This structure is

typically *hierarchical,* with goals, subordinate subgoals, and so on. This hierarchical structure is not unique to problem solving but may be a general characteristic of any directed activity.

4. Increasing competence at any directed activity goes together with an increase in the degree to which the subcomponents of this activity have become chunked and *automatized.* In learning to send and receive Morse code, as in the attainment of many other skills, learning curves exhibit *plateaus* followed by a later rise, suggesting the acquisition of progressively larger units. Similar chunking seems to occur in many forms of mental activity, including problem solving, and differentiates masters and beginners in many endeavors such as mental calculation, musical composition, and playing chess.

5. An influential approach to problem solving comes from work on *computer simulation* of certain aspects of human thinking. A number of solution strategies have been incorporated into several computer programs, including *algorithms* and *heuristics.* Some recent attempts feature provisions for loosening the computer's single-mindedness, in the hope that a certain imperfection may produce an artificial intelligence more similar to our own.

6. Problem solving is not always successful. One reason may be a strong, interfering *mental set* which makes the subject *rigid,* and which is especially hard to overcome under conditions of intense motivation.

7. The solution of certain problems often involves a radical restructuring in which a misleading set is overcome. Such restructurings may be an important feature of much of *creative thinking.* Accounts by prominent writers, composers, and scientists, suggest that restructuring often occurs after a period of *incubation.* Restructuring may also play a role in *humor,* which often occurs when an unexpected cognitive organization turns out to make sense after all.

8. All humans go through a process of *cognitive development.* According to Jean Piaget, they do so by passing through the same sequence of *developmental stages.*

9. In Piaget's account, the first stage is the period of *sensory-motor intelligence,* and lasts until about two years of age. During this period, the infant develops the concept of *object permanence,* becomes capable of *coordinated sensory-motor schemas,* and acquires increasingly complex mental *representations.*

10. The next period lasts till about five or six. It is the *preoperational period* during which children are capable of representational thought but lack mental operations that order and organize these thoughts. Characteristic deficits include an inability to *conserve* number and quantity, *egocentrism,* a very concrete approach to moral judgment, and preoperational conceptions of reality, including *animism.*

11. At about six, children have begun to acquire a system of mental operations that allows them to manipulate their representations with consequent success in conservation tasks and similar tests. But until they are about eleven, they are still in the period of *concrete operations* which lack an element of abstractness. After eleven, they enter the period of *formal operations.* As a result, they can consider hypothetical possibilities and become capable of scientific thought.

12. Piaget's views on cognitive development have come in for some serious criticisms. Some involve issues of fact. Examples are studies which suggest the pre-schoolers' abilities have been underestimated by Piaget: Their egocentrism is much less than Piaget assumed and they are capable of certain forms of conservation, such as those which pertain to number. Other issues concern the causes of cognitive growth. Is it based on maturation, on learning, or on the interplay between *assimilation* and *accommodation* proposed by Piaget?

CHAPTER 10

Language

By Lila R. Gleitman and Henry Gleitman

When we consider the social forms and physical artifacts of human societies, we are struck by the diversity of cultures in different times and places. Some humans walk on foot, others travel on camels, still others ride rockets to the moon. But in all communities and all times, humans are alike in having oral languages. This essential connection, between *having language* and *being human,* is one reason why those interested in the nature of human minds have always been particularly intrigued with how people learn and use language.

To philosophers such as Descartes, language was that function which most clearly distinguished between beasts and humans, and was "the sole sign and only certain mark of thought hidden and wrapped up in the body." He wrote,

> Now all men, the most stupid and the most foolish, those even who are deprived of the organs of speech, make use of signs, whereas the brutes never do anything of the kind; which may be taken for the true distinction between man and brute (Descartes, 1649; in Eaton, 1927).

Descartes' claim comes up against an immediate objection: There are about 5,500 languages now in use on earth. Obviously, these are different from each other, for the users of one cannot understand the users of another. In what sense, then, can we talk about "language in general" rather than about French or English or Hindi?

The answer is that human languages are at bottom much more alike than they seem at first glance to be. One similarity is in the means that they have for expressing thoughts. For instance, all languages have words, sounds, and sentences. In contrast, animal communications often have something like sounds or words (for instance a cat can make happy purrs and angry meows), but they never have complicated sentences (such as "I'm going to stop purring and start meowing if you don't give me that catnip immediately!").

353

Another similarity is in the thoughts human languages can express. When the United Nations ambassador from France makes a speech at the UN, numerous translators immediately whisper its equivalent in English, Russian, Hebrew, and so on to the listening ambassadors from other countries. The fact that the French speech can readily be translated suggests that, by and large, the same things can be said in English, Russian, and other languages that can be said in French. This is true despite the fact that the Russian or English listeners may disagree with what the Frenchman is saying. The point is that the translation allows them to *know* that they disagree, so they are in a position to stomp out of the room in a rage or make a counterspeech—which will also be translatable. In this chapter, we use English as our main example of a human language. But it is important to realize that what we say about English generally goes for the other human languages as well.

Some Properties of Language

There are five major properties of all human languages that psychology must describe: language is ***creative*** (or ***novel***), it is highly ***structured*** (or ***rule-governed***), it is ***meaningful,*** it is ***referential*** (that is, it refers to and describes things and events in the real world), and it is ***interpersonal*** (involving the thoughts of more than one person at a time).

LANGUAGE USE IS CREATIVE

The early associationist psychologists (as well as modern behavior theorists such as Skinner) believed that language is in principle no different from any other kind of learned task that humans and animals can master. In their view, all such skills are based on networks of associations (see Chapters 4 and 8).

Some of these psychologists emphasized associative connections between sounds and mental images (having a mental picture of a dog, on hearing the word *dog*); others stressed the association between certain stimuli and responses (saying "You're welcome" on hearing "Thanks"). But all were agreed that, details aside, language is merely a complicated habit, a set of acts by ear and mouth that have been acquired by memorization and practice. On this view, the explanation of talking is simple: Each of the memorized speech acts is simply performed whenever the appropriate circumstances arise. Our mothers said "That's a rabbit" when they saw a rabbit. Having observed this, we now say "That's a rabbit" when we see a rabbit.

This general position is hard to maintain, because of the intricacy and variety of speech in everyday life. To see this problem, it is only necessary to realize that, in addition to "That's a rabbit," each of us has also learned how to say and understand

> *"That's a rabbit over there."*
> *"A rabbit is what I see over there."*
> *"Obviously, that is a rabbit."*
> *"How clearly I recall that the word for that animal is* rabbit.*"*
> *"Well, bless my soul, if that isn't a rabbit!"*

And so on, with hundreds of other examples. A little child who has memorized all these sentences must be industrious indeed. And he must also be lucky to have a mother so talkative that she said all these rabbit sentences while the child was around listening. But the situation is really incredibly more complicated than this, for surely we learn to talk about objects and creatures other than rabbits, including aardvarks, Afgans, apples, armies, and proceeding all the way to zyzogetons.

A related point has to do with the sheer number of English sentences. A good estimate of the number of reasonably short (20 words or fewer) English sentences is 10^{30}. Considering the fact that there are only 3×10^9 seconds in a century, a learner memorizing a new one every second would have learned only a minute fraction of them in the course of a lifetime. But the fact is that we all can understand and say most of them (Postal, 1968).

In sum, we effortlessly create and interpret new sentences on the spot. Only a very few, such as "How are you?", "What's new?", and "Have a nice day" are said and heard with any frequency. All the rest are at least partly new. Thus memorization cannot explain how we learned our language.

LANGUAGE IS STRUCTURED

People make up their new sentences in lawful, not accidental ways. They do not sometimes say "Is rabbit that a" or "A rabbit that's," even though these are fairly comprehensible ways to say "That's a rabbit." Speakers construct their sentences in accordance with certain general principles which are often called ***rules of grammar.***

THE EFFECT OF WELL-FORMEDNESS ON COMPREHENSION AND RECALL

Sentences that are not ***well-formed*** (are ***ungrammatical***) are rarely uttered. But neither for that mattter are they readily understood or remembered. This was shown in several studies in which subjects listened to sequences of words that varied in meaningfulness and in grammaticality

1. *Furry wildcats fight furious battles* (grammatical and meaningful)
2. *Furry fight furious wildcats battles* (meaningful but ungrammatical)
3. *Furry jewelers create distressed stains* (meaningless and grammatical)
4. *Furry create distressed jewelers stains* (meaningless and ungrammatical)

In one experiment, subjects had to detect these sequences in the presence of a loud background noise (Marks and G. Miller, 1964). In another experiment, they were asked to memorize and recall them (G. Miller and Isard, 1963). In both situations, the results were the same. Well-formed meaningful sentences (such as 1 above) were easiest; and scrambled, meaningless, sentences (such as 4) were hardest. The other two types fell in between.

That meaningful material is easier to detect and recall is hardly surprising. What is more impressive is that grammatical patterning had similar effects. Thus sequences that are meaningless but well-formed (such as 3) were easier to deal with than those that were both meaningless and ungrammatical (such as 4). Such demonstrations show that grammar is not just something one does at school; it is a part of ordinary psychological functioning.

GRAMMATICAL RULES AS ORGANIZING PRINCIPLES

How can we account for the fact that, while people could not possibly have stored all English sentences in memory, they can nevertheless recognize good sentences whenever the occasion calls for it (and will thus succeed on Miller's tests)? The answer is that language involves something much more than stored lists of words or sentences. Each of us learns organizing principles, laws or rules of grammar and of meaning. These rules tell us how to create and understand boundless new instances. This system is generally not known consciously, but is implicit. Even so, it governs our use of language and allows us to compose and understand an infinite number of new sentences.

Language is not unique in being unlimited and rule-governed, for a number of other behavior patterns also have a similar potential for systematic and novel use. Consider arithmetic. We have not stored in our minds what every two numbers sum up to. Surely we don't know the sum of, say, 5,384 and 9,253 offhand. But we can readily calculate it, for we know a set of laws—the rules of arithmetic. Similarly, we can drive cars to destinations where we have never traveled before, solve chess problems we have never encountered before, and blush at embarrassments we have never experienced before. Thus many behavioral systems have the limitless character we have just shown for language.

Notice, then, that language use is not a **habit,** for the term *habit* applies to tasks in which one does the same thing again and again. Skills whose use is lawful and yet allows novelty must be accounted for in a different way, in terms of some general principles, or **rules.**

DESCRIPTIVE VERSUS PRESCRIPTIVE RULES

Before proceeding, we have to make a distinction. We have been discussing **descriptive rules** of language. These describe our natural speech. But these

The power of an "H" *In a scene from the film version of* My Fair Lady, *the cockney flower girl, Liza (Audrey Hepburn), is taught by Henry Higgins (Rex Harrison) how to pronounce an "H." She thus becomes a lady. (Courtesy The Museum of Modern Art/Film Stills Archive)*

rules in many ways are at variance with the ***prescriptive rules*** we painfully learned in the sixth grade (and thankfully forgot in the seventh), such as "Never say ain't" or "A sentence cannot end with a preposition." These latter rules are recipes (or social "prescriptions") from certain authorities about how they believe we *ought* to speak. Our primary interest in this chapter will be in the descriptive rules, for these are fundamental in understanding language as a universal human skill. In fact, many cultures do not even have any prescriptive rules of language.

Even so, we may well ask how the prescriptive rules sometimes arise. In some cultures, a particular dialect of the language is elevated for professional, literary, and other formal purposes, and called the prescribed or "standard" dialect. This is the case for English, which has marvelously many dialects depending on geographical area (regional dialects) and ethnic and social grouping (social-class dialects). A standard form is useful for the joint intercommunications of these many subgroups. However, it is often argued that the standard dialect is also in some ways the "best" style of speaking (Bernstein, 1967), a claim that is much harder to defend on objective grounds.

Consider certain inner-city black dialects of American English. These are often called "substandard," rather than merely "nonstandard," and attacked as "illogical" (Bereiter and Engelmann, 1966). One reason given is that speakers of these dialects often omit the present tense ***copula*** (the verb *be*). yielding such sentences as "He a fool" rather than the standard "He is a fool" or "He's a fool." But which style is the more logical? It has been shown that speakers of both dialects are expressing the same ideas and understand each other equally well (Labov, 1970*a*). Moreover, many prestigious languages of the world, including Russian, Hungarian, and Arabic, are like black English in omitting the present tense of the copula, but never are called illogical. This suggests that the black American dialects are frowned upon as a matter of convention, or even prejudice, and not because they are poorer vehicles for expressing meaning or thinking logically.

Such considerations do not stop each dialect group from disdaining the speech of the next group. Long before the English language was born, the ancient Athenians were laughing at the "rude vowels" of Ionian farmers. More recently, Henry Higgins changed the "H" of Eliza Doolittle, whereupon she was welcomed into the British upper classes and called "My Fair Lady." Such social prejudices can scarcely be justified by claiming one style of speech is more logical or beautiful (What, after all, is so beautiful about an "H"?). Still, speaking the standard dialect, just like wearing the right clothes to a cocktail party, may be a requirement for some coveted job or social status. Scientific study demonstrates, however, that each language and dialect is as rule-governed, as complex, and as meaningful as the next (Labov, 1970*b*).

LANGUAGE IS MEANINGFUL

Each word in a language expresses a meaningful idea, about some thing (e.g., *camera* or *rabbit*), action (*run* or *hit*), abstraction (*justice* or *fun*), relation (*similar* or *and*), quality (*red* or *altruistic*), and so on. The purpose of language is to express all these meanings, so we have no choice but to learn a conventional word for each. Our memory for all these words is really quite amazing, considering the fact that some words may not be encountered for years, and yet are recollected quite effortlessly. For example, even such seemingly common words as *strangler, yodel, backache, wormy,* and *abrasive* occur less than once per million words (Thorndike and Lorge, 1944), but we do not forget them. Each is stored forever in the brain, against the rare day when we might want to "mean" them.

But we also discovered in the previous section that people learn to talk in terms of word patterns (grammatical sentences) rather than just stringing out meaningful words in a row. This is because we wish to talk about whole events and situations, rather than just to name things or actions. To do so, we must put words together. More than this, we must get across to the listener the logic that holds these words together, how they are meaningfully related to each other in this sentence in particular. For example, the words *dogs, cats, bite,* express very different logical thoughts, depending on how they are put together: *dogs bite cats* or else *cats bite dogs.*

To realize that these two sentences mean different things, despite the fact that they are composed of exactly the same words, the listener must attend to grammatical patterns. In English, as we see here, these rules take account of the order in which the words are said (or written). For some other languages, inflections (case endings) perform these functions instead. But for all languages, grammatical rules of some kind are necessary so that people can understand, not only words, but the myriad relationships among words that sentences can express. Every human language has the property that it can express simple meanings with words, and complicated meanings with sentences.

LANGUAGE IS REFERENTIAL

Language users know more than how to put words together into sentences. They also know which words refer to which things, events, and scenes in the world. If a child said, "That's a box" (a sentence whose grammatical form is impeccable and whose meaning is transparent) but did so while pointing to a rhinoceros, we would not think she had learned English very effectively. This is the problem of ***reference;*** how to use language to describe the world of real things and events.

THE ASSOCIATIONIST THEORY OF CONNECTING WORDS AND THINGS

How do we learn to relate each word to its correct referent (the real thing, out there in the world)? One theory (associationism) asserts that various events in the world act as direct stimuli to speech responses. On this view, word learning would go something like this: An adult sees a lemon, whereupon he says "lemon." On hearing the adult, the child forms an association between the sight of a lemon and the sound "lemon." Hence, when this child next sees a lemon, she too cries out "lemon" in response.

Even if this description has some truth to it, it cannot be in anything like the sense of stimulus and response connections as we have studied them in the animal laboratory (see Chapters 4 and 5). In the real-life use of language, we often cannot even identify a particular stimulus that evoked some sentence from a speaker. As an example, consider the sentence *Public morality isn't what it used to be.* This sentence can be uttered appropriately upon seeing litter scattered on the highway, on hearing that the Republican candidate has won the election, on hearing that the Republican candidate has *lost* the election, on musing about dormitory life at Smith College or Harvard, on meeting a used-car salesman, or watching strip mining. That is, the possible "stimuli" that could appropriately draw forth this language "response" are practically infinite. Therefore, a stimulus-response theory of language use really tells the scientist almost nothing. All it can say is that, once some sentence is uttered, there is a list of five hundred thousand or so situations that might be "associated" with it, and thus could have been the stimulus for it.

This situation looks even worse when viewed from the other way round: if we consider some external stimulus in the world, and ask which word or sentence can now be uttered that is appropriate to it. Suppose we see a lemon. It would now surely be appropriate to say, "That's a lemon." But an enormous variety of other utterances would be just as appropriate, including, "Lemons hurt my teeth," "Fruits are very expensive these days," "Yellow is an ugly color," "Martinis are better with olives," "My uncle George had a face like that," and so on and on. One is even free to say something quite unrelated to lemons, upon seeing a lemon, such as "Let's go to the movies." And one is free to talk of lemons in the absence of lemons; for example, one might say, "Harvey, go next door to grannie and borrow a lemon." In short, it is impossible to believe that utterances of English are associates of particular past events or are evoked as direct responses to specifiable stimuli (Chomsky, 1959).

The source of language events has to do with the contents of the mind, what one is thinking about. Of course, if one sees a lemon, the probability that one is thinking about lemons is increased; but it is by no means a certainty. Seeing a lemon does not evoke the cry "lemon" in anything like the sense that seeing a lemon evokes salivation from a hungry viewer, or in the sense that seeing a lemon in bright light evokes a bluish afterimage. Salivation and visual afterimages are direct psychophysiological reactions (responses) to identifiable events (stimuli). But sentences about lemons are not automatic reactions to seeing lemons. Sentences are expressions of our state of mind, and this can vary with relatively little regard to what is going on "out there in the real world."

LANGUAGE IS INTERPERSONAL

We have so far given an overview of properties of language knowledge in a single human mind. But there is something bloodless about description of language as a property of the individual. The primary uses of languages are in functions that cross from one individual to another. To accomplish these social ends, speakers must know not only a language, but rules for using language appropriately in successful communication.

CONVERSATIONAL RULES

Suppose, for example, one sees a lion in the parlor and wants to tell a companion about this. It is not enough that both parties speak English. One has to estimate the listener's mental state, capacities, motivations, and relations to oneself in order to speak appropriately. If the companion is a sharpshooter with a rifle, one might say,

> *"Quick, shoot! There is a lion in the parlor."*

But if the companion is an artist,

> *"Quick, draw! Lion of a gorgeous shade of ochre is in the parlor."*

To a biologist,

> *"Quick, look! Member of the genus* Felis leo *in the parlor."*

And to an enemy,

> *"Lovely morning, isn't it? See you later."*

Clearly, what one says about a situation is not just a description of that situation. What one says depends upon one's knowledge, beliefs, and wishes about the listener. To speak appropriately, then, one must build a mental picture of "the other" to whom speech is addressed (Austin, 1962; Clark and Clark, 1977).

The same problem arises for the listener, of course. To determine the sense of what one has heard, one must make an estimate of the speaker and the circumstances of her utterance. Suppose, for example, someone said, "Can you pass me the salt?" To know how to respond appropriately, one must ask oneself (implicitly, of course), "Does this speaker think my arms are broken?" (in which case, the answer should be "Yes, I can" or "No, I can't," depending presumably on whether one's arms *are* broken). But if one is hale and hearty, the normal supposition would be, "The speaker must *know* that I can, physically, pass the salt; therefore she is not asking me whether I *can* pass it, but rather this is a polite way of requesting me *to* pass it" (and now the answer might be "Sure. Here!" accompanied by the action of passing the salt) (Searle, 1969).

ADJUSTING TO CONVERSATIONAL PARTNERS

Listeners have a variety of abilities to adjust their speech styles in response to the ways they perceive their listeners. For instance, speech is simplified to foreigners and to young children who are perceived not to understand the language well (Freed, 1980; Newport, 1977; Snow, 1972). One particularly interesting example was shown in a study of four-year olds who had to teach someone else how to use a new toy. Sometimes these children had to teach an adult. Sometimes they had to teach a two-year-old child. The investigators showed that the four-year olds used their most sophisticated speech to instruct the adults, but that they "talked down" to the two-year olds, using a four-year old's version of baby talk. It is amazing that even four-year olds, who have barely mastered English themselves, should be able to monitor and adjust their speech in response to the needs and abilities of even younger children (Shatz and Gelman, 1973; 1977; see also Sachs and Devin, 1976).

In sum, the actual speech acts that pass between people are merely hints about the thoughts that are being conveyed. Talking would take forever if one literally had to say all, only, and exactly what one meant. Rather, the communicating pair takes the utterance and its context as a basis for making a series of complicated inferences about the meaning and intent of the conversation. A listener who fails to make these inferences is taken for an incompetent at worst and a bore at best. A person who blandly answers "Yes" when you say "Could you tell me the time?" has failed to obey the normal **rules of conversation** that make communication possible (Grice, 1968).

Linguistic Organization

Language is organized as a hierarchy of structures (Figure 10.1). At the bottom of the hierarchy, a language consists of little snippets of sound; and at the other end, of sentences and conversations. In the discussion that follows, we

10.1 The hierarchy of linguistic structures Every sentence is composed of phrases, which are composed of words, which are composed of morphemes (simpler units of meaning such as strange *and the plural* -s), which in turn are composed of phonemes (the units of speech sound, such as p *and* ə). The phonemes are described by symbols from the phonetic alphabet because English spelling is not always true to the sounds of words.

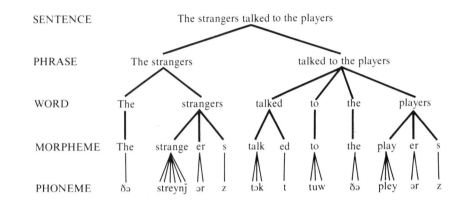

will be describing how humans, through a highly organized chain of mental processes, turn their thoughts into sounds for the sake of talking, and turn the sounds back into thoughts for the sake of understanding. We begin by describing the low-level sound units of which speech is composed, its phonemes. We then progress up the linguistic hierarchy to the morpheme, word, phrase, and sentence units that carry the language meanings. It is important to see that at each level of the linguistic hierarchy, the language units are tightly organized into a structure. And each person who knows the language responds to this structure in everyday speech, without any noticeable effort, and in fact without being aware of the structure itself.

PHONEMES, THE UNITS OF SOUND

To speak, we move the various parts of the vocal apparatus (Figure 10.2) from one position to another in a rapid sequence, while expelling a column of air up

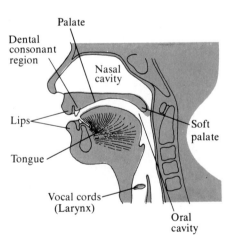

10.2 The human vocal tract Speech is produced by the air flow from the lungs which passes through the larynx (popularly called the voice box) containing the vocal cords and from there through the oral and nasal cavities which together make up the vocal tract. Different vowels are created by movements of the lips and tongue which change the size and shape of the vocal tract. Consonants are produced by various articulatory movements which temporarily obstruct the air flow through the vocal tract. For some consonants the air flow is stopped completely. Examples are p, *where the stoppage is produced by bringing both lips together; and* t *where it is produced by bringing the tip of the tongue to the back of the upper teeth. Some other consonants are created by blocking the air sound only partially, for example* th (as in there), *produced by bringing the tip of the tongue close to the upper teeth but without actually touching. (After Lieberman, 1975)*

361

from the lungs and out through the mouth. Each of these movements "shapes" the column of air from the lungs differently, and thus produces a distinctive speech sound. Many of these differences among speech sounds are ignored by the listener. Consider the word *bus* which may be pronounced with more or less of a hiss in the *s*. This difference is irrelevant to the listener, who interprets what was heard to mean "a large vehicle" in either case. But some sound distinctions do matter, for they signal differences in meaning. Thus, neither *butt* nor *bum* will be taken to mean "large vehicle." This suggests that the distinction between *s* sounds and *t* and *m* sounds is relevant to speech perception. Speech sounds that are perceived to matter in this way are called **phonemes.** They are the perceptual units of which different speech sequences are composed.

To get a rough idea of how phonemes are defined, consider the words *din, dun,* and *den.* Each of these begins with a sound that is different from those that begin the words *kin, bun,* and *pen;* but is more or less the same as the sound that ends *lid, mud,* and *bed.* The common element is the phoneme which we designate by the symbol *d.*

ANALYZING THE SPEECH SOUNDS

In normal conversation, the speech sounds are produced very rapidly. In a real utterance, there are no gaps or silences that mark off one speech unit from the next. This holds not only for successive phonemes but also for words and phrases; all the units run into each other so that it is often impossible to tell where one ends and the other starts. Yet listeners hear utterances not as a single complicated noise, but rather as a sequence of phonemes that seem to occur one after another, like beads on a string (Liberman et al., 1967).

Hearing an utterance as a sequence of phonemes, rather than as the big mushy blob it often is, partly depends on knowing the language that is spoken. This is why foreign speech often sounds "too fast" and like a vague and undifferentiated muddle without separable sounds at all: The foreign language uses phonemes partly different from our own. Because of the construction of the human speech apparatus, children can learn to **articulate** (pronounce) a couple of hundred different speech sounds clearly and reliably. But each language restricts itself to using only some of them. English uses about forty.* Other languages select differently from among the possible phonemes. For instance, German uses certain gutteral sounds that are never heard in English, and French uses some vowels that are different from the English ones.

Once learners have acquired the system of sounds used in their mother tongue, they usually become quite rigid in their phonemic ways; it is hard for them to utter or perceive any others. This is why foreigners speak with accents. We tear out our hair trying to say German *R*s and French *U*s. It is irritating that even four-year-old German and French children can do better. Symmet-

---

* The English alphabet provides only twenty-six symbols (letters) to write these forty phonemes, so it often uses the same symbol for more than one. Thus the letter *O* stands for two different sounds in *hot* and *cold*, an "ah" sound, and an "oh" sound. This fact contributes to the difficulty of learning to read English.

rically, the Japanese language does not distinguish between our phonemes *L* and *R*, so a Japanese adult has great trouble learning to hear or make them in learning English as a second language.

RULES FOR COMBINING PHONEMES

As speakers of a language, we have learned the phonemes that constitute its sound elements. But we have learned something further as well—the ways these phonemes can be combined in words. Every language has some **phonological rules** that specify which phonemes can and which cannot go together.

To demonstrate how such phonological rules operate, consider the task of an advertising executive who tries to find a name for a new breakfast food. She will have to find some arrangement of phonemes that has not already been used to mean something else. Will any new sequence of phonemes do? The answer is no. To begin with, some, such as *gogrs* or *fpips*, would be hard to pronounce. But even among phoneme sequences that can be pronounced, some seem somehow un-Englishlike. Consider the following possibilities: *Pritos, Glitos* and *Tlitos*. They can all be pronounced, but one seems wrong: *Tlitos*. English speakers sense intuitively that English words never start with *tl*, even though this sequence is perfectly acceptable in the middle of a word (as in *motley* or *battling*). So the new breakfast food will be marketed as tasty, crunchy *Pritos* or *Glitos*. Either of these two names will do, but *Tlitos* is out of the question. The restriction against *tl-* beginnings is not a restriction on what human tongues and ears can do. For instance, one Northwest Indian language is named *Tlingit,* obviously by people who are perfectly willing to have words start with *tl*. This shows that the restriction is a rule of English specifically. Few of us are conscious of this rule, but we have learned it and similar rules exceedingly well, for we honor them in our actual language use.

MORPHEMES AND WORDS, THE UNITS OF MEANING

At the next level of the linguistic hierarchy (see Figure 10.1) fixed sequences of phonemes are joined into **morphemes**. The morphemes are the smallest language units that carry bits of meaning. They are approximately the units we usually call roots, stems, prefixes, and suffixes. Some words consist of a single morpheme, such as *strange*, meaning *alien* or *odd*. Some morphemes cannot stand alone as words, but can be joined with other morphemes to make complex words. Examples are *er* (meaning *one who*) and *s* (meaning *more than one*). When these are joined in the complex word *strangers* (*strange + er + s*), the meaning becomes correspondingly complex (*one + s + who are + alien*).

Just as for the case of phonemes, the morpheme patterns in a language are restricted in precise ways. Thus we would not re-order our example morphemes to get *erstranges* rather than *strangers*. Each morpheme has fixed positions within English words. Intelligent English speakers know about 50,000 morphemes along with a meaning for each. And if we count vocabulary in terms of whole words rather than morphemes, each adult has a vocabulary of hundreds of thousands of them, for then the items *strange, stranger, strangers, strangest,* and so forth, would all be counted separately.

PHRASES AND SENTENCES

The words of a language in their turn are organized into patterned sequences, called phrases and sentences, which convey complex meaning relationships. As we have repeatedly noted, the number of sentence units in English (or any other language) is titanically large. If one is impressed by the human ability to deal with, say, 50,000 morphemes, one ought to be positively stupefied by our capacity to deal with this staggering number of sentences. And at this level of the linguistic hierarchy, too, there are rules of combination. It is appropriate to string words together into such sequences as "That's a rabbit," in forming sentences; but it is inappropriate to form the sequence "A that's rabbit." For all the billions of English sentences, speakers and listeners recognize quite effortlessly whether they are well-formed sequences (i.e., grammatical sentences) and what they mean.

THE LINGUISTIC HIERARCHY AND RULE SYSTEMS

We have seen that language consists of a small number of sound units (the 40 phonemes) organized into fixed sequences (the 50,000 morphemes and 200,000 or so words), which in turn are organized into the boundless number of sentences. In sum, as we ascend the linguistic ladder there are more and more units at every level. How can the human mind deal with this ever-expanding number of items? There is only one possible answer: We don't learn the billions of sentences in the first place. Instead, we acquire general rules that tell us how to construct any sentence. Thus it is the fact that linguistic rules exist at each of the levels of the hierarchy that makes language use possible in the first place. Without such rules, we would not be able to learn, speak, or understand a language—there would simply be too much to learn.

But why do humans go to the trouble of acquiring language? The answer, of course, is just that it allows us to convey our boundless thoughts from one human mind to another human mind. Of primary interest, then, are the higher level units and systems of language, the meaningful words and phrases and the meaningful sentences made up out of these words and phrases. In the following sections, therefore, we will take up the questions of word meaning and sentence meaning in detail.

The Meaning of Words

The question, "What do words mean?" is one of the knottiest in the whole realm of language (see J. D. Fodor, 1977, for a general discussion). The subfield that deals with this question, **semantics,** has thus far been able to give only a few, rather tentative answers. As so often, the first step is to eliminate some of the answers that appear to be false.

WHAT MEANING IS NOT

Meaning as reference   One of the oldest approaches to the topic equates word and phrase meaning with **reference.** According to this position, the meaning of a word or phrase is whatever it refers to in the world. Thus this view asserts that words and certain phrases are essentially names. Proper names such as *Billie Jean King, Australia,* and the *Eiffel Tower* are labels for a particular person, place, and object. The reference theory of meaning claims that expressions such as *tennis player, continent,* and *building* function in a similar manner. On this view, the only difference between such expressions and true proper names is that the former are more general: *tennis player* refers to various male and female players and to champions as well as duffers: *Billie Jean King* refers to one player and no one else.

The reference theory of meaning runs into several difficulties. One is that some words or phrases are perfectly meaningful even though it is hard to know exactly what they refer to. Some of these are abstract expressions such as *justice, infinity,* and *historical inevitability.* One cannot point to a real "infinity" somewhere out there in the world. Others are imaginary, such as *unicorn* and *the crown prince of South Dakota,* which presumably have no real-world referents at all.

Further problems arise from the fact that words or phrases that have the same referent are not necessarily substitutable for each other in a sentence. As an example, consider the phrases

> *Franklin D. Roosevelt*
> *Eleanor Roosevelt's husband*
> *The most eminent citizen from Hyde Park, N.Y.*
> *The most famous victim of polio*

There is no doubt that all of these expressions have one and only one referent: the man who was the thirty-second president of the United States, Franklin D. Roosevelt. But do they really "mean the same thing," as the reference theory of meaning asserts? If they do, we should be able to use them interchangeably in a sentence without changing its meaning. But this is clearly not the case. Consider the sentence

> *When I grow up, I want to be the most eminent citizen from Hyde Park, N.Y.*

A person might very well want to say this, without committing herself to a host of other desires, such as

> *When I grow up, I want to be Franklin D. Roosevelt*
> *When I grow up, I want to be Eleanor Roosevelt's husband*
> *When I grow up, I want to be the most famous victim of polio*

The fact is that all of these expressions mean different things, so that one can truly want some of them and not others. But this shows that there must be more to the meaning of a word or phrase than all of the things it refers to. In short, *meaning* is not the same as *reference.*

Meaning as image   A variant of the reference theory argues that meanings are mental images. According to this theory, the meaning of a word or phrase is a mental image of whatever the word or phrase refers to. Thus the meaning of *triangle* is a mental picture of a triangle.

On closer analysis, this theory faces many of the same difficulties that beset

365

the reference theory. One problem was pointed out three centuries ago by the philosopher Bishop Berkeley (1710). The meaning of a word is necessarily more general and abstract than any mental image can possibly be. Suppose we conjure up a mental image of a triangle. If this imagined triangle is really a visual experience, it has to have some particular triangular shape (say, a right triangle), and probably also has a specific size (say, an altitude of three inches). But if so, how could we possibly recognize a ten-inch, isosceles triangle as a triangle when we come across it? To do so, we presumably have to say, "The exact shape and length of the triangle in my head are irrelevant. What matters is whether the external object is similar to the image in the appropriate regards. So long as it is a closed, two-dimensional figure with three straight sides whose angles add up to 180 degrees, it is a triangle all the same." But given this mental statement, who needs the mental image? Its work—in recognizing triangles—is entirely done by the statement.

THE FEATURE THEORY OF MEANING

The preceding arguments show that the meaning of a word is neither just the thing it refers to nor a mental picture of that thing. But then what can word meaning be?

One proposal tries to analyze word meaning into a set of subcomponents. This approach starts out with the fact that there are various meaning relationships among different words and phrases. Some words are similar in meaning (*wicked-evil*), others are opposites (*wicked-good*), still others seem virtually unrelated (*wicked-ultramarine*). According to one proposal, these relationships can be explained by assuming that words are **bundles of semantic features** (Katz and Fodor, 1963; Katz, 1972). As an example, take the word *bachelor*. This word clearly has something in common with *uncle, brother, gander,* and *stallion.* As speakers of English, we know that all of these words carry the notion *male.* This point is forcefully made by considering various sentences that most English speakers will regard as odd (or, to use the technical term, **anomalous**). Thus, the sentence *My _____ is pregnant* sounds very peculiar if the missing word is any of the members of the bachelor-related group listed below:

$$My \begin{Bmatrix} uncle \\ brother \\ gander \\ stallion \\ bachelor \end{Bmatrix} is\ pregnant$$

Demonstrations of this sort suggest that words like *stallion* and *bachelor* are not simple in meaning, but rather are composed of a number of meaning atoms—the semantic features. Further demonstrations with anomalous sentences show that *bachelor* contains additional features such as *unmarried* and *adult.* This explains why the following sentences are also odd in meaning:

My sister is married to a bachelor
I met a two-year-old bachelor yesterday.

The ultimate aim of this kind of analysis is to describe the meaning of words and phrases as packages of features (Katz, 1972). According to this view, each word bundles up a limited set of primitive semantic attributes. For *bachelor* these might be *never married, human, adult,* and *male;* for *stallion,* they would include *adult, male,* and *horse.* Words like *stallion* and *bachelor* will be perceived to be similar because when an individual looks up the features for each word in her mental dictionary, she will find that the meaning atom *male* is listed for both of them.

THE PROTOTYPE THEORY OF MEANING

The feature theory faces a problem, for some members of a meaning category appear to exemplify that category better than others do. Thus, a German Shepherd seems to be a more doglike *dog* than a Pekinese, and an armchair seems to be a better example of the concept of *furniture* than a reading lamp. This seems to be at odds with the feature analysis we have described thus far, which is similar to the entries in a standard dictionary. The aim of feature analysis was to specify the necessary and sufficient attributes that *define* a given concept. When a dictionary says that a bachelor is "an adult human male who has never married" it claims to have said it all. Whatever fits under the umbrella of this feature list is a bachelor; whatever does not, is not. But if so, how can one bachelor be more bachelorlike (or one dog more doglike) than another?

The question is whether the meaning categories described by words are really as all-or-none as the feature theory would have it. Eleanor Rosch and her colleagues have made a strong case for an alternative view, the theory of **prototypes** (Rosch, 1973; Rosch and Mervis, 1975).

The facts that the prototype theory tries to account for can be easily illustrated. Close your eyes and try to imagine a bird. It is pretty safe to guess that you just imagined something like a robin or a sparrow, not a buzzard, ostrich, or partridge. There is something quintessentially *birdy* about a robin, while a partridge does not seem such a very good example of a bird. The theory of features would have great trouble accounting for the fact that most people think a robin is a "better bird" than a partridge or an ostrich. Whatever the features mentally associated with the concept *bird* (possibly, *has feathers, flies, lays eggs, chirps*), these are said in the feature theory to be **defining:** each of them is necessary and all together are sufficient to pick out all birds. If both partridges and robins are said to be birds because they share these necessary and sufficient features, what makes the robin more birdy than the partridge?

According to Rosch, the answer is that the meaning of many words is described by a whole set of features, no one of which is individually either necessary or sufficient. The concept is then held together by what some philosophers call a **family resemblance structure** (Wittgenstein, 1953). Consider the way in which members of a family resemble each other. You may look like your father to the extent that you have his eyes. Your sister may look like your father to the extent that she has his nose. But your sister and you may have no feature in common (you have your grandfather's nose and she has Aunt Fanny's eyes), and so the two of you do not look alike at all. Still, you two are physically related through a family resemblance, for each of you has some resemblance to your father. In sum, a family resemblance structure is like a

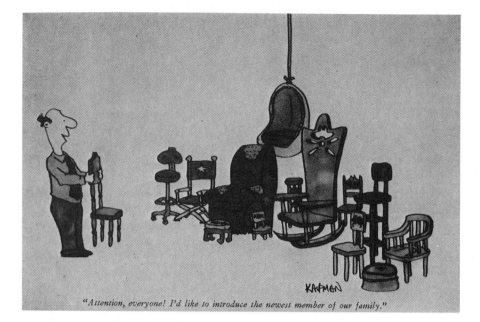

(Drawing by Kaufman; © 1977 The New Yorker Magazine, Inc.)

"Attention, everyone! I'd like to introduce the newest member of our family."

collection of attributes. No single member of the family will have them all. Nor will any two members of a family have the same ones (except for identical twins). But all will have at least some. Some individuals will have many of the family attributes and these are often called the "real Johnsons" or "prototypical Smiths." They are the "best" exemplars of the family resemblance structure because they have, say, the most Johnson-attributes and the least Jones-attributes. Other family members are marginal. They have only the nose, or the little freckle behind the left ear, but nothing else (Figure 10.3).

Rosch believes that what holds for the Smiths and the Johnsons may hold for many word concepts, such as *bird*, as well. For in fact, there is little doubt that except for professional biologists, most people don't really know what all birds have in common. Thus, contrary to our first guess, not all birds fly (ostriches can't fly). And not everything that lays eggs is a bird (giant tortoises lay eggs). Not all birds chirp (crows do not chirp, they caw), and some chirpers (crickets) are not birds. What are we left with from our list of defining features? Nothing but a pile of feathers! But feathers alone do not make something a bird. Hats have feathers too. And, after all, if one plucked all the feathers out of a robin, it would be a mutilated robin, but it is still a bird for all that. (You think this unfair? What would *you* call it? A hippopotamus?)

According to Rosch, birdyness is largely a matter of the total number of bird features a given creature exhibits. No one of these features is necessary and none is sufficient, but animals that have few (such as penguins and ostriches) will be judged to be poor members of the bird family while those that have many (such as robins) will seem to be exemplary members. In Rosch's view, these judgments are based on a comparison with the internal

10.3 The Smith brothers and their family resemblance *The Smith brothers are related through family resemblance, though no two brothers share all features. The one who has the greatest number of the family attributes is the most prototypical. In the example, it is Brother 9, who has all the family features: brown hair, large ears, large nose, moustache, and eyeglasses. (Courtesy Sharon Armstrong)*

prototype of the concept. Such prototypes represent mental averages of all the various examples of the concept the person has encountered. In the case of birds, people have presumably seen far more robins than penguins. As a result, something that resembles a robin will be stored in their memory system and will then be associated with the word *bird.* When the person later sees a new object, he will judge it to be a bird to the extent that it resembles the prototype in some way. A sparrow will resemble it in many ways and will be judged to be a "good bird"; a penguin resembles it just a little and hence is a "marginal bird."

Evidence for Rosch's view comes from the fact that when people are asked to come up with typical examples of some category, they generally produce instances that are close to the presumed prototype (e.g., *robin* rather than *ostrich*). A related result concerns the time required to verify category membership. Subjects respond more quickly to the sentence *A robin is a bird* than to the sentence *An ostrich is a bird* (Rosch et al., 1976; for a related discussion, see Chapter 8).

COMBINING FEATURE AND PROTOTYPE DESCRIPTIONS

It appears that both approaches to word meaning have something to offer. The prototype view helps us to understand why robins are better birds than ostriches. But the feature theory explains why an ostrich is nevertheless recognized as a bird. Perhaps we can combine both views of meaning rather than choosing between them.

Consider the word *grandmother.* This word designates people who are *mothers of a parent.* Thus *grandmother* clearly has a set of necessary and sufficient attributes that neatly define it. The feature theory seems just right for words like this. But now reconsider. Everyone knows that a grandmother is a person who bakes cookies, is old and gray, and has a kindly twinkle in her eye. When we say that someone is *grandmotherly,* we are referring to such prototypical attributes of grandmothers, not to geneology. Of course, some grandmothers lack these typical properties. Zsa Zsa Gabor is a mother of a parent, but she is hardly gray or twinkly. And we all know some kindly lady who is gray and twinkly but never had a child; she may be grandmotherly but she is not a grandmother.

The most plausible assumption is that people have two partly independent mental representations for the meaning of a word. They know about prototypical attributes that are good symptoms of being a grandmother, such as being old and gray. They probably store a list (or perhaps a picture) of such symptoms as a handy way of picking out likely grandmother candidates. But they also store defining grandmother features (e.g., *mother of a parent*). These features determine grandmother limits, and tell one how to use the prototype appropriately. (Armstrong, Gleitman and Gleitman, 1980).

Combining the two approaches allows us to deal with the disparate phenomena of meaning we have been discussing. The prototype description enables us to understand why people are surprised to hear that Elizabeth Taylor is a grandmother. The featural description enables us to laugh at the little boy who bought his grandmother a birthday card whose legend read "You have been just like a grandmother to me" (Landau, 1980).

369

Noam Chomsky

Syntax: Organizing Words into Sentences

We have now seen that the system of words in a language is very rich indeed and allows us to express a bewildering variety of meanings with great precision. Given the richness of this system, one might wonder why languages do not simply stop at the level of words—why they have yet another level of organization that combines the words into sentences. That is, one might well wonder why we do not simply have a new word for each new meaning, rather than having both words and sentences. For example, we might have a word meaning "dog"; another word, such as *nard,* meaning "I saw a dog"; and another word, *blitso,* meaning "my brother saw a dog." This would spare humans the trouble of learning rules for combining words lawfully (that is, grammar rules).

The answer again lies in the unending novelty of language use. There are hundreds of millions of thoughts that we want to, and do, express in language, but no one could memorize a separate word for the infinities of events that could take place. Thus language is a system that from finite means (a stock of memorized meaningful words) gives us the capacity to speak of infinitely many meaningful events, by combining the old words in lawful, but always different, ways. *Syntax* (from the Greek, "arranging together") is the general name for the system that arranges words together into phrases and sentences. This topic has been investigated extensively by the American linguist, Noam Chomsky and his colleagues (1957; 1965; 1975).

PHRASE STRUCTURE

Just as a morpheme is an organized grouping of phonemes, and a word is an organized grouping of morphemes, so a ***phrase*** is an organized grouping of words. Consider, for example, the phrases in the following two sentences:

> *The French bottle smells good.*
> *The French bottle good smells.*

Clearly these two sentences mean different things. This is because, though they consist of the same words, these words are ordered differently and are grouped differently into phrases; roughly, either

> *(The French bottle) (smells) (good).*

or

> *(The French) (bottle) (good smells).*

Thus, by the choice of phrasing, the word *bottle* comes out a noun in the first sentence, so that sentence is telling us something about *French bottles;* but the word *bottle* comes out a verb in the second sentence, and so this sentence tells us about what the French put into bottles—namely, *good smells* (that is, perfumes).

The phrase is thus the unit of which sentences are composed. Each sentence is an appropriate sequence of phrases. Just as for phoneme sequences and morpheme sequences, some phrase sequences are acceptable while others are outlawed—or ungrammatical.

The meaning of a sentence depends not only on the phrases it contains, but also on the way these are put together. But the rules whereby phrase combinations yield meaning are by no means simple. Consider the sentence *The boy hit the ball* which, grouped into phrases, becomes *(The boy) (hit) (the ball)*. If we now switch the first noun phrase (that is, *the boy*) with the second (that is, *the ball*), the result is *(The ball) (hit) (the boy)* which obviously means something else entirely.

This example shows that there are some cases when meaning is drastically affected by switching the position of the first and second noun phrases in a sentence. But this isn't always true. Consider the sentence with which we started—*(The boy) (hit) (the ball)*—and the further sentence *(The ball) (was hit by) (the boy)*. Here, the first and second noun phrases of the sentence *(the boy)* and *(the ball)* are switched around and yet much of the meaning of the sentence is kept intact.

How can we explain the fact that some arrangements of phrases mean very different things while other arrangements have much the same meaning? Many linguists believe that the reason is that each sentence in a language is mentally represented in two different ways. Both of these mental representations are phrase structures, but they are organized quite differently. One is the **surface phrase structure** of a sentence. This is the organization that describes the sequence of phrases in a sentence as it is actually spoken or read. Thus all three of our example sentences have different surface structures, for each is a different sequence of spoken or written English phrases. The second kind of mental organization of a sentence is its **underlying phrase structure.** This underlying structure pertains to sentence meaning. Two sentences may be very different in their surface structure but much alike in the underlying structure, as in *The boy hit the ball* and *The ball was hit by the boy* which sound quite different (that is, differ in surface structure) and mean much the same thing (that is, are much alike in their underlying structure).

SURFACE PHRASE STRUCTURE

Consider again the simple sentence *The boy hit the ball.* This sentence seems to be naturally organized into two main phrases. One is a so-called **noun phrase** *(the boy)*. The other is a **verb phrase** *(hit the ball)*. Even young schoolchildren can demonstrate their knowledge of these sentence parts by, say, enclosing the phrase units within parentheses: *(The boy) (hit the ball)*. Modern linguists use a different notation to convey this same partitioning of sentences into their natural parts. It is a **tree diagram,** so called because of its branching appearance, and similar to those we have encountered in the discussion of hierarchical plans in directed thinking (see Chapter 9):

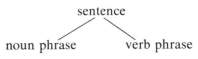

This tree-diagram notation is a useful way of showing that sentences can be thought of as a hierarchy of structures, of the kind we discussed previously

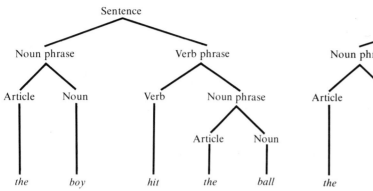

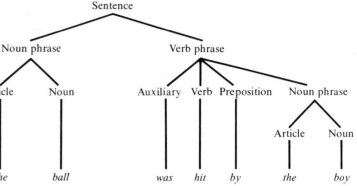

10.4 The surface structure of the sentence The boy hit the ball *This surface-structure tree is called a phrase-structure description for it shows how the sentence can be analyzed into phrase units. Notice particularly that there are two noun phrases in this sentence: one noun phrase* (the ball) *is part of the verb phrase* (hit the ball); *the other noun phrase* (the boy) *is not part of the verb phrase. A description of this kind also shows the word class types (e.g.,* article, noun, verb) *of which each phrase consists. Finally, it shows the words of the sentence. Reading these (the bottom row in the tree) from left to right, we get the actual sequence of words in the sentence being described. Thus (in its bottom row) a surface-structure tree describes the actual words that speakers say and listeners hear.*

10.5 The surface structure of the sentence The ball was hit by the boy *Notice that the surface phrase descriptions in Figures 10.4 and 10.5 look quite different: The words in the bottom row are arranged in a different way. Thus the two surface-structure trees succeed in describing the fact that the active sentence and the passive sentence sound quite different (even though, to be sure, they have quite a few words in common).*

(see Figure 10.1). Each sentence can be broken down into phrases, which can be broken down into words, which can be broken into morphemes, and so on. The descending branches of the tree correspond to the smaller and smaller units of sentence structure.

A complete description of such structural parts, for all the sentences of a language, is called a ***phrase-structure description*** of that language. It consists of a set of rules which progressively analyze each sentence into smaller and smaller units. The details of these rules will not concern us here. But it is important to get an idea of what surface phrase-structure descriptions of simple English sentences look like. Figure 10.4 shows the surface phrase structure of the example sentence *The boy hit the ball.* At the very top of the tree this description asserts that the example is a sentence; at the bottom it is a string of words, and in between, it is a sequence of phrases, subphrases, and word class names (e.g., "noun" and "verb"). Similarly, Figure 10.5 shows the surface phrase structure of the passive sentence *The ball was hit by the boy.* Clearly, these two figures look very different: The surface phrase structures of the two sentences are not the same, despite the fact that both mean about the same thing.

THE PSYCHOLOGICAL REALITY OF SURFACE PHRASE STRUCTURE

The fact that even schoolchildren with little formal training can analyze sentences into the phrase-sized pieces of Figures 10.4 and 10.5 suggests that this analysis is not unnatural. Further evidence comes from various laboratory studies. One investigator asked whether recall is helped if the subject is enabled to think of the item in phrase-sized units. To find out, he asked subjects to memorize strings of nonsense words. One kind of string had almost no structure at all: *The yig wur vum rix hum in jag miv.* The second kind was identical to the first, except that English suffixes such as *s, ly,* and so on, were added to some of the nonsense syllables, resulting in sequences such as: *The yigs wur vumly rixing hum in jagest miv.*

On the face of it, the second sequence should be harder to memorize than the first, for it is longer. But in fact, the opposite was true. The English suffixes allowed the subject to organize the sequence of items in terms of a phrase structure so that they were easier to memorize (Epstein, 1961). Compare

>   *(The dogs) (were sadly serenading Naomi) (in mellowest tone)*
> and
>   *(The yigs) (wur vumly rixing hum)   (in jagest miv).*

This of course is the method that Lewis Carroll used in the poem "Jabberwocky" to make such nonsense as " 'Twas brillig, and the slithy tove" appear to be meaningful. The mere existence of language structure gives the illusion of meaningfulness. In the nonsense-word experiment, the subjects were able to learn the suffixed versions more easily than the unsuffixed versions, because the suffixes give clues for performing a phrase analysis; and the phrase unit seems to be an efficient package for storing languagelike information.

UNDERLYING PHRASE STRUCTURE

Underlying phrase structure, or the structure of sentence meaning, has two aspects: proposition and attitude. The ***proposition*** is the basic thought that a sentence expresses, what it is about. Therefore, the proposition is the same in all the different sentences below, for they are all about the idea *boy-hitting-ball:*

> 1. *The boy hit the ball.*
> 2. *The boy did not hit the ball.*
> 3. *Did the boy hit the ball?*
> 4. *The ball was hit by the boy.*

To the extent that all these sentences contain the same proposition, they are related in sentence meaning. But clearly they are not identical to each other in sentence meaning.

What differs for these four sentences is the stance or ***attitude*** the speaker (or writer) is adopting toward the proposition. Namely, sentence (1) asserts the truth of the proposition about boy-hitting-ball; sentence (2) denies it; sentence (3) questions it; and sentence (4) again asserts it, but shifts the main focus of attention onto *the ball,* rather than *the boy.*

The whole logic of the sentence meaning, its underlying structure, is the proposition and attitudes taken together. Again, phrase-structure trees will describe these underlying forms. This is because the meaning of the sentence (as well as its outward surface form) is still naturally organized as phrase-sized units: A word group (or phrase) such as *the boy* acts as a coherent whole in the meaning of sentences.

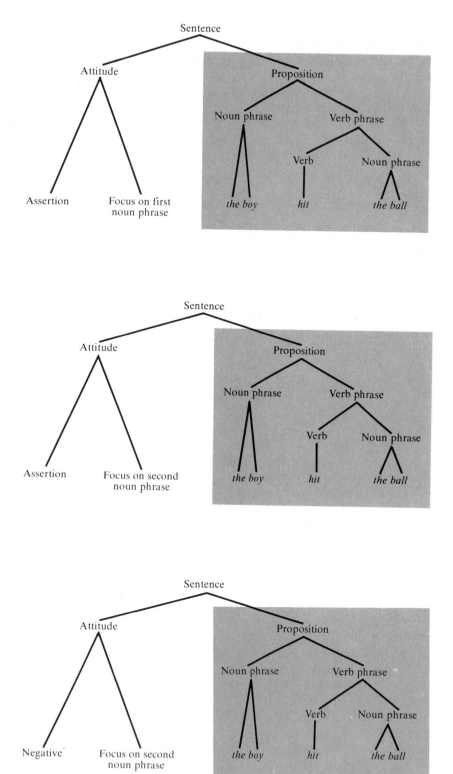

10.6   Underlying structure of The boy hit the ball   *Notice that the actual English sentence.* The boy hit the ball *looks exactly like the proposition* the boy hit the ball *as it appears in this underlying structure. But as the diagram shows, the real sentence is something more than the proposition: It is an assertion of the truth of the proposition. In informal wording, when a person says, "The boy hit the ball," he really means, "I assert that it is true that the boy hit the ball." The tree diagram here describes both aspects of the thought: its proposition and the attitude about it. (Since our discussion focuses on phrases particularly, we leave out here, and in the succeeding figures, some details such as word-class names—e.g., noun, article.)*

10.7   Underlying structure of the passive sentence The ball was hit by the boy   *The similarity of meaning of this sentence to the one shown in Figure 10.6 is that both have the same proposition. The difference is that their list of attitudes is partly different.*

10.8   Underlying structure of the negative-passive sentence The ball was not hit by the boy   *Notice that again the proposition is shown identically to the way it appeared in Figures 10.6 and 10.7. This makes clear that the sentence is related to the previous two figures: It has the same proposition. But it does not mean the same thing: It denies the truth of the proposition, rather than asserting the truth of the proposition. Notice particularly, from this example, that a sentence can express many of the attitudes at once. It is possible to switch focus onto the second noun phrase of a proposition (i.e., to say a passive sentence) and also express denial (i.e., to say "not").*

Figures 10.6, 10.7, and 10.8 are tree diagrams of the underlying phrase structure of three related sentences. One is in the active form: *The boy hit the ball.* Another is passive: *The ball was hit by the boy.* A third is negative-passive: *The ball was not hit by the boy.* The figures are a compact way of describing the two aspects of sentence meaning—proposition and attitude. To begin with, they graphically show that all three sentences are related in meaning; for all contain the same proposition organized in the same way (the part of each diagram that is shaded brown). But these diagrams also show the ways these sentences differ in meaning; each has a different list of attitudes it expresses toward the proposition—focus, assertion, negation.

THE PSYCHOLOGICAL REALITY OF UNDERLYING STRUCTURE

There are many convincing demonstrations that what people remember primarily is the underlying structure, rather than the surface structure, of sentences. This is not surprising for we usually care about what someone meant to say to us, not the exact way it was phrased. One investigator asked adult subjects to listen to stories. Afterward, she presented some isolated sentences and asked if these exact ones had appeared in the stories heard earlier (Sachs, 1967). For instance, a sentence in the original story might be

(1) *He sent a letter about it to Galileo.*

The later, test sentences were

(2) *Galileo sent a letter about it to him.*

and also

(3) *A letter about it was sent to Galileo by him.*

Neither (2) nor (3) had ever appeared in the original story. While the subjects generally knew that (2) was never presented, they often believed that (3) was. This is because the underlying structures of the two sentences (1) and (3) contain the same proposition *(He sent a letter about it to Galileo).* In contrast, sentence (2) contains a different proposition *(Galileo sent a letter about it to him).* In short, people remember the plot, but they often forget its exact presentation. They are more likely to recall propositions than the surface shapes of sentences (see also Bransford and Franks, 1971, for evidence that subjects can forget how information is packaged into sentences, but still remember the gist).

THE RELATIONS AMONG SENTENCE MEANINGS

We have sketched the two aspects of a dual theory of syntax. According to this theory, humans organize each sentence in terms of a hierarchical phrase structure whose bottommost units are the actual words of the sentence, as it is spoken and heard. This is called the surface structure. But the theory shows that humans also organize the sentence into a rather different-looking hierarchical phrase structure. This structure represents the meaningful organization of the sentence, and is called the underlying structure.

Paraphrase The fact that sentences have both a surface and an underlying structure allows us to describe certain ways in which sentences are related. One such relation we have discussed already. It occurs whenever two sentences have the same proposition in their underlying structure. In which case, as we have seen, the two are related in meaning. But the precise nature of this relation depends on the sentence attitudes as well. If the only difference between two sentences is in the focus from which the action is regarded, as in the active versus the passive form, then the two sentences are **paraphrases**—their meanings are essentially equivalent. Thus (1) *Wellington defeated Napoleon* and (2) *Napoleon was defeated by Wellington* say the same thing in different words. Some differences in sentence attitude, on the other hand, alter the meaning radically, as in the case of assertion versus denial. The two sentences (3) *Wellington defeated Napoleon* and (4) *Wellington did not defeat Napoleon* clearly do not mean the same thing. They are opposites. But this is not to say that they are unrelated in meaning, for they both take a stand (to be sure, an opposite stand) on the same proposition. They are related in meaning in a different way than the two sentences (5) *Wellington defeated Napoleon* and (6) *Wellington ate hard-boiled eggs.* A negative sentence attitude describes the difference in meaning between sentences (3) and (4) but a propositional difference describes the meaning difference between (5) and (6).

Ambiguity Some of the preceding examples described sentences that differ in their surface structure but have the same proposition in their underlying structure. These turn out to be paraphrases, opposites, and so on. What happens when the conditions are reversed, when the two sentences have the same surface structure but contain different propositions in their underlying structures? In this case, we will have two sentences that look for all the world as if they were a single sentence—on the surface they surely are, for they consist of the identical string of words. But this single sentence has two meanings depending on its two possible underlying structures. As a result, it is **ambiguous**—a single form that can be interpreted in two ways.

As examples, consider *Visiting relatives can be boring* and *Smoking volcanoes can be dangerous.* Each of these sentences has more than one meaning.

10.9 Underlying structure ambiguity

A
SURFACE: Smoking volcanoes can be dangerous

UNDERLYING PROPOSITIONS:
Volcanoes smoke This can be dangerous

B
SURFACE: Smoking volcanoes can be dangerous

UNDERLYING PROPOSITIONS:
Someone smokes volcanoes This can be dangerous

The first can mean either "Going to visit relatives can be boring" or else "Relatives who come and visit can be boring." The more interesting case is the second example, because sheer sanity leads us to believe it can mean only one thing: "A volcano with smoke billowing out of it is potentially dangerous since it might erupt" (Figure 10. 9A). But another interpretation comes to mind. One can envision a deranged giant smoking away on a volcano, with effects the surgeon-general might claim are dangerous to his health (Figure 10.9B).

How does one single physical event (the actual sequence of words, *smoking-volcanoes-can-be-dangerous*) lead to two different ideas in the listener's mind? The answer is that the surface sequence *smoking volcanoes* goes back to two different underlying propositions: *Volcanoes smoke* (as in Figure 10.9A) or *Someone smokes volcanoes* (as in Figure 10.9B). In sum, the identical sequence of words can come from different underlying structures. When listeners hear the sequence, they attempt to understand it by constructing its surface structure and underlying structure representations. In this instance, there was more than one choice for what the underlying structure might have been. Here, our listeners construct both these possible underlying propositions, and thus come up with two possible meanings.

SURFACE STRUCTURE: Make me a milkshake

SURFACE STRUCTURE: Make me a milkshake

10.10 A child's joke that turns on underlying structure ambiguity

UNDERLYING STRUCTURE: Make a milkshake for me

UNDERLYING STRUCTURE: Make me into a milkshake

Kinds of ambiguity **Underlying structure ambiguity,** as in the smoking volcano example, is appreciated even by young school-age children, and is the basis for much of their verbal humor (Figure 10.10). But ambiguity of underlying structure is only one of several kinds of ambiguity that exist in language. Another kind is **surface structure ambiguity,** which arises when the surface sentence can be marked off into phrases in several ways (Figure 10.11). The sentence *Harvey saw a man eating fish* can be marked off into phrases in either of two ways, including *(man) (eating fish)* or *(man-eating) (fish)*. Of course the sentence can be pronounced so as to eliminate the ambiguity—but in verbal humor, pronunciation will be carefully neutral to maintain the ambiguity.

A   B

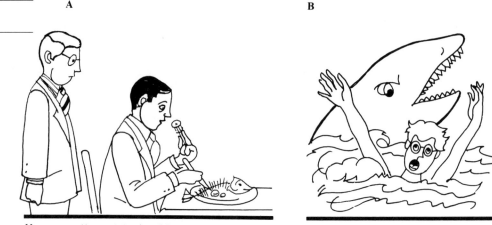

10.11   A child's joke that turns on surface-structure ambiguity

Harvey saw ((a man) (eating fish))

Harvey saw ((a man-eating) (fish))

A similar phenomenon of ambiguity arises in quick speech, even when dividing a sentence into its component words (e.g., *eight teacups* versus *eighty cups).* Finally, of course, there is **word meaning ambiguity.** This occurs whenever words have double meanings. Thus *Someone stepped on his trunk* will give rise to two different mental pictures depending on whether *his* refers to a traveler with a suitcase or to a kneeling elephant. As may have been noticed, word meaning ambiguity accounts for yet a third interpretation of the smoking volcano sentence. To say "volcanoes smoke" could mean "volcanoes have smoke billowing from them" or else "volcanoes puff on pipes or cigarettes" (Shultz and Horibe, 1974; Hirsh-Pasek, Gleitman, and Gleitman, 1978).

THE MEANING OF PROPOSITIONS

The dual theory of syntax has described many meaning relationships among sentences. At bottom, the claim has been that a particular proposition is represented in a uniform way in the mental underlying structure (as in Figures 10.6, 10.7, and 10.8). It is in terms of this uniform representation that propositions are recognizably the same despite their surface disguises (Figures 10.4 and 10.5). What has been left aside in our discussion so far is what sense the comprehender makes of the particular proposition itself.

A simple proposition is most easily thought about as a sort of miniature drama, in which the verb is the action and the nouns are the performers, each playing a different role.* For example, in our proposition about *boy-hitting-ball, the boy* is the "doer" of the action, *the ball* is the "done-to," and *hit* is the action itself. The job of a listener is much like that of a playgoer. First she must recover the plot of the story, regardless of the many ways it might have been staged. This is analogous to the listener's recovery of the underlying structure which renders the plot (the proposition) in a uniform way. But then the playgoer must determine which actors are portraying the various roles in this drama. Similarly, for each of the millions of heard sentences, the listener must discover exactly who did what to whom. This is a matter of interpreting the propositional structure itself (Healy and G. A. Miller, 1970).

* Our informal terminology, e.g., doer and done-to, really oversimplifies the variety of semantic roles that noun phrases play in sentences. For a linguistic description, see Fillmore, 1968.

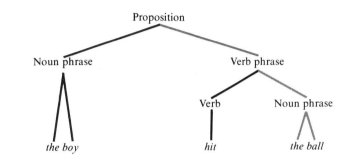

10.12   The underlying proposition in The boy hit the ball, The ball was hit by the boy, *and so on*   *This reproduces the shaded areas of Figures 10.6, 10.7, and 10.8. The emphasis here is on the propositional aspect of sentence meaning. Here, the doer is shown in brown, the done-to in light brown, and the action in black. Thus the basic plot line of the proposition is recoverable from its underlying structure representation.*

If the proposition in our example sentences is in some ways like the diagram in Figure 10.12, the listener could identify the characters and action by inspecting the subparts of the diagram. The doer is whoever played this role:

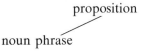

Looking at this part of the tree in Figure 10. 12 (brown) we see that *the boy* was the doer. The done-to is whoever played this role:

$$\text{verb phrase} \diagdown \text{noun phrase}$$

Looking at this part of the tree in Figure 10.12 (light brown) we find that *the ball* was the done-to. But what was the action? Whatever occupies this place in the tree in Figure 10.12 (black):

$$\text{verb phrase} \diagup \text{verb}$$

This part of the tree refers to the action, so *hit* is what happened.*

In sum, we can begin to explain how the listener reconstructs the logical meaning of propositions from varying (surface) forms of sentences: The listener reconstructs a uniform (underlying) representation of the proposition, and then analyzes that proposition into doer, done-to, and action.

---

* It is interesting to compare this modern psychological syntax with the informal traditional grammars we were exposed to at school. It was usually claimed there that the first noun phrase (or subject) of the sentence was the doer and the second noun phrase (or direct object) was the done-to. Most of us were uncomfortably aware that this description worked pretty well for active sentences, but failed miserably for passive sentences (where the doer is the second noun phrase). This problem is a major reason why a dual theory is now generally accepted. The theory we have been discussing approaches this problem by extracting the proposition from both active and passive, and describing them in a uniform way. Now it seems that the first noun phrase is the doer. (To see this point clearly, inspect again Figures 10.6, 10.7, and 10.8). In short, the idea of the first noun phrase as doer seems to be true of propositions but false of some sentences—it is false of a passive sentence, but true of the proposition in that sentence. The facts about propositional structure and theories of grammar have necessarily been oversimplified in this discussion, and we have presented only one of several competing accounts (for recent theoretical perspectives see, e.g., Bresnan, 1978; Chomsky and Lasnik, 1977).

379

THE ROAD TO UNDERLYING STRUCTURE: COMPREHENSION

How do listeners go about discovering the underlying structures of sentences (and hence their meanings) from what is said to them? After all, they receive only the surface sequence of words. These sequences don't usually look much like the underlying structures. That is, people don't usually say, "Denial: focus on the done-to: The boy hit the ball," or "Assertion: focus on the doer: The boy hit the ball." But rather, "The ball was not hit by the boy" or "The boy hit the ball."* Then how do listeners recover the underlying structure so as to get at the meaning of the sentences?

In one regard, the problem of the listener is similar to that of the visual perceiver who has to determine the real size of an object given its retinal image. This retinal image changes with the object's distance from the eye. But the observer can nevertheless perceive the object's actual size for he has a number of **cues**, such as perspective, that tell him about the distance from which the object was viewed. Given these cues, the observer can now reconstruct the actual size of the object perceptually (see Chapter 7).

Something analogous happens with language. Here, the underlying structures give rise to various surface forms. But these surface forms still bear telltale traces of the underlying structures to which they are related. An example is the presence of a pattern such as *is* verb-*ed by,* as in *is pushed by, is complimented by,* and so on. This particular pattern is a good hint that we are dealing with a passive surface structure, and that the focus of the underlying structure is on the done-to.

All of this shows that the road to the underlying structure goes through the overt surface form. The listener tries to reconstruct the underlying structure from cues in the surface word strings he actually hears. But what specific procedures does he employ to this end? So far we only have some tentative answers.

CLAUSE ANALYSIS

According to some investigators, one of the first steps in sentence comprehension is analysis into proposition-sized pieces. Many sentences contain two or more propositions. For instance, *The boy hit the ball and the ball broke the window* obviously has two complete thoughts, or propositions, within it. The first job of the would-be comprehender is to chop this surface sentence into its smaller, proposition-sized, pieces or **clauses.**

Evidence that listeners really do break up surface forms in this way comes from the so-called click method. Subjects listen to spoken sentences. At various points during the presentation of the sentence, a brief burst of noise, the click, appears. When asked where in the sentence they heard the click, subjects reveal systematic misperceptions. If the click is objectively within a clause, it tends to be perceived between clauses. Consider the two-clause sentence that contains our old friend, the proposition about *boy-hitting-ball,* together with another proposition about *boy-bothering-Shirley: The boy who bothered Shirley hit the ball.* What happens when this sentence is presented along with a click that objectively occurs right in the middle of the word *Shirley?* The most

---

* There are certain partial exceptions. Foreigners and young children sometimes seem to talk in ways closer to these underlying forms, as in "No I go sleep" or "Why Mommie hit Billie?" It is as if these novices knew something of the underlying sentence meanings, but not the surface grammatical forms of the language (McNeill, 1966).

likely result is that the subjects will report that the click occurred just after *Shirley*. That is, they will hear the click at the boundary between the clauses.

$$\boxed{\text{objective location of click}}$$
$$\downarrow$$
The boy who bothered Shirley hit the ball
$$\uparrow$$
$$\boxed{\text{subjective location of click}}$$

According to several psycholinguists, this is because a clause represents a cognitive unit, and such a unit resists disruption. As a result, the click tends to "migrate" toward a clause boundary, to be heard as a kind of mental comma between clauses rather than as an intrusion within them (Fodor, Bever, and Garrett, 1974). Since this work was done, much effort has been devoted by psycholinguists to the questions of how listeners extract the various units of sentences, such as phrase and word, and the relations among these, from the incoming acoustic signal (see, e.g., Wanner and Maratsos, 1978; Forster, 1976) and how they organize their thoughts into these units so as to speak (Fromkin, 1973; Garrett, 1975.)

WHO DID IT? ACTIVE VERSUS PASSIVE FORMS

Once the sentence is subdivided into clauses, the listener has to take the next step in deciphering sentence meaning—extracting the two components of the underlying structure, the proposition and the attitude (e.g., active versus passive). It appears that listeners use several strategies to accomplish this.

The first-noun-phrase-did-it strategy One fairly common strategy seems to be based on a preliminary guess (or prejudice) that any clause is in the active form (Bever, 1970). This means that the first noun phrase is tentatively cast in the role of the doer and the second in that of the done-to. This strategy is useful, for in practice active sentences are by far the most frequent; but it obviously fails on the rarer occasions when the sentence is really in the passive form. The listener will eventually find the clues to this effect in the surface form; that is, in words such as *was* and *by* that occur in the passive sentences. The listener's mental sentence analyzer will now do a quick about-face. It will revise its first guess and reassign the roles of doer and done-to.

How can we test whether listeners really use this strategy for assigning doer status? One procedure uses reaction time. The-first-noun-phrase-did-it strategy necessarily implies that it will take a bit longer to understand a passive sentence than its corresponding active form. To comprehend the passive, one presumably must first revise one's initial guess, and this takes some time. To determine whether this is true, one investigator had subjects listen to sentences such as *The dog is chasing the cat* and *The cat is chased by the dog*. Immediately after hearing the sentence, the subjects were shown one of two pictures—a dog chasing a cat or a cat chasing a dog. Their job was to decide whether the sentence did or did not describe the picture. Both children and adult subjects reached the decision faster when the sentence was in the active rather than the passive form (Slobin, 1966; see Figure 10.13).*

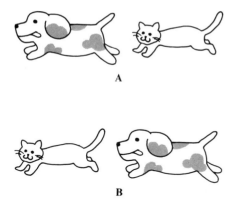

10.13 Deciding who is doer and who is done-to *Subjects were presented with sentences such as* The cat chases the dog *and* The dog is chased by the cat. *They were then shown either (A) or (B) and had to decide whether the sentence described the picture. Reaction times were faster for active than passive sentences. (Slobin, 1966)*

* It is important to realize that we are speaking of tiny differences in time (about 30 milliseconds more for passive than active). So one does not realize consciously that passives are a mite harder, or slower, to understand, but these small differences are experimentally demonstrable.

Analysis by direct meaning   The preceding result suggests that people often go through a fairly elaborate grammatical analysis of word strings to understand the underlying proposition. But there is some evidence that they don't always do this. At least sometimes, listeners use shortcuts. Consider the sentences *The girl is watering the flowers* and *The flowers are watered by the girl.* In this sentence pair, the passive is understood just as quickly as is its active counterpart (Slobin, 1966). The reason is that listeners have nongrammatical clues for finding the doer. All they have to do is to consider the meaning of the separate words; in this case: *girl, water, flowers.* Sheer plausibility will tell them that while girls may very well water flowers, it is unlikely that flowers will water girls. As a result, listeners don't have to go through the time-consuming job of analyzing the structure of the passive sentence *The flowers are watered by the girl.* They can quite confidently guess who is doer and done-to by the meaning of the words in isolation. This situation is quite different from that in sentences such as *The cat is chased by the dog.* Here, the two roles are reversible. Since cats are just as likely to chase dogs as to be chased by them (or nearly so), the listener has to perform a structural analysis of the sentence to discover its intent. In this case the only way of uncovering propositional meaning is to recognize that it is in the passive form.

Language Learning

Language quite clearly is a far more complex human skill than we might have thought at first glance. But how is language acquired by young children? Three kinds of facts about acquiring one's native tongue suggest that this is a very unusual kind of learning:

Children hear utterances, but learn rules   As we have seen, speaking and understanding require the use of a complex set of rules, for putting sounds together, interpreting words, and arranging the words into sentences. But nobody teaches rules to babies. Children just naturally learn to talk in informal settings, where adults and older children talk to them, using the surface forms of language. How can children learn the rule system if they only hear individual words and sentences? As an example, consider the difference between surface and underlying structure, which is so critical in language use and comprehension. How do children manage to learn about underlying structure when all they are exposed to are the surface forms their parents and other speakers utter? No one ever "says an underlying structure" to a child. In sum, children hear only utterances, but somehow manage to extract a deeper rule system that relates all of the utterances possible in their native tongue (Chomsky, 1965; Wexler and Culicover, 1980).

Each child hears different sentences, but all in a language community come up with the same knowledge in the end   A language has infinitely many sentences of which each young learner will hear only some during the period of learning. In one home a child will hear, "Believe in the Lord and you will be saved," while a child in another home hears, "Religion is the opiate of the poor." But both learn the same language nevertheless. If the two meet later in life, though surely they will argue about religion, each will argue in English and they will understand each other even though they disagree. Thus the same language knowledge is acquired from different utterances children happen to hear.

All children succeed in language learning Normal human children all acquire their native tongue at a high level of proficiency by the age of four or five years. The learning is much the same for Greek and Chinese as it is for English or Hungarian; as true for dull children as for wiser ones; as true for children of kind and talkative mothers as for children of nasty or taciturn ones; and as true for children from intellectually primitive backgrounds as for those from more sophisticated ones. In sum, we find for language learning a uniform and early success with a complex task, despite differences in the learners, their motivations, their environments, and the languages they have to learn (Blount, 1972; Bowerman, 1973; Newport, 1977; Williamson, 1979).

It seems that, for all its complexity, language is an irrepressible human activity. The child's success at talking is the more surprising because the simplest mechanics for learning from the environment, such as imitation, reinforcement, and correction, will not explain how we come to talk and understand (for a general discussion, see Pincker, 1979).

LANGUAGE LEARNING AND IMITATION

The first mechanism that comes to mind to explain language learning is **imitation.** But it is also the first hypothesis that has to be discarded, for even very young children say sentences they have never heard and thus have had no opportunity to imitate. For instance, a mother may say to her child "I love you, Jane." But in response the child may very well say "I hate you, Mommie" or " I'm going to crayon a face on this wall." These sentences are clear, though unwelcome, creative language acts of Jane's. They could not possibly have been learned by imitation.

Further evidence comes from studies of children who differ in their degree of normal imitativeness. Some spontaneously repeat much of what they hear; others do not (Bloom, Hood, and Lightbown, 1974). If imitation plays an important role in language learning, one would expect the imitative children to acquire language more quickly than the nonimitative ones. But in fact, no clear difference is found.

Similar considerations apply to word learning. Children surely learn to call dogs *dog* in English—and *perro* in Spanish—by directly copying the usage of adults. But the real trick in word use is again creative: The word *dog* must apply to new dogs that language learners see. What served as a name for the neighborhood poodle and the pet bulldog must apply to the birthday terrier as well. Since language learners soon come to name new dogs with the appropriate label, we must acknowledge that the process of single word learning involves much more than imitation. Children must realize that Fido and Spot and Pluto share some essential doggish properties; and hence that Rover seen for the first time is a dog too, while Bambi is emphatically not. In short, to use language appropriately, we must name new creatures with old names, and new situations with old sentence types (Carey, 1981).

(Photograph by Ken Heyman)

LANGUAGE LEARNING AND REINFORCEMENT

Similar arguments show that **reinforcement** cannot account for language learning. Suppose that Jane is complimented, or otherwise reinforced, for saying a good English sentence such as "I colored the wall blue." If she likes this compliment (i.e., *is* reinforced) should she now find it proper to say "I see the wall blue" or "I colored the wall beautiful"? Both these new sentence attempts are grammatically peculiar, despite their gross similarity in form and meaning to the one that was previously reinforced. Even though our learner was reinforced for saying *certain* good English sentences, this does not tell her which *other* sequences of words will also be good sentences.

To solve this problem, children must learn general rules, and parents cannot reinforce rules. For one thing, children never say a rule, so the opportunity to reinforce one never occurs; for another thing, most parents—unless they are professional linguists—do not even consciously know what the right rules are! In practice, parents rarely reinforce their children just because the latter used grammatical sentences. It should come as no surprise to learn that mothers do not usually answer "Oh, what a beautifully grammatical sentence you just said, dear Jane" to reinforce Jane who just said (all too correctly) "I colored the wall blue." Quite the contrary, such wondrous talking feats from Jane are likely to be followed by a frown or a smack. In contrast, a systematic study of child/parent speech has shown that mothers will happily beam and hug the child who says "Me wuvs yer, mom," or similar true and socially acceptable things, no matter how poor the grammar (Brown and Hanlon, 1970).

LANGUAGE LEARNING AND CORRECTION

Another popular hypothesis about language learning is that it is based on explicit **correction** by parents. According to this view, grammatical mistakes are immediately pointed out to the young language learner who subsequently avoids them. But in fact, this hypothesis is false. In actual practice, mistakes in grammar generally go uncorrected, as in the following exchange:

2-YEAR OLD:	Mama isn't boy, he a girl.
MOTHER:	That's right.

The situation is quite different if the child makes an error of fact. In that case, the mother often does correct:

2-YEAR OLD:	And Walt Disney comes on Tuesday.
MOTHER:	No, he does not.
	(Brown and Hanlon, 1970, p. 49)

These findings are perfectly reasonable. Parents are out to create socialized and rational beings, not little grammarians, and so they correct the facts and the rules of conduct, not the rules of grammar. Another reason for the adults' tolerance of poor language forms is less obvious. Correction doesn't work, as shown by the following interchange:

CHILD:	Nobody don't like me.
MOTHER:	No, say "Nobody likes me."

CHILD:	Nobody don't like me.
MOTHER:	No, say "Nobody likes me."
CHILD:	Nobody don't like me.
	[seven more repetitions of this same exchange]
MOTHER:	No, now listen carefully: "Nobody likes me."
CHILD:	Oh! Nobody don't likes me.

(McNeill, 1966, p. 69)

Despite selective reinforcement, correction, and opportunities to practice and imitate, this child sticks to his own speech patterns. Clearly, he has some rules of his own that he *cannot* violate even when, as in this instance, he is earnestly trying to do so.

It appears that such formal teaching techniques as correction and reinforcement do not play a major role in language learning. To be sure, parents tend to speak in rather simple ways to children: their speech to youngsters is short, clear, and grammatical (Snow, 1972; Cross, 1977). But this still leaves many problems for children to figure out by themselves without explicit instructions. And in fact, those parents who simplify their speech most carefully do not produce children who learn to talk faster than do parents who are more careless in this regard (Newport, 1977; Newport, Gleitman, and Gleitman, 1977).

Language Development in the Young Child

The preceding discussion suggests that children do not come to language learning as little robots who copy what they hear, repeat what they are reinforced for, and omit errors their elders correct. Rather, children seem to organize incoming linguistic stimulation according to some preexisting notions of their own. The question is how. As a first step toward an answer, we will describe the normal course of language development in young children.

THE PRELINGUISTIC CHILD

Children begin to vocalize from the first moments of life. They cry, they coo, and at about four months of age they begin to babble. They make sounds such as "ga" and "bagoo" that sound much like real words—only, insofar as anyone can tell, these babbles have no real or intended meaning. (To be sure, such cries often signal some affective state such as joy or fretfulness and will cause the caretaker to respond; but it cannot be said that children cry or babble so as to get someone to do something for them.) Even deaf children will babble during the period from about four to twelve months of age. Since they can't hear the sounds they produce, communication is probably not the motive at this stage; babies just naturally make noises (Lenneberg, 1967). But in hearing children, these "gagas" and "googoos" soon take on a social quality; children are more likely to babble and coo when an adult vocalizes to them (Collis, 1975; de Villiers and de Villiers, 1978). This is quite different in deaf children who progressively lapse into silence.

Though speech is absent in the first year of life, prelinguistic children have their own ways of making contact with the minds, emotions, and social behaviors of others. Quite early in life, babies begin to exchange looks, caresses, and touches with caretakers. Several investigators have suggested that these gestures are precursors and organizers of the language development to follow. The idea is that the gesture-and-babble interaction helps children to become linguistically socialized; to realize, for instance, that each participant in a conversation "takes a turn," and responds to the other (Bruner, 1974/1975; Sinclair, 1970, 1973).

A further important function of preverbal communication is to allow babies and adults to make reference to the same things, events, and scenes in view (Bruner, 1974/1975). Parents and infants begin to establish a mutuality of reference as they both gaze at the same object, wave it about, and point at it. At an earlier stage of life, this mutuality is absent. A six-month old who evidently wants some toy merely peers at it and cries. An older baby reaches toward the toy and often tries to drag the parent toward it. True speech begins just when gestures of this kind become increasingly focused and precise. To speak to another, one has to have an idea—no matter how primitive—that the other lives in the same, mutually perceived, world (Bates, 1976).

The relationship between mutual gesturing and the onset of language makes a lot of sense, for as the parent and child point and wave, the parent naturally accompanies the interaction by naming and talking about objects and situations. Surely, this naming of items in the here-and-now helps the child discover which word means *Joey,* which *hit,* and which *rabbit.* Even so, we do not precisely know how children realize that words "stand for" or refer to things and actions (Bruner, 1974/1975). But by the end of the first year of life, children seem to know that language is a vehicle for human communication—a means for getting another person's attention so as to comment on the world and make one's wishes known; and hence it is worth learning.

THE ONE-WORD SPEAKER

Children begin to talk sometime between about 10 to 20 months of age. Almost invariably, their first utterances are one word long. Some first words refer to simple interactions with adults, such as *Hi* and *peekaboo.* Others are names, such as *Mama* and *Fido.* Most of the rest are simple nouns, such as *duck* and *spoon,* adjectives such as *hot* and *big,* and action verbs such as *give* and *push.* And lest one think that child-rearing is all pleasure, one of the first words is almost always a resounding *No.* The early vocabulary tends to refer to things that can be moved around and manipulated or move themselves in the child's environment; for example, children are less likely to talk about ceilings than about rolling balls. And this early vocabulary refers more often to attributes and actions children can perceive in the outside world, such as shape or size than to internal states or feelings such as pain or thought (Nelson, 1973).

Missing totally are certain words and suffixes called **functors.** Examples are *the, and, can, be,* and *-ed.* These are among the items the child hears most frequently from adults, but they are never said even so. This is not really surprising, however, for these functors are important to syntax (that is, the arrangements of words into a sentence). Since these youngsters say only one word at a time they presumably have little use for items whose central function is to organize groups of words into sentence form.

10.14   Some difficulties for a child trying to learn the connections between words and things   *The child's helpful mother points out a rabbit to the child, saying "rabbit." Even so, the child still has a big job to do. She sees the rabbit, indeed, but she also sees a paw, a left ear, a left-ear-and-paw-together, a rabbit-plus-a-piece-of-the-floor, and so on, as she follows her mother's pointing gesture. Which one does the mother mean to refer to by the word* rabbit? *Some of these problems may be solved through the child's perceptual biases: rabbit-plus-a-piece-of-the-floor is not a good visual Gestalt (see Chapter 7). But other possibilities can't be ruled out so easily. For example, a paw is a good visual Gestalt (and, indeed, the child will eventually have to learn the word* paw *somehow) just as the rabbit is. Every time the child sees a whole rabbit, it simultaneously sees a paw. So how does the child figure out which word refers to paws and which word refers to the whole rabbit? This is one of the central topics in the study of language learning today.*

WORD MEANING AT THE ONE-WORD STAGE

It is hard to know just what very young children mean by the words they say. Even if a child says "rabbit" on seeing a rabbit, he may mean "tail" or "animal" or "white" or even "runs-by," for all we know (Figure 10.14). There is a good reason for our relative ignorance about these earliest word-meanings: It is murderously hard to get babies to cooperate in psychological experiments (or anything else). Keep in mind that one-word speakers are toddling infants, still in diapers, easily distracted, and quickly bored; they are not interested in the march of science.

Despite such difficulties, developmental psychologists have made a number of attempts to learn something about the child's earliest word meanings. Some investigators take a ***functional approach.*** They believe that children use words to classify things together that act alike in their world—a ball is that which one throws and bounces in the playground (Nelson, 1973). Others argue for a ***featural approach.*** These investigators believe that children use words to designate things that look alike in at least some regards, things which share certain perceptual features. Thus, a ball is anything that is round, including balls, moons, and faces (Clark, 1973). Still others believe that early word meanings are based on ***prototypes.*** In their view, children call things *ball* to the extent that they resemble a particular ball which serves as the model (prototype) for the entire concept (Anglin, 1975; de Villiers, J., 1980; Bates and MacWhinney, 1981). And yet others believe that the child's word meanings are about the same as those of adults (Carey, 1978; 1981). All of these views probably have some truth to them. Different aspects of vocabulary may be acquired differently and children's word learning is probably different at different developmental moments.

PROPOSITIONAL MEANING AT THE ONE-WORD STAGE

There is another question about children's first words: Are these little foreshortened sentence attempts? That is, do children have a proposition and attitude in mind when they say "Doggie!" as a dog runs by? To listening adults, it does seem as though children have in mind a comment, request, question, or command. Thus adults are inclined to interpret "Eat" as "The duck is eating" when it is said as the child watches a duck eat; but as "Eat this cookie!" if it is said as the child forces a cookie into a stuffed duck's beak. Many investigators of child language believe young children have propositional ideas in mind, even when they are speaking only one word at a time.

One basis for this belief is that one-word speakers seem to fill out their spoken words with accompanying gestures (Greenfield and Smith, 1976). A child may say "rabbit" and also reach toward a rabbit at the same time, so the meaning "Give me that rabbit" or "I want that rabbit" comes across to the watching-listening adult. Further evidence is that one-word speakers have been shown to respond with good comprehension to some sentences said by their mothers or by experimenters (Huttenlocher, 1974; Sachs and Truswell, 1978). For example, a child told to "Kiss doggie" will sometimes carry out this whole act, though he could say only "Kiss" or "Doggie" himself.

We see then that one-word speakers have some inkling that the two words *Kiss doggie* take their meaning together, rather than being two separate thoughts. Still, these babies give no evidence that they know anything about syntax, about how the specific arrangement of the two words contributes to meaning. That is, the children seem not to realize that "Kiss doggie" and "Doggie kiss" would mean different things in English (Bloom, 1973; Gleitman, Shipley, and Smith, 1978).

UNIFORMITIES IN EARLY ACQUISITION PATTERN

Children from about one to two years are acquiring a stock of content words to refer to their small world and they use these to render simple thoughts in one-word utterances. To be sure, there is some individual difference in the rate of vocabulary learning. Some children will speak only ten to twenty words by the age of two, while others will speak many hundreds. Such differences are apparently not significant for the child's future development; there is almost no correlation between size of early vocabulary and, say, the eventual IQ of the child (McCarthy, 1954). So while parents may be vexed because Gertie next door says more in this period than their own Bella or Rodney, there really is no cause for alarm. Perhaps Bella will walk sooner and Rodney may get a tooth first.

A similar pattern of early language acquisition is found in children all over the world who learn different languages under different conditions; they all show about the same developmental time frame as English-speaking children (Bowerman, 1973; Lenneberg, 1967; Slobin, 1973; Williamson, 1979). In each language community, children speak no intelligible words until ten or fifteen months of age. Then for some period of time, most children will say only one word at a time. The meanings of the early vocabulary items grow and deepen in this one-word period, the words referring more and more appropriately and precisely to the world as adults know it. And then, one day, the child of two or two and a half years begins to put words together into primitive sentences, and then we are aware most poignantly that another human mind is among us.

THE TWO-WORD (TELEGRAPHIC) SPEAKER

Around the age of two, drastic changes take place in young children's speech. Their vocabulary begins to spurt, rising to many hundreds of words. And little sentences, usually two words in length, begin to be said—haltingly at first, and then with growing confidence. The functor words and suffixes are still missing, and so these sentences sound like the short ones we often use in telegrams and newspaper headlines: "Throw ball," "Mommy sock," "No eat" (R. Brown, and Bellugi, 1964).

THE ORIGIN OF SYNTAX

From the earliest moments of two-word speech, the words seem to be serially ordered according to the propositional roles they assume in the simplest (active-declarative) sentences—doer, action, done-to.* The child who says "Throw ball" usually does not say "Ball throw" to mean the same thing (Braine, 1963; 1976; R. Brown, 1973). With rare exceptions, the word order for two-word English speakers is the right one for the simplest sentences of English (and the word order for French speakers is right for French, etc.). Thus English-speaking children put the doer of the action first, and so will say "Mommie throw" if they want the mother to throw the ball; and they put the done-to last, and so will say "Throw ball!" in approximately the same circumstances. Such facts lead to the conclusion that these children now know something about English syntax, as well as knowing something about meaning. (In fact, since the two-word sentence now expresses propositions so well, one might wonder why children bother to learn anything further; see Figure 10.15 for a demonstration of why two-word speech is not sufficient for full human communication.)

*The terms used in the language development literature to refer to these relational meaning roles in sentences are more specific and elaborate than the informal terms (e.g., *doer*) used in this chapter. In general, descriptions and terms adapted from Fillmore (1968) are used by psychologists. But these more technical terms are used for reasons that go beyond the scope of this chapter.

10.15   The ambiguities of two-word speech   *The two-word utterances of young children, while systematic and meaningful, are quite ambiguous. The three panels from the children's story* Higgledy Piggledy Pop, *by Maurice Sendak, show why one young child might want to learn more about adult syntax. (A) An adventurous dog takes a job as nurse to Baby. He must get Baby to eat, or he will be fed to the lion down in the basement. Here Baby refuses the food, saying "No eat!" (I will not eat). (B) Here, the dog eats up the food Baby has refused. Baby finds this objectionable, and so cries out "No eat!" (Don't eat my porridge!). (C) Baby has angrily pushed the button so the dog-nurse will fall down to the waiting lion; but Baby has accidentally fallen also. To avoid being eaten by the lion, Baby cries out "No eat!" (Don't eat me up!). (From Maurice Sendak, 1979)*

A

B

C

Two-word speakers of English evidently know about doers of action and that these come first in simple sentences; about actions, which come second; and about done-to's, which come last. There are thus three parts to their propositional ideas, much as for adults. But since they are *two*-word speakers, they cannot utter all *three* words in a single sentence. Our belief that two-word speakers have propositional ideas much as adults do comes from the fact that they appropriately order the two words they do utter. But if they can grasp all three components of the proposition, why can't the children express them all? Many investigators suppose that the reason is a memory problem, caused by the two-word speakers' tender age and by his relative lack of practice with the language. He may have three words in mind; but by the time he gets two salient words out of his mouth, any third is long forgot.

There is some interesting evidence in favor of this hypothesis. One investigator asked what would happen when such children got around to saying three-word sentences. The first finding is that then, indeed, they do say doer action done-to ("Mommy throw ball," and the like). Another finding is more intriguing. Sometimes, and for obvious reasons, a word like *no* appears in a child's sentence. Suppose a three-word speaker continues to have some memory problems—she can now get out three words in a sentence, but still not four. She can now say "Mommy throw ball." But if she wishes to express the negative of this, the sentence will be over the memory limit ("Mommy no throw ball"). Now the child says "No throw ball" or "No Mommy throw." We know that she can conceive of the whole proposition "Mommie throw ball," for she has said this under other circumstances. The child presumably has this proposition in mind, but must discard a piece of it in order to fit the word *no* into the three-word sentence (Bloom, 1970).

The idea that two-word speakers "know" full underlying propositions (even though they don't fully express them) is bolstered by studies of children's responses to language from adults. One experiment showed that two-word speakers appreciate well-formed adult sentences, even though they never speak them. They obey more frequently if the mother says "Throw me the ball!" (Using the mother's own normal speech forms) than if she says "Throw ball!" (mimicking the child's own normal speech; Shipley, Smith, and Gleitman, 1969). In sum, there is good evidence that two-year olds have picked up the ideas that a proposition has such parts as doer, action, and done-to; and that word order is the clue—for talking and listening, in English—as to which words are playing which of these roles in English sentences. The earliest sentences spoken by children fail to display this knowledge fully just because the sheer problems of memory, arranging the tongue properly, and so on, make the task too hard.*

---

* An intriguing example of a similar phenomenon, as children learn the sounds of their language, comes from P. de Villiers (1978). His child at age 2 could not say *s* and *p* together, so he said "poon" instead of "spoon." A few months later, he could and did say "spoon." But in a complicated situation he fell back to his earlier ways: he said, "table-poon" instead of "table-spoon." Again, this shows that the child may have certain knowledge but be unable to show the full knowledge when the task situation is complex.

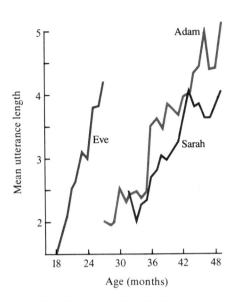

10.16   The average length of the utterances produced by three children   *The mean utterance length in three children between 1½ and 4 years of age. The utterance length is measured in morphemes, where* dolls *counts as two morphemes* (doll + s). *Note the variations among the children, who were all within a normal range. (After Brown, Cazden, and Bellugi-Klima, 1969)*

LATER STAGES OF LANGUAGE LEARNING

By two-and-a-half or so, children progress beyond the two-word stage. Their utterances now become longer (Figure 10.16). They can now say little sentences that contain all three terms of a basic proposition and functors have begun to appear. Their utterances are still short and simple, but—at least initially—they are quite correct as far as they go. Soon, however, a new phenomenon appears. Children start to make various kinds of errors. Does this mean that they are unlearning English?

OVERGENERALIZATION

An example concerns the *-ed* suffix which represents "pastness." At the age of two or so, many children use correct irregular forms of the past tense, such as *ran, ate,* and *hit.* But at the age of three or four, these same children often begin to say *runned, eated,* and *hitted.* What has happened? The answer seems to be that the child is now seeking general rules that operate over the whole vocabulary or set of sentence structures. If some words choose to be exceptions, so much the worse for those words. Such **overgeneralizations** are rampant in child speech. (Ervin, 1964; Ervin-Tripp, 1973; Klima and Bellugi, 1973).

A further example is plural formation. The general rule is to add *-s,* so the little learner says *foots* and *mouses.* Another example is the use of nouns as verbs. The child has heard "John bats the ball," where *bat* means "hit with a bat," so he invents "John *broomed* Mary" to mean *John hit Mary with a broom* (Clark, 1981). A more complicated case is the invention of so-called **causative verbs** (Bowerman, 1981). Children apparently notice that there are many ways to express "cause" in English syntax. Given a sentence like "The ship sank," one can express the causal agent in this affair by saying either, "John caused the ship to sink" or else "John sank the ship." So since children know sentences like "She eats," they make an analogy from *sink* and say "Don't eat her" to mean "Don't cause her to eat" (feed her).

LANGUAGE BASICS AND ELABORATIONS

Children are rule seekers and so they overgeneralize and ignore irregularities. But initially, they can only extract the relatively simple rules of the language. As a result, their speech and comprehension are for a while confined to certain **language basics.** More refined **language elaborations** will come later. The basics include the use of words and rules for arranging them sequentially into propositions. The elaborations include the use of so-called functor words, the "little" words and morphemes such as *and, but,* or *is -ed by,* which enable us to combine two or more propositions or interweave them with the various sentence attitudes (as in the use of *is -ed by* in the passive; Brown, 1973).

An example of children's initial failure to deal with language elaborations is their lack of comprehension of sentences that are in the passive voice. They are as yet unable to appreciate the complexity of surface structures which mirror underlying meanings in complex ways. Instead, they take the one simple rule they know and apply it across the board: the first noun phrase is

391

the doer and the second is the done-to. This rule works well enough for active sentences, and three- and four-year olds can therefore understand them. When supplied with appropriate toys and asked to act out sentences such as *The cat kicked the giraffe,* the children gleefully comply and perform correctly. But when asked to act out the passive sentence *The cat was kicked by the giraffe,* the children err. They overgeneralize the first-noun-is-the-doer rule and assume that the two sentences mean the same thing—so that the unfortunate giraffe ends up as the victim in both cases (Bever, 1970; de Villiers and de Villiers, 1973).

LANGUAGE LEARNING AND LANGUAGE CHANGE

Our discussion of language acquisition has shown that children are not merely *learners* of the language. In the process of extracting language rules, they overgeneralize and become active and creative contributors to the learning process, arranging language to their fancy as they acquire it. As a result, the children of the world can change their language whether their parents like it or not. And in fact, they not only can but do. The evolution of different languages is partially produced by children's failure to learn what is "hard," thus transforming the language into an easier one.

Languages change with the passage of time. Once Latin was spoken in Rome, but now the language spoken there has changed so it would be unintelligible to the ancient Romans; this new language is called Italian. Latin was also spoken in other parts of Europe, including Spain, France, and Roumania. There it has also evolved and changed, and has new forms (Spanish, French, and Roumanian) that again would be unintelligible to the early Romans. One reason for this continual change of languages has to do with errors in learning them, made by children (Kiparsky, 1968).

As an example of what is going on here, let us reconsider the formation of English past tense by adding *-ed.* Clearly this rule fails very often. In fact, for the most frequently used verbs of English, this "rule" works only about 40 percent of the time. Still, children learn the rule; poor as it is, there is no better one in English that works more often. Children apply the rule correctly to the common verbs that require it, but they apply it to the other "irregular verbs" as well (Ervin, 1964). Over the passage of the next five or ten years of life, children will memorize the irregular forms for most common verbs. But what about the uncommon ones? The child must be excused if she fails to remember that a word she hears once every two or three years (e.g., *wring,* meaning "squeeze," and its past tense *wrung*) has a particular irregular ending. If she forgets, she will go with the general rule, and say "wringed." If such a process is at work in English, through the imperfect learning of its speakers, we should expect the rare and irregular words to undergo the regularization, but the commonest words (heard often, so their irregular forms are easily memorized) to stay irregular, over the passing generations. This turns out to be true. While only relatively few of the most common English verbs have the regular *-ed* ending today, fully 98 percent of a sample of uncommon English verbs follow the regular rule. So English moves inexorably, over time, toward the general use of *-ed* as the mark of pastness.

In sum, language in a very real sense becomes what language learning makes it. Humans constantly seek general principles to order their behavior, rather than learning things one at a time. Hence, as any parent can tell you, we hear creative, highly patterned inventions from the small child. Naïvely, we take such innovations to be errors or inelegancies which, if they go uncorrected, will alter our language to its detriment. One is free, of course, to look down one's nose at this kind of language creativity and call it childish, slangy, barbaric, or ignorant. But even so, one must also accept the facts: No matter how dearly we love old plurals such as *hooves* (hoofs) and *celli* (cellos) and old verb forms such as *dove* (dived) and *wrought* (worked), these are doomed by the organizational aspects of human minds. The learner seeks to acquire his native tongue "on the cheap." Everything that he goes to the trouble of memorizing has to extend to hundreds or thousands of new circumstances, to minimize the rote labor. The effect of this central fact about learning is that irregular variations are lost with the passage of time (Bloomfield, 1933).

Given these phenomena of language learning, one might well expect new languages, such as modern English, to have become more regular than old languages, such as ancient Greek, by this time in history. But in fact they are not. Modern languages have not evolved to be neater, more regular, or more rule-bound than older ones. The reason is that language learning by children is not the only factor that influences language change.

There are other influences which work in the direction of irregularity. One such factor has to do with **rhetoric**—the desire for elegant variation and alternative forms in poetry and oratorical discourse. A more important factor is **language mixture**—the influence of foreign speakers, whose own native language usages impose themselves on the new language. Though each of the original languages (say, English and Spanish, as they intermix on the streets of New York and Los Angeles today) may have some simple and regular form, the two individual regularities are different from each other. The end product of mixing them is two forms—in short, a new irregularity.

Roughly, language learning tends to level old irregularities (by overgeneralization of single rules) while language mixing (by speakers of different languages or different dialects) tends to create new irregularities. Hence, the language moves in two directions at once. As one author put it, the overall effect is that the more language changes, the more it stays the same (Slobin, 1975).

Language Learning in Changed Environments

Thus far, our focus has been on language development as it proceeds normally. Under these conditions, language seems to emerge in much the same way in virtually all children. They progress from babbling to one-word speech, advance to the two-word telegraphic stage, and eventually graduate to complex sentence forms. The fact that this progression is so uniform and so universal has led many psycholinguists to the view that children are somehow biologically pre-programmed to acquire human language. Further evidence for this view stems from studies of language development under certain unusual conditions. We will begin by considering what happens to language when children grow up in environments that are radically different from those in which language development usually proceeds.

10.17 A modern wolf boy *Ramu, a nine-year-old boy discovered in India in 1954, was said to have been reared among animals. He was deformed, apparently from lying in cramped positions, as in a den. He could not walk, was unable to speak, and drank by lapping with his tongue. His favorite food was raw meat, which he seemed to be able to smell at a distance. (Courtesy Wide World Photos)*

LANGUAGE WITHOUT OTHER PEOPLE

Which aspects of the early environment are essential for language learning? One line of evidence comes from reports of children who grew up in the wild or under conditions of virtual social isolation.

WILD CHILDREN

There are some remarkable examples of children who wandered (or were abandoned) in the forest, and who somehow survived, reared by bears or wolves. Some of these cases have been discussed by the psycholinguist Roger Brown (1958). In 1920, some Indian villagers discovered a wolf mother in her den together with four cubs. Two were baby wolves, but the other two were human children, subsequently named Kamala and Amala. No one knows how they got there and why the wolf adopted them. Brown tells us what these children were like:

> Kamala was about eight years old and Amala only one and one-half. They were thoroughly wolfish in appearance and behavior: Hard callus had developed on their knees and palms from going on all fours. Their teeth were sharp edged. They moved their nostrils sniffing food. Eating and drinking were accomplished by lowering their mouths to the plate. They ate raw meat. . . . At night they prowled and sometimes howled. They shunned other children but followed the dog and cat. They slept rolled up together on the floor. . . . Amala died within a year but Kamala lived to be eighteen. . . . In time, Kamala learned to walk erect, to wear clothing, and even to speak a few words (Brown, 1958, p. 100).

The outcome was much the same for the thirty or so other wild children about whom we have reports. When finally found, they were all shockingly animal-like. None of them could be rehabilitated so as to use language at all normally, though some, including Kamala, learned to speak a few words (Figure 10.17).

Initially, such cases were regarded as crucial to the nature-nurture controversy. Quite a few authors believed that the knowledge and behavior displayed by such wild children provides an index of what is innately given. But as Brown points out, the findings can be interpreted to fit either a nativist or an environmentalist bias. Nativists can claim that the children were retarded in the first place (which may be why they were abandoned). They may also argue that the children were somehow damaged in their early life so that their natively given capacities never had a chance to emerge. The damage may have been psychological (by living in a predatory society), or perhaps nutritional (by eating a carnivore diet). Environmentalists will take a different tack. They will admire the plasticity of these children (which enabled them to adapt to the ways of wolves) and their partial recovery, in gait and a little primitive speech. All we can say for sure is that having a wolf or a bear for a mother is not conducive to learning human language.

ISOLATED CHILDREN

Kamala and Amala were removed from all human society. Some other children have been raised by humans, but under conditions that were almost unimaginably inhumane. Very occasionally, a child's parents are both vicious and deranged. Sometimes, they will deprive a baby of all human contact. Isabelle was hidden away, apparently from early infancy, and given only the minimal attention necessary to sustain her life. Apparently no one spoke to her (in fact, her mother was a deaf mute). She was six years old when discovered. Of course she had no language, and her cognitive development was below that of a normal two-year old. But within a year, this girl learned to speak. Her tested intelligence was normal and she took her place in an ordinary school (Davis, 1947; Brown, 1958). Thus Isabelle at seven years, with one year of language practice spoke about as well as her peers in the second grade, all of whom had had seven years of practice.

Rehabilitation from isolation is not always so successful. A child, Genie, discovered in California a few years ago, was fourteen years old when found. Since about twenty months, apparently, she had lived tied to a chair, was frequently beaten, and never spoken to—but sometimes barked at, for her father said she was no more than a dog. Since then, she has been taught by psychologists and linguists (Fromkin et al., 1974). But Genie has not become a normal language user. She says many words, and puts them together into meaningful propositions, as young children do, such as "No more take wax" and "Another house have dog." Thus she has some basics of language, and indeed in semantic sophistication, what she means by what she says, is far beyond young children. Yet, even after many years of instruction, Genie is not learning the little functor words, pronouns and auxiliary verbs, and so on that appear in mature English sentences, nor does she combine propositions together in elaborate sentences (Curtiss, 1977).

Why is Genie not progressing to full language learning while Isabelle did? The best guess is that the crucial factor is the age at which language learning began. Genie was discovered after she had reached puberty while Isabelle was only six. As we shall see later, there is some reason to believe that there is a *critical period* for language learning. If the person has passed this period, language learning proceeds with greater difficulty.

LANGUAGE WITHOUT SOUND

The work on wild and isolated children argues that a necessary condition for learning human language is some contact with other humans. If one's early life was spent entirely among animals, the effect may be irreversible. If it was spent among people who never used language, language may still be acquired later on if a critical learning period has not been passed as yet. Our next question concerns the more specific factors of the language learner's human environment. What aspects of this environment are essential for language to emerge?

It has sometimes been suggested that an important ingredient is exposure to language sounds. According to this view, language is intrinsically related to the way in which we organize what we hear. If so, language cannot develop in the absence of sound.

This hypothesis is false. For there is one group of humans that is totally cut off from the auditory-vocal language—the deaf, who cannot hear it. Yet this doesn't mean that they have no language. Most deaf people eventually learn to read and write the language of the surrounding community of persons who can hear. But they usually learn it as a second language; the result is that they are generally less expert at this than are their hearing peers (Gibson, Shurcliff,

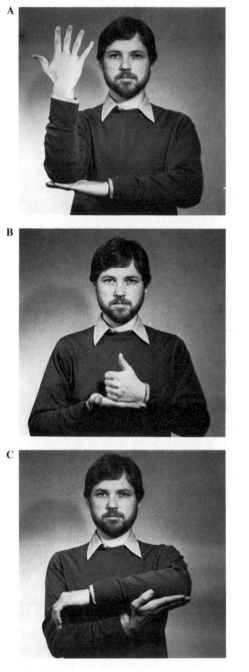

and Yonas, 1970). But most deaf persons also have a first language, a **manual system.** A widely used system of this kind is **American Sign Language** or **ASL.** If their parents are also deaf, deaf children pick up the manual system from the adults around them, through informal interaction rather than by explicit instruction, just as we learn our spoken language (Newport and Ashbrook, 1977).

Is the manual system of the deaf a genuine language? Evidence comes from similarities to the structure and development of spoken languages (Figures 10.18 and 10.19). ASL has hand shapes and positions of which each word is composed, much like the tongue and lip shapes that allow us to fashion the sounds of spoken language (Stokoe, 1960; Stokoe, Casterline, and Croneberg, 1965). It has morphemes, devices for building complex words out of simple ones, and it has grammatical rules for combining such words into sentences that are similar to those of English (Supalla and Newport, 1978; Klima, Bellugi et al., 1979; Newport, 1981). Finally, babies who acquire this communication system go through the same stages as hearing infants who are learning English. They first sign one word at a time, then two, and so on (Newport and Ashbrook, 1977). It is hard to avoid the conclusion that ASL and similar manual systems have the status of human languages.

It appears that language does not depend on the auditory-vocal channel. When the usual modes of communication are denied to humans of normal mentality, they come up with an alternative that reproduces the same contents and structures as other language systems. It seems that language is an irrepressible trait: deny it to the mouth and it will dart out through the fingers.

LANGUAGE WITHOUT A MODEL

The evidence we have reviewed thus far shows that language emerges despite many environmental deprivations. Still, each case seemed to have one requirement—some adults who knew a language and could impart it to the young. But this must leave us puzzled about how language originated in the first place. Is it a cultural artifact (like the internal-combustion machine) rather than a basic property of human minds? Should we regard it as just one more invention, that took place in prehistoric times? Our bias has been the opposite, for we have argued that humans are biologically pre-programmed to communicate. But our case would have been much better if Kamala and Amala had invented a human language of their own, down there in the wolf's den. Why didn't they? There are many ways to write off or ignore this case—maybe they were too busy learning to be good wolves, and maybe a human language is of no special use for learning to devour raw chickens. Is there a better test?

10.18 Some common signs in ASL (A) *The sign for* tree. *One difference between ASL and spoken language is that many of the signed words physically resemble their meanings. This is so for* tree, *in which the upright hand stands for the trunk and the outstretched fingers for the branches. But in many cases, such a resemblance is not present. Consider (B) which is the modern sign for* help, *whose relation to its meaning seems as arbitrary as that between most spoken words and their meaning. Even so, such a relation was once present, as shown in (C), a nineteenth-century sign for* help. *At that time, the sign was not arbitrary; it consisted of a gesture by the right hand to support the left elbow, as if helping an elderly person across a street. (B) grew out of (C) by a progressive series of simplifications in which signs tend to move to the body's midline and use shorter, fewer, and more stylized movements. All that remains of (C) is an upward motion of the right palm. (Frishberg, 1975; photographs of and by Ted Supalla)*

MEANING	STAGES IN DEVELOPMENT			
	1	2	3	4
Bird				
Ox				
Sun				

10.19 Stylization in the evolution of writing *Some parallels to the evolution of manual systems are found in the development of writing. Here, too, there was an increasing tendency toward conventional symbols that bear no physical resemblance to the objects or events they signify. An example is the development of an early writing system (cuneiform, in which symbols were scratched on clay tablets) from an initial pictorial version to a later, more abstract one. Note that here, as in signed language, the tendency is toward simplification. The original pictorial symbols were rounded. They gave way to a more stylized, angular form that could be executed by a few strokes of a stylus. The figure shows several stages in the development of the cuneiform signs for* bird, ox, *and* sun. *(After Gelb, 1952)*

It would certainly be interesting if we could find a case of mentally normal humans, living in a socially human (not wolf) way but not taught any language. The easy way would be to maroon some spare infants on a desert island (while providing them with life's necessities). If they invented a language, we would have strong evidence of a human urge to communicate. People have dreamed of this "ultimate" language-learning experiment from earliest times, and this of course is why Kamala, Genie, and Isabelle so intrigued all psychologists. The trouble is that these cases are so contaminated by brutish mistreatment that they cannot be interpreted easily.

We will instead consider an experiment which the ancients claim to have performed and will then turn to a modern study that reproduces some of its theoretically important properties. Herodotus, an ancient Greek historian, reports a tale told to him when he visited Egypt, in about 460 B.C.:

> [The Egyptian king] Psammeticus ... made an attempt to discover what men were most ancient [of mankind]. ... He took two children of the common sort, and gave them over to a herdsman to bring up at his folds, strictly charging him to let no one utter a word in their presence, but to keep them in a sequestered cottage ... see that they got their fill of milk, and in all other respects look after them. His object herein was to know, after the first indistinct babblings of infancy were over, what word they would first articulate. The herdsman obeyed his orders for two years, and at the end of that time ... the children both ran up to him with outstretched arms, and distinctly said *Becos*. ... Psammeticus ... learnt that *becos* was the Phrygian word for bread. In consideration of this circumstance the Egyptians ... admitted the greater antiquity of the Phrygians (Herodotus, ca. B.C. 460).

Feldman, Goldin-Meadow, and Gleitman (1978) found six children who were in many ways in a situation similar to that created by King Psammeticus. These children were deaf, so they had not learned spoken language. But their parents, who could hear, had decided not to allow the children to learn a manual language. This is because they shared the belief (held by some groups of educators) that deaf children can achieve an adequate knowledge of spoken language by special training in lip-reading and vocalization. The investigators looked at these children before they had acquired any knowledge of English, for a number of prior studies had shown that under these circumstances deaf children will spontaneously begin to gesture to others (Tervoort, 1961; Fant, 1972). This informal gesturing pattern, called *home sign,* is initially a rough-and-ready pantomime, like the earliest communication systems of the deaf. The question was which aspects of communication these youngsters would come up with as they developed. Unlike Herodotus, the investigators did not expect this self-made language to be Egyptian or Phrygian. But they expected it to have some of the general properties of human language, because even though these children were totally isolated from any language, they were human nevertheless. And unlike Kamala and Amala, Genie, or Isabelle, these children had not been socially mistreated. They were living with loving parents, in normal homes.

The results showed that the children invented something much like language, using hand gestures rather than sounds produced by moving the mouth. This finding was all the more surprising since the investigators found that the parents, true to their word, were doing very little complicated gesturing of their own (though, to be sure, they waved and pointed to their deaf children in simple ways). The development of this self-made language showed many parallels to the course of language development in hearing children. The deaf children all began by simple pointing to express their thoughts and desires. They gestured one sign at a time, in the period when hearing language learners speak one word at a time. They pointed to ducks and bouncing balls, rather than to sofas and ceilings; that is their "vocabularies" too looked like those of the children who learn spoken language from their parents. The children then began to invent pantomimic gestures; for example, flapping their arms to express *bird* and fluttering their fingers to express *snow*. (Figure 10.20). Eventually, the children started to put the pointings and pantomimes together into little two- and three-word sentences. This was in the same developmental period during which hearing children (in the presence of a received spoken language) begin to say two- and three-word sentences.

In sum, the early stages of a self-made first language, in these deaf children without adult models, looked remarkably similar to the early stages of a first language, acquired by hearing children with parents "teaching them how." In later years, the deaf children went on to say longer and longer sentences in their homemade language. But in these deprived circumstances, certain further developments that are found in four- and five-year olds did not appear. By now, these are familiar. They are the functor words (or gestures to take their place) and a number of complicated methods for putting propositions together into single sentences. Such refinements did not appear in the gesture system of the untutored children. These findings remind us of the distinction between the two aspects of language structure found in the language growth of normal children: its basics and its elaborations. The **basics** include the use of words (or signs) and some means of putting them together to express propositions. These seem to emerge without instruction and without a model. In contrast, the **elaborations** (such as the use of functor words) do not crop up on their own, but depend upon exposure to a well-developed spoken or manual language (Goldin-Meadow, 1981).

The home-sign study provides us with a fairly pure case of a group of children who were isolated from language but not from society. The results showed that something like language emerged even so. This finding, together with other evidence we considered earlier, suggests that language is a deep-seated property of the human mind—at least in its basics, if not its elaborations. We thus have no need to ask further, with Psammeticus, about the origins of human language. Our best guess is that as human nature originated in evolutionary history, language necessarily and inevitably made its appearance too.

Language Learning with Changed Endowments

The preceding discussion showed what happens to language learning when the normal environment in which humans grow up is drastically altered. How is language learning affected if we alter the learner's normal endowment? We will begin by looking at language in persons who are mentally retarded.

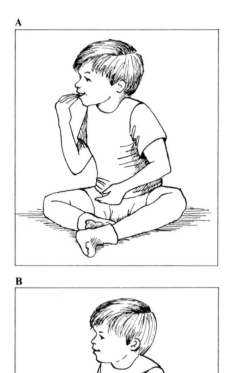

10.20 Self-made signs in a deaf boy never exposed to sign language *A two-sign sequence. (A) The first sign means "eat" or "food." Immediately before, the boy had pointed to a grape. (B) The second sign means "give." The total sequence presumably means "give me the food." (Goldin-Meadow, 1981; drawing courtesy Noel Yovovich)*

LANGUAGE IN THE MENTALLY RETARDED

About 1 in 10,000 Americans is severely mentally retarded. They have a measured IQ below 35 (see Chapter 15) and have considerable difficulty with some of the simplest problems of ordinary existence. For example, the most severely retarded individuals don't have the slightest sense of number even as adults, though normal three-year olds do (Gelman and Gallistel, 1978; Fowler, Gelman, and Gleitman, 1980). In light of such extreme deficits, it is surprising that language—surely a highly complex skill—is rather advanced in some retardates. To find a retarded person who cannot learn to talk and understand simple sentences, one has to go below a measured IQ of about 20. Above this level, most retardates are distinguished from normals more by what they say than by how they say it. Although the rate of language learning is much slower in retardates than in normals, they find the same aspects of language easy as normals do, and learn these first; and they find the same things hard, and learn these last or not at all (Morehead and Ingram, 1976; Lackner, 1976). Such findings further support the view that language learning is a heavily pre-programmed skill: While the difference between normals and retardates in intellectual function is enormous, the difference in language attainment is much less obvious.

Not surprisingly, the retarded individuals show the largest language difference from normals in what we have previously called language elaborations. Specifically, retardates have some trouble with functor words and with joining two or more propositions into one sentence (Lenneberg, 1967). They have what three-year olds have, what Genie has, the language basics which seem to be the most direct manifestation of the human language capacity—expressing single propositions by arranging words in a sequence. To varying extents, the retardates lack what these others also lack—the complex system of elaborations that requires more subtle language learning.

LANGUAGE IN APHASICS

The belief that language learning is partially pre-programmed by our biological makeup finds further support in some facts about brain function. There is little doubt that certain areas of the brain are specialized to control various language functions (Figure 10.21; there are also some peripheral specializations that involve the external speech apparatus, shown in Figure 10.2.) In most right-handers, the language areas are in the left cerebral hemisphere (see Chapter 2). When these areas are damaged—by a stroke, a blow on the head, or some other traumatic event—language capacities are diminished and sometimes totally lost. The resulting condition is called **aphasia.** Its victims lose the ability to talk, to understand, or both. There is no question that damage to these areas has an effect on language specifically rather than on the use of the apparatus (the lips, tongue, and so on) that carries out speech functions. Aphasia patients can still move their jaws and tongues to bite and swallow. What they have lost (in whole or part) is the ability to employ these organs to produce speech. Such findings leave little doubt that particular areas of the brain have evolved for the special functions of language.

A more detailed analysis of certain kinds of aphasia shows deficits similar to

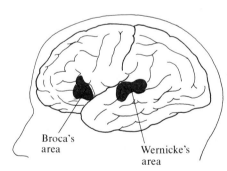

10.21 **The language areas of the brain** *Certain areas of the cerebral cortex (in most right-handers, in the left hemisphere) are devoted to language functions. These include Broca's, whose damage produces deficits in speech production (expressive aphasia), and Wernicke's area, whose damage leads to deficits in comprehension (receptive aphasia). For more details, see Chapter 2. (After Geschwind, 1972)*

399

those that are found in very young children and in severely retarded persons. In ***expressive aphasia,*** the patient has enormous difficulty in saying things even though the speech apparatus is not paralyzed. Sometimes the deficit is total and the patient can say virtually nothing. But in less severe cases, some words come out. What is missing are the functor words and complex syntactic elaborations. The patient speaks in single words or in foreshortened sentences that omit the functor words (Bradley, Garrett, and Zurif, 1979; Kean, 1977; Marin, Saffron, and Schwartz, 1976; Zurif and Blumstein, 1978). Once again, we note the difference between language basics and language elaborations. The elaborations appear last as language develops and are the first to go as it is impaired.

LANGUAGE IN CHIMPANZEES

We have considered the role of the human biological endowment in language learning and language use. What happens when this endowment is no longer human? To answer this question, we will look at attempts to teach language to our closest animal relative, the chimpanzee.

A number of early studies asked whether chimpanzees could learn to speak. Two investigators raised a young chimpanzee, Viki, in their home and patiently tried to get her to utter human speech sounds, initially manipulating her lips to produce "Mama." Their efforts failed. After six years of such heroic labors, Viki's total speech output consisted of only three words: "mama," "papa," and "cup" (Hayes, 1952).

Such results show that chimpanzees can't talk, but this doesn't necessarily mean that they are unable to acquire language. Several investigators reasoned that Viki's failure was a mere consequence of her inability to articulate human speech sounds. To overcome this obstacle, they employed various visual languages. Some were artificial visual systems based on colored plastic chips or signs on a computer screen (Premack, 1976; Rumbaugh, 1977). Other studies used a natural language already employed by humans, American Sign Language (Gardner and Gardner, 1969; 1971; 1978; Terrace et al., 1979). While the interpretation of these studies is still a matter of controversy, there is no doubt that apes taught by such visual means give a much better account of themselves than Viki (see Chapter 5).

VOCABULARY

There is general agreement that chimpanzees can learn a substantial number of visual "words," whether these are ASL signs or artificial tokens. Consider Washoe, a chimpanzee introduced to a modified version of ASL at eleven months of age by Allen and Beatrice Gardner. Washoe was raised in an environment not too different from that of a human child, with scheduled meals and naps, baths, and diapers. She was taught some ASL signs by having her hands physically molded into the desired position; others were acquired by imitation (Fouts, 1972). After four years of this, she had learned about 130

10.22 Chimpanzees signing *(A) Washoe making the sign for "bird." (Courtesy Roger Fouts) (B) Nim, a young chimpanzee studied by another research group, making the sign for "hug." (Terrace et al., 1979; photograph courtesy Herbert Terrace)*

A

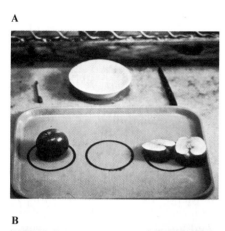

B

10.23   A test for propositional thought in chimpanzees   *(A) A chimpanzee is shown a whole apple and two halves of an apple. Its task is to place one of three alternatives between them: a pencil, a bowl of water, or a knife. (B) The animal chooses the knife, the instrument which produced the change from the uncut to the cut state. In other trials, when the animals were shown a blank piece of paper and a scribbled-upon piece of paper, in general, they would put the pencil in the middle. When shown a dry sponge and a wet sponge, they chose the bowl of water. (From Premack, 1976; photographs courtesy David Premack)*

signs, including signs for objects *(banana, hand)*, actions *(bite, tickle)*, attributes *(different, green)*, and action modifiers *(enough, more)* (Figure 10.22).

To check whether Washoe's vocabulary was genuine, the Gardners devised a special test. They showed Washoe pictures of various objects and asked her to sign what she saw. One observer saw the signs but not the pictures. A second observer saw the pictures but not the signs. By this arrangement, Washoe could serve as a communicating link between the two observers. The first had to tell the second what Washoe "told" him she had seen. Washoe did rather well, performing correctly on 72 percent of the trials. Nor were her errors random. When shown a picture of a dog, she would sometimes give the sign for other animals, such as a cat or a cow (Gardner and Gardner, 1971).

These results suggest that chimpanzees can learn words. They learn fewer than human children and learn them more slowly. (A four-year-old child has a vocabulary of over 3,000 words, impressively more than Washoe's 130.) They are also less spontaneous in their word acquisition than human children (including deaf children who learn sign language from deaf parents); apes' hands have to be molded and they are constantly encouraged to imitate. But even so, their achievements are impressive enough, and are probably greater than most of us would have expected from a "dumb" animal.

PROPOSITIONAL THOUGHT

As we have seen, one of the important functions of human language is that it expresses propositional meanings such as the relation between doer, action, and done-to. Are chimpanzees capable of any such propositional thought? We know that they have mental representations of various objects and events in the world, for they have words for them. But do they have mental representations of the relations between these objects and events? Do they have anything like a notion of this-does-something-to-that?

One line of evidence comes from some of David Premack's studies on the concept of causation in chimpanzees. Premack showed his animals pairs of objects. In each pair the second object was the same as the first but had undergone some change. One pair consisted of a whole apple and an apple that was cut in pieces, another pair was a dry towel and a wet towel, a third was an unmarked piece of paper and a piece of paper covered with pencil marks. The chimpanzees' task was to place one of several alternatives between the objects. Among the alternatives were a knife, a bowl of water, and a pencil. The question was whether the animals would choose the item that caused the change (Figure 10.23). On this and similar tests, Premack's star pupil, Sarah, performed correctly on 77 percent of the trials. Premack regards this as evidence that the animals have some primitive notions of the relation between certain objects, acts, and outcomes—knives cut up things, water wets them, and pencils mark them. To the extent that the apes have these concepts, they have the germs of propositional thought (Premack, 1976).

SYNTAX

Can chimpanzees learn rules for putting words together in sentences in order to express propositional meanings? We know that they can learn words for, say, *cat, bite,* and *dog.* Can they arrange or modify these words to distinguish

401

between the two different meanings *the cat bites the dog* and *the dog bites the cat?* Put another way, the question is whether the animals can acquire syntax. This is one of the most controversial issues in the area, which is hardly surprising since syntax is generally regarded as one of the hallmarks of human language.

A number of investigators, including the Gardners, believe that Washoe, and many primates in other laboratories, have acquired some elements of syntax, perhaps on a par with children at the two-word (or two-sign) stage of language development. As evidence, they refer to a number of novel combinations of words or signs produced by the animals. Washoe has apparently come up with a few sign sequences of her own, such as *listen eat* on hearing an alarm clock that signals mealtime, *open key* when confronting a locked door and *water bird* upon seeing a duck.

A number of critics feel that such observations prove little or nothing. They are in the nature of anecdotes which can be interpreted in several ways. Take the sequence *water bird,* signed in the presence of a duck. On the face of it, it seems like a remarkable achievement—a chimpanzoid equivalent of a compound noun which presumably means something like *bird that lives in water.* But is this interpretation justified? Or did Washoe merely produce an accidental succession of two signs: *water* (perhaps water was seen just before) and *bird* (because of the duck)? Since all we have is an anecdote, we cannot be sure.

There are further methodological problems. Washoe and other signing apes often produce repetitive sequences such as *me banana you banana me you give.* Many of the investigators eliminate such repetitions from their reports of what the animal "says," much as a court stenographer ignores coughs and "er's" when taking a verbatim transcript. But the result can be misleading. For one thing, this sort of random repetition is not at all characteristic of early childhood speech; eliminating these repetitions may also create an unjustified impression of meaningfulness. If *me banana you banana me you give* is rendered as, say, *me banana you give,* the result makes a bit more sense (it might mean "you give me a banana"). But this sense is the experimenter's rather than the ape's (Seidenberg and Petitto, 1979).

Current evidence, then, is that chimpanzees can learn words and show some propositional thought. But there is no satisfactory evidence that they can acquire syntax, a system of rules that allows them to recognize different arrangements of the same words so as to express different propositional meanings. And even if they do have some sense of **sequence** (and many investigators doubt it), this by itself is not enough. The hallmark of syntax is a hierarchical structure in which units are organized at many levels of complexity, each with its rules—phonemes, morphemes, words, phrases, sentences. There is not the slightest evidence as yet that chimpanzees can acquire such a hierarchical structure, that they can learn, say, that sentences consist of phrases. While two-year-old humans give only slight evidence of such syntactic knowledge, they soon turn into three-year olds and then they do. But even adult chimpanzees have never yet shown any such capacity.

To sum up, the chimpanzees' linguistic abilities are probably greater than that of any other nonhuman animal, but they are very much less than our own. All of which makes perfectly good sense on the assumption that language learning is a biologically pre-programmed activity. If so, it should not be too surprising that the animal biologically closest to us shows some rudiments of this capacity. Whether these rudiments are enough to warrant the title *language* depends on one's definition. We can choose to say that the apes use language. But in so doing, we have changed the ordinary meaning of the term. For one thing is certain: If any of our children learned language the way Washoe did, we would be terror-stricken and rush them to the nearest neurologist.

Language Learning and Critical Periods

There is an important and familiar phenomenon we have ignored thus far—language learning is very much easier in children than in adults. This and related facts are often regarded as evidence that there is a **critical period** for language learning. This period is thought to extend from roughly three months to puberty. According to the hypothesis, some characteristics of the brain change as the critical period draws to its close so that later language learning (both of the first language and of later ones) becomes more difficult (Lenneberg, 1967).

Critical periods seem to govern the acquisition of a number of important behavior patterns in many animals. One example is the attachment of the infant to its mother which generally can only be formed in early childhood (see Chapter 11). Another example is bird song. Male birds of many species have a song that is characteristic of their own kind. They learn this song by listening to adult males of their own species. But this exposure will only be effective if it occurs at a certain period in the bird's life. This has been extensively documented for the white-crowned sparrow. To learn the white-crowned sparrow song in all its glory (complete with special trills and grace notes), the baby birds must hear an adult's song sometime between the seventh and sixtieth day of their life. The next forty days are a marginal period. If the fledgling hears his species song during that interval but hasn't heard it before, he learns some limited basics of the sparrow song, without the full elaborations heard in normal adults (Figure 10.24). If the exposure comes still later, it has no effect at all. The bird will never sing (Marler, 1970).

Evidence for a critical period in language learning comes from various sources. Taken alone, none of these is particularly convincing. But considered as a whole, they seem to make a rather good case.

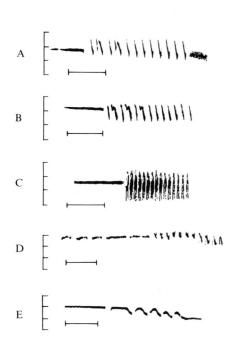

10.24   Critical period in the development of bird song   (A) A graphic presentation of the song of an adult, male white-crowned sparrow. The figure, a so-called sound spectrograph, plots the frequency region of the bird's vocal output over time. Frequency is indicated by the vertical axis, in steps of 2,000 hertz. The horizontal time marker indicates ½ second. The figure shows that the normal song begins with a whistle or two, continues with a series of trills, and ends with a vibrato. (B) The song of a bird raised in acoustic isolation but exposed to four minutes of normal song between the ages of 35 and 56 days. His adult song was almost normal. (C) The song of an isolated bird exposed to normal song between days 50 and 71. The adult song of this bird has some crude similarities to normal white-crowned sparrow song. There is a whistle followed by trills, but the details are very different. (D) and (E) show the songs of birds whose exposure to normal song occurred very early in life (days 3 to 7) or very late (after 300 days of age) respectively. Training at either of these times had no effect. (After Marler, 1970)

FIRST LANGUAGE LEARNING

The most direct test of the hypothesis involves first language learning. Can one learn to speak (or sign) after childhood has passed? We have already discussed the few cases that bear on this question—children who grew up in the wild or who were isolated from language contact by insane parents. As we have seen, these cases are hard to interpret. We don't know what the children were like at birth, and we cannot determine whether their deficits are a direct consequence of their language deprivation or a more general result of their mistreatment. Still, some of the results are suggestive.

Consider Isabelle who was deprived of language until six and Genie whose isolation lasted until age fourteen. As we saw, Isabelle became a normal English speaker while Genie's speech never progressed beyond the basics and still lacks such elaborations as functor words and pronouns. It is tempting to suppose that when Isabelle was discovered she was still in the midst of the critical period for language learning and so could still develop into a normal human language speaker. But Genie had just entered puberty and was thus at the critical period's margin. This may be why she was only able to learn the language basics and never acquired its elaborations. This may be analogous to the performance of young white-crowned sparrows whose first exposure to adult song comes in the marginal period: they learn the sparrow song basics but not its elaborations (Goldin-Meadow, 1981).

SECOND LANGUAGE LEARNING

Cases like Isabelle and Genie are (fortunately) extremely rare, so we have very little information about first language learning in the years after childhood. In contrast, we know quite a bit about second language learning. Whether learning a second language is comparable to learning the first is debatable, but it probably taps some of the same capacities. In any case, there is little doubt that children and adults differ in their ability to learn a second language. Children pick up a foreign language very rapidly and soon speak it just like natives. This is much less common in adults. Consider immigrants from another country who acquire the language of their new home. Many of them continue to speak this language with an accent and may have occasional lapses on subtle points of grammar, even after thirty or forty years in the new language community. The general impression is that the cutting line is at puberty. If immigration occurred before then, there will probably be no accent; if afterward, an accent is very likely. Once again, we have a suggestion of a critical period. If this period is passed, language learning is more difficult, at least for the language elaborations.

RECOVERY FROM APHASIA

Further support for the critical period hypothesis comes from studies of aphasia. We have seen that damage to certain regions of the left cerebral hemisphere leads to marked disturbances of language functions called aphasia. Do aphasia patients ever recover?

The answer depends on the patient's age. If the damage to the brain was suffered in adulthood, recovery will rarely be complete. The outlook is much better if the injury occurred during childhood. If so, language use is often regained entirely. This means that children can relearn language even after they have lost most of it but adults cannot, which certainly fits in with the hypothesis that there is a critical period for language learning (see Chapter 2).

IS THE CRITICAL PERIOD SPECIFIC TO LANGUAGE?

In the light of all this, the notion of a critical period seems fairly plausible. What is less clear is whether such a critical period is specific to language. One can take a broader view, which simply asserts that children are better at picking up any and all complex skills of which language is only one. As of now, we have insufficient evidence to choose between the narrow and the broad conceptions of the critical period. It may be specific to language alone. Or it may be nonspecific—so much so, perhaps, that to assert that such a period exists amounts to little more than the statement that you can't teach an old dog (or an old language learner) new tricks (for discussions that emphasize the relations between cognitive stage and language stage, see Macnamara, 1972; Cromer, 1976).

THE INGREDIENTS FOR LANGUAGE LEARNING

When we consider the whole range of the evidence, we find much value in Descartes' claim that language is an inevitable part of human nature. There is reason to believe that human children come equipped with a species-specific urge to communicate in certain uniquely human ways. This biological predisposition enables them to acquire language basics—a simple system for arranging words to form propositions.

As children get older, they learn more and more language elaborations. They use functor words and combine propositions. They eventually appreciate the complex ways in which underlying structure is expressed in surface forms. But this progression from language basics to language elaborations is not universal. If language learning does not take place during some critical period, many elaborations will never appear, as in Genie's case. The same holds for persons whose endowments are drastically impaired, such as certain retardates and aphasics. As for nonhuman language users such as Washoe and Sarah, the best guess is that—while these animals may have interesting thoughts which they can embody in words—they cannot learn even the human language basics.

To sum up, children find it easy to acquire language because they are predisposed to organize language inputs in certain ways. They assume that language must contain meaningful words lawfully arranged into propositions. Such rock-bottom assumptions are guiding principles that make language learning possible. Children organize what they hear in terms of these assumptions and then put it together with what they observe in the real world. Armed with these biases about what language is and with their experiences in the world around them, children learn the words of their language and then proceed to invent its sentences.

Structure in Language and Other Cognitive Realms

We have seen structures and substance in human language organization that differ from those in other cognitive realms. But there are also some overarching similarities between language and cognition that we should consider. For example, perception, no less than language, is structured and organized, often in complex and hierarchical ways. Another similarity is less obvious. Language is organized according to a dual system, in which the listener is exposed to surface forms that reflect an underlying meaning structure. To understand what is said, the listener has to cut through the surface to the meaning underneath. One of the key questions for psychology is how people manage to do this when all they are given is the outward form. But this problem is not unique to language, for a distinction analogous to that between surface and underlying structure also exists in other psychological domains.

PERCEPTUAL CONSTANCY AND PARAPHRASE

As an example, let us return to a phenomenon we have already described in our discussion of visual perception (see Chapter 7). Suppose we look at a table. The table "out there" has a particular shape which is rectangular. But the image that actually falls on the retina of the eye is rarely rectangular. It is almost always a trapezoid whose exact shape depends upon the particular angle from which the tabletop is viewed (Figure 10.25A). Since that shape necessarily varies as the observer moves around, the trapezoid also varies. But despite the continual changes in the retinal image, what we perceive is something that remains the same: the constant, underlying true rectangular shape of the table out there in the world. Our perceptual system is somehow able to operate on all of the various trapezoidal images that the tabletop gives rise to, take account of the angle from which the table was viewed, and interpret them all as the same rectangle. In the terminology of visual perception, the observer transcends the changes in the **proximal stimulus** (the retinal image) and perceives the unchanging quality of the **distal stimulus** (the rectangular tabletop) thus achieving **perceptual constancy** (see Chapter 7).

Perceptual constancy effects of this sort are roughly analogous to certain forms of **paraphrase.** Consider the sentences *the boy hit the ball* (focus on doer) and *the ball was hit by the boy* (focus on done-to). These two sentences are paraphrases. They differ in surface form but have the same underlying propositional meaning. To this extent they are analogous to two different retinal images that correspond to the same tabletop. The surface forms are different because of a difference in focus. This is analogous to the visual difference in angle of regard which produces different trapezoidal images (Figure 10.25B). We previously noted that listeners seem to remember the meaning of what was heard rather than its specific forms; when asked to recall, they tend to recollect the underlying meaning while often ignoring the surface forms (Sachs, 1967). This is the linguistic equivalent of perceptual constancy in vision. We perceive the true, unchanging, rectangular shape of the real table and pay little attention to the shifting trapezoidal shapes of the images it casts on the retina. In short, both eye and ear (or more precisely, both the visual and linguistic perceivers) tend to hold onto the underlying structure and let go of the surface form.

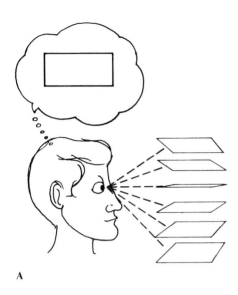

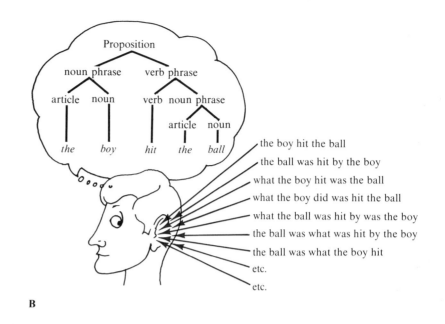

A   **B**

10.25   An analogy between perceptual constancy and verbal paraphrase
(A) Shape constancy. The eye literally senses a variety of different trapezoids, but the visual system interprets them all as one rectangle. (B) Paraphrase. The ear literally hears a variety of surface sentences, but the linguistic perceptual system interprets them all as the same proposition.

Of course this does not mean that the surface structures themselves do nothing for the perceiver. The visual perceiver wants to know the angle from which he viewed the table or he will soon bump into it. But he notes this as a separate attribute, independent of the table itself which he perceives to be "the same" from every angle. Similarly, the listener wants to know the focus of interest of the speaker, but she stores this idea separately from the proposition which she takes to be "the same one" in all its surface guises (Savin and Perchonock, 1965; Foss and Hakes, 1978).

Few viewers and hearers are especially conscious of the surface structure. One has to go to art school to notice the surface forms of tables (and draw in perspective) or to grammar school to notice the surface forms of sentences (and draw phrase structure diagrams). While we respond to surface forms, we are rarely aware of doing so. For most everyday purposes our consciousness is primarily directed at the real shape of the object we see or the meaning of the sentence we hear.

AMBIGUITY IN LANGUAGE AND IN VISION

A similar analogy can be drawn for certain kinds of ambiguity. For example, two sentences can have the same surface structure but different underlying structures. They thus appear identical but can be interpreted in two different ways. Similar cases are found in visual perception—the so-called ambiguous figures (see Chapter 7). The classical example is the Necker cube which can be seen in either of two ways (Figure 10.26). The perceptual system tries to determine what the image corresponds to outside in the world. In effect, it tries to find the underlying structure of which the image is the surface form. It does this by asking what external object could have produced this retinal image. It now comes up not with one, but rather two answers. As a result, there is an ambiguity—the pattern can be seen two different ways. This situation is analogous to the one produced by such linguistic ambiguities as *smoking volcanoes can be dangerous.* In both cases there is a single surface form which has two

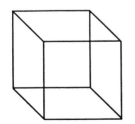

10.26   The Necker Cube   A classical example of an ambiguous figure which can be seen in either of two ways.

407

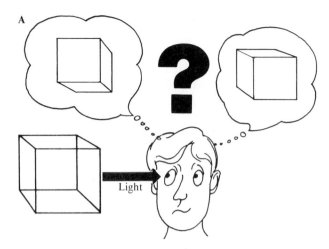

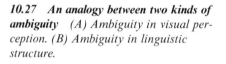

10.27 An analogy between two kinds of ambiguity (A) Ambiguity in visual perception. (B) Ambiguity in linguistic structure.

possible interpretations at a deeper and more meaningful level (see Figure 10.27).

SURFACE AND UNDERLYING STRUCTURE IN BEHAVIOR

The same analogy that relates certain aspects of language and visual perception may apply to yet further domains. As we saw previously, behavioral acts can be considered in both a *molecular* and a *molar* sense (Chapters 4 and 5). At a relatively molecular level, an act is described as a series of particular movements. At a more molar level, what counts is not the specific motor reactions but rather the goal or intention. There is no doubt that any particular molar behavior pattern can be expressed in a number of different molecular forms. A man may try to hurt another in any number of ways—by hitting, snubbing, or insulting. Here, we have a number of different expressions of the same underlying intention—to make the other person come to harm. This response equivalence is the behavioral analogue of paraphrase—different molecular responses, the same underlying goal direction. The opposite is also found—two acts that are more or less alike superficially but which have two different underlying goal directions. This is the behavioral analogue of ambiguity. An example is violently shoving someone who is standing in the middle of the road. This could be the expression of intense hostility or an attempt to push him out of the path of a runaway truck.

To the extent that language, visual perception, and goal-directed behavior are all organized according to the surface form and underlying structure distinction, they all pose a similar problem to the observer, who must somehow peer beneath what he is overtly given to grasp the meaningful structure that lies below. He must comprehend the underlying meaning of a sentence when he is given only its surface form; he must perceive the stable properties of a real object in the world when all he has is its retinal image; he must determine another person's intention when all he sees is that person's overt act.

Such feats indicate that in all of these psychological domains there are rules that relate the surface to the underlying structure and ways in which observers can come to know these rules and make use of them. These rule systems surely differ. So do the means whereby they become known to the observer. Some of these means are built in (perceiving whether an object is light or dark). Others seem to depend on learning (perceiving whether an object is large or small). But in all realms of cognition, there seem to be rule systems and hierarchical structures. A major task of the psychology of knowledge is to spell out precisely what these rule systems are.

Summary

1. Among the most important properties of language are that it is *creative* and *rule-governed.* The creative aspect of language use allows us to utter and understand an unlimited number of sentences we have never heard before. This potential infinity is produced by organizing rules of grammar and meaning which permit ever-new sentences to be spoken and understood.

2. Other characteristics of language are that it can express *meaning* and *refer* to the real world. It is also *interpersonal,* a system that allows one human mind to contact another human mind.

3. Any language is organized as a hierarchy of structures, going from *sentence,* down to *phrases,* to *words,* to *morphemes,* with *phonemes* at the bottom level. Each level of the hierarchy is governed by its own system of rules, as in the case of *phonological rules* that specify which phonemes can and cannot go together in a given language.

4. The field of *semantics* is concerned with the meaning of words. There is wide agreement on what meaning is not: It is not the same as *reference* and it is not a *mental image.* Two current approaches are the *feature theory* and the *prototype theory.* While neither seems to be an adequate description of word meaning when taken alone, the combination of the two looks promising.

5. *Syntax* is a system of rules for organizing words into sentences. The words are first grouped into *phrases.* Sentences are mentally represented in two different ways. One is the *surface phrase structure,* the sequence of phrases as it is actually spoken or read. The second is the *underlying phrase structure,* which more directly pertains to sentence meaning. A convenient way to describe both the surface and the underlying phrase structures is by way of a *tree diagram.*

6. Underlying phrase structure has two aspects: *proposition* and *attitude.* Many sentences that differ greatly in their surface structure, such as sentences in *active* and *passive form,* have very similar underlying structures, sharing the same proposition and differing only in the speaker's attitude to it. A number of studies indicate that listeners attend to and remember the underlying structure rather than its surface manifestation.

7. The difference between surface and underlying structure is highlighted by various relationships between surface sentences. Some sentences are *paraphrases:* They are essentially the same in meaning (in underlying structure) but have different surface structures. Other sentences exhibit *ambiguity:* They consist of one surface structure that can go back to two different underlying structures.

8. The meaning of propositions can be described as a set of relationships exhibited in their underlying phrase structure. In English, the *doer* is described by the first noun phrase, the *action* by the verb, the *done-to* by the noun phrase that is contained in the verb phrase.

9. The listener's task in comprehension is to reconstruct the underlying structure from *cues* in the surface structures. One of the first steps in this process seems to be *clause analysis,* as shown by studies on perceived location of clicks presented within sentences. Further studies show that listeners utilize various strategies to determine which noun phrase is the doer of the sentence; among these strategies are an initial bias toward the active form, the use of syntactic cues such as *-ed by,* and analysis by semantic meaning.

10. Any theory of language acquisition in children has to explain (a) how children learn rules when all they hear are utterances, (b) how all children in a given language community end up knowing the same rules even though they all hear different sentences, and (c) why all normal children succeed at language learning. Certain simple principles of learning, specifically, *imitation, reinforcement,* and *correction,* cannot account for these phenomena.

11. The normal course of early language development goes through a number of stages. At about four months, the infants will *babble,* and will then begin to talk between ten and twenty months. Initially, infants talk in *one-word utterances.* At about two years they become *telegraphic speakers,* uttering *two-word,* and a bit later, *three-word sentences.* At this point, the child has acquired *language basics,* a simple syntax that expresses propositional ideas but lacks most of the *functors* and devices for combining propositions into complex sentences.

12. At about three years *language elaborations* are developed, including an increasing use of functors. Proof that language rules are being learned comes from *errors of overgeneralization.* These overgeneralizations may be one of the main factors that lead to *language change.*

13. There has been considerable interest in how language acquisition proceeds in radically altered environments, as in the case of *wild children* reared by animals, *isolated children* raised in human company but under monstrous conditions, and *deaf children who have no language model* because they are raised by nonsigners. The results indicate that children isolated from language but not from human society learn at least language basics, including deaf children without a language model who may invent an elementary language system. Deaf children with signing parents learn a manual language as elaborate as spoken language. These facts have been interpreted as evidence for a biologically pre-programmed language learning capacity.

14. Similar theoretical interests have led to studies of language under conditions of changed endowments, including work on language in *mentally retarded persons* and in *aphasics.* Almost all retardates acquire language basics; what is lacking or impaired are the elaborations. The work on aphasia gives further support to the hypothesis of biological pre-programming, since certain areas of the brain are clearly specialized for language functions. In *expressive aphasia,* the deficit is in language production rather than comprehension, a deficit that hits language elaborations first and language basics second.

15. There have been several attempts to teach language to chimpanzees. The techniques include the use of a modified form of sign language and several artificial visual systems. The results suggest that chimpanzees can acquire a respectable vocabulary and are capable of some rudiments of propositional thought. There is as yet no evidence, however, that they can learn syntactic rules. To this extent, the results are in line with the view that language is characteristic of humans only.

16. Several phenomena suggest that there is a *critical period* for language learning in humans, just as there is for the development of bird song in certain sparrows. Evidence comes from studies of isolated children, of second-language learning, and of recovery from aphasia.

17. The distinction between surface and underlying structure, that is so basic to language, has analogues in other cognitive domains. In visual perception it is related to the distinction between the proximal stimulus and the perception of the distal stimulus; in the interpretation of behavior it corresponds to the molecular-molar distinction. As a result, there are further analogies. For example, *paraphrase* is a linguistic version of *size* and *shape constancy,* while *ambiguous sentences* have perceptual analogues in *ambiguous figures.*

PART III

Social Behavior

In the preceding chapters, we have asked what organisms do, what they want, and what they know. But thus far we have raised these questions in a somewhat limited context, for we have considered the organism as an isolated individual, abstracted from the social world in which it lives. For some psychological questions this approach may be perfectly valid. Robinson Crusoe's visual system was surely no different on his lonely island than back home in London. But many other aspects of behavior are impossible to describe by considering a single organism alone, without reference to its fellows. Consider a male parrot feeding a female in a courtship ritual, a monkey mother clasping her infant closer at a stranger's approach, two stags locking antlers during the rutting season, or the front runner of a band of wild hunting dogs cutting off a fleeing zebra's escape—all of these activities are social by definition. Courtship, sex, parental care, competition, and cooperation are not merely actions. *They are* interactions *in which each participant's behavior is affected by the behavior of the others.*

Social interactions are vital in the lives of most animals; after all, successful reproduction (that is, sex and parental care) is what species survival is all about. In humans, the role of social factors is even more powerful than in animals, for our world is fashioned not only by our contemporaries but by generations preceding whose vast cultural heritage structures the very fabric of our lives. Most of our motives are social for they concern other people—the desire to be loved, to be accepted, to be esteemed, perhaps to excel, and in some cases, unhappily, to inflict pain and hurt. The all-importance of social factors extends even to motives that, on the face of it, seem to involve only the isolated organism, motives such as hunger, thirst, and temperature maintenance. These motives as such may pertain primarily to the individual, but the ways in which they are satisfied are enormously affected by the social context in which we live. We eat food that is raised by a complex agricultural technology based on millenia of human discovery, and we eat it, delicately, with knife and fork, according to the etiquette of a long-dead king. Even the isolated Robinson Crusoe was no exception. In Defoe's tale, Crusoe's survival depended upon a few items of valuable debris he managed to salvage from his sunken ship. Thus his existence was not truly solitary; he was still bound to a world of others—by a few nails, a hammer, and a plank or two. Robinson Crusoe was on an island, but even he was not an island entire to itself.

In the following chapters we will discuss these social factors in some detail, as they bear on our actions, motives, thoughts, and knowledge.

CHAPTER 11

The Biological Basis
of Social Behavior

A classic question posed by philosophers is, "What is the basic social nature of man?" Are greed, competition, and hate (or, for that matter, charity, cooperation, and love) unalterable components of the human makeup, or can they be instilled or nullified by proper training? To answer these questions, we will have to consider not just humankind but some of its animal cousins as well.

The Social Nature of Humans and Animals

Are human beings so built that social interaction is an intrinsic part of their makeup? Or are they essentially solitary creatures who turn to others only because they need them for their own selfish purposes? The English social philosopher Thomas Hobbes (1588–1679) argued for the second of these alternatives. In his view, man is a self-centered brute who, left to his own devices, will seek his own gain regardless of the cost to others. Except for the civilizing constraints imposed by society, men would inevitably be in an eternal "war of all against all." According to Hobbes, this frightening "state of nature" is approximated during times of anarchy and civil war. These were conditions Hobbes knew all too well, for he lived during a time of violent upheavals in England when Stuart royalists battled Cromwell's Puritans, when commoners beheaded their king in a public square, and when pillage, burning, and looting were commonplace. In such a state of nature, man's life is a sorry lot. There are "no Arts; no Letters; no Society; and which is worst of

Thomas Hobbes *(After a painting by William Dobson; courtesy The Granger Collection)*

Charles Darwin *(Courtesy The American Museum of Natural History)*

all, continuall feare, and danger of violent death; And the life of man solitary, poore, nasty, brutish, and short" (Hobbes, 1651, p. 186). Hobbes argued that under the circumstances, men had no choice but to protect themselves against their own ugly natures. They did so by entering into a "social contract" to form a collective commonwealth, the State.

Hobbes' psychological starting points are simple enough: Man is by nature asocial and destructively rapacious. Society is a means to chain the brute within. Only when curbed by social fetters does man go beyond his animal nature, does he become truly human. Given this position, the various social motives that bind us to others (that is, love, loyalty) presumably are imposed through culture and convention. They are learned, for they could not possibly be part of our intrinsic makeup.

NATURAL SELECTION AND EVOLUTION: CHARLES DARWIN

During the nineteenth century, Hobbes' doctrine of inherent human aggression and depravity was garbed in the mantle of science. The Industrial Revolution seemed to give ample proof that life is indeed a Hobbesian battle of each against all, whether in the marketplace, in the sweatshops, or in the far-off colonies. Ruthless competition among men was regarded as just one facet of a more general struggle for existence that is waged among all living things. This harsh view of nature had gained great impetus at the start of the nineteenth century when Thomas Malthus announced his famous law of population growth. According to Malthus, human and animal populations grow by geometrical progression (for example, 1, 2, 4, 8, 16, . . .) while the food supply grows arithmetically (for example, 1, 2, 3, 4, 5, . . .). As a result, there is inevitable scarcity and a continual battle for survival.

When Charles Darwin (1809–82) read Malthus' essay, he finally found the explanatory principle he had been seeking to account for the evolution of living things. He, as others before him, believed that all present-day plants, animals, and even humans, were descended from prior forms. The evidence came from various sources such as fossil records that showed the gradual transformation from long-extinct species to those now living. But what had produced these changes? Within each species there are individual variations; some horses are faster, others are slower. Many of these variations are part of the animal's hereditary makeup and thus are bequeathed to its descendants. But will an individual animal have descendants? That depends on how it fares in the struggle for existence. As a matter of fact, most organisms don't live long enough to reproduce. Only a few seedlings grow up to be trees; only a few tadpoles achieve froghood. But certain characteristics may make survival a bit more likely. The faster horse is more likely to escape predatory cats than its slower fellow and it is thus more likely to leave offspring. This process of **natural selection** does not guarantee survival and reproduction; it only increases their likelihood. In consequence, evolutionary change is very gradual and proceeds over eons. (Darwin, 1872a).

INHERITED PREDISPOSITIONS TO BEHAVIOR

The inherited characteristics that increase the chance for biological survival (that is, reproduction) may concern bodily structures, such as the horse's hooves. But Darwin and his successors pointed out that natural selection may also involve behavior. Squirrels bury nuts and beavers construct dams; these behavior patterns are characteristic of the species and depend on the animals' *genes,* the basic units of heredity. Whether these genes are selected for or not depends upon the *adaptive value* (that is, the biological survival value) of the behavior they give rise to. A squirrel who has a genetic predisposition to bury nuts in autumn is presumably more likely to survive the winter than one who doesn't. As a result, it is more likely to have offspring who will inherit the nut-burying gene (or genes). The end product is an increase in the number of nut-burying squirrels.

Granted that behavior can be shaped by evolution, what kind of behavior is most likely to evolve? And, most important to us, what kind of built-in predispositions are most likely to characterize humankind? Many nineteenth-century thinkers answered in Hobbesian terms. They reasoned that man is an animal and that in the bitter struggle for existence all animals are shameless egoists by sheer necessity. At bottom, they are all solitary and selfish, and man is no exception. To the extent that humans act sociably and on occasion even unselfishly—mating, rearing children, living and working with others—they have learned to do so in order to satisfy some self-centered motive such as lust or hunger.

On the face of it, this Hobbesian view seems to fit evolutionary doctrine. But on closer examination, Darwinian theory does not imply anything of the sort. It holds that there is "survival of the fittest," but "fittest" only means most likely to survive and to have offspring; it says nothing about being solitary or selfish. Darwin himself supposed that certain predispositions toward cooperation might well be adaptive and would thus be selected for. We now know that something of this sort is true, for animals as well as human beings. As we shall see, there is considerable evidence that, Hobbes to the contrary, humans and animals are by nature social rather than asocial and that much of their social behavior grows out of natively given predispositions rather than running counter to them.

Konrad Lorenz *(Photograph by Nina Leen)*

INSTINCTIVE SOCIAL PATTERNS AND ETHOLOGY

Most systematic studies of built-in social behavior have been conducted within the domain of ***ethology,*** a branch of biology that studies animal behavior under natural conditions. Led by the Europeans Konrad Lorenz and Niko Tinbergen, both Nobel Prize winners, ethologists have analyzed many behavior patterns that are characteristic of a particular species and seem to be primarily built-in or instinctive. Many of these instinctive, ***species-specific*** behavior patterns are social; they dictate the way in which creatures interact with others of their own kind. Some involve a positive bond between certain members of the same species—courtship, copulation, care of the young. Others concern reactions of antagonism and strife—the struggle for social dominance, competition for a mate, and dispute over territory.

SPECIES-SPECIFIC BEHAVIOR: A CASE STUDY

An example of species-specific social patterns is provided by the three-spined stickleback, an innocuous little fish that is common in North European fresh waters. In early spring, both sexes become ready to mate. But how will they

Niko Tinbergen *(Photograph by Nina Leen)*

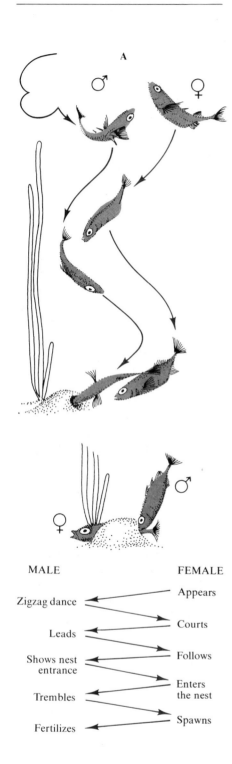

11.1   The mating ritual of the three-spined stickleback   *(A) The figure illustrates the steps in the male and female stickleback's pre-programmed mating pattern. The female appears, which triggers the male's zigzag dance, which leads her to swim toward him, and so on until fertilization. Each step in this reaction chain is a fixed-action pattern which serves as a releasing stimulus for a fixed-action pattern by the mate. (After Tinbergen, 1951) (B) Three-spined stickleback. (Courtesy Animals Animals/ Oxford Scientific Films)*

get together and meet at the right time? This synchronization is achieved by an intricately tuned system of built-in reactions. Each member of the pair acts in turn and its action provides the stimulus for the other to take the next step in the sequence.

The mating cycle begins as the male stickleback stakes out a territory for himself from which he chases all intruders. He then builds a small nest at the water bottom—a small depression in the sand covered with a bridge of weeds. His belly now turns bright red, an unmistakable advertisement: "Mature male, ready and anxious to mate." Sooner or later, a female stickleback will enter his territory. As she does, she displays her egg-swollen abdomen by adopting a head-up posture. This triggers the male's next response, a back-and-forth, zigzag dance which prompts her to swim toward him. This stimulus makes the male turn round and swim toward the nest. She now follows and this prompts him to poke his head into the nest opening. Having "shown" her the nest he withdraws and she enters it with her entire body. At this point, the male starts to quiver and prods her rhythmically at her tail base. This is her stimulus to lay the eggs, after which she quickly leaves the nest. The male now enters, releases his sperm and thus fertilizes the eggs (Figure 11.1).

FIXED-ACTION PATTERNS

Stereotyped, species-specific movements such as the female stickleback's head-up posture or the male's zigzag dance are called *fixed-action patterns.* According to ethologists, these fixed-action patterns are just as much a part of the animal's genetic makeup as are its bodily structures.

Ethologists believe that fixed-action patterns are largely elicited by genetically pre-programmed *releasing stimuli.* For example, newly hatched herring gull chicks beg for food by pecking at the tips of their parents' beaks. The parent will then regurgitate some food from its crop and feed it to the young. But what is the critical stimulus that elicits the begging response? To answer the question, Tinbergen offered newly hatched gull chicks various cardboard models of gull heads and observed which of these they pecked at the most. The most successful model was one that was long and thin and had a red patch at its tip. These are the very characteristics of an adult herring gull's beak, but the newly hatched chicks had never encountered a parent's beak previously. Evolution has evidently done a good job in pre-programming the chick to respond to certain critical stimulus features so as to recognize the parent's beak at first sight.

Among the most important of all releasing stimuli are those which are produced by an animal's own behavior. Such response-produced stimuli are called **displays.** They produce an appropriate reaction in another animal of the same species and are thus the basis of a primitive, built-in communication system. The stickleback's zigzag dance is an example of such a display, as is the gull chick's begging peck. One elicits an approach movement in the egg-carrying female; the other leads to feeding by the parent (Tinbergen, 1951).

THE SURVIVAL VALUE OF FIXED-ACTION PATTERNS

An instinctive pattern presumably has survival value, since if it didn't it would have been bred out long ago. An interesting study by Tinbergen and his associates provides an example of how the survival argument can be experimentally tested in a given case. There are several species of gulls who are remarkably tidy. Shortly after their young are hatched, the parents pick up the empty eggshells and drop them at some distance from the nest. Tinbergen supposed that this behavior tends to make the nest less conspicuous; the outer shell of the egg is camouflaged with irregular dots, but the open insides are white and clearly visible to would-be predators. To test this hypothesis, Tinbergen left some broken eggshells near some gull nests but not near others. The nests with nearby eggshell litter were robbed much more often. It appears that Tinbergen's conjecture was correct; an unlittered nest is less subject to predation. It seems that cleanliness can be a built-in virtue (Tinbergen, Kruuk, and Paillette, 1962).

FIXED-ACTION PATTERNS: INNATE OR ACQUIRED?

What is the basis for the belief that fixed-action patterns have a genetic basis? One line of evidence comes from the fact that certain stimulus releasers provoke the relevant response on the very first occasion the animal is exposed to them, as in the case of the newly hatched gull chick that pecks at its parent's beak. The same point is made by **deprivation experiments** in which animals are reared in specially restricted conditions. Male sticklebacks raised in isolation will attack a red-bellied (and hence male-looking) wooden model even though they have never seen a male stickleback before (Hinde, 1974, p. 38).

Even more persuasive are the results of studies in which animals were bred for this or another behavior pattern. An example is a study of lovebirds. These animals forage for nesting materials such as bark, which they cut into thin strips and then bring back to the nesting site. One species carries the strips in its beak. Another transports them by tucking them into its rump feathers. When these two species were mated, the hybrid offspring behaved in an intermediate manner. When they reached the age of nest-building they

419

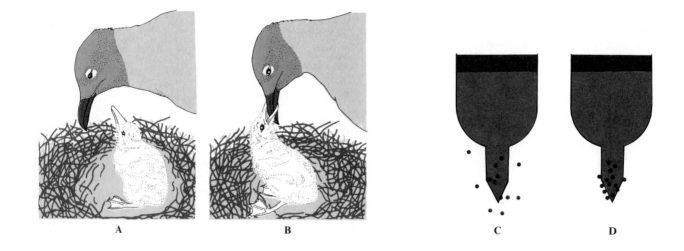

A   B   C   D

11.2　The modification of built-in behaviors　*(A) and (B) show the normal feeding behavior of a laughing gull chick. As the parent lowers its head (A), the chick pecks at the parent's beak, grasps it and bends it downward (B). As a result, the parent regurgitates some food which the chick then eats. When chicks were presented with painted models of an adult gull's head, the results showed that the pecking response is not initially perfect. (C) shows the pecks of a newly hatched chick: (D) shows those of the same chick two days later. The figures clearly indicate that pecking accuracy improves considerably, a demonstration that some fixed-action patterns can become further developed through learning. (Hailman, 1969)*

seemed thoroughly confused. They cut strips of nesting material and then tried to tuck them into their rumps but almost always without success. Eventually they used their beaks. But even then they acted as if they really preferred the other method; they raised their rump feathers and made incompetent tucking motions, in inefficient homage to a now useless genetic heritage (Dilger, 1962).

Such results are evidence for the claim that some species-specific behavior patterns are inherited. But this does not mean that learning plays no part in their further development. A given action may be built-in, but it often becomes elaborated and refined through learning. An example is the gull chick's begging peck. Initially, these pecks are quite clumsy and they often miss. But after only two days, the chick becomes an accomplished beak-pecker and strikes unerringly (Figure 11.2).

The Biological Sources of Aggression

The preceeding discussion provided a general introduction to built-in social patterns. The stickleback's mating behavior shows many facets of its social nature: the aggression between competitors, the attraction between male and female, the provision for future generations. We will begin our more detailed examination of these social processes by considering the biological basis of aggression.

That brutality and aggression form a recurrent theme throughout human history needs little documentation. Men have clubbed, axed, speared, stabbed, strangled, shot, burned, and otherwise demolished each other as far back as records go. Human aggression is clearly a fact. The question is, "What are its causes?" Some presumably are events in the immediate present, such as threats and frustrations that provoke anger and hostility. Others stem from the individual's own past and prior learning. Our present concern is with sources that lie in our inherent makeup, the biological roots of aggression that derive from our evolutionary past. To uncover these, we have to study animals as well as humans, for the biological sources of human aggression are often obscured by cultural factors and tradition.

CONFLICT BETWEEN SPECIES: PREDATION AND DEFENSE

Most psychobiologists restrict use of the term *aggression* to conflict between members of the same species. When an owl kills a mouse, it has slaughtered for food rather than murdered in hatred. As Lorenz points out, the predator about to pounce upon his prey does not look angry; the dog who is on the verge of catching a rabbit never growls nor does it have its ears laid back (Lorenz, 1966). Neurological evidence leads to a similar conclusion. Rat-stalking (predatory attack) and arched-back hissing (aggression or self-defense) are elicited by the stimulation of two different areas of a cat's hypothalamus (Wasman and Flynn, 1962). Predatory attack is an outgrowth of the hunger motive and not of aggression; the hypothalamic site whose stimulation gives rise to rat-stalking also elicits eating (Hutchinson and Renfrew, 1966).

Somewhat closer to true aggression is the counterattack lodged by a prey animal against a predatory enemy. Flocks of birds sometimes *mob* an intruding cat or hawk. A colony of lovebird parrots will fly upon a would-be attacker in a body, flapping their wings furiously and uttering loud, shrill squeaks. In the face of this commotion, the predator often withdraws to look for a less troublesome meal (Dilger, 1962). Defense reactions may also occur when a hunted animal is finally cut off from retreat. Even normally reticent creatures may then become desperate fighters, as in the case of the proverbial cornered rat.

Aside from these defense behaviors, aggression is the exception rather than the rule among members of different species. In an aquarium filled with tropical fish, like attacks like but leaves unlike alone. Vicious fights between unrelated species such as tigers and pythons have been photographed for wild-life films, but they are rare; the animals involved are either half-starved or they are goaded into the unnatural contest by having their escape route blocked (Lorenz, 1966).

Atypical interspecies conflicts may be engineered in the laboratory. Two animals of different species—a ferret and a rat, or a hamster and an opossum—are placed in a small, enclosed chamber with a wire floor. When the floor is suddenly electrified, each beast immediately attacks the other, as if to retaliate for the incomprehensible electric shock (Figure 11.3). This effect is known as *pain-induced aggression* and is by no means fully understood. For example, shock does not have this effect on animals that are normally ferociously aggressive, such as fighting cocks and Siamese fighting fish; no one knows why. In any case, it is reasonable to suppose that when the effect does occur, one factor is the animal's inability to escape from an enclosure that has suddenly become dangerous. So again the fight between different species seems more like a case of self-defense than like true aggression.

A

B

11.3 Pain-induced aggression *In part (A) a raccoon and a laboratory rat are peacefully together in a cage. Suddenly the cage floor is electrified. Now the raccoon immediately pounces on the rat (B). (From Azrin, 1967)*

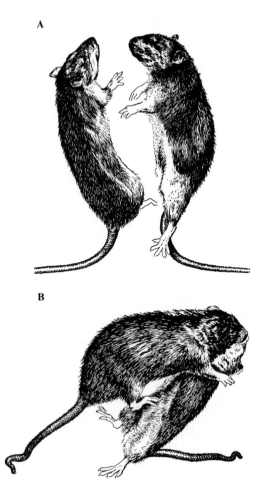

11.4 Aggression in the rat *Male rats generally fight in fairly stereotyped ways, including a "boxing position" (A) that often escalates into a leaping, biting attack (B). (From Barnett, 1963)*

CONFLICT BETWEEN LIKE AND LIKE

There is probably no group among the animal kingdom that has foresworn aggression altogether; fighting has been observed in virtually all species. Fish chase and nip each other; lizards lunge and push; birds attack with wing, beak, and claw; sheep and cows butt heads; deer lock antlers; rats adopt a boxing stance and eye each other warily, until one finally pounces upon the other and begins a furious wrestling match, with much kicking and leaping and occasionally serious bites (Figure 11.4).

Among vertebrates, the male is generally the more aggressive sex. In some mammals, this difference in combativeness is apparent even in childhood play. Young male rhesus monkeys, for instance, engage in more vigorous rough-and-tumble tusslings than do their sisters (Harlow, 1962). A related result concerns the effect of **testosterone,** a male sex hormone. High testosterone levels in the bloodstream accompany increased aggressiveness in males; the reverse holds for decreased levels. This generalization seems to hold over a wide range of species including fish, lizards, turtles, birds, rats and mice, monkeys, and human males (for instance, Davis, D. E., 1964). Stags, as indeed the males of many other species, battle most ferociously during the mating season (when testosterone levels are at their maximum) and even the wildest bull becomes a placid ox after castration (which leads to a drastic reduction of testosterone).

This is not to say that the female is always more pacific than the male. In a few species, she is by far the more combative. An example is the female hamster, who is both larger and much more aggressive than the male. In courting, the male is risking injury or even death if the female proves to be unwilling (Hediger, 1965). But more important is the fact that there are various situational factors that may produce intense aggression in even the most peaceable female. An example is an intrusion on her young, which is likely to provoke a vehement counterattack by the mother.

TERRITORIALITY IN ANIMALS

What do animals fight about? Their struggles are about scarce **resources**—something valuable in their world that is in short supply. Such a resource may be a food source or a water hole; very often it is a mate.

To secure a modicum of such resources many animals stake out a claim to a particular region which they will then defend as their exclusive preserve, their private **territory.** In many species this territory is held by an individual male; in some it is owned and defended by both members of a mating pair; in still others it is held by a more or less organized group, such as a wolf pack or a troop of monkeys.

We have already encountered one example of this territorial pattern in the male stickleback, who selects a few square feet which he then guards jealously against all other stickleback males. Another example is provided by male songbirds. In the spring, they endlessly patrol their little empires and furiously repel all male intruders who violate their borders. Contrary to the poet's fancy, the male bird who bursts into full-throated song is not giving vent to inexpressible joy, pouring out his "full heart in profuse strains of unpremeditated art." His message is more prosaic. It is a warning to male trespassers and an invitation to unattached females: "Have territory, will share."

One biological benefit of territoriality is that it secures an adequate supply of resources for the next generation. The stickleback male who chases his rivals away will probably leave more offspring than the one who doesn't, for his progeny will have a better start in life. Once his claim is staked out he can entice the female, offering his territory as a kind of dowry. Another important effect of this territorial pattern is the dispersal of the species over a wider geographical range. The male who has no territory of his own is forced to stake out a claim farther away.

LIMITING AGGRESSION

A certain amount of aggression may be biologically adaptive. For example, a more aggressive songbird will conquer a larger or more desirable territory and bequeath this advantage to his progeny. As a result, we would expect some selection for aggressiveness. But this only holds up to a point. Aggressiveness may confer some benefits, but it also has its costs. Combat is dangerous and can lead to death or serious injury. In addition, it distracts the animal from other vital pursuits. The male who is continually fighting with his sexual rivals will have little time (let alone energy) left to mate with the female even after his competitors have fled. Under the circumstances, natural selection strikes a compromise; there is aggression, but it is kept firmly in hand. Many animals have evolved built-in codes for conflict that set limits to the violence they do to their own kind.

One means of minimizing actual combat is territoriality. While this is an aspect of aggression, it also serves to hold it in bounds. Good fences make good neighbors, at least in the sense that they keep the antagonists out of each other's hair (or fins or feathers). When two troops of howling monkeys get within a few hundred yards of each other, they don't engage in physical battle. Instead, they defend their territories as befits their name by defiantly howling at each other from the safety of their treetops for hours on end (Carpenter, 1965).

The mechanism whereby territoriality limits combat is rather simple. Once a territory is established, its owner has a kind of home-court advantage in further disputes. On his home ground, he is courageous; if he ventures beyond it, he becomes timid and is readily repulsed. As a result, there are few actual conflicts other than occasional border skirmishes. This phenomenon is utilized by circus trainers who make sure that they are the first to enter the training ring; the animals come in later. As a result, the ring becomes the trainer's territory and even the big cats are more readily cowed (Hediger, 1968).

Dominance hierarchies Potential combatants can be kept at peace by means more subtle than mere physical separation. Animals that live in groups often develop a stable social order in which overt struggle is kept at a minimum. There are lasting distinctions of rank which produce a ***dominance hierarchy.*** The dominant individual has usually achieved his status in one or more prior encounters. After that his status is settled and he no longer has to confirm it, at least for a while. Lower-ranking baboons generally step aside to let the

A   B

11.5   Some characteristic threat displays
*Some species threaten by making them-
selves appear larger and more impressive.
(A) Some types of lizards expand a
throat skin fold. (Courtesy Animals
Animals/J. H. Robinson) (B) Other
species threaten by displaying their
weapon, as a baboon baring his teeth.
(Photograph by Irven DeVore/Anthro-
Photo)*

"alpha-male" pass and they nervously scatter if he merely stares at them. The
result is lessened aggression—everyone "knows his place" (Rowell, 1966).
Whatever fighting occurs is mainly among the younger males who have yet to
determine who outranks whom. Rank has its privileges: The alpha-male has
first choice of sleeping site and has priority in mating. But there are also
obligations. The alpha-male baboon takes the lead in group defense. He also
has some of the functions of a policeman. When younger animals quarrel, he
often intervenes to restore law and order.

Bluffs, ritual fighting, and appeasement   The limitation on violence appears in
other ways as well. Many conflicts are settled by blustering diplomacy before
they erupt into actual war. For example, male chimpanzees try to intimidate
each other by staring, raising an arm, shaking some branches, or uttering
fearsome shouts. This approach is found throughout the entire animal kingdom: Whenever possible, try to get your way by threat and bluff rather than
by actual fighting. This holds even for creatures as large as elephants or as
fierce as tigers. Both these, and other, species have ***threat displays*** which often
represent a compromise between an expression of fierce vehemence and one
of submission (Figure 11.5).

Of course, fighting sometimes occurs in spite of these mechanisms. When it
does, it is often conducted in a ritualized manner, as though it were some kind
of tournament with rigid rules of fair play. The combatants behave as if under
an internal compulsion not to inflict serious damage. For example, male
antelopes rarely gore each other with their horns, only engaging in head-
pushing contests. This is not because they can't use their horns as weapons;
when attacked by lions, they certainly do (Figure 11.6).

Wolves have an even more complex dueling code. They snap and bite at
each other until one "admits defeat" by adopting a special submissive posture,
such as begging like a puppy or rolling on his back (Figure 11.7). This is an

11.6 Ritualized combat *Male impalas (an African antelope) fight by pushing heads, with little danger of one goring the other. (Courtesy Animals Animals/ Stefen Meyers)*

11.7 Appeasement signals in wolves *Wolves adopt submissive postures, by begging like a puppy or rolling on their back. (Courtesy I. Eibl-Eibesfeldt)*

appeasement signal that is functionally equivalent to our white flag of surrender. Unlike some human warriors, the victorious wolf is without rancor. He generally accepts the loser's submission and all fighting stops. According to Lorenz, the appeasement signal is a built-in device that is very adaptive in an animal whose natural weapons are so lethal that the species might very well kill itself off if it didn't have some sort of arms control (Lorenz, 1966).

TERRITORIALITY IN HUMANS

Is any of this relevant to human behavior? At least on the surface there are parallels which have led some writers to suppose that concepts such as territoriality, dominance hierarchy, and the like, apply to humans as well as to animals. There are certainly some aspects of human behavior that resemble territoriality. Even within the home, different members of a family have their private preserves—their own rooms or corners, their places at the dinner table, and so on. Other territorial claims are more temporary, such as a seat in a railroad car, whose possession we mark with a coat, a book, or a briefcase if we have to leave for a while.

A related phenomenon is *personal space,* the physical region all around us whose intrusion we guard against. On many New York subways, passengers sit on long benches. Except during rush hour, they will carefully choose their seats so as to leave the greatest possible distance between themselves and their nearest neighbor (Figure 11.8).

In one study, personal space was deliberately violated. Experimenters went to a library and casually sat next to a person studying there, even though a more distant chair was available. After some fidgeting, the victim tried to move away. If this was impossible, books and rulers were neatly arranged so as to create a physical boundary (Felipe and Sommer, 1966). A desire to maintain some minimum personal space is probably nearly universal, but the physical dimensions seem to depend upon the particular culture. In North America, acquaintances stand about two or three feet apart during a conversation; if one moves closer, the other feels crowded or pushed into an un-

425

A

B

11.8 Personal space *Many species try to maximize the distance between themselves and their neighbors. Birds will peck at a neighbor who comes too close. (A) A result is the relatively even spacing of these herring gulls. (Courtesy Animals Animals/Leonard Lee Rue III) (B) A number of ethologists believe that the maintenance of personal space in humans is a related phenomenon. (Photograph by Wallace Litwin)*

wanted intimacy. For Latin Americans, the acceptable distance is said to be much less. Under the circumstances, misunderstanding is almost inevitable. The North American regards the Latin American as overly intrusive; the Latin American in turn feels that the North American is unfriendly and cold (Hall, 1959).

How seriously should we take such parallels between humans and animals? There is no doubt that many people—though not all—care deeply about private ownership, whether of things, of real estate, or more subtle private preserves. The question is whether this concern stems from the same evolutionary roots as does the territoriality of the songbird or of the howling monkey, whether humans really respond to a built-in "territorial imperative" that, according to some writers, is part of our genetic ancestry and cannot be disobeyed (Ardrey, 1966). There are good reasons to doubt that this is so.

The best guess is that while the overt behaviors may sometimes be similar, the underlying mechanisms are not. Territoriality in robins is universal and innately based; but in humans it is enormously affected by learning. For example, there are some societies in which private ownership is relatively unimportant, which certainly suggests that cultural factors play a vital role. There are also cognitive factors. Consider personal distance in a railroad car. Suppose you are all alone in the car and a stranger approaches and sits down next to you. Your reaction depends upon your interpretation of his action. Is it an attempt to start a conversation, an unwelcome intrusion, a sexual invitation? Or is it simply a response to the fact that all other seats in the car happen to be covered with soot? The point is that humans don't respond to other people's actions automatically; they respond to those actions as they interpret them. The robin has no such subtle problems. Compared to us, his life is simple; any other male that crosses the territory boundary has to be repelled and that's that.

The Biological Basis of Love: Sexual Behavior

The preceding discussion has made it clear that there is some biological foundation for strife and conflict. The tendencies toward destruction are kept in bounds by a set of counteracting tendencies such as territoriality and ritualized fighting. As we shall see, they are also controlled and modified by learning, especially during childhood in humans, and their expression is greatly affected by situational factors (Chapters 12, 13, and 14).

But over and above these various inhibiting checks on aggression, there is a positive force which is just as basic and deeply rooted in the biological makeup of animals and humans. The poets call it love. Scientists use the more prosaic term *bonding,* the tendency to affiliate with others of one's own kind. Such attractive forces are most obvious in the various facets of the reproductive cycle—between mate and mate, between child and parent. But positive bonds occur even outside of mating and child care. An example is *grooming* in monkeys and apes, who sit in pairs while the groomer meticulously picks lice and vermin out of the groomee's fur (Figure 11.9). The animals evidently like to groom and be groomed over and above considerations of personal hygiene; it is their way of "relating to one another." A comparable human practice may be small talk, in which we exchange no real information but simply talk for the sake of talking to the other person. Other people are part of our universe and we need them and want their company. Much the same is probably true for most animals.

SEXUAL BEHAVIOR IN ANIMALS

In some very primitive organisms, reproduction is asexual; thus amoebas multiply by a process of simple division. But the vast majority of animal species reproduce sexually. Sexual reproduction may or may not be more enjoyable than the asexual varieties, but its biological advantage goes beyond mere pleasure—it assures a greater degree of genetic variability. An amoeba who splits into two has created two replicas of its former self. Here natural selection has no differences to choose between; the second amoeba can be neither better nor worse in its adaptation to the environment than the first, for the two are genetically identical. Things are quite different in sexual reproduction in which specialized cells, *sperm* and *ovum,* must join to create a new individual. This procedure amounts to a kind of genetic roulette. To begin with, each parent donates only half of the genetic material; and, within some limits, it is a matter of chance that determines which genes are contained in any one sperm or ovum. Chance enters again to determine which sperm will join with which ovum. As a result there must be differences among the offspring. Now natural selection can come into play, perhaps favoring the offspring with the sharper teeth or the one with the more frightening aggressive display, and thus enhancing the survival of the gene that produced these attributes.

For sexual reproduction to occur, sperm and ovum must meet in the appointed manner, at the proper time, and in the proper place. The resulting fertilized egg, or *zygote,* requires a favorable environment in which it can develop as an embryo. Many structures have evolved to accomplish these ends and so have many behavior patterns.

11.9 Grooming in chimpanzees
(Courtesy Animals Animals / Miriam Austerman)

SEXUAL CHOICE

Advertising one's sex   Many animals have structures whose primary purpose is to display their owner's sex; for example, the comb and the wattle of the rooster. These structures are often crucial for appropriate mating behavior. In one species of woodpecker, the male has a moustache of black feathers while the female does not. An unkind ethologist trapped a female and attached a moustache. When she later flew back to her nest, her mate attacked her mercilessly, presumably under the impression that he was warding off an intruding male (Etkin, 1964).

In humans, structural displays of sex differences are less pronounced but they are present nonetheless. A possible example is the enlarged female breast whose adipose tissue does not really increase the infant's milk supply. According to some ethologists, it evolved as we became erect and lost our reliance upon smell, a sense which provides the primary information about sex and sexual readiness in many mammals. Under the circumstances, there had to be other ways of displaying one's sex. The prominent breasts of the female may be one such announcement among hairless, "naked apes" (Morris, 1967).

Announcing one's intention   In many animals, sexual display involves various species-specific behavior patterns. Some are mainly a means to exhibit the structural sex differences, as in the male peacock who spreads his magnificent tail feathers. Others are more complex **courtship rituals.** Penguins bow deeply to each other while rocking from side to side and certain gulls complete an elaborate aquatic ballet by exchanging gifts of seaweed (Figure 11.10). In some species such rituals also serve as a form of mutual stimulation and are a precondition for ovulation. Sometimes it is sufficient that the female merely watch the male's ritual without herself participating in it. In one study, male pigeons were allowed to court females—but a plate-glass window separated them. After seven days of watching the males go through their genetically prescribed ritual of bowing and cooing, most of the females ovulated—ready for the next step, should the experimenter relent and raise the glass partition (Lehrman, 1964).

11.10   Courtship rituals in birds   *The courtship ceremonials of the great crested grebe, a European water fowl, are quite elaborate. Part (A) depicts a head-shaking ritual in which both birds face each other, display their head feathers, and solemnly shake their heads from side to side. Part (B) shows an acquatic ballet in which the male swims toward the female with his head submerged and then suddenly shoots high out of the water just in front of her. And Part (C) illustrates a mutual gift exchange in which both partners dive to the bottom and then emerge simultaneously to present each other with gifts of water weeds. (After Etkin, 1964)*

A   B   C

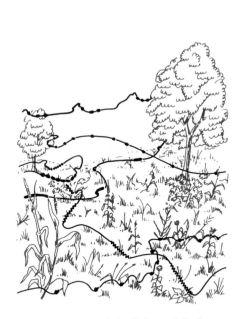

11.11 Characteristic flight and flash patterns of different firefly species
Firefly males advertise their presence by emitting light flashes until a female of their own species flashes back. Different species have different flight and flash codes as illustrated in the figure which shows a few selected ones. (After Bermant and Davidson, 1974)

In many animals, courtship involves alternating bouts of approach and withdrawal, of coy retreat and seductive flirtation. What accounts for these apparent oscillations between yes and no? There is an underlying conflict between attraction and fear; neither animal can really be sure that the other is not hostile. Each must therefore inform the other that its intentions are not aggressive. This is especially true of the male who in many species performs various appeasement rituals that allay the female's fears. The appeasement gestures are often derived from the animal's infancy. Thus many birds woo their intended mates by offering bits of food, as parents do to their fledglings. In effect, the courting animal announces that its feelings are gentle, as those of a parent to its young. In many cases, the rituals are only vestigial remnants of the parent-infant feeding patterns. Courting finches only touch each others' beaks—they "bill."

Indicating one's species Courtship patterns have a further function. They not only increase the likelihood that boy meets girl, but they virtually guarantee that the two will be of the same species. This is because the courtship rituals are so highly species-specific, as in the case of the gift-exchanging gulls. Differences between the courtship patterns of related species are found at all levels of the animal kingdom. An elegant example is provided by fireflies. These are beetles whose males fly around emitting light flashes until a female flashes back. Different species of fireflies have their own characteristic codes, using different flashing rates and rhythms (Figure 11.11). The important fact is that both sexes respond only to the flash pattern of their own kind. As a result, there are no attempts to mate between different species. Certain fireflies use this flash system to provide themselves with food as well as love. The females answer both their own males and the males of other species. For the latter, they mimic the appropriate flash patterns and then eat the would-be suitors when they arrive (Smith, 1977).

The effect of these species-specific courtship codes is that they maintain the integrity of the species. Contrary to popular view, different species can interbreed if they are related closely enough. They do not do so under natural conditions, but they are occasionally mated in captivity. The offspring of such "unnatural" unions are often infertile; an example is the mule, a result of crossing a horse with a donkey. But in other cases, fertile offspring may ensue. If this cross-species mating occurred with any frequency, the two original species would merge into a new form, which would, on the whole, probably be maladaptive. Different courtship patterns are a way of preserving what evolution has wrought by keeping populations in **reproductive isolation** thus maintaining them as separate species, each adapted to its own ecological niche.

Who makes the choice? The preceding discussions have centered on the various factors that bring male and female together. But, interestingly enough, the two don't have an equal voice in the ultimate decision. In most species, the female finally decides whether or not to mate. The biological reason is simple—the female shoulders the major cost of reproduction. If she is a bird, she supplies not only the ovum but also the food supply for the developing embryo. If she is a mammal, she carries the embryo within her body and later provides it with milk. In either case, her biological burden is vastly greater than the male's. If a doe's offspring fails to survive, she has lost a whole

11.12 Plumage pattern in the male and female phalarope *The phalarope male hatches and feeds the chicks. Since he carries a larger share of the biological cost of reproduction, he is more coy and choosy than the female. As the drawing indicates schematically, the female phalarope (bottom) is larger and more colorfully plumaged than the male (top). (After Hohn, 1969)*

breeding season. In comparison, the stag's loss is minimal—a few minutes of his time and some easily replaced sperm cells. Under the circumstances, natural selection would favor the female who is particularly choosy about picking the best possible male; that is, the male whose genetic contribution will best ensure their offsprings' survival. From the male's point of view, the female seems coy or "plays hard to get." But in fact this is not just playacting for, to the female, reproduction is serious business. According to our Victorian ancestors, "It is always the woman who pays." In part, they were simply describing the then-prevailing double standard of sexual morality. But their adage also summarizes a phenomenon that goes much deeper—a difference in the biological costs of reproduction.

There are a few interesting exceptions. One example is the sea horse, whose young are carried in a brood pouch by the male. In this animal, the male exhibits greater sexual caution and discrimination than the female. A similar effect is found in the phalarope, an arctic seabird whose eggs are hatched and whose chicks are fed by the male (Figure 11.12). Here a greater part of the biological burden falls on the male and we should expect a corresponding increase in his sexual choosiness. This is just what happens. Among the phalaropes, the female does the wooing. She is brightly plumaged, and aggressively pursues the dull-colored, coyly careful male (Williams, 1966).

REPRODUCTION AND TIMING

Once male and female have met, the next step is to arrange for the union of their respective sperm and ovum. Terrestrial animals have evolved a variety of sexual mechanics to accomplish this end. In general, the male introduces his sperm cells into the genital tract of the female where the ovum is fertilized. The problem is synchronization. The sperm has to encounter a ready ovum and the fertilized egg can develop only if it is provided with the appropriate conditions. Under these circumstances, timing is of the essence. In birds and mammals, the timing mechanism depends on a complex feedback system between brain centers and hormones.

Hormonal cycles For both birds and butterflies, spring is the time for love. Some mammals can conceive throughout the year, but many others have a **mating season.** The mechanism that governs the timing seems to depend upon the duration of daylight. As the days change in length, they somehow reset an internal clock. This in turn affects hormone production in both males and females. An example is the growth of testes. If male birds are caged in late fall but exposed to an artificial spring by gradually increasing periods of "daylight," their testicles will grow, and so will their sexual inclinations, which are normally dormant during the winter months (Marler and Hamilton, 1966).

Quite apart from seasonal variations, there are other cyclic factors that determine whether mating will occur. Except for the primates, mammals mate only when the female is in heat, or *estrus.* For example, the female rat goes through a fifteen-hour estrus period every five days. At all other times, she will resolutely reject any male's advances. If he nuzzles her or tries to mount, she will kick and bite. But during estrus, the female responds quite differently to the male's approach. She first retreats in small hops, then stops to look back, and wiggles her ears provocatively (McClintock and Adler, 1978). Eventually she stands still, her back arched upward, her tail held to the side, in all respects a willing sexual partner.

What accounts for the difference between the female's behavior during estrus and at other times? The crucial fact is a simple matter of reproductive biology. The time of estrus is precisely the time when the female's ova are ripe for fertilization. Evolution has obviously provided a behavioral arrangement that is exactly tuned to reproductive success.

The mechanism is an interlocking system of hormonal and neurological controls which involves the pituitary gland, the hypothalamus, and the ovaries. In effect, there are three phases: (1) During the first, follicles in the ovary mature under the influence of pituitary secretions. The follicles produce the female sex hormone *estrogen.* As the concentration of estrogen in the bloodstream rises, the hypothalamus responds by directing the pituitary to change its secretions. In consequence, follicle growth is accelerated until the follicle ruptures and releases the mature ovum. (2) This triggers the second phase during which the animal is in estrus. Estrogen production climbs to a steep maximum and stimulates certain structures in the hypothalamus which make the animal sexually receptive. (3) The third phase is dominated by the action of another female sex hormone, *progesterone,* which is produced by the ruptured follicle. Its secretion leads to a thickening of the uterus lining, a first step in preparing the uterus to receive the embryo. If the ovum is fertilized, there are further steps in building an appropriate womb. If it is not, the thickened uterus walls are reabsorbed and another cycle begins. In humans and some primates, too much extra tissue is laid on to be easily reabsorbed; the thickened uterus lining is therefore sloughed off as *menstrual flow* (Figure 11.13).

Hormones and behavior   Some hormonal changes affect behavior dramatically. When male rats are castrated, they soon lose all sexual interest and capacity, as do female rats without ovaries. Sexual behavior is quickly restored by injections of testosterone or estrogen respectively.

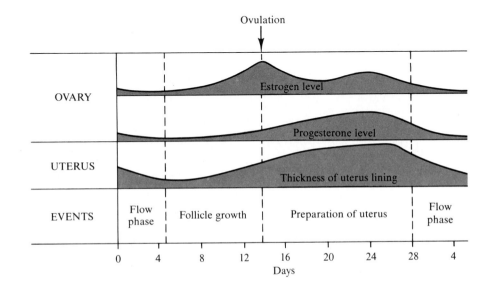

11.13   The main stages of the human menstrual cycle   *The figure shows estrogen and progesterone levels and thickness of the uterus lining during the human menstrual cycle. The cycle begins with the growth of a follicle, continues through ovulation and a maximum estrogen level, which is followed by a phase during which the uterus becomes prepared to receive the embryo and, in humans, ends with a flow phase during which the thickened uterus lining is sloughed off. (After Keeton, 1980)*

431

Many investigators believe that behavioral effects of hormone levels are caused by cells in the hypothalamus which can sense the concentration of sex hormones in the bloodstream. These "hormone receptors" are increasingly aroused with increasing hormone concentration and they trigger sexual appetite and behavior. This hypothesis has been tested by injecting minute quantities of various hormones into several regions of the hypothalamus. The total amounts were negligible and could hardly affect the overall hormone concentration in the blood. Will the hypothalamic sexual control system be fooled by the local administration of the hormone, as is its thermostatic counterpart when it is locally cooled or heated (see Chaper 2)? It evidently is. A spayed female cat will go into estrus when estrogen is implanted in her hypothalamus (Harris and Michael, 1964). Analogous effects have been obtained with **androgens** (that is, male hormones) administered to castrated male rats (Davidson, 1969).

Hormones affect behavior, but the relation can also work the other way around. What an animal does and what it sees and feels will often have drastic effects on its hormonal secretions. An example is the effect of copulation on progesterone secretion in female rats. Some progesterone is secreted during the normal cycle, but not enough to permit the implantation of the fertilized egg in the uterus. Yet more progesterone is released as a reflex response to sexual stimulation. In rats, the male evidently has two reproductive functions. He supplies the sperm but he also supplies the necessary stimulation which triggers the extra progesterone secretion without which there can be no pregnancy. This is shown by the fact that when the male rat ejaculates too quickly no pregnancy results. There has been too little stimulation to set off the female's hormonal reflex (Adler, 1969).

HUMAN SEXUALITY

The major difference between animal and human sexuality concerns the flexibility of sexual behavior. When does it occur, how, and with whom? Compared to animals, we are much less automatic in our sexual activities, much more varied, much more affected by prior experience. Human sexuality is remarkably plastic and can be variously shaped by experience, especially early experience, and by cultural patterns (see Chapters 12 and 13). This flexibility is evidently part of an evolutionary trend, for the sexual behavior of lower mammals such as rats and cats is much more stereotyped than that of primates. Virgin male and female rats who have never even seen another rat since weaning copulate quite competently on their very first encounter, if the female is in estrus. Sexual behavior in primates is another matter. Here experience plays a larger role. Inexperienced chimpanzees of either sex fumble clumsily at first until they gradually learn what to rats comes naturally, either by trial and error, or by appropriate instruction from a more sophisticated partner (Nissen, 1953).

EMANCIPATION FROM HORMONAL CONTROL

The difference between animal and human sexual behavior is especially marked when we consider the effects of hormones. In rats and cats, sexual behavior is highly dependent upon hormone levels; castrated males and spayed females stop copulating a few months after the removal of their

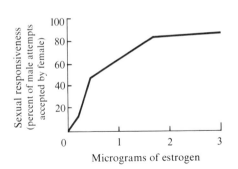

11.14 The effect of estrogen on the sexual behavior of female rats *The effect of estrogen injections on the sexual responsiveness of female rats is measured by the number of male attempts at mounting that were accepted by the female. The females' ovaries had been removed, so they could not produce estrogen themselves. The hormone was injected daily in the doses shown above. Sexual behavior was measured eight days after hormone treatment began. (After Bermant and Davidson, 1974)*

gonads (Figure 11.14). In humans, on the other hand, sexual activity may persist for years, even decades, after castration or ovariectomy, provided that the operation was performed after puberty (see Chapter 13; Bermant and Davidson, 1974).

The liberation from hormonal control is especially clear in human females. To be sure, women are subject to a physiological cycle, but this has relatively little impact on sexual behavior, at least when compared to the profound effects seen in animals. The female rat or cat is chained to an estrus cycle that commands her to be receptive during one period and prevents her from being so at all other times. There are no such fetters on the human female who is capable of sexual behavior at any time during her cycle, and also capable of refusing.

Although we are evidently not the vassals of our hormones that most animals are, this is not to say that hormonal factors have no effect. Androgen injections into men with abnormally low hormone levels will generally increase their sex drive. An important demonstration of this concerns the effects of androgen administration on male homosexuals. The androgen-injected homosexual becomes more sexually active; but, contrary to a common misconception, his renewed sexual vigor is toward homosexual partners just as before (Kinsey, Pomeroy, and Martin, 1948).

Another demonstration of hormonal effects comes from studies of the menstrual cycle. While women can respond sexually at virtually all points of their cycle, there are still some variations within that period. Sexual desire and activity tend to be highest during the middle of the cycle, when ovulation occurs (Hamburg, Moos, and Yalom, 1968). These effects are not very pronounced; they probably represent a small remnant of the old animal estrus cycle, buried under layers of evolutionary change.

EVOLUTION AND SEXUAL ACTIVITY

What evolutionary factors have led to this downgrading of hormonal control in humans? In part, it probably reflects a general trend toward increasing flexibility in most areas of behavior. Humans are less stereotyped than monkeys, who in turn are less so than rats, whether we consider how they mate, how they feed, or how they try to escape from their enemies.

There may have been some factors, however, that are specific to the sexual sphere. Some anthropologists suggest that the abolition of the female estrus period was an aspect of the evolution of human society. About a million years ago, our primitive ancestors embarked on a radically new way of life. They became **hunter-gatherers,** adopting a mode of existence that required a larger and much more complex social structure than any found among primates up to then. The males—stronger and faster than the females, and unencumbered by pregnancy—formed into hunting bands that pursued big game with spears and axes. The women stayed at a homesite, took care of the infants, and gathered whatever edibles were available nearby. What held these groups together? In particular, what led the men to return from their far-ranging hunting trips so as to share their kill with the women and children back home? Some authors believe that one inducement was sex. But the strength of this inducement would presumably be less if fulfillment could occur only a few days in each month. Under the circumstances, there may well have been a selective advantage that favored the disappearance of the estrus period.

This general line of reasoning suggests that one of the roots of human social organization is sexual behavior. In humans, sex had become a vital motive that went beyond simple lust. With the disappearance of estrus, sex could be less frenzied, more personal—more human. It became part of a deeper relation between the partners, which ethologists call a *pair-bond* and which most of us call love.

The fact of human sexual love is one of the most important aspects of our existence; it cannot be traced to one simple, single source, for it doubtless has many roots apart from sexuality: the built-in tenderness between parent and infant which eventually extends to the relation between mate and mate, social learning in infancy, and cultural patterns (see Chapters 12 and 13). For now, we will mention only one factor in the development of sexual love. It has to do with anatomy. When our ancestors adopted a fully erect position there were various anatomical side-effects. One consequence was a forward shift in the vaginal opening. This allowed the possibility of a face-to-face position during the sexual intercourse. Animals mount from the rear. Humans of course can do so too; in fact, they can employ any one of countless other positions. But interestingly enough, their preferred position is face-to-face. This preference is not unique to our culture; it is found in virtually all other cultures that have been studied in this regard, from Greenland Eskimos to Pacific Islanders. In part, the reason is that in this position the woman's clitoris receives more stimulation. But another reason is that the face-to-face position allows each partner to perceive the other's unique humanity, to see and feel who the partner is, so that sexual intercourse is not just copulation, not just a reproductive act, but is—making love.

The Biological Basis of Love: The Parent-Child Bond

There is another bond of love whose biological foundations are no less basic than the sexual tie—the relation between mother and child (and, in many animals, the relation between father and child as well). In birds and mammals some kind of parental attachment is almost ubiquitous. In contrast to many fish and reptiles that lay eggs by the hundreds and then abandon them, birds and mammals invest in quality rather than quantity. They have fewer offspring, but they then see to it that most of their brood survives into maturity. They feed them, clean them, shelter them, and protect them during some initial period of dependency. This period of protection allows the young animal to acquire some facts about the world into which it must soon enter and some of the skills that will help it to survive in that world. Not surprisingly, then, this period of initial dependency is longest in animals that live by their wits such as monkeys and apes; it is longest of all in humans.

MATERNAL ATTACHMENT

The mother-child relation grows out of a number of built-in reaction patterns, of child to mother and of mother to child. The human infant begins life with a few relevant reflex patterns, including some that help it find the mother's nipple and suck at it once it is found. It also has an essentially innate signal system through which it tells the mother that it is in distress: It cries. Analogous *distress calls* are found in many animals. When the young chirp, bleat, mew, or cry, the mother immediately runs to their aid and comforts them.

Why does the mother mother her infant? After all, it is surely a nuisance in many ways as well as a serious drain on her energy. Many ethologists believe that to some extent the mother simply can't help herself. In their view, evolution has equipped the infant with a set of stimulus features that function as innate releasers of parental, and especially maternal, feelings. The cues that define "babyness" include a large, protruding forehead, large eyes, an upturned nose, chubby cheeks, and so on. Endowed with these distinctive properties, the baby looks "cute" and "cuddly," something to be picked up, fussed over, and taken care of. The case is similar for the young of various animals who share aspects of the same "baby schema". Various commercial enterprises are devoted to the deliberate manufacture of cuteness. Dolls and Walt Disney creatures are designed to be babied by children, while certain lap dogs are specially bred to be babied by adults (Figure 11.15).

11.15   The stimulus features of "babyness"   "Cute" characteristics of the "baby schema" are common to humans and a number of animals. (A) These include a rounded head shape, protruding forehead, and large eyes below the midline of the head. (After Lorenz, 1943) These properties, as well as a rounded body shape and large head-to-body ratio, produce cuteness in a lap dog (B) and a cartoon animal (C). (Photograph by Wallace Litwin [B]; © Walt Disney Productions [C])

B

A

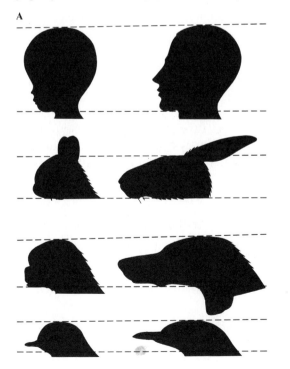

C

Nature has provided the infant with yet another trick to disarm even the stoniest of parental hearts: the smile. In some fashion, smiling may begin within the first month; it is often considered a built-in signal by which humans tell each other, "I wish you well. Be good to me." There is reason to believe that it is innate. Infants who are born blind smile under conditions that also produce smiling in sighted children, as when they hear their mother's voice. They obviously could not have learned this response by imitation.

THE INFANT'S ATTACHMENT TO THE MOTHER

Countless generations of parents have known that an unhappy infant is comforted by the sight, sound, and touch of its caretaker.* The infant wants its mother and wants to be sure that she is always there. As the child grows and develops, it ventures further away from the mother, gaining courage for ever-more-distant expeditions. But the child can achieve its ultimate independence only when assured that there is a secure home base, a place to run back to should unmanageable threats be encountered.

Separation anxiety (*Photograph by Tana Hoban/DPI)*

The attachment to the mother has a corollary: A separation from her evokes distress. For the first five or six months, the infant may still accept a substitute. There is as yet no clear-cut conception of the mother that differentiates her from all other persons. But after this early point, separation has drastic effects. Infants of seven months or older who are placed in a hospital for a short stay fret and protest and seem negative and frightened. After returning home, they remain anxious for a while, as if terrified of another separation. They continually cling to their mother, scream when left alone by her, are unusually afraid of strangers, and are even suspicious of such familiar persons as fathers and siblings (Schaffer and Callender, 1959). Similar effects are often seen in older children. One study dealt with two- and three-year olds who were placed in a residential nursery for some weeks. During the first few days, they cried frequently and desperately clung to some favorite toy they had brought along. After a while their crying abated, but not their distress. They became apathetic and hostile and lost previously acquired bowel control (Heinicke and Woestheimer, 1965).

As children get older, they become increasingly secure in the knowledge that the mother will be there when needed; they can therefore accept increasingly longer separations. According to some psychologists, this emotional knowledge provides a basic trust which then serves as the foundation for further attachments and allows the child to become independent, to become an adult (Erikson, 1963).

However firm our basic trust, eventually all of us must face the grim reality of irrevocable separation. The English psychiatrist John Bowlby argues that the grief experienced by adults at the death of someone they love is in many ways akin to the separation anxiety of a child away from the mother. But unlike the child, bereaved adults don't just fear irretrievable loss; they are

---

* Since the caretaker is typically the child's mother (which was certainly so in earlier eras), we will from here on refer to the child's caretaker by the traditional term *mother,* despite the fact that the actual caretaker may well be another person entirely, such as the father or a babysitter.

11.16 Grief in apes and humans *(A) Two orphans, a young champanzee after losing his mother and an orphaned nineteenth-century boy. (Photograph by Jane von Lawick-Goodall, top; courtesy Barnardo Photo Library, below) (B) A mother baboon cuddling a dying infant. (Photograph by Timothy W. Ransom © National Geographic Society)*

actually suffering it (Bowlby, 1973). The first symptoms of grief are often crying, as in the mother-separated infants. Following this—again similar to the isolated newborns—the symptoms are those of hopeless despair: numb apathy, withdrawal, and profound depression. Similar effects are sometimes seen in ape and monkey mothers whose infants have died. They refuse to abandon the dead body and carry it with them until it is only skin and skeleton (Figure 11.16).

IS THE NEED FOR THE MOTHER PRIMARY?

What accounts for the infant's attachment to the mother (or to some other person), an attachment so powerful that the mere threat of the loved one's departure leads to panic? Until fairly recently, most theorists believed that the love for the mother is a secondary consequence of her association with basic creature satisfactions such as the alleviation of hunger, thirst, and pain. Sigmund Freud believed that the infants's upset at the mother's absence is based on the crass fear that its bodily needs will now go unsatisfied. John Bowlby has called this the "cupboard theory" of mother love; it boils down to the view that the first love object is the mother's breast or the bottle.

The cupboard theory of the infant's tie to its mother has been criticized in various ways. One problem concerns the fact of separation anxiety. Children in hospitals are presumably well-fed and well-diapered and all of their bodily needs are taken care of. If that is all a child wants, why the intense depression at the mother's absence? Another issue concerns the great interest babies show in other people, even those who have never fed them or satisfied other bodily needs. They seem to enjoy seeing others smile or play peek-a-boo. Does

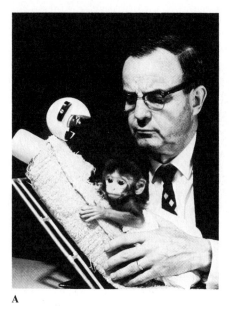

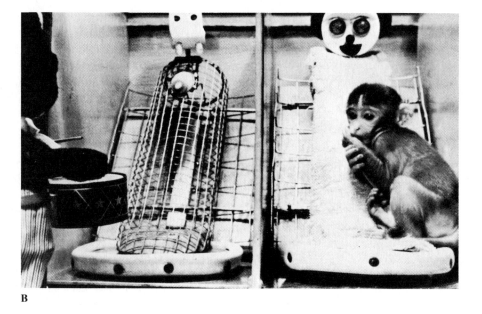

A

B

11.17 The need for contact comfort
(A) Harry Harlow with an infant rhesus monkey and a terry-cloth mother (which here, atypically, has a bottle). (Photograph by Nina Leen) (B) A baby rhesus, frightened of a mechanical toy animal, clings to its terry-cloth mother for contact. (Courtesy Harry Harlow, Wisconsin Primate Laboratory)

anyone seriously propose that the infant wants someone to play peek-a-boo with another person because this has previously been associated with food? It seems much more reasonable to assume that the infant comes predisposed to seek social stimulation which is rewarding in and of itself.

Another demonstration that love of mother goes beyond bodily need comes from the experiments of Harry Harlow. Harlow raised newborn rhesus monkeys without their mothers. Each young monkey lived alone in a cage that contained two stationary figures. One of these models was built of wire; the other was made of soft terry cloth. The wire figure was equipped with a nipple that yielded milk but no similar provision was made for the terry-cloth model. Even so, the monkey infants spent much more time on the terry-cloth "mother" than on the wire figure. The terry-cloth figure could be clung to and could provide what Harlow calls ***contact comfort*** (Figure 11.17). This was especially clear when the infants were frightened. When placed in an unfamiliar room or faced by a mechanical toy that approached with clanking noises, they invariably rushed to the terry-cloth mother and clung to her tightly. The infants never sought similar solace from the wire mothers, who were their source of food and nothing more (Harlow, 1958).

These results are in complete opposition to the cupboard theory. The monkey infant evidently loves its mother (whether real or terry cloth) not because she feeds it but because she feels so "comforting." Some characteristics of the figure toward whom the infant can direct its attachment are evidently preprogrammed. In monkeys, these apparently include cues to touch. Whether touch is equally important for human infants is as yet unclear, but very likely it plays some role. Frightened young humans run to their mothers and hug them closely just as rhesus infants do. Children also like stuffed, cuddly toys such as teddy bears, whom they hold tightly when they feel apprehensive. Perhaps Linus's security blanket is a kind of terry-cloth mother. It may or may not be; but, contrary to the cupboard theory, it is surely not a substitute tablecloth.

What is the alternative to the cupboard theory? According to Bowlby, the young of most birds and mammals become afraid when they are away from some familiar object (typically, their mother) to which they have become attached. In consequence, they do everything they can to stay nearby. Bowlby believes that this built-in fear has a simple survival value. Infants that lack it are more easily victimized by predators, who are much more likely to attack weak animals that are isolated from their fellows.

Of course infants could scarcely know enough about the world to fear specific predators. On the contrary, the built-in fears are probably quite unspecific. Bowlby conjectures that the fear of mother's absence is analogous to what psychiatrists call *free-floating anxiety,* a state in which the patient doesn't know what he is afraid of but which is all the more intense for that. Given this anxiety, even mild external threats become enormous to the child; the increased need for reassurance leads to wild clinging and "childish" dependency, as in the dark or during a thunderstorm. This may occur even when the threat comes from the parents themselves. A child who is severely punished by its parents often becomes even more clinging and dependent than before. The parents caused the fear but they are the ones approached for reassurance. This is analogous to the dog who licks the hand that whipped him. The whipping led to fear and pain but who can the dog approach for solace but his master?

THE DEVELOPMENT OF ATTACHMENTS: IMPRINTING

Who (or what) does the young animal become attached to? Harlow's studies show that the focus of filial devotion is not rigidly predetermined by the genes, as witness the love borne for the terry-cloth mother. Initially, many objects are capable of eliciting the infant's affections, though there are some limitations even at the outset; wire mothers will not do. As time proceeds, the range of acceptable attachment figures narrows further and further. In nature, this progressive focusing of filial attachment ends up exactly where it should, with the infants' parents, especially the mother. What is the process whereby this comes about?

Some interesting suggestions stem from the study of *imprinting* in birds, a kind of learning that occurs very early in life and that provides the basis for the chick's attachment to its mother. When a newly hatched duckling is first exposed to a moving stimulus, it will approach and follow the stimulus as soon as it is able to walk (at about twelve hours after hatching). If the chick follows the object for as little as ten minutes, an attachment is formed; the bird is imprinted. In nature, the moving stimulus is the duckling's mother and all is well. But in the laboratory it need not be. The duckling may be exposed to a wooden duck on wheels, or to a rectangle sliding back and forth behind a glass window, or even to Konrad Lorenz' booted legs. In each case the result is the same. The duckling becomes imprinted on the wooden duck or the rectangle or Lorenz; it follows these objects as if they were its mother, uttering piteous distress calls whenever they are not nearby (Figure 11.18). Imprinting is hard to reverse. The attachment remains despite the fact that the inanimate objects give neither food nor comfort. The real mother may quack enticingly so as to woo her lost offspring back, but to no avail; the imprinted duckling continues to follow Lorenz (Hess, 1959, 1973).

Imprinting occurs most readily during a so-called *critical period* which in

A

B

11.18 Imprinting in ducklings *(A) A duckling is imprinted by exposure to a moving wooden male duck. The duckling is then tested for imprinting by noting whether it follows the moving model. The more effort the duckling expended in the initial exposure—for example, by scaling an obstacle—the stronger the imprinting. (After Hess, 1958) (B) Imprinted ducklings following Konrad Lorenz. (Courtesy Nina Leen)*

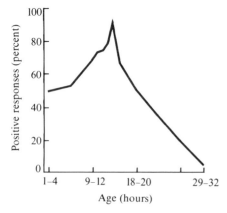

ducklings lasts for two days after hatching with a maximum sensitivity at about fifteen hours (Hess, 1959). Subsequent to this period, imprinting is difficult if not impossible to achieve. According to one interpretation, this is because now the young bird has become afraid of all strange objects. When exposed to the wooden duck, it flees from it instead of following. Having lived for two or three days, it has learned something about what is familiar and it can therefore appreciate—and fear—what is strange (Figure 11.19).

To test this hypothesis, several experimenters have raised chicks and ducklings under conditions of minimal visual stimulation between the time of hatching and the imprinting test. Since the animals couldn't see, no visual form could have become familiar, so that none should be strange and fright-

11.19 Imprinting and the critical period *The curve shows the relation between imprinting and the age at which a duckling was exposed to a male moving model. The imprinting score represents the percentage of trials on which the duckling followed the model on a later test. (From Hess, 1958)*

ening. As predicted, this procedure did indeed extend the critical period (Sluckin, 1965). But the extension was relatively minor, no more than a few days. Thus the fear-of-the-unfamiliar hypothesis can only partly explain why the older chicks don't imprint. Perhaps there is a critical period in the maturation of the nervous system which makes it especially responsive to some environmental events at that time.

Analogous behaviors have been found in various mammals. Lambs raised with a dog accompany it everywhere and bleat continuously upon separation (Cairns and Johnson, 1965) and one- or two-month-old puppies readily approach and follow people. Older animals do not bestow their affections so generously. Puppies who first meet humans when they are four months or older are generally quite wary; they can be tamed, but they tend to remain timid and unresponsive to people (Scott, 1963).

Whether the underlying mechanisms that produce attachments in birds and mammalian animals (let alone ourselves) are actually the same is still an open question. But at least on the surface there are some striking similarities. A lasting attachment is formed during a critical period in the animals's youth, such that proximity to the attachment figure provides comfort and security, while separation from it leads to distress. This attachment seems to be crucial for the creature's subsequent social development. Given these similarities, it is reasonable to suppose that studies of the development of attachment in mammals and birds may have some bearing on our understanding of analogous phenomena in human childhood.

SEXUAL IMPRINTING

Imprinting not only cements the mother-child relationship but sometimes has a further function. It enables the animal to recognize its own species and thus directs its future choice of a mate. *Sexual imprinting* is illustrated by birds who were raised with other species and then become cases of persistent unrequited love. If imprinted on geese, ducks will try to copulate with geese in later life; if imprinted on Lorenz, they will court Lorenz. Imprinting is evidently one means of maintaining species identity, but it is not the only means. In some animals, species recognition is clearly pre-programmed. An example is birds who lay their eggs in the nests of other species. If cuckoos depended on sexual imprinting there would soon be no cuckoos left, since none of them ever sees its own mother.

FILIAL AND SEXUAL LOVE

What is the relation between the human child's attachment to its parent and an adult's attachment to his or her sexual mate? On the face of it, there seems to be some connection. We use the same word, *love,* to describe both bonds, and we experience the same grief when either bond is severed. But what exactly is the relation between the two? A very influential hypothesis was proposed by Sigmund Freud, the father of psychoanalysis. As he saw it, mating and parental bonds serve the same basic urge, whose ultimate nature is sexual. On this view, the love between man and woman is a more adult version of the love the child bears to its parent, so that sexuality and filial love are at bottom the same (see Chapter 12).

441

A

B

11.20 Huddling and cradling
(A) A rhesus mother and older child.
(B) Human children. (Courtesy
I. Eibl-Eibesfeld)

Modern developmental psychologists agree with Freud's assertion that there are precursors of adult sexuality in childhood. Erections of the penis are observed in newborns, and the phenomenon of masturbation in both male and female preschool children surely proves (if proof were needed) that genital stimulation is pleasurable long before puberty. There is also little doubt that adult sexual partners often act with one another as though one were the parent and the other the child, often switching roles while doing so; they seek comfort and are comforted. But the fact that both filial and sexual tendencies are found throughout the life-span does not prove that the two spring from the same biological roots, as Freud had thought. The best guess is that they do not.

One line of evidence comes from the development of filial and sexual patterns in animals. As we have seen, many birds imprint upon maternal figures and also imprint sexually. However, these two processes are not the same. They seem to have two different critical periods. In ducks, maternal imprinting is restricted to the first two days after hatching, while sexual imprinting can wait as long as three weeks (Bowlby, 1973). Such findings suggest that filial and sexual reactions represent two different behavioral systems, with different biological origins.

Further evidence concerns behavior patterns that characterize parental care. These include sheltering and reassuring gestures, as when a monkey mother embraces her infant or gently touches it with her hands. Such gestures are widely used among adults in many animal species. They are a way of cementing a social bond and are not restricted to sexual partners. These gestures derive from the parent-child interaction; to call them *sexual* is to stretch, and thus distort, the meaning of that word (Figure 11.20).

Such considerations suggest that adult love represents the conjunction of two separate biological systems, sex and parental-filial attachment. In humans, the two often merge to create a powerful bond between lovers, cemented both by lust and affection. The two strands are woven into one fabric but they are still distinguishable. At one moment, there is intense sexual passion; at another there is a sweet feeling of tenderness.

THE ABSENCE OF ATTACHMENT

What happens when the initial attachment of the child to the mother is not allowed to form? The effects are drastic.

MOTHERLESS MONKEYS

We have considered Harlow's studies on rhesus monkeys raised with substitute mothers made of terry cloth. In some later work, monkey infants were reared without any contact whatsoever from birth on. The infants were isolated for periods that ranged from three months to one year. During this time, the infants saw no living creature, not even a human hand.

After their period of solitary confinement, the animals' reactions were observed in various test situations. A three-month isolation had comparatively little effect. But longer periods led to dramatic disturbances. The animals huddled in a corner of the cage, clasped themselves, and rocked back and forth. When they were brought together with normally reared age-mates, the

A   B

11.21 Motherless monkeys (A) A monkey reared in isolation, huddling in terror in a corner of its cage. (B) An isolated monkey biting himself at the approach of a stranger. (Courtesy Harry Harlow, University of Wisconsin Primate Laboratory)

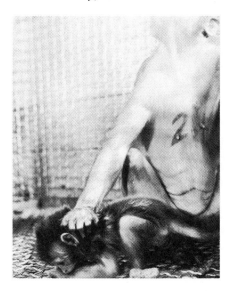

results were pathetic. There was none of the active chasing and playful romping that is characteristic of monkeys at that age. Whenever the normals took an aggressive lunge at them, the monkeys reared in isolation were unable to fight back. They withdrew, huddled, rocked—and bit *themselves* (Figure 11.21).

This social inadequacy persisted into adolescence and adulthood. One manifestation was a remarkable incompetence in sexual and parental matters. Formerly isolated males were utterly inept in the business of reproduction: "Isolates may grasp other monkeys of either sex by the head and throat aimlessly, a semi-erotic exercise without amorous achievements." Formerly isolated females resisted the sexual overtures of normal males. Some were eventually impregnated, in many cases by artificial means. When these motherless monkeys became mothers themselves, they seemed to have no trace of love for their offspring. Most of them just ignored their infants. In a few cases, there was hideous abuse. The mothers crushed the infant's head to the floor, chewed off its toes or fingers, or bit it to death (Figure 11.22).

Early social deprivation evidently wrecked the animals' subsequent social and emotional development. The evidence indicates that in monkeys the important age is between three and nine months. These results have been viewed as evidence that there is a critical period for the establishment of social attachment and affection, analogous to the critical periods found for imprinting in birds, for the acquisition of birdsong, and for language development in humans (see Chapter 10). The critical period hypothesis asserts that the relevant behavior system is either established at a particular time or not at all.

11.22 Motherless monkeys as mothers Female monkeys raised in isolation may become mothers by artificial impregnation. They usually ignore their infants. Sometimes, as shown here, they abuse them. (Courtesy Harry Harlow, University of Wisconsin Primate Laboratory)

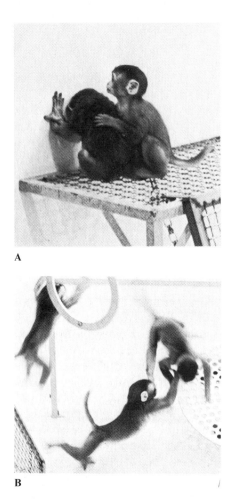

A

B

11.23 Therapy to undo the effects of early isolation (A) A young, would-be therapist tenaciously clings to an unwilling isolate. (B) Some weeks later, there are strong signs of recovery as both patient and therapist engage in vigorous play. (Courtesy Harry Harlow, University of Wisconsin Primate Laboratory)

There is, however, some evidence that things are not quite so all-or-none for the development of social relations in primates. It appears that some of the effects of early isolation in monkeys are reversible. In one study, young rhesus monkeys were rehabilitated for social life after six months of isolation (Suomi, Harlow, and McKinney, 1972). They were placed together with monkey "therapists." These therapists were carefully chosen. They were normally reared and were three months *younger* than their patients. They were thus too young to display aggression but old enough to seek and initiate social contact. At first, the previously isolated monkeys withdrew and huddled in their corners. But they hadn't counted on the persistence of their little therapists who followed them and clung to them. After a while, the isolates clung back, and within a few weeks patient and therapist were vigorously playing with each other (Figure 11.23). Six months later, the patients seemed to be completely recovered.

HUMANS REARED IN INSTITUTIONS

Can we generalize from infant monkeys to human children? There is reason to suspect that there are some important similarities. After all, the monkey is related to *Homo sapiens,* however distantly; and like humans, monkeys go through a long period of development before they attain adulthood. In any case, it appears that human infants reared under conditions of comparative social deprivation (though needless to say, not as drastic as that imposed on the monkeys) suffer somewhat analogous deficits.

The evidence comes from studies of infants reared in institutions. In many cases, the infants received perfectly adequate nutrition and bodily care; the problem was that there was very little social stimulation. In one institution the infants were kept in separate cubicles for their first eight months or so as a precaution against infectious disease. Their brief contacts with adults were restricted to the times when they were fed or diapered. Feeding took place in the crib with a propped-up bottle. There was little social give and take, little talk, little play, and little chance that the busy attendant would respond to any one baby's cry (Provence and Lipton, 1962).

When these infants were compared to others who were raised normally, there were no differences for the first three or four months. Thereafter, the two groups diverged markedly. The institutionalized infants showed serious impairments in their social development. Their reactions to people were apathetic. They rarely tried to approach adults, either to hug and caress them or to get reassurance when in distress. Some of these infants were reminiscent of Harlow's monkeys; they sat in a corner of their cribs, withdrawn and expressionless, and rocked their bodies. Given this failure to relate to others, an impairment of language development was almost inevitable. There was no one in their worlds for these infants to communicate to. The cubicles were nearly silent; there was no cooing or babbling, little crying, and not a single word had appeared at the end of the first year of life.

The parallels to Harlow's monkeys are striking. As with monkeys, social deprivation in early life (though not at the very outset) led to serious disruptions of subsequent social development. We have seen that in monkeys this effect is to some extent reversible. Is a similar rehabilitation possible for deprived human children?

The evidence is by no means clear-cut, but the results of one study give some grounds for optimism. The subjects were children at an overcrowded orphanage. There were few staff members and little individual attention. After about one and a half years, some of the children were transferred out of the orphanage to an institution for the mentally retarded. Ironically, this institution provided the necessary means for emotional and intellectual rehabilitation. There was a richer and more stimulating environment, but most important, there were many more adult caretakers. Each of the transferred children was "adopted" by one adult who became especially attached to it. This new emotional relationship led to improvements in many spheres of behavior. While the intelligence test scores of the children who remained in the orphanage dropped during the succeeding years, those of the transferred children rose considerably. Similarly for social adjustment. When they reached their thirties, the transferred subjects had attained an educational and occupational level that was about average for the country at that time. In contrast, half of the subjects who remained behind never finished the third grade (Skeels, 1966).

HOW DOES THE PAST AFFECT THE PRESENT?

The studies of early social deprivation in human and monkey infants suggest that the normal mother-infant tie provides a vital foundation upon which further social relationships are built. But this early experience probably does not affect adult behavior directly. Harlow's investigations suggest how the process works in monkeys. Each step in a sequence of social developments paves the way for the next. The mother's presence during the first six months allays the infants' fears of approaching other monkeys. As a result, they can play with their age-mates and enter the social apprenticeship of childhood and adolescence. In interacting with their peers they gradually acquire the various social skills of adult monkeyhood; they can chase and be chased, can cope with aggression and if necessary inhibit their own. These skills allow both sexes to mate when they reach maturity and also enable them to respond appropriately to their own offspring. Each stage is a preparation for the next: the mother-infant tie enables the infant to enjoy peer relations which lead to mating and so on. Given this step-by-step progression, the motherless infants can be redeemed by introducing them to the subsequent peer-stage through special means—the unthreatening young therapists.

Something of a similar nature probably holds for human social development as well. Life after six is not a reenactment of earlier events. The early years are crucial in the sense that certain social patterns are much more likely to be acquired then, such as the capacity to form attachments to other people. These early attachments are a prerequisite for the formation of later ones; the child who never enjoyed some sense of being loved as an infant will be frightened by its peers and probably hampered in its further social development. But while the earlier attachments (to mother and father) are a necessary stage for the formation of later ones (to friends, to lovers) the two are nevertheless quite different. The first floor of a house can only be built after the foundations are up, but this does not mean that the first floor is another version of the basement.

SELF-SACRIFICE AND EVOLUTION

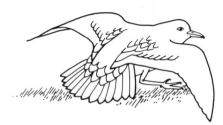

11.24 A misleading display *In feigning injury, the Kentish plover, a shore bird, runs erratically from predators that approach its nest, often flopping about as if it had a broken wing. (After W. J. Smith, 1977)*

PARENTS AND OFFSPRING

Many animals go to considerable lengths to defend their offspring. Various birds have evolved characteristic ways of feigning injury such as drooping one wing and paddling around in circles to draw a predator away from their nests. On the face of it, such acts appear heroically unselfish for they decrease the parent's chances of personal survival. But what seems unselfish from the vantage of the individual looks different from a biological point of view (Wilson, 1975). The mother bird who does not divert a potential attacker may very well live longer because she has played it safe. But from an evolutionary perspective what counts is not her own survival but the survival of her genes. And these are more likely to perish if she flies off to safety; while she hides in the bushes, the marauding cat will eat her chicks. As a result, she will have fewer offspring to whom she can pass on her genes, including the very gene or genes which underlie her maternal indifference. Those of her offspring that do survive will in turn have fewer offspring and so on until her genetic attributes disappear (Figure 11.24).

ALTRUISM IN ANIMALS

Seen in this light, parental self-sacrifice can be understood in evolutionary terms. Can a similar analysis be applied to unselfish actions that benefit individuals who are not one's own children? Such apparently altruistic acts are found in various animal species.* A case in point is the warning signal sounded by many species at the approach of a predator. When a robin sees a hawk overhead, it gives an ***alarm call,*** a special cry that impels all members of the flock to seek cover. This alarm call is based on a built-in, inherited tendency and is essentially unlearned. All robins emit this cry when in danger, and they do so even if raised in complete isolation from their fellows. There is no doubt that this alarm benefits all robins who hear it. They crouch low and hide, so their chances of escape are enhanced. But what does it gain the bird who sounds the alarm? Doesn't it place him in greater danger by increasing the likelihood that the hawk will detect *him?* Why does the robin play the hero instead of quietly stealing away and leaving his fellows to their fate?

One possible answer is that this act of avian heroism may well turn out to be a winning bet (Trivers, 1971). It may increase the warner's own chance of personal survival in the longer run. If a particular robin spies a hawk but remains quiet, then there is a greater chance that some bird in the flock will be captured, most likely another bird. But what about tomorrow? A hawk who has seized a prey in a particular location will probably return to the same place in search of another meal. And this meal may be the very same robin who originally minded its own business and stayed uninvolved.

---

* In modern biological usage, the term *altruism* is reserved for cases in which the good deed benefits neither the doers nor their own offspring.

But there is a more fundamental factor yet. Let us assume that our heroic robin is unlucky, is seized by the hawk, and dies a martyr's death. While this act may have caused the robin to perish as an individual, it may well have served to preserve some of that bird's genes. This may be true even if none of the birds in the flock are the hero's own offspring. They may be relatives who carry some of the hero's genes, brothers or sisters who share half the same genes or first cousins who share one-fourth. If so, the alarm call may have saved several relatives who carry the alarm-calling gene and will pass it to future generations of robins. These will eventually sound the alarm when their time comes. From an evolutionary point of view, the alarm call had survival value—if not for the alarm caller or its own direct offspring, then for the alarm-calling gene (Maynard Smith, 1965).

ALTRUISM AND HUMANS

Can human altruism be understood in similar terms? According to Edward Wilson, the founder of *sociobiology,* the answer is yes, at least to some extent. While Wilson emphasizes the enormous variations among human social systems, he still notes certain common themes which he regards as grounded in our genetic heritage. One example is the great human capacity for loyalty to a group and the heroic self-sacrifices this can inspire. Examples are soldiers on suicide missions or religious martyrs burning at the stake. Wilson suspects that such heroic acts are rooted in one built-in element—the hero's ability to subordinate himself to a group. The genes that underlie this capacity enable the individual to risk death in battle or in martyrdom. Wilson suggests that by doing so the individual helps to ensure the survival of the group (and thus of his own genes since the group probably includes his own kin). As with the robin, the individual hero may die but his genes will survive.

This sociobiological analysis is highly controversial. Some of its critics argue that human social behavior depends crucially on culture. To understand human self-sacrifice, we have to understand it in its own social terms (Blurton Jones, 1976). The ancient Romans fell on their swords when defeated not to save their brothers' genes but to save their honor; the early Christians defied death because of a religious belief rather than to maintain a particular gene pool. We cannot comprehend the ancient Romans without considering their concept of honor, nor can we explain the martyrdom of the early Christians without reference to their belief in a hereafter. This is not to say that in unravelling the cultural contexts of these acts we have explained them fully. We surely have not. After all, not all defeated Romans fell on their swords, nor did all early Christians choose martyrdom. There is much about human altruism that is still a mystery. But any attempt to solve this mystery must include some reference to the cultural conditions in which such human acts occur. Our human genetic makeup is relevant, but this relevance is probably indirect. Our genes allow us to have a culture, they make us sociable, they give us the capacity for language, they endow us with the enormous gift for learning on which culture rests. But they don't explain the products of culture directly. And according to Wilson's critics, one such product is altruism, as we normally encounter it.

Communicating Motives

The preceding discussion has given ample testimony that animals exist within a social framework in much the same way as humans do. What one creature does often has a crucial effect on the behavior of another of its own kind. As we have seen among animals, the major means for exerting such social influences is signaling display. What is the origin of this largely built-in mode of communication?

EXPRESSIVE MOVEMENTS: ANIMAL DISPLAY

Displays represent a simple mode of communication whereby animals inform each other of what they are most likely to do in the immediate future. The crab waves its claws and the wolf bares its fangs; these threat displays may save both sender and receiver from bodily harm if the message is heeded. In effect, displays communicate the animal's present motive state—its readiness to fight or to mate, its need for food, or parental attention, and so forth. For this reason, displays are sometimes said to "express" the animal's inner state and are therefore described as *expressive movements.* In humans, such built-in social displays are relegated to a lesser place. After all, we have the much richer communication system provided by human language. But even so, we still possess a sizable repertory of built-in social displays that tell others about our feelings and needs.

DECIPHERING THE MESSAGE

How do ethologists determine what message is conveyed by a given display? If the sender is an animal, we cannot ask it directly. We can, however, infer the message by noting the correlation between a given display and the animal's behavior just before and after its occurrence. For example, if a certain posture is generally followed by attack, then it is often called a threat display; if it is usually followed by mating, it is probably a courtship signal, and so on.

In actual fact, displays often convey not one motive, but several conflicting ones. This is especially true of threat displays which occur when the animal is torn between the tendency to attack and the tendency to flee. If there were only aggression or only fear, there would be no conflict and the animal would either attack or run away without hesitation. Because it is in conflict, it does neither, at least for a while. Instead, it threatens. Some evidence for this view comes from the fact that threat displays are most frequent in situations in which attack and flight tendencies are nearly equal; for example, at territory boundaries (Hinde, 1970). Some investigators have argued that the intensities of the two conflicting motives are directly mirrored in the expressive movement patterns. For instance, certain facial "expressions" of cats have been analyzed as mixtures of separate rage and fear components (Figure 11.25).

There is reason to believe that displays do not mirror the animal's inner motives directly. In such cases, the meanings of the message are not given by the display alone; to decipher the message, the recipient must also note the context in which it occurs. One investigator studied a special call uttered by a flycatching bird, the Eastern phoebe. This call is given in a wide variety of

Increasing aggressiveness ⟶

Increasing fear ⟶

11.25   Expressions of fear and aggression in cats   *Various mixtures of fear and aggression are manifested in a cat's bodily stance. In the figure, fear increases from top to bottom and aggressiveness from left to right. Thus the cat at the lower right corner is the one most in conflict, torn by equally strong tendencies to flee and to attack. (After Hinde, 1966)*

circumstances which undoubtedly involve very different motive states. But there is a common factor: Whenever the bird gives this call, it is likely to change its present locomotion. The call apparently indicates some conflict between two opposing motor patterns. Should it continue to fly straight ahead or veer off to one side, should it keep on flying or stop on a perch? The motives that underly this locomotor hesitancy may be aggression and fear ("Do I dare attack him?"), sex and fear ("Will she reject me if I approach her?"), or food begging and fear ("Will my father peck at me if I ask to be fed?"). Which of these motives is actually involved can be determined only by noting the context in which the message is given (W. J. Smith, 1977).

THE EVOLUTIONARY ORIGIN OF DISPLAYS

What is the origin of social displays? One answer dates back to Charles Darwin, who suggested that various gestures which seem to convey an emotional state have evolved from preparatory movements for an action the animal is about to take. Darwin gives the example of an angry dog's snarl. The lips are retracted from the sharp canines which are now ready for action (Figure 11.26). Analogous ***intention movements*** are seen in the threat postures of many species. For example, herring gulls threaten by pointing their beaks downward (preparatory to striking) and slightly raising their wings from their bodies (preparatory to beating another herring gull with them).

While some displays may represent preparatory movements of the sort that Darwin envisaged, many do not and seem to have no function apart from communication. An example is provided by certain species of birds who lower their tail feathers as part of a threat display. In effect, they are announcing that they are about to fly at an antagonist with beak and claw. But the lowered tail feathers are not appropriate as the first preparatory movement for a

11.26   Emotional expressions as intention movements   *The drawing is taken from Darwin's own work, "The expression of the emotions in man and animals," and shows a dog's snarl. Darwin regarded this as a kind of preparation for the aggressive action the animal is about to take—the dog is now ready to bite. (Darwin, 1872b)*

449

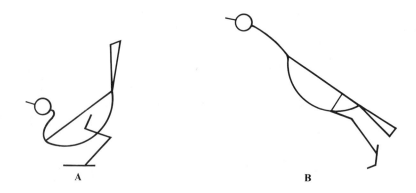

11.27 Displays that are not preparatory movements *The figure shows two phases of a bird's take-off leap as it is about to fly. (A) It crouches and raises its tail, and then (B) reverses these movements and springs off. Many aggressive displays of birds resemble (B) rather than (A), a strong argument that such displays evolved as signals in their own right. (After Hinde, 1974)*

takeoff. A bird that is about to take flight must first raise its tail feathers and then lower them (Figure 11.27). The display is out of sequence for proper takeoff and is therefore useless as a preparatory motion. Thus, whatever its evolutionary origin, the lowering of the tail feathers is now a signal and nothing more.

Phenomena of this sort can tell us something about the function that a display movement serves now. But how can we do more than idly speculate about its evolutionary history? Displays leave no fossils, so there is no direct method for reconstructing their biological past. One approach is to compare built-in displays in related species. By noting their similarities and differences, the ethologist tries to infer the evolutionary steps in their history, much as a comparative anatomist charts the family tree of fins, wings, and forelegs.

An example of how this **comparative method** has been applied to species-specific behaviors is a study of an odd courtship ritual in a predatory insect, the dancing fly (Kessel, 1955). At mating time, the male dancing fly secretes a little ball of silk which he brings to the female. She plays with this silk ball while the male mounts her and copulates.

How did this ritual arise? The courtship patterns in a number of related species give a clue. Most flies of related species manage with a minimum of precopulatory fuss; the trouble is that the female may decide to eat the male rather than mate with him. However, if she is already eating a small prey animal, the male is safe. Some species have evolved a behavior pattern that capitalizes on this fact. The male catches a small insect and brings it to the female for her to eat while he mates with her. In still other species, the male first wraps the prey in a large silk balloon. This increases his margin of safety, for the female is kept busy unwrapping her present. The dancing fly's ritual is probably the last step in this evolutionary sequence. The male dancing fly wastes no time or energy in catching a prey animal, but simply brings an empty ball of silk, all wrapping and no present. Copulation can now proceed unimpeded since the female is safely occupied—perhaps the first creature in evolutionary history to realize that it is the thought and not the gift that matters (Figure 11.28).

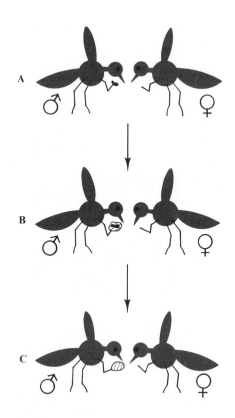

11.28 Some possible stages in the evolution of courtship in dancing flies *(A) In some species, the male catches a prey animal and gives it to the female to eat during copulation; this keeps her busy so she is less likely to eat him. (B) In other species, the male first wraps the prey in a balloon of secreted silk. This keeps the female even busier since she has to unwrap the prey. (C) Finally, in the dancing fly, the male gives the female a ball of silk without anything in it. (After Klopfer, 1974)*

EXPRESSIVE MOVEMENT IN HUMANS

If animals possess built-in display signals, why shouldn't humans? We obviously have a sizable repertory of emotional expressions, mostly facial. We smile, laugh, weep, frown, snarl, and grit our teeth. Are any of these expressions essentially equivalent to displays? If so, they should be universal to all humans and innately determined. This is what Charles Darwin believed, and some recent investigations suggest that his belief was justified.

In one study, photographs were posed by American actors to convey such emotions as fear, anger, and happiness. These pictures were then shown to members of different cultures, both literate (Swedes, Japanese, Kenyans) and preliterate (members of an isolated New Guinea tribe barely advanced beyond Stone-Age culture). When asked to identify the portrayed emotion, all groups came up with quite similar judgments. The results were much the same when the procedure was reversed. The New Guinea tribesmen were asked to portray the emotions appropriate to various simple situations such as happiness at the return of a friend, grief at the death of a child, and anger at the start of a fight. Photographs of their performances were then shown to American college students who readily picked out the emotions the tribesmen had tried to convey (Figure 11.29).

These results indicate that there may be some emotional expressions that are common to all humans. This conclusion fits with the observations with children born blind. As already noted, these children cry, smile, and laugh under essentially the same conditions that elicit these reactions in sighted

11.29 Attempts to portray emotion by New Guinea tribesmen Acting out emotions appropriate to various situations: (A) "Your friend had come and you are happy" (B) "Your child has died" (C) "You are angry and about to fight" (D) "You see a dead pig that has been lying there for a long time." (From Ekman, 1973)

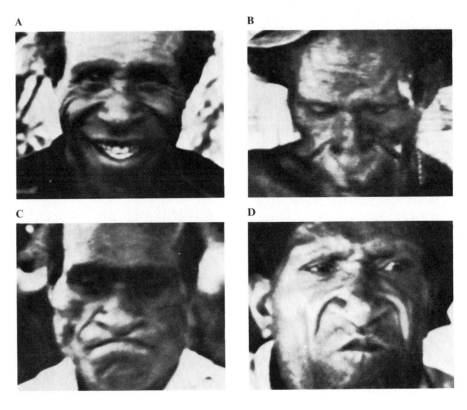

A

B

C

D

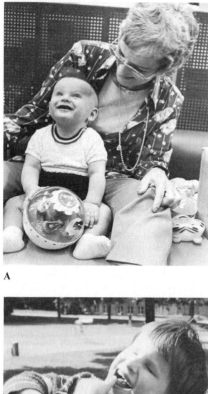

A

B

11.30   The smile in children born blind
(A) Smiling in a child born blind.
(Courtesy New York Lighthouse for
the Blind) (B) Smiling in a child
born both blind and deaf. (Courtesy
I. Eibl-Eibesfeldt)

children. In fact, much the same is true even of children born both blind and deaf (Figure 11.30). It would be hard to argue that these children had *learned* the emotional expressions when the sensory avenues of both sight and sound were blocked off.

These results do not imply that smiling and other expressive movements are unaffected by cultural conventions. According to some accounts, Melanese chieftains frown fiercely when greeting each other at a festive occasion, and Samurai mothers are said to have smiled when hearing that their sons had fallen in battle (Klineberg, 1940). But such facts do not disprove the claim that facial expressions are built-in social signals; they only show that such signals can be artificially modified later on. The Japanese child is taught to maintain an outward smile of politeness whatever it may feel inside. The smile has come under voluntary control, at least in part. It can be held back artificially and can be produced artificially. How and when such artifice comes in depends upon the culture.

That *voluntary* control of emotional expression depends upon learning is demonstrated by some further studies on blind children. We have noted that congenitally blind children are like sighted ones in their spontaneous emotional expressions. But they are much less competent than their sighted agemates when asked to act out fear or anger or delight (Charlesworth and Kreutzer, 1973). This makes good sense. To "put on the face of fear" may well require some model in memory, such as a memory of what other people look like when they are afraid, which is, of course, just what blind children lack.

DISPLAY AND HUMAN LANGUAGE

How are display repertoires different from the communication achieved by human language? There is an obvious similarity. In both cases, the behavior of one organism affects that of its fellows. But the differences between these two communication systems far outweigh the similarities.

NUMBER OF POSSIBLE MESSAGES

One obvious difference is in the complexity and flexibility of the two communicative systems. Consider the relative size of the two "vocabularies." Most mammals have some twenty to forty distinguishable display signals. This contrasts with an estimated vocabulary size of at least 50,000 words for the average human adult. The contrast is even sharper when we compare the way in which these vocabulary items are combined. Human language is based on a *productive* principle. Given the rules for putting words together (syntax), the speaker can construct any number of new messages he has never heard before (see Chapter 10). Not so for animal displays. The display system is rigid. Each stickleback, robin, and rhesus monkey sends only messages that were sent by previous sticklebacks, robins, and rhesus monkeys. There is no room for originality in the language of display.

One reason is that in animal display systems there is no provision for rearrangements of parts so as to make a new whole. Consider the messages of the jackdaw. This bird has two distinct calls that beckon others to fly with it—a high-pitched call that sounds like *kia,* uttered when the jackdaw migrates southward in the fall, and a lower-pitched call that sounds like *kiaw* uttered when the bird returns home in the spring. Yet another jackdaw call is *zick-zick-zick* which occurs during courtship. There is also an angry, *rattle*like sound, emitted when the jackdaw is about to attack an enemy (Lorenz, 1952). These various calls are useful in helping the jackdaw communicate with its fellows, but they should not be considered as the analogues of words in a language. If they were, the jackdaw should be able to shuffle the individual calls around to create new and ever more complex messages. They might produce a sentence in Jackdawese: *"Kia, rattle-rattle; Kiaw, zick-zick-zick."* Freely translated, this sentence might read, "Let us fly south to fight the enemy and then fly home to make love." No jackdaw—or indeed, any animal but man—has ever achieved such a linguistic feat.

THE CONTENT OF THE MESSAGES

Thus far, we have looked at the difference in the ways display and true language systems express their messages. But there is also a difference in the content of these messages. Displays are ways of telling a fellow creature what one is about to do. In effect, they are statements about the sender's interpersonal motives at a given time and place. If this is indeed what displays are about we can understand why the relative poverty of the system is no barrier to communication. There is no need for a large vocabulary or a productive combinatorial system, because there is a limit on the number of things an animal wants to do to (or with) another of its own kind: flee, attack, feed or be fed by, copulate, and a few others.

In contrast, human language must describe precisely the world outside and is thus virtually unlimited in its topics. For this, a productive system is absolutely crucial. The variety of possible events and relationships in the world is infinite, and only a system that is capable of an infinite number of utterances can do justice to this variety.

Some evidence for the claim that the messages of display and of human language differ fundamentally in their content comes from our own experience. We obviously don't use our display systems to tell others about the external world. We don't smile, blush, or embrace so as to inform each other about the Pythagorean theorem or the leak in the upstairs toilet. But conversely, we sometimes feel "at a loss for words" to express emotion and motive (the proper content of display messages). Such matters are often difficult to put into words, or at least words seem inadequate when we finally manage to do so. "I love you" is hard to say and, even if said, is somehow not enough. "I'm very sorry" is pallid as an expression of grief or consolation. In these situations the more primitive display system is more appropriate because the signal to be sent concerns interpersonal feelings. The beloved is touched, the bereaved is cradled, and these "simple" gestures seem somehow right. Nothing more is gained by speech, because what matters has already been displayed.

(Photograph by Benny Ortiz)

Ethology and Human Nature

Over three hundred years have passed since Hobbes described the War of All against All which he regarded as the natural state of all mankind. We are still far from having anything that even resembles a definite description of our

453

basic social nature. But at least we know that some of Hobbes' solutions are false or oversimplified. Humans are not built so as to be solitary. Other people are a necessary aspect of our lives, and a tendency to interact with others is built into us at the very outset. What holds for humans holds for most animals as well. The stickleback is pre-programmed to deal with other sticklebacks, the robin with other robins, the baboon with other baboons. Some of these interactions are peaceful, while others are quarrelsome; what matters is that there is always some intercourse between like and like. This social intercourse is an essential aspect of each creature's existence, as shown by an elaborate repertory of built-in social reactions that govern reproduction, care of offspring, and intraspecies competition at virtually all levels of the animal kingdom. No man is an island; neither is any other animal.

Summary

1. Are humans inherently asocial and self-centered? Thomas Hobbes believed that they are. An alternative position, championed by Charles Darwin among others, is that both humans and animals have built-in social dispositions. The study of such innate bases of social reactions has largely focused on animal behavior and has been undertaken by *ethologists.*

2. Most animals exhibit various stereotyped behaviors that are specific to their species, such as the mating pattern of the stickleback. Many of these reactions are *displays,* which serve as communicative signals. To determine whether such behavior patterns are innately given, ethologists have used various procedures, including breeding studies and *deprivation experiments.*

3. One realm of social behavior that has important biological roots is *aggression,* a term generally reserved for conflict between members of the same species. To secure a supply of resources for themselves and their descendants, many animals (usually the males) stake out a *territory* which they then defend. Various methods have evolved to keep aggression within bounds, including *territoriality* which separates potential combatants in space and *dominance hierarchies* which separate them in social status. Further limitations on aggression include *ritualized fighting,* as well as *threat* and *appeasement displays.*

4. While there are certain parallels between aggression among animals and among humans—for example, *territoriality* and *personal space*—there is reason to suppose that most of the underlying mechanisms are different, in that human aggression depends in great part upon learning and culture.

5. Built-in predispositions figure heavily in various aspects of sexual reproduction. Various displays advertise the animal's sex, its readiness to mate, and its species. Examples are *courtship rituals* which are highly species-specific and tend to prevent animals from interbreeding with members of other species.

6. Sexual behavior is partially controlled by several sex hormones. In mammalian animals, the male hormone, *testosterone,* or the female hormone, *estrogen,* stimulate cells in the hypothalamus which trigger sexual activity. Female animals only mate when they are in *estrus,* the time during which the ovum is ready for fertilization. The female's *estrus cycle* depends on the interplay of estrogen, which stimulates the development of the ovum and makes the animal sexually receptive, and *progesterone,* another female hormone, which prepares the uterus to receive the embryo.

SUMMARY

7. In humans, sexual behavior is less dependent upon hormonal conditions. Thus human females are capable of sexual behavior at any time in their cycle.

8. In birds and mammals, innate factors are an important determinant of another bond, that between parents and children. Parental reactions are elicited, at least in part, by various stimulus releasers produced by the young, such as *distress calls* and the human infant's smile.

9. Studies of *separation anxiety* in humans and monkeys indicate that the infant's attachment to its mother is not primarily caused by the fact that she feeds it. Instead, this attachment seems to grow out of a (perhaps built-in) fear of being away from a familiar object, typically the mother. Experiments on *imprinting* in birds suggest that the attachment to this mother-object can only be formed during a *critical period* early in life. If this early attachment is not formed, later social development may be seriously impaired, as shown by studies of motherless monkeys and institution-reared children.

10. Some inherited behavior patterns, such as the *alarm calls* of certain birds, seem to be unselfish. Their survival value may depend on the fact that such acts may save a number of relatives who carry the "altruist's" genes. Some authors have tried to explain human altruism in similar, *sociobiological* terms, an attempt that is highly controversial.

11. The key to most animal social behavior is communication by means of displays. Attempts to explain the evolutionary origin of such displays go back to Darwin who proposed that emotional expressions are a preparation for certain actions. Such *intention movements* underlie only some displays. Many others have evolved to serve a signal function but nothing more.

12. Displays are found in humans as well as animals. The major example is *emotional expression*. Many facial expressions seem to be partially based on built-in predispositions; one demonstration is smiling in children born blind. But such facial expressions are also affected by cultural conventions and can be voluntarily inhibited or "faked."

13. While both display repertories and human language are communications systems, they differ in some important regards. Display systems have a much smaller vocabulary, have no system for rearranging the individual signals to create new "sentences," and convey something about the sender's present intentions. In contrast, human languages have a large vocabulary, have some syntactic system that can rearrange words to form an infinite number of sentences, and can convey messages about just about anything in the world.

CHAPTER 12

Personality Development I: The Contributions of Sigmund Freud

Sigmund Freud *(Courtesy National Library of Medicine)*

In the preceding chapter, we considered the basic social nature of human beings. We tried to understand the effects of our evolutionary past by looking at the built-in social dispositions of humans and animals. We now turn to the effects of a much more recent and personal past—our own childhoods. This is the period in which we first encounter the force of society as embodied in the way in which we are reared; in which we are introduced to that web of shared knowledge, of common do's and don'ts, that is called culture; in which we learn our different native tongues; in which we take the first and most important steps toward becoming the persons we finally are as adults. The emphasis on this childhood period of *socialization* goes back for millenia. The poets who declared that "the child is the father of the man," and that "as the twig is bent, the tree's inclined," were echoing a belief held by generations before them, whether Hebrews, or Spartans, or medieval churchmen.

The botanical analogy to twigs and trees tells us little about how the socialization process actually takes place. How is the twig bent? Who does the bending? Does the twig resist? We will organize our account of the socialization process by considering the views of the man who revolutionized all subsequent concepts of what human beings are really like and how they become what they are—the founder of psychoanalysis, Sigmund Freud (1856–1939).

The Origins of Psychoanalytic Thought

Freud's basic conception holds that man is divided against himself. This view is in many ways a reflection of the world in which Freud lived. Most of his long life was spent in Vienna, the capital of the Austro-Hungarian Empire, an empire of warring factions and nationalities, of Austrians, Hungarians, Czechs, Slovaks, Poles, and Croatians, that finally disintegrated in 1918 at the end of World War I.

More directly relevant than the clash between nationalities was the nineteenth-century conflict between two major intellectual movements. The dominant view was a faith in reason, formulated by several generations of European thinkers, from such men of the French Enlightenment as Voltaire to such heirs of Locke in England as John Stuart Mill. These men preached that reason will ultimately lead to human happiness, that evil and misery are always caused by ignorance and superstition, and that education and understanding will eventually create a world of peace and contentment for all. Their creed of reason found justification in the accomplishments of nineteenth-century science and technology which promised ever-increasing progress in all spheres of human endeavor.

But this faith was not shared by all. The followers of the Romantic movement sounded another note. They championed feeling over reason, instinct over intellect. At first, these sentiments were in an optimistic vein. Philosophers like Rousseau and poets like Byron and Shelley insisted that man is intrinsically good and should therefore always follow the dictates of the heart. But as the century wore on, as wars of liberation failed and as revolutions only brought disappointment, the mood of Romanticism turned grim and despairing. The heroes of Dostoevsky's novels gain comfort from neither heart nor intellect. They may be brilliant and well-educated but they still become murderers without knowing why, victims of dark forces that well up from some mysterious depths inside. As the century ended, the grounds for optimism became fewer and fewer. Reason had promised much but had delivered little, a failure that was ultimately climaxed by the mad slaughter of World War I.

Freud's intellectual contribution was an attempt to understand the forces of human irrationality through reason and science. The son of a lower middle-class Jewish wool merchant, he studied medicine and began his career as a physiologist and neurologist. His training imbued him with an unshakable faith in the power of rationality as expressed through the methods of science. But when he later dealt with psychiatric patients, he found himself face to face with irrationality magnified manifold; his patients' symptoms were bizarre and incomprehensible by any ordinary criterion. His attempt to decipher these symptoms and the underlying disorder that produced them led to a new conception, not only of psychopathology, but of human nature in general.

In some ways, Freud can be regarded as a modern Hobbesian. Hobbes had insisted that at bottom men are savage brutes whose natural impulses would inevitably lead to murder, rape, and pillage if left unchecked (see Chapter 11). To curb this beast within, they had formed a social contract in some distant past and subordinated themselves to a larger social unit, the state. Like Hobbes, Freud regarded the basic human instincts as a "seething cauldron" of pleasure-seeking that blindly seeks gratification regardless of the consequences. This savage, selfish human nature had to be tamed by civilization.

The Dream of Reason Produces Monsters
An engraving by Franciso Goya (1799) suggesting that the same mind that is capable of reason also produces unknown terrors. (Courtesy National Library of Medicine)

457

Unlike Hobbes, Freud did not believe that the subjugation of the brute in man was a onetime event in human political history. It occurs in every lifetime for the social contract is renewed in the childhood of every generation. Another difference concerns the nature of the taming process. According to Hobbes, men's baser instincts are curbed by *external* social sanctions; they want to rob their neighbors but don't do so because they are afraid of the king's men. According to Freud, the restraints of society are incorporated internally during the first few years of childhood. The first curbs on behavior are based on a simple (and quite Hobbesian) fear of direct social consequences—of a scolding or spanking. But eventually the child inhibits his misdeeds because he feels that "they are bad," and not just because he fears that he will be caught and punished. At this point, the taming force of society has become **internalized.** The king's men are now within us, internalized embodiments of society's dictates whose weapons—the pangs of conscience—are no less powerful for being mental.

According to Freud, the taming process is never fully complete. The forbidden impulses cannot be ruled out of existence. They may be denied for a while, but eventually they will reassert themselves, often through new and devious channels, leading to yet further repressive measures which will probably fail in their turn as well. As a result, there is constant conflict between the demands of instinct and of society, but this war goes on underground, within the individual and usually without his or her own knowledge. As a result, man is divided against himself, and his **unconscious conflicts** express themselves in thoughts and deeds that appear irrational.

HYSTERIA AND HYPNOSIS

When Freud began his medical practice, many of his patients suffered from a disorder called **hysteria.** The symptoms of hysteria presented an apparently helter-skelter catalogue of physical and mental complaints—total or partial blindness or deafness, paralysis or anesthesia of various parts of the body, uncontrollable trembling or convulsive attacks, distortions and gaps in memory. Except for these symptoms the patients were in no sense "insane"; they were generally lucid and did not have to be institutionalized. Was there any underlying pattern that could make sense of this confusing array of complaints?

The first clue came with the recognition that hysterical symptoms are **psychogenic,** the results of some unknown psychological cause rather than the product of organic damage to the nervous system. This discovery was made by Jean Charcot (1825–93), a French neurologist, who noticed that many of the bodily symptoms of hysteria make no anatomical sense. For example, some patients suffered from anesthesia of the hand but lost no feeling above the wrist. This **glove anesthesia** could not possibly be caused by any nerve injury, since it is known that an injury to any one of the relevant nerve trunks must affect a portion of the arm above the wrist (Figure 12.1). This rules out a simple organic interpretation and suggests that glove anesthesia has some psychological basis. While such findings showed that the hysterical symptoms are somehow psychological, this does not mean that they are therefore unreal. The patients weren't simply faking; their symptoms were real enough to them and often caused considerable suffering.

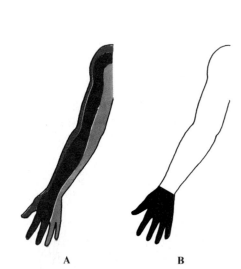

12.1 Glove anesthesia *(A) Areas of the skin of arms and hands that supply sensory information to different nerves. (B) A typical region of anesthesia in a hysterical patient. Anatomically, the anesthesia makes no sense. If there were nerve injury (in the spinal cord) the anesthesia would extend the length of the arm, as in (A).*

A   B

Charcot and other French psychiatrists of the period tried to relate hysteria to *hypnosis.* This is a temporary, trancelike state which can be induced in normal people but which may produce effects that resemble hysterical symptoms. The hypnotized person is exceedingly *suggestible.* If told that she cannot move her arm, she will act as if paralyzed. Similarly for suggestions of blindness, deafness, or anesthesia. If the trance is deep enough, the hypnotist can induce hallucinations in which the subject "sees" or "hears" imaginary objects. There are also effects on memory. If the subject is asked to forget everything that happened during the trance she generally complies. During this period of *posthypnotic amnesia* she will respond to suggestions planted during the trance. She might, for example, take off her shoes when the hypnotist gives the previously arranged signal. Such characteristics of the hypnotized state, especially those that involve paralysis and sensory deficit, buttressed the suspicion that hypnosis and hysteria were somehow related.

One of Charcot's contemporaries, Hippolyte Bernheim, thought that the link between the two phenomena is suggestion. In his view, the hysterical symptom was caused by suggestion, usually produced under conditions of intense emotional stress. If so, couldn't one fight fire with fire and remove the suggested symptom by a countersuggestion made during hypnosis? Bernheim and his colleagues tried to do just that. There were occasional successes but in many cases the symptom proved obdurate. Sometimes the hysterical symptoms disappeared upon direct posthypnotic suggestion but were then replaced by others; a patient might regain the use of her legs but lose her sight.

In collaboration with another physician, Josef Breuer (1842–1925), Freud took an important further step. Both men came to believe that removing hysterical symptoms by suggestion is essentially futile; it was an attempt to erase a symptom without dealing with its underlying cause, like trying to cure measles by painting the spots. Their own efforts were based on the notion that hysterical symptoms are a disguised means of keeping certain emotionally

Charcot demonstrating hypnosis
(Courtesy National Library of Medicine)

A commemorative stamp issued in honor of Anna O. *In the annals of psycho-analysis, Anna O. figures only as a famous case history. But in real life, Anna—or to use her true name, Bertha Pappenheim—was much more than that. After she recovered from her various disorders, she became a distinguished pioneer in the field of social work, as well as a militant and effective champion of women's rights in Eastern Europe. (Courtesy the Ministry of Post, Bonn, West Germany)*

charged memories under mental lock and key. When such memories are finally recovered, there is ***catharsis,*** an explosive release of previously dammed up emotions that has therapeutic effects.

Initially Breuer and Freud probed for these memories while the patients were in a hypnotic trance. One of Breuer's cases was Anna O., a twenty-one-year-old girl who was a walking collection of assorted symptoms: various paralyses, hysterical squints, coughs, occasional disorders of speech, and so on. When hypnotized, she was able to recall certain crucial events in her past that seemed to be at the root of this or the other symptom. Many of these events dated back to a particularly traumatic period during which she nursed her dying father. An example is a nervous cough which she traced to an occasion at her father's bedside. She heard the sound of dance music coming from a neighbor's house, felt the wish to be there, and was immediately struck by guilt and self-reproach. She covered up her feelings with a nervous cough, and thereafter coughed uncontrollably whenever she heard rhythmic music. The symptom disappeared when the forgotten episode was remembered (Freud and Breuer, 1895).

RESISTANCE AND REPRESSION

Eventually Freud abandoned hypnosis altogether, in part because not all patients were readily hypnotized. He found that crucial memories could be recovered even in the normal, waking state through the method of ***free association.*** The patients are told to say anything that enters their mind, no matter how trivial and unrelated it might seem, or how embarrassing, disagreeable, or indiscreet. Since all ideas are presumably related by an associative network, the emotionally charged "forgotten" memories should be evoked sooner or later. At first, this procedure seemed to work and yielded results similar to those obtained through hypnotic probes. But a new difficulty arose, for it became clear that the patients did not really comply with Freud's request. There was ***resistance*** of which the patient was often unaware:

> The patient attempts to escape . . . by every possible means. First he says nothing comes into his head, then that so much comes into his head that he can't grasp any of it. Then we observe that . . . he is giving in to his critical objections, first to this, then to that; he betrays it by the long pauses which occur in his talk. At last he admits that he really cannot say something, he is ashamed to. . . . Or else, he has thought of something but it concerns someone else and not himself. . . . Or else, what he has just thought of is really too unimportant, too stupid and too absurd. . . . So it goes on, with untold variations, to which one continually replies that telling everything really means telling everything (Freud, 1924, pp. 298–99).

Freud noticed that the intensity of resistance was often an important clue to what was really important. When a patient seemed to struggle especially hard to change a topic, to break off a train of thought, she was probably close to the recovery of an emotionally charged memory. Eventually it would come, often to the patient's great surprise. But if this was so, and if the recovery of these memories helped the patient to get better (as both Freud and his patients believed) why then did the patients resist the retrieval of these memories and thus obstruct their own cure? Freud concluded that the observed phenomenon of resistance was the overt manifestation of some powerful force that opposed the recovery of the critical memories into consciousness. Certain experiences in the patient's life—certain acts, impulses, thoughts, or memories—were pushed out of consciousness, were *repressed,* and the same repressive forces that led to their original expulsion were mobilized to oppose their reentry into consciousness during the psychiatric session.

What are the ideas whose recollection is so vehemently resisted, which have to be repressed and kept out of mental sight? According to Freud, they are always connected with some wish or impulse that the person is unable to face without suffering intense anxiety. Repression is a defense; the unacceptable wish and various thoughts associated with it are pushed out of consciousness to ward off intolerable pain. The repressed wishes are invariably linked to the basic biological urges, especially the sexual ones, whose full expression is forbidden by society.

Freud also concluded that the critical repressions date back to early life when the instinctual urges of the child first clash with the restraints imposed by society as embodied in its parents. As evidence he cited his clinical observations. In patient after patient, the eventual recovery of a repressed memory merely led to further resistance which ultimately gave way to reveal a repressed memory earlier on, and so on back to the early years of childhood. Further evidence came from his patients' emotional reactions toward *him.* They began to love him or hate him intensely, as if he were some significant figure in their own personal life, typically their father. Freud called this phenomenon *transference,* a transfer of emotional reactions that were originally directed to crucial individuals in the patient's own early life and that are then redirected toward the person of the therapist.

Freud believed that the repressed material is not really eradicated but remains in the *unconscious.* This is a metaphorical expression which only means that the repressed ideas still exert a powerful effect. Again and again, they push up from below, like a jack-in-the-box, fueled by the biological urges that gave rise to them in the first place, or triggered by associations in the here and now. As these repressed ideas well up again, they also bring back anxiety and are therefore pushed down once more. The result is a never-ending unconscious conflict. This conflict often leads to a compromise in which the rejected wishes are expressed, but in a censored form. According to Freud, many symptoms of psychopathology represent conflict solutions of this kind. An example is a patient who repeatedly pulls off her blouse with one hand and pulls it back on with the other. Freud would probably argue that this is a dramatized sexual fantasy in which the patient plays two roles—a lover who is trying to undress her and that part of herself that tries to resist.

Freud's subsequent career was a continued exploration of the same basic phenomenon that he first inferred from his patients' resistance—unconscious conflict. The task he set for himself was the analysis (as he called it, the *psychoanalysis*) of these conflicts, the discovery of their origins, of their effects in the present, of their removal or alleviation. He soon came to believe that the same mechanisms which produce the symptoms of psychopathology also operate in normal persons, that his discoveries were not just a contribution to psychiatry, but were a foundation for a general theory of human personality.

Freud's Theory of Personality

Our sketch of Freud's theory of the nature and development of human personality will concentrate on those aspects that seem to represent the highlights of a complex theoretical formulation that was continually revised and modified during the course of Freud's long career. In this description, we will separate two aspects of Freudian theory. We will begin with the conception of the **mechanisms of unconscious conflict.** We will then deal with Freud's theory of the **origins of these conflicts** in the individual's life history, and of their relation to the development of sex identity and of morality. Except for occasional asides, we will postpone criticism for later sections. We will also postpone a discussion of psychoanalysis as a form of therapy, concentrating on Freud's theories of what people are like rather than upon his proposed techniques for making some people better. (For a discussion of psychotherapy, see Chapter 18.)

UNCONSCIOUS CONFLICT

Freud's theories concern the forces whose antagonism produces unconscious conflict and the effects produced when they clash. We will frame our discussion around two major questions. First, who fights whom in unconscious conflict? Second, what are the general laws that describe such conflicts?

THE ANTAGONISTS OF INNER CONFLICT

When conflict is external, the antagonists are easily identified: David and Goliath, St. George and the Dragon, and so on. But what are the warring forces when the conflict is inside of the individual? In essence, they are different behavior tendencies, such as Anna O's sexually tinged desire to be at a dance and her conflicting reactions of guilt at leaving a dying father. One of the tasks Freud set himself was to classify the tendencies that participate in such conflicts, to see which of them are usually arrayed together and fight on the same side. The result was a threefold classification of conflicting tendencies within the individual which he regarded as three more or less distinct subsystems of the human personality: the *id,* the *ego,* and the *superego.* In some of Freud's writings, there is a tendency to treat these three systems as if they were three separate persons that inhabit the mind. But this is only a metaphor that must not be taken literally; *id, ego,* and *superego* are just names for three sets of very different reaction patterns. They are not persons in their own right (Freud, 1923).

The id   The id is the most primitive portion of the personality, from which the other two are derived. It contains all of the basic biological urges: to eat, drink, eliminate, be comfortably warm and, most of all, to gain sexual pleasure.* The

---

* These urges are sometimes called instincts, but that is a misnomer caused by an unfortunate translation of Freud's original term.

id's sole law is the ***pleasure principle***—satisfaction now and not later, regardless of circumstances and whatever the cost.

The id's blind strivings for pleasure know no distinction between self and world, between fantasy and reality, between wishing and having. Its insistent urges spill out into reflex motor action, like emptying the bladder when it is full. If that doesn't work, the clamoring for pleasure leads to primitive thoughts of gratification, fantasies of wish fulfillment that cannot be distinguished from reality.

The ego   At birth, the infant is all id. But the id's shrill clamors are soon met by the harsh facts of external reality. Some gratifications come only after a delay. The breast or the bottle are not always present; the infant has to cry to get them.

The confrontations between hot desire and cold reality lead to a whole set of new reactions that are meant to reconcile the two. Sometimes the reconciliation is by appropriate action (saying "please"), sometimes by self-imposed delay (going to the bathroom), sometimes by suppression of a forbidden impulse (not touching one's genitals). These various reactions become organized into a new subsystem of the personality—the ego. The ego is derived from the id and is essentially still in its service. But unlike the id, the ego obeys the ***reality principle.*** It tries to satisfy the id (that is, to gain pleasure) but it does so pragmatically, in accordance with the real world and its real demands. As time proceeds, the opposition between need and reality leads to the emergence of more and more skills, all directed to the same end, as well as a whole system of thought and memories that grows up concurrently. Eventually, this entire system becomes capable of looking at itself and now deserves the name Freud gave it, ego or self. Until this point, there was no "I" but only a mass of undifferentiated strivings (appropriately named after the Latin impersonal pronoun *id,* literally "it").

There is an interesting similarity—as well as many differences—between Freud's view of the formation of the ego and some of Piaget's conceptions of early cognitive development considered previously (see Chapter 7 and 9). Both Freud and Piaget believe that the young infant does not distinguish between itself and the world outside, let alone between itself and others. They both assert that these distinctions are achieved through the infant's active intercourse with its environment. The difference is one of emphasis. Piaget is primarily concerned with the child's *cognitive* development, with the growth of intelligence. He therefore focuses on the intellectual achievements of early childhood, such as the way in which the child actively manipulates various objects and thus attains object permanence (see Chapter 9). Freud's emphasis was on the development of motives and emotions, and so he concentrated upon the emerging distinction between desire and actual goal attainment, on the child's growing awareness that he or she has to do something to make a wish come true.

The superego   The id is not the ego's only master. As the child grows older, a new reaction pattern develops from within the ego that acts as a kind of judge that decides whether the ego has been "good" or "bad." This new mental agency is the ***superego*** which represents the internalized rules and admonitions of the parents, and through them, of society. Initially, the ego only had to worry about external reality. It might inhibit some id-inspired action, but only to avert some future trouble: You don't steal cookies because you might be caught. But a little later, the forbidden act is suppressed even when there can never be any real punishment. This change occurs because the child starts to act and think as if he himself were the parent who administers praise and reproof. A three-year old is often seen to slap his own hand as he is about to play with mud or commit some other heinous deed; he sometimes mutters some self-righteous pronouncement like "Dirty. Bad." This is the beginning of the superego, the ego's second master, which praises and punishes just as the parents did. If the ego lives up to the superego's dictates, the reward is pride. But if one of the superego's rules is broken, the superego metes out punishment just as the parents scolded or spanked or withdrew their love. There is then self-reproach and a feeling of guilt.

The formation of the superego puts the ego in a difficult position, for its two masters often issue conflicting commands. The promptings of the id are all too often in forbidden directions; if the ego gives in, the superego will punish it. What's worse is that both masters are essentially infantile. We have seen that the id's demands are blind and unreasoning, but the superego's strictures are also rooted in childish irrationality. The superego was formed when the child's cognitive abilities were still quite primitive. At that time, it could only internalize what it understood then—blind do's and don'ts. As a result, the superego is essentially irrational; Freud regarded it as largely unconscious. It issues absolute imperatives that are not accessible to reason. If the ego obeys, it must throttle various urges of the id, even if those are merely expressed in a thought or a memory. To accomplish this feat, the ego must resort to repression.

The superego represents the internalized rules and prohibitions of society as these are transmitted to the young child by its parents. But what makes the parents issue their decrees? According to Freud, many parental commands grow out of the irrational absolutes that were handed down to them by their parents in their own childhood. The superego thus becomes the vehicle of a conservative moral tradition. As Freud put it, "The past, the tradition of the race and of the people, lives on in the ideology of the superego; and . . . plays a powerful part in human life" (Freud, 1933, p. 60).

In summary, Freud's threefold division of the personality is just a way of saying that our thoughts and actions are determined by the interplay of three major factors: our biological drives, the various ways through which we have learned to satisfy these drives and master the external world, and the commands and prohibitions of society. Freud's contribution is his insistence that the conflicts among these three forces are inside the individual, that they are derived from childhood experiences, and that they are waged without the individual's conscious awareness.

Inner conflicts as envisaged by Plato
The Greek philosopher Plato anticipated Freud's tripartite division of the mind by over two thousand years. In one of his Dialogues, *he likened the soul to a chariot with two horses that often pull in opposed directions. The chariot's driver is Reason, the two horses are Spirit (our nobler emotions) and Appetite. This Renaissance medallion depicts Plato's image of the internal conflict. (Courtesy the British Museum)*

THE MECHANISMS OF UNCONSCIOUS CONFLICT

We now turn to Freud's formulation (here drastically simplified) of the rules by which these inner wars are waged. In rough outline, the conflict begins as id-derived urges and various associated memories are pushed underground, are repressed. But the forbidden urges refuse to stay down. They find substitute outlets whose further consequence is a host of additional defenses that are erected to reinforce the original repression, hold off the id-derived flood, and allow the ego to maintain its self-regard (S. Freud, 1917, 1926; A. Freud 1946).

Repression and anxiety   What is the mechanism that underlies repression? Freud believed that the crucial factor is intense **anxiety,** an emotional state akin to fear (see Chapter 3). According to Freud, various forbidden acts become associated with anxiety as the child is scolded or disciplined for performing them. The parents may resort to physical punishment or they may merely register their disapproval with a frown or reprimand; in either case, the child is threatened with the loss of their love and becomes anxious. The next time he is about to, say, finger his penis or pinch his baby brother, he will feel a twinge of anxiety, an internal signal that his parents may leave him, and that he will be abandoned and alone.

Since anxiety is intensely unpleasant, the child will do everything he can in order to remove it or to ward it off. If the cause is an external stimulus, the child's reaction is clear. He runs away and thus removes himself from the fear-inducing object. But how can he cope with a danger that comes from within? As before, he will flee from whatever evokes fear or anxiety. But now the flight is from something inside himself. To get rid of anxiety, the child must suppress that which triggers it—the forbidden act.

This kind of reasoning may explain why the child refrains from an overt action that the parents condemn. But Freud's concept of repression obviously pertains to more than outward behavior; it applies to the thought no less than the deed. We can understand that a four-year-old boy who is punished for kicking his baby brother will refrain from such warlike acts in the future. But why does the boy stop *thinking* about them and why does he fail to remember the crucial incident, as Freud maintains? One answer is that thinking about an act is rather similar to performing it. A modern behavior theorist might suggest that if anxiety becomes associated to the act, it will also be evoked by the thought, through stimulus generalization (see Chapter 4). Another interpretation concerns the young child's limited cognitive abilities. He has not as yet fully mastered the distinction between thought and action. Nor does he know that his father can't really "read his mind," that his thoughts are private and thus immune from parental prosecution. Whatever the reasons, the inhibition applies not just to overt action, but to related thoughts, memories, and wishes.

Displacement   When a geyser is dammed up, its waters usually penetrate other cracks and fissures and eventually gush up elsewhere. According to Freud, the same holds for repressed urges, which tend to find new and often disguised outlets. An example is **displaced aggression** that develops when fear of retaliation blocks the normal direction of discharge. The child who is reprimanded by her parent turns on her playmate or vents her anger on the innocent household cat. According to many social psychologists, the same mechanism underlies the persecution of minority groups. They become convenient scapegoats for aggressive impulses fueled by social and economic unrest. Freud's own emphasis was on the displacement of sexual urges. In particular, he was concerned with the redirection of infantile sexual longings blocked by incest taboos (of which more later). In his view, the selection of adult sex partners can always be understood as a displaced wish for the mother or father.

465

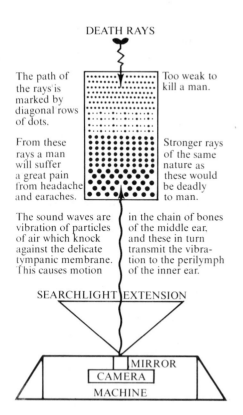

DEATH RAYS

The path of the rays is marked by diagonal rows of dots.

Too weak to kill a man.

From these rays a man will suffer a great pain from headache and earaches.

Stronger rays of the same nature as these would be deadly to man.

The sound waves are vibration of particles of air which knock against the delicate tympanic membrane. This causes motion

in the chain of bones of the middle ear, and these in turn transmit the vibration to the perilymph of the inner ear.

SEARCHLIGHT EXTENSION

MIRROR
CAMERA
MACHINE

12.2 An influencing machine *This diagram was drawn by a paranoid patient and depicts a mysterious "machine" by which he insists his "enemies" have influenced his thoughts and actions since his birth. By means of this influencing machine, they read and control his feelings, induce all kinds of evil sexual and other forbidden desires, and can cause him to suffer pain, illness, or even death. This delusion is an extreme manifestation of the mechanism of projection. The patient denies that his evil thoughts and desires are really his, but instead imputes them to outside agents who force these thoughts and feelings on him by mechanical means. (After Masserman, 1946)*

Mechanisms of defense   If a dam doesn't hold the geyser back, it has to be reinforced and new dams must be erected to keep the water from erupting at other points. According to Freud, this is precisely what happens when the original repression does not keep the forbidden impulses down. Various *mechanisms of defense* come into play. They are mobilized for the same reason that prompted the original repression, to get rid of anxiety.

Some defense mechanisms are yet further attempts to block the forbidden impulse altogether. An example is *reaction formation* in which the repressed wish is warded off by its diametrical opposite. The young girl who jealously hated her sister and was punished for hostile acts may turn her feelings into the very opposite; she now showers her sister with an exaggerated love and tenderness, a desperate bulwark against aggressive wishes that she cannot accept. But the repressed hostility can still be detected underneath the loving exterior; her love is overly solicitous and stifling and the sister probably feels smothered by it. According to psychoanalytic writers, a similar mechanism accounts for the vehemence of some crusaders against vice, who are thought to be prompted by a reaction formation against their own repressed sexual longings.

In reaction formation, there is an attempt (albeit not too successful) to keep the forbidden wishes at bay. Some other mechanisms represent a different line of defense; the repressed thoughts break through but they are reinterpreted and are not recognized for what they are. An example is *rationalization* in which the person interprets some of his own feelings or actions in more acceptable terms. The cruel father beats his child mercilessly but is sure that he does so "for the child's own good." Countless atrocities have been committed under the same guise of altruism; heretics have been tortured to save their immortal souls and cities have been razed to protect the world against barbarism. Rationalization is also employed at a more everyday level, as a defense not only against repressed wishes but against any thought that would make the individual feel unworthy and anxious. An example is the sour-grapes phenomenon. The jilted lover tells his friends that he never really cared for his lost love; eventually he believes it himself.

Another example of a defense mechanism in which cognitive reorganization plays a major role is *projection.* Here the forbidden urges well up and are recognized as such. But the person does not realize that these wishes are his own; instead, he attributes them to others. "I desire you" becomes "You desire me," "I hate you" becomes "You hate me"—desperate defenses against repressed sexual or hostile wishes that can no longer be banished from consciousness (Freud, 1911).

An extreme form of projection is characteristic of *paranoid schizophrenia,* a disorder in which the patient loses contact with reality and is generally institutionalized (see Chapter 17). The paranoid schizophrenic often suffers from delusions of persecution, accusing various people—his wife, the doctor, the grocer next door, the pope—of conspiring against him. His own feelings of rage terrify him and he therefore imputes them to people in the outside world. But his projected rage recoils and makes things even worse. If all those people really hate him, how can he help but hate them all the more? His feelings of rage are now intensified, which leads to an increase in the hostility he projects outside, and so on, in a vicious cycle (Figure 12.2).

UNCONSCIOUS CONFLICT IN NORMAL LIFE

Freud arrived at his theory of unconscious conflict by studying the behavior of disturbed individuals, usually hysterics. But he soon concluded that the same clash of unconscious forces that results in neurotic symptoms is also found in the life of normal persons. Their inner conflicts are under control, with less resulting anxiety and no crippling effects, but they are present nonetheless. We will consider two areas to which Freud appealed for evidence: lapses of memory and slips of the tongue in everyday life, and the content of dreams.

Errors of speech and memory   Freud drew attention to what he called the psychopathology of everyday life, in which we momentarily forget a name that might call up embarrassing memories or in which we suffer a slip of the tongue that unwittingly reveals an underlying motive (Freud, 1901). Shakespeare's Portia is obliged by her father's will to be impartial among her several suitors and to select her husband essentially by lot. Before the final choice is made, she tells her favorite suitor:

> One half of me is yours, the other half yours—
> Mine own I would say . . .
>
> (*The Merchant of Venice*, Act III, Scene ii)

thus committing a "Freudian slip" nearly three hundred years before Freud was born. Suppressed intentions sometimes emerge to make us become "absentminded" about things we don't really want to do. Freud cites the example of a friend who wrote a letter which he forgot to send off for several days. He finally mailed it, but it was returned by the post office for there was no address. He addressed it and sent it off again only to have it returned once more because there was no stamp.

This is not to say (though psychoanalytic writers often seem to say it) that all slips of the tongue, all mislayings of objects, and all lapses of memory are *motivated* in Freud's sense. The host who cannot call up a guest's name when he has to introduce him to another guest is unlikely to have some hidden reason for keeping that name out of his consciousness. The name is probably blocked because of simple, and quite unmotivated, memory interference (see Chapter 8).

The theory of dreams   One of Freud's most influential works was his theory of dreams (Freud, 1900). He argued that dreams have a meaning which can be deciphered if one looks deeply enough. In his view, the dream concerns the dreamer's past and present and it arises from unknown regions within. He saw the dream as somewhat analogous to a hysterical symptom. On the surface they both appear meaningless and bizarre, but they become comprehensible when understood as veiled expressions of an unconscious clash between competing motives.

Freud began with the assumption that at bottom every dream is an attempt at **wish fulfillment.** While awake, a wish is usually not acted upon right away for there are considerations of both reality (the ego) and morality (the superego) that must be taken into account: "Is it possible?" and "Is it allowed?"

The Prisoner's Dream *A painting by Moritz von Schwind (1836) that Freud used as a frontispiece in one of his books on dreams. Here, the dream expresses the dreamer's wish directly, for the gnomes clambering up the wall and sawing through the bars do just what he would like to do. (Courtesy The Schack Galerie)*

But during sleep these restraining forces are drastically weakened and the wish then leads to immediate thoughts and images of gratification. In some cases the wish fulfillment is simple and direct. Starving explorers dream of sumptuous meals; men stranded in the desert dream of cool mountain streams. According to a Hungarian proverb quoted by Freud, "Pigs dream of acorns and geese dream of maize."

Simple wish-fulfillment dreams are comparatively rare. What about the others, the strange and illogical nightly narratives that are far more usual? Freud argued that the same principle of attempted wish fulfillment could explain these as well. But here a new process comes into play. The underlying wish touches upon some forbidden matters that are associated with anxiety. As a result, various mechanisms of defense are invoked. The wish cannot be expressed directly; it is ***censored*** and is only allowed to surface in symbolic disguise. The dreamer never experiences the underlying ***latent dream*** that represents his own hidden wishes and concerns. What he does experience is the carefully laundered version that emerges after the defense mechanisms have done their work—the ***manifest dream.*** The end product is reminiscent of hysterical symptoms and various pathologies of everyday life. It represents a compromise between forbidden urges and the repressive forces that hold them down. The underlying impulse is censored but it surreptitiously emerges in a veiled disguise.

Two examples will suffice to show how fragments of the same day's events *(day residues)* are interwoven with disguised urges to produce the manifest-dream content. The first was reported during World War I by a middle-aged woman whose son was in the army. In this dream, the underlying sexual wish is readily discernible and the censorship is expressed by gaps in the stream of events. She dreamed of volunteering some unspecified patriotic service for the benefit of the troops:

> She approached a staff surgeon with her request, and he understood her meaning after she had said only a few words. The actual wording of her speech in the dream was: "I and many women and girls in Vienna are ready to . . ." At this point in the dream her words turned into a mumble ". . . for the troops—officers and other ranks without distinction." . . . There followed an awkward silence of some minutes. The staff surgeon then put his arm around her waist and said: "Suppose, madam, it actually came to . . . (mumble)" . . . She replied: "Good gracious, I'm an old woman and I might never come to that. . . . It must never happen that an elderly woman . . . (mumble) . . . a mere boy. That would be terrible." "I understand perfectly," replied the staff surgeon. Some of the officers, and among them one who had been a suitor of hers in her youth, laughed out loud (Freud, 1917, p. 137).

In other dreams, the disguise is achieved by more elaborate means. The underlying wish finds expression in various displaced forms. There is ***symbolism*** in which one thing stands for another. Some symbols are widely shared because certain physical, functional, or linguistic similarities are perceived by most people (for example, screwdriver and box for penis and vagina). But there is no simple cipher that can be generally applied. After all, many physical objects are either long and pointed or round and hollow; a pat equation with male and female genitals will be of little use. Most symbolic relationships

Dreams and symbolism *The 1927 German silent film* The Secrets of a Soul *by Georg Pabst tried to depict a case history in psychoanalytic terms. Its subject was a middle-aged man suffering from impotence. The film portrays several of the patient's dreams. In this one, he tries to plant a tree, a symbol for impregnating his wife. (Courtesy The Museum of Modern Art/Film Stills Archive)*

depend upon the dreamer's own life experience and can only be interpreted by noting his free associations to the dream. An example is the dream of a woman who had been married for many years and had just learned that her friend Elise had become engaged:

> She was at the theater with her husband. One side of the stalls was completely empty. Her husband had told her that Elise L. and her fiance had wanted to go too, but had only been able to get bad seats—three for 1½ florins—and of course they could not take those. She thought it would not really have done any harm if they had (Freud, 1917, p. 122).

Upon free association, it became clear that the dream incorporated still other recent incidents in the dreamer's life. The half-empty theater was an allusion to a recent occurrence when she paid a special fee to buy some theater tickets in advance; it was an unnecessary expense because there were still many empty seats on the day of the performance and her husband had teased her for being too much in a hurry. The cost of the tickets in the dream seemed to be an indirect reference to a present of 150 florins her sister-in-law had received from her husband; the silly woman had then rushed out immediately to spend the whole sum on jewelry. Freud was struck by a repeated theme, the idea of buying too quickly and not well. The crucial point concerned her friend Elise, a woman of her own age, who had not hurried but had waited all this time and had nevertheless found a fine husband all the same. In Freud's analysis, the latent dream expressed the wish that she too had waited. The husband she got was worth very little; by waiting, she might have found a much better one, perhaps one a hundred times better (1½ versus 150 florins).

FREUD'S THEORY OF DEVELOPMENT

Freud believed that the unconscious conflicts he uncovered—in dreams, in memory lapses, in neurotic symptoms—always referred to certain critical events in the individual's early life. These crucial events seemed to be remarkably similar from person to person. He concluded that all human beings go through a largely similar sequence of significant emotional events in their early lives, that some of the most important of these involve infantile sexual urges, and that it is this childhood past that shapes their present (Freud, 1905).

STAGES OF PSYCHOSEXUAL DEVELOPMENT

Freud's theory of psychosexual development (like Piaget's account of cognitive growth) emphasizes different stages, each of which is built upon the achievements of those before. In Freud's view, the child starts life as a bundle of pleasure-seeking tendencies. Pleasure is obtained by the stimulation of certain zones of the body that are particularly sensitive to touch: the mouth, the anus, and the genitals. Freud called these regions *erogenous zones* for he believed that the various pleasures associated with each of them have a common element which is sexual.* As the child develops, the relative importance of the zones shifts. Initially, most of the pleasure seeking is through the mouth

---

* One of his arguments for regarding oral and anal stimulation in infancy as ultimately sexual was the fact that such stimulation sometimes precedes (or replaces) sexual intercourse in adulthood.

(the **oral stage**). With the advent of toilet concerns, the emphasis shifts to the anus (the **anal stage**). Still later, there is an increased interest in the pleasure that can be obtained from stimulating the genitals (the **phallic stage**). The culmination of **psychosexual development** is attained in adult sexuality in which pleasure involves not just one's own gratification but also the social and bodily satisfaction brought to another person (the **genital stage**) (Table 12.1).

Table 12.1 SKETCH OF FREUD'S STAGES OF PSYCHOSEXUAL DEVELOPMENT OF BOYS

Stage	Approximate age	Main characteristics of that period	Consequences
Oral	1	Stimulation of mouth (sucking; later: biting, chewing)	Fixation → "Oral character" (passive, dependent) Reaction-formation → Vehement denial of dependence (tough, sarcastic, etc.)
Anal	1–3	Pleasurable stimulation of bowels. Later: requirement to control this pleasure during toilet training	Fixation → Disorderly, tempestuous Reaction-formation → "Anal character" (compulsively orderly, stingy, obstinate)
Phallic	3–5	Stimulation of genitals, as in infantile masturbation	→ Oedipus complex ↓ Sexual desire directed toward mother ↓ Hostility and fear of father ↓ Renunciation of mother, identification with father ↓ Formation of superego
Latency	6–13	Sexuality repressed	
Genital	Puberty on	Rearousal of sexuality	→ Sexual desire with interest in partner's erotic and social satisfaction: love

How does the child move from one stage to the next? In part, it is a matter of physical maturation. For example, bowel control is simply impossible at birth, for the infant lacks the necessary neuromuscular readiness. But there is another element. As the child's bodily maturation proceeds, there is an inevitable change in what the parents allow, prohibit, or demand. Initially, the child nurses, then it is weaned. Initially, it is diapered, then it is toilet trained. Each change automatically produces some frustration and conflict as former ways of gaining pleasure are denied. Under the circumstances, many of the dynamics of conflict we have previously discussed come into play.

Obstacles to smooth progression Freud emphasized certain general kinds of reactions that occur at each changeover point. The first is *fixation,* which simply refers to a lingering attachment to an earlier stage of pleasure-seeking even after a new stage has been attained. Some remnants of the earlier pattern may hang on for a while, such as thumb-sucking in weaned infants. Fixation has a further effect. If there is considerable conflict or frustration at a later point, the child may *regress* to a mode characteristic of an earlier stage at which she found considerable satisfaction (and was therefore fixated). The four-year old who is forced to cede center stage to a baby sister may regress to infantile patterns; she may throw temper tantrums, suck her thumb, or lose bowel control.

Still another mode of response to frustration during development is *reaction formation*. At a given point in his development, a child will be asked to forgo certain pleasures. During toilet training, he must not relax his sphincter however much he would like to. Similarly for a whole set of related activities, such as being dirty, playing in the mud, and so on. His urge is to relax his sphincter. Given his parent's clearly expressed disapproval, this urge leads to anxiety. One means of dealing with the conflict is to do the exact opposite of what he really wants. This reaction formation may be manifested by constipation, or, in a more general sense, by excessive neatness.

ORAL AND ANAL CHARACTERS

Freud believed that residues of early fixations and reaction formations continue into adulthood. The degree varies. Adult oral fixations might range from the common desire to give and receive oral caresses, to a fondness for sweets, to such extremes as compulsive orgies of overeating during periods of serious anxiety.

Eventually Freud became convinced that what is really important in these early stages is not the particular anatomical region, whether mouth or anus, through which the child gains pleasure at the time. More crucial are certain ways of relating to other persons that are characteristic of a given stage and leave residues in adult behavior. According to this view, the degree to which the early social patterns persist is one important determinant in the shaping of different adult personalities (Freud, 1940).

An example is the so-called *oral character* which is said to go back to oral fixation. During the oral stage, the infant is utterly dependent upon the mother. It feels warm, well-fed, and protected, leading an idyllic existence in which all is given and nothing is asked in return. According to Freud and Abraham, certain adults are oral characters whose relations to others recapitulate the passive dependency they enjoyed while sucking at the mother's breast (Abraham, 1927).

Freud believed that there is also an **anal character** whose personality derives from severe conflicts during toilet training (Freud, 1908). Since toilet training often begins before the child is physically capable of voluntary sphincter control, it is a difficult task. A frequent result is considerable anxiety, which in turn leads to various defenses. One of these is reaction formation in which the child inhibits rather than relaxes his bowels. This broadens and becomes manifest in more symbolic social terms. The child becomes compulsively clean and orderly ("I must not soil myself").

Freud believed that there are several other effects (some of which are by now regarded as rather implausible). One is obstinacy. The child asserts himself by holding back when on his potty ("You can't make me if I don't want to"), a stubbornness which may become a more generalized "no." A final characteristic is stinginess. According to Freud, this is a general form of withholding, a refusal to part with what is one's own (that is, one's feces). This refusal generalizes, and the child becomes obsessed with property rights and jealously hoards his possessions. Freud believed that excessive conflicts during the anal stage may lead to an adult personality that displays the three symptomatic attributes of the anal character—compulsive neatness, stubbornness, stinginess. These attributes seemed to occur together more often than chance would allow and Freud took this as evidence for a common underlying motif.

THE OEDIPUS COMPLEX

We now turn to that aspect of the theory of psychosexual development that Freud himself regarded as the most important—the family triangle of love and jealousy and fear that is at the root of internalized morality and out of which grows the child's identification with the parent of the same sex. This is the **Oedipus complex,** named after the mythical king of Thebes who unknowingly

Oedipus Rex *From a 1955 production directed by Tyrone Guthrie with Douglas Campbell in the title role, at Stratford, Ontario. (Courtesy Billy Rose Theatre Collection, The New York Public Library at Lincoln Center, Astor, Lenox and Tilden Collections)*

committed the two most awful crimes—killing his father and marrying his mother. According to Freud, an analogous family drama is reenacted in the childhood of all men and women. Since he came to believe that the sequence of steps is somewhat different in the two sexes, we will take them up separately. We will start with his theory of how genital sexuality emerges in males (Freud, 1905).

First Act: Love and hate   At about three or four years of age, the **phallic stage** begins. The young boy becomes increasingly interested in his penis, which becomes a source of both pride and pleasure. He masturbates and this brings satisfaction, but it is not enough. His erotic urges seek an external object. The inevitable choice is his mother (or some mother substitute). After all, he has already become attached to her through the various gratifications she provided during the oral stage. It seems only logical to direct his phallic urges to this source of all other pleasure. In some cases, this tendency is intensified by the mother herself who takes a special interest in her "little man." (An analogous pattern is seen in fathers who very often are especially fond of their daughters.) The little boy wants to be near his mother, wants to touch and caress her. In addition, he perhaps has some vaguely erotic fantasies about her when he touches his penis. He has found his first sexual partner.

But there is an obstacle—the boy's father. The little boy wants to have his mother all to himself, as a comforter as well as an erotic partner, but this sexual utopia is out of the question. His father is a rival and he is bigger. The little boy wants his father to go away and not come back—in short, to die. This is not to say that the child's wish for his father's death is in any sense the same as a murderous wish in an adult, for the boy has as little conception of death as he has of adult sexuality. As Freud remarks, all of this may not be much when compared to the tragic acts of Oedipus, but it is enough. The family drama is played in the small arena of the nursery but the basic pattern is the same: a love of mother and a jealousy of father.

Second Act: Fear and renunciation   At this point, a new element enters into the family drama. The little boy begins to fear the father he is jealous of. What brings this fear about? Freud suggests several causes. To begin with, the parents have by now probably discovered and condemned their son's masturbational practices. They may have done so quite severely; in Freud's day there were often threats of dire consequences. As a result, the pleasurable sensations from the penis and their associated thoughts become connected with anxiety. In addition, there is the son's jealous hate of his father which ultimately recoils back upon him. The little boy is sure that the father knows of his son's hostility and that the father will surely answer hate with hate.

With childish logic the little boy suspects that his punishment may be all too horribly appropriate to his crime. The same organ by which he sinned will be the one that is made to suffer. The result is **castration fear** which is aggravated by whatever threats the parents may have issued when they saw him masturbate. As a result, the boy tries to push the hostile feelings underground but they refuse to stay buried. They return and the only defense that is left is projection: "I hate father" becomes "Father hates me." This can only increase the boy's fear, which increases his hate, which is again pushed down, comes

Freud at age sixteen with his mother, Amalie Nathanson Freud *Freud was his mother's first-born and her favorite; a fact that may have affected his theory of the human family-drama. As he put it, "A man who has been the indisputable favorite of his mother keeps for life the feeling of a conqueror, that confidence of success that often induces real success." (E. Jones, 1953, p. 5, photograph courtesy Mary Evans Picture Library)*

back up, and leads to yet further projection. This process spirals upward, until the father is finally seen as an overwhelming ogre who threatens to castrate his son.

Third Act: Renunciation and final victory   As the vicious cycle continues, the little boy's anxiety eventually becomes unbearable. At this point, he throws in the towel, renounces his mother as an erotic object, and more or less renounces genital pleasures, at least for a while. Instead, he ***identifies*** with his father. He concludes that by becoming like him, he will eventually enjoy an erotic partnership of the kind his father enjoys now, if not with his mother, then at least with someone much like her.

According to Freud, the renunciation of the Oedipal problem is accomplished by the repression of all the urges, feelings, and memories of the family drama. One lasting residue is the superego, the internalized voice of the father admonishing his son from within.

Freud believed that once the tumult of the Oedipal conflict dies down, there is a period of comparative sexual quiet which lasts from about five to twelve years of age. This is the ***latency period*** during which phallic sexuality lies dormant; boys play only with boys, devote themselves to athletics and want to have nothing to do with the opposite sex. All of this changes at puberty. The hormone levels rise, the sex organs mature rapidly, and the repressed sex impulses can no longer be denied. But as these urges come out of their closet, parts of the Oedipal family skeleton come out as well, dragging along many of the fears and conflicts that had been comfortably hidden away for all these years.

According to Freud, this is one of the reasons why adolescence is so often a period of deep emotional turbulence. The boy is now physically mature and he is strongly attracted to the opposite sex, but this very attraction frightens him and he doesn't know why. Sexual contact with women arouses the unconscious wishes and fears that pertain to mother and father. In healthy individuals, the Oedipus complex has been resolved well enough so that these fears can be overcome without generating still further defenses. The boy can eventually accept himself as a man and achieve ***genital sexuality,*** in which he loves a woman as herself rather than as some shadowy substitute for his mother, and in which his love involves giving as well as taking.

Some men are less fortunate. In them, the infantile sexual conflicts were never satisfactorily resolved and form the basis of later disturbances emerging in adulthood. The symptoms are sometimes quite blatant. Freud described a case of a man who suffered from various ***obsessions;*** bizarre and frightening ideas that intrude themselves into waking consciousness and interfere with ordinary living. Many of the patient's obsessions involved death wishes directed at his father. They were evidently triggered by erotic urges. Whenever the patient fell in love during adolescence he could not help thinking of his father's death. When he first engaged in sexual intercourse, there was a sudden thought that came out of nowhere: "This is glorious! One might murder one's father for this!" (Freud, 1909, p. 339).

Other dramas, same old theme   The family drama often has a cast that is larger than three. As a result, the basic loves and jealousies and fears may be more complex. There may be some erotic feeling between brother and sister; there may also be **sibling rivalry.** The legends of mankind are ample testimony to the enduring grudges of the child who thinks it has been less favored: Esau and Jacob, Cinderella and her stepsisters. In each case, we have the jealous child's fantasy of ultimate ascendance over its hated rivals: Jacob gets his father's blessing and Cinderella wins the prince.

According to Freud, the patterns of infantile love, fear, and hate developed in the early family constellation lay the groundwork for everything that follows. In his view, the essentials of the adult personality are determined during these first five or six years. Unless drastic events intervene, all persons are destined to reenact their own childhood drama over and over again for the rest of their lives—the dialogue may be more sophisticated, but the underlying plot is always the same.

THE ELECTRA COMPLEX

We have traced Freud's account of the male psychosexual odyssey to adult sexuality. What about the female? In Freud's view, she goes through essentially identical oral and anal phases as does the male. And in many ways, the development of her phallic interests (Freud used the same term for both sexes) is symmetrical to the male's. As he focuses his erotic interests on the mother, so she upon the father. As he resents and eventually comes to fear the father, so she the mother. In short, there is a female version of the Oedipus complex (sometimes called the **Electra complex** after the Greek tragic heroine who goaded her brother into slaying their mother). But there is a theoretical difficulty. How does the little girl get to desire her father in the first place? Her first attachment was to the mother. According to Freud, this initial attachment was ultimately sexual. But if so, what accounts for the little girl's switch of sex objects?

Electra   In Eugene O'Neill's tragedy, Mourning becomes Electra, *the Electra myth is set in the period of the American Civil War. Like the Greek plays from which it derives, O'Neill's tragedy focuses on the murderous hatred a daughter bears her mother. From the 1947 film based on the play, with Rosalind Russell, Katina Paxinov, and Raymond Massey. (Courtesy The Museum of Modern Art/Film Stills Archive)*

To answer this question, Freud elaborated a far-fetched scheme that is widely regarded as one of the weakest aspects of his whole theory. The shift of attachments begins as the little girl discovers that she does not have a penis. According to Freud, she regards this lack as a catastrophe and develops **penis envy.** Her little brother might fear that he *will* be castrated; she believes that she already *is,* and feels unworthy. One consequence is that she withdraws her love from the mother, whom she regards as equally unworthy. The little girl wants a penis, but how can she get one? She turns to her father who does have the desirable organ and who she believes can help her obtain a penis substitute—a child. (Why *child* equals *penis* requires even more far-fetched arguments.) At this point, she directs her affections toward the father. From here on, the rest of the process unfolds more or less analogously to its counterpart in the boy: love of father, jealousy of mother, increasing fear of mother, eventual repression of the entire complex, and identification with the mother (Freud, 1925; 1933).

This theory of psychosexual development has been widely attacked on both scientific and political grounds. Its faults are many: Why does the girl want a penis? (And if she does, why does she blame her mother for the lack of it?) That she envies her little brother's social role in a culture in which men have more power and status is not surprising (of this more later, see pp. 483–85). But there is no evidence she really envies the particular male organ as such rather than the role and status which maleness confers in many cultures.

We conclude that Freud's theory of female psychosexual development is inadequate. Freud began with the basic premise that the *initial* attachment to one's mother is sexual. Given this belief, he was forced to find an explanation for the eventual shift in the girl's sexual choice. But we have already seen that this first premise is very suspect, for filial and sexual attachments probably do not stem from the same biological source (see Chapter 11). In consequence, there is no need to postulate any intrinsic difference in the pattern of psychosexual development of males and females. By and large, males choose females and females choose males, mostly because of built-in tendencies which are probably reinforced by cultural factors. Under the circumstances, the development is symmetrical. Whether Freud was right about the basic family triangle is still an open question (see p. 486). But if he was right, the drama unfolds in the same way regardless of whether the starring role is played by a boy or a girl.

A Reexamination of Freudian Theory

Thus far, we have presented Freud's views with a minimum of critical comment. We now shift our perspective to consider some of his assertions in the light of present-day thought and evidence.

TESTING FREUD'S THEORIES

By what criteria can one determine whether Freud's assertions are in fact correct? Freud's own criterion was the evidence from the couch. He considered the patient's free associations, his resistances, his slips of the tongue, his dreams, and then tried to weave them into a coherent pattern that somehow made sense of all the parts. But can one really draw conclusions from this kind of clinical evidence alone? Clinical practitioners cannot be totally objective no matter how hard they try. As they listen to a patient, they are more likely to hear and remember those themes that fit in with their own views than those that do not. (This point is especially pertinent to Freud who never took notes during psychoanalytic sessions.) Would another clinician with different biases have remembered the same themes?

The issue goes deeper than objective reportage. For even if the analyst could be an utterly objective observer, he cannot possibly avoid affecting that which he observes. His own theoretical preconceptions are inevitably noticed by his patients, whose dreams and free associations will very likely be colored by them. The trouble is that there is no way of disentangling the effect of the analyst (and of his theories) upon the patient's mental productions (which we want to use as evidence for or against these theories).

CONCEPTUAL DIFFICULTIES

Yet another problem is conceptual. Scientific theories lead to certain predictions; if these fail, the theory is refuted. But are Freud's assertions theories in this sense? What specific predictions do they lead to? Consider the hypothetical case of a boy raised by a harsh, rejecting mother and a weak, alcoholic father. What will the boy be like as an adult? Will he seek dominating women who will degrade him as his mother did? Will he try to find a warm, comforting wife upon whom he can become dependent and thus make up for the mothering he never had as a child? Will he become a homosexual because his father was so weak that he could not identify with him because his only feeling was contempt? There is no way of predicting on psychoanalytic grounds. Each outcome makes perfectly good sense—*after* it has occurred.

Another problem with many psychoanalytic arguments is that the analyst's theory often determines whether a patient's statement should or should not be accepted at face value. Suppose a woman insists that she hates her mother. The analyst will probably believe her. But if she swears that she loves her mother, the analyst may conclude that she, like Shakespeare's lady, "doth protest too much." He may then interpret her protestations of love as meaning the exact opposite, as reflecting a reaction formation against her "real" feelings of hate. The trouble with this kind of two-way reasoning is that it becomes difficult to find any sort of disproof.

Such considerations suggest that if we want to test Freud's assertions, we must look for more objective evidence and must be more rigorous in the way in which we interpret it. We will begin by considering some work that bears on Freud's theories of unconscious conflict.

REPRESSION AND DEFENSE

According to Freud, human beings are impelled by inner conflicts, of which they mostly are unaware. Unacceptable impulses are kept out of consciousness by elaborate devices of internal censorship: the mechanisms of defense, headed by repression. This notion of repressive forces is the cornerstone of psychoanalytic thought. What does modern psychology have to say about this notion? Our primary concern will be with cases that involve memory and are thus akin to what Freud called repression.

CLINICAL EVIDENCE

A recent study tried to provide some objective evidence for a repressionlike effect during psychoanalytic sessions. During such sessions (as of course, in ordinary life) patients sometimes have a momentary lapse of memory. They say, "I just had a thought, but it slipped my mind." Eventually they think of what they had wanted to say, often within the same session. Are these memory lapses related to the patient's emotional preoccupations? Freud would certainly have guessed that they are, that they occur when the patient is thinking (or is about to think) of something that is especially charged with emotion.

In a test of this hypothesis, several hundred tape-recorded psychoanalytic sessions were examined for instances of such momentary forgetting (Luborsky, 1973). When did such lapses occur? The investigator examined the topics the patient talked about just before and just after the memory lapse. He then compared these topics with those dealt with during control intervals (taken from other sessions in which there were no lapses). The results indicate that the lapses did not occur at random; they were much more likely during periods when the patient dealt with a crucial emotional theme.

COMBAT NEUROSIS

More dramatic examples of emotion-induced memory failure are cases of **combat neurosis** produced by the catastrophic stress of the battlefield. An occasional symptom is the inability to remember the events of that period. If pressed to recall (often under drugs) the patients stutter, tremble, and become intensely anxious. They often remember the details eventually, and when they recount them, their anxiety seems only too horribly justified:

> I got right up, and went over to the hole. Two men were in there, our First Sergeant and a Staff Sergeant was on top. He was dead, with his head blown open. There wasn't any top to his head. The other man was underneath. He was still alive, but the side of his chest was open, and I could see part of his lung. He was crying; God, I can still hear him crying. I felt sick, and my mind was funny, I couldn't think. I was shaking so I could hardly move (Grinker and Spiegel, 1945, p. 100).

The interpretation of such combat-produced memory disturbances is by no means simple. There are often brain concussions or other head injuries which may cause retrograde amnesia quite apart from the patients' emotional distress (see Chapter 8). But the case histories do suggest that at least some facets of the memory deficits may be traceable to the anxiety itself, and to this extent they resemble repression.

LABORATORY EVIDENCE

Anxiety and recall There have been many efforts to produce repression and related effects in the laboratory (see Eriksen and Pierce, 1968). But this task is

Combat fatigue *A World War II soldier suffering from a traumatic combat reaction. (Courtesy The Bettmann Archive)*

far from easy. According to psychoanalytic theory, motivated forgetting is a defense against anxiety. One would therefore expect that materials that are associated with anxiety will be recalled less readily than neutral items. But how can the experimenter be sure that the critical material is really anxiety-provoking for the subject? If it isn't, there is no reason to expect repression or any other form of defense.

To cope with this problem, several investigators have pre-selected their items to fit each subject's own pattern of anxieties. One way of doing this is by an initial word-association test. The subject is given a list of words; she has to reply to each with the first word that comes to mind. If her reaction to any one stimulus word is unusually slow or if it is accompanied by increased heart rate or a marked galvanic skin response, that word is presumably emotion-arousing for her. Using this method, one experimenter selected a set of neutral and emotional words for each subject (Jacobs, 1955). When these were later used as the responses in a paired-associate task, the subject had more trouble in producing the emotional than the neutral items. One way of explaining the result is to assume that as the emotionally loaded word was about to be retrieved from memory, it triggered anxiety which blocked further efforts at retrieval.

Seen in this light, repression may turn out to be a special case of retrieval failure. We have previously seen that recall is enormously dependent upon the presence of an appropriate retrieval cue. We forget the street names of the city we grew up in, but most of them come back when we revisit the city after many years. The same may hold for memories that Freud said are repressed. Perhaps they are not really held back by some imperious censor; perhaps they are rather misfiled under a hard-to-reach rubric and cannot be retrieved for this reason. One might want to add some further assumptions about the role of anxiety in maintaining this state of affairs. Perhaps anxiety blocks refiling; perhaps it impedes the use of appropriate retrieval cues.

Perceptual defense   A somewhat similar process may operate in recognition as well as in recall. This effect is often called ***perceptual defense.*** An example is provided by a study in which subjects were shown a series of nonsense syllables at very brief exposures. The task was to report the syllables which they saw. Some of the syllables were anxiety-arousing; they had previously been paired with a painful electric shock. These syllables were recognized less readily than neutral items—as if the subject "tried not to see" the syllable that reminded him of pain (Lazarus and McCleary, 1951). But at another level, the subject did seem to recognize the item. The investigators measured the subjects' autonomic arousal by obtaining their galvanic skin response as each of the items was presented. The critical, shock-associated syllables evoked a larger GSR than did the control syllables, despite the fact that the subject did not recognize them. The authors concluded that the anxiety-provoking items were recognized "subconsciously," a process of subterranean recognition which they called ***subception.*** Subception triggered anxiety (as indicated by the GSR) which blocked conscious recognition (as indicated by the subjects' verbal report).

The subception hypothesis has drawn various criticisms. What does it mean to see a stimulus at one level and not to see it at another? One possible interpretation is that the verbal report and the GSR measure the recognition of two different aspects of the same stimulus. When paired with shock, a syllable such as XAT becomes conditioned to autonomic fear reactions. But this connection may hold not just for the full-fledged syllable but also with its component parts, such as one or two of the individual letters, X, A, or T. These components would not suffice for recognition of the whole syllable (as indexed by the verbal report), but they might well elicit the fear response (as measured by the GSR). According to this interpretation, perceiving something is not an all-or-none affair, but a process that occurs in stages: a shape, a human figure, a woman . . . oh, it's mother! If anxiety is evoked at an early stage, further recognition processes are impeded and the later stages may never emerge (Erdelyi, 1974).*

Repressors and sensitizers Such evidence indicates that repressionlike phenomena can occur under laboratory conditions. But further studies suggest that these effects are not found in everyone. Some individuals are **repressors:** When presented with materials that arouse anxiety, they tend not to recall or recognize them. But other persons seem to lack this convenient ability to shut the door on their own anxieties. They are **sensitizers** who are unable to overlook or to forget that which worries them; in fact, they pay special attention to it. Interestingly enough, the repressors seem to have some of the personality characteristics (to be sure, in a milder form) of hysterics. For example, they are more likely to complain about various minor bodily ills (Byrne, 1964). According to Freud and other analysts, hysterics adopt repression as their major defense mechanism. In other neuroses, other defense mechanisms such as reaction formation play a larger role (see Chapter 17).

DREAM CONTENT

The preceding discussion suggests that unconscious conflict and defense are probably genuine phenomena. To this extent, Freud's general position has been upheld. But the verdict has been less favorable on some of his more specific assertions. An example is his theory of dreams. According to Freud, dreams provide us with one of the main windows into the workings of unconscious defense processes.

DREAMS AND EMOTIONS

Stated in the most general terms, Freud's theory asserts that dreams tend to reflect the current emotional preoccupations of the dreamer, including those of which he is unaware, often portrayed in a condensed and symbolic form. This is probably quite true. Thus patients who await major surgery reveal their fears in what they dream about during the two or three nights before the operation. Their fears are rarely expressed directly; few, if any, of their dreams are about scalpels or operating rooms. The reference is indirect, in condensed and symbolized form, as in dreams about falling from tall ladders

---

* Such a stage analysis avoids some of the logical problems that are posed by Freud's repression concept. According to Freud, threatening items are excluded from consciousness. But in order to know which items are to be excluded, we must first recognize them. This leads to a paradox. We have to recognize an item in order to determine whether it is an item we must not recognize. By assuming that there are several stages of recognition this problem is circumvented.

or standing on a high, swaying bridge, or about a decrepit machine that needs repair (Breger, Hunter, and Lane, 1971).

A similar point is made by a recent study that related dream content to the hormonal changes during the menstrual cycle (Baron, 1977). The second half of this cycle is characterized by a high level of progesterone, the pregnancy hormone that prepares the uterus to receive the fertilized ovum, regardless of whether fertilization has in fact occurred (see Chapter 11). One might expect a greater preoccupation with maternal concerns during this progesterone-dominated phase of the cycle. An analysis of the dreams of female college sophomores bore out this expectation. Dreams about childbirth, babies, and baby-related topics were more frequent during this phase of the cycle than during others.

DREAMS AND WISH FULFILLMENT

Such evidence indicates that dreams do express whatever motives are currently most important. But Freud's theory went much further than this. As we saw, he believed that the manifest dream is a censored and disguised version of the latent dream that lies underneath and represents a wish fulfillment. This conception of dreams has been much criticized. To begin with, there is considerable doubt that all (or even many) dreams are attempts at wish fulfillments, whether disguised or open. In one study, subjects were made extremely thirsty before they went to sleep. Since thirst is hardly a forbidden urge, there is no reason to suppose an internal censorship. However, none of the subjects

The Nightmare *This painting by Henry Fuselli (painted in 1783 and said to have decorated Freud's office) highlights what seems to be one of the difficulties of Freud's dream theory. If all dreams are wish-fulfillments, what accounts for nightmares? According to Freud, they are often dreams in which the latent dream is not sufficiently disguised. The forbidden wish is partially recognized, anxiety breaks through, and the sleeper suffers a nightmare. (Courtesy The Detroit Institute of Arts)*

reported dreams of drinking. Since they were so thirsty, why didn't they gratify themselves in their dreams (Dement and Wolpert, 1958)?

Another problem is the fact that the same urge is sometimes freely expressed in dreams, but heavily disguised on other occasions. Tonight, the sleeper dreams of unabashed sexual intercourse; tomorrow night, she dreams of riding a team of wild horses. For sake of argument, let us agree that riding is a symbol for intercourse. But why should the censor disguise tomorrow what is so freely allowed tonight?

One investigator, C. S. Hall, has come up with a plausible suggestion (Hall, 1953). According to Hall, the dream symbol does not *disguise* an underlying idea; on the contrary, it *expresses* it. In Hall's view, the dream is a rather concrete mental shorthand that embodies a feeling or emotion. Riding a horse, plowing a field, planting a seed—all of these may be concrete renditions of the idea of sexual intercourse. But they are not meant to hide this idea. Their function is much the same as the cartoonist's picture of Uncle Sam or John Bull. These are representations of the United States and of England, but they are certainly not meant as disguises for them. During sleep, more specifically during REM sleep (see Chapter 3), we are incapable of the extreme complexity and abstractness of waking mental life. We are thus reduced to a more concrete and archaic form of thinking. The wishes and fears of our waking life are still present at night and we dream about them. But the way in which these are now expressed tends to be more primitive, a concrete pictorialization that combines fragments of various waking concerns and serves as a kind of symbolic cartoon.

This hypothesis may explain why a given idea (say, sexual intercourse) is sometimes dreamed about overtly and sometimes in symbolic form. If there is no attempt to mask an idea, one may express it either directly or in visual metaphor. There may be some uniformities of dream symbolism; after all, there are perceptual similarities between the genital organs and various physical objects and we may express these similarities in our dreams. (These very similarities are expressed in the many slang terms for penis and vagina; Hall 1964.) But dream symbolism is far from universal, for it necessarily depends upon our own experiences and preoccupations. Suppose an architect dreams about a collapsing steeple. Does his dream reveal a fear of impotence or a gnawing worry about an actual building he has recently designed? As some writers point out, an explicit sex dream may itself symbolize something else (an idea that would have been wholly foreign to Freud). This notion goes back to the ancient Greeks: "If a Greek dreamed that his mother enticed him into her bed, he would probably conclude that his motherland . . . was going to bestow some exceptional honor upon him" (Eysenck and Wilson, 1973, p. 390).

BIOLOGY OR CULTURE

While many psychologists agree with Freud's thesis that there is unconscious conflict, they are more skeptical of his particular assertions of what these conflicts are. One of their major quarrels is with Freud's insistence that the pattern of these conflicts is biologically based and will therefore be found in essentially the same form in all men and all women.

THE EMPHASIS ON SOCIAL FACTORS

Since Freud believed that the key to emotional development is in biology, he assumed that its progression followed a universal course. In his view, all humans pass through oral, anal, and phallic stages and suffer the conflicts appropriate to each stage. This conception has been challenged by various clinical practitioners, many of whom used Freud's own psychoanalytic methods. These critics felt that Freud had overemphasized biological factors at the expense of social ones. This point was first raised by one of Freud's own students, Alfred Adler (1870–1937). It was later taken up by several like-minded authors who are often grouped together under the loose label **neo-Freudians,** including Erich Fromm (1900–80), Karen Horney (1885–1952), and H. S. Sullivan (1892–1949).

According to the neo-Freudians, human development cannot be properly understood by focusing on the particular anatomical regions—mouth, anus, genitals—through which the child tries to gratify its instinctual desires. In their view, the important question is how humans relate, or try to relate, to others—whether by dominating, or submitting, or becoming dependent, or whatever. Their description of our inner conflicts is therefore in social terms. For example, if they see a mother who toilet trains her child very severely, they are likely to interpret her behavior as part of an overall pattern whereby she tries to push the child to early achievement; the specific frustrations of the anal stage as such are of lesser concern to them. Similarly for the sexual sphere. According to Freud, the neurotic conflict centers on the repression of erotic impulses. According to the neo-Freudian critics, the real difficulty is in the area of interpersonal relationships: Neurosis often leads to sexual symptoms, not because sex is a powerful biological motive that is pushed underground, but rather because it is one of the most sensitive barometers of interpersonal attitudes. The man who can only relate to other people by competing with them may well be unable to find sexual pleasure in his marriage bed; but the sexual malfunction is an *effect* of his neurotic social pattern rather than its *cause*.

The same emphasis on social factors highlights the neo-Freudian explanation for how these conflicts arise in the first place. In contrast to Freud, it denies that these conflicts are biologically pre-ordained; they rather depend upon the specific cultural conditions in which the child is reared. According to the neo-Freudians, the conflicts that Freud observed may have characterized *his* patients, but this does not mean that these same patterns will be found in persons who live at other times and in other places.

The neo-Freudian position became especially prominent in the United States during the 1930s and 1940s. In part this is because it fit in with the general tenor of the times. Various movements of reform, such as the New Deal, were based on the belief that social ills like war and depression are not an unalterable consequence of man's inherent nature: They are caused by environmental conditions and can be cured by appropriate changes. A basic optimism of this kind resonated to the neo-Freudian denial of a universal Oedipus complex or of a universal female tendency toward penis envy. There was a ready audience for the belief that human social development is essentially plastic and does not have the implacable inevitability of an insect's

Margaret Mead *(Courtesy The American Museum of Natural History)*

metamorphosis (for overviews, see Munroe, 1955, and Hall and Lindzey, 1970, Chapter 10).

THE REJECTION OF CULTURAL ABSOLUTISM

One set of relevant findings came from another discipline, **cultural anthropology,** which concerns itself with the practices and beliefs of different peoples throughout the world. There are evidently considerable variations in these patterns, with accompanying variations in the kind of person who is typical in each setting. Personality characteristics that are typical in our culture are by no means universal, a result that was beautifully tuned to the antibiological bias of the neo-Freudians.

A well-known example concerns cultural variations in the roles that different societies assign to the two sexes. An influential study by the American anthropologist Margaret Mead, "Sex and Temperament," compared the personality traits of men and women in three New Guinea tribes that lived within a hundred-mile radius. Among the Arapesh, both men and women were mild, cooperative, and, so to speak, "maternal" in their attitudes to each other and especially to children. Among the neighboring Mundugomor, both sexes were ferociously aggressive and quarrelsome. In yet another tribe, the Tchambuli, the usual sex roles were reversed. The women were the hale and hardy breadwinners who fished and went to market unadorned. While the women managed the worldly affairs, the men gossiped and pranced about, adjusted elaborate hairdos, carved and painted, and practiced intricate dance steps (Mead, 1935, 1937). The neo-Freudians took such findings as a strong argument against the cultural absolutism which regards the patterns of modern Western society as the built-in givens of human nature.

Several anthropologists have criticized Mead's account as an oversimplification. They point out that there are probably some universal sex roles after all; for example, warfare is generally conducted by the men, even among the Tchambuli. They argue that some of the difference between male and female aggressiveness may very well be due to biological factors. As we have previously seen, aggression is in part under hormonal control; as androgen levels rise, both human and animal males become more aggressive (see Chapter 11). What culture does is to determine how this aggression is to be channeled and against whom, whether it is to be valued, and how much of it is allowed.

FREUD'S THEORIES OF DEVELOPMENT

The enormous impact of psychoanalytic theory led many investigators to concentrate on the childhood events that Freud and his students considered so crucial. By and large, the findings do not seem to bear out Freud's specific hypotheses (for an overview, see Zigler and Child, 1972).

CHILD-REARING PRACTICES

Toilet training An example concerns the effects of toilet training. Some mothers begin training when the infant is as young as five months; others wait until the child is two years old. There are some slight indications that starting later makes the whole process simpler and may minimize certain childhood disorders of elimination such as bed-wetting (Brazelton, 1962). But what about the more interesting long-term effects that Freud had in mind when he described the "anal character"?

On the whole, the verdict is negative. There is little if any evidence that shows any long-term effects from toilet-training practices, either in our own or other cultures (Orlansky, 1949). For example, there seems to be no relationship between the severity of toilet training in different cultures and the degree of hoarding or economic competition (Cohen, 1953). There is thus little evidence for Freud's claim that the toilet is a prep school for becoming a banker or a captain of industry.

Cultural differences and the Oedipus complex   The most influential of Freud's assertions about early childhood concerns sexuality and the Oedipus complex. Our major source of information in this area comes from studies of other cultures. On the whole, the evidence was welcome grist to the neo-Freudian mill: The Oedipus conflict is not universal but depends upon cultural variations in the family constellation.

This point was first raised some fifty years ago by the English anthropologist Bronislaw Malinowski on the basis of his observations of the Trobriand Islanders of the Western Pacific (Malinowski, 1927). The family pattern of the Trobriand Islanders is quite different from our own. Among the Trobrianders, the biological father is not the head of the household. He spends time with his children and plays with them, but he exerts no authority. This role is reserved for the mother's brother who acts as a disciplinarian. The Trobriand Islanders thus separate the roles that in Freud's Vienna were played by one and the same person.

According to Freud, this different family pattern should make no difference. There should still be an Oedipus complex in which the father is the hated villain for, after all, it is he who is the little boy's sexual rival. But this did not turn out to be the case. Malinowski saw no signs of friction between sons and fathers, though he did observe a fair amount of hostility directed at the maternal uncle. The same held for dreams and folk tales. The Trobriand Islanders believe that there are prophetic dreams of death; these generally involve the death of the maternal uncle. Similarly there are no myths about evil fathers or stepfathers; again, the villain is typically the mother's brother. If we accept Freud's notion that dreams (and myths) involve unconscious wishes and preoccupations, we are forced to conclude that the Trobriand boy hates his uncle, not his father. In sum, the child has fears and fantasies about the authoritarian figure in his life, the man who bosses him around. This is the father in Freud's Austria, but the uncle on the Trobriand Islands. His fears are not about his mother's lover as such, for the Trobriand boy does not hate the father who plays this role.

THE HOME ATMOSPHERE

The cross-cultural findings show that while the emotional relations between the child and members of the family may exert long-lasting effects, the specific factors that enter into the equation are not those that Freud had made so much of. The same holds true for our own culture. The results of many studies suggest that parents influence their children, not so much by this or the other specific practice (say, early toilet training), but rather by the general social atmosphere in which the child is raised. The parents communicate their attitudes about the child, about the world, about the role they expect the child to fill. These attitudes have an important effect on the child at each stage of its development. A given child-rearing practice may be less important than the attitude with which it is carried out.

Parental warmth An example is parental discipline. Some parents are restrictive; they set up many rules and prohibitions. Others are more permissive and impose fewer constraints. What effects are produced by this difference? According to one review, the effect depends upon yet another factor—the "warmth" of the parents, especially of the mother (Becker, 1964). In a warm home atmosphere, the parents tend to be affectionate, are likely to use praise, try to explain the reasons for the household do's and don'ts, are less likely to use physical punishment, and are less severe when they resort to it—all in all, they act as if they *like* the child. At the other extreme is a hostile atmosphere which is characterized by the opposite conditions. In several studies, judges rated the home atmosphere along both of these dimensions: restrictive-permissive, and hostile-warm. The child's behavior was then observed independently outside of the home situation; for example, in a nursery school. The results depended upon both dimensions. Permissiveness coupled with parental warmth seems to induce a greater level of self-reliance; the children were described as more active, outgoing, and self-assertive. But when permissiveness occurs in a context of parental hostility the results are very different. Such children tend to be extremely aggressive and destructive; in fact, they may become delinquents. Put another way, hostile parents who let their children do pretty much what they please are not really permissive; they are neglectful.

The "anal character" and culture A similar point is made by a study that was directed at Freud's concept of the "anal character" (Beloff, 1957). According to Freud, this personality pattern is composed of several attributes that he believed go together—neatness, obstinacy and parsimony. A number of undergraduates were asked to rate their own and their friends' characteristics. Their ratings showed that these attributes do form a coherent cluster. Those students who judged themselves (or were judged by others) to be obstinate were also those who tended to be orderly and a bit stingy. More important, the students with these anal characteristics tended to have mothers with similar attributes, as shown by questionnaires administered to the mothers. These results seem to vindicate Freud's theory, for it appears that anal children have anal mothers. But a further finding runs counter to the theory. The mothers were asked at what age they toilet trained their children. There was no correlation whatever between this factor and the personality attributes that define anal character.

Our best guess is that Freud's developmental hypothesis is false. Obstinacy, parsimony, and orderliness are indeed transmitted from parents to child. But they are transmitted as part of a general pattern of middle-class values and attitudes, instilled as one facet of what the parents want the child to become. They are not by-products of getting the child out of diapers.

It appears that "anal" character traits have little to do with the anus. But such a relation might have existed in the group from which Freud drew his patients. Obstinacy, orderliness, and parsimony are probably a result of the parents pushing their child toward independence and achievement. It may be that at the turn of the century some mothers regarded early toilet training as the first sign of success and accomplishment, competing with other mothers to see whose child would be ready first. If so, early toilet training would be correlated with anal characteristics, and this perhaps is the correlation that Freud observed in his Viennese parents.

SOCIAL DEVELOPMENT AFTER FIVE

Contrary to Freud's beliefs, personality does not seem to be frozen rigidly in early childhood, but keeps on developing until adulthood and beyond. Nor are the parents the only agents that shape their children's social reactions. As they grow up, their personal drama is enacted on an ever-expanding stage with an ever-increasing cast of characters. There are siblings to be emulated or envied with whom one has to learn to share. There are peers who with time become increasingly important and whose approval is then sought as eagerly (if not more eagerly) than that of the parents. As a teen-ager, the child enters adolescent society with its quickly changing fashions, slang, and slogans; this is a convenient mid-point between the simple social structure of the family and the complex adult twentieth-century world. Here sports, clubs, cliques, and dating serve as preparation and practice for adulthood (Campbell, 1969). Peer groups undoubtedly affect social behavior, and some of the experiences of that period have lasting effects.

The socialization process does not stop even at this point. Various social institutions continue to shape us, for better or for worse: schools, colleges, the army, various professional and political organizations, to name a few. Finally, there are the important personal relations of adulthood: friendships, love affairs, marriage, one's own children and one's children's children. To be sure, there is some loss of flexibility with increasing age, for previous choices limit the choices that are still open, but development never really stops until the grave.

Erikson's psychosocial stages   A very influential modern psychoanalyst, Erik Erikson, has tried to reconcile the belief in continued human growth with the basic themes of Freudian thought. According to Erikson, humans pass through a series of major **crises** as they go through the life cycle. At each stage there is a critical confrontation between the self the individual has achieved thus far and the various new demands posed by his or her social and personal setting. In all, there are "eight ages of man," of which the first few occur in early childhood and more or less correspond to Freud's oral, anal, and phallic stages (Table 12.2).

Identity crisis   Of primary interest is Erikson's description of the crises that occur after childhood. The best known of these is the **identity crisis** of late adolescence or early adulthood. One characteristic of the period is an attempt

Erik H. Erikson   *(Photograph by Jon Erikson)*

Table 12.2 ERIKSON'S EIGHT AGES OF MAN

Approximate age	Developmental task of that stage	Psychosocial crisis of that stage
0–1½ years	Attachment to mother, which lays foundations for later trust in others	Trust versus mistrust
1½–3 years	Gaining some basic control of self and environment (e.g., toilet training, exploration)	Autonomy versus shame and doubt
3–6 years	Becoming purposeful and directive	Initiative versus guilt
6 years– puberty	Developing social, physical, and school skills	Competence versus inferiority
Adolescence	Making transition from childhood to adulthood; developing a sense of identity	Identity versus role confusion
Early adulthood	Establishing intimate bonds of love and friendship	Intimacy versus isolation
Middle age	Fulfilling life goals that involve family, career, and society; developing concerns that embrace future generations	Productivity versus stagnation
Later years	Looking back over one's life and accepting its meaning	Integrity versus despair

SOURCE: Based on Erikson, 1963.

to establish a separation from the world of one's parents. To accomplish this end, the adolescent adopts all kinds of external trappings of what's "now" and what's "in," such as distinctive tastes, in dance steps, clothing, and idiom. These change with bewildering rapidity as yesterday's adolescent fads diffuse into the broader social world and become today's adult fashions (as witness men's hair styles). New adolescent styles spring up to maintain the differentiation (Douvan and Adelson, 1958).

But the separation from the adult's sphere is only one manifestation of what adolescents are really trying to achieve. Their major goal throughout this entire period is to find their own identity. In our complex culture, there are many social roles, and adolescence is a time to try them on to see which one fits best—which vocation, which ideology, which group membership. The adolescent's primary question is, "Who am I?" and to answer it he strikes a succession of postures, in part for the benefit of others, who then serve as a mirror in which he can see himself. Each role, each human relationship, each world view, is temporarily adopted on an all-or-none basis with no room for compromise. Each is at first a costume. When the adolescent finds that some costume fits, it becomes the clothes of his adult identity. Most adolescents eventually succeed, but the process of identity seeking has its difficulties:

The danger of this stage is role confusion. . . . To keep themselves together they temporarily overidentify, to the point of apparent loss of identity, with the heroes of cliques and crowds. This initiates the stage of "falling in love," which is by no means entirely, or even primarily, a sexual matter . . . To a considerable extent adolescent love is an attempt to arrive at a definition of one's identity by projecting one's diffuse ego image on another and by seeing it thus reflected and gradually clarified. This is why so much of young love is conversation (Erikson, 1963, p. 262).

According to Erikson, the adolescent crisis is essentially *psychosocial* rather than biological. Its primary cause is the fact that the individual has to switch from a set of rather simple social roles to a vastly more complex role constellation. Biological factors such as hormonal spurts at puberty play a part but they alone are not responsible for the emotional upheavals that so often accompany this period. Some evidence in favor of this view comes from certain preliterate cultures in which the transition from childhood to adulthood is very gradual. Among the Arapesh of New Guinea, the young participate increasingly in adult activities as they get older. The child begins by tilling her parents' garden and eventually tills her own. Given the relatively simple social and economic structure of Arapesh life, the change is not very drastic. Correspondingly, there seems to be no psychological crisis among the Arapesh during adolescence (Mead, 1939). However enviable, such a gentle transition is hard to achieve in our modern industrial society. It's hard to see how a five-year old can help his father at his job if that job happens to be computer programming.

Some of the difficulties of the adolescent crisis in our society are further compounded by the fact that the youth's elders may be unclear about *their* roles and *their* values. Adults are shaky in their beliefs because the enormous social and technological changes of the last few decades have rendered many of the convictions of their own youth obsolete. Is education really the road to success? And what is success anyway? Under the circumstances, the adolescent's rebellion against her parents' control may go beyond the quest for personal autonomy and become a more general struggle against an older and (as she sees it) oppressive world view.

Later crises   In Erikson's scheme, there are still further stages of personality development. In young adulthood, the healthy individual has to achieve the capacity for closeness and intimacy through love, or else suffer a sense of isolation that will permit only shallow human relationships. In early middle age, she has to develop a sense of personal creativity that extends beyond her own self. This includes a concern for others, for her work, for the community of which she is part. And toward the end of life there is a final crisis during which each person has to come to terms with his or her own life and accept it for what it was, with a sense of integrity rather than of despair. Erikson eloquently sums up this last reckoning, "It is the acceptance of one's own and only life cycle as something that had to be and that, by necessity, permitted of no substitutes . . . healthy children will not fear life if their elders have integrity enough not to fear death" (Erikson, 1963, pp. 268–69).

It is hard to know how to evaluate Erikson's developmental scheme. It is a literary and moving account of the human odyssey through life, but in what sense is it a true description? Erikson holds that there are eight ages of man.

Why not seven or nine? Erikson picks certain undeniably important turning points of life, but one can argue that there are others. Entering upon a career (which usually happens after adolescence), becoming a grandparent, adjusting to menopause—isn't each of these a psychosocial crisis that poses a further question of self-definition? As yet, there is no proof that Erikson picked *the* significant milestones in the road of life. His contribution is in his insistence that the student of human development consider the entire stretch of this road and not only its very beginning.

Psychoanalytic Interpretation of Culture, Myth, and Literature

Thus far, our primary focus has been on Freud's theories of human personality, both from his own perspective and from that of his critics. But in Freud's hands, psychoanalysis had become a world view with still broader implications. He and his followers tried to extend its scope to shed light, not only on human nature but on humanity's important accomplishments: its civilization, its religions, its myths, its works of art. Partially because of these extensions, Freud's views had an enormous impact not only within psychiatry and psychology, but also on fields outside such as anthropology and literature.

THE ORIGIN OF SOCIETY AND THE INCEST TABOO

One extension of psychoanalytic thinking is provided by Freud's speculations about the origin of human society. In his view, the Oedipus complex is a universal human experience and society is at bottom an outgrowth of this basic struggle between parents and children. He supposed that early humans lived in "primal hordes" dominated by one strong male who was the father of all the young and who had exclusive sexual rights to all the females. The sons who rebelled were killed, castrated, or expelled from the group. Eventually, the exiled sons banded together and defeated and killed their father. But after the patricide, they quarreled among themselves, each trying to achieve the father's primal eminence. They finally decided to form a sexual social contract whose basic law was the ***incest taboo.*** The war of all against all was averted and brothers could live in harmony, for no mating was allowed within the family (Freud, 1913*a*).

Modern anthropologists regard this account as a quasi-Hobbesian fairy tale, for they doubt that there were ever any primal hordes under one male's exclusive dominion. But they share Freud's interest in the incest taboo which is certainly one of the very few universal thou-shalt-nots; it is found in all human societies. Its origin is unknown, though there are some plausible speculations. It is clear that the taboo is not based on an aversion. After all, the taboo is sometimes violated, especially among those who are regarded as semidivine and thus exempt from mortal laws, such as Egyptian pharaohs and their sisters. Another argument against the view that the taboo is based on an aversion is the fact that there are no taboos against acts that no one wants to perform anyway (there is no taboo against sleeping with crocodiles).

What then can account for the taboo? The best guess is that those groups who developed it had a better chance to survive and prosper than those who did not. The prohibition against incest avoids the deleterious genetic effects of inbreeding. If parents are closely related, there is a good chance that they will bequeath their offspring the same harmful recessive gene. Another advantage is social and economic. If there is a prohibition against incest, the children of one family are necessarily forced to select their mates from among the sons and daughters of another family. This tends to create an enlarged network of emotional ties; as a result the small band expands to a larger tribe. Such tribes have a selective advantage over smaller ones. They can hunt and gather more efficiently and, upon confrontation, they can defeat the smaller group in warfare. As the group survived, so did its taboo (Aberle et al., 1963).

This line of reasoning is certainly far from the historical speculations that Freud proposed. But anthropologists still find much of interest in Freud's description, if it is taken as a kind of metaphor. Their views of culture have been much affected by many aspects of Freud's theories, such as his emphasis on the family as the medium through which society transmits its rules and prohibitions, and as the cornerstone upon which all further social organization is built.

PSYCHOANALYTIC THEORY OF MYTHS

Freud and his students contended that as dreams are a window into the individual's unconscious, so myths, legends, and fairy tales allow us a glimpse into those hidden concerns that are shared by whole groups of men, if not all of humanity. Indeed, psychoanalysts found an ample supply of Oedipal themes. There are numerous ogres, dragons, and various monsters whom the hero must slay if he wants to reach the fair maid. The part of the villain is often taken by a cruel stepparent, a fairly transparent symbol of Oedipal hostilities.

As an example of a psychoanalytic interpretation of a fairy tale, consider Snow White and the seven dwarfs (J. F. Brown, 1940). Snow White is a child princess who is persecuted by her stepmother, the wicked queen. The queen is envious of Snow White's beauty and tries to have her killed. The child escapes and lives with seven dwarfs who work in an underground mine. The queen finally discovers Snow White and persuades her to eat part of a poisoned apple. Snow White falls as if dead. The dwarfs place her in a beautiful coffin in which she lies motionless for seven years. At this point, a handsome prince appears, opens the casket with his sword, awakens Snow White from her long sleep, and the two live happily ever after.

According to psychoanalytic authors, this fairy tale is a veiled allegory of the Oedipal sequence. The wicked queen is the mother on whom the child projects her own hate and sexual jealousy. The Oedipal conflict is temporarily resolved as the child's erotic urges go underground and remain dormant for the seven years of the latency period, symbolized both by Snow White's long sleep and by the seven dwarfs. At the end of this period, her sexuality is reawakened in adult form by the young prince. (The meaning of the sword is left as an exercise for the reader.)

Is this interpretation valid? It is hard to know by what ground rules validity can be judged. There are undoubtedly many alternative (and perhaps more plausible) interpretations of this and many other legends that psychoanalysts have tried to squeeze into their scheme. Death and resurrection are old themes in mythology which probably refer to many important natural cycles such as the daily succession of darkness and light and the yearly alternation of winter's desolation and spring's green rebirth. Myths may also embody dim folk memories of long-past wars, dynastic conflicts, previously held religions, and various catastrophes. The psychoanalytic view may throw some further light on a fascinating aspect of our cultural heritage, but it is just one light among many others and it may not be the brightest one.

PSYCHOANALYSIS AND LITERATURE

Freud's approach to the interpretation of works of art and literature was very similar to the way in which he tried to understand the hidden meaning of dreams and myths. The artistic production reflects the artist's own inner conflicts and has impact upon others because it strikes the same unconscious chords in them. Perhaps the most famous example of psychoanalytic literary interpretations is Freud's analysis of *Hamlet,* later elaborated by his student Ernest Jones (Jones, 1954). The central puzzle of the play is Hamlet's indecisiveness. He waits until the end of the fifth act before he finally avenges his father's death upon his hated uncle, a delay that causes his own death as well as the death of virtually everyone else in the play, innocent as well as guilty. To Freud and Jones, the clue to Hamlet's inaction is the Oedipus complex. Hamlet is paralyzed because he must kill a man who did precisely what he himself unconsciously wants to do, kill his father and marry his mother. According to Freud and Jones, the play grips the audience because it stirs the same latent conflicts in them.

Shakespearean scholars are by no means agreed on the virtues of this interpretation, though some find it interesting. But the issue goes further than that. Suppose we accept the interpretation that Freud and Jones offer. Is this *the* key to Hamlet, which is then shorn of all its mysteries, like a completed

Hamlet confronting his mother in her bedroom A scene from Laurence Olivier's 1948 film Hamlet. Olivier's conception of the role of Hamlet was seriously affected by Ernest Jones' psychoanalytic interpretation of the play. His casting of a young attractive actress, Eileen Herlie, for the part of Hamlet's mother helped to underscore the Oedipus theme. (Courtesy Universal Pictures)

crossword puzzle that is discarded once it is solved? The truth is that there is no one key, there is no one meaning of *Hamlet*, for a work of art is necessarily ambiguous. As with myths and legends, this or the other interpretation may help to illuminate them, but it does not explain them away. *Hamlet* may be about Oedipal conflicts, but many hack novels have the same theme. What makes the one a great literary treasure while the others are forgotten almost immediately?

These points argue against the overenthusiastic application of psychoanalytic interpretation to literary works. But for good or ill (probably for both) Freud's impact on literature and literary criticism has been enormous. Most literary critics today have at least a passing acquaintance with Freud's basic works and many major authors have been consciously affected by him. By now, his insights have become part of our culture and Freudian lore (often vulgarized) is a staple of our popular literature, our stage, and our screen.

Freud's Contributions in Retrospect

We have seen that many of Freud's beliefs have not been confirmed. There are good grounds to doubt Freud's essentially Hobbesian view of human nature. There is little evidence for his general theory of psychosexual development and even less for his male-centered conception of feminine psychology. He overemphasized biological givens at the expense of cultural factors, and there are strong arguments against his belief that personality is for all intents and purposes fixed by the age of five or six. We have also seen that Freud can be criticized not just for what he asserted but for the way in which he tried to prove his claims. By now, there is general agreement that the psychoanalytic couch is not a source of objective fact. But even if it were, there

Freud looking at a bust of himself sculpted for his seventy-fifth birthday by O. Nemon (Courtesy Wide World Photos)

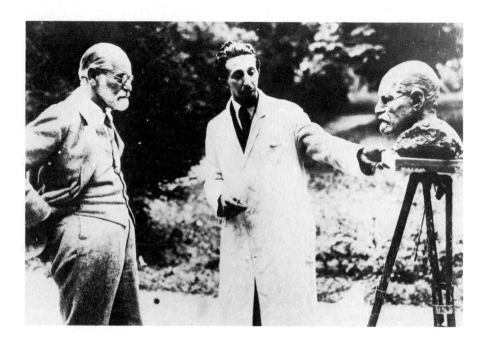

is the further problem that many of Freud's theoretical proposals are a bit vague and metaphorical, that it is not clear how one can decide whether they are right or wrong. In addition, there are many questions about the efficacy of his psychoanalytic method as a form of therapy, a matter we will discuss later on (see Chapter 18).

All in all, this is a formidable set of criticisms. But even so, many psychologists would maintain that, wrong as he probably was in any number of particulars, Sigmund Freud must nevertheless be regarded as one of the giants of psychology, one of the few our field has known thus far. There are at least two reasons.

The first concerns one major conception of Freud's that still stands, however much it may have to be modified and reinterpreted—the notion that there is internal conflict of which we are often unaware. Freud was not the first to recognize that we are often torn in opposite directions and that we frequently deceive ourselves about what we want. But he was the first for whom this insight was the cornerstone of an entire point of view. Whether his own therapeutic procedure, psychoanalysis, is an appropriate tool to make the unknown known and thus to restore a measure of free choice to the emotionally crippled victims of inner conflict is still debatable (see Chapter 18). But whether his therapy works or not, Freud's contribution remains. He saw that we do not know ourselves, that we are not masters of our own souls. By pointing out how ignorant we are, he set a task for later investigators who may ultimately succeed, so that we may then be able to follow Socrates' deceptively simple prescription for a good life, "Know thyself."

The other major reason why Freud has a lasting place among the greats of intellectual history is the sheer scope of his theoretical conception. His was a view of human nature that was virtually all-embracing. It tried to encompass both rational thought and emotional urges. It conceived of neurotic ailments as a consequence of the same psychological forces that operate in everyday life. It saw humans as biological organisms as well as social beings, as creatures whose present is rooted in their past and who are simultaneously children and adults. The range of psychological phenomena that Freud tried to comprehend within his theory is staggering—neurotic symptoms, personality patterns, social groupings, family relations, humor, slips of the tongue, dreams, artistic productions, aspects of religious thought. This catalogue is by no means complete. Freud's theory has many faults, but this long list highlights some of its virtues. It dealt with matters of genuine human significance, it concerned both human beings and their works, it was an account that was about humanity as a whole. To this extent Freud provided a goal for posterity. He showed us the kinds of questions that we have to answer before we can claim to have a full theory of human personality.

Summary

1. Human behavior is partially determined by childhood *socialization*. A very influential theory of this socialization process was advanced by Sigmund Freud who asserted that all persons experience *unconscious conflicts* originating in childhood. His theories grew out of studies of *hysteria*, a *psychogenic* mental disorder whose symptoms are similar to some effects observed in *hypnosis*. Freud proposed that hysterical symptoms are a means of keeping *repressed* thoughts or wishes unconscious. He

believed that the symptoms would be eliminated once the repressed materials are recovered, and devised a procedure, *psychoanalysis,* directed toward this end.

2. Freud distinguished three subsystems of the human personality. One is the *id,* a blind striving toward biological satisfaction that follows the *pleasure principle.* The second is the *ego,* a system of reactions that tries to reconcile the id-derived needs with the actualities of the world, in accordance with the *reality principle.* A third is the *superego,* which represents the internalized rules of the parents and punishes deviations by feelings of guilt. The struggles between these three subsystems often occur outside of consciousness.

3. Internal conflict is initially prompted by anxiety, which becomes associated with forbidden thoughts and wishes, usually in childhood. As a *defense* against anxiety, the child represses the forbidden materials. But these materials surface again, sometimes in new and disguised form, as in *displaced aggression.* To push such thoughts and wishes down again, further *mechanisms of defense* come into play, including *reaction formation, rationalization,* and *projection.*

4. Freud tried to apply his theory of unconscious conflict to many areas of everyday life. An example is his theory of dreams. To Freud, all dreams are attempts at wish fulfillment. Since many of these wishes prompt anxiety, their full expression is *censored.* As a result, the underlying *latent dream* is transformed into the *manifest dream* in which the forbidden urges emerge in a disguised, sometimes *symbolic* form.

5. Freud believed that most adult unconscious conflicts are ultimately sexual in nature and refer back to events during childhood *psychosexual development.* This passes through three main stages which are characterized by the *erogenous zones* through which gratification is obtained: *oral, anal,* and *phallic.* At each stage, socialization thwarts some of these gratifications, as in weaning and toilet training. The smooth course of development from one stage to another may be impeded by *fixation* or *reaction formation.* These help to shape adult personality, as in the case of *oral* and *anal characteristics.*

6. During the phallic stage, the male child develops the *Oedipus complex.* He directs his sexual urges toward his mother, hates his father as a rival, and comes to dread him as he suffers increasing *castration fear.* He finally renounces his sexual urges, identifies with his father, and represses all relevant memories which then become the nucleus of the superego. At adolescence, repressed sexual urges surface, are redirected toward adult partners, and the person generally achieves *genital sexuality.* In female children, a similar complex develops, with love toward father and rivalry toward mother.

7. Attempts to find evidence for repression and unconscious conflict outside of the psychoanalytic session have met with some moderate success, for example in work on *combat neurosis* and studies of *motivated forgetting* and *subception.* The verdict on Freud's more specific hypotheses about the nature of such conflicts is less favorable. An important challenge comes from the *neo-Freudians* who emphasize social and cultural factors rather than biological ones and from *cultural anthropology* which has shown that personality patterns typical of our own culture are not universal.

8. Some critics of Freud's theories of emotional development have studied child-rearing and found little evidence for long-lasting effects of weaning and toilet-training practices, or for a universal Oedipus complex, independent of culture. Other authors, such as Erik Erikson, have focused on personality development after five, noting certain psychosocial *crises* that may be widely shared.

9. Psychoanalytic thinking extends to fields beyond psychiatry and psychology. Its extensions include Freud's theory of the origin of society and psychoanalytic interpretations of myths and literature.

CHAPTER 13

Personality Development II: Modern Conceptions of Socialization

In the preceding chapter we considered some aspects of socialization, the way the child is transformed into a full-fledged member of the society into which it is born. Our discussion there was organized primarily around Freud's theoretical proposals. We now turn to some more recent conceptions of how socialization works. We will first consider various theories about the way in which society shapes the child. We will then look at the outcome of the socialization process by considering two aspects of human personality in some detail. One is a motive that is largely the product of social forces—the desire for achievement. The other is created by an interaction of biological givens with socialization—the fact that we see ourselves as male or female and behave accordingly.

The Process of Socialization

How is the child taught to become a member of society? Is it taught rote responses that are maintained by reward and the fear of punishment? Is it taught to follow the leader and to imitate? Or is it taught to achieve a gradual understanding of what it is supposed to do and why? There is little doubt that

Socialization *Most authors agree that parents exert some effect on the personality development of their children. What is at issue are the effects they have and how they achieve them.*

children are taught in all three of these ways, but different psychologists have emphasized one or the other of these socialization mechanisms in their analysis of how the child comes to be an adult social being.

SOCIALIZATION AND REINFORCEMENT

Freud believed that the socialization process is essentially one of taming. The seething instinctual urges of the id are blocked and rechanneled and the parental do's and don'ts are ultimately internalized. Some aspects of this position are similar to those of S-R reinforcement theory. Both views share one basic tenet: The child is socialized by a calculus of pain and pleasure. She will continue to do (or to wish or think or remember) whatever previously brought her gratification and she will refrain from whatever led to punishment and anxiety.

SOCIAL LEARNING THEORY

Many psychologists believe that a learning theory exclusively based on classical and instrumental conditioning cannot possibly do justice to the socialization process. We are animals with a culture. This makes us altogether unlike any of the animals studied in the learning laboratory. Thorndike's cats had to discover how to get out of the puzzle box by themselves (see Chapter 4). No other cat told them how to do it; no other cat could. But in the course of a lifetime, human beings learn a multitude of problem solutions that were discovered by those who came before them. They do not have to invent spoken language or the alphabet; they do not have to discover fire or the wheel or even how to eat baby food with a spoon. Other people show them.

A group of psychologists who are sometimes called ***social learning theorists*** regard ***observational learning*** (and its more complex relative, ***learning by listening***) as one of the most powerful mechanisms of socialization. The child observes another person who serves as a ***model*** and then imitates her. That this phenomenon occurs requires no documentation, for it is a commonplace of everyday life. The real question is how and why.

MODELING

By watching a model's behavior, a person (or for that matter, a monkey) can learn how to do something he didn't know before (Figure 13.1). The child sees an adult hammer a nail into a board and tries to duplicate the same feat (with any luck, not on the new dining room table). Many cultures explicitly use such imitative patterns as a way of inducting the child into adult ways. In one Central American society, young girls are presented with miniature replicas of a water jar, a broom, and a grinding stone. They observe how their mothers use the real objects and through constant imitation they acquire the relevant skills themselves. Providing models is clearly a means of speeding up what might otherwise be a very tedious learning process. In some cases, it is absolutely essential, for alternative learning procedures would entail too high a risk. Learning to drive by trial and error would cost too much in terms of upended pedestrians (Bandura and Walters, 1963).

13.1 Learning by imitation *Skills as diverse as clay work and ballet are learned by imitating an accomplished model. (Photograph by Yoram Kahana © Kahana Film Productions/Peter Arnold, Inc., top; photograph © Jill Krementz, bottom)*

How does a person learn a new response by imitation? There is little doubt that imitative learning is not a species of instrumental conditioning. As social learning theorists point out, imitation may occur even though the observer does not copy the model's actions at the time he sees them (learning without performance) and even though he neither receives a reward himself nor sees the model receive one (learning without reinforcement).

But what can we say about imitative learning beyond indicating what it is *not?* As yet, the answer is unclear. As various writers such as Piaget point out, there is reason to believe that imitative learning involves considerable cognitive complexity (see Chapter 9). One of the requirements seems to be a realization of the correspondence between one's own body and that of the model's. Consider the boy who imitates his father hitching up his trousers. In order to do so he has to relate his own clothes and body to those of his father: my trouser belt is to my hands as his trouser belt is to his hands, and so on. In effect, the imitator "takes the model's role." But he can do so only if the model's behavior fits into a well-developed "schema" (to use Piaget's term). A trained dancer who is shown a new step by a colleague may very well be able to imitate it at first sight. But the novice will be completely helpless. Her problem is not that she lacks the physical prowess. Her main difficulty is that she never really *saw* the dance step in the first place. She hasn't yet learned how to observe well enough so that she can imitate properly.

IMITATION AND PERFORMANCE

Imitation may involve a response one already knows. In this case, what is learned by watching others is whether a response should or should not be performed. Consider a foreign visitor who is invited to a feast on some south sea island. At the end of the meal, her hosts belch thunderously and then look at her. She pauses, gulps, and finally belches too. She obviously didn't learn how to belch by watching her hosts. But she learned that it was acceptable (in fact, demanded) that she do so now. In this example, a previously learned but generally inhibited response is disinhibited by observational learning. A similar effect is the inhibition of responses by imitation. When others lower their voices, we generally do the same. Such imitative effects sometimes happen without any conscious awareness, as when we start to whisper to a person with laryngitis.

Social learning theorists have conducted a number of experiments which show that the performance of an observed act depends in part upon the characteristics of the model. Not surprisingly, subjects are more likely to imitate people they like, respect, and regard as competent (Lefkowitz, Blake, and Mouton, 1955). In general, performance of an observed act will also depend upon the consequences that seem to befall the model. In a widely cited study, several groups of nursery-school children were shown a film that featured an adult and a large plastic "Bobo doll." The adult walked over to the doll and ordered it out of the way. When the doll did not comply, the adult punched it, hit it with a mallet, and kicked it around the room, punctuating her attacks with suitable phrases such as "Right on the nose, boom, boom" and "Sockeroo, stay down." One group of subjects saw the film up to this point but no further. Another group saw a final segment in which villainy was

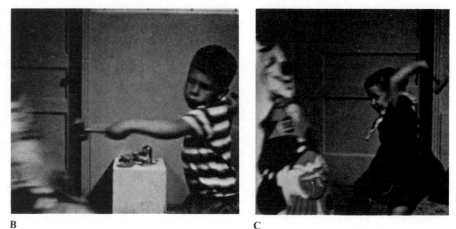

A   B   C

13.2 Copying a model   *Children watch an adult strike an inflated rubber doll with a mallet and promptly strike it too. (From Bandura and Walters, 1963)*

shown to come to a bad end. A second adult arrived on the scene, called the aggressor a big, bad bully, spanked her, and threatened further spankings if she should ever do such bad things again. After seeing the films, all children were brought into a room that contained various toys, including a Bobo doll. They were left alone but were watched through a one-way screen. The children who never saw the villain's comeuppance imitated the model's aggressive acts and the Bobo doll came in for a hard time (Figure 13.2). In contrast, those children who had seen the model's punishment behaved much more pacifically (Bandura, 1965).

SOCIAL LEARNING AND OBSERVED VIOLENCE

Physical punishment in child-rearing   The results of the Bobo-doll study and similar investigations make it clear that an aggressive model may induce aggressive behavior in the observer. According to some social learning theorists, these results bear on important issues of everyday life. One implication concerns the effect of physical punishment in child-rearing. Parents who beat their child severely do not merely punish him for a transgression; they also provide an unwitting model for how one goes about enforcing one's will upon others. The spanked child sees how the parent treats *him*. According to modeling theory, he will imitate the parent's behavior and wreak all kinds of havoc upon his unfortunate playmates. If this hypothesis is true, there should be a correlation between the frequent use of physical punishment and the aggressiveness of the child. Such a correlation has in fact been found by several investigators (Sears, Maccoby, and Levin, 1957; Lefkowitz, Walder, and Eron, 1963). This finding is clearly consistent with modeling theory but, as we shall see, there are some alternative interpretations.

Violence on television   Another implication concerns the effect of violence on the television screen. In this country, children watch TV for hours on end; in one sample, the average was a viewing time of some 25 hours per week (Stein, Friederich, and Vondracek, 1972). Much of what they see is violence. The antagonists may be cartoon figures or real persons, they may be "good guys" or "bad guys," ultimate winners or eventual losers—whichever they are, they solve their problems by beating, kicking, shooting, or other violent acts. If children learn by observation, what is the effect of continued exposure to violence in their own living room? Many investigators have tried to show that this massive electronic mayhem increases the likelihood of aggression in the child.

One line of evidence comes from correlational studies. The investigators determined how much time the child spends watching televised violence and also assessed the child's own aggressiveness as rated by his peers. In all such studies, there was a positive correlation: The children who watched more aggression behaved more aggressively (for example, Eron, 1963). This correlation held up even when the children were equated for social class, school performance, and total amount of time spent in front of the television set. Moreover, the effect was remarkably stable over time. Children who preferred violent TV shows at the age of nine were more overtly aggressive when studied ten years later (Lefkowitz, Eron, Walder, and Huesmann, 1972).

The trouble with these correlational results is that they don't establish a cause-and-effect relationship. For all we know, aggressive children may enjoy watching violent TV programs because they are aggressive instead of becoming aggressive because they watch TV violence. The fact that early TV habits predict later behavior may only indicate that there is some stable disposition that lasts over time. To get around this problem, several investigators have tried to manipulate TV exposure experimentally. In one study, several groups of nursery-school children were systematically exposed to different TV diets over a four-week period. For one group, the twenty-minute-long daily program featured violence (for instance, "Batman"); for another group, the material was innocuous. When observed during subsequent play sessions, the

Children watching violence on TV
(Photograph by George Roos/Peter Arnold, Inc.)

Say that crime is rising

Say their neighborhoods are only
somewhat safe or not safe at all

Say their chances of being involved
in violence are 10 in 100

Percent of persons who give that answer

**13.3 TV viewing and beliefs about
violence** *The figure gives results for
a sample of about 2,500 subjects in a
representative sample of United States
residents, all of whom had at least some
college. All subjects were asked various
questions that pertain to violence. Heavy
TV viewers (here defined as watching
TV for more than four hours per day,
and shown in black) were more inclined
to feel that crime is rising, that their
own neighborhoods are not too safe, and
that their own chances of becoming involved in violence were "10 in 100" or
more, than light TV watchers (here defined as watching less than two hours
per day and shown in color). The authors argue that, at least in part, this
difference stems from the greater exposure to TV and its disproportionate emphasis on violence. (Gerbner, Gross,
Morgan, and Signorielly, 1980)*

children who had been exposed to violence were more aggressive than were
those who were shown innocuous selections. In part, this effect seemed to
depend upon the initial predisposition of the subject. TV violence led to an
increase in aggression in only those children who were more aggressive than
average to begin with (Stein, Friederich, and Vondracek, 1972). This suggests
that the TV program serves as a catalyst for tendencies that are already there
(Liebert and Baron, 1972).

In sum, we can only say that as yet the issue is undecided. Exposure to
violence on TV may lead to a long-term enhancement of personal aggressiveness or it may not. On this point the jury is still out. But according to some
authors, there are other results of prolonged TV viewing that are even more
important than its direct effects on the individual's behavior. What TV seems to
provide is a picture of the world and what is acceptable in it. Both adults and
children get much of their information (both right and wrong) from what they
see on the TV screen. People who frequently watch violent TV programs come
to believe that what they see on the screen is a normal occurrence in the real
world. When asked to guess various statistics about crime, they overestimate
its incidence, are more likely to believe that they themselves might be victimized, and so on. Persons of similar social class and education who watch TV
less often are not as inclined to believe that violence is so rampant (Figure
13.3). This result suggests that exposure to TV violence has a subtler effect
than the enhancement of one's own overt aggressiveness. It seems to produce
a distorted conception in which violence is a common and legitimate part of
ordinary life. This cognitive distortion may ultimately lead to even graver
consequences than an induced change in overt aggression. If social reality is
misperceived, public policy is likely to be misdirected, as in exaggerated calls
for law and order and failure to enact gun controls (Gerbner and Gross, 1976).

COGNITIVE PROCESSES IN SOCIALIZATION

Psychologists who emphasize social learning are clearly at odds with those
theorists who argue that socialization is simply a process of **molding,** whether
through the taming of instinctual urges (Freud), through classical conditioning (Pavlov), or instrumental learning (Skinner). The social learning approach
focuses on processes like observational learning that operate much less blindly
than the mechanisms in which Freud, Pavlov, and Skinner put their trust. But
there is yet another point of view which argues that social learning theory has
not gone far enough in its opposition to blind molding. This is the **cognitive
approach to socialization** which emphasizes the role of understanding in the
development of interpersonal conduct and morality. Adherents of this approach admit that certain aspects of social behavior and morality have a blind
and even irrational quality. Some involve the emotional factors that Freud
had stressed, as when a girl is brought up to regard parts of her body as "dirty"
and then, as an adult, dreads her own sexual feelings. In other cases, the child
acquires some automatic routines either by reward or by uncomprehending
imitation, perhaps in saying "please" and "thank you" or in reciting the
Pledge of Allegiance. But cognitive theorists argue that there are many other
situations in which the child behaves neither as a creature impelled by irra-

tional forces, nor as a puppet controlled by schedules of reward and punishment, nor as a sheep that follows an adult leader. For whatever else the child may be, she is also a rational person who has some understanding of her own actions, who not only knows that some things are "bad" and others "good" but has some sense of why. Initially her understanding is quite dim, but as her mental development unfolds so does her rational comprehension of how one does (and should) relate to others.

THE SENSIBLE SIDE OF IMITATION

Vicarious reinforcement   To illustrate the cognitive approach to socialization, let us go back to the topic of imitation. We have already seen that cognitive factors play a major role in *learning* by imitation. But they are also relevant in determining why observational learning leads to *performance*. Why does the child perform a response he has learned by watching another person? According to social learning theorists, the child sees that the model is rewarded or punished and so he is ***vicariously reinforced*** himself. He later performs the model's action in accordance with the reinforcement he has seen the model receive. According to this position, while observational learning may be a cognitive process, its utilization is governed by the laws of reinforcement and does not involve comprehension.

Imitation through understanding   Cognitive theorists such as Lawrence Kohlberg take a different view. One difference concerns the child's motive for imitation. In Kohlberg's view, the child is not only interested in getting cookies or receiving praise. A no less important reason for copying his elders is that he wants to be able to do some of the many things the all-powerful adults are capable of. In this sense, imitation is its own reward. The child wants to master his universe, wants to attain some sense of competence. Once he can copy an adult's action he wants to be observed in his own turn, to be an actor and not just a passive watcher, and so he clamors eagerly, "Watch *me* do it. Watch!"

Given this view of what the child wants, his imitation of adult models seems no longer blind and illogical. The novice mountain climber who follows a guide is in no way like a sheep that runs after a leader; he follows because he knows that the guide will bring him safely up and down. The child who imitates is not irrational. He operates according to a reasonable rule: By and large, adult models know more than he does (Kohlberg, 1969).

Prestige suggestion   A similar effect was demonstrated some time ago by Solomon Asch in relation to the phenomenon of ***prestige suggestion.*** Previous investigators had found that people are more likely to agree with statements about various social issues if these are attributed to persons who are admired rather than disapproved. As an example, take the following quotation: "I hold it, that a little rebellion, now and then, is a good thing, and as necessary in the political world as storms in the physical." This statement was shown to American subjects who were asked to indicate how strongly they agreed or disagreed with it. Some of the subjects were told that the statement was made by Thomas Jefferson (it was). Other subjects were told that the author was V. Lenin, the leader of the Communist Revolution in Russia. The effect was dramatic. If the subjects thought that Jefferson said so, they agreed; if they believed that the author was Lenin, they strongly disagreed (Lorge, 1936).

Does this phenomenon prove that people are sheep who blindly follow prestigious authorities? Asch believed not. He argued that the subjects who agreed with Jefferson reacted to a different statement than did those who disagreed with Lenin. Of course both groups read the identical prose passage. But this doesn't mean that they interpreted it in the same way. To demonstrate this point, Asch asked different groups of subjects to explain the meanings of various statements of this kind, sometimes attributed to an author who was approved, sometimes to one who was disapproved. The results bore out his hypothesis. Given the statement about the "little rebellion," subjects who thought that it was made by Jefferson took it for granted that the rebellion referred to the American Revolution, an insurrection against a tyrannical government on behalf of democratic freedom. If they thought that the statement was made by Lenin it meant something else entirely—a Communist world revolution, the overthrow of democratic institutions, and so on. The subjects judged two different statements and, given their political values, judged reasonably. They were not blind sheep but rational human beings (Asch, 1948).

MORAL DEVELOPMENT

Cognitive theorists such as Kohlberg have stressed the role of understanding in socialization. But the crucial point for them is that the level of this understanding changes as the child's mental development proceeds. In this regard they have been strongly influenced by the work of Jean Piaget who argued that the mind of the child passes through several successive stages of cognitive development. There are qualitative differences in the way in which the child comprehends the physical world around him (see Chapters 7 and 9). But there are also changes in the way in which he understands interpersonal relations and the moral rules that govern them.

Moral reasoning　We have already sketched Piaget's description of the child's changing conception of morality as development proceeds (see Chapter 9). Kohlberg has elaborated this account and has tried to extend it to adolescence and adulthood (Kohlberg, 1969). His basic method is to confront subjects with a number of stories that pose a moral dilemma. An example is a story about a man whose wife will die unless treated with a very expensive drug costing $2,000. The husband scraped together all the money he could, but it was not enough. The pharmacist refused to give him the drug and to let him pay the balance later. In desperation, the husband broke into the pharmacy and stole the drug. The subjects were asked whether the husband's act was right or wrong and why.

According to Kohlberg's analysis of the subjects' answers, moral reasoning proceeds through a series of successive stages. Roughly speaking, there is a progression from a primitive morality guided by personal fear of punishment or desire for gain ("If you let your wife die, you will get in trouble"), through stages in which right or wrong are defined by convention, by what people will say ("Your family will think you're an inhuman husband if you don't"), to the highest stage in which there are internalized moral principles that have be-

Table 13.1   KOHLBERG'S STAGES OF MORAL REASONING

Stage of moral reasoning	Moral behavior is that which:
Preconventional morality	
Level 1	Avoids punishment
Level 2	Gains reward
Conventional morality	
Level 3	Gains approval and avoids disapproval of others
Level 4	Is defined by rigid codes of "law and order"
Postconventional morality	
Level 5	Is defined by a "social contract" generally agreed upon for the public good
Level 6	Is based on abstract ethical principles that determine one's own moral code

SOURCE: Adapted from Kohlberg, 1967.

come one's own ("You wouldn't be blamed and you would have lived up to the outside rule of the law but you wouldn't have lived up to your own standards of conscience"). As one would expect, there is a rough correlation between Kohlberg's levels and age. But even in adulthood only a small proportion of the subjects give answers that correspond to Kohlberg's highest level. Considering that Kohlberg regards this as the level that characterized such moral giants as Mahatma Gandhi and Dr. Martin Luther King, the failure of most of his subjects (and no doubt, most of us) to attain it is perhaps not surprising (Figure 13.4; Table 13.1).

Moral conduct   Are Kohlberg's stages of moral development related to ethical conduct? To some extent they may be. Kohlberg found that college students with higher, principled levels of moral reasoning were less likely to cheat in an ambiguous situation in which they were unobserved. In further support of a relation between moral reasoning and moral conduct, Kohlberg cites the justifications offered by Adolf Eichmann who supervised the deportation of millions to the Nazi death camps of World War II. Eichmann's defense certainly exhibits a primitive level of moral reasoning: "In actual fact, I was merely a little cog in the machinery that carried out the directives of the German Reich.... I carried out my orders.... I would like to stress again, however, that my department never gave a single annihilation order.... We were responsible only for deportation" (Kohlberg, 1969, p. 383).

Such evidence suggests that there may be some relation between moral reasoning and moral conduct but it is unlikely that the relation is very strong.

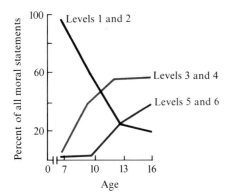

13.4   Level of moral reasoning as a function of age   *With increasing age, the level of moral reasoning changes. In this figure, the percent of all moral judgments made by children at various ages fall into one of three general categories defined by Kohlberg. At seven, virtually all moral judgments are in terms of avoiding punishment or gaining reward (Kohlberg's levels 1 and 2). At ten, about half the judgments are based on criteria of social approval and disapproval or of a—rigid—code of laws (Kohlberg's levels 3 and 4). From thirteen on, some of the children refer to more abstract rules—a generally agreed upon social contract or a set of abstract ethical principles (Kohlberg's levels 5 and 6). (After Kohlberg, 1963)*

The trouble is that Kohlberg's stages do not specifically pertain to conduct. They concern the ability to *describe* certain moral principles by which the individual may or may not be ruled. That the ability to describe such rules increases with mental development (and thus with age) is not surprising. The same holds for the ability to describe and to reason about various other rules—those of space, or causality, or language.

THE CHILD'S EFFECT ON THE PARENTS

Thus far, we have discussed socialization as something that is done *to* the child. But socialization is a two-way street. The child is more than a lump of psychological clay that is acted upon by various social agencies. In actual fact, she actively participates in her own rearing. Her own behavior affects that of the parents who in turn affect the child. To the extent that this is true, the parents don't just socialize the child. They are also socialized by her.

One of the main reasons why socialization works in both directions is that infants differ from the very day they are born. For example, there are differences in **temperament,** which probably have a built-in, genetic basis (see Chapter 16). One infant may be relatively placid and passive; another will be more active and assertive. These differences persist over at least the first two years of life and probably much beyond (Thomas, Chess, and Birch, 1970). The mother will necessarily respond quite differently to these two infants. If we later study the relation between what the mother did and how the child acts, we will find a correlation. But in this case, the order of cause and effect is the reverse of the one that is actually expected. A difference in the child led to a difference in the way her parents treated her.

Such reversed cause-and-effect relations can never be ignored as possible (perhaps partial) explanations of correlations between child-rearing patterns and personality. An example is a finding we already described. Children whose parents frequently resorted to physical punishment were more aggressive (Sears, Maccoby, and Levin, 1957). One interpretation is that the parents provide a model for the child who learns to do to others what his parents had done unto him. But there is an alternative. Some children may be more aggressive to begin with and they are the ones who are more likely to be spanked. In fact, the relation may be even more complex. The more aggressive child will probably be punished more severely, but this in turn will produce more aggression in the child, which then provokes yet further parental punishment. The point is that the cause-and-effect relation can go in either direction or even in both.

The Products of Socialization: The Need to Achieve

The preceding discussion has centered on *how* socialization comes about, the kinds of learning through which the child comes to adopt the ways of the adult world into which it is born. We now turn to some of the products of the socialization process. One general result is the establishment of certain *motives* that characterize the members of a given society. A Comanche boy during the early part of the last century was brought up to become a hunter and a warrior but his socialization was not just a matter of being taught the relevant skills for this way of life. He also acquired the appropriate motives for this existence, such as loyalty to his own band and a passionate craving for honors gained in battle (Kardiner, 1945). Other societies instill other motives. We will consider one such socially derived motive that is relevant to our own Western culture—the need for achievement. This motive has been studied intensively for over two decades and it is an excellent illustration of the way in which cultural values and child-rearing practices interact to make the child a functioning member of his or her society.

ASSESSING THE ACHIEVEMENT MOTIVE

For many persons, the need for achievement is a compelling desire that dominates their entire existence. They pit themselves against some standard of excellence, whether in their own vocation or in some other area, and they then strain to attain as high a level as they can. This need for achievement is not just a desire for fame or fortune. To be sure, the achievers may obtain such tangible rewards (they often do) and they will probably welcome them. But they are not the primary goals. The sprinter who is trying to beat a record and the physicist who is trying to find a new subatomic particle are trying to be the best possible sprinter or physicist they can possibly be. They will be happy to receive their gold medal or their Nobel Prize, but what they really wanted was the knowledge that they achieved what they wanted to achieve.

People obviously differ in the strength of their achievement motive. How can we measure this? It clearly won't do to look merely at their actual accomplishments, for these depend not only on desire but also upon aptitude and opportunity. The technique for assessing the intensity of the achievement motive was developed by David McClelland and his co-workers (McClelland, Atkinson, Clark, and Lowell, 1953). The procedure is based on an assumption which Freud would have been happy to endorse—that a person's motives will influence his or her fantasies. The subject is shown a set of pictures and is asked to write a story about each of them. These stories are then analyzed somewhat in the manner in which Freud analyzed dreams. The question is how many of the story themes involve achievement and to what extent. (For other clinical uses of this so-called *Thematic Apperception Test* or *TAT*, see Chapter 16.)

As an example of how this method works, consider the story fragments elicited by a picture that shows an eighteen-year-old boy sitting at a classroom desk with an open book in front of him. Such a picture might evoke a story that contains several achievement themes, as in the following fragment: "The boy is taking an hour written. . . . The test is about two-thirds over and he is doing his best to think it through. . . . He knows he has studied the answers he can't remember and is trying to summon up the images and related ideas to remind him of them. . . . He will try hard until five minutes are left." On the other hand, the same picture may also evoke a story that is comparatively barren of achievement fantasy: "A boy in a classroom who is daydreaming about something. He is recalling a previously experienced incident. . . . He is thinking about the experience and is now imagining himself in the situation. He hopes to be there. He will probably be called on by the instructor and will be embarrassed" (McClelland, 1961, p. 41; see Figure 13.5).

Achievement motivation   Roger Bannister breaking the four-minute barrier in the one-mile run in 1954, an example of extraordinary achievement motivation and of extraordinary actual achievement. (Photograph by Ralph Moore/ Life Magazine © 1954 Time Inc.)

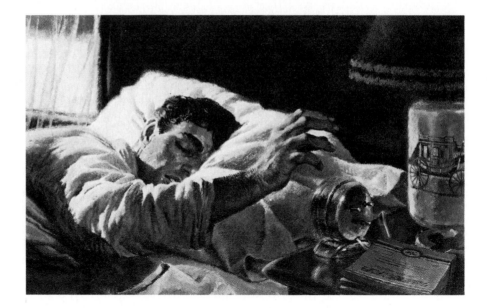

13.5   Stimulus card for assessing the need for achievement   *Cards like the one shown at right may or may not elicit stories with achievement themes—themes such as getting up to face the new day's challenges or turning off the alarm to get more sleep. (Courtesy David C. McClelland)*

Do these fantasy-derived measures really indicate the person's inner motive? Several studies suggest that they do. An example is a comparison of the grades and intelligence test scores of high-school students (Strodtbeck, 1958). The investigators calculated the average grades obtained at each level of intelligence as measured by the intelligence test. Some boys did better than predicted on this basis; others did worse. When achievement motivation was now assessed by McClelland's method, the results were as expected. Boys with a high need for achievement attained higher grades than would have been predicted on the basis of their intelligence test scores alone. They were "overachievers."

There are some further indications that McClelland's measure taps some genuine tendencies that transcend the specific test situation. For example, persons with a high achievement score are more willing to tackle fairly difficult tasks, rather than easy ones; they evidently like the challenge. Such people are willing to take risks, provided that success depends upon skill rather than luck (McClelland, 1961). When they win, their reward is simply the sense of having done something well.

PARENTAL INFLUENCE AND ACHIEVEMENT

How does the achievement need come about? In all likelihood, some rudiments are part of our biological makeup. The toddler wants to feed herself instead of having mother do it, to walk over to daddy without help, and to explore and manipulate an ever-increasing region of her world. Such facts are at variance with the notion (held by Freud, among others) that the child's only concern is with the gratification of his or her primary tissue needs. Quite the contrary. Some primitive desire to understand, to master the world, seems to be given almost from the start (R. White, 1959).

But while the need for achievement has roots in our native endowment, its further development is clearly affected by the way in which the child is raised.

Several investigations have shown that the child's parents are an important factor in determining the child's later strivings. In the first place, they may set standards of performance. Secondly, they will affect his belief that he can attain these standards by his own acts.

In one study, two groups of ten-year-old boys were selected, equated for social class and intelligence test score, but differing in the level of their achievement need; one was high, the other was low. The investigators visited the boys' homes and asked the parents to watch while their sons tried to perform a rather difficult task. They had to build a tower out of irregularly shaped blocks while blindfolded and restricted to the use of one hand. The parents were told that they could do or say whatever they wanted but that they could not touch the blocks. They were also told the height of the tower the "average boy" would erect and were asked to predict (confidentially) how well their own son would do.

The parents of the two groups of boys behaved quite differently. To begin with, parents of high-scoring boys predicted a better level of performance than did the other parents. This is probably what they do in general, setting higher standards of excellence for the child to strive for. Further differences showed up while the boy was busy piling block upon block. The parents of sons with high achievement needs were more encouraging and more likely to reward accomplishment with warm praise. An interesting further difference concerns the fathers. Fathers of high-achievement-oriented boys were warm and friendly while their sons were working but remained in the back seat. They left their sons free to make their own decisions, perhaps giving a hint or two, but rarely telling them how to do it. The fathers of low-achievement-oriented sons were more domineering. They gave specific directions from the sidelines and were more likely to show irritation when things went awry (Rosen and D'Andrade, 1959). An authoritarian father evidently casts a long shadow over his son which inhibits the son's own striving for excellence.

We have noted that parents whose children have a high level of achievement motivation set high standards of excellence for them. But these standards must not be too high. There are indications that when the achievement standard is set at an unrealistic level, the effect is the opposite of that intended. Children who are expected to do well on tasks they are too young to cope with tend to end up with a *lower* level of achievement motivation. They have learned to give up. The desire to achieve is evidently created by a series of *optimal challenges*—not so hard so that there is no hope of success nor so easy that there is no chance of failure, and thus no meaningful sense of accomplishment (McClelland, 1961).

CULTURAL VALUES AND CHILD-REARING PRACTICES

What the parents do evidently has some effect on the kinds of motive that the child eventually adopts as its own. But what makes the parents rear their children as they do? In part, their child-rearing practices reflect the dominant values of the culture of which they are a part. This is hardly surprising. The child is socialized to become a member of a *particular* society, whether it be a band of nomad herdsmen, a medieval village, or a tribe of Polynesian fishermen; each of these societies will inevitably try to instill different characteristics in its young members-to-be. This point is especially clear when we consider the economy on which the society is based. Cultures that make their living through agriculture or animal husbandry tend to stress compliance, conformity, and responsibility as they raise their children. These attributes fit the adult role which the child must eventually assume—the patient, cooperative life of a farmer or herder who must plough his soil or milk his cows at specified times and in specified ways so as to protect and augment an accumulated food supply. In contrast, hunting and fishing societies emphasize self-reliance, and initiative—reasonable values for people who have to wrest their food from nature in day-to-day individual encounters (Barry, Child, and Bacon, 1959).

Achievement motivation and the Protestant ethic   McClelland and his coworkers have searched for analogous cultural factors in the development of achievement motivation. They were influenced by a famous hypothesis proposed at the turn of the century by the German sociologist Max Weber (1864–1920). Weber saw a connection between the Protestant Reformation and the rise of modern capitalism. He argued that the personal attributes valued by Protestant preachings were precisely those that would lead to success in the new capitalist economy. The religious precepts of the early Calvinist businessman led him to adopt an austere existence in which self-indulgence and display were not allowed. He could thus do little with his profits except to reinvest them in his business. As a result, he prospered; but what did he gain from his long hours in the shop or office? According to Weber, the motive behind this Protestant work ethic was simply the "irrational sense of having done his job well." To McClelland this was just another way of describing the achievement motive. McClelland now took a bold step. He argued that the new religious outlook led to a changed pattern of child-rearing that emphasized self-reliance, self-denial, and personal achievement. Raised according to this outlook, the children would then become achievement-oriented adults who would be more likely to attain economic success in a world of private enterprise (Figure 13.6).

Several studies have tried to find evidence for McClelland's position by linking various aspects of the Protestant work ethic to achievement need. One necessary attribute of an entrepreneur is the willingness to forgo immediate gratification for the sake of a later (and presumably, larger) profit. In one study, Trinidad children had a choice between getting a small candy bar immediately or waiting a week for a much larger one (Mischel, 1961). In line with McClelland's thesis, the children who were willing to defer immediate reward were those who obtained a higher score on the achievement-motive test. Another study employed a cross-cultural comparison. Forty-five preliterate societies were rated according to the extent to which their members engaged in entrepreneurial occupations such as being traders or independent

Achievement themes in children's books   *An illustration from McGuffey's Reader, widely used in U.S. schools between 1880 and 1910, which shows one boy lazily watching another split firewood: "'Don't you hate splitting wood?' asked Charlie.... 'No, I rather like it.... I pretend it's a lesson, or a tough job of any kind, and it's nice to conquer it.'" The end of the story underlines the difference between the two by asking: "Now, which of these boys, do you think, grew up to be a rich and useful man, and which of them joined a party of tramps before he was thirty years old?" (From McGuffey's Third Eclectic Reader, 1879)*

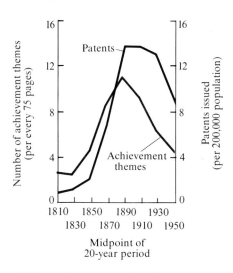

13.6 Achievement motivation and economic innovation *The colored curve plots the need for achievement as measured by the number of achievement themes found in American children's readers typical of each twenty-year period between 1800 and 1960. The black curve plots the number of patents issued in the United States during the same periods, adjusted by population (patents per 200,000 persons). As the figure shows, there is a marked relationship—an early wave of achievement motivation followed shortly after by a sharp increase in patents issued. (After de Charms and Moeller, 1962)*

artisans. In such occupations one doesn't consume one's entire produce but instead exchanges all or part of it for some form of income. To determine the characteristic level of achievement motivation, folktales from these cultures were analyzed by a scoring system analogous to McClelland's. The results fit the hypothesis—entrepreneurial occupations were more prevalent in societies whose folktales were rich in achievement themes (Child, Storm, and Veroff, 1958).

McClelland has tried to extend his ambitious scheme even further. He argued that as a society's children become more achievement-oriented, that society's general level of productivity will rise in the subsequent decades when these children are adults. His particular concern was with economic growth as assessed through such indices as per capita electrical output. He obtained these indices from 23 different nations over the period 1925–50. But how could he measure the characteristic achievement needs of these countries at these times? His solution was to turn to the standardized children's readers used in these nations' school systems in the early grades. He assumed that the stories in these readers reflect the child-rearing values held in the various nations at the time in which the readers were in use, and so he scored these stories for achievement motivation in the usual way. The results were impressive. The level of achievement motivation in 1925 was a good predictor of the economic growth attained by 1950. Interestingly enough, there was no such correlation between economic growth during this period and achievement motivation in 1950. In short, the achievement orientation of the children predicts what will happen later on as these children become the adult members of the society and determine how it is shaped (McClelland, 1961; see Figure 13.6).

Achievement motivation and social class We have seen that achievement motivation varies in different societies. The same holds for subgroups within our own society. The most important example is social class. Sociologists have employed various criteria for establishing such categorizations; among the most important are income, occupation, and educational level. There is no doubt that class structure as thus defined is correlated with ethnic origin and with race. For example, while blacks make up about 11 percent of the U.S. population, they constitute 25 percent of those at the very bottom income level (Havighurst, 1970).

There is evidence that the lower socioeconomic groups have less achievement motive as assessed by McClelland's procedure (Rosen, 1956). In part, this may be traceable to child-rearing. Middle-class parents tend to place earlier stress on self-reliance and independence, while lower-class parents emphasize neatness and conformity. But even more important are factors outside of the family, in the real world the disadvantaged child encounters. If he fails to develop a strong desire for achievement, one important reason is that he learns not to expect any success. He grows up surrounded by overcrowding, malnutrition, unemployment, and family instability. Nor will his school experience give him more encouragement. It often has little to do with his own life outside of school. In addition, many of his teachers are not very helpful; by and large, teachers of lower-class children are more rigid and dominating than those of middle-class children (Yee, 1968). Under these circumstances, the child learns that his own efforts are of little avail; what happens to him seems to be caused by circumstances beyond his own control.

In line with this general argument is the fact that lower-class children are more likely to externalize the locus of responsibility for whatever befalls them. Middle-class children tend to accept the responsibility for their own successes or failures. If they pass a test, they assume it is because they studied for it. Lower-class children interpret the outcome differently. If they fail, they think this is because the test was too hard. If they pass, they assume the test was especially easy (Crandall, Kratkovsky, and Crandall, 1965). Given this background, it is not surprising that lower-class children fail to develop a strong achievement motive. If you don't expect to succeed, why try? (We have previously encountered a related, though probably more extreme, version of this general attitude, **learned helplessness,** Chapter 5.)

The same argument applies to the willingness to defer gratification, which is related to the desire for achievement. There is some evidence that this willingness is lower in lower-class than in middle-class children. But given the lower-class child's experiences, her choice of immediate gain seems perfectly rational. To forgo the satisfactions of the moment for the sake of a larger profit at some later time makes little sense if one has no confidence in the ultimate attainment of the greater reward. If this trust is lacking—and it probably is in the poor—one might as well elect the short-term goal, to take the cash and let the credit go. The slow route to success through saving pennies or attending night school seems doomed from the outset when there are so many unpredictable catastrophes along the way.

THE USES OF THE INTERDISCIPLINARY APPROACH

McClelland's general scheme has encountered various criticisms. There is some question whether his measure of achievement motivation correlates with actual achievement (Lazarus, 1966); there is some contradictory evidence about the child-rearing patterns that have been said to produce this motive (Zigler and Child, 1969); there is some question about the appropriate indices to assess economic growth. But whatever the ultimate verdict on McClelland's theories, he has provided a remarkable example of how one might bring together a concern with the individual's motives and personality structure, her own past, and her cultural setting. His work demonstrates that such an attempt has to call upon the insights and methods of several disciplines—psychology, anthropology, sociology, economics, and even history.

The Products of Socialization: Sex Roles

Our discussion of the achievement motive considered the ways in which socialization affects what we *want.* But perhaps more important are the ways in which socialization determines who we *are,* in our own eyes and in those of others. Perhaps the best example is our sense of sexual identity and all that goes with it. Our sexual identities develop through the interaction of various socializing factors and our biological makeups. Virtually all of us have a clear, inner sense of being male or female *(gender identity)* which is generally accompanied by a whole host of external behavior patterns that our culture deems appropriate for each sex *(gender role).** Our choice of a sexual partner *(sexual orientation)* is by and large—though, of course, not always—directed toward the opposite sex. Gender identity, gender role, and sexual orientation are among the most important determinants of a person's social existence. How do they come about?

GENDER ROLES

The recent resurgence of feminism has focused attention on the pervasive influence of gender roles on all facets of social life. The induction into one or the other of these roles begins with the very first question that is asked when a human being enters the world: "Is it a boy or a girl?" As soon as the answer is given, the process of *sex typing* starts the infant along one of two different social paths. Some of the patterns of sex typing have undoubtedly changed in the wake of the woman's movement of the sixties and seventies, but many differences in child-rearing persist. The stereotype is simple enough: The infant is dressed in either pink or blue; the child plays with either dolls or trucks; the adult woman's place is in the home while man's is in the marketplace—or buffalo-hunting grounds, or whatever (Figure 13.7).

* It has become customary to distinguish between *sex* and *gender*. The term *sex* is reserved for the biological aspects of the male-female difference that pertain to reproductive function (for example, ovaries versus testes, vagina versus penis) or to designate erotic feelings, inclinations, or practices (for example, heterosexual, homosexual). The term *gender* refers to social and psychological aspects of being seen as male or female or regarding oneself to be so. It is one thing to be a male, it is another to be a man. The same holds for being female and being a woman (Stoller, 1968).

Figure 13.7 **Gender stereotypes as reflected in children's books** *(A) Themes in over a hundred popular children's books and the sex they are associated with. As the figure shows, more boys than girls tend to be depicted as adventurous, brave, and clever, more girls than boys as passive and dependent. (Data from Women on Words and Images, 1972) (B) The conception of the relative helplessness of girls compared to the competence of boys is shown even in their relation to pets. A little girl's dog is small but she can barely manage him; the little boy's dog is enormous but the boy has him under firm control. (Weitzman et al., 1972; Women on Words and Images, 1972; illustrations from Kasilovsky, 1953 [top] and 1962 [bottom])*

B

She was bigger than her dog!

He was bigger than his dog!

A

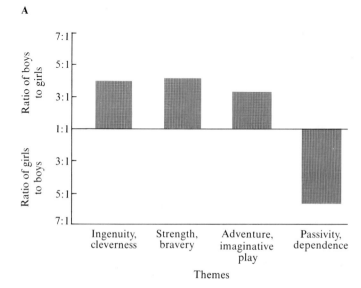

Society not only has different expectations of what the two sexes should *do;* it also has different conceptions of what they should *be.* In our own culture, the male is expected to be more aggressive and tough, more restrained emotionally, more interested in things than in people. The contrasting expectations for females are greater submissiveness, greater emotional expressiveness, and an interest in people rather than in things. On the average, these expectations tend to be met, though of course there are many exceptions. Some men do cry easily and some women are competitive professional athletes. The point is that these two descriptions represent a cultural ideal, a valued *norm* laid down by society. If a child seriously departs from this norm, there will be repercussions. The boy who plays with dolls is laughed at as a sissy.

Deviations in later life lead to internal turmoil as well as external censure. An example is the drive for achievement in women. In this society, women who strive for success in the "man's world" are often caught in conflict; they lose if they fail but they also lose if they succeed. In one study, college men and women were asked to complete stories given a few opening lines that featured either a hero or a heroine: "After the first term, Anne (John) finds herself (himself) at the top of her (his) medical school class." In writing about a male protagonist, men foresaw a bright and happy future. Women were much less sanguine about the prospects for the heroine. About 65 percent of them wrote stories that betrayed an underlying *fear of success.* They described Anne's future life as friendless, lonely, and unfulfilled. A gnawing worry was winning out in competition over men: "Anne will deliberately lower her academic standing the next term, while she does all she subtly can to help Carl. . . . His grades come up and Anne soon drops out of med school. They marry and he goes on in school while she raises their family" (Horner, 1970, p., 60).

Departure from the norm has its costs, but, especially for women, so does adherence to it. One need not have read feminist literature to realize that in this society—as indeed in most others—females occupy a social status of less power and lower prestige. The world is run by men who head governments, lead armies, control industries, direct churches, and pray to an omnipotent male God for protection against a male devil. By now, women in the United States vote, hold property, and represent a significant proportion of the labor force, but they are still paid considerably less than men who are doing the same job and they are much less likely to hold positions of social prestige. A concurrent effect is a prejudice of women against their own sex when considering accomplishments outside the traditional woman's sphere. In one study, women were asked to judge the same scholarly articles said to be authored by "Joan T. McKay" for one group and "John T. McKay" for another. John's articles received a significantly higher rating of excellence than did Joan's (Goldberg, 1968).

NATURE, NURTURE, AND SEX DIFFERENCES

What accounts for the difference in current sex roles? We will consider both constitutional and cultural factors in an attempt to understand how biology and society conspire to make boys into men and girls into women.

Which of the differences between the sexes are based on constitutional makeup? Apart from the obvious anatomical and physiological differences that pertain to reproduction, there are of course differences in average size, strength, and physical endurance. But what about psychological differences? There is no doubt that such differences do exist and that some of them fit cultural stereotypes. The question is whether any of these differences—in aggression, in dependency, in emotional expressiveness, in social sensitivity— are biologically given, whether they accompany the sexual anatomy the way menstruation goes along with a female's XX chromosome pair.

Before proceeding we should note two preliminary cautions. The first is that any psychological difference between the sexes is one between *means*. The *average* three-year-old girl seems to be more dependent than her male age-mate; she is more likely to ask for help, to cling, and to seek affection (Emmerich, 1966). But this doesn't mean that the two groups don't overlap. There are certainly many three-year-old girls who are less dependent than many three-year-old boys. After all, the same holds true even for certain physical differences. There is no doubt that men are, on the average, taller than women. But it is equally clear that a sizable number of women are taller than many men.

A second caution concerns interpretation. What accounts for whatever difference is obtained? The fact that a difference in dependency shows up as early as three could reflect different biological predispositions. But it doesn't really prove that the difference is intrinsically sex-linked. In our society, boys are encouraged to be independent, to be "little men," beginning at a very early age, and the obtained difference may simply reflect this cultural fact. Here, as in so many other areas, nature and nurture are very difficult to disentangle.

CONSTITUTIONAL FACTORS

Aggression There are a few psychological sex differences that do seem to be constitutional in origin, at least in part. One of these is aggression. Males tend to be more active and assertive than females. This difference is apparent from the very outset; male infants are more irritable and physically active than females. The divergence continues through childhood and beyond. At two or three, boys are more likely to engage in rough-and-tumble play and mock fighting than girls (a difference also seen in apes and monkeys; see Figure 13.8). At five or so, they are more ready to exchange verbal insults and to repel aggression by counterattack. Similar results have been obtained in such widely different cultural settings as Ethiopia, India, Kenya, Mexico, Okinawa, and Switzerland (Maccoby and Jacklin, 1974). The fact that this sex difference is found so early in life, is observed in so many different cultures, and is also seen in apes and monkeys, suggests a constitutional origin, all the more so given the fact that aggressiveness is enhanced by the administration of the male sex hormone (see Chapter 11).

Cognitive orientation There is another psychological difference between the sexes that appears to be based on biological givens—***cognitive orientation.*** There seems to be a difference in the pattern of intellectual aptitudes. The

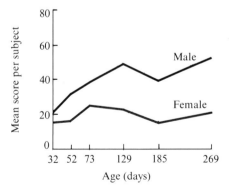

13.8 *The development of rough-and-tumble play in male and female rhesus monkeys* Roughhouse play in two male and two female rhesus monkeys during the first year of life. The scores are based on both frequency and vigor of this activity, in which monkeys wrestle, roll, or sham bite—all presumably in play, since no one ever gets hurt. Roughhouse play is considerably more pronounced in males than in females, a difference that increases during the first year of life. (After Harlow, 1962)

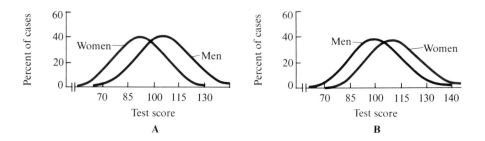

13.9 Sex differences in cognitive ability
Characteristic performance curves of men and women on tests of spatial-mathematical and verbal ability. Men are generally superior on the first, women on the second. (A) Results on a spatial-mathematical test which included questions such as, "How many times between three and four o'clock do the hands of a clock make a straight line?" The curve plots the percentage of subjects who receive a particular score (with men in black, women in color). As the figure shows, the men perform better than the women, though the two curves overlap considerably. (B) Results on a vocabulary test asking for synonyms. Here, the women (again in color) do better than the men (again in black), though here, too, there is a great deal of overlap. (Data from Very, 1967. To make the figures comparable, the test scores were adjusted by a method called normalization, as if they were based on two tests which had the same mean and variance.)

general finding is that, on the average, women do better on tests of verbal rather than spatial or mathematical ability while the reverse holds for men (Figure 13.9). There is some evidence that one component of this difference is constitutional. There seems to be a recessive gene that contributes to spatial ability and is sex-linked. If boys have it, its effects will be manifest; if girls have it, there is a 50:50 chance that a second sex-linked dominant gene will suppress the effect of the first. As a result, there is a greater average genetic potential for the acquisition of various spatial skills in men than in women (Maccoby and Jacklin, 1974).

The adaptive value of sex differences   Most modern biologists would argue that built-in characteristics generally have survival value or they would have been bred out of the species by natural selection. What is the biological value of sex differences in aggression and spatial ability, granting that they are indeed of constitutional origin? One guess is that these attributes, coupled with the greater strength of the male, went along with the basic division of labor that characterized our primitive ancestors. The women were gatherers who stayed near home and cared for the children while the men hunted big game miles away from the campsite. Strength, aggressiveness, and the ability to think in spatial terms must have been useful traits to the males who had to track down and face dangerous animals, had to find their way back home, and were probably often forced to defend their home territory against marauding fellowmen. One would guess that this built-in pattern of sexual differentiation was incorporated into our ancestors' social institutions, which led to the exaggeration of whatever differences were initially there. The origin of social sex roles may well lie in such beginnings. For our ancestors this general arrangement made sense; the sex-role distinction was grounded in their way of keeping themselves alive. The irony is that these differences are still with us, more than half a million years later. Our modern economy puts little special premium on strength or physical courage but we continue to adhere to sex-role patterns that have by now outlived their usefulness.

SOCIAL FACTORS

While some of the roots of different gender roles may be biological, even more important is the way in which boys and girls are socialized. We will reconsider the same two characteristics for which there is some evidence of a biologically based sex difference: aggression and cognitive orientation.

Aggression There may well be a greater initial predisposition toward aggressiveness in boys than in girls, but cultural pressures serve to magnify whatever sex differences exist at the outset. Parents will generally allow (and even foster) a degree of aggressiveness in a boy that they would not countenance in a girl. Thus fathers often encourage their sons to fight back when another boy attacks them (Sears et al., 1957). The result of such differential social training is that the initial built-in bias toward a sex difference in behavior is considerably exaggerated.

An interesting demonstration of the way in which social factors modulate the effect of constitutional predispositions comes from a longitudinal study of seventy men and women who were observed as infants and as children and were interviewed years later in their early twenties (Kagan and Moss, 1962). The question was whether one could predict the adult's behavior from his or her behavior in childhood or infancy. For some attributes, the answer was yes. In men there was a definite correlation between temper tantrums in childhood and the ease with which anger was aroused in adult life. This result suggests that there is some stable component of personality that is probably based on constitutional predisposition and is related to aggressiveness. But interestingly enough, there was no such correlation between the childhood and adult behavior of the women. We have seen that women tend to be less aggressive than men. But why should this tendency be less stable over time? The answer may be that the two gender roles make different demands. Unlike her brother, the young girl is taught not to express her aggression directly. She therefore inhibits such tendencies and channels them in other directions. As a result, there is a diminished correlation between her aggressiveness in childhood (when she was not yet fully socialized) and in later life (when she is). The underlying predisposition toward aggressiveness is still there but it manifests itself in other ways. In adulthood, it is expressed not as anger but rather as a greater motivation for scholastic or professional success. These motives are (somewhat) greater in women who had more temper tantrums in their childhood. This may be an indirect manifestation of personal continuity, disguised by the pressures of a gender role that, at least through the sixties, frowned upon the direct expression of aggression in females from childhood on.

Cognitive orientation Similar considerations may apply to differences in cognitive orientation. The genes may contribute to a sex difference, but they tell only part of the story. For social factors again magnify whatever differences may have been there to start with. In our society, girls are expected to do better in English than in math. This belief is shared by teachers, parents, and pupils who all help to make it come true. As a result, even the girl who does have the appropriate genetic potential may do worse on spatial and mathematical tests than her ability warrants. An interesting demonstration of this interaction between biological and social factors comes from studies of boys whose father was absent during some or all of the formative years of their childhood, usually because of wartime military service. These boys were raised without a male role model. As a result, they tended to be less "masculine" in their interests. One manifestation was an aptitude pattern that resembled that of girls—higher scores in verbal than in mathematical ability (Carlsmith, 1964). Girls may be better at reading poetry and boys at reading maps, but this difference is not simply genetic. Parents augment it by their own views of which skill is most important for each sex.

Sex reassignment in childhood   The most dramatic examples of the effect of social factors in the determination of gender identity and gender role come from studies of children who at birth were declared to be of one sex but who were later reassigned to the other. This sometimes occurs if the newborn is a **hermaphrodite,** with reproductive organs that are anatomically ambiguous so that they are not exclusively male or female (Money and Ehrhardt, 1972). In such cases, parents and physicians sometimes decide to reverse the initial sex assignment. Corrective surgery is undertaken, the sex is officially reassigned, and the child is raised accordingly. The results show that if the reassignment occurs before the age of three or four, the child adjusts to a remarkable degree. It becomes a he or a she, in part because that is how other people now regard it (Hampson and Hampson, 1961).

The reports of parents leave no doubt that the child is seen very differently before and after the reassignment. One case involved a child that was genetically male. It had a male's XY chromosome pair and testes. But the external genital organs were otherwise more similar to a female's than to a male's. At birth, the baby was pronounced a boy but the decision was reversed seventeen months later, at which time there was corrective surgery. According to the parents, there was an immediate change in the way the newly female child was treated. Even her three-year-old brother reacted differently, showing "a marked tendency to treat her much more gently. Whereas, before, he was just as likely to stick his foot out to trip her as he went by, he now wants to hold her hand to make sure she doesn't fall" (Money and Ehrhardt, 1972, p. 124).

Even more startling is the case of two normally born, male, identical twins one of whom suffered a surgical accident at the age of seven months—his penis was amputated flush with the abdominal wall. After lengthy medical consultation, the parents decided upon sex reassignment. In a case like this, there is considerable plastic surgery to construct female genitals. There is also endocrine treatment to produce pubertal growth and femininization. The end result is a person who looks exactly like a female and can enjoy female sexual function (the remnant of the penis becomes the clitoris). Since she lacks ovaries she obviously cannot have children and is told that as an adult she can become a mother through adoption.

Following sex reassignment and surgery, the two twins were treated very differently. The newly created girl was dressed in frilly blouses and her hair was allowed to grow long. She was encouraged to be neat and to help her mother with the housekeeping. She was also reproved for being too rough and noisy, qualities that were regarded as perfectly natural in the boy. The different conceptions of what is right and proper show up clearly in two incidents related by the mother. One episode dealt with the boy when he was four and a half: "In the summer time, one time I caught him—he went out and he took a leak in my flower garden in the front yard, you know. He was quite happy with himself. And I just didn't say anything. I just couldn't. I started laughing and I told daddy about it." The mother felt differently about corresponding acts on the part of the girl: "I've never had a problem with her. She did once when she was little, she took off her panties and threw them over the fence. . . . But I just,

I gave her a little swat on the rear, and I told her that nice little girls didn't do that, and she should keep her pants on. . . . And she didn't take them off after that" (Money and Ehrhardt, 1972, p. 120).

By four and a half, the twins behaved very differently and in accordance with their sex roles. The girl was neat and tidy, helped with the housework, played with dolls, and spent hours admiring herself in a new dress or curling her hair. The boy was sloppy, always forgot to wash his face, played with toy cars in a toy garage, and said that he wanted to be a fireman when he grew up. These differences are all the more impressive considering that the twins are identical. Genetically, they are both males—an excellent demonstration of the fact that gender identity is not a simple function of one's chromosomes.

These results point to the importance of social factors in determining one's sense of being male or female and of what being male or female means. Needless to say, constitutional factors also enter. In the case of the genetically male identical twin who was turned into a female, there was some effect of the male genetic blueprint. For example, the child was unusually active physically when compared to girls of that age. Related results come from a study of girls who were exposed to an abnormally high level of male hormone in the womb. (In some of the cases this condition was brought about by a now obsolete hormone substance which was administered in an effort to prevent miscarriage.) These girls were often hermaphrodites at birth, with ambiguous external genitals. After appropriate surgery, all was well and they were raised as females. But follow-up studies showed that the excess androgen during pregnancy had some long-term psychological effects. When compared to a control group, the androgenized girls were much more likely to be "tomboys" during childhood. They chose trucks over dolls, loved to play in energetic team sports, especially with boys, preferred functional slacks to feminine dresses, and had little interest in jewelry or perfume. As adolescents, they looked forward to a future in which marriage and maternity were subordinated to a career. Interestingly enough, this masculinization of interests did not apply to the choice of a sex partner (a point that is relevant to the interpretation of homosexuality; see below). The androgenized girls embarked upon their sex life at a later age than the controls, but their sexual fantasies were about men and not about women.

According to many investigators, these psychological effects are produced by a prenatal masculinization of some system in the brain (probably the hypothalamus). The masculinization is presumably triggered by the excess androgen during the mother's pregnancy. This hypothesis fits in with results of prenatal hormone administration in animals. For example, prenatally androgenized female monkeys act somewhat like human "tomboy" girls. Unlike normal monkey females, they engage in rough-and-tumble play with mutual chasing and mock fighting (Goy, 1968). Since monkeys have no culture that tells them about the assigned female role, these effects are presumably based on constitutional changes during the prenatal period.

THEORIES OF SEX TYPING

Social factors are evidently of great importance in fashioning our sense of being men or women and shaping our behavior accordingly. But exactly how

519

do these social factors exert their effects? Each of the three main theories of socialization—psychoanalysis, social learning theory, and the cognitive developmental approach—has tried to offer an answer.

Psychoanalytic theory According to Freud, the basic mechanism is **identification.** The child models itself on the same-sexed parent in an effort to become like him or her. In Freud's view, identification is the end product of the Oedipus conflict at age five or six. The little boy is unable to cope with the mounting anxieties aroused by his sexual longing for the mother and his resentment of the father. He therefore represses both incestuous love and patricidal hate. But his renunciation of the mother is only for the time being. He identifies with the all-powerful father to propitiate him, (if I am like him, he won't want to hurt me), and also in the hope that he will thereby gain the mother's sexual love in some blissful future (if I am like him, she will love me). By means of this identification process, which Freud thought to be largely unconscious, the boy incorporates many aspects of the father's personality, including those that pertain to sex role. At the same time, he also adopts his father's moral strictures which become internalized as the superego. By a roughly analogous process, the little girl comes to identify with her mother (see Chapter 12).

Male and female models *(Courtesy Suzanne Szasz)*

Social learning theory A very different position is held by social learning theorists, who argue that gender role and identity do not arise from the sex drive. In their view, children behave in sex-appropriate ways for the simplest of possible reasons: They are rewarded if they do so and are punished when they don't. For the most part, they learn what each sex is supposed to do by imitation. But whom shall they imitate? They quickly discover that they must choose a model (usually the parent) of their own sex. The girl imitates her mother and is rewarded for rocking the baby (for the time being a doll will have to do), for prettying herself up, for becoming mother's little helper. The boy who imitates these maternal acts will be ridiculed and called a sissy. He will do better by imitating his father who rewards him for doing boylike things (Mischel, 1970).

According to this view, the sex drive has little to do with the matter and anatomy enters only indirectly. The penis and vagina are relevant only in determining whether the child is a boy or a girl in the parents' eyes. From this point on, differential rewards and punishments do the rest.

Why do parents push their sons and daughters into different social molds? A social learning theorist would probably reply that the parents' behavior (as well as that of peers, teachers, and so on) is also shaped by various reinforcers, all of which act to maintain a particular social structure. In effect, the socialization of children is simply an apprenticeship into the roles they will adopt as adults.

Cognitive developmental theory Yet another proposal has been offered by Lawrence Kohlberg who regards sex-typing in the context of the child's growing cognitive development (Kohlberg, 1966). Kohlberg's emphasis is on the child's emerging awareness of its gender identity, the sense of being male or female and of being so irrevocably.

Kohlberg points out that the concept of gender is quite vague until the child is five or six. The four-year old has only a shadowy notion of what the categories "male" and "female" mean. He has no real comprehension of how these categories pertain to genital anatomy, no matter how diligently his parents may have tried to enlighten him in this regard. In one study, children were presented with clothed and unclothed figures of boys, girls, men, and women, that were cut up into head, trunk, and below-the-trunk sections. Their task was to put the sections together correctly and to identify their gender. Three- and four-year olds did reasonably well when the figures were clothed but were confused when they were not (Katcher, 1955). More important is the fact that the four-year old doesn't understand that gender is one of the permanent and (for all intents and purposes) unchangeable attributes of the self. When shown a picture of a girl, four-year olds say that she could be a boy if she wanted to, or if she wore a boy's haircut, or wore a boy's clothes. This shaky understanding of *gender constancy* is also shown by the fact that the four-year old is not clear that the categories "male" and "female" extend across generations. An example is a young boy who consoled his mother for the fact that she didn't own a bicycle: "When you grow up to be a Daddy, you can have a bicycle too." In a similar vein is a conversation between a four-year-old boy and his rather more sophisticated four-and-a-half-year-old friend (Kohlberg, 1966, p. 95):

JIMMY: When I grow up, I'll be a Mommy.
JOHNNY: No, you can't be a Mommy. You have to be a Daddy.
JIMMY: No, I'm going to be a Mommy.
JOHNNY: No, you're not a girl, you can't be a Mommy.
JIMMY: Yes, I can.

Why should the concept of gender constancy be so hard to comprehend? According to Kohlberg, the problem is not with gender as such. The difficulty is a more general consequence of the young child's failure to understand the stability of many attributes during this period of its cognitive development, which Piaget called the stage of *preoperational thought.* At this stage, the child does not conserve liquid quantity, mass, or number (see Chapter 9). Similar effects pervade many other aspects of the four-year old's thinking. When asked whether a cat would be a dog if it wanted to, or if its whiskers were cut off, the majority of four-year olds say yes. Such considerations suggest that lack of gender constancy is just one more facet of a general failure to comprehend the underlying constancies of the universe. Kohlberg quotes a four-year-old boy who is sure that airplanes get small when they fly away in the sky and that the people in them shrink when this happens. If a child can believe that people can shrink and expand, why shouldn't he believe that a mommy can change into a daddy?

Kohlberg's views on gender identity lead him to a different hypothesis about identification from that entertained by social learning theorists. According to social learning theorists, the choice of the same-sexed model *precedes* the attainment of gender identity. Sex typing occurs because of differential rewards and punishments. The girl is rewarded for doing girl-like things and for modeling herself on her mother. As a result, she wants to be a girl and act like one. In Kohlberg's view, the sequence is reversed. Identification *follows* the acquisition of gender identity. The child first has to recognize its own gender identity, to understand that he is a boy or she is a girl and that these attributes define him or her forever. Once they have this realization, boys and girls try to live up to it, to act in a manner that fits in with their own self-concept. They now look for appropriate models that can show them how to get better and better at being a male or a female, for their concept of gender has expanded to include father and mother in the categories of "us men" and "us women" (Figure 13.10).

Sexual feeling, gender role, and gender identity   The three approaches to sex typing we have just discussed—psychoanalytic theory, social learning theory, and cognitive developmental theory—differ in many particulars. But details aside, the real difference among the three approaches is in their emphases. According to Freud, the roots of sex typing are sexual in the erotic sense of that term—they grow out of the child's erotic feelings and the direction in which they are aimed. To social learning theorists the critical factor is gender role. Their emphasis is on the cultural forces that impinge upon the individual and shape his or her behavior by suitable rewards and punishments until it fits into the appropriate social mold. According to Kohlberg and other cognitive developmental theorists, the emphasis is on gender identity, an individual's self-concept as a he or a she.

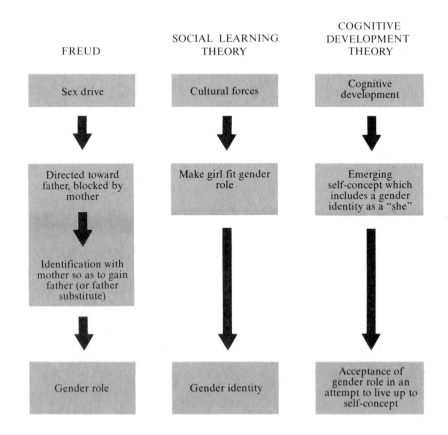

13.10   Three theories of sex typing
The figure summarizes the three major theories of sex typing (for females).

James Morris, who at the age of 46 had a transsexual operation and became Jan Morris (Courtesy United Press International, top; photograph by Henry Grossman, bottom)

According to a common-sense view, gender identity, gender role, and sexual feeling and orientation are essentially equivalent as definitions of maleness and femaleness. And indeed they are for most of us. The great majority of human beings are male or female in all three senses. The person who regards himself as a man is also so regarded by others and he will choose women as his sexual partners. But as we have repeatedly pointed out, the three facets of sex and gender are in principle independent. As a final illustration, consider James Morris, a man whose sex was surgically altered in adulthood from male to female. Prior to the operation, he had all the external trappings of a masculine gender role. Among other things, he was a member of Sir Hilary's expedition to climb Mt. Everest. (Greater machismo hath no man!) He also had the appropriate credentials of a masculine sexual orientation. He was married and had fathered three children. What was discordant was the sense of gender identity. From early childhood on, he felt that he was really a woman who was somehow trapped in the body of a man (J. Morris, 1974). Sexual orientation, gender role, and gender identity are not really one and the same, despite the fact that they usually go together. What we need is a theory that describes their interrelations. Thus far we have only the barest beginnings of an answer, for until recently the subject of human sexuality was a forbidden topic, shrouded by superstition and taboo.

SEXUAL ORIENTATION

The majority of men and women are **heterosexual.** They seek a partner of the opposite sex. But for a significant minority, the sexual orientation is otherwise; their erotic and romantic feelings are directed primarily (or exclusively) toward members of their own sex. What can we say about the factors that determine which sexual orientation is adopted?

THE INCIDENCE OF HOMOSEXUALITY

According to a survey made in the forties, 4 percent of American males are exclusively homosexual during their lifetime (Kinsey, Pomeroy, and Martin, 1948). The comparable incidence of exclusive homosexuality among women seems to be lower—about 2 percent (Kinsey, Pomeroy, Martin, and Gebhard, 1953)—though its prevalence may have been underestimated, since women are probably more reticent than are men in describing their sex life in an interview with a stranger. In any case, a substantial number of men and women are erotically oriented toward a partner of their own sex despite the fact that our society sharply stigmatizes such behavior. This cultural taboo is by no means universal. According to one cross-cultural survey, two-thirds of the societies studied regarded homosexuality as normal and acceptable, at least for some persons or for some age groups (Ford and Beach, 1951). In some historical periods the practice was glorified and extolled, as in classical Greece where Pericles, the great Athenian statesman, was regarded as rather odd because he was *not* attracted to beautiful boys.

Homosexuality is yet another illustration of the fact that sexual orientation, gender identity, and gender role are in principle independent. Most male homosexuals think of themselves as men and are so regarded by others; the analogous point holds for female homosexuals. There is a widespread popular

523

belief that homosexuals fall into "active" and "passive" categories and act like "husband" or "wife" in their erotic liaisons. This conception is false. Most homosexuals adopt both passive and active roles. Nor does there seem to be a correlation between physical appearance, social mannerisms, and preferred sexual practice. A particular male homosexual may be "effeminate," but this does not mean that he necessarily prefers the passive sexual role (Marmor, 1975).

HOMOSEXUALITY: DISEASE OR DIFFERENT LIFE STYLE?

Is homosexuality an illness that requires a cure if any can be found? Or is it simply a different form of sexual expression that happens to be disapproved of in this culture at this time? Few issues in the area of human sexuality have been more hotly debated than this.

According to one psychiatric view, homosexuality is pathological, based on incapacitating fears of the opposite sex and "incompatible with life" (Bieber, 1965). The primary evidence for this view comes from a widely cited study of 106 male homosexuals under psychiatric treatment (Bieber et al., 1962). Their therapists described them as more deeply disturbed and unhappy than a group of heterosexual patients with whom they were compared. But this study suffers from several flaws. One concerns the sample of homosexuals upon which the conclusions were based. This sample is biased since it only included persons who sought psychiatric help. Such people are almost certain to be more disturbed than the population at large and are not representative of the many homosexuals who never enter a psychiatrist's office.

In an effort to meet these objections, several investigators have compared nonpatient homosexuals to nonpatient heterosexuals of equal age, educational level, and intelligence. The results of such studies show that the differences in personal adjustment between homosexuals and heterosexuals are much less than had been supposed. Some investigators found no difference whatever (Hooker, 1957; Thompson, McCandless, and Strickland, 1971). Others found that homosexuals (especially male homosexuals) were somewhat more likely to lack confidence, to suffer from low self-esteem, and to clown at their own expense (Saghir and Robins, 1973). But such differences are probably best explained by the fact that homosexuals in our society are members of a rejected minority group. Self-hatred and protective clowning are common characteristics in any persecuted minority (Hooker, 1965).

In any case, the real issue is not whether homosexuals as a group are happier or better adjusted than heterosexuals as a group. Given the stigma attached to their sexual orientation, it would be surprising if they were. The question is whether homosexuality as such necessarily implies personal disturbance and neurosis. The answer seems to be no. Under the circumstances, there is no reason to maintain that homosexuality is a psychological disorder. In 1974 this view became part of the official position of the American Psychiatric Association. The Association voted that "homosexuality by itself does not necessarily constitute a psychiatric disorder" (Marmor, 1975, p. 1,510).

Needless to say, some homosexuals may want to change their sexual orientation, and if they do, a therapist might try to help them. But this undertaking is by no means easy, especially for persons who have been exclusively homosexual. Freud himself was doubtful that it could be done. Later psychoanalysts were more optimistic, but even they rarely reported lasting changes in more than about one-third of the cases treated.

The safest conclusion seems to be that sexual orientation—both heterosexual and homosexual—is a fairly stable condition. It can be changed in some cases but not easily. Homosexuality is not a disease or a personality disturbance. But neither is it a simple matter of personal choice that can be done and undone more or less at will.

WHAT CAUSES HOMOSEXUALITY?

What leads to homosexuality? So far there is no clear answer. It may well be that this question simply represents the other side of the question, "What leads to heterosexuality?" This second question is rarely asked because we take the heterosexual preference for granted. But if we did know how to explain the origin of heterosexuality, we would probably be much closer to an understanding of how homosexuality comes about as well.

Genes and Hormones   One approach has looked to biology. For a while, it seemed as if there might be a **genetic predisposition** (Kallman, 1952). The evidence came from a study that showed that the correlation between homosexual tendencies in pairs of twins is much greater if the twins are **identical** (formed from the same egg and thus possessed of the same genetic makeup) than if they are **fraternal** (formed from two different eggs and thus no more alike than any two ordinary siblings). This result is impressive, but its significance is undermined by the failure of later investigators to find the same effect.

Other investigators have concentrated upon sex hormones. Some recent studies indicate that the levels of certain male hormones tend to be lower in male homosexuals than in heterosexuals (Kolodny et al., 1971). The trouble is that stress and illness produce a similar effect in male heterosexuals. Since homosexuals live under considerable social stress because of their deviant status, their hormonal balance may be an indirect effect of their homosexuality rather than its cause.

In any case, there is a final argument against male hormone levels as a cause of homosexuality. As has been mentioned, when androgen is administered to male homosexuals, it enhances sexual vigor but does not change its direction—the renewed interest is still toward homosexual partners (Kinsey, Pomeroy, and Martin, 1948). Male homosexuality is evidently not caused by an insufficiency of male hormones. It seems plausible to assume that an analogous statement applies to female homosexuals.

Childhood experience   A different approach dates back to Freud, who accepted the then-prevailing belief that there are some constitutional factors that predispose persons toward homosexuality. But he believed that this potential is only translated into actuality by certain environmental events. In his view, homosexuality is often a response to fears aroused during the Oedipal conflict. The little boy is too terrified to compete with his father for his mother's affections and his terror generalizes to other women. He therefore tries to propitiate the father by identifying with the mother instead (after all, father loves *her*).

525

Some modern psychoanalysts have tried to find evidence in line with Freud's emphasis on the early family constellation. According to one study the homosexuals tend to have "close-binding, intimate" mothers and "hostile, detached" fathers.* As the authors describe it, the pattern is somewhat as follows: The mother was usually extremely close to her son whom she dominated, babied, and overprotected. She was openly hostile to and contemptuous of the boy's father. She made her son her confidant, overtly preferred him to her husband, and pitted son against father in countless arguments. The father himself was emotionally detached or hostile to his son and never tried to counteract the mother's all-engulfing influence over the boy. All of this took place against a backdrop of sexual prudery. The mother regarded sex as dirty, strictly prohibited masturbation, and often interfered with any heterosexual interests her son might have shown, from childhood until early adult life (Bieber et al., 1962).

Do such results show that male homosexuality is caused by close-binding mothers and hostile-detached fathers? Many critics argue that this conclusion is unwarranted. One objection concerns the fact that the sample only included homosexuals who were psychiatric patients. It is not clear whether male homosexuals whose own personal adjustment is reasonably healthy have a similar family background, though some authors argue that they do to some extent (Thompson and McCandless, 1976). Another methodological problem is that the descriptions of childhood were retrospective accounts offered in adulthood. A definitive study requires a longitudinal study in which parents and children are studied independently over perhaps a twenty-year period. But such a study has not been performed.

THE ACQUISITION OF SEXUAL ORIENTATION

The preceding discussion suggests that homosexuality may be at least partially learned. In some cases, the primary learned reaction may be a fear of the opposite sex; in others, it is a more strongly developed attraction to members of one's own. But whatever is learned must be acquired at a fairly early age. The majority of homosexual men and women have homosexual dreams, fantasies, and romantic attachments prior to adolescence. Many of them state that they have been that way "all of my life" (Saghir and Robins, 1973). And as we have already seen, once the homosexual orientation is learned (if indeed it is learned) it is hard to unlearn.

What is the mechanism through which this rather early, hard-to-reverse kind of learning is established? As mentioned, there seems to be a critical period during which this process—which may be akin to imprinting—occurs. But how and why this happens we simply do not know. As a matter of fact we know embarrassingly little about the causes of the heterosexual orientation. Ninety-six percent of men and 98 percent of women (to take Kinsey's figures) are sexually "turned on" by the opposite sex. Is heterosexuality learned? If so, shouldn't there be more variability in sexual orientation, shouldn't the number of homosexuals be much greater than it is?

---

* We omit a discussion of the family antecedents of female homosexuality because the evidence is meager and contradictory.

An alternative possibility is that heterosexuality is built-in, but that it can be inhibited through learning, with homosexuality as one result. While this hypothesis also has some problems, it has a certain plausibility. The best argument in its favor is a simple faith in the power of natural selection. Reproduction seems too important to be left in the hands of such a chancy mechanism as learning. There probably is a critical period during which the developing child's sexual orientation becomes imprinted on this or the other kind of sex object. There may be a built-in bias, or "preparedness" (see Chapter 5) for heterosexual objects. Perhaps those children who eventually become homosexuals have less of this initial bias and are thus more likely to be affected if they encounter environmental conditions that might tip sexual orientation toward members of their own sex.

The subject of sexual orientation, and the broader topic of sex roles of which it is a part, provide a fitting conclusion to the discussion of socialization. They are an example of what true socialization involves. They show the powerful effect of the social environment in which the child grows up, but they also illustrate that this development can only take place within the limits imposed by our biological makeup.

Summary

1. A modern attempt to explain the mechanisms which underlie socialization is *social learning theory*. This emphasizes the effect of *modeling*, both upon the acquisition of new responses and on the performance of responses that are already known. This theory may have implications on such issues as the effect of observing TV violence.

2. The *cognitive developmental approach* to socialization emphasizes the role of understanding rather than imitation. The nature of this understanding is believed to change as the child's mental development proceeds. This approach is exemplified by Kohlberg's analysis of progressive stages in *moral reasoning*.

3. Socialization depends not only on the social agents that act on the child but also upon the child itself. The child's own characteristics partially determine the way the parents treat it, as suggested by studies on infant *temperament*.

4. Socialization can instill various motives characteristic of a given society. An example is the *need for achievement* as assessed by various fantasy measures. McClelland has tried to relate this need for achievement to a set of interlocking factors, including economic forces, sociocultural values, and patterns of child-rearing.

5. Socialization plays a role in determining various senses of being male or female, including *gender identity, gender role,* and *sexual orientation*.

6. Certain psychological differences between the sexes may be based on biological differences. One is *aggression* which tends to be more pronounced in men. Another is a tendency for males to perform better on spatial rather than verbal tests of mental ability, with the opposite pattern characteristic of females. Such biologically based differences—if any—are undoubtedly magnified by socially imposed sex roles. The importance of such roles is illustrated by the effects of *sex reassignment* in childhood.

7. Each of the three main theories of socialization—psychoanalysis, social learning theory, and the cognitive developmental approach— tries to explain how social factors

shape our sense of being male or female. Psychoanalysis asserts that the basic mechanism is *identification*. Social learning theory proposes that it is *imitation* of the parent of the same sex. Cognitive developmental theorists believe that identification comes after the child acquires gender identity which presupposes an understanding of *gender constancy*. Some of these theoretical differences grow out of differences of emphasis: Psychoanalysis focuses on sexual orientation, social learning theory concentrates on gender role, and cognitive developmental theory is most interested in gender identity.

8. While some psychiatrists regard homosexuality as a psychological disorder, the presently dominant view is that it is not. Its causes are still unclear. Constitutional factors may play a role, as well as childhood learning. Whatever its causes, this sexual orientation (no less than heterosexuality) is a fairly stable condition that can be changed only with difficulty if at all.

CHAPTER 14

Interpreting the
Social Situation

The preceding chapters have explored the ways in which social behavior is shaped by our *past*. We began by considering certain social reactions that stem from an evolutionary past that predates our own by many eons—the built-in facets of filial, sexual, and aggressive behavior, and various signals such as the distress cry and the smile that seem to be part of our biological heritage (see Chapter 11). We then looked at social patterns that are rooted in our own personal past and considered the effects of childhood socialization upon later personality (see Chapters 12 and 13). Thus genetic makeup and socialization experience clearly provide necessary preconditions for social life.

But these effects of our biological and personal past cannot by themselves account for our adult social behavior. They do not explain why we vote for one candidate or for another, why we join or don't join a protest demonstration, why we help or ignore a stricken passerby, why we believe a rumor or discount it, why we buy one detergent and not another. These are the kinds of choices that are the stuff of social life. When millions of individuals make one of these choices rather than another, they affect the general condition of our social, political, or economic world.

The way in which these choices are made seems to depend more upon the *present* situation than upon factors in our past. If we are convinced that a certain bank is failing, we withdraw our money; the particulars of our childhood history have little effect. To be sure, we have to be socialized into the cultural patterns in the first place. A Mundugomor or an Arapesh would probably not understand our monetary system and would therefore not join in

Solomon E. Asch *(Courtesy Swarthmore College)*

a rush on the bank. But socialization provides only the initial entry into the social drama, especially in adulthood. Once we are upon that stage, our behavior depends upon the present situation as we see it now. Do we see others running to the teller's window? Is the bank insured? It is these situational factors in the present that are the province of modern *social psychology*.

The main purpose in this chapter is to give some sense of what modern social psychologists do and how they do it. We will organize our account around a central question: How does an individual interpret social events and how does this interpretation affect his or her actions?

Interpreting the Social World

An individual's response to a social situation depends upon what he understands it to be. Romeo killed himself in front of Juliet's tomb because he thought that Juliet was dead; had he known that she was only drugged, the play would have had a happy ending. This simple point forms the basis for much of modern social psychology. But many modern social psychologists make an important further assertion: The way in which we interpret such social events is in principle no different from the way in which we interpret and try to comprehend any event, whether social or not. Seen in this light, many facets of social psychology are simply an aspect of the psychology of thinking and cognition in general.

THE INTERPERSONAL NATURE OF REALITY

WHAT IS REAL?

Much of what we know, we know because of others. The primary medium of this cognitive interdependence is, of course, human language which allows us to share our discoveries and to pass them on to the next generation. As a result, we look at the world not just through our own eyes but also through the eyes of others. To some extent, we all realize that this is so; for example, we are quite aware that our ideas about many foreign lands and cultures are based on what we have heard or read. But the shared aspects of human knowledge go deeper than this, for our very notion of physical reality is at least in part a matter of mutual agreement. This point is made very dramatically in a classic study performed by Solomon Asch (Asch, 1956).

In Asch's experiment, nine or ten subjects are brought together in a laboratory room and shown pairs of cards placed a few feet in front of them. On one card is a black line, say, 8 inches long. On the other card are three lines of varying length, say 6½, 8, and 9 inches (Figure 14.1). The subjects are asked to make a simple perceptual judgment. They have to indicate which of the three lines on the one card is equal in length to the one line on the other card.

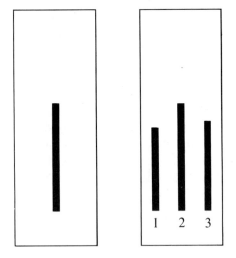

14.1 The stimulus cards in Asch's social pressure experiment *The cards are drawn to scale. In the actual experiment, they were generally placed on the ledge of a blackboard, separated by forty inches. (Asch, 1956)*

A   B   C

14.2 The subject in a social pressure experiment *(A) The true subject (center) listens to the instructions. (B) On hearing the unanimous verdict of the others, he leans forward to look at the cards more carefully. (C) After twelve such trials, on all of which he remained independent, he explains that "he has to call them as he sees them." (Photographs by William Vandivert; courtesy* Scientific American*)*

Then the experimenter tells the subjects that this procedure is only a minor prelude to another study and casually asks them, in the interest of saving time, to indicate their judgments aloud by calling them out in turn (the three comparison lines are designated by the numbers 1, 2, and 3 printed underneath them). This procedure continues for a dozen or so pairs of cards.

Considering the sizable differences among the stimuli, the task is absurdly simple except for one thing: There is only one "real" subject. All of the others are the experimenter's secret confederates. They have arranged their seating order so that most of them will call out their judgments before the real subject's turn comes around. After the first few trials, they unanimously render false judgments. For example, the confederates might declare that a 6½-inch line equals an 8-inch line, and so on, for a dozen or more trials. What does the real subject do now? (See figure 14.2.)

Asch found that the chances were less than 1 in 3 that the real subject would be fully independent and would stick to his guns on trials on which the group disagreed with him (Figure 14.3). Most of them yielded to the group on at least some occasions, in fine disregard of the evidence of their senses—a result with rather uncomfortable implications for the democratic process. When interviewed after the experiment, the yielding subjects made it clear that the group didn't really affect how they saw the lines. No matter what everyone else said, the 8-inch line still looked bigger than the 6½-inch line. But the subjects wondered whether they were right, became worried about their vision or sanity, and were exceedingly embarrassed at expressing their deviance in public.

But the really important question is not why some subjects outwardly complied with the group while others stood their ground. For our present purposes, there is an even more important result of Asch's study that pertains to how the subjects *felt*. In this regard, most of them were alike. Some yielded and some were independent; but, assuming they did not suspect a trick (and few of them did), they were generally very much disturbed. Some thought that their sight had become impaired, others that they were "going mad." Why all the furor?

The answer is that Asch's procedure had violated a basic premise of the subjects' existence: However people may differ, they all share the same phys-

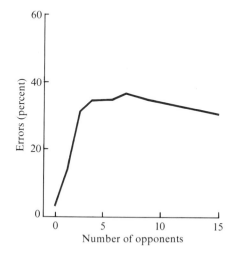

14.3 The effect of social pressure *The extent to which the subject yielded against the size of the group pitted against him is demonstrated by this figure. In this situation, the effect of group size seems to reach a maximum at three, though other studies (such as Gerard, Wilhelmy, and Connolley, 1968) have found that conformity continues to rise beyond this point as the number of opponents increases. (After Asch, 1955)*

ical reality. Under the circumstances, it is small wonder that Asch's subjects were deeply alarmed by a discrepancy they had never previously encountered. (Needless to say, the whole experiment was carefully explained to them immediately thereafter.) There is an old movie, *Gaslight,* in which the villainous husband of a wealthy heiress cleverly stage-manages various physical occurrences such as inexplicably flickering gaslights, which he then denies having seen. His object is to have his wife doubt her own sanity so he can gain control of her fortune. Both Asch and the movie make the same point. Our belief in physical reality is tied up with our assumption that it is shared by others.

What accounts for this assumption of a socially shared reality? To answer this question we must first ask what we mean when we say that an object is "real." One criterion is that the various senses provide *consistent* information. Macbeth sees a dagger but cannot touch it and therefore regards it as "a dagger of the mind, a false creation proceeding from the heat-oppressed brain." Another criterion is consistency across time. Real objects provide what one philosopher called a "permanent possibility of a sensation." You may look away from a tree but it is still there when your gaze returns to it a moment later (J.S. Mill, 1865). To be sure, the appreciation of these coherences—across different senses and over time—may develop with age; as we have seen in our discussion of Piaget's work, a very young infant lacks the concept of object permanence (see Chapter 7). But eventually, the general notion of a fixed reality that is "out there" and independent of our momentary point of view becomes a rock-bottom concept which is accepted without question. If it is challenged, we become deeply disturbed. A man who can't touch what he can see is in a bad way even if he has *not* murdered the king of Scotland.

A similar consistency principle may account for the fact that our reality is shared with others. If reality is initially defined by agreement among different perceptions and memories within one person, it may well be that this definition is eventually expanded to include agreement among different persons. The belief that others see, feel, and hear pretty much as we do will then become a cognitive axiom of our everyday existence. When this axiom is violated, as it is in Asch's experiment, a vital prop is knocked out from under us, a prop so basic that we never even knew that it was there.

How many people have to share our perception of the world if we are to maintain our faith in its reality? We can tolerate (or ignore) some disagreement with others if we are not completely devoid of social support. In a pinch, one lone supporter is enough. In a variation of Asch's experiment, one of the experimenter's confederates acted as the real subject's ally; all other confederates gave unanimous false judgments while the one ally's judgments were true. Under these conditions, the real subject yielded very rarely and was not particularly upset. The moral is simple: One person who believes as we do can sustain us against all others. Two against all is a valiant band; one against all is a crackpot (Figure 14.4).

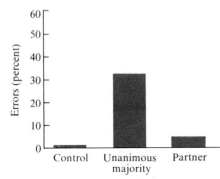

14.4 The effect of social pressure when the subject has a partner *The figure shows the errors when there is no social pressure, when there is a unanimous majority (here, of eight), and when the subject has a partner. It is clear that the amount of yielding drops markedly when the subject is no longer alone. (Data from Asch, 1958)*

SOCIAL COMPARISON

The Asch study shows what happens when the clear evidence of one's own senses is contradicted by the verdict of a unanimous group. But suppose that our own perception does not provide a clear-cut answer. This would happen for example if the lines differed by only a small amount. If left to our own devices, we would try to obtain some further sensory evidence. We might look at the lines once more but from a different angle, or try to measure them with a ruler. But if we can't do that, it is only reasonable to listen to what others say. Their judgment can then be used in lieu of further information provided by our own eyes or hands. If the others should now disagree with us, we might well change our own answer on their say-so. Several studies have shown that this is precisely what occurs in an Asch-type experiment in which the discrimination is fairly difficult. There is more yielding and very little emotional disturbance (Crutchfield, 1955).

This general line of reasoning may explain why people seek the opinion of others whenever they are confronted by a situation which they do not fully comprehend. To evaluate the situation, they need more information. If they cannot get it at firsthand, they will try to compare their own reactions to those of others (Festinger, 1954). The need for *social comparison* is especially pronounced when the evaluations pertain to social issues, such as the qualifications of a political candidate or the pros and cons of fluoridating the water supply, questions that are obviously much more ambiguous than those which pertain to our everyday physical universe.

Comparison groups Whose opinion will we seek out if we ourselves are unsure? Not everyone serves equally well. If we have to judge which of two very similar tones is of higher pitch, we are more likely to ask a musician than a friend whom we know to be tone deaf. But to whom do we turn when we want to evaluate what to do or to think about social matters? Here the tendency is to refer to persons who share some common sentiments and social assumptions and who will then represent our *comparison group.* The adolescent who is in doubt about what to wear to a dance wants to know what his friends think; his parents' views on this matter (and many others) have little effect.

Group support A widely quoted demonstration of the social comparison process is provided in a study by Stanley Schachter (1959). Schachter's subjects were told that the experiment for which they volunteered was about the effects of electric shock on human physiology. Some subjects were made to feel extremely apprehensive by being informed that the shocks they were to receive "will be quite painful but, of course, . . . will do no permanent damage." Others were assured that the shocks would produce only a mild tingle and would not be painful at all. Not surprisingly, the first group of subjects was much more frightened than the second, as shown by subsequent questioning.

In actual fact, no shocks were ever administered. The key part of the experiment occurred just prior to an initial ten-minute delay while the subjects were waiting (so they thought) for the equipment to be set up. The experimenter explained that the subject could wait in one of several rooms outside of the laboratory. As an afterthought, he added that some people might prefer to wait alone while others might like to spend the ten minutes in the company of other subjects who were also waiting to participate in the same experiment. The results were clear-cut. The more frightened subjects were much more likely to choose the company of others than were subjects who had been reassured that the shocks would be of little consequence.

Fear evidently leads to a desire to be with others, but why? According to Schachter, one reason is social comparison. The fearful subject is unsure whether his own emotional reactions are really appropriate. One way of evaluating his own feelings is to talk to others who are about to suffer a similar fate. To paraphrase Schachter's own summary, misery loves company—especially if it is miserable company.

COGNITIVE CONSISTENCY

The preceding discussion has shown that people try to make sense of the world they encounter. In effect, they do so by looking for consistencies among their own experiences and memories, turning to others for comparison and confirmation. But suppose they become aware of some inconsistency among some of their own experiences, beliefs, attitudes, or feelings? They will generally tend to reinterpret what they saw or heard (or believed or felt) so as to restore some sense of coherence. According to Leon Festinger, this is because any perceived inconsistency among various aspects of knowledge, feelings, and behavior sets up an unpleasant internal state—***cognitive dissonance***—which people try to reduce whenever possible (Festinger, 1957).

COGNITIVE CONSISTENCY AND BELIEFS

We will start with an example that concerns **beliefs,** that is, sets of expectations about the world. Suppose you read a newspaper headline, "Citizens of Moscow Denounce Communism at Mass Rally." At first you are puzzled by this new bit of information, for it doesn't fit in with what you already know and believe. Is it a joke? You look at the date and find out that it is not April 1. Was there another revolution in Russia? You haven't read a paper for a week, but surely someone would have told you. The whole business makes no sense. Unless . . . You suddenly find the reinterpretation that sets your cognitive world aright—it was Moscow, *Idaho.*

Cognitive dissonance is not always reduced so easily. An example is provided by a study of a sect that was awaiting the end of the world. The founder of the sect announced that she had received a message from the "Guardians" of outer space. On a certain day, there would be an enormous flood. Only the true believers were to be saved and would be picked up at midnight of the appointed day in flying saucers. (Technology has advanced considerably since the days of Noah's Ark.) On doomsday, the members of the sect huddled together, awaiting the predicted cataclysm. The arrival time of the flying saucers came and went; tension mounted as the hours went by. Finally, the leader of the sect received another message: To reward the faith of the faithful, the world was saved. Joy broke out and the believers became more faithful than ever (Festinger, Riecken, and Schachter, 1956).

Given the failure of a clear-cut prophecy, one might have expected the very opposite. A disconfirmation of a predicted event should presumably lead one to abandon the beliefs that produced the prediction. But cognitive dissonance theory says otherwise. By abandoning the belief that there are Guardians, the person who had once held this belief would have to accept a painful dissonance between her present skepticism and her past beliefs and actions. Her prior faith would now appear extremely foolish. Some members of the sect

(Drawing by Rea; © 1955 The New Yorker Magazine, Inc.)

had gone to such lengths as giving up their jobs or spending their savings; such acts would lose all meaning in retrospect without the belief in the Guardians. Under the circumstances, the dissonance was intolerable. It was reduced by a belief in the new message which bolstered the original belief. Since other members of the sect stood fast along with them, their conviction was strengthened all the more. They could now think of themselves, not as fools, but as loyal, steadfast members of a courageous little band whose faith had saved the earth.

COGNITIVE CONSISTENCY, ATTITUDES AND PREJUDICE

Many social psychologists argue that the notion of cognitive consistency applies not only to beliefs ("The earth is round") but also to **attitudes** ("Communism is a menace"). While beliefs need not necessarily be evaluative, attitudes always are. They are defined as fairly stable evaluative dispositions that make a person think, feel, or behave positively or negatively about some person ("Jane is a warm and friendly woman"), a group ("Doctors are unfeeling and only care about money"), or a social issue ("Marihuana should be legalized").

People tend to interpret various items of relevant information to fit into their preexisting attitudes. For example, we are generally more likely to assume the best when our friends are involved and to believe the worst about our enemies. Similarly, citizens of warring nations are likely to believe stories that reflect well on their own side and to reject those that don't as enemy propaganda. This phenomenon probably has held true throughout the history of warfare, whether between the Greeks and the Trojans or between the Americans and the Vietcong, though its statistical documentation had to await the development of twentieth-century public-opinion surveys. A representative example is a study performed in the United States in 1940 when some Americans still supported the German cause. The subjects were asked to judge the truth or falsity of statements about the combatants, such as "The Germans have deliberately bombed the residential districts of defenseless cities in Poland and England," "British airplanes have willfully violated the neutrality of Belgium and other neutrals." The responses were in line with the subjects' sympathies (Coffin, 1941).

The reinterpretation of the world to maintain a coherent scheme of values and attitudes may be facilitated by a social group (a political party, a social class, a nation) that often provides a ready-made system to explain away some otherwise painful inconsistencies. Consider the ideology of the European colonialists of the nineteenth century. They created colonies that served their own economic interests at the expense of the native populations which were used as pools of convenient, cheap labor. This system ultimately had to be propped up by military force. The colonialists subscribed to values of Christian morality and of fair play. But if so, how could they justify their policies?

The answer is simple. The natives were seen as lazy and indolent, in contrast to the virtuous colonialists who were self-denying and industrious. This explained why the one was and should be governed by the other. It also justified the natives' ridiculously low wages; being so lazy, they had no right to expect any more. The use of repressive force was also justified. The natives were regarded as foolish and childlike, as people who had to be protected against their own impulsiveness. When rebellion did occur, it was generally attributed to "outside agitators," for under normal conditions the childlike natives were thought to be happy and contented (Memmi, 1967). The similarity between the European colonialists' ideology and that which was used to justify slavery and the subsequent black-white relationship in the South after the Civil War needs no comment (Sampson, 1976).

Prejudice and self-perception Several social psychologists have pointed out that the victim of oppression often accepts the ideology of his oppressor. After all, he too needs a coherent understanding of the social world in which he lives; the colonialist's (or the slaver's) ideology provides one explanation of why his state is what it is. Several investigations have shown that victims of group prejudice become prejudiced against their own group. A classic demonstration used subjects who were black children, aged three to seven. They were shown several dolls, some black and some white, and were asked which of the dolls they preferred to play with. They were also asked which doll was "nice" and which "looked bad." The majority of the children preferred the white doll, described the white doll as "nice" and the black doll as "bad" (Clark and Clark, 1958). This result suggests that the black children were growing up to reject their own group and in a sense to reject themselves. (For evidence of self-derogation in another "minority group," women, see Chapter 13.) But this study was performed in 1939. Since then, there has been a major social movement, one aim of which is to abolish black self-hatred and instill a positive sense of group identification in its stead ("Black is beautiful"). Given this social backdrop, it is encouraging to note that when the 1939 study was repeated recently, the results were quite different. A majority of the black children now preferred the black doll (Hraba and Grant, 1970). It seems that American blacks are turning to a new ideology to make sense of their world.

WHY DID I DO WHAT I DID?

According to Festinger, one of the most important sources of cognitive dissonance involves a person's own acts. All of us operate on the unstated assumption that, given a free choice, we choose what we like rather than what we don't. But what if the choice is between two alternatives each of which has both positive and negative features? After the choice is made, there is bound to be cognitive dissonance for, whichever alternative is chosen, one has to forgo some positive aspects and to accept some negative ones.

Festinger's general hypothesis is supported by a number of experimental demonstrations. In one study, subjects were offered a choice between two attractive gifts. Prior to the choice, they had rated the attractiveness of two objects (such as a toaster and a coffee maker) along with several other items. When asked to rate the objects after the choice was made, the results were in line with dissonance reduction. Compared to the object that was rejected, the one that was chosen seemed more attractive now than it had been before (Brehm, 1956).

A related finding concerns the retrospective justification of effort. People often make considerable sacrifices to attain a goal—backbreaking exertion to scale a mountain, years and years of study to become a cardiologist. Was it worth it? According to dissonance theory, the goal will be esteemed more highly the harder it was to reach. If it were not, there would be cognitive dissonance. Support comes from common observation of the effects of harsh initiation rites, such as fraternity hazing or the rigors of Marine bootcamp. After the ordeal is passed, the initiates seem to value their newly found membership all the more. Similar effects have been obtained in the laboratory. Subjects admitted to a discussion group after going through a fairly harsh screening test put a higher value on their new membership (Aronson and Mills, 1959; Gerard and Mathewson, 1966).

A related result is the effect of *forced compliance.* The basic idea is simple. Suppose someone agrees to give a speech in support of a view that is contrary to his own position, as in the case of a bartender arguing for prohibition. Will his public act change his private views? The answer seems to depend upon why he agreed to make the speech in the first place. If he was bribed by an enormous sum, there will be little effect. As he looks back upon his public denunciation of alcohol, he knows why he did what he did; $500 in cold cash is justification enough. But suppose he gave the speech with lesser urging and received only a trifling sum. If we later ask what he thinks about prohibition, we will find that he has begun to believe in his own speech. According to Festinger, the reason is cognitive dissonance. If the bartender asks himself why he took a public stand so contrary to his own attitudes, he can find no adequate justification; the few dollars he received are not enough. To reduce the dissonance, the compliant bartender does the only thing he can: He decides that what he said wasn't really all that different from what he believes.

A number of experimental studies have demonstrated such forced compliance effects in the laboratory. Subjects have been asked to inveigle another person (as usual, a confederate) to perform a monotonous task they themselves have just completed by informing that person that the task was really very interesting. In one study, they were paid either $1 or $20 for lying in this way. When later asked how enjoyable they themselves had found the task, the well paid subjects said that it was boring while the poorly paid subjects said that it was fairly interesting (Figure 14.5).

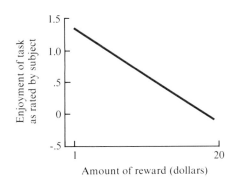

14.5 The effect of forced compliance on attitude *After being paid either $1 or $20 to tell someone that a boring task they just performed was very interesting, subjects were asked to rate their own true attitude. As the figure shows, subjects who were only paid $1 gave a much higher rating than those paid $20. (After Festinger and Carlsmith, 1959)*

SOME DISSONANCE ABOUT DISSONANCE

The cognitive consistency approach has come in for various criticisms (Chapanis and Chapanis, 1964). One objection is the fact that there is no way of predicting in advance just how cognitive inconsistency will be resolved in any particular case. As an example, suppose you are a devout Catholic and hear that the Pope has endorsed the use of LSD. How do you square this with your attitudes on both the drug and the papacy? You could choose to believe that the report is untrue. You could decide that the Pope didn't really mean to endorse LSD in general but only meant to approve of its use in special, medically sanctioned contexts. You could conclude that you might have been wrong about LSD all this time; perhaps it's not much worse than alcohol. You could decide that the Pope was in error, a difficult cognitive step but still possible because he was not speaking *ex cathedra.* No doubt there are many other alternatives as well. The point is that it is impossible to predict just exactly what the person will do to reduce the inconsistency. All one can predict is that there will be a tendency to reduce it in some way (Abelson, 1959).

Does there have to be a tendency to reduce inconsistency (or dissonance) altogether? Consider the person who has just made an irrevocable choice and finds that she chose incorrectly. Festinger and his followers argue that she will try to persuade herself that she chose well after all. But at least sometimes, some of us are willing to admit that we made an error. Under some circumstances we simply can't do otherwise. The man who decided to sail on the *Titanic* instead of another ship will surely have more than a bit of regret. The same holds for simple beliefs that don't involve our own actions. We don't always aim for cognitive consistency. A world that is completely predictable and comprehensible will generate no cognitive inconsistency, but it will be a bore. We enjoy a magician's tricks even though we can't figure out how he accomplishes them and know that we will never find out (for magicians never tell).

Social Perception

Thus far our discussion of how people interpret the social world has focused upon the way in which they try to harmonize various events with their attitudes and beliefs. A similar approach has been applied to find out how we form impressions of other people and how we try to understand why they do what they do..

PERCEIVING OTHERS

In the course of ordinary life we encounter many other people. The vast majority of them play the role of anonymous extras in each of our private dramas, especially in the big cities where we briefly cross the paths of countless strangers of whom we will never know anything. But a sizable number of other persons do impinge upon our lives, as bit players (a traffic cop of whom we ask directions), supporting cast (a casual acquaintance), and starring leads (friends, lovers, bosses, enemies). These we cannot help but evaluate and try to understand as they, in their turn, evaluate and try to understand us. Much of the plot of our own dramas (and of theirs) depends upon the outcome of these mutual social attempts at understanding. How are they achieved?

Perceiving the characteristics of another person is in some ways analogous to perceiving certain stable attributes of a physical object, such as its shape or size. In our previous discussion of visual perception, we saw that to do this the observer must extract certain invariant properties from the stimulus pattern (see Chapter 7). She must abstract the crucial relationships within the stimulus input so that she can see the form of the object, say, a catlike shape. She must also disregard various features of the stimulus pattern that tend to obscure the stable characteristics of the object; examples are illumination, distance, and angle of regard. By doing all this, the observer attains perceptual constancy and can answer such life-and-death questions as whether she is dealing with a kitten nearby or a tiger far away. She has managed to perceive the real, distal stimulus through the masking surface manifestations of the ever-changing proximal stimulus.

Something analogous occurs when we perceive—or rather, infer—such attributes of a person as his violent temper or warmth, and so on. In effect, we are making a judgment as to what the person is "really" like, a judgment independent of the particular moment and occasion. His personal attributes (often called **traits**) are inferred invariant properties that seem to characterize his behavior in different situations. When we say that a person is irascible, we don't mean that he will utter an impolite expletive when someone deliberately steps on his toe. We mean that he will generally be short-tempered over a wide range of circumstances. To put it another way, the attempt to understand what another person is like boils down to an effort to note the *consistencies* in what he does over time and under different circumstances.

The question is how this consistency is abstracted from the few bits of behavior of the other person that are all we can actually observe. Several authors have dealt with different facets of this question, using much the same analogy to visual perception as the one here presented (Heider, 1958).

IMPRESSIONS OF OTHERS AS PATTERNS

The most fundamental fact of form perception is that perceived form depends upon the *relations* among the elements of which the form is composed; it is a Gestalt which does not depend upon these elements in isolation. Thus a triangle can be composed of dots or crosses and remain the same triangle. The same holds for certain auditory patterns. A melody remains the same even if every one of its notes is changed when there is a transposition to another musical key (see Chapter 7). According to Solomon Asch, a similar principle describes our conceptions of other people. In his view, these conceptions of others are not a simple aggregate of the attributes we perceive them to have. Instead, they form an organized whole whose elements are interpreted in relation to the overall pattern (Asch, 1952).

Impressions of others as wholes To test his hypothesis, Asch performed several experiments on how people form impressions of others. His technique was to give subjects a list of attributes which they were told described the same person. Their task was to write a short sketch of the person so characterized and to rate this person on a checklist of antonyms (generous/ungenerous, good-natured/irritable). In one study, some subjects were given a list of seven traits: *intelligent, skillful, industrious, warm, determined, practical, cautious.*

539

Other subjects received the same list except that *cold* was substituted for *warm.* The resulting sketches were quite different. The "warm person" was seen as "driven by the desire to accomplish something that would be of benefit" while the "cold person" was described as "snobbish . . . calculating and unsympathetic." The checklist results were in the same direction. The person described as warm was seen as generous, happy, and good-natured. The "cold person" was characterized by the appropriate antonyms (Asch, 1946). It appears that the warm/cold trait acted as a focus around which the total impression of the person was organized. To use Asch's term, it was a **central trait** that determined the perception of the whole.

Some other findings give further credence to the patterning hypothesis. One group received a list in which *warm* was embedded in a rather unflattering context: obedient, weak, shallow, *warm,* unambitious, vain. Given this backdrop, the attribute *warm* acquired a different and less favorable meaning. It was seen as "a dog-like affection . . . passive and without strength." (For some methodological criticisms, see Wishner, 1960.)

First impressions   New items of information are often incorporated into patterns of organization that are already there. A familiar example is the effect of **mental set.** If subjects expect to be shown the name of an animal, then a very brief presentation of D-CK will be seen as DUCK rather than as DOCK (see Chapter 9). Our everyday experience suggests that a similar phenomenon occurs in person perception. Our first impression of someone often determines how we interpret what we find out about him later on.

This point was illustrated by Asch in another version of his experiment with trait lists. One group of subjects was told to describe their impressions of a person who is *intelligent, industrious, impulsive, critical, stubborn,* and *envious.* Another group received the same traits in reverse order. The results suggest that it pays to put one's best foot forward. If the list began on a positive note, it set up a favorable evaluative tone that seemed to overpower the later negative attributes; the opposite effect occurred when the unfavorable traits came first (Asch, 1946). Similar **primacy effects** have been obtained by other investigators, but their explanation is still a matter of debate. According to Asch, the later attributes take on different shades of meaning depending upon the context provided by the traits encountered earlier in the sequence (Figure 14.6).

Primacy effects can be considerable, but they can of course be overcome just as mental set can be broken. We sometimes do change our minds and come to respect or even love a person whom we detested on first meeting. The primacy effect only means that such alterations in judgment encounter a certain inertia. In old Hollywood movies, the fact that the hero and heroine took an instant dislike to each other was a tip-off to the audience that they would clinch by the final frame. But in real life, first impressions generally make more of a difference. If nothing else, they often preclude the chance of a later reevaluation.

ATTRIBUTION

As previously pointed out, the attempt to understand what another person is like is really an attempt to find the pattern, the consistency, in what he does.

14.6   The primacy effect in forming impressions of personality   *Subjects were presented with sets of six adjectives describing a person, and then had to rate that person on a scale ranging from highly favorable to highly unfavorable. (The complete scale is not shown.) The results showed that the judgment was more favorable if positive adjectives were presented early rather than late in the list. The figure shows ratings for two adjective lists presented in two orders, one starting with the positive adjectives (color) and the other the reverse (black). (Data from Anderson and Barrios, 1961)*

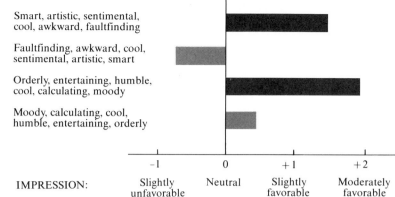

ADJECTIVE LIST:

Smart, artistic, sentimental, cool, awkward, faultfinding

Faultfinding, awkward, cool, sentimental, artistic, smart

Orderly, entertaining, humble, cool, calculating, moody

Moody, calculating, cool, humble, entertaining, orderly

IMPRESSION:

	−1	0	+1	+2
	Slightly unfavorable	Neutral	Slightly favorable	Moderately favorable

An important step is to infer what *caused* his behavior, for the meaning of any given act depends upon its cause. Consider a football player who bumps an opponent in the course of a game. If the bumping occurred while a play was in progress, not much is revealed about the bumper's personality; he was behaving according to the rules of the game. But if the bump occurred some seconds after the official blew his whistle and the play was over, the situation is different. Now the act is more revealing, suggesting a grudge or a nasty disposition. The bumpee will conclude that the bumper's action was *internally caused* and he will self-righteously become bumper in his turn.

In such examples, the observer has to decide to which of several possible causes the behavior of the person should be attributed. An influential recent approach, often called ***attribution theory,*** takes the study of how such decisions are reached as its special concern (Heider, 1958; Jones and Davis, 1965; Jones et al., 1971). According to some adherents of attribution theory, the way in which the observer infers why someone acted as he did is analogous to the manner in which a scientist tracks down the cause of a physical event (Kelley, 1967). An effect (for instance, an increase in gas pressure) is attributed to a particular condition (such as a rise in temperature) if the effect occurs when that condition is present but does not occur when that condition is absent. When people try to explain the behavior of others, they seem to refer implicitly to a similar principle of the covariation of cause and effect. To answer the question "Why did he bump me?" one considers the conditions under which bumping is known to occur. Does it generally occur in circumstances just like now? Would most other people do the same under similar circumstances? If the answer is yes, the behavior will be attributed to essentially external causes, such as the social pressures of team play. But if the answer is no, the act will be attributed to an internal disposition of the actor. He is a dirty player who took a "cheap shot."

Situations versus dispositions   These everyday observations are supported by several laboratory investigations which show that people consider ***situational factors*** when trying to infer the ***dispositional qualities*** (abilities, motives, and so on) of another person. In one study, subjects were asked to rate the personality traits of job applicants on the basis of a (specially prepared) taped job interview. When the applicant described himself in terms that fit the position's requirements, the subjects had little confidence that they learned what the job-seeker was really like. But when the applicant's self-description was discrepant from what the job called for, the subjects usually took him at his word (Jones, Davis, and Gergen, 1961). We apparently feel that we find out more about a person when he does something that does *not* fit into his social role or situation; a waiter who smiles at a guest tells us less about himself than one who is surly.

But while we take account of situational factors in judging the behavior of others, we do so less than we really should. There seems to be a powerful bias to attribute behavior to dispositional qualities in the person while underrating the role of the external situation. The person on welfare is often judged to be lazy (a dispositional attribute) when he is really unable to find work (a situational attribute). Similarly for our interpretation of public affairs. We look for heroes or scapegoats and tend to praise or blame political leaders for acts they had little control over.

This general underemphasis of situational factors in interpreting why another person does what he does is illustrated in an experimental study in which subjects were asked to estimate a debater's own attitudes on a public issue, specifically his views on Castro. All the subjects had to go on was a written text of a speech the debater had (allegedly) written taking either a pro or a con position. The subjects were informed that the debaters did not choose the side they were arguing for but were randomly assigned to one or the other. Even so, there was a tendency to judge the debaters' attitudes by the position they took in their speeches. They knew that this position was determined by external factors, but they did not sufficiently take this into account (Jones and Harris, 1967). To put this in terms of our previous perceptual analogy, it appears that there is imperfect "person constancy." Our visual system does an excellent job at discounting illumination, distance, and orientation, thus yielding the perceptual constancies of brightness, size, and shape. Social perception is nowhere as accurate as this. We are too prone to view acts as caused by something within an actor, so that all too often, the question "Why did it happen?" becomes "Whose fault was it?"

PERCEPTION OF THE SELF

We have discussed some of the ways in which we see various qualities in others. What about the ways in which we see such qualities in ourselves? We all have a conception about our own selves, what we are really like and why we do what we do: "I am a certain kind of person with such and such capacities, beliefs, and attitudes." But before we can deal with this matter, there is a prior question. What is this *I* about which such assertions are made?

THE ORIGINS OF THE SELF-CONCEPT

The bodily self All of us have a sense of "I," of "me" and "mine." But how does that notion arise? Our present interest is with the most rudimentary aspect of this notion, the recognition that one's own body is fundamentally different from all other objects in the universe. How is this discovery made?

A

B

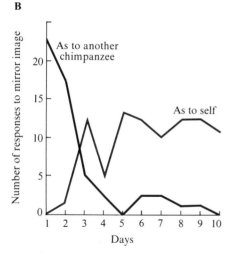

14.7 Self-recognition in chimpanzees
(A) A home-raised chimpanzee looking at herself in a mirror. (Courtesy Keith Hayes). (B) Responses to their mirror image in chimpanzees after a mirror is placed in front of their cage. Initially, the responses to the mirror image are social as if the image were another chimpanzee. Later on, the responses to the mirror image seem to be directed toward the self (e.g., picking food from teeth). The figure shows the number of responses to the mirror image as if it were another ape (black) and the responses as if it were one's own self (color). (After Gallup, 1968)

One way is through vision. Unlike all other objects, the child's own body does not change in retinal size as she moves through the world. A similar discovery can come through touch. As the infant explores the world with mouth and fingers, she will surely note that some things feel quite different from all others. When they are touched, they "touch back." This feeling of "double touch" occurs whenever the child touches a part of her own body, but not otherwise; it provides yet another means for differentiating one's own body from the outside. Still further sources of the bodily self-concept are the numerous sensations that arise from within. There are feelings of muscular movement and strain, of visceral aches and pleasures. All of these sensations eventually become linked as part of a more general concept—one's own body. This in turn becomes the foundation upon which our complex self-concept is built.

Some recent evidence suggests that a rudimentary sense of a bodily self may be present in apes (Gallup, 1970). Several chimpanzees were individually housed in cages outside of which a full-length mirror was placed. Initially, the animals responded with some agitation. They screamed at their own reflection, made threatening gestures, and generally acted as if they were confronting another chimpanzee. But after a few days, their behavior changed. They no longer behaved as if the reflection was another animal. Instead, they seemed to use it as a guide for self-directed body grooming, much as we do when we shave or comb our hair. For example, they carefully watched their mirror image while picking bits of food from between their teeth (Figure 14.7). To establish this point more firmly, the investigators removed the chimpanzees from their cages, anesthetized them, and painted a red spot over one eye and on one ear. Thus marked, the animals were brought back to their cages, initially without the mirror. A few hours after they woke up and recovered, the mirror was brought back. The effect was dramatic. When the chimpanzee saw his reflection, he immediately touched himself and fingered the marked regions, much like a human who looks in a mirror and discovers some soot on his cheeks. But this capacity to recognize oneself seems to require a reasonably advanced intellect. Monkeys showed no comparable effect, even after hundreds of hours of exposure to their own mirror reflection (Gallup, 1968).

The rudimentary sense of one's own body is probably soon linked with certain other characteristics that we take as basic to the notion of "self." One is its relation to goal-directed striving, which Freud emphasized when discussing the ego (Chapter 12). We feel ourselves to be active agents who want and will and who experience pains and pleasures. However, little is known about how this connection is made. One guess is that the child learns to associate the feeling of being-about-to-move with sensations of the movement that follows. If this association is generalized, it might give rise to a broader conception of will or intention which would then be related to the sense of the bodily self (W. James, 1890).

Many philosophers have been preoccupied with yet a further attribute of the self. We experience it as continuous over time (e.g., Shoemaker, 1963). There is a continuity of memories which joins our past to our present. A similar continuity of wishes and expectations links our present to our future. As a result, we feel personal continuity: *I* am *I* and always was and always will be as long as *I* shall exist, for no matter how much *I* may change, there is always an underlying self that stays the same.

The social self   Thus far we have considered the sense of self without any reference to other people. But there is little doubt that there can be no full-fledged "I" without a "you" or "they"; for a crucial component of the self-concept is social. According to many authors, the child begins to see herself through the eyes of the important figures in her world and thus acquires the idea that she is a person, albeit at first a very little person, just as they are (Mead, 1934). As the social interactions become more complex, more and more details are added to the self picture. In effect, the child sees herself through the mirror of the opinions and expectations of those others—mother, father, siblings, friends—who matter to her. Her later behavior cannot help but be shaped by this early "looking-glass self" (Cooley, 1902). Examples of such effects include the roles in which society casts children from the moment of birth: black, white, male, female, and so on (see Chapter 13).

A striking example of the effects of other people's views on the self-concept and on later behavior concerns a West African tribe, the Ashanti. These people believe that a person's character depends upon the day of the week on which he is born and they tend to name the child according to that day. Thus Monday's children are often named Kwadwo and are expected to become quiet and peaceful citizens. Children born on Wednesday are called Kwaku and have a more ominous prognosis. They are thought to be potential troublemakers. According to one investigator, the prediction held true. Police records showed that violent crime and delinquency were unusually low for Kwadwos and high for Kwakus—an excellent example of a self-fulfilling prophecy (Jahoda, 1954).

WHO AM I?

The preceding discussion has sketched some of the hypotheses about the ways in which we come to know ourselves—as a body bounded in space, as an active agent continuous in time, as a person who is much like other persons. How do we find out what kind of person we really are? In part, as we have seen, we find out from others. But isn't there a more direct method? Can't we discover who we are and what we feel simply by observing ourselves?

According to some authors, the answer is no. In their view, our conceptions of self are attained through an attribution process no different in kind from that which allows us to form conceptions of other people. Advocates of this *self-perception theory* maintain that, contrary to commonsense belief, we do not know our own selves directly (Bem, 1972). In their view, self-knowledge can only be achieved indirectly, through the same attempts to find consistencies, discount irrelevancies, and interpret observations that help us to understand other people.

Behavior and attitude   One line of evidence concerns the relation between attitude and behavior. Common sense argues that attitudes cause behavior, that our own actions stem from our feelings and our beliefs. To some extent, this is undoubtedly true. The pro-segregationist is unlikely to join a civil rights demonstration. But under some circumstances, the cause-and-effect relation is reversed. Sometimes, our feelings or beliefs are the *result* of our own actions. A simple example is our liking for people. Naturally enough, we are more prone to do favors for the people we like than for those we do not. But occasionally there is a reverse effect This is the basis of Benjamin Franklin's cynical advice on how to win someone's good graces: Get that person to do you a small favor, such as lending you a book, and he will end up beholden to *you.*

Whether Franklin's advice was ever followed by any of his revolutionary colleagues is unknown, but his suggestion was recently tested in a study in which subjects were made to act either kindly or harshly to someone else. The subjects had to supervise two "learners" (naturally, confederates) in a learning task. They were told to compliment one of the learners whenever he made a right response. In contrast, they had to criticize the other learner harshly for any error. After the session was over, the subjects were asked to rate the learners' personalities. Benjamin Franklin would have been pleased to know that the subjects had a more favorable judgment of the learner they had praised than the one to whom they issued reproofs (Schopler and Compere, 1971). The subjects were presumably unable to attribute their own acts entirely to the instructions imposed by the experimenter. Under the circumstances, they had to find some additional reasons within themselves: "I couldn't have been that unpleasant unless I disliked him."

A similar effect involves the "foot-in-the-door" technique, originally perfected by traveling salesmen. In one study, suburban homeowners were asked to comply with an innocuous request, to put a 3-inch square sign in their window advocating auto safety. Two weeks later, another experimenter came to visit those homeowners who agreed to display the small sign. This time they were asked to grant a much greater request, to permit the installation of an enormous billboard on their front lawns, proclaiming "Drive Carefully" in huge letters while obstructing most of the house. The results showed that agreement depended upon prior agreement. Once having complied with the first, small request, the subjects were much more likely to give in to the greater one (Freedman and Fraser, 1966).

One interpretation of this and similar findings is a change in self-perception (Snyder and Cunningham, 1975). Having agreed to put up the small sign, the subjects now thought of themselves as active citizens involved in a public issue. Since no one forced them to put up the sign, they attributed their action to their own convictions. Given that they now thought of themselves as active, convinced, and involved, they were ready to play the part on a larger scale. Fortunately for their less involved neighbors, the billboard was in fact never installed—after all, the request was only part of an experiment. But in real life we may not be let off so easily. The foot-in-the-door approach is a common device for persuading the initially uncommitted; it can be used to sell encyclopedias or political convictions. Extremist political movements generally do not demand violent actions from newcomers. They begin with small requests like signing a petition or giving a distinctive salute. But these may lead to a changed self-perception that ultimately may ready the person for more drastic acts.

This line of argument may have some bearing on our understanding of how social systems function. The social world casts people in different roles that prescribe particular sets of behaviors; representatives of labor and management will obviously take different positions at the bargaining table. But the roles determine attitudes as well as behavior. If one has to act like a union representative, one starts to feel like one. The same holds for the corporation

Commitment by doing *The competent political organizer gets volunteers involved in some activity, even if that activity is not especially useful at the time. The important thing is to get the person committed, and the best means to accomplish this is through some form of action. (Photograph by Charles Harbutt © 1970 Magnum Photos)*

executive. This point has been verified in a study of factory workers both before and after they had become union stewards or were promoted to foreman (Lieberman, 1956).

In short, our attitudes are affected by what we do and are expected to do. To some extent at least, the role makes the man or the woman. If one is appointed a judge, one begins to feel judicious.

SUBJECTIVE EMOTION: A SPECIAL CASE OF SELF-PERCEPTION?

An intriguing extension of the self-perception approach concerns the way in which we recognize our own emotions. We have seen that there is evidence that we come to know our own attitudes by a process of self-attribution. A similar process may be involved in the production of the subjective experience of emotion. We say that we feel love, joy, grief, or anger. But are we always sure exactly which emotion we experience? In one of Gilbert and Sullivan's operettas a character notes that the uninitiated may mistake love for indigestion. The point may be valid for most of us. We often have to interpret our own internal states, have to decide whether the knot in our stomach is fear (say, of an examination) or is impatient anticipation (say, of a lover's meeting). According to some psychologists, such interpretative processes are involved whenever we experience an emotion (Schachter and Singer, 1962; Mandler, 1975). To put their views in perspective, we will begin with a discussion of some earlier theories of emotion.

THEORIES OF EMOTION

The topic of emotion has vexed generations of investigators. Psychologists and biologists have had reasonable success in uncovering some of the objective, bodily manifestations of emotional states; examples are the physiological concomitants of fear and rage (see Chapter 3) and emotional expressions such as the smile (see Chapter 11). But what can we say about the way our emotions are experienced subjectively, how they feel "inside"?

The James-Lange theory Many nineteenth-century psychologists tried to catalogue various emotional experiences, much as they had classified the different sensations provided by the senses (such as red, sour, A-flat). But their efforts were not too successful. There were simply too many emotional experiences that people reported and the classification schemes that were proposed did not seem to do justice to the richness of these subjective feelings. In addition, there were disagreements about the precise meanings of emotional terms. How does sadness differ from dolor or weariness or dejection? Different people reported different shades of meaning and there was little hope of agreement so long as the description was confined to the subjective experience alone (which is private by definition).

A different approach to the problem was proposed by William James. To James, the crucial facet of emotion was that it is an aspect of what a person *does*. In fear, we run; in grief, we weep. The commonsense interpretation is that the behavior is caused by the emotion. James stood common sense on its head and maintained that the causal relation is reversed; we are afraid *because* we run:

Common-sense says, we lose our fortune, are sorry and weep; we meet a bear, are frightened and run; we are insulted by a rival, are angry and strike. The hypothesis here . . . is that we feel sorry because we cry, angry because we strike, afraid because we tremble. . . . Without the bodily states following on the perception, the latter would be purely cognitive in form, pale, colorless, destitute of emotional warmth. We might then see the bear, and judge it best to run, receive the insult and deem it right to strike, but we should not actually *feel* afraid or angry (James, 1890, v. II, p. 449).

These phrases are the core of what is now known as the **James-Lange theory of emotions.** (Carl Lange was a contemporary of James' who offered a similar account.) In effect, the theory asserts that the subjective experience of emotion is neither more nor less than the awareness of our own bodily changes in the presence of certain arousing stimuli. According to James, these bodily changes might be produced by skeletal movements (running) or visceral reactions (pounding heartbeat), though later adherents of his theory emphasized the visceral responses and the activity of the autonomic nervous system that underlies them (Figure 14.8).

14.8   The sequence of events as conceived by the James-Lange theory of emotions   *According to the James-Lange theory, the subjectively experienced emotion is simply our awareness of our own response to the anger- or fear-arousing situation. We see a dangerous object (an attacking dinosaur will do as well as any other), this triggers a bodily response (running, pounding heart), and the awareness of this response is the emotion (here, fear).*

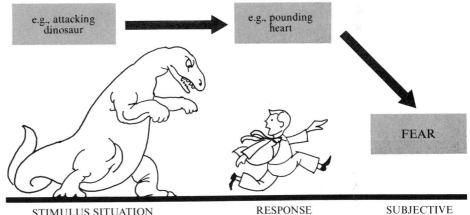

e.g., attacking dinosaur

e.g., pounding heart

FEAR

STIMULUS SITUATION   RESPONSE   SUBJECTIVE EMOTION

Objections to the James-Lange theory   The James-Lange theory has been the focus of considerable controversy. One of the major criticisms was raised by Walter Cannon, the pioneer in the study of autonomic functioning (see Chapter 3). Cannon pointed out that sympathetic reactions to arousing stimuli are pretty much the same, while our emotional experiences vary widely. So if subjective emotions are really nothing but the awareness of our own visceral responses, how could we possibly tell the difference between them when we are unable to distinguish among these visceral reactions? Cannon pointed out that fear and rage, for example, are accompanied by much the same pattern of violent sympathetic discharge (Cannon, 1927). Since we can certainly distinguish these two emotions, the James-Lange theory must have a flaw.*

* Several later investigators have tried to show that, contrary to Cannon, there are some differences in the autonomic patterns that accompany such different emotions as fear and rage (for instance, Ax, 1953; Funkenstein, 1956). This point is still a matter of debate (for instance, Mandler, 1975).

A different objection concerns the effect of artificial autonomic arousal. In several early studies, this was accomplished by injecting subjects with adrenalin (Landis and Hunt, 1932). This triggered sympathetic activation with all its consequences—palpitations, tremor, and sweaty palms. According to the James-Lange theory, these are the internally produced stimuli that give rise to the intense emotions of fear and rage. But in fact, the subjects did not experience these emotions. Some simply reported the physical symptoms. Others said that they felt "as if" they were angry or afraid, a kind of "cold emotion" that the subjects knew was not the real thing. These findings represent a further argument against the James-Lange theory. The visceral reactions are evidently not a sufficient condition for the emotional experience.

EMOTIONS AND THE ATTRIBUTION PROCESS

A different conception of the relation between autonomic arousal and emotional experience suggests that autonomic arousal provides only the raw materials for an emotional experience, a state of undifferentiated excitement and nothing more (Schachter and Singer, 1962). This excitement is shaped into a specific emotional experience by an attribution process. A person's heart beats rapidly and her hands are trembling—is it fear, rage, joyful anticipation, or a touch of the flu? If the individual has just been insulted, she will interpret her internal reactions as anger and feel and act accordingly. If she is confronted by William James' bear, she will attribute her visceral excitement to the bear and experience fear. If she is at home in bed, she will probably assume that she is sick. And if she knows that she has just been injected with adrenalin and is aware of the drug's bodily consequences, she will feel no emotion at all (or at best, will feel an "as if" emotion). In short, according to Schachter and Singer, emotional experience is produced, not by autonomic arousal as such, but rather by the interpretation of this arousal in the light of the total situation as the subject sees it (Figure 14.9).

14.9 The sequence of events as conceived by Schachter and Singer's cognitive evaluation theory of emotions According to Schachter and Singer, subjectively experienced emotion is the result of an evaluation process in which the subject interprets his own bodily reactions in the light of the total situation. Any number of external stimuli (ranging from attacking dinosaurs to competition in a race) may lead to the same general bodily reaction pattern—running and increased heart rate. The subjective emotion depends upon what the subject attributes these bodily responses to. If he attributes them to a danger signal (the dinosaur) he will feel fear. If he attributes them to the race, he will feel excitement.

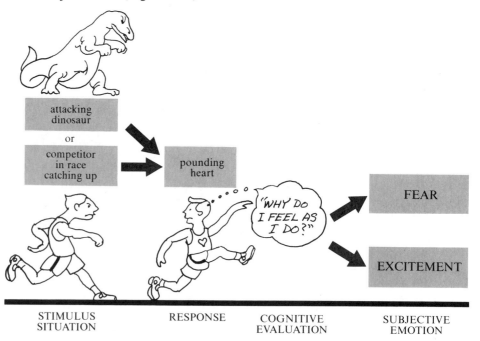

STIMULUS SITUATION   RESPONSE   COGNITIVE EVALUATION   SUBJECTIVE EMOTION

To test this conception, subjects were injected with a drug they thought was a vitamin supplement but which was really adrenalin. Some subjects were informed of the drug's real effects such as increase in heart rate, flushing, tremor, and so on. Other subjects were misinformed. They were told that the drug might have some side-effects such as numbness or itching but were not informed of its actual bodily consequences. After the drug had been administered, the subjects sat in an anteroom while waiting for what they thought was a test of vision. In actual fact, the main experiment was conducted in this waiting room with a confederate posing as another subject while the experimenter watched through a one-way screen. One condition was set up to produce anger. The confederate was sullen and irritable and eventually stalked out of the room. Another condition provided a context for euphoria. The confederate was ebullient and frivolous. He threw paper planes, played with a hula hoop, and tried to engage the subject in an improvised basketball game with paper wads. Following their stay in the waiting room, the subjects were asked to rate their emotional feelings. (Schachter and Singer, 1962).

The critical question was whether the prior information about the drug's effects had influenced the subject's emotional reaction. Schachter and Singer reasoned that those subjects who had been correctly informed about the physiological consequences of the injection would show less of an emotional response than those who were misinformed. The informed subjects could attribute their tremors and palpitations to the drug rather than to the external situation. In contrast, the misinformed subjects had to assume that their internal reactions were caused by something outside, the elation of the euphoric confederate or the sullenness of the angry one. Given this external attribution, their emotional state would be in line with the environmental context, euphoric or angry as the case might be. The results were as predicted. The misinformed subjects in the euphoria condition were more joyful than their correctly informed counterparts. They said that they were in a happier mood, and they were more likely to join in the confederate's mad antics. Analogous results were obtained in the anger condition. The misinformed subjects behaved more angrily in the waiting room and described themselves as more irritable than did the subjects who were correctly informed.

Schachter and Singer's experiments have come in for some sharp criticisms; some important controls were omitted and some of the results were by no means as neat as they initially appeared (Plutchik and Ax, 1970). In addition, a recent experiment which partially replicated their original study suggests that subjective emotion is not as labile as Schachter and Singer had presumed. If the drug dosage is high enough, adrenalin seems to induce an unpleasant mood even though the subject is misinformed about the symptoms and is in the presence of a euphoric confederate (Marshall, 1976). These objections are serious enough to make one wish for further and more extensive replications. But even so, there are reasons for holding onto Schachter and Singer's general approach, at least for the time being. One reason is simply that their attempt to treat subjective emotional experience as an aspect of self-attribution is very plausible. It reconciles the James-Lange emphasis on bodily facets of emotion with the fact that these bodily manifestations are very diffuse and do not by themselves suffice to produce a genuine emotional experience.

Another argument for the Schachter and Singer interpretation comes from further studies which have shown analogous misinterpretations of internal sensations in different situations. In one study, male subjects were allowed to listen to an amplification of their own heartbeats while looking at slides of nude females (Valins, 1966). These amplified heartbeats were in fact rigged by the experimenter; they were sometimes faster and sometimes slower than the subject's own. The subject's task was both pleasant and simple. He had to rate the attractiveness of each nude. The results showed that the subjects based their judgments not only upon what they saw but also on what they heard—or thought they heard. If their heartbeat was rapid, they were more likely to judge the nude as especially attractive. She had to be, for she made their heart race. It appears that in erotic situations we listen to our heart in a more than figurative sense.

EMOTION AND THE THEATER

There is a certain emotional experience that is in some ways quite unlike those we encounter in everyday life—the emotion we feel when watching a play or a movie. Is it a real emotion? Sometimes it seems to be. Some plays or movies can obviously move us to tears. As children we weep at Lassie's illness; as adults, at Juliet's death. In retrospect, we may insist that while watching the play or the movie, we were "really in it" and had come to accept the characters' joys and sorrows as though they were real. But did we truly? Consider a great performance of "Oedipus Rex," climaxed by that awesome scene in which Oedipus blinds himself. We may say that while watching the play we believed that what happened on stage was reality. In fact, we did no such thing. If we had, we would have experienced horror instead of tragic awe; we would have rushed for help, perhaps shouting, "Is there an ophthalmologist in the house?" In fact, we never believe that the stage Oedipus is real; at best, we are willing to suspend our *dis*belief, as the poet Coleridge put it so aptly. But in the fringes of our consciousness there is always the feeling that we are sitting in a comfortable theater armchair. We may suspend disbelief, but this does not mean that we believe.

The emotion we experience in the theater cannot be identical to the one we feel in the real world. But then, what is it? One possibility is that the experience is analogous to the "cold fear" produced by injecting adrenalin, an "as if" emotion that occurs in subjects who cannot attribute their arousal to any external cause. Let us assume that when we witness certain events that befall others in real life—a tearful reunion, a fistfight, a death scene—we experience real emotions. When analogous events occur on stage or on the screen, they trigger a similar arousal. But the cognitive context is quite different, for we still know that we are sitting in a darkened theater hall, so our experience necessarily has an "as if" quality.

The special esthetic flavor of the theatrical experience probably depends upon just this "as if." But this quality requires a delicate balance between disbelief and belief, between too little arousal and too much. On the one hand, there must be some sense of "being in it," or the experience will be cold and dispassionate, like that of the bored usher who has seen the same show over and over again. On the other hand, too much arousal will also defeat the esthetic goal to the point that the "as if" feeling is lost altogether. A theatrically naïve audience may believe that what happens on stage is the real thing, as in children's theater where the four- and five-year olds shout fearful warnings at Snow White when the evil old witch approaches. Their seven-year-old cousins are less naïve and thus more capable of enjoying a genuine dramatic

Emotion and the actor *A scene from Shakespeare's* King Lear *in which the old king, half-crazed with impotent fury, screams at the world during a raging storm. Lear was surely in a state of vehement frenzy. But was the actor who portrayed him? (Paul Schofield and Alec McCowen in a Royal Shakespeare production; photograph by Zoë Dominic)*

Children at a Punch-and-Judy show
One child, upset over the fate of one of the puppets, is reassured by her older brother. (Courtesy Suzanne Szasz)

experience. They feel aroused and excited, but can reassure their younger friends with an air of theater-wise sophistication, "Don't worry. It's not really real."

When a performance threatens to become too real, sophisticated adults may protect themselves by laughing nervously and thus breaking the spell altogether. This reaction to the loss of "psychical distance" (Bullough, 1912) is sometimes seen in in-the-round theaters, where the audience surrounds the playing area and those in the front row can almost touch the actors. If the play is a blood-and-guts melodrama, in-the-round staging may become too close for comfort. Suppose there is a well-acted scene in which a man almost murders his wife with an ax. The members of the audience directly adjacent to the two actors are very likely to avert their heads. The scene has become too real and the emotion too genuine. The audience responds by breaking contact.

The "as if" experience may be an important ingredient in the appreciation emotion the actor feels as he plays his part. Many dramatic critics have asked the question, "What does the actor feel when he portrays the jealousy of an Othello or the rage of a Lear?" According to some schools of acting (such as the famous Actors' Workshop of New York which teaches "method" acting), the actor's job is to bring emotional reality to his role. In practice, the actor accomplishes this by vividly recalling some emotion-filled fragments of his own life that are appropriate to his present role and scene. The result is often a sense of genuine dramatic truth, felt by both actor and audience. But admirable as this may be, is it real in the sense in which everyday emotion is real? Again, the answer is almost surely no. No sane actor who ever played Othello really wanted to strangle the actress who portrayed Desdemona. Yet there is nevertheless this "as if" experience, a state of arousal, perceived and interpreted against a cognitive context that includes both the situation of the character and that of the actor who plays that character.

The "as if" experience may be an important ingredient in the appreciation of several art forms. In theater, it is the simultaneous awareness of events that may move us deeply and are yet known to be unreal. In the visual arts, it is the simultaneous awareness of a scene or object that looks real and lifelike but is nonetheless seen to be a flat, painted canvas (see Chapter 7).

PERCEIVING OTHERS WHILE BEING SEEN

The preceding discussion has shown that the means whereby we interpret the social world are in many ways analogous to those that underlie the perception of our physical environment. In both cases, we try to abstract some intrinsic characteristic of an object from the welter of distorting stimulus features in which it appears; to perceive the real size of a distal object independent of its distance, to infer the real feelings or motives of a person independent of her role, even when that person happens to be our own self.

But this analogy to visual perception can be pushed too far, for social perception is more complex. It is a two-way process in which all participants are potential stimuli as well as observers, are capable of being seen as well as of seeing. And most important, each participant knows this and knows that the others know it too. As a result, perceiving people is in one sense very different from perceiving a physical object like a rock. The rock doesn't know that we are looking at it and it surely isn't trying to make a particular impression. People are considerably more troublesome than this.

Since you can't go around saying you're terrific, let our clothes do it for you. *Country Set*

Impression management *The advertising industry spares no effort to tell us that we can be who we want to be by wearing the appropriate clothes, makeup, eye glasses, and so on and so on. (Courtesy Country Set)*

SELF-PRESENTATION

In contrast to rocks, people are constantly working at ***impression management,*** a term coined by the sociologist Erving Goffman (1959). As Goffman sees it, much of social interaction is akin to a theatrical performance in which the actors are "putting on a front." Some "play hard to get," others wear elaborately contrived "casual looks," still others try to appear "above it all." Many of these impressions go along with social or professional roles. The medical student soon discovers that there is more to becoming a doctor than acquiring certain medical skills. He must also learn how to look like a doctor, how to instill confidence, how to develop a proper "bedside manner." The audience for whom such productions are staged often includes the actors themselves. The would-be-healer gradually comes to believe his own role, as one patient after another greets him as "Doctor" and treats his pronouncements with reverential awe.

Goffman points out that many of these social performances are jointly produced. To begin with, the actor is often supported by a team. The doctor's image is maintained not only by his own behavior but by that of various aides and nurses as well. Further support comes from the audience itself. We often go to considerable lengths to preserve another person's self-presentation, to allow her to "save face." If we want to break off an encounter at a cocktail party, we pretend that we are going to the bar for another drink. The other person knows that we have no intention of returning, and we know that he knows, but this doesn't matter. Both participants tactfully play along. This kind of tact can reach consummate heights as in the case of the legendary English butler who accidentally surprised a lady in her bath and hurriedly mumbled, "I beg your pardon, Sir."

KEYS

There is yet another dimension to social perception that adds to its already awesome complexity. A particular pattern of social interaction can have different meanings depending upon how it is *keyed,* to use Goffman's term (1974). A ***key*** is a signal (analogous to keys in musical notation) that indicates the sense in which some act or utterance should be taken. Consider a nude model at an art class. The situation is keyed to make nudity nonsexual. To preserve this key, both model and art students will avoid each other's eyes. The model is looked at, but as a sort of statue, as an anatomical specimen, not as a person who could be a potential sexual partner.

Our ability to see social interaction in terms of the appropriate key is reminiscent of some effects of context in linguistic communication. A well-known example is the use of certain questions as implied imperatives (Searle, 1969). "Do you have a cigarette?" is not a question about possession. It is very different from questions like "Do you have a two-car garage?" or "Do you have a hippopotamus?" It is a polite way of asking for a cigarette and there are only two possible answers. One is "No. I'm sorry" and the other is the offer of a cigarette. The reply "Yes" without any accompanying action is either a joke or an insult (see Chapter 10).

Some Apparent Failures of Rationality: Blind Obedience and Crowd Behavior

Thus far our focus has been on the way in which the individual interprets social situations and events. To the extent that she acts in accordance with her interpretation (which may or may not be correct), her behavior is often described as rational. But there are various social behavior patterns that on first sight seem not to be rational in this sense. They usually involve actions that people perform as members of a group and which they would rarely commit alone. An example is looting while in a rioting crowd. Can social psychology contribute to our understanding of such actions? We will consider two examples. One is obedience to orders that violate one's own conscience. Here the individual subordinates her own rationality to the presumed rationality of some authority. Another example concerns the apparently irrational behavior of people who are members of violent or panicky crowds.

BLIND OBEDIENCE

Obedience *The commandant of a concentration camp in Germany stands amid some of his prisoners who were burned or shot as the American army approached the camp during the last days of World War II. Most Nazis who held such positions insisted that they were "just following orders." (Courtesy United Press International)*

In any society, no matter how primitive, some individuals have authority over others, at least within a limited sphere. Obedience is particularly relevant as societies get more complex, where the spheres within which authority can be exerted become much more differentiated. Teachers assign homework, doctors order intravenous feedings, and policemen stop automobiles. The pupils, nurses, and motorists generally obey. Their obedience is based on an implicit recognition that the persons who issued the orders were operating within their legitimate domain of authority. If this domain is overstepped, obedience is unlikely. Policemen can't order motorists to recite lists of irregular French verbs or to take two aspirins and go to bed.

Some tendency to obey authority is a vital cement that holds society together; without it, there would be chaos. But the atrocities of this century—the slaughter of the Armenians, the Nazi death camps, the My Lai massacre—give terrible proof that this disposition to obedience can also become a corrosive poison that destroys our sense of humanity. Some of these atrocities could not have been committed without the obedience of tens or hundreds of thousands and the acquiescence of many more. How could such obedience have come about? Attempts to answer this question have focused on either of two factors. One concerns the personality structure of the blindly obedient individual; the other emphasizes the social situation in which the obedient person finds himself.

OBEDIENCE AND PERSONALITY STRUCTURE

What made people obey and thus participate in any of the unspeakable acts of which history tells us? One interpretation is that some personalities are more prone to obey than others, that the crucial determinant is *within* the person rather than in the situation.

An influential version of the person-centered hypothesis was presented in the decade after World War II by a research group at the University of

California at Berkeley. These investigators believed they had discovered a personality type who was predisposed toward totalitarian dogma and might thus be more ready to obey unquestioningly (Adorno, Frenkel-Brunswik, Levinson, and Sanford, 1950). Their evidence came from the responses of American subjects in clinical interviews and on various attitude tests. According to the investigators, some of the subjects could be aptly described as **authoritarian personalities.** Such persons were prejudiced against various minority groups and also held certain sentiments about authority, including submission to those above, harshness to those below, and a general belief in the importance of power and dominance. These authoritarian attitudes were indicated by a tendency to agree emphatically with such statements on the attitude scales as, "Obedience and respect for authority are the most important virtues children should learn," "Most of our social problems would be solved if we could somehow get rid of the immoral, the crooked and feeble-minded people," and "People can be divided into two distinct classes: the weak and the strong."

The Berkeley investigators believed that this constellation of attitudes was an expression of underlying personality patterns formed in childhood. They found that people who scored high on minority prejudice and authoritarianism described their childhoods as dominated by a stern and harshly punitive father who insisted on absolute obedience. According to the investigators, the children thus reared had little choice but to repress their hostility of the all-powerful father. They developed a reaction formation (see Chapter 12) in which obedience and submission to all authority became exalted virtues. But the hostility was not repressed completely; it found new outlets through displacement upon safer targets, such as minority groups. In addition, there was a glorification of toughness and a kind of taboo on tenderness. Yet another consequence was the projection of the repressed hostility upon the outside world, which was seen as populated by dangerous enemies who had to be crushed before one was crushed by them (such as the "International Jewish Conspiracy").

The Berkeley studies have been the target of considerable criticism (Christie and Jahoda, 1954). Some critiques focused on the way in which the items were worded, others on the fact that the information about the subjects' childhoods was mainly based upon the subjects' own recollections. But while the original claims of the Berkeley group may have been too extravagant, their studies did focus on an important set of relationships between political and social attitudes (Brown, 1965). Minority prejudice probably does tend to go together with authoritarian sentiments, and these in turn are often accompanied by certain ways of remembering and idealizing one's parents and a belief in stern childhood discipline. Whether this constellation of attitudes is caused by childhood experiences in a psychoanalytic sense is still debatable. There is evidence that authoritarianism is more pronounced among persons of lower socioeconomic status, of lower education, and of lower intelligence (Christie, 1954). As one writer put it, "Authoritarianism may be the world-view of the uneducated in western industrialized societies" (Brown, 1965, p. 523).

OBEDIENCE AND THE SITUATION

Can the person-centered hypothesis explain the atrocities of recent times? Were those who obeyed the order to massacre countless innocents sick minds

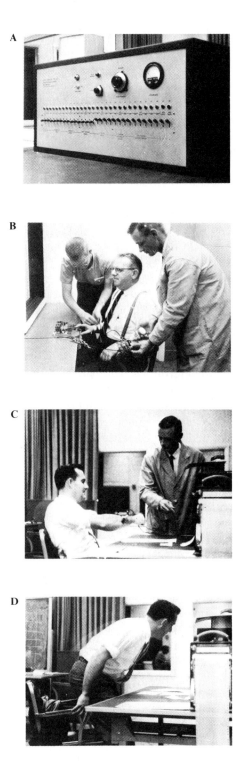

or abnormal personalities, completely different from the rest of us? Some of them probably were (Dicks, 1972). But the frightening fact is that many of these men seemed to be cast in a much more ordinary mold; what is horrifying about them is what they did and not who they were. An example is a convicted war criminal who had personally murdered dozens of persons. He obtained his position as a guard so as to get ahead in the world. According to the psychiatric interview, he was a rather average man who "could have lived his life in quieter days unnoticed, a respectable craftsman and probably harming nobody" (Dicks, 1972, p. 141). In a well-known account of the trial of Adolf Eichmann, the man who supervised the deportation of six million Jews to the Nazi gas chambers, the author comments on this grotesque "banality of evil": "The trouble with Eichmann was precisely that so many were like him, and that the many were neither perverted nor sadistic, that they were, and still are, terribly and terrifyingly normal" (Arendt, 1965, p. 276).

It appears that obedience to inhuman orders is in part a function of the total situation in which a person finds himself. Under some social systems—Hitler's Germany, Stalin's Russia—the conditions for compliance or tacit acceptance are so powerful that an outsider might well pause to wonder whether "there but for the grace of God go I."

The importance of situational factors in producing obedience is highlighted by the results of one of the best-known (and most controversial) experiments of modern social psychology, a study conducted by Stanley Milgram (1963). Milgram's subjects were drawn from a broad spectrum of socioeconomic and educational levels; they were recruited by a local newspaper ad offering $4.50 per hour to persons willing to participate in a study of memory. Milgram's subjects arrived at the laboratory where a white-coated experimenter told them that the study in which they were to take part concerned the effect of punishment on human learning.

The subjects were run in pairs and drew lots to determine who would be the "teacher" and who the "learner." The task of the learner was to master a list of paired associates. The task of the teacher was to present the stimuli, record the learner's answers, and—most important—to administer punishment whenever the learner responded incorrectly. The learner was conducted to a cubicle where the experimenter strapped him in a chair, to "prevent excess movement," and attached the shock electrodes to his wrist—all in full view of the teacher. After the learner was securely strapped in place, the teacher was brought back to the main experimental room and seated in front of an imposing looking shock generator. The generator had 30 lever switches with labeled shock intensities, ranging from 15 volts to 450 volts in 15-volt increments. Below each of the levers there were also verbal descriptions ranging from "Slight Shock" to "Danger: Severe Shock." (The labels below the last two levers were even more ominous; they were devoid of any verbal designation and were simply marked "XXX" (Figure 14.10).

The teacher presented the items that had to be memorized. He was instructed to move on to the next item on the list whenever the learner re-

14.10 The obedience experiment (A) The "shock generator" used in the experiment. (B) The learner is strapped into his chair and electrodes are attached to his wrist. (C) The teacher receives a sample shock. (D) The teacher breaks off the experiment. (Copyright 1965 by Stanley Milgram. From the film Obedience, *distributed by the New York University Film Library*)

sponded correctly but to administer a shock whenever an error was made. He was told to increase the level of punishment with each succeeding error, beginning with 15 volts and going up by one step for each error thereafter until 450 volts was reached. To get an idea what the learner experienced, the teacher first submitted to a sample shock of 45 volts, the third of the 30-step punishment series, which gave an unpleasant jolt. During the experiment, all communications between teacher and learner were conducted over an intercom, since the learner was out of sight, strapped to a chair in the experimental cubicle.

Needless to say the shock generator never delivered any shocks (except for the initial sample) and the lot drawing was rigged so that the learner was always a confederate, played by a mild-mannered, middle-aged actor. The point of the experiment was simply to determine how far the subjects would go in obeying the experimenter's instructions. Since the learner made a fair number of errors, the shock level of the prescribed punishment kept on rising. By the time 120 volts was reached, the victim shouted that the shocks were becoming too painful. At 150 volts he demanded that he be let out of the experiment. At 180 volts, he cried out that he could no longer stand the pain. At 300 volts, he screamed that he would give no further answers and insisted that he be freed. On the next few shocks there were agonized screams. After 330 volts, there was silence.

The learner's responses were of course predetermined. But the real subjects—the teachers—did not know that, so they had to decide what to do. When the victim cried out in pain or refused to go on, the subjects usually turned to the experimenter for instructions. In response, the experimenter told the subjects that the experiment had to go on, indicated that he took full responsibility, and pointed out that "the shocks may be painful but there is no permanent tissue damage."

How far do subjects go in obeying the experimenter? When the study was described to several groups of judges, including a group of forty psychiatrists, all predicted considerable defiance. In their view, only a pathological fringe of at most 2 percent of the subjects would go to the maximum shock intensity. But these predictions were far off the mark. In fact, about 65 percent of Milgram's subjects continued to obey the experimenter to the bitter end. This proportion was unaffected even when the learner mentioned that he suffered from a mild heart condition. This isn't to say that the objedient subjects had no moral qualms. Quite the contrary. Many of them were seriously upset. They bit their lips, twisted their hands, sweated profusely—and obeyed even so.

Is there a parallel between obedience in these artificial laboratory situations and obedience in the all-too-real nightmares of Nazi Germany or My Lai? In some ways, there is no comparison, given the enormous disparities in scope and degree. But Milgram believes that some of the underlying psychological processes may be the same in both cases.

Being another person's agent   In Milgram's view, one of the crucial factors is a socialization history that stresses obedience to legitimate authority, first within the family, then in the school, and still later within the institutional settings of the adult world. The good child does what he is told; the good employee may raise a question but will accept the boss's final decision; the good soldier is not even allowed to question why. As a result, all of us are well practiced in adopting the attitude of an agent who performs an action that is initiated by

14.11   Obedient subject pressing the learner's hand upon the shock electrode (*Copyright 1965 by Stanley Milgram. From the film* Obedience, *distributed by the New York University Film Library*)

someone else. The responsibility belongs to that someone else, and not to us.

This feeling of being another person's agent was repeatedly encountered in Milgram's obedient subjects. When interviewed after the experiment, they said that they felt they had no choice, that the responsibility was not theirs but the experimenter's. Very similar statements were made by the Nazi guards, by Adolf Eichmann, and by Lt. Calley (of the My Lai massacre).

The sense of not being personally responsible is enhanced by any factor that minimizes the awareness of one's own personal identity. An example is a military uniform which tends to make its wearer feel anonymous; if he pulls the trigger, he does so as a faceless agent of his government and not of his own volition. According to one writer, tribal masks serve a similar function in certain primitive cultures. They announce that the wearer is not "personally involved" (Redl, 1973).

Another way of reducing the sense of personal responsibility is by increasing the psychological distance between one's own actions and their end result. This phenomenon has been observed in Milgram's laboratory. In one variation, two teachers were used. One was a confederate who was responsible for administering the shocks; the real subject was engaged in a subsidiary task. In this new role, the subject was still essential to the smooth functioning of the experimental procedure. If he stopped, the victim would receive no further shocks. But he felt much further removed from the ultimate consequence of the procedure, like a minor cog in a bureaucratic machine. Under these conditions, over 90 percent of the subjects went all the way.

In another experimental manipulation, Milgram tried to decrease the psychological distance between what the subject did and its effect upon the victim. Rather than being out of sight in an experimental cubicle, the victim was seated next to the subject who had to administer the shock in a brutally direct manner. He had to press the victim's hand upon a shock electrode, holding it down by force if necessary (Figure 14.11). Compliance dropped considerably, in analogy to the fact that it is easier to drop bombs on an unseen enemy than to plunge a knife into his body when he looks you in the eye. But even so, 30 percent of the subjects reacted with perfect obedience.

Cognitive reinterpretations   To cope with the moral dilemma posed by compliance with immoral orders the obedient person develops an elaborate set of cognitive devices to reinterpret the situation and his own part in it. One of the most common approaches is to put on psychic blinders and try to shut out the awareness that the victim is a living, suffering fellow-being. According to one of Milgram's subjects, "You really begin to forget that there's a guy out there, even though you can hear him. For a long time I just concentrated on pressing the switches and reading the words" (Milgram, 1974, p. 38). This *dehumanization* of the victim is a counterpart to the obedient person's self-picture as an agent of another's will, someone "who has a job to do" and who does it whether he likes it or not. The obedient person sees himself as an instrument; by the same token, he sees the victim as an object. In his eyes, both have become dehumanized.

The dehumanization of the opponent is a common theme in war and mass atrocity.Victims are rarely described as people, but only as bodies, objects, numbers. The process of dehumanization is propped up by euphemisms and bureaucratic jargon. The Nazis used terms such as "final solution" (the mass murder of six million persons) and "special treatment" (death by gassing); the

557

Dehumanizing the victim *As Joseph Goebbels, Hitler's infamous minister of propaganda, put it, "I keep on hearing voices that assert that Jews are also humans. To this I can only reply that bedbugs are also animals, but extremely disagreeable ones." (From a radio broadcast heard in 1938 in Germany; photograph courtesy Photo World)*

nuclear age contributed "fallout problem" and "preemptive attack"; the Vietnam War gave us "free-fire zone" and "body count"—all dry, official phrases that are admirably suited to keep all thoughts of blood and human suffering at a reasonably safe distance.

This cognitive shift of focus allows men to deal inhumanly with other men. But the same mental device is sometimes employed to serve humane and decent goals; for example, by rescue workers at the site of a jetliner crash who have to steel themselves to ignore the mangled remains of the dead while searching for survivors (Bernard, Ottenberg, and Redl, 1965).

By dehumanizing the victim, moral qualms are pushed into the background. But for all but the most brutalized, these qualms can't be banished forever. To justify continued obedience, such queasy feelings may be suppressed by reference to some higher, overriding moral ideology. In Milgram's study, the subjects convinced themselves that science had to be served regardless of the victim's cries; in Nazi Germany, the noble cause was to cleanse humanity by ridding it of Gypsy and Jewish "vermin." In a related kind of self-justification, the fault is projected on the victims; they are subhuman, dirty, evil, and only have themselves to blame. In part, this cognitive reorientation may stem from a primitive belief that by and large the world is "just"; if someone is punished, there is probably a good reason. This general conception has been tested in several laboratory experiments. The results suggest that persons who suffer some misfortune are judged to have deserved it (Lerner, 1971). An extreme example of the same phenomenon was reported when the British forced a group of German civilians to march through a nearby Nazi death camp in the days just after the war. One of the civilians was overheard to remark, "What terrible criminals these prisoners must have been to get such punishment" (Cohn, in Dicks, 1972, p. 262).

The cognitive reorientation by which a person no longer feels responsible for his own acts is not achieved in an instant. Usually, inculcation is by gradual steps. The initial act of obedience is relatively mild and does not seriously clash with the person's own moral outlook. Escalation is gradual so that each step seems only slightly different from the one before. This of course was the pattern in Milgram's study. A similar program of progressive escalation was evidently used in the indoctrination of death-camp guards. The same is true for the military training of soldiers everywhere. Draftees go through "basic training," in part to learn various military skills, but much more important, to acquire the habit of instant obedience. Raw recruits are rarely asked to point their guns at another person and shoot. It's not only that they don't know how; most of them probably *wouldn't* do it.

EVALUATIONS OF OBEDIENCE RESEARCH

Some questions of method Studies of obedience have been attacked on several grounds; some involve questions of methodology. Martin Orne raises serious doubts about the way in which the subjects in a social psychology experiment interpret the situations in which they are placed. The trouble is that in so many social psychology experiments things aren't really what they seem to be; the "learner" isn't really shocked, the 8-inch line isn't really shorter than the 6½-inch line, and so on. Instead, there is an elaborately staged production with props (the shock generator) and actors (confederates) to create a particular impression. But is this desired impression really created? Some subjects may become suspicious and catch on to the trick. Others may not see through the deception, but they may nevertheless fail to make the interpretation the experimenter wants them to make.

According to Orne, subjects try to guess the purpose of the study in which they are participating by using all available cues, including campus rumors, the total setting, the experimenter's behavior, and so on. The totality of these cues, the **demand characteristics** of the situation, are used by the subject to determine what is really demanded. One result is that an experimenter's hypothesis is sometimes confirmed, not because it is true, but because the subject picked up a cue about what the experimenter expected (Orne, 1962). An illustration is provided by so-called **experimenter effects.** These have been studied by an investigator who asked different graduate students to serve as experimenters for the same experiment. He told some that he expected one outcome while informing others that he expected the very opposite. The results showed that there was a small but reliable bias in line with the experimenters' expectations (Rosenthal, 1967).

Orne argues that a related interpretation applies to the obedience studies. The demand characteristics of the Milgram experiment might have shown the subjects that no serious hurt is really inflicted (Orne and Holland, 1968). If so, the behavior of one of Milgram's subjects is comparable to that of a member of an audience who is asked to come on stage and help the magician saw a lady in two. He complies and dutifully does what the magician tells him to because he has no doubt that, whatever the trick, the lady will still be in one piece after the curtain comes down.

This hypothesis may explain the behavior of some of Milgram's subjects, but it probably does not apply to all or even most of them (Milgram, 1972). Milgram's subjects were not college students who might be expected to be wise in the ways of psychological experiments; they were a cross-section of the population. When questioned after the study, the majority of them seemed to have no doubts about the genuineness of the situation and their tendency to comply was not much different from that of subjects who expressed some skepticism (Milgram, 1972; Rosenhan, 1974). Some of the obedient subjects later wrote to Milgram to tell him that the experience had shaken them deeply. One became a conscientious objector because of it. Surely he must have thought that the situation was real enough. A further point concerns Milgram's finding that better educated people were somewhat more defiant. A demand-characteristics hypothesis might be expected to produce the opposite result; the more sophisticated subjects would be more likely to see through the ruse and hence more likely to comply. In any case, results much like Milgram's have been obtained in an obedience study with an authentic victim; about 50 percent of a group of college students went all the way in administering genuine electric shock to a cute, little puppy whose distress and howls of pain they could see and hear (Sheridan and King, 1972).

Some questions of ethics Once one assumes that subjects accept the experiment as genuine, the Milgram study raises serious ethical issues. To be sure, the victim received no shocks, but the subjects thought he did and that they inflicted them. Many of them were horrified at what they had done. Did the investigator have the right to subject them to this kind of anguish (Baumrind,

1964)? Milgram countered that he thoroughly "debriefed" the subjects after the experiment was completed. He explained the point of the study, arranged for a "reconciliation" meeting with the victim, and so on. But can this debriefing really erase the memory of what the subject did; might there not be some lasting changes in self-perception and self-esteem despite the fact that the subject later found out that it was "all a trick"? In response, Milgram reports the results of a follow-up questionnaire he gave to his subjects. Less than 2 percent indicated that they were sorry to have participated. In fact, some of them said that they had gained some important personal insights and thought that they would be less likely to yield in blind obedience thereafter (Milgram, 1964). But did the investigator have the right to change any other person—even if for the better—without that person's prior consent (Kelman, 1967)? After all, the laboratory is not a therapist's office nor were the subjects patients who had previously said that they wanted to be changed.

Yet another argument concerns the ultimate value of the research to scientific understanding. Such understanding may ultimately help all of us, and this benefit may offset the harm (if any) to the individual subject. But how do we estimate these values? And more important yet, how do we balance them against each other, to decide how much potential scientific gain is worth a particular personal cost to an individual subject? If Milgram's study were about a trivial matter, the answer might be easy. But it obviously isn't; it concerns a topic that is all too relevant to us today. Under the circumstances there are no easy answers; but then moral questions are generally the most difficult ones.

It is obvious that these ethical concerns are not unique to obedience studies. Similar issues arise in considering many other experiments in psychology, some of which are likely to produce pain or discomfort and sometimes involve a form of deception. Under these conditions subjects are really deprived of their free choice; they do not know what they are letting themselves in for. Many psychologists are painfully aware of the moral dilemma posed by research of this sort. One prescription is an increased emphasis on the postexperimental session in which the true purpose of the experiment is explained to the subjects and every attempt is made to have them feel good about themselves and about their role in the experiment, a not unreasonable repayment for their contribution to the scientific enterprise (Aronson, 1972).

Some implications of objedience research In summary, Milgram's results show—if various methodological qualms can be set aside—that for a large proportion of people, obedience to legitimate authority seems to take precedence over the demands of their own consciences. By obeying, the subjects show that social behavior isn't always appropriate to one's own interpretation of the situation; there are occasions when one relinquishes the effort to make sense of the world and delegates this responsibility to others, accepting their definition of what is and what ought to be. This is not to say that the obedient person has stopped cognitive functioning. Of course he continues to think and to try to interpret events; but he thinks about subsidiary matters like how to proceed when the victim no longer answers, about means rather than ends. The end itself—the experiment which requires that the victim be punished—is not questioned. It has been formulated by someone else—the experimenter.

The Milgram studies, let alone the horrible real-life events on which they were modeled, demonstrate the evils that can result from obedience. But there is a grim irony in the fact that some degree of obedience to legitimate authority is probably a necessary prerequisite for any organized social order. Our society depends upon an intricate network of authority relationships and many of them make excellent sense, as when a doctor tells a nurse what medication to give to a patient. But this very facility for obedience may become the instrument for our ultimate destruction. As Milgram puts it, "It is ironic that the virtues of loyalty, discipline, and self-sacrifice that we value so highly in the individual are the very properties that create destructive organizational engines of war and bind men to malevolent systems of authority" (Milgram, 1974, p. 188).

THE BEHAVIOR OF CROWDS

The obedient person may perform acts that he would never engage in as a private individual, but we have seen that we can nevertheless explain some aspects of his behavior by asking how he interprets the situation in which he is placed. A similar point applies to the behavior of crowds in riots or panics. On the face of it, their behavior appears irrational. But here too, cognitive factors play a vital role.

There is little doubt that under some circumstances people in crowds behave differently from the way they do when alone. They occasionally express aggression at a level of bestial violence that would be inconceivable if they acted in isolation. A gruesome example was the lynch mob of the American South. These mobs murdered some two thousand persons, mostly blacks, in the first fifty years of this century, often after hideous tortures. On other occasions, crowds may become frantically fearful. An example is the panic that may sweep a tightly packed theater auditorium when someone shouts "Fire." The resulting stampede will often claim many more victims than the fire as such. One such case occurred when a fire broke out in a Chicago theater in 1903. There were 602 victims. Many of them died because they blocked the exits or jammed the stairways in their frightened rush to escape; they were smothered or trampled to death by the surging mass of those behind them. Others jumped to their deaths off the packed fire escapes or were pushed off by the fear-frenzied crowd. When the firemen later disentangled the bodies, "the heel prints on the dead faces mutely testified to the cruel fact that human animals stricken by terror are as mad and ruthless as stampeding cattle" (Foy and Harlow, 1928, quoted in Brown, 1965, p. 715).

What does the crowd do to the individual to make him act so differently from his everyday self? According to one view, it transforms him completely until his behavior is no longer describable by the usual laws that apply to individual functioning. He becomes wild, stupid, and irrational as he gives vent to primitive impulses that are normally suppressed. The foremost exponent of this position was Gustav Le Bon (1841–1931), a French journalist of conservative political leanings whose disdain for the masses was reflected in his theory of crowd behavior. According to Le Bon, persons in a crowd become alike. They infect each other with whatever emotion they may feel. This emotion rises to an ever-higher pitch as more and more crowd members are affected. In consequence, fear becomes panic and hostility turns into murderous rage. In the grip of such intense passions, the crowd members become creatures of impulse rather than reason. As Le Bon put it,

By the mere fact that he forms part of an organized crowd, a man descends several rungs in the ladder of civilization; in a crowd, he is a barbarian—that is, a creature acting by instinct. . . . [He can be] induced to commit acts contrary to his most obvious interests and best known habits. An individual in a crowd is a grain of sand amid other grains of sand, which the wind stirs up at will (Le Bon, 1895).

THE PANICKY CROWD

A cognitive analysis of panic   Is crowd behavior really as irrational as Le Bon held it to be? The example of panic described above testifies to the fact that people in groups sometimes act in ways that have disastrous consequences which none of them foresaw or desired. This shows that crowd behavior can be profoundly maladaptive, but does it prove that the individual members of the crowd acted irrationally? Several social psychologists have argued that it does not (Brown, 1965). They point out that in certain situations such as fires in crowded auditoriums the optimum solution for all participants (that is, escape for all) can only come about if they all trust one another to behave cooperatively (that is, not to run for the exits). If this trust is lacking, each individual will do the next best thing given her motives and her expectations of what others will do. She will run to the exit because she is sure that everyone else will do the same, hoping that if she runs quickly enough she will get there before them. The trouble is that all others make the same assumption that she does, and so they all arrive more or less together, jam the exit, and perish.

According to this cognitive interpretation, intense fear as such will not produce crowd panic, contrary to Le Bon's assertion. What matters are people's beliefs about escape routes. If they think that the routes for escape (the

theater exits) are open and readily accessible, they will not stampede. Nor will panic develop if all escape routes are thought to be completely blocked, as in a mine collapse or a submarine explosion. Such disasters may lead to terror or apathetic collapse; but there will be none of the chaos that characterizes a panicky crowd. For panic to occur, the exits from danger must be seen to be limited or closing. In that case, each individual may well think that he can escape only if he rushes ahead of the others. If everyone thinks this way, panic may ensue (Smelser, 1963).

The prisoner's dilemma   Roger Brown believes that some facets of escape panic can be understood in terms of a problem taken from the mathematical theory of games (Brown, 1965). It is generally known as the **prisoner's dilemma** (Luce and Raiffa, 1957). Consider the hypothetical problem of two men arrested on suspicion of bank robbery. The district attorney needs a confession to guarantee conviction. He hits on a diabolical plan. He talks to each prisoner separately and offers each a simple choice—confess or stay silent. But he tells each man that the consequences will depend not just on what he does, but also on his partner's choice. If both confess, he will recommend an intermediate sentence of, say, eight years in prison for each. If neither confesses, he will be unable to prosecute them for robbery but he will charge them with a lesser crime such as illegal possession of a gun and both will get one year in jail. But suppose one confesses and the other does not? In this case the two men will be dealt with very differently. The one who confesses will be treated with extra leniency for turning state's evidence; he will receive a suspended sentence and won't go to jail at all. But the one who remains silent will feel the full force of the law. The D.A. will recommend the maximum penalty of twenty years.

As the situation is set up, there are four possible combinations of what the prisoners may do. Both may remain silent; Prisoner A may confess while B does not; B may confess while A does not; both may confess. Each of the four sets of decisions has a different consequence or *payoff* for each of the two prisoners. The four sets of decisions and the payoffs associated with each are presented in the payoff matrix in Table 14.1. (For a discussion of payoff matrices in the context of detection experiments, see the Appendix to Chapter 6.)

Table 14.1   PAYOFF MATRIX FOR PRISONERS' DILEMMA

		Prisoner B:	
		Stays silent	Confesses
Prisoner A:	Stays silent	1 year for *A* 1 year for *B*	20 years for *A* No jail for *B*
	Confesses	No jail for *A* 20 years for *B*	8 years for *A* 8 years for *B*

Given this payoff matrix, what can the prisoners do? If both remain silent, the consequence is reasonably good for each of them. But how can either be sure that his partner won't double-cross him? If A remains silent while B tells all, B is even better off than he would be if both kept quiet; he stays out of jail entirely, while poor, silent A gets 20 years. Can A take the chance that B will not confess? Conversely, can B take this chance on A? The best bet is that they will *both* confess. The D.A. will get his conviction and both men will get eight years.

In a sense, the prisoners' behavior is maladaptive, for the outcome is far from optimum for each. But this doesn't mean that either of the two men behaved irrationally. On the contrary. Paradoxically enough, each picked the most rational course of action considering that he couldn't be sure how his partner would decide. Under the circumstances, each man had to act so as to maximize his own payoff regardless of what the partner does. Consider Prisoner A. Confession will yield him a better outcome than silence, whatever decision B might make—no jail instead of one year if B stays silent, eight years instead of twenty if B confesses. The same holds for B. Each individual acted as rationally as possible; the ironic upshot was an unsatisfactory outcome for each. In the best of all possible worlds they would have been able to trust each other, would have remained silent, and been in jail for a much shorter period.

Prisoner's dilemma and panic The underlying logic of the prisoner's dilemma applies to various social interactions whose payoff matrix is formally analogous. Brown has shown how it pertains to panic. Here there are more than two participants, but the essential ingredients are much the same. Each individual in the burning auditorium has two choices—she can wait her turn to get to the exit or she can rush ahead. What are the probable outcomes? As in the case of the prisoners, they partially depend upon what others in the auditorium (especially those nearby) will do. If the individual rushes to the exit and everyone else does too, they will all probably suffer severe injuries and run some risk of death. If she takes her turn and others decorously do the same, the outcome is better; they will probably all escape, though they may suffer some minor injuries. The best outcome for the individual is produced if she ruthlessly pushes herself ahead of the others while the others continue to file out slowly. In this case *she* will surely escape without a blister, but the chances for the others to escape are lessened. Suppose the situation is reversed so that the individual waits her turn while everyone near her runs ahead? Now the others may very well get out without injury while she herself may die. These sets of decisions and their associated outcomes represent just another version of the prisoner's dilemma, which are shown in the payoff matrix of Table 14.2.

Given the payoff matrix of Table 14.2, most persons will probably opt to rush ahead rather than wait their turn. As in the case of the two prisoners, this solution is grossly maladaptive, but from the point of view of each separate individual it is, sadly enough, quite rational. We again face the peculiar irony of the prisoner's dilemma. As Brown notes, "This irony about escape behavior . . . is always worked over by newspaper editorialists after panic occurs. 'If only everyone had stayed calm and taken his turn, then . . .'" (Brown, 1965, p. 741).

Brown's model of panic applies only if certain qualifications are met. As already noted, the danger must seem serious enough and the escape routes must appear to be inadequate. Another factor is the strength of certain social inhibitions. Most of us have been socialized to act with some modicum of respect for others; pushing ahead is socially disapproved and would therefore

Table 14.2 PAYOFF MATRIX FOR AN INDIVIDUAL *(I)* AND OTHERS *(O)* IN A BURNING AUDITORIUM

		Others (O):	
		Take turns	Rush ahead
Individual (I):	Takes turn	Minor injuries for *I* Minor injuries for *O*	Increased change of death for *I* No injuries for *O*
	Rushes ahead	No injuries for *I* Increased chance of death for *O*	Severe injuries for *I* Severe injuries for *O*

contribute a negative value to the relevant cells in the payoff matrix. The weight of this factor depends on the situation. If the fire seems minor enough, the embarrassment at behaving discourteously (or acting like a coward) might outweigh the fear of being the last to escape. If so, the payoff matrix will not be that of the prisoner's dilemma and no panic will ensue. Another factor is the person's role. Consider the sinking ship which appears not to have enough lifeboats. There is a long socialization history that insists on "women and children first." For many adult males, the idea of shoving women and children aside to secure a place in the lifeboat is repugnant; its negative value may overpower the fear of drowning. Under the circumstances, the payoff matrix is not one that would produce panic.

Some economic applications A similar analysis can be applied to certain patterns of economic behavior. An example is a run on the bank. In the days before the New Deal, the payoff matrix was such that individual rationality led to collective disaster. Each depositor who crowded up to the teller's window to withdraw his savings was acting sensibly enough. Had he waited until

A run on the Nineteenth Ward Bank in New York City in the early 1900s
(*Courtesy Library of Congress*)

tomorrow, the bank might have failed and he would have been left without a cent. Since most depositors felt the same way, the bank finally did fail; and so of course did countless others throughout the country, with catastrophic effects on the entire economy. Here was a prisoner's dilemma that affected an entire nation. Its essential nature was captured in Franklin D. Roosevelt's famous slogan, "We have nothing to fear but fear itself." As in a theater fire, one way of minimizing fear was to assure everyone of a guaranteed exit. In the case of the banks, it was a federal insurance plan for bank deposits.

A final example is the speculative boom in which people vie furiously with each other to obtain some scarce commodity such as a share of stock or a piece of real estate. As individuals compete, the prices rise higher and higher. Once again, here is crowd behavior that at first glance appears irrational. But again, each individual acts rationally. The true villain is another prisoner's dilemma. It differs from those we have discussed before in only one regard. In the previous payoff matrices the choice was between a negative outcome and one that is even worse—one or eight years in prison, third- or first-degree burns. In the speculative boom, the choice (or so the speculators think) is between a smaller and a larger gain—getting a moderate profit or making a killing. Each investor tries to buy the stock or the piece of land ahead of everyone else, while it is still a bargain. But since many others have the same idea, the net effect is to drive the price ever-higher. The boom finally reaches a crest and is then followed by a bust, as more and more persons realize that the actual worth of the items is much less than their price. The effect is reversed. Panic results as each stock- or landowner tries to sell before the price falls even lower. The inevitable result is a complete price collapse (Smelser, 1963).

THE HOSTILE CROWD

The preceding discussion has shown that there is a plausible explanation for crowd panic, based on the laws of individual behavior. There is thus no need to appeal to some new principles of "mob psychology" according to which men are transformed into savage beasts as Le Bon had claimed. Can the same be said about the behavior of violent crowds whose frenzy is turned either against defenseless victims (as in lynchings or pogroms) or against another group that fights back (as in many riots)? Can such hostile group acts also be understood by reference to the laws of individual behavior?

Most modern social psychologists believe that the answer is yes. Of course, the specific explanation must be different from that which handles panic. In panic, the members of the group are essentially all competing with one another. If there is a fire or a run on the bank, their governing philosophy is to "Let the Devil Take the Hindmost"; in consequence, he often takes them all. In lynching or rioting mobs, there is no such within-group competition. On the contrary, the members of the crowd are united, against others outside of their group. We will consider one example taken from a shameful page of American history—the lynching of blacks in the rural South.

The motives for lynching What motives impelled the lynchers, who often tortured and mulilated their victims and finally burnt them alive? There is little doubt that one major purpose was to maintain the unequal status of blacks. While lynching has an early history that goes back to the frontier days

A lynching in the South, 1882 (Courtesy The Bettmann Archive)

of the West, blacks did not become its primary victims until some time after the Civil War. From then on, lynching became a bloody instrument to maintain social and economic control over the newly freed slaves, to "keep them in their place." It was a response to threatening signs of defiance and assertion; the mere suspicion of an attack on a white person was often grounds enough. The horrible fate of the victim would then serve as a warning to other blacks. It is probably no accident that lynchings were comparatively uncommon in Southern counties run on the plantation system in which blacks worked as tenant farmers and wage hands. Here the caste system was so sharply drawn that whites saw little threat. Lynchings were more prevalent in poor rural communities in which blacks were a minority who often competed economically with lower-class whites (Brown, 1954).

Many authors believe that an additional motive for lynching was displaced aggression (see Chapter 12). The life of the poor white in the rural South was filled with many social and economic frustrations. As we have previously seen, frustration often begets aggression (see Chapter 5). But toward whom should this aggression be directed? The black was an all too convenient target.

Overcoming social prohibitions However intense the individual mob member's hatred, it would probably not suffice to make him kill and torture were he alone. There are various social restraints on violence, some based on fear of retribution, others on internalized moral qualms. The presence of others somehow weakens these restraints. The question is how.

One of the key factors is the perception of unanimity. This enhances each crowd member's belief in the righteousness of his actions. More important, it produces a sense of ***diffusion of responsibility.*** There is a diminished fear of retribution. When there are dozens of participants, it becomes harder to determine what each of them actually did. The same applies to the person's own sense of guilt, which becomes diluted by the fact that there are so many others. (A similar diffusion effect occurs in a firing squad whose members know that only some of the rifles are loaded with real bullets while the rest contain blanks.)

14.12 The apparent homogeneity of a crowd *(A) A long-shot view of a crowd of students surrounding Nelson Rockefeller during a 1964 campaign address. (B) An enlargement of a part of the photograph shows that the crowd is not as homogeneous as it may appear at first. Some members of the crowd look at Rockefeller, others look away, and so on. (Milgram and Toch, 1969; Wide World Photos)*

A

Yet another effect of the appearance of unanimity is that it leads to ***pluralistic ignorance*** among the waiverers in the crowd. In actuality, the crowd is not as homogeneous as it seems (few crowds are; see Figure 14.12). But the waiverers don't know that. They hear only the vociferous clamors for violence, assume that they are alone in their opposition, and therefore go along, in ignorance of the fact that there are others who feel as they do.

THE APATHETIC CROWD

Diffusion of responsibility helps to allay moral misgivings in a crowd bent on violence; everyone feels that if all join in, none can be blamed. A similar effect may explain why city dwellers sometimes ignore a stranger's cry for help. The classic example is the tragic case of Kitty Genovese who was attacked and murdered on an early morning in 1964 on a street corner in Queens, New York. The assault lasted over half an hour, during which time she screamed and struggled while her assailant stabbed her repeatedly until she finally died. It later developed that thirty-eight of her neighbors had watched the episode from their windows. But none of them came to her aid; no one even called the police (Rosenthal, 1964). Why this appalling inactivity?

To answer this question we must first ask how the individual interprets the situation he confronts. Consider the passerby who sees a man lying unconscious on a city street. How can he tell whether the man is ill or is merely drunk? A similar confusion troubled some of the witnesses to the Genovese slaying. They later reported that they weren't quite sure what was going on. Perhaps it was a joke, a drunken bout, or a lovers' quarrel; were it any of these, intervention might have proven very embarrassing. One reason for failure to act in an emergency is that the emergency is not recognized as such.

But suppose the emergency *is* recognized, as it probably was by many of those who watched Kitty Genovese die. To understand why they failed to act

(Photograph by Susan Shapiro)

even so, we have to realize that they were all in an implicit crowd situation. Like the passerby on the city street, they knew that many others watched the same scene. As a result, they felt a diffusion of responsibility. The witness or the passerby may want to help but they also have self-centered motives that hold them back. Some of the witnesses of the Genovese murder later explained that they didn't want to get involved, that they were afraid of the assailant, or that they were apprehensive about dealing with the police. The conflict between the desire to help and to mind one's own business was finally resolved in favor of inaction through the knowledge that others witnessed the same event. Everyone assumed that someone else would do something or had already done it (such as calling the police); as a result, no one did anything.

Responsibility diffusion has essentially the same effect in the violent crowd and in the implicit crowd situation produced by the city dweller's cry for help. In both cases it tips the scale against personal morality. In the violent crowd, it leads all mob members to join in a hideous act of *commission*—the lynching. In the crowd of onlookers, it makes all witnesses perform an unfeeling act of *omission*—the failure to help.

This general line of thinking has been tested in several experiments on **bystander intervention.** In one study, subjects were asked to participate in what they thought was a group discussion about college life with either one, three, or five other persons. The subjects were placed in individual cubicles and took turns in talking to each other over an intercom system. In actuality, there was only one subject; all the other discussants were tape recordings. The discussion began as one of the (tape-recorded) confederates described some of his personal problems, which included a tendency toward epileptic seizures in times of stress. When he began to speak again during the second round of talking, he feigned a seizure and gasped for help. The question was whether the subjects would leave their own cubicles to assist the stricken victim (usually, by asking the experimenter's help). The results were in accord with the diffusion of responsibility hypothesis. The larger the size of the group which the subject thought he was in, the less likely he was to come to the victim's assistance (Darley and Latané, 1968).

Some further studies have shown that the effect of other bystanders depends on what the subject thinks about their competence in the situation. In one experiment, the subject was convinced that the only other person who knew about the emergency was in another building, too far to help. The result was that the subject responded as quickly as if he had been alone; under the circumstances, there was no one to whom he could pass the buck (Bickman, 1971). Conversely, the subject will tend to do nothing if he believes that another bystander is better qualified to handle the problem. Thus subjects in a variation of the epileptic-seizure experiment were less likely to intervene if they thought that one of the other members of the discussion group was a medical student (Schwartz and Clausen, 1970).

The Generality of Social Psychology

In the preceding pages we considered some of the situational factors of the present that are the concern of social psychology: how the individual interprets the social world, how he tries to render it meaningful and consistent, how

569

he perceives the motives and acts of others and of his own self. We then turned to several phenomena that at first glance seemed incompatible with a cognitive approach—blind obedience to inhuman commands and various crowd reactions. But on closer inspection, we saw that some of the same cognitive factors still apply. To understand obedience one has to ask how the individual reinterprets what he is asked to do; to comprehend a panic one must consider the crowd members' assumptions about the availability of exits and about the behavior of others around them.

It appears that social psychology has contributed to our understanding of social behavior. But how broadly applicable is this understanding? Does it bring us closer to an understanding of basic human nature or is it necessarily limited to our own time and place? Could it be that the discoveries of modern social psychology reveal something only about our own social and cultural circumstances and cannot be generalized beyond them?

Some authors believe that this is indeed the case. In their view, many of the assertions of modern social psychology hold true only for our own present-day culture. Perhaps consistency, attribution of motives, self-perception, obedience, diffusion of responsibility, and so on, are patterns of behavior that are specific to twentieth-century industrialized society, and don't describe how people act and think in other places and other times (Gergen, 1973). This culture-specific critique may be a valuable corrective to the notion that a genuine science of the psychology of social behavior can be developed in isolation from other social disciplines such as anthropology, sociology, economics, political science, and history. To understand the social situation the individual confronts, one has to refer to many cultural (or sociological or historical or political or economic) factors that transcend the individual. As a result, social psychology cannot prosper as a self-contained island of knowledge.

Many modern social psychologists subscribe to similar anti-isolationist sentiments (Pepitone, 1976). But this does not mean that they hold the pessimistic belief that there are no general laws of social behavior (Schlenker, 1974). Perhaps some of the formulations of modern social psychology are indeed culture-specific. But if so—and this is an empirical issue that requires cross-cultural research—it shows only that our existing formulations are not general enough and that we must look for some deeper regularities of human social life.

In any case, there are reasons to believe that human social nature is not as unstable as the culture-specific critique assumes it to be. Such diverse political theorists as Aristotle, Hobbes, and Machiavelli are still read despite the fact that they lived many centuries ago and under very different political systems than our own; they wrote about characteristics of human social behavior that we can recognize even today. History provides many other examples of enduring social reactions. There are records of panics in Roman amphitheaters when the stands collapsed, of riots during sports events in Byzantium, and of murderous mobs in medieval Europe. The cast and costumes differ, but the basic plots were much the same as now. Some of the ancients even used certain of our modern propaganda devices. When the city of Pompeii was destroyed by a volcano in 79 A.D., it was evidently in the midst of a municipal election. Modern archeologists have found some of the election slogans on the excavated walls: "Vote for Vatius, all the whoremasters vote for him" and

"Vote for Vatius, all the wife-beaters vote for him." While the techniques of the anti-Vatius faction may be a bit crude for our modern taste, they certainly prove that the psychology of the smear campaign has a venerable history (Raven and Rubin, 1976).

Phenomena of this sort suggest that there are some invariant properties of human social behavior which can provide the foundation for a genuine science of social psychology.

Summary

1. Social behavior depends in part on how people interpret situations they encounter. The processes that lead to such interpretations are in many ways similar to those that underlie cognitive processes in general.

2. Our conception of what is real is heavily affected by confirmation from others, as shown by Asch's study on the effects of group pressure and by the need for *social comparison,* especially in ambiguous or frightening situations.

3. To make sense of the world, people look for *cognitive consistency.* According to *dissonance theory,* they will do what they can to reduce any inconsistency (dissonance) they perceive by reinterpreting information to fit in with their *beliefs, attitudes,* and *prejudices.* They will also reevaluate their own motives to fit in with their own acts, as shown by studies on *forced compliance.*

4. The way we perceive others is in some ways similar to the way we perceive inanimate objects or events. *Impressions of others* can be regarded as Gestalt patterns whose elements are interpreted in terms of the whole, thus accounting for related phenomena such as *primacy effects* in impression formation.

5. *Attribution theory* tries to explain how we infer the causes of another person's behavior by attributing them either to *situational factors* or *dispositional qualities.* In judging others, we tend to underestimate the role of the first and to overestimate that of the second.

6. According to *self-perception theory* similar attribution processes determine how we perceive our own selves. An example is Schachter and Singer's revision of the *James-Lange theory of emotions.* This revision argues that the emotion we feel is an interpretation of our own autonomic arousal in the light of the situation to which we attribute it.

7. Our perception of people is further complicated by the fact that they know they are being perceived which may create attempts at *impression management.* Further complications arise because social communications are often *keyed* to provide the context in which the message should be taken.

8. Some social behaviors seem irrational. An example is *blind obedience.* This has sometimes been ascribed to factors within the person, as in studies on the *authoritarian personality.* But situational factors may be even more important, as shown by Milgram's obedience studies. His findings suggest that obedience is partially caused by *depersonalization* and *cognitive reinterpretation,* though some of his results may have been a side product of the *demand characteristics* of his experimental situation.

9. Another kind of apparent irrationality characterizes the *behavior of crowds,* as in *panics.* Such social behavior may not be as irrational as it appears. The *prisoner's dilemma* shows that under certain conditions there can be collective irrationality even

571

though all of the participants behave rationally as individuals. This analysis probably applies to many group panics.

10. Other forms of apparently irrational crowd behavior are violent *group hostility* and *apathy*. Here, too, part of the explanation lies in the way the individual members of the group interpret the situation. An important factor is *diffusion of responsibility* which applies both to sins of commission (as in rioting mobs) and sins of omission (as in *bystander apathy*).

PART IV

Individual Differences

People are different. They vary in bodily characteristics such as height, weight, strength, and hair color. They also vary along many psychological dimensions. They may be proud or humble, adventurous or timid, gregarious or withdrawn, intelligent or dull—the list of psychological distinctions is very large. Thus far such individual differences have not been our main concern. Our emphasis has been on attempts to find general psychological laws that apply to all persons, whether in physiological function, perception, memory, learning, or social behavior. To be sure, we have occasionally dealt with individual differences, as in the discussions of handedness, color blindness, variations in imagery, and differences in the need for achievement. But our focus was not on these differences as such; it was rather on what they could tell us about people in general—on how color blindness could help to explain the underlying mechanisms of color vision or how variations in the strength of the achievement motive could help us understand some aspects of socialization. In effect, our concern was with the nature of humankind, not with particular men and women.

We now change our emphasis and will consider individual differences as a topic in its own right. We will first deal with the measurement of psychological attributes, specifically intelligence and personality traits. We will then turn to the discussion of psychopathology and attempts to treat it, a field in which the fact that people are in some ways different—sometimes all too different—is starkly clear.

CHAPTER 15

Intelligence: Its Nature and Measurement

In twentieth-century industrialized society, especially in the United States, the description of individual differences is a flourishing enterprise that has produced a multitude of psychological tests to assess various personal characteristics, especially those that pertain to intellectual aptitude. This effort is a relatively recent phenomenon, for until the turn of the century most psychologists preferred to study the "generalized human mind" without worrying about the fact that different minds are not identical.

As we will see, the interest in individual differences grew in part from an effort to apply evolutionary ideas to humanity itself. But even more important was the social climate of the times which provided a fertile soil for such concerns. The study of individual differences makes little sense in a society in which each person's adult role is fully determined by the social circumstances of his or her birth. In a caste society there is no need for vocational counselors or personnel managers. In such a society farmers beget farmers, soldiers beget soldiers, and princes beget princes; there is no point in administering mental tests to assist in educational selection or job placement. The interest in human differences arises only if such differences matter, if there is a social system that will accommodate them.

In a complex, industrialized society like our own, with its many different socioeconomic niches and some mobility across them, we have the precondition for a systematic assessment of human characteristics. Such a society will try to find a means, however imperfect, for selecting the proper person to occupy the proper niche.

Mental tests were meant to supply this means. They were devised as an instrument to help in educational and occupational selection, for use in various forms of personal guidance and diagnosis. As such, they are often regarded as one of the major contributions of psychology to the world of practical affairs. However, for this very reason, the discussion of test results and applications necessarily touches upon social and political issues that go beyond the usual confines of scientific discourse. Under the circumstances, it is hardly surprising that some of the questions raised by testing, especially intelligence testing, are often debated in an emotionally charged atmosphere. Should a student be denied admission to a college because of his or her scholastic aptitude test score? Are such tests fair to disadvantaged ethnic or racial groups? Are scores on such tests determined by heredity, by environment, by both? This chapter will not be able to provide definitive answers to all of these questions. Some involve value judgments about social and political matters; others hinge on as yet unresolved issues of fact. Our primary purpose is to provide a background against which such questions have to be evaluated.

The Basis of Mental Tests

Mental tests come in different varieties. Some are tests of *achievement;* they measure what an individual can do *now,* his present knowledge and competence in a given area—how well he understands computer language or how well he can draw. Other tests are tests of *aptitude;* they predict what an individual will be able to do *later,* given the proper training and the right motivation. An example is a test of mechanical aptitude, which tries to determine the likelihood that an individual will do well as an engineer after an appropriate training period. *Intelligence tests* are sometimes considered as tests of a very general cognitive aptitude, including the ability to benefit from schooling. Still another kind of test is a *test of personality,* which tries to assess an individual's characteristic behavior dispositions—whether she is generally outgoing or withdrawn, placid or moody, and so on.

We will begin our discussion by considering the nature of mental tests in general, regardless of what in particular they try to measure. We must begin by realizing that mental tests are in many ways different from tests used in medicine and the physical sciences. To be sure, there is a similarity on the face of it. A high score on a psychological test, such as a mechanical aptitude test, suggests a better than average ability for work in engineering; a certain reaction on chemical tests used by obstetricians indicates pregnancy. But there are some important differences as well. For one thing, the relation between the test result and what it signifies is much more tenuous in psychology than in the physical or biological sciences. To begin with, there is a difference in predictive accuracy. A high mechanical aptitude test score makes it more likely that the individual will succeed in engineering, while a certain chemical reaction on the obstetrician's test makes pregnancy a virtual certainty. More important yet is the fact that for most medical tests we have a much better understanding of why the test result signifies what it does. When a physician diagnoses the heart's condition from an electrocardiogram, the inference is fairly direct, for the test provides a graphic record of the heartbeat. Mental testers are usually

Table 15.1 QUETELET'S
DISTRIBUTIONS OF CHEST MEASURES
OF SCOTTISH SOLDIERS

Measures of the chest in inches	Number of men per 1,000
33	4
34	31
35	141
36	322
37	732
38	1,305
39	1,867
40	1,882
41	1,628
42	1,148
43	645
44	160
45	87
46	38
47	7
48	2

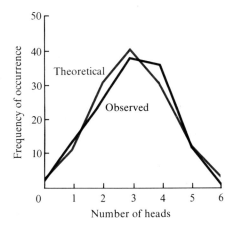

15.1 *Theoretical and observed distribution of number of heads in 128 throws of six coins* (After Anastasi, 1958)

in a less fortunate situation, for they can point to few theoretical links between their tests and what these tests try to measure. To understand the reasoning that underlies the construction and use of mental tests, we will have to take a detour and look at the general problem of variability and of its measurement.

VARIATION AND COVARIATION

The study of how individuals vary from each other grew up in close association with the development of statistical methods. Until the nineteenth century, the term *statistics* meant little more than the systematic collection of various state records (*state*-istics) such as birth and death rates or the physical measurements of army recruits. In poring over such figures, the Belgian scientist Adolphe Quetelet (1796–1874) saw that many of them fell into a pattern. From this, he determined the ***frequency distribution*** of various sets of observations, that is, the frequency with which individual cases are distributed over different intervals along some measure. For example, he plotted the frequency distribution of the chest expansion of Scottish soldiers, noting the number of cases that fell into various intervals, from 33 to 33.9 inches, 34 to 34.9 inches, and so on (Table 15.1).

VARIABILITY

Two facts are immediately apparent. The scores tend to cluster around a central value. One of the most common measures of this central tendency is the ***mean,*** or average, which is obtained by summing all of the values and dividing by the total number of cases. But the clustering tendency is by no means perfect, for there is variability around the average. All Scottish soldiers are not alike, whether in their chest sizes or anything else. An important measure of variability in a distribution is the ***variance*** (V). This is computed by taking the difference between each score and the mean, squaring this difference, and then taking the average of these squared differences. For many purposes, a more useful measure of variability is the ***standard deviation*** (SD) which is simply the square root of the variance.*

Quetelet's main contribution was the realization that, when put on a graph, the frequency distributions of various human physical attributes have a characteristic bell-shaped form. This symmetrical curve approximates the so-called ***normal curve*** which had already been studied by mathematicians in connection with games of chance. The normal curve describes the probability of obtaining certain combinations of chance events. Suppose, for example, that someone has the patience to throw six coins for over a hundred trials. How often will the coins fall to yield six heads, or five, four, three, two, one, or none? The expected distribution is shown in Figure 15.1, which also indicates what happened when a dedicated statistician actually performed the experiment. As more and more coins are thrown on any one trial, the expected distribution will approach the normal curve (Figure 15.2).

According to Quetelet, the variability found in many human characteristics can be explained in similar terms. He believed that nature aims at an ideal

---

* For a fuller description of these and other statistical matters which will be referred to in this chapter, see the Appendix, "Statistics: The Collection, Organization, and Interpretation of Data."

15.2   The normal curve   *(A) The probability of the number of heads that will occur in a given number of coin tosses is easily determined. (B) When the number of coins tossed approaches infinity, the resulting distribution is the normal curve. The fact that this curve describes the distribution of many physical and mental attributes suggests that these attributes are affected by a multitude of independent factors, some pulling one way and some another.*

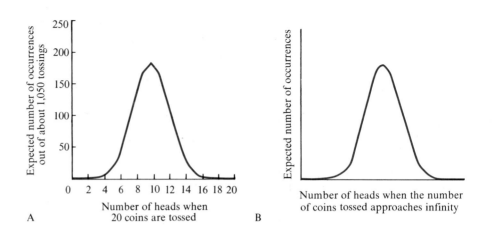

A

B

value—whether of height, weight, or chest size—but that it generally misses the mark, sometimes falling short and sometimes overshooting. The actual value of an attribute such as height depends upon a host of factors, some of which lead to an increase, others to a decrease. But each of these factors is independent and their operation is determined by chance. Thus nature is in effect throwing a multitude of coins to determine any one person's height. Each head adds, say, a millimeter to the average, and each tail subtracts one. The result is a frequency distribution of heights that approximates a normal curve.

VARIABILITY AND DARWIN

After Darwin published his *Origin of the Species,* variability within a species was suddenly considered in a new perspective. Darwin showed that it provides the raw material on which natural selection could work. Suppose that the average finch on a particular island has a fairly long and narrow beak. There is some variability; a few finches have beaks that are shorter and wider. These few would be able to crack certain hard seeds that the other finches could not open. If these hard seeds suddenly become the primary foodstuffs in the habitat, the short-beaked finches might find themselves at a reproductive advantage. They would outlive and thus outbreed their long-beaked comrades and eventually a new species might be born (or more precisely, hatched). Seen in this light, variability is far from being an error of nature that missed the ideal mark as Quetelet had thought. On the contrary, it is the very stuff of which evolution is made (Figure 15.3).

CORRELATION

Can this line of reasoning be applied to variations in human characteristics? It might, if these characteristics could be shown to be hereditary, at least in part.

15.3   Darwin's finches   *In 1835 Charles Darwin visited the Galapagos Islands in the Pacific Ocean and observed a number of different species of finches. They eventually provided an important stimulus to his theory of natural selection, as he supposed that "one species had been taken and modified for different ends." The figure shows two of these finches. One has a rather narrow beak and is a woodpeckerlike bird that lives in trees and feeds on insects. The other is a large-beaked seed-eater. (After Lack, 1953)*

Francis Galton *(Courtesy National Library of Medicine)*

This assumption seemed reasonable enough for physical attributes of the kind that Quetelet had tabulated, but is it appropriate for mental characteristics such as intellectual ability? A half-cousin of Darwin's, Francis Galton (1822–1911) spent much of his life trying to prove that it is. Most of the subsequent work in the area rests on the statistical methods he and his followers developed to test his assertions.

An important part of Galton's program called for the assessment of the similarity among relatives. The trouble is that such relationships are not perfect. Children tend to be like their parents but only to some extent. The problem was to find some measure of this relationship. Put more generally, the question was how one could determine whether a variation along one characteristic could be accounted for by variation along another. The two characteristics might be the height of a father and that of his son. They might also be characteristics within the same individual such as a person's height and the same person's weight.

Take as an example an individual's weight. How is this related to his height? The first step is to construct a **scatter diagram** in which one axis represents weight and the other height. Each person will be represented by one point corresponding to his position along the weight and height axes (Figure 15.4). Inspection of the scatter diagram reveals that the two variables are related for they covary: that is, as height goes up, so does weight. But this covariation, or **correlation,** is far from perfect. We can draw a **line of best fit** through the points in the scatter diagram which allows us to make the best prediction of a person's weight given his height. But this prediction is relatively crude, for there is considerable variability around the line of best fit.

Galton and his students developed a mathematical expression which summarizes both the direction and the strength of the relationship between the two measures. This is the **correlation coefficient** which varies between + 1.00 and − 1.00 and is symbolized by the letter *r*. The plus or minus sign of the correlation coefficient indicates the direction of the relationship. In the case of height and weight this direction is positive: as height increases so does weight. With other measures, the direction is negative: as the score on one measure increases, the score on the other declines (Figure 15.5).

15.4   A positive correlation *(left)   A scatter diagram of the heights and weights of 50 male undergraduates. Note that the points fall within an ellipse which indicates the variation around the line of best fit. The correlation for these data was* + *.70.*

15.5   A negative correlation *(right)   A scatter diagram of the test performances of 70 students in an introductory psychology course. The diagram plots number of errors in a midterm against number of correct answers on the final. The correlation was* −*.53. If errors (or correct answers) had been plotted on* both *exams, the correlation would of course have been positive.*

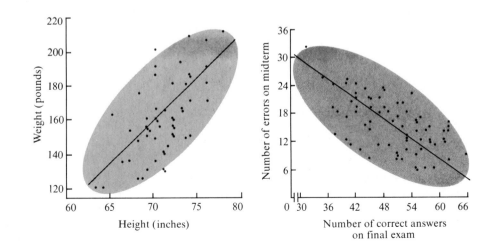

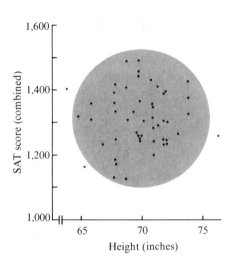

15.6 A correlation of zero *A scatter diagram of the scholastic aptitude scores and the heights of 50 undergraduate males. Not surprisingly, there was no relation as shown by the fact that the points fall within a circle. The actual correlation was +.05, which for all essential purposes is equivalent to zero.*

The strength of the correlation is expressed by its absolute value (that is, its value regardless of sign). A correlation of $r = .00$ indicates no relation whatsoever. An example might be the relation between a man's collar size and his yearly income. If we plot the scatter diagram, the points will be arranged in a circle. There is no way of predicting income from collar size, so there is no single line of best fit (Figure 15.6). As the absolute value of r increases, the dots on the scatter diagram form an ellipse around the line of best fit. As the correlation goes up, the ellipse gets thinner and thinner. The thinner the ellipse, the less error there is as we try to predict the value of one variable (say, weight) when given the value of the other (say, height). When the absolute value of r reaches 1.00 (whether + 1.00 or − 1.00), the ellipse finally becomes a straight line. There is no more variation at all around the line of best fit; the correlation is perfect and prediction is error-free. However, such perfect correlations are virtually never encountered in actual practice; even in the physical sciences there is bound to be some error of measurement.

While correlations are a useful index of the degree to which two variables are related, they have a limitation. The fact that two variables are correlated says nothing about the underlying causal relationship between them. Sometimes, there is none at all. Examples are correlations that are produced by some third factor. The number of umbrellas one sees on a given day is surely correlated with the number of people who wear raincoats. A Martian observing the human scene might conclude that umbrella-carrying causes raincoat-wearing or vice versa; our own earthly wisdom tells us that both are caused by the rain.

ASSESSING PEOPLE

While the correlation techniques developed by Galton and his students were initially meant to investigate the extent to which relatives resemble each other, they were soon extended to other problems. One important application was to mental testing, for which they provided the underlying statistical methodology.

A mental test is meant to be an objective yardstick to assess some psychological trait or capacity on which people differ. But how can one tell that a given test actually accomplishes this objective? In many penny arcades there is a contraption that claims to provide a test of driving skill. For a quarter or two, one can handle a steering wheel, gear stick, and accelerator and thereby guide a "car" through a tortuous maze of "roads" on a video screen, accumulating a score based on the car's total progress. When the time is up, this score tells whether the "driver" is an expert, reasonably good, a beginner, or an incompetent whose license should be revoked. However, with the possible exception of the proud six-year old whose score proclaims him a race car champion, no one would seriously argue that getting a driver's license should depend on one's performance on this electronic "driving test." Common sense tells us that driving skill is not properly measured in this way. But can we justify this intuition more precisely? Are there are any objective criteria against which the test itself can be tested? (See Figures 15.7, 15.8, and 15.9 for examples of aptitude tests in actual use.)

15.7   A test of manual dexterity   *This and the next two figures illustrate some representative aptitude tests in present use. The test of manual dexterity shown in this figure features a tray that contains metal pegs which have to be picked up with pliers and placed in small holes in the correct order. Similar tests have been shown to correlate .46 with speed of work in sewing-machine operators. (Cronbach, 1970a; photograph from Freeman, 1962)*

15.8   A test of art aptitude   *The person tested is presented with (A). Using the lines in this card as a start, he has to make a completed drawing. (B) A completed sample. The test score is based on ratings by an experienced art teacher. These scores correlated quite well (.66) with grades in a special art course for high-school seniors. (Cronbach, 1970a. Test item from the Horn Art Aptitude Inventory, 1953; courtesy Stoelting Co., Chicago)*

A

B

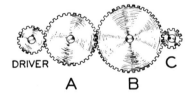

15.9   A test of mechanical comprehension   *One of the items asks, "Which gear will make the most turns in a minute?" (From the Bennett Test of Mechanical Comprehension; courtesy The Psychological Corporation)*

RELIABILITY

One important criterion of the adequacy of a test is its **reliability,** the consistency with which it measures what it measures. Consider a spring balance. If the spring is in good condition, the scale will give virtually identical readings when the same object is repeatedly weighed. But if the spring is gradually losing its elasticity, repeated weighings will give different values. If it does this, we throw away the scale. It is unreliable.

The same logic underlies test reliability. One way of assessing this is by administering the same test twice to the same group of subjects. The correlation between test and retest scores will be an index of the test's reliability. If the same person gets a champion's score today and a beginner's score tomorrow, the electronic driving test is unreliable in essentially the sense in which the poor scale proved to be.

581

One trouble with the ***test-retest method*** is that the performance on the retest may be affected by what the subject learned the first time around. For example, some people may look up the answers to questions they missed. To avoid this problem, testers sometimes develop ***alternative forms*** of a test; if the two alternate forms are exactly equivalent, reliability can be assessed by using one form on one occasion and another on a second. Since any two halves of a single test can be considered "alternate forms," reliability is often measured by the ***split-half technique*** (correlating subjects' scores on, say, all of the odd items with their scores on all of the even items). If both halves correlate highly, we consider the test reliable; if they don't, we regard it as unreliable.

Most standard psychological tests now in use have ***reliability coefficients*** (that is, test-retest or split-half correlations) in the .90s or in the high .80s. Tests with lower reliability are of little practical use.

VALIDITY

High reliability alone does not guarantee that a test is a good measuring rod. Even more critical is a test's ***validity,*** which is most simply defined as the extent to which it measures what it is supposed to measure.

Again consider the spring scale. If the spring is made of good steel, the scale may be highly reliable. But suppose someone decides to use this scale to measure *length*. This bizarre step will produce an instrument of high reliability but virtually no validity. It measures some attribute very precisely and consistently but that attribute is not length. As a test of length, the scale is invalid.

In the case of the scale, we can readily define the physical attribute that it is meant to measure and this lets us assess validity. But how can we define the psychological attribute which a mental test tries to assess?

Predictive validity One approach is to consider the test as a ***predictor*** of future performance. If a test claims to measure scholastic aptitude, a score on that test should predict later school or college performance. The same holds for tests of vocational aptitude, which ought to predict how persons later succeed on the job. One index of a test's validity is the success with which it makes such predictions. This is usually measured by the correlation between the test score and some appropriate ***criterion.*** For scholastic aptitude, a common criterion is the grade-point average the student later attains. For vocational aptitude, it is some measure of later job proficiency. For example, aptitude tests for salespersons might be validated against their sales records.

Validity coefficients (that is, the correlations between test scores and criteria) for scholastic aptitude are generally in the neighborhood of .50 or .60, which means that the prediction is far from perfect. This is hardly surprising. For one thing, the tests probably don't provide a perfect index of one's "capacity" (ignoring for the time being just what this capacity might be). But even if they did, we would not expect validity coefficients of 1.00, for we all know that school grades depend on many factors in addition to ability.

An important fact about validity coefficients is that their magnitude depends upon the ***range of ability*** within the group in which they are determined. As this range is narrowed, the correlation between test score and criterion declines. This relationship holds for all correlation coefficients. Consider the correlation between height and weight. If we choose to narrow the range by

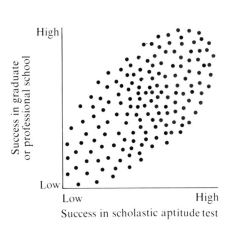

15.10 The effect of preselection upon correlation *Hypothetical data which show the relation between some scholastic aptitude test taken in high school and success in graduate or professional school. When we look at the records of those who actually entered postgraduate schools (color), we find little if any relation to aptitude scores in high school. If there had been no preselection—that is, if every high school student eventually ended up in graduate or professional school—the resulting scatter diagram would include all dots (both black and color) and would indicate a sizable correlation. (After Cronbach, 1970b)*

excluding jockeys and basketball players, the height-weight correlation will be reduced. If we narrow the range more drastically by, say, looking only at persons between 5'7" and 5'8", the correlation will become virtually insignificant.

The same phenomenon occurs in the field of testing. Scholastic aptitude tests do a reasonably good job in predicting high school and college grades. However, they tend to be less useful in predicting how a student will perform in graduate or professional school. The reason is that the postgraduates are already preselected. They have survived many years of schooling and are thus screened for academic ability, at least to some extent. As a result, the range of scholastic aptitude within this group is necessarily less than that found within the population at large. Since the differences in scholastic aptitude within this preselected group are relatively small, they are of less value in predicting future academic performance (Figure 15.10). But this does not mean that the test has no bearing on the prediction of future performance. It may not be able to predict success in graduate or professional school for those who are already admitted. But it can be used for the larger, unselected population. For example, it may help a vocational guidance counselor in advising a high school student who considers, say, a career in medicine (Cronbach, 1970b).

Construct validity Predictive validity is not the only way of assessing whether a test measures what it claims to. Another approach is to establish that the test has **construct validity** (Cronbach and Meehl, 1955). This is the extent to which performance on the test fits into a theoretical scheme—or construct—about the attribute the test tries to measure. As an example, consider the test for achievement motivation developed by McClelland and his associates (see Chapter 13). The validity of this test was not established by correlating it with any *one* criterion measure, such as over- or under-achievement in school. Instead, the investigators asked whether the test results fit into a whole network of hypotheses about the achievement motive, its relation to child-rearing, to the ability to defer gratification, to social class structure, and so on. To the extent that the results do indeed fit into this larger pattern, they confer construct validity on the test. In terms of the medical analogy we used before, present-day chemical tests of pregnancy have both construct and predictive validity. They have construct validity because modern medical science knows enough about the hormonal changes during pregnancy to understand why the chemical reacts as it does. They also have predictive validity, for they correlate almost perfectly with the highly visible manifestations of pregnancy which appear a short time later.

STANDARDIZATION

To evaluate a test, we need one further item of information in addition to its reliability and validity. We have to know something about the group on which the test was **standardized.** A person's test score by itself provides little information. It can, however, be interpreted by comparing it with the score obtained by other people. These other scores provide the **norms** against which an individual's test scores are evaluated. To obtain these norms, the test is first administered to a large sample of the population on which the test is to be used. This initial group is the **standardization sample.**

A crucial requirement in using tests is the comparability between the subjects who are tested and the standardization sample that yields the norms. If these two are drawn from different populations, the test scores may not be interpretable. Consider a scholastic aptitude test standardized on ten-year olds in 1920. Its norms will surely not apply today to ten-year olds whose schooling undoubtedly differs in many ways. Under the circumstances, there is no way of evaluating a particular test score, for the desired comparison is with ten-year olds today rather than sixty years ago. No less important is the fact that the reliability and validity coefficients obtained for the original standardization sample are probably also obsolete. A particular set of test items may have predicted school performance in 1920. But there is no way of knowing whether the same items would yield the same correlation with school grades today.

The preceding example represents a hypothetical case; in actual practice scholastic aptitude tests are updated rather frequently. But a similar issue crops up when tests are administered to persons whose cultural backgrounds are different from that of the standardization sample. This problem is by no means hypothetical; examples are the cultural differences between ethnic and racial groups and between rural and urban dwellers. Some test items clearly discriminate in favor of one group or another. When urban school children were asked questions like "What is the largest river in the United States?" or "How can banks afford to pay interest on the money you deposit?" they did considerably better than rural school children of the same age. The difference was reversed for questions like "Name a vegetable that grows above ground" or "Why does seasoned wood burn more easily than green wood?" (Shimberg, 1929).

USING TESTS FOR SELECTION

Suppose we have a test of good reliability and reasonable validity. How is it used? One important application in our society is as a selection device. A well-known example is an aptitude test for pilot training developed by the Army Air Force during World War II. A large number of separate subtests were constructed for this purpose, including tests of motor coordination, reaction time, perceptual skills, and general intellectual ability. These subtests were administered to over 185,000 men who went through pilot training. The initial question was how each of these subtests correlated with the criterion—success or failure in training. The scores of each subtest were then weighted to produce a composite score that gave the best estimate of the criterion. The use of this composite pilot aptitude test score led to an appreciable improvement in trainee selection. Without the test, the failure rate was 24 percent. By using the test, the failure rate was cut to 10 percent. This was accomplished by setting a *cutoff score* on the test below which no applicant was accepted (Flanagan, 1947).

Given a reasonable validity coefficient, the use of tests evidently helps to reduce the number of selection errors. The overall number of such errors declines as the validity coefficient of the test increases. But some errors will always be present, for validity coefficients are never at 1.00; in fact, most vocational aptitude testers count themselves lucky if they manage to obtain validity correlations of .40 or .50.

15.11 Selection errors and cutoff scores
Applicants to pilot training are selected on the basis of an aptitude test. The line of best fit indicates the prediction of trainee performance from aptitude test score; the ellipse shows the variation around this line. The choice of a cutoff aptitude score, below which no applicant is accepted, determines the nature of selection errors. (A) A high cutoff score will increase the proportion of false rejects relative to false accepts. (B) A low cutoff score has the reverse effect.

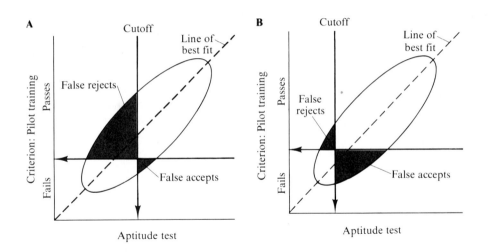

The important point is that selection errors are of two kinds. On the one hand, there are "false accepts," persons who are accepted but who will fail. On the other hand, there are "false rejects," people who are rejected but who would have performed adequately. What determines which of the two kinds of errors will predominate? The answer depends upon the choice of the cutoff score. Suppose we decide to use a very stringent cutoff point. The result will be a marked reduction in the number of false accepts; but there is a price, an increased frequency of false rejects. We can reduce the number of false rejects by picking a lower cutoff score; but again there is a trade-off, a concomitant increase in the number of false accepts (Figure 15.11).

What cutoff score is the appropriate one? The answer hinges on the costs and benefits the selector assigns to each of the four possible outcomes: false accepts, false rejects, correct accepts (accepted applicants who succeed), and correct rejects (rejected applicants who would not have succeeded). These costs and benefits yield a *payoff matrix* similar to some we have already encountered (see Chapters 6 and 14).

Just what these costs and benefits are depends upon a number of social, economic, and institutional values. Let us consider only the selection errors. Which is the more harmful? It obviously depends. In selecting combat pilots, there is a premium on avoiding false accepts. Pilot training is extremely costly. A trainee who doesn't make the grade represents a serious loss: in instruction time, in tying up expensive equipment, and—in case of really extreme failure—in life and limb. From the point of view of the Air Force, a false reject is much less serious: a rejected applicant who would in fact have succeeded as a pilot is still perfectly useful as a member of the ground crew. Under the circumstances, a high cutoff score makes good sense. In other selection situations, however, the payoff matrix may be very different. Suppose that there is a serious shortage in a particular occupation, say, engineering. If the number of applicants to engineering schools is relatively low, the schools would be well advised to set a lower cutoff point on an engineering aptitude test. Given the increased need for engineers and the reduced pool of applicants, there are good reasons to minimize false rejects. Graduating a few additional engineers may now be worth the price of a larger number of student dropouts.

The payoff matrix that underlies a selection procedure obviously varies with the situation. It also varies according to one's perspective. The best example is the contrast between the institution that does the selecting and the applicant. A college with a large number of applicants might well decide to reduce the number of false accepts. But many applicants will see things very differently, especially if they have applied only to this one school. From their point of view, the worst error is to be falsely rejected (Table 15.2). This is not to say that the payoff matrices of selector and potential selectee are always different. Occasionally they are in harmony. In picking combat pilots, the Air

Table 15.2   TWO PAYOFF MATRICES FOR ACCEPTING COLLEGE APPLICANTS (IN ARBITRARY UNITS)

A. *From the perspective of the college*

Performance in college

		Passes	Fails
Decision	Accept	*Correct accept:* Fine all around +5	*False accept:* Waste of resources, lowers general intellectual level, etc. −5
	Reject	*False reject:* Too bad, but not really serious for there are more applicants than openings −1	*Correct reject:* Satisfaction in having decided correctly +1

B. *From the perspective of the applicant*

Performance in college

		Passes	Fails
Decision	Accept	*Correct accept:* Delighted +10	*False accept:* A wasted year but not completely since something was gained anyway −1
	Reject	*False reject:* A calamity −10	*Correct reject:* Ok, if really so +1

Force wants to minimize the number of false accepts. But so do the applicants. When poor job performance may mean a fiery death, a high cutoff score is in the best interest of both parties.*

To conclude, the use of tests in selection involves several factors. To begin with, there is the question of how well the test predicts performance, whether in school or on the job. To answer this question we need to know the test's reliability and validity. But since prediction is necessarily imperfect, we have the further question of where to set the cutoff point. And this decision cannot be settled on the basis of the test alone. It is inextricably tied up with all kinds of value judgments that determine the payoff matrix for the possible outcomes.

Intelligence Testing

What is *intelligence?* In a crude sense, of course, we all have some notion of what the term refers to. The dictionary is full of adjectives that distinguish levels of intellectual functioning such as *bright* and *dull, quick-witted* and *slow.* Intelligence tests try to get at some attribute (or attributes) that roughly correspond to such distinctions. But the test constructors did not begin with a precise conception of what it was they wanted to test. There was no consensus as to a definition of intelligence, and those definitions that were offered were usually so broad and all-inclusive as to be of little use. Intelligence was said to be a capacity, but what is it a capacity for? Is it for learning, for transfer, for abstract thinking, for judgment, comprehension, reason, or perhaps all of these? There was no agreement. One author suggested a first approximation according to which intelligence was to be defined "as that quality of mind . . . in respect to which Aristotle, Plato, Thucydides, and the like, differed most from Athenian idiots of their day." While this seemed sensible enough, it hardly went beyond the intuitive notions people had long before psychologists appeared on the scene (Heim, 1954).

Given the difficulty in defining intelligence, devising tests for this hard-to-define attribute was an undertaking of a rather different sort from constructing a specialized aptitude test for prospective pilots. The pilot aptitude test has a rather clear-cut validity criterion. But what is the best validity criterion for intelligence tests? Since the nature of intelligence is unclear, we can't be sure of what the appropriate validity criterion might be.

But our theoretical ignorance notwithstanding, we do have intelligence tests, and many of them. They were developed to fulfill certain practical needs. We may not understand exactly what it is that they assess, but the test consumers—schools, armies, industries—want them even so. The fact is that for many practical purposes these tests work quite well.

---

* There is a formal similarity between the selection problem just discussed and the decision subjects have to make in a detection experiment. In a detection study, a subject can make two kinds of errors: "false alarms" (reporting a stimulus when in fact there is none) and "misses" (failing to report a stimulus when in fact there is one). False alarms are analogous to false accepts, while misses are analogous to false rejects. In both the selection problem and the detection experiment, the choice between yea and nay is partially determined by a cutoff value which in turn depends on a payoff matrix (see the Appendix to Chapter 6).

MEASURING INTELLIGENCE

The first attempts to measure intelligence were made by Galton and some of his immediate successors. Their efforts were based on the psychological theories of the time which held that the "higher mental processes" of reasoning and problem solving are ultimately based on more elementary components such as sensation and association. Accordingly, these investigators developed tests for sensory acuity, motor ability, reaction time, and rote memory. They found considerable individual differences, many of which proved to be fairly stable. But it was soon discovered that these various tests did not correlate with each other. Nor did they correlate with school grades. It appeared that tests of simple psychological processes do not suffice to assess a complex attribute like intelligence.

TESTING INTELLIGENCE IN CHILDREN

The major advance was made by a French psychologist, Alfred Binet (1857–1911). As so often in the field of individual differences, the impetus came from the world of practical affairs. By the turn of the century, compulsory elementary education was the rule among the industrialized nations. Large numbers of school children had to be dealt with and some of them seemed mentally retarded. If they were indeed retarded, it appeared best to send them to special schools. But mere backwardness was not deemed sufficient to justify this action; perhaps a child's prior education had been poor, or perhaps the child suffered from some illness. In 1904, the French minister of public instruction appointed a special committee, including Binet, and asked it to look into this matter. The committee concluded that there was a need for an objective diagnostic instrument to assess each child's intellectual state. Much of what we now know about the measurement of intelligence comes from Binet's efforts to satisfy this need.

Intelligence as a general cognitive capacity   Binet and his collaborator, Théodore Simon, started with the premise that intelligence is a rather general attribute that manifests itself in many spheres of cognitive functioning. This view led them to construct a test that ranged over many areas. It included tasks that varied in both content and difficulty—copying a drawing, repeating a string of digits, recognizing coins and making change, explaining absurdities. The child's performance on this potpourri of subtests yielded a composite score. Later studies showed that this composite measure correlated with the child's school grades and with the teacher's evaluations of the child's intelligence. To this extent, the test evidently tapped something that corresponds with some of our intuitive notions of what intelligence is.

Binet and other intelligence testers have sometimes been criticized on the ground that some—perhaps all—of their test items depend upon prior knowledge. One obviously cannot define a word without having seen or heard it, nor can one make change for a franc without exposure to arithmetic and French currency. But Binet did not regard this as a drawback. He felt that there is no such thing as pure, disembodied intelligence which develops independently of environmental input. In constructing his tests he tried to use only items whose

Alfred Binet   *(Courtesy National Library of Medicine)*

content was in principle familiar to all of the children that he tested. He believed that once this condition is met, the test score makes sense. Each child has had some contact with a common culture; one assesses the children's underlying capacity by noting what they have picked up from this environment and how they can put it together in different ways.

The intelligence quotient, IQ Binet made another assumption about intelligence. He believed that it develops with age until maturity is reached. Here too his ideas fit our intuitive notions. We know that an average group of six-year olds is no intellectual match for an average group of eight-year olds. It's not just that they know less; they're not as smart. This conception provided the basis for the test's scoring system.

Binet and Simon first gave the test to a standardization sample composed of children of varying ages whose test performance provided the norms. Binet and Simon noted which items were passed by the average six-year old, which by the average eight-year old, and so on. (Items that were passed by younger but not by older children were excluded.)

The resulting classification of the test items generated a ladder of tasks in which each rung corresponds to a number of subtests that were successfully passed by the average child of a given age. Testing a child's intelligence was thus tantamount to a determination of how high the child could ascend this ladder before the tasks finally became too difficult. The rung she attained indicated her **mental age** (usually abbreviated MA). If she successfully coped with all items passed by the average eight-year old and failed all those passed by the average nine-year old, her MA was said to be eight years. Appropriate scoring adjustments were made when the performance pattern did not work out quite as neatly; for example, if a child passed all items at the seven-year-old level, 75 percent of those at the eight-year-old level, 25 percent of those at the nine-year-old level, and none beyond. Table 15.3 (p. 590) presents representative test items for the Stanford-Binet, a widely used American adaptation of the Binet-Simon test.

The MA assesses an absolute level of cognitive capacity. To determine whether a child is "bright" or "dull" one has to compare her MA with her chronological age (CA). To the extent that her MA exceeds her CA, we regard the child as "bright" or advanced; the opposite is true if the MA is below the CA. But a particular lag or advance clearly has different import depending upon the child's age. A six-year old with an MA of three is obviously more retarded than a ten-year old with an MA of seven. To cope with this difficulty, a German psychologist, William Stern (1871–1938), proposed the use of a ratio measure, the **intelligence quotient** or **IQ.** This is computed by dividing the MA by the CA. The resulting quotient is multiplied by 100 to get rid of decimal points. Thus,

$$IQ = \frac{MA}{CA} \times 100$$

By definition, an IQ of 100 indicates average intelligence; it means that the child's MA is equivalent to its CA and thus to the average score attained by its age-mates in the standardization sample. By the same token, an IQ greater

Table 15.3 REPRESENTATIVE TASKS FROM THE STANFORD-BINET

Age	Task
2½	Points to toy object that "goes on your feet" Names *chair, flag* Can repeat two digits
4	"In daytime it is light, after night it is . . . ?" "Why do we have houses?"
6	"What is the difference between a bird and a dog?" "An inch is short; a mile is . . . ?" "Give me _____ blocks" (up to ten)
9	"Tell me a number that rhymes with *tree.*" "If I buy 4 cents worth of candy and give the store keeper 10 cents, how much money will I get back?" Repeats four digits in reversed order

12	Defines *skill, muzzle*
	"The streams are dry _____ there has been little rain."
	". . . 'In an old graveyard in Spain, they have discovered a small skull
	  which they believe to be that of Christopher Columbus when he
	  was about ten years old.' . . . What is foolish about that?"
	Repeats 5 digits in reversed order

SOURCE: Modified from Terman and Merrill, 1972.

than 100 indicates that the child is above average; an IQ of less than 100 that it is below average.

Stern's quotient measure has various drawbacks. The major problem is that the top rung of Binet's mental age ladder was sixteen (in some later revisions of the Stanford-Binet, the ceiling was higher). In some ways, this makes good sense, for intelligence does not grow forever, any more than height does. But since CAs keep on rising beyond the MA ceiling, the IQ (defined as a quotient) cannot help but decline. Consider the IQ of an adult. If her CA is 48 and her MA is 16, the use of the standard computation results in an IQ of 33 ($16/48 \times 100 = 33$), a score that indicates severe mental retardation. To get around such absurdities, mental testers tried various stratagems, including provisions for higher rungs on the MA scale and the use of a CA of 16 as the maximum denominator in the computation of the IQ. But none of these procedures proved quite satisfactory.

Eventually a new approach was adopted. In the last analysis, an intelligence score indicates how an individual stands in relation to an appropriate comparison sample—his own age-mates. The intelligence quotient expresses this comparison as a ratio, but there are more direct measures for getting at the same thing. One example is an individual's **percentile rank;** that is, the proportion of persons in his comparison group whose score is below his. A more commonly used measure that provides the same information is the ***deviation IQ.*** We will not go into the details of how this measure is arrived at; suffice it to say that an IQ of 100 indicates a score equal to the average of the comparison sample (and thus a percentile rank of 50); that for most standard tests, IQs of 85 and 115 indicate percentile ranks of about 16 and 84, while IQs of 70 and 130 correspond to percentile ranks of 2 and 98. Note that as the IQs deviate more and more from the mean, they become increasingly rare. An IQ of 160 or better is obtained in only 3 cases out of 10,000.*

TESTING INTELLIGENCE IN ADULTS

Binet's methods were enthusiastically received, especially in America, where a modified version of the Binet-Simon scale won instant popularity. Overworked teachers and educational counselors welcomed these tests as diagnostic instruments that were sufficiently objective to be, as Binet put it, "affected neither by the bad humor nor the bad digestion of the examiner."

Although the Binet scales were originally meant for children, demands soon arose for the diagnosis of adults' intelligence. Binet's tests for children were obviously inadequate. One reason was the nature of the test items, most of which were unsuitable for adults. In addition, the Binet scale had not been standardized on an adult population so that there were no appropriate norms. Such considerations led David Wechsler to construct an intelligence test for adults—the Wechsler Adult Intelligence Scale (Wechsler, 1958).

Performance versus verbal tests One of Wechsler's objections to the Binet scales was that they were too heavily loaded with items that require verbal skills. Wechsler argued that there are intellectual abilities that are not predominantly verbal (a view that has found later confirmation in studies of hemispheric function; see Chapter 2). In addition, there is the fact that verbal items discriminate against persons with a language handicap—people who have learned English late in life, have had a limited education, are illiterate, have reading difficulties, or are hard of hearing.

To cope with these difficulties, Wechsler divided his test into a verbal and a performance subtest. The verbal test includes items that assess general information, vocabulary, comprehension, and arithmetic. The performance test includes tasks that require the subject to assemble the cut-up parts of a familiar object so as to form the appropriate whole, to complete an incomplete drawing, or to rearrange a series of pictures so that they are in the proper sequence and tell a story (Figure 15.12, page 592).

Group tests Both the Binet and the Wechsler scales are administered individually. This has the advantage of permitting a more careful evaluation of the person who is tested. An experienced test administrator does not just come

---

* One might reasonably ask why deviation IQs are called IQs at all, considering that they are not really quotients. The answer is that the term *IQ* has become part of everyday language. Teachers and counselors had become so accustomed to the IQ scale that later test makers felt obliged to convert their deviation scores into comparable expressions, equivalent only in the sense that a given deviation IQ has the same percentile rank as a ratio IQ of the same magnitude.

INFORMATION

1. Who wrote *Huckleberry Finn*?

2. Where is Finland?

3. At what temperature does paper burn?

4. What is entomology?

COMPREHENSION

1. Why should we obey traffic laws and speed limits?

2. Why are antitrust laws necessary?

3. Why should we lock the doors and take the keys to our car when leaving the car parked?

4. What does this saying mean: "Kill two birds with one stone."

ARITHMETIC

1. How many 15¢ stamps can you buy for a dollar?

2. How many hours will it take a cyclist to travel 60 miles if he is going 12 miles an hour?

3. A man bought a used stereo system for ¾ of what it cost new. He paid $225 for it. How much did it cost new?

4. Six men can finish a job in ten days. How many men will be needed to finish the job in two and a half days?

A. Verbal tests

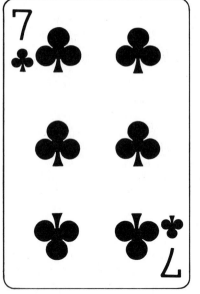

B. Picture completion

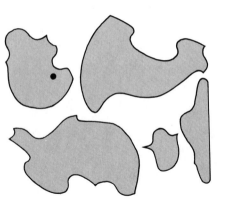

C. Object assembly

15.12   Test items similar to some in the Wechsler Adult Intelligence Scale *(A) Verbal tests. These include tests of information, comprehension, and arithmetic. (B) Picture completion. The task is to note the missing part. (C) Object assembly. The task is to arrange the cut-up pieces to form a familiar object. (D) Block design. The materials consist of four blocks, which are all red on some sides, all white on other sides, and half red and half white on the rest of the sides. The subject is shown a pattern and has to arrange the four blocks to produce this design. (Courtesy The Psychological Corporation)*

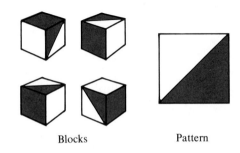

Blocks   Pattern

D. Block design

up with a quantitative score, but can also note how the individual approaches the problems the test sets forth—whether the subject exerts maximum effort, whether he is anxious, and so on. Such qualitative observations are often very important in judging a particular case. But there is the obvious drawback that individual testing is a lengthy and expensive business. If the object is to assess a large number of persons—army recruits, potential employees in large industrial organizations, myriads of children in a city's schools, college applicants— the cost of administering tests individually becomes prohibitive.

Such economic facts of life led to the development of group tests of intelligence, usually of the paper-and-pencil multiple-choice format. Some important examples of such group tests are the Lorge-Thorndike Test, often used in schools up to the twelfth grade, the Scholastic Aptitude Test (SAT) taken by many college applicants, and the Graduate Record Examination, a more difficult version of the SAT designed for applicants to graduate schools. A test that emphasizes abstract, nonverbal intellectual ability is the Progressive Matrices Test (Figure 15.13).

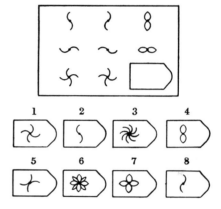

15.13 An example item from the Raven Progressive Matrices Test *The task is to select the alternative that fits into the empty slot above. (Courtesy The Psychological Corporation)*

AN AREA OF APPLICATION: MENTAL DEFICIENCY

Binet's original purpose was to design an instrument for the diagnosis of mental retardation. How well did he and his followers succeed? On the whole, the tests seem to perform their diagnostic function rather well; they certainly provide one of the main bases for classification. The usual line of demarcation for retardation is an IQ of about 70 or below. Thus defined, 3 percent of the population of the United States would be regarded as retarded (Cytryn and Lourie, 1975). But the test performance criterion is by no means the only one. Equally important is social and cultural competence, the ability to learn and to cope with the demands of society, to take care of oneself, to earn a living. This competence obviously depends in part upon the nature of the society in which a person lives. A complex technological culture like ours puts a higher premium on various intellectual skills than an agrarian society. Someone classified as mildly retarded in the twentieth-century United States probably would have managed perfectly well in, say, feudal Europe.

Table 15.4 CHARACTERISTICS OF THE MENTALLY RETARDED

Degree of retardation	IQ range	Level of functioning at school age (6–20 years)	Level of functioning in adulthood (21 years and over)
Mild	52–67	Can learn academic skills up to approximately sixth-grade level by late teens; can be guided toward social conformity.	Can usually achieve social and vocational skills adequate to minimum self-support, but may need guidance and assistance when under unusual social or economic stress.
Moderate	36–51	Can profit from training in social and occupational skills; unlikely to progress beyond second-grade level in academic subjects; may learn to travel alone in familiar places.	May achieve self-maintenance in unskilled or semiskilled work under sheltered conditions; needs supervision and guidance when under mild social or economic stress.
Severe	20–35	Can talk or learn to communicate; can be trained in elemental health habits; profits from systematic habit training.	May contribute partially to self-maintenance under complete supervision; can develop self-protection skills at a minimum useful level in controlled environment.
Profound	below 20	Some motor development present; may respond to minimal or limited training in self-help.	Some motor and speech development; may achieve very limited self-care; needs nursing care.

SOURCE: Adapted from Cytryn and Lourie, 1975.

CLASSIFYING RETARDATION

A widely used classification system distinguishes several degrees of mental deficiency: "mild" (IQ of 52 to 67), "moderate" (IQ of 36 to 51), "severe" (IQ of 20 to 35), and "profound" (IQ below 20). The more severe the retardation, the less frequently it occurs in the population; in 100 retarded persons, one would expect that the degree of retardation would be "mild" in 90, "moderate" in 6, "severe" in 3, and "profound" in 1 (Robinson and Robinson, 1970).

Table 15.4 presents a description of the general level of intellectual functioning in each of the categories at various ages. The table shows that mentally retarded persons do not have to be precluded from useful participation in society. This is especially true for those whose degree of retardation is mild, and they account for almost 90 percent of all the cases. If provided with appropriate education and training, such persons can ultimately achieve an acceptable level of adjustment in adult life (Tyler, 1965).

THE CAUSES OF RETARDATION

Retardation is not a condition that has one single cause. It is a symptom that can reflect any number of underlying conditions, many of which are as yet unknown. Some forms of retardation are produced by certain known genetic disorders or by aberrations in the chromosome structure (see pp. 613–14). Others are produced by brain damage suffered in the womb, during delivery, or after birth. Still others may reflect the composite effect of hundreds of genes. And yet others may be the result of impoverished environmental conditions, especially during early life.

A number of investigators have tried to order this hodgepodge of known and unknown causal factors by arguing that cases of mental retardation can be classified into two main types—those that are produced by one factor and those that are produced by many. According to this hypothesis, **unifactor** forms correspond to the more severe varieties of retardation; these are thought to result from a major pathology, such as a gene defect, chromosomal aberration, or brain damage. In contrast, mild retardation is believed to be a **multifactor** phenomenon. According to this view, mild retardation simply represents the lower portion of the distribution of intelligence. Seen in this light, intelligence in normals as well as mild retardates is produced by the joint action of numerous separate factors, some genetic and some environmental. Their composite effect determines the degree of intelligence. Adherents to this view believe that the lower end of the distribution consists of those unlucky cases for whom the large majority of causal factors fell in the wrong direction (Zigler, 1967).

The Nature of Intelligence

We have seen that there is no consensus on a definition of intelligence and thus no clear-cut validity criterion for a test that claims to measure it. But even so, many psychologists would agree that such instruments as the Stanford-Binet and the Wechsler tests do distinguish people in ways that have a rough correspondence with our initial, intuitive conceptions of the term *intelligence*. There is no doubt that with appropriate modifications, either scale would easily differentiate between Aristotle and the Athenian village idiot. Can we get any further than this?

THE PSYCHOMETRIC APPROACH

According to one group of investigators, the starting point for further inquiries into the nature of intelligence is just the fact that intelligence tests do make some distinctions between people that fit our initial sense of what intelligence is about. They believe that we can refine our knowledge of the nature of intelligence by a careful further study of these distinctions. This line of reasoning underlies the **psychometric approach** to the study of intelligence. In effect, it amounts to a bootstrap operation. One looks at the results the measuring instrument provides in order to find out what the instrument really measures.

THE STRUCTURE OF MENTAL ABILITIES

When we use the term *intelligence*, we imply that it is a unitary ability. But is it really? In principle, one could imagine several kinds of mental ability that are quite unrelated. Perhaps different intellectual tasks draw on distinctly different cognitive gifts. It may also be that the truth is in between. Perhaps human intellectual abilities are composed of both general and more particular capacities. How can we decide among these alternatives?

All we have to go on are people's scores on various tests. These scores presumably reflect some underlying abilities—perhaps one, perhaps several. But these underlying capacities are not observable directly; they can only be inferred. Students of psychometrics have tried to perform this inference by looking at the intercorrelations among different tests.

To get an intuitive idea of this general approach, consider a man who looks at a lake and sees what appear to be serpentlike parts:

He can entertain various hypotheses. One is that all visible parts belong to one huge sea monster (a hypothesis that is analogous to the assumption that there is a unitary intellectual ability):

He might also assume that there are several such beasts (analogous to separate mental abilities):

Or finally, he might believe that there are as many sea animals as there are visible parts (analogous to the hypothesis that every test measures a totally different ability):

How can he choose among these alternatives, given that he has no way of peering below the waters? His best bet is to wait and watch how the serpentine parts change over time and space. If he does this, he can find out which parts go together. If all parts move jointly (B), the most reasonable interpretation is that they all belong to one huge sea monster. (For the purposes of our example, we will assume sea serpents are severely arthritic and are unable to move their body portions separately.) If the first part goes with the second, while the third goes with the fourth (C), there are presumably two smaller creatures. If all parts move separately (D), the best bet is that there are as many sea serpents as there are visible parts. In effect, our sea-serpent watcher studied a correlation pattern on the basis of which he inferred the invisible structure (or structures) under the sea.

Spearman and the concept of "general intelligence"   The psychometric equivalent of the joint movements of sea-serpent portions is the correlation pattern among different tests of mental abilities. As an example, consider the correlations among four subtests of the Wechsler Adult Scale: Information *(I),* comprehension *(C),* arithmetic *(A),* and vocabulary *(V).* These intercorrelations are all quite high. The correlation between *I* and *C* is .70, that between *I* and *A* is .66, and so on. These results can be presented in the form of a **correlation matrix,** in which the intercorrelations can be read off directly (Table 15.5).

Table 15.5   CORRELATION MATRIX OF FOUR SUBTESTS
ON THE WECHSLER ADULT SCALE

	I	*C*	*A*	*V*
I (Information)	—	.70	.66	.81
C (Comprehension)		—	.49	.73
A (Arithmetic)			—	.59
V (Vocabulary)				—

SOURCE: From Wechsler, 1958.

NOTE: The matrix shows the correlation of each subtest with each of the other three. Note that the left-to-right diagonal (which is here indicated by the dashes) can't have any entries because it is made up of the cells that describe the correlation of each subtest with itself. The cells below the dashes are left blank because they would be redundant.

An inspection of this correlation matrix suggests that there is a common factor that runs through all four of these subtests. The positive correlations indicate that people with a greater fund of information are also people who get higher scores in comprehension, who are better at arithmetic, and who have a larger vocabulary. Given the fact that all of these measures are correlated it is plausible to assume that they share something in common, that they all measure the same underlying attribute. This was exactly the conclusion reached by the English psychologist Charles Spearman (1863–1945), who developed the first version of **factor analysis,** a statistical technique by which one can "extract" this common factor that all of the various tests share. In his view, this factor was best described as **general intelligence,** or **g,** a mental attribute that is called upon in any intellectual task a person has to perform.

Spearman pointed out that this *g*-factor alone cannot explain the intercorrelations among mental tests. If test performance were determined by *g* and only *g,* then the correlations between any two subtests should be perfect except for errors of measurement. But in fact the intercorrelations fall far short of this. To explain why this is so, Spearman proposed that any test taps not only *g* but also some other ability, *s,* that is completely specific to the particular test used. Thus performance on an arithmetic subtest depends in part on *g* and in part on numerical skills *(s)* that are specific to that subtest. Since people vary along both general intelligence, *g,* and these different specific factors, the *s*'s, the intercorrelations among different tests cannot be perfect (Spearman, 1927).

Group-factor theories   Spearman described his theory of intelligence as "monarchic." As he saw it, there is one and only one underlying factor, *g,* that reigns supreme over all intellectual functions. But his position was soon challenged by other investigators who argued that the intercorrelations among test scores are better explained by a set of underlying mental abilities than by one overarching *g*-factor. Spearman called this **group-factor theory** an "oligarchic" conception of intelligence, since it viewed intelligence as just the composite of separate abilities without a sovereign capacity that enters into each. As an illustration of the kind of evidence that led to the multiple-factor theory, consider the hypothetical (and idealized) correlation matrix in Table 15.6 among four tests: digit span *(D)*, paired-associate learning *(P)*, vocabulary *(V)*, and comprehension *(C)*.

Table 15.6 HYPOTHETICAL CORRELATION MATRIX
BETWEEN FOUR TESTS

	D	*P*	*V*	*C*
D (Digit span)	–	.65	.40	.25
P (Paired associates)		–	.35	.30
V (Vocabulary)			–	.75
C (Comprehension)				–

In looking over the matrix, we see that all of the tests are positively correlated; this of course is the phenomenon that led Spearman to insist on *g*. But we also see that some of the tests form clusters. Scores on *D* tend more to go with those on *P* than with the scores on the other tests; the same holds for *V* and *C*. An adherent of the oligarchic view would interpret this pattern by postulating two underlying factors: The first is an ability tapped mostly by tests *D* and *P*, while the second enters primarily into tests *V* and *C*. To identify these two abilities, we look at the tests that enter into each and try to determine what they have in common. A reasonable guess is that the first factor (digit span and paired-associate learning) corresponds to a capacity for rote memory, while the second (vocabulary and comprehension) pertains to verbal ability.

Needless to say, this illustration is a drastic oversimplification. In actual practice, group-factor analysts operate on correlation matrices that are based on many tests deliberately selected to be as varied as possible. L. L. Thurstone (1887–1955), who originated most of the concepts and techniques that underlie group-factor theory, started with a set of 56 tests, yielding a matrix of 1,540 intercorrelations. Thurstone invented powerful new statistical techniques to extract the underlying factors, which he called "primary mental abilities." Some of the more important of these are spatial, numerical, verbal, and reasoning abilities.

Later investigators have come up with increasingly refined ways of classifying the mental abilities that underlie test performance. One of the most influential recent attempts was undertaken by J. P. Guilford, who proposed an ambitious three-dimensional classification of intellectual functions containing 120 factors in all. But Guilford's proposal amounts to more than just a new way of slicing up the intellectual pie. His scheme is based on a theory of how

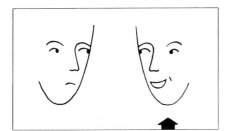

1 I'm glad you're feeling a little better.

2 You make the funniest faces!

3 Didn't I tell you she'd say "No"?

15.14 Testing for social intelligence
An item on one of Guilford's tests of social intelligence. The task is to decide what the person marked by the arrow is most probably saying to the other. (The answer is number 3). Thus far, there is relatively little evidence concerning the validity of this and similar tests of social intelligence. (From Guilford, 1967)

15.15 An ability profile based on group factors *An ability profile for a hypothetical male college student considering a career in architecture. The profile indicates his percentile scores on some important group factors. These are verbal ability (vocabulary, synonyms), numerical ability (arithmetic), spatial ability (reassembling cut-up objects), reasoning ability (interference problems), word fluency (give as many five-letter words as you can that start with* T*), and perceptual speed (rapid visual recognition). As the profile shows, the student is quite superior on the verbal and reasoning factors, but only average on the spatial and perceptual factors. Under the circumstances, a counselor might suggest a shift in career plans.*

intellectual tasks can be classified: by the kind of operation the thinker is asked to perform (e.g., evaluation, memory), by the materials on which she has to operate (e.g., visual figures, verbal meanings), and by the end result that is asked for (e.g., relations, implications). An attractive aspect of Guilford's approach is an unusually broad conception of what intelligence is. Some of his factors pertain to a kind of social intelligence, including the ability to infer another person's state of mind or to predict her probable behavior (Figure 15.14). Another example is a set of factors probably related to creativity, an attribute largely ignored in traditional tests of intelligence.

But despite these virtues, Guilford's system has not gone unchallenged. One major objection is that he has gone to the opposite extreme from Spearman. Where Spearman had one sole monarch, Guilford has an oligarchy of 120 separate and distinct factors. Guilford's critics contend that this carries the fractionation of human abilities too far, that 120 separate fragments are too narrow and specific to predict human behavior in any actual situation (Vernon, 1964).

The hierarchical theory Group-factor theories emphasize the fact that there are components of human ability that have a considerable range. While narrower than Spearman's *g*, they are much broader than his *s*'s. The identification of such group factors helped to explain the intercorrelations among tests of ability. But there was also a practical advantage. Group factors made it possible to interpret an individual's test results as a ***profile*** of different abilities that was often useful for vocational or educational guidance (Figure 15.15).

But such advantages notwithstanding, the group-factor theorists faced a troublesome problem: Spearman's *g* refused to go away. Consider Thurstone's Test of Primary Mental Abilities briefly described previously. It yielded several separate scores, each representing a different factor. But these factors are not as neatly independent as Thurstone might have wished. The person who obtained a high score on, say, spatial ability, also tended to do well in verbal tasks. To be sure, the correlation between these factors was not as great as the correlation among the subtests that measured each of them. But some correlation among the factors was still there. Spearman's monarch had returned from exile.

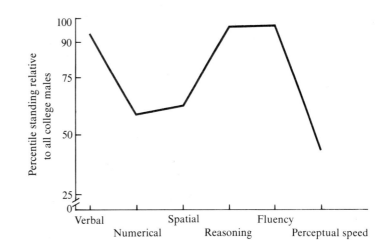

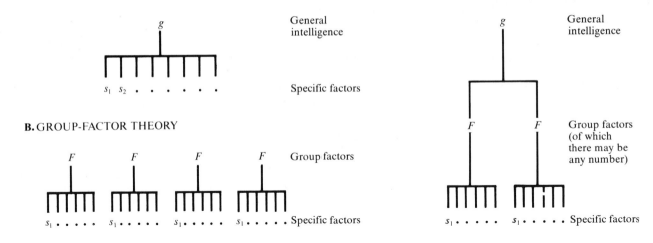

A. SPEARMAN'S THEORY

g

General intelligence

s_1 s_2 . . . . . .

Specific factors

B. GROUP-FACTOR THEORY

F   F   F   F   Group factors

s_1 . . . . s_1 . . . . s_1 . . . . s_1 . . . . Specific factors

C. HIERARCHICAL THEORY

g

General intelligence

F   F   Group factors (of which there may be any number)

s_1 . . . . s_1 . . . . Specific factors

15.16   A schematic review of three theories of the structure of human intelligence   *(A) Spearman's monarchic theory. (B) Group-factor theory. (C) The hierarchical theory.*

Some way had to be found for general intelligence and for narrower group abilities to coexist. The answer was a compromise between the monarchic and the oligarchic views: the ***hierarchical theory*** of human abilities (Vernon, 1950). According to the hierarchical theory, there is a broad, general ability, *g*, that manifests itself in every intellectual performance. But even after all people have been equalized on this *g*-factor (and this can be done by statistical means), there still are variations in their performance. These reflect abilities of intermediate generality: the group factors, of which the most important are those that distinguish verbal and nonverbal performance. Finally, there are aptitudes of a much more task-specific variety, equivalent to Spearman's *s*'s (Figure 15.16).

INTELLIGENCE AND AGE

Factor analysts tried to get some insight into the nature of intelligence by studying how scores on various subtests correlate with one another. Another psychometric approach is to relate test performance to other attributes on which people vary. An obvious candidate is age, which after all was the basis on which the first intelligence tests were standardized. But Binet used only the age range of three to sixteen years. Numerous later studies have asked about the development of intelligence throughout the entire life-span.

Intelligence in the infant   Several investigators have constructed scales to test the mental development of infants and young preschoolers. Such scales provide norms for representative behaviors at various ages; say, between four weeks and thirty-six months. The items measure visual-motor coordination, manipulative skills, imitation and comprehension, social responsiveness, and language functions (Table 15.7). These tests are a fair enough measure of developmental rate in early life, but they do not predict what happens in later years. Except in cases of severe retardation, there is no way of extrapolating what IQ a person will have at the age of ten or sixteen from information about how well she performed at eighteen months. Very little can be foretold about school-age intelligence until a child is three or four (Figure 15.17).

15.17   Correlations of boys' IQs at 16 to 18 with their mental test scores at earlier ages   *Correlations between adult intelligence and mental-test scores in infancy are negligible, until the child is about three or four. From that time on, they begin to predict later intelligence-test performance fairly well. (Bayley and Schaefer, 1964)*

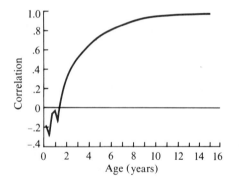

Table 15.7 SOME CHARACTERISTIC ITEMS TO TEST MENTAL DEVELOPMENT IN INFANTS AND YOUNG CHILDREN

Item	Average age at which item is passed (months)
Turns eyes to light	2
Turns to sound	4
Lifts cup	6
Recognizes voices	8
Puts cube in cup	10
Imitates words	12
Makes tower of two cubes	14
Makes tower of three cubes	16
Puts cover on box	18
Turns door knob	20
Names three objects	22
Names five pictures	24
Selects "big" object when asked	26
Understands three prepositions	28
Buttons one button	31
Names seven pictures	33

SOURCE: From Bailey, 1933.

Why is this so? The best guess is that tests designed for infants and young preschoolers tap different abilities than those measured by the Stanford-Binet or the Wechsler. This is not the fault of the tests; it is inherent in the nature of early childhood. The infant who is precocious in reaching for objects displays an earlier development of what Piaget called sensory-motor schemas (see Chapter 9). The development of these schemas is a necessary precondition for later levels of intellectual functioning that are built upon them. But these later levels are qualitatively different from the earlier ones; they involve symbolic and conceptual skills of an altogether different order. By the time children are three or four, they have some of the rudiments of the cognitive skills that make up adult intelligence. To this extent, a test of intelligence administered at this age draws on similar abilities as a test given in the late teens. This similarity becomes even greater by the age of seven, at which time the correlations with adult intelligence are quite respectable (about .70 to .80). This is reasonable enough, since there is considerable overlap between the cognitive demands made upon school-age children at seven and a decade later. It appears that whatever *g* may be, it doesn't become manifest until children are about three or four. In infants, *g* is only a potentiality, and their performances reveal very little about their probable intellects as adults.

Intelligence in later life Many investigators have tried to plot the growth of intelligence from middle childhood to old age. The procedure was straightforward. The same test was administered to different age groups matched by sex and socioeconomic level. Figure 15.18 presents a composite curve based on several investigations. The figure should hearten the young and bring gloom to all who are past twenty: There is a sharp increase in mental ability between ten and twenty, and an accelerating decline thereafter.

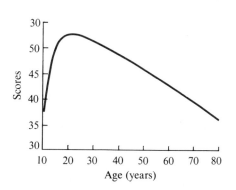

15.18 Mental test scores as related to age *The scores are based on comparisons of different age groups. They are expressed in units that allow comparisons of different tests and are based on averaged results of three different studies. (After Jones and Kaplan, 1945)*

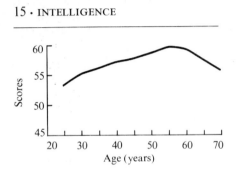

15.19 Mental test scores as related to age when studied by the longitudinal method *The scores, which cover a fifty-year age range, were obtained over a seven-year period from several adult populations, the youngest of which was twenty at the beginning of the study and the oldest in their sixties. (After Schaie and Strother, 1968)*

Later investigators (perhaps prompted by the fact that they were over thirty) concluded that the situation could not be as bleak as that. They argued that the steep decline in intelligence could have resulted from an artifact, a by-product of an irrelevant factor: On the average, the older age groups had a lower level of education. Such a difference might have been present even if the groups were matched by years of schooling, for curricula have probably improved over time. One way of getting around this difficulty is through a *longitudinal* study in which the same persons are tested at different ages. The results of such longitudinal studies show a continued *rise* on tests for verbal meaning, for reasoning, and for educational aptitude until about fifty. After this, there is a moderate decline (Figure 15.19).

Further studies have shown that the age curves are different depending upon the particular ability that is tested. Many facets of verbal intelligence show no decline until seventy. Tests of vocabulary are even more encouraging to those of later years; they show no drop even at eighty-five (Blum, Jarvik, and Clark, 1970). In contrast, nonverbal abilities that are tapped by such tests as the Progressive Matrices decline earlier, usually around forty (Green, 1969). The most pronounced drops are found for tests that depend on quick recall, especially when there is no memory organization that can aid in retrieval (see Chapter 8). An example is the word fluency test, in which the subject has two minutes to write down as many words as he can think of which start with a particular letter. Such mental calisthenics are best left to the young; declines in word fluency are very steep and are seen as early as thirty (Schaie and Strother, 1968).

Some authors believe that the different age curves found for different subtests of intelligence scales reflect an important distinction between two underlying intellectual abilities (Cattell, 1963). One is *fluid intelligence* which is the ability to deal with essentially new problems. The other is *crystallized intelligence* which is the repertoire of information, cognitive skills, and strategies acquired by application of fluid intelligence to various fields. According to the theory, fluid intelligence declines with age, beginning in middle adulthood or earlier. But crystallized intelligence does not drop off. On the contrary, it will continue to grow until old age if the person is in an intellectually stimulating environment. From the point of view of actual functioning in middle age and beyond, the drop in the one ability may be more than compensated for by the increase in the other.* The older person has "appropriated the collective intelligence of the culture for his own use" (Horn and Cattell, 1967). By so doing, he has not only amassed a store of knowledge larger than the one he had when he was younger, but he has also developed better ways of organizing this knowledge, of approaching problems, of filing new information away for later use.

These cognitive achievements are similar to those we discussed in Chapter 9 in which we considered the distinction between "masters" and "apprentices." The masters have chunked and organized the material at a different level than the apprentices. On balance, then, the slight loss in fluid intelligence can be tolerated if made up for by an increase in crystallized intelligence. Still, there are drawbacks. If the problem is really new, the older person may not be able

---

* Some of these issues are still a matter of debate (e.g., Horn and Donaldson, 1976; Baltes and Schaie, 1976).

to tackle it as capably as he once might have. This is especially true if speed of recall is a factor. As Wechsler put it, "Wisdom and experience are necessary to make the world go round; creative ability to make it go forward" (Wechsler, 1958, p. 143).

The distinction between fluid and crystallized intelligence has a practical side, for it can help in the diagnosis of mental deterioration. A pronounced difference between a vocabulary score and some appropriate performance test is often very revealing. Suppose a high vocabulary score is accompanied by a drastically lower score on a test that is a fair index of fluid intelligence (such as the Progressive Matrices). Since vocabulary reflects crystallized intelligence, it is relatively unaffected by changes in the person's present level of intellectual functioning. It operates like a marker on certain thermometers. As the mercury column climbs, the marker is pushed up. But it doesn't fall down even after the mercury drops; as a result, its position shows the maximum temperature attained on the preceding day. The vocabulary score can be interpreted in an analogous fashion. It measures the level of fluid intelligence a person once had. A serious discrepancy between the vocabulary score and some appropriate performance test will thus suggest a deterioration of intellectual ability. This decline may be temporary as in cases of severe emotional disturbance. But it may also be essentially permanent, as in brain damage and senile decay.

THE SEARCH FOR UNDERLYING PROCESSES

What has the psychometric approach taught us about intelligence? We know that the instruments devised by Binet and his successors can diagnose the extreme form of intellectual deficit we call mental retardation; they can also predict school success, at least as defined in a middle-class, twentieth-century industrial world. We have considered the hypothesis that these instruments measure an underlying set of abilities, of which some are more and some less general; the whole structure probably is arranged according to a hierarchical scheme. Finally, these tests show marked changes in performance over age— an initial sharp improvement followed by a moderate decline on some subtests in later years. Many of these results are of considerable practical importance. Since tests are used in diagnosis, guidance, and selection, they often have an important impact on individual lives. But has any of this helped us to understand the processes that underlie more or less intelligent behavior? Does it explain why individuals fail (or succeed) on a particular problem? The psychometric approach provides tools whereby we can compare how people perform relative to each other; their relative standing gives us a measure of a presumed attribute we call intelligence. But it provides little insight into the mechanisms that lead to problem solution or to failure.

By way of analogy, consider how the psychometric approach might be extended to measure the performance of automobiles. The purchaser wants to predict how the car she considers buying today will perform some years hence, say, in power or in the number of required repairs. We can imagine a Binet of the future applying his talents to the vehicular field. He takes many different models, presumably in the same price category, and measures their performance along with a large number of subtests—acceleration, braking, number of rattles in a standardized test ride, and so on. All of these indices are

603

correlated with the cars' performance two years later. Those that correlate highly are kept in the scale. Some future Spearman might even go further and use the intercorrelations among the subtests to extract a common factor, *a,* corresponding to "general automotive competence."

Such a psychometric (or, rather, autometric) approach might have some practical usefulness; if the test works, consumer advocates would surely be delighted. But the measures will not provide much theoretical insight. We would know that a particular car gets a high score, but this alone will not tell us why it functions as well as it does. To answer that question, we have to say something about the mechanisms that determine how an automobile operates and why it breaks down; how an internal combustion engine works and what the brake disks do.

For automobiles, of course, the mechanisms are known. But in the case of intelligence the situation is different. To understand intelligent (or unintelligent) performance, we need a reasonable theory of thinking and problem solving, including their relationships to language function and to various other cognitive processes such as memory, attention, and perception. But as we have seen, we are still far from having such a theory (see Chapters 7–10).

There have been some efforts in this direction. They generally involve two steps. To begin with, the investigator takes two or more groups that differ markedly in what we intuitively mean by intelligence and that also differ in their measured test scores. Examples are groups of young and older children or of mentally retarded and normal persons. These groups are then compared in task situations which tap processes that experimental psychologists have studied in other contexts and for which some theories already exist. Examples might be classical conditioning, discrimination learning, short- and long-term memory tasks, and Piagetian conservation problems. If groups that have previously been defined as more or less intelligent perform differently on some but not all of these, we have an initial hint about the difference in underlying processes that distinguish the two.

INTELLIGENCE TESTING AND PIAGET

One line of inquiry grows out of the work of Jean Piaget, which we have considered in a previous section (see Chapter 9). To recapitulate briefly, Piaget distinguished four main stages of intellectual development: *sensory-motor intelligence* (0–2 years) during which children achieve the conception of a stable physical world; the *preoperational stage* (2–7 years) during which they develop an increasing capacity to "represent" mentally objects and events that are not actually in the physical here and now; the *stage of concrete operations* (7–11 years) during which they develop an initial primitive set of rules for manipulating such representations; and the *stage of formal operations* (from 11 years on) in which these rules have become more systematic and permit genuinely abstract thought. An important test for the presence of such rules (which Piaget called *operations*) is the child's understanding that certain properties of an object stay unchanged despite various transformations—they are *conserved.* An example is *conservation of liquid quantity,* a test for the presence of concrete operations, which is shown when the child realizes that the amount of liquid remains the same when poured from a wide beaker into a tall, narrow glass.

Piaget and the mental-test movement parted company over fifty years ago, at the very start of Piaget's long career. At that time, Piaget worked in a laboratory supervised by Binet's collaborator Simon. However, his interests soon diverged from Simon's. Where Simon (as Binet) tried to determine whether a child passed or failed a given item, Piaget wanted to know *why* the child answered as it did, especially when the answer was wrong. Since then, Piaget's primary concern has been with those aspects of intellectual development that are the same in every child. But Piaget's system can be adjusted to allow for at least some individual differences. Some of his co-workers have suggested that there are different rates of development and that some stage (or even stages) may never be reached in some children. This line of reasoning led to the construction of diagnostic tests using tasks—mainly conservation problems—that check some of Piaget's developmental mileposts. On the evidence provided by such tests, Piaget's main collaborator, Bärbel Inhelder, concluded that mildly retarded persons eventually attain concrete operations, though at a later age than normals, but that they never acquire formal operational thought. More severely retarded persons never progress beyond the preoperational level, as shown by their inability to conserve mass, not recognizing that a clay ball contains the same amount of clay even when flattened into a pancake. Similar findings have been obtained by other investigators (Wilton and Boersma, 1974).

The Piagetian approach may shed some light on mental retardation, but how successful is it in explaining variations in intelligence among normals? The results look promising for work in the five- to eight-year range. Here, Piagetian tasks correlate respectably (at least .50) with standard tests of intelligence and also with school achievement (Jensen, 1980). One advantage of these tasks, according to their proponents, is that they are relatively "culture-free": They seem less dependent on particular learned skills that are more likely to be picked up in one cultural milieu rather than another. Even so, there are some difficulties. One problem is that the last of Piaget's mental stages, that of formal operations, has not been as extensively investigated as the earlier ones. This makes it harder to assess differences among older children, let alone adults, who have presumably reached this rung on the Piagetian ladder (Figure 15.20).

INTELLIGENCE AND HUMAN COGNITIVE PROCESSES

A somewhat different line of attack has been taken by psychologists whose primary concern is with such cognitive processes as learning, memory, and attention. Can differences in intelligence-test scores be attributed to differences in these more fundamental domains?

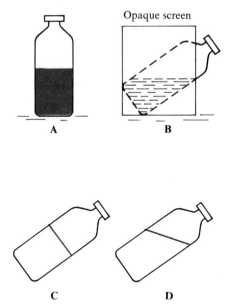

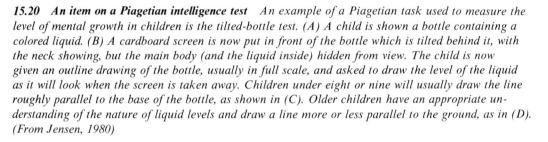

15.20 An item on a Piagetian intelligence test An example of a Piagetian task used to measure the level of mental growth in children is the tilted-bottle test. (A) A child is shown a bottle containing a colored liquid. (B) A cardboard screen is now put in front of the bottle which is tilted behind it, with the neck showing, but the main body (and the liquid inside) hidden from view. The child is now given an outline drawing of the bottle, usually in full scale, and asked to draw the level of the liquid as it will look when the screen is taken away. Children under eight or nine will usually draw the line roughly parallel to the base of the bottle, as shown in (C). Older children have an appropriate understanding of the nature of liquid levels and draw a line more or less parallel to the ground, as in (D). (From Jensen, 1980)

The search for elementary capacities The most tempting hypothesis is that there are a few (ideally, just one) differences in some elementary capacity such as the rate at which associations are formed and/or forgotten. But in fact, there is little evidence that variations in intelligence can be attributed to rock-bottom differences of this kind. Retarded subjects acquire a classically conditioned response in just about the same number of trials as do normals. Much the same holds for forgetting. There is no evidence that retarded persons, once having learned a skill, are more prone to forget it over time than people of normal IQ (Estes, 1970).

More recent studies have focused on various operations in short- and long-term memory. An example is the recognition that the characters *A* and *a,* though not identical physically, share the same name, while *A* and *e* do not. The reaction time to reach this judgment is reliably faster in college students who do well on conventional tests of verbal ability than it is in students whose test performance is inferior (E. Hunt, Lunneborg, and Lewis, 1975). Some authors interpret this result as evidence for the view that one of the basic factors underlying verbal intelligence is the speed with which name tags are looked up in the long-term store. In their view, this and some other related cognitive factors are the elements on which differences in intelligence-test performance rest (E. Hunt, 1976). But thus far, these claims are still in the realm of conjecture. To bolster the view that such cognitive functions are really more basic than those that have been proposed by previous investigators—from Binet and Spearman to Piaget—one would require some evidence that performance on tasks that tap these functions, such as the *A-a* recognition test, is an especially powerful predictor of some relevant validity criterion. Thus far no such evidence has been offered.

The role of strategies It would appear that, thus far at least, no one has found a difference in some elementary capacity that provides an adequate explanation for the enormous discrepancies in the intellectual performance of normal and retarded subjects, or of older and younger children. A normal adult can master tasks (such as memorizing a 16-place number) that are generally beyond the reach of a retarded adult or of a normal six-year old. The main reason does not seem to be that the normal adult has a better grade of mental glue. It is rather that she uses a well-developed repertoire of strategies for solving problems, for learning, and for remembering. When asked to memorize unrelated items, she rehearses and tries to organize the material by imposing some kind of structure upon it, by rhythmic grouping, syntactic order, or semantic categories. Similar strategies come into play at the time of retrieval, as shown by the fact that the order in which the items are recalled reflects the category clusters under which they were filed in memory (see Chapter 8).

Strategies of this kind, if they exist at all, are much more primitive in retardates, who attack tasks with little or no resort to organization. Mentally retarded persons are less likely to group the items in a list, or to use mnemonic aids such as meaningful connections between items, or to show category clustering (A. Brown, 1974). Similar results have been found in young children (Flavell, 1970; Flavell and Wellman, 1976).

A related effect concerns the use of rehearsal in recall. When presented with a list of nine items, the retardates' recall of the earlier items is much inferior to

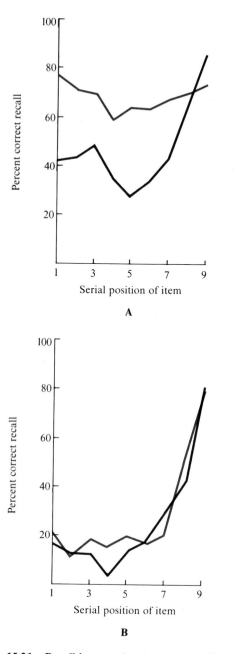

A

B

that of normals. This is presumably because retarded persons do not rehearse, or rehearse less efficiently (Ellis, 1970). Further evidence comes from the effects of varying the rates at which the items are presented. We know that a slower rate increases the opportunity for rehearsal and should thus enhance the *primacy effect* (recall of the earlier items) without affecting the *recency effect* (recall of the later items, which depends on short-term memory; see Chapter 8). This is what happens in normals. But the results are different in retardates. As Figure 15.21 shows, a slower rate of presentation augments the primacy effect in normals but makes virtually no difference to the recall performance of retardates. The mentally retarded person is not helped by an increase in the available study time for he does not know how to study.

Is there any way of teaching retardates or young children some of the strategies for problem solving and remembering that they so grossly lack? This question has important implications; if the answer is yes, then some aspects of retardation may be remediable. The results of several investigations provide a glimmer of hope. There is evidence that retarded subjects can be trained to rehearse; for example, by being required to repeat the items cumulatively and aloud (A. Brown et al., 1973). This induced rehearsal procedure leads to recall performance virtually identical to that of normal adults.

These results would be extremely encouraging except for one discordant note. According to many investigators, the newly acquired strategies are often abandoned shortly after they are taught. Furthermore, they tend not to be generalized to tasks other than the one in which they were acquired. An example is training in the use of semantic categories, which shows little transfer to new lists with different verbal materials (Bilsky, Evans, and Gilbert, 1972). Other investigators take a more optimistic view. They cite evidence that retardates can retain a rehearsal strategy over a six-month interval (Brown, Campione, and Murphy, 1974). Further studies indicate that when the original training is extensive enough, various mnemonic organizational strategies will show some transfer to new situations (Nye, McManis, and Haugen, 1972; Turnure and Thurlow, 1973). It is clear that all of the facts are not yet in. But the bulk of the evidence suggests that while young children and retarded persons can be taught some strategies for learning and remembering, the strategies tend to help mostly in the specific situation of the particular problem.

Strategies for using strategies How is it that retarded persons and young children are generally so narrow in their use of the strategies they are taught? If retardates learn to remember a set of names by rehearsing them aloud, why don't they apply the same principle to a shopping list? According to several

15.21 Recall in normal and retarded subjects *(A) A group of normal subjects had to remember the location of nine digits that were presented, one at a time, in nine different places. In one condition, there was a two-second pause between digits; in the other, there was no pause. The figure plots recall against the item's serial position on the list: that is, presented first, second, and so on. The pause condition (color) produces better recall than the no-pause condition (black), a superiority that is most pronounced toward the beginning and middle of the list. This marked enhancement of the primacy effect is caused by the opportunity for rehearsal during the pause. (B) The same experiment was performed on a group of adult retarded subjects with an average IQ of 61. The figure shows that their recall was poorer than that of the normal subjects, and that the pause condition (color) was virtually identical with the no-pause condition (black), indicating that the retarded subjects did not make use of the opportunity to rehearse. Note that the recall of the last one or two digits—which does not depend on rehearsal—is no worse in the retardate than in the normal group. (After Ellis, 1970)*

writers, what is lacking is a "master plan" for dealing with memory tasks in general, a strategy for using strategies (Flavell, 1970). Normal adults adopt this higher-order strategy as a matter of course whenever they try to learn. They know that remembering telephone numbers, or traffic directions, or the names of the twelve cranial nerves, are at bottom similar memory tasks. They also know that trying to learn them means to use some aids to learning—the lower-order strategies of rehearsal, rhythmic and semantic grouping, or whatever. Both young children and retardates lack this general insight. They don't recognize what all memory tasks have in common and what they all require for their mastery. Young children will get it in time; retardates may never attain it.

Some relevant evidence comes from studies that contrast the results of intentional and incidental learning. In such investigations, some subjects are intentional learners; they are asked to memorize a list and expect to be tested later on. Other subjects are incidental learners. They are exposed to the identical list while performing some extraneous "cover task" that forces them to attend to the list, such as crossing out all the *e*'s in every word; to their surprise, they are later asked to recall the items. In normals, the result is a sizable superiority in the recall performance of intentional learners. But in preschool children, recall is no different after intentional or incidental learning instructions (Appel et al., 1972). The same holds for retarded adolescents (Shif, 1969). It seems reasonable to conclude that normal adults benefit from the intention to learn because this intent leads to an active utilization of organizational strategies (see Chapter 8). The young and the retarded have few such strategies if any (Figure 15.22).

This strategy for using strategies displayed by normal intentional learners is an instance of a general class of higher-order cognitive processes. Human adults can reflect on the cognitive operations whereby they gain knowledge. They know, and they also know that they know. They perceive and know that they perceive; this allows them to understand that some perceptual experiences are illusions, to become artists or art connoisseurs. They communicate through language and know that they do; this permits them not only to talk and understand but also to play with language, as in puns and word games, to recognize that some sentences are ill-formed, and to become linguists. They can remember and often know that they remember; this provides the awareness of a personal past that still lives in the present. The ability to learn intentionally requires a similar higher-order process. It is based upon the recognition that all learning tasks call for something similar from the learner and it requires the ability to utilize a common overall plan to master them. Such higher-order cognitive processes are generally subsumed under the general label ***metacognition,*** knowing that one knows and how one gets to know. It

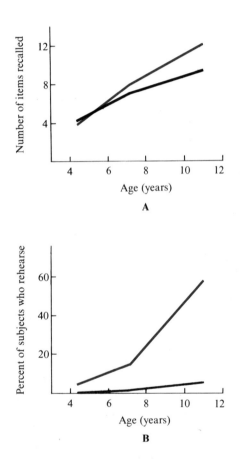

15.22 Strategies for memorizing in children *(A) Nursery-school children, first graders, and fifth graders were shown a number of pictures. In one condition, they were merely asked to look at the stimuli. In another, they were asked to look and to try to remember. Recall was tested after both conditions. In the oldest children, the try-to-remember condition (color) produced better recall than the just-look condition (black), but no such difference was found for the youngest group. (B) While the subjects watched the stimuli, the experimenters observed them for signs of rehearsal—naming the pictures, moving the lips while watching, and so on. The figure shows the proportion of all children who rehearsed in the just-look (black) and in the try-to-remember condition (color). In the older children, there was quite a bit of rehearsal in the try-to-remember condition. But there was very little for the first graders and virtually none for the nursery-school children. Very similar results have been found for retarded subjects. (Data from Appel et al., 1972)*

may well be that such metacognitive processes are one of the distinguishing hallmarks of adult human intelligence.

THE LACK OF A PROCESS THEORY

As we look back, it is clear that we are still far from an understanding of the processes that underlie intelligence. To put it another way, we have taken only a few tentative steps toward the construct validation of intelligence tests. Piaget and other developmental psychologists have given us some insight into its growth from childhood origins; psychologists concerned with learning and memory have provided us with some leads, including the role of various strategies that young children and retardates lack. But these are only guideposts for the future. Thus far, we have no general theory of intelligence. We may be able to measure intelligence, but we don't know what it really is.

Heredity, Environment, and IQ

While it is far from clear just what intelligence tests really measure, this state of affairs has not deterred psychologists—nor indeed, the general public—from making intelligence-test performance one of the major foci of the nature-nurture controversy, debating it with a stormy passion rarely found in any other area of the discipline.

The vehemence of the debate is understandable considering that mental testing is a field in which the concerns of the scientist impinge drastically upon those of the practical world. In our society, those who are well off tend to do better on intelligence tests than those who are disadvantaged. The same holds for their children. Why is this so? There is some tendency for social groups to be biased in favor of different answers. This bias was especially marked some sixty years ago when the prevailing social climate was much more conservative. Then—and to a lesser extent even now—advantaged groups were more likely to believe that intelligence is largely inherited. This assertion was certainly comforting to those who benefited from the status quo since it suggested they got what they "deserved."

In contrast, spokesmen for the disadvantaged took a different view. To begin with, they often disparaged the tests themselves, arguing that the tests are not fair to their own subculture. In addition, they argued that intellectual aptitudes are much more determined by nurture than nature. In their view, differences in intelligence, especially those between different ethnic and racial groups, are determined predominantly by environmental factors such as early home background and schooling. Seen in this light, the children of the poor obtain lower test scores, not because they inherit deficient genes, but rather because they inherit poverty.

These contrasting views lead to different prescriptions for social policy. An example of the impact of a hereditarian bias is the rationale behind the United States immigration policy between the two World Wars. The Immigration Act of 1924 set definite quotas to minimize the influx of what were thought to be biologically "weaker stocks," specifically those from Southern and Eastern Europe. To prove the genetic intellectual inferiority of these immigrants, a congressional committee pointed to their army intelligence-test scores, which were indeed substantially below those attained by Americans of Northern European ancestry.

In actual fact, the differences were primarily related to the length of time that the immigrants had been in the United States prior to the test; their average test scores rose with every year and became indistinguishable from native-born Americans after twenty years of residence in the United States. This result undermines the hypothesis of a hereditary difference in intelligence between, say, Northern and Eastern Europeans. But the congressional proponents of differential immigration quotas did not analyze the results so closely. They had their own reasons for restricting immigration, such as fears of competition from cheap labor; the theory that the excluded groups were innately inferior provided a convenient justification for their policies (Kamin, 1974).

A more contemporary example of the relation between psychological theory and social policy is the argument over the value of compensatory education programs for preschool children from disadvantaged backgrounds. Such programs have been said to be failures because they generally do not lead to improvement in later scholastic performance. The question is why. A highly controversial paper by Arthur Jensen suggests that heredity may be a significant contributing factor. According to Jensen, the fact that the average intelligence-test score of American blacks is lower than that of whites may be due in part to genetic differences between these groups. Given this hereditarian position, Jensen argues that environmental alterations such as compensatory education programs can at best mitigate the group difference; they cannot abolish it (Jensen, 1969). Jensen's thesis has been vehemently debated on many counts, some of which we will discuss below. For now, we will only note that the failure of a given compensatory program (assuming that it was really a failure) does not prove the hereditarians' claim. Perhaps the preschool experience that was provided was not of the right sort; perhaps it was inadequate to counter the overwhelming effects of ghetto life* (J. McV. Hunt, 1961).

Our emphasis thus far has been on the social and political aspects of the nature-nurture issue in intelligence, the considerations that bias people to take one or another side of the issue. But while it is interesting to know what people prefer to believe about the world, our primary concern is with what that world is really like. What is the evidence about the contributions of heredity and environment in producing differences *within* groups (for instance, among American whites) and *between* groups (for instance, between American whites and blacks)?

GENETICS AND INTELLIGENCE

Before turning to the relationship between intelligence-test performance and genetic endowment, we must say a few words about the mechanisms that underlie the transmission of genetic characteristics from one generation to the next.

* While the effects of preschool education on intelligence-test scores is debatable, there is evidence that this early experience does have a positive effect on school performance in later years. Low-income children who have participated in preschool programs seem to perform more acceptably in later grades (from 4th to 12th) than children who did not, as measured by not being held back in grade, not dropping out of school, and so on (Lazar and Darlington, 1978).

THE MECHANISM OF GENETIC TRANSMISSION

Every organism starts life with a genetic blueprint, a set of instructions that steers its development from fertilized cell to mature animal or plant. The genetic commands are carried by the *chromosomes* in the cell's nucleus. In organisms that reproduce sexually, the chromosomes come in corresponding pairs, with one member of each pair contributed by each parent. In humans, there are 23 such chromosome pairs.

Every chromosome stores thousands of genetic commands, each of which is biologically engraved in a *gene,* the unit of hereditary transmission. Any given gene is located at a particular place (its *locus*) on a given chromosome. Since chromosomes come in pairs, each member of the pair has corresponding loci at which there are genes that carry instructions about the same bodily characteristic (for example, eye color). These two related genes or *alleles*—one contributed by each parent—may or may not be identical. Consider eye color. If both alleles are identical (blue-blue or brown-brown), there is no problem; the eye color will follow suit. But suppose they are different. Now the overt expression of the genetic blueprint depends upon still other relationships between the members of the gene pair. One such relationship is dominance. In humans, the brown-eyed allele is *dominant;* it will exert its effect regardless of whether the other member of the gene pair calls for brown or blue eyes. In contrast, the blue-eyed allele is *recessive.* The recessive blue-eyed allele will lead to blue eyes only if there is an identical, that is, blue-eyed, allele on the corresponding locus of the paired chromosome.

Phenotype versus genotype The phenomenon of gene dominance illustrates a crucial distinction in the study of heredity. On the one hand, there is the overt appearance of an organism—its visible structure and behavior. This is the *phenotype,* the characteristic we actually observe in a given individual. But this phenotype is by no means equivalent to the organism's genetic blueprint, or *genotype.* As we have seen, two people who have brown eyes may well have different genotypes for eye color; one may be brown-brown, the other brown-blue. The phenotypes are the same, for if a blue-eyed allele is present it will be masked by its brown-eyed counterpart. To uncover the actual genotype one has to perform an appropriate breeding experiment. One possibility is to mate the brown-eyed person with a blue-eyed one (whose genotype has to be blue-blue since blue is a recessive), and examine the eye color of their children. (The father of genetics, Gregor Mendel, performed analogous experiments in a Czech monastery over a hundred years ago; he, however, found it more convenient to breed peas than people). If the brown-eyed parent's genotype is brown-brown, none of the children will have blue eyes. If his or her genotype is brown-blue, one-fourth of the children will be blue-eyed (Figure 15.23, page 612). The crucial point is that the genotype cannot be directly assessed from a knowledge of the phenotype alone; it is obtained by inference from the results of breeding experiments.

The underlying genotype thus may be masked by the interaction between alleles. Another way in which a genotype may be kept from overt expression is by the interaction between genotype and environment. This interaction is especially important during earlier stages in the organism's development. A

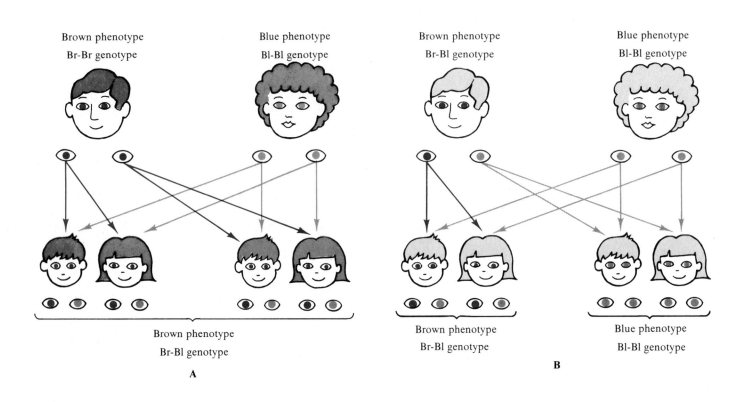

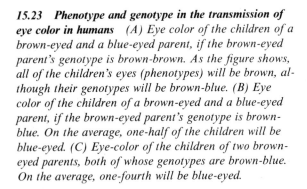

15.23 Phenotype and genotype in the transmission of eye color in humans *(A) Eye color of the children of a brown-eyed and a blue-eyed parent, if the brown-eyed parent's genotype is brown-brown. As the figure shows, all of the children's eyes (phenotypes) will be brown, although their genotypes will be brown-blue. (B) Eye color of the children of a brown-eyed and a blue-eyed parent, if the brown-eyed parent's genotype is brown-blue. On the average, one-half of the children will be blue-eyed. (C) Eye-color of the children of two brown-eyed parents, both of whose genotypes are brown-blue. On the average, one-fourth will be blue-eyed.*

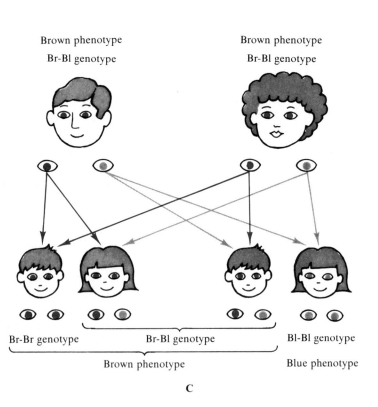

particular genetic command can only be executed if certain characteristics (oxygen concentration, temperature) both within and outside of the developing body are within a certain range.

As an example, consider the dark markings on the paws, tail, and eartips of a Siamese cat. These markings are not present at birth, but appear gradually as the kitten matures. The genealogical records kept by cat breeders leave no doubt that these markings in the mature animal are determined by heredity. But this does not mean that this characteristic emerges independently of the environment. In Siamese cats, the critical environmental variable turns out to be temperature. The dark markings will only appear if the kitten's extremities are kept at their normal temperature, which happens to be lower than that of the rest of the animal's body. If the extremities are deliberately warmed during early kittenhood by such devices as leggings and tail- and earmuffs, they will not turn darker—in apparent defiance of the creature's genotype (Ilyin and Ilyin, 1930).

This example underlines the fact that genes do not operate in a vacuum. They are instructions to a developing organism, instructions that will be followed only within a given range of environmental conditions. It therefore makes no sense to talk of heredity alone or environment alone, for there is no trait that does not depend upon both. There can be no organism without a genotype, and this genotype cannot ever express itself independently of the environment.

The inheritance of behavior   So far, our examples have concerned the inheritance of bodily attributes, but there is ample evidence that many behavioral characteristics are also a matter of heredity. Different strains of dogs vary in their emotional dispositions. Basset hounds are relatively lethargic, German shepherds are relatively excitable, and the offspring of their cross-matings have temperaments in between (W. T. James, 1941). Some behavioral tendencies seem to be determined by a single gene. An example is the response to intense, high-pitched noises in mice. Some mice are relatively unaffected, while others react with violent epileptic seizures. Breeding experiments analogous to Mendel's have shown that this proneness to seizures is carried by a single recessive allele (Collins and Fuller, 1968).

An illustration of a human psychological characteristic that is determined by a single gene is a severe form of mental retardation, ***phenylketonuria*** or ***PKU***. In the United States, about one baby in every fifteen thousand is born with this defect. PKU is caused by a deficiency in an enzyme which allows the body to transform ***phenylalinine,*** an amino acid (a building block of proteins) into another amino acid. When this enzyme is absent, phenylalinine accumulates and is converted into a toxic agent that accumulates in the infant's bloodstream and damages its developing nervous system. Analyses of the incidence of PKU among the siblings of afflicted children and of their family trees indicate that this disorder is produced by a single recessive allele.

Although PKU is of genetic origin, it can be treated by appropriate environmental intervention. (Its detection in the newborn is a simple matter of a blood test.) The trick is a special diet that contains very little phenylalinine. If this diet is introduced at an early enough age, retardation can be minimized, or even eliminated.

This result demonstrates the fallacy of the popular belief that the consequences of what is inborn is necessarily unchangeable. The genes lay down certain biochemical instructions that determine the development of a particular organ system; if we understand the genetic command clearly enough, we may eventually find ways to circumvent it. In the case of PKU, we can already do so (McClearn and deFries, 1973).

Polygenic inheritance Characteristics determined by a single gene are generally of an either-or character: brown-eyed or blue-eyed, seizure-prone or not seizure-prone, and so on. But what can we say about attributes that vary continuously, like stature or IQ? To the extent that these are genetically determined, the determination is probably not by a single gene, as for height and intelligence which are obviously not all-or-none in nature. The answer is **polygenic inheritance,** in which the expression of the trait is controlled by many gene pairs. As an example, let us assume that height is determined by, say, ten gene pairs. At each of the ten gene loci, there can be either of two alleles, which we will call T or t. Any one T allele will add, say, an inch to some average value; a t allele has no effect (for the sake of simplicity, we will assume that there is no dominance relationship). The resulting set of genotypes will then range from one that has a total of 20 Ts (every gene pair is TT) to one that has no Ts at all (every gene pair is tt). If we assume that a genotype of 10 Ts produces a phenotype of average height, say, 5′6″, the resulting distribution of phenotypes will approximate a normal curve, with a mean of 5′6″ and a range that extends from 4′8″ to 6′4″. The reason there are so many more individuals in the region of the mean than at the extreme is simple enough: There are many more combinations that produce a genotype of 10 T/10 t than genotypes of more extreme values; say, 18 T/2 t. This polygenic conception of inheritance brings us back to our discussion of Quetelet and nature's coin tossings. In our present example, nature throws twenty genetic coins to generate a frequency distribution of heights that is approximately normal (Figure 15.24).

In the light of the preceding analysis, the fact that a given trait is normally distributed is sometimes taken as evidence for its polygenic inheritance. But this conclusion does not follow. A normal distribution implies that there is a multitude of independent factors each of which contributes a small share to the final value. But it does not tell us whether these factors are genetic or environmental. All we can conclude from the distribution is that, *if* there is a hereditary contribution, it is likely to be polygenic.

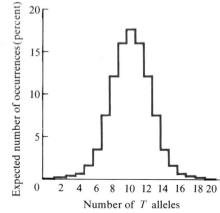

15.24 Polygenic inheritance *Expected number of genotypes given twenty independent chances of obtaining T rather than t. The figure shows the probability of obtaining O T/20t, 1T/19 t, and so on, which approximates a normal curve, as explained in the text.*

GENETIC CONTRIBUTIONS TO INTELLIGENCE

How can we find out whether human intelligence (at least as measured by intelligence-test performance) has a genetic basis? To do so, we have to infer the underlying genotypes from the observable phenotypic behavior. In animals, this task is accomplished by suitable breeding experiments. But outside of science fiction novels, such studies cannot be performed on humans, since people stubbornly refuse to cooperate with behavior geneticists and insist on picking their own mates. Under the circumstances, how can we proceed?

Disentangling genetic and environmental factors One basic strategy is to examine the similarities between relatives, an approach that dates back to

Francis Galton. Galton found that eminence (which he measured by reputation) runs in families; eminent men were more likely to have eminent relatives than the average person (Galton, 1869). Similar results have been repeatedly obtained with intelligence-test scores. For example, the correlation between the IQs of children and parents, or between the IQs of siblings, runs in the neighborhood of .50 (Erlenmeyer-Kimling and Jarvik, 1963). From Galton's perspective, such findings document the inheritance of mental ability. But the environmentalist has a ready reply. Consider eminence. The relatives of an eminent person obviously share his or her social, educational, and financial advantages. As a result, there is a similarity of environmental background, as well as an overlapping set of genes. The same argument applies to the interpretation of the correlations between the IQs of close relatives.

A similar problem arises in another connection. As we've previously seen, IQs tend to be fairly stable; the ten-year old with an IQ of 130 will probably get a roughly similar score at fifteen. Supporters of the genetic theory of intelligence have often interpreted this constancy of the IQ as evidence for their views. As they see it, this constancy shows that intelligence tests measure an inborn capacity, "native intelligence," which is an essentially unalterable characteristic of an individual and is genetically based. This belief has been used as a justification of such educational practices as early assignment to one or another school track. But IQ constancy is no proof that intelligence is fixed or inborn. To the extent that this constancy occurs, it only demonstrates that a child tends to maintain his relative standing among his age-mates over time. This may be because of a genetically given attribute that remains unchanged with age. But it may also be because the child's environmental advantages stay pretty much the same as time goes on. If a child is born in a slum, the odds are pretty good that she will still be there at twelve; the same holds if she is born in a palace. Once again, the evidence is inconclusive.

During the last fifty years, psychologists have developed a variety of research designs that were meant to disentangle hereditary and environmental factors. We will consider two main attempts to accomplish this end: (1) the study of twins and (2) the study of adopted children.

Twin studies Twins must have been especially created for the benefit of human behavior geneticists, for one could hardly imagine a more ideal group for the investigation of the nature-nurture issue. There are two kinds of twins—***identical*** and ***fraternal.*** Identical twins originate from a single fertilized egg that splits into two exact replicas which then develop into two genetically identical individuals. In contrast, fraternal twins arise from two different fertilized eggs. Each of two eggs in the female reproductive tract is fertilized by a different sperm cell. Under the circumstances, the genetic similarity between fraternal twins is no greater than that between ordinary siblings. Since this is so, a comparison between identical twins and fraternal twins of the same sex is of considerable interest, if one is willing to assume that the twins' environments are no more similar if they are identical than if they are fraternal. Given this premise, it follows that if identical twins turn out to be more similar on some trait than fraternals, one can conclude that this trait is in part genetically determined.

The relevant comparisons have been performed in over a dozen studies. In each case, the essential result was the same. The correlation between the IQs

15.25 Correlations between intelligence-test performance of children and other members of the family with whom they live *The figure is a summary of a large number of studies of correlations between intelligence-test performance of children and other members of the family with whom or by whom they were reared. Every point represents the correlation obtained in an individual U. S. study. The vertical slashes indicate the averages for the studies in each condition, weighted according to the number of cases.*

The results point to a genetic contribution to intelligence-test performance. The correlations between identical twins are higher than those between fraternal twins, siblings, and children with natural parents. The lowest correlations are those between unrelated children reared together and between children and unrelated adoptive parents.

There are also indications of environmental effects. The best evidence is the moderate correlation between intelligence-test scores of unrelated children reared together. In addition, there is some suggestion that the correlation between fraternal twins is somewhat greater than that between ordinary siblings.

While the results as a whole make reasonable sense, there are some puzzles. For example, it is not clear why the correlations between unrelated children reared together are greater than those between adopted children and their (unrelated) adoptive parents. (The format of presentation is that of Erlenmeyer-Kimling and Jarvik, 1963; but the data included in the figure are limited to studies performed in the U.S. as summarized by Jencks et al., 1972)

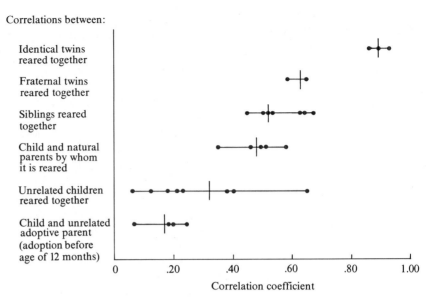

Correlations between:

Identical twins reared together

Fraternal twins reared together

Siblings reared together

Child and natural parents by whom it is reared

Unrelated children reared together

Child and unrelated adoptive parent (adoption before age of 12 months)

Correlation coefficient

of identical twins was substantially larger than that between the IQs of fraternal twins. Considering only twins in the United States, the average correlation is .89 for identicals, and .63 for fraternals (Jencks et al., 1972, p. 292). A summary of these and related findings is presented in Figure 15.25.

On the face of it, this pattern of results seems like clear-cut evidence for a genetic component in the determination of IQ. But during recent years, a number of criticisms have been leveled at these and related studies. One argument bears on the assumption that the similarity in the environments of identical and fraternal twins is essentially equal. But is it really? Since identical twins look alike, there may be a tendency to treat them the same way. Ultimately, parents and teachers may develop the same expectations for them. In contrast, fraternal twins are no more or less similar in appearance than ordinary siblings and may thus evoke a more differentiated reaction from others. If this is so, the comparison of the IQ correlations between identical and fraternal twins is not as neat a test of the nature-nurture issue as it seemed at first (Anastasi, 1971; Kamin, 1974).

A recent study was designed to meet this criticism. Over three hundred twins were classified as identical or fraternal according to two criteria. One was by a comparison of twelve blood-type characteristics. This is as objective a method for assessing genotype identity as is now available. To be judged identical, both members of a twin pair must correspond on all of the twelve indices. Another criterion involved the subjects' own belief in whether they are identical or fraternal. This belief is presumably based on how similar the twins think they are and how similarly they feel that they are treated. In a sizable number of twins this subjective judgment did not correspond to the biological facts as revealed by the blood tests. Which of the two ways of classifying a twin is a better predictor of the similarity in intelligence-test scores? The results suggest that the primary determinant is the true genotype. When the classification was by blood tests, there was the usual effect; identical twins scored more similarly than did fraternals. But when the classification was based on the twins' own judgments, this effect was markedly reduced.

This result suggests that the greater intellectual similarity of identical as compared to fraternal twins is not an artifact of different environments. The best guess is that the effect occurs because intelligence-test performance is in part genetically determined (Scarr and Carter-Saltzman, 1979).

Adoptive children   Another line of evidence comes from studies of adopted children. One study was based on two hundred children who were adopted immediately after birth (Horn, Loehlin, and Wellerman, 1975). When these children were later tested, the correlation between their IQs and those of their *biological* mothers (whom they had never seen) was greater than the corresponding correlation with the IQs of their *adoptive* mothers (.32 versus .15). Other investigators have shown that this pattern persists into adolescence. When the adopted child is tested at age fourteen, the correlation between its IQ and that of the biological mother's education is greater than that between the child's IQ and the educational level of the adoptive mother (.31 versus .04; Skodak and Skeels, 1949).

These results seem like strong evidence for the genetic view, but they have not remained unchallenged. One criticism concerns **selective placement.** Adoption agencies generally try to place infants in homes that are similar in social and educational backgrounds to those of their biological parents. This leads to a problem. To the extent that IQ is determined by the environment and that the adoption agency is successful in matching those environments, there is an inevitable—and quite spurious—correlation between the IQs of the children and those of their biological parents (Kamin, 1974). This environmentalist argument is plausible except for one thing: it does not readily explain why there is a smaller correlation between the children and the adoptive parents.

There may be a way of circumventing this problem. The trick is to estimate the degree of selective placement directly; one way of doing this is to compute the correlation between the biological and adoptive parents' IQs. (If placement were random, this correlation should be zero.) Given this estimate, one can correct for statistically selective placement. When this was done using data from a recent study, the corrected correlations between the IQs of children and their biological parents was .30, while the corresponding correlation with the IQs of the adoptive mother was .10 (Horn et al., 1975). In light of this, there seems little reason to accept the environmentalists' reinterpretation of the results of the adoption studies.

THE EFFECT OF ENVIRONMENT

There is evidently a genetic component in the determination of intelligence-test performance. But heredity alone does not account for all of the variance in intellectual performance. There is little doubt that environmental factors also play a role.

Enriched and impoverished environments   Evidence for environmental effects comes from several sources. One is the comparison of mean IQs of whole populations following some significant change in cultural life or of educational practices. An example is a community in East Tennessee that was quite isolated from the United States mainstream in 1930 but became less and less

15.26 Heritability *Consider the group of evergreen trees shown in (A). They vary in height, and the degree to which they vary from each other is measured by the variance. What produces this variance? (B) Some is presumably caused by genetic factors. To determine how much, we equate environmental conditions—the soil, water, light, and so on (here indicated by different shadings of the ground). We now take a group of seedlings randomly chosen from (A), plant them in this equated environment, and patiently wait until they reach maturity. We note that the size variation in (B) is less than that in (A). This reduction in the variance reflects the fact that environmental conditions are equal for (B), so that one important source of variation has been removed. The remaining variance in (B) is entirely produced by genetic factors. We can now determine the heritability of height for (A). It is the variance in (B) (that is, the variation attributable to genetic factors), divided by the variance in (A) (that is, the total variation in the population).*

so during the following decade with the introduction of schools, roads, and radios. Between 1930 and 1940, the average IQ of individuals in this community rose by 10 points, from 82 to 92 (Wheeler, 1942).

Enriching the environment is evidently beneficial. Impoverishing it has the opposite effect. Evidence comes from children who worked on canalboats in England during the 1920s and hardly attended school at all (Gordon, 1923), or who lived in remote regions of the Kentucky mountains (Asher, 1935). These are poor environments for the development of the intellectual skills tapped by intelligence tests. If so, exposure to such an environment should have a cumulative effect; the longer the child has been in it, the more depressed its IQ should be. This is precisely the result that was obtained. There was a sizable *negative* correlation between IQ and age. The older the child, the longer it had been in the impoverished environment, and thus the lower its IQ.

More adoption studies Further evidence comes from adoption studies. We have previously seen that they show the importance of genetic factors. But they also document the contribution of environment. One group of investigators studied the mean IQ of adopted children, most of whom were placed in foster homes before they were three months old (Skodak and Skeels, 1945, 1947, 1949). At age four, their mean IQ was 112; at age 13 it was 117. The authors argue that these values are considerably higher than the mean IQ that would have been predicted for this group of children, given the fact that the occupational and educational level of the biological parents was known to be below average. Since the adopting parents were above average on these indices as well as on IQ, it seemed only natural to assume that the home background they provided led to an increase in their adopted children's IQs.

HERITABILITY

The evidence as a whole dictates the conclusion that both genetic and environmental factors play a role in determining IQ variations within groups. On this point there is wide agreement. What is at issue is the relative weight exerted by each of these factors.

Just what is meant by the relative importance of heredity and environment in determining the variation of any given trait? To answer this question, we must refer to a technical expression developed by geneticists, the **heritability ratio (H)**. This is the proportion of the variance of the phenotypic expression of a trait in a given population that is attributable to genetic variation among the individuals within that population* (Figure 15.26).

To get a feeling for what H means, suppose that all children born in the U.S. (within a given racial-ethnic group) were raised in completely identical environments. When this environmentally equalized group is later tested, there

---

* The idea is that the total variance of the trait (V_T)—be it height, weight, or IQ—can be considered as the sum of several constituents: the variance produced by genetic differences (V_G), the variance produced by different environments (V_E), and some others. The heritability ratio, H, is then given by

$$H = \frac{V_G}{V_T}$$

The actual value of H for IQ (in industrialized populations like ours) is still a matter of debate, though most experts would probably agree that it falls within the range of .4 to .8.

will still be variations in IQ. These will be entirely attributable to genetic variation for environment is no longer a factor. Under these conditions, H would necessarily equal 1.00.

There are some widely held misconceptions about the nature of heritability. Perhaps the worst is the notion that the heritability ratio applies to individuals. In popular discussions it is sometimes said that 80 percent—or 70 percent or 40 percent, depending on the value of H the author accepts—of a person's intelligence is determined by heredity, the rest by environment. This is sheer nonsense. Heritability is a concept that applies only to trait variations within a particular population; it does not apply to individuals. For any given person, both heredity and environment are equally important in determining whatever he or she is. As an example, consider height, for which heritability is about .90. This means that if genotype variation were eliminated (in other words, if all subjects were derived from the same fertilized egg) the remaining variance would be only 10 percent of what it is in the normal population. But it does not mean that a man whose height is six feet can thank heredity for sixty-five of his inches and credit environment with the remaining seven.

GROUP DIFFERENCES

Thus far, we have focused on IQ differences *within* groups and have considered the nature-nurture debate as it pertained to these. But the real fury of the controversy rages over another issue—the differences in average IQ that are found between groups such as socioeconomic classes or racial-ethnic groups.

Numerous studies have shown that the average score of American blacks is about 15 IQ points below the average of the white population (Loehlin, Lindzey, and Spuhler, 1975). The fact that there is such a difference is not in dispute. What is at issue is what this difference means and how it comes about.

Before proceeding, we should emphasize that the differences are between *averages*. There is considerable overlap between the two distributions. From 15 to 25 percent of the blacks score higher than half of the whites (Shuey, 1966). Clearly the numerical IQ variations *within* either group are much greater than those between groups.

ARE THE TESTS "CULTURE FAIR"?

Some psychologists have tried to deal with the between-groups difference by explaining it away. They suggested that it is primarily an artifact of a cultural bias built into the tests themselves (Sarason, 1973). According to this view, the intelligence tests now in use were designed to assess the cognitive skills of the white middle class. When these tests are administered to another group with different customs, values, and even dialects—such as inner-city black children—there cannot help but be a cultural bias which makes the yardstick no longer applicable. This point is obvious when the test item calls for verbal information, as in vocabulary or analogy tests. If different subgroups have different degrees of exposure to the relevant information, any difference in test scores becomes uninterpretable. We have already noted evidence for some such effects when discussing the test results obtained with rural and urban children; it is very likely that a similar point applies to comparisons between children from white suburbs and black ghettos. Further problems stem from different motivations in the test-taking situation and to different attitudes toward the tester. Yet another complication is posed by different degrees of language comprehension. According to some linguists, many American blacks speak a dialect of English—black English—the syntax, phonology, and lexicon of which differ in some important ways from standard English (e.g., Labov, 1970; see Chapter 10). Since intelligence tests are usually administered in standard English, the black children who take them are under a linguistic handicap.

Such considerations suggest that some component of the black-white test score difference is attributable to cultural bias, either in the tests themselves, in their administration, or both. The question is whether this accounts for all of the difference. There are reasons to believe that it does not. The evidence comes from studies in which one or another possible source of cultural bias has been eliminated or at least minimized. An example is an attempt to test American blacks in black English. To this end, the Stanford-Binet was translated into black English and was then administered orally to black children by black examiners (Quay, 1971). The performance of these children was virtually identical to that of a group that was tested with the regular version. The dialect difference is evidently not the crucial variable.

Related results come from comparisons of verbal and nonverbal items on various intelligence tests. At least on the face of it, one would expect verbal items to be more culturally biased than nonverbal ones. In fact, such tests as the Progressive Matrices are sometimes said to be relatively "culture free." If this is so, the black-white difference should be greater on the verbal than the nonverbal tests. But the results prove otherwise. The group difference remains undiminished in tests of spatial ability, of numerical reasoning, or on the Progressive Matrices. The same apparently holds for Piagetian conservation tests (Jensen, 1980).

Still further evidence comes from the fact that various intellectual aptitude tests predict later academic performances just about as successfully for whites as for blacks. A case in point is the widely used Scholastic Aptitude Test (SAT) taken by high-school seniors applying for college. Its correlations with high-school and college grades are nearly identical for white and black students (Cleary, 1968). Such findings suggest that the black-white difference in average IQ is not simply the result of a test artifact. We may not know exactly what intelligence tests measure (though it is evidently related to scholastic performance in twentieth-century United States schools), but they probably measure more or less the same thing in both racial-ethnic groups.

BETWEEN-GROUP DIFFERENCE: HEREDITY OR ENVIRONMENT

The between-group difference in average IQ is evidently not just an artifact. But what accounts for it? In the thirty years before 1965, the consensus among social scientists in the United States was that the effect results from the massively inferior environmental conditions that were (and in many ways, still are) the lot of most blacks—systematic discrimination, poorer living conditions, lower life expectancies, inadequate diets and housing, and inferior schooling. But the issue was reopened in the sixties and early seventies, by among others, Arthur Jensen, who felt that the hypothesis of a genetic contribution to the between-group difference had been dismissed prematurely (Jensen, 1969, 1973).

As currently conceived, human racial groups (some authors prefer the term *racial-ethnic* groups) are populations whose members are more likely to inter-breed than to mate with outsiders. This restriction on the gene flow between different subgroups may be imposed by geographical barriers, such as oceans or mountains, or by social taboos, such as prohibitions on intermarriage. The restrictions are not complete, but if they last long enough, they may result in a population that differs from other groups in the statistical frequency of various genes. That this is the case for genes that determine such characteristics as eye and skin color, pattern of hair growth, various blood groups, and so on, is undeniable. But does the same hold for behavioral traits like intelligence-test performance? More specifically, is the difference in average black and white IQs partially attributable to different frequencies of IQ-determining genes in the two populations?

Within-group heritability   One of Jensen's arguments was based on the finding that IQ has a substantial within-group heritability. Jensen suggested that, given this fact, it was plausible to suppose that the between-group difference (that is, the difference between the black and white averages) could be interpreted in similar terms. A number of critics disagreed. They countered by saying that the fact that within-group heritability is high does not imply that between-group differences are genetically determined (Layzer, 1972).

One writer gave an example of two samples of seed, randomly drawn from a bag that contains several genetically different varieties. One sample is placed in barren soil and the other in soil that is extremely fertile. When the plants are fully grown they will differ in height. There will be within-group differences as measured by the variance within each of the two samples. There will also be a between-group difference as indicated by a difference in the average height of the plants in the two samples. The within-group difference can be attributed to genetic variation; the samples were drawn from a genetically mixed bag so that there is high within-group heritability. But the between-group variation must be primarily of environmental origin since the two sets of seeds were planted in soils of different fertility (Lewontin, 1976; see Figure 15.27).

15.27 Between-group and within-group differences *Between-group differences may be caused by very different factors than within-group differences. Here, the between-group difference reflects an environmental factor (soil) while the difference within each group reflects genetic variation (seed).*

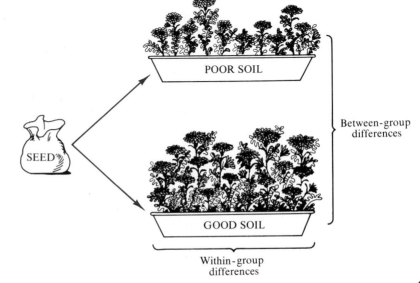

POOR SOIL

SEED

GOOD SOIL

Between-group differences

Within-group differences

621

The moral is simple: Differences within and between groups may be produced by very different causal factors. This holds for plants and the heights they attain at maturity. And it may also apply to human racial-ethnic groups and IQ.

Matching for environment　If the black-white difference in IQs is really a result of environmental factors, that difference should disappear if one compares black and white groups who are equated in these regards. It is reasonable to suppose that the relevant factors include socioeconomic variables like parents' education, income, occupational level, and so on. A number of studies have tried to match black and white children on indices of this kind and then compared the IQ averages of the two matched groups. The general result was that the black-white difference was markedly reduced (Loehlin, Lindzey, and Spuhler, 1975).

On the face of it, such results seem like vindications of the environmentalists' view: equate the soil and the two sets of seeds will grow up much alike. But hereditarians will emphasize another finding. While equalizing socioeconomic variables diminishes the black-white difference, it does not abolish it. In their view, this residual difference makes the genetic hypothesis all the more plausible. Environmentalists reply that the environments of the black and white children were not truly matched, despite the social scientists' very best efforts. For matching parental education, income, and occupational level is not enough. The very fact that one child is black and the other white means that they grow up in different environments, since our society is riddled with racial discrimination that will hit the one child but not the other.

A somewhat better approximation to an equalized environment is found in a study of the illegitimate offspring of United States servicemen stationed in Germany after World War II. The investigators compared two groups of such children whose white, German mothers were roughly similar in socioeconomic background. One group of children was fathered by black soldiers and the other by white ones. When the children were tested with a German version of the Wechsler scale, the main finding was that both groups had about the same average IQ. This result seems to contradict the genetic interpretation of the black-white difference, for the children received half of their genes from a black father. To maintain the genetic hypothesis, one would have to postulate a special kind of mating selection—for example, that the black fathers had considerably higher IQs than white fathers. This possibility cannot be ruled out, but it does not seem very plausible (Loehlin, Lindzey, and Spuhler, 1975).

The effect of environmental change　Some investigators have taken another tack. Instead of trying to match environments, they have tried to see what happens when the environment is changed. In particular they looked at the effects of migration from the South to the (relatively) more benign North during the thirties and forties. They found that migration led to a moderate increase in the IQ of black children; the longer their stay in the North (and in Northern schools), the greater this increase (Lee, 1951).

A more drastic environmental change is interracial adoption. One group of investigators studied ninety-nine black children who were adopted at an early age by white middle-class parents, most of whom were college-educated (Scarr-Salapatek and Weinberg, 1975). The mean IQ of these children was

110. This value exceeds the national average for black children by about 25 IQ points. Some of this increase may well have been an artifact of selective placement by the adoption agency, but a part of it may represent a genuine environmental effect.

SOME TENTATIVE CONCLUSIONS

How can we summarize? Perhaps the fairest thing to say is that there is not a single study whose results or interpretations cannot be challenged, nor is there a single argument (whether genetic or environmental) for which there is no counterargument. Under the circumstances, no conclusion can be anything but tentative. Even so, the weight of the evidence seems to tilt toward the environmentalist side, especially when one's intuitions about the effects of three hundred years of slavery and racist oppression are thrown into the balance.

But suppose that the genetic interpretation is correct after all. Suppose that some significant fraction of the black-white IQ difference is in fact determined by the genes. What then? What effects should this have on our thinking about social issues and socioeconomic policy? In our view, relatively little. There are several reasons for this.

First, the genetic interpretation does not imply that environmental intervention—in home or school—will have no effect. There is no one who denies that environmental factors are responsible for some proportion of the between-group variance. There are thus no grounds for abandoning appropriate educational efforts for improving cognitive skills (and presumably raising IQs). The trouble is that thus far we have only the skimpiest ideas about the kinds of environmental changes that would do the trick.

Second, what about the portion of the variance that, according to the hereditarians, is determined by the genotype? Is that unchangeable? Some participants on both sides of the controversy seem to feel that, almost by definition, environmentally determined traits are alterable while genetically determined ones are fixed. But this is far from true. Some environmentally produced effects are almost impossible to change, including some that are acquired through certain forms of learning. Examples are the long-lasting effects of imprinting (see Chapter 11) and the difficulty most adults have in shedding the phonological system of their mother tongue when trying to speak another language without an accent (see Chapter 10). Nor is it true that genetically determined traits are necessarily unchangeable. The widely cited counterexample is PKU, an inherited form of mental retardation which, as we have seen, can be treated by an appropriate diet. Conceivably, other approaches may be found to alter the effects of some of the genes that underlie the polygenic distribution of IQ.

Third, there are reasons to believe that the black-white IQ difference, regardless of what causes it, is not a major factor in producing the economic inequality between whites and blacks. To be sure, IQ is correlated with adult income, but according to at least some writers, this correlation accounts for only 12 percent of the total variance in individual incomes in the United States (Jencks et al., 1972). Given this relatively low value, the emphasis on IQ in discussions of social inequality may well be misplaced.

623

We should make a final point (which has been stressed by Jensen no less than by his environmentalist critics). In a democratic society the emphasis is on *individuals* and their own abilities and attributes. A given individual's subgroup may have a greater or smaller average gene frequency for this or the other trait, but this has no bearing on how this particular person should be judged. When people are assessed according to the average characteristics of the group to which they belong rather than according to the characteristics that they themselves possess, one of the most essential premises of a democratic society is violated.

Summary

1. Many physical and psychological characteristics vary from one individual to another. This pattern of variation is often displayed by *frequency distributions.* The scores in a frequency distribution tend to cluster around a central tendency, often measured by the *mean.* The *variability* around this central tendency is indicated by the *variance,* or its square root, the *standard deviation.* The graphed frequency distributions of many physical and psychological characteristics has a shape approximating that of the *normal curve,* which describes the probability of combinations of chance events.

2. The extent to which two characteristics vary together, is measured by the *correlation coefficient,* or *r*. Perfect correlation is indicated by an *r* of $+1.00$ or -1.00; zero correlation by an *r* of .00.

3. An important application of the correlation technique was the development of mental testing. A *mental test* is meant to be an objective yardstick to assess some psychological trait or capacity about which people differ. One criterion of a test's adequacy is its *reliability,* the consistency with which it measures what it measures, as given by *test-retest* correlations and similar indices. An even more important criterion is the test's *validity,* the extent to which it measures what it is supposed to measure. *Predictive validity* is assessed by determining the correlation between the test and an appropriate *criterion. Construct validity* is the extent to which performance on a test fits into some relevant theoretical scheme.

4. Tests with good reliability and reasonable predictive validity may be useful as a selection device. But since validity coefficients are less than 1.00, there are inevitable selection errors, some of which are "false accepts" while others are "false rejects." The relative proportion of these two errors depends on the choice of a *cutoff point* below which no applicant is selected. The choice of this cutoff value depends on the selector's *payoff matrix.*

5. Binet, the originator of intelligence tests, was primarily interested in assessing children. His tests measured *mental age,* or *MA.* The relative standing of a child relative to its age-mates was determined by comparing its MA with its *chronological age,* or *CA.* A widely used measure of this relative position is the *intelligence quotient,* or *IQ,* which equals MA/CA × 100. Modern testers prefer another measure, the *deviation IQ.* This is based on a comparison between an individual's score and that of his age-mates and can be used with adults.

6. Intelligence tests can be used to diagnose several levels of *mental retardation* varying from mild to profound. According to one hypothesis, the more severe forms of retardation are caused by one factor such as major brain pathology, while the milder forms are produced by the joint effect of many factors.

7. Investigators using the *psychometric approach* try to discover something about the underlying nature of intelligence by studying the pattern of results provided by intelligence tests themselves. One issue is the *structure of mental abilities.* To determine whether intelligence is one unitary ability or is composed of several unrelated abilities, investigators have looked at the correlations between different subtests. *Factor analysis* of these correlations led to a number of competing theories of mental structure, including *Spearman's theory of general intelligence,* or *g; group factor theory;* and *hierarchical theory.*

8. Another psychometric issue is the relation between intelligence-test performance and age, throughout the life span. Studies on infants indicate that performance on infant scales predicts very little about IQ at school age or beyond. Studies of intelligence in later life suggest that for some—though not all—facets of test performance there is a drop after middle age. Several authors believe that there is an important distinction between two kinds of intellectual abilities. One is *fluid intelligence* which declines with age—the ability to deal with essentially new problems. The other is *crystallized intelligence* which does not drop off—the repertoire of mental skills and information originally acquired by means of fluid intelligence.

9. Yet another approach tries to relate intelligence to the psychology of cognitive processes. One line of inquiry grows out of the work of developmental psychologists who regard mental retardation as a failure to reach certain Piagetian stages. Another tries to relate intellectual deficits to the failure to acquire and use various cognitive *strategies.*

10. Intelligence-test performance has become one of the major foci of the nature-nurture controversy, fueled in great part by various social and political forces. The factual questions concern the relative contributions of heredity and environment in producing differences within and between groups in contemporary America.

11. A key distinction in any discussion of heredity transmission is that between *phenotype* which describes some overt characteristic of an organism, and *genotype,* which describes the organism's set of relevant *genes.* Each genetic instruction is issued by two corresponding genes, one from each parent. If one member of a gene pair is *dominant* while the other is *recessive,* the first will mask the effect of the other leading to a difference between phenotypic expression and underlying genotype. Attributes of an either-or character are generally determined by a single gene; attributes that vary continuously, such as height, tend to be based on *polygenic* inheritance. Contrary to popular view, what is inborn is not necessarily immutable. An example is *phenylketonuria,* or *PKU,* a hereditary form of mental retardation that can be treated by a special diet.

12. Human intelligence-test performance seems to be determined by both environmental and genetic factors, though the issue is not regarded as fully settled by all psychologists. Evidence for the role of genetic factors comes from the fact that the correlation between IQs of *identical twins* are higher than those for *fraternal twins.* Further evidence for a hereditary contribution comes from *adopted children* whose IQs correlate more highly with those of their biological than their adopted parents. Evidence for environmental effects is provided by increases and decreases in the mean IQ of populations whose cultural or educational level has been raised or lowered. A similar point is made by adoption studies which show IQ increases in adopted children after being placed in superior foster homes.

13. The relative weight of genetic and environmental factors in determining the variation of a given characteristic is given by the *heritability ratio,* or *H.* The value of *H* depends in part upon the given population, for *H* only describes the degree to which the variability within this population can be attributed to genetic variance.

14. In recent years, much interest (and polemic) has focused on IQ differences *between* different racial-ethnic groups. The mean IQ of American blacks is about 15 points lower than that of American whites. Some authors have argued that this is in part a consequence of a genetic difference between the two groups. Environmentalists reply that the difference is markedly reduced by various environmental changes such as interracial adoption. A similar point is made by the fact that the mean IQs of illegitimate children of white German mothers fathered by US soldiers after World War II are just about the same whether the fathers were black or white. While none of these arguments and counterarguments is conclusive, the author's bias tilts toward the environmentalist side on the between-group issue.

CHAPTER 16

Personality Assessment

In the preceding chapter, our focus was on differences in cognitive ability. But people also differ in nonintellectual attributes. They differ in their predominant desires, in their characteristic feelings, and in their typical modes of expressing these needs and feelings. All of these distinctions fall under the general heading of *personality differences.* The specific attributes that define these distinctions (for example, energetic versus lazy) are called *personality traits.*

The fact that personality differences exist is hardly a recent discovery. In the fourth century B.C., the Greek philosopher Theophrastus (ca. 370–287 B.C.) wrote a series of sketches, "The Characters," that featured such diverse types as the Coward, the Flatterer, the Boor, and so on. At least some of his types are as recognizable today as they were in ancient Greece:

> The Garrulous man is one that will sit down close beside somebody he does not know, and begin talk with a eulogy of his own life, and then relate a dream he had the night before, and after that tell dish by dish what he had for supper. As he warms to his work he will remark that we are by no means the men we were, and the price of wheat has gone down, and there's a ship of strangers in town. . . . Next he will surmise that the crops would be all the better for some more rain, and tell him what he is going to grow on his farm next year, adding that it is difficult to make both ends meet . . . and "I vomited yesterday" and "What day is it today?" . . . And if you let him go on he will never stop (Edmonds, *The Characters of Theophrastus,* 1929, pp. 48–49).

There is an implicit assumption that underlies Theophrastus' sketches, and that assumption is shared by subsequent authors who have written about personality, even to the present. The personality patterns they ascribed to

Theophrastus *(Courtesy Villa Albani, Rome.)*

their characters were presumed to be essentially consistent from time to time and from situation to situation. The hero was generally heroic, the villain villainous, and the garrulous man kept on talking regardless of who listened (or rather, tried not to listen). Some of the traits by which modern students of personality describe people are more subtle than those that Theophrastus wrote about, but for many investigators the key assumption of this *trait theory* still exists. They presume that these traits characterize a person's behavior in a variety of situations. This is just another way of saying that knowledge of an individual's personality traits will permit us to predict what he is likely to do, even in situations in which we have never observed him (Allport, 1937). Personality tests were devised in an attempt to supply the information that makes such predictions possible.

Methods of Assessment

Psychologists have developed several approaches to the problem of describing and assessing different personalities. We will discuss two of the major ones: those that are structured and objective ("paper-and-pencil tests") and those that are relatively unstructured ("projective techniques").

STRUCTURED PERSONALITY TESTS: TESTING BY "SELF-REPORT"

As in the case of intelligence measurement, the impetus for the development of personality tests came from the world of practical affairs. But the parallel is even closer than that, for both kinds of tests began as instruments to determine certain undesirable conditions. Binet's test was originally designed to identify mentally retarded children. The first personality test had a parallel diagnostic aim. It was meant to identify emotionally disturbed United States Army recruits during World War I. This test was an "adjustment inventory" consisting of a list of questions that dealt with various symptoms or problem areas (for instance, "Do you daydream frequently?" and "Do you wet your bed?"). If the subject reported many such symptoms, he was singled out for further psychiatric examination (Cronbach, 1970a).

The parallel between tests of intelligence and those of personality ends when we turn to the question of how these tests are validated. Binet and his successors had various criteria of validity: teachers' evaluations, academic performance, and, perhaps most important, chronological age. It turns out that validity criteria are much harder to come by in the field of personality measurement.

VALIDITY BY ASSERTION

One approach to validation is to deny its necessity. This is sometimes done by test constructors who assert that their test is valid on the face of it. They argue that the content of the test items makes it plausible to assume that they tap the trait they were meant to tap. The originators of the first personality inventories took just this line. They merely wanted their tests to serve as a screening device to determine who should undergo a psychiatric interview. Given this modest purpose, they felt justified in supposing that there was no need for further validation. After all, a recruit who describes himself as an incessant daydreamer and bed-wetter is on the face of it a reasonable candidate for more serious psychiatric study. But this is not enough when the tester has more ambitious aims and wants to use the inventory as a diagnostic tool in its own right rather than merely as a screening device. One problem is that the subject may lie. He may claim symptoms he doesn't have (to stay out of the army) or deny symptoms that he does have (to stay out of a mental hospital). But even if the subject answers honestly, we still need more solid evidence that the test really measures what it is supposed to measure. The fact that it *seems* to do so is no substitute for an objective validity criterion.

THE MMPI: CRITERION GROUPS FROM THE CLINIC

To provide such an objective validity criterion, some later investigators turned to the diagnostic categories developed in clinical practice. Their object was to construct a test that could assess a person's similarity to this or the other psychiatric criterion group—hysterics, depressed patients, schizophrenics, and so on. The best-known test of this sort is the ***Minnesota Multiphasic Personality Inventory,*** or ***MMPI,*** which first appeared in 1940 and is still one of the most widely used personality tests on the current scene, especially in clinical practice. It was called multiphasic because it was developed to assess a number of psychiatric patterns simultaneously.

Constructing the MMPI The authors of the MMPI began by compiling a large set of test items taken from previously published inventories, from psychiatric examination forms, and from their own clinical hunches. These items were then administered to several patient groups with different diagnoses as well as to a group of normal subjects. The next step was to eliminate all items that did not discriminate between the patients and the normal controls and to retain those items that did. The end result was the MMPI in substantially its present form—an inventory of 550 items, the responses to which can be analyzed by reference to ten major scales. The score on each of these scales indicates how the subject's answers compare with those of the relevant criterion group (Table 16.1, page 630).

It is hard to overemphasize the essential difference in outlook between the originators of the early personality inventories and the authors of the MMPI. The former stressed plausibility; they wanted the items to "look right." The latter didn't care too much whether the items seemed plausible; what mattered to them was whether they discriminated between the criterion group and normal subjects.

One can readily see why members of a certain diagnostic group would answer many of the MMPI questions as they did. But for some items, the reasons are more obscure. As an example, consider two items that differentiate a group of patients diagnosed as paranoids. One identifying characteristic of such patients is the presence of delusions, which may be of persecution or of grandeur (see Chapter 17). It is easy enough to see why such patients would be especially likely to agree with the statement, "I believe I am being plotted against." But why do these same patients tend to say, "False" when presented with the statement, "Most people are honest chiefly through fear of

Table 16.1   SOME MMPI SCALES WITH REPRESENTATIVE EXAMPLE ITEMS*

Scale	Criterion group	Example items
Depression	Patients with intense unhappiness and feelings of hopelessness	"I often feel that life is not worth the trouble."
Paranoia	Patients with unusual degree of suspiciousness, together with feelings of persecution and delusions of grandeur	"Several people are following me everywhere."
Schizophrenia	Patients with a diagnosis of schizophrenia, characterized by bizarre or highly unusual thoughts or behavior, by withdrawal, and in many cases by delusions and hallucinations	"I seem to hear things that other people cannot hear."
Psychopathic deviance	Patients with marked difficulties in social adjustment, with histories of delinquency and other asocial behaviors	"I often was in trouble in school, although I do not understand for what reasons."

* In the example items here shown, the response appropriate to the scale is "True." For many other items, the reverse is true. Thus, answering "False" to the item "I liked school" would contribute to the person's score on the psychopathic deviance scale.

being caught." A paranoid person, who presumably suspects the motives of all around him, might have been expected to endorse this statement rather than to reject it. Perhaps one can come up with some after-the-fact hypothesis to explain this result, but within the conceptual framework that governed the construction of the MMPI it really doesn't matter. The critical point is that the item differentiates a particular criterion group from normal persons. Exactly why it does so is another question.

Using the MMPI   In actual practice, interpreting an MMPI record is a complicated business. Clinicians don't merely look at the absolute scores obtained on any one scale. Instead, they consider the various scale values in relation to each other. This is most easily done by inspecting **score profiles** which present the scores on every scale in graphic form (Figure 16.1). An example is the interpretation of scores on the so-called depression scale. This consists of items which differentiated a group of patients diagnosed to be in a depressive state from normal persons. But a high score on this scale alone tells little more than that the patient is very unhappy. If we want to know more about the nature of this disturbance (for example, whether the patient suffers from a severe neurosis or a psychosis), we have to look at the profile as a whole (Meehl, 1956).

Check-up scales   We have mentioned that the old personality inventories ran into the problem that subjects could easily misrepresent themselves. To cope with this and related problems, the originators of the MMPI added a set of

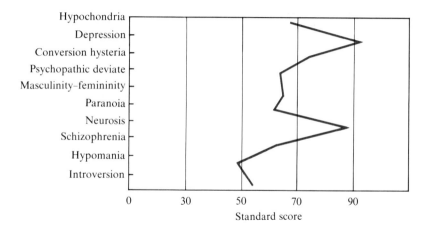

16.1 MMPI profile *The profile is of an adult male seeking help in a community health center. The scales are those described in Table 16.1. The scores are based on the performance of the standardization group. Scores above 70 will occur in about 2.5 percent of the cases; scores above 80 in about .1 percent. The profile strongly suggests considerable depression and neurotic anxiety. (After Lanyon and Goodstein, 1971)*

further items that make up several "check-up" scales. One is a simple lying scale. It contains items like "I gossip a little at times" and "Once in a while I laugh at a dirty joke." The assumption is that a person who denies a large number of such statements is either a saint (and few of those take personality tests) or is lying. Another check-up scale consists of a number of bizarre statements like "There are persons who are trying to steal my thoughts and ideas" and "My soul sometimes leaves my body." To be sure, some of these statements are accepted by severely disturbed psychiatric patients, but even they endorse only a small proportion of them. As a result, we can be reasonably sure that a person who checks an unusually large number of such items is either careless, or has misunderstood the instructions, or is trying to fake psychiatric illness. If the score on these and similar check-up scales is too high, the test record is discarded as invalid.

THE CPI: CRITERION GROUPS FROM NORMAL LIFE

While the MMPI can be employed to test normal subjects, it has some limitations when used in this way. The main problem is that the criterion groups that defined the scales were composed of psychiatric patients. One can't help but feel a bit uneasy when interpreting the test results of a reasonably normal high-school student by reference to scales that differentiated, say, a number of paranoid patients from normal persons. Additional difficulties are posed by the relatively large number of items that test for the presence of major psychiatric symptoms. An average person is likely to become more than a little suspicious when confronted by a personality test that inquires whether he is possessed by evil spirits, is being followed, is plotted against, has his mind controlled by others, hears strange things when he is alone, is afraid of using a knife or anything very sharp or pointed, and at times becomes aware of peculiar odors.

Considerations of this sort prompted the development of several new inventories constructed according to the same logic that led to the MMPI, but with normal rather than with pathological criterion groups. One of the best known of these is the **California Psychological Inventory,** or **CPI.** The CPI is especially aimed at high-school and college students. It tests for various per-

631

sonality traits such as dominance, sociability, responsibility, sense of well-being, and so on.

As an example of how scales for these and other traits were derived, consider *dominance*. High-school and college students were asked to name the most and the least dominant persons within their social circles. The persons who comprised these two extremes were then used as the criterion groups that defined the dominance-submission dimension. From here on, the procedure paralleled that which led to the construction of the MMPI. A large set of items (many of them taken from the MMPI) was administered to both groups, and those items that differentiated between the groups were kept to make up the dominance scale. Other traits were defined in a similar manner and several check-up scales were added to assess the subjects' test-taking attitudes (Gough, 1957).

THE VALIDITY OF PERSONALITY INVENTORIES

The originators of the MMPI, the CPI, and other personality inventories based on criterion groups, took considerable pains to provide their instruments with a solid, empirical foundation. To evaluate the success of their efforts, we must look at the validity of these tests.

Predictive validity The usual way to assess validity is to determine the degree to which a test can predict some real-world events. There is evidence that personality tests do indeed have some predictive power. For instance, among college women during the fifties and sixties, the sociability scale of the CPI correlated with how often the subject went out on dates and whether she joined a sorority. Other scales correlate with how subjects are rated by their peers (Hase and Goldberg, 1967).

The trouble is that while personality inventories can predict, their efficiency in doing so is discouragingly low. The correlations between test scores and validity criteria are generally in the neighborhood of +.30. This contrasts poorly with the validation coefficients of intelligence tests (usually assessed by correlating IQ and academic performance), which are about +.50. The contrast is even sharper if we compare the usefulness of these personality tests with the predictive efficiency of common-sense measures such as relevant past behavior in related situations. The result is simple. The best predictor of future performance (for example, psychiatric breakdown, delinquency) is past performance. A dramatic and widely cited example is provided by a study which showed that the thickness of a mental patient's file folder correlates +.61 with the probability of his rehospitalization following his release (Lasky et al., 1959).

Construct validation The low validity coefficients of personality inventories may not be grounds for as much chagrin as one might assume at first. One line of defense is an attack on the criterion measures. Many validation studies of the MMPI rely on correlations with psychiatric diagnoses. But how good are these diagnoses, which are sometimes made after only a brief interview? Similar comments apply to validation studies with normal subjects. Consider peer ratings, dating frequency, and sorority joining as criterion measures of sociability. Could peer ratings be in error? Is (or was) sorority joining really an appropriate criterion? One can surely think of many reasons why a very sociable college woman might never want to become a sorority sister (even in the fifties and before).

Arguments of this sort suggest that the best index for evaluating a test is not necessarily given by its correlation with *one* criterion measure. To be sure, this correlation (that is, the predictive validity) may sometimes be all that counts, as when the primary concern is pragmatic forecasting. An example is aptitude tests for pilot training. Here, the object is not to discover what pilot aptitude really is; all we want to do is to minimize the number of training failures and airplane crashes (see Chapter 15). But our interest in assessing personality is not so narrowly practical. What most personality tests try to get at is some hypothesized psychological entities, such as traits, that are presumed to underlie overt behavior. In effect, the trait—whether sociability, or psychopathic deviance, or whatever—is a theoretical concept devised by the psychologist in an effort to make sense, not just of one set of observations, but of many. To validate such a construct, one has to devise and test hypotheses about the relation between the underlying trait and various behavioral effects. This is **construct validation,** an approach we have discussed previously, in the context of intelligence testing (see Chapter 15).

Construct validation is often built upon a set of diverse relationships between the test scores and rather different behavioral manifestations. An example is provided by the psychopathic deviance scale (Pd) of the MMPI, a scale originally based upon those items that differentiated a group of delinquents from other groups (see Table 16.1). Not too surprisingly, normal (that is, nondelinquent) high-school students who are regarded as "least responsible" by their classmates have much higher Pd scores than students rated as "most responsible." A related fact is that high Pd scores are characteristic of school dropouts. Another set of findings shows that high Pd scorers tend to be relatively aggressive. For example, nurses with high Pd scores are judged to be "not shy" and "unafraid of mental patients" while persons with low Pd scores are considered "good-natured." Rather further afield is the fact that high Pd scores are also characteristic of professional actors. Still more remote is the finding that hunters who have "carelessly" shot someone in a hunting accident have higher Pd scores than other hunters. On the face of it, many of these findings seem unrelated, but they do fit together if understood as different manifestations of the same underlying personality trait, psychopathic deviance. In its extreme form, this trait is characterized by shallow social and emotional ties, a disregard of social mores and conventions, a failure to consider potential dangers and to worry about the consequences of one's own actions—in short, an attitude that says, "I just don't give a damn" (Cronbach and Meehl, 1955).

The various correlations just described are all fairly small. None of these effects—being rated "irresponsible," having hunting accidents, and so on—correlate strongly enough with the Pd scale to provide a decent single criterion for predictive validity. But when they are considered together, they fit into a network of relationships that does seem to give some validity to the underlying construct. Seen in this light, the fact that the individual correlations are not very strong is not surprising. "If they were, we would find the same person dropping out of school, being ill-natured, becoming a Broadway actor and shooting a fellow hunter. . . . Personality structure, even if perfectly measured, represents only a disposition rather than a determining force" (Cronbach, 1970*a*, p. 555). How that disposition will manifest itself depends upon the particular circumstances the person is in.

UNSTRUCTURED PERSONALITY TESTS: TESTING BY "PROJECTION"

The 1940s and 1950s saw the increasing popularity of a new approach to personality assessment, an approach which is an offshoot of psychoanalytic thought—the use of ***projective techniques.*** These techniques present the subject with a relatively unstructured task, such as making up a story to fit a picture or describing what one sees in an inkblot. In part, this approach was a protest against the highly structured paper-and-pencil tests of personality discussed above. Exponents of the projective approach granted that the MMPI and similar tests contained various safeguards to assure that the subject would not lie to the test administrator. But they pointed out that these tests give no guarantee that the subjects would not lie to themselves.

As they saw it, paper-and-pencil personality inventories can only reveal those aspects of the subject's personality of which she herself is conscious. But in their view this was little more than the tip of the iceberg. Following Freud, they were convinced that the deeper layers of any individual's personality contain repressed wishes, unconscious conflicts, and various hidden defense maneuvers that are not accessible by ordinary means. But how can one penetrate below the surface to find out what the subject does not know herself?

The trick was to find a technique that could circumvent the subject's own defenses against threatening impulses and ideas. Freud himself had pointed the way. He regarded dreams as the "royal road to the unconscious." In his view, the ordinary demands of the "reality principle" are much diminished while dreaming, when the person's defenses are sufficiently relaxed to allow the repressed material to break through the normal barricades, even if only in disguised and symbolic form (see Chapter 12). Projective techniques were devised to provide a similar opportunity for self-revelation during the waking state. The basic idea is that when structuring unstructured materials the subject cannot help but unveil some deeper facets of his personality makeup. The test materials are thus considered as a kind of screen upon which the subject "projects" his inner feelings, wishes, conflicts, and ideas. In this optimistic view, projective techniques provide what amounts to an "X-ray of the personality" (Frank, 1939).

The number and variety of projective techniques invented during the past fifty years is remarkable. Some require the subject to give word associations or to complete sentences; others to draw a person or to copy designs; yet others ask subjects to state "three wishes." Where Freud was satisfied with just one royal road to the unconscious, the projective practitioners tried to map several hundred. We will consider only the two that are used most widely—the Rorschach inkblot technique and the Thematic Apperception Test.

THE RORSCHACH INKBLOTS

Hermann Rorschach, a Swiss psychologist, used the perception of unstructured forms as a diagnostic tool. That unstructured forms can be perceived in many different ways was well known before Rorschach's inkblots became part of every clinical psychologist's tool kit. An illustration is provided by Prince Hamlet:

HAMLET   Do you see yonder cloud that's almost in the shape of a camel?
POLONIUS   By the mass, and 'tis like a camel, indeed.
HAMLET   Methinks it is like a weasel.
POLONIUS   It is backed like a weasel.
HAMLET   Or like a whale?
POLONIUS   Very like a whale.

(Hamlet, Act III, scene ii)

In 1921, Rorschach published an "experimental study of form perception." This study used ten symmetrical inkblots, some colored and some black and white, that he had presented to various groups of psychiatric patients. When the patients were asked what they saw in the inkblots, their responses seemed to differ depending upon the diagnostic group to which they belonged. Rorschach regarded these findings as tentative, but he nevertheless used them to devise a system for scoring and interpretation. (Zubin, Eron, and Shumer, 1965).

Administration and scoring   An example of a card similar to those employed by Rorschach is shown in Figure 16.2. The subject is presented with each of ten cards, one at a time, and is asked to tell what she sees, what the blots might be. After all ten of the cards have been presented, the examiner queries the subject about each response to find out which part of the blot was used and which of its attributes determined its nature.

The scoring is according to three categories: location, determinants, and content. **Location** concerns the portion of the blot that is used in the response. Is it the whole blot, a large detail, or small detail? **Determinants** are the attributes of the stimulus that are the basis of the response, such as form, shading, or color. Also classed as a determinant is movement, a scoring category which is used whenever the subject describes a person, animal, or object

16.2 An inkblot of the type used in the Rorschach test Because familiarity with the cards makes it difficult to evaluate a person's first reaction, most psychologists prefer not to print the actual inkblots used in the test. Five of the actual cards are in black and white, five others are colored.

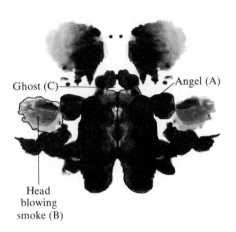

16.3   Sample responses and scoring on a Rorschach-type inkblot.   *(A) Two angels with wings, flying among clouds.* Where are they? *The whole thing? Here are the angels; here are their wings. The rest is clouds.* What makes them look like that? *Their shape. The shaded parts are clouds.* Scoring: Location—Whole; Determinants—Human movement, shading. (B) A man's head blowing smoke Scoring: Location—Large detail; Determinants—Human movement, shading. (C) A ghost in a shroud. In white. Scoring: Location—Small detail; Determinant—White space.*

that is said to be in motion. The final scoring category, **content,** refers to what the subject sees, rather than where or how he sees it. Among the major content categories are human figures or parts of human figures, animals or parts of animals, inanimate objects, plants, blood, X rays, and so on (Figure 16.3).

Interpretation   Rorschach experts insist that the interpretation of a Rorschach record cannot be performed in a simple cookbook fashion, for it demands the interrelation of all of its various features in all their complexity. In their view, interpretation is a subtle art which requires much talent and even more experience. Nevertheless, we can at least sketch a few of the major hypotheses about certain Rorschach signs. For example, using the entire inkblot is said to indicate integrative, conceptual thinking, whereas the use of a high proportion of small details suggests compulsive rigidity, and a relatively frequent use of the white space (which then serves as figure rather than as ground) is supposed to be a sign of rebelliousness and negativism. Responses that describe humans in movement are said to indicate imagination and a rich inner life; responses that are dominated by color suggest emotionality and impulsivity.

Traditional approaches to Rorschach interpretation hold that content is less important for diagnosis than the formal categories of location and determinants. But even so, most interpreters use content to some extent. That knives and mutilated bodies are generally regarded as indicators of hostility is not surprising. In some cases, the content analysis becomes more esoteric. For example, some Rorschach experts may regard it as quite significant if a male subject does *not* give the response *vagina* (or *channel, canyon,* etc.) to a portion of a certain card that is often seen this way. The expert would be especially interested if the subject describes this region of the card in terms that seem to refer to female sexuality while simultaneously denying it; for example, as a "statue of a draped female figure." Given this response, some experts might find it hard to resist the interpretation that the subject has strong sexual inhibitions and a tendency to "put women on a pedestal."

Assessing the validity of Rorschach interpretation is a difficult task. We will consider this issue together with similar ones raised by the other major projective technique in current use, the **Thematic Apperception Test,** or **TAT** developed by Henry Murray and his associates (Morgan and Murray, 1935).

THE THEMATIC APPERCEPTION TEST (TAT)

To Rorschach, content was a secondary concern. To the originators of the TAT, it was the primary focus, for their emphasis was on a person's major motives and preoccupations, defenses, conflicts, and ways of interpreting the world.

Administration and scoring   The TAT test materials are a number of pictures of various scenes (Figure 16.4). The subject is asked to tell a story about each picture, to describe what is happening, what led up to the scene, and what the outcome will be. One of the pictures represents the ultimate in unstructuredness—it is completely blank.

Most clinicians score the test in a rather impressionistic manner, with special attention to recurrent themes. Some systematic scoring procedures do

16.4   A picture of the type used in the TAT

exist and have been used mostly for research purposes. They involve such measures as the number of times a given motive comes up (for example, the need for achievement; see Chapter 13), the ratio of positive to negative outcomes, the frequency with which "mother figures" or "father figures" are seen as threatening or supportive, and so on. But thus far, none of these scoring systems has gained wide acceptance in actual clinical use.

Interpretation   In clinical practice, TAT interpretation is usually a rather freewheeling affair. Each story suggests a hypothesis which is then checked and elaborated (or discarded) by looking at later stories. The desired end product is a picture of the person's major motives and conflicts, pieced together by interpreting the TAT stories in the light of all previously available information, of which the case history is probably the most important.

An illustration of this impressionistic and global approach to TAT interpretation is provided by the case of Morris, a twenty-six-year-old securities salesman, one of whose conflicts centered upon his sex life. He was puzzled why sex was relatively unimportant to him and he had at least as many homosexual as heterosexual experiences. Condensations of two of his TAT stories are presented below:

> *Picture of a naked man . . . in the act of climbing a rope up or down:* The man is a eunuch in Ethiopia . . . and there this man Ahab, as he was called by the Arabs, lived for 20 years as servant in the sheik's harem. Surprisingly, instead of developing the usual lackadaisical castrated attitude that comes to eunuchs . . . this Ahab was constantly tormented by the presence of all the women and his complete inability to do anything about it . . . he decided he must escape . . . threw a rope out of the window . . . and let himself down. . . . Fate was against him. He got to the bottom: four of the servants of the Arab chief were there, ready to grab him. . . . He died in the most unique way the chief could think up . . . in a room with a couple of colonies of red ants.

> *Picture of a young man standing with downcast head buried in his arm. Behind him is the figure of a woman lying in bed:* "Jesus, what a shape! Positively indecent! . . ." His first thought was that the man was "going to the bathroom to make sure he doesn't catch anything!" He then said that the scene was in Hawaii, where a man and girl were "sitting and drinking on a terrace." After "six drinks, they stagger upstairs and land on the bed"; a couple of minutes later, the man goes to the bathroom to throw up. (Janis, Mahl, Kagan, and Holt, 1969, pp. 700–701)

In both these stories heterosexual love comes to an unhappy end. The same holds true for two other stories in this person's TAT record which contained heterosexual themes. There is also the fact that each of these four stories was set in such distant places as Ethiopia and Hawaii. To the TAT interpreter this meant that Morris was unable to imagine any heterosexual involvement in the here and now. In contrast, homosexual themes occurred in contemporaneous settings close to home. A related fact concerns another TAT picture which shows a male embracing a female. But in Morris' story, the sexes are misperceived. The male is seen as a mother, the female as the mother's weak and pudgy son who has to lean on her. This confusion of sexual identity goes together with the theme of castration that is quite explicit in one of the two stories summarized here. According to the TAT interpreter, this theme is linked to Morris' life history. His father deserted the family when Morris was

637

only eight, a fact which may have contributed to Morris' unsure sense of being a heterosexual male (Janis et al., 1969).

Interpretations of this sort are very beguiling. They suggest facets of an individual's personality which might never have been revealed otherwise. But are these facets actually there? To what extent can we trust the projective tester's interpretations? Are these interpretations equally astute when the tester does not have the benefit of hindsight, when she does not know the salient facts of the subject's life history?

THE VALIDITY OF PROJECTIVE TECHNIQUES

By now, there are probably seven thousand published articles that are explicitly devoted to the Rorschach and the TAT. Considering all of this effort, the upshot has been disappointing. According to some experts, these techniques have some limited validity; according to others, they have none. But by no stretch of the imagination could either qualify as an X ray of the personality.

Validity and the Rorschach Individual Rorschach indices—especially those that don't refer to content—show little or no relation to external validity criteria. In one study of psychiatric patients, over thirty different measures from the Rorschach records (for instance, the number of responses using the whole inkblot) were studied to see whether there was any relation to later diagnosis. There was none. Similar results apply to nonpsychiatric populations. For example, a preponderance of human movement responses is said to indicate creativity, but a group of eminent artists were no different from ordinary persons in this regard. Another example concerns the use of white space. Such responses are said to reflect rebelliousness and negativism, but when a large number of juvenile delinquents were compared to a matched group of nondelinquents, the proportion of white space responses was about the same (Zubin, Eron, and Shumer, 1965).

Studies of this kind have sometimes been criticized as too "atomistic," for they compare individual indices one by one in various criterion groups. Wouldn't it be better to use the test as a whole, and to allow the judge to read the entire record verbatim (or even to administer the test) and then predict the criterion on the basis of this overall, "global" knowledge? One study that meets these conditions used twelve eminent Rorschach experts who tried to assess various aspects of the personalities of various patients on the basis of their complete Rorschach records. The external criterion was the pooled judgment of a number of psychiatrists who read each patient's case history, obtained in six or so interviews of several hours each. The mean correlation between the Rorschach experts' predictions and the psychiatrists' judgments was a mere +.21 (Little and Shneidman, 1959).

Global assessment on the basis of the verbatim record evidently has some modest validity. Some authors believe that this is because some important information is provided by the specific content of the subject's responses (Zubin, 1954). This fits in with other evidence which shows moderate relationships between Rorschach content and external criteria. For example, hostile Rorschach content (knives) correlates with hostility as rated by judges (Zubin, Eron, and Shumer, 1965). Thus, contrary to traditional Rorschach lore, *what* subjects see in the inkblots seems to be more revealing than *how* they see it.

Validity and the TAT   If content is the crucial variable, then one should have high hopes for the validity of the TAT, which aims for little else but thematic content. But in fact, the TAT has fared no better than the Rorschach in those validity studies that assessed its ability to predict psychiatric diagnosis. In one case study, the TAT was administered to over a hundred male veterans, some in mental hospitals and others in college. There was no difference between normals and patients, let alone between different psychiatric groups (Eron, 1950).

While such results indicate that the TAT may have drawbacks as a diagnostic tool for psychiatric classification, the test does seem to have some validity for more limited purposes. A number of studies have shown that the TAT may be a fair indicator of the presence of certain motives, though probably not of all. One group of investigators worked with subjects who had not eaten for various periods of time. When presented with TAT-like pictures, some of which suggested food or eating, hungry subjects came up with more stories whose plots concerned hunger or food-seeking than a control group of sated subjects (Atkinson and McClelland, 1948). Related findings have been obtained with various other motives including aggression, sexual arousal, the desire for power, and so on. Thus far, the most impressive work has centered on the achievement motive. The success of these efforts represents a kind of construct validation of the TAT as an assessment device for at least some motives.

Projective techniques and incremental validity   Given the verdict of these various validation studies, many projective experts have become convinced that their devices are not really tests at all, but instead are important adjuncts to a clinical interview (Zubin, Eron, and Shumer, 1965). Rorschach and TAT scores make little sense to a practitioner who has not administered the tests personally or at least read the verbatim records. They are also hard to interpret without a knowledge of the subject's background and life history. But proponents of these techniques argue that when they are used as part of the total clinical evaluation, they help to provide a richer understanding of the person (Figure 16.5).

16.5   Projective techniques for use with children   *Special projective techniques have been developed for use with children. An example is the Children's Apperception Test, CAT, that consists of ten pictures in which all characters are animals. (Courtesy Bellak and Bellak, 1980)*

We have seen that when the Rorschach or TAT are used in this manner, they do indeed have some modest predictive validity for diagnosis. But according to some critics, predictive validity is not enough; the real issue is whether these tests have ***incremental validity*** (Meehl, 1959). The question is how much additional information these techniques provide over and above that which is contained in case histories and similar data that have to be gathered anyway. To give and score a Rorschach and/or a TAT is very time-consuming; since this is so, these tests ought to provide a reasonable increment in information. But the available evidence suggests otherwise. Several studies have shown that when clinical psychologists were asked to make inferences about a subject's personal characteristics, they were just as accurate with only the case history to go on as they were when provided with additional data in the form of the Rorschach or TAT records (Kostlan, 1954; Winch and More, 1956.)

Traits versus Situations

The preceding discussion has shown that personality tests are not particularly accurate probes into the human psyche. What accounts for this state of affairs? One possibility is that the fault lies with the tests themselves, that the tests have somehow failed to uncover those traits (or inner motives, conflicts, or whatever) that characterize the difference between one human personality and another. But there is another possibility that is more disquieting. Perhaps the tests do so poorly because that which they are trying to measure—a set of stable personality traits—isn't really there. To put it another way, perhaps Theophrastus was wrong, and there is no real consistency in the way people behave at different times and on different occasions.

THE DIFFICULTIES WITH TRAIT THEORY

The concept of stable personality traits was seriously challenged by Walter Mischel, whose survey of the research literature led him to conclude that people behave much less consistently than a trait theory would predict (Mischel, 1968). A classic study concerns honesty in children (Hartshorne and May, 1928). Grade-school children were given the opportunity to lie, cheat, or steal in a wide variety of settings: in athletic events, in the classroom, at home, alone, or with peers. The important finding was that the child who was dishonest in one situation (cheating on a test) was not necessarily dishonest in another setting (an athletic contest). There was some consistency, but it was rather unimpressive; a recent reanalysis of the results came up with an average intercorrelation of +.30 (Burton, 1963). The correlations were greater the greater the similarity between the two situations in which honesty was assessed. Honesty in one classroom situation was more consistent with honesty in another classroom situation than with honesty assessed at home.

Mischel argued that a similar lack of cross-situational consistency is found for many other behavior patterns. Examples are aggression, dependency, rigidity, and reactions to authority. The intercorrelations among different measures of what seems to be the same trait are often low and sometimes nonexistent. In Mischel's view, the fact that personality tests have relatively low validities is just another demonstration of the same phenomenon. A personality test taps behavior in one situation while the criterion assesses behavior in another context. Since cross-situational consistency tends to be low, so are validity coefficients.

If this view is right, the underlying consistency of the personalities of our friends and acquaintances (as well as our own) is more or less illusory. But if so, how can one explain the fact that most people have held this particular illusion since Theophrastus' time and no doubt much before? Mischel's answer was that personality traits are largely mental constructions devised by the observer who watches another person's actions and tries to make sense out of them. To do so, the observer *attributes* the act to some inner, stable characteristic of the actor (see Chapter 14 for a discussion of this attribution process).

SITUATIONISM

The failure to find behavioral consistency has been taken as an argument against the importance of personality characteristics in determining what a person will do. But if these are not relevant, what is? One answer is ***situationism,*** the notion that human behavior is largely determined by the characteristics of the situation rather than by those of the person. That this is so for some situations is indubitable. Given a red light, most drivers stop; given a green light, most go—regardless of whether they are friendly or unfriendly, stingy or generous, dominant or submissive, and so on. Situations of this sort produce predictable reactions in virtually all of us. But according to situationism, the same principle applies to much or nearly all of human behavior. Consider the

In some situations, most people behave the same way (Photograph by Hiroji Kubota, Magnum Photos)

In other situations, most people behave differently A major task of personality psychologists is to discover whether they behave consistently across different situations. (Photograph by Elliott Erwitt, Magnum Photos)

enormous effect of social roles which often define what an actor must do with little regard to who the actor is (see Chapter 14). To predict how someone will act in a courtroom, there is little point in asking whether she is sociable or extravagant with money or whether he gets along with his father. What we really want to know is the role that he or she will play—judge, prosecutor, defense attorney, or defendant. Seen in this light, what we do depends not on who we are, but on the situation in which we find ourselves.

This is not to say that situationists deny the existence of individual differences. They certainly agree that various demographic and socioeconomic factors are powerful determinants of human behavior. Examples are age and sex, marital status, ethnic background, occupation, and income. Nor do they dispute the important effect of differences in ability, especially cognitive ability. As they see it, all of these factors determine the kinds of situations a person is likely to encounter or to have encountered (and thus learned from). But in their view, it is these situations, rather than personality traits, that determine what people actually do.

PERSONALITY AND MENTAL DISORDER

The situationist perspective may help explain why the study of personality has so often been linked to the field of mental disorder. This link exists for personality theory: Freud's conception of human nature grew out of his observations of severely disturbed neurotics. It also exists for personality assessment: Some of the most widely used personality tests are validated on criterion groups drawn from the psychiatric clinic. In part, the link between the two fields arose because of various historical accidents. For instance, Freud made his living as a practicing psychiatrist, and personality tests were initially devised to help psychiatric diagnosis.

There was probably a deeper reason as well. One of the characteristics of mentally disturbed persons is that they are generally less responsive to the demands of a situation than are normals. As a result, they show more behavioral consistency across situations. Normal people smile about births and cry about deaths; psychiatrically depressed patients may cry about both. The same applies to other forms of mental illness. The patients' responses are governed more by factors within themselves—depressions, violent elations, delusions—than by the situation that confronts them. As a result, their behavior is often viewed by others as inappropriate to the occasion (which is one of the reasons why they are in the psychiatric ward). But in consequence, they also manifest more cross-situational consistency and thus provide more evidence for personality traits than do the rest of us (for some relevant research findings, see Moos, 1969). This may explain why the study of abnormal behavior has had such an enormous influence on the way in which psychologists think about normal personality.

IN DEFENSE OF TRAITS

The emphasis on situations provided a useful corrective to those who sought to explain everything people do as a manifestation of their own inner nature. But if pushed to the extreme, this position becomes just as questionable as the one it had tried to correct. For in this form it can be interpreted as asserting that personality does not exist at all. Whether any psychologist has actually gone to this extreme is doubtful; certainly Mischel never did. But the very possibility that someone might climb all the way out on this particular theoretical limb, and argue that personality is a myth, produced a spirited counterreaction against Mischel's attack on the trait concept.

EVIDENCE FOR BEHAVIORAL CONSISTENCY

The reaction to the situationist position took several forms. Some authors felt that it amounts to an overstatement. For example, they argued that there is considerable personal consistency over time (a point explicitly made by Mischel himself; Mischel, 1968; 1973). This fact is familiar enough from everyday experience; after meeting an old acquaintance whom we haven't seen for many years, we say that she hasn't changed at all. More formal demonstrations are provided by longitudinal studies which document a fair degree of behavioral consistency over sizable stretches of the life-span and across different situations. To give one example, in males, dependability as judged in high school correlates quite well with ratings of the same attribute made by different judges some ten or more years later ($r = +.55$; Block, 1971).

REINTERPRETING BEHAVIORAL INCONSISTENCY

A somewhat different argument was sounded by critics who insisted that behavioral inconsistency is often more apparent than real. They argued that on closer examination, two reactions that are superficially quite dissimilar may turn out to be a manifestation of the same underlying source. An example is aggression. In males, this is fairly consistent between childhood and adolescence, but it takes different overt forms at different ages. Young boys pummel each other with their fists; young men rarely do more than shout in anger (Kagan and Moss, 1962). Another example concerns the distinction between the attributes *happy/outgoing* and *somber/reserved*. When different judges were asked to assess this trait in persons first studied at age six and then again at age fifteen, their ratings were quite similar, yielding correlations of about +.60. This consistency disappeared, however, when the judges were asked to rate overt behavior only. The five-year old who is reserved and somber shows this by a low level of physical vitality. At ten, the same underlying attribute manifests itself as cautiousness and emotional vulnerability. Still later, during adolescence, this basic pattern goes together with a sense of inferiority (Bronson, 1966). We are reminded of the molar-molecular distinction in the area of animal behavior (see Chapters 4 and 5). Here, as in many other facets of the behavior of organisms, a superficial difference may disguise a deeper sameness.

THE INTERACTION BETWEEN PERSON AND SITUATION

Yet another group of commentators felt that the debate between situationists and trait theorists had harped on the wrong distinction. As originally formulated, the question was whether an individual's actions are better predicted by the situation or by his or her own personal characteristics. But there is a third alternative: The critical factor may be the ***interaction*** between person and situation.

643

The term *interaction* is used here in a technical sense. To explain what is meant by interaction in this context, let us consider a hypothetical experiment in which we study the reactions of several pairs of individuals to two different situations. The response will be anxiety as indicated by the galvanic skin response (GSR); the two situations are waiting to take a test and being threatened with electric shock. Let's call the subjects Jane and Carol, Mary and Claire, and let us assume that the GSR scale runs from 0 (no anxiety) to 12 (maximal anxiety). Two extreme outcomes are displayed in Tables 16.2 and 16.3.

Table 16.2   EFFECT OF SITUATION

		Situation		Average for each person
		Test	Shock	
Person	Jane	3	9	6
	Carol	3	9	6
Average for situation		3	9	

Table 16.3   EFFECT OF INDIVIDUAL DIFFERENCES

		Situation		Average for each person
		Test	Shock	
Person	Mary	3	3	3
	Claire	9	9	9
Average for situation		6	6	

The pattern of results shown in Tables 16.2 and 16.3 is diametrically opposed. Table 16.2 depicts a powerful effect of the situation. For these two subjects, Jane and Carol, shock is evidently much more frightening than the test. But there is no effect of individual differences since Jane and Carol behave identically. In Table 16.3 we see the reverse. Here, there is a massive effect of individual differences; Claire is evidently much more fearful than is Mary. But in this second example, the two situations are essentially equivalent in the fear they provoke.

These two illustrations fit the extreme positions that ascribe all behavior either to the situation or to personality differences. Needless to say, there are much more plausible intermediate outcomes in which both factors play a role. But our concern is with another alternative, which has quite different theoretical implications. Consider the pattern of results shown by yet another pair of subjects as indicated in Table 16.4.

Table 16.4   AN EFFECT OF SITUATION AND INDIVIDUAL DIFFERENCES INTERACTING

		Situation		Average for each person
		Test	Shock	
Person	Anne	3	9	6
	Donna	9	3	6
Average for situation		6	6	6

What is important about the results of Table 16.4 is that they do not exhibit effects of the situations as such nor of the individual differences as such. When we look at average GSRs, Anne and Donna prove equally fearful. The same holds for the difference between the situations; *on the average,* the test and the threatened shock produce equal GSRs. But there is a new twist which is obscured by the averages. The two situations produce radically different effects in the two persons. Anne is evidently much more afraid of the shock than of the test, while the opposite holds for Donna. In statistical language, a relationship of this kind, in which the effect of one variable (fear-evoking situation) depends upon another variable (individual differences) is called an *interaction.*

The test-shock experiment here described is a highly simplified version of a large number of studies that have actually been carried out. An example is a study in which subjects were asked to describe their usual reaction to various threats (Endler and Hunt, 1969). Some of these perils involved loss of self-esteem (failing an examination), others physical danger (being on a high ledge on a mountaintop), still others a threat whose nature was still unclear (getting a police summons). The results showed that both individual differences and situations affected behavior to some extent. Some people seemed more generally fearful than others, and some situations ("being approached by cars racing abreast") evoked more fear than others ("sitting in a restaurant").

What is more interesting is that the bulk of these effects were produced by the person-by-situation interaction. Put in other words, people tend to be frightened (or angered or reassured) by different things. A simple situationism is evidently untenable; the man who is terrified of heights may well be a passionate scuba diver. But this finding also undercuts the usefulness of general traits such as "anxiety." To predict behavior better, such traits should be qualified; for example, "anxiety in an interpersonal setting," "anxiousness when facing physical danger," "anxiety in the face of the unknown." By this utilization of the person-by-situation interaction, the notion of stable personality differences can be maintained. But there is a price, for the process of qualification may be endless. Consider interpersonal anxiety. It probably depends on whether the situation involves members of the same or the opposite sex. If it does, should we subdivide the trait still further? The end result can only be an enormous proliferation of ever more finely drawn traits.

PERSON CONSTANCY

In the light of all this, what can we say about the assumption that there is an underlying unity in how any one individual acts and thinks and feels, a basic consistency that we now call personality? The evidence indicates that this assumption—which goes back to Theophrastus—still stands. To be sure, behavioral consistency may be obscured by the demands of the situation. In addition, it is generally too subtle to be captured by a few simple trait descriptions; a list of highly qualified mini-traits is often the best we can do. But there is no reason to discard our intuitive belief in something like "person constancy," a phenomenon analogous to "object constancy" in perception (see Chapter 7). A chair is perceived as a stable object whose size remains the same whether we are near to it or far away and whose shape stays unchanged regardless of our visual orientation. These constancies are not illusions; they

reflect a genuine stability in the external world. The constancy of personality is not as sturdy as that of chairs but it has some reality even so. Jane remains Jane whether she is at home or at the office, whether it is today or yesterday or the day after tomorrow.

To this extent, Theophrastus is upheld. But on reflection, his character sketches—and the modern trait theory of personality—imply more than person constancy. Trait theorists assume not only that a particular person will behave consistently but that this person can be categorized along with others whose behavior is in some respects equivalent. There is the hitch, for the question now becomes how these categories are to be defined. Theophrastus picked a few attributes that were easy to caricature—loquaciousness, boorishness, stinginess, and so on. But are these the proper traits by which personalities should be classified?

In a way, much the same question is faced during the early stage of any science. At this point, a major task is the development of a useful *taxonomy,* or classification system. Consider the early biologists. They recognized that the various creatures differ in a multitude of ways—their size and color, the absence or presence of a skeleton, the number and kind of appendages, and so on. The biologists had to decide which of these distinctions provide the most useful classification categories. Exactly the same issue faces the psychologist who studies personality differences. The dictionary lists eighteen thousand trait names (Allport and Odbert, 1936). But without some kind of taxonomy how can we decide by which of these many traits to classify people?

We have seen that personality inventories rarely generate validity coefficients much above $+.30$. In part, this reflects various shortcomings of the tests. In part, it reflects the fact that personal differences are often obscured by the demands of the situation. But in part, it probably also reflects our failure to find the proper classification scheme that tells us which personality traits to assess.

Wanted: A Taxonomy

The preceding discussion has highlighted the major lack in the field of personality differences—a taxonomy that tells which personality distinctions really matter. But while such a classification scheme seems a far-off hope, we can at least sketch a few of the approaches that have been taken toward this end.

CLASSIFICATION BY INTERNAL CONSISTENCY

One approach tries to discover the basic dimensions of personality by means of factor analysis, a method already discussed in connection with tests of intelligence (see Chapter 16). The basic idea is to find out which test items

An early taxonomy of personality   *A medieval illustration of one of the earliest attempts to classify human personality, Hippocrates' four temperaments: sanguine (cheerful and active), melancholic (gloomy), choleric (angry and violent), and phlegmatic (calm and passive). According to Hippocrates, these temperaments reflected an excess of one of four bodily humors; thus sanguine persons were thought to have relatively more blood. Today the humor theory is a mere historical curiosity, but some aspects of Hippocrates' classification are still with us. (Courtesy the Bettmann Archive)*

Table 16.5   FACTOR DESIGNATIONS FOR TWENTY TRAIT-RATING SCALES

Factor names	Scale dimensions
Extroversion	Talkative/Silent Frank, open/Secretive Adventurous/Cautious Sociable/Reclusive
Agreeableness	Good-natured/Irritable Not jealous/Jealous Mild, gentle/Headstrong Cooperative/Negativistic
Conscientiousness	Fussy, tidy/Careless Responsible/Undependable Scrupulous/Unscrupulous Perservering/Quitting, fickle
Emotional stability	Poised/Nervous, tense Calm/Anxious Composed/Excitable Not hypochondriacal/Hypochondriacal
Culture	Artistically sensitive/Artistically insensitive Intellectual/Unreflective, narrow Polished, refined/Crude, boorish Imaginative/Simple, direct

SOURCE: Adapted from Norman, 1963.

correlate highly with one another while correlating little or not at all with others. The resulting item clusters are then inspected to see what they have in common. Such efforts have led to several contending lists of personality factors. An example is a hierarchical model in which several lower-level traits (tidy/careless, persevering/fickle) are seen as manifestations of a higher-order factor (conscientiousness) (Table 16.5).

NEUROTICISM AND EXTRAVERSION-INTROVERSION

We will begin by considering the work of Hans Eysenck, a British psychologist who has tried to encompass personality differences in a space defined by only two dimensions—neuroticism and extraversion-introversion. *Neuroticism* is equivalent to emotional instability and maladjustment. It is assessed by affirmative answers to questions like "Do you ever feel 'just miserable' for no good reason at all?" And "Do you often feel disgruntled?" *Extraversion-introversion* are terms that refer to the main direction of a person's energies, toward the outer world of material objects and other people or toward the inner world of one's own thoughts and feelings. The extravert is sociable, impulsive, and enjoys new experiences while the introvert tends to be more solitary, cautious, and slow to change. Extraversion is indicated by affirmative answers to questions such as "Do you like to have many social engagements?" and "Would you rate yourself as a happy-go-lucky individual?"

As Eysenck sees it, neuroticism and extraversion-introversion are independent dimensions. To be sure, both introverts and neurotics have something in common; they are both unsociable and withdrawn. But, in Eysenck's view,

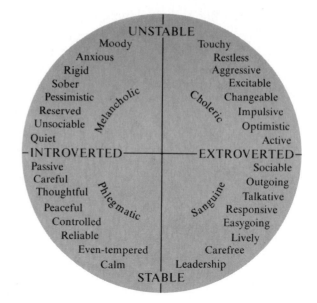

16.6 Eysenck's two-dimensional classification of personality *Two dimensions of personality—neuroticism (emotional instability) and extraversion-introversion—define a space into which various trait terms may be fitted. Eysenck points out that the four quadrants of this space seem to fit Hippocrates' temperaments. Introverted and stable—phlegmatic; introverted and unstable—melancholic; extraverted and stable—sanguine; extraverted and unstable—choleric. (Eysenck and Rachman, 1965)*

their lack of sociability has different roots. The healthy introverts are not afraid of social activities; they simply do not like them. In contrast, neurotically shy persons keep to themselves because of fear; they want to be with others but are afraid of joining them (Figure 16.6).

TEST FACTORS AND LABORATORY PHENOMENA

Can we be sure that the factors extracted by these statistical methods are the "real" dimensions of personality? Unfortunately, the answer has to be no. To begin with, factor analysts disagree with each other on too many points; they often come up with different classification systems to order the same set of data. Even more important is the fact that the end product of the analysis has to depend on what is fed into it. The factors describe the coherence among a certain set of items; if some items are added and others subtracted, the pattern of coherence (and thus the factors) will usually be different. In short, factor analysis is a technique that helps us understand how subparts of a test hang together. It is not a magic shortcut toward a taxonomy of personality traits.

Some of these objections can be partially met by formulating and testing some theoretical notions about the nature of the dimensions extracted through factor analysis. Eysenck and his associates have tried to provide this kind of construct validation for extraversion-introversion by relating it to many psychological phenomena outside of the personality domain.

As Eysenck sees it, introversion corresponds to a higher level of central nervous system arousal than does extraversion; in effect, introverts are thought to be more awake than extraverts (see Chapter 3). As a result, they are less distractable and better able to attend to the task at hand. For example, they do better at signal-detection tasks (Harkins and Green, 1975) and perform a monotonous tapping task with fewer involuntary rest pauses than persons with high extraversion scores (Eysenck, 1967). A related finding is that they are more reactive to external stimuli than extraverts; according to Eysenck, this is one of the reasons why they shy away from the world while extraverts embrace it enthusiastically. For example, introverts have lower pain tolerance (Lynn and Eysenck, 1961). On the other hand, people with high extraversion scores tend to seek out sensations; they enjoy taking off on trips without preplanned routes and say that they might like to try parachute jumping (Farley and Farley, 1967). They need external stimulation more than do the naturally aroused introverts.

Whether Eysenck's formulations will stand the test of time is a matter of debate. For example, it is still unclear whether the extraversion-introversion dimension is really independent of neuroticism (Carrigan, 1960). In addition, some of the laboratory effects are not as sturdy as one might have hoped (for example, Purohit, 1966). But whatever the ultimate verdict on Eysenck's specific hypotheses, future investigators will probably accept his more general thesis that a taxonomy of personality differences can only be successful if it makes contact with the rest of psychological and biological fact.

CLASSIFICATION THROUGH BIOLOGY

Other approaches to the development of a taxonomy of personality also try to build it within the framework of the more established biological sciences. We will consider two different lines of attack. One tries to relate personality differences to body build; the other focuses on the contribution of heredity.

PERSONALITY AND BODY BUILD

The notion that personality is somehow related to bodily physique probably goes back to antiquity. Shakespeare must have echoed the views of his contemporaries (and of the Roman writer, Plutarch, from whom he took several of his plots) when he linked Cassius' "lean and hungry look" with the fact that "he thinks too much." Is there any evidence to support this belief in a substantial correlation between temperament (that is, basic and presumably built-in personality characteristics) and physique? A number of investigators have thought that there is, and that it provides an appropriate starting point for a taxonomy of personality.

Physique and temperament   The most widely known exponent of this position is William Sheldon, who classified body types (or **somatotypes**). According to Sheldon, a person's somatotype can be described in terms of three components: **endomorphy, mesomorphy,** and **ectomorphy.** A person who is high in endomorphy and low in the other two components is soft and round; one who is high in only mesomorphy is hard, rectangular, and well muscled; one who is high in ectomorphy alone is thin, of delicate build, and lightly muscled. Needless to say, such extremes are rare; in actuality most people have intermediate somatotypes, although one component usually predominates (Figure 16.7). Somatotypes are determined by a combination of judges' ratings (based on nude photographs) and various physical measurements (Sheldon, 1940).

The next step was to decide on the personality traits to which these somatotypes might be related. Three clusters of traits were chosen. One is **viscerotonia,** which includes a love of food and comfort, relaxed tolerance, sociability, and a need for affection. A second is **somatotonia,** which is characterized by a desire for power and dominance, a zest for physical activity and adventure,

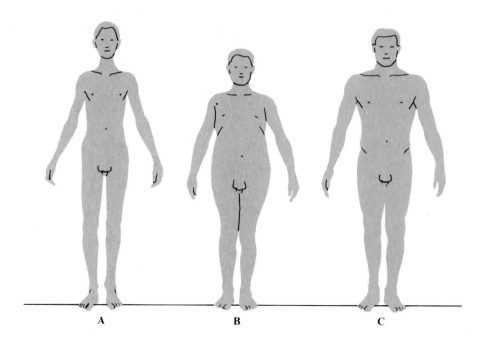

16.7   Sheldon's dimensions of physique
*Three extreme somatotypes: (A) Ecto-
morph; (B) endomorph; (C) mesomorph.*

A   B   C

and a relative indifference to other people. Finally, there is **cerebrotonia,**
which includes self-consciousness, overreactiveness, and a preference for privacy. Sheldon's hypotheses about the relations of these temperaments and
body build are implicit in the names he gave each cluster. The names indicate
the body regions which he believed to be most relevant for these personality
attributes. Thus endomorphy should go along with viscerotonia, mesomorphy
with somatotonia, and ectomorphy with cerebrotonia.

Testing the relations between physique and temperament   To test these hypotheses, Sheldon studied two hundred young men over a five-year period
and then determined their somatotypes. The direction of the relationships
were exactly as he had predicted. What is more, the correlations were huge,
with an average of about +.80 (Sheldon, 1942). There was only one trouble.
The results were too good to be true, for correlations of this size are unheard of
in personality research. Several critics soon pointed out a basic flaw in the
procedure. The same person—Sheldon himself, who presumably believed his
own theory—had rated both the temperaments and the somatotypes. Under
the circumstances, it is not surprising that his ratings of temperament were
contaminated by his observation of the subjects' physiques (Humphreys,
1957).

Sheldon and other investigators tried to meet this criticism by having physique and temperament assessed by different judges. The resulting correlations were in line with Sheldon's hypotheses but much lower than those he
had originally reported, with an average of +.26 (Child, 1950).

A more impressive set of findings concerns juvenile delinquency. Here is a
behavior pattern that presumably involves some of the characteristics of somatotonia: physical action, aggressiveness, and a disregard of what others
think or want. One would therefore expect a relationship with mesomorphy
and this is just what the data show. When five hundred male delinquents were

compared to five hundred matched nondelinquents, about 60 percent of the delinquents were found to be predominantly mesomorphic, compared to 30 percent of the nondelinquent group (Glueck and Glueck, 1956). A similar relationship seems to characterize female delinquents (Epps and Parnell, 1952).

All in all, there is little doubt that Sheldon's initial claims were overstated. But even so, there seems to be a core of truth to his (and other writers') assertion that physique and temperament are related. The underlying factors may turn out to be somewhat different from those that Sheldon had proposed. For instance, several authors believe that the critical dimensions for body type are skeletal height and width and that the proportion of fat to muscle makes no difference (Rees and Eysenck, 1945). The result is a two-dimensional classification that ignores endomorphy. It apparently yields a better fit to the facts. One relevant finding concerns the constancy of body build over age. For the mesomorphy and ectomorphy components, the constancy is quite good. When these components were measured at age seventeen and then again at age thirty-three, the average correlation for both men and women was +.78. In contrast, endomorphy shows little constancy. The correlation between age seventeen and age thirty-three was a negligible +.14 (Zuk, 1958).

Accounting for the relation between physique and temperament What explains the relation between body build and personality, if it indeed exists? One possibility is that certain physiques foster some behavior patterns rather than others. If a boy wants to bully his peers, he had better have the musculature with which to back it up. If he has, he is more likely to succeed (and thus be reinforced) than if he hasn't; the end product is an association between physical action and mesomorphy. Another possibility is that the relation between physique and temperament is a by-product of popular stereotypes. Such stereotypes are very prevalent; they are already found in five-year olds (Lerner and Korn, 1972). If a chubby boy learns that others think of him as easygoing and compliant, he may come to see himself the same way and behave accordingly. This hypothesis does not explain how the stereotype arose in the first place, but it does suggest how it is perpetuated.

In sum, there probably is a relation between body build and personality attributes. This relationship is relatively weak and its origins are still a matter of speculation. It is of considerable interest all the same, for it may provide a clue about the way in which some personality differences develop from childhood origins. But thus far at least, the correlations between physique and temperament are too small and too poorly understood to provide the basis of a viable taxonomy of personality differences.

PERSONALITY AND GENETICS

In principle, there are several other ways in which biology might provide some clues for the development of a classification system. One promising approach centers on certain consistencies of behavior beginning in infancy. This holds for attributes like sociability and activity level, which seem to be remarkably stable from early childhood to adolescence (Kagan and Moss, 1962). Such consistencies have been observed beginning from the first weeks of life. An example comes from a study of 141 children, observed for about a decade following birth.

Donald exhibited an extremely high activity level almost from birth. At three months . . . he wriggled and moved about a great deal while asleep in his crib. At six months he "swam like a fish" while being bathed. At twelve months he still squirmed constantly while he was being dressed or washed. . . . At two years he was "constantly in motion, jumping and climbing." At three, he would "climb like a monkey and run like an unleashed puppy." . . . By the time he was seven, Donald was encountering difficulty in school because he was unable to sit still long enough to learn anything (Thomas, Chess, and Birch, 1970, p. 104).

Consistencies of this sort suggest the operation of genetic factors. The evidence comes from the same methods used to study hereditary effects in the determination of intelligence: the comparison of twins. In general, identical twins have proved to be more alike than fraternal twins on various personality attributes. Examples are extraversion-introversion, emotionality, and activity level (Scarr, 1969; Buss and Plomin, 1975). These results argue for some contribution of heredity to personality makeup. But, as one might have expected, the proportion of the variance accounted for by genetic factors is considerably lower for personality than for intelligence.

Still, such facts might provide the basis of the long-sought taxonomy. The idea is simple: Those traits that are especially heritable are presumably more basic and should therefore serve as the primary categories for classification. But which traits are the basic ones? For a while it seemed as if extraversion-introversion was one, since it seemed to have higher heritabilities than all the rest (Loehlin, 1969). But later research argues otherwise.

In a recent study, 850 twins of high-school age took a standard personality test, the California Psychological Inventory. As expected, the scores of the identical twins were more alike than those of the fraternal twins. The trouble was that this difference was just about the same on each of the tests' eighteen scales. This suggests that all of these traits are about equally heritable (Loehlin and Nichols, 1976). This result is surprising; perhaps it reflects something about the test rather than the nature of the underlying attributes. But, at least for the time being, it rules out any classification scheme based on the belief that some traits are more heritable than others.

CLASSIFICATION THROUGH LANGUAGE

Yet another approach to the development of a taxonomy involves an examination of the language we use to describe personality attributes. Advocates of this procedure argue that the adjectives used to describe people embody the accumulated observations of many previous generations. A systematic sifting of dictionary trait-words may then give clues about individual differences whose description was important enough to survive the test of time. This line of reasoning led to the development of a widely used personality inventory by one of the major proponents of the factor-analytic approach to personality, Raymond Cattell (1957). Cattell's starting point was a set of 4,500 terms taken from the 18,000 trait-words in the unabridged dictionary (Allport and Odbert, 1936). This list was drastically reduced by throwing out difficult or uncommon words and eliminating synonyms. Finally, 171 trait names were left. A group of judges was then asked to rate subjects in terms of this list. Their ratings were factor analyzed to discover how the trait-words were related to each other. The results yielded what Cattell thought were some 15 to 20 primary factors of personality.

A number of other psychologists share Cattell's belief that personality measurement must be grounded upon the trait-words of the language, but they feel that he turned away from the dictionary too soon. In their view, factor analysis is not the key to getting a taxonomy. What is necessary is a deeper analysis of the trait-words themselves. One question is whether a given word has many synonyms or near-synonyms. If so, it probably concerns a dimension of individual differences which the language community regards as important. After all, why else would they want to talk about it with so many different nuances of meaning (Goldberg, 1972)? Another question concerns the generality of the trait-word. If it is found in many languages, it presumably describes a rather basic attribute of human behavior (Goldberg, 1975).

Still another question pertains to the separation of descriptive and evaluative aspects of trait-words. Consider the terms *thrifty* and *extravagant.* They differ in the behavior they describe—unlikely to spend money versus likely to do so. But they also differ in the evaluation they place on these behaviors: the first is good, the second is bad. To separate the descriptive and evaluative aspects, one has to find a pair of words in which these relations are reversed, such as *stingy* and *generous* (Peabody, 1967). If subjects are rated on all four of these adjectives, we can separately determine the extent to which the judge believes that the subject will spend his money and the extent to which she likes or dislikes him for doing so. Such procedures may help to eliminate some of the defects in traditional testing procedures (Goldberg, 1975). But it is too early to tell whether they will also provide some major advance in the classification of personality differences.

IS A CLASSIFICATION SYSTEM POSSIBLE?

In addition to those we've discussed, there have been several other approaches to a taxonomy of personality differences. One is based on the similarity to various forms of mental illness. For example, normal persons might be classified by how closely their behavior resembles that found in mania, depression, or schizophrenia. Some of the early interpretations of normals' responses to the MMPI or the Rorschach were essentially in this vein. A very different taxonomy might be based on certain crucial events in childhood; Freud's theory of fixation at various stages of psychosexual development is a famous example. No doubt there are many other possibilities as well.

Have any of them worked? Some may have, to a limited extent. But the kind of taxonomy on which a science can really build, the kind that biologists have known for centuries, is not as yet in sight, although some of the developments we have surveyed are promising.

Summary

1. *Personality traits* are attributes that define distinctions in the predominant desires and feelings and the typical modes of expressing these, which are characteristic of different persons. The underlying assumption of *trait theory* is that such traits are fundamentally consistent over time and situations.

2. One approach to personality assessment is by *objective personality inventories*. An example is the *Minnesota Multiphasic Personality Inventory*, or *MMPI*. It assesses traits by means of a number of different *scales,* each of which measures the extent to which a person's answers approximate those of a particular psychiatric *criterion group*. In actual practice, MMPI records are interpreted by inspecting the person's *score profile*, including his response to various *check-up scales*. A number of other personality inventories such as the *California Psychological Inventory*, or *CPI*, were constructed in an analogous manner but using normal rather than pathological criterion groups.

3. The validity of personality inventories has been evaluated by using indices of *predictive validity*. The results show that while these tests predict, they predict not too well, for their *validity coefficients* are relatively low. When the evaluation is based on *construct validity,* the results look somewhat more promising.

4. A very different way of assessing personality is by means of *projective techniques*. Two prominent examples are the *Rorschach inkblot test* and the *Thematic Apperception Test,* or *TAT*. While these tests are often used in clinical practice, they have been criticized because of their relatively low predictive validity and even lower *incremental validity* coefficients.

5. The concept of stable personality traits has been seriously challenged by *situationism* which argues that people behave much less consistently than a trait theory would predict, their behavior being largely determined by the situation in which they find themselves. This critique led to a reassessment in which some commentators opted for a third alternative—what is consistent is an *interaction* between person and situation.

6. A major problem of modern personality theory is the absence of an established *taxonomy* for personality traits. One attempt to develop such a taxonomy depends on *factor analysis* and has led to a number of contending lists of personality factors. An example is Eysenck's scheme which is based on two dimensions—*neuroticism* and *extraversion-introversion*.

7. Other investigators have tried to build a taxonomy by relating personality traits to bodily physique. The major example is Sheldon's classification of *somatotypes* according to the dimensions of *endomorphy, mesomorphy,* and *ectomorphy*. Sheldon asserted that these dimensions of body type go together with three clusters of personality traits, *viscerotonia, somatotonia,* and *cerebrotonia*. The evidence indicates that the correlations between somatotype and personality are very much smaller than Sheldon had claimed initially, though some modest relation between physique and temperament may well be present.

8. Another approach centers on genetic factors. The existence of inherited dispositions which affect personality is suggested by consistencies in temperament, from early infancy through adulthood. Further evidence comes from studies that show that the scores on many personality inventories are more similar for identical than for fraternal twins.

9. Still another attempt to impose a classification scheme upon the myriad ways in which we can describe personality comes through an analysis of the language used for such descriptions. The assumption is that commonly used trait words embody the accumulated observations of previous generations which may provide clues to the dimensions which really matter.

CHAPTER 17

Psychopathology

In the preceding chapter, we considered differences in human personality traits. We now turn to conditions in which such differences go beyond the range of normal functioning and take on the appearance of psychological disorder. The study of such disorders is the province of **psychopathology** or, as it is sometimes called, **abnormal psychology.** There is considerable debate about how the subject matter of abnormal psychology is to be defined. Is it simply a problem of statistical deviance, of behavior that is markedly different from the norm? Or should we take the term *psychopathology* more literally and regard its manifestations as something akin to illness? But if these manifestations are illnesses, of what kind are they? Are they caused by some bodily disorder, such as a defect in brain function or a biochemical imbalance? Or are they better conceived of as *mental* illnesses whose origin is psychological, such as a learned defense against anxiety?

As we shall see, there is no one answer to these questions. The reason is that the various conditions that are generally subsumed under the rubric of psychopathology are a very mixed lot. For some, the term *illness* seems quite appropriate; for others, this is not so clear. In any case, there is little doubt that many of the conditions that come to the attention of the psychopathologist—the psychiatrist, the clinical psychologist, or other mental-health specialists—often cause considerable anguish and may seriously impair the afflicted person's functioning. Two examples will suffice here.

The first is a case of an **obsessional neurosis** (plural, **neuroses**): "A farmer developed obsessive thoughts of hitting his three-year-old son over the head with a hammer. The father was completely unable to explain his 'horrible thoughts.' He stated that he loved his son very much and thought he must be going insane to harbor such thoughts" (Coleman, 1972, p. 233). In neurosis, the patient has not lost contact with reality. He can generally hold on to a job, maintain a household, and so on, no matter how miserable he may feel. The situation is different in a *psychosis* (plural, *psychoses*), a broad category that includes some of the most severe mental disorders.* In psychoses, the patient's thoughts and deeds no longer meet the demands of reality. An example is a thirty-two-year-old woman with bizarre delusions and a diagnosis of schizophrenia:

> DR. When did you come here?
> PT. 1416, you remember, doctor . . .
> DR. Do you know why you are here?
> PT. Well in 1951 I changed into two men. President Truman was judge at my trial. I was convicted and hung . . .
> DR. Can you tell me the name of this place?
> PT. I have not been a drinker for 16 years. I am taking a mental rest after a "carter" assignment or "quill." You know, a "penwrap." I had contracts with Warner Brothers Studios and Eugene broke phonograph records but Mike protested. . . . I am made of flesh and blood—see, doctor (pulling up her dress) (Coleman, 1972, pp. 280–81).

We will begin our discussion of psychopathology by considering some of the historical roots of our conceptions of what "madness" is and how it should be dealt with.

Different Conceptions of Madness

An early example of mental disorder
King Nebuchadnezzer as depicted by William Blake (1795). (Courtesy the Tate Gallery, London)

Mental disorders existed for many millenia before psychiatrists appeared on the scene. Early mythological and religious writings are proof enough. The Greek hero, Ajax, slew a flock of sheep which he mistook for his enemies; King Saul of Judea alternated between bouts of murderous frenzy and suicidal depressions; and the Babylonian King Nebuchadnezzar walked on all fours in the belief that he was a wolf. Such phenomena were evidently not isolated instances. According to the Bible, young David feigned madness while seeking refuge from his enemies at the court of a Philistine king. This king had obviously encountered insanity before and upbraided his servants, "Do I lack madmen, that you have brought this fellow to play the madman in my presence?"

INSANITY AS DEMONIC POSSESSION

What leads to mental disorder? One of the earliest theories held that the afflicted person was possessed by evil spirits. It followed that the cure for the

---

* Some psychiatrists doubt that the distinction between neurosis and psychosis is as clear-cut as it was once believed to be, and they advocated that one or both of these terms be dropped from the official diagnostic catalogue of their profession (*The Diagnostic and Statistical Manual of Mental Disorders,* or *DSM*). Nevertheless, we will use these two terms in the present account, at least in an informal way. To avoid them altogether is difficult, given the fact that they have become part of common parlance.

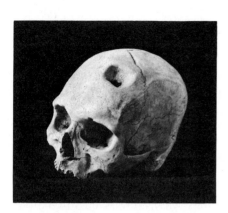

17.1 Trephining *A trephined prehistoric skull found in Peru. The patient apparently survived the operation for a while, for there is some evidence of bone healing. (Courtesy The American Museum of Natural History)*

17.2 Witch hunts in sixteenth-century Europe *A witch about to be burned at the stake. (Courtesy the Bettmann Archive)*

malady was to drive the devils out. If the patient was lucky, the exorcism procedures were fairly mild; the unruly demons were calmed by music or were chased away by prayers and religious rites. More often the techniques were less benign. One approach was to provide a physical escape hatch for the devils. According to some anthropologists, this may explain why Stone Age men sometimes cut large holes into their fellows' skulls; many such **trephined** skulls have been found, often with signs that the patient managed to survive the operation (Figure 17.1). The plausibility of this hypothesis is enhanced by the fact that trephining is still performed by some preliterate tribes, and for much the same reasons (Stewart, 1957). Yet another idea was to make things as uncomfortable for the devil as possible so as to induce him to escape. Accordingly, the patient was chained, immersed in boiling hot or ice-cold baths, was starved, flogged, or tortured. That such procedures usually drove the patient into worse and worse derangement is hardly surprising.

According to some medical historians, the demonological approach to mental disorder reached its culmination during the witch hunts of the sixteenth and seventeenth centuries (Zilboorg and Henry, 1942). This was a period marked by a host of social, political, and religious upheavals, of wars, famines, and pestilence, all of which triggered a search for scapegoats whose punishment might alleviate these ills. Persons accused of witchcraft were doomed to this role; according to most theological authorities of the times they had become possessed by striking a bargain with the devil, which gave them power to cause effects ranging from plagues and floods to sexual impotence and the souring of milk (Figure 17.2).

Since such people were clearly a menace to society, no measures were too stern to deal with them. As a result, there was an unrelenting series of witch hunts that involved most of Europe and whose bonfires claimed about 500,000 lives (Harris, 1974). Some of these unfortunates were undoubtedly deranged in one way or another; many were senile, some suffered from various delusions, from hysteria, or mania, and so on. Some may have experienced hallucinations under the influence of LSD-like drugs, taken either wittingly or by accident. Such hallucinogenic substances are now known to occur in grains that have been invaded by a certain fungus; it is quite possible that the girls whose visions sparked the Salem witchcraft trials had eaten bread made of such hallucinogenic rye. But many of those accused of witchcraft seem not to have suffered from any mental disorder. Some may have participated in various local cults derived from pagan origins which orthodox Christianity condemned as a form of Satanism. Others probably fell prey to some neighbor's avarice, since a considerable proportion of a condemned person's property was awarded to his or her accuser (Kors and Peters, 1972).

INSANITY AS A DISEASE

The demonological theory of mental disorder is a thing of the past. Even in its heyday there was an alternative conception which attributed such conditions to natural causes. The difficulty was in specifying these causes. The great physicians of antiquity assumed that the key to mental derangement was an imbalance between the main body fluids or **humors,** a position that dominated medical thought until a few centuries ago. Later writers proposed different hypotheses. Some felt that the cause of mental disorder was an imbalance of nervous energy produced by overexcitement; others believed that such conditions depended upon the condition of the blood vessels of the brain (Mora, 1975).

HOSPITALS THAT WERE PRISONS

The belief that mental disorders have natural causes does not, however, automatically lead to a more humane treatment of the afflicted. It might if a ready cure were available but, until recently, there was little hope of that. As a result, the "madmen" were treated with little sympathy for they seemed to have no common bond with sane humanity, and there was little likelihood that they ever would have. They were seen as a nuisance at best and a menace at worst. In either case, the interests of society seemed best served by "putting them away."

To this end, a number of special hospitals were established throughout Europe. But until the beginning of the nineteenth century (and in some cases, much later still), most of these were hospitals in name only. Their real function was to serve as a place of confinement in which all kinds of social undesirables were segregated from the rest of humankind—criminals, idlers, old people, epileptics, incurables of all sorts, and the mentally disturbed (Rosen, 1966). After they had been in the "hospital" for a few years, it became hard to distinguish among them. Their treatment was barbaric. One author describes conditions in the major mental hospital for Parisian women at the end of the eighteenth century: "Madwomen seized by fits of violence are chained like dogs at their cell doors, and separated from keepers and visitors alike by a long corridor protected by an iron grille; through this grille is passed their food and the straw on which they sleep; by means of rakes, part of the filth that surrounds them is cleaned out" (Foucault, 1965, p. 72).

To most of their contemporaries, this treatment seemed only natural; after all, the so-called madmen were like dangerous animals and had to be caged. But since such animals are interesting to watch, some of the hospitals took on another function—they became a zoo. At London's Bethlehem hospital (whose name was slurred until it was popularly known as Bedlam), the patients were exhibited to anyone curious enough to pay the required penny per visit. In 1814, there were 96,000 such visits (Figure 17.3).

A number of reformers gradually succeeded in eliminating the worst of these practices. Historians have given much of the credit to the French physician, Phillipe Pinel (1745–1826), who was put in charge of the Parisian hospital system in 1793 when the Revolution was at its height. Pinel wanted to remove the inmates' chains and fetters, but the government gave its permission only grudgingly. A high functionary argued with Pinel, "Citizen, are you mad yourself that you want to unchain these animals?" (Zilboorg and Henry, 1941, p. 322).

Within a few decades, Pinel's efforts were followed by similar reforms elsewhere, primarily in England and the United States. This is not to say that all forms of physical restraint were abolished. Far from it. Patients considered violent were often put in straitjackets, wrapped in wet sheets, strapped to special confinement chairs, and held by various belts, straps, and locked

17.3   The mentally disturbed on exhibit
*(A) An eighteenth-century engraving by
Hogarth of a tour of Bedlam. (Courtesy
Philadelphia Museum of Art) (B) An
admission ticket to view the insane.*

gloves. The extent to which such devices were used depended upon the hospital's resources. Many of these hospitals were crowded by "pauper lunatics," who had the double misfortune of being both mentally disordered and poor. Their care was paid for by the community, whose taxpayers had even less patience for "budgetary frills" than their modern counterparts today. The result was serious overcrowding, far too few attendants, and a consequent resort to physical restraint. The policy of nonrestraint was regarded as an ideal, but this ideal was difficult to attain for any but the well-to-do (Hunter and Macalpine, 1974).

Pinel ordering the removal of the inmates'
*fetters   From a nineteenth-century
painting by Charles Muller. (Courtesy
the Bettmann Archive)*

MENTAL DISORDER AS AN ORGANIC ILLNESS

Pinel and other reformers sounded one main theme: Madness is a disease. By this assertion, they transformed the inmates from prisoners to patients for whom a cure had to be found. To find such a cure, one first had to discover the cause of the disease (or rather, diseases, since it was already known that there were several varieties of mental disorder). Today, almost two hundred years after Pinel, we are still searching for the causes of most of them.

At least initially, the notion of mental disorder as an illness implied a bodily cause, most likely some disease of the brain. Proponents of this *somatogenic* hypothesis (from *soma,* "body") could point to such relevant discoveries as the effects of cerebral strokes in impairing speech (see Chapter 2). But the somatogenic position gained its greatest impetus at the end of the nineteenth century from the discovery of the organic cause of a once widely prevalent psychosis, *general paresis.* This psychosis is characterized by a general decline in physical and psychological functions culminating in marked personality aberrations which may include childish delusions ("I am the Prince of Wales") or wild hypochondriacal depressions ("My heart has stopped beating"). Without treatment, there is increasing deterioration, progressive paralysis, and death within a few years (Dale, 1975).

By the end of the nineteenth century, the conviction had grown that general paresis has its roots in a syphilitic infection contracted many years prior to the appearance of overt symptoms. In some untreated syphilitics (according to recent estimates, perhaps 5 percent), the infection seems to be cured, but the spirochete that caused it remains, invading and damaging the nervous system. Experimental proof came in 1897. Several paretic patients were inoculated with matter taken from syphilitic sores, but none of them developed any of the earlier symptoms of syphilis.* This was a clear sign that they had contracted the disease previously. Once the cause of the disease was known, the discovery of its cure and prevention was just a matter of time. The preferred modern treatment is with penicillin. Its effectiveness is unquestioned. While paresis at one time accounted for more than 10 percent of all admissions to mental hospitals, today it accounts for less than 1 percent (Dale, 1975; Coleman, 1972).

The conquest of paresis reinforced the beliefs of somatogenicists that ultimately all mental disorders would be traced to some organic cause. They could point to some successes. Several psychoses had been explained as brain malfunctions. In the case of senile patients, the cause is atrophy of cortical cells; in the case of chronic alcoholics, the cause is a change in cerebral structures brought on by the dietary deficits that often accompany alcoholism. The question was whether this view could account for all mental disorders.

MENTAL DISORDER AS A PSYCHOLOGICAL ILLNESS

Psychogenic disorders The achievements of the somatogenic approach were very impressive, but by the end of the nineteenth century it became clear that

---

* Modern medical and scientific practitioners are considerably more sensitive than our forebears to the ethical issues raised by this and similar studies. Today such a procedure would require the patients' informed consent.

it could not include the full spectrum of mental disorders. One of the main stumbling blocks was neurosis, especially in the form of hysteria.

The story of hysteria is part of the background that led to psychoanalytic theory (see Chapter 12). For now, we will only reiterate the key discoveries. Hysteria featured a variety of symptoms that seemed to be organic but really were not; for example, paralyzed limbs that moved perfectly well during hypnosis. This suggested that hysteria is a **psychogenic** disorder; that is, a disorder whose origin is psychological rather than organic. A number of cases studied by French hypnotists of the nineteenth century seemed to have their origins in a traumatic incident. A patient trapped in a derailed railroad car developed hysterical paralysis of his legs; the legs were actually in perfect physical condition but the patient's belief that they were crushed ultimately produced his hysterical symptoms. Freud's theories were cast in a similar psychogenic mold, but they were much more elaborate, focusing on repressed sexual fantasies in early childhood that threatened to break into consciousness and could only be held back by drastic defense maneuvers, of which the somatic symptom was one.

Exactly what produced the hysteria is not our present concern. The important point is that by the turn of the century most theorists had become convinced that the disorder was psychogenic. This was another way of saying that there are illnesses that have mental *causes* as well as mental *symptoms*.

Evaluating the somatogenic-psychogenic distinction   The distinction between somatogenic and psychogenic disorders is sometimes criticized as artificial. The argument is that all behavior is ultimately based on organic processes in the nervous system. But if so, what remains of the distinction? Doesn't it then simply boil down to the difference between conditions whose organic basis has already been discovered and those for which it is as yet unknown?

The answer is no. There is no doubt that all psychological processes—whether in psychosis, neurosis, or normalcy—have a neurophysiological underpinning. But this doesn't necessarily mean that the proper scientific explanation of all psychological phenomena is necessarily at this neurophysiological level. As an example, consider two persons who can speak and see but who are unable to read. One of the two has a certain combination of brain lesions that disconnect the regions that control vision from those that handle language functions. The other person can't read because she was never taught. One can maintain that in a way both conditions are organically caused. In one case, the organic basis is the set of brain lesions; in the other, it consists of the failure to establish the various neurological changes that are brought about by learning to read. But it is perfectly obvious that while the organic account is a useful explanation in the one case, it provides no illumination in the other. This is not just because we don't yet know much of anything about the neurological basis of learning. Even if we did, to explain why someone is illiterate in terms of, say, a specification of millions of synaptic connections that were or were not formed is a much more cumbersome account than the simple statement that she can't read because she never learned.

The same analysis applies to the distinction between somatogenic and psychogenic disorders. To say that a disorder is somatogenic is to claim that the most direct explanation of the malfunction is at the organic level, as in the case of the syphilitic infection in paresis. To say that the disorder is psychogenic is to assert that the most direct explanation of what ails the patient is at the psychological level, such as a learned mode of coping with anxiety in hysteria. This is not to deny that all psychological events are ultimately based on some underlying neurological processes. Of course they are, but for many purposes this fact is of little relevance.

The Pathology Model

Psychiatrists might debate about the somatogenic or psychogenic origins of a particular mental disorder, but they were all agreed on one thing: these conditions are illnesses that are in principle analogous to illnesses such as tuberculosis and diabetes. They are called *mental* illnesses because their primary symptoms are psychological; but they are illnesses all the same. Given this assumption, it was only logical to propose that such diseases should be dealt with by the same broad set of rules that describe the treatment of disease in general. We will call this general class of rules the **pathology model.** According to this model, various overt symptoms are produced by an underlying cause—the disease or pathology. The main object of the would-be healer is to remove the underlying pathology. After this is done, the symptoms will presumably disappear. As here used, the term *pathology model* makes no particular assumptions about the kind of pathology that underlies a particular mental disorder. It might be somatogenic or psychogenic or perhaps a little of both.

Some authors endorse a particular version of the pathology model, the so-called **medical model.** This is a pathology model that makes certain further assumptions. To begin with, it assumes that the underlying pathology is organic and its practitioners therefore employ various forms of somatic therapy such as drugs. In addition, it takes for granted that the would-be healers are members of the medical profession (Siegler and Osmond, 1974). In contrast, the pathology model is much broader. It includes any conception of mental disorder that holds (1) that we can generally distinguish between symptoms and underlying causes, and (2) that these causes may be regarded as a form of pathology. Whether the causes are somatogenic or psychogenic is another question. The same holds for questions of how the disorder should be treated and by whom.*

MENTAL DISORDER AS PATHOLOGY

To get a better understanding of how mental disorder is viewed from the perspective of the pathology model, we must first ask what is meant by disease in general. A moment's reflection tells us that the concept of disease is both a scientific and an evaluative notion. To say that measles and rickets are diseases is to say something about the kinds of causes that produce such conditions—infections, dietary insufficiencies, and so on. But it also says that such conditions are undesirable. They produce pain and disability, and sometimes

---

* The medical model is often distinguished from the **psychoanalytic model** in which the practitioner seeks psychogenic causes and practices some form of psychotherapy based on psychoanalytic principles. The broader term, *pathology model*, includes both the medical and psychoanalytic models.

they lead to death. Speaking most generally, they are conditions that interfere with the organism's proper functioning as a biological system.

The extension of the disease concept to the psychological realm is based on certain parallels between the effects of psychopathology and those of non-psychiatric, organic disorders. Where ordinary organic illnesses are often associated with physical pain, many mental disorders are accompanied by psychological distress in the form of anxiety or depression. (Some may lead to death, as in the case of suicidal depression.) But the most important criterion is the interference with proper psychological functioning. The mentally disordered person may be unable to form or maintain gratifying relationships with others. Or she may be unable to work effectively. Or she may be unable to relax and play. According to advocates of the pathology model of mental disorder, the inability to function properly in these psychological areas is the behavioral analogue of the malfunctions in such biological domains as respiration, circulation, digestion, and so on that characterize ordinary organic illnesses.

Some special questions arise from the fact that the terms *psychopathology* and *abnormal psychology* are often used interchangeably. Does this mean that psychopathology necessarily involves behavior that deviates from some statistical norm? Advocates of the pathology model would answer no. They would concede that in actual practice mental disorder often involves aberrations from what people usually do in a given situation; the disordered person may hear voices, suffer from severe mood swings, or behave in ways that are clearly bizarre. It was surely for reasons of this sort that the term *abnormal* has become a near-synonym for *psychopathological.* But within the framework of the pathology model, deviation from a statistical norm is not what defines psychopathology. Consider the Black Death which wiped out half of the population in the fourteenth century. At that time, having the plague may well have been statistically normal. But this did not change the plague's status as a disease. The same applies to behavior. Certain behavior patterns may be pathological no matter how common they are.

CLASSIFYING DISORDERS

The ways in which we decide what is and what is not a mental disorder are by no means settled. But no less controversial is the issue of classifying these disorders. How do we decide whether two patients have the same disorder or two different ones?

THE PSYCHIATRIC CLASSIFICATION SYSTEM

To answer this question, practitioners have tried to set up classificatory schemes for mental disorders analogous to the diagnostic systems in other branches of medicine. Here, as elsewhere in science, the purpose of a taxonomy is to bring some order into what at first seem a host of diverse phenomena. If the taxonomy is valid, then conditions that have been grouped together will turn out to have the same cause, and better yet, the same cure.

As in other branches of medicine, the diagnostic process begins with a consideration of the overt **symptoms.** In nonpsychiatric disorders, these might be such complaints as fever or chest pains. Examples of symptoms in psycho-

Emil Kraepelin (1855–1925) *The major figure in psychiatric classification, Kraepelin distinguished between two groups of severe mental disorders, schizophrenia and manic-depressive psychosis (now called bipolar effective disorder). (Courtesy Historical Pictures Service)*

663

pathology would be anxiety or a profound sense of worthlessness. The trouble is that an individual symptom is rarely enough for diagnosis; fever occurs in a multitude of organic illnesses and anxiety is found in many different mental disorders. As a result, the diagnostician often looks for a pattern of symptoms that tend to go together, a so-called *syndrome.* An example of such a syndrome in psychopathology is a set of symptoms that includes disorganization of thinking, withdrawal from others, and hallucinations. This syndrome is characteristic of schizophrenia.

By groupings of this kind, psychiatrists have set up a taxonomy of mental disorders. The list covers an enormous range which includes mental deficiency, senile deterioration, schizophrenia, affective disorders such as mania and depression, various neuroses, psychophysiological disorders such as hypertension produced by emotional stress, antisocial personality (certain kinds of delinquents), alcoholism and drug addiction, and various forms of sexual deviation.

THE RELIABILITY OF PSYCHIATRIC CLASSIFICATION

How reliably are patients assigned to the various diagnostic filing categories provided by the American Psychiatric Association's *Diagnostic and Statistical Manual of Mental Disorders (DSM)* or by similar classification schemes? Thus far, the reliability is only fair. Diagnostic reliability can probably be improved by correcting some deficiencies in the classification system. Among other problems, some distinctions may not really exist or may be too subtle (Ward et al, 1962). Psychiatry is not the only field of medicine plagued by problems of diagnostic reliability. Among experienced radiologists, 30 percent have been found to disagree in their interpretation of chest X rays (Garland, 1960). One way to reduce observer errors of this kind is to spell out diagnostic criteria much more clearly. The American Psychiatric Association has recently revised its diagnostic manual in an attempt to do just that (*DSM*-III, 1980).

EXPLAINING DISORDER

Adherents of the pathology model believe that all—or at least many—mental disorders will ultimately prove to result from underlying causes, some organic and others psychological, that mirror the pathological processes found in other diseases. But since many of these pathologies are still unknown, how can we evaluate the assertion that they are actually there? One approach is to analyze a disease that is already well understood. This can then provide a standard against which the claims of the model's advocates can be judged. Our illustrative example will be an organic illness, diabetes.

The first step in the analysis of this, as of other medical disorders, is to look at the overt symptoms. In diabetes, these include declining strength, a marked increase in the quantity of urine passed, enormous thirst, and, in many cases, voracious appetite. The next step is to look for the underlying physiological pathology of which this syndrome is a manifestation. This pathology was discovered to be a disorder of carbohydrate metabolism which is produced by an insufficient secretion of insulin (see Chapter 3). These pathological conditions represent the immediate cause of the symptoms. But a full understanding of the disease requires a further step, an inquiry into the more remote

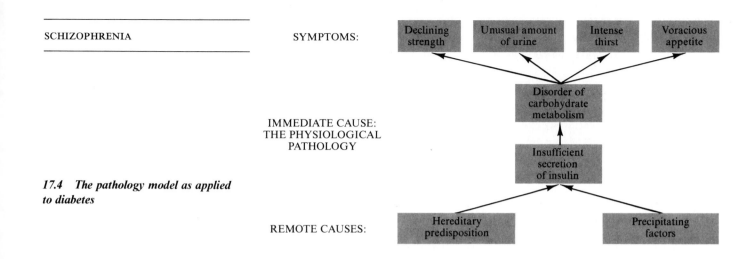

SYMPTOMS:

Declining strength | Unusual amount of urine | Intense thirst | Voracious appetite

Disorder of carbohydrate metabolism

IMMEDIATE CAUSE:
THE PHYSIOLOGICAL
PATHOLOGY

Insufficient secretion of insulin

17.4 The pathology model as applied to diabetes

REMOTE CAUSES:

Hereditary predisposition | Precipitating factors

causes that led to the present pathology. When the causal chain is traced backward, two general factors emerge. One is a set of conditions that help to precipitate the defective insulin mechanism; an example is obesity. The other is a hereditary predisposition. In diabetes, as in a number of other disorders, the genetic constitution provides a marked susceptibility to the disease, which is then triggered by the precipitating factors.

The treatment follows from the analysis. Since the diabetic's pancreas does not secrete enough insulin, this substance is supplied from the outside. Further control of the faulty metabolism is imposed by an appropriate diet.

A schematic outline of this analysis of a nonpsychiatric ailment is presented in Figure 17.4. The figure gives us an idea what an analysis of a disease looks like when the disease is reasonably well understood. This is the framework we will use when we ask whether a particular mental disorder is an illness, and if so, in what sense. How such disorders are treated will be taken up in the next chapter.

Schizophrenia

One of the most serious conditions in the whole field of psychopathology is **schizophrenia** (from the Greek *schizo,* "split" and *phrene,* "mind").* The term was coined in 1911 by the Swiss psychiatrist, Eugen Bleuler (1857–1939) to designate what he regarded as the main attribute of this disorder—a fragmentation of mental functions (Bleuler, 1911).

Schizophrenia is quite prevalent. According to one estimate, about one in a hundred Americans will need treatment for this disorder at some period during his or her lifetime, typically between the ages of fifteen and forty. At any one time, about four hundred thousand persons are hospitalized with this

Eugen Bleuler *(Courtesy National Library of Medicine)*

* This etymological derivation is responsible for a widespread confusion between schizophrenia, which is a psychosis, and **multiple (or split) personality,** which may be regarded as a rare kind of neurosis. While both fall under the general rubric of psychopathology, the two conditions have little in common.

condition, about half of all of the beds in the country's mental hospitals. The total cost to society, including the indirect costs of time lost from employment and so on, has been estimated at around $14 billion a year (Babigian, 1975). The total cost in human anguish to patients and their families is incalculable.

Many investigators believe that schizophrenia is a disease, in the straightforward, somatogenic, sense of the term. To evaluate this position, we will discuss the disorder within the same framework we used when we considered the interpretation of the organic disease, diabetes—the symptom pattern, the underlying pathology, the less immediate causes such as genetic predisposition, and the precipitating factors.

THE SYMPTOMS

The fragmentation of mental life characteristic of schizophrenia can be seen in disorders of cognition, of motivation and emotion, and of social relationships. Few patients who are diagnosed as schizophrenics show all of these signs. How many symptoms must be present, and in what degree, to justify this diagnosis depends upon the clinician's judgment. Under the circumstances, it is not surprising that diagnostic agreement is far from perfect.

DISORDERS OF COGNITION

Disturbance of thought A key symptom is a pervasive thought disturbance. The schizophrenic doesn't "think straight"; he can't maintain one unified guiding thought, but rather skips from one idea to the next. An example is a fragment of a letter written by one of Bleuler's patients:

> I am writing on paper. The pen I am using is from a factory called "Perry & Co." This factory is in England. I assume this. Behind the name of Perry Co., the city of London is inscribed; but not the city. The city of London is in England. I know this from my school-days. Then, I always liked geography. My last teacher in that subject was Professor August A. He was a man with black eyes. I also like black eyes. There are also blue and gray eyes and other sorts too. I have heard it said that snakes have green eyes. All people have eyes. There are some, too, who are blind. These blind people are led about by a boy (Bleuler, 1950, p. 17).

This kind of simple idea-hopping sometimes leads to an endless cataloguing of associated items:

> I wish you, therefore, a very happy, pleasant, healthy, blessed and fruit-crop-rich year; and also many good wine-harvest years thereafter, as well as good potato-crop years; as well as fine potato years, and sauerkraut years, and sprouts years, and cucumber years, and nut years; a good egg-year, and also a good cheese year (Bleuler, 1950, p. 28).

Disturbance of attention Such examples show that the schizophrenic may have difficulty in suppressing irrelevant ideas that come from within. Similar problems arise with irrelevant stimuli that assail her from without. We have seen that in ordinary perception one focuses on some aspects of the world while de-emphasizing others. We somehow filter out the irrelevant stimuli so that we can follow a conversation without being continually distracted by other people's voices or radiator clankings or whatever (see Chapter 7). But schizophrenics seem to be less efficient in attending selectively. They hear (and see and feel) too much, perhaps because they can't exclude what is extraneous. Some patients (only mildly disordered or recovered) describe what this feels like:

> During the last while back I have noticed that noises all seem louder to me than they were before. It's as if someone turned up the volume. . . . I notice it most with background noises. . . . Now they seem to be just as loud and sometimes louder than the main noises that are going on. . . . it makes it difficult to keep your mind on something when there's so much going on that you can't help listening to (McGhie and Chapman, 1961, p. 105).

> By the time I was admitted to the hospital I had reached a stage of "wakefulness" when the brilliance of light on a window sill or the colour of blue in the sky would be so important it could make me cry. I had very little ability to sort the relevant from the irrelevant. The filter had broken down. Completely unrelated events became intricately connected in my mind (MacDonald, 1960, p. 176).

Given these subjective reports, it is hardly surprising that experimental tests of selective attention (see Chapter 7) show greater deficits in schizophrenics than in normal persons. This is especially pronounced during the early, acute stage of the disorder. When asked to listen to one message while simultaneously exposed to another, acute schizophrenics are more distracted by the competing voice than are normals (Rappaport, 1967).

LOSING CONTACT

Social withdrawal A common facet of schizophrenia is a withdrawal from contact with other people. In some patients this withdrawal begins quite early; they have had few friends and little or no contact with the opposite sex. What brings on this withdrawal is still unknown. One possibility is that it is a defense against the overstimulation to which they are exposed because of their inability to filter out the irrelevant. Another possibility is that it grows out of pathological family relations during childhood and adolescence.

Autism Whatever the reason that led up to it, the schizophrenic's withdrawal from social contacts has drastic consequences. He starts to live in a private world of his own. This condition becomes increasingly worse. The withdrawal from others provides fewer and fewer opportunities for *social-reality testing* in which one's own ideas are checked against those of others and corrected when necessary. As a result, the schizophrenic's ideas become ever more idiosyncratic, until the patient may have trouble communicating with others even if he wants to; they may very well rebuff him because they can't understand him and and think he's "weird." The result is further withdrawal, which leads to further idiosyncracy, still further withdrawal, and so on. The final consequence of this vicious cycle is a condition which Bleuler called *autism,* in which the patient can no longer distinguish between his own thoughts and fantasies and external reality. He has lost contact.

Disturbance in communication   Once this state is reached, it becomes extremely difficult to understand what a patient is trying to say. To begin with, there is the basic thought disturbance in which irrelevant ideas crowd each other out in fast succession. But, in addition, there is a whole set of private fantasies, personal symbolisms, and special words invented by the patient himself *(neologisms).* As an example, consider a patient's answer to the question "Who is the doctor in charge of your ward?"

> A body just like yours, sir. They can make you black or white. I say good morning, but he just comes through there. At first it was a colony. They said it was heaven. These buildings were not solid at the time, and I am positive this is the same place. They have others just like it. People die, and all the microbes talk over there, and *prestigitis* you know is sending you from here to another world. . . . I was sent by the government to the United States to Washington to some star, and they had a pretty nice country there. Now you have a body like a young man who says he is of the prestigitis (White, 1932, p. 228).

ELABORATING THE PRIVATE WORLD

The private world of some schizophrenics is organized in elaborate detail. They have strange beliefs, and may see and hear things that aren't there. In Bleuler's view, such symptoms are secondary effects that follow from the basic thought disturbance and the withdrawal from reality.

Delusions   Once having initiated the break with the social world, many schizophrenics develop *ideas of reference.* They begin to believe that external events are specially related to them, personally. The patient observes some strangers talking and concludes that they are talking about *her;* she sees people walk by and decides that they are following *her;* she hears a radio commercial and is sure that it contains a specially disguised message aimed at *her.* Eventually, these ideas become systematized in the form of false beliefs or *delusions.* Such delusions are especially common in the subcategory called *paranoid schizophrenia.*

An example of paranoid schizophrenia is a delusion of persecution. The patient is sure that *they*—the Communists or the FBI or the Jews or the members of the American Medical Association or whoever—are spying on him and plotting against him. This delusion gradually expands as the patient gathers further evidence which convinces him that his wife and children, the ward psychiatrist, and the man in the bed near the door, are all part of the conspiracy (Figure 17.5).

Hallucinations   Delusions result from misinterpretations of real events. In contrast, *hallucinations* are perceived experiences that occur in the absence of actual sensory stimulation. This phenomenon is fairly common in schizo-

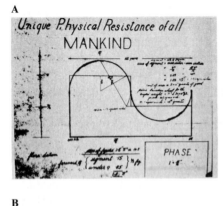

A

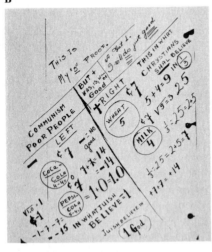

B

17.5   Schizophrenic thought systems   *(A) This figure, drawn by a schizophrenic engineer after ten years of hospitalization, shows the patient's retention of his engineering skills but also shows the intrusion of many unrelated ideas that the patient tries to fit together into one comprehensive scheme. (B) Another patient's production. Here the schizophrenic tendency toward overinclusiveness is even clearer. All kinds of diverse ideas—religious, political, economic, arithmetical, and so on—are subsumed under one quite odd and highly abstract scheme that makes little sense to anyone except the patient. (From Lehmann, 1975)*

phrenia. The patient "hears" voices, or, less commonly, "sees" various persons or objects. The voices may be of God, the devil, relatives, or neighbors. If the patient can make out what they say, she hears that they are talking about her, sometimes threateningly and sometimes obscenely.

The best guess is that such hallucinations reflect an inability to distinguish between one's own memory images and perceptual experiences that originate from without. Some evidence for this view comes from a study in which hallucinating patients were asked to press a key whenever they heard one of their voices. At the same time, the investigator recorded muscular activity in the patient's larynx. The results showed that the patients generally experienced auditory hallucinations when their larynx became especially active. It appears that the patients were talking to themselves and then interpreted their own inner speech as originating from outside. They "heard themselves talk" and thought they heard voices (McGuigan, 1966). Just what these voices said presumably reflected the patient's own fears and wishes.

To explain these events, the patient weaves them into the delusional system if he has one. Once again, he refers to the ever-present *they*. He concludes that *they* make the voices, that *they* induce certain unacceptable sensations like the tingling between his legs, and that *they* compel him to think certain thoughts and to commit certain acts. To explain how *they* manage all this, the patient refers to special powers through which *they* can transmit their thoughts into other people's minds. This idea illustrates Freud's concept of **projection,** a mechanism by which one's own unacceptable impulses are denied and assigned to external agents. An example is one paranoid schizophrenic, hospitalized for many years, who describes his "pursuers":

> They are able to carry on a conversation with a person over a mile away and out of sight, by ascertaining the person's unspoken thoughts, and then by means of their so-called "radio voices" answer these thoughts aloud audibly to the person. . . . It feels good to certain mind-reading pursuers to have patients masturbate. This is how certain pursuers go about it. . . . [They] make love to them, offering to sleep with them, have illicit intercourse with them . . . or pretend they are being raped or other such sex story. Then, if all this fails to bring results, certain pursuers, from the distance without corporeal contact, tickle the patients between their legs and in their erogenous zones or coax them to masturbate. This sort of thing has been going on for over twenty years (White, 1956, pp. 83–84).

DISORDERS OF MOTIVATION AND EMOTION

Thus far our focus has been on the schizophrenic's thoughts. When we look at his motives and feelings, we find similar evidence of disruption and fragmentation. In the early phase of the disorder, there is often a marked emotional oversensitivity. The slightest rejection may trigger an extreme response, as in the case of the patient who committed suicide because his psychiatrist told him he couldn't see him right away but would do so three hours later (Lehman, 1975). As time goes on, this sensitivity declines. In many patients it dips below normal until there is virtual indifference to their own fate or that of others. This apathy is especially pronounced in long-term schizophrenics, who stare vacantly, their faces expressionless, and answer questions in a flat and toneless voice. While most writers believe that this emotional blunting is an important facet of the schizophrenic disorder itself, the sheer length of insti-

669

tutionalization (which for some patients is reckoned in decades) probably contributes to it as well.

In some cases, emotional reaction is preserved but the emotion has become strikingly inappropriate to the situation. A patient may break into happy laughter at the news of a brother's death "because she was so pleased at receiving letters with black borders"; another becomes enraged when someone says hello (Bleuler, 1950, p. 52). This mismatch between emotional expression and the external situation may be caused by a number of factors. One possibility is some malfunction in the neurological structures that control various aspects of the emotions. Another possibility is that the patient has somehow misinterpreted the stimulus, incorporating it into her own private world in some special manner. (For all we know, *hello* might be viewed as a threat.) Yet another possibility is that the psychiatric observer has misinterpreted the patient's response. The schizophrenic who smiles broadly when he talks about his child's death may perhaps feel the appropriate emotion inside but can no longer express this emotion overtly in a socially comprehensible way, or does not choose to do so.

DISORDERS OF BEHAVIOR

Given the disruptions in the schizophrenics' thoughts, motives, and feelings, it is hardly surprising that there are often concomitant disorders in how they act. Some patients develop bizarre mannerisms. They may grimace, or make odd, repetitive gestures; they may imitate the movements they are observing. Other patients remain virtually motionless for long periods of time. They may be standing or sitting or they may adopt some unusual posture which they often maintain for hours on end (Figure 17.6). While in this state, the patient seems to be completely oblivious to everything around him. In actual fact, this is not the case. When questioned later, the patient shows excellent recall of conversations that were carried on in front of him while he was immobile.

According to some theorists, the patient's immobility is another secondary reaction to the basic disturbance of thought and attention. The schizophrenic is overstimulated as it is, but this stimulation becomes even greater when she is in motion. So she stops moving, in sheer self-defense. As one patient put it, "I did not want to move, because if I did everything changed around me and upset me horribly so I remained still to hold on to a sense of permanence" (quoted in Broen, 1968, p. 138).

17.6 Patient with a diagnosis of catatonic schizophrenia who spent virtually all waking hours in this crouched position *(Photograph by Bill Bridges, Globe Photos)*

SUBCATEGORIES OF SCHIZOPHRENIA

Psychiatrists have found it convenient to distinguish among several subtypes of schizophrenia which are defined by the kind of symptoms that are predominant. We will consider the four originally described by Bleuler.

THE CLASSICAL SUBTYPES

Hebephrenia In **hebephrenia,** the predominant symptoms are incoherence of thought and marked inappropriateness of affect. In many ways, the hebephrenic conforms to the popular stereotype of insanity. His speech is often

17.7 Hebephrenia *In hebephrenic schizophrenia (in the language of DSM-III, the disorganized type of schizophrenia) there is frequent incoherence; the expression of emotions appears blunted, inappropriate, or silly; and there are no systematized delusions. The condition is often accompanied by grimaces and odd mannerisms. (From Lehman, 1975)*

bizarre or incoherent and his behavior is strange and silly; there are meaningless smiles, odd posturings and grimaces, childish giggles, and sudden fits of laughing and crying (Figure 17.7). The patient often deteriorates profoundly and loses all concern over his personal appearance and ignores the most elementary rules of social conduct; for example, he may urinate and defecate in public.

Catatonia   In catatonia, the most conspicuous symptom involves peculiar motor activity or inactivity, such as **catatonic stupor,** in which the patient is immobile and can maintain strange positions for lengthy periods. On other occasions, there may be frenzied **catatonic excitement,** sometimes accompanied by extreme violence with serious danger of harm both to the patient and to others.

Paranoid schizophrenia   This is the most common form of schizophrenia. Its dominant symptom is a set of delusions, often organized into an elaborate system. Paranoid schizophrenics tend to deteriorate less than catatonics and hebephrenics. They are tense and suspicious but their social behavior is often passable. In matters that don't touch on their delusions, their intelligence may be relatively unimpaired. The great nineteenth-century American chess master, Paul Morphy, was hospitalized with this condition, but if someone managed to get him to the chessboard, he still played a champion's game.

Simple type   In contrast to the other subcategories, the **simple type** of schizophrenia is remarkably colorless. There are few of the dramatic symptoms of schizophrenia such as delusions, hallucinations, or bizarre actions. Instead, there is a gradual loss of interest in other people and a quiet, isolated existence. With time, there is increasing shallowness of emotion as the person drifts through life, aimless and alone. Many—perhaps most—simple schizophrenics are never recognized as such but live on the fringe of society, as vagrants, hoboes, prostitutes, or in other marginal ways.

PROCESS VERSUS REACTIVE SCHIZOPHRENIA

Some of the classical subtypes are still used in modern diagnosis, but there has been a growing suspicion about their usefulness. In many cases, the symptoms overlap; in others, they change from one pattern to the other as time goes on.

Recent investigators have cast about for some better ways of distinguishing among schizophrenics than those provided by the classical subtypes. One possibility centers on the hypothesis that schizophrenic symptoms may arise in either of two ways—as a *reaction* to some major personal blow such as bereavement or as a gradually developing *process* that is not so patently instigated from without (Garmezy, 1967). A schizophrenic patient is classified as **reactive** if his symptoms developed suddenly, if his prior social and personal adjustment seemed reasonably normal, and if there was some obvious precipitating stress. His disorder is said to be **process schizophrenia** if he has a long prior history of social withdrawal and poor personal adjustment, if his symptoms came on gradually, and if there was no obvious precipitating factor at the time of his hospitalization. There is evidence that the prognosis is much better for reactive than for process schizophrenics. In one study, about 150 patients

671

were classified according to these two categories while in the hospital and were then reevaluated between five and thirteen years later. In the cases where schizophrenia was reactive, only 3 percent were unimproved, in contrast to 49 percent of the cases with process schizophrenia (Stephens and Astrup, 1963).

THE SEARCH FOR THE UNDERLYING PATHOLOGY

We have described the various symptoms that define schizophrenia. As in diabetes or in any other organic disease, the next step is to look for the underlying malfunction from which these symptoms spring. But since schizophrenia is not an ordinary (so to speak, orthodox) disease, in as much as its main symptoms are behavioral, any attempt to discover its pathology has to involve two steps. To begin with, one has to specify the underlying *psychological malfunction* of which the symptoms are a manifestation. This done, then—if there is reason to suspect that the disorder is somatogenic—one searches for the organic pathology of which this psychological malfunction is an expression.

WHAT IS THE PSYCHOLOGICAL DEFICIT?

A widely held view is that the schizophrenic's primary trouble is cognitive. The details of the proposed explanations vary, but most of them agree that the patient's major deficit is an inability to keep things in proper focus. Normal people focus in both space and time. They perceive objects without being distracted by extraneous stimuli; they execute plans without interference by irrelevant responses. Not so the schizophrenic who has considerable difficulty in holding onto one line of thought or action and is forever lured off the main path.

An example is provided by experiments on reaction time in which the subject has to respond to a stimulus as quickly as he can. If the procedure includes a warning signal (say, a light) that always precedes the stimulus (say, a tone) by a constant interval, a normal subject's reaction time will be decreased. This is because the warning signal alerts the subject and this alertness rises to a peak just when the stimulus appears. The advantage conferred by the warning signal is considerably greater if the interval between that signal (the light which warns the subject) and the stimulus (the tone to which he must respond) stays the same from trial to trial rather than being changed irregularly. If it remains constant, the subject can develop a mental set that he can apply across trials. This is true for normals but not for schizophrenic patients. To the patients it doesn't seem to matter whether the warning interval remains the same or is changed irregularly (Shakow, 1963). To benefit from the regular warning, one must be able to hold on to a mental set for a period of time during which all extraneous thoughts and reactions are inhibited. But this seems to be precisely what the schizophrenic cannot do (Figure 17.8).

Given this deficit, the patient's many disturbances of language and thought follow. His speech is marked by one tangent after another; sometimes the sheer sound of a word is enough to trigger a series of rhyming associations, as in "How are you today by the bay as a gay, doctor?" (Davison and Neale, 1974, p. 330). His inability to disregard irrelevant attributes leads to strange conceptualizations in which incongruous items are grouped together. One patient explained that Jesus, cigar boxes, and sex are all identical. This was

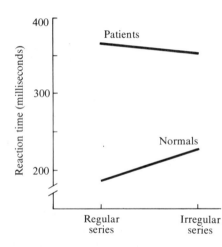

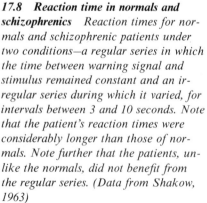

17.8 Reaction time in normals and schizophrenics *Reaction times for normals and schizophrenic patients under two conditions—a regular series in which the time between warning signal and stimulus remained constant and an irregular series during which it varied, for intervals between 3 and 10 seconds. Note that the patient's reaction times were considerably longer than those of normals. Note further that the patients, unlike the normals, did not benefit from the regular series. (Data from Shakow, 1963)*

because all three are encircled—the head of Jesus by a halo, a cigar box by the tax band, and a woman by a man's sexually interested glance (Von Domarus, 1944).

It is tempting to believe that the other main symptoms of schizophrenia—social withdrawal and emotional inappropriateness—are consequences of the primary cognitive disturbance, though whether this is actually so is still unknown. We have previously sketched some possible routes through which the one could lead to the others. Social withdrawal, at least initially, may be a defense against overstimulation. The relative absence or inappropriateness of emotional feeling may reflect yet another aspect of the fragmentation of the schizophrenic's mental life. The precedent for regarding certain other symptoms, such as delusions and hallucinations, as secondary consequences of the basic thought disturbance was set by Bleuler himself. He saw these symptoms as elaborations of the autistic world of a person who has lost contact with other people and can no longer distinguish between his private fantasies and external reality.

WHAT IS THE ORGANIC PATHOLOGY?

Many investigators are convinced that the psychological deficit that underlies schizophrenia is an expression of an organic pathology. This belief persists despite the fact that we still don't know just what this organic pathology is. Under the circumstances, what accounts for this belief?

Arguments for an organic basis One argument is the pattern of results obtained by cross-cultural studies. It turns out that there is a remarkable similarity in what different peoples consider insane. One investigator studied Eskimo villagers on an Arctic island and a group of Yorubas, a tribe in West Africa. Both groups had a word for "being crazy." Among the Yorubas, a person is called *were* if he hears voices where there are none, laughs when there is nothing to laugh at, talks all the time or not at all, picks up sticks and leaves for no reason except to put them in a pile, tears off his clothes, defecates in public, or suddenly attacks others with a weapon. This pattern of bizarre symptoms would probably lead to a diagnosis of schizophrenia in a Western society.

Similar patterns of behavior characterize people that the Eskimos consider "crazy" (their word happens to be *nuthkavihak*). Interestingly enough, the prevalence of such conditions is roughly comparable to that found in Western societies. Among samples collected in Canadian and Swedish villages, the rate of schizophrenia was 5.6 per 1,000. Among the Yorubas, 6.8 per 1,000 were described as *were* by local village headmen; among the Eskimos, 4.4 per 1,000 were regarded as *nuthkavihak* by neighbors or friends (Murphy, 1976).

On the face of it, these results suggest that schizophrenia has a biological basis, at least in part. A psychogenic theory would emphasize factors in the social environment, most likely some aspect of the way the patient was treated as a child. Since different cultures differ widely in their child-rearing practices, we would expect rather different rates of incidence. The fact that a disorder that resembles schizophrenia is found in many different cultures, and occurs with about the same rate of incidence in all of them, suggests that some of the causal factors lie elsewhere.

Another line of evidence that is sometimes used to buttress a somatogenic interpretation of schizophrenia is the therapeutic effect of a group of drugs called *phenothiazines.* The effect of these drugs seems to be fairly specific to schizophrenia. They lead to a marked alleviation of primary schizophrenic symptoms, that is, thought disorder, social withdrawal, and autistic behaviors. On the other hand, they have little or no effect on nonschizophrenic symptoms such as anxiety, depression, and guilt (Klein and Davis, 1969). Some authors regard these results as an argument for an organic basis of the disorder, reasoning by analogy to the effects of drugs on many ordinary diseases, as in the case of insulin and diabetes. Whether this line of reasoning is valid is debatable; the fact that an organic treatment alleviates—or even cures—a disorder does not really prove that the disorder has an organic cause.

Perhaps the strongest argument of all comes from genetic studies. Their results have convinced most investigators that schizophrenia has an important hereditary component. But how would such a genetic factor exert its influence? The most reasonable hypothesis is that it does so by some modification of normal neurological functioning. We will present the details of the genetic evidence in a later section; for now, we only note that such a genetic factor exists and that it—together with the cross-cultural evidence and the effects of antischizophrenic drugs—is an argument for a somatogenic theory of schizophrenia.

Schizophrenia and hallucinogenic drugs   Considerations of this sort prompted a flood of studies trying to discover the organic pathology in schizophrenia. Many investigators were convinced that the key was a biochemical defect, a conviction which led to endless analyses of schizophrenic blood, cerebrospinal fluid, and urine to see whether there were any ways in which they differed from those of normals. In fact, numerous differences were obtained. The trouble is that on subsequent examination many of them proved to be artifacts (that is, by-products of other conditions not directly related to the disorder). Some results could be attributed to the fact that the patients had been on a long regimen of drug therapy or had lived on an institutional diet. An example is a study in which a difference in the urine composition of normals and schizophrenics was traced to the fact that the patients drank more coffee than the controls (Kety, 1965).

One interesting attempt was to link schizophrenia with the effect of *hallucinogenic drugs,* so-called because they produce hallucinations. Examples are mescaline and lysergic acid diethylamide, better known as LSD. On the face of it, there is some similarity between the effects such drugs produce on normal subjects and aspects of a psychosis. There are perceptual alterations, hallucinations, and sometimes distortions of thought and feeling. While these drug effects may mimic schizophrenia in some respects, they differ from it in some important ways. The primary effect of LSD is that it makes people see things; the primary effect of schizophrenia is that it disturbs thinking and feeling. There are also differences in the hallucinations produced by the two conditions; under LSD these are mostly visual, while in schizophrenia they tend to be auditory and involve voices (Snyder, 1974). These points suggest that the discovery of the ultimate basis of LSD effects, while undoubtedly interesting in its own right, may not tell us too much about the underlying organic pathology of schizophrenia.

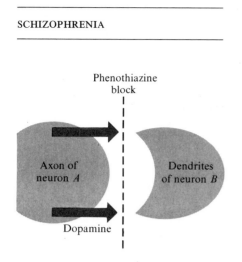

Phenothiazine block

Axon of neuron *A*

Dendrites of neuron *B*

Dopamine

17.9   The dopamine block hypothesis of phenothiazine action

Malfunctioning neurotransmitters   Most recent investigators believe that the underlying organic pathology is some malfunction of neurotransmitters, the substances whose secretion by one neuron may either trigger or inhibit an impulse in another neuron on the other side of the synapse. A likely candidate is ***dopamine.*** This is one of the ***catecholamines,*** transmitters liberated by neurons which have an arousing function in various parts of the brain (see Chapter 3). According to the dopamine hypothesis, many neurons in the schizophrenic's brain have become oversensitive to dopamine. One line of evidence comes from the effect of the group of drugs called ***phenothiazines.*** As mentioned before, phenothiazines are known to block dopamine at the synapse (Figure 17.9). This dopamine blockade is more pronounced in some phenothiazine drugs than in others. As predicted by the dopamine hypothesis, the stronger the blockade, the more therapeutic the drug (Snyder, 1976).

If a decrease of dopamine activity makes schizophrenics better, an increase should presumably make them worse. This is indeed the case. One group of investigators injected small doses of a drug that increases dopamine activity into the veins of schizophrenics who were in a comparatively mild state. Within a minute, the patients' symptoms became wild and extreme. One started to shred a pad of paper, announcing that he had been sending and receiving messages from ancient Egypt. Others became catatonic (Davis, 1974). Related effects are seen in normals who take overdoses of amphetamines. These are stimulants which enhance dopamine activity. If taken often enough and in large enough doses, they produce a temporary ***amphetamine psychosis*** that is in many ways quite similar to paranoid schizophrenia (Angrist et al., 1974). As the dopamine hypothesis would predict, phenothiazines that block dopamine activity at the synapse will also reduce the psychotic symptoms that follow amphetamine overuse.

Why should an oversensitivity to dopamine produce the psychotic reactions characteristic of schizophrenia? One possibility is that a hyperreactive dopamine system is equivalent to chronic overstimulation. When dopamine-releasing neurons in the limbic system of the brain are destroyed, the animals ignore sensory stimuli (Ungerstedt and Ljungberg, 1974). Perhaps the opposite is true when dopamine tracts are overreactive. This may cause an inability to ignore anything, whether sensory messages from the outside or irrelevant thoughts from the inside, leading to that jangling, screaming cognitive overload which some schizophrenics describe in retrospective accounts of their condition (Carlson, 1977).

Despite some intriguing evidence in its favor, as yet the dopamine hypothesis is still what its name implies—a hypothesis. Not all investigators subscribe to it; for example, some authors believe that the transmitter malfunctioning lies elsewhere, specifically in an insufficiency of ***norephinephrine*** (Stein and Wise, 1971). But whatever the final verdict on issues of detail, it is very likely that our eventual understanding of schizophrenia will include some reference to a biochemical defect.

MORE REMOTE CAUSES OF SCHIZOPHRENIA

We have considered several analyses of the basic pathology in schizophrenia, including hypotheses about the underlying psychological deficit and some guesses about organic malfunctions. These hypotheses about pathological processes—at either the psychological or the physiological level—are about the *immediate causes* of the disorder. The next question concerns causes that are less immediate and further back in time. As we have seen in our discussion of diabetes, any attempt to understand a disease involves both an analysis of its immediate causes (a metabolic malfunction brought on by insulin insufficiency) and a search for causes that are more remote (genetic factors, environmental effects). We will follow the same approach in our discussion of schizophrenia, beginning with the effect of heredity (a remote cause).

HEREDITARY PREDISPOSITION

Evidence for a genetic factor   Does schizophrenia have a hereditary basis? This question has been studied by the same means used to assess the role of heredity in other human traits such as intelligence. The basic approach is to consider family resemblance. In schizophrenia, as in intelligence, this resemblance is considerable. For example, the likelihood that a person who has a schizophrenic sibling is schizophrenic himself or will eventually become so is about 8 percent; this compares to a 1 percent risk of schizophrenia in the general population (Rosenthal, 1970). But again, as in the area of intelligence, such family resemblances don't settle anything about the nature-nurture issue, for they can be interpreted either way. For more conclusive evidence we have to turn to the familiar methodological standbys that are used to disentangle the contributions of heredity and environment—studies of twins and of adopted children. A widely used method focuses on twins, one of whom is schizophrenic. The question is whether the schizophrenic's twin is schizophrenic as well. The probability of this event, technically called ***concordance,*** is 44 percent if the twins are identical, compared to only 9 percent if they are fraternal and of the same sex (averaged over eleven studies; Rosenthal, 1970). Further evidence comes from adoption studies. Children born to schizophrenic mothers and placed in foster homes within a week or so after birth, are much more likely to become schizophrenic than persons in a matched control group of adoptees born to normal mothers (Heston, 1966).

The specificity of the genetic factor   There is evidently an inherited predisposition to schizophrenia. But how specific is this predisposition? Is it specific for schizophrenia only? Or is it a more general susceptibility that renders its possessor liable to other mental disorders as well?

The evidence suggests that there is some specificity. For example, schizophrenia and bipolar affective disorder (see p. 683) are genetically distinct (Rosenthal, 1970). Furthermore, there is some genetic specificity in the classical schizophrenic subtypes. Relatives of hebephrenics who become schizophrenics are more likely to be hebephrenics than catatonics or paranoids, a result which suggests that the subtypes may have more genuine clinical reality than is sometimes thought (Slater and Cowie, 1971). But the genetic effect seems to have a more general side. Adoptees born of schizophrenic mothers are almost three times more likely than those born to normal mothers to exhibit serious social or psychological problems in later life, quite apart from schizophrenia. Some have police records for assault or other impulsive, antisocial acts; others are alcoholics; still others are emotionally unstable (Heston and Denney, 1968).

One interpretation of these results is that the underlying predisposition toward schizophrenia is determined by many genes. The greater the number of pathological genes carried by an individual, the greater his chance of becoming schizophrenic. If this number is smaller, it tends to predispose the person to various lesser psychological malfunctions. These probably have to be within a schizophrenia-related spectrum which includes some of the characteristics found in schizophrenia proper, such as looseness of thought, withdrawal, and so on. The schizophrenic genes would presumably have no effect on the likelihood of developing disorders outside of this spectrum, such as bipolar affective disorder or hysteria.

ENVIRONMENTAL STRESS

The preceding discussion indicates that schizophrenia has a genetic basis. But there is no doubt that environmental factors also play a role. The proof is simple: The concordance for schizophrenia among identical twins, while considerable, is appreciably less than 100 percent. Since identical twins have the same genotype, there must be some nongenetic factors that also have a say in the determination of who becomes schizophrenic and who does not.

What are these nongenetic factors? As yet, there is no concensus. We will consider a few lines of evidence that relate to various potentially stress-producing conditions. Some involve the person's social class; others concern his family. According to many modern investigators, these or other stress-producing environmental factors may bring out the latent pathology in a person with a genetic predisposition toward schizophrenia and will eventually precipitate the actual disorder, much as obesity precipitates diabetes (Meehl, 1962).

Social class In searching for environmental causes, sociologically minded investigators have focused upon social class. They have found a sizable relationship. The proportion of schizophrenics is much higher at the bottom of the socioeconomic hierarchy than it is at the top. According to one study the ratio is 9 to 1 (Hollingshead and Redlich, 1958). The prevalence of schizophrenia is highest in the poorest and most delapidated areas of the city and diminishes progressively as one moves outward toward the higher status regions (Figure 17.10). This general relation between social class and schizophrenia has been found in city after city, from New York, Omaha, New Haven, and Milwaukee in the United States to Oslo, Helsinki, London, and Taiwan abroad (Kohn, 1968).

Some critics argue that this finding is an artifact. Incidence rates of schizophrenia are usually based on admissions to mental hospitals, and lower-class psychotics may be more likely to be hospitalized in such institutions than are psychotics from higher strata. To get around this problem, some investigators studied a representative sample of all persons in a community—whether inside

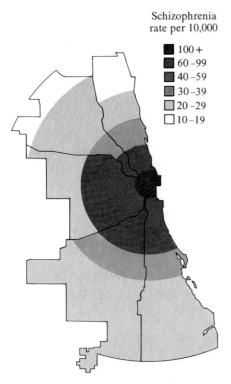

Schizophrenia
rate per 10,000

■ 100+
■ 60–99
■ 40–59
▨ 30–39
▧ 20–29
☐ 10–19

17.10 The prevalence of schizophrenia in different regions of a city *A map of Chicago (1922–34) represented by a series of concentric zones. The center zone is the business and amusement area, which is without residents except for some transients and vagabonds. Surrounding this center is a slum region inhabited largely by unskilled laborers. Further out are more stable regions: a zone largely populated by skilled workers, followed by zones of middle- and upper-middle-class apartment dwellers and, furthest out, the upper-middle-class commuters. The map shows clearly that the incidence of schizophrenia increases the closer one gets to the city's center. (After Faris and Dunham, 1939)*

a hospital or not—and had psychiatrically trained interviewers rate their mental health. The same general result was found; the poor are more likely to become schizophrenic than the rich.

One interpretation of this result is that poverty, inferior status, and low occupational rank lead to increased environmental stresses which sooner or later convert a genetic susceptibility toward schizophrenia into the actual disorder. According to this view, given the predisposition, one becomes a schizophrenic because one is at the lowest rung of the social ladder. But there is a theoretical alternative, for the causal direction may be reversed. Perhaps one falls to the bottom of the ladder because one is a schizophrenic. The evidence to date suggests that both factors play a role. If so, schizophrenia is an effect of lower socioeconomic status as well as a cause, although the issue is by no means settled (Kohn, 1968).

Pathology in the family A different emphasis pervades the work of more psychoanalytically oriented investigators. True to their general outlook, they have concentrated upon the schizophrenic's family. They paint a gloomy picture. As they describe them, schizophrenics' mothers are rejecting, cold, dominating, and prudish, while their fathers are detached, humorless, weak, and passive (Arieti, 1959). Later studies concentrated on the relationships within the family. In general, they found a high degree of instability. Many schizophrenics come from homes in which a parent was lost early in the patient's life through death or divorce. In homes with both parents, there is often serious discord. In many such families the children become directly involved in the marital schism, with each parent trying to undercut the other in continual attempts to enlist the child as an ally (Lidz et al., 1957).

Later critics argued that this family portrait of the schizophrenics is inaccurate. The descriptions of the parents were often sketched by the same psychiatrists who treated the children and who were probably guilty of partisanship as they saw the parents through the patients' eyes (Hill, 1955). In addition, many of the older studies lacked appropriate control groups, without which there is no way of telling whether the proportion of, say, detached, weak, and passive fathers is any greater for schizophrenic patients than for some other group matched by age, socioeconomic level, and the like. When such procedural flaws are eliminated, the schizophrenic's family doesn't appear to be quite as pathological as it did at first. But enough signs of pathology remain even so. Objective studies in which the families of schizophrenic patients are observed in discussions of various topics (such as "When should teenagers begin dating?") have shown more within-family conflicts than normal controls (Fontana, 1966).

Communication in the family Several authors feel that one source of the patient's difficulties is a confused pattern of communication within the family. Compared to normals, the members of the patient's family are less likely to give each other clear and unambiguous signals, a possible prelude to the patient's own communicative difficulties (Wynne and Singer, 1963*a* and *b*). Of particular interest is the continual employment of self-contradictory communications. A parent may tell a child one thing while simultaneously conveying the message that what is really meant is the very opposite. The child is in a **double bind;** she is damned if she does and damned if she doesn't. According to some writers, schizophrenia is the residue of a long exposure to such double-bind situations. An example is provided by a young schizophrenic who was visited by his mother:

> He was glad to see her and impulsively put his arms around her shoulders whereupon she stiffened. He withdrew his arm and she asked, "Don't you love me any more?" He then blushed and she said, "Dear, you must not be so easily embarrassed and afraid of your feelings." The patient was able to stay with her only a few minutes more and following her departure he assaulted an aide (Bateson et al., 1956, p. 258).

As the authors see it, the patient was placed in an impossible dilemma: To secure his mother's love, he had to show his own affection; but if he did so, he would lose her love.

The double-bind hypothesis is intriguing, but it can claim little in the way of empirical support. Some parents no doubt put their children into double-bind situations and some may do so more frequently than others. But there is no evidence that double-binding parents are more likely to have schizophrenic offspring than anyone else (Ringuette and Kennedy, 1966). While schizophrenics and nonschizophrenics may have different family environments, it seems premature to pin down the difference to so subtle a communication problem as double-binding.

Disentangling cause and effect Schizophrenics evidently come from a less benign family background than normal children. In part, this relationship may simply be yet another manifestation of the genetic factor. But it appears that this is not all. Some pertinent evidence comes from a study of adoptees who were hospitalized for schizophrenia. An appropriately matched control group consisted of nonschizophrenic adoptees. As judged by a special psychiatric interview, the *adoptive* parents of the schizophrenics were in poorer mental health than the adoptive parents of the normals (Wender, Rosenthal, and Kety, 1968).

The work on adoptees shows that there is a relation between schizophrenia and family environment. But this does not prove that the familial environment is a *cause* of the patient's disorder. It may also be an effect; after all, having a schizophrenic in the family is probably quite disturbing. Some recent studies of mother-child interactions suggest that something of this sort does play a role (Mishler and Waxler, 1968). The investigators studied mothers who had both a schizophrenic and a healthy daughter. When observed with their schizophrenic daughters, the mothers seemed aloof and unresponsive. But when seen with their healthy daughters, the mothers behaved more normally. Their unresponsiveness may then not be a general characteristic of their personality (and thus perhaps a *cause* of the child's disorder) but rather a reaction to the schizophrenic daughter (and thus an *effect* of the child's disorder upon the mother's behavior).

All in all, there is evidently a relation between schizophrenia and various psychological characteristics of the family. This relationship is probably caused by three contributing factors. One is genetic; both the parents and their schizophrenic offspring may share some pathological genes. A second factor is environmental; the parents' psychopathology precipitates the disorder of the child. A third factor involves the reversed causal relation; having a schizophrenic child produces psychopathological reactions in the rest of the family.

THE PATHOLOGY MODEL AND SCHIZOPHRENIA

We have considered schizophrenia under the same headings that are used to analyze nonpsychiatric illnesses—the symptom patterns, the underlying pathology, the role of more remote causes such as genetic predisposition, and precipitating factors. What can we conclude? To guide our evaluation, we will refer to a schematic diagram of the main factors in the schizophrenic disorder that is analogous to the one we used to analyze diabetes (Figure 17.11).

It appears that the main symptoms of schizophrenia can be regarded as the manifestations of an underlying psychological deficit, perhaps a defect in the ability to focus in space and time. The best guess is that this psychological malfunction reflects an underlying organic pathology whose exact nature is still unknown. Many investigators suspect that it is a biochemical defect, most likely one that involves some neurotransmitter system. The pathology that represents the immediate cause of the disorder is in turn produced by more remote causes. One is a hereditary predisposition. Another is a set of environmental stresses, including socioeconomic and familial pressures, which trigger the pathological process in persons with the initial predisposition.

A final word. Schizophrenia, like most other disorders, varies in severity. In describing it, we have necessarily concentrated on the most clear-cut examples, and these tend to be quite severe. But this should not blind us to the fact that there are some schizophrenics whose affliction is relatively mild and who may be able to function reasonably well in the ordinary world. There are also cases in which the symptoms are present mostly during acute psychotic episodes; at other times, the patient may be nearly symptom free. Total disability is relatively rare (Bernheim and Lewine, 1979).

17.11 The pathology model as applied to schizophrenia *The diagram shows that the causal analysis by which nonbehavioral disorders such as diabetes are described (see p. 665) can be applied to mental disorders such as schizophrenia. The basic logic applies regardless of whether the disorder ultimately turns out to be in part somatogenic or not.*

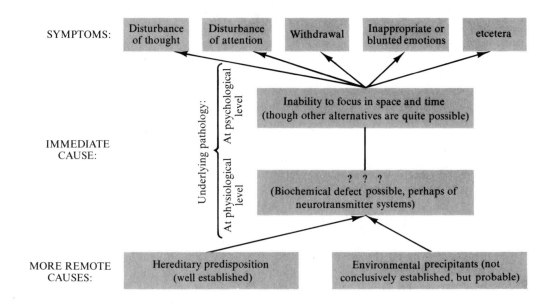

Affective Disorders

While schizophrenia can be regarded as essentially a disorder of thought, in another group of disorders the dominant disturbance is one of *mood*. These are the **affective disorders** that are characterized by two emotional extremes—the vehement energy of **mania,** the despair and lethargy of **depression,** or both. (The term *affective* is a synonym for emotional feeling.)

THE SYMPTOM PATTERNS

Affective disorders are often periodic. The episodes are of varying durations. In some cases, they are as short as one or two days; more often, they last for several months or more. In one variety of the condition, **bipolar affective disorder** (formerly called **manic-depressive psychosis**), the patient swings from one emotional extreme to the other, sometimes with intermittent periods of normalcy, experiencing both manic and depressive episodes. Other cases are **unipolar;** in these, the mood extremes are of one kind only. Patients who suffer from only manic episodes are very rare. The bulk of the unipolar disorders consists of people who suffer from deep depressions.

MANIA

In their milder form, manic states are often hard to distinguish from normal high spirits. The person seems to have shifted into some form of mental high gear; she is more lively and infectiously merry, is extremely talkative and always on the go, is charming, utterly self-confident, and indefatigable. It is hard to see that something is wrong unless one notices that she jumps from one plan to another, seems unable to sit still for a moment, and quickly shifts from unbounded elation to intense irritation if she meets even the smallest frustration. These pathological signs become greatly intensified as the manic episode becomes more severe *(acute mania).* Now the motor is racing and all brakes are off. There is an endless stream of talk that runs from one topic to another and knows no inhibitions of social or personal (or for that matter, sexual) propriety. Patients are incessantly busy. They rarely sleep, burst into shouts of song, smash furniture out of sheer overabundance of energy, do exercises, conceive grandiose plans for rebuilding the hospital or redirecting the nation's foreign policy or making millions in the stock market—a ceaseless torrent of activity that continues unabated over many days and sleepless nights and will eventually sap the patients' health (and that of those around them) if they are not sedated.

An example of a manic episode is described in an autobiography by Clifford Beers, a man who lived through three years of a severe bipolar disorder, recovered, and went on to become a crusader for mental hospital reform. Beers started to write letters about everything that was happening to him. He soon ran out of stationery so he obtained large rolls of wrapping paper which he cut into one-foot strips and pasted together into long rolls, writing letters that were twenty to thirty feet long, and continuing to write at the rate of twelve feet per hour. He eventually tried to take charge of the hospital, was put in a small cell, and soon tried his hand at inventions. He decided to overcome the force of gravity. He tore a carpet into strips and used the makeshift ropes to suspend his bed (with himself in it) off the floor. "So epoch-making did this discovery appear to me that I noted the exact position of the bed so that a wondering posterity might ever afterward view and revere the exact spot on the earth's surface whence one of man's greatest thoughts had winged its way to immortality" (quoted in White and Watt, 1973, p. 486).

DEPRESSION

In many ways, depression is the polar opposite of mania. The patient's mood is utterly dejected, his outlook is hopeless; he has lost his interest in other people and regards himself as completely worthless. In many cases, both thought and action slow down to a crawl:

> The patient appears dejected and cheerless; everything he says and does is with effort.... He speaks only in response to questions and even then answers in a word, not a sentence.... He speaks in such a low tone that one finds oneself moving close to him and speaking more loudly as if he were the one who could not hear. He says that everything is hopeless, that he is a disgrace to his family; he recalls that when he was a boy he took a paper from the newsstand and did not pay for it (Cohen, 1975, p. 1,019).

In severe cases, there may be delusions or even hallucinations. Most are variations on the same theme of personal worthlessness: "I must weep myself to death. I cannot live. I cannot die. I have failed so. It would be better if I had not been born.... I am the most inferior person in the world.... I am subhuman" (Beck, 1967, p. 38).

Sometimes the patient believes that she has committed some horrible crime for which she is about to be punished, with torture and execution imminent. Occasionally she hears voices that speak of sin and death and utter condemnation.

Depression and suicide   Given the depressive's bottomless despair, it is not surprising that suicide is a very real risk. Probably no patient in real life has described his preoccupation with death, suicide, and dissolution as eloquently as that greatest depressive in all of English literature, Prince Hamlet:

> O that this too too sullied flesh would melt,
> Thaw, and resolve itself into a dew,
> Or that the Everlasting had not fixed
> His canon 'gainst self-slaughter. O God, God,
> How weary, stale, flat, and unprofitable
> Seem to me all the uses of this world!
> Fie on 't, ah fie, 'tis an unweeded garden
> That grows to seed.
>
> (*Hamlet*, Act I, Scene ii)

Like Hamlet, many depressives think of suicide. Some attempt the act, and more than a few succeed. The suicide rate among depressives is high; according to some estimates, it is about twenty-five times greater than that found in the population as a whole. But contrary to what one might expect, the risk of

Depression   *(Photograph by Wayne Miller, Magnum Photos)*

suicide is relatively low while the patient is still in the trough of the depressive phase. At that point his gloom is deepest, but so too is his apathy. The risk increases as the patient comes out of his depression. Suicide rates are greatest during weekend leaves from the hospital and shortly after discharge (Beck, 1967). Then the patient's mood may still be black, but he has regained some of his energy and ability to act. He has recovered just enough to do the one thing that will prevent all further recovery.

ORGANIC FACTORS

What produces the mood extremes that are characteristic of affective disorders? According to one view, some of these conditions—especially the bipolar variety—are *endogenous,* that is, produced by some internal, organic pathology.

GENETIC COMPONENTS

The belief that such an organic pathology exists is based on several considerations. As in schizophrenia, there is the rather specific therapeutic effect of certain drugs (described below). And again, as in schizophrenia, there is good reason to suppose that at least some forms of the disorder have an important hereditary component. This is almost certainly true for the bipolar condition. The average concordance for identical twins of whom one suffers from bipolar affective disorder is 67 percent, while the comparable figure for fraternal twins is 16 percent (based on Slater and Cowie, 1971). The evidence suggests that the genetic factor is much weaker or perhaps altogether absent in unipolar cases.

BIOCHEMICAL HYPOTHESES

The genetic evidence is a strong argument for the view that there is some biological factor that underlies bipolar affective disorders. This view is further bolstered by the fact that in bipolars, the switch from one mood to the other is generally quite divorced from external circumstances. The most plausible interpretation is that there is some internal, biological switch.

One hypothesis is that the disorder is based on a biochemical defect that involves the supply of various neurotransmitters, specifically, the *catecholamines,* at certain critical sites in the brain. When there is an oversupply, there is mania; when there is a shortage, there is depression (Schildkraut, 1965). Some evidence comes from the study of certain therapeutic drugs. Drugs which deplete various catecholamines lead to mood depressions in normal persons. Conversely, drugs which increase the available amount of these transmitters act as *antidepressants.* An example is *imipramine,* a drug widely used in the treatment of depression. Imipramine leads to an increase in the available supply of certain catecholamines.

The catecholamine hypothesis of affective disorder has a certain plausibility. As we have seen, catecholamines serve as transmitters for the tracts that activate the brain. Under the circumstances, it seems reasonable enough to suppose that an increase in these transmitters will lead to overactivation (that is, mania), and a decrease to underactivation (that is, depression). But, as so often, the actual state of affairs is probably not as simple as originally envisaged. According to a number of investigators, the catecholamine hypothesis alone is not a sufficient account of the biochemistry of affective disorders and of their alleviation by various drugs (Shopsin et al., 1974). It appears that, as yet, the organic basis of affective disorders is still in doubt.

PSYCHOGENIC FACTORS

The organic pathology—whatever it may turn out to be—might account for the extremes of some patients' mood, the fact that they are speeded up or slowed down in virtually all respects. But can it explain *what* the patient thinks or does, the manic's glow of overweening self-satisfaction and the depressive's hopeless despair and self-loathing? How does an inadequate supply of catecholamines lead to the belief that one is "the most inferior person in the world?"

MOOD OR COGNITION?

What comes first, mood or cognition? The question is again one of cause and effect. Theorists who regard the disorder as primarily somatogenic believe that what the patient thinks *follows* from her mood. If a catecholamine insufficiency (or some other biochemical state) makes her feel sluggish and gloomy, she looks for reasons to explain her own mood. Eventually she will find them: the world is no good, and nor is she. The end result is that her cognitions match her feelings. (For an analogous approach to the nature of emotional feelings in normals, see Chapter 14).

Does this approach really do justice to the phenomenon? Theorists who believe in a psychogenic interpretation think not. They grant that affective disorders—especially those that are bipolar—involve a constitutional predisposition toward mood excess but they insist that psychological factors play a vital role. In their view, the patient's belief that he and the world are no good comes first and his depression comes second—as an *effect* of these cognitions rather than as their cause.

One such view has been proposed by Aaron Beck, who feels that the patient's condition can be ultimately traced to a number of intensely negative beliefs about himself and the world around him: that he is utterly worthless, that his future is bleak, and that whatever happens around him is sure to turn out to be for the worst (Beck, 1967).

LEARNED HELPLESSNESS AND DEPRESSION

Where Beck's cognitive theory grew out of clinical observations of depressed patients, a related cognitive account, proposed by M. E. P. Seligman, had its source in studies of animal learning (Seligman, 1975). The initial findings that led to Seligman's approach concerned **learned helplessness,** first observed in the animal laboratory (see Chapter 5).

When normal dogs are placed in a shuttle box in which they have to jump from one compartment to another in order to escape an electric shock, they learn to do so with little difficulty. This is in contrast with a second group of dogs who have first been exposed to a series of painful shocks about which they could do absolutely nothing. When this second group was later placed in the shuttle box, their performance was drastically different from that of nor-

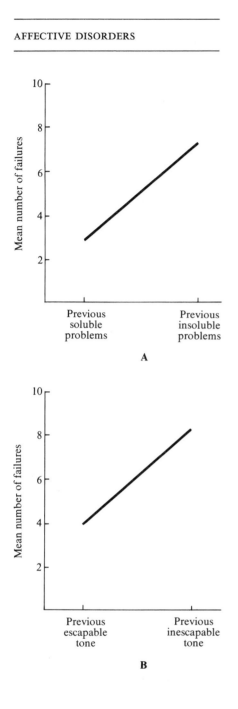

A

B

mal dogs. Unlike normal animals, they did not run around frantically looking for some means of escape. Nor did they ever find the correct response—jumping over the hurdle. Instead, they simply gave up: they layed down, whimpered, and passively accepted their fate. They had learned to become helpless (Seligman, Maier, and Solomon, 1971).

Seligman argues that learned helplessness in animals is in many ways similar to at least some forms of human depression. Like the helpless dogs, depressed patients have given up. They just sit there, passively, unable to take any initiative that might help them cope. Some further similarities concern the effects of certain antidepressant drugs (see Chapter 18). These drugs alleviate the symptoms of many depressive patients. They have a similar effect on animals rendered helpless: the helplessness disappears and the animals behave much like normals (Porsolt, LePichon, and Jalfre, 1977).

In an attempt to buttress the analogy, Seligman and his collaborators have tried to demonstrate something akin to learned helplessness in human laboratory subjects. In one such study, subjects were exposed to loud, unpleasant noises through earphones. One group of subjects was able to escape the noises by performing a simple response; a second group received the same number of noises as the first but was unable to do anything about them. When later tested in a variety of situations, the subjects pretreated with inescapable noise behaved somewhat like the dogs who had received inescapable shock. They became impaired in their ability to solve rather simple problems, such as anagram puzzles, that posed little difficulty for the control subjects. Seligman argues that this manipulation had induced a temporary sense of helplessness, a feeling that there was no point in trying, since one's actions would have no effect. This analogy is supported by a further finding. Subjects who were already depressed before the experiment started, performed poorly on the anagram puzzles whether they experienced inescapable noise or not. These subjects presumably required no special technique to render them helpless. They were already helpless—and hence depressed—before the experiment began (Klein and Seligman, 1976; Miller and Seligman, 1975; see Figure 17.12).

Seligman believes that the parallels between learned helplessness in animals and in humans point to a common factor which may help to explain depression. Both the dogs who suffered inescapable shock and the humans who experienced inescapable noises developed an expectation that their own acts would be of no avail. As a result, both became unable to initiate responses, or to recognize that something they do has a desirable effect. Something similar may happen in human depression. The precipitating factor may be some personal catastrophe—rejection, bankruptcy, physical disease, the death of a loved one. This leads to a generalized sense of impotence: a belief that there is nothing one can do to shape one's destiny, that one is a passive victim with no control over events—that one is helpless.

17.12 Learned helplessness in laboratory subjects   *(A) College students were given several discrimination tasks. For one group, the tasks were solvable; for the other, they were arranged so that there was no solution. After this, both groups were given 20 anagrams that had to be unscrambled to make a word. Each anagram was solvable. If a subject failed to solve an anagram within 100 seconds, it was scored as a failure. The figure shows that the number of failures was considerably greater for the group that had previously received the unsolvable discrimination tasks. The authors regard this as a human analogue to learned helplessness in animals. (B) Similar results were found for two groups of human subjects previously exposed to escapable or inescapable loud tones. If the tones were inescapable, the subjects' ability to solve the anagrams was impaired. (After Hiroto and Seligman, 1975)*

Whether learned helplessness theory can adequately account for the phenomena of depression, is still a matter of debate (Abramson, Seligman, and Teasdale, 1978; Costello, 1978; Depue and Monroe, 1978). But whatever the outcome of this debate, the parallels that Seligman has pointed to will have to be considered by any future theory of the disorder.

REACTIVE DEPRESSION

Some authors believe that while psychological factors are probably involved in all affective disorders, they are of greatest relevance in cases of *reactive depression.* These are episodes that occur in people who have no history of prior depression nor any known genetic susceptibility to affective disorders. The onset of these episodes usually occurs shortly after a major personal loss—the death or departure of a loved one, a debilitating organic illness, a severe setback in work and career. Such episodes are sometimes called reactive because they seem like reactions to the stressful event, rather than arising endogenously from within the individual.

The reactive-endogenous distinction has led to some controversy. Many recent investigators believe that the distinction is not genuine. Some believe that the two terms simply describe a difference in severity, with reactive depressions being less severe. Others hold that once a major depression has developed, its course and response to treatment are the same whether its onset was associated with some stressful event or not. This view is reflected in the most recent psychiatric diagnostic system in which the distinction has been dropped (*DSM*-III, 1980).

In any case, precipitating stress cannot be the whole story in depression. After all, there are many people who suffer major setbacks but don't fall into a depressive collapse. One possibility is that the person who becomes depressive has been sensitized by prior experiences, perhaps in early life. When she later encounters similar situations, these reactivate the panic of helplessness she felt earlier. Some support for this view comes from the finding that, compared to normals, depressed patients are more likely to have lost a parent in childhood or adolescence (Beck, 1967), though this result has been disputed by other investigators (Pitts et al., 1965).

THE DEPRESSIVE'S SELF-HATRED

There is one facet of depression that does not follow from any of the theoretical positions we have described thus far—the depressive's violent self-hatred. Hopelessness, helplessness, or a shortage of catecholamines might well lead him to feel that the world is a terrible place, but why does he blame himself? One possible explanation involves the patient's upbringing. Several authors have suggested that the parents of depressives made unusually strict demands upon them when they were children, insisting on high achievement and a rigid code of morality, with severe punishments for failure to live up to these standards (Gibson, Cohen, and Cohen, 1959). Reared in this manner, the child might well develop a marked tendency toward self-blame, setting off torrents of self-directed abuse in times of misfortune. The idea seems plausible enough, but the evidence is still unclear, for many of the investigations whose results seem to support it can be criticized for failure to control age, social class, and similar factors.

Neuroses

In affective disorders, as we have seen, it is still unclear whether the underlying pathology is best regarded as somatic or psychogenic or as both. There is much more agreement about another class of disorders in which both the main symptoms and underlying pathology are generally considered to be primarily mental—the **neuroses.** As used here, the term *neurosis* describes conditions whose primary symptoms are either anxiety or defenses that ward off anxiety. While such symptoms often cause serious distress and impair the person's functioning, they generally do not render him incapable of coping with external reality. He is neurotic, not psychotic.

It is worth noting that there is no sharp line that demarcates neurosis from normalcy (nor for that matter, from psychosis). As a result, it is hard to determine how widespread neurosis is, for different investigators use different criteria. According to one study of a metropolitan population, the incidence of moderately severe disturbance may be as high as 22 percent (Srole et al., 1962). Other authors give lower figures, with estimates of 5 to 10 percent (Coleman, 1972).

PHOBIAS

In some neuroses, the primary symptom is a **phobia,** an intense and irrational fear of some object or situation. During the nineteenth century, some of these irrational fears were catalogued and assigned high-sounding Greek or Latin names. Examples are fear of high places (acrophobia), or open places (agoraphobia), or enclosed places (claustrophobia), or of crowds (ocholophobia), or germs (mysophobia), or cats (ailurophobia)—the list is potentially endless. The crucial point in the definition is that the fear must be *irrational,* that there really is no danger or that the danger is exaggerated out of all proportion. An African villager who lives at the outskirts of the jungle and is worried about leopards has an understandable fear; a San Francisco apartment dweller with a similar fear has a phobia (which would presumably be called *pardalisophobia*). In many cases, this irrationality is quite apparent to the sufferer, who knows that the fear is groundless but continues to be afraid all the same.

In phobia, the irrational fear exerts an enormous effect on every aspect of the sufferer's life, for he is always preoccupied with his phobia. On the face of it, it is not entirely clear why this should be so. Why can't the phobic simply avoid the situations that frighten him? If he is afraid of leopards and snakes, he should stay away from the zoo; if he is terrified of heights, he should refrain from visits to the top of the Sears Tower. Some phobias may be minor enough to be handled this easily, but most cannot. In many cases this is because the phobia tends to expand. The fear of leopards becomes a fear of the part of the city where the zoo is located, of all cats and catlike things, or of all spotted objects, and so on. Other phobias may be more wide-ranging to begin with.

Fear of heights *A scene from the Alfred Hitchcock film* Vertigo. *Here the camera tries to recreate the sensation the phobic experiences even in everyday circumstances. (Courtesy the Museum of Modern Art/Film Stills Archive)*

An example is agoraphobia, a fear of open spaces that really amounts to a dread of leaving the safety of one's own home:

> "He was crossing the Place de la Concorde (alone, it should be noted) when he felt a strange sensation of dread. His breathing became rapid and he felt as if he were suffocating: his heart was beating violently and his legs were limp as if half-paralyzed. He could go neither forwards nor backwards, and he had to exert a tremendous effort, bathed in sweat, to reach the other side of the square." As time went on, the patient's phobic condition expanded. He was no longer able to go out except in the company of his wife: "His wife had to hold him tightly by his arm, and then he would calm down and cross the square without further incident. His wife has to accompany him absolutely everywhere now, even when he goes to the toilet" (Janet, quoted in Nemiah, 1975a, p. 1,234).

THE CAUSE OF PHOBIAS

What is the mechanism that underlies phobias? One notion goes back to John Locke who believed that such fears are produced by a chance association of ideas, as when a child is told stories about goblins that come by night and is forever after terrified of the dark (Locke, 1689). Several modern authors express much the same idea in the language of conditioning theory. In their view, phobias result from classical conditioning; the conditioned stimulus is the feared object (open spaces) and the response is the autonomic upheaval (increased heart rate, cold sweat, and so on) characteristic of fear (Wolpe, 1958).

A number of phobias may indeed develop in just this fashion. Examples include fear of dogs after dog bites, fear of heights after a fall down a flight of stairs, and fear of cars or driving after a serious automobile accident (Marks, 1969). Conditioning theorists can readily explain why phobias acquired in this manner expand and spread to new stimuli. The fear response is initially conditioned to a particular stimulus. If this stimulus subsequently occurs in a new context, the fear will be evoked and thus conditioned to a whole set of new stimuli. An example is a woman who developed a fear of anesthetic masks after experiencing a terrifying sensation of suffocation while being anesthetized. This same sense of suffocation reoccurred later when she was in a stuffy, crowded elevator. This in turn led to a dread of elevators, whether empty or crowded. The phobia generalized to any and all situations in which she could not leave at will, even playing cards (Wolpe, 1958, p. 98).

According to many writers, many phobias cannot be explained quite as simply as the classical conditioning account would have it. The point is that phobias sometimes have a twisted sort of function. The patient gets some devious benefit from his fear, a fact which is hard to explain if classical conditioning is all that is involved. Psychoanalysts believe that one such benefit is **displacement.** The patient is afraid of something that he cannot face consciously. As a protective measure, he displaces his fear to a conceptually related object, but without recognizing the relationship. Thus a husband's phobia about knives may be a displaced fear of his own impulse to stab his wife. The phobia is a defense in which the patient trades a greater fear for a lesser one.

Another potential function of the phobia is that it can serve as a roundabout way to control others. The patient can play the role of an invalid; this may

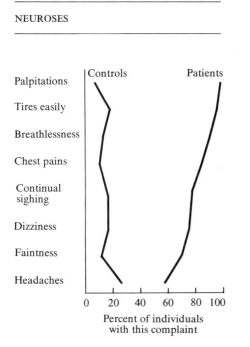

Palpitations
Tires easily
Breathlessness
Chest pains
Continual sighing
Dizziness
Faintness
Headaches

Controls   Patients

0   20   40   60   80   100

Percent of individuals
with this complaint

17.13   The symptoms of anxiety neurosis
Incidence of various symptoms in persons with anxiety disorders and in a control group. (Data from Marks and Lader, 1973)

gain sympathy, attention, and relief from unpleasant responsibilities. According to some authors, such motives are a critical factor in many phobias (Andrews, 1966). An example is the agoraphobic Parisian described before. One suspects that he derived a certain benefit from his crippling phobia; it gave him a valid reason for allowing himself to become totally dependent upon his wife, to the point where she even had to accompany him to the toilet.

ANXIETY NEUROSIS

In phobias, anxiety is focused on a particular object or situation; in *anxiety neurosis,* it is all-pervasive or, as it is sometimes called, free-floating. The patient is constantly tense and worried, feels inadequate, is oversensitive, can't concentrate or make decisions, and suffers from insomnia. This state of affairs is generally accompanied by any number of physiological concomitants—rapid heart rate, irregular breathing, excessive sweating, frequent urination, and chronic diarrhea. As if this weren't bad enough, this chronically anxious state peaks to become an acute anxiety attack, a terrifying episode of incomprehensible panic and sense of impending catastrophe that may last a few seconds or over an hour (Figure 17.13).

According to one interpretation, anxiety neurosis shows what happens when there are no defenses against anxiety or when those defenses are too weak and collapse. This sometimes occurs when unacceptable impulses break into consciousness and precipitate a panic reaction.

Conditioning theorists offer another account. In their view, anxiety neurosis is much like a phobia. The difference is that the anxiety is conditioned to a very broad range of stimuli so that avoidance is virtually impossible (Wolpe, 1958). The trouble is that the stimuli to which anxiety is said to be conditioned are not easily specified. Since this is so, the conditioning interpretation of anxiety neurosis is hard to evaluate.

OBSESSIVE-COMPULSIVE NEUROSIS

In phobias, anxiety is aroused by external objects or situations. In contrast, anxiety in *obsessive-compulsive neurosis* is produced by internal events, certain persistent thoughts or wishes that intrude into consciousness and cannot be stopped. An example of such an *obsession* is a mother who has frightening thoughts of strangling her children. To ward off the anxiety produced by such obsessions, the patient often feels compelled to perform a variety of ritualistic acts. Such *compulsions* are attempts to counteract the anxiety-producing impulse that underlies the obsessive thought; in Freud's terms, a way of *undoing* what should not have been done. Examples of such compulsions are ritualistic cleaning, handwashing, and incessant counting. The mother with uncontrollable thoughts of committing infanticide might feel compelled to count her children over and over again, as if to check that they are all there, that she hasn't done away with any. The obsessive-compulsive patient is aware that his behavior is irrational but he can't help himself even so. Lady Macbeth knew that "what's done cannot be undone," but she nevertheless continued to wash the invisible blood off her hands.

Minor and momentary obsessional thoughts or compulsions are commonplace. After all, most people have had the occasional feeling that they ought to check whether the door is locked even when they are perfectly sure that it is. But in obsessive-compulsive neurosis, such thoughts and acts are the patient's major preoccupation and are crippling:

> A man in his 30's, fearing lest he push a stranger off the subway platform in the path of an oncoming train, was compelled to keep his arms and hands glued rigidly to his sides. . . . [He] was on one occasion obsessed with the idea that, despite his stringent precautions, he had, after all, inadvertently knocked some-one off the subway platform. He struggled with himself for weeks to dispel what he rationally knew was a foolish notion but was at length compelled to call the transport authority to reassure himself that there had not in fact been any such accident. The same patient was for a time preoccupied with the concern that, when he walked on the streets, he was dislodging manhole covers so that strang-ers passing by would fall into the sewer and be injured. Whenever he passed a manhole in the company of friends, he would be compelled to count his com-panions to make sure that none was missing (Nemiah, 1975*b*, p. 1,245).

HYSTERIA AND RELATED CONDITIONS

The defenses against anxiety set up by obsessive-compulsive neurotics are cumbersome and never work completely. Try as they may, these patients are always encumbered with guilt and vacillation. But there is another neurotic reaction which apparently does a better job at managing anxiety. This is *hysteria* in which the primary defense is repression. The patient shoves all anxiety-evoking materials out of consciousness. This allows him to deny that there is anything to be anxious about. The hysteric is a virtuoso at refusing to take responsibility for his own unacceptable behavior. Some forbidden im-pulse may break through or some forbidden act may get performed, but the hysteric saves the situation—he simply insists that it wasn't really his fault.

CONVERSION HYSTERIA

One way of escaping responsibility is by being sick. This is the path chosen by *conversion hysterics* who resolve some intolerable internal conflict by develop-ing a hysterical bodily ailment, such as paralysis of a limb (see Chapter 12).*
The soldier who is terrified of going into battle but cannot face the idea of being a coward may become hysterically paralyzed. This allows him to give in to his impulse of refusing to march. But it also lets him do so without guilt or shame—he is not marching because he *can't* march.

DISSOCIATIVE STATE

Another way in which a person can deny responsibility for some acts (or thoughts or wishes) is by insisting that they were never committed, or at least not by her. This approach is characteristic of a subgroup of hysterias called *dissociative reactions.* In these disorders, a whole set of mental events—acts,

---

* The term *conversion* was coined by Freud who believed that the repressed energies that power the patient's unconscious conflict are "converted" into a somatic symptom much as a steam engine converts thermal energy into mechanical energy.

thoughts, feelings, memories—is shoved out of ordinary consciousness. One example is psychogenic *amnesia* in which the individual is unable to remember some period of her life, or sometimes all events prior to the amnesia, including her own identity. In other cases, the dissociation involves a *fugue state,* in which the individual wanders away from home, and then, days, weeks, or even years thereafter, suddenly realizes that he is in a strange place, doesn't know how he got there, and has total amnesia for the entire period of the fugue.

Still more drastic are cases of *multiple personality.* Here the dissociation is so massive that it results in two or more separate personalities. The second—and sometimes third or fourth—personality is built upon a nucleus of memories that already had some prior separate status. An example is a shy and inhibited person who has had fantasies of being carefree and outgoing from childhood on. These memories eventually take on the characteristics of a separate self. Once formed, the new self may enter upon the scene quite suddenly, as in the famous case of Eve White:

> After a tense moment of silence, her hands dropped. There was a quick, reckless smile and, in a bright voice that sparkled, she said, "Hi there, Doc.". . . There was in the newcomer a childishly daredevil air, an erotically mischievous glance, a face marvelously free from the habitual signs of care, seriousness, and underlying distress, so long familiar in her predecessor. This new and apparently carefree girl spoke casually of Eve White and her problems, always using *she* or *her* in every reference, always respecting the strict bounds of a separate identity. When asked her own name she immediately replied, "Oh, I'm Eve Black" (Thigpen and Cleckley, 1957, as described in Coleman, 1972, p. 246).

A movie recreation of a case of multiple personality Joanne Woodward in The Three Faces of Eve *portraying Eve White (left) and Eve Black (right) (Courtesy the Museum of Modern Art/ Film Stills Archive)*

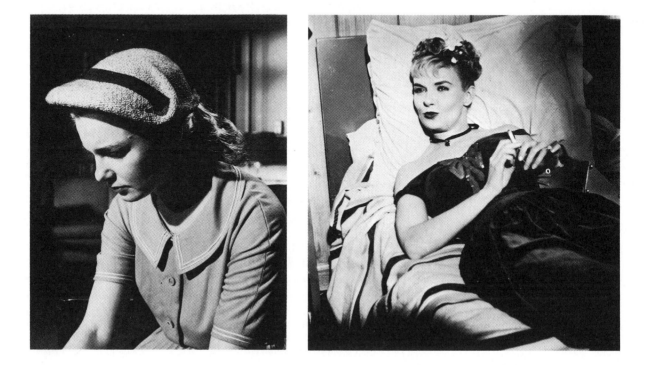

THE UNDERLYING MECHANISM OF HYSTERIA

The mechanism by which hysterical symptoms develop is still obscure. Freud believed that such symptoms are a defense against anxiety. Conditioning theorists hold a similar position, translated into their own conceptual framework. But this anxiety hypothesis only accounts for the hysteric's motives. It may explain why she wants not to see or not to walk or to develop an alternate personality; it does not explain how she accomplishes these feats, especially the wholesale alterations of consciousness that characterize dissociations.

Some authors suggest that such phenomena may represent an unusual form of self-dramatization in which the person acts *as if* she were blind or *as if* she were Eve Black without any consciousness that any playacting is going on (Sarbin and Allen, 1968; Ziegler, Imboden, and Rodgers, 1963). According to this view, the hysteric is like an actor who becomes so involved in his role that he is no longer aware that he is on stage. In actuality of course, no actor ever completely forgets that he is playing a part; if he did, he would be unable to leave the stage when the play calls for his exit. But by the same token, no hysteric is ever completely paralyzed or blind and so on—his "paralyzed" leg still responds to reflex stimulation and will probably serve quite well in emergencies such as a fire.

Much the same kind of as-if behavior characterizes a deeply hypnotized patient who is given a suggestion, say, not to see a chair in the middle of the room. When asked whether she sees it, she answers no; but when she walks across the room, she somehow never bumps into it; she manages to circle around it, as if to see it so as not to see it. The important point is that the hysteric, the hypnotized person, and—to a lesser extent—the deeply involved actor, are not aware of what they are aware of.

THE UNDERLYING PATHOLOGY OF NEUROSES

We have looked at some of the major patterns of neurosis. Their symptoms vary widely. But are they nevertheless similar in sharing a common underlying pathology?

As we have seen, many modern practitioners follow Freud in believing that there is a pathology underlying neurosis, but that it is behavioral (that is, mental) rather than organic. In their view, the symptoms of neurosis are primarily a defense against some intolerable anxiety. This view fits some neuroses rather well. For example, compulsive acts can be understood as responses that block an anxiety-related obsessive thought, even if only temporarily. But in some other cases, the relation between symptom and underlying pathology is a matter of debate.*

Suppose a person has a crippling phobia about water that makes it hard to drink, wash, and so on. A psychoanalyst would argue that this water phobia is only the visible part of the neurosis. To understand this symptom, we have to

* As mentioned before, this is one of the reasons why some psychopathologists prefer to abandon the general category *neurosis* altogether. In their view, diagnostic categories should be based on observed symptoms rather than on a theory about underlying causes. This position is now embodied in the recent revision of the *DSM* in which the general rubric *neurosis* is dropped and the various symptom clusters that were formerly described as neurotic subtypes (phobias, conversion disorders, and so on) are listed separately.

dig deeper and find out what he is "really" afraid of, what water stands for in his private symbolism. But a behavior theorist would probably take a different tack. He would argue that the patient's trouble is a conditioned fear of water, no more and no less, and that there are no hidden conflicts of which this fear of water is a devious manifestation. In his view, the neurotic symptom *is* the disease and it is the removal of this symptom toward which treatment—or as he would call it, ***behavior therapy***—should be directed. Having rejected the distinction between symptom and underlying pathology as applied to neurosis, some behavior therapists go the rest of the way: They reject the entire pathology model that insists on this distinction.

Is the pathology model really inapplicable to neurosis? The question is primarily relevant to issues that concern psychotherapy (see Chapter 18). For now, we merely point out that cases in which a symptom *is* the pathology are not unheard of in ordinary, organic medical practice. An example is a broken bone that is visible to the naked eye. Here symptom and pathology seem to be one and the same, so that to heal the one is equivalent to healing the other. But this in itself does not seem to be an adequate reason for abandoning the pathology model as a general conceptual framework.

MORE REMOTE CAUSES OF NEUROSIS

Whatever their differences, all psychopathologists agree that neurosis is largely based on learning. The defenses against anxiety may represent the immediate cause of the symptoms, but they in turn are based on some learned experiences farther back in the individual's life.

In many cases, the disorder can be traced to a stressful event in the just-preceding past, some traumatic episode that led to a phobia, some harrowing war experience that precipitated a conversion hysteria, or a marital breakup that initiated an anxiety attack. Oddly enough, there is usually a lag of a few days between the trauma and the onset of the neurotic symptoms. During this lag, the individual thinks about the traumatic event and relives the fearful emotions which keep on increasing and finally erupt into the neurotic symptom pattern.

Upon investigation, it turns out that in many cases the trauma was only a precipitant; the patient had some prior adjustment problems. In effect, the trauma served to reevoke some earlier reactions to anxiety acquired in a more distant past. An example is psychiatric breakdown during combat. Soldiers who collapse under relatively minor stress are more likely to have a history of prior psychiatric difficulties, signs of neurosis in childhood, and so on (Slater, 1943).

What are the events of the more remote past that are reevoked by the current stressful situation? Most investigators assume that the relevant factors involve the patient's family. Some evidence comes from studies of the neurotic patient's parents. One group of investigators administered a number of personality tests to the parents of neurotic and of normal veterans and found more signs of psychopathology in the parents of neurotics (Fisher et al., 1959). Other studies showed that this familial similarity extends to the kind of neurosis. Thus parents and siblings of anxiety neurotics are more likely to suffer from anxiety neurosis than from some other neurotic disorder. The same holds for hysteria and obsessive-compulsive neurosis (Slater and Cowie, 1971). Related evidence pertains to phobias. For example, fearful mothers tend to have fearful children. In fact, the fears tend to be the same; mothers and daughters often have the same phobias (Marks, 1969).

Neurosis evidently runs in families. Could this be an effect of heredity? As in other areas, attempts to answer this question have focused on identical and fraternal twins. Given that one twin was diagnosed as neurotic, what was the diagnosis for the other twin? The results show that, on the average, the concordance was only 1.6 times larger in identical than in fraternal twins. This suggests that heredity plays a comparatively minor role in the development of neurosis, at least as compared to its role in schizophrenia where the average concordance in identical twins is 4.2 times larger than in fraternal twins (Pollin et al., 1969). Under the circumstances, the most plausible interpretation is that the family resemblance in neurosis is attributable largely to the effects of a common familial environment.

Neurotic symptoms probably have roots in the past and may be related to something in the familial environment. But this does not bear on the question of whether a given symptom has a hidden symbolic meaning or has not. A water phobia might be traceable to a childhood experience of being caught under a waterfall and then being punished by parents for wetting a new party dress. Or it might have originated in a childhood fantasy of shoving one's mother into a swimming pool and then watching her drown; here the phobia is presumably an unconscious defense against repressed murderous wishes. In either case, the past experience determines the present pathology. But thus far we neither know what aspects of the past are relevant nor how they exert their present effects.

Psychophysiological Disorders

Thus far, our concern has been with psychopathological conditions whose primary symptoms are psychological. But certain other conditions can lead to genuine organic damage. For example, peptic ulcer or asthma may be produced by organic causes, as in the case of an asthmatic allergic reaction. Yet they may also be caused by emotional factors. If so, they are called *psychophysiological conditions* (or, to use an older term, *psychosomatic disorders*). But whether their origin is organic or mental makes no difference to the victim; they are equally real in either case.

In this regard, the symptoms of psychophysiological disorders are quite different from the somatic complaints of the conversion hysteric. The hysteric's paralysis of the legs will probably disappear shortly after his underlying conflict is resolved; after all, his locomotor machinery is still intact. But the patient with a psychophysiological ulcer (or asthma, or high blood pressure) has a disorder that often plays for keeps. His ulcer will bleed and hurt just as much as an ulcer caused by a gastric disease, and if it perforates his stomach wall he will suffer the same case of peritonitis and, if he dies, his death will be no less final.

ESSENTIAL HYPERTENSION

We will consider one psychophysiological disorder in some detail—*essential hypertension.* This is a chronic elevation of blood pressure that can lead to serious disability and premature death. While some cases of hypertension result from various organic pathologies, essential hypertension is at least partially psychogenic.

THE EFFECT OF CONTINUED AUTONOMIC AROUSAL

Blood pressure is the pressure exerted by the blood as the heart pumps it through the body's arteries. One way in which this pressure can rise is by the constriction of the arteries. This occurs in fight-or-flight emergencies, as when a zebra suddenly sees a hungry lion (see Chapter 3). The sympathetic branch of the autonomic nervous system is aroused and, among other things, this leads to the contraction of the muscles of the arterial walls. The effect is much like squeezing on a water hose. There is an immediate increase in the force of the liquid spurting out. As a result, the skeletal muscle, and the heart muscles themselves, get blood more quickly—a vital necessity in life-or-death situations which call for sudden, violent exertions.

Such extraordinary measures are all very well for zebras trying to get away from lions. The emergency really does call for increased muscular effort; when it is over, the muscles inform the nervous system that they no longer need the same supply of food. When this happens, the circulatory system soon returns to normal. The situation is quite different for us today. We rarely encounter emergencies that call for violent muscular effort. But our lives are filled with any number of fear- and anger-producing situations. An unfair grade, a neighbor's snub, a near-miss on the superhighway—all trigger the sympathetic emergency reaction, even though a sudden spurt of muscular energy is of no avail. But our autonomic nervous system doesn't know that. And so we are put on an emergency basis, some of us more than others, but all to some extent. As a result, our blood pressure goes up, again and again, in the daily stress of living. Since the emergency does not lead to any extra muscular effort, the autonomic nervous system never gets the proper message that signals the end of the emergency. As a result, the blood pressure remains up for a while after the incident has passed.

In some people, continued autonomic overactivity eventually takes its toll—the elevated blood pressure no longer comes down to normal. One reason is a gradual thickening of the arterial muscle walls. This, together with an increased sensitivity to stimulation, makes these muscles overreact to normal neural impulses. As a result, they are in an almost continual state of constriction. The more constricted they are, the thicker and more sensitive they get. The ultimate effect of this vicious cycle is *hypertension,* a condition that afflicts twenty-three million Americans and represents a major public-health problem. Among its relatively minor symptoms are headaches and dizziness. If serious and prolonged, the disorder leads to lesions in the arteries that supply the kidneys, the brain, and the heart. The final results include kidney failure, cerebral stroke, coronary disease, and heart attacks (Lipowski, 1975).

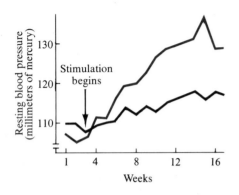

17.14 Chronic autonomic arousal and hypertension *A group of rats was exposed to continued electrical stimulation of the hypothalamic defense area. The electric stimulation was mild; it merely produced alerting reactions such as sniffing. But the stimulation was chronic, with one stimulus every minute for 12 hours every day over the better part of a four-month period. The figure shows the average resting blood pressure of the rats in this group (color) compared to the blood pressure of a control group that suffered no hypothalamic stimulation (black). The toll exacted by the continued defense reaction is shown by the difference between the two groups after four months. (After Folkow and Rubinstein, 1966)*

HYPERTENSION AND EMOTIONAL STRESS

Hypertension is evidently a residue of continued sympathetic arousal. Thus, we would expect its incidence to go up with increasing emotional stress. This is indeed the case. For example, there was a marked increase in the rate of hypertension among the inhabitants of Leningrad during the siege and bombardment of that city during World War II (Henry and Cassel, 1969). Similar effects are produced by socioeconomic stress. Hypertension is much more common among blacks than whites in the United States; and it is especially prevalent in metropolitan regions marked by high population density, poverty, and crime (Lipowski, 1975). Still other studies show that hypertension is more prevalent among persons whose occupations impose unusual emotional stress. An example is provided by air-traffic controllers, especially those who work in airports in which traffic density is high (Cobb and Rose, 1973).

In all of these cases, the critical element is not environmental stress as such, but rather the individual's reaction to it. What the besieged citizen of Leningrad, the unemployed inner-city black, and the overburdened air-traffic controller have in common is unremitting sympathetic arousal; they are continually afraid or angry or harassed and eventually their bodies pay the price in the form of hypertension (Figure 17.14).

OTHER PSYCHOPHYSIOLOGICAL DISORDERS

Emotional stress also leads to an increase in the rate of other psychophysiological disorders. While air-traffic controllers are unusually prone to hypertension, they are also more likely to develop peptic ulcers (Cobb and Rose, 1973). Is there any way to predict which disorder stress will produce in any one person? What determines whether "she will eat her heart out" or whether "she'll tie her stomach into knots?"

THE WEAKEST-LINK THEORY

According to the ***weakest-link hypothesis,*** the locus of the psychophysiological disorder depends on a preexisting somatic susceptibility that may be of genetic origin. Given enough emotional stress, the body will cave in at its most vulnerable point.

Some evidence for this view comes from studies which show that elevated blood pressure tends to run in families, in mice as well as men. In humans, a blood-pressure correlation between children and parents is seen as early as infancy. The best guess is that there is a genetic factor which is partially responsible for the initial blood-pressure elevation. This may bias the individual to respond to stress with his arterial muscles rather than with his lungs or stomach. If the stress is prolonged enough, the individual will become a hypertensive rather than an asthmatic or an ulcer patient (Henry and Cassel, 1969).

A somewhat similar account applies to psychogenic peptic ulcer. This is a lesion in the lining of the stomach or duodenum whose immediate physiological cause is an oversecretion of gastric acid; in effect, the stomach or duodenum digests itself. A number of studies have shown that in some individuals, emotional stress leads to gastric oversecretion and ultimately to ulcer formation (Wolf, 1971). Similar results have been reported for various animals (Sawrey, Conger, and Turrell, 1956).

Once again the question is why certain individuals respond to tension in this way. And again the answer is that one of the factors is an initial predisposition. One group of investigators measured gastric secretion levels in army recruits just prior to the stressful months of basic training. After several months some of these men developed ulcers. Everyone who did had very high gastric secretion levels before he entered basic training (Weiner et al., 1957).

SPECIFIC REACTION THEORY

The weakest-link hypothesis assumes that the emotional stress reaction is essentially the same in everybody; what differs is which organ system collapses under it. An alternative conception is that different psychophysiological disorders are produced by different *specific emotional reactions.* In this view, the hypertensive, the asthmatic, and the ulcer-ridden are characterized by different emotional conflicts. Since the underlying emotions are different, the visceral organs through which they are expressed differ also.

Most of the evidence for this view comes from clinical descriptions of the personalities of patients who suffer from one or another psychophysiological disorder. According to such accounts, hypertensives feel threatened and always on guard (Graham, 1962). Many of them seem to be unable to handle their own hostility; they can't express it openly, but are constantly seething inside. They are always in a silent rage that is never discharged, for its manifestations are autonomic rather than skeletal. The patient's "blood is boiling over"; his arteries perpetually constrict as his autonomic nervous system keeps on preparing him for a physical combat that never takes place. The inevitable consequence is hypertension (Saul, 1939).

Ulcer patients are described quite differently. They tend to be outwardly strong, independent, and aggressive. Inside, however, they are said to have a suppressed desire to be loved and taken care of. But the wish to be dependent is not allowed to break through the external facade; as the patient sees it, surrendering to such longings would be weak and shameful. Under the circumstances, he can only give in with his viscera. According to a (rather controversial) psychoanalytic theory, early associations between being fed and taken care of now call various food-related conditioned responses into play. One of these is gastric secretion, which eventually becomes hypersecretion and finally produces a peptic ulcer (Alexander, 1934).

THE NEED FOR A DUAL THEORY

By now, most investigators are convinced that both weak-link and specific-reaction factors play a role. There is no doubt that there are somatic susceptibilities. A man may be torn between an intense wish to appear like a cowboy hero and an overwhelming desire to be cuddled like a baby. But if he does not have the predisposition toward gastric hypersecretion, he will not contract a peptic ulcer. At the same time, there is some evidence that people cope with emotional stress in somewhat different ways. These different reaction patterns, coupled with different initial predispositions, determine which—if any—psychophysiological toll the body will exact if hit by stress.

A Categorizing Review

We have looked at a number of different mental disorders. The pathology model provides a convenient framework to review the way in which these disorders are generally considered today. This review is summarized in Table 17.1 which classifies disorders by the nature of their main symptoms and of their presumed underlying pathology (which in many cases is still controversial). Either the main symptoms or the pathology or both, can be organic. But they can also be mental, that is, defined by behavioral rather than by organic attributes.

Table 17.1 A CLASSIFICATION OF MENTAL DISORDERS

		Symptoms	
		Primarily organic	Primarily mental
Presumed underlying pathology	Primarily organic	Diabetes Measles Rickets etc.	General paresis Schizophrenia* Bipolar affective disorders*
	Primarily mental	Psychophysiological disorders	Most neuroses (e.g., phobias, obsession-compulsion, etc.)

* The underlying pathology of these disorders is still a matter of some debate.

The Sociological Critique of the Pathology Model

Thus far, our focus has been on the psychological and biological aspects of mental disorder. But psychopathological conditions can also be looked at from a sociological perspective which emphasizes how disordered people are viewed and dealt with by society. This sociological approach has led to several recent and influential attacks on the pathology model.

WHAT SOCIETY DOES TO THOSE IT CALLS MAD

The sociological critique of the pathology model is among other things a form of social protest. One of its recurrent themes is that mentally disordered persons are treated as outcasts, even today. Social historians point out that this has been their role since before medieval times. During the late Middle Ages, many European towns placed their "madmen" into special boats, "ships of fools," that dumped their deranged human cargo on far-off foreign shores. Later, the madmen were caged like beasts. Although their fate has improved considerably in modern times, even today they are still largely exiles from the rest of the world.

Some critics of the way in which mental disorder is dealt with in modern society accuse psychiatrists of acting more like jailors than like physicians. Many mentally disordered people are relegated to mental hospitals whose function is custodial rather than therapeutic. Such hospitals are similar to prisons in that they are "total institutions" with round-the-clock control by attendants who train and regiment the inmates in virtually all aspects of daily life (Goffman, 1961). There is little time or money left for psychiatric treatment. This is partially due to extreme understaffing. For instance, in 1969, the ratio of patients to psychiatrists in the mental hospitals of Pennsylvania was so large that the average patient could expect to see a psychiatrist for no more than a fifteen-minute interview every ten days (Kittrie, 1971). The inevitable consequence is boredom, apathy, and despair. The best the patient can do is to learn to play the part of the "good mental patient" as the attendants and psychiatrists want her to; if she does, she may gain various little favors such as coffee, cigarettes, and access to TV or a sunlit dayroom (Figure 17.15).

Until fairly recently, the inmates of such institutions had few legal rights, especially if they were committed. In 1949, only 10 percent of the admissions to mental hospitals in the United States were voluntary. Today, this proportion is much higher, but involuntary institutionalizations are still more common than voluntary ones. Like many other social ills, involuntary institutionalization befalls the poor more often than the well-to-do. The mental patient whose family can keep him at home or put him in a private hospital is less likely to be legally committed (Kittrie, 1971). A number of recent patients' rights campaigns have led to the establishment of more stringent safeguards on commitment procedures. But while such measures have curbed some abuses, they have not changed the fact that mentally disturbed people are still more or less banished and live under a social stigma that is hard to remove. In

17.15 The condition of mental patients *(A) As recently as 1946 and 1947, the conditions in many state mental hospitals led Albert Deutsch to entitle a book on the subject* The Shame of the States. *(From Deutsch, 1948; courtesy the Lucy Kroll Agency) (B) Conditions have improved considerably, but in many cases the mental hospital is still more of a custodial than a therapeutic institution, and the patient's life there is often empty and barren. (Photographs by Ken Heyman)*

A

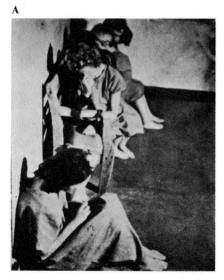

B

retrospect, it is ironic that some of the first mental asylums in Europe were set up in former leper houses that had become empty. Leprosy had disappeared, so now the "madman" took over the part of the pariah which the leper had played in former times (Foucault, 1965).

WHOM DOES SOCIETY CALL MAD?

The treatment society metes out to mentally disordered persons is grim even with enlightened attitudes. The sociological critics of the pathology model ask who the people are who are treated in this way. To the mental health practitioner, the answer is obvious: Those who demonstrate mental illness by a variety of signs and symptoms. The sociological critics reply that in many ways the causal chain works in reverse; sometimes the label creates the symptoms. The fact that a person is called mentally ill makes others see and treat him differently. Eventually, the labeled individual may change his own self-perception; then he and others will behave so as to make the label fit more and more.

To the extent that this is true, it is another demonstration of a self-fulfilling prophecy (see Chapter 14). This sometimes has paradoxical effects. To the hospital authorities—attendants, nurses, psychiatrists—the very fact that a person is an inmate is virtual proof that there must be something wrong with her. If a mental patient proclaims her sanity, this is merely evidence that she is even more deranged than anyone had suspected; she doesn't even "have insight." The patient has a better chance of getting discharged if she first admits that she is sick. She can then announce that she is getting better; now the authorities will tend to look at her more kindly, for she is obviously "responding to treatment" (Goffman, 1961).

The labeling notion does not logically imply any hypothesis about why a given person was stuck with the label in the first place. It only points out that once the label is attached—and for whatever reason—it is hard to peel off. But some critics of the pathology model go considerably further, attacking the underlying concepts of mental illness itself. Some of them argue that mental disorder does not really exist, except as a label pinned on the victim (for instance, Szasz, 1974); others suggest that it is not really a pathology, but rather a form of personal rediscovery (for instance, Laing, 1967); still others propose that the pathology does not inhere in any one individual but in a group of interacting persons (for instance, Cooper, 1967). Despite important differences of emphasis, all of these critics share a general point of view. They all emphasize social and sociological factors, they all use schizophrenia as their main example of mental disorder, and they all see themselves as mavericks, fighting the battle against psychiatric orthodoxy.

MENTAL ILLNESS AS A MYTH

Some critics maintain that the key to mental disorder is the label; without this, there would be no disorder at all. A prominent exponent of this position is psychiatrist Thomas Szasz. According to Szasz, mental illness is a myth (Szasz, 1974). He and other critics charge that it is merely a term by which we designate people whose behavior deviates from the norms of their society but

Are those whom society calls mad merely those of whom society disapproves? *The film* One Flew over the Cuckoo's Nest *with Jack Nicholson dramatizes this question. (Courtesy the Museum of Modern Art/Film Stills Archives)*

does not fall into any of the recognized categories of nonconformity. They are neither criminals, nor prostitutes, nor heretics, nor revolutionaries, and so on. To account for their deviance, only one explanation is left—they are mentally ill (Scheff, 1966). Seen in this light, mental disorder is not a condition that is inherent in the individual; instead, it depends upon how the individual is seen by others. According to this position, madness (like beauty) is in the eye of the beholder.

THE EVIDENCE ON THE ROLE OF LABELING

Cross-cultural comparisons What evidence supports the labeling theory? One line of argument comes from the study of different cultures. There is no doubt that what is deviant in one culture is not necessarily deviant in another. The Kwakiutl Indian who burns valuable blankets at a potlatch ceremony to shame his rivals is honored by his fellow chiefs; the Los Angeles executive who decides to dynamite his speedboat and swimming pool to prove that he can afford to do so is quietly sent off to a private sanitorium. To labeling theorists this suggests that what is meant by *mental disorder* is entirely relative to the culture and is therefore essentially arbitrary.

This point does not follow. Even if it were true that all mental disorders are culturally determined, this would not prove that these disorders are caused by labeling. Such a result might support the notion that the disorders are psychogenic and are somehow caused by the cultural pattern. But this is quite different from the statement that the disorder does not really exist except as a label attached by others.

In any case, there is good evidence that shows that there is less cultural relativism in psychiatric matters than is sometimes supposed. To be sure, some kinds of disorders may be more prevalent in a given culture. An example is hysteria, which appears to be much less common today than it was in the nineteenth century; according to some authors this is because of a less restrictive family atmosphere and more permissive child-rearing, especially in sexual areas (Chodoff, 1954). But the fact that some disorders may be culturally determined does not prove that all disorders are. The best evidence suggests that schizophrenia and bipolar affective disorders are found throughout the world. As we have seen, the symptom patterns of schizophrenia have been observed among Greenland Eskimoes and West African villagers, as well as among ourselves.

Being sane in insane places   Proponents of labeling theory often appeal to the results of a study by David Rosenhan to support their position. Rosenhan arranged to have himself and seven other normal persons admitted as patients to various psychiatric hospitals across the country. Each pseudopatient came to the hospital admissions office with the same complaint—he or she heard voices that said "empty," "hollow," or "thud." They employed a pseudonym and sometimes misrepresented their professions, but in all other respects they reported their own life histories and their true present circumstances. All pseudopatients were admitted to the psychiatric ward, all but one with the diagnosis of schizophrenia. Once on the ward, the pseudopatients' behavior was completely normal. They said that they no longer heard voices and that they felt perfectly fine.

There was not a single case in which a hospital staff member detected the deception. The fact that pseudopatients behaved quite normally did not help, for whatever they did was generally interpreted in line with the original diagnosis. For example, all of the pseudopatients took extensive notes. At first, they did so surreptitiously, but they soon found out that there was no need for circumspection. The note-taking was seen as just one further manifestation of the disorder. A typical nurse's report read, "Patient engaged in writing behavior." No one ever asked what was written and why; presumably it was an aspect of being schizophrenic.

Once labeled in this way, the pseudopatients suffered much the same neglect that was the lot of the other patients. They felt depersonalized and powerless. They received many pills (which they flushed down the toilet), but had little access to members of the professional staff. Their average daily contact with psychiatrists, psychologists, residents, and physicians combined was 6.8 minutes.

Prior to the study, all of the pseudopatients had agreed that they would try to get discharged without outside help by convincing the hospital staff that they were sane, but without admitting the original deception. They found that it was easier to get in than out. On the average, it took nineteen days; in one case, it took fifty-two. When they were finally discharged, it was with the diagnosis "Schizophrenia, in remission." In lay terms, this means that there are no symptoms, at least for now. The validity of the original diagnosis was never questioned (Rosenhan, 1973).

The Rosenhan findings paint an unflattering picture of current conditions in mental hospitals and add legitimate fuel to social protests and cries for reform. They also show that a diagnostic label may reinforce a preexisting conception of what a patient is like. But do they really show that the distinction between sane and insane depends *only* upon the label and that mental illness is a myth?

The answer is no. Consider the situation from the psychiatrist's point of view. A patient had auditory hallucinations on entering the hospital. This symptom promptly disappears. What are the psychiatrists to do? The idea of deception never occurs to them. (After all, who would be paranoid enough to suspect that it was all part of a psychological experiment?) Under the circumstances, they must conclude that the patient is or was suffering from some psychotic disorder, probably schizophrenia, and should be kept under further observation. The fact that the patient's later acts are interpreted in terms of the original diagnosis is now quite understandable. He did hear voices a few days ago, so his present sanity is probably more apparent than real. Seen in this light, the psychiatrists' acts don't seem all that irrational (Wishner, 1974).

MENTAL ILLNESS AS MENTAL REBIRTH

A rather different approach to mental disorder, and especially to schizophrenia, is associated with the Scottish psychiatrist, R. D. Laing. Laing does not believe that schizophrenia is a *dis*order. On the contrary, he regards it as in some ways preferable to what we ordinarily call normality. His thesis is as old as Western literature: The sane are mad, and the mad are sane. He argues that what we call normality is a web of hypocracies and contradictions which stunt our potential for self-awareness and genuine love: "By the time the new human being is fifteen or so, we are left with a being like ourselves, a half-crazed creature more or less adjusted to a mad world. This is normality in our present age" (Laing, 1967, p. 58).

In Laing's view, schizophrenia is not a *mal*function, is not a reflection of a pathology. It is rather a kind of "voyage of self-discovery," at least for some patients, which represents an attempt to heal the wounds a sick society has inflicted on them. Laing therefore believes that schizophrenics don't need therapy in any of the traditional forms that psychiatry has to offer. They may, however, need compassionate understanding as well as guidance on the journey into their own inner life. To provide these, Laing and his associates set up a special haven in an old house in London where therapists and patients lived and worked together as equal members of a democratically run commuinity. Laing feels he helped many of those who came to live there, but his claims have been criticized on several counts. Among other things, his patients seem to have been primarily reactive schizophrenics. The prognosis for such cases is quite good regardless of which therapy is used; in fact, they often get better without any therapy at all.

But whether Laing's treatment works or not, there is another issue: his belief that schizophrenia is not a pathological condition but an attempt at a mental rebirth. This suggests that schizophrenia is in some ways a desirable state. But schizophrenics do not seem to think that it is. Those who recover sufficiently to tell us about their experience in retrospect leave little doubt that they felt in desperate straits—they did not think of themselves as intrepid Marco Polos exploring some inner space.

The romantic view of mental disorder *The idea that madness makes a person better, or purer, or confers a deeper understanding of the world, has a long history in Western thought. One example is Cervantes' Don Quixote who tilted with windmills but was more kindly and noble than the sane people around him. (Engraving by Gustave Dore, courtesy the Bettmann Archive)*

703

Some critics have likened Laing's view of schizophrenia to the romanticizing of tuberculosis in a prior era. Many nineteenth-century plays and operas featured ethereal, consumptive heroines who were spiritually purified by their suffering and proclaimed their undying love for the hero while gently expiring at the end of Act V. But in fact, tuberculosis is not a romantic condition; it is a slow, insidious, ugly killer, now fortunately robbed of its horror because physicians learned to understand it as an illness and then went about the unromantic business of finding its cure (Siegler and Osmond, 1974). Much the same is true for schizophrenia. No amount of romantic prose can change the fact that it is a scourge. Perhaps the next few decades will lead to its elimination through the discovery of a definite cure.

SOCIAL DEVIANCE

It is rather ironic that the sociological critics of the pathology model have concentrated most of their fire on a mental disorder which the pathology model handles reasonably well, namely schizophrenia. A similar critique might have found more appropriate targets had it been directed at certain other diagnostic categories that also huddle under the psychiatric umbrella. The psychiatric classification system includes a number of human conditions that are certainly deviant and usually undesirable, such as antisocial personality, alcoholism, drug addiction, and various sexual deviations. But it is by no means clear that all of these are really mental disorders. Nor is it clear that the pathology model is the most appropriate framework within which they should be viewed.

Society calls some forms of deviance criminal while calling others mad and it has set up institutions to deal with each—the judicial system for the first and the mental health system for the second. In actual fact, the two classifications overlap and both shade off into normality. As Figure 17.16 shows, there are

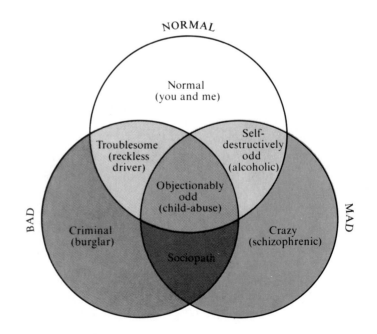

17.16   The three labels, BAD, MAD, and NORMAL, and their areas of overlap   (After Stone, 1975)

some people who occupy a gray area between normality and lawlessness. An example might be a person who is a habitual reckless driver. Others are on the boundary between mental disorder and normality. An example would be a man with a serious drinking problem. Still others are in the region of overlap between criminality and mental disorder. They are somehow both mad and bad at the same time. Our present concern is with one such group of individuals, the so-called *antisocial personalities* or, as they have also been called, *sociopaths.* *

THE SOCIOPATH

The clinical picture   The sociopath is an individual who gets into continual trouble with others and with society. He is grossly selfish, callous, impulsive, and irresponsible. His—or, somewhat less frequently, her—difficulties generally start with truancy from school, runaway episodes, and a "wild adolescence" marked by belligerence and precocious sexual experience and promiscuity (Robins, 1966). Later on there are various minor scrapes which often escalate into increasingly serious legal and social offenses. But the distinguishing characteristics of sociopathy go deeper than this. One feature is the lack of any genuine feeling of love or loyalty for any person or any group. Another characteristic is that there is relatively little guilt or anxiety. As a result, the sociopath is a creature of the present whose primary object is to gratify the impulses he feels now, with little concern about the future and even less remorse about the past.

All of this is another way of saying that sociopaths are not truly socialized. They are not pack animals; they are genuine loners. They are often quite adept at the outward skills of social living; they are frequently charming and of greater than average intelligence. In these regards, sociopaths are quite different from ordinary criminals and delinquents. These too are in conflict with established society, but unlike sociopaths, they generally have a society of their own, such as a juvenile gang or a crime syndicate, whose code they try to honor and to which they have some sense of loyalty.

Another contrast is that between sociopaths and neurotics. Most neurotics are overcontrolled. They are guilt-ridden, anxious, and unable to express their impulses except in devious, roundabout ways. The sociopath on the other hand is undercontrolled and readily yields to the fleeting impulse of the moment (McCord and McCord, 1964). An illustration is the case of a forty-four-year-old man:

> [Roger] was reared in a well-to-do family, the only child of a doting mother. In the past ten years, Roger squandered a substantial inheritance and was beginning to "fall on hard times." Handsome, well-educated and suave in manner, he had always been skillful in charming and exploiting others, especially women. Faced with economic adversity, Roger allied himself with a group of stock promoters involved in selling essentially worthless shares of "sure-bet" Canadian mining stock. This led to other "shady deals"; and in time Roger became a full-fledged "love swindler" who intrigued, lived off, and "borrowed" thousands of dollars from a succession of wealthy and "lonely" mistresses (Millon, 1969, p. 434).

* An earlier designation was *psychopath.* Some versions of this term are still in current use. An example is the MMPI scale which attempts to measure *psychopathic deviance.*

705

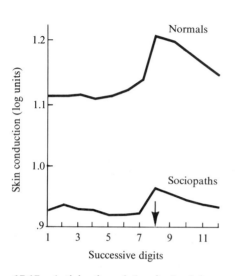

17.17   Anticipation of electric shock in normals and sociopaths   *Normals and sociopaths were repeatedly presented with a series of 12 consecutive digits from 1 to 12. Whenever the digit 8 appeared, the subjects suffered an electric shock. To determine whether there were any differences in anticipatory anxiety prior to the advent of shock, the galvanic skin response (GSR) was measured. The results are shown in units of log conductance (a measure of GSR activity) for each of the 12 digits in the series. The sociopaths showed a much lower base-response level. In addition, they showed less anticipatory reaction to the digits just prior to the critical digit. (After Hare, 1965)*

Some possible causes of sociopathy   What accounts for the inadequate socialization that characterizes sociopaths? A number of investigators have focused on the sociopath's lack of concern about the future consequences of his actions. Sociopaths are comparatively fearless. This is especially true when the danger is far off. One investigator told sociopaths and normals that they would receive a shock at the end of a ten-minute period. The subjects' apprehensiveness was assessed by their galvanic skin response (GSR). As the time grew closer, the control subjects grew increasingly nervous. In contrast, the sociopaths showed little anticipatory fear (Lippert and Senter, 1966). If future pain had just as little import when the sociopath was young, his inadequate socialization becomes partially comprehensible. Whoever tried to teach him the don'ts of childhood had no effective deterrents (Figure 17.17).

The strange fearlessness of sociopaths has been observed by several writers who have noted their "extraordinary poise," their "smooth sense of physical being," and their "relative serenity" under conditions that would produce agitation in most of us (Cleckley, 1964). How does this difference between sociopaths and normals come about? Several investigators believe that there is a difference in some underlying physiological functions. One line of evidence concerns the EEG (electrical recordings from the brain; see Chapter 3). It appears that a fairly high proportion of sociopaths have abnormal EEGs which resemble those of children. One possible interpretation is that this cortical immaturity of sociopaths is the physiological counterpart of their essential childishness—their desire for instant gratification and their belligerent tantrums when thwarted.

Another hypothesis is that the sociopath is cortically underaroused, as if he were not fully awake under normal conditions (see Chapter 3). Proponents of this hypothesis argue that because of this underarousal, sociopaths actively seek stimulation—they court thrills and danger to rouse themselves to some optimal level of stimulation, much as the rest of us might pinch our arms to keep ourselves from dozing off (Hare, 1970).

Such physiological differences suggest that there may be a constitutional predisposition toward sociopathy. This predisposition may well be genetic, as shown by the fact that identical twins have higher concordance rates on sociopathy than fraternal twins. Early environment also plays a role. There is considerable evidence that sociopaths are more likely to have a sociopathic or alcoholic father than are normals (Figure 17.18). An additional factor is dis-

17.18   Sociopaths' perceptions of their fathers   *Sociopaths and normals were asked to describe the concept "my father" by reference to a series of bipolar adjectives (such as good-bad, weak-strong). The figure shows that sociopaths evaluated their fathers much more negatively than normal controls. (After Marks, 1965)*

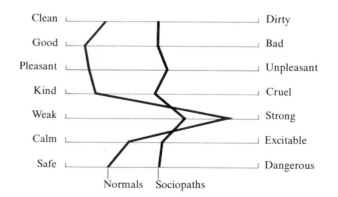

cipline; inconsistent discipline in childhood or no discipline at all correlates with sociopathy in adulthood (Robins, 1966).

Sociopathy and the pathology model By now, we are starting to get some understanding of how sociopathy might come about. But does that justify our calling it a mental disorder? Put another way, does this mean that the pathology model applies to this condition? There is some doubt whether it really does. In what sense is sociopathy a mental disorder? To be sure, the sociopath often comes to grief, but so do ordinary criminals and for the same reason: they get caught. Why should we call the one mad and the other bad? Why should one be the province of the mental-health system while the other is the business of the courts?

The question is especially pertinent given the fact that many modern psychiatrists and psychologists are pessimistic about the possibility of therapy for sociopaths. An additional difficulty is caused by problems of differential diagnosis, for in actual practice it is by no means easy to distinguish criminals and sociopaths. Under the circumstances, it is not obvious what is gained by classifying sociopathy as a psychiatric condition. To be sure, there is some evidence that the sociopath is a distinctive kind of person with a particular set of factors that make him so. But then so is the ordinary criminal. It is also true that sociopathy is an undesirable condition—if not for the sociopath himself, then for those around him. But so again is ordinary criminality.

SOME CONTRIBUTIONS OF LABELING THEORY

Sociopathy is only one of the questionable categories in the psychiatric catalogue. Similar questions can be raised about drug addiction or alcoholism or a number of other deviant patterns. Are these really mental disorders in the sense in which schizophrenia and obsessive-compulsive neurosis are? By stretching the meaning of the term so wide as to include virtually all forms of human behavior that cause personal unhappiness, psychopathologists court the danger of proving their critics right after all. When defined so broadly, mental illness may indeed become the myth that Szasz has claimed it to be.

The imperialism of modern psychopathology that makes it continually try to subsume more conditions is not the fault of an overambitious psychiatric establishment. Instead, it is the product of a society that insists on quick and simple solutions. We think that by designating a given human or social problem a *mental disorder* we have somehow taken a stride toward its solution. But we've really done nothing of the sort. For calling a problem—alcoholism, sexual exhibitionism, drug addiction, or whatever—a psychiatric disorder does not necessarily make it so. Nor does it mean that we therefore know what to do about it.

Critics like Thomas Szasz and R. D. Laing may have overstated their cases against the pathology model, but they have nevertheless performed several vital functions. One comes from their insistence on the social role of labeling. This provides a constant reminder that terms such as *schizophrenia* are not merely diagnostic categories. In many cases, they are also applied as stigmatizing labels that impede the patient's path to recovery and make his eventual return to the community difficult and frightening (Bernheim and Lewine, 1979). A related contribution of labeling theory is that it serves as a brake against the tendency to apply the term *mental disorder* to more and more forms of deviancy. These critics of the pathology model have also served as watchdogs against various forms of psychiatric tyranny. In this capacity, they have pointed to certain abuses that grow out of civil commitment procedures and they have raised public concern about the far from optimum conditions that still prevail in many mental hospitals.

As we have seen, Szasz and Laing are primarily interested in patients diagnosed as schizophrenics. But their humane concerns apply with even greater force to several other groups. Examples are patients who are said to suffer from **senile dementia** and related problems of aging. While many such patients in mental hospitals have trouble in remembering recent events and experience disorientation, their main difficulties often lie elsewhere. As one writer put it in describing a 1966 court decision:

> The superintendent of St. Elizabeth's at the time testified that "only 50 percent of the patients ... require hospitalization in a mental institution" and that "for many older patients, the primary need was found to be for physical rather than psychiatric care." ... Nor was this need well met at the hospital. The court recognized that long-term hospitalization debilitates patients, and that the last thing an aged person needs is the depersonalization of a large institution, further isolation, loss of dignity, and boredom" (Stone, 1975, p. 172).

Less frequent now, but fairly common a few decades ago, is the institutionalization of another group of persons who have even less business in a mental hospital but who were put there nevertheless. These were deaf people who do not speak. Today we know that the deaf can communicate perfectly well by means of sign language if they are in the company of other deaf people. In fact, if there is no such community, they sometimes invent a sign system of their own (see Chapter 10). But until recently, they were regarded as mutes and "dummies," as people who were retarded or mentally disordered, and who were therefore often placed in special institutions. Once there, their fate was even worse than in the outside world; their inability to speak was seen as further proof that they were mentally defective. Given the label, they were treated accordingly. One report tells of a deaf child who was in a mental institution for 5 years before he was finally recognized for what he was and released (Vernon and Brown, 1964; Sullivan and Vernon, 1979).

THE SCOPE OF PSYCHOPATHOLOGY

We have seen that an enormous range of conditions are encompassed within psychiatric classification schemes. Most of these conditions cause personal distress and some impair social functioning. But what else do they have in common? Some are somatogenic disorders while others seem to be psychogenic. Still others are in a murky borderland between criminality and psychopathology, or between normality and psychopathology. Still others may simply be deviant behavior patterns that our own society doesn't approve of. But since they are all categories of the same psychiatric classification scheme, they must have something in common. What exactly is it?

There is really only one answer. What all of these conditions share is that they are all dumped into the lap of the same group of mental-health professionals who are then told, "They are your responsibility. You take care of them. If at all possible, you cure or treat or rehabilitate them. If you can't, then confine them. But whatever you do or don't do, they are yours." In a way this is very similar to what our ancestors did when they threw criminals, ne'er-do-wells, seniles, psychotics, neurotics, and political dissenters into the same asylum dungeons.

Under the circumstances, we must not expect to find one set of principles that accounts for all conditions that psychopathologists deal with. There may be some principles that underlie schizophrenia, some others that underlie neurosis, still others for drug addiction, and so on. But these principles may very well be quite different. For the simple fact is that the field of psychopathology is not a scientifically coherent enterprise. Its coherence comes from a social need that asks that a certain set of problems be taken care of. But these problems are very heterogeneous and so the same conceptual and curative models will almost surely not apply to all.

Summary

1. The field of *psychopathology,* which is sometimes called *abnormal psychology,* deals with a wide assortment of behavioral conditions that generally cause considerable anguish and seriously impair the person's functioning. Examples are cases of *neurosis,* in which contact with reality is maintained, and *psychosis,* in which it often is not.

2. In certain periods of history, mental disorder was seen as a form of demonic possession. In others, as in our own, it was regarded as a form of illness. Some of these disorders are *somatogenic,* being the result of a bodily malfunction. An example is *general paresis,* which was discovered to result from a syphilitic infection contracted years before. Other mental disorders are thought to be *psychogenic,* resulting from psychological rather than organic causes, a view which seemed to apply to many cases of neurosis, especially *hysteria.*

3. A very general conception of the cause of mental disorder is the *pathology model* which states that mental disorder is analogous to an organic disease. A given disorder has various *symptoms* which often form a pattern or *syndrome;* these are the bases for diagnosis and classification. The symptom patterns are thought to result from some underlying and relatively immediate cause, the pathology. This in turn is often produced by more remote causes, including various predispositions and precipitating triggers. As here formulated, the pathology model is largely descriptive and makes no assertions about the nature of the symptoms, their psychogenic or somatogenic causes, or of the appropriate mode of treatment. This is in contrast to the so-called *medical model,* a more restricted version of the pathology model, which assumes that the underlying pathology is organic and recommends largely somatic forms of treatment administered by physicians.

4. One of the most serious conditions in the realm of psychopathology is *schizophrenia.* Its main symptoms are disorders of thought and attention, social withdrawal, disruption of emotional responding, and in many cases, the construction of a private world accompanied by *delusions* and *hallucinations.* Psychiatrists often distinguish among four subtypes of *schizophrenia: hebephrenia, catatonia, paranoid schizophrenia,* and the *simple type.* A more recent distinction is between *reactive* schizophrenia in which the symptoms develop suddenly, and *process* schizophrenia, in which the onset is very gradual.

709

5. One question about the pathology is how best to characterize the schizophrenic's underlying psychological malfunction. Many authors believe that it is fundamentally a disorder of thought, based on an inability to focus mentally in space and time. A different question concerns the cause of this psychological deficit. This is widely believed to be an expression of an organic pathology. Evidence comes from studies which show that the incidence of what appears to be schizophrenia is roughly the same in different cultures, from genetic studies which show that it has a substantial heredity component, and from the fact that a certain class of drugs, the *phenothiazines,* have a specific therapeutic effect on schizophrenic symptoms.

6. Exactly what the underlying organic pathology of schizophrenia is—assuming that there is one—is still unknown. According to one hypothesis, the critical malfunction is an oversensitivity to *dopamine,* a neurotransmitter that has an arousing function in the brain. Supporting evidence derives from the therapeutic effect of the phenothiazines, which are known to block dopamine at neuron synapses.

7. More remote causes of schizophrenia include a genetic factor. The evidence is provided by *concordance* studies of identical and fraternal twins and by studies of children of schizophrenic mothers adopted shortly after birth. But this genetic factor is only a predisposition; its conversion into the actual schizophrenic disorder depends on some precipitating environmental stress. Some investigators believe that the critical environmental factors include socioeconomic class. Others emphasize various pathological interactions within the family, including confusing patterns of communication such as the *double bind.*

8. In another group of conditions, *affective disorders,* the dominant disturbance is one of mood, as in the frenzied energy of *mania* or the despair and lethargy of *depression.* Affective disorders are generally periodic, and may be *bipolar,* with recurrent swings from one emotional extreme to the other, or *unipolar,* in which the mood extreme is of one kind only, generally depression. According to one view, affective disorders, especially the bipolar ones, are produced by an organic pathology, a belief bolstered by evidence that such conditions have a genetic component. One hypothesis has it that there is a defect in the supply of certain neurotransmitters, the *catecholamines.* Other investigators stress the role of psychogenic factors, such as cognitive outlook, especially in cases of *reactive depression.* An influential example of a psychogenic approach is the *learned helplessness theory* of depression.

9. In still another class of disorders, the *neuroses,* both the main symptoms and the underlying pathology are primarily psychological. Examples include *phobia, anxiety hysteria, obsessive-compulsive neurosis, conversion hysteria,* and various *dissociative states* including cases of *multiple personality.* Many practitioners believe that the symptoms of neurosis are either anxiety or learned reactions to ward off anxiety.

10. In *psychophysiological conditions,* psychogenic causes have genuinely organic consequences. Examples are *essential hypertension* and *psychophysiological ulcers.* Hypertension is evidently a residue of continual sympathetic arousal brought about by chronic emotional stress.

11. A contemporary critique of the pathology model takes a *sociological perspective,* emphasizing the fact that those whom society calls "mad" are socially *deviant.* This position has led to *labeling theory,* a view which finds some—controversial—support from studies of *pseudopatients.* An extreme version of labeling theory was proposed by Szasz who holds that mental illness is a myth. A related conception is Laing's, who goes further and regards certain disorders such as schizophrenia as voyages of mental rediscovery. The evidence suggests that while labeling may make a patient's condition worse, it has little bearing on how it arose in the first place, nor does it undermine the view that many mental disorders reflect genuine pathologies.

12. The problem of defining psychopathology is especially acute for conditions such as *sociopathy* in which the deviance overlaps mental disorder and criminality. The causes of sociopathy are still unknown; hypotheses include cortical immaturity, a chronic state of underarousal that leads to attempts to seek continued stimulation, and a genetic predisposition.

13. Labeling theory has made some important contributions by pointing to various abuses in psychiatric commitment procedures. It has also called attention to many questionable categories in the psychiatric catalogue whose status as mental disorders is highly debatable, including drug addiction, alcoholism, and *senile dementia.*

CHAPTER 18

Psychopathology: Treatment

What can be done about mental disorders? There is no scarcity of proposed remedies, each with its adherents. Some rely on biological interventions such as drugs. Others approach the condition at the psychological level; the classical example is psychoanalysis. Unfortunately, the proven accomplishments are thus far relatively modest. In a way, this is hardly surprising. Considering that we know so little about the causes of the various mental disorders, can we expect to know much more about their cures?

Somatic Therapies

One approach to treatment is through various manipulations of the body. Such *somatic therapies* constitute medicine's classical attack on any disease. Thus, once mental disorder was cast as an illness, it was only natural to try to heal it with the traditional tools of the physician's trade. But in fact, until fairly recently, most such attempts were unsuccessful. In some cases, the would-be cures were worse than the disease. We already mentioned a very early example: trephining, the removal of sections of the skull, a prehistoric practice that persisted into medieval times. Other early procedures involved a relentless succession of bloodlettings and purgatives, all in the hope of restoring a proper harmony among the bodily humors. Later developments were hardly milder. For example, Benjamin Rush (1745–1813), one of the signers of the Declaration of Independence and the acknowledged father of American psy-

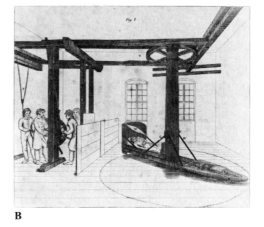

A

B

C

18.1 Early methods for treating mental disorder *(A) A crib for violent patients. (Courtesy Historical Pictures Service) (B) A centrifical-force bed. (Courtesy National Library of Medicine) (C) A swinging device. (Courtesy Culver Pictures)*

chiatry, dunked patients into hot or cold water and kept them under just short of drowning, or twirled them on special devices at speeds that often led to unconsciousness (Figure 18.1). Such methods were said to reestablish the balance between bodily and mental functions. They almost certainly had no such salutary effects, although they were probably welcomed by hospital attendants since such methods undoubtedly terrified the inmates and thus helped to "keep order" (Mora, 1975).

DRUG THERAPIES

The bleak outlook for somatic therapy did not appreciably brighten until the beginning of this century. The first step was the conquest of general paresis, a progressive deterioration of physical and psychological functioning, by an attack on the syphilitic infection that caused it (see Chapter 17). But the major breakthrough came only during the last thirty years or so with the discovery of a number of drugs that seemed to control, or at least to alleviate, schizophrenia and affective disorders.

MAJOR PSYCHIATRIC DRUGS

Antischizophrenic drugs As already noted, a widely used agent in combatting schizophrenia is **chlorpromazine** which belongs to the family of drugs called **phenothiazines** (see Chapter 17). Chlorpromazine and some of its pharmacological relatives tend to reduce many of the major symptoms of schizophrenia, such as thought disorder, withdrawal, and hallucinations. The impact of these antischizophrenic drugs (together with drugs aimed at affective disorders) upon psychiatric practice has been enormous. In 1955, there were about 560,000 patients in the mental hospitals of the United States; about half of these were schizophrenics. Based on the rate at which that population had increased prior to 1955, a reasonable projection for 1970 was about 738,000. But the actual figure for 1970 was 340,000, less than half of that estimate. One reason for this was the psychiatric revolution produced by the new drugs which appeared during the mid-fifties. These drugs made it possible to dis-

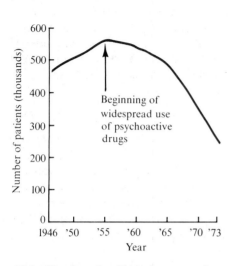

18.2 *Number of residents in state and local government mental hospitals between 1946 and 1973 in the United States* *(After Davis and Cole, 1975)*

charge schizophrenic patients more quickly than ever before, with average hospital stays of about two months. The result was a drastic reduction in the total hospital population (Figure 18.2).*

It has sometimes been argued that drugs like chlorpromazine are not really antischizophrenic agents at all, but merely fancy sedatives that quiet patients down. This position does not square with the facts. While chlorpromazine and other phenothiazines alleviate schizophrenic symptoms, such powerful sedatives as phenobarbital have no such effect. Furthermore, the antischizophrenic drugs seem to improve the behavior both of patients who are highly agitated and of those who are apathetic and withdrawn; they calm the frenzy of the first and help bring the second out of their stupor. Still other evidence suggests that the phenothiazines have a *specific drug effect.* They work on the symptoms that characterize schizophrenia but not on symptoms that are not specific to that disorder. For example, they help to clear up the patient's disordered thought but have little effect on depression or anxiety. It is thus hardly surprising that chlorpromazine and other phenothiazines do not calm down normals or anxious neurotics (Davis and Cole, 1975).

Antidepressants Shortly after the introduction of the antischizophrenic agents, several other drugs were found that acted as *antidepressants.* An example is *imipramine,* which belongs to the family of drugs called *tricyclic antidepressants.* Just as the phenothiazines are not mere sedatives, so the tricyclics are not mere stimulants; they appear to have a specific effect on depression. Evidence comes from the fact that imipramine and related drugs do not produce euphoria in normals; they evidently have little effect on mood if there is no depression to begin with (Cole and Davis, 1975).

Lithium A more recent development is the use of *lithium carbonate* in the treatment of mania. Manic patients are said to show remarkable improvement within five to ten days after starting lithium therapy. According to some authors, the drug can counteract both manic and depressive episodes in bipolar affective disorders (see Chapter 17). Perhaps most important is the possibility that in such patients the drug acts to prevent future episodes of either mania or depression, though the evidence is as yet far from conclusive (Fieve, 1975).

EVALUATING A DRUG

How can we assess the effectiveness of a drug? We will consider how this is done in detail, for some of the issues raised by drug evaluation methods are not limited to tests of drug therapy. In principle, they apply to the evaluation of any therapeutic procedure whatever, including psychotherapy.

Suppose we want to find out whether a given drug, say, chlorpromazine, has the curative effects its advocates claim. The most obvious approach is to administer the drug to a group of schizophrenic patients for some period and then make a before-and-after assessment. In fact, many of the clinical studies reported in the literature are of just this kind. But a little reflection shows that this procedure is not adequate.

---

* Another factor was a change in social policy, prompted in part by economic considerations, which stressed discharge rather than long-term hospitalization.

Controlling for spontaneous improvement   One problem with the simple before-and-after test is that it ignores the possibility that the patient's condition would have cleared up without treatment, whether permanently or just for a while. Such spontaneous improvements occur in many disorders. To control for this factor one has to compare two groups of patients drawn from the same population. One group would receive the drug for, say, six weeks; a control group would not. Both groups would be judged at the start and the end of the study (and perhaps during periods in between). Initially, they ought to be equivalent. The question is whether they will be judged to be different when the six weeks are up.

Controlling for placebo effects   Suppose that after six weeks the patients who were given chlorpromazine seem to be less disoriented and withdrawn than the untreated controls. The fact that the untreated control group improved less or not at all rules out the possibility that this change for the better was produced by spontaneous improvement. So can we now conclude that the lessening of schizophrenic symptoms was caused by the drug as such? The answer is no, for we have not controlled for the possibility that the result is a so-called **placebo effect.**

In medicine, the term *placebo* refers to some inert (that is, medically neutral) substance that is administered to a patient who believes that this substance has certain therapeutic powers, although it actually has none. Numerous studies have shown that, given this belief, a sizable proportion of patients suffering from many disorders will show some kind of improvement after ingesting what are actually sugar pills or receiving injections of harmless salt solutions. Such placebo effects probably account for many of the cures of ancient physicians whose medications included such items as crocodile dung, swine teeth, and moss scraped from the skull of a man who died a violent death (Shapiro, 1971).

Given the power of the placebo effect, how can we be sure that the improvement in the drug-treated group of our example is caused by the properties of the drug itself? Perhaps a sugar pill—or a bit of crocodile dung—would have done as well. To rule out this possibility, we must administer a placebo to the control patients. They will thus no longer be "untreated." On the contrary, they will receive the same attention, will be told the same thing, and will be given the same number of pills at the same time as the patients in the true drug group. There will be only one difference between the two groups: the control patients will swallow pills that, unbeknownst to them, contain only inert materials. As a result of this stratagem, we achieve simultaneous control for two factors—spontaneous improvement and placebo effects. Now that these two factors are controlled, a difference in the way the two groups appear after treatment can finally be attributed to the effect of the drug itself. Figure 18.3 shows the results of such a study, comparing the effects of chlorpromazine and a placebo control after 1, 3, and 6 weeks of treatment. As the figure shows, chlorpromazine is clearly superior. But as the figure also shows, some slight improvement is found in the placebo group as well, thus highlighting the need for such a control in the evaluation of drug effectiveness.

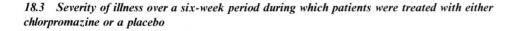

18.3   *Severity of illness over a six-week period during which patients were treated with either chlorpromazine or a placebo*

Controlling for the doctor's expectations By definition, a placebo control implies that all of the patients in the group think that they are being treated with the real drug. But to guarantee this desired state of ignorance, the doctors—and the nurses and attendants—must also be kept in the dark about who is getting a placebo and who the real drug, for the true information may affect their ratings of the patients' progress. If they believe in the drug's effectiveness, they may exaggerate signs of improvement in members of the drug-treated group.

The staff members' knowledge may also have a more indirect effect. They may unwittingly communicate it to the patients, perhaps by observing the drug-treated ones more closely or by being less concerned if a placebo-treated patient fails to take her morning pill. By such signals, the patients may find out whether the doctors expect them to get better or not. If so, there is no genuine placebo control. To guard against such confounding effects of expectation, modern drug evaluators use the ***double-blind technique*** in which neither the staff members nor the patients know who is assigned to which group. The only ones who know are the investigators who run the study.

LIMITATIONS OF DRUG THERAPY

The preceding discussion may have suggested that present-day psychiatric drugs are an unqualified boon which provide a definitive cure for schizophrenia or affective disorders. At least as yet, this is not the case. To begin with, these drugs can have side-effects. For example, phenothiazines may produce various disruptions of autonomic functioning that range from chronic dryness of the mouth to blurred vision, difficulty in urination, and cardiac irregularities. In addition, there are sometimes disturbances of posture and involuntary movement, with symptoms such as tremors, a shuffling gait, and a curiously inexpressive, masklike face. Individuals react differently to the drugs. For some, the side-effects are great, for others only minimal.

These side-effects can be regarded simply as a kind of cost exacted by the use of the drugs. But how great are the drugs' benefits? Critics of drug therapy contend that currently the beneficial results of drug therapy are still rather limited. This is especially so for the antischizophrenic drugs. To be sure, the phenothiazines have made it possible to discharge schizophrenic patients much sooner than in predrug days. But this doesn't mean that these patients are fully cured. For one thing, they have to stay on a ***maintenance dose*** of the drug outside of the hospital, which they often prefer not to do, given the drug's unpleasant side-effects. If they discontinue taking the drug, they may relapse. But even with a maintenance dose, there is no guarantee that the discharged patients will become normal members of the community. This is especially unlikely for patients whose social adjustment was poor before they developed psychotic symptoms. Such patients will probably make only a marginal adjustment to the external world. The picture is brighter for drug therapy of the affective disorders, especially in the case of lithium treatment. But even here patients must usually be kept on a maintenance dose and the cure is not always complete.

Despite these limitations, modern drug therapies do represent a major step forward. They have restored some patients to normal functioning and have allowed those who would otherwise have spent much of their lives in hospital wards to manage, however imperfectly, in a family or community setting. No less important is the fact that these drugs—especially the phenothiazines—have completely changed the atmosphere in mental hospitals. Until a few decades ago, straitjackets were common, as were feces-smeared and shriek-filled wards; today, such things are comparatively rare because the drugs do diminish the more violent symptoms of many mental ailments. As a result, the mental hospital can function as a therapeutic center. It can provide important social and psychological services, including psychotherapy, all of which would have been unthinkable in the "snake-pit" settings of former times.

OTHER SOMATIC THERAPIES

PSYCHOSURGERY

Until the advent of the major psychiatric drugs, psychiatrists relied on several other somatic therapies, all of which involved more drastic assaults on the nervous system. Some of these consisted of brain surgery. An example is *prefrontal lobotomy,* in which the neurological connections between the thalamus and the frontal lobes are severed, in whole or in part. This operation was meant to liberate the patient's thoughts from the pathological influence of his emotions, on the dubious neurological assumption that thought and emotion are localized in the frontal lobes and the thalamus respectively.

Evaluation studies of these surgical procedures have come up with largely ambiguous results (Robbin, 1958). Furthermore, there is a serious possibility that such operations produce some impairment of higher intellectual functions, such as foresight and the ability to sustain attention. Therefore these procedures are now used only rarely in the United States. Irreversible damage to the brain is a stiff price to pay, whatever the therapeutic benefits; if one can't even be sure that such benefits exist, the price appears exorbitant (Maher, 1966).

CONVULSIVE TREATMENTS

Other attempts at somatic therapy involve the deliberate production of massive convulsive seizures. This procedure was an outgrowth of an assumption that was later found to be in error; it appeared that people with epilepsy rarely suffered from schizophrenia. This suggested that convulsions somehow counteract the psychotic process. If so, perhaps one could treat schizophrenia by inducing convulsions deliberately. Originally, this was accomplished by injecting the patient with high doses of certain drugs, such as insulin.

Today, the most widely used form of the convulsive method is *electroconvulsive shock treatment,* or *ECT*. A current of moderate intensity is passed between two electrodes attached to each side of the patient's forehead; it is applied for about half a second. The result is immediate loss of consciousness, followed by a convulsive seizure similar to that seen in epilepsy (Figure 18.4). When this treatment first came into use, patients sometimes suffered serious bruises or bone fractures while thrashing about during their convulsions. To prevent this, modern practitioners usually administer muscle relaxants prior to the treatment (Redlich and Freedman, 1966).

While ECT was originally meant as a treatment of schizophrenia, appro-

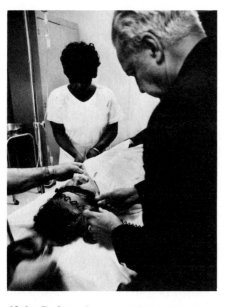

18.4 Patient about to undergo electroconvulsive shock treatment (Photograph by Paul Fusco, Magnum Photos)

priate evaluation studies soon showed that its area of primary effectiveness is depression. Here, its efficacy is considerable. It may well be more effective than imipramine and it works for a sizable proportion of patients who don't respond to any antidepressant drugs. In addition, it seems to act more quickly than the drugs usually do (Cole and Davis, 1975). But despite these advantages, physicians tend to use ECT only reluctantly. The main reason for this hesitancy is the possibility of brain damage. After all, a current intensity great enough to set off convulsions may well be sufficient to injure nervous tissue; this danger is all the greater since ECT is usually administered to the patient repeatedly (Maher, 1966). Under the circumstances, ECT is generally used only after drug therapy has failed or when there seems to be a serious chance of suicide. In the latter case, the fast-acting quality of ECT treatment may be an overriding advantage (Kalinowsky, 1975).

What accounts for the therapeutic effect of ECT? The plain fact is that we don't know. The early notion that the effect is related to epilepsy turned out to be false; but what other theory is there? One hypothesis emphasizes the role of ECT-produced amnesia: a side-effect of ECT is that the patient loses memory for events that preceded it, especially those events within a few days preceding treatment. This might have beneficial consequences, on the assumption that the lost memories are linked to guilt and anxiety. The trouble is that the therapeutic effects of ECT show up after only a few sessions, while amnesia sets in after quite a few more. Still another interpretation is that ECT affects some neurotransmitters in the brain; for example, by increasing the amount of available norepinephrine (see Chapter 3). But this, too, is little more than a speculation. As so often in medicine, ECT is used because it works even though we don't understand the reasons. In some ways, its action is reminiscent of what happens when we kick a recalcitrant TV set; the kick may help but we certainly don't know why.

Psychotherapy

Biological manipulation represents one approach to the treatment of psychopathology. But as we have already seen, there is another approach to the treatment of such disorders that forgoes all ministrations to the patient's body. Instead, it relies on psychological means alone. Such attempts to treat mental disturbance by psychological rather than somatic methods can be grouped under the general label *psychotherapy.*

There are many different schools of psychotherapy. According to one author, there were thirty-six such systems in 1959 (Harper, 1959). The chances are that this number has doubled in the interim. One difference among the schools is in their theories about the nature of psychopathology. These range from a Freudian emphasis on unconscious conflicts rooted in childhood to a humanistic concern for free will and the need to imbue life with coherent meaning to models of neurosis based on S-R theories of animal avoidance learning. No less different are the techniques of therapy which are often dictated by these different theories of psychopathology.

We will distinguish among four subtypes of psychotherapy conducted with individual patients: (1) orthodox psychoanalysis, (2) modern off-shoots of psychoanalysis, (3) behavior therapy, and (4) humanistic approaches to psychotherapy.*

CLASSICAL PSYCHOANALYSIS

Classical psychoanalysis is the method Freud developed at the start of this century. According to some writers, this technique is the ancestor of virtually all forms of modern psychotherapy, whether they acknowledge this heritage or not (London, 1964).

As we have previously seen, Freud's basic assumption was that the neurotic's ills stem from unconscious defenses against unacceptable urges that date back to early childhood. The neurotic has drawn a mental blanket over his head and is unable to see either the outer or the inner world as it really is. His symptoms are an indirect manifestation of his unconscious conflicts (see Chapter 12). To overcome his neurosis, the patient must drop the blanket, must achieve access to his buried thoughts and wishes, and gain insight into why he buried them. By so doing, he will master the internal conflicts that crippled him for so long. Once these are resolved, his symptoms will presumably wither away by themselves. In effect, Freud's prescription for the neuroses is the victory of reason over passion: "Where id was, there shall ego be."

THE RECOVERY OF UNCONSCIOUS MEMORIES

Free association The origin of psychoanalytic technique dates back to Freud's attempts to treat hysteria by helping the patient recover some emotionally charged memories (see Chapter 12). Initially, Freud and his then collaborator, Josef Breuer, probed for these memories while their patients were hypnotized. Later on it became clear that such memories could be dug up even in the normal waking state by the method of *free association.* The patient was asked to say whatever came into his mind, and sooner or later the relevant memory was likely to emerge. Various forms of *resistance,* usually unconscious, by which the patient tried to derail a given train of thought—by changing the topic, forgetting what he was about to say, and so on—often gave important clues that the patient was about to remember something he had previously tried to forget.

In popularized movie or TV versions, this dredging up of forgotten memories is often presented as the essence of psychoanalysis. The distraught heroine finally remembers a childhood scene in which she was spanked for a little sister's misdeed; suddenly a weight lifts from her shoulders, she rises from the couch reborn, is ready to face life and love serenely, and will live happily—or

---

* Many practitioners use the term *psychotherapy* to describe only a subset of the full range of psychological treatments. The problem is that these subsets are different for different writers. Freudian psychoanalysts speak of psychotherapy when they want to describe briefer, and in their view, more diluted versions of psychoanalysis. Conversely, behavior therapists use the term to embrace virtually all forms of psychological treatment that try to help patients gain insight into their own inner thoughts and wishes rather than deal with the undesirable behavior patterns by themselves. The result of these divergent usages is considerable terminological confusion. The usage here adopted treats the term as a simple nonevaluative category label that embraces all forms of psychological treatment and makes no further statements about their methods, theories, or therapeutic effectiveness (White and Watt, 1973).

at least unneurotically—ever after. But as Freud described it, what actually happens is much less dramatic. The discovery of the patient's unconscious conflicts comes bit by bit, as a memory surfaces here, a dream or a slip of the tongue suggests a meaning there, and as the analyst offers an occasional interpretation of the resistances that crop up on a given session. To help the patient see how all of these strands of her mental life are woven together is one of the analyst's main tasks.

Interpretation How does one decide whether a particular interpretation is correct? According to Freud, the best test is the patient's reaction. If she genuinely accepts it, perhaps with a sense of "Aha!" the interpretation is probably right. But many psychoanalysts contend that an interpretation is not necessarily wrong even if the patient rejects it; her "No" may simply be a sign of resistance and the very vehemence of her denial a hint that the analyst's assertion is really true. Given this "Heads, I win; tails, you lose" style of argument, how can we possibly decide?

Freud felt that there was a way. In this view, psychoanalysis is a bit like solving a jigsaw puzzle. By the time the puzzle is completed, each piece can fit into one and only one place. In a similar way, one can judge the correctness of an interpretation by noting how it fits into the overall picture (Fenichel, 1945). This analogy is interesting but not altogether convincing. Is it really true that the dreams, memories, and thoughts of a patient will make sense in one and only one arrangement?

EMOTIONAL INSIGHT

Psychoanalysts want their patients to attain insight into the motives of which they were formerly unaware, but they don't want that insight to be merely intellectual. The patient must regain access, not just to various repressed thoughts and memories, but also and more importantly, to the feelings that go along with them. Freud was emphatic that recollections without emotions have little therapeutic effect. Genuine self-discovery is only achieved when the patient rids himself of the repressive forces that had kept the insights from him, and this typically requires a good deal of emotional involvement. Without this involvement, the psychoanalytic process is an intellectual exercise rather than a therapy (Freud, 1913b).

Catharsis What would produce the necessary emotional involvement? Originally, Freud put his faith in the **catharsis** which accompanied the recovery of certain long-lost memories. When these surfaced, a host of associated emotions followed in their wake and were explosively discharged in fits of sobbing or in bursts of sharp anger. Such an emotional release is generally experienced as a kind of relief.* It turned out, however, that dramatic reactions of this kind were fairly rare. Moreover, even when they did occur, their benefits proved

---

* It is by no means clear why this should be so (or whether it always is). But right or wrong, the notion that catharsis helps goes back to antiquity. The Greeks used the term to describe both the purging of the body (by an emetic or strong laxative) and the purification of the emotions (by watching a deeply moving event, as in a tragedy on stage). In effect, they drew an analogy between indigestible foods and troubling, unexpressed emotions. They evidently believed that both ought to be expelled, as if voiding and vomiting were to the body as weeping is to the soul.

rather short-lived; after a while, the symptoms reappeared. If emotions are a necessary ingredient of analytic therapy, they have to be evoked by another means.

Transferences As Freud saw it, that means is the **transference** relationship between patient and analyst (see Chapter 12). The patient starts to respond to the analyst in increasingly personal terms. He reacts to him as he had reacted to the major figures in his own life, and he will therefore love or hate the analyst as he had loved or hated his mother, father, siblings and, more recently, his lovers and friends. All of these feelings are transferred to the analyst, as a kind of emotional reliving of the unresolved problems of the patient's childhood.

Freud argued that this transference relation can be a powerful therapeutic tool. It lets the analyst hold up a mirror to the patient, to show him how he really feels and acts toward the important people in his life. As an example, take a person who expresses violent anger at the psychiatrist, and then is immediately seized by a feeling of total terror. What is going on? A psychoanalytic interpretation is that the patient had equated the analyst with his own tyrannical father. Having transgressed against him, he could not help but expect some awful retribution. But needless to say, the analyst will not retaliate. Instead, he may say something mildly reassuring, such as "That was hard to get out, wasn't it?" After that he will probably interpret the patient's outburst and subsequent fear and will point out the discrepancy between the actual present and the long-dead past.

Through many such experiences, the patient's anxieties are gradually extinguished. The analyst's role in all of this is to serve as a temporary stand-in for the significant characters in the patient's early family drama. But he won't let himself be drawn into the play. He will let the patient say the same old lines and go through the same old motions, but he won't respond to them as the patient's father (or mother, brother, or whoever) did. The analyst's job is to let the patient see what he is really doing, what is really happening on his private stage. The effect is a gradual process of emotional reeducation.

MODERN VERSIONS OF PSYCHOANALYSIS

A sizable number of present-day psychotherapists still use techniques that bear Freud's imprint. Although some practice psychoanalysis just as Freud did, this is becoming less frequent. The majority of practitioners have modified Freud's theories and procedures in various ways. Many of them subscribe to *neo*-Freudian views; their emphasis is on interpersonal and cultural factors rather than on psychosexual development, and on the patient's problems in the present rather than on the origin of these problems in his early past (see Chapter 12). But like Freud, they believe that the key to neurosis is unconscious conflict, and that therapy requires emotional insight into these unconscious processes.

These variations on Freud's theoretical themes are accompanied by corresponding alterations of therapeutic technique. In classical analysis, sessions are scheduled for five times per week, and may continue for five or more years. This obviously restricts psychoanalysis to the affluent few, and whether it is all that beneficial even to them is debatable. According to some critics, a five-

18.5 A picture of Freud's consultation room *In classical psychoanalysis, the patient reclines on the couch while the analyst sits behind him, out of sight. Freud adopted this method to avoid influencing the patient's flow of associations by his own facial expressions. He also had a personal motive: "I cannot bear to be gazed at for eight hours a day." (Freud, 1913b; photograph by Edmund Engleman)*

times-a-week, five-years-or-more analysis can easily become a patient's last-ditch defense against getting well; she escapes from her real problems in the present by hiding in a never-ending stream of free associations about her past. In effect, she has become couch-ridden.

To counter this trend, many psychoanalytically oriented therapists are adopting a schedule of fewer sessions per week. They believe that this helps to keep the sessions from becoming routine and intellectualized (Alexander and French, 1946). Others have tried to condense the whole process into a few months or one year, sometimes by defining therapeutic goals in advance or setting definite time limits (Malan, 1963). One casualty of these modifications is that venerable instrument of Freudian orthodoxy, the psychoanalytic couch. Many practitioners have dispensed with it in favor of the simpler face-to-face interview. One reason is that a prone position encourages a feeling of dependency on the all-powerful analyst from which the patient may be hard to wean (Figure 18.5).

Yet other modifications concern the relation between what goes on in the therapist's office and what happens in the outer world. Freud believed that the crucial theater of operations is the analysis itself. He argued that it is there that the patient is shown how he reacts to the analyst, how that reaction mirrors his childhood responses to his mother or father, and how these childish patterns have been endlessly repeated in his dealings with the important figures in his later life. Once the patient gains emotional insight into these transference patterns, the beneficial results will automatically generalize to the interpersonal relations of his real-life world. But many modern therapists prefer to help the generalization along by encouraging external activities that they regard as healthy. They point out that the transference relation is an enormously valuable sort of rehearsal of how to relate to others. But they believe that this rehearsal must be followed by actual performance and that the therapist has some responsibility to help bring this performance about (Alexander and French, 1946).

BEHAVIOR THERAPY

Not all psychotherapists use techniques that are as directly affected by psychoanalytic thinking as those we have just described. The last two or three decades have seen the emergence of two major movements. Both are reactions against psychoanalysis, but for reasons that are diametrically opposed. The first is **behavior therapy** which maintains that the theoretical notions underlying psychoanalysis are vague and untestable, while its therapeutic effectiveness is a matter of doubt. The other group consists of various **humanistic therapies,** who regard psychoanalysis as too mechanistic and too rational in its approach. Freud, who had a fine sense of irony, would have been wryly amused to find himself in the middle of this two-front war in which one side accuses him of being too scientific and the other of not being scientific enough.

Behavior therapists hold that neurosis is caused by maladaptive learning and that its remedy is a form of reeducation. Taken by itself, this view is hardly original. What makes it different is that the behavior therapists take the emphasis on learning and relearning much more seriously than anyone had before them. They see themselves as applied scientists whose techniques for reeducating troubled people are adapted from principles of learning and conditioning discovered in the laboratories of such investigators as Pavlov, Thorndike, and Skinner (see Chapter 4).

Like the learning theorists to whom they trace their descent, behavior therapists have a basically tough-minded and pragmatic outlook. They emphasize overt, observable behavior rather than hypothetical underlying causes, such as unconscious thoughts and wishes, which they regard as hard to define and even harder to observe. Their concern is with what a person does, especially if it causes him distress. If so, the behavior therapists want to modify such behaviors—to get the agoraphobic over his fear of open places, to help the compulsive overcome his hand-washing rituals that threaten to rub his skin away. To accomplish these ends, behavior therapists resort to various techniques for learning and unlearning—extinction of fear responses, conditioning of incompatible reactions, or whatever. But their treatment does not include any attempt to have the patient gain insight into the origin of these neurotic symptoms. As these therapists see it, such insights into the past have no therapeutic effect even if they happen to be valid. What is wrong is the patient's behavior in the here and now, and it is this that has to be righted.

Before turning to details, there is a broader question. The principles of learning on which behavior therapeutic techniques are based are themselves derived from studies of animals. Can we be sure that the same principles apply to human beings? Behavior therapists are not seriously troubled by this issue since most of them believe that the same laws of learning apply to rats as to humans. But suppose that the laws do not apply equally across the species (as much recent evidence does in fact suggest; see Chapter 5). Behavior therapists might argue that this is irrelevant to their purposes. The main difference in the ways rats and people learn concerns complex cognitive relationships, as in playing chess or writing poetry. But according to most behavior therapists, the essence of neurotic behavior is not in its cognitive complexity. There is something irrational, and unthinking, about neurotic acts. So it may just be that the laws that account for conditioning in dogs, rats, and pigeons apply to those aspects of human behavior that seem most impervious to human reason—aspects of behavior of which neurosis is one example.

THERAPIES BASED ON CLASSICAL CONDITIONING

The major target of most behavior therapists is unrealistic fear or anxiety, as in the case of a morbid dread of heights. The basic hypothesis is that this fear is a classically conditioned response that is evoked by various eliciting stimuli such as looking down a flight of stairs or being on a rooftop (see Chapters 4 and 17). Exactly how the original conditioning took place is not our present concern. It may have been produced by a single traumatic incident or by a series of cumulative experiences. The present issue is how this connection between stimulus and fear can be broken, regardless of how it was originally forged.

Systematic desensitization   The most widely used behavior therapeutic technique for unlearning such fears is **systematic desensitization,** a procedure developed by the psychiatrist Joseph Wolpe. The basic idea is to fight the original conditioning by **counterconditioning,** to connect the stimuli that now evoke fear to a new response that is incompatible with fear and will therefore displace it (Wolpe, 1958). The competing response is usually **muscular relaxation,** a pervasive untensing of the body's musculature that is presumably incompatible with the autonomic and muscular reactions that underlie the fear response. This relaxation has to be learned. The usual method is to focus the patient's full attention on each of his major muscle groups in turn by asking him to first tense and then untense them. After several training sessions, the patient can achieve this deep-relaxation state whenever the therapist asks him to. Once this point is reached, the trick is to condition the relaxation to such fear-evoking stimuli as stairs and rooftops (Figure 18.6).

To establish the desired link between relaxation and the fear-evoking stimuli, one must somehow bring these stimuli into the behavior therapist's office. But how can this be done? Some phobics are afraid of heights, others of enclosed places, or snakes, or meeting strangers; there is no practicable way of physically presenting many of these stimuli in a clinic room. Wolpe hit on a simple alternative. He asked the patients to *imagine* these situations as vividly as possible while in deep relaxation. It turned out that such imagined encounters had enough reality for most patients to evoke a reasonable amount of anxiety (Wolpe and Lazarus, 1966).

There is another problem. The presumption is that as the link between the relaxation response and the feared stimuli gets stronger and stronger, the old fear will gradually be displaced and the phobia will be overcome. But unfortunately, things are not quite so simple. The trouble is that just as muscular relaxation competes with fear, fear competes with muscular relaxation. Since this is so, how can one get the phobic person to perform the relaxation response in the first place when the fear-evoking stimuli are around, even if only in imagination.

Wolpe's answer is a deliberate policy of gradualism. The therapist sneaks up on the fear response, step by step. The therapist first asks the patient to construct an **anxiety hierarchy** in which feared situations are arranged from least to most anxiety-provoking. The patient then starts out by imagining the

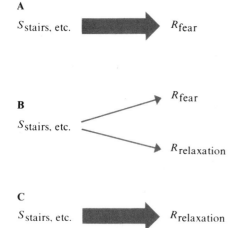

18.6   Behavior therapy through counter-conditioning   *(A) The state of affairs in phobia. Various stimuli such as flights of stairs arouse the response of fear. (B) These stimuli are conditioned to the response of relaxation. As this connection becomes stronger, the connection between the stimulus and the fear response is weakened. (C) The state of affairs when counterconditioning is complete. The relaxation response has completely displaced the old fear response.*

first scene on the hierarchy (for instance, being on the first floor of the Empire State Building). He imagines this scene while in a state of deep relaxation. He will stay with this scene—imagining it and relaxing—until he no longer feels any qualm. After this, the next scene is imagined and thoroughly counterconditioned, and so on, until the patient finally can imagine the most frightening situation of all (leaning over the railing of the observation tower above the 102nd floor) and still be able to relax.

According to Wolpe and his followers, this procedure of taking the sting out of imagined horrors carries over almost completely into the actual world. But other investigators argue that the transfer into real life is less than Wolpe claims and generally lags behind the desensitization of the images. A plausible guess is that the shift from image to actuality is not automatic but requires some active participation on the part of the patient. In effect, the patient gives himself "homework assignments" in which he actively exposes himself to progressively more fear-evoking stimulus situations in the real world.

While the desensitization method is most directly applicable to simple phobias, many behavior therapists believe that it is useful whenever anxiety is a major factor in the disorder and when the stimuli that trigger this anxiety are known. Examples are sexual disturbances such as impotence and frigidity (Brady, 1972).

Flooding   In recent years, some behavior therapists have experimented with a technique that is the very opposite of desensitization. Instead of having the patient inch his way up an anxiety hierarchy, they ask him to imagine the most fear-evoking situations from the very start. The woman with a fear of dogs must imagine herself surrounded by half a dozen snarling Dobermans; the man who is plagued by an obsessive fear of contamination that he tries to allay by endless washing rituals must imagine himself immersed in a stinking sewer. The patients are told to lose themselves in these scenes and to experience them with full emotion, an approach rather reminiscent of the cathartic method of Freud's early years. The result is that they are **flooded** with anxiety. The idea is to extinguish the conditioned link between the stimulus and the fear response. According to some theorists, this is most readily achieved if the fear response is actually evoked. Putting it another way, the trick is to have the patient become so terrified that he can see how silly his terror really is.

The proponents of this flooding procedure argue that it is considerably more efficient than desensitization, with marked improvement after fewer sessions (Stampfl and Levis, 1967). Other behavior therapists are more skeptical. They admit that the flooding technique often works as well as desensitization, but they feel that it is potentially dangerous. In the view of such critics, flooding can be much like throwing a child into a swimming pool to get him over his fear of water. It's fine if it works, but if it doesn't, the child's fear will be greater than ever before.

Aversive therapy   Another behavior therapy technique, **aversive therapy,** tries to attach negative feelings to stimulus situations that are initially very attractive so that the patient will no longer want to approach them. The object of this endeavor is to eliminate behavior patterns that both patient and therapist regard as undesirable. Examples are overeating, excessive drinking, or engaging in certain sexual deviations such as exhibitionism.

The basic procedure of aversion therapy is very simple. One pairs the stimulus that one wants to render unpleasant with some obnoxious unconditioned stimulus. An example is aversion therapy for excessive drinking. The patient takes a sip of alcohol while under the effect of a nausea-producing drug. He tastes the liquor while he desperately wants to vomit.

Whether aversive therapy works is debatable. No one doubts that it works in the therapist's office; the question is whether it is effective outside when the shocking device is no longer attached or the nausea-producing drugs are no longer administered. The evidence on this point is as yet meager (Rachman and Teasdale, 1969).

COGNITIVE THERAPY

Desensitization, flooding, and aversion treatments focus on behaviors that are more or less overt and try to modify them by techniques based on the principles of simple learning. In desensitization and flooding, the emphasis is on some external stimulus (such as heights) that is connected with anxiety, a connection the therapy tries to sever. In aversion treatment, it is on some overt response (such as excessive drinking), a response the therapy tries to eliminate. But what treatment is appropriate when the patient's problems cannot be so readily described by referring to fear-evoking stimuli or to overt, undesirable responses? There are many patients whose difficulties stem from anxiety that is triggered by their own thoughts and feelings. An example is the obsessive-compulsive whose own obsessional thoughts lead to an intense panic that can be relieved only by ever more frantic compulsive rituals. Here the critical features of the disorder derive from covert rather than overt sources: thoughts and feelings that go on "within the patient's head." How does behavior therapy handle cases such as these?

A number of therapists deal with such problems by a frontal attack on the way the patient thinks. They try to replace the patient's irrational beliefs and attitudes that caused his emotional stress by a more appropriate mode of thinking that is better in accord with reality. This general form of therapy goes under various labels; we will call all such approaches *cognitive therapy* (see Beck, 1976).

On the face of it, the goal of cognitive therapy seems similar to the psychoanalytic quest for emotional insight. But cognitive therapists see themselves as more closely allied to behavior therapy. While they make little use of conditioning principles and concentrate on what the patients think rather than on what they do overtly, their techniques share many of the characteristics of behavior therapy. They are extremely *directive.* They are primarily concerned with the patient in the here and now rather than with his history, and they focus on beliefs that affect what the patient actually does.

The basic technique of cognitive therapists is to confront the patients with the contradictions inherent in their neurotic beliefs. To accomplish this end, the therapist adopts an active, dominant role throughout the proceedings, and often gives the patient "homework assignments." Albert Ellis, one of the founders of this general approach (he calls his own method *rational-emotive psychotherapy*) asks his patients to discover the illogical phrases or sentences they say to themselves in various anxiety-provoking situations. Once these irrational conceptions are ferreted out, the patients have to tell themselves repeatedly that they are false (Ellis, 1962). The way this treatment deals with irrational thoughts indicates its close affinity to behavior therapy. A fear-evoking thought is regarded as a form of behavior: the response of saying an illogical sentence to oneself.

THERAPY AS SOCIAL EDUCATION

Most of the therapeutic techniques we have discussed thus far have goals that are essentially negative—to eliminate irrational fears, suppress unwanted behaviors, and root out illogical beliefs. These goals are certainly admirable but do they go far enough? There is no doubt that, say, agoraphobia or compulsive drinking are millstones around a person's neck. But what happens after they are removed? Is the therapist's task to help the patient find new and more appropriate behavior patterns to take the place of the unhealthy ones he has finally managed to shuck off?

Many therapists feel that the answer is yes. They point out that the neurotic's fears had kept him from learning all kinds of interpersonal skills that are by no means easy to acquire: how to conduct an initial approach to the opposite sex, how to assert oneself without being overly aggressive, and so on. These skills have to be learned and practiced in the real world, but the patient can get a modest start in the therapist's office.

A number of techniques have been developed to help the therapist conduct this tutorial course in interpersonal relations. One technique employs **graded task assignments,** in which the patient is asked to take progressively larger steps in the real-life social interactions that give him trouble. We have already discussed an application of this step-by-step approach in the treatment of phobias. Another example is training in assertiveness, which would progress from tasks like maintaining eye contact with other people to asking directions from a stranger, to complaining to a waiter about an overdone steak (Lazarus, 1971). Another technique is **modeling** in which the therapist shows the patient some effective ways of handling a particular situation. Yet another is **role-playing** in which the patient and therapist act out some scenes, such as a marital confrontation, that are likely to take place at some future time.

An illustration of the use of role-playing is provided by a patient who was unable to make a genuinely affectionate statement to his wife:

> [The therapist] says "Tom, do you really care for me?" Tom says "I would say to her that I do, but she'd complain." Therapist: "Don't tell me what you *would* do. I'm Jane. Talk to me. Tom, do you really care for me?" Tom (turning away, looking slightly disgusted): "Yes." Therapist (still as Jane): "You don't say it like you mean it." Tom: "Yeah, that's what she says, and I usually . . ." Therapist (interrupting): "You're again telling me *about* what you'd say. I'm Jane. Tom, you don't say it like you mean it." Tom: "It's very hard for me to answer her when she says that." Therapist: "How do you feel when she says it?" Tom: "Angry, pushed." Therapist: "OK, I'm Jane. Tell me how you feel." Tom: "Jane, when you do that it really turns me off. Maybe if you didn't ask me so often I'd be able to say it spontaneously without feeling like a puppet . . . (then, in a tone that indicates he is now talking to the therapist as therapist) Gee, I wonder what would happen if I really said that to her" (Wachtel, 1977, pp. 234–35).

Carl Rogers *(Photograph by Nozizwe S.)*

HUMANISTIC THERAPIES

A number of practitioners charge that behavior therapy (and to a lesser extent, psychoanalysis) describes human beings too atomistically, explains them too mechanistically, and treats them too manipulatively. These *humanistic therapists* try to deal with the individual at a more global level, not as a bundle of conditioned fear responses to be extinguished, nor as a collection of warring, unconscious strivings to be resolved, but rather as a whole person, who must be "encountered and understood" in his own "living, suffering actuality."

One example of a humanistically oriented approach is *client-centered therapy.* This psychotherapeutic system was initially developed by the psychologist Carl Rogers during the early 1940s. One of its main premises is that the process of personality development is akin to growth. Rogers followed theorists like Abraham Maslow (1908–70) in believing that all persons have a native impulse toward the full realization of their human potentialities (Maslow, 1968). In this sense, he holds that human nature is inherently good. But, alas, such self-actualization is fairly rare, for personality growth is often stunted. There are many people who dislike themselves, are out of touch with their own feelings, and are unable to reach out to others as genuine fellow beings. Rogers' remedy is to provide the appropriate psychological soil in which personal growth can resume; this soil is the therapeutic relationship.

Rogers believes that therapy should be essentially democratic. The Rogerian therapist does not act as an omniscient authority who sagely interprets what the patient says or dreams (as does a psychoanalyst) or who tells him what to do for his own good (as does a behavior therapist). Instead, he tries to help the patient—whom he calls a client—help himself.

Rogers initially tried to achieve this client-centered quality by a variety of *nondirective techniques* (Rogers, 1942). He would never advise or interpret directly, but would only try to clarify what the client really felt, by echoing or restating what the client himself seemed to say or feel.

In later formulations, Rogers decided that there is no way of being truly nondirective. Despite one's best intentions one can't help but convey some evaluation with even the blandest nod. But more important, Rogers came to believe that the main contribution of the therapist does not lie in any particular approach or technique; it is rather to supply the one crucial condition of successful therapy, *himself* or *herself,* as a genuinely involved, participating fellow person. The Rogerian therapist's main job is to let the client know that she understands how the world looks through *his* eyes; that she can empathize with his wishes and feelings; and, most important of all, that she accepts and values him as a human being. In Rogers' view, this awareness that another person unconditionally accepts and esteems him, ultimately helps the client to accept and esteem himself (Rogers, 1961). Perhaps this is just a modern restatement of the old idea that love can redeem us all.*

---

* Rogers' humanistic approach has often been attacked by behavior therapists who regard him as "antiscientific." Under the circumstances, it is somewhat ironic that Rogers was one of the pioneers of psychotherapy evaluation, the first major figure in the field of psychotherapy who looked for evidence that his techniques were actually having some effect.

SOME COMMON THEMES

Our emphasis thus far has been on the differences among the various therapeutic schools. But despite all of their divergences, some underlying common themes run through their beliefs and practices:

Emotional defusing All psychotherapies aim at some kind of emotional reeducation. They try to help the patient rid himself of various intense and unrealistic fears. To this end, these fears, and other strong emotions such as anger, are evoked during the therapeutic session. Since this happens in the presence of an accepting, noncondemning therapist, the fear is weakened.

Interpersonal learning All major schools stress the importance of interpersonal learning and follow Freud in believing that the therapeutic relationship is an important tool in bringing this about. This relationship shows the patient how she generally reacts to others and also provides a vehicle through which she can discover and rehearse new and better ways for doing so.

Insight Most psychotherapists try to help their patients achieve greater self-knowledge, though different therapeutic schools differ in what kind of self-knowledge they try to bring about. For psychoanalysts, the crucial emotional insights the patient must acquire refer to his own past; for Rogerians, they concern one's feelings in the present; for behavior therapists, the relevant self-understanding is the correct identification of the stimuli to which fear has been conditioned.

Therapy as a step-by-step process There is general agreement that therapy is a gradual affair and that this is so regardless of whether the therapy emphasizes cognitive insight, feelings, or behaviors. There are few sudden flashes of insight or emotional understanding which change a patient overnight. Instead, each new-found insight and freshly acquired skill must be laboriously applied in one life situation after another before the patient can call it her own.

Therapy as a socially accepted practice Most psychotherapists operate within a social context that gives them the status of officially designated healers for emotional ills. As a result, the stage is set for a number of nonspecific gains of psychotherapy. One is an intimate, confiding relation with another person. This alone may be a boon to some persons who have no close bonds to anyone and for whom psychotherapy may amount to what one author calls "the purchase of friendship" (Schofield, 1964). Another nonspecific gain is the hope that one will get better. This may lead the patient to think better of himself, which may lead to small successes in the outside world, which may fuel further hope, and increase the chances of yet other successes.

Psychotherapy—the purchase of friendship?
(© 1950, 1952 United Feature Syndicate Inc.)

Evaluating Therapeutic Outcome

We have just surveyed what different kinds of therapists do. We now ask whether what they do does any good. This question often arouses indignant protests from therapists and patients alike. For many of them feel utterly certain that they help or have been helped; they therefore see no point in questioning what to them is obvious. But their testimonials alone are not convincing. For one thing, both patients and therapists have a serious stake in believing that psychotherapy works. If it doesn't, the patient has wasted his money and the therapist has wasted his time. Under the circumstances, neither may be the most objective judge in assessing whether there was a significant change. But even granting that change occurred, what caused this change? Was it produced by the therapeutic situation, or would it have come about in any case? And, assuming that the therapy did play a role, was the improvement caused by the therapy as such or was it produced by nonspecific, placebolike factors such as hope, expectations of cure, and the decision to "turn a new leaf"?

These questions are very similar to those encountered in the evaluation of drug therapies. It is therefore not surprising that investigations that try to determine whether psychotherapy works use rather similar research plans.

DOES PSYCHOTHERAPY WORK?

Much of the impetus for discussions of psychotherapeutic outcomes came from a sharp attack on the efficacy of psychoanalysis and similar "insight therapies" launched by the British psychologist Hans Eysenck (Eysenck, 1961). Eysenck surveyed some two dozen articles that reported the number of neurotic patients who improved or failed to improve after psychotherapy. Overall, about 60 percent improved, a result that might be considered fairly encouraging. But Eysenck argued that there was really nothing to cheer about. According to Eysenck's analysis, the spontaneous recovery rate in neurotics who received *no* treatment was, if anything, even higher—about 70 percent. If so, psychotherapy apparently has no curative effects.

More recent reviews suggest that Eysenck's appraisal was unduly harsh. In particular, he apparently overestimated the rate of spontaneous improvement. On the basis of more recent data, this rate seems to be closer to 40 percent. While the difference between this figure and 60 percent (the average improvement rate in neurotics who receive psychotherapy) is not exactly staggering, it is at least in the right direction and thus constitutes what one author calls "some modest evidence that psychotherapy 'works' " (Bergin, 1971, p. 229).

The preceding comments applied to averages. When we look at individuals, we find that while psychotherapy may have an effect, this effect is not always for the better. A certain proportion of patients seem to get worse. One line of evidence comes from an inspection of the variability of post-treatment test scores (for example, self-rating). After psychotherapy, the scores on such tests are more spread out than the scores of an untreated control group. This suggests that while some patients are improving, some others—fortunately a smaller number—become worse than they were to start with. The cause of this so-called **deterioration effect** is still unclear. One hypothesis is that psychotherapy sometimes disturbs an unstable neurotic equilibrium without supplying an appropriate substitute (Bergin, 1967).

COMPARING DIFFERENT THERAPIES

Comparisons of improvement across different studies (of the kind just described) have certain limitations. Different studies are often not strictly comparable: The patient groups may differ in age, socioeconomic background, and severity of disorder, and different therapists may use different criteria to assess improvement. As a result, it is often difficult to make specific comparisons that would allow us to distinguish between genuine effects of treatment and placebo effects, or to decide whether different forms of therapy produce different results. But it is just these specific comparisons that are of the greatest interest. For the general question "Does psychotherapy work?" is probably not the most important one. It is like asking "Does drug therapy work?" without specifying either the drug or the disease for which it is recommended. Several recent investigators argue that, instead, the right question is "*What* treatment, by *whom,* is most effective for *this* individual with *that* specific problem, and under *which* set of circumstances?" (Paul, 1967a, p. 111). During the last decade, work on psychotherapy outcome has been increasingly addressed to more specific questions of this sort.

A STUDY OF THERAPEUTIC OUTCOME

An elegant study by Gordon Paul has set a model for much of the subsequent research in the area. We will describe it in some detail because it highlights the methodological issues that any investigation of the effectiveness of psychotherapy has to face (Paul, 1966).

Paul's "patients" were ninety-six undergraduates who suffered from rather severe anxiety when they had to talk in front of others. This disability was especially distressing since they were currently enrolled in a required course in public speaking. All of these students had accepted an offer of free treatment and were randomly assigned to one of several groups:

Insight therapy The subjects in this group received five sessions of insight-oriented pyschotherapy. The therapists tried to reduce the subjects' stage fright and related anxieties by helping them to understand their own fears and the way these related to other problem areas in their lives.

Desensitization therapy The subjects in this group received five sessions of systematic desensitization, in which a hierarchy of speech-related anxieties was progressively worked through.

Placebo control This group was run to control for placebo effects. The subjects were seen for five sessions during which they took what they thought was a potent tranquilizer (it actually was a bicarbonate capsule) and performed a boring discrimination task. They were told that this task was ordinarily very stressful but would not be so for them because of the "tranquilizer." If repeated often enough, this experience would then inoculate them against anxiety-provoking situations in ordinary life. Needless to say, all of this was a ruse, but the subjects accepted it and believed that the treatment would help them. As a result they did for Paul what a sugar-pill group does for a pharmacologist—they controlled for placebo effects.

No-treatment control   A final group was the usual nontreatment control. This group received the identical before-and-after tests that were administered to the other three groups. The subjects were drawn from the same population that had volunteered for treatment. They were told that they could not be accommodated just then but were promised treatment some time in the future (a promise that was kept).

All subjects were assessed before and after the first three groups received their five treatment sessions. The assessments included both objective and subjective indices. The subjects were observed while speaking in front of a class and were rated for behavioral signs of anxiety such as trembling hands and quivering voice. Additional objective measures included physiological indices, such as sweating and pulse rate. The subjects also rated their own anxiety on several questionnaires.

The results showed that the two groups that received treatment improved significantly as compared to the no-treatment control. But the same was true of the placebo control: They also improved, despite the fact that all they had been given was faith and bicarbonate of soda. This finding is a clear demonstration of a placebo effect in psychotherapy. People get better because they believe they will and because someone pays special attention to them.

The critical question was whether there was some specific effect of psychotherapy over and beyond the placebo. To answer this question, Paul compared the improvements observed in the two real treatment groups with those found for subjects in the placebo control. The results were clear-cut. Desensitization produced considerably more improvement than the placebo treatment, but insight treatment did not (Table 18.1). These effects were still present on a follow-up two years later in which all subjects were again questioned about their speech anxiety. Relative to the statements they had made two years earlier, improvement was shown by 85 percent of the desensitization subjects and by 50 percent of both the insight and placebo subjects (Paul, 1967*b*).

Table 18.1   PSYCHOTHERAPY FOR STAGE FRIGHT

Group	Percentage of cases "significantly improved"		
	Self-report of anxiety	Objective behavior	Physiological indices
Desensitization	100	100	87
Insight	53	60	53
Placebo control	47	73	47
No treatment control	7	24	28

SOURCE: Data from Paul, 1967*b*.

Paul's results show that desensitization is a more effective means of combating stage fright and related anxieties than are insight therapies. But what is the story on more serious conditions? To answer this question a group of investigators selected about a hundred clinic outpatients whose psychiatric complaints were of moderate severity. The complaints included anxiety attacks, depression, obsessive thoughts, and so on. One third of these patients was treated by behavior therapy (which usually included a heavy dose of desensitization), another third by traditional insight therapy, and a final third was assigned to an untreated control group that received therapy later on. Both treatment groups improved more than the untreated control, with a slight edge in favor of behavior therapy. An interesting finding concerns the match between patients and therapies. Insight-oriented therapy only helped patients who were relatively young, had more education, and were financially better off. In contrast, behavior therapy was effective for a wider patient spectrum, but was slightly more helpful for older, less educated, and financially worse off persons (Sloane et al., 1975).

It appears that psychotherapy works, but not too dramatically. It works to a modest extent. It is too early to tell whether one particular therapeutic method is better than the others. But one thing at least seems clear. The very fact that behavior therapy comes off quite well when compared to other methods—sometimes just as well, sometimes even better—suggests that emotional insight is not always a necessary ingredient for therapeutic success. What seems to matter is much simpler. The patient learns. He extinguishes anxieties and he acquires new ways of thinking, feeling, and behaving.

Will these new learned patterns help the patient when he leaves the therapist's office? The answer depends on the similarity between what he learned there, during therapy, and the situation he has to face outside. The more similar the two, the greater the transfer. It is probably for these reasons that behavior therapy is sometimes found to be more effective than other therapeutic methods. Behavior therapists often give their patients "homework" and ask them to apply their therapeutic lessons in their own, real world.

Some psychoanalytically oriented therapists have cautioned that the behavior therapists' emphasis on symptoms may backfire. In their view, when therapy concentrates on symptoms (as does behavior therapy) the symptom may subside but at a cost—there will be **symptom substitution** because the underlying conflict is still there. The facts suggest, however, that this is not the case. When symptoms get better during behavior therapy, they are not replaced by other symptoms. If anything, the reverse is true: As particular symptoms disappear, the patient starts to improve in other areas as well (Sloane et al., 1975).

Extensions of Psychotherapy

In Freud's time, psychotherapy was still considered a somewhat arcane art, practiced by a few initiates and limited to a selected group of well-educated

18.7 Play therapy, an extension of psychotherapy adapted for children *In play therapy, the therapist tries to help the child understand his feelings about his parents and other family members through play with various toys. (Photograph by Sybil Shelton, Monkmeyer Press)*

adult patients. Since then, psychotherapy has been broadened and extended to cover increasingly more terrain. One set of extensions widened the patient population to include children, retarded persons, various kinds of sociopaths, and psychotics (Figure 18.7). Another extension was a shift from the original one-therapist, one-patient formula to various modes of **group therapy** that feature all conceivable permutations: one therapist and several patients, several therapists and several patients, several patients and no therapist, and so on. Some practitioners went beyond treating patients in groups to defining the group itself as the patient. Examples are **family therapists** whose primary interest is in the "pathological" interaction patterns within the family, rather than the individual family members as such. An even broader sociocultural perspective led other therapists to an interest in community mental health, to questions of prevention, and to problems of social reform. But perhaps most drastic of all has been a change in treatment goals. At first the goal was cure or alleviation of distress. Now some therapists aim at broader and more diffuse objectives such as happiness or the discovery of "meaning" in life.

GROUP THERAPY

One of the fastest growing movements in the mental health field is treatment in groups. One reason is economic. The per-patient cost of therapy can be much less when patients are treated in groups rather than individually. Another reason is scarcity of personnel. There simply aren't enough trained therapists for all the people who want their services; seeing clients in groups is one way of making the supply fit the demand. But the appeal of group therapy may have some deeper reasons as well. For instance, the new therapeutic groups seem to fill a void, at least temporarily, left by the weakening of family and religious ties in modern urbanized society.

SHARED-PROBLEM GROUPS

One approach is to organize a group of people all of whom have the same problem: They may all be alcoholics, or drug addicts, or ex-convicts. The members meet, share relevant advice and information, help newcomers along, exhort and support each other in their resolve to overcome their handicaps. The classic example is **Alcoholics Anonymous,** which provides the alcoholic with a sense that he is not alone and helps him weather crises without suffering a relapse. In such we-are-all-in-the-same-boat groups, the primary aim of the group is to *manage* the problem that all members share. No specific therapy is provided for emotional problems that are unique to any one individual.

THERAPY GROUPS

The rules of the game are very different in groups explicitly organized for the purpose of **group therapy.** Here, a group of selected patients, usually around ten, are treated together under the guidance of a trained therapist. Economic considerations aside, this form of therapy may have some advantages that individual treatment lacks. According to its proponents, in group therapy the therapist does not really treat the members of the group; instead, he helps them to treat each other. The specific techniques of the therapist may vary from psychoanalytically oriented insight therapy to various forms of behavior therapy to Rogerian client-centered approaches. But whatever techniques the therapist favors, the treatment of each group member really begins as he realizes that he is not all that different from the others. He learns that there are other people who are painfully shy, who have hostile fantasies about their parents, or whatever. Further benefits come from a sense of group belongingness, of support, and of encouragement. But most important of all is the fact that the group provides a ready-made laboratory in interpersonal relations. The patient can discover just what he does that rubs others the wrong way, how he can relate to certain kinds of people more effectively, and so on (Sadock, 1975).

It is hard to evaluate the effectiveness of group psychotherapy for emotional disorders. One major problem in assessing effectiveness is that in group therapy, all group members are considered to be informal co-therapists. Since this is so, who they are and how they relate to each other may well be expected to affect the outcome. This factor is very hard to control, which makes outcome evaluation difficult. Still, the available evidence suggests that group therapy does lead to some moderate improvement (Figure 18.8).

THE EXPANSION OF THERAPEUTIC GOALS

Group methods and other extensions made psychotherapy available to a much larger number of people. But did all of them really need it? The answer depends on what one believes the goals of therapy to be.

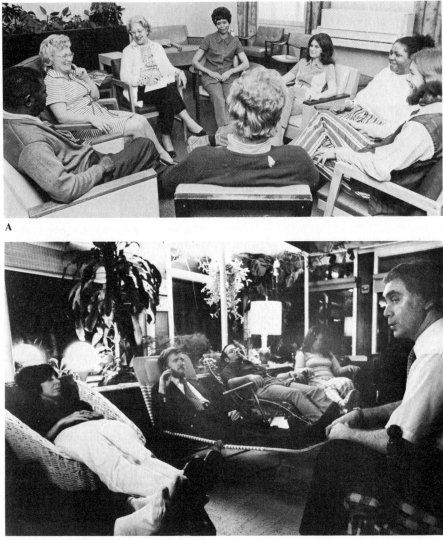

18.8   The extension of psychotherapy to groups   (A) A structured group therapy session. (Courtesy the National Institutes of Mental Health) (B) Systematic desensitization conducted for a group. (© Van Bucher, Photo Researchers)

To Freud, the matter was simple. Most of the neurotics he saw were incapable of any kind of healthy life. They were crippled by terrorizing phobias or all-consuming compulsions and were thus unable to work and love. Freud wanted to cure these pathologies so that his patients could once again deal with their everyday existence. But he never regarded this cure as equivalent to happiness or fulfillment or the discovery of a meaning in life. These the patients had to find for themselves and they might very well fail to do so even when no longer saddled with their neuroses.

Later therapists broadened the treatment goals. This is especially true of humanistic therapists such as Rogers. To be sure, Rogerian therapists try to remove or alleviate their clients' distress. But their ambitions go further. They aim at more than a cure (the goal of psychoanalysts, at least in their early days) and at more than the modification of unwanted behavior patterns (the goal of behavior therapists). Their ultimate object is to help their clients to "grow" and to "realize their human potentialities." But with this expansion of the therapeutic goal, there is a concomitant widening of the group to which the therapeutic enterprise may be said to apply. Now therapy can be appropriate for just about anyone, regardless of whether he suffers some form of psychopathology or does not (Orne, 1975). After all, who among us can claim to have achieved his full potential?

Rogers' emphasis on growth represents one expansion of the goals of therapy. We will discuss some related extensions of therapeutic aims by considering two futher offshoots of the humanistic movement, existential therapy and the encounter group movement.

EXISTENTIAL THERAPY

Rogers' approach to therapy is distinctively American in its optimistic faith in an almost limitless human capacity for growth and self-improvement. Another humanistic approach to therapy originates in Europe and takes a more somber view. This is *existential therapy,* a movement that echoes some of the major themes sounded by a group of philosophers called *existentialists.* Existential therapists are primarily concerned with what they regard as the major emotional sickness of our times, an inability to endow life with meaning. In their view, this condition is a by-product of the rootless, restless anonymity of twentieth-century Western life; it is especially prevalent in modern Europe, in the wake of the despair that followed two bloody world wars and the Nazi terror. It is marked by a sense that one is alienated, lost, and dehumanized; that one is nothing but a cog in a huge, impersonal machine; and that one's existence is meaningless. According to existential therapists, this feeling that everything is pointless is a common facet of many modern emotional disorders. It is this, rather than the specific symptoms of neurosis—the phobias, the obsessions, and the like—that they want to rectify.

In essense, existential therapists try to help people achieve a personal outlook that gives meaning to their lives. How do they do this? It turns out that most existential therapists have no distinctive technique. Some use the couch and ask the patient to free-associate, while others sit face to face and have lengthy philosophical discussions. What is distinctive about them is their underlying attitude. They try to make their patients aware of the importance of free choice. They insist that people are persons and not objects, that human acts spring from within rather than being imposed from without, that there are always choices—even in jail, even in a concentration camp—and that what one is is ultimately what one chooses to do. The therapist's job is to help the patient realize that the responsibility for finding and for making her life's choices is hers and hers alone. If and when the patient accepts this responsibility, she will no longer be plagued by the vacuum of her own existence but will begin to feel "authentic."

Like practitioners of most other schools, existential therapists stress the role of the therapeutic relationship in affecting the changes they want to bring about. In their view, the key element of this relationship is what they call the *encounter,* in which two individuals meet as genuine persons of whose independent human existence neither has any doubt. According to existential therapists, the experience derived from this encounter will ultimately transfer to the way in which the patient sees himself and others (May, 1958).

In the past, the task which existential therapists have set themselves was generally held to be the province of clergymen. It was priests and parsons and rabbis who tried to help people find some meaning in their existence. They did so within a religious framework that defined the spiritual dimension of human life. As religious values have eroded, other social institutions have stepped in and have tried to take the clergy's place. One of these is modern humanistic psychotherapy, especially the existentialist school. It is no accident that an influential book by a prominent existential therapist bears the title *The Doctor and the Soul* (Frankl, 1966).

No one would dispute that the spiritual goals of existential therapy are admirable. To help people find some meaning to their existence is surely a worthwhile task. The question is whether success at this task can be properly evaluated as we have tried to evaluate that of other therapies. The trouble is that the goals of existential therapy are so broad that we don't know how to judge whether they have been achieved.

ENCOUNTER GROUPS

Existential therapists often ask their patients to concentrate on the concrete feelings of the moment, especially as they pertain to the person-to-person encounter within the therapeutic relationship. Somewhat similar aims are characteristic of various ***encounter groups***, the proliferation of which in the United States during the last two decades has assumed the dimensions of a major social movement (Back, 1972). These groups are formed for just one purpose—to provide each member with the opportunity to interact with others in an open manner while dropping the conventional masks and abandoning the habitual defenses of everyday life. The idea was that such experiences would carry over into the individual's life outside, that they would increase his interpersonal sensitivity, make him more aware of himself, and make him more authentic in his relations with significant persons in his world. These aims are quite similar to those of group therapy. But in contrast to therapy groups, encounter groups are not typically composed of patients. Their members are generally normal persons who want to function better than they do. They want a personal education, not a cure.

Encounters as a road to growth   The ways in which encounter groups (sometimes called sensitivity training groups, or ***T-groups*** for short) try to provide this "education for life" vary considerably. Group leaders may be highly dominant or relatively passive; they may be provocative or gently supporting. But there are some common themes. In most encounter groups, there is a good deal of vigorous give-and-take in which members reveal themselves to each other, tell others what they think of them, and hear how they are perceived in turn. The resulting group atmosphere tends to become quite emotional. There are episodes of confrontation and hostility, as well as of warmth and intense affection.

As the encounter group movement developed, verbal methods were supplemented by a variety of nonverbal exercises (Schutz, 1967). Encounter group leaders feel that these often help to warm up a group and to cut through verbal defenses. Examples are falling backward, eyes closed, into the steady arms of another group member (this is said to develop a sense of trust) and allowing oneself to be lifted, passed from one member to another, and then slowly rocked (this is said to develop the ability to accept affection). Later developments featured more drastic techniques to reach "gut feelings." One

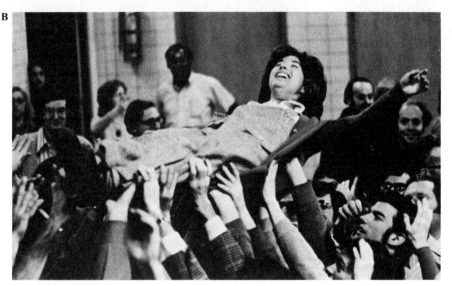

18.9   Encounter groups   *(A) Group exercises to remove inhibitions. (Photograph by Ken Heyman) (B) Exercise to develop a sense of trust. (Photograph by Bob Nadler, DPI)*

method is the ***marathon encounter***, which may last for forty-eight hours or so with hardly any time for sleep. The notion is that this forced, no-exit group exposure, coupled with sheer fatigue, will lead to an accelerated abandonment of social masks. A widely publicized variant of this technique is the nude marathon which is based on the premise that it is easier to strip off people's interpersonal facades if one has first stripped off their clothes (Figure 18.9).

A description of events that are likely to occur in certain encounter groups follows:

> There is a silence and the group waits. [Another] member says . . . he doesn't ever get along well with authority and that's what he's here to work on. He falters and stops. . . . The leader wonders if the member would like to try an encounter with his father. Two chairs are found and sit facing each other. The leader directs the

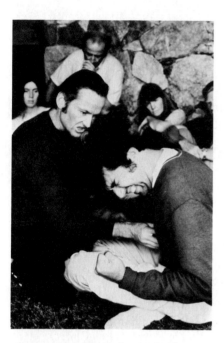

An encounter group therapy leader encourages a group member to express his suppressed rage (Photograph by Arthur Schatz, © Time Inc)

member to sit in one. The group rings the chairs, watching. . . . [The leader] instructs the member to visualize his father sitting in the empty chair and to speak to him. . . . [Later] the leader puts a cushion on father's chair and instructs the member to kneel in front of it and pound it while shouting out his anger. The member complies. The pounding starts mildly and there are no words. The leader urges him to hit harder. A couple of other members echo the urging. The pounding becomes stronger, the angry words come, and the whole thing crescendoes into a screaming paroxysm of rage culminating in weeping and then near collapse. Two of the women hold him and rock him gently, cooing to him and caressing him. After a time he talks briefly about the feelings of release and about his profound astonishment at having such violence in himself. He smiles ruefully at the leader and embraces him. For now, at least, he seems not to have an "authority problem" (Kahn, 1973, pp. 399–400).

Evaluating encounter groups   Do any of these encounters really lead to personal growth? The best study to date involved about two hundred Stanford undergraduates who joined various encounter groups. To assess the effects, the investigators looked at a number of before-and-after indices of emotional well-being, such as self-esteem and relations to others. They found a greater proportion of positive changes in students who had the encounter experience than in control subjects who had not. These results should probably be regarded with some reservation; the effects were relatively modest and they were only obtained when the subjects judged themselves, rather than being judged by others (Lieberman, Yalom, and Miles, 1973).

Such beneficial changes as did occur seemed to be a function of the general group climate, rather than the theoretical framework within which the group was run. In particular, groups and group leaders who were especially warm and supportive had a greater than average proportion of members who felt that they had changed for the better.

But the impact can be for the worse as well. About 8 percent of the participants were classified as "casualties"; they were adversely affected by the group experience and still suffered some ill-effects half a year later, as judged by themselves, by others, and by an outside interviewer. Many of them sought some form of psychotherapeutic help subsequent to the group sessions. They generally blamed the group or the group leader, usually for vehement personal attacks that they were unable to handle.

The paradoxes of the encounter movement   The encounter movement is a product of the relentless extension and popularization of the psychotherapeutic enterprise. In many ways it is a bundle of ironic contradictions. To begin with, take the goals. On the one hand, the encounter is said to be a therapy for normals that leads to regeneration and fulfillment. But on the other hand, its goals are often described as the experience in itself. If so, the encounter might well be regarded as a special kind of entertainment, perhaps profoundly moving but with no objective over and beyond itself (Serber, 1972). Another contradiction involves the movement's ambivalent attitude toward science, technology, and intellectual matters in general. Adherents of the encounter movement usually reject science as "mechanistic," decry an "engineering approach" to human concerns, regard words with suspicion because they tend to falsify experience, and prefer to rely on immediate feelings and "vibes" as the ultimate reality. But this anti-intellectualism is often clothed in the language of science. Telling another person what one really thinks of her is "feedback," touching her is "nonverbal communication," and various bodily exercises are justified by vague appeals to the "psychosomatic unity of body and mind."

A further contradiction is probably related to current conditions in America. The deeply felt communion of the encounter is an intimacy between strangers. They are strangers when they meet and revert to being strangers when they part, no matter how much they may have opened themselves to each other during the encounter weekend. This aspect of the encounter movement may reflect the enormous geographical mobility of American society, in which one is here today and gone tomorrow, and in which one quickly forms attachments and just as quickly lets them go. In such a setting, people tend to become interchangeable, like motels on a superhighway or modular units in a TV set. Seen in this light, the encounter group movement mirrors the contemporary American scene. If this is true, it "may be more a symptom of what ails society than a cure for its ills" (Back, 1972).

A Century of Psychotherapy

Where does all of this leave us? What can we say today about psychological treatments of mental disorders, now that almost a hundred years have passed since Freud and Breuer conducted their classic studies of hysteria?

To begin with, there is little doubt that psychotherapy produces some non-specific benefits. It helps people by providing someone in whom they can confide, who can give them advice about troubling matters, who listens to them, and instills new hope and the expectation that they will get better. The critic will reply that such gains merely reflect placebo effects and similar factors. In this view, the benefits are not produced by any specific psychotherapeutic technique, but might just as easily have been provided by a wise uncle or an understanding family doctor. Perhaps so, but the point may not be relevant. For wise uncles are in short supply today. The extended family in which uncles, nieces, and grandparents lived in close proximity is largely a thing of the past. The same holds for the family doctor who has vanished from the scene, together with his bedside manner. All of this suggests that psychotherapy has come to fill a social vacuum. Some of its effects may well be placebolike, but until a definitive treatment comes along a placebo may be better than nothing. And for the present, the psychotherapeutic professions seem to be the officially designated dispensers of such placebos.

This is not to say that there are no genuine specific psychotherapeutic effects. As we have seen, there is reasonable evidence for a modest, positive effect—improvement, though rarely complete cure. The specific ingredients that bring these effects about have not been identified with certainty but they probably include emotional defusing, interpersonal learning, and some insight—all acquired within the therapeutic situation and somehow transferred to the patient's life beyond.

Summary

1. One major form of treatment of mental disorder is by *somatic therapies*. Of these, *drug therapies* seem to be the most promising. Psychiatric drugs in current use include the *phenothiazines* such as *chlorpromazine,* which seem to reduce the major symptoms of schizophrenia, *antidepressants* such as *imipramine,* and *lithium carbonate* for the treatment of mania.

2. The effectiveness of drug treatment—as indeed of all therapies—requires careful evaluation procedures that control for *spontaneous improvement* and *placebo effects,* and that also guard against both the physicians' and the patients' expectations by use of *double-blind techniques.* Such studies have demonstrated genuine effects of certain psychiatric drugs, some of which are quite specific to a particular disorder. But thus far these drugs have not produced complete cures, especially in schizophrenia. Without a *maintenance dose,* a discharged patient may relapse; even with it, his adjustment may be only marginal.

3. Other somatic therapies include *prefrontal lobotomy,* a procedure now widely suspect, and *electroconvulsive shock treatment* or *ECT,* which is sometimes used in cases of severe depression.

4. Another approach to mental disorder, *psychotherapy,* relies on psychological means alone. It derives from *classical psychoanalysis* as developed by Freud. Psychoanalysts try to help their patients to recover repressed memories and wishes so that they can overcome crippling internal conflicts. Their tools are *free association* and the *interpretation* of the patient's *resistance.* The goal is emotional rather than mere intellectual insight, an achievement made possible by an analysis of the *transference* relationship between analyst and patient.

5. Many modern psychoanalysts practice modified variants of Freud's technique. They generally place greater emphasis on interpersonal and social problems in the present than on psychosexual matters in the past. They also tend to take a more active role in helping the patient extend the therapeutic experience to the world outside.

6. A different approach is taken by *behavior therapists* whose concern is with unwanted, overt behaviors rather than with hypothetical underlying causes. Many of the behavior therapists' techniques are derived from the principles of classical and instrumental conditioning. An example is *systematic desensitization* which tries to *countercondition* irrational fears by a policy of gradualism. Another is *flooding* which attempts to extinguish the patient's fear by evoking the fear response in full force. Yet another is *aversive therapy* in which undesired behavior patterns are coupled with unpleasant stimuli.

7. Some recent offshoots of behavior therapy share its concrete and *directive* orientation but not its emphasis on conditioning. One example is *cognitive therapy* which tries to change the way the patient thinks about his situation. Others include various attempts to advance the patient's social education, using techniques such as *graded task assignments, modeling,* and *role-playing.*

8. Behavior therapists regard psychoanalysis as too subjective and not scientific enough. Another group of practitioners, the *humanistic therapists,* take the very opposite position. They charge that both behavior therapy and psychoanalysis are too mechanistic and manipulative and that they fail to deal with their patients as "whole persons." An example of such a humanistic approach is Roger's *client-centered therapy* which is conducted along democratic lines, is largely *nondirective,* and is based on the idea that therapy is a personal growth process rather than a form of reeducation supervised by the therapist.

SUMMARY

9. Evaluation studies suggest that psychoanalysis and other insight therapies such as Roger's have a modest effect: On the average, they produce improvement in about 60 percent of the patients in contrast to a 40 percent spontaneous recovery rate. Comparing the effectiveness of different therapies is enormously difficult. Such evidence as there is suggests that desensitization is more effective than insight therapy for certain phobias, especially milder ones. The story on more serious conditions is still unknown.

10. The last few decades have seen an enormous extension of psychotherapy. One extension was of method. An example is *group therapy* in which patients are treated in groups rather than individually. Another extension concerns the therapeutic goals. The original purpose was to cure a pathology. As time went on, the goal was broadened to include personal growth and the discovery of meaning in life. This last is the special concern of *existential therapists* who try to help their patients recognize the importance of personal responsibility and free choice.

11. One consequence of the increasing proliferation of therapeutic goals together with the continued popularization of psychotherapy was the *encounter group* movement. Encounter groups try to "help people get in touch with their own feelings." Their accomplishments vary depending upon the group and its leader; in some cases, the effect may be harmful.

Epilogue

We have come to the end of our journey. We have traveled through the sprawling fields of psychology, a loosely federated intellectual empire that stretches from the domains of the biological sciences on one border to those of the social sciences on the other. We have considered some aspects of human and animal action: how it is based on certain biological underpinnings, how it is directed and purposive, how it is modified and shaped through various forms of learning. We have looked at some problems in the psychology of knowledge: how it is acquired, interpreted, stored, retrieved, thought about, and communicated to others. We have asked about the sources of social interaction: how some are based on our ancestral, biological past; how some grow out of our childhood rearing; and how still others depend upon the conditions of the social present. We finally took up how people differ from each other: in intelligence, in personality, and occasionally in ways that are so extreme and so disabling that they are considered pathological. We have gone from one end of psychology to another. What have we learned?

In looking back over our journey, there is little doubt that we have encountered many more questions than answers. To be sure, more is known today about mind and behavior than was known in the days of, say, Thorndike and Köhler, let alone those of Descartes, Locke, and Kant. But this does not change the fact that what we know today is just a tiny clearing in a vast jungle of ignorance.

What can we say? We can point at what we know and congratulate ourselves. Or we can consider what we do not know and bemoan our ignorance. Perhaps a wiser course is one recommended by Sigmund Freud on thinking about some aspects of human intellectual history (Freud, 1917).

Freud suggested a parallel between the psychological growth of each human child and the intellectual progress of humanity as a whole. As he saw it, the infant is initially posessed by an all-pervading sense of his own power and importance. He cries and his parents come to change or feed or rock him and so he feels that he is the cause of whatever happens around him, the sole center of a world that revolves around him alone. But this happy delusion of his own omnipotence cannot last forever. Eventually the growing infant discovers that he is not the hub of the universe. This recognition may come as a cruel blow, but he will ultimately be the better for it. For the child cannot become strong and capable without some awareness that he is not so as yet, without first accepting the fact that he can't have his way just by wishing. His first achievements will be slight—as he lifts his own cup or a bit later says his first word—but they are real enough and will lay the foundations for his later mastery of his environment.

Freud thought that a similar theme underlies the growth of humankind's awareness of the world in which we live. On two crucial occasions in our history, we had to give up some cherished beliefs in our own power and importance. With Copernicus, we had to cede our place in the center of the physical universe: the sun doesn't circle us, but we the sun. With Darwin, we had to perform a similar abdication in the biological sphere: we are not specially created but are descended from other animals. Each of these intellectual revolutions ran into vehement opposition; in large part because each represented a gigantic blow to humanity's self-love and pride. They made us face our own ignorance and insignificance. But however painful it may have been initially, each recognition of our weakness ultimately helped us gain more strength, each confession of ignorance eventually let to deeper understanding. The Copernican revolution forced us to admit our minute place in the celestial scheme of things, but this admission was the first step in a journey of ever-increasing physical horizons, a journey which in our own time brought human beings to the moon. The Darwinian revolution made us aware that we are just one biological species among millions, the product of the same evolutionary process that brought forth sea urchins and penguins as well as us. But this awareness opened the way for continually expanding explorations of the biological universe, explorations that have already given us much greater control of our own bodily condition and of the fragile environment in which humans and other species exist.

In this century we have had to suffer yet another blow to our self-pride. We learned that we are not sure of what goes on in our own minds. Modern psychology, for all its accomplishments, has made it utterly clear that thus far we know even less about our own mental processes and behavior than we know about the physical and biological world around us. Here, too, we have to confess that we are weak and ignorant. We can only hope that this confession will have some of the effects of our previous ones, that here again strength will grow out of weakness and knowledge out of folly and ignorance. If so, we may finally understand why we think and do what we think and do, so that we may ultimately master our inner selves as we have learned to master the world around us.

We can only hope. There are few goals in science that are worthier than this.

Statistics: The Collection, Organization, and Interpretation of Data

By Neil A. Macmillan

A large body of psychological knowledge has been summarized in this book, and a good part of the discussion was devoted to the ways in which this knowledge was obtained. But there are certain methodological issues that were dealt with only in passing. These concern *statistical methods,* the ways in which investigators gather, organize, and interpret collections of numerical data.

Suppose some investigators want to find out whether three-year-old boys are more aggressive than three-year-old girls. To answer this question is a very big job. To start with, the investigators will have to come up with some appropriate measure of aggression. They will then have to select the subjects. The investigators presumably want to say something about three-year-olds in general, not just the particular three-year olds in their study. To make sure that this can be done, they have to select their subjects appropriately. Even more important, their groups of boys and girls must be as comparable as possible, so that one can be reasonably sure that any differences between the two groups is attributable to the difference in sex rather than to other factors (such as intellectual development, social class, and so on).

The investigators are now ready to collect their data. But having collected them, they will have to find some way of organizing these data in a meaningful way. Suppose the study used two groups of, say, 50 boys and 50 girls, each observed on 10 separate occasions. This means that the investigators will end up with at least 1,000 separate numerical entries (say, number of aggressive acts for each child on each occasion), 500 for the boys and 500 for the girls. Something has to be done to reduce this mass of numbers into some manageable, summarized form. This is usually accomplished by some process of averaging scores.

The next step involves statistical interpretation. Suppose the investigators find that the average aggression score is greater for the boys than for the girls (it probably will be). Can they be sure that the difference between the groups is large enough not to be dismissed as a fluke, a chance event? For it is just about certain that the data contain *variability.* The children in each group will not perform equally; furthermore, the same child may very well behave differently on one occasion than another. As a result, the scores in the two groups will almost surely overlap; that is, some girls will get a higher aggression score than some boys. Could it be that the difference *between* the groups (that is, the difference between the two averages) is an accidental chance product of the variability that is seen to hold *within* the two groups? One of the key functions of the statistical methods is to deal with questions of this sort, to help us draw useful and general conclusions about organisms despite the unavoidable variability in their behavior.

The preceding example indicates the main tasks to which statistical methods have been applied. In this appendix, we will sketch the logic that underlies these methods as psychologists use them.

Describing the Data

The data with which statistics deals are numerical, so a preliminary step in statistical analysis is the reduction of the actual results of a study to numbers. Much of the power of statistics results from the fact that numbers (unlike responses to a questionnaire, videotapes of social interactions, or lists of words recalled by a subject in a memory experiment) can be manipulated with the rules of arithmetic. As a result, scientists prefer to use response measures that are in numerical form. Consider our hypothetical study of aggression and sex. The investigators who watched the subjects might rate their aggression in various situations (from, say, "extremely aggressive" to "extremely docile") or they might count the number of aggressive acts (say, hitting or insulting another child), and so on. This operation of assigning numbers to observed events (usually, a subject's responses) is called *scaling.*

There are several types of scales that will concern us. They differ by the arithmetical operations that can be performed upon them.

CATEGORICAL AND ORDINAL SCALES

Sometimes the scores assigned to individuals are merely *categorical,* (also called *nominal*). For example, when respondents to a poll are asked to name the television channel they watch most frequently, they might respond "4," "2," or "13." These numbers serve only to group the responses into categories. They can obviously not be subjected to any arithmetic operations.

Ordinal numbers convey more information, in that their relative magnitude is meaningful—not arbitrary, as in the case of categorical scales. If individuals are asked to list the ten people they most admire, the number 1 can be assigned to the most admired person, 2 to the runner-up, and so on. The smaller the number assigned, the more the person is admired. Notice that no such statement can be made of television channels: Channel 4 is not more anything than channel 2, just different from it.

Scores which are ordinally scaled cannot, however, be added or subtracted. The first two persons on the most-admired list differ in admirability by 1; so do the last two. Yet the individual who has done the ranking may admire the first person far more than the other nine, all of whom might be very similar in admirability; in other words, given an ordinal scale, differences of 1 are not necessarily equal psychologically. Imagine a child who, given this task, lists his mother first, followed by the starting lineup of the Chicago Cubs baseball team. In this example, the difference of 8 between person 2 and person 10 probably represents a smaller difference in judged admirability than the difference of 1 obtained between persons 1 and 2 (at least so the mother hopes).

INTERVAL SCALES

Scales in which equal differences between scores, or intervals, *can* be treated as equal units are called **interval scales.** Reaction time is a common psychological variable which is usually treated as an interval scale. In some memory experiments, a subject must respond as quickly as possible to each of several words, some of which he has seen earlier in the experiment; the task is to indicate whether each word has appeared before by pressing one of two buttons. An unknown, but possibly constant, part of the reaction time is simply the time required to press the response button; the rest is the time required for the decision-making process:

$$\text{reaction time} = \text{decision time} + \text{button-press time.} \qquad (1)$$

Suppose a subject requires an average of 2 seconds to respond to nouns, 3 seconds for verbs, and 4 seconds for adjectives. The difference in decision time between nouns and verbs ($3 - 2 = 1$ second) is the same as the difference in decision time between verbs and adjectives ($4 - 3 = 1$ second). We can make this statement—which in turn suggests various hypotheses about the factors that underlie such differences—precisely because reaction time can be regarded as an interval scale.

RATIO SCALES

Scores based on an interval scale allow subtraction and addition. But they do not necessarily allow multiplication and division. Consider the centigrade scale of temperature. There is no doubt that the difference between 10 and 20 degrees centigrade is equal to that between 30 and 40 degrees centigrade. But can one say that 20 degrees centigrade is *twice* as high a temperature as 10 degrees centigrade? The answer is no, for the centigrade scale of temperature is only an interval scale. It is not a **ratio scale** which allows statements such as

10 feet is 1/5 as long as 50 feet, or 15 pounds is 3 times as heavy as 5 pounds. To make such statements one needs a true zero point. Such a ratio scale with a zero point does exist for temperature—the Kelvin absolute temperature scale, whose zero point is about −273 degrees centigrade.

Some psychological variables can be described by a ratio scale. This is true of various forms of sensory intensity—brightness, loudness, and so on. For example, it makes sense to say that the rock music emanating from your neighbor's apartment is four times as loud as your roommate singing in the shower. But there are many psychological variables which cannot be so readily described in ratio terms. Let's go back to reaction time. This cannot be considered a ratio scale for the decision process. In our previous example we saw that the reaction time for adjectives was 4 seconds, while that for nouns was 2 seconds. But we cannot say that the 4-second response represents twice as much *decision* time as the 2-second response, because of the unknown time required to press the response button. Since this time is unknown, we have no zero point.

The fact that very few variables are ratio scaled does not, of course, prevent people from describing ordinal- or interval-scaled variables in ratio terms. A claim by an advertiser that drug *A* is "twice as effective" as drug *B* may mean that *A* works twice as fast, or for twice the time, or is successful on twice as many people, or requires only half the dose. A potential consumer needs to know the advertiser's meaning of "effective" to evaluate the claim. Similarly, a 4-second reaction time in the word-recognition experiment is certainly twice as long as a 2-second reaction time; there is no harm in saying so, as long as it is understood that we are not talking about decision time but rather about the total reaction time.

Collecting the Data

The kinds of scales we have just discussed concern the ways in which psychological variables are described in numerical terms. The point of most psychological investigations is to see how such variables are related to various factors that may produce them. Psychologists—and most other scientists—employ three major methodological tools to achieve this end: the experiment, the observational study, and the case study.

THE EXPERIMENT

An *experiment* is a study in which the experimenter deliberately manipulates one or more variables to determine the effect of this manipulation on another variable. As an example, consider an experiment conducted to determine whether visual imagery aids memory. Participants in the experiment listen to a list of words, which they are instructed to memorize; later they are asked to recall as many words as possible. Two groups of subjects are chosen. One is the *experimental group;* this is the group to which the experimenter's manipulation is applied. It consists of subjects who are instructed to form visual images that connect each word to the preceding word. Other subjects form the

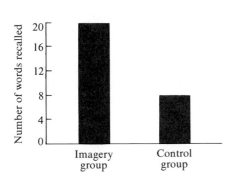

A.1 The results of a memory experiment. *Subjects in the imagery group, who formed visual images of the words they were to memorize, recalled an average of 20 words. Subjects in the control group, who received no special instructions, recalled an average of 8 items.*

control group, a group to which the experimenter's manipulation is not applied. These control subjects are not given imagery instructions. Many experiments have more than one experimental group (in this example, different groups might be told to do their visual imagining in different ways), or more than one control group (here, a second control group might be instructed to rehearse by repeating each word over and over).

Like many other experiments, this one can be thought of as a situation in which the experimenter varies something (here the instructions given to the subjects) and observes the effect of this variation on certain responses of the subjects (the number of words they correctly recall). The variable which is manipulated by the experimenter (imagery instructions) is called the **independent variable.** The subject's response (number of words recalled) is called the **dependent variable,** since the investigator wants to know whether it is dependent upon his manipulation of the independent variable. Speaking loosely, independent variables are sometimes regarded as causes, dependent variables as effects.

The results of our experiment are graphically presented in Figure A.1. The values of the independent variable are plotted on the horizontal, or *x*-axis, and the values of the dependent variable on the vertical, or *y*-axis. The figure displays the average number of items recalled for subjects who used visual imagery in memorizing and for those who did not. We will have more to say about this experiment presently.

OBSERVATIONAL STUDIES

Much psychological research departs from the experimental method in that investigators do not produce the effects directly, but only observe them. They do not so much design the experiment as discover it. Such an investigation is called an **observational study.** Consider the question "What is the effect of prenatal malnutrition on IQ?" This question can only be answered by locating children whose mothers were malnourished during pregnancy and measuring their IQs; to deliberately provide pregnant women with inadequate diets is obviously worse than unethical. But even though the investigators do not manipulate the mother's diet (or indeed, anything else), some of the methodological terms used before can still be applied. We can consider the mother's diet as the independent variable, and the child's IQ as the dependent variable. A group analogous to the experimental group would consist of children whose mothers were malnourished during pregnancy. An analogue to the control group is a group of children whose mothers' diet was adequate.

Observational studies like this one are sometimes called "experiments of nature." Because nature does not always provide exactly those control groups which the investigator might have wished for, observational studies can be difficult to interpret. For example, children whose mothers were malnourished during pregnancy are often born into environments which might also be expected to have negative effects on IQ. Women whose diet is inadequate during pregnancy are likely to be poor; they are therefore less likely to provide some of the physical advantages (like good food and health care) and educational advantages (like books and nursery schools) which may well be helpful in developing intelligence.

THE CASE STUDY

In many areas of psychology, conclusions are based on only one person who is studied intensively. Such an investigation is called a *case study*. Individuals who display unusual psychological or physiological characteristics, such as rare forms of color blindness, exceptionally good or poor memory, or brain injuries, can sometimes provide information about normal vision, memory, or brain function that would be difficult or impossible to obtain from normal individuals. Take the patient known as H.M., who suffered severe amnesia after brain surgery (see Chapter 8). Before the operation his memory was normal; afterward he could remember virtually nothing about events that occurred after the operation. This patient has been very extensively studied because of his unusual memory disorder. Since his amnesia is apparently the result of the destruction of a particular structure in the brain, the hippocampus, a comparison of H.M.'s performance with that of normal individuals allows us to make inferences about the role of the hippocampus in normal memory.

Some of the most famous case studies in psychology are those described by Sigmund Freud, whose extensive psychoanalytic interviews of his patients led him to develop theories of dreams, defense mechanisms, and other psychological processes (see Chapter 12).

Selecting the Subjects

How does one select the subjects for a psychological study? To answer this question, we have to consider the difference between a population and a sample.

SAMPLE AND POPULATION

Psychologists—again like other scientists—usually want to make statements about a larger group of persons (or animals) than the particular subjects they happen to use in their study. They want their conclusions to apply to a given *population*: all members of a given group—say, all three-year old boys, all schizophrenic patients, all U.S. voters, and in some cases, all humans. But they obviously can't study all members of the population. As a result, they have to select a *sample,* that is a subset, of the population they are interested in. Their hope is that the results found in the sample can be generalized to the population from which the sample is drawn.

It is important to realize that generalizations from a given sample to a particular population can only be made if the sample is representative (that is, typical) of the population to which one wants to generalize. Suppose one does a study on memory using college students. Can one generalize the results to adults in general? Strictly speaking one cannot, for college students are on the average younger than the population at large and are more accustomed to memorizing things. Under the circumstances, the safest course may be to restrict one's generalizations to the population of college students.

Most experimenters would probably argue that college students don't differ too greatly from the general population (at least in memory skills) so that results obtained with them do apply in general, at least approximately. But there are many cases in which inadequate sampling leads to gross blunders. The classic example is a 1936 poll which predicted that Franklin D. Roosevelt would lose the presidential election. In fact, he won by a landslide. This massive error was produced by a *biased sample*—all persons polled were selected from telephone directories. But in 1936 having a telephone was much more likely among persons of higher than of lower socioeconomic status. As a result, the sample was not representative of the voting population as a whole. Since socioeconomic level affected voting preference, the poll predicted falsely.

RANDOM AND STRATIFIED SAMPLES

To ensure that one can generalize from sample to population, investigators use a *random sample.* This is a sample in which every member of the population has an equal chance to be picked—as in a jury drawn by lot from all the voters of a given district (if none are disqualified or excuse themselves). The random sampling procedure applies with special force to the assignment of subjects in an experiment. Here every effort has to be made to assign subjects randomly to the various experimental or control groups.

For some purposes, even a random sample may not be good enough. While every member of the population has an equal chance to be selected, the sample may still turn out to be atypical by chance alone. This danger of chance error becomes less and less the greater the size of the sample. But if one is forced to use a small sample (and one often is because of lack of time or money), other sampling procedures may be necessary. Suppose we want to take a poll to determine the attitudes of American voters toward legalized abortion. We can expect peoples' attitudes to differ depending on (at least) their age, sex, and religion. If the sample is fairly small, it is important that each subgroup of the population be (randomly) sampled in proportion to its size. This procedure is called *stratified sampling,* and is common in studying psychological traits or attitudes which vary greatly among different subgroups of the population.

SAMPLING RESPONSES

The distinction between sample and population does not only apply to subjects. It also applies to the subjects' responses. Consider the investigators who studied aggressive behavior in 50 three-year-old boys. Each of these boys was observed on 10 occasions. Those 10 occasions can be regarded as a sample of all such occasions, just as the 50 boys can be regarded as a sample of all three-year-old boys (or at least of all middle-class U.S. boys). The investigators will surely want to generalize from this sample of occasions to the population of all such occasions. To make sure that such a generalization is warranted, one has to see to it that the occasions are not atypical—that the child isn't especially tired, or sick, and so on.

Organizing the Data: Descriptive Statistics

We have considered the ways in which psychologists describe the data provided by their subjects by assigning numbers to them (scaling) and the ways in which they collect these data in the first place (experiments, observational studies, case studies). Our next task is to see how these data are organized.

THE FREQUENCY DISTRIBUTION

Suppose we have designed and performed an experiment such as the imagery study described previously. The data will not automatically arrange themselves in the form shown in Figure A.1. Instead, investigators will first be faced with a list of numbers, the scores (number of words recalled correctly) for each subject in a given group. For example, if there were 10 subjects in the control group, their scores (in words correct) might have been

$$8,11,6,7,5,9,5,9,9,11$$

A first step in organizing the data is to list all the possible scores and the frequency with which they occurred, as shown in Table A1. Such an arrangement is called a ***frequency distribution.***

Table A.1   FREQUENCY DISTRIBUTION

Score	Frequency
11	2
10	0
9	3
8	1
7	1
6	1
5	2

The frequency distribution can be expressed graphically. A common means for doing this is a ***histogram*** which depicts the frequency distribution by a series of contiguous rectangles (Figure A.2). The values of the dependent variable (here, number of words recalled) are shown by the location of each rectangle on the horizontal or *x*-axis. The frequency of each score is shown on the vertical or *y*-axis, that is, by the height of each rectangle. This is simple enough for our example, but in practice graphic presentation often requires a further step. The number of possible values the dependent variable can assume is often very large. As a result, exactly equal values rarely occur, as when reaction times are measured to the nearest millisecond (thousandth of a second). To get around this, the scores are generally grouped by intervals for purposes of graphic display. The histogram might then plot the frequency of all reaction times between, say, 200 and 225 milliseconds, between 226 and 250 milliseconds, and so on.

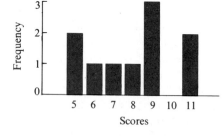

A.2 Histogram *In a histogram, a frequency distribution is graphically represented by a series of rectangles. The location of each rectangle on the x-axis indicates a score value, while its height shows how often that score value occurred.*

MEASURES OF CENTRAL TENDENCY

A frequency distribution is a more concise description of the result of the experiment than the raw list of scores from which it was derived, but for many purposes we may want a description that is even more concise. We often wish to summarize an entire distribution by a single, central score; such a score is called a *measure of central tendency.* Three measure of central tendency are commonly used to express this central point of a distribution: the mode, the median, and the mean.

The *mode* is simply the score that occurs most frequently. In our example, the mode is 9. More subjects (to be exact, 3) recalled 9 words than recalled any other number of words.

The *median* is the point that divides the distribution into two equal halves, when the scores are arranged in increasing order. To find the median in our example, we first list the scores:

$$5,5,6,7,8,9,9,9,11,11.$$
$$\uparrow$$

Since there are 10 scores, the median lies between the fifth and sixth scores, that is, between 8 and 9, as indicated by the arrow. Any score between 8 and 9 would divide the distribution into two equal halves, but it is conventional to choose the number in the center of the interval between them, that is, 8.5. When there is an odd number of scores, this problem does not arise.

The third measure of central tendency, the *mean, (M),* is the familiar arithmetic average. If N stands for the number of scores, then

$$M = \frac{\text{sum of scores}}{N}$$

$$= \frac{5+5+6+7+8+9+9+9+11+11}{10} = \frac{80}{10} = 8.0$$

Of these three measures, the mode is the least helpful, because the modes of two samples from the same population can differ greatly even if the samples have very similar distributions. If one of the 3 subjects who recalled 9 words recalled only 5 instead, the mode would have been 5 rather than 9. But the mode does have its uses. For example, in certain elections, the candidate with the most votes—the modal candidate—wins.

The median and the mean differ most in the degree to which they are affected by extreme scores. If the highest score in our sample were changed from 11 to 111, the median would be unaffected, whereas the mean would jump from 8.0 to 18.0. Most people would find the median (which remains 8.5) a more compelling "average" than the mean in such a situation, since most of the scores in the distribution are close to the median, but are not close to the mean (18.0).

Distributions with extreme values at one end are said to be *skewed.* A classic example is income, since there are only a few very high incomes but many low ones. Suppose we sample 10 individuals from a neighborhood, and find their yearly incomes (in thousands of dollars) to be:

$$5, 5, 5, 5, 10, 10, 10, 20, 20, 1,000.$$

The median income for this sample is 10 ($10,000), since both the fifth and sixth scores are 10, and this value reflects the income of the typical individual. The mean income for this sample, however, is $(5+5+5+5+10+10+10+20+20+1,000)/10 = 109$, or $109,000. A politician who wants to demonstrate that his neighborhood has prospered might—quite honestly—use these data to claim that the average (mean) income is $109,000. If, on the other hand, he wished to plead for financial aid, he might say—with equal honesty—that the average (median) income is only $10,000. There is no single "correct" way to find an "average" in this situation, but it is obviously important to know which average (that is, which measure of central tendency) is being used.

When deviations in either direction from the mean are equally frequent, the distribution is said to be **symmetric**. In such distributions, the mean and the median are equal. Many psychological variables have symmetric distributions, but for variables with skewed distributions, like income, measures of central tendency must be chosen with care.

MEASURES OF VARIABILITY

In reducing an entire frequency distribution to an average score, we have discarded a lot of very useful information. Suppose we (or the National Weather Service) measure the temperature every day for a year in various cities, and construct a frequency distribution for each city. The mean of this distribution tells us something about the city's climate. That it does not tell us everything is shown by the fact that the mean temperature in both San Francisco and Albuquerque is 56 degrees Fahrenheit. But the climates of the two cities nonetheless differ considerably, as indicated in Table A.2.

Table A.2   TEMPERATURE DATA FOR TWO CITIES (DEGREES FAHRENHEIT)

City	Lowest month	Mean	Highest month	Range
Albuquerque, New Mexico	35	56	77	42
San Francisco, California	48	56	63	15

The weather displays much more variability in the course of a year in Albuquerque than in San Francisco. A simple measure of variability is the **range,** the highest score minus the lowest. The range of temperatures in San Francisco is 15, while in Albuquerque it is 42.

A shortcoming of the range as a measure of variability is that it reflects the values of only two scores in the entire sample. As an example, consider the following distributions of ages in two college classes:

Distribution A: 19, 19, 19, 19, 19, 20, 25
Distribution B: 17, 17, 17, 20, 23, 23, 23

Each distribution has a mean of 20. Intuitively, distribution A has less variability, since all scores but one are very close to the mean. Yet the range of scores is the same (6) in both distributions. The problem arises because the range is determined by only two of the seven scores in each distribution.

A better measure of variability would incorporate every score in the distribution rather than just two scores. One might think that the variability could be measured by the average difference between the various scores and the mean, that is, by:

$$\frac{\text{sum of (score} - M)}{N}.$$

This hypothetical measure is unworkable, however, because some of the scores are greater than the mean and some are smaller, so that the numerator is a sum of both positive and negative terms. (In fact, it turns out that the sum of the positive terms equals the sum of the negative terms, so that the expression shown above always equals zero.) The solution to this problem is simply to square all the terms in the numerator, thus making them all positive.[1] The resulting measure of variability is called the *variance* (V):

$$V = \frac{\text{sum of (score} - M)^2}{N}. \tag{2}$$

The calculation of the variance for the control group in the memorization experiment is shown in Table A.3. As the table shows, the variance is obtained by subtracting the mean (M, which equals 8) from each score, squaring each result, adding all the squared terms, and dividing the resulting sum by the total number of scores (N, which equals 10), yielding a value of 4.4.

Table A.3   CALCULATING VARIANCE

Score	Score—mean	(Score—mean)²
8	$8 - 8 = 0$	$0^2 = 0$
11	$11 - 8 = 3$	$3^2 = 9$
6	$6 - 8 = -2$	$(-2)^2 = 4$
7	$7 - 8 = -1$	$(-1)^2 = 1$
5	$5 - 8 = -3$	$(-3)^2 = 9$
9	$9 - 8 = 1$	$1^2 = 1$
5	$5 - 8 = -3$	$(-3)^2 = 9$
9	$9 - 8 = 1$	$1^2 = 1$
9	$9 - 8 = 1$	$1^2 = 1$
11	$11 - 8 = 3$	$3^2 = 9$

Because deviations from the mean are squared, the variance is expressed in units different from the scores themselves. If our dependent variable were a distance, measured in centimeters, the variance would be expressed in square

---

1. An alternative solution would be to sum the absolute value of (score $- M$), that is, consider only the magnitude of this difference for each score, not the sign. The resulting statistic, called the *average deviation,* is little used, however, primarily because absolute values are not too easily dealt with in certain mathematical terms that underlie statistical theory. As a result, statisticians prefer to transform negative into positive numbers by squaring them.

centimeters. As we will see in the next section, it is convenient to have a measure of variability which can be added to or subtracted from the mean; such a measure ought to be expressed in the same units as the original scores. To accomplish this end, we employ another measure of variability, the *stan-dard deviation,* or *SD.* The standard deviation is derived from the variance (V); it is obtained by taking the square root of the variance. Thus

$$SD = \sqrt{V}$$

In our example, SD is about 2.1, the square root of the variance which is 4.4.

CONVERTING SCORES TO COMPARE THEM

Suppose a person takes two tests. One measures her memory span—how many digits she can remember after one presentation. The other test measures her running ability—how fast she can run 100 yards. It turns out that she can remember 8 digits and runs 100 yards in 17 seconds. Is there any way to decide whether she can remember digits better (or worse or equally well) than she can run 100 yards? On the face of it, the question seems absurd; it seems to be like comparing apples and oranges. But in fact, there is a way, for we can ask where each of these two scores is located on the two frequency distributions of other persons (presumably women of the same age) who are given the same two tasks.

PERCENTILE RANKS

One way of doing this is by transforming each of the two scores into *percentile ranks.* The percentile rank of a score indicates the percentage of all scores that lie below that given score. Let's assume that 8 digits is the 78th percentile, which means that 78 percent of the relevant comparison group remembers fewer digits. Let's further assume that a score of 17 seconds in the 100-yard dash is the 53rd percentile of the same comparison group. We can now answer the question with which we started. Our subject can remember digits better than she can run 100 yards. By converting into percentile ranks we have rendered incompatible scores compatible, allowing us to compare the two.

STANDARD SCORES

For many statistical purposes there is an even better method of comparing scores or of interpreting the meaning of individual scores. This is to express them by reference to the mean and standard deviation of the frequency distribution of which they are part, by converting them into *standard scores* (often called *z-scores*).

Suppose you take a test that measures aptitude for accounting and are told your score is 36. In itself, this number cannot help you decide whether to pursue or avoid a career in accounting. To interpret your score you need to know both the average score and how variable the scores are. If the mean is 30, you know you are above average, but how far above average is 6 points? This might be an extreme score, or one attained by many, depending on the variability of the distribution.

Let us suppose that the standard deviation of the distribution is 3. Your score of 36 is therefore 2 standard deviations (6 points) above the mean (30). A score which is expressed this way, as so many standard deviations from the mean, is called a standard score, or z-score. The formula for calculating a z-score is:

$$z = \frac{(\text{score}-M)}{SD} \tag{3}$$

Your aptitude of 36 has a z-score of $(36 - 30)/3 = 2$; that is, your score is 2 standard deviations above the mean.

The use of z-scores allows one to compare scores from different distributions. Still unsure whether to become an accountant, you take a screen test to help you decide whether to be an actor. Here your score is 60. This is a larger number than the 36 you scored on the earlier test, but it may not reveal much acting aptitude. Suppose the mean score on the screen test is 80, the standard deviation 20; then your z-score is $(60 - 80)/20 = -1$. In acting aptitude, you are 1 standard deviation below the mean; in accounting aptitude, 2 standard deviations above. The use of z-scores makes your relative abilities clear.

Notice that scores below the mean have negative z-scores, as in the last example. A z-score of 0 corresponds to a score which equals the mean.

Percentile rank and a z-score give similar information, but one cannot be converted into the other unless we know more about the distribution than just its mean and standard deviation. In many cases this information is available, as we shall now see.

THE NORMAL DISTRIBUTION

Frequency histograms can have a wide variety of shapes, but many variables of psychological interest have a *normal distribution,* (often called *normal curve*) which is a symmetric distribution of the shape shown in Figure A.3. The graph is smooth, unlike the histogram in Figure A.2, because it approximates the distribution of scores from a very large sample. The normal curve is bell-shaped, with most of its scores near the mean; the farther a score is from the mean, the less likely it is to occur. Among the many variables whose distributions are approximately normal are IQ, scholastic aptitude test scores (SAT), and women's heights (see Table A.4).[2]

A.3 Normal distribution *Values taken from any normally distributed variable (such as those presented in Table A.4) can be converted to z-scores by the formula z = (score − mean)/(standard deviation). The figure shows graphically the proportions that fall between various values of z.*

Table A.4 NORMALLY DISTRIBUTED VARIABLES

			z-scores				
Variable	Mean	Standard deviation	−2	−1	0	1	2
IQ	100	15	70	85	100	115	130
SAT	500	100	300	400	500	600	700
Height (women)	160 cm	5 cm	150	155	160	165	170

2. Men's heights are also normally distributed, but the distribution of the heights of all adults is not. Such a distribution would have two peaks, one for the modal height of each sex, and would thus be shaped quite differently from the normal curve. Distributions with two modes are called *bimodal.*

These three variables, IQ, SAT score, and height, obviously cannot literally have the "same" distribution, since their means and standard deviations are different (Table A.4 gives plausible values for them). In what sense, then, can they all be said to be normal? The answer is that the distribution of z-scores for all these variables is the same. For example, an IQ of 115 is 15 points, or 1 standard deviation, above the IQ mean of 100; a height of 165 centimeters is 5 centimeters, or 1 standard deviation, above the height mean of 160 centimeters. Both scores, therefore, have z-scores of 1. Furthermore, the percentage of heights between 160 and 165 centimeters is the same as the percentage of IQ scores between 100 and 115—34 percent. This is the percentage of scores which lie between the mean and one standard deviation above the mean for any normally distributed variable.

THE PERCENTILE RANK OF A z-SCORE

When a variable is known to have a normal distribution, a z-score can be converted directly into a percentile rank. A z-score of 1 has a percentile rank of 84—that is, 34 percent of the scores lie between the mean and $z = 1$, and (because the distribution is symmetric) 50 percent of the scores lie below the mean. A z-score of -1 corresponds, in a normal distribution, to a percentile rank of 16: only 16 percent of the scores are lower. These relationships are illustrated in Figure A.3 and Table A.4.

HOW THE NORMAL CURVE ARISES

Why should variables such as height or IQ scores—and many others—form distributions that have this particular shape? Mathematicians have shown that whenever a given variable is the sum of many smaller variables, its distribution will be close to that of the normal curve. An example is height (see Chapter 15, pp. 614). Height can be thought of as the sum of the contributions of the many genes (and some environmental factors) which influence this trait; it therefore satisfies the general condition.

The basic idea is that the many different factors that influence a given measure (such as the genes for height) operate independently. A given gene will pull height up or push it down; the direction in which it exerts its effort is a matter of chance. If the chances are equal either way, then a good analogy to this situation is a person who tosses a coin repeatedly and counts the number of times the coin comes up heads. In this analogy, a head corresponds to a gene that tends to increase height, a tail to a gene that tends to diminish it. The more often the genetic coin falls heads, the taller the person will be.

What will the distribution of the variable "number of heads" be? Clearly, it depends on the number of tosses. If the coin is tossed only once, then there will be either 0 heads or 1 head, and these are equally likely. The resulting distribution is shown in the top panel of Figure A.4.

If the number of tosses (which we will call N) is 2, then 0, 1, or 2 heads can arise. However, not all these outcomes are equally likely: 0 heads come up only if the sequence tail-tail (TT) occurs; 2 heads only if head-head (HH) occurs; but 1 head results from either HT or TH. The distribution of heads for $N = 2$ is shown in the second panel of Figure A.4. The area above 1 head has

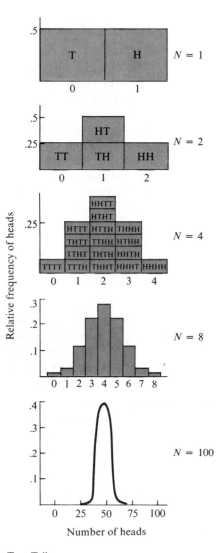

T = Tail
H = Head

A.4 Histograms showing expected number of heads in tossing a fair coin N times. *In successive panels, N = 1, 2, 4, 8, and 100.*

been subdivided into two equal parts, one for each possible sequence containing a single head.[3]

As N increases, the distribution of the number of heads looks more and more like the normal distribution, as the subsequent panels of Figure A.4 show. When N becomes as large as the number of factors that determine height, the distribution of the number of heads is virtually identical to the normal distribution. Similar arguments justify the assumption of normality for many psychological variables.

Describing the Relation between Two Variables: Correlation

The basic problem facing the psychological investigator is to account for observed differences in a variable of interest. Why, for example, do some people display better memory than others? The experimental approach to the problem, described earlier, is to ask whether changes in an independent variable produce systematic changes in the dependent variable. In the memory experiment, we asked whether subjects using visual imagery as an aid to memorizing would recall more words on the average than those without. In an observational study, however, our approach must be different, for in such a study we do not manipulate the variables. What is often done here is to observe the relationship between two—sometimes more—variables as they occur naturally, in the hope that differences in one variable can be attributed to differences in a second.

POSITIVE AND NEGATIVE CORRELATION

Imagine that a taxicab company wants to identify drivers who will earn relatively large amounts of money (for themselves and, of course, for the company). The company's officers make the plausible guess that one relevant factor is the driver's knowledge of the local geography, so they devise an appropriate test of street names, routes from place to place, and so on, and administer the test to each driver. The question is whether this test score is related to the driver's job performance as measured by his weekly earnings. To decide, one has to find out whether the test score and the earnings are *correlated*—that is, whether they tend to vary together.

In the taxicab example, the two variables will probably be ***positively correlated***—as one variable (test score) increases, the other (earnings) will generally increase too. But other variables may be ***negatively correlated***—when one increases, the other will tend to decrease. An example is a phenomenon called Zipf's law, which states that words that occur frequently in a language tend to be relatively short. The two variables word length and word frequency are negatively correlated, since one variable tends to increase as the other decreases.

---

3. The distribution of the number of heads is called the ***binomial distribution***, because of its relation to the binomial theorem: the number of head-tail sequences which can lead to k heads is the $(k + 1)$st coefficient of $(a + b)^N$.

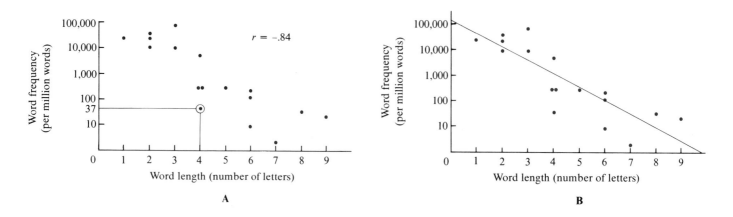

A

B

A.5 Scatter plot of a negative correlation between word length and word frequency

Correlational data are often displayed in a **scatter plot,** (or scatter diagram) in which values of one variable are shown on the horizontal axis and variables of the other on the vertical axis. Figure A.5A is a scatter plot of word frequency versus word length for the words in this sentence.[4] Each word is represented by a single point. An example is provided by the word *plot,* which is 4 letters long and occurs with a frequency of 37 times per million words of English text (and is represented by the circled dot). The points on the graph display a tendency to decrease on one variable as they increase on the other, although the relation is by no means perfect. It is helpful to draw a straight line through the various points in a scatter plot which comes as close as possible to all of them (Figure A.5B). The line is called a **line of best fit,** and it indicates the general trend of the data. Here, the line slopes downward because the correlation between the variables is negative.

The three panels of Figure A.6 are scatter plots showing the relation between other pairs of variables. In Figure A.6A hypothetical data from the taxicab example show that there is a positive correlation between test score and earnings (since the line of best fit slopes upward), but that test score is not a perfect predictor of on-the-job performance (since the points are fairly widely scattered around the line). Points above the line represent individuals who earn more than their test score would lead one to predict, points below the line individuals who earn less.

The examples in Figures A.5 and A.6A each illustrate moderate correlations; panels B and C of Figure A.6 are extreme cases. Figure A.6B shows data from a hypothetical experiment conducted in a fourth-grade class to illustrate the relation between metric and English units of length. The heights of five children are measured twice, once in inches and once in centimeters; each point on the scatter plot gives the two height measurements for one child. All the points in the figure fall on the line of best fit, because height in centimeters always equals 2.54 times height in inches. The two variables, height in centimeters and height in inches, are perfectly correlated—one can be perfectly predicted from the other. Once you know your height in inches, there is no information to be gained by measuring yourself with a meterstick.

4. There is no point for the "word" *A.5A* in this sentence. The frequencies of the other words are taken from H. Kucera and W. N. Francis, *Computational Analysis of Present-Day American English* (Providence, R. I.: Brown University Press, 1967).

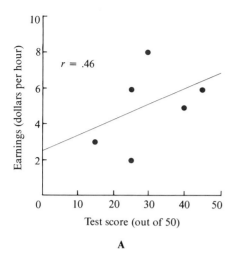

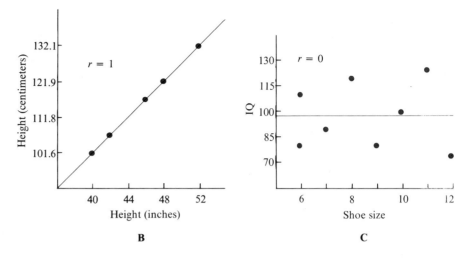

A.6   Scatter plots of various correlations
(A) The scatter plot and line of best fit show a positive correlation between a taxi-driving test and earnings. (B) A perfect positive correlation. The line of best fit passes through all the points. (C) A correlation of zero. The line of best fit is horizontal.

Figure A.6c presents a relation between IQ and shoe size. These variables are unrelated to each other; people with large shoes have neither a higher nor a lower IQ than people with small ones. The line of best fit is therefore horizontal, because the best guess of an individual's IQ is the same no matter what his or her shoe size—it is the mean IQ of the population.

THE CORRELATION COEFFICIENT

Correlations are often described by a ***correlation coefficient***, denoted **r,** a number that can vary from +1.00 to −1.00 which expresses the strength and the direction of the correlation. For positive correlations, r is positive; for negative correlations, it is negative; for variables which are completely uncorrelated, $r = 0$. The largest positive value r can have is +1.00, which represents a perfect correlation (as in Figure A.6B); the largest possible negative value is −1.00, which is also a perfect correlation. The closer the points in a scatter plot come to falling on the line of best fit, the nearer r will be to +1.00 or −1.00, and the more confident we can be in predicting scores on one variable from scores on the other. The values of r for the scatter plots in Figures A.5 and A.6A are given on the figures.

The method for calculating r between two variables, X and Y, is shown in Table A.5. The formula is

$$r = \frac{\text{sum } (z_x z_y)}{N}. \tag{4}$$

The variable z_x is the z-score corresponding to X; z_y is the z-score corresponding to Y. To find r, each X and Y score must first be converted to a z-score by subtracting the mean and then dividing by the standard deviation. Then the product of z_x and z_y is found for each pair of scores. The average of these products (the sum of the products divided by N, the number of pairs of scores) is the correlation coefficient r.

Table A.5 CALCULATION OF THE CORRELATION COEFFICIENT

1. Data (from Figure A.6A).

Test Score (X)	Earnings (Y)
45	6
25	2
15	3
40	5
25	6
30	8

2. Find the mean and standard deviation for X and Y.

For X, mean = 30, standard deviation = 10
For Y, mean = 5, standard deviation = 2

3. Convert each X and each Y to a z-score, using $z = \dfrac{(\text{score}-M)}{SD}$

X	Y	z-score for X (z_x)	z-score for Y (z_y)	$z_x z_y$
45	6	1.5	0.5	0.75
25	2	−0.5	−1.5	0.75
15	3	−1.5	−1.0	1.50
40	5	1.0	0.0	0.00
25	6	0.5	0.5	−0.25
30	8	0.0	1.5	0.00
				2.75

4. Find the product $z_x z_y$ for each pair of scores.

5. $r = \dfrac{\text{sum }(z_x z_y)}{N} = \dfrac{2.75}{6} = .46$

Figure A.7 illustrates why this procedure yields positive values of r for positively related variables and negative values of r for negatively related variables. For positively correlated variables, most points are either above or below the mean on both variables. If they are above the mean, both z_x and z_y

A.7 Correlation coefficients (A) Two positively correlated variables. Most of the points lie in the upper right and lower left quadrants, where $z_x z_y$ is positive, so r is positive. (B) Two negatively correlated variables. Most of the points lie in the upper left and lower right quadrants, where $z_x z_y$ is negative, so r is negative.

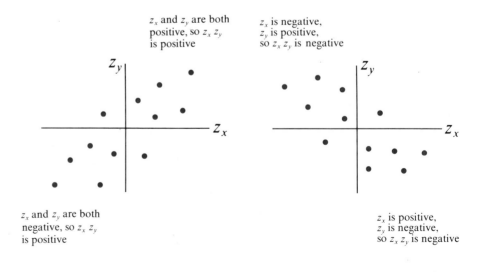

z_x and z_y are both positive, so $z_x z_y$ is positive

z_x is negative, z_y is positive, so $z_x z_y$ is negative

z_x and z_y are both negative, so $z_x z_y$ is positive

z_x is positive, z_y is negative, so $z_x z_y$ is negative

will be positive; if they are below, both z_x and z_y will be negative. (This follows from the definition of a z-score.) In either case the product $z_x z_y$ will be positive, so r will be positive. For negatively correlated variables, most points which are above the mean on one variable are below the mean on the other—either z_x is positive and z_y is negative, or vice versa. The product $z_x z_y$ is therefore negative, and so is r.

INTERPRETING AND MISINTERPRETING CORRELATIONS

It is tempting, but false, to assume that if two variables are correlated, one is the cause of the other. There is a positive correlation between years of education and annual income in the population of North American adults; many people, including some educators, argue from these data that students should stay in school as long as possible in order to increase their eventual earning power. The difficulty with this reasoning is not the existence of counterexamples (such as Andrew Carnegie, the American industrialist and millionaire who never finished high school), which merely show that the correlation is less than 1.00. It is rather that it is difficult to infer causality from this correlation because both variables are correlated with yet a third variable. Years of schooling and income as an adult are not only correlated with each other, they are also correlated with a third variable—the parents' income. Given this fact, can we make any assertions about what causes adult income? Perhaps income is determined by one's education (it probably is, in part). But perhaps the relationship between income and education is a spurious by-product of the parents' income. Perhaps this third factor partially determines both one's education and one's income, and there is no real causal connection between the two.

Another demonstration of the fact that correlation is not equivalent to causation occurs while waiting for a bus or a subway whose schedule is unknown. There is a negative correlation between the number of minutes a rider will have to wait for the next subway and the number of people waiting when the rider enters the station: the more there are waiting, the sooner the subway will arrive. This negative correlation is fairly substantial, but even so, one would hardly try to cut down one's waiting time by arriving at the station with fifty friends. Here, the third, causal variable (time since the last train or bus left) is fairly obvious.[5] But even when it is harder to imagine just what the third variable might be, it is still possible that such a third variable exists and is responsible for the correlation. As a result, correlations can never provide solid evidence of a causal link.

Interpreting Data: Inferential Statistics

We have seen that a psychologist collecting data encounters variability. In memory experiments, for example, different individuals recall different numbers of items, and the same person is likely to perform differently when tested twice. An investigator wishes to draw general conclusions from data in spite of this variability, or to discover the factors which are responsible for it.

5. I thank Barry Schwartz for this example.

ACCOUNTING FOR VARIABILITY

As an example of how variability may be explained, consider a person shooting a pistol at a target. Although he always aims at the bull's eye, the shots scatter around it (Figure A.8A). Assuming that the mean is the bull's eye, the variance of these shots is the average squared deviation of the shots from the center; suppose this variance is 100.

Now we set about explaining the variance. If the shooting was done outdoors, the wind may have increased the spread; moving the shooter to an indoor shooting range produces the tighter grouping shown in Figure A.8B. The new variance is 80, a reduction of 20 percent—this means that the wind accounts for 20 percent of the original variance. Some of the variance may result from the unsteady hand of the shooter, so we now mount the gun. This yields a variance of 50 (Figure A.8C), a reduction of 50 percent, so 50 percent of the variance can be attributed to the shaky hand of the shooter. To find out how much of the variance can be accounted for by either the wind *or* the shaking, we mount the gun *and* move it indoors; now we may find a variance of only 30 (Figure A.8D). This means we have explained 70 percent of the variance, leaving 30 percent unaccounted for.[6] Not all changes in the situation will reduce the variance. For example, if we find that providing the shooter with earmuffs leaves the variance unchanged, we know that none of the original variance was due to the noise of the pistol.

6. I am grateful to Paul Rozin for suggesting this example.

A.8 Results of target shooting under several conditions In each case, the bull's eye is the mean and the variance is the average squared deviation of the shots from the bull's eye. (A) Outdoors, no mount. Variance = 100. (B) Indoors, no mount. Variance = 80. (C) Outdoors, mount. Variance = 50. (D) Indoors, mount. Variance = 30.

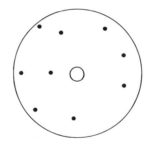

A. Outdoors, no mount. Variance = 100.

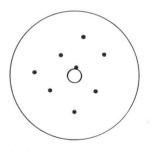

C. Outdoors, mount. Variance = 50.

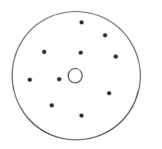

B. Indoors, no mount. Variance = 80.

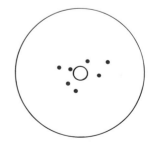

D. Indoors, mount. Variance = 30.

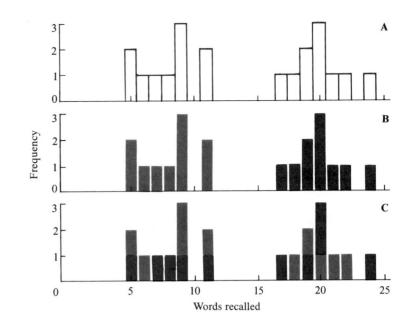

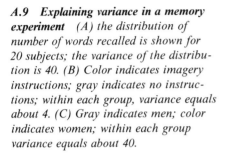

A.9 Explaining variance in a memory experiment *(A) the distribution of number of words recalled is shown for 20 subjects; the variance of the distribution is 40. (B) Color indicates imagery instructions; gray indicates no instructions; within each group, variance equals about 4. (C) Gray indicates men; color indicates women; within each group variance equals about 40.*

VARIANCE AND EXPERIMENTS

Figure A.9 shows how this approach can be applied to the experiment on memory and visual imagery, described earlier. Figure A.9A shows the distribution of scores for all 20 subjects in the experiment (that is, both groups); the total variance of this distribution is 40. But 10 of these subjects had been instructed to use visual imagery in memorizing, whereas the other 10 were given no special instructions. How much of the variance can be accounted for by instructions? In Figure A.9B, the histograms for the two groups are distinguished by shading; clearly there is less variability within the imagery group (and within the control group) than in the overall distribution. In fact, the variance within a group averages only 4.0. The instructions given the subjects therefore account for 90 percent of the variance; 10 percent (4 ÷ 40) still remains unexplained.

Figure A.9C shows a situation in which an independent variable (in this case, sex) explains little of the variance. The overall distribution is the same, but here the shading indicates which scores were obtained by women and which by men. Now the variance of women's scores alone, and the men's scores alone, is about 40, the same as the total variance. The subject's sex evidently accounts for none of the overall variance in memorizing ability.

VARIANCE AND CORRELATION

The technique of explaining the variance in one variable by attributing it to the effect of another variable can also be applied to correlational studies. Here, the values of one variable are explained (that is, accounted for) when the values of the other variable are known. Recall the taxicab example. In it a correlation of .46 was found between taxi drivers' earnings and their scores on a screening test. Since the correlation is neither perfect nor zero, some but not all of the variance in job performance can be explained by the aptitude test scores. The greater the magnitude of the correlation coefficient, r, the more variance is accounted for. The rule is that the proportion of variance which is explained equals r^2: If $r = .46$, one variable accounts for $(.46)^2 = .21$ of the variance of the other. (Just why this proportion is r^2 is beyond the scope of this discussion.) To put this another way, suppose all the cab drivers were identical on the one variable, their performance on the geographical test. This means that the variance on that variable would be zero. As a result, the variability on the second variable, earnings, would be reduced. The formula tells us by how much. The original variance on earnings can be determined from the hata in Table A.5. It is 4. Its correlation with the geography test is .46. Since the effect of this variable, the geography test, is completely controlled, the variability on earnings will be $4 - (.46)^2 \times 4 = 3.16$. The drop in the variance from 4 to 3.16 is a reduction of 21 percent. The aptitude test does help us to predict taxicab earnings, for it accounts for 21 percent of the variance. But a good deal of the variance—79 percent—is still unexplained.

HYPOTHESIS TESTING

Much behavioral research attempts to answer two-alternative questions. Does the amount of food a person eats depend on the effort required to eat it? Can people learn while they are sleeping? Is drug X more effective than aspirin? Each of these questions suggests an experiment, and the procedures described in the previous section could be used to discover how much of the variance in the dependent variable could be accounted for by the independent variable. But how can the results of such experiments lead to simple yes-or-no answers to the questions that inspired them?

TESTING HYPOTHESES ABOUT SINGLE SCORES

We will begin by testing a hypothesis about single scores. Consider the problem iz interpreting a lie-detector test. In such a test, a person is asked a series of questions and various measures of physiological arousal are taken as he answers. An answer which is accompanied by an unusually high degree of arousal is taken as possible evidence that the person is lying. The question is how high is "unusually high?"

To answer this question we will first rephrase it. Can we reject the hypothesis that the given score came from the distribution of responses the same individual gave to neutral questions? (An example is "Is your name Fred?") Suppose the average arousal score to such control questions is 50, that the standard deviation of these neutral responses is 10, and that the arousal scores are normally distributed. We now look at the arousal score to the critical item. Let us say that this is 60. How likely is it that this score is from a sample drawn by chance from the population of responses to neutral questions? To find out, we convert it to a z-score, by computing its distance from the mean and dividing it by the standard deviation. The resulting z-score is $(60-50)/10$ or 1. Since the distribution is normal, Figure A.3 tells us that 16 percent of this person's arousal scores would be as high or higher than this. Under the circumstances we don't feel justified in rejecting the hypothesis that the score in question comes from the distribution of neutral responses. Put another way, we don't feel justified in accusing the person of lying. Our feelings might be different if the score were 70 or above. For now the z-score is $(70-50)/10$, or 2 standard deviations above the mean of the neutral distribution. The chances that a score this high or higher is from a sample drawn from the population of neutral responses is only 2 in a 100. We might now feel more comfortable in rejecting the hypothesis that this score is simply a chance event. We are more likely to assume that it is drawn from another distribution—in short, that the person is lying.

In this example we had to decide between two hypotheses. We look at a given score (or a set of scores) obtained under a particular experimental condition (in this case, a loaded question). One hypothesis is that the experimental condition has no effect, that the score is merely a reflection of the ordinary variability around the mean of a control condition (in this case, neutral questions). This is the so-called **null hypothesis,** the hypothesis that there really is no effect. The **alternative hypothesis** is that the null hypothesis is false, that the score is far enough away from the control mean so that we can assume that the same experimental condition has some effect. To decide between these two hypotheses, the data are expressed as a z-score which in the context of hypothesis testing is called a **critical ratio.** Behavioral scientists generally accept a critical ratio of 2 as a cutting point. If this ratio is 2 or greater, they generally reject the null hypothesis and assume there is an effect of the experimental condition. (Such critical ratios of 2 or more are said to be **statistically significant,** which is just another way of saying that the null hypothesis can be rejected.) Critical ratios of less than 2 are considered too small to allow the rejection of the null hypothesis.

This general procedure is not foolproof. It is certainly possible for a subject in the lie-detection example to have an arousal score of 70 (a critical ratio of 2) or higher even though he is telling the truth. According to Figure A.3, this will happen about 2 percent of the time, and the person administering the test will erroneously "detect" a lie. Raising the cutoff value for the critical ratio of 3 or 4, would make such errors less common, but would not eliminate them entirely; furthermore, such a high critical value might mean failure to discover any lies the subject does utter. One of the important consequences of the variability in psychological data can be seen here: the investigator who has to decide between two interpretations of the data (the null hypothesis and the alternative hypothesis) cannot be correct all the time.

TESTING HYPOTHESES ABOUT MEANS

In the preceding discussion, our concern was with hypotheses about single scores. We now turn to the more commonly encountered problems in which the hypotheses involve means.

In many experiments, the investigator compares two or more groups—subjects tested with or without a drug, with or without imagery instructions, and so on. Suppose we get a difference between the two groups. How do we decide whether the difference is genuine rather than a mere chance fluctuation?

Let us return to the experiment in which memory for words was tested with and without instructions to imagine the items visually. To simplify the exposition, we will here consider a modified version of the experiment in which the same subjects serve in both the imagery and the nonimagery conditions. Each

Table A.6   NUMBER OF ITEMS RECALLED WITH AND WITHOUT IMAGERY INSTRUCTION, FOR 10 SUBJECTS

Subject	Score with imagery	Score without imagery	Improvement
Alphonse	20	5	15
Betsy	24	9	15
Cheryl	20	5	15
Davis	18	9	9
Earl	22	6	16
Fred	19	11	8
Germaine	20	8	12
Hortense	19	11	8
Imogene	17	7	10
Jerry	21	9	12
Mean	20	8	12

$$\text{Variance of improvement scores} = \frac{\text{sum of (score} - 12)^2}{10} = 8.8$$

$$\text{Standard deviation of improvement scores} = \sqrt{8.8} = 2.97$$

subjects memorizes a list of 30 words without instructions, then memorizes a second list of 30 words under instructions to visualize. What we want to know is whether the subjects show any improvement with imagery instructions. There is no separate control group in this experiment, but, because a subject's score in the imagery condition can be compared with his score in the uninstructed condition, each subject provides his own control.

Table A.6 gives data for the 10 subjects in the experiment. For each subject, the table lists the number of words recalled without imagery instructions, the number recalled with such instructions, and the improvement (the difference between the two scores). The mean improvement is 12 words, from 8 words without imagery to 20 words with imagery. Is this difference statistically significant?

To show how this question is answered, we will follow much the same logic as that used in the analysis of the lie-detection problem. We have a mean—the average difference score of 10 subjects. What we must realize is that this mean—12—is really a sample based on the one experiment with 10 subjects we have just run. Suppose we had run the experiment again, with another set of 10 subjects—not just once, but many times. Each such repetition of the experiment would yield its own mean. And each of these means would constitute another sample. But what is the population to which these samples refer? It is the set of all of these means—the average differences between imagery and nonimagery instructions obtained in each of the many repetitions of the experiment we might possibly perform. And the mean of these means—a kind of grand mean—is the mean of the population. Any conclusions we want to draw from our experiment are really assertions about this population mean. If we say that the difference we found is statistically significant, we are asserting that the population mean is a difference score which is greater than zero (and in the same direction as in the sample). Put another way, we are asserting that the difference we found is not just a fluke but is real and would be obtained again and again if we repeated the experiment, thus rejecting the null hypothesis.

The null hypothesis amounts to the claim that the mean we actually obtained could have been drawn by chance from a distribution of sample means (that is, the many means of the possible repetitions of our experiment) around a population mean of zero. To test this claim, we have to compute a critical ratio that can tell us how far from zero our own mean actually is. Like all critical ratios, this is a z-score which expresses the distance of a score from a mean in units of the standard deviation (the SD). Thus, $z = (score - M)/SD$. In our present case, the score is our obtained mean (that is, 12); the mean is the hypothetical population mean of zero (assumed by the null hypothesis). But what is the denominator? It is the standard deviation of the distribution of sample means, the means of the many experiments we might have done.

The standard deviation of such a distribution of sample means is called the **standard error** of the mean (**SE**). Its value is determined by two factors: the standard deviation of the sample and the size of that sample. Specifically,

$$SE = \frac{SD}{\sqrt{N-1}}. \tag{5}$$

It is clear that the variability of a mean (and this is what the standard error measures) goes down with the increasing sample size. (Why this factor turns out to be $\sqrt{N-1}$ is beyond the scope of this discussion.) A clue as to why comes from the consideration of the effects of an atypical score. Purely by chance, a sample may include an extreme case. But the larger the size of that sample, the less the effect of on extreme case on the average. If a sample of 3 persons includes a midget, the average height will be unusually far from the population mean. But in a sample of 3,000, one midget will not affect the average very markedly.

We can now complete our analysis of the memory experiment. The critical ratio to be evaluated is.

$$\text{critical ratio} = \frac{\text{obtained sample mean} - \text{population mean by null hypothesis}}{\text{standard error of the mean}}$$

Since the assumed population mean is zero, this becomes:

$$\text{critical ratio} = \frac{\text{obtained sample mean}}{SE}. \tag{6}$$

This critical ratio expresses the mean difference between the two experimental conditions in units of the variability of the sample mean, that is, the standard error. To compute the standard error, we first find the standard deviation of the improvement scores; this turns out to be 2.97, as shown in Table A.6. Then equation (5) tells us

$$SE = \frac{SD}{\sqrt{N-1}} = \frac{2.97}{\sqrt{10-1}} = .99$$

7. There are several simplifications in this account. One is that the critical ratio described here does not have an exactly normal distribution. When the sample size is large, this effect is unimportant, but for small samples (like the one in the example) they can be material. To deal with these and related problems, statisticians often utilize measures that refer to distributions other than the normal one. An example is the t-test, a kind of critical ratio based on the so-called t-distribution.

The critical ratio is now the obtained mean difference divided by the standard error, or $12/.99 = 12.12$. This is clearly very much larger than 2.0, and we conclude that the observed difference in memory between the imagery and control conditions is much too large to be attributed to chance factors. Thus using visual imagery evidently does improve recall.[7]

SOME IMPLICATIONS OF THE HYPOTHESIS-TESTING PROCEDURE

This method of testing hypotheses, which is routine in psychological research, has three important characteristics which color the interpretation of "significant" results. The conclusions drawn are probabilistic, conservative, and affected by sample size.

The probabilistic nature of statistics is the most important, and the most obvious. Since there is always unexplained variance in a psychological study, there is always some probability that the conclusions are wrong as applied to the population. And even if we have come to a correct conclusion about population means, we cannot generalize to individuals. Thus a study which shows that men have higher scores than women on spatial relations tests is not inconsistent with the existence of brilliant female artists or architects. Sample means for the two groups can differ significantly, even though there is considerable overlap in the two distributions of scores.

The conservative property of hypothesis testing is the great stress it places on the null hypothesis in reaching a decision. It is necessary to be very convinced that the null hypothesis is false before the alternative hypothesis can be entertained. There are other imaginable strategies for making statistical decisions, but this one does have a perfectly rational basis. If there really are differences between groups due to the independent variable, this conservative procedure may force us to conclude that no differences exist. As a result we may have failed to discover a small effect. Still, if the effect is interesting, someone else may well attempt a similar experiment. But if we "discover" that an independent variable has an effect, when it actually does not (that is, if the null hypothesis is true), we will have added an inaccurate "fact" to the store of scientific knowledge, and run the risk of leading other investigators into a blind alley.

Finally, consider how sample size influences our decisions. Suppose that, in the population, a very small difference is produced by a change in the independent variable. As an example, suppose that the population difference between men and women on a spatial relations test is 1 percent. We would probably be unable to reject the null hypothesis (that there are no sex differences on the test) with samples of moderate size. If the sample size were increased sufficiently, however, the null hypothesis could be rejected, since the variance associated with the sample means would decrease (leading to an increase in the critical ratio). Someone reading a report of the experiment would learn that, by using thousands of subjects, we had discovered a "significant" difference of 1 percent. A fair reaction to this bit of intelligence would be that perhaps the null hypothesis can be rejected, but that the size of the effect is so small that its *psychological* significance is slight. Statistical significance is required before a result is considered reliable, but it does not guarantee that the effect discovered is of psychological significance or any practical importance.

Summary

1. Statistical methods concern the ways in which investigators describe, gather, organize, and interpret collections of numerical data. A crucial concern of statistical endeavors is to deal with the variability that is encountered in all research.

2. An early step in the process is *scaling*, a procedure for assigning numbers to psychological responses. Scales can be *categorical, ordinal, interval,* or *ratio scales.* These differ in the degree to which they can be subjected to arithmetical operations.

3. There are three main methods for conducting psychological research: by means of an *experiment,* an *observational study,* and a *case study.* In an experiment, the investigator manipulates one variable, the *independent variable,* to see how it affects the subject's response, the *dependent variable.* In an observational study, the investigator does not manipulate any variables directly but rather observes them as they naturally occur. A case study is an investigation in which one person is studied in depth.

4. An important distinction in psychological research is that between *sample* and *population.* The population is the entire group about which the investigator wants to draw conclusions. The sample is the subset (usually small) of that population that is actually tested. Generalizations from sample to population are only possible if the one is representative of the other. This requires the use of *random samples.* In some cases a special version of the random sample, the *stratified sample,* may be employed.

5. A first step in organizing the data is to arrange them in a *frequency distribution,* often displayed in graphic form, as in a *histogram.* Frequency distributions are characterized by a *central tendency* and by *variability* around this central tendency. The common measure of central tendency is the *mean,* though sometimes another measure, the *median,* may be preferable, as in cases when the distribution is *skewed.* Important measures of variability are the *variance* and the *standard deviation.*

6. One way of comparing two scores drawn from different distributions is to convert both into *percentile ranks.* Another is to transform them into *z-scores,* which express the distance of a score from its mean in standard deviation units. The percentile rank of a *z*-score can be computed if the shape of that score's distribution is known. An important example is the *normal distribution,* graphically displayed by the *normal curve* which describes the distribution of many psychological variables and is basic to much of statistical reasoning.

7. In observational studies, the relation between variables is often expressed in the form of a *correlation* which may be positive or negative. It is measured by the *correlation coefficient,* a number that can vary from +1.00 to −1.00. While correlations reflect the extent to which two variables vary together, they do not necessarily indicate that one of them causes the other.

8. A major task of any investigator is to explain the variability of some dependent variable, usually measured by the variance. One means for doing so is to see whether that variance is reduced when a certain independent variable is controlled. If so, this independent variable is said to account for some of the variability of the dependent variable.

A27

9. One of the main functions of the statistical methods is to help test hypotheses about population given information about the sample. An important example is the difference between mean scores obtained under two different conditions. Here the investigator has to decide between the *null hypothesis* which asserts that the difference was obtained by chance, and the *alternative hypothesis* which asserts that the difference is genuine and exists in the population. The decision is made by dividing the obtained mean difference by the *standard error,* a measure of the variability of that mean difference. If the resulting ratio, called *critical ratio,* is large enough, the null hypothesis is rejected, the alternative hypothesis is accepted, and the difference is said to be *statistically significant.*

Glossary

absolute threshold The lowest intensity of some stimulus that produces a response.

accommodations The process by which the lens is thickened or flattened to focus on an object.

achievement motive The desire to meet or exceed some standard of excellence.

action potential A brief change in the electrical potential of an axon that is the physical basis of the nervous impulse.

active rehearsal Rehearsal in which material is actively reorganized while being held in short-term memory. In contrast to maintenance rehearsal, this confers considerable benefit. *See also* maintenance rehearsal.

active sleep (or REM sleep) A stage of sleep during which the EEG is similar to that of waking, during which there are rapid eye movements (REMs), and during which dreams occur.

adaptive value In biological terms, the extent to which an attribute increases the likelihood of viable offspring. Also, the unit of inheritance.

additive color mixture Mixing colors by stimulating the eye with two sets of wavelengths simultaneously (e.g., by focusing filtered light from two projectors on the same spot).

adrenalin *See* epinephrine.

affective disorders A group of disorders whose primary characteristic is a disturbance of mood. *See also* bipolar disorder, depression, mania, and unipolar disorder.

afferent nerves Sensory nerves that carry messages to the brain.

alarm call Special, genetically pre-programmed cry, mostly in birds, that impels all members of a group to seek cover. A biological puzzle, since it seems to endanger the individual's own survival.

algorithm In computer problem-solving, a procedure in which all of the operations are specified step-by-step. *See also* heuristics.

all-or-none law Describes the fact that once a stimulus exceeds threshold, further increases do not increase the amplitude of the action potential.

alpha blocking The disruption of the alpha rhythm by visual stimulation or by active thought with the eyes closed.

alpha waves Fairly regular EEG waves, between 8–12 per second, characteristic of a relaxed, waking state, usually with eyes closed.

alternative hypothesis In statistics, the hypothesis that the null hypothesis is false; that an obtained difference is so far from zero that one has to assume that the mean difference in the population is greater than zero. *See also* null hypothesis.

altruism As used by sociobiologists, any behavior pattern that benefits individuals that are not one's own offspring (e.g., an alarm call). *See also* alarm call.

ambiguity (in sentence meaning) The case in which a sentence (i.e., one surface structure) has two meanings (i.e., two underlying structures). (E.g., "These missionaries are ready to eat" overheard in a conversation between two cannibals.)

anal character In psychoanalytic theory, a personality pattern derived from severe conflicts during toilet training. It is dominated by a reaction formation against giving in to impulses of elimination, resulting in the characteristic attributes of compulsive orderliness, stubborness, and stinginess.

anal stage In psychoanalytic theory, the stage of psychosexual development during which the focus of pleasure is on activities related to elimination.

androgen Any male sex hormone.

anterograde amnesia A memory deficit suffered after some brain damage. It is an inability to learn and remember any information imparted after the injury, with little effect on memory for information acquired previously. *See also* retrograde amnesia.

antidepressants Drugs (e.g. imipramine) which alleviate depressive symptoms.

antisocial personality Also called psychopath or sociopath. The term describes persons who get into continual trouble with society, are indifferent to others, impulsive, with little concern for the future or remorse about the past.

anxiety An emotional state akin to fear. According to Freud, many mental illnesses center around anxiety and on attempts to ward it off by various unconscious mechanisms.

anxiety hierarchy *See* systematic desensitization.

anxiety neurosis An anxiety disorder in which anxiety is all-persuasive without specific symptoms such as phobias or obsessive-compulsive behavior.

aphagia Refusal to eat (and in an extreme version, to drink) brought about by lesion of the lateral hypothalamus.

aphasia A disorder of language produced by lesions in certain association areas of the cortex. A lesion in Broca's area leads to expressive aphasia, one in Wernicke's area to receptive aphasia.

apparent movement The perception of movement produced by stimuli that are stationary but flash on and off with appropriate time intervals.

artificial intelligence Some aspect of cognitive processing that is carried out by a computer. Examples are computer programs that recognize patterns or solve certain kinds of problems.

assimilation and accommodation In Piaget's theory, the twin processes by means of which cognitive development proceeds. Assimilation is the process whereby the environment is interpreted in terms of the schemas the child has at the time. Accommodation is the way the child changes his schemas as he continues to interact with the environment.

association A linkage between two psychological processes as a result of past experience in which the two have occurred together. A broad term which subsumes conditioning and association of ideas among others.

association areas Regions of the cortex that are not projection areas. They tend to be involved in the integration of sensory information or of motor commands.

attention A collective label for all the processes by which we perceive selectively.

attitude A fairly stable, evaluative disposition that makes a person think, feel, or behave positively or negatively about some person, group, or social issue.

attribution theory A theory about the process by which we try to explain a person's behavior, attributing it to situational factors or to some inferred dispositional qualities or both.

authoritarian personality A cluster of personal attributes (e.g., submission to persons above and harshness to those below) and social attitudes (e.g., prejudice against minority groups) which is sometimes held to constitute a distinct personality.

automatization A process whereby components of a skilled activity become subsumed under a higher-order organization and are run off automatically.

autonomic nervous system (ANS) A part of the nervous system that controls the internal organs, usually not under voluntary control.

aversive therapy A form of behavior therapy in which the undesirable response leads to an aversive stimulus (e.g., patient shocks himself every time he reaches for a cigarette).

avoidance learning Instrumental learning in which the response averts an aversive stimulus before it occurs. This poses a problem: What is the reinforcement for this kind of learning?

A30

axon Part of a neuron which transmits impulse to other neurons or effectors.

basilar membrane *See* cochlea.

behavior therapy A general approach to psychological treatment which (1) holds that the disorders to which it addresses itself are produced by maladaptive learning and must be remedied by reeducation, (2) proposes techniques for this reeducation based on principles of learning and conditioning, (3) focuses on the maladaptive behaviors as such rather than on hypothetical unconscious processes of which they may be expressions.

belongingness in learning The fact that the ease with which associations are formed depends upon the items to be associated. This holds for classical conditioning in which some CS-UCS combinations are more effective than others (e.g. learned taste aversions) and for instrumental conditioning in which some response-reinforcer combinations work more easily than others (e.g., specific defense reactions in avoidance conditioning of species).

between-group heritability The extent to which variation between groups (as in the difference between the mean IQs of U. S. whites and blacks) is attributable to genetic factors. *See also* heritability and within-group heritability.

bipolar disorder Affective disorder in which the patient swings from one emotional extreme to another, experiencing both manic and depressive episodes. Formerly called manic-depressive psychosis.

brightness A perceived dimension of visual stimuli—the extent to which they appear light or dark.

brightness contrast The perceiver's tendency to exaggerate the physical difference in the light intensities of two adjacent regions. As a result, a gray patch looks brighter on a black background, darker on a white background.

brightness ratio The ratio between the light reflected by a region and the light reflected by the area that surrounds it. According to one theory, perceived brightness is determined by this ratio.

British empiricism A school of thought that holds that all knowledge comes by way of empirical experience, that is, through the senses.

Broca's area *See* aphasia.

case study An observational study in which one person is studied intensively.

catatonia One of Bleuler's four subtypes of schizophrenia. Its main symptoms are peculiar motor patterns such as periods in which the patient is immobile and maintains strange positions for hours on end.

catecholamines A family of neurotransmitters which have an activating function, including epinephrine, norepinephrine and dopamine.

categorical scale A scale that divides the responses into categories that are not numerically related. *See also* interval scale, ordinal scale, and ratio scale.

catharsis An explosive release of hitherto dammed-up emotions that is sometimes believed to have therapeutic effects.

censorship in dreams *See* Freud's theory of dreams.

central nervous system (CNS) The brain and spinal cord.

central tendency The tendency of scores in a frequency distribution to cluster around a central value. *See also* median, mean, and variability.

cerebellum Two small hemispheres that form part of the hindbrain and control muscular coordination and equilibrium.

cerebral cortex   The outermost layer of the gray matter of the cerebral hemispheres.

cerebral hemispheres   Two hemispherical structures which comprise the major part of the forebrain in mammals and serve as the main coordinating center of the nervous system.

cerebrotonia   *See* somatotype theory.

chunking   A process of reorganizing (or recoding) materials in memory which permits a number of items to be packed into a larger unit.

classical conditioning   A form of learning in which a hitherto neutral stimulus, the conditioned stimulus (CS) is paired with an unconditioned stimulus (UCS) regardless of what the animal does. In effect, what has to be learned is the relation between these two stimuli. *See also* instrumental conditioning.

client-centered therapy   A humanistic psychotherapy developed by Carl Rogers. *See also* humanistic therapies.

closure   A factor in visual grouping. The perceptual tendency to fill in gaps in a figure so that it looks closed.

cochlea   Coiled structure in the inner ear which contains the basilar membrane whose deformation by sound-produced pressure stimulates the auditory receptors.

cognitive dissonance   An inconsistency among some experiences, beliefs, attitudes or feelings. According to dissonance theory, this sets up an unpleasant state which people try to reduce by reinterpreting some part of their experiences to make them consistent with the others.

cognitive interpretation theory of emotions   A theory proposed by Schachter and Singer which asserts that emotions are an interpretation of our own autonomic arousal in the light of the situation to which we attribute it. *See also* attribution theory.

cognitive map   *See* cognitive theory.

cognitive theory   A conception of human and animal learning which holds that both humans and animals acquire items of knowledge (cognitions) such as what is where (cognitive map) or what leads to what (expectancy). This contrasts with theories of instrumental learning such as Thorndike's or Skinner's which assert that learning consists of the strengthening or weakening of particular response tendencies.

cognitive therapy   An approach to therapy that tries to change some of the patient's habitual modes of thinking. It is related to behavior therapy because it regards such thought patterns as a form of behavior.

combat neurosis   A psychogenic disorder brought on by the catastrophic stress of the battlefield.

complementary colors   Two colors which, when additively mixed with each other in the right proportions, produce the sensation of gray.

compulsions   *See* obsessive-compulsive neurosis.

concordance   The probability that a person who stands in a particular family relationship to a patient (e.g., an identical twin) has the same disorder as the patient.

concrete operational period   In Piaget's theory, the period from ages six or seven to about eleven. At this time the child has acquired mental operations that allow her to abstract some essential attributes of reality such as number and substance; but these operations are as yet applicable only to concrete events and cannot be considered entirely in the abstract.

conditioned reflex   *See* conditioned response.

conditioned response (CR)   A response elicited by some initially neutral stimulus, the conditioned stimulus (CS), as a result of pairings between that CS and an unconditioned stimulus. This CR is typically not identical with the unconditioned response though it often is similar to it. *See also* conditioned stimulus, unconditioned response, and unconditioned stimulus.

conditioned stimulus (CS)   In classical conditioning, the stimulus which comes to elicit a new response by virtue of pairings with the unconditioned stimulus. *See also* conditioned response, unconditioned response, and unconditioned stimulus.

cones   Visual receptors that respond to greater light intensities and give rise to chromatic (color) sensations.

conservation   In Piaget's theory, the understanding that certain attributes such as substance and number remain unchanged despite various transformations (e.g., liquid conservation, the realization that the amount of liquid remains the same when poured from a tall, thin beaker into a wide jar).

construction theory of perception   A theory which asserts that visual patterns are constructions based on visual expectations about the consequences of eye movements or of other acts.

construct validity   The extent to which performance on a test fits into a theoretical scheme about the attribute the test tries to measure.

contiguity   The togetherness in time of two events, which is sometimes regarded as the condition that leads to association.

contingency   A relation between two events in which one is dependent upon another. If the contingency is greater than zero, than the probability of event A will be greater when event B is present than when it is absent.

convergence   The movement of the eyes as they swivel toward each other to focus upon an object.

conversion hysteria   A condition in which there are physical symptoms that seem to have no physical basis but appear linked to psychological factors, serving as a means for reducing anxiety.

corpus callosum   A bundle of fibers that connects the two cerebral hemispheres.

correlation   The tendency of two variables to vary together. If one goes up as the other goes up, the correlation is positive; if one goes up as the other goes down, the correlation is negative.

correlation coefficient   A number, referred to as r, that expresses both the size and the direction of a correlation, varying from $+1.00$ (perfect positive correlation) through 0.00 (absence of any correlation) to -1.00 (perfect negative correlation).

counterconditioning   A procedure for weakening a classically conditioned CR by connecting the stimuli that presently evoke it to a new response that is incompatible with the CR.

criterion groups   Groups whose test performance sets the validity criterion for certain tests (e.g., the Minnesota Multiphasic Personality Inventory, MMPI, which uses several psychiatric criterion groups to define most of its subscales).

critical period   Period in the development of an organism when it is particularly sensitive to certain environmental influences. Outside of this period, the same environmental influences have little effect. (E.g., the period during which a duckling can be imprinted).

critical ratio   A z-score used for testing the null hypothesis. It is obtained by dividing an obtained mean difference by the standard error (SE) so that critical ratio = obtained mean difference/SE. If this ratio is large enough, the null hypothesis is rejected and the difference is said to be statistically significant. *See also* standard error.

crystallized intelligence   The repertoire of information, cognitive skills, and strategies acquired by the application of fluid intelligence to various fields. This is said to increase with age, in some cases into old age. *See also* fluid intelligence.

cultural anthropology A branch of anthropology that compares the similarities and differences among human cultures.

culture fairness of a test The extent to which test performance does not depend upon information or skills provided by one culture but not another.

curare A drug which completely paralyzes the skeletal musculature but does not affect visceral reactions.

cutoff score A score on a test used for selection below which no individual is accepted.

decay A possible factor in forgetting, producing some loss of the stored information through erosion by some as yet unknown physiological process.

defense mechanism In psychoanalytic theory, a collective term for a number of reactions that try to ward off or lessen anxiety by various unconscious means. *See also* displacement, projection, rationalization, reaction formation, and repression.

definition (of a word) A set of necessary and sufficient features shared by all members of a category which are the criteria for membership in that category.

delusion Systematized false beliefs, often of grandeur or persecution.

demand characteristics (of an experiment) The cues which tell a subject what the experimenter expects of him.

dendrites A typically highly branched part of a neuron that receives impulses from receptors or other neurons and conducts them toward the cell body and axon.

dependent variable *See* experiment.

depression A state of deep and pervasive dejection and hopelessness, accompanied by apathy and a feeling of personal worthlessness.

descriptive rule *See* rule of grammar.

deviation IQ A measure of intelligence test performance based on an individual's standing relative to his own age-mates (e.g., an IQ of 100 is average and IQs of 70 and 130 correspond to percentile ranks of 2 and 98 respectively). *See also* Intelligence Quotient.

dichotic listening A procedure by which each ear receives a different message while the listener is asked to attend to one.

difference threshold The amount by which a given stimulus must be increased or decreased so that the subject can perceive a just noticeable difference (j.n.d.).

directed thinking Thinking that is aimed at the solution of a problem.

discrimination A process of learning to respond to certain stimuli that are reinforced and not to others which are unreinforced.

disinhibition An increase of some reaction tendency by the removal of some inhibiting influence upon it (e.g., the increased strength of a frog's spinal reflexes after decapitation).

displacement In psychoanalytic theory, a redirection of an impulse from a channel that is blocked into another, more available outlet (e.g., displaced aggression, as in a child who hits a sibling when punished by her parents).

display Term used by ethologists to describe genetically pre-programmed responses which serve as stimuli for the reaction of others of the same species, and thus serve as the basis of a communication system (e.g., mating rituals).

dissociative reactions Disorders in which a whole set of mental events is stored out of ordinary consciousness. These include psycho-genic amnesia, fugue states and, very rarely, cases of multiple personality.

dissonance theory *See* cognitive dissonance.

distal stimulus An object or event outside (e.g., a tree) as contrasted to the proximal stimulus, which is the pattern of physical energies that originates from the distal stimulus and impinges on a sense organ (e.g., the retinal image of the tree).

doctrine of specific nerve energies The assertion that qualitative differences in sensory experience are not attributable to the differences in the stimuli that correspond to different sense modalities (e.g., light versus sound) but rather to the fact that these stimuli excite different nervous structures.

dominant allele An allele that will exert its effect regardless of the allele on the corresponding locus of the paired chromosome. *See also* genotype, phenotype, and recessive allele.

dopamine (DA) A catecholamine which is the neurotransmitter in various brain structures, including some which control motor action. Some writers believe that schizophrenia is based on an oversensitivity to dopamine in some part of the brain.

dopamine hypothesis of schizophrenia Asserts that schizophrenics are oversensitive to the neurotransmitter dopamine and are therefore in a state of overarousal. Evidence for this view comes from the fact that the phenothiazines, which alleviate schizophrenic symptoms, block dopamine transmission. *See also* phenothiazines.

double bind A conflict set up in a person who is told one thing while simultaneously receiving the message that what is meant is the very opposite.

double-blind technique A technique for evaluating drug effects independent of the effects produced by the expectations of patients (placebo effects) and of physicians. This is done by assigning patients to a drug group or a placebo group with both patients and staff members in ignorance of who is assigned to which group. *See also* placebo effect.

drive-reduction theory A theory that claims that all built-in rewards are at bottom reductions of some noxious bodily state. The theory has difficulty in explaining motives in which one seeks stimulation, such as sex and curiosity.

ectomorphy *See* somatotype theory.

effectors Organs of action; in humans, muscles and glands.

efferent nerves Nerves that carry messages to the effectors.

ego In Freud's theory, a set of reactions that try to reconcile the id's blind pleasure strivings with the demands of reality. These lead to the emergence of various skills and capacities which eventually become a system that can look at itself—an "I". *See also* id and superego.

egocentrism In Piaget's theory, a characteristic of preoperational children, an inability to see another person's point of view.

eidetic memory A relatively rare kind of memory characterized by relatively long-lasting and detailed images of scenes that can be scanned as if they were physically present.

Electra complex *See* Oedipus complex.

electroconvulsive shock treatment (ECT) A somatic treatment, mostly used for cases of severe depression, in which a brief electric current is passed through the brain to produce a convulsive seizure.

electroencephalogram (EEG) A record of the summed activity of cortical cells picked up by wires placed on the skull.

encounter group General term for a large variety of groups set up to develop greater social and personal awareness in group members. Procedures vary widely.

endocrine system The system of ductless glands whose secretions are released directly into the bloodstream and affect organs elsewhere in the body (e.g., adrenal gland).

endomorphy *See* somatotype theory.

epinephrine (adrenalin) A catecholamine released into the bloodstream by the adrenal medulla whose effects are similar to those of sympathetic activation (e.g., racing heart).

episodic memory Memory for particular events in one's own life (e.g., I missed the train this morning). *See also* generic memory.

erogenous zones In psychoanalytic theory, the mouth, anus, and genitals.

escape learning Instrumental learning in which reinforcement consists of the reduction or cessation of an aversive stimulus (e.g., electric shock).

essential hypertension *See* psychophysiological conditions.

estrogen A female sex hormone which dominates the first half of the female cycle through ovulation; in animals, estrus performs this function.

estrus In mammalian animals, the period in the cycle when the female is sexually receptive (in heat).

ethology A branch of biology that studies the behavior of animals under natural conditions.

expectancy *See* cognitive theory.

experiment A study in which the investigator manipulates one (or more than one) variable (the independent variable) to determine its effect on the subject's response (the dependent variable).

expressive movements Movements of the face and body in animals and humans that seem to express emotion. They are usually regarded as built-in social displays.

extinction In classical conditioning, the weakening of the tendency of CS to elicit CR by unreinforced presentations of CS. In instrumental conditioning, a decline in the tendency to perform the instrumental response brought about by unreinforced occurrences of that response.

extraversion-introversion In Eysenck's system, a trait dimension that refers to the main direction of a person's energies: toward the outer world of objects and other people (extraversion) or toward the inner world of one's own thoughts and feelings (introversion).

factor analysis A statistical method for studying the interrelations among various tests, the object of which is to discover what the tests have in common and whether these communalities can be ascribed to one or several factors that run through all or some of these tests.

false alarm *See* payoff matrix.

family resemblance structure Overlap of features among members of a category of meaning such that no members of the category have all of the features but all members have some of them.

feature analyzers Neurons in the retina or brain that respond to specific features of the stimulus such as movement, orientation, and so on.

Fechner's law The assertion that the strength of a sensation is proportional to the logarithm of physical stimulus intensity.

feedback system A system in which some action produces a consequence which affects (feeds back on) the action. In negative feedback, the consequence stops or reverses the action (e.g., thermostat-controlled furnace). In positive feedback, the consequence strengthens the action (e.g., rocket that homes in on airplanes).

figure-ground organization The segregation of the visual field into a part (the figure) which stands out against the rest (the ground).

fixation In psychoanalytic theory, a lingering attachment to facets of some earlier stage of psychosexual development even after a new stage has been attained.

fixed-action patterns Term used by ethologists to describe stereotyped, species-specific behaviors triggered by genetically pre-programmed releasing stimuli (e.g., male stickleback's zigzag dance).

fluid intelligence The ability, which is said to decline with age, to deal with essentially new problems. *See also* crystallized intelligence.

forced compliance effect An individual forced to act or speak publically in a manner contrary to his own beliefs may change his own views in the direction of the public action. But this will happen only if his reward for the false public pronouncement is relatively small. If the reward is large, there is no dissonance and hence no attitude change. *See also* cognitive dissonance.

forebrain In mammals, the bulk of the brain. Its foremost region includes the cerebral hemispheres; its rear includes the thalamus and hypothalamus.

fraternal twins Twins which arise from two different eggs which are (simultaneously) fertilized by different sperm cells. Their genetic similarity is no different than that between ordinary siblings. *See also* identical twins.

free association Method used in psychoanalytic therapy in which the patient is to say anything that comes to her mind, no matter how apparently trivial, unrelated, or embarrassing.

free recall A test of memory that asks for as many items in a list as a subject can recall regardless of order.

frequency distribution An arrangement in which scores are tabulated by the frequency in which they occur.

Freud's theory of dreams A theory that holds that at bottom all dreams are attempts to fulfill a wish. The wish fulfillment is in the latent dream, which represents the sleeper's hidden desires. This latent dream is censored and reinterpreted to avoid anxiety. It reemerges in more acceptable form as the mainfest dream, the dream the sleeper remembers upon awakening.

frontal lobe A lobe in each cerebral hemisphere which includes the motor projection area.

functional fixedness A set to think of objects in terms of their normal function.

functor The short, unstressed grammatical morphemes in a language (e.g., *a, the, is, ing, or*).

galvanic skin response (GSR) A drop in the electrical resistance of the skin, widely used as an index of autonomic reaction.

gender identity The inner sense of being male or female. *See also* gender role and sexual orientation.

gender role The set of external behavior patterns a given culture deems appropriate for each sex. *See also* gender identity and sexual orientation.

generalization gradient The curve which shows the relationship between the tendency to respond to a new stimulus and its similarity to the original CS.

general paresis A psychosis characterized by progressive decline in cognitive and motor function culminating in death, reflecting a deteriorating brain condition produced by syphilitic infection.

generic memory Memory for items of knowledge as such, independent of the occasion on which they are learned (e.g., The capital of France is Paris). *See also* episodic memory.

genital stage In psychoanalytic theory, the stage of psychosexual development reached in adult sexuality in which sexual pleasure involves not only one's own gratification but also the social and bodily satisfaction brought to another person.

genotype The genetic blueprint of an organism which may or may not be overtly expressed by its phenotype. *See also* phenotype.

Gestalt An organized whole such as a visual form or a melody.

Gestalt psychology A theoretical approach which emphasizes the role of organized wholes (Gestalten) in perception and other psychological processes.

glove anesthesia A condition sometimes seen in hysteria, in which there is an anesthesia of the entire hand with no loss of feeling above the wrist. This symptom makes no organic sense given the anatomical arrangement of the nerve trunks and indicates that the condition has a psychological basis.

glucose A form of sugar which is the major source of energy for most bodily tissues. If plentiful, much of it is converted into glycogen and stored away.

glycogen A stored form of metabolic energy derived from glucose. To be used, it must first be converted back into glucose.

good continuation A factor in visual grouping. Contours tend to be seen in such a way that their direction is altered as little as possible.

gradient of reinforcement The curve which describes the declining effectiveness of reinforcement with increasing delay between the response and the reinforcer.

group-factor theory of intelligence A factor-analytic approach to intelligence-test performance which argues that intelligence is the composite of separate abilities (group factors such as verbal ability, spatial ability, etc.) without a sovereign capacity that enters into each. *See also* factor analysis and Spearman's theory of general intelligence.

group therapy Psychotherapy of several persons at one time.

hallucination Perceived experiences that occur in the absence of actual sensory stimulation.

hebephrenia One of Bleuler's four subtypes of schizophrenia, now called disorganized schizophrenia. It is characterized by incoherence of thought, marked inappropriateness of emotional expression, and oddity of behavior.

heritability As measured by H, the heritability ratio, this refers to the relative importance of heredity and environment in determining the variation of a particular trait. More specifically, H is the proportion of the variance of the trait in a given population that is attributable to genetic factors.

hermaphrodite A person whose reproductive organs are anatomically ambiguous so that they are not exclusively male or female.

heterosexuality A sexual orientation leading to a choice of sexual partners of the opposite sex.

heuristics In computer problem solving, a procedure which has often worked in the past and is likely, but not certain, to work again. *See also* algorithm.

hierarchical organization Organization in which narrower categories are subsumed under broader ones which are subsumed under still broader ones and so on. Often expressed in the form of a tree diagram.

higher-order conditioning In classical conditioning, a procedure by which a new stimulus comes to elicit the CR by virtue of being paired with an effective CS (e.g., first pairings of tone and food, then pairings of bell and tone until finally the bell elicits salivation by itself).

hindbrain The most primitive portion of the brain, which includes the medulla and the cerebellum.

histogram A graphic rendering of a frequency distribution which depicts the distribution by a series of contiguous rectangles. *See also* frequency distribution.

homeostasis The body's tendency to maintain the conditions of its internal environment by various forms of self-regulation.

homosexuality A sexual orientation leading to a choice of partners of the same sex.

hue A perceived dimension of visual stimuli whose meaning is close to the term *color* (e.g., red, blue).

humanistic therapies Methods of treatment that emphasize personal growth and self-fulfillment. They try to be relatively nondirective since their emphasis is on helping the clients achieve the capacity for making their own choices. *See also* nondirective techniques.

hyperphagia Voracious, chronic overeating brought about by lesion of the ventromedial region of the hypothalamus.

hypnosis A temporary, trancelike state which can be induced in normal persons, sometimes producing effects that resemble hysterical symptoms by various hypnotic or posthypnotic suggestions.

hypothalamus A small structure at the base of the brain which plays a vital role in the control of the autonomic nervous system, of the endocrine system, and of the major biological drives.

hysteria A psychogenic mental disorder often characterized by various bodily complaints that have no organic basis (e.g., glove anesthesia). Also, a term for a group of neuroses that includes conversion hysteria and dissociative reactions. *See also* conversion hysteria, dissociative reactions, and glove anesthesia.

id In Freud's theory, a term for the most primitive reactions of human personality consisting of blind strivings for immediate biological satisfaction regardless of cost. *See also* ego and superego.

ideas of reference A characteristic of some mental disorders, notably schizophrenia, in which the patient begins to think that external events are specially related to them personally (e.g., "People walk by and follow me").

identical twins Twins that originate from a single fertilized egg which then splits into two exact replicas which develop into two genetically identical individuals. *See also* fraternal twins.

identification In psychoanalytic theory, a mechanism whereby a child models itself (typically) on the same-sexed parent in an effort to become like him or her.

imprinting A learned attachment that is formed at a particular period in life (the critical period) and is difficult to reverse (e.g., the duckling's acquired tendency to follow whatever moving stimulus it encounters 12–48 hours after hatching).

incidental learning Learning without trying to learn (e.g., as in a study in which subjects judge a speaker's vocal quality when she recites a list of words and are later asked to produce as many of the words as they can recall). *See also* intentional learning.

independent variable   *See* experiment.

induced movement   Perceived movement of an objectively stationary stimulus that is enclosed by a moving framework.

information processing   A general term for the presumed operations whereby the crude raw materials provided by the senses are refashioned into items of knowledge. Among these operations are perceptual organization, comparison with items stored in memory, and so on.

insightful learning   Learning by understanding the relations between components of the problem; often contrasted with "blind trial and error" and documented by wide and appropriate transfer if tested in a new situation.

instrumental conditioning (operant conditioning)   A form of learning in which a reinforcer (e.g., food) is given only if the animal performs the instrumental response (e.g., pressing a lever). In effect, what has to be learned is the relationship between the response and the reinforcer. *See* classical conditioning.

insulin   A hormone with a crucial role in utilization of nutrients. One of its functions is to help promote the conversion of glucose into glycogen.

Intelligence Quotient (IQ)   A ratio measure to indicate whether a child's mental age (MA) is ahead or behind its chronological age (CA); specifically IQ = 100 × MA/CA. *See also* deviation IQ and mental age.

intentional learning   Learning when informed that there will be a later test of learning. *See also* incidental learning.

intention movements   A term used by ethologists to describe displays which represent anticipations of an impending response (e.g., the bared fangs of a threatening dog).

interference theory of forgetting   The assertion that items are forgotten because they are somehow interfered with by other items learned before or after.

interneurons   Neurons which receive impulses and transmit them to other neurons.

interval scale   A scale in which equal differences between scores can be treated as equal so that the scores can be added or subtracted. *See also* categorical scale, ordinal scale, and ratio scale.

introversion   *See* extraversion-introversion.

invariant   Some aspect of the proximal stimulus pattern that remains unchanged despite various transformations of the stimulus.

James-Lange theory of emotions   A theory which asserts that the subjective experience of emotion is the awareness of one's own bodily reactions in the presence of certain arousing stimuli.

just noticeable difference (j.n.d.)   *See* difference threshold.

kinesthesis   A general term for sensory information generated by receptors in the muscles, tendons, and joints which informs us of our skeletal movement.

labeling theory of mental disorders   The assertion that the label "mental illness" acts as a self-fulfilling prophecy that perpetuates the condition once the label has been applied. In its extreme form, it asserts that the concept is a myth, mental illness being merely the term by which we designate social deviance that does not fall into other, recognized categories of deviance.

latency   General term for the interval before some reaction occurs.

latency period   In psychoanalytic theory, a stage in psychosexual development in which sexuality lies essentially dormant, roughly from ages 5 to 12.

latent dream   *See* Freud's theory of dreams.

latent learning   Learning which occurs without being manifested by performance.

lateral hypothalamus   A region of the hypothalamus which is said to be a "hunger center" and to be in an antagonistic relation to a supposed "satiety center," the ventro-medial region of the hypothalamus.

lateral inhibition   The tendency of adjacent neural elements of the visual system to inhibit each other; underlies brightness contrast and the accentuation of contours. *See also* brightness contrast.

lateralization   An asymmetry of function of the two cerebral hemispheres. In most right-handers, the left hemisphere is specialized for language functions, while the right hemisphere is better at various visual and spatial tasks.

Law of Effect   A theory which asserts that the tendency of a stimulus to evoke a response is strengthened if the response is followed by reward and is weakened if the response is not followed by reward. Applied to instrumental learning, this theory states that as trials proceed, incorrect S-R bonds will weaken while the correct bond will be strengthened.

learned helplessness   A condition created by exposure to inescapable aversive events. This retards or prevents learning in subsequent situations in which escape or avoidance is possible.

learned helplessness theory of depression   The theory that depression is analogous to learned helplessness effects produced in the laboratory by exposing subjects to uncontrollable aversive events.

learning curve   A curve in which some index of learning (e.g., the number of drops of saliva in Pavlov's classical conditioning experiment) is plotted against trials or sessions.

learning set   The increased ability to solve various problems, especially in discrimination learning, as a result of previous experience with problems of a similar kind.

lightness constancy   The tendency to perceive the lightness of an object as more or less the same despite the fact that the light reflected from these objects changes with the illumination that falls upon them.

limbic system   A set of brain structures including a relatively primitive portion of the cerebral cortex and parts of the thalamus and hypothalamus; believed to be involved in the control of emotional behavior and motivation.

line of best fit   A line drawn through the points in a scatter diagram which yields the best prediction of one variable when given the value of the other variable.

lithium carbonate   A drug used in the treatment of mania and bipolar affective disorder.

Lobotomy   *See* prefrontal lobotomy.

longitudinal study   A developmental study in which the same person is tested at various ages.

long-term memory   A memory system that keeps memories for long periods, has a very large capacity, and stores items in relatively processed form. *See* sensory register and short-term memory.

maintenance rehearsal   Rehearsal in which material is merely held in short-term memory for a while. In contrast to active rehearsal, this confers little benefit. *See also* active rehearsal.

mania Hyperactive state with marked impairment of judgment, usually accompanied by intense euphoria.

manifest dream *See* Freud's theory of dreams.

matching to sample A procedure in which an organism has to choose one of two alternative stimuli which is the same as a third sample stimulus.

maturation A pre-programmed growth process based on changes in underlying neural structures that are relatively unaffected by environmental conditions (e.g., flying in sparrows and walking in humans).

mean (M) The most commonly used measure of the central tendency of a frequency distribution. It is the arithmetical average of all the scores. If M is the mean and N the number of cases, then $M = $ sum of the scores$/N$. *See also* central tendency and median.

median A measure of the central tendency of a frequency distribution. It is the point that divides the distribution into two equal halves when the scores are arranged in ascending order. *See also* central tendency and mean.

medical model A conception of mental disorders that makes the assumptions of the pathology model and also assumes: (1) that the underlying pathology is somatogenic, (2) that it should be treated by somatic means, and (3) that the treatment should be conducted by physicians. *See also* pathology model.

medulla The rearmost portion of the brain, just adjacent to the spinal cord. It includes centers which help to control respiration and muscle tone.

memory span The number of items a person can recall after just one presentation.

memory trace The change in the nervous system left by an experience which is the physical basis of its retention in memory. What this change is, is still unknown.

mental age (MA) A score devised by Binet to represent a child's test performance. It indicates the chronological age at which 50 percent of the children in that age group will perform at the level of the child's performance. If the child's MA is greater than its chronological age (CA), it is ahead of its age mentally; if its MA is lower than its CA, it lags behind.

mental retardation Usually defined as an IQ of 70 and below.

mental set The predisposition to perceive (or remember or think of) one thing rather than another.

mesomorphy *See* somatotype theory.

metacognition A general term for knowledge about knowledge, as in knowing that we do or don't remember something.

midbrain Part of the brain which includes some lower centers for sensory-motor integration (e.g., eye movements) and part of the reticular formation.

middle ear An antechamber to the inner ear which amplifies sound-produced vibrations of the eardrum and imparts them to the cochlea. *See also* cochlea.

Minnesota Multiphasic Personality Inventory (MMPI) *See* criterion groups.

mnemonics Deliberate devices for helping memory. Many of them utilize imagery such as the method of pegs and method of loci (see Chapter 8).

molar description of behavior Behavior analyzed in terms of larger units, such as the environmental effect produced by the response. *See also* molecular description of behavior.

molecular description of behavior Behavior analyzed in relatively small units, such as particular muscle movements. *See also* molar description of behavior.

monocular depth cues Various features of the visual stimulus which indicate depth, even when viewed with one eye (e.g., linear perspective and parallax).

morpheme The smallest significant unit of meaning in a language (e.g., the word *boys* has two morphemes, *boy + s*).

motor projection areas *See* projection areas.

nativism The view that some important aspects of perception and of other cognitive processes are innate.

natural selection The explanatory principle that underlies Darwin's theory of evolution. Some organisms produce offspring which are able to survive and reproduce while other organisms of the same species do not. Thus, organisms with these hereditary attributes will eventually outnumber organisms who lack these attributes.

negative feedback *See* feedback system.

neo-Freudians A group of theorists who accept the psychoanalytic conception of unconscious conflict but who differ with Freud in (1) describing these conflicts in social terms rather than in terms of particular bodily pleasures or frustrations, and (2) maintaining that many of these conflicts arise from the specific cultural conditions under which the child was reared rather than being biologically pre-ordained.

nerve impulse *See* action potential.

neuron A nerve cell.

neurosis Broad term for mental disorders whose primary symptoms are anxiety or various defenses against anxiety.

neuroticism A trait dimension that refers to emotional instability and maladjustment.

neurotransmitters Chemicals liberated at the terminal end of an axon which travel across the synapse and have an excitatory or inhibitory effect on an adjacent neuron (e.g., norepinephrine).

non directive techniques A set of techniques for psychological treatment developed by Carl Rogers. As far as possible, the counselor refrains from offering advice or interpretation but only tries to clarify the patient's own feelings by echoing him or restating what he says.

nonsense syllable Two consonants with a vowel between that do not form a word. Used to study associations between relatively meaningless items.

norepinephrine (NE) A catecholamine which is the neurotransmitter by means of which the sympathetic fibers exert their effects on internal organs. It is also the neurotransmitter of various arousing systems in the brain.

normal curve A symmetrical, bell-shaped curve which describes the probability of obtaining various combinations of chance events. It describes the frequency distributions of many physical and psychological attributes of humans and animals.

normal distribution A frequency distribution whose graphic representation has a symmetric, bell-shaped form—the normal curve. Its characteristics are often referred to when investigators test statistical hypotheses and make inferences about the population from a given sample.

null hypothesis The hypothesis that an obtained difference is merely a chance fluctuation from a population in which the true mean difference is zero. *See also* alternative hypothesis.

obesity A condition of marked overweight in animals and humans; produced by a large variety of factors including metabolic factors (over-secretion of insulin) and behavioral conditions (overeating, perhaps produced by nonresponsiveness to one's own internal state).

object permanence The conviction that an object remains perceptually constant over time and exists even when it is out of sight. According to Piaget, this does not develop until infants are age eight months or more.

observational study A study in which the investigator does not manipulate any of the variables but simply observes their relationship as they occur naturally.

obsessions *See* obsessive-compulsive neurosis.

obsessive-compulsive neurosis A disorder whose main symptoms are obsessions (persistent and irrational thoughts or wishes) and compulsions (uncontrollable, repetitive acts that seem to be defenses against anxiety).

occipital lobe A lobe in each cerebral hemisphere which includes the visual projection area.

Oedipus complex In psychoanalytic theory, a general term for a whole cluster of impulses and conflicts which occur during the phallic phase, at around age five. In boys, a fantasied form of intense sexual love is directed at the mother, which is soon followed by hate and fear of the father. As the fear mounts, the sexual feelings are pushed underground and the boy identifies with the father. An equivalent process in girls is called the Electra complex.

operant In Skinner's system, an instrumental response. *See also* instrumental conditioning.

operant conditioning *See* instrumental conditioning.

opponent-process theory of color vision A theory of color vision which asserts that there are three pairs of color antagonists: red-green, blue-yellow, and white-black. Excitation of one member of a pair automatically inhibits the other member.

oral stage In psychoanalytic theory, the earliest stage of psychosexual development during which the primary source of bodily pleasure is stimulation of the mouth and lips, as in sucking at the breast.

ordinal scale A scale in which responses are rank-ordered by relative magnitude but in which the intervals between successive ranks are not necessarily equal. *See also* categorical scale, interval scale, and ratio scale.

orienting response In classical conditioning, an animal's initial reaction to a new stimulus (e.g., turning toward it and looking attentive).

paired-associate method A procedure in which subjects learn to provide particular response terms to various stimulus items.

paranoid schizophrenia One of Bleuler's four subtypes of schizophrenia. Its dominant symptom is a set of delusions which are often elaborately systematized, usually of grandeur or persecution.

paraphrase The relation between two sentences whose meanings (underlying structures) are the same but whose surface structures differ (e.g., *The boy hit the ball/The ball was hit by the boy*).

parasympathetic overshoot A rebound effect in which the parasympathetic system responds above its normal level after the inhibition from its sympathetic antagonist is suddenly lifted (e.g., weeping).

parasympathetic system A division of the autonomic nervous system which serves vegetative functions and conserves bodily energies (e.g., slowing heart rate). Its action is antagonistic to that of the sympathetic system.

parietal lobe A lobe in each cerebral hemisphere which includes the somatosensory projection area.

partial reinforcement A condition in which a response is reinforced only some of the time.

partial-reinforcement effect The fact that a response is much harder to extinguish if it was acquired during partial rather than continuous reinforcement.

pathology model A term adopted here to describe a conception of mental disorders that holds (1) that one can generally distinguish between symptoms and underlying causes, and (2) that these causes may be regarded as a form of pathology. *See also* medical model.

payoff matrix A table which shows the costs and benefits for each of the four outcomes in a detection experiment: a hit, reporting the stimulus when it is present; a correct negative, reporting it as absent when it is absent; a miss, failing to report it when it is present; and a false alarm, reporting it when it is absent.

percentile rank The percentage of all the scores in a distribution that lie below a given score.

perceptual adaptation The gradual adjustment to various distortions of the perceptual world, as in wearing prisms which tilt the entire visual world in one direction.

perceptual defense The tendency to perceive anxiety-related stimuli less readily than neutral stimuli.

perceptual differentiation Learning to perceive features of stimulus patterns that were not perceptible at first. A phenomenon central to the theory of perceptual learning proposed by J. J. Gibson and E. J. Gibson.

period of formal operations In Piaget's theory, the period from about age eleven on, when genuinely abstract mental operations can be undertaken (e.g., the ability to entertain hypothetical possibilities).

personality inventories Paper-and-pencil tests of personality that ask questions about feelings or customary behavior. *See also* projective techniques.

phallic stage In psychoanalytic theory, the stage of psychosexual development during which the child begins to regard its genitals as a major source of gratification.

phenothiazines A group of drugs including chlorpromazine which seem to be effective in alleviating the major symptoms of schizophrenia.

phenotype The overt appearance and behavior of an organism, regardless of its genetic blueprint. *See also* genotype.

phenylketonuria (PKU) A severe form of mental retardation determined by a single gene. This disorder can be treated by means of a special diet (if detected early enough), despite the fact that the disorder is genetic.

pheromones Special chemicals secreted by many animals which trigger particular reactions in members of the same species.

phobia An intense and, at least on the surface, irrational fear.

phoneme The smallest significant unit of sound in a language. In English, it corresponds roughly to a letter of the alphabet (e.g., *apt*, *tap*, and *pat* are all made up of the same phonemes).

phonology The rules in a language that govern the sequence in which phonemes can be arranged.

phrase   A sequence of words within a sentence that function as a unit (e.g., *The ball/rolled/down the hill*).

phrase structure   The organization of sentences into phrases. Surface structure is the phrase organization of sentences as they are spoken or written. Underlying structure is the phrase organization that describes the meaning of parts of the sentence, such as do-er, action, and done-to.

pituitary gland   An endocrine gland heavily influenced by the hypothalamus. A master gland because many of its secretions trigger hormone secretions in other glands.

placebo effect   A beneficial effect of a treatment administered to a patient who believes it has therapeutic powers even though it has none.

pluralistic ignorance   A situation in which individuals in a group don't know that there are others in the group who share their feelings.

polygenic inheritance   Inheritance of an attribute whose expression is controlled not by one but by many gene pairs.

population   The entire group of subjects (or test trials) about which the investigator wants to draw conclusions. *See also* sample.

positive feedback   *See* feedback system.

predictive validity   A measure of a test's validity based on the correlation between the test score and some criterion of behavior the test predicted (e.g., a correlation between a scholastic aptitude test and college grades).

prefrontal lobotomy   A somatic treatment for severe mental disorders by surgically cutting the connections between the thalamus and the frontal lobes; now only rarely used in the U.S.

preoperational period   In Piaget's theory, the period from about ages two to six during which children come to represent actions and objects internally but cannot systematically manipulate these representations or relate them to each other; the child is therefore unable to conserve quantity across perceptual transformations and also is unable to take points of view other than her own.

prescriptive rule   *See* rule of grammar.

prestige suggestion   Approving some statement because a high-prestige person has approved it.

primacy effect (in impression formation)   In forming an impression of another person, the phenomenon whereby attributes first noted carry a greater weight than attributes noted later on.

primacy effect (in recall)   In free recall, the recall superiority of the items in the first part of a list compared to those in the middle. *See* recency effect.

prisoner's dilemma   A particular arrangement of payoffs in a two-person situation in which each individual has to choose between two alternatives without knowing the other's choice. The payoff structure is so arranged that the optimal strategy for each person depends upon whether he can trust the other or not. If trust is possible, the payoffs for each will be considerably higher than if there is no trust.

proactive inhibition   Disturbance of recall of some material by other material learned previously. *See* retroactive inhibition.

progesterone   A female sex hormone which dominates the latter phase of the female cycle during which the uterus walls thicken to receive the embryo.

projection   In psychoanalytic theory, a mechanism of defense in which various forbidden thoughts and impulses are attributed to another person rather than the self, thus warding off some anxiety (e.g., "I hate you" becomes "You hate me").

projection areas   Regions of the cortex that serve as receiving stations for sensory information or as dispatching stations for motor commands.

projective techniques   Devices for assessing personality by presenting relatively unstructured stimuli which elicit subjective responses of various kinds. Their advocates believe that such tasks allow the person to "project" her own personality into her reactions (e.g., the TAT and the Rorschach inkblot test). *See also* personality inventories.

prototype   The typical example of a category of meaning (e.g., robin is a prototypical bird).

proximal stimulus   *See* distal stimulus.

psychoanalysis   (1) A theory of human personality formulated by Freud whose key assertions include unconscious conflict and psychosexual development. (2) A method of therapy that draws heavily on this theory of personality. Its main aim is to have the patient gain insight into his own, presently unconscious, thoughts and feelings. Therapeutic tools employed toward this end include free association, interpretation, and the appropriate use of the transference relationship between patient and analyst. *See also* free association and transference.

psychogenic disorders   Disorders whose origins are psychological rather than organic (e.g., phobias). *See also* somatogenic disorders.

psychometric approach to intelligence   An attempt to understand the nature of intelligence by studying the pattern of results obtained on intelligence tests.

psychopathology   The study of psychological disorders.

psychophysics   The field which tries to relate the characteristics of physical stimuli to the sensory experience they produce.

psychophysiological conditions   In these disorders (formerly called psychosomatic), the primary symptoms involve genuine organic damage whose ultimate cause is psychological (e.g., essential hypertension, a condition of chronic high blood pressure brought about by the bodily concomitant of chronic emotional stress).

psychosexual development   In psychoanalytic theory, the description of the progressive stages in the way the child gains its main source of pleasure as it grows into adulthood, defined by the zone of the body through which this pleasure is derived (oral, anal, genital) and by the object toward which this pleasurable feeling is directed (mother, father, adult sexual partner). *See also* anal stage, genital stage, oral stage, and phallic stage.

psychosis   A broad category that describes some of the more severe mental disorders in which the patient's thoughts and deeds no longer meet the demands of reality.

psychosocial crises   In Erik Erikson's theory, a series of crises through which all persons must pass as they go through their life cycle (e.g., the identity crisis during which adolescents or young adults try to establish the separation between themselves and their parents).

psychotherapy   As used here, a collective term for all forms of treatment that use psychological rather than somatic means.

quiet sleep   Stages 2 to 4 of sleep during which there are no rapid eye movements and during which the EEG shows progressively less cortical arousal. Also known as non-REM sleep.

random sample   *See* sample.

rationalization   In psychoanalytic theory, a mechanism of defense by means of which unacceptable thoughts or impulses are reinterpreted in more acceptable and thus less anxiety-arousing terms (e.g., the jilted lover who convinces himself he never loved her anyway).

ratio scale An interval scale in which there is a true zero point thus allowing ratio statements (e.g., this sound is twice as loud as the other). *See also* categorical scale, interval scale, and ordinal scale.

reaction formation In psychoanalytic theory, a mechanism of defense in which a forbidden impulse is turned into its opposite (e.g., hate toward a sibling becomes exaggerated love).

reaction time The interval between the presentation of a signal and the observer's response to that signal.

recall A task in which some item must be produced from memory. *See* recognition.

recency effect In free recall, the recall superiority of the items at the end of the list compared to those in the middle. *See* primacy effect (in recall).

receptive field The retinal area in which visual stimulation affects a particular cell's firing rate.

receptors A specialized cell that can respond to various physical stimuli and transduce them.

recessive allele An allele that will only exert its effect if the allele on the corresponding locus of the paired chromosome calls for the same effect. *See also* dominant allele, genotype, and phenotype.

reciprocal inhibition The arrangement by which excitation of some neural system is accompanied by inhibition of that system's antagonist (as in antagonistic muscles).

recognition A task in which a stimulus has to be identified as having been previously encountered in some context or not. *See also* recall.

reference The relations between words or sentences and objects or events in the world (e.g., "ball" refers to ball).

reflex A simple, stereotyped reaction in response to some stimulus (e.g., limb flexion in withdrawal from pain).

regression In psychoanalytic theory, a reversion to a mode of satisfaction characteristic of an earlier stage of psychosexual development.

rehearsal *See* active rehearsal and maintenance rehearsal.

reinforced trial In classical conditioning, a trial on which the CS is accompanied by UCS. In instrumental conditioning, a trial in which the instrumental response is followed by reward, cessation of punishment, or other reinforcement.

releasing stimulus Term used by ethologists to describe a stimulus which is genetically pre-programmed to elicit a fixed-action pattern (e.g., a long, thin, red-tipped peak which elicits a herring gull chick's begging response). *See also* fixed-action pattern.

reliability The consistency with which a test measures what it measures, as assessed, for example, by the test-retest method.

REM sleep *See* active sleep.

representational thought In Piaget's theory, thought that is internalized and includes mental representations of prior experiences with objects and events.

repression In psychoanalytic theory, a mechanism of defense by means of which thoughts, impulses, or memories that give rise to anxiety are pushed out of consciousness.

resistance In psychoanalysis, a collective term for the patient's failures to associate freely and say whatever enters his head.

response bias A preference for one or another response in a psychophysical experiment, independent of the stimulus situation.

restructuring A reorganization of a problem, often rather sudden, which seems to be a characteristic of creative thought.

retention The survival of the memory trace over some interval of time.

reticular activating system (RAS) A system that includes the upper portion of the reticular formation and its ascending branches to much of the brain. Its effect is to arouse the brain.

reticular formation A network of neurons extending throughout the midbrain with ramifications to higher parts of the brain. This plays an important role in sleep and arousal.

retina The structure which contains the visual receptors and several layers of neurons further up along the pathway to the brain.

retinal image The image of an object that is projected on the retina. Its size increases with the size of that object and decreases with its distance from the eye.

retrieval The process of searching for some item in memory and of finding it. If retrieval fails, this may or may not mean that the relevant memory trace is not present; it simply may be inaccessible.

retrieval cue A stimulus that helps to retrieve a memory trace.

retroactive inhibition Disturbance of recall of some material by other material learned subsequently. *See* proactive inhibition.

retrograde amnesia A memory deficit suffered after head injury or concussion in which the patient loses memory of some period prior to the injury. *See also* anterograde amnesia.

ROC curve A curve which shows the relationship between hits and false alarms in a detection experiment.

rods Visual receptors that respond to lower light intensities and give rise to achromatic (colorless) sensations.

Rorschach inkblot test A projective technique which requires the person to look at inkblots and say what she sees in them.

rule of grammar A formula that describes how words are arranged into sentences. Prescriptive rules are rules of grammar prescribed by "authorities" and are not the subject matter of linguistics. Descriptive rules are rules of grammar that describe how native speakers actually organize their sentences and are known only unconsciously (implicitly). Sentences that follow these rules are called well-formed or grammatical.

sample A subset of a population selected by the investigator for study. A random sample is one so constructed that each member of the population has an equal chance to be picked. A stratified sample is one so constructed that every relevant subgroup of the population is randomly sampled in proportion to its size. *See also* population.

saturation A perceived dimension of visual stimuli that describes the "purity" of a color—the extent to which it is rich in hue (e.g., green rather than olive).

scaling A procedure for assigning numbers to a subject's responses. *See also* categorical scale, interval scale, ordinal scale, and ratio scale.

schedule of reinforcement A rule that determines the occasions when a response is reinforced. An example is a fixed-ratio schedule, in which reinforcement is given after a fixed number of responses.

schema In Piaget's theory, a mental pattern.

schizophrenia A group of psychotic disorders characterized by at least some of the following: marked disturbance of thought, withdrawal, inappropriate or flat emotions, delusions, and hallucinations. *See also* catatonia, hebephrenia, paranoid schizophrenia, and simple type of schizophrenia.

secondary reinforcement   An initially neutral stimulus that acquires reinforcing properties through pairing with another stimulus that is already reinforcing.

self-perception theory   The assertion that we don't know ourselves directly but rather infer our own states and dispositions by an attribution process analogous to that we use when we try to explain the behavior of other persons. *See also* attribution theory.

semantic feature   The smallest significant unit of meaning within a word (e.g., male, human, and adult are semantic features of the word "man").

semantic memory   The component of generic memory that concerns the meaning of words and concepts.

semantics   The organization of meaning in language.

sensation   According to the British empiricists, the primitive experiences that the senses give us (e.g., green, bitter).

sensorimotor intelligence   In Piaget's theory, intelligence during the first two years of life which consists mainly of sensations and motor impulses with, at first, little in the way of internalized representations.

sensory adaptation   The decline in sensitivity found in most sensory systems after continuous exposure to the same stimulus.

sensory coding   The process by which the nervous system translates various aspects of the stimulus into dimensions of our sensory experience.

sensory projection areas   *See* projection areas.

sensory register   A system of memory storage in which material is held for a second or so in its original, unprocessed, sensory form. *See also* long-term memory and short-term memory.

Set   *See* mental set.

sexual orientation   The direction of a person's choice of a sexual partner, which may be heterosexual or homosexual. *See also* gender identity and gender role.

shape constancy   The tendency to perceive the shape of objects as more or less the same despite the fact that the retinal image of these objects changes its shape as we change the angle of orientation from which we view them.

short-term memory   A memory system that keeps material for intervals of a minute or so, that has a small storage capacity (sometimes said to be 7 ± 2), and that holds material in relatively less processed form than long-term memory. *See also* long-term memory and sensory register.

signal detection theory   A theory which asserts that observers who are asked to detect the presence or absence of a stimulus try to decide whether an internal sensory experience should be attributed to background noise or to a signal added to background noise.

simple type of schizophrenia   One of Bleuler's four subtypes of schizophrenia. It lacks the dramatic symptoms of the other forms such as hallucinations but has some of the others such as withdrawal and emotional shallowness, though in less extreme form.

situationism   The view that human behavior is largely determined by the characteristics of the situation rather than those of the person. *See also* trait theory.

size constancy   The tendency to perceive the size of objects as more or less the same despite the fact that the retinal image of these objects

changes in size whenever we change the distance from which we view them.

social comparison   A process of reducing uncertainty about one's own beliefs and attitudes by comparing them to those of others.

socialization   The process whereby the child acquires the patterns of behavior characteristic of its society.

social learning theory   A theoretical approach which is midway between S-R reinforcement theory and cognitive approaches. It stresses learning by observing others who serve as models for the child's behavior. The effect of the model may be to allow learning by imitation and also may be to show the child whether a response he already knows should or should not be performed.

sociobiology   A recent movement in biology that tries to trace social behavior to genetically-based predispositions; an approach that has led to some controversy when extended to humans.

somatic therapies   A collective term for any treatment of mental disorders by means of some organic manipulation. This includes drug administration, any form of surgery, convulsive treatments, etc.

somatogenic mental disorders   Mental disorders that are produced by an organic cause. This is the case for some disorders (e.g., general paresis) but almost surely not for all (e.g., phobias). *See also* psychogenic theory.

somatotonia   *See* somatotype theory.

somatotype theory   A theory proposed by Sheldon who suggested that there are three body-type (or somatotype) components: endomorphy (soft and round), mesomorphy (hard, rectangular, and well muscled), and ectomorphy (delicate build and lightly muscled). These body types are asserted to go with certain clusters of personality traits, specifically: endomorphy with viscerotonia (loves food and comfort, is sociable, needs affection); mesomorphy with somatotonia (desire for power, delight in physical activity, an indifference to people); and ectomorphy with cerebrotonia (self-consciousness, overreactiveness, desire for privacy).

sound waves   Successive pressure variations in the air which vary in amplitude and wave length.

Spearman's theory of general intelligence (g)   Spearman's account, based on factor analytic studies, ascribes intelligence test performance to one underlying factor, general intelligence *(g)* which is tapped by all subtests, and a large number of specific skills (*s*'s) which depend on abilities specific to each subtest. *See also* factor analysis and group-factor theory.

split brain   A condition in which the corpus callosum and some other fibers are cut so that the two cerebral hemispheres are isolated.

spontaneous recovery   An increase in the tendency to perform an extinguished response after a time interval in which neither CS nor UCS are presented.

stabilized image technique   A procedure by which the retina receives a stationary image even though the eye is moving.

standard deviation (SD)   A measure of the variability of a frequency distribution which is the square root of the variance. If *V* is the variance and *SD* the standard deviation, then $SD = \sqrt{V}$. *See also* variance.

standard error of the mean   A measure of the variability of the mean whose value depends both on the standard deviation *(SD)* of the distribution and the number of cases in the sample *(N)*. If *SE* is the standard error, then $SE = SD/\sqrt{N-1}$.

standardization group   The group against which an individual's test score is evaluated.

standard score Also called *z*-score. A score which is expressed as a deviation from the mean in standard deviation units, which allows a comparison of scores drawn from different distributions. If *M* is the mean and *SD* the standard deviation, then $z = (score - M)/SD$.

Stevens' power law An equation that links psychological magnitude *(S)* and physical intensity *(I)* by asserting that $S = kI^n$ where *k* is a constant and *n* is an exponent, usually smaller than *I*.

stimulus Anything in the environment which the organism can detect and respond to.

stimulus generalization In classical conditioning, the tendency to respond to stimuli other than the original CS. The greater the similarity between the CS and the new stimulus the greater this tendency will be. An analogous phenomenon in instrumental conditioning is a response to stimuli other than the original discriminative stimulus.

S-R theory The stimulus-response theory of learning which holds that the basic components of learning are S-R bonds—stimuli and responses which become forged together as learning proceeds.

subtractive color mixture Mixing colors by subtracting one set of wavelengths from another set (as in mixing colors on a palette or superimposing two colored filters).

superego In Freud's theory, a set of reaction patterns within the ego that represent the internalized rules of society and that control the ego by punishing with guilt. *See also* ego and id.

surface structure *See* phrase structure.

sympathetic system A division of the autonomic nervous system which mobilizes the body's energies for emergencies (e.g., increasing heart rate). Its action is antagonistic to that of the parasympathetic system.

symptoms The outward manifestations of an underlying pathology.

synapse The juncture between the axon of one neuron and the dendrite or cell body of another.

syndrome A pattern of symptoms that tend to go together.

systematic desensitization A behavior therapy that tries to remove anxiety connected to various stimuli by a gradual process of counter-conditioning to a response incompatible with fear, usually muscular relaxation. The stimuli are usually evoked as mental images according to an anxiety hierarchy whereby the less frightening stimuli are counterconditioned before the more frightening ones.

taste buds The receptor organs for taste.

taxis An automatic orienting response of the entire body to some stimulus energy. Generally found only in lower organisms (e.g., positive phototaxis in moths).

taxonomy A classification system.

temperament In modern usage, a characteristic level of reactivity and energy, often thought to be based on constitutional factors.

temporal lobe A lobe in each cerebral hemisphere which includes the auditory projection area.

territory Term used by ethologists to describe a region a particular animal stakes out as its own. The territory holder is usually a male, but in some species the territory is held by a mating pair or by a group.

testosterone The principal male sex hormone (androgen) in mammals.

test profile A graphic indication of an individual's performance on several components of a test. This is often useful for guidance or clinical evaluation because it indicates which abilities or traits are relatively high or low in that person.

thalamus A part of the lower portion of the forebrain which serves as a major relay and integration center for sensory information.

Thematic Apperception Test (TAT) A projective technique in which persons are shown a set of pictures and asked to write a story about each.

threshold Some value a stimulus must reach to produce a response.

token economy An arrangement for operant behavior modification in hospital settings. Certain responses (e.g., talking to others) are reinforced with tokens which can be exchanged for desirable items.

trace consolidation hypothesis The hypothesis that newly acquired traces undergo a gradual change that makes them more and more resistant to any disturbance.

trait theory The view that people differ in regard to a number of underlying attributes (traits) that partially determine behavior and that are presumed to be essentially consistent from time to time and from situation to situation. *See also* situationism.

transduction The process by which a receptor translates some physical stimulus (e.g., light or pressure) to give rise to an action potential in another neuron.

transference In psychoanalysis, the patient's tendency to transfer emotional reactions that were originally directed to one's own parents (or other crucial figures in one's early life) and redirect them toward the analyst.

transfer of training The effect of having learned one task on learning another. If learning the first task helps in learning the second, the transfer is called positive. If it impedes in learning the second, the transfer is said to be negative.

transposition The phenomenon whereby visual and auditory patterns (i.e., figures and melodies) remain the same even though the parts of which they are composed are changed.

two-factor theory of avoidance learning A theory which claims that avoidance learning is based on both classical and instrumental conditioning. The reinforcement for the instrumental response is said to be a reduction of fear.

unconditioned reflex *See* unconditioned response.

unconditioned response (UCR) In classical conditioning, the response which is elicited by the unconditional stimulus without prior training. *See* conditioned response, conditioned stimulus, and unconditioned stimulus.

unconditioned stimulus (UCS) In classical conditioning, the stimulus which elicits the unconditioned response and the presentation of which acts as reinforcement. *See* conditioned response, conditioned stimulus, and unconditioned response.

unconscious inference A process postulated by Helmholtz to explain certain perceptual phenomena such as size constancy. An object is perceived to be in the distance and is therefore unconsciously perceived or inferred to be larger than it appears to be retinally. *See also* size constancy.

underlying structure *See* phrase structure.

unipolar affective disorder Affective disorder (usually depression) in which there is no back-and-forth swing between the two emotional extremes.

validity   The extent to which a test measures what it is supposed to measure. *See also* construct validity and predictive validity.

variability   The tendency of scores in a frequency distribution to scatter away from the central value. *See also* central tendency, standard deviation, and variance.

variance (V)   A measure of the variability of a frequency distribution. It is computed by finding the difference between each score and the mean, squaring the result, adding all the squared deviations obtained in this manner and dividing it by the number of cases. If V is the variance, M the mean, and N the number of scores, then $V =$ sum of (score $- M)^2/N$.

vasoconstriction   The constriction of the capillaries brought on by activation of the sympathetic division of the autonomic nervous system in response to excessive cold.

vasodilatation   The dilating of the capillaries brought on by activation of the parasympathetic division of the autonomic nervous system in response to excess heat.

ventromedial region of the hypothalamus   An area in the hypothalamus that is said to be a "satiety center" and in an antagonistic relation to a supposed "hunger center," the lateral hypothalamus.

vestibular sense   A set of receptors that provide information about the orientation and movements of the head, located in the semicircular canals and the vestibular sacs of the inner ear. *See also* inner ear, semicircular canals, and vestibular sacs.

vicarious reinforcement   According to social learning theorists, a form of reinforcement said to occur when someone watches a model being rewarded or punished.

viscerotonia   *See* somatotype theory.

visual cliff   A device for assessing depth perception in young organisms; consists of a glass surface that extends over an apparently deep side (the cliff) and an apparently shallow side.

Weber's law   The observation that the size of the difference threshold is proportional to the intensity of the standard stimulus.

well-formedness   *See* rule of grammar.

Wernicke's area   *See* aphasia.

wishfulfillment in dreams   *See* Freud's theory of dreams.

within-group heritability   The extent to which variation within groups (e.g., among U.S. whites) is attributable to genetic factors. *See also* between-group heritability and heritability.

z-score   *See* standard score.

References

ABELSON, R. P. 1959. Modes of resolution of belief dilemmas. *Journal of Conflict Resolution* 3:343–52.

ABERLE, D. F.; BRONFENBRENNER, U.; HESS, E.H.; MILLER, D.R.; SCHNEIDER, D. M.; AND SPUHLER, J.N. 1963. The incest taboo and the mating pattern of animals. *American Anthropologist* 65:253–65.

ABRAHAM, K. 1927. The influence of oral eroticism on character formation. In Abraham, K., *Selected papers,* pp. 393–406. London: Hogarth Press.

ABRAHAM, S.; COLLINS, G.; AND NORDSIECK, M. 1971. Relationship of childhood weight status to morbidity in adults. *HSMA Health Reports* 86:273.

ABRAMSON, L. Y.; SELIGMAN, M. E. P.; AND TEASDALE, J. D. 1978. Learned helplessness in humans: Critique and reformulation. *Journal of Abnormal Psychology* 87:49–74.

ADELMAN, H. M., AND MAATSCH, J. L. 1956. Learning and extinction based upon frustration, food reward and exploratory tendency. *Journal of Experimental Psychology* 52:311–15.

ADLER, N. 1969. Effects of the male's copulatory behavior on successful pregnancy of the female rat. *Journal of Comparative and Physiological Psychology* 69:613–22.

ADOLPH, E. F. 1947. Urges to eat and drink in rats. *American Journal of Physiology* 151:110–25.

ADORNO, T. W.; FRENKEL-BRUNSWIK, E.; LEVINSON, D. J.; AND SANFORD, R. N. 1950. *The authoritarian personality.* New York: Harper & Row.

ADRIAN, E. D. 1928. *The basis of sensation.* New York: Norton.

ALEXANDER, F. 1934. The influence of psychological factors upon gastro-intestinal disturbances: General principles, objectives and preliminary results. *Psychoanalytic Quarterly* 3:501–39.

ALEXANDER, F., AND FRENCH, T. 1946. *Psychoanalytic theory.* New York: Ronald Press.

ALLPORT, G. W. 1937. *Personality: A psychological interpretation.* New York: Henry Holt.

ALLPORT, G. W., AND ODBERT, H. S. 1936. Trait-names: A psychological study. *Psychological Monographs* 47 (Whole No. 211).

AMSEL, A. 1962. Frustrative nonreward in partial reinforcement and discrimination learning. *Psychological Review* 69: 306–28.

ANASTASI, A. 1971. More on heredity: Addendum to the Hebb and Jensen interchange. *American Psychologist* 26: 1036–37.

ANDERSON, N. H. 1965. Primacy effects in personality impression formation using a generalized order effect paradigm. *Journal of Personality and Social Psychology* 2:1–9.

ANDERSON, N. H., AND BARRIOS, A. A. 1961. Primacy effects in personality impression formation. *Journal of Abnormal and Social Psychology* 63:346–50.

ANDERSSON, B.; GRANT, R.; AND LARSSON, S. 1956. Central control of heat loss mechanisms in the goat. *Acta Physiologica Scandinavica* 37:261–80.

ANDREWS, J. D. W. 1966. Psychotherapy of phobias. *Psychological Bulletin* 66:455–80.

ANGLIN, J. M. 1975. The child's first terms of reference. In Ehrlich, S., and Tulving, E., eds., *Bulletin de Psychologie,* special issue on semantic memory.

ANGRIST, B.; SATHANANTHAN, G.; WILK, S.; AND GERSHON, S. 1974. Amphetamine psychosis: Behavioral and biochemical aspects. *Journal of Psychiatric Research* 11:13–24.

ANREP, G. V. 1920. Pitch discrimination in the dog. *Journal of Physiology* 53:367–85.

ANSTIS, S. M. 1975. What does visual perception tell us about visual coding? In Gazzaniga, M. S., and Blakemore, C., eds., *Handbook of psychobiology* New York: Academic Press.

APPEL, L. F.; COOPER, R. G.; MCCARRELL, N.; SIMS-KNIGHT, J.; YUSSEN, S. R.; AND FLAVELL, J. H. 1972. The development of the distinction between perceiving and memorizing. *Child Development* 43:1365–81.

ARDREY, R. 1966. *The territorial imperative.* New York: Dell.

ARENDT, H. 1965. *Eichmann in Jerusalem: A report on the banality of evil.* New York: Viking Press.

ARIETI, S. 1959. Schizophrenia: The manifest symptomatology, the psychodynamic and formal mechanisms. In Arieti, S., ed., *Ameri-*

can handbook of psychiatry, vol. 1, pp. 455–84. New York: Basic Books.

ARISTOTLE. ca. 330 B.C. On sleep and waking; On dreams; On prophecy in sleep. In The works of Aristotle, vol. 3. London: Oxford University Press, 1931.

ARMSTRONG, S.; GLEITMAN, H.; AND GLEITMAN, L. R. 1980. On what some concepts might not be. Unpublished manuscript, University of Pennsylvania.

ARNHEIM, R. 1974. Art and visual perception, new version. Berkeley, California: University of California Press.

ARONSON, E. 1972. The social animal. San Francisco: Freeman.

ARONSON, E., AND MILLS, J. 1959. The effect of severity of initiation on liking for a group. Journal of Abnormal and Social Psychology 59:177–81.

ASCH, S. E. 1946. Forming impressions of personality. Journal of Abnormal and Social Psychology 41:258–90.

ASCH, S. E. 1948. The doctrine of suggestion, prestige and imitation in social psychology. Psychological Review 55:250–77.

ASCH, S. E. 1952. Social psychology. New York: Prentice-Hall.

ASCH, S. E. 1955. Opinions and social pressure. Scientific American 193:31–35.

ASCH, S. E. 1956. Studies of independence and conformity: A minority of one against a unanimous majority. Psychological Monographs 70 (9, Whole No. 416).

ASCH, S. E. 1958. Effects of group pressure upon the modification and distortion of judgements. In Maccoby, E. E.; Newcomb, T. M.; and Hartley, E. L., eds., Readings in social psychology, pp. 174–81. New York: Henry Holt.

ASHER, E. J. 1935. The inadequacy of current intelligence tests for testing Kentucky Mountain children. Journal of Genetic Psychology 46:480–86.

ATKINSON, J. W., AND MCCLELLAND, D. C. 1948. The projective expression of needs. II. The effect of different intensities of the hunger drive on thematic apperception. Journal of Experimental Psychology 38:643–58.

ATTNEAVE, F. 1971. Multistability in perception. Scientific American 225:62–71.

AUGUSTINE. 397 A.D. The confessions. Translated and annotated by Pilkington, J. G. P. Cleveland: Fine Editions Press, 1876.

AUSTIN, J. L. 1962. How to do things with words. London: Oxford University Press.

AX, A. F. 1953. The physiological differentiation of fear and anger in humans. Psychosomatic Medicine 15:433–42.

AYLLON, T. 1963. Intensive treatment of psychotic behavior by stimulus satiation and food reinforcement. Behavior Research and Therapy 1:53–61.

AYLLON, T., AND AZRIN, N. H. 1968. The token economy: A motivational system for therapy and rehabilitation. New York: Appleton-Century-Crofts.

AZRIN, N. H.; HUTCHINSON, R. R.; AND HAKE, D. F. 1966. Extinction-induced aggression. Journal of the Experimental Analysis of Behavior 10:131–48.

AZRIN, N. H. 1967. Pain and aggression. Psychology Today 1:27–33.

BABIGIAN, H. M. 1975. Schizophrenia: Epidimeology. In Freedman, A. M.; Kaplan, H. I.; and Sadock, B. J., eds., Comprehensive textbook of psychiatry—II, vol. 1, pp. 860–66. Baltimore, Md.: Williams & Wilkins.

BACK, K. W. 1972. Beyond words. New York: Russell Sage.

BADDELEY, A. D. 1966. Short-term memory for word sequences as a function of acoustic, semantic, and formal similarity. Quarterly Journal of Experimental Psychology 18:362–65.

BADDELEY, A. D. 1976. The psychology of memory. New York: Basic Books.

BALL, W., AND TRONICK, E. 1971. Infant responses to impending collision: Optical and real. Science 171:818–20.

BALTES, P. B., AND SCHAIE, K. W. 1976. On the plasticity of intelligence in adulthood and old age. American Psychologist 31:720–25.

BANDURA, A. 1965. Influence of models' reinforcement contingencies on the acquisition of imitative responses. Journal of Personality and Social Psychology 1:589–95.

BANDURA, A., AND WALTERS, R. H. 1963. Social learning and personality development. New York: Holt, Rinehart & Winston.

BARLOW, H. B., AND LEVICK, W. 1965. The mechanism of directionally sensitive units in the rabbit's retina. Journal of Physiology 178: 477–504.

BARNETT, S. A. 1963. The rat: A study in behavior. Chicago: Aldine.

BARNOUW, V. 1963. Culture and personality. Homewood, Ill.: Dorsey Press.

BARON, J. 1977. Menstrual hormone changes and instinctual tendencies in dreams. Motivation and emotion 1:273–82.

BARRY, H., III; CHILD, I. L.; AND BACON, M. K. 1959. Relation of child training to subsistence economy. American Anthropologist 61:51–63.

BARTLETT, F. C. 1932. Remembering: A study in experimental and social psychology. Cambridge, England: Cambridge University Press.

BARTOSHUK, L. M. 1971. The chemical senses. 1. Taste. In Kling, J. W., and Riggs, L. A., eds., Experimental psychology, 3rd ed. New York: Holt, Rinehart & Winston.

BASS, M. J., AND HULL, C. L. 1934. The irradiation of a tactile conditioned reflex in man. Journal of Comparative Psychology 17:47–65.

BATES, E. 1976. Language and context: The acquisition of pragmatics. New York: Academic Press.

BATES, E., AND MACWHINNEY, B. 1981. Functionalist approaches to grammar. In Wanner, E., and Gleitman, L. R., eds. Language acquisition: State of the art. Cambridge, England: Cambridge University Press.

BATESON, G.,; JACKSON, D. D.; HALEY, J.; AND WEAKLAND, J. 1956. Toward a theory of schizophrenia. Behavioral Science 1:251–64.

BAUMRIND, D. 1964. Some thoughts on ethics of research: After reading Milgram's 'Behavioral study of obedience.' American Psychologist 19:421–23.

BAYER, E. 1929. Beiträge zur Zweikomponententheorie des Hungers. Zeitschrift der Psychologie 112:1–54.

BAYLEY, N. 1969. Bayley scales of infant development: Birth to two years. New York: Psychological Corporation.

BAYLEY, N., AND SCHAEFER, E. S. 1964. Correlations of maternal and child behaviors with the development of mental abilities: Data from the Berkeley Growth Study. Monographs of the Society for Research in Child Development 29:1–80.

BECK, A. T. 1967. Depression: Causes and treatment. Philadelphia: University of Pennsylvania Press.

BECK, A. T. 1976. Cognitive therapy and the emotional disorders. New York: International Universities Press.

BECK, J. 1966. Effect of orientation and of shape similarity on perceptual grouping. Perception and Psychophysics 1:300–302.

BECKER, W. C. 1964. Consequences of different kinds of parental discipline. In Hoffman, M. L., and Hoffman, L. W., eds., Review of child development research, vol. 1, pp. 169–208. New York: Russell Sage Foundation.

BÉKÉSY, G. VON. 1951. The mechanical properties of the ear. In Stevens, S. S., ed., Handbook of experimental psychology, pp. 1075–1115. New York: Wiley.

BÉKÉSY, G. VON. 1957. The ear. Scientific American 197:66–78.

BELOFF, H. 1957. The structure and origin of the anal character. Genetic Psychology Monographs 55:141–72.

BEM, D. J. 1967. Self-perception: An alternative interpretation of cognitive dissonance phenomena. *Psychological Review* 74:183–200.

BEM, D. J. 1972. Self-perception theory. In Berkowitz, L., ed., *Advances in experimental social psychology,* vol. 6, pp. 2–62. New York: Academic Press.

BEREITER, C., AND ENGLEMANN, S. 1966. *Teaching culturally deprived children in pre-school.* Englewood Cliffs, N.J.: Prentice-Hall.

BERGIN, A. E. 1967. An empirical analysis of therapeutic issues. In Arbuckle, D., ed., *Counseling and psychotherapy: An overview,* pp. 175–208. New York: McGraw-Hill.

BERGIN, A. E. 1971. The evaluation of therapeutic outcomes. In Bergin, A. E., and Garfield, S. L., eds., *Handbook of psychotherapy and behavior change,* pp. 217–70. New York: Wiley.

BERKELEY, G. 1709. An essay towards a new theory of vision. In Berkeley, G., *Works on vision,* edited by Turbayne, C. M. Indianapolis, Ind.: Bobbs-Merrill, 1963.

BERKELEY, G. 1710. *The principles of human knowledge.* In Berkeley, G., *The principles of human knowledge,* edited by Warnock, G. J. London: Fontana Library, 1962.

BERMANT, G., AND DAVIDSON, J. M. 1974. *Biological bases of sexual behavior.* New York: Harper & Row.

BERNARD, C. 1957. *An introduction to the study of experimental medicine.* New York: Dover.

BERNARD, V. W.; OTTENBERG, P.; AND REDL, F. 1965. Dehumanization: A composite psychological defense in relation to modern war. In Schwebel, M., ed., *Behavioral science and human survival,* pp. 64–82. Palo Alto, Calif.: Science and Behavior Books.

BERNHEIM, K. W., AND LEWINE, R. R. J. 1979. *Schizophrenia: Symptoms, causes, treatments.* New York: Norton.

BERNSTEIN, B. 1967. Social structure, language and learning. In Passow, A. H.; Goldberg, M.; and Tannenbaum, A. J., eds., *Education of the disadvantaged,* New York: Holt, Rinehart & Winston.

BEVER, T. G. 1970. The cognitive basis for linguistic structures. In Hayes, J. R., ed., *Cognition and the development of language,* pp. 279–362. New York: Wiley.

BICKMAN, L. 1971. The effect of another bystander's ability to help on bystander intervention in an emergency. *Journal of Experimental Social Psychology* 7:367–79.

BIEBER, I. 1965. Clinical aspects of male homosexuality. In Marmor, J., ed., *Sexual inversion,* pp. 248–67. New York: Basic Books.

BIEBER, I.; DAIN, H. J.; DINCE, P. R.; DRELLICH, M. G.; GRAND, H. G.; GRUNDLACH, R. H.; KREMER, M. W.; RIFKIN, A. H.; WILBUR, C. B.; AND BIEBER, T. B. 1962. *Homosexuality: A psychoanalytic study.* New York: Basic Books.

BILSKY, L.; EVANS, R. A.; AND GILBERT, L. 1972. Generalization of associative clustering tendencies in mentally retarded adolescents: Effects of novel stimuli. *American Journal of Mental Deficiency* 77:77–84.

BIRCH, H. G. 1945. The role of motivational factors in insightful problem-solving. *Journal of Comparative Psychology* 38:295–317.

BLACK, A. H. 1959. Heart rate changes during avoidance learning in dogs. *Canadian Journal of Psychology* 13:229–42.

BLAKEMORE, C. 1975. Central visual processing. In Gazzaniga, M. S., and Blakemore, C., eds., *Handbook of psychobiology.* New York: Academic Press.

BLEULER, E. 1911. *Dementia praecox, or the group of schizophrenias.* English translation by Zinkin, J., and Lewis, N. D. C. New York: International Universities Press, 1950.

BLOCK, J. 1971. *Lives through time.* Berkeley, Calif.: Bancroft.

BLOCK, N. J., AND DWORKIN, G. 1976. IQ, heritability and inequality. In Block, N. J., and Dworkin, G., eds., *The IQ controversy,* pp. 410–540. New York: Pantheon Books.

BLODGETT, H. C. 1929. The effect of the introduction of reward upon the maze performance of rats. *University of California Publications in Psychology* 4:113–34.

BLOOM, L. 1970. *Language development: Form and function in emerging grammars.* Cambridge, Mass.: MIT Press.

BLOOM, L. 1973. *One word at a time.* The Hague: Mouton.

BLOOM, L.; HOOD, L.; AND LIGHTBOWN, P. 1974. Imitation in language development: If, when and why? *Cognitive Psychology* 6:380–420.

BLOOMFIELD, L. 1933. *Language.* New York: Holt, Rinehart & Winston.

BLOUNT, G. 1972. Parental speech and language acquisition: Some Luo and Samoan examples. *Anthropological Linguist* 14(4):119–30.

BLUM, J. E.; JARVIK, L. F.; AND CLARK, E. T. 1970. Rate of change on selective tests of intelligence: A twenty-year longitudinal study. *Journal of Gerontology* 25:171–76.

BLURTON-JONES, N. G. 1976. Review of Wilson's 'Sociobiology.' *Animal Behavior* 24:701–3.

BOGEN, J. E. 1969. The other side of the brain II: An appositional mind. *Bulletin of the Los Angeles Neurological Societies* 34:135–62.

BOLLES, R. C. 1970. Species-specific defense reactions and avoidance learning. *Psychological Review* 77:32–48.

BOOTH, D. A. 1973. Protein synthesis and memory. In Deutsch, J. A., ed., *The physiological basis of memory,* pp. 27–58. New York: Academic Press.

BORING, E. G. 1930. A new ambiguous figure. *American Journal of Psychology* 42:444–45.

BORING, E. G. 1942. *Sensation and perception in the history of experimental psychology.* New York: Appleton-Century-Crofts.

BORING, E. G. 1950. *A history of experimental psychology,* 2nd edition. New York: Appleton-Century-Crofts.

BORING, E. G. 1964. Size constancy in a picture. *American Journal of Psychology* 77:494–98.

BORKE, H. 1975. Piaget's mountains revisited: Changes in the egocentric landscape. *Developmental Psychology* 11:240–43.

BOUSFIELD, W. A. 1953. The occurrence of clustering in the recall of randomly arranged associates. *Journal of General Psychology* 49:229–40.

BOWER, G. H. 1970a. Organizational factors in memory. *Cognitive Psychology* 1:18–46.

BOWER, G. H. 1970b. Analysis of a mnemonic device. *American Scientist* 58:496–510.

BOWER, T. G. R. 1966. The visual world of infants. *Scientific American* 215:80–92.

BOWER, T. G. R. 1971. The object in the world of the infant. *Scientific American* 225:30–38.

BOWERMAN, M. 1973. *Early syntactic development: A crosslinguistic study with special reference to Finnish.* London: Cambridge University Press.

BOWERMAN, M. 1973. Structural relationships in children's utterances: Syntactic or semantic? In Moore, T. E., ed., *Cognitive development and the acquisition of language.* New York: Academic Press.

BOWERMAN, M. 1981. Reorganizational processes in language development. In Wanner, E., and Gleitman, L. R., eds., *Language development: State of the art.* Cambridge, England: Cambridge University Press.

BOWLBY, J. 1973. *Attachment and loss.* New York: Basic Books.

BRADLEY, D. C.; GARRETT, M. F., AND ZURIF, E. G. 1979. Syntactic deficits in Broca's aphasia. In Caplan, D., ed., *Biological studies of mental processes.* Cambridge, Mass.: MIT Press.

BRADY, J. P. 1972. Systematic desensitization. In Agras, W. S., ed., *Behavior modification: Principles and clinical applications,* pp. 127–50. Boston: Little, Brown.

BRAIN, L. 1965. *Speech disorders: Aphasia, apraxia, and agnosia.* London: Butterworth.

BRAINE, M. D. S. 1963. The ontogeny of English phrase structure: The first phase. *Language* 39:3–13.

BRAINE, M. D. S. 1976. Children's first word combinations. *Monographs of the Society for Research in Child Development* 41(1, Serial No. 164).

BRANSFORD, J. D., AND FRANKS, J. J. 1971. The abstraction of linguistic ideas. *Cognitive Psychology* 2:331–50.

BRAZELTON, T. B. 1962. A child-oriented approach to toilet training. *Pediatrics* 29:121–28.

BREGER, L.; HUNTER, I.; AND LANE, R. W. 1971. The effect of stress on dreams. *Psychological Issues* 7(3, Monograph 27):1–213.

BREHM, J. W. 1956. Postdecision changes in the desirability of alternatives. *Journal of Abnormal and Social Psychology* 52:384–89.

BRELAND, K., AND BRELAND, M. 1951. A field of applied animal psychology. *American Psychologist* 6:202–4.

BRELAND, K., AND BRELAND, M. 1966. *Animal behavior.* New York: Macmillan.

BRESNAN, J. 1978. A realistic transformation grammar. In Halle, M.; Bresnan, J.; and Miller, G., eds., *Linguistic theory and psychological reality.* Cambridge, Mass.: MIT Press.

BROADBENT, D. E. 1958. *Perception and communication.* London: Pergamon Press.

BROEN, W. E., JR. 1968. *Schizophrenia: Research and theory.* New York: Academic Press.

BRONSON, W. C. 1966. Central orientations: A study of behavior organization from childhood to adolescence. *Child Development* 37:125–55.

BROWN, A. L. 1974. The role of strategic memory in retardate memory. In Ellis, N. R., ed., *International Review of Research in Mental Retardation,* vol. 7, pp. 55–108. New York: Academic Press.

BROWN, A. L.; CAMPIONE, J. C.; BRAY, N. W.; AND WILCOX, B. L. 1973. Keeping track of changing variables: Effects of rehearsal training and rehearsal prevention in normal and retarded adolescents. *Journal of Experimental Psychology* 101:123–31.

BROWN, A. L.; CAMPIONE, J. C.; AND MURPHY, M. D. 1974. Keeping track of changing variables: Long-term retention of a trained rehearsal strategy by retarded adolescents. *American Journal of Mental Deficiency* 78:446–53.

BROWN, J. F. 1940. *The psychodynamics of abnormal behavior.* New York: McGraw-Hill.

BROWN, J. S. 1948. Gradients of approach and avoidance responses and their relation to level of motivation. *Journal of Comparative and Physiological Psychology* 41:450–65.

BROWN, J. W. 1972. *Aphasia, apraxia, and agnosia.* Springfield, Ill.: Thomas.

BROWN, R. 1954. Mass phenomena. In Lindzey, G., ed., *Handbook of social psychology,* vol. 2, pp. 833–76. Reading, Mass.: Addison-Wesley.

BROWN, R. 1958. *Words and things.* New York: Free Press, Macmillan.

BROWN, R. 1965. *Social psychology.* New York: Free Press, Macmillan.

BROWN, R. 1970. *Psycholinguistics: Selected papers.* New York: Free Press, Macmillan.

BROWN, R. 1973. *A first language: The early stages.* Cambridge, Mass.: Harvard University Press.

BROWN, R., AND BELLUGI, U. 1964. Three processes in the child's acquisition of syntax. *Harvard Educational Review* 34:133–51.

BROWN, R.; CAZDEN, C.; AND BELLUGI-KLIMA, U. 1969. The child's grammar from 1 to 111. In Hill, J. P., ed., *Minnesota symposium on child psychology,* vol. 2, pp. 28–73. Minneapolis: University of Minnesota Press.

BROWN, R., AND HANLON, C. 1970. Derivational complexity and order of acquisition in child speech. In Hayes, J. R., ed., *Cognition and the development of language,* pp. 11–53. New York: Wiley.

BROWN, R., AND MCNEILL, D. 1966. The tip of the tongue phenomenon. *Journal of Verbal Learning and Verbal Behavior* 5:325–27.

BRUNER, J. S. 1969. Eye, hand and mind. In Elkind, D., and Flavell, J. H., *Studies in cognitive development,* pp. 223–36. New York: Oxford University Press.

BRUNER, J. S. 1974/75. From communication to language—a psychological perspective. *Cognition* 3:255–78.

BRYAN, W. L., AND HARTER, N. 1897. Studies in the physiology and psychology of telegraphic language. *Psychological Review* 4:27–53.

BRYAN, W. L., AND HARTER, N. 1899. Studies on the telegraphic language. The acquisition of a hierarchy of habits. *Psychology Review* 6:345–75.

BUCHSBAUM, R. M. 1948. *Animals without backbones.* Chicago: University of Chicago Press.

BUGELSKI, B. R., AND ALAMPAY, D. A. 1961. The role of frequency in developing perceptual sets. *Canadian Journal of Psychology* 15:205–11.

BULLOUGH, E. 1912. "Psychical distance" as a factor in art and an aesthetic principle. *British Journal of Psychology* 5:87–118.

BURNHAM, R. W.; HANES, R. M.; AND BARTELSON, C. J. 1963. *Color: A guide to basic facts and concepts.* New York: Wiley.

BURTON, R. V. 1963. Generality of honesty reconsidered. *Psychological Review* 70:481–99.

BUSS, A. H., AND PLOMIN, R. 1975. *A temperament theory of personality development.* New York: Wiley.

BYRNE, D. 1964. Assessing personality variables and their alteration. In Worchel, P., and Byrne, D., eds., *Personality Change,* pp. 38–68. New York: Wiley.

CAIRNS, R. B., AND JOHNSON, D. L. 1965. The development of interspecies social attachments. *Psychonomic Science* 2:337–8.

CAMPBELL, E. Q. 1969. Adolescent socialization. In Goslin, D. A., ed., *Handbook of socialization theory and research,* pp. 821–60. Chicago: Rand McNally, 1969.

CANNON, W. B. 1927. The James-Lange theory of emotions: A critical examination and an alternative theory. *American Journal of Psychology* 39:106–24.

CANNON, W. B. 1929. *Bodily changes in pain, hunger, fear and rage,* revised edition. New York: Appleton-Century.

CANNON, W. B. 1932 and 1960 (revised and enlarged). *The wisdom of the body.* New York: Norton.

CANNON, W. B. 1942. "Voodoo" death. *American Psychologist* 44:169–81.

CAPALDI, E. J. 1967. A sequential hypothesis of instrumental learning. In Spence, K. W., and Spence, J. T., eds., *The psychology of learning and motivation,* vol. 1, pp. 67–156. New York: Academic Press.

CAREY, S. 1978. The child as word learner. In Halle, M.; Bresnan, J.; and Miller, G., eds., *Linguistic theory and psychological reality,* pp. 264–93. Cambridge, Mass.: MIT Press.

CAREY, S. 1981. Semantic development: State of the art. In Wanner, E., and Gleitman, L. R., eds., *Language acquisition: State of the art.* Cambridge, England: Cambridge University Press.

CARLSMITH, L. 1964. Effects of early father absence on scholastic aptitude. *Harvard Educational Review* 34:3–21.

CARLSON, N. R. 1977. *Physiology of behavior.* Boston: Allyn and Bacon.

CARPENTER, C. R. 1965. The howlers of Barro Colorado Island. In DeVore, I., ed., *Primate behavior,* pp. 250–91. New York: Holt, Rinehart & Winston.

CARRIGAN, P. M. 1960. Extraversion-introversion as a dimension of personality: A reappraisal. *Psychological Bulletin* 57:329–60.

CARRINGTON, P. 1972. Dreams and schizophrenia. *Archives General Psychiatry* 26:343–50.

CARROLL, L. 1865. *Alice in Wonderland.* Abridged by Frank, J. and illustrated by Torrey, M. M. New York: Random House, 1969.

CASE, R. 1974. Structures and strictures: Some functional limitations on the course of cognitive growth. *Cognitive Psychology* 6:544–74.

CATTELL, R. B. 1957. *Personality and motivation structure and measurement.* New York: Harcourt, Brace and World.

CATTELL, R. B. 1963. Theory of fluid and crystallized intelligence: A critical experiment. *Journal of Educational Psychology* 54:1–22.

CHAPANIS, N. P., AND CHAPANIS, A. 1964. Cognitive dissonance: Five years later. *Psychological Bulletin* 61:1–22.

CHARLESWORTH, W. R., AND KREUTZER, M. A. 1973. Facial expressions of infants and children. In Ekman, P., ed., *Darwin and facial expression: A century of research in review.* New York: Academic Press.

CHASE, W. G., AND SIMON, H. A. 1973. Perception in chess. *Cognitive Psychology* 4:55–81.

CHERRY, E. C. 1953. Some experiments upon the recognition of speech, with one and with two ears. *Journal of the Acoustical Society of America* 25:975–79.

CHILD, I. L. 1950. The relation of somatotype to self-ratings on Sheldon's temperamental traits. *Journal of Personality* 18:440–53.

CHODOFF, PAUL 1954. A reexamination of some aspects of conversion hysteria. *Psychiatry* 17:75–81.

CHOMSKY, N. 1957. *Syntactic structures.* The Hague: Mouton.

CHOMSKY, N. 1959. Review of '*Verbal behavior*' by B. F. Skinner. *Language* 35:26–58.

CHOMSKY, N. 1965. *Aspects of the theory of syntax.* Cambridge, Mass.: MIT Press.

CHOMSKY, N. 1975. *Reflections on language.* New York: Pantheon Books.

CHOMSKY, N., AND LASNIK, H. 1977. Filters and control. *Linguistic Inquiry* 8:425–504.

CHOROVER, L. 1965. Discussion of the effects of electroconvulsive shock on performance and memory. In Kimble, D. P., ed., *The anatomy of memory,* pp. 253–63. Palo Alto, Calif.: Science & Behavior Books.

CHRISTIE, R. 1954. Authoritarianism re-examined. In Christie, R., and Jahoda, M., eds., *Studies in the scope and method of "The authoritarian personality."* New York: Free Press, Macmillan, 1954.

CHRISTIE, R., AND JAHODA, M., eds., 1954. *Studies in the scope and method of "The authoritarian personality."* New York: Free Press, Macmillan.

CLARK, E. V. 1973. What's in a word?: On the child's acquisition of semantics in his first language. In Moore, T. E., ed., *Cognitive development and the acquisition of language.* New York: Academic Press.

CLARK, E. V. 1981. The young word-maker: A case study of innovation in the child's lexicon. In Wanner, E., and Gleitman, L. R., eds., *Language acquisition: State of the art.* Cambridge, England: Cambridge University Press.

CLARK, H. H., AND CLARK, E. V. 1977. *Psychology and language: An introduction to psycholinguistics.* New York: Harcourt Brace Javanovich.

CLARK, K. B., AND CLARK, M. 1958. Racial identification and preference in Negro children. In Maccoby, E. E.; Newcomb, T. M.; and Hartley, E. J., eds., *Readings in social psychology,* revised edition, pp. 602–11. New York: Holt, Rinehart & Winston.

CLEARY, T. A. 1968. Test bias: Prediction of grades of Negro and white students in integrated colleges. *Journal of Educational Measurement* 5:115–24.

CLECKLEY, H. 1964. *The mask of sanity,* 4th edition. St. Louis, Missouri: Mosby.

COBB, S., AND ROSE, R. M. 1973. Hypertension, peptic ulcer and diabetes in air traffic controllers. *Journal of the American Medical Association* 224:489–92.

COFFIN, T. E. 1941. Some conditions of suggestion and suggestibility: A study of certain attitudinal and situational factors influenc-ing the process of suggestion. *Psychological Monographs* 53 (4).

COHEN, H. 1972. Active (REM) sleep deprivation. In Chase, M. H., ed., *The sleeping brain: Perspectives in the brain sciences,* vol. 1, pp. 343–47. Los Angeles: Brain Research Institute, University of California.

COHEN, R. A. 1975. Manic-depressive illness. In Freedman, A. M.; Kaplan, H. I.; and Sadock, B. J., eds., *Comprehensive textbook of psychiatry—II,* vol. 1, pp. 1012–24. Baltimore, Md.: Williams & Wilkins.

COHEN, Y. A. 1953. A study of interpersonal relations in a Jamaican community. Unpublished doctoral dissertation, Yale University.

COLE, J. O., AND DAVIS, J. M. 1975. Antidepressant drugs. In Freedman, A. M.; Kaplan, H. I.; and Sadock, B. J., eds., *Comprehensive textbook of psychiatry—II,* vol. 2, pp. 1941–56. Baltimore, Md.: Williams & Wilkins.

COLEMAN, J. C. 1972 AND 1976. *Abnormal psychology and modern life,* 4th and 5th editions. Glenview, Ill.: Scott, Foresman.

COLLINS, A. M., AND QUILLIAN, M. R. 1969. Retrieval time from semantic memory. *Journal of Verbal Learning and Verbal Behavior* 8:240–47.

COLLINS, R. L., AND FULLER, J. L. 1968. Audiogenic seizure prone (ASP): A gene affecting behavior in linkage group VIII of the mouse. *Science* 162:1137–39.

COLLIS, G., 1975. The integration of gaze and vocal behavior in the mother-infant dyad. Paper presented at Third International Child Language Symposium, London.

CONRAD, R. 1964. Acoustic confusions in immediate memory. *British Journal of Psychology* 55: 75–84.

CONRAD, R. 1972. Speech and reading. In Kavanagh, J. F., and Mattingly, I. G., eds., *Language by ear and by eye: The relationships between speech and reading.* Cambridge, Mass.: MIT Press.

COOLEY, C. H. 1902. *Human nature and the social order.* New York: Scribner.

COOPER, D. 1967. *Psychiatry and anti-psychiatry.* London: Tavistock

COOPER, L. A., AND SHEPARD, R. N. 1973. The time required to prepare for a rotated stimulus. *Memory and Cognition* 1:246–50.

COREN, S.; PORAC, C.; AND WARD, L. M. 1978. *Sensation and perception.* New York: Academic Press.

CORNSWEET, T. M. 1970. *Visual perception.* New York: Academic Press.

COSTELLO, C. G. 1978. A critical review of Seligman's laboratory experiments on learned helplessness and depression in humans. *Journal of Abnormal Psychology* 87:21–31.

COWLES, J. T. 1937. Food-tokens as incentives for learning by chimpanzees. *Comparative Psychology Monographs* 14 (5. Serial No. 71)

CRAIK, F. I. M., AND WATKINS, M. J. 1973. The role of rehearsal in short-term memory. *Journal of Verbal Learning and Verbal Behavior* 12:599–607.

CRANDALL, V. C.; KATKOVSKY, W.; AND CRANDALL, V. J. 1965. Children's beliefs in their own control of reinforcements in intellectual-academic achievement situations. *Child Development* 36:91–109.

CRANDALL, V.; KATKOVSKY, W.; AND PRESTON, A. 1962. Motivational ability determinants of young children's intellectual achievement behaviors. *Child Development* 33:643–61.

CRESPI, L. P. 1942. Quantitative variation of incentive and performance in the white rat. *American Journal of Psychology* 55:467–517.

CROMER, R. F. 1976. The cognitive hypothesis of language acquisition and its implications for child language deficiency. In Morehead, D. M., and Morehead, A. E., eds., *Normal and deficient child language,* pp. 283–334. Baltimore, Md.: University Park Press.

CRONBACH, L. J. 1970a. *Essentials of psychological testing, 3rd edition.* New York: Harper & Row

CRONBACH, L. J. 1970b. Test validation. In Thorndike, R. L., ed., *Educational measurement.* Washington: American Council on Education.

CRONBACH, L. J., AND MEEHL, P. E. 1955. Construct validity in psychological tests. *Psychological Bulletin* 52:281–302.

CROSS, T. G. 1977. Mothers' speech adjustments: The contribution of selected child listener variables. In Snow, C. E., and Ferguson, C. A., eds., *Talking to children: Language input and acquisition.* Cambridge, England: Cambridge Univeristy Press.

CROWDER, R. G. 1976. *Principles of learning and memory.* Hillsdale, N. J.: Lawrence Erlbaum.

CROZIER, W. J., AND HOAGLAND, H. 1934. The study of living organisms. In Murchinson, C., ed., *A handbook of general experimental psychology.* Worcester, Mass.: Clark University Press.

CRUTCHFIELD, R. S. 1955. Conformity and character. *American Psychologist* 10:191–99.

CURTISS, SUSAN. 1977. *Genie: A linguistic study of a modern-day "wild child."* New York: Academic Press.

CYTRYN, L., AND LOURIE, R. S. 1975. Mental retardation. In Freedman, A. M.; Kaplan, H. I.; and Sadock, B. J., et s., *Comprehensive textbook of psychiatry—II,* vol. 1, pp. 1158–97. Baltimore, Md.: Williams & Wilkins.

DALE, A. J. D. 1975. Organic brain syndromes associated with infections. In Freedman, A. M.; Kaplan, H. I.; and Sadock, B. J., eds., *Comprehensive textbook of psychiatry—II,* vol. 1, pp.1121–30. Baltimore, Md.: Williams & Wilkins.

DARLEY, J., AND LATANÉ, B. 1968. Bystander intervention in emergencies: Diffusion of responsibility. *Journal of Personality and Social Psychology* 10:202–14.

DARWIN, C. 1872a. *The origin of species.* New York: Macmillan, 6th edition, 1962.

DARWIN, C. 1872b. *The expression of the emotions in man and animals.* London: Appleton

DARWIN, C. J.; TURVEY, M. T.; AND CROWDER, R. G. 1972. An auditory analogue of the Sperling partial report procedure: Evidence for brief auditory storage. *Cognitive Psychology* 3:255–67.

DAVIDSON, J. M. 1969. Hormonal control of sexual behavior in adult rats. In Raspé, G., ed., *Advances in bioscience,* vol. 1, pp. 119–69. New York: Pergamon

DAVINCI, LEONARDO. ca. 1500. *Treatise on painting.* In Philosophical Library Edition, *The art of painting.* New York: Philosophical Library, 1957.

DAVIS, D. E. 1964. The physiological analysis of aggressive behavior. In Etkin, W., ed., *Social behavior and organization among vertebrates.* Chicago: University of Chicago Press.

DAVIS, J. M. 1974. A two-factor theory of schizophrenia. *Journal of Psychiatric Research* 11:25–30.

DAVIS, J. M., AND COLE, J. O. 1975. Antipsychotic drugs. In Freedman, A. M.; Kaplan, H. I.; and Sadock, B. J., eds., *Comprehensive textbook of psychiatry—II,* vol. 2, pp. 1921–41. Baltimore, Md.: Williams & Wilkins.

DAVIS, K. 1947. Final note on a case of extreme social isolation. *American Journal of Sociology* 52:432–37.

DAVISON, G. C., AND NEALE, J. M. 1974 and 1978. *Abnormal psychology: An experimental clinical approach,* 1st and 2nd editions. New York: Wiley.

DE CHARMS, R., AND MOELLER, G. H. 1962. Values expressed in American children's readers: 1800–1950. *Journal of Abnormal and Social Psychology* 64:136–42.

DEGROOT, A. D. 1965. *Thought and Choice in Chess.* The Hague: Mouton.

DEMENT, W. C. 1974. *Some must watch while some must sleep.* San Francisco: Freeman.

DEMENT, W. C., AND KLEITMAN, N. 1957. The relation of eye movements during sleep to dream activity: An objective method for the study of dreaming. *Journal of Experimental Psychology* 53:339–46.

DEMENT, W. C., AND WOLPERT, E. A. 1958. The relationship of eye-movements, body motility, and external stimuli to dream content. *Journal of Experimental Psychology* 55:543–53.

DENNIS, W., AND DENNIS, M. G. 1940. The effect of cradling practice upon the onset of walking in Hopi children. *Journal of Genetic Psychology* 56:77–86.

DEPUE, R. A., AND MONROE, S. M. 1978. Learned helplessness in the perspective of the depressive disorders: Conceptual and definitional issues. *Journal of Abnormal Psychology* 87:3–20.

DESCARTES, R. 1646. *The passions of the soul.* In *The philosophical works of Descartes,* translated by Haldane, E. S., and Ross, G. R. T. New York: Dover, 1951.

DESCARTES, R. 1649. Letter (to Morus); AT V, 278. In Eaton, R. M., ed., *Descartes selections,* p. 360. New York: Scribner's, 1927. Cited in Vendler, Z., *Res cogitans: An essay in rational psychology.* Ithaca, N.Y.: Cornell University Press, 1972.

DESCARTES, R. 1662. *Traité de l'homme.* Translated by Haldane, E. S., and Ross, G. R. T. Cambridge, England: Cambridge University Press, 1911.

DETHIER, V. G. 1976. *The hungry fly.* Cambridge, Mass.: Harvard University Press.

DEUTSCH, A. 1948. *The shame of the states.* N.Y.: Harcourt and Brace. (Reprint edition, New York: Arno Press, 1973.)

DEVALOIS, R. L. 1965. Behavioral and electrophysiological studies of primate vision. In Neff, W. D., ed., *Contributions of sensory physiology,* vol. 1. New York: Academic Press.

DEVALOIS, R. L., AND DEVALOIS, K. K. 1975. Neural coding of color. In Carterette, E. C., and Friedman, M. P., eds., *Handbook of perception,* vol. 5, pp. 117–62. New York: Academic Press.

DEVILLIERS, J. G. 1980. The process of rule learning in child speech: A new look. In Nelson, K., ed., *Child Language,* vol. 2. New York: Gardner Press.

DE VILLIERS, J. G., AND DE VILLIERS, P. A. 1973. Development of the use of word order in comprehension. *Journal of Psycholinguistic Research* 2:331–41.

DEVILLIERS, J. G., and DEVILLIERS, P. A. 1978. *Language acquisition.* Cambridge, Mass.: Harvard University Press.

DEVILLIERS, P. A. 1978. Speech presented at the Boston Child Language Conference.

Diagnostic and statistical manual of mental disorders, 3rd edition. Washington: American Psychiatric Association, 1980.

DICARA, L. V. 1970. Learning in the autonomic nervous system. *Scientific American* 222:30–39

DICKS, H. V. 1972. *Licensed mass murder: A sociopsychological study of some S.S. killers.* New York: Basic Books.

DILGER, W. C. 1962. The behavior of lovebirds. *Scientific American* 206:88–98.

DI VESTA, F. J.; INGERSOLL, G.; AND SUNSHINE, P. 1971. A factor analysis of imagery tests. *Journal of Verbal Learning and Verbal Behavior* 10:471–79.

DOUVAN, E., AND ADELSON, J. 1958. The psychodynamics of social mobility in adolescent boys. *Journal of Abnormal and Social Psychology* 56:31–44.

DUNCKER, K. 1929. Über induzierte Bewegung. *Psychologische Forschung* 12:180–259.

DUNCKER, K. 1945. On problem solving. *Psychological Monographs* (Whole No. 270): 1–113.

EBBINGHAUS, H. 1885. *Memory.* New York: Teacher's College, Columbia University, 1913. (Reprint edition, New York: Dover, 1964).

ECCLES, J. C. 1965. *The synapse.* Scientific American 212:56–66.

ECCLES, J. C. 1973. *The understanding of the brain.* New York: McGraw-Hill.

EGGER, M. D., AND FLYNN, J. P. 1963. Effect of electrical stimulation of the amygdala on hypothalamically elicited behavior in cats. *Journal of Neurophysiology* 26:705–20.

EIBL-EIBESFELDT, I. 1970. *Ethology: The biology of behavior.* New York: Holt, Rinehart & Winston.

EKMAN, P. 1973. Cross-cultural studies of facial expression. In Ekman, P., ed., *Darwin and facial expression.* pp. 169–222 New York: Academic Press.

ELLIS, A. 1962. *Reason and emotion in psychotherapy.* Secaucus, N. J.: Lyle Stuart.

ELLIS, N. R., ed., 1963. *Handbook of mental deficiency.* New York: McGraw-Hill.

ELLIS, N. R. 1970. Memory processes in retardates and normals. In Ellis, N. R., ed., *International review of research in mental retardation,* vol. 4, pp. 1–33. New York: Academic Press.

EMMERICH, W. 1966. Continuity and stability in early social development, II. Teacher ratings. *Child Development* 37:17–27.

EMMONS, W. H., AND SIMON, C. W. 1956. The non-recall of material presented during sleep. *American Journal of Psychology* 69:76–81.

ENDLER, N. S., AND HUNT, J. M. 1969. Generalization of contributions from sources of variance in the S-R inventories of anxiousness. *Journal of Personality* 37:1–24.

EPPS, P., AND PARNELL, R. W. 1952. Physique and temperament of women delinquents compared with women undergraduates. *British Journal of Medical Psychology* 25:249–55.

EPSTEIN, A. N.; FITZSIMONS, J. T.; AND ROLLS, B. J. 1970. Drinking induced by injection of angiotensin into the brain of the rat. *Journal of Physiology* 210:457–74.

EPSTEIN, A. W., AND TEITELBAUM, P. 1962. Regulation of food intake in the absence of taste, smell, and other oropharyngeal sensations. *Journal of Comparative and Physiological Psychology* 55:753–59.

EPSTEIN, S. M. 1967. Toward a unified theory of anxiety. In Maher, B. A., ed., *Progress in experimental personality research,* vol. 4. New York: Academic Press.

EPSTEIN, W. 1961. The influence of syntactical structure on learning. *American Journal of Psychology* 74:80–85.

ERDELYI, M. H. 1974. A new look at the new look: Perceptual defense and vigilance. *Psychological Review* 81:1–25.

ERIKSEN, C. W., AND PIERCE, J. 1968. Defense mechanisms. In Borgatta, E. F., and Lambert, W. W., eds., *Handbook of personality theory and research,* pp. 1007–40. Chicago: Rand McNally.

ERIKSON, E. H. 1963. *Childhood and society.* New York: Norton.

ERLENMEYER-KIMLING, L., AND JARVIK, L. F. 1963. Genetics and intelligence: A review. *Science* 142:1477–79.

ERON, L. D. 1950. A normative study of the thematic apperception test. *Psychological Monographs* 64 (Whole No. 315).

ERON, L. D. 1963. Relationship of t.v. viewing habits and aggressive behavior in children. *Journal of Abnormal and Social Psychology* 67:193–96.

ERVIN, S., 1964. Imitation and structural change in children's language. In Lenneberg, E. H., ed., *New directions in the study of language,* Cambridge, Mass.: MIT Press.

ERVIN-TRIPP, S. 1973. Some strategies for the first two years. In Moore, T. E., ed., *Cognitive development and the acquisition of language.* New York: Academic Press.

ESTES, W. K. 1970. *Learning theory and mental development.* New York: Academic Press.

ETKIN, W. 1964. Reproductive behaviors. In Etkin, W., ed., *Social behavior and organization among vertebrates,* pp. 75–116. Chicago: University of Chicago Press.

EYSENCK, H. J. 1961. The effects of psychotherapy. In Eysenck, H. J., ed., *Handbook of abnormal psychology,* pp. 697–725. New York: Basic Books.

EYSENCK, H. J. 1967. *The biological basis of personality.* Springfield, Ill.: Thomas.

EYSENCK, H. J., AND RACHMAN, S. 1965. *The causes and cures of neurosis.* San Diego, Calif.: Robert R. Knapp.

EYSENCK, H. J., AND WILSON, G. D. 1973. *The experimental study of Freudian theories.* London: Methuen.

FANT, L. G. 1972. *Ameslan: An introduction to American Sign Language.* Silver Springs, Md.: National Association of the Deaf.

FANTZ, R. L. 1957. Form preferences in newly hatched chicks. *Journal of Comparative and Physiological Psychology* 50:422–30.

FANTZ, R. L. 1961. The origin of form perception. *Scientific American* 204:66–72.

FANTZ, R. L. 1970. Visual perception and experience in infancy: Issues and approaches. In National Academy of Science, *Early experience and visual information processing in perceptual and reading disorders,* pp. 351–81. New York: National Academy of Science.

FARIS, R. E. L., AND DUNHAM, H. W. 1939. *Mental disorders in urban areas.* Chicago: University of Chicago Press.

FARLEY, F., AND FARLEY, S. V. 1967. Extroversion and stimulus-seeking motivation. *Journal of Consulting Psychology* 31:215–16.

FEARING, F. 1930. *Reflex action: A study in the history of physiological psychology.* Baltimore, Md.: Williams & Wilkins.

FELDMAN, H.; GOLDIN-MEADOW, S.; AND GLEITMAN, L. R. 1978. Beyond Herodotus: The creation of language by linguistically deprived deaf children. In Lock, A., ed., *Action, gesture, and symbol: The emergence of language.* London: Academic Press.

FELIPE, N. J., AND SOMMER, R. 1966. Invasions of personal space. *Social Problems* 14:206–14.

FENICHEL, O. 1945. *The psychoanalytic theory of neurosis.* New York: Norton.

FENZ, W. D., AND EPSTEIN, S. 1962. Measurement of approach-avoidance conflict along a stimulus dimension by a thematic apperception test. *Journal of Personality* 30:613–32.

FERSTER, C. B., AND SKINNER, B. F. 1957. *Schedules of reinforcement.* New York: Appleton-Century-Crofts.

FESTINGER, L. 1954. A theory of social comparison processes. *Human Relations* 7:117–40.

FESTINGER, L. 1957. *A theory of cognitive dissonance.* Evanston, Ill.: Row, Peterson.

FESTINGER, L., AND CARLSMITH, J. M. 1959. Cognitive consequences of forced compliance. *Journal of Abnormal and Social Psychology* 58:203–10.

FESTINGER, L.; RIECKEN, H.; AND SCHACHTER, S. 1956. *When prophecy fails.* Minneapolis: University of Minnesota Press.

FIEVE, R. R. 1975. Lithium (antimanic) therapy. In Freedman, A. M.; Kaplan, H. I.; and Sadock, B. J. eds., *Comprehensive textbook of psychiatry—II,* vol. 2, pp. 1982–87. Baltimore, Md.: Williams & Wilkins.

FILLMORE, CHARLES J. 1968. The case for case. In Bach, E., and Harms, R. T., eds., *Universals in linguistic theory,* pp. 1–87. New York: Holt, Rinehart & Winston.

FISHER, S.; BOYD, I.; WALKER, D.; AND SHEER, D. 1959. Parents of schizophrenics, neurotics, and normals. *Archives of General Psychiatry* 1:149–66.

FLANAGAN, J. C. 1947. Scientific development of the use of human resources: Progress in the Army Air Forces. *Science* 105:57–60.

FLAVELL, J. H. 1963. *The developmental psychology of Jean Piaget.* New York: Van Nostrand Reinhold.

FLAVELL, J. H. 1970. Developmental studies of mediated memory. In Reese, H. W., and Lipsitt, L. P., eds., *Advances in child development and behavior,* vol. 5. New York: Academic Press.

FLAVELL, J. H.; BEACH, D. H.; AND CHINSKY, J. M. 1966. Spontaneous verbal rehearsal in a memory task as a function of age. *Child Development* 37:283–99.

FLAVELL, J. H., AND WELLMAN, H. M. 1976. Metamemory. In

Kail, R. V., and Hagen, J. W., eds., *Memory in cognitive development.* Hillsdale, N. J.: Erlbaum.

Fodor, J. A. 1972. Some reflections on L. S. Vygotsky's *Thought and language. Cognition* 1:83–95.

Fodor, J. A. 1975. *The language of thought.* New York: Crowell.

Fodor, J. A., and Bever, T. G. 1965. The psychological reality of linguistic segments. *Journal of Verbal Learning and Verbal Behavior* 4:414-20.

Fodor, J. A.; Bever, T. G.; and Garrett, M. F. 1974. *The psychology of language.* New York: McGraw-Hill.

Fodor, J. D. 1977. *Semantics: Theories of meaning in generative grammar.* New York: Crowell.

Folkow, B., and Rubenstein, E. H. 1966. Cardiovascular effects of acute and chronic stimulations of the hypothalmic defense area in the rat. *Acta Physiologica Scandinavica* 68:48–57.

Fontana, A. F. 1966. Familial etiology of schizophrenia: Is a scientific methodology possible? *Psychological Bulletin* 66:214–77.

Ford, C. S., and Beach, F. A. 1951. *Patterns of sexual behavior.* New York: Harper & Row.

Forster, K. I. 1976. Accessing the mental lexicon. In Wales, R. J., and Walker, E., eds., *New approaches to language mechanisms.* Amsterdam: North-Holland.

Foss, D. J., and Hakes, D. T. 1978. *Psycholinguistics: An introduction to the psychology of language.* Englewood Cliffs, N. J.: Prentice-Hall.

Foster, R. 1968. The reward value of saccharin solution prior to eating experience. *Psychonomic Science* 10:83–84.

Foucault, M. 1965. *Madness and civilization.* New York: Random House.

Foulkes, D. 1966. *The psychology of sleep.* New York: Scribner's.

Fouts, R. S. 1972. Use of guidance in teaching sign language to a chimpanzee *(Pan troglodytes). Journal of Comparative and Physiological Psychology* 80:515–22.

Fowler, A.; Gelman, R.; and Gleitman, L. 1980. Effects of mental retardation on language learning. Unpublished manuscript, University of Pennsylvania.

Frank, L. K. 1939. Projective methods for the study of personality. *Journal of Personality* 8:389–413.

Frankl, V. E. 1966. *The doctor and the soul.* New York: Knopf.

Fraser, C.; Bellugi, V.; and Brown, R. 1963. Control of grammar in imitation, comprehension, and production. *Journal of Verbal Learning and Verbal Behavior* 2:121–135.

Freed, B. 1980. Foreigner talk, baby talk, native talk. *International Journal of the Sociology of Language* 28:2.

Freedman, D. G. 1971. Behavioral assessment in infancy. In Stoeling, G. B. A., and Van Der Weoff Ten Bosch, J. J., eds., *Normal and abnormal development of brain and behavior,* pp. 92–103, Leiden: Leiden University Press.

Freedman, J. L., and Fraser, S. C. 1966. Compliance without pressure: The foot-in-the-door technique. *Journal of Personality and Social Psychology* 4:195–202.

French, J. D. 1957. The reticular formation. *Scientific American* 196:54–60.

Freud, A. 1946. *The ego and the mechanisms of defense.* London: Hogarth Press.

Freud, S. 1900. The interpretation of dreams. In Strachey, J., trans., *The standard edition,* vols. 4–5. London: Hogarth Press, 1953.

Freud, S. 1901. *The psychopathology of everyday life.* Translated by Tyson, A. New York: Norton, 1965.

Freud, S. 1905. *Three essays on the theory of sexuality.* Translated by Strachey, J. New York: Avon Books, 1962.

Freud, S. 1908. Character and anal eroticism. In Freud, S., *Character and culture,* translated by McWatters, C., pp. 27–33. New York: Collier Books, 1963.

Freud, S. 1909. *Notes upon a case of obsessional neurosis* In Strachey, J., and Strachey, A., trans., *Collected papers,* vol. 3, pp. 293–383. London: Hogarth Press, 1949.

Freud, S. 1911. Psychoanalytic notes upon an autobiographical account of a case of paranoia (dementia paranoides). In Strachey, J., and Strachey, A., trans., *Collected Papers,* vol. 3, pp. 390–605 London: Hogarth Press, 1949.

Freud, S. 1913a. *Totem and taboo.* Translated by Strachey, J. New York: Norton, 1950.

Freud, S. 1913b. Further recommendations in the technique of psychoanalysis. Translated by Riviere, J. In Freud, S., *Therapy and technique,* pp. 135–56. New York: Macmillan, 1963.

Freud, S. 1917. *A general introduction to psychoanalysis.* Translated by Riviere, J. New York: Washington Square Press, 1952.

Freud, S. 1923. *The ego and the id.* Translated by Riviere, J. New York: Norton, 1962.

Freud, S. 1925. Some psychological consequences of the anatomical distinction between the sexes. In Strachey, J., and Strachey, A., trans., *Collected Papers,* vol. 5, pp. 189–97. London: Hogarth Press, 1956.

Freud, S. 1926. *Inhibitions, symptoms, and anxiety.* Translated by Strachey, A. New York: Norton, 1959.

Freud, S., 1933. *New introductory lectures on psychoanalysis.* Translated by Strachey, J. New York: Norton, 1965.

Freud, S. 1940. *An outline of psychoanalysis,* Translated by Strachey, J. New York: Norton, 1949.

Freud, S., and Breuer, J. 1895. *Studies on hysteria.* Translated by Strachey, J. New York: Avon Books, 1966.

Friedman, M. I., and Stricker, E. M. 1976. The physiological psychology of hunger: A physiological perspective. *Psychological Review* 83:409–31.

Frishberg, N. 1975. Arbitrariness and iconicity: Historical change in American Sign Language. *Language* 51:696–719.

Fromkin, V. A. 1973. *Speech errors as linguistic evidence.* The Hague: Mouton.

Fromkin, V.; Krashen, S.; Curtiss, S.; Rigler, D.; and Rigler, M. 1974. The development of language in Genie: A case of language acquisition beyond the "critical period." *Brain and Language* 1:81–107.

Funkenstein, D. H. 1956. Nor-epinephrine-like and epinephrine-like substances in relation to human behavior. *Journal of Mental Diseases* 124:58–68.

Gallistel, C. R. 1973. Self-stimulation: The neurophysiology of reward and motivation. In Deutsch, J. A., ed., *The physiological basis of memory,* pp. 175–267. New York: Academic Press.

Gallup, G. G., Jr. 1968. Mirror-image stimulation. *Psychological Bulletin* 70:782–93.

Gallup, G. G., Jr. 1970. Chimpanzees: Self-recognition. *Science* 167:86–87.

Galton, F. 1869. *Hereditary genius: An inquiry into its laws and consequences.* London: Macmillan.

Galton, F. 1883. *Inquiries into human faculty and its development.* London: Macmillan.

Garcia, J., and Koelling, R. A. 1966. The relation of cue to consequence in avoidance learning. *Psychonomic Science* 4:123–24.

Gardner, B. T., and Gardner, R. A. 1971. Two-way communication with an infant chimpanzee. In Schrier, A. M., and Stollnitz, F., eds., *Behavior of nonhuman primates,* vol. 4, pp. 117–84. New York: Academic Press.

Gardner, R. A., and Gardner, B. T. 1969. Teaching sign language to a chimpanzee. *Science* 165:664–72.

Gardner, R. A., and Gardner, B. T. 1978. Comparative psychology and language acquisition. *Annals of the New York Academy of Science* 309:37–76.

Garland, L. H. 1960. The problem of observer error. *Bulletin of the New York Academy of Medicine* 36:570–84.

Garmezy, N. 1967. Process and reactive schizophrenia: Some

conceptions and issues. In Katz, M., and Cole, J., eds., *The role and methodology of classification in psychiatry and psychopathology,* pp. 419–66. Washington D. C.: U. S. Government Printing Office.

GARRETT, M. F. 1975. The analysis of sentence production. In Bower, G. H., ed., *The psychology of learning and motivation,* vol. 9, pp. 133–77. New York: Academic Press.

GAZZANIGA, M. S. 1967. The split brain in man. *Scientific American* 217:24–29.

GELB, J. J. 1952. *A study of writing: The foundations of grammatology.* Chicago: University of Chicago Press.

GELMAN, R. 1972. Logical capacity of very young children: Number invariance rules. *Child Development* 43:75–90.

GELMAN, R. 1978. Cognitive Development. *Annual Review of Psychology* 29:297–332.

GELMAN, R., AND GALLISTEL, C. R. 1978. *The young child's understanding of number: A window on early cognitive development.* Cambridge, Mass.: Harvard University Press.

GERARD, H. B., AND MATHEWSON, G. C. 1966. The effects of severity of initiation on liking for a group: A replication. *Journal of Experimental Social Psychology* 2:278–87.

GERARD, H. B.; WILHELMY, R. A.; AND CONNOLLEY, E. S. 1968. Conformity and group size. *Journal of Personality and Social Psychology* 8:78–82.

GERBNER, G., AND GROSS, L. 1976. Living with television: The violence profile. *Journal of Communication* 26:173–99.

GERBNER, G.; GROSS, L.; MORGAN, M.; AND SIGNORIELLI, N. 1980. *Violence profile No. 11. Trends in network television drama and viewer conceptions of social reality.* Philadelphia, Pa.: Annenberg School of Communications.

GERGEN, K. J. 1973. Social psychology as history. *Journal of Personality and Social Psychology* 26:309–20.

GESCHWIND, N. 1970. The organization of language and the brain. *Science* 170:940–44.

GESCHWIND, N. 1972. Language and the brain. *Scientific American* 226:76–83.

GIBSON, E. J. 1969. *Principles of perceptual learning and development.* New York: Appleton-Century-Croft.

GIBSON, E. J.; SHURCLIFF, A.; AND YONAS, A. 1970. Utilization of spelling patterns by deaf and hearing subjects. In Levin, H., and Williams, J. P., eds., *Basic studies on reading,* pp. 57–73. New York: Basic Books.

GIBSON, J. J. 1950. *The perception of the visual world.* New York: Houghton Mifflin.

GIBSON, J. J. 1966. *The senses considered as perceptual systems.* New York: Houghton Mifflin.

GIBSON, J. J., AND GIBSON, E. J. 1955. Perceptual learning: Differentiation or enrichment? *Psychological Review* 62:32–41.

GIBSON, R. W.; COHEN, M. B.; AND COHEN, R. A. 1959. On the dynamics of the manic-depressive personality. *American Journal of Psychiatry* 115:1101–7.

GINZBERG, L. 1909. *The legends of the Jews,* vol. 1. Translated by SZOLD, H. Philadelphia, Pa.: Jewish Publication Society of America.

GLANZER, M. AND CUNITZ, A. 1966. Two storage mechanisms in free recall. *Journal of Verbal Learning and Verbal Behavior* 5:531–60.

GLASS, A. L.; HOLYOAK, K. J.; AND SANTA, J. L. 1979. *Cognition.* Reading, Mass: Addison-Wesley.

GLEASON, K. K., AND REYNIERSE, J. H. 1969. The behavioral significance of pheromones in vertebrates. *Psychological Bulletin* 71:58–73.

GLEITMAN, H. 1955. Place learning without prior performance. *Journal of Comparative and Physiological Psychology* 48:77–79.

GLEITMAN, H. 1963. Place-learning. *Scientific American* 209:116–22.

GLEITMAN, H. 1971. Forgetting of long-term memories in animals. In Honig, W. K., and James, P. H. R., eds., *Animal Memory,* pp. 2–46. New York: Academic Press.

GLEITMAN, H. 1979. Some trends in the study of cognition. In-

vited paper read at the 1979 meeting of the American Psychological Association, New York.

GLEITMAN, H., AND GILLETT, E. 1957. The effect of intention upon learning. *Journal of General Psychology* 57:137–49.

GLEITMAN, H., AND GLEITMAN, L. R. 1979. Language use and language judgment. In Fillmore, C. J.; Kempler, D.; and Wang, W. S. Y., eds., *Individual differences in language ability and language behavior,* pp. 123–26. New York: Academic Press.

GLEITMAN, H., AND STEINMAN, F. 1964. Depression effect as a function of retention interval before and after shift in reward magnitude. *Journal of Comparative and Physiological Psychology* 57:158–60.

GLEITMAN, L. R., AND GLEITMAN, H. 1971 *Phrase and paraphrase.* New York: Norton.

GLEITMAN, L. R., AND ROZIN, P. 1977. The structure and acquisition of reading. In Reber, A. S., and Scarborough, D. L., eds., *Toward a psychology of reading.* Hillsdale, N. J.: Erlbaum.

GLEITMAN, L. R.; SHIPLEY, E. F.; AND SMITH, C. 1978. Old and new ways not to study comprehension. *Journal of Child Language* 5:501–20.

GLUCKSBERG, S. 1962. The influence of strength of drive on functional fixedness and perceptual recognition. *Journal of Experimental Psychology* 63:36–41.

GLUECK, S., AND GLUECK, E. 1956. *Physique and delinquency.* New York: Harper.

GOFFMAN, E. 1959. *The presentation of self in everyday life.* Garden City, N. Y.: Anchor Books, Doubleday.

GOFFMAN, E. 1961. *Asylums.* Chicago: Aldine.

GOFFMAN, E. 1974. *Frame-analysis.* New York: Harper & Row.

GOLDBERG, L. R. 1972. Some recent trends in personality assessment. *Journal of Personality Assessment* 36:547–60.

GOLDBERG, L. R. 1975. Toward a taxonomy of personality descriptive terms: A description of the O. R. I. Taxonomy Project. *Oregon Research Institute Technical Report,* vol. 15 (2).

GOLDBERG, P. 1968. Are women prejudiced against women? *Trans-action* 5:28–30.

GOLDIN-MEADOW, S. 1981. Fragile and resilient properties of language learning. In Wanner, E., and Gleitman, L. R., eds., *Language acquisition: State of the art.* Cambridge, England: Cambridge University Press.

GOMBRICH, E. H. 1961. *Art and illusion.* Princeton, N.J.: Bollingen Series, Princeton University Press.

GOMBRICH, E. H. 1963. *Meditations on a hobby horse.* Greenwich, Conn.: Phaidon, distributed by N.Y. Graphic Society.

GORDON, H. 1923. Mental and scholastic tests among retarded children. *Educational Pamphlet,* no. 44. London: Board of Education.

GOUGH, H. G. 1957. *California psychological inventory manual.* Palo Alto, Calif.: Consulting Psychologists' Press.

GOY, R. W. 1968. Organizing effect of androgen on the behavior of rhesus monkeys. In Michael, R. P., ed., *Endocrinology and human behavior.* London: Oxford University Press.

GRAFF, H., AND STELLAR, E. 1962. Hyperphagia, obesity and finickiness. *Journal of Comparative and Physiological Psychology* 55:418–24.

GRAHAM, C. H., AND HSIA, Y. 1954. Luminosity curves for normal and dichromatic subjects including a case of unilateral color blindness. *Science* 120:780.

GRAHAM, D. T. 1962. Some research on psychophysiologic specificity and its relation to psychosomatic disease. In Roessler, D., and Greenfield, N. S., eds., *Physiological correlates of psychological disorder.* Madison: University of Wisconsin Press.

GRAY, G. W. 1948. The great ravelled knot. *Scientific American* 179:26–38.

GREEN, D. M. 1976. *An introduction to hearing.* New York: Academic Press.

GREEN, D. M., AND SWETS, J. A. 1966. *Signal detection theory and psychophysics.* New York: Wiley.

GREEN, R. 1969. Age-intelligence relationships between ages sixteen and sixty-four: A rising trend. *Developmental Psychology* 1:618–27.

GREENFIELD, P. M., AND SMITH, J. H. 1976. *The structure of communication in early language development.* New York: Academic Press.

GREGORY, R. L. 1963. Distortion of visual space as inappropriate constancy scaling. *Nature* 199:678–80.

GREGORY, R. L. 1968. Visual illusions. *Scientific American* 219:66–76.

GREGORY, R. L., AND WALLACE, J. G. 1963. Recovery from early blindness: A case study. *Experimental Psychology Society Monograph,* No. 2.

GRICE, H. P. 1968. Utterer's meaning, sentence-meaning and word-meaning. *Foundations of Language* 4:225–42.

GRINKER, R. R., AND SPIEGEL, J. P. 1945. *War neuroses.* New York: Blakiston.

GUILFORD, J. P. 1967. *The nature of human intelligence.* New York: McGraw-Hill.

GUTTMAN, N., AND KALISH, H. I. 1956. Discriminability and stimulus generalization. *Journal of Experimental Psychology* 51:79–88.

HABER, R. N. 1969. Eidetic images. *Scientific American* 220:36–44.

HAILMAN, J. P. 1969. How an instinct is learned. *Scientific American* 221:98–106.

HALL, C. S. 1934. Drive and emotionality: Factors associated with adjustment in the rat. *Journal of Comparative and Physiological Psychology* 17:89–108.

HALL, C. S. 1953. A cognitive theory of dream symbols. *Journal of General Psychology* 48:169–86.

HALL, C. S. 1964. Slang and dream symbols. *Psychoanalytic Review* 51:38–48.

HALL, C. S. 1966. *The meaning of dreams.* New York: McGraw-Hill.

HALL, C. S., AND LINDZEY, G. 1970. *Theories of personality,* 2nd edition. New York: Wiley.

HALL, C. S., AND VAN DE CASTLE, R. 1966. *The content analysis of dreams.* New York: Appleton-Century-Crofts.

HALL, E. T. 1959. *The silent language.* New York: Doubleday.

HAMBURG, D. A.; MOOS, R. H.; AND YALOM, I. D. 1968. Studies of distress in the menstrual cycle and the postpartum period. In Michael, R. P., ed., *Endocrinology and human behavior,* pp. 94–116. London: Oxford University Press, 1968.

HAMPSON, J. L., AND HAMPSON, J. G. 1961. The ontogenesis of sexual behavior in man. In Young, W. C., ed., *Sex and internal secretions,* 3rd edition. Baltimore, Md.: Williams & Wilkins.

HARE, R. D. 1965. Temporal gradients of fear arousal in psychopaths. *Journal of Abnormal Psychology* 70:442–45.

HARE, R. D. 1970: *Psychopathy: Theory and research.* New York: Wiley.

HARKINS, S., AND GREEN, R. G. 1975. Discriminability and criterion differences between extraverts and introverts during vigilance. *Journal of Research in Personality* 9:335–40.

HARLOW, H. F. 1949. The formation of learning sets. *Psychological Review* 56:51–65.

HARLOW, H. F. 1950. Learning and satiation of response in intrinsically motivated complex puzzle performance in monkeys. *Journal of Comparative and Physiological Psychology* 43:289–94.

HARLOW, H. F. 1958. The nature of love. *American Psychologist* 13:673–85.

HARLOW, H. F. 1959. Learning set and error factor theory. In Koch, S., ed., *Psychology: A study of a science,* vol. 2, pp. 492–537. New York: McGraw-Hill.

HARLOW, H. F. 1962. The heterosexual affectional system in monkeys. *American Psychologist* 17:1–9.

HARLOW, H. F., AND ZIMMERMAN, R. R. 1959. Affectional responses in the infant monkey. *Science* 130:421–32.

HARPER, R. A. 1959. *Psychoanalysis and psychotherapy: 36 systems.* Englewood Cliffs, N.J.: Prentice-Hall.

HARRIS, G. W., AND MICHAEL, R. P. 1964. The activation of sexual behavior by hypothalamic implants of estrogen. *Journal of Physiology* 171:275–301.

HARRIS, M. 1974. *Cows, pigs, wars, and witches.* New York: Random House.

HARTMANN, E. L. 1973. *The functions of sleep.* New Haven: Yale University Press.

HARTSHORNE, H., AND MAY, M. A. 1928. *Studies in the nature of character,* vol. 1. New York: Macmillan.

HASE, H. D., AND GOLDBERG, L. R. 1967. Comparative validities of different strategies of constructing personality inventory scales. *Psychological Bulletin* 67:231–48.

HAVIGHURST, R. J. 1970. Minority cultures and the law of effect. In Korten, F. F.; Cook, S. W.; and Lacey, J. I., eds., *Psychology and the problems of society.* Washington, D. C.: American Psychological Association.

HAYES, C. 1952. *The ape in our house.* London: Gollacz.

HAYES, W. N., AND SAIFF, E. I. 1967. Visual alarm reactions in turtles. *Animal Behavior* 15:102–6.

HEALY, A. F., AND MILLER, G. A. 1970. The verb as the main determinant of sentence meaning. *Psychonomic Science* 20:372

HEBB, D. O. 1946. On the nature of fear. *Psychological Review* 53:259–76.

HEBB, D. O. 1949. *The organization of behavior: A neuropsychological theory.* New York: Wiley.

HEDIGER, H. 1965. Environmental factors influencing the reproduction of zoo animals. In Beach, F. A., ed., *Sex and behavior.* New York: Wiley, 1965.

HEDIGER, H. 1968. *The psychology and behavior of animals in zoos and circuses.* New York: Dover.

HEIDBREDER, E. 1933. *Seven psychologies.* New York: Appleton-Century-Crofts.

HEIDER, F. 1958. *The psychology of interpersonal relationships.* New York: Wiley.

HEIM, A. W. 1954. *The appraisal of intelligence.* London: Methuen.

HEINICKE, C., AND WESTHEIMER, I. 1966. *Brief separations.* London: Longmans, Green.

HELD, R. 1965. Plasticity in sensory-motor systems. *Scientific American* 213:84–90.

HELD, R., AND BOSSOM, J. 1961. Neonatal deprivation and adult rearrangement: Complementary techniques for analyzing plastic sensory-motor coordinations. *Journal of Comparative and Physiological Psychology* 54:33–37.

HELD, R., AND HEIN, A. 1963. Movement-produced stimulation in the development of visually guided behavior. *Journal of Comparative and Physiological Psychology* 56:872–76.

HELLER, D. 1968. Absence of size constancy in visually deprived rats. *Journal of Comparative and Physiological Psychology* 65:336–39.

HELMHOLTZ, H. 1883. *Wissenschaftliche Abhandlungen, II,* pp. 764–843.

HESTON, L. L. 1966. Psychiatric disorders in foster home reared children of schizophrenic mothers. *British Journal of Psychiatry* 112:819–25.

HESTON, L. L., AND DENNEY, D. 1968. Interactions between early life experience and biological factors in schizophrenia. In Rosenthal, D., and Kety, S. S., eds., *The transmission of schizophrenia,* pp. 363–76. New York: Pergamon.

HILL, L. B. 1955. *Psychotherapeutic intervention in schizophrenia.* Chicago: University of Chicago Press.

HINDE, R. A. 1966 and 1970. *Animal behavior,* 1st and 2nd editions. New York: McGraw-Hill.

HINDE, R. A. 1974. *Biological bases of human social behavior.* New York: McGraw-Hill.

HINELINE, P. N., AND RACHLIN, H. 1969. Escape and avoidance of shock by pigeons pecking a key. *Journal of the Experimental Analysis of Behavior* 12:533–38.

HINTZMAN, D. L. 1978. *The psychology of learning and memory.* San Francisco: Freeman.

HIROCO, D. S., AND SELIGMAN, M. E. P. 1975. Generality of learned helplessness in man. *Journal of Personality and Social Psychology* 31:311–27.

HIRSCH, J., AND KNITTLE, J. L. 1970. Cellularity of obese and nonobese human adipose tissue. *Federation of American Societies for Experimental Biology: Federation Proceedings* 29:1516–21.

HIRSH-PASEK, K.; GLEITMAN, H.; AND GLEITMAN, L. R. 1978. What did the brain say to the mind? In Sinclair, A.; Jarvella, R. J.; and Levelt, W. J. M., eds., *The child's conception of language.* Berlin: Springer-Verlag.

HOBBES, T. 1651. *Leviathan.* Baltimore, Md.: Penguin Books, 1968.

HOCHBERG, J. E. 1970. Attention, organization and consciousness. In Mostofsky, D. I., ed., *Attention: Contemporary theory and analysis,* pp. 99–124. New York: Appleton-Century-Crofts.

HOCHBERG, J. E. 1978a. *Perception,* 2nd edition. Englewood Cliffs, N.J.: Prentice-Hall.

HOCHBERG, J. E. 1978b. Art and perception. In Carterette, E. C., and Friedman, M. P., eds., *Handbook of perception,* vol. 10, pp. 225–55. New York: Academic Press.

HOCHBERG, J. E. 1980. Pictorial functions and perceptual structures. In Hagen, M. A., ed., *The perception of pictures,* vol. 2, pp. 47–93. New York: Academic Press.

HOFFMAN, J. W. 1979. Maternal employment: 1979. *American Psychologist* 34:859–65.

HOHN, E. O. 1966. The phalarope. *Scientific American* 220:104–11.

HOLLINGSHEAD, A. B., AND REDLICH, F. C. 1958. *Social class and mental illness: A community study.* New York: Wiley.

HONIG, W. K.; BONEAU, C. A.; BURSTEIN, K. R.; AND PENNYPACKER, H. S. 1963. Positive and negative generalization gradients obtained after equivalent training conditions. *Journal of Comparative and Physiological Psychology* 56:111–16.

HOOKER, E. 1957. The adjustment of the male overt homosexual. *Journal of Projective Techniques* 21:18–31.

HOOKER, E. 1965. Male homosexuals and their "worlds." In Marmor, J., ed., *Sexual inversion,* pp. 83–107. New York: Basic Books.

HORN, J. L., AND CATTELL, R. B. 1967. Age differences in fluid and crystallized intelligence. *Acta Psychologica* 26:107–129.

HORN, J. L., AND DONALDSON, G. 1976. On the myth of intellectual decline in adulthood. *American Psychologist* 31:701–719.

HORN, J. L.; LOEHLIN, J.; AND WELLERMAN, L. 1975. Preliminary report of Texas adoption project. In Munsinger, H., The adopted child's IQ: A critical review. *Psychological Bulletin* 82:623–59.

HORNER, M. S. 1970. Femininity and successful achievement: A basic inconsistency. In Bardwick, J. M.; Dorwan, E.; Horner, M. S.; and Gutmann, D., eds., *Feminine personality and conflict,* pp. 45–74. Belmont, Calif.: Brooks/Cole.

HRABA, J., AND GRANT, G. 1970. Black is beautiful: A reexamination of racial preference and identification. *Journal of Personality and Social Psychology* 16:398–402.

HUBEL, D. H. 1963. The visual cortex of the brain. *Scientific American* 209:54–62.

HUBEL, D. H., AND WIESEL, T. N. 1959. Receptive fields of single neurones in the cat's visual cortex. *Journal of Physiology* 148:574–91.

HUBEL, D. H., AND WIESEL, T. N. 1965. Receptive fields and functional architecture in two nonstriate visual areas (18 and 19) of the cat. *Journal of Neurophysiology* 28:229–89.

HUDSON, W. 1960. Pictorial depth perception in sub-cultural groups in Africa. *Journal of Social Psychology* 52:183–208.

HULL, C. L. 1934. The rat's speed of locomotion gradient in the approach to food. *Journal of Comparative and Physiological Psychology* 17:393–422.

HULL, C. L. 1943. *Principles of behavior.* New York: Appleton-Century-Crofts.

HUMPHREY, G. 1951. *Thinking: An introduction to its experimental psychology.* New York: Wiley.

HUMPHREYS, L. G. 1939. The effect of random alternation of reinforcement on the acquisition and extinction of conditioned eyelid reactions. *Journal of Experimental Psychology* 25:141–58.

HUMPHREYS, L. G. 1957. Characteristics of type concepts with special reference to Sheldon's typology. *Psychological Bulletin* 54:218–28.

HUNT, E. 1976. Varieties of cognitive power. In Resnick, L. B., ed., *The nature of intelligence,* pp. 237–60. Hillsdale, N. J.: Erlbaum.

HUNT, E.; LUNNEBORG, C.; AND LEWIS, J. 1975. What does it mean to be high verbal? *Cognitive Psychology* 7:194–227.

HUNT, J. M. 1961. *Intelligence and experience.* New York: Ronald Press.

HUNTER, R., AND MACALPINE, I. 1974. *Psychiatry for the poor.* Folkestone, K.Y.: Dawson.

HURVICH, L. M., AND JAMESON, D. 1957. An opponent-process theory of color vision. *Psychological Review* 64:384–404.

HUTCHINSON, R. R., AND RENFREW, J. W. 1966. Stalking attack and eating behaviors elicited from the same sites in the hypothalamus. *Journal of Comparative and Physiological Psychology* 61:360–367.

HUTTENLOCHER, J. 1974. The origins of language comprehension. In Solso, R. L., ed., *Theories in cognitive psychology.* Hillsdale, N.J.: Erlbaum.

HYDE, D. M. 1959. An investigation of Piaget's theories of the development of the concept of number. Unpublished doctoral dissertation, University of London. (Quoted in Flavell, J. H., *The developmental psychology of Jean Piaget,* p. 383. New York: Van Nostrand Reinhold).

ILJIN, N. A., AND ILJIN, V. N. 1930. Temperature effects on the color of the Siamese cat. *Journal of Heredity* 21:309–318.

INHELDER, B., AND PIAGET, J. 1958. *The growth of logical thinking from childhood to adolescence.* New York: Basic Books.

IVINS, W. M., JR. 1975. *On the rationalization of sight.* New York: Da Capo Press.

JACKSON, J. H. 1884. Evolution and dissolution of the nervous system. In Taylor, J., ed., *Selected writings of John Hughlings Jackson,* vol. 2, pp. 45–75. New York: Basic Books, 1958.

JACOBS, A. 1955. Formation of new associations to words selected on the basis of reaction-time-GSR combinations. *Journal of Abnormal and Social Psychology* 51:371–77.

JACOBSON, A. L.; FRIED, C.; AND HOROWITZ, S. D. 1967. Classical conditioning, pseudoconditioning, or sensitization in the planarian. *Journal of Comparative and Physiological Psychology* 64:73–79.

JACOBSON, E. 1932. The electrophysiology of mental activities. *American Journal of Psychology* 44:677–94.

JAHODA, G. 1954. A note on Ashanti names and their relation to personality. *British Journal of Psychology* 45:192–95.

JAMES, W. 1890. *Principles of psychology.* New York: Henry Holt.

JAMES, W. T. 1941. Morphological form and its relation to behavior. In Stockard, C. R., *The genetic and endocrinic basis for differences in form and behavior,* pp. 525–643. Philadelphia, Pa.: Wistar Institute.

JAMESON, D., AND HURVICH, L. 1975. From contrast to assimilation: In art and in the eye. *Leonardo* 8:125–31.

JANIS, I. L.; MAHL, G. G.; KAGAN, J.; AND HOLT, R. R. 1969. *Personality: Dynamics, development and assessment.* New York: Harcourt, Brace and World.

JENCKS, C.; SMITH, M.; ACLAND, H.; BANE, M. J.; COHEN, D.; GINTIS, H.; HEYNS, B.; AND MICHELSON, S. 1972. *Inequality: A reassessment of the effect of family and schooling in America.* New York: Basic Books.

JENKINS, H. M., AND MOORE, B. R. 1973. The form of the autoshaped response with food or water reinforcers. *Journal of the Experimental Analysis of Behavior* 20:163–81.

JENKINS, J. G., AND DALLENBACH, K. M. 1924. Oblivescence during sleep and waking. *American Journal of Psychology* 35:605–612.

JENSEN, A. R. 1965. Scoring the Stroop test. *Acta Psychologica* 24:398–408.

JENSEN, A. R. 1969. How much can we boost I.Q. and scholastic achievement? *Harvard Educational Review* 39:1–123.

JENSEN, A. R. 1973. *Educability and group differences.* New York: Harper & Row.

JENSEN, A. R. 1980. *Bias in mental testing.* New York: Free Press.

JOHNSON, D. M. 1972. *Systematic introduction to the psychology of thinking.* New York: Harper & Row.

JOHNSON, J. D.; KRETCHMER, N.; AND SIMOONS, F. J. 1974. Lactose malabsorption: Its biology and history. *Advances in Pediatrics* 21:197–237.

JONES, E. 1953. *The life and work of Sigmund Freud.* New York: Basic Books.

JONES, E. 1954. *Hamlet and Oedipus.* New York: Doubleday.

JONES, E. E., AND DAVIS, K. E. 1965. From acts to dispositions: The attribution process in person perception. In Berkowitz, L., ed., *Advances in experimental social psychology,* vol. 2, pp. 219–66. New York: Academic Press.

JONES, E. E.; DAVIS, K. E.; AND GERGEN, K. J. 1961. Role playing variations and their informational value for person perception. *Journal of Abnormal and Social Psychology* 63:302–310.

JONES, E. E., AND HARRIS, V. H. 1967. The attribution of attitudes. *Journal of Experimental Social Psychology* 3:1–24.

JONES, E. E.; KANOUSE, D. E.; KELLEY, H. H.; NISBETT, R. E.; VALINS, S.; AND WEINER, B. 1971. *Attribution: Perceiving the causes of behavior.* Morristown, N.J.: General Learning Press.

JONES, H. E., AND KAPLAN, O. J. 1945. Psychological aspects of mental disorders in later life. In Kaplan, O. J., ed., *Mental disorders in later life,* pp. 69–115. Stanford, Calif.: Stanford University Press.

JOUVET, M. 1967. The states of sleep. *Scientific American* 216:62–72.

JOUVET, M. 1969. Biogenic amines and the states of sleep. *Science* 163:32–41.

KAGAN, J., AND MOSS, H. A. 1962. *Birth to maturity: The Fels Study of psychological development.* New York: Wiley.

KAHN, M. 1973. The return of the repressed. In Aronson, E., ed., *Readings about the social animal,* pp. 389–405. San Francisco: Freeman.

KAHNEMAN, D. 1973. *Attention and effort.* Englewood Cliffs, N.J.: Prentice-Hall.

KALINOWSKY, L. B. 1975. The convulsive therapies. In Freedman, A. M.; Kaplan, H. I.; and Sadock, B. J., eds., *Comprehensive textbook of psychiatry—II,* vol. 2, pp. 1969–75. Baltimore, Md.: Williams & Wilkins.

KALLMAN, F. J. 1952. Comparative twin study of genetic aspects of male homosexuality. *Journal of Mental and Nervous Diseases* 15:283–98.

KAMIN, L. J. 1974. *The science and politics of I.Q.* New York: Wiley.

KAMIYA, J. 1969. Operant control of the EEG and some of its reported effects on consciousness. In Tart, C., ed., *Altered states of consciousness.* New York: Wiley.

KANIZSA, G. 1976. Subjective contours. *Scientific American* 234:48–52.

KARDINER, A. 1945. *The psychological frontiers of society.* New York: Columbia University Press.

KATCHER, A. 1955. The discrimination of sex differences by young children. *Journal of Genetic Psychology* 87:131–43.

KATZ, B. 1952. The nerve impulse. *Scientific American* 187:55–64.

KATZ, J. J. 1972. *Semantic theory.* New York: Harper & Row.

KATZ, J. J., AND FODOR, J. A. 1963. The structure of a semantic theory. *Language* 39:170–210.

KAUFMAN, L., AND ROCK, I. 1962. The moon illusion. *Science* 136:953–61.

KEAN, M. L. 1977. The linguistic interpretation of aphasic syndromes: Agrammatism in Broca's aphasia, an example. *Cognition* 5:9–46.

KEETON, W. T. 1980. *Biological Science,* 3rd edition. New York: Norton.

KEIL, F. C. 1979. *Semantic and conceptual development: An ontological perspective.* Cambridge, Mass.: Harvard University Press.

KELLEY, H. H. 1967. Attribution theory in social psychology. In Levine, D., ed., *Nebraska symposium on motivation,* pp. 192–240. Lincoln: University of Nebraska Press.

KELMAN, H. C. 1967. Human use of human subjects: The problem of deception in social psychological experiments. *Psychological Bulletin* 67:1–11.

KESSEL, E. L. 1955. The mating activities of balloon flies. *Systematic Zoology* 4:97–104.

KETY, S. S. 1965. Biochemical theories of schizophrenia. *International Journal of Psychiatry* 1:409–446.

KEYNES, R. D. 1958. The nerve impulse and the squid. *Scientific American* 199:83–90.

KIMBLE, G. A. 1961. *Hilgard and Marquis' conditioning and learning.* New York: Appleton-Century-Crofts.

KIMBLE, G. A., AND PERLMUTER, L. C. 1970. The problem of volition. *Psychological Review* 77:361–84.

KING, H. E. 1961. Psychological effects of excitation in the limbic system. In Sheer, D. E., ed., *Electrical stimulation of the brain.* Austin: University of Texas Press.

KINSEY, A. C.; POMEROY, W. B.; AND MARTIN, C. E. 1948. *Sexual behavior in the human male.* Philadelphia, Pa.: Saunders.

KINSEY, A.; POMEROY, W.; MARTIN, C.; AND GEBHARD, P. 1953. *Sexual behavior in the human female.* Philadelphia, Pa.: Saunders.

KIPARSKY, P. 1968. Linguistic universals and language change. In Bach, E., and Harms, R. T., eds., *Universals in linguistic theory.* New York: Holt, Rinehart & Winston.

KITTRIE, N. N. 1971. *The right to be different: Deviance and enforced therapy.* Baltimore, Md.: Penguin Books, 1973.

KLEIN, D. C., AND SELIGMAN, M. E. P. 1976. Reversal of performance deficits in learned helplessness and depression. *Journal of Abnormal Psychology* 85:11–26.

KLEIN, D. F., AND DAVIS, J. M. 1969. *Diagnosis and drug treatment of emotional disorders.* Baltimore, Md.: Williams & Wilkins.

KLEITMAN, N. 1960. Patterns of dreaming. *Scientific American* 203:82–88.

KLEITMAN, N. 1963. *Sleep and wakefulness,* revised edition. Chicago: University of Chicago Press.

KLIMA, E. S., AND BELLUGI, U. 1966. Syntactic regularities in the speech of children. In Lyons, J. and Wales, R. J., eds. *Psycholinguistics papers,* pp. 183–208. Edinburgh: Edinburgh University Press.

KLIMA, E., AND BELLUGI, U.; WITH BATTISON, R.; BOYES-BRAEM, P.; FISCHER, S.; FRISHBERG, N.; LANE, H.; LENTZ, E. M.; NEWKIRK, D.; NEWPORT, E.; PEDERSEN, C.; AND SIPLE, P. 1979. *The signs of language.* Cambridge, Mass.: Harvard University Press.

KLINEBERG, O. 1940. *Social psychology.* New York: Henry Holt.

KNITTLE, J. L., AND HIRSCH, J. 1968. Effect of early nutrition on the development of the rat epididymal fat pads: Cellularity and metabolism. *Journal of Clinical Investigations* 47:2091.

KOESTLER, A. 1964. *The act of creation.* New York: Macmillan.

KOFFKA, K. 1935. *Principles of Gestalt psychology.* New York: Harcourt Brace.

A54

KOHLBERG, L. 1963. Development of children's orientations toward a moral order. *Vita Humana* 6:11–36.

KOHLBERG, L. 1966. A cognitive developmental analysis of children's sex-role concepts and attitudes. In Maccoby, E. E., ed., *The development of sex differences,* pp. 82–171. Stanford, Calif.: Stanford University Press.

KOHLBERG, L. 1969. Stage and sequence: The cognitive developmental approach to socialization. In Goslin, D. A., ed., *Handbook of socialization theory of research,* pp. 347–480. Chicago: Rand McNally, 1969.

KOHLER, I. 1964. The formation and transformation of the perceptual world. *Psychological Issues* 3 (Whole No. 4).

KÖHLER, W. 1925. *The mentality of apes.* New York: Harcourt Brace and World.

KÖHLER, W. 1941. On the nature of associations. *Proceedings of the American Philosophical Society* 84:489–502.

KÖHLER, W. 1947. *Gestalt psychology.* New York: Liveright.

KOHN, M. L. 1968. Social class and schizophrenia: A critical review. In Rosenthal, D., and Kety, S. S., eds., *The transmission of schizophrenia,* pp. 155–74. London: Pergamon.

KOLODNY, R.; MASTERS, W.; HENDRYX, J.; AND TORO, G. 1971. Plasma testosterone and semen analysis in male homosexuals. *New England Journal of Medicine* 285:1170–74.

KORS, A. C., AND PETERS, E. 1972. *Witchcraft in Europe: 1100–1700. A documentary history.* Philadelphia, Pa.: University of Pennsylvania Press.

KOSSLYN, S. M. 1973. Scanning visual images: Some structural implications. *Perception and Psychophysics* 14:90–94.

KOSTLAN, A. 1954. A method for the empirical study of psychodiagnosis. *Journal of Consulting Psychology* 18:83–88.

KUFFLER, S. W. 1953. Discharge pattern and functional organization of mammalian retina. *Journal of Neurophysiology* 16:37–68.

LABERGE, D. 1975. Acquisition of automatic processing in perceptual and associative learning. In Rabbitt, P. M. A., and Dormic, S., eds., *Attention and performance,* vol. 5. London: Academic Press.

LABOV, W. 1970a. *Language in the inner city.* Philadelphia: University of Pennsylvania Press.

LABOV, W. 1970b. The logic of nonstandard English. In Williams, F., ed., *Language and poverty: Perspectives on a theme,* pp. 153–89. Chicago: Markham.

LACK, D. 1953. Darwin's finches. *Scientific American* 188:66–72.

LACKNER, J. R. 1976. A developmental study of language behavior in retarded children. In Morehead, D. M., and Morehead, A. E., *Normal and deficient child language,* pp. 181–208. Baltimore, Md.: University Park Press.

LAING, R. D. 1967. *The politics of experience.* New York: Ballantine.

LA METTRIE, J. O. 1748. *Man, a machine.* Translated by Calkins, M. W. LaSalle, Ill.: Open Court, 1961.

LANDAU, B. 1980. Will the real grandmother please stand up: The psychological reality of multiple meaning representations. Unpublished manuscript, University of Pennsylvania.

LANDIS, C., AND HUNT, W. A. 1932. Adrenalin and emotion. *Psychological Review* 39:467–85.

LANYON, R. I., AND GOODSTEIN, L. D. 1971. *Personality assessment.* New York: Wiley.

LANE, H.; BOYES-BRAEM, P.; AND BELLUGI, U. 1976. Preliminaries to a distinctive feature analysis of handshapes in American Sign Language. *Cognitive Psychology* 8:263–89.

LASHLEY, K. S. 1951. The problem of serial order in behavior. In Jeffress, L. A., ed., *Cerebral mechanisms in behavior, the Hixon Symposium.* New York: Wiley.

LASKY, J. J.; HOVER, G. L.; SMITH, P. A.; BOSTIAN, D. W.; DUFFENDECK, S. C.; AND NORD, C. L. 1959. Post-hospital adjustment as predicted by psychiatric patients and by their staff. *Journal of Consulting Psychology* 23:213–18.

LAWRENCE, D. H. 1952. The transfer of a discrimination along a continuum. *Journal of General Psychology* 52:37–48.

LAYZER, D. 1972. Science or superstition: A physical scientist looks at the I.Q. controversy. *Cognition* 1:265–300.

LAZAR, I., AND DARLINGTON, R. B. 1978. *Lasting effects after preschool: 1977–1978 report.* U.S. Department of Health, Education, and Welfare Report (OHDS) 79-30178.

LAZARUS, A. A. 1971. *Behavior therapy and beyond.* New York: McGraw-Hill.

LAZARUS, R. S. 1966. Story telling and the measurement of motivation: The direct versus substitutive controversy. *Journal of Consulting Psychology* 30:483–87.

LAZARUS, R. S., AND MCCLEARY, R. A. 1951. Autonomic discrimination without awareness: A study of subception. *Psychological Review* 58:113–22.

LEASK, J.; HABER, R. N.; AND HABER, R. B. 1969. Eidetic imagery in children: II. Longitudinal and experimental results. *Psychonomic Monograph Supplements* 3(Whole No. 35):25–48.

LE BON, G. 1895. *The Crowd.* New York: Viking Press, 1960.

LEE, E. S. 1951. Negro intelligence and selective migration: A Philadelphia test of the Klineberg hypothesis. *American Sociological Review* 16:227–33.

LEEPER, R. W. 1935. A study of a neglected portion of the field of learning: The development of sensory organization. *Journal of Genetic Psychology* 46:41–75.

LEFKOWITZ, M. M.; BLAKE, R. R.; AND MOUTON, J. S. 1955. Status factors in pedestrian violation of traffic signals. *Journal of Abnormal and Social Psychology* 51:704–706.

LEFKOWITZ, M. M.; ERON, L. D.; WALDER, L. O.; AND HUESMANN, L. R. 1972. Television violence and child aggression: A follow-up study. In Comstock, G. A., and Rubinstein, E. A., eds, *Television and social behavior,* vol. 3, pp. 35–135. Washington, D.C.: U.S. Government Printing Office.

LEFKOWITZ, M. M.; WALDER, L. O.; AND ERON, L. D. 1963. Punishment, identification and aggression. *Merrill-Palmer Quarterly* 9:159–174.

LEHMANN, H. E. 1975. Schizophrenia: Clinical features. In Freedman, A. M.; Kaplan, H. I.; and Sadock, B. J., eds., *Comprehensive textbook of psychiatry—II,* vol. 1, pp. 890–922. Baltimore, Md.: Williams & Wilkins.

LEHRMAN, D. S. 1964. The reproductive behavior of the ring dove. *Scientific American* 211:48–54.

LEMPERS, J. S.; FLAVELL, E. R.; AND FLAVELL, J. H. 1977. The development in very young children of tacit knowledge concerning visual perception. *Genetic Psychology Monographs* 95:3–53.

LENNEBERG, E. H. 1967. *Biological foundations of language.* New York: Wiley.

LEPPER, M. R.; GREENE, D.; AND NISBETT, R. E. 1973. Undermining children's intrinsic interest with extrinsic rewards: A test of the "overjustification" hypothesis. *Journal of Personality and Social Psychology* 28:129–37.

LERNER, M. J. 1971. Observer's evaluation of a victim: Justice, guilt and veridical perception. *Journal of Personality and Social Psychology* 20:127–35.

LERNER, R. M., AND KORN, S. J. 1972. The development of body-build stereotypes in males. *Child Development* 43:908–920.

LETTVIN, J. Y.; MATURAN, H. R.; MCCULLOCH, W. S.; AND PITTS, W. H. 1959. What the frog's eye tells the frog's brain. *Proceedings of the Institute of Radio Engineers* 47:1940–51.

LEVINE, F. M., AND FASNACHT, G. 1974. Token rewards may lead to token learning. *American Psychologist* 29:816–20.

LEVY, J. 1974. Psychobiological implications of bilateral asymmetry. In Dimond, S. J., and Beaumont, J. G., eds, *Hemisphere function in the human brain,* pp. 121–83. New York: Wiley.

LEVY, J. 1979. Author's personal communication with Levy.

LEVY, J.; TREVARTHEN, C.; AND SPERRY, R. W. 1972. Perception of bilateral chimeric figures following hemispheric deconnexion. *Brain* 95:61–78.

LEWONTIN, R. C. 1970. Race and intelligence. *Bulletin of the Atomic Scientist* 26:2–8.

LEWONTIN, R. C. 1976. Race and Intelligence. In Block, N. J., and Dworkin, G., eds., *The IQ controversy*, pp. 78–92. New York: Pantheon.

LIBERMAN, A. M.; COOPER, F. S.; SHANKWEILER, D. P.; AND STUDDERT-KENNEDY, M. 1967. Perception of the speech code. *Psychological Review* 74: 431–61.

LIDZ, T.; CORNELISON, A.; FLECK, S.; AND TERRY, D. 1957. The intrafamilial environment of schizophrenic patients: II. Marital schism and marital skew. *American Journal of Psychiatry* 114:241–48.

LIEBERMAN, M. A.; YALOM, I. D.; AND MILES, M. B. 1973. *Encounter groups: First facts.* New York: Basic Books.

LIEBERMAN, P. L. 1975. *On the origins of language.* New York: Macmillan.

LIEBERMAN, S. 1956. The effects of changes in roles on the attitudes of role occupants. *Human Relations* 9:385–402.

LIEBERT, R. M., AND BARON, R. A. 1972. Some immediate effects of televised violence on children's behavior. *Developmental Psychology* 6:469–75.

LINDSAY, P. H., AND NORMAN, D. A. 1977. *Human information processing*, 2nd edition. New York: Academic Press.

LINDSLEY, D. B. 1960. Attention, consciousness, sleep, and wakefulness. In *Handbook of Physiology,* Sect. 1, *Neurophysiology,* Vol. III. Washington, D.C.: American Physiological Society.

LINDSLEY, D. B.; SCHREINER, L. H.; KNOWLES, W. B.; AND MAGOUN, H. W. 1950. Behavioral and EEG changes following chronic brain stem lesions in the cat. *Electroencephalography and Clinical Neurophysiology* 2:483–98.

LIPOWSKI, Z. J. 1975. Psychophysiological cardiovascular disorders. In Freedman, A. M.; Kaplan, H. I.; and Sadock, B. J., eds., *Comprehensive textbook of psychiatry—II*, vol. 2, pp. 1660–68. Baltimore, Md.: Williams & Wilkins.

LIPPERT, W. W., AND SENTER, R. J. 1966. Electrodermal responses in the sociopath. *Psychonomic Science* 4:25–26.

LITTLE, K. B., AND SHNEIDMAN, E. S. 1959. Congruencies among interpretations of psychological test and anamnestic data. *Psychological Monographs* 73 (Whole No. 476).

LOCKE, J. 1690. *An essay concerning human understanding.* New York: Meridian, 1964.

LOEB, J. 1918. *Forced movements, tropisms, and animal conduct.* Philadelphia, Pa.: Lippincott.

LOEHLIN, J. C. 1969. Psychological Genetics. In Cattell, R. B. *Handbook of modern personality theory.* Chicago: Aldine.

LOEHLIN, J. C.; LINDZEY, G.; AND SPUHLER, J. N. 1975. *Race differences in intelligence.* San Francisco: Freeman.

LOEHLIN, J. C., AND NICHOLS, R. C. 1976. *Heredity, environment and personality: A study of 850 sets of twins.* Austin: University of Texas Press.

LOFTUS, E. F. 1973. Activation of semantic memory. *American Journal of Psychology* 86:331–37.

LOFTUS, E. F. 1975. Leading questions and the eyewitness report. *Cognitive Psychology* 7:560–72.

LOFTUS, E. F., AND ZANNI, G. 1975. Eyewitness testimony: The influence of the wording of a question. *Bulletin of the Psychonomic Society* 5:86-88.

LOGAN, F. 1969. The negative incentive value of punishment. In Campbell, B. A., and Church, R. M., eds., *Punishment and aversive behavior.* New York: Appleton-Century-Crofts.

LONDON, P. 1964. *The modes and morals of psychotherapy.* New York: Holt, Rinehart & Winston.

LORENZ, K. Z. 1952. *King Solomon's ring.* New York: Crowell.

LORENZ, K. Z. 1966. *On aggression.* London: Methuen.

LORGE, I. 1936. Prestige, suggestion and attitude. *Journal of Social Psychology* 7:386–402.

LUBORSKY, L. 1973. Forgetting and remembering (momentary forgetting) during psychotherapy: A new sample. *Psychological Issues* 8(20):29–55.

LUCE, R. D., AND RAIFFA, H. 1957. *Games and decisions.* New York: Wiley.

LUCHINS, A. S. 1942. Mechanization in problem-solving: The effect of Einstellung. *Psychological Monographs* 54 (Whole No. 248).

LUND, F. H. 1930. Why do we weep? *Journal of Social Psychology* 1:136–51.

LURIA, A. R. 1966. *Higher cortical functions in man.* New York: Basic Books.

LYNN, R., AND EYSENCK, H. J. 1961. Tolerance for pain, extraversion and neuroticism. *Perceptual and Motor Skills* 12:161–62.

MCCARTHY, D. 1954. Language development in children. In Carmichael, L., ed., *Manual of child psychology*, pp. 492–630. New York: Wiley.

MCCLEARN, G. E., AND DEFRIES, J. C. 1973. *Introduction to behavioral genetics.* San Francisco: Freeman.

MCCLELLAND, D. C. 1961. *The achieving society.* New York: Van Nostrand.

MCCLELLAND, D. C.; ATKINSON, J. W.; CLARK, R. A.; AND LOWELL, E. L. 1953. *The achievement motive.* New York: Appleton-Century-Crofts.

MCCLINTOCK, M. K., AND ADLER, N. T. 1978. The role of the female during copulation in wild and domestic Norway rats *(Rattus Norvegicus). Behaviour* 67:67–96.

MACCOBY, E. E., AND JACKLIN, C. N. 1974. *The psychology of sex differences.* Stanford, Calif.: Stanford University Press.

MCCORD, W., AND MCCORD, J. 1964. *The psychopath: An essay on the criminal mind.* New York: Van Nostrand.

MACDONALD, N. 1960. Living with schizophrenia. *Canadian Medical Journal* 82:218–21.

MACFARLANE, D. A. 1930. The role of kinesthesis in maze learning. *California University Publications in Psychology* 4:277–305.

MCGAUGH, J. L. 1966. Time dependent processes in memory storage. *Science* 153:1351–58.

MCGHIE, A., AND CHAPMAN, J. 1961. Disorders of attention and perception in early schizophrenia. *British Journal of Medical Psychology* 34:103–116.

MCGUIGAN, F. J. 1966. Covert oral behavior and auditory hallucinations. *Psychophysiology* 3:421–28.

MCKAY, D. G. 1973. Aspects of the theory of comprehension, memory and attention. *Quarterly Journal of Experimental Psychology* 25:22–40.

MACKENZIE, N. 1965. *Dreams and dreaming.* London: Aldus Books.

MACKINTOSH, N. J. 1974. *The psychology of animal learning.* New York: Academic Press.

MACNAMARA, J. 1972. Cognitive basis of language learning in infants. *Psychological Review* 79:1–13.

MCNEILL, D. 1966. Developmental psycholinguistics. In Smith, F., and Miller, G. A., eds., *The genesis of language: A psycholinguistic approach.* Cambridge, Mass.: MIT Press.

MACNICHOL, E. F., JR. 1964. Three-pigment color vision. *Scientific American* 211:48–56.

MAGNUS, O., AND LAMMERS, J. 1956. The amygdaloid-nuclear complex. *Folia Psychiatrica Neurologica et Neurochirurgico Neerlandica* 59:552–82.

MAGOUN, H. W.; HARRISON, F.; BROBECK, J. R.; AND RANSON, S. W. 1938. Activation of heat loss mechanisms by local heating of the brain. *Journal of Neurophysiology* 1:101–114.

MAHER, B. A. 1966. *Principles of psychopathology.* New York: McGraw-Hill.

MAIER, S. F.; SELIGMAN, M. E. P.; AND SOLOMON, R. L. 1969. Pavlovian fear conditioning and learned helplessness: Effects on escape and avoidance behavior of (a) the CS-US contingency and (b) the independence of the US and voluntary responding. In Campbell, B. A., and Church, R. M., ed., *Punishment and aversive behavior,* pp. 299–342. New York: Appleton-Century-Crofts.

MALAN, H. 1963. *A study of brief psychotherapy.* Philadelphia, Pa.: Lippincott.

MALINOWSKI, B. 1927. *Sex and repression in savage society.* New York: Meridian, 1955.

MANDLER, G. 1967. Organization and memory. In Spence, K. W., and Spence, J. T., eds., *The psychology of learning and motivation,* vol. 1, pp. 327–72. New York: Academic Press.

MANDLER, G. 1975. *Mind and emotion.* New York: Wiley.

MANDLER, G., AND PEARLSTONE, Z. 1966. Free and constrained concept learning and subsequent recall. *Journal of verbal learning and verbal behavior* 5:126–31.

MARIN, O.; SAFFRON, E.; AND SCHWARTZ, M. 1976. Dissociations of language in aphasia: Implications for normal function. *Annals of the New York Academy of Sciences* 280:868–84.

MARKS, I. M. 1969. *Fears and phobias.* New York: Academic Press.

MARKS, I. M., AND LADER, M. 1973. Anxiety states (anxiety neurosis): A review. *Journal of Nervous and Mental Disease* 156:3–18.

MARKS, L., AND MILLER, G. A. 1964. The role of semantic and syntactic constraints in the memorization of English sentences. *Journal of Verbal Learning and Verbal Behavior* 3:1–5.

MARLER, P. R. 1970. A comparative approach to vocal learning: Song development in white-crowned sparrows. *Journal of Comparative and Physiological Psychology Monographs* 71(No. 2, Part 2):1–25.

MARLER, P. R., AND HAMILTON, W. J. 1966. *Mechanisms of animal behavior.* New York: Wiley.

MARMOR, J. 1975. Homosexuality and sexual orientation disturbances. In Freedman, A. M.; Kaplan, H. I.; and Sadock, B. J., eds., *Comprehensive textbook of psychiatry—II,* vol. 2, pp. 1510–19. Baltimore, Md.: Williams & Wilkins.

MARQUIS, D. G. 1935. Phylogenetic interpretation of the functions of the visual cortex. *Archives of Neurological Psychology* 33:807–15.

MARSHALL, G. D. 1976. *The affective consequences of "inadequately explained" physiological arousal.* Unpublished doctoral dissertation, Stanford University.

MASLOW, A. 1968. *Toward a psychology of being,* 2nd edition. New York: Van Nostrand.

MASSERMAN, J. H. 1946. *Principles of dynamic psychiatry.* Philadelphia, Pa.: Saunders.

MAX, L. W. 1937. An experimental study of the motor theory of consciousness: IV. Action-curved responses in the deaf during awakening, kinaesthetic imagery and abstract thinking. *Journal of Comparative Psychology* 24:301–344.

MAY, R. 1958. Contributions of existential psychotherapy. In May, R.; Angel, E.; and Ellenberger, H. F., eds., *Existence,* pp. 37–91. New York: Basic Books.

MAYER, J. 1955. Regulation of energy intake and body weight: The glucostatic theory and the lipostatic hypothesis. *Annals of the New York Academy of Sciences* 63:15–43.

MEAD, G. H. 1934. *Mind, self, and society.* Chicago: University of Chicago Press.

MEAD, M. 1935. *Sex and temperament in three primitive societies.* New York: Morrow.

MEAD, M. 1937. *Cooperation and competition among primitive peoples.* New York: McGraw-Hill.

MEAD, M. 1939. *From the South Seas: Studies of adolescence and sex in primitive societies.* New York: Morrow.

MEEHL, P. E. 1956. Profile analysis of the MMPI in differential diagnosis. In Welsh, G. S., and Dahlstrom, W. G., eds., *Basic readings on the MMPI in psychology and medicine,* pp. 291–97. Minneapolis: University of Minnesota Press.

MEEHL, P. E. 1959. Some ruminations on the validation of clinical procedures. *Canadian Journal of Psychology* 13:102–128.

MEEHL, P. D. 1962. Schizotaxia, schizotypy, schizophrenia. *American Psychologist* 17:827–38.

MELTZOFF, A. N. AND MOORE, M. K. 1977. Imitation of facial and manual gestures by human neonates. *Science* 198:75–78.

MELZACK, R. 1973. *The puzzle of pain.* New York: Basic Books.

MEMMI, A. 1967. *The colonizer and the colonized.* Boston: Beacon.

MICHAEL, R. P., AND KEVERNE, E. B. 1968. Pheromones in the communication of sexual status in primates. *Nature* 218:746–49.

MIKAELIAN, H., AND HELD, R. 1964. Two types of adaptation to an optically rotated visual field. *American Journal of Psychology* 77:257–63.

MILGRAM, S. 1963. Behavioral study of obedience. *Journal of Abnormal and Social Psychology* 67:371–78.

MILGRAM, S. 1964. Issues in the study of obedience: A reply to Baumrind. *American Psychologist* 19:848–52.

MILGRAM, S. 1972. Interpreting obedience: Error and evidence. In Miller, A. G., ed., *The social psychology of psychological research,* pp. 138–54. New York: Free Press, Macmillan.

MILGRAM, S. 1974. *Obedience to authority.* New York: Harper & Row.

MILGRAM, S., AND TOCH, H. 1969. Collective behavior: Crowds and Social Movements. In Lindzey, G., and Aronson, E., eds., *Handbook of social psychology,* 2nd edition, vol. 4, pp. 507–610. Reading, Mass.: Addison-Wesley.

MILL, J. S. 1865. *An examination of Sir William Hamilton's philosophy.* London: Longman, Green, Longman, Roberts & Green.

MILLER, G. A. 1956. The magical number seven plus or minus two: Some limits on our capacity for processing information. *Psychological Review* 63:81–97.

MILLER, G. A.; GALANTER, E.; AND PRIBRAM, K. H. 1960. *Plans and the structure of behavior.* New York: Holt, Rinehart & Winston.

MILLER, G. A., AND ISARD, S. 1963. Some perceptual consequences of linguistic rules. *Journal of Verbal Learning and Verbal Behavior* 2:217–28.

MILLER, N. E. 1944. Experimental studies of conflict. In Hunt, J. M., ed., *Personality and the behavior disorders,* pp. 431–65. New York: Ronald Press.

MILLER, N. E. 1959. Liberalization of basic S-R concepts: Extensions to conflict behavior, motivation, and social learning. In Koch, S., ed., *Psychology: A study of a science,* vol. 2, pp. 196–293. New York: McGraw-Hill.

MILLER, N. E. 1969. Learning of visceral and glandular responses. *Science* 163:434–35.

MILLER, N. E.; BAILEY, C. J.; AND STEVENSON, J. A. F. 1950. Decreased "hunger" but increased food intake resulting from hypothalamic lesions. *Science* 112:256–59.

MILLER, N. E., AND DWORKIN, B. R. 1973. Visceral learning: Recent difficulties with curarized rats and significant problems for human research. In Obrist, P. A. et al., eds., *Contemporary trends in cardiovascular psychophysiology.* Chicago: Aldine-Atherton.

MILLER, R. J. 1973. Cross-cultural research in the perception of pictorial materials. *Psychological Bulletin* 80:135–50.

MILLER, W. R., AND SELIGMAN, M. E. P. 1975. Depression and learned helplessness in man. *Journal of Abnormal Psychology* 84:228–38.

MILLON, T. 1969. *Modern psychopathology.* Philadelphia, Pa.: Saunders.

MILNER, B. 1966. Amnesia following aperation on the temporal lobes. In Whitty, C. W. M., and Zangwill, O. L., eds., *Amnesia,* pp. 109–133. London: Butterworth.

MILNER, B.; CORKIN, S.; AND TEUBER, H. L. 1968. Further analysis of the hippocampal syndrome: 14-year follow-up study of H. M. *Neuropsychologia* 6:215–34.

MINAMI, H., AND DALLENBACH, K. M. 1946. The effect of activity upon learning and retention in the cockroach. *American Journal of Psychology* 59:1–58.

MISCHEL, W. 1961. Delay of gratification, need for achievement and acquiescence in another culture. *Journal of Abnormal and Social Psychology* 62:543–52.

MISCHEL, W. 1968. *Personality and assessment.* New York: Wiley.

MISCHEL, W. 1970. Sex-typing and socialization. In Mussen, P. H., ed., *Carmichael's manual of child development,* vol. 1. New York: Wiley.

MISCHEL, W. 1973. Towards a cognitive social learning reconceptualization of personality. *Psychological Review* 80:252–83.

MISELIS, R. R., AND EPSTEIN, A. N. 1970. Feeding induced by 2-deoxy-D-glucose injections into the lateral ventricle of the rat. *The Physiologist* 13:262.

MISHLER, E. G., AND WAXLER, N. E. 1968. Family interaction and schizophrenia: Alternative frameworks of interpretation. In Rosenthal, D., and Kety, S. S., eds., *The transmission of schizophrenia,* pp. 213–22. New York: Pergamon.

MOELLER, G. 1954. The CS-UCS interval in GSR conditioning. *Journal of Experimental Psychology* 48:162–66.

MOELY, B. E.; OLSON, F. A.; HALWES, T. G.; AND FLAVELL, J. H. 1969. Production deficiency in young children's clustered recall. *Child Development* 44:238–46.

MONEY, J., AND EHRHARDT, A. A. 1972. *Man and woman, boy and girl.* Baltimore, Md.: Johns Hopkins University Press.

MOOS, R. H. 1969. Sources of variance in responses to questionnaires and in behavior. *Journal of Abnormal Psychology* 74:405–12.

MORA, G. 1975. Historical and theoretical trends in psychiatry. In Freedman, A. M.; Kaplan, H. I.; and Sadock, B. J., eds., *Comprehensive textbook of psychiatry—II,* vol. 1, pp. 1–75. Baltimore, Md.: Williams & Wilkins.

MORAY, N. 1959. Attention in dichotic listening: Affective cues and the influence of instructions. *Quarterly Journal of Experimental Psychology* 11:56–60.

MOREHEAD, D. M., AND INGRAM, D. 1976. The development of base syntax in normal and linguistically deviant children. In Morehead, D. M., and Morehead, A. E., eds., pp. 209–38. Baltimore, Md.: University Park Press.

MORGAN, C. D., AND MURRAY, H. A. 1935. A method for investigating fantasies: The thematic apperception test. *Archives of Neurological Psychiatry* 34:289–306.

MORGAN, C. L. 1894. *An introduction to comparative psychology.* London: Scott.

MORGANE, P. J., AND STERN, W. C. 1974. Chemical anatomy of brain circuits in sleep and wakefulness. In Weitzman, E. D., ed., *Advances in sleep research,* vol. I., pp. 1–131. New York: Spectrum.

MORRIS, D. 1967. *The naked ape.* New York: McGraw-Hill.

MORRIS, J. 1974. *Conundrum.* New York: Harcourt Brace Jovanovich.

MOSHER, F. A., AND HORNSBY, J. R. 1966. On asking questions. In Bruner, J. S.; Olver, R. R.; and Greenfield, P. M., eds., *Studies in cognitive growth,* pp. 86–102. New York: Wiley.

MOWRER, O. H. 1947. On the dual nature of learning—a reinterpretation of "conditioning" and "problem solving." *Harvard Educational Review* 17:102–148.

MUNROE, R. 1955. *Schools of psychoanalytic thought.* New York: Dryden Press.

MURDOCK, B. 1962. The serial position effect of free recall. *Journal of Experimental Psychology* 64:482–88.

NEISSER, U. 1963. The imitation of man by machine. *Science* 139:193–97.

NEISSER, U. 1967. *Cognitive Psychology.* New York: Appleton-Century-Crofts.

NEISSER, U. *Cognition and Reality.* 1976. San Francisco: Freeman.

NEISSER, U., AND BECKLEN, R. 1975. Selective looking: Attending to visually-specified events. *Cognitive Psychology* 7:480–94.

NELSON, K. 1973. Structure and strategy in learning to talk. *Monographs of the Society for Research in Child Development* 38:(1–2, Serial No. 149).

NEMIAH, J. C. 1975a. Phobic neurosis. In Freedman, A. M.; Kaplan, H. I.; and Sadock, B. J., eds., *Comprehensive textbook of psychiatry—II,* vol. 1, pp. 1231–41. Baltimore, Md.: Williams & Wilkins.

NEMIAH, J. C. 1975b. Obsessive-compulsive neurosis. In Freedman, A. M.; Kaplan, H. I.; and Sadock, B. J., eds., *Comprehensive textbook of psychiatry—II,* vol. 1, pp. 1241–55. Baltimore, Md.: Williams & Wilkins.

NEWELL, A.; SHAW, J. C.; AND SIMON, H. A. 1958. Elements of a theory of human problem solving. *Psychological Review* 65:151–66.

NEWELL, A., AND SIMON, H. A. 1972. *Human problem solving.* Englewood Cliffs, N.J.: Prentice-Hall.

NEWPORT, E. L. 1977. Motherese: The speech of mothers to young children. In Castellan, N. J.; Pisoni, D. B.; and Potts, G. R., eds., *Cognitive theory,* vol. II. Hillsdale, N.J.: Erlbaum.

NEWPORT, E. L. 1981. Task specificity in language acquisition? Evidence from speech perception and American Sign Language. In Wanner, E., and Gleitman, L. R., eds., *Language acquisition: State of the art.* Cambridge, England: Cambridge University Press.

NEWPORT, E. L., AND ASHBROOK, E. F. 1977. The emergence of semantic relations in American Sign Language. *Papers and Reports in Child Language Development* 13.

NEWPORT, E. L.; GLEITMAN, H.; AND GLEITMAN, L. R. 1977. Mother, I'd rather do it myself: Some effects and non-effects of maternal speech style. In Snow, C., and Ferguson, C., eds., *Talking to children: Language input and acquisition.* Cambridge, England: Cambridge University Press.

NISBETT, R. E. 1968. Taste, deprivation, and weight determinants of eating behavior. *Journal of Personality and Social Psychology* 10:107–116.

NISSEN, H. 1953. Instinct as seen by a psychologist. *Psychological Review* 60:287–97.

NORMAN, W. T. 1963. Toward an adequate taxonomy of personality attributes: Replicated factor structure in peer nomination personality ratings. *Journal of Abnormal and Social Psychology* 66:574–83.

NYE, W. C.; MCMANIS, D. L.; AND HAUGEN, D. M. 1972. Training and transfer of categorization by retarded adults. *American Journal of Mental Deficiency* 77:199–207.

ODIORNE, J. M. 1957. Color changes. In Brown, M. E., ed., *The physiology of fishes,* vol. 2. New York: Academic Press.

OLDS, J., AND MILNER, P. 1954. Positive reinforcement produced by electrical stimulation of septal areas and other regions of rat brains. *Journal of Comparative and Physiological Psychology* 47:419–27.

OLDS, J., AND OLDS, M. 1965. Drives, rewards and the brain. In Newcomb, T. M., ed., *New directions in psychology II,* pp. 329–410. New York: Holt, Rinehart & Winston.

ORLANSKY, H. 1949. Infant care and personality. *Psychological Bulletin* 46:1–48.

ORNE, M. T. 1962. On the social psychology of the psychological experiment: With particular reference to demand characteristics and their implications. *American Psychologist* 17:776–83.

ORNE, M. T. 1975. Psychotherapy in contemporary America: Its development and context. In Arieti, S., ed., *American handbook of psychiatry,* 2nd edition, vol. 5, pp. 1–33. New York: Basic Books.

ORNE, M. T., AND HOLLAND, C. C. 1968. On the ecological validity of laboratory deceptions. *International Journal of Psychiatry* 6:282–93.

ORNE, M. T., AND WILSON, S. K. 1978. On the nature of alpha feedback training. In Schwartz, G. E., and Shapiro, D. *Consciousness and self-regulation: Advances in research and theory*, pp. 359–400. New York: Plenum.

OSWALD, I.; TAYLOR, A. M.; AND TREISMAN, M. 1960. Discriminative responses to stimulation during sleep. *Brain* 83:440.

PAI, M. N. 1946. Sleep-walking and sleep activities. *Journal of Mental Science* 92:756–65.

PAUL, G. L. 1966. *Insight vs. desensitization in psychotherapy: An experiment in anxiety reduction.* Stanford, Calif.: Stanford University Press.

PAUL, G. L. 1967a. Strategy of outcome research in psychotherapy. *Journal of Consulting Psychology* 31:109–118.

PAUL, G. L. 1967b. Insight versus desensitization in psychotherapy two years after termination. *Journal of Consulting Psychology* 31:333–48.

PAVLOV, I. 1927. *Conditioned reflexes.* Oxford, England: Oxford University Press.

PEABODY, D. 1967. Trait inferences: Evaluative and descriptive aspects. *Journal of Personality and Social Psychology Monograph* 7(Whole No. 644).

PENFIELD, W. 1975. *The mystery of the mind.* Princeton, N.J.: Princeton University Press.

PENFIELD, W., AND RASMUSSEN, T. 1950. *The cerebral cortex of man.* New York: Macmillan.

PENFIELD, W., AND ROBERTS, L. 1959. *Speech and brain mechanisms.* Princeton, N.J.: Princeton University Press.

PEPITONE, A. 1976. Toward a normative and comparative biocultural social psychology. *Journal of Personality and Social Psychology* 34:641–53.

PERIN, C. T. 1943. A quantitative investigation of the delay of reinforcement gradient. *Journal of Experimental Psychology* 32:37–51.

PETERSON, L. B., AND PETERSON, M. J. 1959. Short-term retention of individual items. *Journal of Experimental Psychology* 58:193–98.

PIAGET, J. 1929. *The child's conception of the world.* New York: Harcourt, Brace.

PIAGET, J. 1930. *The child's conception of physical causality.* London: Kegan Paul.

PIAGET, J. 1932. *The moral judgement of the child.* London: Kegan Paul.

PIAGET, J. 1951. *Play, dreams and imitation in childhood.* New York: Norton.

PIAGET, J. 1952. *The origins of intelligence in children.* New York: International University Press.

PIAGET, J. 1972. *The child's conception of the world.* Totowa, N.J.: Littlefield, Adams.

PIAGET, J., AND INHELDER, B. 1967. *The child's conception of space.* New York: Norton.

PINCKER, S. 1979. Formal models of language learning. *Cognition* 7:217–83.

PITTS, F. N., JR.; MEYER, J.; BROOKS, M.; AND WINOKUR, G. 1965. Adult psychiatric illness assessed for childhood parental loss and psychiatric illness in family members—a study of 748 patients and 250 controls. *American Journal of Psychiatry Supplement* 121:i–x.

PLUTCHIK, R., AND AX, A. F. 1970. A critique of *Determinants of emotional state* by Schachter and Singer (1962). In Arnold, M. B., ed., *Feelings and emotions: The Loyola symposium.* New York: Academic Press.

POLLIN, W.; ALLEN, M. G.; HOFFER, A.; STABENAU, J. R.; AND HRUBEC, Z. 1969. Psychopathology in 15,909 pairs of veteran twins. *American Journal of Psychiatry* 126:597–609.

PORSOLT, R. D.; LE PICHON, M.; AND JALFRE, M. 1977. Depression: A new animal model sensitive to antidepressant treatments. *Nature* 266:730–32.

POSTAL, P. M. 1968. Epilogue. In Jacobs, R. A., and Rosenbaum, P. S., *English transformational grammar,* pp. 253–89. Waltham, Mass.: Blaisdell.

POSTMAN, L. 1961. The present status of interference theory. In Cofer, C. N., ed., *Verbal learning and verbal behavior,* pp. 152–79. New York: McGraw-Hill.

POSTMAN, L. 1969. Mechanisms of interference in forgetting. In Talland, G. A., and Waugh, N. C., eds., *The pathology of memory,* pp. 195–210. New York: Academic Press.

PREMACK, A. J. 1976. *Why chimps can read.* New York: Harper.

PREMACK, A. J., AND PREMACK, D. 1972. Teaching language to an ape. *Scientific American* 227:92–99.

PREMACK, D. 1962. Reversibility of the reinforcement relation. *Science* 136:235–37.

PREMACK, D. 1976. *Intelligence in ape and man.* Hillsdale, N.J.: Erlbaum.

PREMACK, D. 1978. On the abstractness of human concepts: Why it would be difficult to talk to a pigeon. In Hulse, S.H.; Fowler, H.; and Honig, W. K., eds. *Cognitive processes in animal behavior.* Hillsdale, N.J.: Erlbaum.

PREMACK, D., AND WOODRUFF, G. 1978. Does the chimpanzee have a theory of mind? *The Behavioral and Brain Sciences* 4:515–26.

PRITCHARD, R. M. 1961. Stabilized images on the retina. *Scientific American* 204:72–78.

PROUST, M. 1913. *Swann's way.* Translated by Moncrieff, C. K. S. New York: Modern Library, 1928.

PROVENCE, S., AND LIPTON, R. C. 1962. *Infants in institutions.* New York: International Universities Press.

PUROHIT, A. D. 1966. Levels of introversion and competitional paired-associate learning. *Journal of Personality* 34:129–43.

QUAY, L. C. 1971. Language, dialect, reinforcement, and the intelligence test performance of Negro children. *Child Development* 42:5–15.

RACHMAN, S. J., AND TEASDALE, J. 1969. Aversion therapy: An appraisal. In Franks, C. M., ed., *Behavior therapy: Appraisal and status,* pp. 279–320. New York: McGraw-Hill.

RAPPAPORT, M. 1967. Competing voice messages: Effects of message load and drugs on the ability of schizophrenics to attend. *Archives of General Psychiatry* 17:97–103.

RAVEN, B. H., AND RUBIN, J. Z. 1976. *Social psychology: People in groups.* New York: Wiley.

REDL, F. 1973. The superego in uniform. In Sanford, N., and Comstock, C., eds., *Sanctions for evil.* San Francisco: Jossey-Bass.

REDLICH, F. C., AND FREEDMAN, D. X. 1966. *The theory and practice of psychiatry.* New York: Basic Books.

REES, L., AND EYSENCK, H. J. 1945. A factorial study of some morphological and psychological aspects of human constitution. *Journal of Mental Science* 91:8–21.

REITMAN, J. S. 1974. Without surreptitious rehearsal, information in short-term memory decays. *Journal of Verbal Learning and Verbal Behavior* 13:365–77.

REITMAN, W. 1965. *Cognition and thought: An information processing approach.* New York: Wiley.

RESCORLA, R. A. 1967. Pavlovian conditioning and its proper control procedures. *Psychological Review* 74:71–80.

RESCORLA, R. A., AND SOLOMON, R. L. 1967. Two-process learning theory: Relationships between Pavlovian conditioning and instrumental learning. *Psychological Review* 74:151–82.

REYNOLDS, G. S. 1968. *A primer of operant conditioning.* Glenview, Ill.: Scott, Foresman.

RICHTER, C. P. 1957. On the phenomenon of unexplained sudden death in animals and man. *Psychosomatic Medicine* 19:191–98.

RIGGS, L. A.; RATLIFF, F.; CORNSWEET, J. C.; AND CORNSWEET, T. N. 1953. The disappearance of steadily fixated visual test objects. *Journal of the Optical Society of America* 43:495–501.

RINGUETTE, E. L., AND KENNEDY, T. 1966. An experimental study of the double-bind hypothesis. *Journal of Abnormal Psychology* 71:136–42.

ROBBIN, A. A. 1958. A controlled study of the effects of leucotomy. *Journal of Neurology, Neurosurgery and Psychiatry* 21:262–69.

ROBINS, L. R. 1966. *Deviant children grown up: A sociological and psychiatric study of sociopathic personality.* Baltimore, Md.: Williams & Wilkins.

ROBINSON, H. B., AND ROBINSON, N. M. 1970. Mental retardation. In Mussen, P. H., ed., *Carmichael's manual of child psychology,* vol. 2, pp. 615–66. New York: Wiley.

ROCK, I. 1975. *An introduction to perception.* New York: Macmillan.

ROCK, I., AND KAUFMAN, L. 1962. The moon illusion, II. *Science* 136:1023–31.

ROCK, I., AND VICTOR, J. 1964. Vision and touch: An experimentally created conflict between the two senses. *Science* 143:594–96.

RODIN, J. 1977. Bidirectional influences of emotionality, stimulus responsivity and metabolic events in obesity. In Maser, J. D., and Seligman, M. E. P., eds., *Psychopathology: Experimental models.* San Francisco: Freeman.

ROEDER, K. D. 1935. An experimental analysis of the sexual behavior of the praying mantis. *Biological Bulletin* 69:203–220.

ROEDER, K. 1967. *Nerve cells and insect behavior.* Cambridge, Mass.: Harvard University Press.

ROGERS, C. R. 1942. *Counseling and psychotherapy: New concepts in practice.* Boston: Houghton Mifflin.

ROGERS, C. R. 1961. *On becoming a person: A therapist's view of psychotherapy.* Boston: Houghton Mifflin.

ROMANES, G. J. 1882. *Animal intelligence.* London: Kegan Paul.

ROSCH, E. H. 1973. Natural categories. *Cognitive Psychology* 4:328–50.

ROSCH, E. H. 1973. On the internal structure of perceptual and semantic categories. In Moore, T. E., ed., *Cognitive development and the acquisition of language.* New York: Academic Press.

ROSCH, E. H., AND MERVIS, C. B. 1975. Family resemblances: Studies in the internal structure of categories. *Cognitive Psychology* 7:573–605.

ROSCH, E. H.; MERVIS, C. B.; GRAY, W. D.; JOHNSON, D. M.; AND BOYES-BRAEM, P. 1976. Basic objects in natural categories. *Cognitive Psychology* 8:382–439.

ROSEN, B. C. 1956. The achievement syndrome: A psycho-cultural dimension of social stratification. *American Sociological Review* 21:203–211.

ROSEN, B. C., AND D'ANDRADE, R. G. 1959. The psychosocial origins of achievement motivation. *Sociometry* 22:185–218.

ROSEN, G. 1966. *Madness in society.* Chicago: University of Chicago Press.

ROSENHAN, D. L. 1973. On being sane in insane places. *Science* 179:250–58.

ROSENHAN, D. L. 1974. Obedience and rebellion: Observations on the Milgram three-party paradigm. Reported in Milgram, S., *Obedience to authority.* N.Y.: Harper & Row, 1974.

ROSENTHAL, A. M. 1964. *Thirty-eight witnesses.* New York: McGraw-Hill.

ROSENTHAL, D. 1970. *Genetic theory and abnormal behavior.* New York: McGraw-Hill.

ROSENTHAL, R. 1967. Covert Communication in the psychological experiment. *Psychological Bulletin* 67:356–67.

ROSS, J., AND LAWRENCE, K. Q. 1968. Some observations on memory artifice. *Psychonomic Science* 13:107–8.

ROWELL, T. E. 1966. Hierarchy in the organization of a captive baboon group. *Animal Behavior* 14:430–33.

ROZIN, P. 1976a. The evolution of intelligence and access to the cognitive unconscious. In Stellar, E., and Sprague, J. M., eds., *Progress in psychobiology and physiological psychology,* vol. 6. New York: Academic Press.

ROZIN, P. 1976b. The psychobiological approach to human memory. In Rosenzweig, M. R., and Bennett, E. L., *Neural mechanisms of learning and memory,* pp. 3–48. Cambridge, Mass.: MIT Press.

ROZIN, P., AND KALAT, J. W. 1971. Specific hungers and poison avoidance as adaptive specializations of learning. *Psychological Review* 78:459–86.

RUCH, T. C. 1965. The homotypical cortex—the "association areas." In Ruch, T. C.; Palton, H. D.; Woodbury, J. W.; and Towe, A. L., eds., *Neurophysiology,* 2nd edition, pp. 465–79. Philadelphia, Pa.: Saunders.

RUMBAUGH, D. M., ed. 1977. *Language learning by a chimpanzee: The Lana Project.* New York: Academic Press.

RUSSEK, M. 1971. Hepatic receptors and the neurophysiological mechanisms controlling feeding behavior. In Ehrenpreis, S., ed., *Neurosciences research,* vol. 4. New York: Academic Press.

RUSSELL, W. R. 1959. *Brain, memory, learning: A neurologist's view.* Oxford, England: Oxford University Press.

SACHS, J. 1967. Recognition memory for syntactic and semantic aspects of connected discourse. *Perception and Psychophysics* 2:437–42.

SACHS, J., AND DEVIN, J. 1976. Young children's use of age-appropriate speech styles in social interaction and role-playing. *Journal of Child Language* 3:81–98.

SACHS, J., AND TRUSWELL, L. 1978. Comprehension of two-word instructions by children in the one-word stage. *Journal of Child Language* 5:17–24.

SADOCK, B. J. 1975. Group psychotherapy. In Freedman, A. M.; Kaplan, H. I., and Sadock, B. J., eds., *Comprehensive textbook of psychiatry—II,* vol. 2, pp. 1850–76. Baltimore, Md.: Williams & Wilkins.

SAGHIR, M. T., AND ROBINS, E. 1973. *Male and female homosexuality.* Baltimore, Md.: Williams & Wilkins.

SALAPATEK, P. 1975. Pattern perception in early infancy. In Cohen, L. B., and Salapatek, P., eds., *Infant perception: From sensation to cognition,* vol. 1, pp. 133–248. New York: Academic Press.

SALAPATEK, P., AND KESSEN, W. 1966. Visual scanning of triangles by the human newborn. *Journal of Experimental Child Psychology* 3:113–22.

SALTZMAN, I. J. 1949. Maze learning in the absence of primary reinforcement: A study of secondary reinforcement. *Journal of Comparative and Physiological Psychology* 42:161–73.

SAMPSON, E. E. 1976. *Social psychology and contemporary society,* 2nd edition. New York: Wiley.

SARASON, S. B. 1973. Jewishness, blackness, and the nature-nurture controversy. *American Psychologist* 28:926–71.

SARBIN, T. R., AND ALLEN, V. L. 1968. Role theory. In Lindzey, G., and Aronson, E., eds., *The handbook of social psychology,* 2nd edition, vol. 1, pp. 488–567. Reading, Mass.: Addison-Wesley.

SARNOFF, C. 1957. *Medical aspects of flying motivation—a fear-of-flying case book.* Randolph Air Force Base, Texas: U.S. Air Force, Air University, School of Aviation Medicine.

SATINOFF, E. 1964. Behavioral thermoregulation in response to local cooling of the rat brain. *American Journal of Physiology* 206:1389–94.

SAUL, L. J. 1939. Hostility in cases of essential hypertension. *Psychosomatic Medicine* 1:153–216.

SAVIN, H. B., AND PERCHONOCK, E. 1965. Grammatical structure and the immediate recall of English sentences. *Journal of Verbal Learning and Verbal Behavior* 4:348–53.

SAWREY, W. L.; CONGER, J. J.; AND TURRELL, E. S. 1956. An experimental investigation of the role of psychological factors in the production of gastric ulcers in the rat. *Journal of Comparative and Physiological Psychology* 49:457–61.

SCARR, S. 1966. Genetic factors in activity motivation. *Child Development* 37:633–73.

SCARR, S. 1969. Social introversion-extraversion as a heritable response. *Child Development* 40:823–32.

SCARR, S., AND CARTER-SALTZMAN, L. 1979. Twin-method: Defense of a critical assumption. *Behavior Genetics* 9:527–42.

SCARR-SALAPATEK, S., AND WEINBERG, R. A. 1975. When black children grow up in white homes. *Psychology Today* 9:80–82.

SCHACHTEL, E. 1949. On memory and childhood amnesia. In Mullahy, P., ed., *A study of interpersonal relations*, pp. 3–49. New York: Hermitage.

SCHACHTER, S. 1959. *The psychology of affiliation*. Stanford, Calif.: Stanford University Press.

SCHACHTER, S. 1971. Some extraordinary facts about obese humans and rats. *American Psychologist* 26:129–44.

SCHACHTER, S., AND SINGER, J. 1962. Cognitive, social and physiological determinants of emotional state. *Psychological Review* 69:379–99.

SCHAFFER, H. R. 1966. The onset of fear of strangers and the incongruity hypothesis. *Journal of Child Psychology and Psychiatry* 7:95–106.

SCHAFFER, H. R., AND CALLENDER, W. M. 1959. Psychological effects of hospitalization in infancy. *Pediatrics* 24:528–39.

SCHAIE, K., AND STROTHER, C. 1968. A cross-sequential study of age changes in cognitive behavior. *Psychological Bulletin* 70:671–80.

SCHEERER, M. 1963. Problem solving. *Scientific American* 208:118–28.

SCHEFF, T. 1966. *Being mentally ill: A sociological theory*. Chicago: Aldine.

SCHENKEL, R. 1967. Submission: Its features and function in the wolf and dog. *American Zoologist* 7:319–29.

SCHIFF, W. 1965. The perception of imminent collision: A study of visually directed avoidant behavior. *Psychological Monographs* 79(Whole No. 604).

SCHIFFMAN, H. R. 1976. *Sensation and perception: An integrated approach*. New York: Wiley.

SCHILDKRAUT, J. J. 1965. The catecholamine hypothesis of affective disorders: A review of supporting evidence. *American Journal of Psychiatry* 122:509–22.

SCHLENKER, B. R. 1974. Social psychology and science. *Journal of Personality and Social Psychology* 29:1–15.

SCHNEIDERMAN, N., AND GORMEZANO, I. 1964. Conditioning of the nictitating membrane of the rabbit as a function of the CS-US interval. *Journal of Comparative and Physiological Psychology* 57:188–95.

SCHNEIRLA, T. C. 1959. An evolutionary and developmental theory of biphasic processes underlying approach and withdrawal. In Jones, M. R., ed., *Nebraska symposium on motivation*, pp. 1–43. Lincoln: University of Nebraska Press.

SCHOFIELD, W. 1964. *Psychotherapy: The purchase of friendship*. Englewood Cliffs, N.J.: Prentice-Hall.

SCHOPLER, J., AND COMPERE, J. S. 1971. Effects of being kind or harsh to another on liking. *Journal of Personality and Social Psychology* 20:155–59.

SCHUTZ, W. C. 1967. *Joy*. New York: Grove Press.

SCHWARTZ, B. 1974. On going back to nature: A review of Seligman and Hager's *Biological boundaries of learning. Journal of the Experimental Analysis of Behavior* 21:183–98.

SCHWARTZ, B. 1978. *Psychology of learning and behavior*. New York: Norton.

SCHWARTZ, B., AND GAMZU, E. 1977. Pavlovian control of operant behavior. In Honig, W. K., and Staddon, J. E. R., eds., *Handbook of operant behavior*. Englewood Cliffs, N.J.: Prentice-Hall.

SCHWARTZ, S. H., AND CLAUSEN, G. 1970. Responsibility, norms, and helping in an emergency. *Journal of Personality and Social Psychology* 16:299–310.

SCOTT, J. P. 1963. The process of primary socialization in canine and human infants. *Monograph of the Society for Research in Child Development* 28:1–47.

SEARLE, J. R. 1969. *Speech acts: An essay in the philosophy of language*. New York: Cambridge University Press.

SEARS, R. R.; MACCOBY, E. E.; AND LEVIN, H. 1957. *Patterns of child rearing*. Evanston, Ill.: Row, Peterson.

SECHENOV, I. M. 1863. *Reflexes of the brain*. Translated by Belsky, S. Cambridge, Mass.: MIT Press, 1965.

SEIDENBERG, M. S., AND PETITTO, L. A. 1979. Signing behavior in apes: A critical review. *Cognition* 7:177–215.

SELIGMAN, M. E. P. 1970. On the generality of the laws of learning. *Psychological Review* 77:406–418.

SELIGMAN, M. E. P. 1975. *Helplessness: On depression, development and death*. San Francisco: Freeman.

SELIGMAN, M. E. P.; KLEIN, D. C.; AND MILLER, W. R. 1976. Depression. In Leitenberg, H., ed., *Handbook of behavior modification and behavior therapy*. Englewood Cliffs, N.J.: Prentice-Hall.

SELIGMAN, M. E. P., AND MAIER, S. F. 1967. Failure to escape traumatic shock. *Journal of Experimental Psychology* 74:1–9.

SELIGMAN, M. E. P.; MAIER, S. F.; AND SOLOMON, R. L. 1971. Unpredictable and uncontrollable aversive events. In Brush, F. R., ed., *Aversive conditioning and learning*. New York: Academic Press.

SENDEN, M., VON 1932. *Raum—und Gestaltauffassung bei operierten Blindgeborenen vor und nach der Operation*. Leipzig: Barth.

SERBER, M. 1972. The experiential group as entertainment. In Houts, P. S., and Serber, M., eds., *After the turn-on, what? Learning perspectives on humanistic groups*. Champaign, Ill.: Research Press.

SHAKOW, D. 1963. Psychological deficit in schizophrenia. *Behavior Science* 8:275–305

SHAPIRO, A. K. 1971. Placebo effects in medicine, psychotherapy, and psychoanalysis. In Bergin, A. E., and Garfield, S. L., eds., *Handbook of psychotherapy and behavior change*, pp. 439–73. New York: Wiley.

SHATZ, M. 1978. The relationship between cognitive processes and the development of communication skills. In Keasey, C. B., ed., *Nebraska symposium on motivation*. Lincoln: University of Nebraska Press.

SHATZ, M., AND GELMAN, R. 1973. The development of communication skills. *Monograph of the Society for Research in Child Development* 38 (5, Serial No. 152).

SHATZ, M., AND GELMAN, R. 1977. Beyond syntax: The influence of conversational constraints on speech modifications. In Snow, C. E., and Ferguson, C. A., eds., *Talking to children: Language input and acquisition*. Cambridge, England: Cambridge University Press.

SHEFFIELD, F. D., AND ROBY, T. B. 1950. Reward value of a non-nutritive sweet taste. *Journal of Comparative and Physiological Psychology* 43:471–81.

SHEFFIELD, F. D.; WULFF, J. J.; AND BACKER, R. 1951. Reward value of copulation without sex drive reduction. *Journal of Comparative and Physiological Psychology* 44:3–8.

SHELDON, W. H. 1940. *The varieties of human physique*. New York: Harper.

SHELDON, W. H. 1942. *The varieties of temperament*. New York: Harper.

SHERIDAN, C. L., AND KING, R. G., JR. 1972. Obedience to authority with an authentic victim. *Proceedings of the 80th Annual Convention of the American Psychological Association*, pp. 165–66.

SHERRINGTON, C. S. 1906. *The integrative action of the nervous system*, 2nd edition. New Haven, Conn.: Yale University Press, 1947.

SHIF, Z. I. 1969. Development of children in schools for the mentally retarded. In Cole, M., and Maltzman, I., eds., *A handbook of contemporary Soviet psychology*, pp. 326–53. New York: Basic Books.

SHIMBERG, M. E. 1929. An investigation into the validity of norms with special reference to urban and rural groups. In *Archives of Psychology*, No. 104.

SHIPLEY, E. F.; SMITH, C. S.; AND GLEITMAN, L. R. 1969. A study in the acquisition of language: Free responses to commands. *Language* 45: 322–42.

SHOEMAKER, S. 1963. *Self-knowledge and self-identity.* Ithaca, N. Y.: Cornell University Press.

SHOPSIN, B.; WILK, S.; SATHANANTHAN, G.; GERSHON, S.; AND DAVIS, K. 1974. Catecholamines and affective disorders revised: A critical assessment. *Journal of Nervous & Mental Disease* 158:369–83.

SHUEY, A. 1966. *The testing of Negro intelligence.* New York: Social Science Press.

SHULTZ, T., AND HORIBE, F. 1974. Development of the appreciation of verbal jokes. *Developmental Psychology* 10:13–20.

SIEGEL, S. 1977. Morphine tolerance acquisition as an associative process. *Journal of Experimental Psychology: Animal Behavior Processes* 3:1–13.

SIEGLER, M., AND OSMOND, H. 1974. *Models of madness, models of medicine.* New York: Harper & Row.

SINCLAIR, H. 1970. The transition from sensory-motor behavior to symbolic activity. *Interchange* 1:119–26.

SINCLAIR, H. 1973. Language acquisition and cognitive development. In Moore, T. E., ed., *Cognitive development and the acquisition of language.* New York: Academic Press.

SKEELS, H. 1966. Adult status of children with contrasting early life experiences. *Monograph of the Society for Research in Child Development* 31 (No. 3).

SKINNER, B. F. 1938. *The behavior of organisms.* New York: Appleton-Century-Crofts.

SKINNER, B. F. 1948. Superstition in the pigeon. *Journal of Experimental Psychology* 38:168–72.

SKODAK, M., AND SKEELS, H. M. 1945. A follow-up study of children in adoptive homes. *Journal of Genetic Psychology* 66:21–58.

SKODAK, M., AND SKEELS, H. M. 1947. A follow-up study of the development of one-hundred adopted children in Iowa. *American Psychologist* 2:278.

SKODAK, M., AND SKEELS, H. 1949. A final follow-up study of children in adoptive homes. *Journal of Genetic Psychology* 75:85–125.

SLATER, E. 1943. The neurotic constitution. *Journal of Neurological Psychiatry* 6:1–16.

SLATER, E., AND COWIE, V. 1971. *The genetics of mental disorders.* London: Oxford University Press.

SLOANE, R. B.; STAPLES, F. R.; CRISTOL, A. H.; YORKSTON, N. J.; AND WHIPPLE, K. 1975. *Psychotherapy vs. behavior therapy.* Cambridge, Mass.: Harvard University Press.

SLOBIN, D. I. 1966. Grammatical transformations and sentence comprehension in childhood and adulthood. *Journal of Verbal Learning and Verbal Behavior* 5:219–27.

SLOBIN, D. I. 1973. Cognitive prerequisites for the development of grammar. In Ferguson, C., and Slobin, D., eds., *Studies of child language development,* pp. 175–208. New York: Holt, Rinehart & Winston.

SLOBIN, D. I. 1975. The more it changes: On understanding language by watching it move through time. In *Papers and reports on child language development,* no. 10. Stanford, Calif.: Department of Linguistics, Stanford University.

SLUCKIN, W. 1965. *Imprinting and early learning.* Chicago: Aldine.

SMEDSLUND, J. 1961. The acquisition of conservation of substance and weight in children. *Scandinavia Journal of Psychology* 2:11–20.

SMELSER, N. J. 1963. *Theory of collective behavior.* New York: Free Press, Macmillan.

SMITH, MAYNARD J. 1965. The evolution of alarm calls. *American Naturalist* 99:59–63.

SMITH, M. C.; DiLOLLO, V.; AND GORMEZANO, I. 1966. Conditioned jaw movement in the rabbit. *Journal of Comparative and Physiological Psychology* 62:479–83.

SMITH, S. M.; BROWN, H. O.; TOMAN, J. E. P.; AND GOODMAN, L. S. 1947. The lack of cerebral effects of d-tubocurarine. *Anaesthesiology* 8:1–14.

SMITH, W. J. 1977. *The behavior of communicating.* Cambridge, Mass.: Harvard University Press.

SNOW, C. E. 1972. Mother's speech to children learning language. *Child Development* 43:549–65.

SNYDER, F. W., AND PRONKO, N. H. 1952. *Vision with spatial inversion.* Wichita, Kansas: University of Wichita Press.

SNYDER, M., AND CUNNINGHAM, M. R. 1975. To comply or not comply: Testing the self-perception explanation of the "foot-in-the-door" phenomenon. *Journal of Personality and Social Psychology* 31:64–67.

SNYDER, S. H. 1974. *Madness and the brain.* New York: McGraw-Hill.

SNYDER, S. H. 1976. The dopamine hypothesis of schizophrenia. *American Journal of Psychiatry* 133:197–202.

SNYDER, S. H.; BANERJEE, S. P.; YAMAMURA, H. I.; AND GREENBERG, D. 1974. Drugs, neurotransmitters and schizophrenia. *Science* 184:1243–53.

SOLOMON, R. L. 1977. An opponent-process theory of acquired motivation: IV. The affective dynamics of addiction. In Maser, J. D., and Seligman, M. E. P., eds., *Psychopathology: Experimental models,* pp. 66–103. San Francisco: Freeman.

SOLOMON, R. L., AND CORBIT, J. D. 1974. An opponent-process theory of motivation: I. Temporal dynamics of affect. *Psychological Review* 81:119–45.

SOLOMON, R. L., AND WYNNE, L. C. 1953. Traumatic avoidance learning: Acquisition in normal dogs. *Psychological Monographs* 67 (Whole No. 354).

SPEARMAN, C. 1927. *The abilities of man.* London: Macmillan.

SPERLING, G. 1960. The information available in brief visual presentations. *Psychological Monographs* 74 (Whole No. 11).

SPIES, G. 1965. Food versus intracranial self-stimulation reinforcement in food deprived rats. *Journal of Comparative and Physiological Psychology* 60:153–57.

SPOONER, A., AND KELLOGG, W. N. 1947. The backward conditioning curve. *American Journal of Psychology* 60:321–34.

SROLE, L.; LANGNER, T. S.; MICHAEL, S. T.; OPLER, M. K.; AND RENNIE, T. A. C. 1962. *Mental health in the metropolis: The midtown Manhattan study.* New York: McGraw-Hill.

STADDON, J. E. R., AND SIMMELHAG, V. L. 1971. The "superstition" experiment: A re-examination of its implications for the principles of adaptive behavior. *Psychological Review* 78:3–43.

STAMPFL, T. G., AND LEVIS, D. J. 1967. Essentials of implosive therapy: A learning-theory-based psychodynamic behavior therapy. *Journal of Abnormal Psychology* 72:496–503.

STEIN, A. H.; FRIEDERICH, L. K.; AND VONDRACEK, F. 1972. Television content and young children's behavior. In Comstock, G. A., and Rubinstein, E. A., eds., *Television and social behavior,* vol. 2, pp. 202–317. Washington, D. C.: U. S. Government Printing Office.

STEIN, L. 1964. Reciprocal action of reward and punishment. In Heath, R. G., ed., *The role of pleasure in behavior.* New York: Hoeber.

STEIN, L., AND WISE, C. D. 1971. Possible etiology of schizophrenia: Progressive damage to the noradrenergic reward system by 6-hydroxydopamine. *Science* 171:1032–36.

STELLAR, E. 1954. The physiology of motivation. *Psychological Review* 61:5–22.

STEPHENS, J. H., AND ASTRUP, C. 1963. Prognosis in 'process' and 'non-process' schizophrenia. *American Journal of Psychiatry* 69:945–54.

STERNBERG, S. 1969. Memory-scanning: Mental processes revealed by reaction-time experiments. *American Scientist* 57:421–57.

STEVENS, S. S. 1955. The measurement of loudness. *Journal of the Acoustical Society of America* 27:815–19.

STEVENS, S. S. 1961a. The psychophysics of sensory function. In Rosenblith, W. A., ed., *Sensory communication*, pp. 1–33. Cambridge, Mass.: MIT Press.

STEVENS, S. S. 1961b. To honor Fechner and repeal his law. *Science* 133:80–86.

STEWART, K. 1951. Dream theory in Malaya. *Complex* 6:21–34.

STEWART, T. D. 1957. Stone age surgery: A general review, with emphasis on the New World. *Annual Review of the Smithsonian Institution.* Washington, D. C.: Smithsonian Institute.

STOKOE, W. C., JR. 1960. Sign language structure: An outline of the visual communication systems. *Studies in Linguistics Occasional Papers* 8.

STOKOE, W. C., JR.; CASTERLINE, D. C.; AND CRONEBERG, C. G. 1955. *A dictionary of American Sign Language on linguistic principles.* Washington, D. C.: Gallaudet College Press.

STOLLER, R. J. 1968. *Sex and gender: On the development of masculinity and femininity.* New York: Science House.

STONE, A. 1975. *Mental health and law: A system in transition.* U.S. Department of Health, Education and Welfare, #75176.

STRATTON, G. M. 1897. Vision without inversion of the retinal image. *Psychological Review* 4:341–60.

STREET, R. F. 1931. *A gestalt completion test.* New York: Teachers College, Columbia Univeristy.

STRICKER, E. M. 1973. Thirst, sodium appetite, and complementary physiological contributions to the regulation of intravascular fluid volume. In Epstein, A. N.; Kissilef, H. R.; and Stellar, E., eds., *The neurophysiology of thirst: New findings and advances in concepts.* Washington, D. C.: Winston.

STRICKER, E. M. 1976. Drinking by rats after lateral hypothalamic lesions: A new look at the lateral hypothalamic syndrome. *Journal of Comparative & Physiological Psychology* 90:127–43.

STRICKER, E. M. 1978. Hyperphagia. *The New England Journal of Medicine* 298:1010–13.

STRICKER, E. M., AND ZIGMOND, M. J. 1976. Recovery of function after damage to catecholamine-containing neurons: A neurochemical model for the lateral hypothalamic syndrome. In Sprague, J. M., and Epstein, A. N., eds., *Progress in psychobiology and physiological psychology,* vol. 6, pp. 121–88. New York: Academic Press.

STRODTBECK, F. L. 1958. Family interaction, values, and achievements. In McClelland, D. C.; Baldwin, A. L.; Bronfenbrenner, U.; and Strodtbeck, F. L., eds., *Talent and society.* Princeton, N. J.: Van Nostrand.

STROOP, J. R. 1935. Studies of interference in serial verbal reactions. *Journal of Experimental Psychology* 18:643–62.

STUNKARD, A. J. 1975. Obesity. In Freedman, A. M.; Kaplan, H. I.; and Sadock, B. J., eds., *Comprehensive textbook of psychiatry—II,* vol. 2. pp. 1648–54. Baltimore, Md.: Williams & Wilkins.

SULLIVAN, P. M., AND VERNON, M. 1979. Psychological assessment of hearing impaired children. *School Psychology Digest* 8(3):271–90. Boys Town Institute for Communication Disorders in Children.

SULS, J. M. 1972. A two-stage model for the appreciation of jokes and cartoons: An information processing analysis. In Goldstein, J. H., and McGhee, P. E., eds., *The psychology of humor,* pp. 81–100. New York: Academic Press.

SUNDBERG, N. D. 1977. *Assessment of persons.* New York: Prentice-Hall.

SUOMI, S. J.; HARLOW, H. F.; AND MCKINNEY, W. T. 1972. Monkey psychiatrist. *American Journal of Psychiatry* 128:41–46.

SUPALLA, T., AND NEWPORT, E. L. 1978. How many seats in a chair? The derivation of nouns and verbs in American Sign Language. In Siple, P., ed., *Understanding language through sign language research.* New York: Academic Press.

SZASZ, T. S. 1974. *The myth of mental illness: Foundations of a theory of personal conduct,* revised edition. New York: Harper & Row.

TEITELBAUM, P., AND EPSTEIN, A. N. 1962. The lateral hypothalamic syndrome: Recovery of feeding and drinking after lateral hypothalamic lesions. *Psychological Review* 69:74–90.

TEITELBAUM, P., AND STELLAR, E. 1954. Recovery from failure to eat produced by hypothalamic lesions. *Science* 120:894–95.

TERMAN, L. M., AND MERRILL, M. A. 1972. *Stanford-Binet intelligence scale—manual for the third revision,* form L-M. Boston: Houghton Mifflin.

TERRACE, H. S.; PETITTO, L. A.; SANDERS, D. L.; AND BEVER, T. G. 1979. Can an ape create a sentence? *Science* 206:891–902.

TERVOORT, B. T. 1961. Esoteric symbolism in the communication behavior of young deaf children. *American Annals of the Deaf* 106:436–80.

THEOPHRASTUS. 319 B.C. *The characters.* Translated by Edmonds, J. M. Cambridge, Mass.: Harvard University Press, 1929.

THIGPEN, C. H., AND CLECKLEY, H. M. 1957. *The three faces of Eve.* New York: McGraw-Hill.

THOMAS, A.; CHESS, S.; AND BIRCH, H. G. 1970. The origin of personality. *Scientific American* 223:102–9.

THOMPSON, N. L. AND MCCANDLESS, B. R. 1976. Homosexuality: Its antecedent conditions. In Davids, A., ed., *Child personality and psychopathology: Current topics,* vol. 3, pp. 157–197. New York: Wiley-Interscience.

THOMPSON, N. L.; MCCANDLESS, B. R.; AND STRICKLAND, B. R. 1971. Personal adjustment of male and female homosexuals and heterosexuals. *Journal of Abnormal and Social Psychology* 78:237–40.

THOMPSON, R. F. 1967. *Foundations of physiological psychology.* New York: Harper & Row.

THOMPSON, T., AND BLOOM, W. 1966. Aggressive behavior and extinction-induced response-rate increase. *Psychonomic Science* 5:535–36.

THORNDIKE, E. L. 1898. Animal intelligence: An experimental study of the associative processes in animals. *Psychological Monographs* 2(Whole No. 8).

THORNDIKE, E. L. 1899. The associative processes in animals. *Biological lectures from the Marine Biological Laboratory at Woods Hole.* Boston: Atheneum.

THORNDIKE, E. L. 1911. *Animal intelligence: Experimental studies.* New York: Macmillan.

THORNDIKE, E. L. 1931. *Human learning.* Cambridge, Mass.: MIT Press.

THORNDIKE, E. L., AND LORGE, I. 1944. *The teacher's word book of 30,000 words.* New York: Teachers College Press, Columbia University.

TINBERGEN, N. 1951. *The study of instinct.* Oxford, England: Clarendon.

TINBERGEN, N. 1952. The curious behavior of the stickleback. *Scientific American* 187:22–38.

TINBERGEN, N.; KRUUK, H.; AND PAILLETTE, M. 1962. Eggshell removal by the blackheaded gull, *Larus r. ridibundus:* II. *Bird Study* 9:123–31.

TINKLEPAUGH, O. L. 1928. An experimental study of representative factors in monkeys. *Journal of Comparative Psychology* 8:197–236.

TOLMAN, E. C. 1932. *Purposive behavior in animals and men.* New York: Century.

TOLMAN, E. C. 1948. Cognitive maps in rats and men. *Psychological Review* 55:189–208.

TOLMAN, E. C., AND GLEITMAN, H. 1949. Studies in learning and motivation: I. Equal reinforcements in both end-boxes, followed by shock in one end-box. *Journal of Experimental Psychology* 39:810–19.

TOLMAN, E. C., AND HONZIK, C. H. 1930. Introduction and removal of reward, and maze performance in rats. *University of California Publications in Psychology* 4:257–75.

TREISMAN, A. M. 1964. Selective attention in man. *British Medical Bulletin* 20:12–16.

TRIVERS, R. L. 1971. The evolution of reciprocal altruism. *Quarterly Review of Biology* 46:35–57.

TULVING, E. 1972. Episodic and semantic memory. In Tulving, E., and Donaldson, W., eds., *Organization and memory.* New York: Academic Press.

TULVING, E., AND PEARLSTONE, Z. 1966. Availability versus accessability of information in memory for words. *Journal of Verbal Learning and Verbal Behavior* 5:381–91.

TURNURE, J. E., AND THURLOW, M. L. 1973. Verbal elaboration and the promotion of transfer of training in educable mentally retarded children. *Journal of Experimental Child Psychology* 15:137–48.

TYLER, L. E. 1965. *The Psychology of human differences.* New York: Appleton-Century-Crofts.

UNDERWOOD, B. J., AND POSTMAN, L. 1960. Extra-experimental source of interference in forgetting. *Psychological Review* 67:73–95.

UNGERSTEDT, U., AND LJUNGBERG, T. 1974. Central dopamine neurons and sensory processing. *Journal of Psychiatry Research* 11:149–50.

VALENTA, J. G., AND RIGBY, M. K. 1968. Discrimination of the odor of stressed rats. *Science* 161:599–601.

VALINS, S. 1966. Cognitive effects of false heart-rate feedback. *Journal of Personality and Social Psychology* 4:400–408.

VERNON, P. E. 1950. *The structure of human abilities.* London: Methuen.

VERNON, P. E. 1964. *Personality assessment.* London: Methuen.

VERNON, P. E. 1970. *Creativity: Selected readings.* Baltimore, Md.: Penguin.

VERNON, M., AND BROWN, D. W. 1964. A guide to psychological tests and testing procedures in the evaluation of deaf and hard-of-hearing children. *Journal of Speech and Hearing Disorders* 29:414–23.

VERY, P. S. 1967. Differential factor structure in mathematical ability. *Genetic Psychology Monographs* 75:169–208.

VIATOR. 1505. *De Artifiali Perspectiva,* Toul 1505. In Ivins, W. M., Jr., *On the rationalization of sight.* New York: Da Capo, 1975.

VIERLING, J. S., AND ROCK, J. 1967. Variations of olfactory sensitivity to exaltolide during the menstrual cycle. *Journal of Applied Physiology* 22:311–15.

VON DOMARUS, E. 1944. The specific laws of logic in schizophrenia. In Kasanin, J., ed., *Language and thought in schizophrenia.* Berkeley, Calif.: University of California Press.

WACHTEL, P. L. 1977. *Psychoanalysis and behavior therapy: Toward an integration.* New York: Basic Books.

WALD, G. 1950. Eye and camera. *Scientific American* 183:32–41.

WALD, G. 1959. The photoreceptor process in vision. In Field, J.; Magoun, H. W.; and Hall, V. E., eds., *Handbook of physiology,* vol. 1, pp. 671–91. Washington, D. C.: American Physiological Society.

WALK, R. D., AND GIBSON, E. J. 1961. A comparative and analytical study of visual depth perception. *Psychological Monographs* 75(Whole No. 519).

WALLACE, R. R. 1970. Physiological effects of transcendental meditation. *Science* 167:1751–54.

WALLACE, R. K., AND BENSON, H. 1972. The physiology of meditation. *Scientific American* 226:84–90.

WALLACE, W. H.: TURNER, S. H.; AND PERKINS, C. C. 1957. Preliminary studies of human information storage. Philadelphia: Signal Corps Project No. 1320, Institute for Cooperative Research, University of Pennsylvania.

WALLACH, H. 1948. Brightness constancy and the nature of achromatic colors. *Journal of Experimental Psychology* 38:310–24.

WALLAS, G. 1926. *The art of thought.* New York: Harcourt, Brace.

WANNER, E., AND MARATSOS, M. 1978. An ATN approach to comprehension. In Halle, M.; Bresnan, J.; and Miller, G. A., eds., *Linguistic theory and psychological reality.* Cambridge, Mass.: MIT Press.

WARD, C. H.; BECK, A. T.; MENDELSON, M.; MOCK, J. E.; AND ERBAUGH, J. K. 1962. The psychiatric nomenclature: Reasons for diagnostic disagreement. *Archives for General Psychiatry* 7:198–205.

WASMAN, M., AND FLYNN, J. P. 1962. Directed attack elicited from the hypothalamus. *Archives of Neurology* 6:220–27.

WATSON, J. B. 1914. *Behavior, an introduction to comparative psychology.* New York: Holt.

WATSON, J. B. 1925. *Behaviorism.* New York: Norton.

WATSON, J. S. 1967. Memory and "contingency analysis" in infant learning. *Merrill-Palmer Quarterly* 13:55–76.

WEBB, W. B. 1972. Sleep deprivation: Total, partial, and selective. In Chase, M. H., ed., *The sleeping brain,* pp. 323–62. Los Angeles: Brain Information Service, Brain Research Institute.

WECHSLER, D. 1958. *The measurement and appraisal of adult intelligence,* 4th edition. Baltimore, Md.: Williams & Wilkins.

WEINER, H.; THALER, M.; REISER, M. F.; AND MIRSKY, I. A. 1957. Etiology of duodenal ulcer: I. Relation of specific psychological characteristics to rate of gastric secretion. *Psychosomatic Medicine* 19:1–10.

WEINSTEIN, S. 1968. Intensive and extensive aspects of tactile sensitivity as a function of body part, sex and laterality. In Kenshalo, D. R., ed., *The skin senses,* pp. 195–218. Springfield, Ill.: Thomas.

WEINSTOCK, S. 1954. Resistance to extinction of a running response following partial reinforcement under widely spaced trials. *Journal of Comparative and Physiological Psychology* 47:318–22.

WEISS, B., AND LATIES, V. G. 1961. Behavioral thermoregulation. *Science* 133:1338–44.

WEITZMAN, L. J.; EIFLEY, D.; HOKADA, E.; AND ROSS, C. 1972. Sex-role socialization in picture books for preschool children. *American Journal of Sociology* 77:1125–50.

WELKER, W. I.; JOHNSON, J. I.; AND PUBOLS, B. H. 1964. Some morphological and physiological characteristics of the somatic sensory system in raccoons. *American Zoologist* 4:75–94.

WENDER, P. H.; ROSENTHAL, D.; AND KETY, S. S. 1968. A psychiatric assessment of the adoptive parents of schizophrenics. In Rosenthal, D., and Kety, S. S., eds., *The transmission of schizophrenia,* pp. 235–50. New York: Pergamon.

WENGER, M. A.; JONES, F. N.; AND JONES, M. H. 1956. *Physiological psychology.* New York: Holt, Rinehart & Winston.

WERTHEIMER, M. 1912. Experimentelle Studien über das Gesehen von Bewegung. *Zeitschrift für Psychologie* 61:161–265.

WERTHEIMER, M. 1923. Untersuchungen zur Lehre von der Gestalt, II. *Psychologische Forschung* 4:301–350.

WERTHEIMER, M. 1945. *Productive Thinking.* New York: Harper.

WERTHEIMER, MICHAEL 1961. Psychomotor coordination of auditory and visual space at birth. *Science* 134:1692.

WEXLER, K., AND CULICOVER, P. 1980. *Formal principles of language acquisition.* Cambridge, Mass.: MIT Press.

WHEELER, L. R. 1942. A comparative study of the intelligence of East Tennessee mountain children. *Journal of Educational Psychology* 33:321–34.

WHITE, R. W. 1956. *The abnormal personality,* 2nd edition. New York: Ronald Press.

WHITE, R. W. 1959. Motivation reconsidered: The concepts of competence. *Psychological Review* 66:297–333.

WHITE, R. W., AND WATT, N. F. 1973. *The abnormal personality,* 4th edition. New York: Ronald Press.

WHITE, W. A. 1932. *Outlines of psychiatry,* 13th edition. New York: Nervous and Mental Disease Publishing Co.

WICKENS, D. D. 1938. Transference of conditioned excitation and conditioned inhibition from one muscle group to the antagonistic muscle group. *Journal of Experimental Psychology* 22:101–123

WILCOXIN, H. C.; DRAGOIN, W. B.; AND KRAL, P. A. 1971. Illness-induced aversions in rat and quail: Relative salience of visual and gustatory cues. *Science* 171:826–28.

WILKINSON, R. T. 1961. Effects of sleep deprivation on performance and muscle tension. In CIBA Foundation, *The nature of sleep.* Boston: Little, Brown.

WILLIAMS, C. D. 1959. The elimination of tantrum behavior by extinction procedures. *Journal of Abnormal and Social Psychology* 59:269.

WILLIAMS, D. R., AND WILLIAMS, H. 1969. Automaintenance in the pigeon: Sustained pecking despite contingent non-reinforcement. *Journal of the Experimental Analysis of Behavior* 12:511–20.

WILLIAMS, G. C. 1966. *Adaptation and natural selection.* Princeton, N. J.: Princeton University Press.

WILLIAMS, H. L.; LUBIN, A.; AND GOODNOW, J. J. 1959. Impaired performance with acute sleep loss. *Psychological Monographs* 73 (No. 14).

WILLIAMS, H. L.; TEPAS, D. I.; AND MORLOCK, H. C. 1962. Evoked responses to clicks and electroencephalographic stages of sleep in man. *Science* 138:685–86.

WILLIAMSON, S. 1979. *Tamil baby talk: A cross-cultural study.* Unpublished Ph.D. dissertation, University of Pennsylvania.

WILSON, E. O. 1975. *Sociobiology.* Cambridge, Mass.: Harvard University Press.

WILTON, K. M., AND BOERSMA, F. J. 1974. Conservation research with the mentally retarded. In Ellis, N. R., *International review of research in mental retardation,* vol. 7, pp. 114–45. New York: Academic Press.

WINCH, R. F., AND MORE, D. M. 1956. Does TAT add information to interviews? Statistical analysis of the increment. *Journal of Clinical Psychology* 12:316–21.

WISHNER, J. 1960. Reanalysis of "impressions of personality." *Psychological Review* 67:96–112.

WISHNER, J. 1974. *Psychopathology: Defective concept or defective practice?* Invited address delivered at the XVIII International Congress of Applied Psychology, Montreal, Canada.

WITTGENSTEIN, L. 1953. *Philosophical Investigations.* Translated by Anscombe, G. E. M. Oxford, England: Blackwell.

WOHLWILL, J. F. 1973. *The study of behavioral development.* New York: Academic Press.

WOLF, S. 1971. Psychosocial influences in gastrointestinal function. In Levi, L., ed., *The psychosocial environment and psychosomatic disease,* vol. 1, 362–68. London: Oxford University Press.

WOLLEN, K. A.; WEBER, A.; AND LOWRY, D. 1972. Bizarreness versus interaction of mental images as determinants of learning. *Cognitive Psychology* 3:518–23.

WOLPE, J. 1958. *Psychotherapy by reciprocal inhibition.* Stanford, Calif.: Stanford University Press.

WOLPE, J., AND LAZARUS, A. A. 1966. *Behavior therapy techniques: A guide to the treatment of neuroses.* Elmsford, N. Y.: Pergamon.

WOLPE, J., AND LAZARUS, A. A. 1969. *The practice of behavior therapy.* New York: Pergamon.

WOLPERT, E. A., AND TROSMAN, H. 1958. Studies in psychophysiology of dreams: I. Experimental evocation of sequential dream episodes. *Archives of Neurology and Psychiatry* 79:603–6.

WOMEN ON WORDS AND IMAGES. 1972. *Dick and Jane as victims: Sex stereotyping in children's readers.* Princeton, N. J.: Women on Words and Images.

WOODS, R. L. 1947. *The world of dreams: An anthology.* New York: Random House.

WOODWORTH, R. S. 1938. *Experimental psychology.* New York: Holt.

WOOLSEY, C. N. 1961. Organization of cortical auditory system. In Rosenblith, W. A., ed., *Sensory communication,* pp. 235–58. New York: Wiley.

WYNNE, L. C., AND SINGER, M. T. 1963a. Thought disorder and family relations in schizophrenics: I. A research strategy. *Archives of General Psychiatry* 9:191–98.

WYNNE, L. C., AND SINGER, M. T. 1963b. Thought disorder and family relations of schizophrenics: II. Classification of forms of thinking. *Archives of General Psychiatry* 9:199–206.

WYRWICKA, W.; DOBRZECKA, C.; AND TARNECKI, R. 1959. On the instrumental conditioned reaction evoked by electrical stimulation of the hypothalamus. *Science* 130:336–37.

YAGI, N. 1927. Phototropism of *Dixippus murosus. Journal of General Physiology* 11:297–300.

YARBUS, A. L. 1965. Eye movements and vision. Translated by Riggs, L. A. New York: Plenum Press, 1967.

YATES, F. A. 1966. *The art of memory.* Chicago: University of Chicago Press.

YEE, A. H. 1968. Source and direction of causal influence in teacher-pupil relationships. *Journal of Educational Psychology* 59:275–82.

ZAHN, T. P., ROSENTHAL, D., AND SHAKOW, D. 1963. Reaction time in schizophrenic and normal subjects in relation to the sequence of series of regular preparatory intervals. *Journal of Abnormal and Social psychology* 67:44–52.

ZENER, K. 1937. The significance of behavior accompanying conditioned salivary secretion for theories of the conditioned response. *American Journal of Psychology* 50:384–403.

ZENTALL, T., AND HOGAN, D. 1974. Abstract concept learning in the pigeon. *Journal of Experimental Psychology* 102: 393–98.

ZIEGLER, F. J.; IMBODEN, J. B.; AND RODGERS, D. A. 1963. Contemporary conversion reactions: III. Diagnostic considerations. *Journal of the American Medical Association* 186:307–311.

ZIGLER, E. 1967. Familial mental retardation: A continuing dilemma. *Science* 155:292–98.

ZIGLER, E., AND CHILD, I. L. 1969. Socialization. In Lindzey, G., and Aronson, E., eds., *The handbook of social psychology,* vol. 3, pp. 450–589. Reading, Mass.: Addison-Wesley.

ZIGLER, E., AND CHILD, I. L. 1972. *Socialization and personality development.* Reading, Mass.: Addison-Wesley.

ZILBOORG, G., AND HENRY, G. W. 1941. *A history of medical psychology.* New York: Norton.

ZOBRIST, A. L., AND CARLSON, F. R., JR. 1973. Advice taking chess-computer. *Scientific American* 228:92–105

ZUBIN, J. 1954. Failures of the Rorschach technique. *Journal of Projective Techniques* 18:303–315.

ZUBIN, J.; ERON, L. D.; AND SHUMER, F. 1965. *An experimental approach to projective techniques.* New York: Wiley.

ZUCKERMAN, C. B., AND ROCK, I. 1957. A reappraisal of the roles of past experience and innate organizing processes in visual perception. *Psychological Bulletin* 54:269–96.

ZUK, C. H. 1958. The plasticity of the physique from early adolescence through adulthood. *Journal of Genetic Psychology* 92:205–214.

ZURIF, E. B., AND BLUMSTEIN, S. E. 1978. Language and the brain. In Halle, M.; Bresnan, J.; and Miller, G. A. *Linguistic theory and psychological reality,* pp. 229–46. Cambridge, Mass.: MIT Press.

Acknowledgments

FIGURES

1.1 Dethier, V. G., *The hungry fly*. Cambridge, Mass.: Harvard University Press, 1976. Adapted by permission of Harvard University Press. 1.2 Dethier, V. G., "The hungry fly," in *Readings in psychology today,* p. 108. Del Mar, Calif.: CRM Books, 1972. In turn reprinted from *Nebraska Symposium on Motivation,* 1966. Adapted by permission of V. G. Dethier. 1.4 and 1.5 Bugelski, B. R., and Alampan, D. A., "The role of frequency in developing perceptual sets," *Canadian Journal of Psychology* 15 (1961):205–211. Adapted by permission of the Canadian Psychological Association. 1.6B Dement, W. C., *Some must watch while some must sleep.* New York: W. W. Norton & Company, Inc., 1974. Illustration is produced with the permission of W. W. Norton & Company, Inc. Copyright © 1972, 1974, 1976 by William C. Dement. 1.7C Kleitman, N., "Patterns of dreaming," *Scientific American* 203 (November 1960):84–85. In turn reprinted from electroencephalograms by William C. Dement. Adapted by permission of William C. Dement.

2.3 Reprinted from *Animals without backbones* by Buchsbaum, R. M., by permission of The University of Chicago Press. Copyright © 1948 by The University of Chicago Press. Also 2.3 Keeton, W. T., *Biological science,* 3rd edition. New York: W. W. Norton & Company, Inc., 1980. Copyright © 1980, 1979, 1972, 1967 by W. W. Norton & Company, Inc. 2.6A Katz, B., "The nerve impulse," *Scientific American* 187 (November 1952):164–65. 2.7 Morgan, C., *Physiological psychology.* New York: McGraw-Hill, 1965. In turn adapted from Evans, C. L., *Starling's principles of human physiology.* Edinburgh, Scotland: Churchill & Livingston, Publishers, 1945. Adapted by permission. 2.8A Eccles, J. C., *The understanding of the brain.* New York: McGraw-Hill, 1973. Adapted by permission of the publisher. 2.8C Keynes, R. D., "The nerve impulse and the squid," *Scientific American* 199 (December 1958):84. Copyright © 1958 by Scientific American, Inc. All rights reserved. 2.9 Thompson, R. F., *Foundations of physiological psychology.* New York: Harper & Row, Inc., 1967. In turn reprinted from Hodgkin, A. L., and Huxley,

A. F., "Action potentials recorded from inside nerve fiber," *Nature* 144 (1939):710–11. Adapted by permission of the author and *Nature*. 2.11 Eccles, J. C., *The understanding of the brain.* New York: McGraw-Hill, Inc., 1973. Adapted by permission of the publisher. 2.12 Sherrington, C. S., *The integrative action of the nervous system.* New Haven, Conn.: Yale University Press, 1961. Adapted by permission of the publisher. 2.17 Roeder, D., *Nerve cells and insect behavior,* p. 198. Cambridge, Mass.: Harvard University Press, 1967. Adapted by permission of Harvard University Press. 2.18 Eccles, J., "The synapse," *Scientific American* 212 (January 1965):56. 2.19 Reprinted from *Animals without backbones* by Buchsbaum, R. M., by permission of The University of Chicago Press. Copyright © 1948 by The University of Chicago Press. 2.20 Keeton, W. T., *Biological science,* 3rd edition. New York: W. W. Norton & Company, 1980. Copyright © 1980, 1979, 1972, 1967 by W. W. Norton & Company, Inc. 2.21 Morgan, C. T., *Physiological psychology,* 3rd edition, p. 40. New York: McGraw-Hill, 1965. In turn adapted from Lickley, J. D., *The nervous system.* New York: Longman, Inc., 1919. Adapted by permission. 2.22B Keeton, W. T., *Biological science,* 3rd edition. New York: W. W. Norton & Company, Inc., 1980. Copyright © 1980, 1979, 1972, 1967 by W. W. Norton & Company, Inc. 2.23 Gray, G. W., "The great ravelled knot," *Scientific American* 179 (October 1948):28–29. 2.24 Thompson, R. F., *Foundations of physiological psychology,* p. 534. New York: Harper & Row, Inc., 1967. Adapted by permission. 2.25 and 2.26 Reprinted with permission of Macmillan Publishing Co., Inc. from *The cerebral cortex of man* by Wilder Penfield and Theodore Rasmussen. Copyright © 1950 by Macmillan Publishing Co., Inc., renewed 1978 by Theodore Rasmussen. 2.27 Morgan, C., *Physiological psychology.* New York: McGraw-Hill, 1965. Reprinted by permission of the publisher. In turn adapted from Cobb, S., *Foundations of psychiatry.* Baltimore, Md.: The Williams & Wilkins Co., 1941. Adapted by permission. 2.28 Thompson, R. F., *Introduction to biopsychology,* p. 7. San Francisco, Calif.: Albion Publishing Company, 1973. Adapted by permission of the publisher. 2.29 Luria, A. R., *Higher cortical functions in man.* New York: Basic Books, Inc., Publishers, 1966. Adapted by permission of the publisher and Tavistock Press, London. 2.32 Gazzaniga, M. S., "The split brain in man," *Scientific American* 217 (August 1967):25. 2.33 Levy, J., Trevarthen, C., and Sperry, R. W., "Perception of chimerical figures following hemispheric disconnection," *Brain* 95 (1972):70. Adapted by permission of Macmillan Journals Ltd. 2.34 After figure "Space Relations" (p. 354) from *Essentials of psychological testing,* 3rd edition, by Lee J. Cronbach. Copyright © 1949 by Harper & Row, Publishers, Inc. Copyright © 1960, 1970 by Lee J. Cronbach. Reprinted by permission of the publisher. 2.35 Geschwind, N., "Language and the brain," *Scientific American* 226 (April 1972):80.

3.5 Keeton, W. T., *Biological science,* 2nd edition. New York: W. W. Norton & Company, Inc., 1972. Copyright © 1972, 1967 by W. W. Norton & Company, Inc. 3.6 Keeton, W. T., *Biological science,* 3rd edition. New York: W. W. Norton & Company, Inc., 1980. Copyright © 1980, 1979, 1972, 1967 by W. W. Norton & Company, Inc. 3.8 Cannon, W. B., *Bodily changes in pain, hunger, fear and rage,* revised edition. New York: Appleton-Century, 1929. Adapted by permission of Elsevier/Nelson Books. 3.10B Inbau, F. E., and Reid, J. E., *Lie detection and criminal investigation.* Baltimore, Md.: The Williams & Wilkins Company, 1953. 3.11 Keeton, W. T., *Biological science,* 3rd edition. New York: W. W. Norton & Company, Inc., 1980. Copyright © 1980, 1979, 1972, 1967 by W. W. Norton & Company, Inc. 3.12 Data in diagram form from "Infants' responses to strangers during the first year" by Morgan, G. A., and Ricciuti, H. N., in *Determinants of infant behavior,* vol. IV, edited by Foss, B. M. New York: Methuen and Company Ltd., 1969. Copyright © 1969 by Tavistock Institute of Human Relations. 3.13 French, J. D., "The reticular formation," *Scientific American* 196 (May 1957):55. 3.15 Guyton, A. C., *Textbook of medical physiology.* Philadelphia, Pa.: W. B. Saunders Company, 1966. Adapted by permission of the publisher. 3.16 Kleitman, N., "Patterns of dreaming," *Scientific American* 203 (November 1960):82–88. In turn reprinted from electroencephalograms by William C. Dement. Adapted by permission of William C. Dement. 3.17B Kleitman, N., "Patterns of dreaming," *Scientific American* 203 (November 1960):82–88. 3.17C From Kleitman, N., "Patterns of Dreaming," *Scientific American* 203 (November 1960):88. Copyright © 1960 by Scientific American, Inc. All rights reserved. 3.18 Data from "Active (REM) sleep deprivation" by Cohen, H., in *The sleeping brain: Perspectives in the brain sciences,* vol. I, edited by Chase, M. H., pp. 343–347. Berkeley, Calif.: University of California Press. Adapted by permission of the publisher. 3.20 Hart, B. L., *Experimental neuropsychology.* San Francisco. Calif.: W. H. Freeman, 1969. Adapted by permission. 3.21B Teitelbaum, P., "Sensory control of hypothalamic hyperphagia," *Journal of Comparative and Physiological Psychology* 48 (1955):156–63. Copyright 1955 by the American Psychological Association. Reprinted by permission. 3.22 Nisbett, R. E., "Taste, deprivation and weight determinants of eating behavior," *Journal of Personality and Social Psychology* 10 (1968):107–116. Copyright 1968 by the American Psychological Association. Reprinted by permission. 3.23 Harlow, H. F., "Learning and satiation of response in intrinsically motivated complex puzzle performance in monkeys," *Journal of Comparative and Physiological Psychology* 43 (1950):289–94.

4.1 Yerkes, R. M., and Morgulis, S., "Method of Pavlov in animal psychology," *Physiological Bulletin* 6 (1909):264. 4.3 Anrep, G. V., "Pitch discrimination in the dog," *Journal of Physiology* 53 (1920):367–85. 4.3B Smith, M. C., DiLollo, V., and Gormezano, I., "Conditioned jaw movements in the rabbit," *Journal of Comparative and Physiological Psychology* 62 (1966):479–83. Copyright 1966 by

the American Psychological Association. Reprinted by permission. 4.5 Spooner, A., and Kellogg, W. N., "The backward conditioning curve," *American Journal of Psychology* 60 (1947):321–34. 4.6 Pavlov, I. P., *Lectures on conditioned reflexes,* vol. I. New York: International Publishers Co., Inc., 1928. Adapted by permission of International Publishers Co., Inc. 4.7 Bass, M. J., and Hull, C. L., "The irradiation of tactile conditioned reflex in man," *Journal of Comparative Psychology* 17 (1934):47–65. 4.8 Thorndike, E. L., *Animal intelligence: Experimental studies.* New York: Macmillan, 1911. 4.9 Thorndike, E. L., "Animal intelligence: An experimental study of the associative processes in animals," *Psychological Monographs* 2 (1898):Whole No. 8. 4.12 Ralph Gerbrands Company, Arlington, Mass. Reprinted by permission. 4.15 Perin, C. T., "A quantitative investigation of the delay of reinforcement gradient," *Journal of Experimental Psychology* 32 (1943):37–51. 4.16 Hull, C. L., "The rat's speed of locomotion gradient in the approach to food," *Journal of Comparative and Physiological Psychology* 17 (1934):393–422. 4.17 Miller, N. E., "Experimental studies of conflict," in Hunt, J. McV., ed., *Personality and the behavior disorders,* pp. 431–65. Ronald Press, 1944. Adapted by permission of N. E. Miller. 4.18 Wickens, D. D., "Transference of conditioned excitation and conditioned inhibition from one muscle group to the antagonistic muscle group," *Journal of Experimental Psychology* 22:101–123. 4.20C and D Skinner, B. F., *The Behavior of organisms: An experimental analysis,* © 1938, renewed 1966, pp. 67, 79. Reprinted by permission of Prentice-Hall, Inc., Englewood Cliffs, N. J. 4.22, 4.23 and 4.24 Ferster. C. B., and Skinner, B. F., *Schedules of reinforcement,* © 1957, pp. 56, 146, 399. Reprinted by permission of Prentice-Hall, Inc., Englewood Cliffs, N. J. 4.25 Weinstock, S., "Resistance to extinction of a running response following partial reinforcement under widely spaced trials," *Journal of Comparative and Physiological Psychology* 47 (1954):318–22. Copyright 1954 by the American Psychological Association. Reprinted by permission. 4.26 From *A primer of operant conditioning* by G. S. Reynolds. Copyright © 1968 by Scott, Foresman and Company. Reprinted by permission. 4.27A DiCara, L. V., "Learning in the automatic nervous system," *Scientific American* 222 (January 1970):33. 4.27B From DiCara, L. V., "Learning in the automatic nervous system," *Scientific American* 222 (January 1970):34. Copyright © 1970 by Scientific American, Inc. All rights reserved. 4.28 Ayllon, T., "Intensive treatment of psychotic behavior by stimulus satiation and food reinforcement," *Behavior Research and Therapy* 1 (1963):53–61. Adapted by permission.

5.4 Gleitman, H., "Place-learning," *Scientific American* 209 (October 1963):116–22. 5.5 Tolman, E. C., and Gleitman, H., "Studies in learning and motivation," *Journal of Experimental Psychology* 39 (1949):810–819. 5.6 Tolman, E. C., and Honzik, C. H., "Introduction and removal of reward, and maze performance in rats," *University of California Publications in Psychology* 4 (1930):257–75. 5.7 Data from Crespi, L. P., "Quantitative variation of incentive and performance in the white rat," *American Journal of Psychology* 55 (1942): 467–519. Copyright © 1942 by The University of Illinois Press. 5.8 and 5.9 Solomon, R. L., and Wynne, L. C., "Traumatic avoidance learning: Acquisition in normal dogs," *Psychological Monographs* 67 (1953): Whole No. 354. 5.11 Maier, S. F., Seligman, M. E. P., and Solomon, R. L., "Pavlovian fear conditioning and learned helplessness: Effects on escape and avoidance behavior of (a) the CS-US contingency and (b) the independence of the US and voluntary responding," in Campbell, B. A., and Church, R. M., ed., *Punishment and aversive behavior,* © 1969, p. 328. Adapted by permission of Prentice-Hall, Inc., Englewood Cliffs, N.J. 5.15 and 5.16 Harlow, H. F., "The formation of learning sets," *Psychological Review* 56 (1949):51–65. Adapted by permission. 5.17C and 5.18 Premack, A. J., and Premack, D., "Teaching language to an ape," *Scientific American* 227 (October 1972):93. 5.20 and 5.21 Premack, A. J., *Why chimps can read.* New York: Harper &

Row, 1976. Copyright © 1976 by Ann J. Premack. Reprinted by permission of Harper & Row, Publishers, Inc. 5.22 Premack, A. J., and Premack, D., "Teaching language to an ape," *Scientific American* 227 (October 1972):92–99. 5.23 Premack, D., and Woodruff, G., "Chimpanzee problem-solving: A test for comprehension," *Science* 202 (3 November 1978):533–534. Copyright 1978 by the American Association for the Advancement of Science.
6.1 Coren, S., Porac, C., and Ward, L., *Sensation and perception.* New York: Academic Press, 1978. Adapted by permission of the author and publisher. 6.3A Krech, D., and Crutchfield, R., *Elements of psychology.* New York: Knopf, Inc., 1958. Adapted by permission of Hilda Krech. 6.3B Conrad G. Mueller, *Sensory psychology,* © 1965, p. 106. Reprinted by permission of Prentice-Hall, Inc., Englewood Cliffs, N.J. 6.4 Schiffman, H. R., *Sensation and perception: An integrated approach.* New York: Wiley & Sons, Inc., 1976. Adapted by permission of the publisher. 6.5 Boring, E. G., *Sensation and perception in the history of experimental psychology,* p. 452. New York: Appleton-Century-Crofts, 1942. Adapted by permission of Mrs. Edwin G. Boring. 6.6 From Weinstein, S., "Intensive and extensive aspects of tactile sensitivity as a function of body part, sex and laterality," in Kenshalo, D. R., ed., *The skin senses,* pp. 195–218, 1968. Courtesy of Charles C. Thomas, Publisher, Springfield, Illinois. 6.7 Boring, E. G., Langfeld, H. S., and Weld, H. P., *Introduction to psychology,* pp. 613, 617. New York: Wiley & Sons, Inc., 1939. Adapted by permission. 6.8 Geldard, F. A., *The human senses,* p. 444. New York: Wiley & Sons, Inc., 1972. Adapted by permission. 6.9 *The senses considered as perceptual systems* by James J. Gibson. Copyright © 1966 by James J. Gibson. Reprinted by permission of Houghton Mifflin Company. 6.10 Thompson, R. F., *Introduction to biopsychology.* San Raphael, Calif.: Albion Publishing Company, 1973. Adapted by permission of the publisher. 6.11 Boring, E. G., Langfeld, H. S., and Weld, H. P., *Introduction to psychology,* p. 565. New York: Wiley & Sons, Inc., 1939. Adapted by permission. 6.12, 6.13A and 6.14A Lindsay, P. H., and Norman, D. A., *Human information processing,* 2nd ed., pp. 126, 133, and 136. New York: Academic Press, 1977. Adapted by permission of author and publisher. 6.13B and 6.14B Corem, S., Porac, C., and Ward, L. M., *Sensation and perception,* pp. 103, 105. New York: Academic Press, 1978. Adapted by permission of the author and publisher. 6.15 Wald, G., "Eye and camera," *Scientific American* 183 (August 1950):33. 6.16, 6.17, 6.18, and 6.20 Cornsweet, T. M., *Visual perception.* New York: Academic Press, 1970. Adapted by permission of the author and publisher. 6.19 Hecht, S., and Shlaer, S., "An adaptometer for measuring human dark adaptation," *Journal of the Optical Society of America* 28(1938):269–75. Adapted by permission. 6.21 Alpern, M., Lawrence, M., and Wolsk, D., *Sensory processes,* p. 28. Monterey, Calif.: Brooks College Publishing Company, 1967. Adapted by permission of the publisher. 6.22 Pritchard, R. N., "Stablized images on the retina," *Scientific American* 204 (June 1961):73. 6.24 Hering, E., *Outlines of a theory of the light sense,* Hurvich, L. M., and Jameson, D., pp. 150–51. Cambridge, Mass.: Harvard University Press, 1920, 1964. Adapted by permission of Harvard University Press. 6.25 Coren, S., Porac, C., and Ward, L. M., *Sensation and perception,* p. 155. New York: Academic Press, 1978. Adapted by permission of the author and publisher. Also 6.25 Cornsweet T. M., *Visual perception,* p. 276. New York: Academic Press, 1970. Adapted by permission of the author and publisher. 6.26 Schiffman, H., *Sensation and perception.* New York: Wiley and Sons, Inc., 1976. Adapted by permission of the publisher. 6.27 Kuffler, S. W., "Discharge pattern and functional organization of mammalian retina," *Journal of Neurophysiology* 16(1953):37–68. Adapted by permission. 6.41A and 6.41B ·Braun, J., and Linder, D., *Psychology today: An introduction,* 4th ed., p. 279. New York: Random House, Inc., 1979. Copyright © 1975, 1979 by Random House, Inc. Reprinted by permission of the publisher. 6.42 MacNichol, E. F., "Three-pigment color vision," *Scientific American* 211 (December 1964):49. 6.43 Hurvich, L.

M., and Jameson, D., "An opponent-process theory of color vision," *Psychological Review* 64 (1957):384–404. Copyright 1957 by the American Psychological Association. Reprinted by permission. 6.45 DeValois, R. L., and DeValois, K. K., *Neural coding of color,* in Carterette, E. C., and Friedman, M. P., eds., *Handbook of perception,* vol. 5, New York: Academic Press, 1975. Adapted by permission of the author and the publisher. 6.47 Guilford, J. P., *Psychometric methods,* p. 38, Figure 2.90. New York: McGraw-Hill, Inc., 1954. Adapted by permission of the publisher. 6.48 Reprinted from Stevens, S. S., "The psychophysics of sensory function," in Rosenblith, W. A., ed., *Sensory communication,* p. 11, by permission of the MIT Press, Cambridge, Massachusetts. Copyright © 1961 by the Massachusetts Institute of Technology.

7.7 Kohler, W., *Gestalt psychology.* New York: Liveright Publishing Company, 1947. Adapted by permission. 7.12 Koffka, K., *Principles of Gestalt psychology,* p. 185. New York: Harcourt Brace Jovanovich, Inc., 1935. Adapted by permission of the publisher and Routledge & Kegan Paul Ltd. 7.14 Julian E. Hochberg, *Perception,* 2nd ed., © 1978, p. 56. Reprinted by permission of Prentice-Hall, Inc., Englewood Cliffs, N.J. 7.19A, 7.20A and B *The perception of the visual world* by James J. Gibson. Copyright © 1950, renewed 1978, by James J. Gibson. Reprinted by permission of Houghton Mifflin Company. 7.21 Hudson, W., "Pictorial depth perception in sub-cultural groups in Africa," *Journal of Social Psychology* 52 (1960):186. Adapted by permission of the publisher. 7.22 Coren, S., Porac, C., and Ward, L. M., *Sensation and perception,* p. 225. New York: Academic Press, 1978. Adapted by permission of the author and the publisher. 7.23 *The perception of the visual world* by James J. Gibson. Copyright © 1950, renewed 1978, by James J. Gibson. Reprinted by permission of Houghton Mifflin Company. 7.25 Dunker, K., "Uber induzierte Bewegung," *Psychologische Forschung* 12 (1929):180–259. Adapted by permission of Springer-Verlag New York, Inc. 7.28 Salapatek, P., "Pattern perception in early infancy," in Cohen, L. B., and Salapatek, P., eds., *Infant perception: From sensation to cognition,* vol. 1, pp. 133–248. New York: Academic Press, 1975. Adapted by permission of the author and the publisher. 7.29 Hubel, D. H., "The visual cortex of the brain," *Scientific American* 209 (November 1963):54-8. 7.32 Held, R., "Plasticity in sensory-motor systems," *Scientific American* 213 (November 1965):85. 7.34 Julian Hochberg, "Attention, organization, and consciousness," in *Attention: Contemporary theory and analysis,* David Mostofsky, ed., © 1970, p. 115. Reprinted by permission of Prentice-Hall, Inc., Englewood Cliffs, N.J. 7.35 Gibson, J. J., and Gibson, E. J., "Perceptual learning: Differentiation or enrichment?" *Psychological Review* 62 (1955):32–41. Copyright 1955 by the American Psychological Association. Reprinted by permission. 7.39 Selfridge, O. G., "Pattern recognition and modern computers," in *Proceedings of Western Joint Computer Conference,* Los Angeles, Calif., 1955. Adapted by permission of the author. 7.40 Reprinted with permission of Macmillan Publishing Co., Inc. from *An introduction to perception* by Irvin Rock. Copyright © 1975, Irvin Rock. 7.43 *The perception of the visual world* by James J. Gibson. Copyright © 1950, renewed 1978, by James J. Gibson. Reprinted by permission of Houghton Mifflin Company. 7.45 Bower, T. G. R., "The visual world of infants," *Scientific American* 215 (December 1966):80–92. 7.46A and B Kaufman, L., and Rock, I., "The moon illusion," *Scientific American* 207 (July 1962):128. 7.46C Rock, I., and Kaufman, L., "The moon illusion II," *Science* 136 (June 1962):1023–31, Figure 22. Copyright 1962 by the American Association for the Advancement of Science. 7.47 Gregory, R. L., "Visual illusions," *Scientific American* 219 (November 1968):67, 68, and 70. 7.48A Gregory, R. L., "Visual illusions," *Scientific American* 219 (November 1968):70.

8.1 Sperling, G., "The information available in brief visual presentations," *Psychological Monographs* 74 (1960):(Whole No. 11). Copyright 1960 by the American Psychological Association. Reprinted by permission.   8.2   Peterson, L. B., and Peterson, M. J., "Short-term retention of individual items," *Journal of Experimental Psychology* 58 (1959):193–98. Copyright 1959 by the American Psychological Association. Reprinted by permission.   8.3   Murdock, B., "The serial position effect of free recall," *Journal of Experimental Psychology* 64 (1962):482–488. Copyright 1962 by the American Psychological Association. Reprinted by permission.   8.4   Glanzer, M., and Cunitz, A., "Two storage mechanisms in free recall," *Journal of Verbal Learning and Verbal Behavior* 5 (1966):351–60. Adapted by permission of the author and Academic Press, New York.   8.5   Murdock, B., "The serial position effect of free recall," *Journal of Experimental Psychology* 64 (1962):483–88. Copyright 1962 by the American Psychological Association. Reprinted by permission.   8.8   Sternberg, S., "Memory scanning: Mental processes revealed by reaction time experiments," in Antrobus, J. S., *Cognition and affect,* pp. 13–58. Boston, Mass.: Little, Brown & Company, 1970. Adapted by permission of Saul Sternberg.   8.9   Chrover, L., "Discussion of the effects of electroconvulsive shock on performance and memory," in Kimble, D. P., ed., *The anatomy of memory,* pp. 253–263. Palo Alto, Calif.: Science & Behavior Books, 1965. Adapted by permission of the publisher. 8.10 and 8.11 Ebbinghaus, H., *Memory,* p. 47. New York: Dover Publications, 1964. Originally published in 1885. Adapted by permission of the publisher.   8.12   Mandler, G., "Organization and memory," in Spence, K. W., and Spence, J. T., eds., *The psychology of learning and motivation,* vol. 1, pp. 327–372. Adapted by permission of the author and the publisher.   8.14   Bartlett, F. C., *Remembering,* p. 180. Cambridge, England: Cambridge University Press, 1932. Adapted by permission of the publisher.   8.16   Bower, G. H., "Analysis of a mnemonic device," *American Scientist* 58:496–510. 8.17   Gleitman, H., and Steinman, F., "Depression effect as a function of retention interval before and after shift in reward magnitude," *Journal of Comparative and Physiological Psychology* 57 (1964):158–60. Copyright 1964 by the American Psychological Association. Reprinted by permission.   8.19   Collins, A. M., and Quillian, M. R., "Retrieval time from semantic memory," *Journal of Verbal Learning and Verbal Behavior* 8 (1969):240–47. Adapted by permission of the author and Academic Press, New York.   8.21   Kosslyn, S. M., "Scanning and visual images: Some structural implications," *Perception and Psychophysics* 14 (1973):90–94. Adapted by permission of the author and the Psychonomic Society, Inc.

9.4   Bryan, W. L., and Harter, N., "Studies of the telegraphic language. The acquisition of a hierarchy of habits," *Psychology Review* 6 (1899):345–75.   9.7 and 9.8   Scheerer, M., "Problem-solving," *Scientific American* 208 (April 1963):119, 124, and 126. 9.9   Cohen, J., *Thinking (from the Eyewitness Series in Psychology),* pp. 28–29. Chicago: Rand McNally, 1971. Adapted by permission of the author.   9.10 and 9.11   Duncker, K., "On problem solving," *Psychological Monographs* (1945):(Whole No. 270) 1–113. 9.12   Hearst, E., "Psychology across the chessboard," in *Readings in psychology today,* 2nd ed., p. 24. DelMar, Calif.: CRM Books, 1972. Reprinted by permission of CRM Books, a division of Random House, Inc.   9.13   After Figure 73 (p. 109) from *Productive thinking,* enlarged edition, edited by Max Wertheimer and Michael Wertheimer. Copyright © 1945, 1959 by Valentin Wertheimer. Reprinted by permission of the publisher.   9.15, 9.16, and 9.17   Luchins, A. S., "Mechanization in problem-solving: The effect of Einstellung," *Psychological Monographs* 54 (1942):(Whole No. 248).   9.18, 9.19A and B, 9.21, and 9.22   Scheerer, M., "Problem-solving," *Scientific American* 208 (April 1963):119 and 126. Copyright © 1963 by Scientific American, Inc. All rights reserved.   9.24   Suls, J. M., "A two-stage model for the appreciation of jokes and cartoons," in Goldstein, J. H., and McGhee, P. E., eds., *The psychology of humor,* p. 85. New York: Academic Press, 1972. Adapted by permission of the author and publisher.   9.28   Piaget, J., and Inhelder, B., *The child's conception of space.* Humanities Press Inc., New Jersey 07716. Adapted by permission of the publisher and Routledge & Kegan Paul Ltd.

10.2   Reprinted with permission of Macmillan Publishing Co., Inc. from *On the origins of language: An introduction to the evolution of human language* by Philip Lieberman. Copyright © 1975 by Philip Lieberman.   10.13   Slobin, D. I., "Grammatical transformation and sentence comprehension in childhood and adulthood," *Journal of Verbal Learning and Verbal Behavior* 5 (1966):219–27. Adapted by permission.   10.16   R. Brown, C. Cazden, and Bellugi-Klima, U., "The child's grammar from 1 to 3," in J. P. Hill (ed.) *Minnesota Symposium on Child Psychology* by The University of Minnesota Press, Minneapolis. Copyright © 1969 by the University of Minnesota.   10.19   Reprinted from *A study of writing: The foundations of gramatology,* 2nd edition, p. 31, by Gelb, J. J., by permission of The University of Chicago Press. Copyright © 1963 by The University of Chicago Press.   10.21   Geschwind, N., "Language and the brain," *Scientific American* 226 (April 1972):78.   10.24   Marler, P. R., "A comparative approach to vocal learning: Song development in white crowned sparrows," *Journal of Comparative and Physiological Psychology Monograph* 71 (May 1970):(No. 2, Part 2), pp. 1–25. Copyright 1970 by the American Psychological Association. Reprinted by permission.

11.1   Tinbergen, N., *The study of instinct.* Oxford, England: Oxford University Press, 1951. Adapted by permission of the publisher. 11.2   Hailman, J. P., "How an instinct is learned," *Scientific American* 221 (December 1969):99–100. Copyright © 1969 by Scientific American, Inc. All rights reserved.   11.10   Reprinted from "Reproductive behaviors" by Etkin, E., in *Social behavior and organization among vertebrates* by Etkin, W., by permission of The University of Chicago Press. Copyright 1964 by The University of Chicago. 11.11   Bermant, G., and Davidson, J. M., *Biological bases of sexual behavior.* New York: Harper & Row, 1974. In turn adapted from Lloyd, J. E., "Studies on the flash communication system in Photinus Fireflies," *Miscellaneous Publications of the Museum of Zoology* 130 (1966). Published by University of Michigan Press. Adapted by permission of J. E. Lloyd.   11.12   From Höhn, E. O., "The phalarope," *Scientific American* 220 (June 1969):104. Copyright © 1969 by Scientific American, Inc. All rights reserved.   11.13   Keeton, W. T., *Biological science,* 3rd ed. New York: W. W. Norton & Company, Inc., 1980. Copyright © 1980, 1979, 1972, 1967 by W. W. Norton & Company, Inc.   11.14   Bermant, G., and Davidson, J. M., *Biological bases of sexual behavior.* New York: Harper & Row, 1974. In turn adapted from data of Davidson, J. M., Rodgers, C. H., Smith, E. R., and Bloch, G. J., "Relative thresholds of behavioral and somatic responses to estrogen," *Physiology and Behavior* 3 (1968):227–229. 11.15A   Lorenz, K., "Die angeborenen Formen moeglicher Erfahrung," *Zeitschrift Für Tierpsychologie* 5 (1943):276. Adapted by permission of Paul Parey Verlagsbuchhandlung, Hamburg and Berlin.   11.18A and 11.19   Hess, E. H., " 'Imprinting' in animals," *Scientific American* 198 (March 1958):82. Copyright © 1958 by Scientific American, Inc. All rights reserved.   11.24   Smith, W. J., *The behavior of communicating.* Cambridge, Mass.: Harvard University Press, 1977. Adapted by permission of Harvard University Press. 11.25   Hinde, R. A., *Animal behavior,* p. 262. New York: McGraw-Hill, 1966. Adapted by permission of the publisher. 11.27   Hinde, R. A., *Biological basis of human social behavior,* p. 271. New York: McGraw-Hill, Inc., 1974. Adapted by permission of the publisher.   11.28   Peter H. Klopfer, *An introduction to animal behavior: Ethology's first century,* © 1974, p. 208. Reprinted by permission of Prentice-Hall, Inc., Englewood Cliffs, N.J.

12.2   Masserman, J. H., *Principles of dynamic psychiatry,* p. 76. Philadelphia: W. B. Saunders & Company, 1946. Adapted by permission of the publisher.

13.3   Gerbner, G., Gross, L., Morgan, M., and Gisnorielli, N., *Violence profile No. 11. Trends in network television drama and viewer conceptions of social reality.* Philadelphia, Pa.: Annenberg School of Communications, 1980. Adapted by permission of the publisher. 13.4   Kohlberg, L., "Development of children's orientation towards a moral order in sequence in the development of moral thought," *Vita Humana* 6 (1963):11–36. Adapted by permission.   13.6   De Charms, R., and Moeller, G. H., "Values expressed in American children's readers: 1800–1950," *Journal of Abnormal and Social Psychology* 64 (1962):136–42. Adapted by permission.   13.7A and B   Women on Words and Images, *Dick and Jane as victims: Sex stereotyping in children's readers."* Princeton, N.J.: Women on Words and Images, 1972. Adapted by permission. Also 13.7B   Reprinted from "Sex-role socialization in picture books for preschool children," *American Journal of Sociology* 77 (1972):1125–50, by Weitzman, L. J., Eifley, D., Hokada, E., and Ross, C., by permission of The University of Chicago Press. Copyright © 1972 by The University of Chicago Press.   13.8B   Harlowe, H. F., "The heterosexual affectional system in monkeys," *American Psychologist* 17 (1962):1–9. Copyright 1962 by the American Psychological Association. Reprinted by permission.   13.9   Very, P. S., "Differential factor structure in mathematical ability," *Genetic Psychology Monographs* 75 (1967):169–208. Adapted by permission.

14.3   Asch, S. E., "Opinions and social pressure," *Scientific American* 193 (1955):31–35. Copyright 1955 by Scientific American, Inc. All rights reserved.   14.4   Asch, S. E., "Effects of group pressure upon the modification and distortion of judgements," in Macoby, E. E., Newcomb, T. M., and Hartley, E. L., eds., *Readings in social psychology,* pp. 174–81. New York: Henry Holt, 1958. Adapted by permission of Carnegie Press, Pittsburgh, Pa.   14.5   Festinger, L., and Carlsmith, J. M., "Cognitive consequences of forced compliance," *Journal of Abnormal and Social Psychology* 58 (1959):203–10. Copyright 1959 by the American Psychological Association. Reprinted by permission.   14.6   Anderson, N. H. and Barrios, A. A., "Primacy effects in personality impression formation," *Journal of Abnormal and Social Psychology* 63 (1961):346–50. Copyright 1961 by the American Psychological Association. Reprinted by permission.   14.7   Gallup, G. G., Jr., "Mirror-image stimulation," *Psychological Bulletin* 70:782–93. Adapted by permission.

15.1   Reprinted with permission of Macmillan Publishing Co., Inc. from *Differential psychology,* 3rd edition, p. 57, by Ann Anastasi. Copyright © 1958 by Macmillan Publishing Co., Inc.   15.3   Lack, D., "Darwin's finches," *Scientific American* 188 (1953):66–72. 15.10   Figure 13.7 (p. 432) from *Essentials of psychological testing,* 3rd edition, by Lee J. Cronbach. Copyright © 1949 by Harper & Row, Publishers, Inc. Copyright © 1960, 1970 by Lee J. Cronbach. Reprinted by permission of the publisher.   15.17   Reprinted from "Correlations of maternal and child behaviors with the development of mental abilities: Data from the Berkeley Growth Study," *Monographs of the Society for Research in Child Development* 29 (1964):1–80, by Bayley, N., and Schaeffer, E. S., by permission of The University of Chicago Press. Copyright © 1964 by The University of Chicago Press.   15.18   Jones, H. E., and Kaplan, O. J., "Psychological aspects of mental disorders in later life," in Kaplan, O. J., ed., *Mental disorders in later life,* 72. Stanford, Calif.: Stanford University Press, 1945. Adapted by permission of the publisher.   15.19   Schaie, K., and Strother, D., "A cross sequential study of age changes in cognitive behavior," *Psychological Bulletin* 70 (1968):671–80. Copyright 1968 by the American Psychological Association. Reprinted by permission.   15.20   Reprinted with permission of Macmillan Publishing Co., Inc. from *Bias in mental testing,* p. 671, by Arthur R. Jensen. Copyright © 1980, Arthur R. Jensen.   15.21A and B   Ellis, N. R., "Memory processes in retardates and normals," *International Review of Research in Mental Retardation,* vol. 4, Ellis, N. R., ed., p. 9. New York: Academic Press, 1970. Adapted by permission of the author and the publisher.   15.22   Appel, L. F., Cooper, R. G., McCarrell, N., Sims-Knight, J., Yussen, S. R., and Flavell, J. H., "The development distinction between perceiving and memorizing," *Child Development* 43 (1972):1365–81. Copyright © 1972 by The Society for Research in Child Development, Inc.   15.25   Jencks, C., Smith, M., Acland, H., Bane, M. J., Cohen, D., Gintis, H., Heyns, B., and Michelson, S., *Inequality: A reassessment of the effect of family and schooling in America.* New York: Basic Books, 1972. Adapted by permission of the publisher.

16.1   Lanyon, R. I., and Goodstein, L. D., *Personality assessment,* p. 79. New York: John Wiley & Sons, Inc., 1971. Adapted by permission of the publisher.   16.6   Eysenck, H. J., and Rachman, S., *The causes and cures of neurosis,* p. 16. San Diego, Calif.: Robert R. Knapp, 1965. Adapted by permission of the publisher.   17.8   Data from Shakow, D., "Psychological deficit in schizophrenia," *Behavior Science* 8 (1963):275–80. Adapted by permission of the author and the publisher.   17.10   Data from Faris, R. E. L., and Dunham, H. W., *Mental disorders in urban areas.* Chicago: University of Chicago Press, 1939. Adapted by permission of the author.   17.12A and B   Hiroto, D. S., and Seligman, M. E. P., "Generality of learned helplessness," *Journal of Personality and Social Psychology* 31 (1975):311–27. Copyright 1975 by The American Psychological Association. Reprinted by permission.

TABLES

6.1   Schiffman, H., *Sensation and perception,* p. 15. New York: Wiley & Sons, Inc., 1976. In turn reprinted from Geldard, F. A., *Fundamentals of psychology,* p. 93. New York: Wiley & Sons, Inc., 1962. Adapted by permission of the publisher.   12.2   Erikson, E. H., *Childhood and society.* New York: W. W. Norton & Company, Inc., 1963. Adapted by permission.   13.1   Kohlberg, L., "Stage and sequence: The cognitive developmental approach to socialization," in Goslin, D. A., ed., *Handbook of socialization theory of research,* pp. 347–480. Chicago: Rand McNally, 1969. Adapted by permission. 15.3   Terman, L. M., and Merrill, M. A., *Stanford-Binet intelligence scale—manual for the third revision,* form L-M. Boston: Houghton Mifflin, 1972. Adapted by permission.   15.4   Adapted from table by Cytryn, L., and Lourie, R. S., in Freedman, A. M., Kaplan, H. I., and Sadock, B. J., eds., *Comprehensive textbook of psychiatry-II,* vol. 1, p. 116. Baltimore, Md.: The Williams & Wilkins Co., 1975. Copyright © The Williams & Wilkins Co., Baltimore.   15.5   Wechsler, D., *The measurement and appraisal of adult intelligence,* 4th edition. Baltimore, Md.: The Williams & Wilkins Co., 1958. Copyright © The Williams & Wilkins Co., Baltimore.   15.7   Bayley, N., "Mental growth during the first three years," *Genetic Psychology Monographs* 14 (1933):1–92.   17.13   Marks, I. M., and Lader, M., "Anxiety states (anxiety neurosis): A review," *Journal of Nervous and Mental Disease* 156 (1973) 3–18. Published by The Williams & Wilkins Co., Baltimore. © 1973 by the Williams & Wilkins Co., Baltimore. 17.14   Folkow, B., and Rubinstein, E. H., "Cardiovascular effects of acute and chronic stimulations of the hypothalamic defense area in the rat," *Acta Physiologica Scandinavica* 68 (1966):48–57. Adapted by permission.   17.16   Stone, A., "Mental health and law: A system in transition," U.S. Department of Health, Education and Welfare, #75176, p. 7, 1975. Adapted by permission.   17.17   Hare, R. D., "Temporal gradient of fear arousal in psychopaths," *Journal of Abnormal Psychology* 70 (1965):442–45. Copyright 1965 by the American Psychological Association. Reprinted by permission. 17.18   Marks, I., "Patterns of meaning in psychiatric patients: Semantic differential responses in obsessives and psychopaths," *Maudsley Monograph* 13 (1966). Adapted by permission of Oxford University Press, Oxford, England, and the Institute of Psychiatry, Oxford University.   18.2 Davis, J. H., and Cole, J. P., "Anti-psychotic drugs," in Freedman, A. M., Kaplan, H. I., and Sadock, B. J., eds., *Comprehensive Textbook of Psychiatry—II,* 2nd ed., vol. 2, pp. 1921–41. Baltimore, Md.: Williams & Wilkins Company, 1975. Copyright © 1975, The Williams & Wilkins Co., Baltimore.   16.5 Norman, W. T., "Toward an adequate taxonomy of personality attributes: Replicated factor structure in peer nomination personality ratings," *Journal of Abnormal and Social Psychology* 66 (1963):577. Adapted by permission.   18.1 and 18.2 Wolpe, J., *Psychotherapy by reciprocal inhibition,* 142–43. Stanford, Calif.: Stanford University Press, 1958. Adapted by permission of the publisher.   18.3 Paul, G. L., "Insight versus desensitization in psychotherapy two years after termination," *Journal of Consulting Psychology* 31 (1967):333–348.

PHOTOS

Page 8 Sendak, M. 1963. *Where the wild things are.* New York: Harper & Row.   Figure 1.10 Lehmann, H. E. 1975. "Schizophrenia: Clinical features." In Freedman, A. M., Kaplan, H. I., and Sadock, B. J., eds., *Comprehensive textbook of psychiatry—II,* vol. 1. Baltimore, Md.: Williams & Wilkins.   Figures 2.16A–C Reproduction by permission of the publishers from Roeder, K. D. 1967. *Nerve cells and insect behavior.* Cambridge, Mass.: Harvard University Press.   Figure 2.18A Lewis, E. R. et al. "Study neural organization in aplysia with the scanning electron microscope," *Science,* vol. 165, pp. 1140–43, Fig. 12, September 1969. Copyright © 1969 by the American Association for the Advancement of Science. Figure 2.29 Luria, A. R. 1966. *Higher cortical functions in man.* New York: Basic Books.   Figure 3.7 Weiss, B., and Laties, V. G. 1961. "Behavioral thermoregulation," *Science,* vol. 133, pp. 1338–44, Fig. 1, 28 April 1961. Copyright © 1961 by the American Association for the Advancement of Science.   Figures 5.1A–D, 5.2 Reproduction by permission of the publishers from Kohler, W. 1976. *The mentality of apes.* London: Routledge & Kegan Paul Ltd.   Figure 5.14A, B Photos courtesy of Bruce Moore.   Figure 5.23A, B Photos courtesy of D. Premack.   Figure 6.30 Lindsay, P. H., and Norman, D. A. 1977. *Human information processing,* 2nd edition. New York: Academic Press.   Figure 7.1A, B Photos courtesy of Harvard University. Boring, E. G. 1964. "Size constancy in a picture," *American Journal of Psychology.* 77:494–98.   Figure 7.10A, B Kanizsa, G. 1976. "Subjective contours," *Scientific American,* 234:48–52.   Figure 7.19C Gibson, J. J. 1950. *The perception of the visible world.* New York: Houghton Mifflin.   Figure 7.33A, B Street, R. F. 1931. Reprinted by permission of the publisher from *A gestalt completion test.* New York: Teachers College Press, Columbia University. All rights reserved.   Figure 7.36A, B Yarbus, A. L. 1965. *Eye movements and vision.* Translated by Riggs, L. A. New York: Plenum Press, 1967. Copyrighted and reprinted with the permission of Plenum Press.   Figure 7.37A–C Neisser, U., and Becklen, R. 1975. "Selective looking: Attending to visually-specified events," *Cognitive Psychology* 7:480–94.   Figure 7.38A–C Boring, E. G. 1930. "A new ambiguous figure," *American Journal of Psychology.* 42:444–45; and Leeper, R. W. 1935. "A study of a neglected portion of the field of learning: The development of sensory

organization," *Journal of Genetic Psychology* 46:41–75.   Figure 7.48B, C Gregory, R. L. 1966. *Eye and brain.* New York: McGraw-Hill, Inc.   Figure 7.50 Lewis, H. P. 1966. *Child art: The beginnings of self-affirmation.* Emoryville, Calif.: Diablo Press. Reproduced by permission of the publisher.   Figure 7.51 Ivins, W. M., Jr. 1975. *On the rationalization of sight.* New York: Da Capo Press. Figure 7.52 Gombrich, E. H. 1961. *Art and illusion.* Princeton, N.J.: Bollingen Series, Princeton University Press.   Figure 8.13 Gombrich, E. H. 1961. *Art and illusion.* Princeton, N.J.: Bollingen Series, Princeton University Press. From Da Vinci, L. ca 1500. *Treatise on painting.*   Figure 8.15 Yates, F. A. 1966. *The art of memory.* Chicago: University of Chicago Press.   Figure 8.20 Carroll, L. 1865. *Alice in wonderland.* Abridged by Frank, J. and illustrated by Torrey, M. M. New York: Random House, 1969. Figure 9.29 Borke, H. 1975. "Piaget's mountains revisited: Changes in the egocentric landscape," *Developmental Psychology* 11:240–43.   Page 354 Ginzberg, L. 1906. *The legends of the Jews,* vol. 1. Translated by Szold, H. Philadelphia, Pa.: Jewish Publication Society of America.   Figure 10.15 Sendak, M. 1979. *Higglety pigglety pop! or There must be more to life.* New York: Harper & Row. Copyright M. Sendak. Published in the U.K. and Commonwealth by the Bodley Head: London. Copyright 1976.   Figure 10.18 Frishberg, N. 1975. "Arbitrariness and iconicity: Historical change in American sign language," *Language* 51:696–719.   Figure 10.22B Terrace, H. S.; Petitto, L. A.; Sanders, D. L.; and Bever, T. G. 1979. "Can an ape create a sentence?," *Science* 206:891–902.   Figures 10.23A, B Premack, D. 1976. *Intelligence in ape and man.* Hillsdale, N.J.: Erlbaum.   Page 417 Both photos by Nina Leen, Life Magazine, © Time Inc.   Figures 11.3A, B Azrin, N. H. 1967. Pain and aggression. *Psychology Today.* 1:27–33.   Figures 11.4A, B Barnett, S. A. 1963. *The rat: A study in behavior.* Chicago: The University of Chicago Press. Reprinted by permission of The University of Chicago Press.   Figures 11.17, 11.18 Photos by Nina Leen, Life Magazine, © Time Inc.   Figure 11.26 Darwin, C. 1965. *The expression of the emotions in man and animals.* Chicago: The University of Chicago Press. Reprinted by permission of the University of Chicago Press. Originally published 1872. London: Appleton and Company, courtesy of the Meredith Publishing company.   Figures 11.29A–D Ekman, P. 1971. "Universals and cultural differences in facial expression," *Nebraska Symposium on motivation.* University of Nebraska Press.   Figures 13.2A–C Bandura, A.; Ross, D.; and Ross, S. A. 1963. Imitation of film-mediated agressive models. *Journal of Abnormal and Social Psychology* 66:8.   Figure 13.17B Krasilovsky, P. 1953. *The very little girl.* Pictures by Ninon. New York: Doubleday & Company, Inc. And: 1962. *The very little boy.* Pictures by Ninon. New York: Doubleday & Company. Reproduced by permission of Doubleday & Company, Inc.   Figure 14.12A Milgram, S., and Toch, H. 1969. Collective behavior: Crowds and Social Movements. In Lindzey, G., and Aronson, E., eds., *Handbook of social psychology,* 2nd edition, vol. 4, pp. 507–610. Reading, Mass.: Addison-Wesley.   Figure 15.14 Guilford, J. P. 1967. *The nature of human intelligence.* New York: McGraw-Hill, Inc.   Figure 16.5 Reprinted by permission of C.P.S., Inc., P. O. Box 83, Larchmont, New York, from the *Children's apperception test (C.A.T.).*   Figures 17.5A, B and 17.7 Lehmann, H. E. 1975. Schizophrenia: Clinical features. In Freedman, A. M., Kaplan, H. I., and Sadock, B. J., eds. *Comprehensive textbook of psychiatry—II,* vol. 1, pp. 890–922. Baltimore, Md.: Williams & Wilkins.

Name Index

White, W. A., 668
Whytt (Scottish physician), 27–28
Wickens, D. D., 117
Wiesel, Torsten, 52, 241
Wilbur, C. B., 524, 526
Wilcox, B. L., 607
Wilcoxin, H. C., 152
Wilde, Oscar, 332
Wilhelmy, R. A., 531
Wilk, S., 675, 684
Williams, C. D., 124
Williams, D. R., 153
Williams, G. C., 430
Williams, H., 153
Williams, H. L., 78
Williamson, S., 383, 388
Wilson, E. O., 446
Wilson, Edward, 447
Wilson, G. D., 483
Wilson, S. K., 77
Wilton, K. M., 605

Winch, R. F., 640
Winokur, G., 686
Wise, C. D., 675
Wishner, J., 703
Wittgenstein, L., 367
Wohlwill, J. F., 348
Wolf, S., 697
Wollen, K. A., 297
Wolpe, Joseph, 127, 688, 689, 724–25
Wolpert, E. A., 80, 483
Wolsk, D., 193
Woodruff, G., 161
Woods, R. L., 10
Woodworth, R. S., 214, 217, 227
Wulff, J. J., 91
Wundt, Wilhelm, 11
Wynne, L. C., 141, 142, 678

Yalom, I. D., 433, 740
Yarbus, A. L., 249

Yates, F. A., 296
Yee, A. H., 511
Yerkes, R. M., 98
Yonas, A., 396
Yorkston, N. J., 733

Zanni, G., 295
Zener, K., 105
Zentall, T., 158
Ziegler, F. J., 692
Zigler, E., 485, 512, 595
Zigmond, M. J., 87
Zilboorg, G., 657, 658
Zimmerman, R. R., 70
Zobrist, A. L., 326
Zubin, J., 635, 638, 639
Zuckerman, C. B., 240
Zuk, C. H., 651
Zurif, E. G., 400

Subject Index

abnormal psychology, *see* psychopathology
absolute threshold, 173–74, 175*n*, 194, 222
   defined, 172
   duplicity theory and, 191–92
   response bias and, 217
abstract concepts, formation and use of, 154–60, 162, 163
accessory structures, senses and, 184, 187, 188–89, 222
accommodation (in cognitive development), 349–50, 352
accommodation (in vision), 189
achievement motive, 55, 506–12, 527
   assessment of, 507–8, 583
   in women, 514
achievement tests, 576, 583
acquisition curves, *see* learning curves
ACTH (adrenocorticotropic hormone), 62
action:
   biological bases of behavior and, 15–54
   directed, in sensory-motor period, 335
   hierarchical organization of, 318
   learning and, 96–163
   motivation and, 55–95
   thought as descended from, 314–15, 337–38
action potential, 23–25, 26, 34, 35
   defined, 23
activation, motivation and, 55, 65–83, 88, 94–95
active rehearsal, 291, 311
active sleep, *see* rapid eye movements
adaptation:
   aftereffect of, 244
   feature analyzers and, 242–43, 269
   perceptual, 244–46, 269
additive mixture, 210, 223

complementary hues and, 205–6
   defined, 205
adolescence, 519, 608, 617
   identity crisis in, 488–90
   in psychoanalytic theory, 471, 475, 496
adoption:
   intelligence studies and, 617, 618, 625, 626
   schizophrenia and, 676, 679
adrenal glands, 62, 63, 66, 67
adrenalin, 62, 67, 68, 548, 549
adrenocorticotropic hormone (ACTH), 62
affective disorders, 664, 681–86, 742
   bipolar, 663, 677, 681, 683, 702, 710
   defined, 681
   organic factors in, 683–84, 710
   psychogenic factors and, 684–86, 710
   symptoms of, 681–83, 710
   unipolar, 681, 683, 710
   see also depression; mania
afferent nerves, 17, 28, 35, 37
aggression, 55, 141
   biological aspects of, 415–17, 420–26, 454, 485
   displaced, 465, 496
   limiting of, 423–25, 454
   modeling and, 499–502
   pain-induced, 421
   predation and defense vs., 421
   sex differences and, 515, 516–17, 527
   use of term, 421
agnosia, 44, 45, 54
agoraphobia, 688, 689
alarm calls, 446–47, 455
Alcoholics Anonymous, 735
alcoholism, 281, 660, 664, 676, 711
algorithms, 325–26, 352

alleles, 611, 613, 614, 625
all-or-none law, 25
   stimulus intensity and, 25–27, 53
alpha waves, 76–77
   blocking of, 77
alternative hypothesis, A23, A26, A28
altruism, 446–47, 455, 466
   biological use of term, 446*n*
ambiguity:
   in language, 3, 376–78, 409
   in vision, 3, 252, 407–8
American behaviorism, *see* behavior theory of learning
American Psychiatric Association, 524, 664
American Sign Language (ASL), 396, 400–401, 410
amnesia, 281–83, 479, 691
   anterograde, 281–82, 310
   posthypnotic, 459
   retrograde, 282–83, 310–11
amoebas, 18, 427
amphetamines, 75, 93, 94, 675
amphibians, increasing encephalization in, 37
anagram puzzle, 320, 321
anal character, in psychoanalytic theory, 471, 473, 486, 496
   culture and, 487–88
anal stage, in psychoanalytic theory, 471, 484, 488, 496
androgens, 62, 422, 431, 432, 433, 454, 485, 519
anesthesia, 458, 459
animal behavior, *see specific animals*
animistic thinking, 15, 19
   in preoperational period, 342, 352
ANS, *see* autonomic nervous system

incubation process, in thinking, 331–32, 352
incus (anvil), 184, 185
individual differences, 11–12, 306
    dreams and, 10–11
    growth of interest in, 575
    in intelligence, 575–626
    personality assessment and, 627–54
    psychopathology and, 655–743
infants, 434–45, 455
    absence of maternal attachment in, 442–45, 455
    intelligence of, 600–601, 625
    perceptual organization in, 237–39, 257–58, 260–61, 269
    response control in, 147
    sensory-motor period in, 261, 270, 334–38, 352, 601, 604
    temperament of, 506, 527
inferential statistics, A19–A26
information processing systems:
    in computers vs. humans, 324–27
    memory and, 274, 275, 310, 324
    see also thinking and thought
inhibitions:
    defined, 32, 103
    lateral, 198–200, 212, 223
    proactive, 299–300, 311
    reciprocal, 31–32, 54
    retroactive, 299–300, 311
inhibitory postsynaptic potentials (IPSP), 35
insects, 172, 450
    feeding patterns of, 1–2
    inhibition and disinhibition in, 32–33
    phototaxes of, 58
insightful learning, 132–36, 141
    evidence for, 134–35
instincts:
    internal vs. external control of, 458
    misuse of term, 462*n*
    see also species-specific dispositions
instrumental conditioning, 97, 106–16, 130, 162–63
    in behavior therapy, 128–30, 131
    classical conditioning vs., 106–7, 112, 118, 124–25
    cognitive learning theory compared to, 138, 140, 147
    contingency in, 147–49, 163
    of involuntary responses, 125–27, 131
    methods for studying of, 110–12
    operant approach to, 111, 116, 118–25, 128–30, 131, 136, 147–49
    response-outcome relations in, 152
    in two-factor theory, 143
insulin, 62, 63, 89, 95, 664–65
integration, *see* transmission-integration system
integration centers of brain, 38, 40
intelligence, 575–626
    age and, 600–603, 625
    artificial, 324–27, 352
    cognitive processes and, 605–9, 625
    fluid vs. crystallized, 602–3, 625
    as general cognitive capacity, 588–89, 595–600, 625
    as g factor, 597–98, 625
    group factor analysis of, 597–99, 600, 625

hierarchical theory of, 599–600, 625
longitudinal studies of, 602
of mentally retarded, 399, 593–95, 600, 605, 606–8, 624, 625
monarchic vs. oligarchic theories of, 597–99, 600
problems in defining of, 587
psychometric approach to, 595–604, 625
role of strategies in, 606–8, 625
underlying processes of, 603–9, 625
intelligence quotient (IQ), 589–91, 624
    constancy of, 615
    deviation, 591, 624
    environmental vs. genetic factors and, 609–24, 625–26
    group differences in, 619–24, 626
    use of term, 591*n*
intelligence tests, 576, 587–95
    achievement motives and, 508, 509, 583
    in adults, 591–93, 601–3, 624
    in children, 588–91, 600–601, 624
    early attempts at, 588
    group, 591–93
    mental retardation and, 593–95, 605, 625
    performance vs. verbal elements in, 591
    personality tests compared to, 628
    Piaget and, 604–5, 609, 620, 625
intention, moral judgment and, 342
intention movements, 449, 455
interaction:
    among memory systems, 308–9
    between person and situation, 643–45, 654
    of senses, 178, 187, 194–200, 223
interference, 277, 299–301, 311
    extraexperimental, 300
interneurons, 17, 22, 28, 35
interposition, as pictorial cue, 232, 262, 269
introverts, 647–49, 654
invertebrates, increasing impulse velocity in, 27
IPSP (inhibitory postsynaptic potential), 35
IQ, *see* intelligence quotient
irises, 188, 189, 223

jackdaws, messages of, 452–53
James-Lange theory of emotions, 546–48, 549, 571
    objections to, 547–48
jokes, 332–33
just-noticeable-difference (j.n.d.), 173, 222

keys, as signals, 552, 571
kidneys, 62, 65, 127
kinesthesis, 175
    vestibular senses and, 176–77, 222
Korsakoff syndrome, 281

language, 44, 52–53, 353–411, 528
    aphasia as disorder of, 45–47, 54, 399–400, 404–5, 410
    association areas and, 44, 54
    basics vs. elaborations, 391–92, 398, 400, 404, 410
    chimpanzees and, 156–60, 400–403, 410–11
    creative use of, 354–55, 409

dialects of, 357
displays and, 446, 450–51, 453
in intelligence testing, 591, 602, 620
interpersonal property of, 354, 359–61, 409
manual system of, 396, 400, 410
of mentally retarded, 399, 410
personality classification through, 652–53, 654
phrase-structure description of, 372
productive principle in, 450, 451
referential property of, 354, 358–59, 409
in relationship to thought, 338
schizophrenia and, 666, 668, 670–71, 672–73
spatial organization vs., 50–51
as species-specific disposition, 154, 411
structure of, 317, 354, 355–57, 361–64, 370–82, 391, 392, 406–9, 410
Zipf's law and, A15
see also grammatical rules; meaning; phrases and phrase structures; sentences
language learning, 154, 382–405, 410–11
    with changed endowments, 398–403, 410
    in changed environments, 393–98, 410
    correction in, 384–85, 410
    critical periods and, 395, 403–5, 411
    general characteristics of, 382–83, 410
    hypotheses of, 383–85
    imitation in, 383, 410
    language change and, 392–93, 410
    later stages of, 391–92, 410
    modeling and, 396–98, 410
    one-word speaker and, 386–88, 410
    without other people, 394–95, 410
    overgeneralization in, 391, 392, 410
    prelinguistic child and, 385–86, 410
    reinforcement in, 384, 385, 410
    second, 404
    without sound, 395–96, 410
    two-word (telegraphic) speaker and, 389–90, 410
    in wild children, 394, 396, 410
latency period, in psychoanalytic theory, 471, 475
latent learning effects, 139, 141, 144, 162
lateral inhibition, 198–200, 212, 223
lateralization, 47–50
law of effect, 109–10, 112–16, 118, 125, 130
learned helplessness, 148–49, 163, 512
    affective disorders and, 684–85
learned taste aversions, 150–52, 163
learning, 96–163
    aggression and, 426, 427, 454
    association in, 97, 103, 143, 149–54, 170*n*, 221, 283–87
    avoidance, 141–44, 162–63
    in cognitive development, 348–49
    cognitive theory of, 137–41, 144, 147, 162
    imprinting as, 439–42
    insightful, 132–36, 141
    intentional vs. incidental, 290–91, 311
    lightness constancy and, 254
    by listening, 498
    memory and, 283–87, 290–91, 298, 311
    motivation and, 55, 85–86
    neuroses and, 693–94
    perceptual, 244–53, 254, 257–58, 268, 269

pain:
aggression and, 421
sensitivity to, 179–80
paired associates, method of, 285, 311
pancreas, 62, 63, 665
panic, 561, 562–66, 570
prisoner's dilemma and, 564–65, 571–72
parallel search, memory retrieval by, 279–80, 310
paralysis, 351, 458, 459
paraphrases, 375–76, 409
perceptual constancy and, 406–7, 411
parasympathetic nervous system, 62, 64, 66–67, 88, 94–95
overshoots of, 71–73, 83
parent-child bond, 434–47, 455
parents, 498
achievement motives influenced by, 508–9
children in socialization of, 506
children's IQ linked to, 616, 617
home atmosphere and, 486–87
homosexuality and, 525–26
infant's attachment to, 436–42, 455
irrationality in commands of, 464
in psychoanalytic thought, 464, 465, 470, 474–75, 476–77, 486–88, 496, 520
see also fathers; mothers
paresis, 660, 709, 713
parietal lobes, 40, 42
aphasia and, 47
partial reinforcement, 122–24, 131
pathology model, 662–65, 709
explaining disorders in, 664–65
neuroses and, 692–94
psychiatric classification system and, 663–64
schizophrenia and, 666–80, 710
sociological critique of, 698–709, 710
sociopaths and, 707
payoff matrix:
in detection theory, 218, 587n
for prisoner's dilemma, 563–65
in selection procedures, 585–87, 624
peg method, mnemonics and, 296, 311
penicillin, 660
penis, 469, 513n
erections of, 28, 66, 442
penis envy, in psychoanalytic theory, 477, 484
percentile ranks, 590, A12, A13
of z-score, A14
perception, 224–69, 351
adaptation and, 244–46, 269
construction and, 246–47, 253, 269
of depth, 231–35, 237–38, 262–64, 268–69
differentiation and, 248, 253, 269
feature analyzers and, 240–43, 269
of form, 227–31, 238–40, 243–44, 247, 268, 539
grouping and, 228–29, 268
in infants, 237–39, 257–58, 260–61, 269
innate factors in, 237–44, 253, 269
interpersonal nature of reality and, 530–34
learning and, 244–53, 254, 257–58, 268, 269
of movement, 235–37, 241, 242–43, 269
problems of, 224–26
of reality, 253–61
selective attention and, 248–52, 269

self-produced movement and, 245–46
after sensory deprivation, 239–40, 269
of size and shape, 225–26, 256–59, 268, 269
social perception compared to, 539, 542, 551
see also social perception
perceptual constancy, 253–61
lightness constancy and, 254–56, 269
object permanence and, 260–61, 269
paraphrase and, 406–7, 411
person constancy compared to, 645–46
peripheral nervous system, 37, 54
see also autonomic nervous system
peristalsis, 28, 37, 62, 66, 67, 143
persecution complex, 668
personality, 456–528, 627–54
of anal character, 471, 473, 486, 487–88, 496
antisocial, 664, 676, 705–7, 710
assessment, methods of, 628–40, 654
authoritarian, 554, 571
biology in classification of, 649–52, 654
differences, defined, 627
Freudian theories of, 456–96
internal consistency in classification of, 646–49
language in classification of, 652–53, 654
mental disorders and, 642
modern conceptions of, 497–528
multiple (or split), 666n, 691, 710
of oral character, 471, 472–73, 496
situationism and, 641–42, 643–45, 654
taxonomy needed for, 646–53, 654
personality tests, 576, 628–40
CAT, 639
CPI, 631–32, 652, 654
early use of, 628
MMPI, 629–32, 633, 634, 654, 705n
Rorschach, 634–36, 638, 639–40, 654
structured, 628–34, 654
TAT, 507, 634, 636–38, 639–40, 654
unstructured, 628, 634–40, 654
personality traits, 627–46
criticism of theory, 640–42, 654
defense of, 642–45, 654
defined, 627, 653
vs. situations, 640–46
phalaropes, sexual behavior in, 430
phallic stage, in psychoanalytic theory, 471, 474, 488, 496
phenobarbital, 714
phenothiazines, 674, 675, 710, 717
chlorpromazine, 713–16, 742
side effects of, 716
phenotypes, 611–13, 614, 625
phenylalinine, 613
phenylketonuria (PKU), 613–14, 625
pheromones, 180–81, 222
phobias, 127–28, 131, 687–89, 694, 743
causes of, 688–89
defined, 100
systematic desensitization of, 724–25
phonemes, 361–63, 409
phonological rules, 363, 409
photographic memory, see eidetic imagery
phototaxes, 58–60
phrases and phrase structures, 361, 370–81
defined, 364, 370

noun, 371–72, 373–75, 378–79, 381, 391–92, 410
surface, 371–73, 376, 377, 380, 407–8, 409–10
underlying, 371, 373–81, 407–8, 409–10
verb, 371–72, 373–75, 378–79, 410
pictorial cues, 232–34, 262, 269
pigeons:
courtship rituals of, 428
learning theories and, 121–23, 125, 152–53, 154, 158, 160–61, 162
piloerection, 61, 64, 68, 69
pineal body, 16–17, 28
pitch, perception of, 185–87
pituitary gland, 62, 63, 65, 431
PKU (phenylketonuria), 613–14, 625
placebo effects, controlling for, 715–16, 731–32, 742
place theory of pitch, 185–87, 222
play therapy, 734
pleasure principle, in psychoanalytic theory, 463, 496
points of view (egocentrism), 341–42, 344–45
polarization, 23, 25, 34–35
polygenic inheritance, 614, 625
population, sample and, A6–A7, A26, A27, A28
positive afterimage, color and, 207n
postsynaptic membranes, 34
praying mantis, disinhibition in, 32–33
predictive validity, in testing, 582–83, 620, 624, 632, 654
preoperational period, in Piaget's theory, 334, 338–43, 344–46, 352, 521, 604
prestige suggestion effect, in imitation, 503–4
presynaptic membranes, 34
primacy effects:
memory and, 278–79, 310, 607
social behavior and, 540, 541, 571
primates, sexual behavior in, 430, 431, 432
Principia (Newton), 15
prisoner's dilemma, 563–566, 571–72
economic applications of, 565–66
proactive inhibitions, 299–300, 311
problem solving, 316–27, 352
chunking in, 320–24, 352
mechanization in, 328–29
mental set and, 328–30, 352
perceptual restructuring in, 330–33, 352
of well-defined vs. ill-defined problems, 326–27
profiles, test:
based on group factors, 599
MMPI and, 630, 631, 654
progesterone, 62, 431, 432, 454, 482
Progressive Matrices Test, 593, 602, 603, 620
projection, 466, 474–75, 496
in schizophrenia, 669
projection areas, 41–44, 54
functions of, 41
motor, 41–42, 44
sensory, 41, 42–44, 52
projective techniques, in personality testing, 628, 634–40
propositions, conceptual, 352
chimpanzees and, 401, 411
defined, 315–16, 373

286, 465
STM, *see* short-term memory
stroboscopic (apparent) movement, 235, 269
Stroop effect, 319
subception, 480–81, 496
subjective contours, 229–30
subtractive mixture, 204, 206, 223
successive approximations method, 121, 131
suicide, depression and, 663, 682–83
summation, 30–31, 32, 34, 35
    spatial, 31, 54
    temporal, 30–31, 54
superego, in psychoanalytic theory, 462, 463–64, 467, 471, 475, 496, 520
superstitious behavior, 121–22, 131
surface structure, 371–73, 376, 409–10
    ambiguity, 377, 409
    defined, 371, 409
    psychological reality of, 372–73
    traces of underlying structure in, 380
symbolism in dreams, 9–10, 468, 469–70, 481–83, 496
sympathetic nervous system, 62, 64, 66–69, 71–73, 95, 143
    James-Lange theory and, 547–548
    RAS compared to, 74–75
synapses, 22, 28–35, 40
    anatomy of, 34
    defined, 18, 21, 28, 54
    inferring of, 28–33, 54
    mechanism of, 34–35, 54
    reflex latency argument for transmission of, 29–33
    summation arguments for transmission of, 30–31
syntax, 157, 370–81, 452, 455
    of chimpanzees, 401–3, 411
    defined, 370, 409
    origin of, 389
syphilis, 660, 709, 713

taste, 171–72, 175, 177–78
    basic qualities of, 177, 222
    hunger and, 85, 95
    sensory interaction and, 178, 187, 194
TAT, *see* Thematic Apperception Test
taxes (orientation responses), 58–60, 94
taxi drivers, problem solving and, 317–18
t-distributions, A26*n*
television:
    color, 205
    violence on, 500–502, 527
temperature regulation, homeostatic balance and, 60–61, 64, 94
temporal lobes, 40, 43, 53
    aphasia and, 47
terminal endings, 21, 38
territoriality, 422–26
    in animals, 422–25, 454
    in humans, 425–26, 454
testes, 62, 430, 513*n*, 518
testosterone, 62, 422, 431, 454
Test of Primary Mental Abilities, 598, 599
test-retest method, 581–82, 624
tests and testing, 575–95, 628–40
    achievement, 576, 583

alternative forms of, 582
basis of, 576–87
criterion in, 582, 583, 587, 624, 628–32, 654
cultural differences in, 584, 589, 619–20
men vs. women and, 516, 527
recognition, 272
reliability of, 576, 583–84, 624
as social selection device, 584–87, 624
standardization of, 583–84
types of, 576
validity of, 582–83, 624, 628–29, 632–34, 638–40, 654
    see also aptitude tests; intelligence tests; personality tests; scores, test; statistical methods
texture gradients, as pictorial cue, 232, 233, 269
T-groups (sensitivity training groups), *see* encounter groups
thalamus, 54
    functions of, 36, 39
theater, emotion and, 550–51
Thematic Apperception Test (TAT), 507, 634, 636–38, 654
    validity of, 639–40, 654
therapy, *see* behavior therapy; drug therapy; psychotherapy; somatic therapy
thinking and thought, 44, 54, 312–52
    animistic, 15, 19, 342, 352
    as central activity, 315–16, 352
    creative, 330–32, 352
    defined, 312
    directed, 312, 352
    disturbance of, schizophrenia and, 666, 672–73, 674, 709, 710
    hypotheses on elements of, 312–16, 351–52
    as mental imagery, 313, 316, 351
    mental set and, 327–33, 352
    as motor action, 313–15, 337, 351
    organization in, 316–18, 321–24, 352
    problem solving and, 316–27, 328–30, 352
    representational, 335, 337–38, 352
    skill development in, 318–20, 352
    two modes of, 50–51
thirst, 65, 94, 143, 482–83
threat displays, 424, 454
thresholds, 23–25, 53
    CES and, 30–31
    defined, 23
    relative refractory period and, 26–27
    two-point, 178
    see also absolute threshold
thyroid, 62
thyroxin, 62
time, sensory interaction in, 194–95, 223
tip-of-the-tongue experience, in memory search, 293, 311
toilet training, 471, 472, 473, 484, 485–86, 496
token economies, 129, 131
tolerance, 93, 94
touch, *see* skin senses
transduction, 21, 22, 172, 187, 221
    in cochlea, 184–85
    vision and, 187, 188–94, 208–9
transference, in psychoanalysis, 461, 721, 742
transfer of training, 135, 162, 311
    defined, 280

paradigms of, 286–87
stimulus generalization as, 104, 112, 130, 154–55, 286, 465
transmission-integration system, 17–18, 22, 25, 53
    synapses and, 28–35, 40, 54
transmission tracts, 38, 40
transsexual operations, 523
treatment, *see* behavior therapy; drug therapy; psychotherapy; somatic therapy
tree diagrams, in linguistics, 371–72, 374–75, 409
Trobrianders, family pattern of, 486
twins:
    homosexuality in, 525
    in intelligence studies, 615–17, 625
    in personality studies, 652, 654
    psychopathology and, 676, 677, 683, 694, 710
    types of, 615, 625
two-factor theory of avoidance learning, 141–44, 162–63

UCR, *see* unconditioned response
UCS, *see* unconditioned stimulus
ulcers, 72, 696–97, 710
uncertainty interval, 174
unconditioned reflexes, 99
unconditioned response (UCR), 99, 105, 130
unconditioned stimulus (UCS), 100–103, 105–7, 143
    belongingness and, 149, 150–52
    contingency and, 145–46, 149, 163
    defined, 99
    reinforcement and, 101, 103, 106–7, 112, 113, 130
unconscious conflict, 458, 461, 462–70, 495–96, 719–22
    antagonists of, 462–64, 496
    mechanisms of, 462, 464–66, 496
    in normal life, 467–70
    origin of, 462
    recovery of, 719–20
    reevaluation of Freudian theory of, 478–84
unconscious inference, in perception, 226, 254, 268
underlying structure, 373–81, 407–10
    comprehension and, 380–81
    defined, 371, 409
    psychological reality of, 375
    relations among sentence meanings and, 375–78, 410
unifactor theory of retardation, 595
uterus, 62, 431, 432, 454, 482

vagina, 469, 513*n*
validity:
    coefficients, 582–83, 584, 654
    construct, 583, 624, 632–34, 654
    predictive, 582–83, 620, 624, 632, 654
variability, A2
    accounting for, A19–A20
    measures of, A10–A12, A27
variable-interval schedule (VI), 123, 131
variable-ratio schedule (VR), 123, 131
variables: